Date Issued		No.	Title
June	1975	No. 7	Accounting and Reporting by Development Stage Enterprises
Oct.	1975	No. 8	Accounting for the Translation of Foreign Currency Transactions and Foreign Financial Statements (superseded)
Oct.	1975	No. 9	Accounting for Income Taxes—Oil and Gas Producing Companies (superseded)
Oct.	1975	No. 10	Extension of "Grandfather" Provisions for Business Combinations
Dec.	1975	No. 11	Accounting for Contingencies—Transition Method
Dec.	1975	No. 12	Accounting for Certain Marketable Securities
Nov.	1976	No. 13	Accounting for Leases (amended, interpreted, and partially superseded)
Dec.	1976	No. 14	Financial Reporting for Segments of a Business Enterprise (amended)
June	1977	No. 15	Accounting by Debtors and Creditors for Troubled Debt Restructurings
June	1977	No. 16	Prior Period Adjustments
Nov.	1977	No. 17	Accounting for Leases—Initial Direct Costs
Nov.	1977	No. 18	Financial Reporting for Segments of a Business Enterprise—Interim Financial Statements
Dec.	1977	No. 19	Financial Accounting and Reporting by Oil and Gas Producing Companies (amended)
Dec.	1977	No. 20	Accounting for Forward Exchange Contracts (superseded)
April	1978	No. 21	Suspension of the Reporting of Earnings per Share and Segment Information by Nonpublic Enterprises
June	1978	No. 22	Changes in the Provisions of Lease Agreements Resulting from Refundings of Tax-Exempt Debt
Aug.	1978	No. 23	Inception of the Lease
Dec.	1978	No. 24	Reporting Segment Information in Financial Statements That Are Presented in Another Enterprise's Financial Report
Feb.	1979	No. 25	Suspension of Certain Accounting Requirements for Oil and Gas Producing Companies
April	1979	No. 26	Profit Recognition on Sales-Type Leases of Real Estate
May	1979	No. 27	Classification of Renewals or Extensions of Existing Sales-Type or Direct Financing Leases
May	1979	No. 28	Accounting for Sales with Leasebacks
June	1979	No. 29	Determining Contingent Rentals
Aug.	1979	No. 30	Disclosure of Information about Major Customers
Sept.	1979	No. 31	Accounting for Tax Benefits Related to U.K. Tax Legislation Concerning Stock Relief
Sept.	1979	No. 32	Specialized Accounting and Reporting Principles and Practices in AICPA Statements of Position and Guides on Accounting and Auditing Matters (amended and partially superseded)
Sept.	1979	No. 33	Financial Reporting and Changing Prices (amended and partially superseded)
Oct.	1979	No. 34	Capitalization of Interest Cost (amended)
Mar.	1980	No. 35	Accounting and Reporting by Defined Benefit Pension Plans (amended)
May	1980	No. 36	Disclosure of Pension Information
July	1980	No. 37	Balance Sheet Classification of Deferred Income Taxes
Sept.	1980	No. 38	Accounting for Preacquisition Contingencies of Purchased Enterprises
Oct.	1980	No. 39	Financial Reporting and Changing Prices: Specialized Assets—Mining and Oil and Gas
Nov.	1980	No. 40	Financial Reporting and Changing Prices: Specialized Assets—Timberlands and Growing Timber
Nov.	1980	No. 41	Financial Reporting and Changing Prices: Specialized Assets—Income-Producing Real Estate
Nov.	1980	No. 42	Determining Materiality for Capitalization of Interest Cost
Nov.	1980	No. 43	Accounting for Compensated Absences
Dec.	1980	No. 44	Accounting for Intangible Assets of Motor Carriers
Mar.	1981	No. 45	Accounting for Franchise Fee Revenue
Mar.	1981	No. 46	Financial Reporting and Changing Prices: Motion Picture Films
Mar.	1981	No. 47	Disclosure of Long-Term Obligations
June	1981	No. 48	Revenue Recognition When Right of Return Exists
June	1981	No. 49	Accounting for Product Financing Arrangements
Nov.	1981	No. 50	Financial Reporting in the Record and Music Industry
Nov.	1981	No. 51	Financial Reporting by Cable Television Companies
Dec.	1981	No. 52	Foreign Currency Translation
Dec.	1981	No. 53	Financial Reporting by Producers and Distributors of Motion Picture Films
Jan.	1982	No. 54	Financial Reporting and Changing Prices: Investment Companies
Feb.	1982	No. 55	Determining Whether a Convertible Security is a Common Stock Equivalent
Feb.	1982	No. 56	Designation of AICPA Guide and SOP 81-1 on Contractor Accounting and SOP 81-2 on Hospital-Related Organizations as Preferable for Applying APB Opinion 20
Mar.	1982	No. 57	Related Party Disclosures
April	1982	No. 58	Capitalization of Interest Cost in Financial Statements that Include Investments Accounted for by the Equity Method
April	1982	No. 59	Deferral of the Effective Date of Certain Accounting Requirements for Revision Plans of State and Local Governmental Units
June	1982	No. 60	Accounting and Reporting by Insurance Enterprises (amended)
June	1982	No. 61	Accounting for Title Plant

Refer to Index for page citations

Refer to Index for page citations

(Listing continued on inside of back cover.)

INTERMEDIATE ACCOUNTING

NINTH EDITION

INTERMEDIATE ACCOUNTING

VOLUME 1

Donald E. Kieso PH.D., C.P.A.

KPMG Peat Marwick Emeritus Professor of Accounting
Northern Illinois University
DeKalb, Illinois

Jerry J. Weygandt PH.D., C.P.A.

Arthur Andersen Alumni Professor of Accounting
University of Wisconsin
Madison, Wisconsin

JOHN WILEY & SONS, INC.
New York • Chichester • Weinheim
Brisbane • Singapore • Toronto

ACQUISITIONS EDITOR: Rebecca H. Hope
DEVELOPMENTAL EDITOR: Rachel Nelson
SUPPLEMENTS EDITOR: David B. Kear
MARKETING MANAGER: Wendy Goldner
PHOTO EDITOR: Hilary Newman
ILLUSTRATION COORDINATOR: Anna Melhorn
COVER AND TEXT DESIGNER: Dawn L. Stanley
PROJECT MANAGEMENT: Elm Street Publishing Services, Inc.
COVER PHOTOS: Circuit board graphic: Louis Bencze/Tony Stone
Images Chip and logo: Courtesy Intel Corporation

All "Perspectives On" photographs provided courtesy of featured individuals.

This book was set in Palatino by Ruttle, Shaw & Wetherill, Inc. and printed and bound by Von Hoffmann Press. The cover was printed by Phoenix Color.

Recognizing the importance of preserving what has been written, it is a policy of John Wiley & Sons, Inc. to have books of enduring value published in the United States printed on acid-free paper, and we exert our best efforts to that end.

Material from the Uniform CPA Examinations and Unofficial Answers, copyright © 1965, 1966, 1967, 1968, 1969, 1970, 1971, 1972, 1973, 1974, 1975, 1976, 1977, 1978, 1979, 1980, 1981, 1982, 1983, 1984, 1985, 1986, 1987, 1988, 1990, 1991, 1992, and 1993 by the American Institute of Certified Public Accountants, Inc., is adapted with permission.

This book contains quotations from *Accounting Research Bulletins*, *Accounting Principles Board Opinions*, *Accounting Principles Board Statements*, *Accounting Interpretations*, and *Accounting Terminology Bulletins*, copyright © 1953, 1956, 1966, 1968, 1969, 1970, 1971, 1972, 1973, 1974, 1975, 1976, 1977, 1978, 1979, 1980, 1981, 1982 by the American Institute of Certified Public Accountants, Inc., 1211 Avenue of the Americas, New York, NY 10036.

This book contains citations from various FASB pronouncements. Copyright © by Financial Accounting Standards Board, 401 Merritt 7, P.O. Box 5116, Norwalk, CT 06856 U.S.A. Reprinted with permission. Copies of complete documents are available from Financial Accounting Standards Board.

Material from the Certificate in Management Accounting Examinations, copyright © 1975, 1976, 1977, 1978, 1979, 1980, 1981, 1982, 1983, 1984, 1985, 1986, 1987, 1988, 1989, 1990, 1991, 1992, and 1993 by the Institute of Certified Management Accountants, 10 Paragon Drive, Montvale, NJ 07645, is adapted with permission.

Material from the Certified Internal Auditor Examinations, copyright © May 1984, November 1984, May 1986 by The Institute of Internal Auditors, 249 Maitland Ave., Altemonte Springs, FL 32701, is adapted with permission.

The financial statements and accompanying notes reprinted from the 1995 Annual Report of Intel Corporation are courtesy of Intel Corporation, copyright © 1996, all rights reserved.

Library of Congress Cataloging in Publication Data:
Kieso, Donald E.
    Intermediate accounting / Donald E. Kieso, Jerry J. Weygandt.—
9th ed.
     p.   cm.
    Includes bibliographical references.
    ISBN 0-471-15775-9 (cloth : main : alk. paper).—ISBN
0-471-19121-3 (v. 1 : cloth : alk. paper).—ISBN 0-471-19123-X (v.
2 : cloth : alk. paper)
    1. Accounting. I. Weygandt, Jerry J. II. Title.
HF5635.K5 1998
657'.046—DC21   97-24249
                                           CIP

Printed in the United States of America

10 9 8 7 6 5 4 3 2 1

Dedicated to
Donna and Enid
for their
Love, Support, and Understanding
and
to the many
dedicated and talented teachers
who have brought our textbook
to life for their students.

Donald E. Kieso, Ph.D., CPA, received his bachelor's degree from Aurora University and his doctorate in accounting from the University of Illinois. He has served as chairman of the Department of Accountancy and is currently the KPMG Peat Marwick Emeritus Professor of Accountancy at Northern Illinois University. He has public accounting experience with Price Waterhouse & Co. (San Francisco and Chicago) and Arthur Andersen & Co. (Chicago) and research experience with the Research Division of the American Institute of Certified Public Accountants (New York). He has done postdoctorate work as a Visiting Scholar at the University of California at Berkeley and is a recipient of NIU's Teaching Excellence Award and four Golden Apple Teaching Awards (1986, 1990, 1992, and 1994). Professor Kieso is the author of other accounting and business books and is a member of the American Accounting Association, the American Institute of Certified Public Accountants, and the Illinois CPA Society. He has served as a member of the Board of Directors of the Illinois CPA Society, the Board of Governors of the American Accounting Association's Administrators of Accounting Programs Group, the AACSB's Accounting Accreditation and Visitation Committees, the State of Illinois Comptroller's Commission, as Secretary-Treasurer of the Federation of Schools of Accountancy, and as Secretary-Treasurer of the American Accounting Association. Professor Kieso is currently serving as vice-chairman of the Board of Trustees and Executive Committee of Aurora University, the Boards of Directors of Castle BancGroup Inc., the Sandwich State Bank, Treasurer and director of Sandwich Community Hospital and committees of the Illinois CPA Society. From 1989 to 1993 he served as a charter member of the national Accounting Education Change Commission. In 1988 he received the Outstanding Accounting Educator Award from the Illinois CPA Society, in 1992 he received the FSA's Joseph A. Silvoso Award of Merit and the NIU Foundation's Humanitarian Award for Service to Higher Education, and in 1995 he received a Distinguished Service Award from the Illinois CPA Society.

Jerry J. Weygandt, Ph.D., CPA, is Arthur Andersen Alumni Professor of Accounting at the University of Wisconsin–Madison. He holds a Ph.D. in accounting from the University of Illinois. Articles by Professor Weygandt have appeared in the *Accounting Review, Journal of Accounting Research*, the *Journal of Accountancy*, and other professional journals. These articles have examined such financial reporting issues as accounting for price-level adjustments, pensions, convertible securities, stock option contracts, and interim reports. He is the author of three other textbooks, *Accounting Principles, Financial Accounting*, and *Cases in Financial Accounting*. He is a member of the American Accounting Association, the American Institute of Certified Public Accountants, and the Wisconsin Society of Certified Public Accountants. He has served on numerous committees of the American Accounting Association, including Chair of the Financial Reporting Standards Committee. Professor Weygandt has also served as Secretary-Treasurer and President of the American Accounting Association and has been a member of the editorial board of the *Accounting Review*. In addition, he has been a member of the Accounting Standards Executive Committee of the American Institute of Certified Public Accounting and has served on task forces of that organization related to income taxes, stock options, and impairments. Presently he is chair of the AICPA's Financial Reporting Coordinating Committee related to business reporting. Professor Weygandt is currently serving as a trustee of the Financial Accounting Foundation, as a member of the Board of Directors of M&I Bank of Southern Wisconsin and the Board of Directors of the Dean Foundation. He has received various teaching awards including the Chancellor's Award for Excellence in Teaching. Recently he received the Wisconsin Institute of CPA's Outstanding Educator's Award and Lifetime Achievement Award.

I n early 1996 we began working on the ninth edition of *Intermediate Accounting*. One of the many changes that we considered was finding and including a new, modern set of specimen financial statements for students to refer to and analyze. Out of the stack of hundreds of companies we examined one jumped out—Intel.

As Intel releases each new microchip, you can be sure that it reflects the industry's rapid-fire pace of change and increasingly diversified needs. This is also true of this new edition of *Intermediate Accounting*. We have conducted extensive market research, including instructor focus groups, student focus groups, telesessions, direct mail surveys, and one-on-one discussions with practitioners to help us focus on how this text should evolve. As a result, we have thoroughly revised and updated the text to include all the latest developments in the accounting profession. We have also addressed the important recommendations of the Accounting Education Change Commission for involving students more in the learning process.

Continuing to keep pace with the complexities of the modern business enterprise and professional accounting pronouncements, we have added new topics, deleted some obsolete material, clarified some of the existing coverage, added numerous illustrations, and updated material where necessary. To provide the instructor with greater flexibility in choosing topics to cover or omit, we have continued the use of judiciously selected appendices. The appendices are concerned primarily with complex subjects, less commonly used methods, or specialized topics.

Benefiting from the comments and recommendations of adopters of our eighth edition, we have made significant revisions. Explanations have been expanded where necessary, complicated discussions and illustrations have been simplified; realism has been integrated to heighten interest and relevancy; and new topics and coverage have been added to maintain currency. We have even deleted some eighth edition coverage and condensed the coverage of other topics.

Accountants must act as well as think; therefore, we believe it is important for students to understand the *how* as well as the *why*. The study of concepts develops an understanding of procedures, and the performance of procedures enriches an understanding of the concepts. We have therefore balanced our coverage so the conceptual discussion and procedural presentation are mutually reinforcing.

We believe that individuals learn to account for and analyze financial events and phenomena best if they fully understand the nature of the business transactions and comprehend the behavioral and economic consequences of the events for which firms account and report. The ability to critically evaluate accounting alternatives and their consequences is important. Throughout this revision, we have provided coverage to help students develop a real understanding of how accounting can be used to make effective financial decisions.

❖ NEW FEATURES

Based on extensive reviews, focus groups, and interactions with other intermediate accounting instructors and students, we have developed a number of new pedagogical features and content changes designed both to help students learn more effectively and to answer the changing needs of the course.

New Chapter Openings: We have revised the chapter openings to increase student interest and to draw readers into the chapter more quickly. These openings consist of two parts:

Chapter-opening vignettes: The chapter openings, most of which are new in this edition, tell stories about accounting experiences of real-world companies. These stories provide a real-world context that helps motivate student interest in the chapter topic.

Chapter preview and outline: A chapter preview further ties the chapter topic to the opening story and explains the importance of the chapter topic. A graphic outline presents a visual "roadmap" of the important topics covered in the chapter.

New "Using Your Judgment" Features:

In the eighth edition, we introduced a new Using Your Judgment section in the end-of-chapter assignment materials. This section contains assignments that help develop students' analytical, critical thinking, and interpersonal communication skills. These materials met with wide acceptance and praise in the market, and in this edition we have added some new features, which will give instructors even more choice of materials with which to develop student abilities. These include the following:

Financial Statement Analysis Case: Each case introduces a real-world company and discusses how financial transactions affect their financial statements. Often, an assessment of the company's liquidity, solvency, or financial profitability is performed.

Comparative Analysis Case: The Coca-Cola Company and PepsiCo, Inc., are compared in relation to the topic(s) discussed in the chapter. Each comparative analysis case provides an opportunity to analyze two well-known companies. The Coca-Cola and PepsiCo. financial statements are available on our Web site encouraging students to use the Internet in this course.

Research Case: Each research case provides an opportunity for the student to conduct independent research into an accounting topic related to the chapter content. In many cases, the student must access a data base (sometimes involving use of the Internet) to find the necessary information.

Integration of Financial Statement Analysis:

By understanding the accounting processes that generate statements and the tools required to analyze these statements, students learn to look beyond the numbers. Financial ratios are covered early in the text in an appendix to Chapter 5 to enhance teaching flexibility and enable instructors who want earlier coverage to have access to it when they need it. Ratio analysis is also woven throughout the text to expose students to the significance of economic events.

Conceptual Overview of the Statement of Cash Flows:

An early conceptual overview of the statement of cash flows emphasizes the increasingly important role this statement is taking in today's business and explains to students the reasons behind the mechanics, that is, the "why" behind the "how." In addition, students will find comprehensive coverage of the statement in Chapter 24, "Statement of Cash Flows."

Internet Resources:

Together with Wiley, we have developed a new Web site dedicated to our users, both students and instructors. Using the address **http://www.wiley.com/college/kieso** you can access an array of valuable resources, including, but not limited to, the following:

Real company disclosures: Denoted by our Web site icon in the margin of the text, additional disclosures can be viewed and downloaded from our Web site. These disclosures relate directly to and help to illustrate topics discussed throughout the text.

Coca-Cola Company and PepsiCo, Inc.: Pertinent financial information related to these two companies can be found on our Web site for comparison and analysis purposes.

Expanded discussions: Amplified discussions of such subjects as interest capitalization and transfer of receivables can be found on our Web site.

Additional homework problems: Students will find additional problems to work, as well as their solution, on our site. Our Web site icon appears in the margin of the end-of-chapter material when additional problems are available on site.

Instructor's course management system: This system, provided by Of Course!, includes an on-line gradebook, a national bench marking and recognition system, a course opinion survey tool, and a web-based feedback mechanism that allows the instructor to collect feedback from students.

The Accounting Workshop: An on-line magazine aimed at the interests of both college students and professors, this feature is designed to entertain, stimulate, and inform by providing original articles relating to various accounting topics and current events.

Whitepeak Corporation Module: One of the recommendations of the Accounting Education Change Commission is that students become more involved in their own learning process. We thoroughly embrace this concept and provide a new simulation to address AECC recommendations. Several paragraphs at the end of most chapters tie into a computer simulation of a company called Whitepeak Corporation. This brief presentation explains Whitepeak's accounting situation as it relates to the chapter topic. Students can then complete the Whitepeak module on their own disk, applying intermediate accounting concepts to prepare, correct, adjust, analyze, and extend accounting procedures at Whitepeak. The simulation's programming allows instructors easily to grade and track students' progress from their own PC, making the assignment of computer problems simple to manage and flexible enough to use as group or individual self-paced exercises.

Brief Exercises: New exercises that focus students on one study objective or topic have been added to the end-of-chapter material.

❖ ENHANCED FEATURES

Real-World Emphasis: We believe that one of the goals of the Intermediate Accounting course is to orient students to the application of accounting principles and techniques in practice. Accordingly, we have continued our practice of using numerous examples from real corporations throughout the text. Many illustrations and exhibits are excerpts from actual financial statements of existing firms, including the 1995 annual report of Intel Corporation, in Appendix 5B. We believe Intel's financial statements are packed with important—and interesting—information that students will be motivated to analyze. We thought it appropriate to include Intel's newest product, the MMX pentium chip, on the cover of our text. In doing so, we welcome Intel to the book.

"Perspectives": We have retained the interviews with prominent accounting and business personalities on relevant accounting topics, which give a real-world emphasis so important for students in the intermediate accounting course who are getting more serious about choosing accounting as a career. In the ninth edition, we have updated a number of interviews from the eighth edition and added new interviews with accounting professionals as well as with young accountants who describe their transitions from school into the business world in interviews entitled "From Classroom to Career."

International Insights: In the eighth edition, we added marginal International Insight paragraphs that describe or compare the accounting practices in other countries. In this edition, we have continued this feature to bring them up to date with changing international accounting practices.

Streamlined Presentation: We have continued our efforts to keep the topical coverage of *Intermediate Accounting* in line with the way instructors are currently teaching the course. Accordingly, we have moved some optional topics into appendices and have omitted altogether some topics that formerly were covered in appendices, moving them to our Web site. Details are noted in the list of specific content changes below.

Currency and Accuracy: Accounting continually changes as its environment changes; an up-to-date book is therefore a necessity. As in past editions, we have striven to make this edition the most up-to-date and accurate text available.

❖ CONTENT CHANGES

The following list outlines the revisions and improvements made in chapters of the ninth edition.

Chapter 1 Financial Accounting and Accounting Standards

- ❖ New section on accounting and capital allocation
- ❖ New section on challenges facing accounting
- ❖ Revised and expanded discussion of international accounting standards

Chapter 2 Conceptual Framework Underlying Financial Accounting

- ❖ Increased emphasis on fair value accounting

Chapter 3 The Accounting Information System

- ❖ Revised discussion of the trial balance
- ❖ Revised and streamlined discussion of adjusting entries.

Chapter 4 Income Statement and Related Information

- ❖ New section on the statement of stockholders' equity, including subsections on the retained earnings statement and appropriations of retained earnings, and new material on other comprehensive income, with presentation of alternative formats

Chapter 5 Balance Sheet and Statement of Cash Flows

- ❖ New section on the usefulness of the cash flows statement, including two financial ratios and coverage of free cash flows
- ❖ Simplified discussion of contingencies
- ❖ Expanded discussion of disclosure of accounting policies, including addition of a sample disclosure of significant risks and uncertainties
- ❖ New chapter-ending appendix on ratio analysis

Chapter 6 Accounting and the Time Value of Money

- ❖ Variables standardized to be consistent with the notations used in finance and terminology simplified

Chapter 7 Cash and Receivables

- ❖ Discussion of cash controls moved to chapter appendix
- ❖ New integrated discussion of analysis of receivables (accounts receivable turnover ratio)
- ❖ Revised discussion of sales of receivables (specifically, transfers with recourse), with new illustration of accounting for transfers of receivables to reflect FASB 125

Chapter 8 Valuation of Inventories: A Cost Basis Approach

- ❖ LIFO reserve coverage moved from chapter appendix and integrated into the body of the chapter

Chapter 9 Inventories: Additional Valuation Issues

- ❖ New section on analysis of inventories

Chapter 10 Acquisition and Disposition of Property, Plant, and Equipment

- ❖ Appendix on special situation of interest capitalization has been deleted

Chapter 11 Depreciation, Impairments, and Depletion

- ❖ Simplified presentation of special depreciation methods by deleting the inventory method, the retirement and replacement methods (now covered in a footnote), and the compound interest methods
- ❖ Coverage of income tax depreciation moved to chapter appendix
- ❖ New (updated) illustration of disclosure of property, plant, and equipment
- ❖ New (updated) illustration of presentation of disclosure of natural resources
- ❖ New discussion of the effect of FASB No. 121 on U.S. oil companies

Chapter 12 Intangible Assets

- ❖ New vignette addressing the hot issue of valuing soft assets, such as knowledge
- ❖ Deleted section on property rights
- ❖ Deleted example of balance sheet presentation of intangibles with contra valuation account
- ❖ Updated appendix for new exposure draft on software accounting

Chapter 13 Current Liabilities and Contingencies

- ❖ Simplified discussion and coverage of short-term debt expected to be refinanced
- ❖ New material on gain contingencies, including an illustration
- ❖ Expanded discussion of self-insurance, including an illustration of self-insurance disclosure (merged from Chapter 16)
- ❖ Merged coverage of contingent liabilities from Chapter 5

Chapter 14 Long-Term Liabilities

- ❖ Streamlined coverage by deleting discussion of defeasance (in-coverage defeasance reduced and moved into a footnote) and moving coverage of financial instruments and derivatives to Chapter 18
- ❖ Revised presentation of long-term debt, including new headings for income statement and balance sheet presentation and note disclosure
- ❖ Added section on ratio analysis of long-term debt

Chapter 15   Stockholders' Equity: Contributed Capital

* ❖ Discussion of the corporate form of organization moved to the beginning of the chapter
* ❖ New illustration on corporate buybacks
* ❖ Revised and expanded discussion of cost method of accounting for treasury stock
* ❖ Par value method moved to chapter appendix; new illustrations to show stockholders' equity with and without treasury stock under par value method
* ❖ Simpler illustration of balance sheet presentation of redeemable preferred stock

Chapter 16   Stockholders' Equity: Retained Earnings

* ❖ Integrated analysis of stockholders' equity
* ❖ New, updated data on dividend payouts added as an illustration
* ❖ Section on self-insurance moved out of this chapter and combined with coverage in Chapter 13
* ❖ Added section on ratio analysis related to stockholders' equity
* ❖ New example of the columnar format for the statement of stockholders' equity

Chapter 17   Dilutive Securities and Earnings Per Share

* ❖ Chapter coverage updated for FASB No. 123, "Accounting for Stock-Based Compensation" and FASB No. 128 "Earnings per Share."

Chapter 18   Investments

* ❖ Moved transfers of investment securities between categories to appendix
* ❖ New appendix on financial instruments with emphasis on derivatives

Chapter 19   Revenue Recognition

Chapter 20   Accounting for Income Taxes

* ❖ Updated illustration of income taxes disclosure (PepsiCo)
* ❖ Updated to emphasize new research findings

Chapter 21   Accounting for Pensions and Postretirement Benefits

* ❖ Updated discussion of pensions plans, including updated statistical data
* ❖ New illustration of note disclosure for pensions
* ❖ Discussion of disclosure effectiveness related to pensions

Chapter 22   Accounting for Leases

* ❖ Discussion of sale-leaseback moved to chapter appendix
* ❖ Deleted appendix on leveraged leases

Chapter 23   Accounting Changes and Error Analysis

* ❖ Updated research and statistical data on types and disclosures of changes

Chapter 24   Statement of Cash Flows

* ❖ Condensed introductory historical discussion

Chapter 25 Full Disclosure in Financial Reporting

❖ New discussion of segment reportings, disaggregations
❖ Enhanced coverage of safe harbor provisions and financial instruments
❖ New coverage of nonfinancial measures of performance

❖ END-OF-CHAPTER ASSIGNMENT MATERIAL

At the end of each chapter we have provided a comprehensive set of review and homework material consisting of questions, exercises, problems, and short cases. For this edition, many of the exercises and problems have been revised, and a new feature—a separate category of brief exercises—has been added to each chapter. In addition, the Using Your Judgment sections, which include financial reporting problems, writing assignments, group assignments, and ethics cases, have been substantially revised and expanded with the addition of three new types of case studies: financial statement analysis cases, comparative analysis cases, and research cases. All of the assignment materials have been class tested and/or double checked for accuracy and clarity.

The questions are designed for review, self-testing, and classroom discussion purposes as well as homework assignments. Typically, a brief exercise covers one topic, an exercise one or two topics. Exercises require less time and effort to solve than cases and problems. The problems are designed to develop a professional level of achievement and are more challenging and time consuming to solve than the exercises. Those exercises and problems that are contained in the *Lotus Problems* supplements are identified by a blue computer disk icon in the margin. The cases generally require essay as opposed to quantitative solutions; they are intended to confront the student with situations calling for conceptual analysis and the exercise of judgment in identifying problems and evaluating alternatives. The Using Your Judgment assignments are designed to develop students' critical thinking, analytical, interpersonal, and communication skills.

The new Whitepeak Corporation computer-based simulation also provides an opportunity for students to apply intermediate accounting concepts to prepare, correct, adjust, analyze, and extend accounting procedures at Whitepeak, a fictional conglomerate. A narrative at the end of applicable chapters reminds the student to complete the computer module. The simulation's programming allows instructors to grade and track students' progress easily from their own PC, providing enough flexibility for use as group or individual self-paced exercises.

Probably no more than one-fourth of the total case, exercise, and problem material must be used to cover the subject matter adequately; consequently, problem assignment may be varied from year to year.

❖ COLOR DESIGN

The color design not only enlivens the textbook's appearance, but, through planned and consistent usage, eases learning. Note that financial statements are presented in blue-toned color with a beige header. Trial balances, work sheets, and large schedules and exhibits are presented in beige with blue headings. Most small illustrations, demonstrations, and excerpts from notes accompanying financial statements are beige colored/blue trim boxes. Significant amounts and descriptions within either blue or beige colored boxes are highlighted in solid blue color. All pages containing assignment material are tabbed with a color bar, while the five interest and annuity tables in Chapter 6 have a beige triangle tab to make it easy to locate and identify them. The names of real-world companies as part of illustrations are red. The color design is summarized as follows:

Red—Real-world company names, secondary headings, and accents

Blue—Financial statements, highlighted amounts and descriptions in boxed illustrations

Beige—Exhibits, schedules, trial balances, work sheets, illustrations, and list of definitions

❖ SUPPLEMENTARY MATERIALS

Accompanying this textbook is an improved and expanded package of student learning aids and instructor teaching aids.

Instructor's Manual: Chs. 1–14
Instructor's Manual: Chs. 15–25

❖ Lecture outlines keyed to text learning objectives
❖ Updated Bibliography
❖ Teaching Transparancy Masters
❖ Section on "How to assign and evaluate ethical issues in the course"
❖ Sections on "How to incorporate writing" and "How to incorporate group (collaborative) work"

Solutions Manual, Vol. I: Chs. 1–14
Solutions Manual, Vol. II: Chs. 15–25

❖ Answers to all questions, brief exercises, exercises, problems and case material provided
❖ Classification Tables categorize the end-of-chapter material by topic to assist in assigning homework
❖ Assignment Tables (characteristics) describe the end-of-chapter material, its difficulty level, and estimated completion time
❖ All solutions triple-checked to ensure accuracy

Test Bank, Vol. I: Chs. 1–14
Test Bank, Vol. II: Chs. 15–25

❖ Essay questions with solutions help you test students' communication skills
❖ Estimated completing times facilitate test planning
❖ Computations for multiple-choice problems assist you in giving partial credit

Computerized Test Bank IBM 3.5"

❖ A large collection of objective questions and exercises with answers for each chapter in the text
❖ Generate questions randomly or manually, and modify/customize tests with your own material
❖ Create multiple versions of the same text by scrambling by type, character, number, or Study Objective

Test Preparation Service
Simply call Wiley's Accounting Hotline (800)541-5602 with the questions you have selected for an exam. Wiley will provide a master exam within 24 hours.

Solution Transparencies, Vol. I: Chs. 1–14
Solution Transparencies, Vol. II: Chs. 15–25

❖ Provided in organizer box with chapter file folders
❖ Large, bold type size for easier class presentation
❖ Provided for all exercises, problems, and cases

Teaching Transparencies

❖ Over 100 color figure illustrations and exhibits
❖ 90% from outside the text

Checklist of Key Figures

Student Study Guide, Vol. I: Chs. 1–14
Student Study Guide, Vol. II: Chs. 15–25

❖ Chapter Learning Objectives
❖ Chapter Outline—a broad overview of general chapter content with space for note-taking in class
❖ Chapter Review with summary of key concepts
❖ Glossary of key terms
❖ Review Questions and Exercises—self-test items with supporting computations

Workpapers, Vol. I: Chs. 1–14
Workpapers, Vol. II: Chs. 15–25
Self-Study Problems/Solutions Book, Vol. I: Chs. 1–14
Self-Study Problems/Solutions Book, Vol. II: Chs. 15–25

❖ Provides additional questions and problems to develop students' problem-solving skills
❖ Explanations assist in the approach, set-up, and completion of problems
❖ Tips alert students to common pitfalls and misconceptions

Lotus Problems 3.5"
Excel Problems 3.5"

❖ Spreadsheet requirements range in difficulty (from data entry to developing spreadsheets)
❖ Review of immediate accounting and Lotus and Excel concepts
❖ Each chapter consists of a basic tutorial, a more advanced tutorial, and two or three problems from the text
❖ Each problem followed by "what-if" questions to build students' analytical skills

Rockford Corporation Computerized Practice Set

❖ This practice set has been designed as a students' review and update of the accounting cycle and the preparation of financial statements

PowerPoint Presentations

❖ Designed to enhance presentation of chapter topics and examples
❖ Separate presentation for each chapter

Instructor's Manual on Disk
Solutions Manual on Disk

❖ Allows you to project, print, and modify material for your course

Instructor's Resource System on CD-ROM

❖ Resource manager with friendly interface for course development and presentation
❖ Includes all instructor supplements, text art, and transparencies

❖ ACKNOWLEDGMENTS

We thank many users of our eighth edition who contributed to this revision through their comments and instructive criticism. Special thanks are extended to the primary reviewers of and contributors to our ninth edition manuscript:

Diana Adcox
University of North Florida

Noel Addy
Mississippi State University

James Bannister
University of Hartford

Kathleen Bauer
Midwestern State University

John C. Borke
University of Wisconsin—Platteville

Eric Carlsen
Kean College of New Jersey

Larry R. Falcetto
Emporia State University

Richard Fern
Eastern Kentucky University

Richard Fleischman
John Carroll University

Clyde Galbraith
West Chester University

Gary Heesacker
Central Washington University

Wayne M. Higley
Buena Vista College

Danny Matthews
Midwestern State University

John Mills
University of Nevada, Reno

Jeffrey D. Ritter
St. Norbert College

James Sander
Butler University

Douglas Sharp
Wichita State University

Keith Smith
George Washington University

Dick Wasson
Southwestern College

Kenneth Wooling
Hampton University

Other colleagues in academe who have provided helpful criticisms and made valuable suggestions as members of a focus group or adopters of the previous edition or reviewers of selected topics include:

Charlene Abendroth
California State University—Hayward

Jon A. Booker
Tennessee Technical University

Suzanne M. Busch
California State University—Hayward

Patrick Delaney
Northern Illinois University

Dean S. Eiteman
Indiana University—Pennsylvania

Larry R. Falcetto
Emporia State University

Stephen L. Fogg
Temple University

Lynford E. Graham
Rutgers University

Marcia L. Halvorsen
University of Cincinnati

Geoffrey R. Horlick
St. Francis College

Cynthia Jeffrey
Iowa State University

Douglas W. Kieso
University of California—Irvine

Paul D. Kimmel
University of Wisconsin—Milwaukee

Martha King
Emporia State University

Henry Le Clerc
Suffolk Community College—Selden Campus

Daphne Main
University of New Orleans

Mohamed E. Moustafa
California State University—Long Beach

Kermit Natho
Georgia State University

Obeau S. Persons
Rider University

John R. Simon
Northern Illinois University

Billy S. Soo
Boston College

Terry Warfield
University of Wisconsin—Madison

Frank F. Weinberg
Golden Gate University

William H. Wilson
Oregon Health University

Shari H. Wescott
Houston Baptist University

Stephen A. Zeff
Rice University

Focus Group Participants

Richard Banham
Tennessee State University

Hank Davis
Eastern Illinois University

Gadis Dillon
Oakland University

David O'Bryan
Pittsburgh State University

Patricia Parker
Columbus State Community College

Barbara Stewart
Towson State University

Bob Turner
Babson College

Dick Wasson
Southwestern College

Telesession Participants

Robert Benjamin
Taylor University

Lee Cartwright
Santa Fe Community College

Michael Doran
Iowa State University

Tom Gilday
Thomas Moore College

Ann Hamilton
University of Oklahoma

LeBrone Harris
University of South Florida

Kathy Heltzel
Luzerne Community College

Barbara Leonard
Loyola University

C. Tommy Moores
University of Nevada—Las Vegas

Claire Purvis
California State University at San Bernadino

David Rees
Southern Utah State College

Jeffrey Ritter
St. Norbert College

Lynn Saubert
Radford University

Keith Smith
Arkansas State University

Rich Sarkisian
Camden Community College

Howard Shapiro
Eastern Washington University

Katherene P. Terrell
University of Central Oklahoma

Phil Thornton
Metropolitan State College

Student Focus Group Participants

University of Kansas
Melissa Hoffman
Sichang Li
Daniel Philips
Brian Sandels
Craig Stebor
Paul Stephens

Baruch College, CUNY
Ann Alverez
Christopher Forczak
Ying Q. Liu
Besa Markovic
Lissette Miranda
Maria Roldan

Quing Samuel
Lian yi Zhu

We would also like to thank those colleagues who contributed to several of the unique features of this edition:

International Notes

Judith Ramaglia, Pacific Lutheran University

Ethics Cases

Bill N. Schwartz, Virginia Commonwealth University
Larry Ponemon, Bentley College
Bruce W. Stuart and Iris Stuart, Concordia College

Underlying Concepts

John Cheever, California State Polytechnic University—Pomona

Writing Assignments

Susan Smith, Northern Illinois University
Katherene P. Terrell and Robert L. Terrell, University of Central Oklahoma

Group Cases/Assignments

Katherene P. Terrell and Robert L. Terrell, University of Central Oklahoma
Terry Warfield, University of Wisconsin—Madison

Perspectives and "From Classroom to Career" Interviews

Stuart Weiss, Stuart Weiss Business Writing, Inc.

Financial Analysis Cases and Problems

Martha King, Emporia State University
Carol M. Fischer, University of Wisconsin—Waukesha

Research Cases

Marc Bauman, University of Wisconsin—Madison

Whitepeak Corporation Modules

Timothy M. Lindquist and Ronald J. Abraham, University of Northern Iowa

Web Site Advisors

Stephen L. Fogg
Temple University

Cynthia Jeffrey
Iowa State University

C. Tommy Moores
University of Nevada—Las Vegas

Elizabeth A. Murphy
DePaul University

Siva Nathan
Georgia State University

Michael G. Welker
Drexel University

Practicing Accountants and Business Executives

From the field of corporate and public accounting, we owe thanks to the following practitioners for their technical advice and for consenting to interviews:

Dennis R. Beresford
Financial Accounting Standards Board

Ron Bernard
NFL Enterprises

Sarah Blake
Technology Management & Development, Inc.

Michael Crooch
Arthur Andersen & Co.

Penelope Flugger
J.P. Morgan & Co.

Darien Griffin
S.C. Johnson Wax

Michelle Lippert
Clifton, Gunderson, & CO.

L. Marton Miller
Cogen Sklar, LLP

David Miniken
Seeney Conrad

Tom Mulflur
Mt. Hood Chemical Corporation

Robert Sack
University of Virginia

Claire Schulte
Deloitte & Touche

Willie Sutton
Mutual Community Savings Bank—Durham, NC

Gary Valenzuela
Yahoo!

Arthur Wyatt
*Arthur Andersen & Co. and
the University of Illinois—Urbana*

Sabina Zaman
Coopers Lybrand—Chicago

Terry D. Warfield of the University of Wisconsin—Madison assisted in the preparation of accounting for stock options and earnings per share (Chapter 17), income taxes (Chapter 20), and accounting for pensions (Chapter 21).

We appreciate the exemplary support and professional commitment given us by the development, marketing, production, and editorial staffs of John Wiley & Sons, including Susan Elbe, Wendy Goldner, Rebecca Hope, David Kear, Rachel Nelson, Cecilia Andersen, Charlotte Hyland, Hilary Newman, Anna Melhorn, Dawn Stanley, and the management and staff at Ruttle, Shaw & Wetherill, Inc. (especially Michael Klinman). A special note of thanks also to Ann Torbert (editorial and content assistance) and Elm Street Publishing Services (specifically Martha Beyerlein, Barb Lange, and Ingrid Mount) for facilitating the production of the manuscript. We also wish to thank Dick Wasson of Southwestern College for coordinating the efforts of the supplements authors and checkers.

We appreciate the cooperation of the American Institute of Certified Public Accountants and the Financial Accounting Standards Board in permitting us to quote from their pronouncements. We thank Intel Corporation for permitting us to use its 1995 Annual Report for our specimen financial statements. We also acknowledge permission from the American Institute of Certified Public Accountants, the Institute of Management Accounting, and the Institute of Internal Auditors to adapt and use material from the Uniform CPA Examinations, the CMA Examinations, and the CIA Examinations, respectively.

If this book helps teachers instill in their students an appreciation for the challenges, worth, and limitations of accounting, if it encourages students to evaluate critically and understand financial accounting theory and practice, and if it prepares students for advanced study, professional examinations, and the successful and ethical pursuit of their careers in accounting or business, then we will have attained our objective.

Suggestions and comments from users of this book will be appreciated.

Somonauk, Illinois   **Donald E. Kieso**
Madison, Wisconsin   **Jerry J. Weygandt**

Brief Contents

Contents

CHAPTER 12
Intangible Assets, *593*

CHAPTER 13
Current Liabilities and Contingencies, *645*

INTERMEDIATE ACCOUNTING

CHAPTER 1

Financial Accounting and Accounting Standards

We've Come a Long Way!

Imagine that you received an annual report from Microsoft, listing net income for the year but not mentioning total revenues. Or that you were looking at IBM's financial statements and saw that it deducted expenses directly from stockholders' equity, thereby transforming a loss for the year into net income. Or that a company like Intel did not provide an annual report at all, and to determine its income, total assets, and other important financial indicators, you would have to ask the company directly for the information.[1]

Impossible? Unheard of? Wouldn't happen? Today, that's true, but these types of shenanigans occurred in the early 1900s. It was not until after the Great Depression, when Congress established the Securities and Exchange Commission, that formal reporting requirements were adopted. Even when activated, the Securities and Exchange oversight was limited to selected companies. For example, over-the-counter companies were not subject to extensive disclosure rules until 1964.

Before financial reporting laws came along in the 1930s, many companies followed the practice of reporting net income without even hinting at gross revenue; among them were Alcoa, Standard Oil of New York (now Mobil), Union Carbide, and United Fruit (now United Brands). Amoskeag Manufacturing, then the largest cotton mill in the world, showed an income statement largely in yards rather than dollars. Although some people find weaknesses in today's financial reporting practices, remember they used to be a lot worse—and still are in some foreign lands.

---

[1]Adapted from Laura Jereski, "You've Come a Long Way, Shareholder," *Forbes,* July 13, 1987.

As the opening story indicates, our financial reporting system has changed greatly in this century. It will continue to change in the future. The business world is experiencing unprecedented challenges, such as globalization, deregulation, and computerization, to name just a few. In the middle of this changing business world is the accounting profession which needs, and is expected, to provide relevant and reliable information so that our capital markets work efficiently.

The purpose of this chapter is to explain the environment of financial reporting and the many factors affecting it. The content and organization of the chapter are as follows:

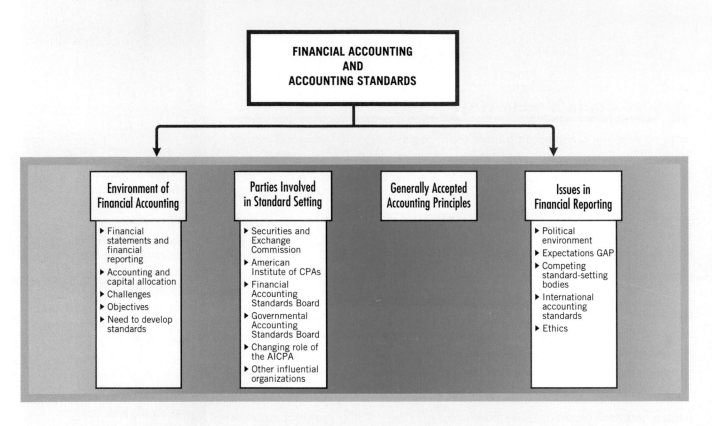

❖ THE ENVIRONMENT OF FINANCIAL ACCOUNTING

Like other human activities and disciplines, accounting is largely a product of its environment. The environment of accounting consists of social-economic-political-legal conditions, restraints, and influences that vary from time to time. As a result, accounting objectives and practices are not the same today as they were in the past. **Accounting theory has evolved to meet changing demands and influences.**

Accounting may best be defined by describing the three essential characteristics of accounting: (1) **identification, measurement, and communication of financial information about** (2) **economic entities to** (3) **interested persons**. These characteristics have described accounting for hundreds of years. Yet, in the last 60 years economic entities have increased so greatly in size and complexity, and the interested persons have increased so greatly in number and diversity, that the responsibility placed on the accounting profession is greater today than ever before.

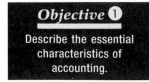

Objective ❶

Describe the essential characteristics of accounting.

Financial Statements and Financial Reporting

Financial accounting is the process that culminates in the preparation of financial reports on the enterprise as a whole for use by parties both internal and external to the enterprise. Users of these financial reports include investors, creditors, managers, unions, and government agencies. In contrast, managerial accounting is the process of identifying, measuring, analyzing, and communicating financial information needed by management to plan, evaluate, and control an organization's operations.

Financial statements are the principal means through which financial information is communicated to those outside an enterprise. These statements provide the firm's history quantified in money terms. The financial statements most frequently provided are (1) the balance sheet, (2) the income statement, (3) the statement of cash flows, and (4) the statement of owners' or stockholders' equity. In addition, note disclosures are an integral part of each financial statement.

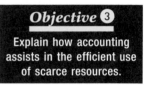

Objective ❷

Identify the major financial statements and other means of financial reporting.

Some financial information is better provided, or can be provided only, by means of financial reporting other than formal financial statements. Examples include the president's letter or supplementary schedules in the corporate annual report, prospectuses, reports filed with government agencies, news releases, management's forecasts, and descriptions of an enterprise's social or environmental impact. Such information may be required by authoritative pronouncement, regulatory rule, or custom; or because management wishes to disclose it voluntarily. The primary focus of this textbook concerns the development of two types of financial information: the basic financial statements and related disclosures.

Accounting and Capital Allocation

Because resources are limited, people try to conserve them, to use them effectively, and to identify and encourage those who can make efficient use of them. Through an efficient use of resources, our standard of living increases.

Objective ❸

Explain how accounting assists in the efficient use of scarce resources.

Markets, free enterprise, and competition—not a committee of social engineers—determine whether a business is to be successful and thrive. This fact places a substantial burden on the accounting profession to measure performance accurately and fairly on a timely basis, so that the right managers and companies are able to attract investment capital. For example, accounting enables investors and creditors to compare the income and assets employed by such companies as IBM, McDonald's, Microsoft, and Ford. As a result, they can assess the relative return and risks associated with investment opportunities and thereby channel resources more effectively. This process of capital allocation works as follows:

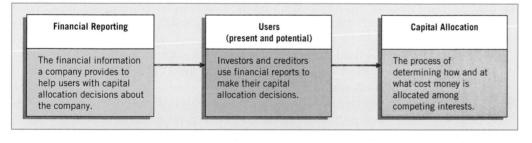

ILLUSTRATION 1-1
Capital Allocation
Process

Financial Reporting	Users (present and potential)	Capital Allocation
The financial information a company provides to help users with capital allocation decisions about the company.	Investors and creditors use financial reports to make their capital allocation decisions.	The process of determining how and at what cost money is allocated among competing interests.

An effective process of capital allocation is critical to a healthy economy, which promotes productivity, encourages innovation, and provides an efficient and liquid market for buying and selling securities and obtaining and granting credit.[2] To provide unreliable and irrelevant information leads to poor capital allocation which adversely affects the securities markets.

---

[2]AICPA Special Committee on Financial Reporting, "Improving Business Reporting—A Customer Focus," *Journal of Accountancy*, Supplement, October 1994.

The accounting numbers that are reported affect the transfer of resources among companies and individuals. Consider the following example: Companies recently were required to record retirement benefits as liabilities. As a result of this new requirement, General Motors (GM) had to record a new liability of $36 billion for health care costs, which reduced its stockholders' equity from $42 billion to $6 billion! It is no surprise that GM and many other companies resisted the new requirement and that, once it was adopted, they are now making changes to their medical benefit plans.

Accounting for investment securities provides another illustration. Prior to 1993, these securities were often carried at historical cost on the balance sheet. Under this standard, the savings and loan (S&L) industry reported a positive stockholders' equity of approximately $38 billion. If the S&L industry had reported the investment securities at market value, it is estimated the stockholders' equity could have been as low as a *negative* $118 billion. If Congress had known these figures, it is quite possible that the industry would not have been deregulated, and U.S. taxpayers would have been saved the cost of the eventual $200 billion bailout of the S&L industry.

The Challenges Facing Financial Accounting

Much is right about financial reporting in the United States. We presently have the most liquid, deep, secure, and efficient public capital markets of any country at any time in history. One reason for this success is that our financial statements and related disclosures have captured and organized financial information in a useful and reliable fashion. However, much still needs to be done. For example, you were probably surprised to learn in reading the opening story that early in this century many companies did not report revenue numbers. Now, suppose you could move to the turn of the next century, say 2100, and look back at financial reporting today. Here is what you might read:

❶ *Non-financial Measurements.* Financial reports in the late 1990s failed to provide some key performance measures widely used by management. For example, non-financial measures such as customer satisfaction indexes, backlog information, and reject rates on goods purchased, all now used to evaluate the long-term stability of the company, were provided on an ad hoc basis, if at all.

❷ *Forward-looking Information.* Financial reports failed to provide forward-looking information needed by present and potential investors and creditors. One individual noted that financial statements in the 1990s ought to start with the phrase, "Once upon a time," to signify their use of historical cost and their accumulation of past events.

❸ *Soft Assets.* Financial reports focused on hard assets (inventory, plant assets) but failed to provide much information on a company's soft assets (intangibles). For example, Microsoft, whose market value was in excess of $30 billion, reported less than $5 billion in total hard assets. Drug companies, such as Baxter, did not report any assets related to their new product breakthroughs. The value of the human resources for companies was not reported.

❹ *Timeliness.* Financial statements were prepared only quarterly, and audited financials were provided annually. Little to no real-time financial statement information was available.

We believe each of these challenges must be met for the accounting profession to continue to provide the type of information needed for an efficient capital allocation process. Already a blue-ribbon committee has suggested that in the future financial statements should include the following:[3]

---

[3]AICPA Special Committee on Financial Reporting, *op. cit.*

ILLUSTRATION 1-2
Financial Reporting in
the Future

Financial and nonfinancial data
- Financial statements and related disclosures.
- High-level operating data and performance measurements that management uses to manage the business.

Management's analysis
- Reasons for changes in the financial, operating, and performance-related data, and the identity and past effects of key trends.

Forward-looking information
- Opportunities and risks, including those resulting from key trends.
- Management's plans, including critical success factors.
- Comparison of actual business performance to previously disclosed forward-looking information.

Information about management and shareholders
- Directors, management, compensation, major shareholders, and transactions and relationships among related parties.

Background about the company
- Broad objectives and strategies.
- Scope and description of business and properties.
- Impact of industry structure on the company.

Changes in these directions would broaden the focus from financial reporting to business reporting.

Objectives of Financial Reporting

In an attempt to establish a foundation for financial accounting and reporting, the accounting profession identified a set of objectives of financial reporting by business enterprises. Financial reporting should provide information:

(a) that is useful to present and potential investors and creditors and other users **in making rational investment, credit, and similar decisions**. The information should be comprehensible to those who have a **reasonable understanding** of business and economic activities and are willing to study the information with reasonable diligence.

(b) to help present and potential investors and creditors and other users **in assessing the amounts, timing, and uncertainty of prospective cash receipts** from dividends or interest and the proceeds from the sale, redemption, or maturity of securities or loans. Since investors' and creditors' cash flows are related to enterprise cash flows, financial reporting should provide information to help investors, creditors, and others assess the amounts, timing, and uncertainty of prospective net cash inflows to the related enterprise.

(c) about the economic resources of an enterprise, the claims to those resources (obligations of the enterprise to transfer resources to other entities and owners' equity), and the effects of transactions, events, and circumstances that change its resources and claims to those resources.[4]

In brief, the objectives of financial reporting are to provide (1) information that is useful in investment and credit decisions, (2) information that is useful in assessing cash flow prospects, and (3) information about enterprise resources, claims to those resources, and changes in them.

The emphasis on "assessing cash flow prospects" might lead one to suppose that the cash basis is preferred over the accrual basis of accounting. That is not the case. Information based on **accrual accounting generally provides a better indication of an**

Objective 5
Identify the objectives of financial reporting.

**INTERNATIONAL
INSIGHT**

The objectives of financial reporting differ across nations. Traditionally, the primary objective of accounting in many continental European nations and in Japan was conformity with the law. In contrast, Canada, the U.K., the Netherlands, and many other nations have shared the U.S. view that the primary objective is to provide information for investors. Insights into international standards and practices will be presented throughout the text.

---

[4]"Objectives of Financial Reporting by Business Enterprises," *Statement of Financial Accounting Concepts No. 1* (Stamford, Conn.: FASB, November 1978), pars. 5–8.

enterprise's present and continuing ability to generate favorable cash flows than does information limited to the financial effects of cash receipts and payments.[5]

Recall from your first accounting course that the objective of accrual basis accounting is to ensure that events that change an entity's financial statements are recorded in the periods in which the events occur, rather than only in the periods in which the entity receives or pays cash. Using the accrual basis to determine net income means recognizing revenues when earned rather than when cash is received, and recognizing expenses when incurred rather than when paid. Under accrual accounting, revenues, for the most part, are recognized when sales are made so they can be related to the economic environment of the period in which they occurred. Over the long run, trends in revenues are generally more meaningful than trends in cash receipts.

The Need to Develop Standards

Objective ❻

Explain the need for accounting standards.

The main controversy in setting accounting standards is "Whose rules should we play by, and what should they be?" The answer is not immediately clear because the users of financial accounting statements have both coinciding and conflicting needs for information of various types. To meet these needs, and to satisfy the fiduciary[6] reporting responsibility of management, a single set of **general-purpose financial statements** is prepared. These statements are expected to present fairly, clearly, and completely the economic facts of the existence and operations of the enterprise. **In preparing financial statements, accountants are confronted with the potential dangers of bias, misinterpretation, inexactness, and ambiguity.** In order to minimize these dangers, the accounting profession has attempted to develop a set of standards that is generally accepted and universally practiced. Without these standards, each enterprise would have to develop its own standards, and readers of financial statements would have to familiarize themselves with every company's peculiar accounting and reporting practices. As a result, it would be almost impossible to prepare statements that could be compared.

The accounting profession has adopted a common set of standards and procedures called **generally accepted accounting principles (GAAP)**. The term "generally accepted" can mean either that an authoritative accounting rule-making body has established a principle of reporting in a given area or that over time a given practice has been accepted as appropriate because of its universal application.[7] Although principles and practices have provoked both debate and criticism, most members of the financial community recognize them as the standards and procedures that over time have proven to be most useful. A more extensive discussion of what constitutes GAAP is presented later in this chapter.

🌐 INTERNATIONAL INSIGHT

Nations also differ in the degree to which they have developed national standards and consistent accounting practices. One indicator of the level of a nation's accounting is the nature of the accounting profession within the country. Professional accounting bodies were established in the Netherlands, the U.K., Canada, and the U.S. in the nineteenth century. In contrast, public accountancy bodies were established in Hong Kong, Singapore, and Korea only in the last half century.

❖ PARTIES INVOLVED IN STANDARD SETTING

A number of organizations are instrumental in the development of financial accounting standards (GAAP) in the United States. The major organizations are as follows:

Objective ❼

Identify the major policy-setting bodies and their role in the standard-setting process.

❶ Securities and Exchange Commission (SEC)
❷ American Institute of Certified Public Accountants (AICPA)

---

[5]*SFAC No. 1*, p. iv. As used here, cash flow means "cash generated and used in operations." The term **cash flows** is frequently used also to include cash obtained by borrowing and used to repay borrowing, cash used for investments in resources and obtained from the disposal of investments, and cash contributed by or distributed to owners.

[6]Management's responsibility to manage assets with care and trust is its **fiduciary** responsibility.

[7]The terms **principles** and **standards** are used interchangeably in practice and throughout this textbook.

❸ Financial Accounting Standards Board (FASB)
❹ Governmental Accounting Standards Board (GASB)
❺ Other influential organizations

Securities and Exchange Commission (SEC)

As indicated in the opening story, the disclosure of financial information prior to 1930 was limited. Prior to 1900, for example, single ownership was the predominant form of business organization in our economy. Financial reports emphasized solvency and liquidity and were limited to internal use and scrutiny by banks and other lending institutions. From 1900 to 1929, the growth of large corporations, with their absentee ownership, led to increasing investment and speculation in corporate stock. Unfortunately, after a couple of days on which stock prices dropped rapidly, both individual and institutional investors panicked, and sold over 16 million shares of stock at huge losses. The stock market crashed in 1929 and contributed to the Great Depression.

As a result of these events, the federal government established the **Securities and Exchange Commission (SEC)** to help develop and standardize financial information presented to stockholders. The SEC is a federal agency. It administers the Securities Exchange Act of 1934 and several other acts. Most companies that issue securities to the public or are listed on a stock exchange are required to file audited financial statements with the SEC. In addition, the SEC has broad powers to prescribe, in whatever detail it desires, the accounting practices and standards to be employed by companies that fall within its jurisdiction. As a result, the SEC exercises oversight over 12,000 companies that are listed on the major exchanges (such as the New York Stock Exchange and the American Stock Exchange). The SEC filing requirements[8] and accounting opinions are published in: (1) its Financial Reporting Releases (FRRs),[9] (2) Regulation S-X, which contains instructions and forms for filing financial statements, and (3) decisions on cases coming before the SEC.

> 🌐 **INTERNATIONAL INSIGHT**
>
> The International Organization of Securities Commissions (IOSCO) is a group of more than 100 securities regulatory agencies or securities exchanges from all over the world. IOSCO has existed since 1987. Collectively, its members represent about 85% of the world's capital markets. The SEC is a member of IOSCO.

Public/Private Partnership

At the time the SEC was created, no group—public or private—was issuing accounting standards. The SEC encouraged the creation of a private standard-setting body because it believed that the private sector had the resources and talent to develop appropriate accounting standards. As a result, accounting standards have generally developed in the private sector either through the American Institute of Certified Public Accountants (AICPA) or the Financial Accounting Standards Board (FASB).

The SEC has affirmed its support for the FASB by indicating that financial statements conforming to standards set by the FASB will be presumed to have substantial authoritative support. In short, the SEC requires registrants to adhere to GAAP. In addition, it has indicated in its reports to Congress that "it continues to believe that the initiative for establishing and improving accounting standards should remain in the private sector, subject to Commission oversight."

---

[8]The Securities Acts require that companies issuing securities file registration statements and periodic reports with the SEC. Most commercial and industrial companies file a *Form S-1* registration statement upon the initial issuance of securities. (Forms S-2 through S-18 are filed by companies in certain specialized industries.) *Form 10-K* is the annual report form required to be filed and *Form 10-Q* the report that must be filed for the first three quarters of each fiscal year. *Form 8-K* must be filed after the occurrence of a material event. Regulation S-K requires nonfinancial information, such as the Management Discussion and Analysis, to be reported.

[9]Prior to 1982 these pronouncements were referred to as Accounting Series Releases (ASRs). The SEC has changed the title of new releases to better reflect their nature and to differentiate FRRs (nonenforcement, nondisciplinary type releases) from the new AAERs (accounting and auditing enforcement releases, which are disciplinary in nature).

SEC Oversight

The SEC's partnership with the private sector has worked well. The SEC has acted with remarkable restraint in the area of developing accounting standards. Generally, it has relied on the AICPA and FASB to regulate the accounting profession and develop and enforce accounting standards.

Over its history, however, the SEC's involvement in the development of accounting standards has varied. In some cases the private sector has attempted to establish a standard, but the SEC has refused to accept it. In other cases it has prodded the private sector into taking quicker action on certain reporting problems, such as accounting for investments in debt and equity securities and the reporting of financial derivatives. In still other situations the commission communicates problems to the FASB, responds to FASB exposure drafts, and provides the FASB with counsel and advice upon request.

The SEC has the mandate to establish accounting principles. The private sector, therefore, must listen carefully to the views of the SEC. In some sense the private sector is the formulator and the implementor of the standards.[10] The partnership appears to be a good one.

Enforcement

As indicated earlier, companies listed on a stock exchange are required to submit their financial statements to the SEC. If the SEC believes that an accounting or disclosure irregularity exists regarding the form or content of the financial statements, it sends a deficiency letter to the company. Usually these deficiency letters are resolved quickly. However, if disagreement continues, the SEC has the power to issue a "stop order," which prevents the registrant from issuing securities or trading securities on the exchanges. Criminal charges may also be brought by the Department of Justice for violations of certain laws. The SEC program, private sector initiatives, and civil and criminal litigation help to ensure the integrity of financial reporting for public companies.

American Institute of Certified Public Accountants (AICPA)

As indicated earlier, the American Institute of Certified Public Accountants (AICPA), the national professional organization of practicing Certified Public Accountants (CPAs), has been vital to the development of GAAP. Various committees and boards established since the founding of the AICPA have contributed to this effort.

Committee on Accounting Procedure

At the urging of the SEC, the AICPA appointed the Committee on Accounting Procedure in 1939. The Committee on Accounting Procedure (CAP), composed of practicing CPAs, issued 51 Accounting Research Bulletins (see list on inside of front cover) dealing with a variety of timely accounting problems during the years 1939 to 1959. But this problem-by-problem approach failed to provide the structured body of accounting principles that was both needed and desired. In response, in 1959 the AICPA created the Accounting Principles Board.

Accounting Principles Board

The major purposes of the Accounting Principles Board (APB) were (1) to advance the written expression of accounting principles, (2) to determine appropriate practices, and (3) to narrow the areas of difference and inconsistency in practice. To achieve these

---

[10]One writer has described the relationship of the FASB and SEC and the development of financial reporting standards using the analogy of a pearl. The pearl (financial reporting standard) "is formed by the reaction of certain oysters (FASB) to an irritant (the SEC)—usually a grain of sand—that becomes embedded inside the shell. The oyster coats this grain with layers of nacre, and ultimately a pearl is formed. The pearl is a joint result of the irritant (SEC) and oyster (FASB); without both, it cannot be created." John C. Burton, "Government Regulation of Accounting and Information," *Journal of Accountancy* (June, 1982).

objectives, its mission was to develop an overall conceptual framework to assist in the resolution of problems as they become evident and to do substantive research on individual issues before pronouncements were issued.

The Board's 18 to 21 members, selected primarily from public accounting, also included representatives from industry and the academic community. The Board's official pronouncements, called **APB Opinions**, were intended to be based mainly on research studies and be supported by reasons and analysis. Between its inception in 1959 and its dissolution in 1973, the APB issued 31 opinions (see complete list inside front cover).

Unfortunately, the APB came under fire early, charged with lack of productivity and failing to act promptly to correct alleged accounting abuses. Later the APB tackled numerous thorny accounting issues, only to meet a buzz saw of industry and CPA firm opposition and occasional governmental interference. In 1971 the accounting profession's leaders, anxious to avoid governmental rule-making, appointed a Study Group on Establishment of Accounting Principles. Commonly known as the **Wheat Committee** for its chair Francis Wheat, this group was to examine the organization and operation of the APB and determine what changes would be necessary to attain better results. The Study Group's recommendations were submitted to the AICPA Council in the spring of 1972, adopted in total, and implemented by early 1973.

Financial Accounting Standards Board (FASB)

The Wheat Committee's recommendations resulted in the demise of the APB and the creation of a new standard-setting structure composed of three organizations—the Financial Accounting Foundation (FAF), the Financial Accounting Standards Board (FASB), and the Financial Accounting Standards Advisory Council (FASAC). The **Financial Accounting Foundation** selects the members of the FASB and the Advisory Council, funds their activities, and generally oversees the FASB's activities.

The major operating organization in this three-part structure is the **Financial Accounting Standards Board (FASB)**. Its mission is to establish and improve standards of financial accounting and reporting for the guidance and education of the public, which includes issuers, auditors, and users of financial information. The expectations of success and support for the new FASB were based upon several significant differences between it and its predecessor, the APB:

❶ *Smaller Membership.* The FASB is composed of seven members, replacing the relatively large 18-member APB.

❷ *Full-time, Remunerated Membership.* FASB members are well-paid, full-time members appointed for renewable 5-year terms, whereas the APB members were unpaid and part-time.

❸ *Greater Autonomy.* The APB was a senior committee of the AICPA, whereas the FASB is not an organ of any single professional organization. It is appointed by and answerable only to the Financial Accounting Foundation.

❹ *Increased Independence.* APB members retained their private positions with firms, companies, or institutions; FASB members must sever all such ties.

❺ *Broader Representation.* All APB members were required to be CPAs and members of the AICPA; currently, it is not necessary to be a CPA to be a member of the FASB.

In addition to research help from its own staff, the FASB relies on the expertise of various task force groups formed for various projects and on the **Financial Accounting Standards Advisory Council (FASAC)**. FASAC has responsibility for consulting with the FASB on both major policy and technical issues and also for helping select task force members.

Due Process

Two basic premises of the FASB are that in establishing financial accounting standards: (1) it should be responsive to the needs and viewpoints of the entire economic community, not just the public accounting profession, and (2) it should operate in full view

INTERNATIONAL INSIGHT

The United States' legal system is based on English common law, whereby the government generally allows professionals to make the rules. These rules (standards) are, therefore, developed in the private sector. Conversely, most of continental Europe follows codified law, which leads to government-run accounting systems.

of the public through a "due process" system that gives interested persons ample opportunity to make their views known. To ensure the achievement of these goals, the following steps are taken in the evolution of a typical FASB Statement of Financial Accounting Standards:

❶ A topic or project is identified and placed on the Board's agenda.
❷ A task force of experts from various sectors is assembled to define problems, issues, and alternatives related to the topic.
❸ Research and analysis are conducted by the FASB technical staff.
❹ A **discussion memorandum** is drafted and released.
❺ A public hearing is often held, usually 60 days after release of the memorandum.
❻ The Board analyzes and evaluates the public response.
❼ The Board deliberates on the issues and prepares an **exposure draft** for release.
❽ After a 30-day (minimum) exposure period for public comment, the Board evaluates all of the responses received.
❾ A committee studies the exposure draft in relation to the public responses, reevaluates its position, and revises the draft if necessary.
❿ The full Board gives the revised draft final consideration and votes on issuance of a **Standards Statement**

The passage of a new FASB Statement requires the support of five of the seven Board members. FASB Statements are considered GAAP and thereby binding in practice. All ARBs and APB Opinions that were in effect in 1973 when the FASB became effective continue to be effective until amended or superseded by FASB pronouncements. In recognition of possible misconceptions of the term "principles," the FASB uses the term **financial accounting standards** in its pronouncements.

Types of Pronouncements

The major types of pronouncements that the FASB issues are:

❶ Standards and Interpretations.
❷ Financial Accounting Concepts.
❸ Technical Bulletins.
❹ Emerging Issues Task Force Statements.

Standards and Interpretations. Financial accounting standards issued by the FASB are considered generally accepted accounting principles. In addition, the FASB also issues **interpretations** that represent modifications or extensions of existing standards. The interpretations have the same authority as standards and require the same votes for passage as standards. However, interpretations do not require the FASB to operate in full view of the public through the due process system that is required for FASB Standards. The APB also issued interpretations of APB Opinions. Both types of interpretations are now considered authoritative support for purposes of determining GAAP. Since replacing the APB, the FASB has issued 131 standards and 42 interpretations (see list inside front cover).

UNDERLYING CONCEPT

The contents of *Concepts Statement No. 1*, detailing the objectives of financial reporting, were presented earlier in this chapter.

Financial Accounting Concepts. As part of a long-range effort to move away from the problem-by-problem approach, the FASB in November 1978 issued the first in a series of **Statements of Financial Accounting Concepts** (see list inside back cover) as part of its conceptual framework project. The purpose of the series is to set forth fundamental objectives and concepts that the Board will use in developing future standards of financial accounting and reporting. They are intended to form a cohesive set of interrelated concepts, a conceptual framework, that will serve as tools for solving existing and emerging problems in a consistent manner. Unlike a Statement of Financial Accounting Standards, **a Statement of Financial Accounting Concepts does not establish GAAP.** Concepts statements, however, pass through the same due process system (discussion memo, public hearing, exposure draft, etc.) as do standards statements.

FASB Technical Bulletins. The FASB receives many requests from various sources for guidelines on implementing or applying FASB Standards or Interpretations, APB Opinions, and Accounting Research Bulletins. In addition, a strong need exists for timely guidance on financial accounting and reporting problems. For example, in a recent tax law change, certain income taxes that companies had accrued as liabilities were forgiven. The immediate question was: How should the forgiven taxes be reported—as a reduction of income tax expense, as a prior period adjustment, or as an extraordinary item? A technical bulletin was quickly issued that required the tax reduction be reported as a reduction of the current period's income tax expense. Note that a technical bulletin is issued only when (1) **it is not expected to cause a major change in accounting practice for a number of enterprises,** (2) **its cost of implementation is low, and** (3) **the guidance provided by the bulletin does not conflict with any broad fundamental accounting principle.**[11]

Emerging Issues Task Force Statements. In 1984 the FASB created the Emerging Issues Task Force (EITF). The EITF is composed of 13 members, representing CPA firms and preparers of financial statements. Also attending EITF meetings are observers from the SEC and AICPA. The purpose of the task force is to reach a consensus on how to account for new and unusual financial transactions that have the potential for creating differing financial reporting practices. Examples include how to account for pension plan terminations; how to account for unusual construction loans by savings and loans; and how to account for excessive amounts paid to takeover specialists.

We cannot overestimate the importance of the EITF. In one year, for example, the task force examined 61 emerging financial reporting issues and arrived at a consensus on approximately 75% of them. The SEC has indicated that it will view consensus solutions as preferred accounting and will require persuasive justification for departing from them.

The EITF helps the FASB in many ways. For example, emerging issues often attract public attention. If they are not resolved quickly, they can lead to financial crises and scandal and can undercut public confidence in current reporting practices. The next step, possible governmental intervention, would threaten the continuance of standard setting in the private sector. In addition, the EITF identifies controversial accounting problems as they arise and determines whether they can be quickly resolved or whether the FASB should become involved in solving them. In essence, it becomes a "problem filter" for the FASB. Thus, it is hoped that the FASB will be able to work on more pervasive long-term problems, while the EITF deals with short-term emerging issues.

Governmental Accounting Standards Board (GASB)

Financial statements prepared by state and local governments are not comparable with financial reports prepared by private business organizations. For example, many state and local governments use a simple cash basis and do not include such items as depreciation in their income statements. This lack of comparability was highlighted in the 1970s when a number of large U.S. cities such as New York and Cleveland faced potential bankruptcy. As a result, a new Governmental Accounting Standards Board (GASB), under the oversight of the Financial Accounting Foundation, was created in 1984 to address state and local governmental reporting issues.

The operational structure of the GASB is similar to that of the FASB. That is, it has an advisory council called the Governmental Accounting Standards Advisory Council (GASAC), and it is assisted by its own technical staff and task forces.

The creation of GASB was controversial. Many believe that there should be only one standard-setting body—the FASB. It was hoped that partitioning standard setting

---

[11]"Purpose and Scope of FASB Technical Bulletins and Procedures for Issuance," *FASB Technical Bulletin No. 79-1* (Revised) (Stamford, Conn.: FASB, June 1984).

between the GASB, which deals only with state and local government reporting, and the FASB, which reports for all other entities, would not lead to conflict. Since we are primarily concerned with financial reports prepared by profit-seeking organizations, this textbook will focus on standards issued by the FASB only.

The formal organizational structure as it currently exists for the development of financial reporting standards is presented in Illustration 1-3.

ILLUSTRATION 1-3
Organizational Structure for Setting Accounting Standards

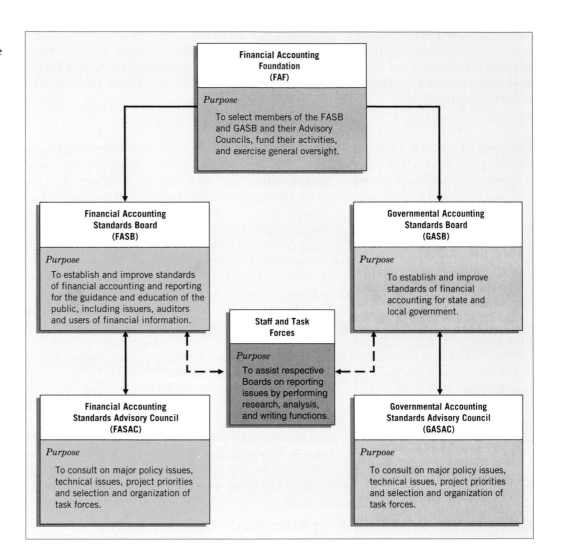

Changing Role of the AICPA

For several decades the AICPA provided the leadership in the development of accounting principles and rules; it regulated the accounting profession and developed and enforced accounting practice more than did any other professional organization. When the Accounting Principles Board was dissolved and replaced with the FASB, the AICPA established the Accounting Standards Division to act as its official voice on accounting and reporting issues.

The **Accounting Standards Executive Committee (AcSEC)** was established within the Division and was designated as the senior technical committee authorized to speak for the AICPA in the area of financial accounting and reporting. It does so through various written communications:

Audit and Accounting Guidelines summarize the accounting practices of specific industries and provide specific guidance on matters not addressed by the FASB and

GASB. Examples are accounting for casinos, airlines, colleges and universities, banks, insurance companies, and many others.

Statements of Position (SOP) provide guidance on financial reporting topics until the FASB or GASB sets standards on the issue in question. SOPs may update, revise, and clarify audit and accounting guides or provide free-standing guidance.

Practice Bulletins indicate AcSEC's views on narrow financial reporting issues not considered by the FASB or GASB.

The AICPA is still the leader in developing auditing standards through its Auditing Standards Board, in regulating auditing practice, in developing and enforcing professional ethics, and in providing continuing professional education programs. The AICPA also develops and grades the CPA examination, which is administered in all 50 states.

Other Influential Organizations

Several other organizations also have been influential in the development of accounting theory and standard setting. Illustration 1-4 provides an overview of these organizations.

Organization	Members	Purpose
American Accounting Association	Primarily accounting academics	Furthers the development of accounting theory by encouraging and sponsoring accounting research.
Institute of Management Accountants (IMA)	Primarily internal accountants	Conducts research and provides input on cost and managerial accounting issues.
Financial Executives Institute (FEI)	Financial executives generally of large corporations (treasurers, financial vice presidents, chief financial officers)	Conducts research and makes recommendations on the impact of financial reporting at the corporate level.

ILLUSTRATION 1-4
Overview of Other Influential Organizations

In addition, the **Internal Revenue Service (IRS)**, which derives its authority from the Internal Revenue Code and its amendments and legal interpretations, constitutes one of the strongest influences on accounting practice. In an effort to lessen the impact of taxes, and to avoid keeping two sets of books, business managers frequently adopt "acceptable" accounting procedures that minimize taxable income. Because the objectives of the tax law differ from the objectives of financial accounting, however, "good tax accounting" is not necessarily "good financial accounting." As noted throughout this textbook, tax laws and "tax effects" are a pervasive influence in business decision making and on the selection of accounting methods. Differences between tax accounting and financial accounting are generally permissible; however, in the preparation of financial statements, tax considerations must give ground to the requirements of sound accounting.

❖ GENERALLY ACCEPTED ACCOUNTING PRINCIPLES

Generally accepted accounting principles are those principles that have "substantial authoritative support." The AICPA's Code of Professional Conduct requires that members prepare financial statements in accordance with generally accepted accounting principles. Specifically, Rule 203 of this Code prohibits a member from expressing an opinion that financial statements conform with GAAP if those statements contain a material departure from a generally accepted accounting principle, unless the member

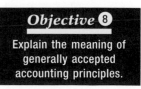

Objective ❽
Explain the meaning of generally accepted accounting principles.

can demonstrate that because of unusual circumstances the financial statements would otherwise have been misleading. Failure to follow Rule 203 can lead to loss of a CPA's license to practice.

The meaning of generally accepted accounting principles is defined by *Statement on Auditing Standards (SAS) No. 69*, "The Meaning of 'Present Fairly in Conformity With Generally Accepted Accounting Principles' in the Independent Auditor's Report." Under this standard, generally accepted accounting principles covered by Rule 203 are construed to be FASB Standards and Interpretations, APB Opinions, and AICPA Accounting Research Bulletins.

Oftentimes, however, a specific accounting transaction occurs that is not covered by any of these documents. In this case, other authoritative literature is used. Major examples are: FASB Technical Bulletins; AICPA Industry Accounting and Auditing Guides; and Statements of Position that have been "cleared" by the FASB.[12] These documents are considered to have substantial authoritative support because the recognized professional bodies, after giving interested and affected parties the opportunity to react to exposure drafts and respond at public hearings, have voted their issuance. If these pronouncements are lacking in guidance, then other sources might be considered. The hierarchy of these sources is presented in Illustration 1-5.[13] If the accounting treatment of an event is not specified by a category (a) pronouncement, then categories (b) through (d) should be investigated. If there is a conflict between pronouncements in (b) through (d), the higher category [for example (b) is higher than (c)] is to be followed.

In the event that none of these pronouncements addresses the event, the support is sought from other accounting literature. Examples of other accounting literature include FASB Concepts Statements, International Accounting Standards, and accounting articles.

ILLUSTRATION 1-5
The House of GAAP

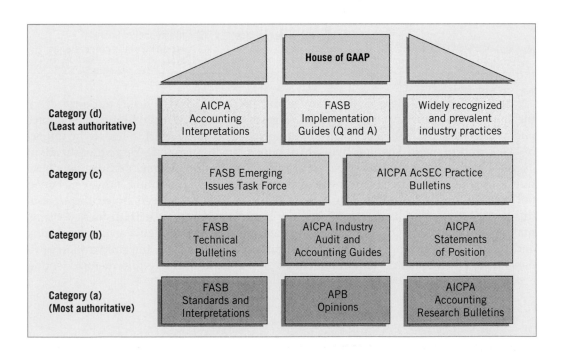

House of GAAP

Category (d) **(Least authoritative)**	AICPA Accounting Interpretations	FASB Implementation Guides (Q and A)	Widely recognized and prevalent industry practices
Category (c)	FASB Emerging Issues Task Force		AICPA AcSEC Practice Bulletins
Category (b)	FASB Technical Bulletins	AICPA Industry Audit and Accounting Guides	AICPA Statements of Position
Category (a) **(Most authoritative)**	FASB Standards and Interpretations	APB Opinions	AICPA Accounting Research Bulletins

---

[12]*SAS No. 69* states that Audit Guides and Statements of Position are assumed to be cleared (approved) by the FASB unless the pronouncement states otherwise.

[13]See for example, "Remodeling the House of GAAP," by Douglas Sauter, *Journal of Accountancy* (July 1991), pp. 30–37.

❖ ISSUES IN FINANCIAL REPORTING

Since many interests may be affected by the implementation of an accounting standard, it is not surprising that there is much discussion about who should develop these standards and to whom they should apply. Some of the major issues are discussed below.

Standard Setting in a Political Environment

Possibly the most powerful force influencing the development of accounting standards is user groups. User groups consist of the parties who are most interested in or affected by accounting standards, rules, and procedures. Like lobbyists in our state and national capitals, user groups play a significant role. **Accounting standards are as much a product of political action as they are of careful logic or empirical findings.**

User groups may want particular economic events accounted for or reported in a particular way, and they fight hard to get what they want. They know that the most effective way to influence the standards that dictate accounting practice is to participate in the formulation of these standards or to try to influence or persuade the formulator of them. Therefore, the FASB has become the target of many pressures and efforts to influence changes in the existing standards and the development of new ones.[14] To top it off, these pressures have been multiplying. Some influential groups demand that the accounting profession act more quickly and decisively to solve its problems and remedy its deficiencies. Other groups resist such action, preferring to implement change more slowly, if at all. Illustration 1-6 shows the various user groups that apply pressure.

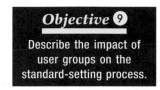

Objective ❾

Describe the impact of user groups on the standard-setting process.

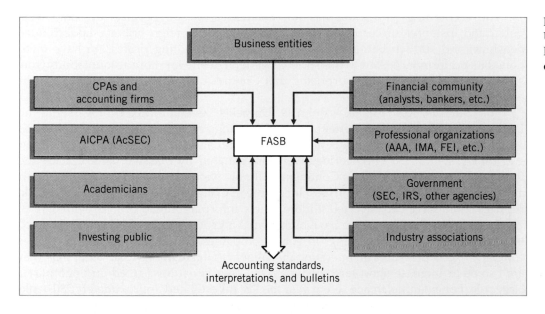

ILLUSTRATION 1-6
User Groups that Influence the Formulation of Accounting Standards

Should there be politics in setting financial accounting and reporting standards? We have politics at home; at school; at the fraternity, sorority, and dormitory; at the office; at church, temple, and mosque—politics is everywhere. The FASB does not exist in a vacuum. Standard setting is part of the real world, and it cannot escape politics and political pressures.

---

[14]All the FASB chairmen have acknowledged that many of the Board's projects, such as "Accounting for Contingencies," "Accounting for Pensions," "Statement of Cash Flows," and "Accounting for Income Taxes," were targets of political pressure.

That is not to say that politics in standard setting is evil. Considering the **economic consequences**[15] of many accounting standards, it is not surprising that special interest groups become vocal and critical (some supporting, some opposing) when standards are being formulated. The Board must be attentive to the economic consequences of its actions. What the Board should *not* do is issue pronouncements that are primarily politically motivated. While paying attention to its constituencies, the Board should base its standards on sound research and a conceptual framework that has its foundation in economic reality. Even so, the FASB can continue to expect politics and special interest pressures, since as T. S. Eliot said, "Humankind cannot bear very much reality."

An illustration of an economic consequence issue is the recent turmoil caused by the FASB's proposal that stock options granted to executives be charged as an expense on the income statement. The consequences of the proposed actions, executives argued, would be disastrous. Big companies would reduce their investment in research and development and equipment. Small companies, being cash starved, would go bankrupt. They would not be able to attract top executives because stock option plans involve too high a charge to income. Employment in the United States would plummet because small companies (who create most of the job growth) would not hire additional workers. The FASB, however, notes that options are compensation, the cost of which should be recorded.

Expectations Gap

All professions have come under increasing scrutiny by the government, whether it be the investment banking profession because of insider trading, the medical profession because of high costs and Medicare or Medicaid frauds, or engineers because of their failure to consider environmental consequences in their work.

The accounting profession has not escaped criticism. Because of some well-publicized instances of corporate fraud, domestic and foreign bribery, underfunded pensions, and sudden bankruptcies, critics of the accounting profession have questioned its performance. Add to this society's general desire for more accountability from all institutions, and it is not surprising that Congress has turned its attention on the accounting profession.

For example, Representative John D. Dingell's Subcommittee on Oversight and Investigation (**Dingell Committee**) has held hearings on a number of accounting and auditing matters. One of these is whether the FASB and the SEC are issuing effective and timely standards. The hearings were precipitated by massive bankruptcies and frauds involving firms such as Continental Illinois National Bank, Penn Square Bank, and Drysdale Government Securities, Inc. Some in Congress contended that such bankruptcies could have been averted if more timely information had been provided.

In addition, these hearings have highlighted a growing concern about "white collar" crime in financial reporting. In some companies, for example, the culture of a company exerts pressures on operating managers "to make things look better than they are" so as to increase short-term earnings. In other situations, greed and ego play a large role. For example, in one recent year the FBI investigated approximately 280 banks suspected of fraud, an increase of approximately 30% over the preceding year. It was estimated that banks lose eight times as much money to insiders as they do to "bank robbers."

The accounting profession recognizes that it must play an important role in combatting "white collar" fraud, and its response to criticisms in this area has been direct

---

[15]"Economic consequences" in this context means the impact of accounting reports on the wealth positions of issuers and users of financial information and the decision-making behavior resulting from that impact. The resulting behavior of these individuals and groups could have detrimental financial effects on the providers (enterprises) of the financial information. For a more detailed discussion of this phenomenon, see Stephen A. Zeff, "The Rise of 'Economic Consequences'," *Journal of Accountancy* (December 1978), pp. 56–63. Special appreciation is extended to Professor Zeff for his insights on this chapter.

and immediate. For example, the AICPA established a new Accounting Firms Division with two sections: one for firms auditing SEC clients (called the **SEC Practice Section**) and the other for firms auditing privately owned, non-SEC clients (called the **Private Companies Section**).[16] And, to help assure the public that the SEC Practice Section is meeting its responsibilities, the AICPA established as part of this structure an independent **Public Oversight Board**. The Board, composed of distinguished nonaccountants, has its own staff and is free to conduct its own inquiries and to report publicly as it wishes. The Private Companies Section also has its own quality control standards and peer review requirements.

More recently, the profession has issued new auditing standards on internal control, fraud and illegal acts, and auditors' communications. It has supported and begun to act on recommendations made by the **National Commission on Fraudulent Financial Reporting (the Treadway Commission)**, chaired by former SEC Commissioner James C. Treadway. And it is developing guidelines in relation to proper disclosures of reasons why auditors resign from audit engagements, particularly when there are questions about management's integrity.

But is it enough? The expectations gap—what the public thinks accountants should be doing and what accountants think they can do—is a difficult one to close. The instances of fraudulent reporting have caused some to question whether the profession is doing enough.[17] Although the profession can argue rightfully that they cannot be responsible for every financial catastrophe, it must continue to strive to meet the needs of society.

Competing Standard-Setting Bodies

As a prominent accountant recently noted, "the FASB is literally unique: it is a private sector institution performing a public function that is defined in the federal statutes." It is not surprising therefore that the right of the FASB to establish accounting standards continues to be challenged. Some of the major challenges come not only from outside the profession, but from within as well.

AICPA

The AICPA started issuing Statements of Position because it believed that more immediate guidance was needed for specific reporting problems. Although the AICPA has reduced its issuance of SOPs, it continues to be concerned about timely financial reporting. In addition, support exists within the AICPA for two sets of GAAP—one for large companies and one for small companies. Small companies complain that the detailed reporting required by GAAP is too costly and not needed by them. This is often referred to as the BIG GAAP–LITTLE GAAP issue.

GASB

As indicated earlier, the GASB is a separate governmental accounting standards board established to regulate state and local governmental reporting. It is modeled after the FASB. The two organizations continue to debate who should set standards in certain not-for-profit accounting areas.

Congress

From time to time Congress becomes active in the standard-setting process, particularly when the issue becomes highly political. For example, Senator Joseph Lieberman (D-Connecticut) introduced legislation that would permit companies not to follow any

---

[16]CPA firms that audit SEC registered firms must join the SEC Practice Section and therefore must comply with more comprehensive practice requirements (such as compulsory peer practice review) than those of the Private Companies Section.

[17]The accounting and auditing profession has designed a new tool to close this expectation gap in the form of a recently issued auditing standard entitled Statement on Auditing Standards (SAS) 82, *Consideration of Fraud in a Financial Statement Audit*. This new 1997 standard "raises the bar" on the performance of financial statement audits by explicitly requiring auditors to assess the risk of material financial statement misstatement due to fraud and misappropriation of assets.

FASB standard that requires a new expense charge for stock options. Senator Lieberman believes that a standard which results in a substantial expense for stock options would be disastrous to the national economy. Such political reaction is unfortunate and raises serious issues about who should be developing accounting standards.

Business Community

Members of the business community have registered numerous complaints about accounting standards. They contend that FASB standards are too complex and costly to implement and that some standards introduce volatility into reported income numbers. Further, they contend that standards requiring disclosures put their companies at a competitive disadvantage in world markets. As a result, this group lobbied hard—and won—for a change in the voting rules of the FASB, from a simple majority (4-3) to a supermajority (5-2). By requiring a supermajority, it is hoped that standards will be less controversial and will be issued only if truly "generally accepted." In addition, the business world argues for more representation on the FASB and the Financial Accounting Foundation.[18]

These developments are viewed by some with alarm. They believe that the supermajority will only lead to a delay in the issuances of standards. And, if the business community dominates the standard-setting process, the regulated will have too much influence on the regulations (leading to a "fox in the chicken coop" situation) and, thus, undermine the credibility of financial reports.

International Accounting Standards

In Germany, the amortization period for an intangible asset is 5 years. In the United States, a maximum period of 40 years is allowed. In Mexico, assets are adjusted for price-level changes. In the United States, assets are generally valued at historical cost. In Japan, income smoothing is permitted because firms are allowed discretionary charges to income for such items as depreciation and bad debts. In the United States, arbitrary charges to income are not permitted. These are just some of the ways in which reporting practices in the United States differ from reporting practices in other countries.

Most countries recognize the need for more uniform standards. As a result, the **International Accounting Standards Committee (IASC)** was formed in 1973—the same year the FASB was born—to attempt to narrow the areas of divergence. The objective of the IASC in terms of standard setting is "to work generally for the improvement and harmonization of regulations, accounting standards and procedures relating to the presentation of financial statements." Eliminating differences is not easy because the objectives of financial reporting in the United States often differ from those in foreign countries, the institutional structures are often not comparable, and strong national tendencies are pervasive. Nevertheless, much headway has been made since IASC's inception, and international standards may gradually supplant national standards.

Recently the SEC indicated that it would allow foreign companies to use IASC standards in securities offerings in the United States, if the IASC met the following three conditions:

❶ The core standards must constitute a comprehensive generally accepted basis of accounting.
❷ The standards must be of high quality.
❸ The standards must be rigorously interpreted and applied.

INTERNATIONAL INSIGHT

Many developing and newly industrialized nations, e.g., Nigeria, Singapore, and Malaysia, have adopted IASC standards as their national standards.

INTERNATIONAL INSIGHT

The IASC has reached agreement with IOSCO to complete a set of core international standards for use in cross-border offerings and listings. The target completion date is March 1998. The SEC supports the IASC's work and has said that it would consider allowing the use of international standards by foreign issuers when they offer securities in the U.S.

---

[18]To date, that argument has not prevailed. In fact, the exact opposite has occurred at the FAF. The SEC recently demanded that the FAF have more public-interest representatives on its board. The SEC argued that more individuals with a strong track record of independence and public service (free of conflicts and committed to the interests of investors) be selected. As a result of the SEC's insistence, the composition of the Foundation board has changed dramatically in favor of more "public-interest" members.

These three conditions will be difficult to meet, but the IASC is making substantial progress. It is entirely possible that the SEC will accept IASC standards before the turn of the century. Once that happens, many U.S.-based companies will petition to use IASC standards instead of U.S.-based standards. They will argue that for competitive purposes it is better that all companies follow the same standards.

Would this change be good or bad? We believe it has the potential to be both: It is good because a common set of standards is needed to measure and recognize economic events. Under international standards, users of financial information will find it easier to make comparisons among companies in different countries—for example, to compare Ford Motor Co. (U.S.) to Daimler Benz (German) to Toyota Motor Co. (Japan). It is bad because the United States is generally viewed as having the most rigorous and comprehensive reporting standards in the world. It is highly likely that international standards will initially not be of the same quality as U.S. standards, nor will enforcement procedures be as strong.

It should be emphasized that the United States has a major voice in how international standards are being developed. As a result, there are many similarities between IASC- and U.S.-based standards.

Ethics in the Environment of Financial Accounting

Robert Sack, a commentator on the subject of accounting ethics, noted that "Based on my experience, new graduates tend to be idealistic . . . thank goodness for that! Still it is very dangerous to think that your armor is all in place and say to yourself 'I would have never given in to that.' The pressures don't explode on us; they build, and we often don't recognize them until they have us."

> **Objective ⑩**
> Understand issues related to ethics and financial accounting.

These observations are particularly appropriate for anyone entering the business world. In accounting, as in other areas of business, ethical dilemmas are encountered frequently. Some of these dilemmas are simple and easy to resolve. Many, however, are complex, and solutions are not obvious. Businesses' concentration on "maximizing the bottom line," "facing the challenges of competition," and "stressing short-term results" places accountants in an environment of conflict and pressure. Basic questions such as: "Is this way of communicating financial information good or bad?" "Is it right or wrong?" "What should I do in the circumstance?" cannot always be answered by simply adhering to GAAP or following the rules of the profession. Technical competence is not enough when ethical decisions are encountered.

Doing the right thing, making the right decision, is not always easy. Right is not always evident. And, the pressures "to bend the rules," "to play the game," "to just ignore it," can be considerable. For example, "Will my decision affect my job performance negatively?" "Will my superiors be upset?" "Will my colleagues be unhappy with me?" are often questions faced in making a tough ethical decision. The decision is more difficult because a public consensus has not emerged to formulate a comprehensive ethical system to provide guidelines.

However, "applied ethics" is still necessary and possible. Here are the steps that you might apply in the process of ethical awareness and decision making:

❶ *Recognize an ethical situation or ethical dilemma.* The first step is to know when you have a problem. To do that, you must develop your own personal ethics or conscience. Your ethics are a subset of society's values. They come from family, educational, and religious institutions as well as from social movements and your own reactions to all of these inputs. Being sensitive to and aware of the effects (potential harm or benefit) of one's actions and decisions on individuals or groups is a first step in resolving ethical dilemmas.

❷ *Move toward an ethical resolution by identifying and analyzing the principal elements in the situation.* Seek answers to the following questions in this sequence:
  (a) What parties (*stakeholders*) may be harmed or benefited?
  (b) Whose rights or claims may be violated?
  (c) Which specific interests are in conflict?
  (d) What are my responsibilities and obligations?

This step involves **identifying and sorting out the facts**.

❸ *Identify the alternatives and weigh the impact of each alternative on various stakeholders.* For instance, in financial accounting, which alternative methods are available to measure or report the transaction, situation, or event? What is the effect of each alternative on the various stakeholders? Which stakeholders are harmed or benefited most?

❹ *Select the best or most ethical alternative, considering all the circumstances and the consequences.* Some ethical issues involve one right answer; and what must be done is to identify the one right answer. Other ethical issues involve more than one right answer; these require an evaluation of each and a selection of the best or most ethical alternative.

This whole process of ethical sensitivity and selection among alternatives can be complicated by pressures that may take the form of time pressures, job pressures, client pressures, personal pressures, and peer pressures. Throughout this textbook, **ethical considerations are presented for the purpose of sensitizing you** to the type of situations you may encounter in the performance of your professional responsibility.

Conclusion

The FASB is in its twenty-fourth year as this textbook is written. Will the FASB survive in its present state, or will it be restructured or changed as its predecessors were? As indicated, some people in government, some in the financial community, and some in the profession itself are continually challenging the accounting profession to assume more responsibility and to be more responsive to the needs of its constituencies.

At present, we believe that the accounting profession is reacting responsibly and effectively to remedy identified shortcomings. Because of its substantive resources and expertise, the private sector should be able to develop and maintain high standards. But it is a difficult process requiring time, logic, and diplomacy. By a judicious mix of these three ingredients, and a measure of luck, the profession may be able to continue to develop its own standards and regulate itself with minimal intervention.

SUMMARY OF LEARNING OBJECTIVES

❶ *Describe the essential characteristics of accounting.* The essential characteristics of accounting are: (1) identification, measurement, and communication of financial information about (2) economic entities to (3) interested persons.

❷ *Identify the major financial statements and other means of financial reporting.* The financial statements most frequently provided are (1) the balance sheet, (2) the income statement, (3) the statement of cash flows, and (4) the statement of owners' or stockholders' equity. Financial reporting other than financial statements may take various forms. Examples include the president's letter or supplementary schedules in the corporate annual report, prospectuses, reports filed with government agencies, news releases, management's forecasts, and descriptions of an enterprise's social or environmental impact.

❸ *Explain how accounting assists in the efficient use of scarce resources.* Accounting provides reliable, relevant, and timely information to managers, investors, and creditors so that resources are allocated to the most efficient enterprises. Accounting also provides measurements of efficiency (profitability) and financial soundness.

❹ *Identify some of the challenges facing accounting.* Financial reports fail to provide (1) some key performance measures widely used by management, (2) forward-looking information needed by investors and creditors, (3) sufficient information on a company's soft assets (intangibles), and (4) real-time financial information.

5 *Identify the objectives of financial reporting.* The objectives of financial reporting are to provide (1) information that is useful in investment and credit decisions, (2) information that is useful in assessing cash flow prospects, and (3) information about enterprise resources, claims to those resources, and changes in them.

6 *Explain the need for accounting standards.* In preparing financial statements, accountants are confronted with the potential dangers of bias, misinterpretation, inexactness, and ambiguity. In order to minimize these dangers, the accounting profession has attempted to develop a set of standards that is generally accepted and universally practiced. Without this set of standards, each enterprise would have to develop its own standards, and readers of financial statements would have to familiarize themselves with every company's peculiar accounting and reporting practices. As a result, it would be almost impossible to prepare statements that could be compared.

7 *Identify the major policy-setting bodies and their role in the standard-setting process.* The *Securities and Exchange Commission (SEC)* is an agency of the federal government that has the broad powers to prescribe, in whatever detail it desires, the accounting standards to be employed by companies that fall within its jurisdiction. The *American Institute of Certified Public Accountants (AICPA)* issued standards through its Committee on Accounting Procedure and Accounting Principles Board. The *Financial Accounting Standards Board (FASB)* establishes and improves standards of financial accounting and reporting for the guidance and education of the public. The *Governmental Accounting Standards Board (GASB)* establishes and improves standards of financial accounting for state and local governments.

8 *Explain the meaning of generally accepted accounting principles.* Generally accepted accounting principles are those principles that have substantial authoritative support, such as FASB Standards and Interpretations, APB Opinions and Interpretations, AICPA Accounting Research Bulletins, and other authoritative pronouncements.

9 *Describe the impact of user groups on the standard-setting process.* User groups may want particular economic events accounted for or reported in a particular way, and they fight hard to get what they want. Therefore, the FASB has become the target of many pressures and efforts to influence changes in the existing standards and the development of new ones. Because of the accelerated rate of change and the increased complexity of our economy, these pressures have been multiplying. As a result, accounting standards are as much a product of political action as they are of careful logic or empirical findings.

10 *Understand issues related to ethics and financial accounting.* Financial accountants in the performance of their professional duties are called on for moral discernment and ethical decision making. The decision is more difficult because a public consensus has not emerged to formulate a comprehensive ethical system that provides guidelines in making ethical judgments.

❖ QUESTIONS ❖

1 Differentiate broadly between financial accounting and managerial accounting.

2 Differentiate between "financial statements" and "financial reporting."

3 Explain how accounting helps users of the financial statement make capital allocation decisions.

4 What are some of the major challenges facing the accounting profession?

5 Why is it important to measure performance accurately and fairly when productive resources are privately owned?

6 Provide some examples of how accounting information influences its environment.

7 What are the major objectives of financial reporting?

8 Of what value is a common set of standards in financial accounting and reporting?

9 What is the likely limitation of "general-purpose financial statements"?

10 What are some of the developments or events that occurred between 1900 and 1930 that helped bring about changes in accounting theory or practice?

11 In what way is the Securities and Exchange Commission concerned about and supportive of accounting principles and standards?

12 What was the Committee on Accounting Procedure and what were its accomplishments and failings?

13 For what purposes did the AICPA in 1959 create the Accounting Principles Board?

14 Distinguish between Accounting Research Bulletins, Accounting Research Studies, Opinions of the Accounting Principles Board, and Statements of the Financial Accounting Standards Board.

15 If you had to explain or define "generally accepted accounting principles or standards," what essential characteristics would you include in your explanation?

16 In what ways was it felt that the statements issued by the Financial Accounting Standards Board would carry greater weight than the opinions issued by the Accounting Principles Board?

17 How are FASB discussion memorandums and FASB exposure drafts related to FASB "statements"?

18 Distinguish between FASB "statements of financial accounting standards" and FASB "statements of financial accounting concepts."

19 What is Rule 203 of the Code of Professional Conduct and what relationship does it have to the standard-setting process?

20 Rank from the most authoritative to the least authoritative, the following three items: FASB Technical Bulletins, AICPA Practice Bulletins, and FASB Standards.

21 The chairman of the FASB at one time noted that "the flow of standards can only be slowed if (1) producers focus less on quarterly earnings per share and tax benefits and more on quality products and (2) accountants and lawyers rely less on rules and law and more on professional judgment and conduct." Explain his comment.

22 What is the purpose of FASB Technical Bulletins? How do FASB Technical Bulletins differ from FASB Interpretations?

23 Explain the role of the Emerging Issues Task Force in establishing generally accepted accounting principles.

24 What is the purpose of the Governmental Accounting Standards Board?

25 What is AcSEC and what is its relationship to the FASB?

26 What are the sources of pressure that change and influence the development of accounting principles and standards?

27 Some individuals have indicated that the FASB must be cognizant of the economic consequences of its pronouncements. What is meant by economic consequences? What dangers exist if politics plays an important role in the development of financial reporting standards?

28 What are some possible reasons why another organization, such as the Governmental Accounting Standards Board, should not issue financial reporting standards?

29 If you were given complete authority in the matter, how would you propose that accounting principles or standards should be developed and enforced?

30 One writer recently noted that 99.4% of all companies prepare statements that are in accordance with GAAP. Why then is there such concern about fraudulent financial reporting?

31 What is the "expectations gap"? What is the profession doing to try to close this gap?

32 A number of foreign countries often have reporting standards that differ from those in the United States. What are some of the main reasons why reporting standards are often different among countries?

33 How are financial accountants challenged in their work to make ethical decisions? Is not technical mastery of GAAP sufficient to the practice of financial accounting?

34 What significant steps might one apply in the process of moral discernment and ethical decision making?

❖ CONCEPTUAL CASES ❖

C1-1 (Financial Accounting)   Rudolph Fisher has recently completed his first year of studying accounting. His instructor for next semester has indicated that the primary focus will be the area of financial accounting.

Instructions
(a) Differentiate between financial accounting and managerial accounting.
(b) One part of financial accounting involves the preparation of financial statements. What are the financial statements most frequently provided?
(c) What is the difference between financial statements and financial reporting?

C1-2 (Objectives of Financial Reporting) Celia Cruz, a recent graduate of the local state university, is presently employed by a large manufacturing company. She has been asked by Angeles Ochoa, controller, to prepare the company's response to a current Discussion Memorandum published by the Financial Accounting Standards Board (FASB). Cruz knows that the FASB has issued six *Statements of Financial Accounting Concepts*, and she believes that these concept statements could be used to support the company's response to the Discussion Memorandum. She has prepared a rough draft of the response citing *Statement of Financial Accounting Concepts No. 1*, "Objectives of Financial Reporting by Business Enterprises."

Instructions
  (a) Identify the three objectives of financial reporting as presented in *Statement of Financial Accounting Concepts No. 1 (SFAC No. 1)*.
  (b) Describe the level of sophistication expected of the users of financial information by *SFAC No. 1*.

(CMA adapted)

C1-3 (Accounting Numbers and the Environment) Hardly a day goes by without an article appearing on the crises affecting many of our financial institutions in the United States. It is estimated that the Savings and Loan (S&L) debacle may end up costing $500 billion ($2,000 for every man, woman, and child in the United States). Some argue that if the S&Ls were required to report their investments at market value instead of cost, large losses would have been reported earlier, which would have signaled regulators to close those S&Ls and, therefore, minimize the losses to American taxpayers.

Instructions
Explain how reported accounting numbers might affect an individual's perceptions and actions. Cite two examples.

C1-4 (Need for Accounting Standards) Some argue that having various organizations establish accounting principles is wasteful and inefficient. Rather than mandating accounting standards, each company could voluntarily disclose the type of information it considered important. In addition, if an investor wants additional information, the investor could contact the company and pay to receive the additional information desired.

Instructions
Comment on the appropriateness of this viewpoint.

C1-5 (AICPA's Role in Standard Setting) One of the major groups involved in the standard-setting process is the American Institute of Certified Public Accountants. Initially it was the primary organization that established accounting principles in the United States. Subsequently it relinquished most of its power to the FASB.

Instructions
  (a) Identify the two committees of the AICPA that established accounting principles prior to the establishment of the FASB.
  (b) Speculate as to why these two organizations failed. In your answer, identify steps the FASB has taken to avoid failure.
  (c) What is the present role of the AICPA in the standard-setting environment?

C1-6 (FASB Role in Standard Setting) A press release announcing the appointment of the trustees of the new Financial Accounting Foundation stated that the Financial Accounting Standards Board (to be appointed by the trustees) "... will become the established authority for setting accounting principles under which corporations report to the shareholders and others" (AICPA news release July 20, 1972).

Instructions
  (a) Identify the sponsoring organization of the FASB and the process by which the FASB arrives at a decision and issues an accounting standard.
  (b) Indicate the major types of pronouncements issued by the FASB and the purposes of each of these pronouncements.

C1-7 (Government Role in Standard Setting) Recently an article stated "the setting of accounting standards in the United States is now about 60 years old. It is a unique process in our society, one that has undergone numerous changes over the years. The standards are established by a private sector entity that has no dominant sponsor and is not part of any professional organization or trade association. The governmental entity that provides oversight, on the other hand, is far more a friend than a competitor or an antagonist."

Instructions

Identify the governmental entity that provides oversight and indicate its role in the standard-setting process.

C1-8 (Meaning of Generally Accepted Accounting Principles) At the completion of Bloom Company's audit, the president, Judy Bloom, asks about the meaning of the phrase "in conformity with generally accepted accounting principles" that appears in your audit report on the management's financial statements. Judy observes that the meaning of the phrase must include something more and different than what she thinks of as "principles."

Instructions

   (a) Explain the meaning of the term "accounting principles" as used in the audit report. (Do not discuss in this part the significance of "generally accepted.")
   (b) President Bloom wants to know how you determine whether or not an accounting principle is generally accepted. Discuss the sources of evidence for determining whether an accounting principle has substantial authoritative support. Do not merely list the titles of publications.

C1-9 (Politicalization of Standard Setting) Some accountants have said that politicalization in the development and acceptance of generally accepted accounting principles (i.e., standard setting) is taking place. Some use the term "politicalization" in a narrow sense to mean the influence by governmental agencies, particularly the Securities and Exchange Commission, on the development of generally accepted accounting principles. Others use it more broadly to mean the compromising that takes place in bodies responsible for developing generally accepted accounting principles because of the influence and pressure of interested groups (SEC, American Accounting Association, businesses through their various organizations, Institute of Management Accountants, financial analysts, bankers, lawyers, etc.).

Instructions

   (a) The Committee on Accounting Procedures of the AICPA was established in the mid to late 1930s and functioned until 1959, at which time the Accounting Principles Board came into existence. In 1973, the Financial Accounting Standards Board was formed and the APB went out of existence. Do the reasons these groups were formed, their methods of operation while in existence, and the reasons for the demise of the first two indicate an increasing politicalization (as the term is used in the broad sense) of accounting standard setting? Explain your answer by indicating how the CAP, the APB, and the FASB operated or operate. Cite specific developments that tend to support your answer.
   (b) What arguments can be raised to support the "politicalization" of accounting standard setting?
   (c) What arguments can be raised against the "politicalization" of accounting standard setting?

(CMA adapted)

C1-10 (Models for Setting Accounting Standards) Presented below are three models for setting accounting standards.

   1. The purely political approach, where national legislative action decrees accounting standards.
   2. The private, professional approach, where financial accounting standards are set and enforced by private professional actions only.
   3. The public/private mixed approach, where standards are basically set by private sector bodies that behave as though they were public agencies and whose standards to a great extent are enforced through governmental agencies.

Instructions

   (a) Which of these three models best describes standard setting in the United States? Comment on your answer.
   (b) Why do companies, financial analysts, labor unions, industry trade associations, and others take such an active interest in standard setting?
   (c) Cite an example of a group other than the FASB that attempts to establish accounting standards. Speculate as to why another group might wish to set its own standards.

C1-11 (Standard-Setting Terminology) Andrew Wyeth, an administrator at a major university, recently said, "I've got some CDs in my IRA, which I set up to beat the IRS." As elsewhere, in the world of accounting and finance, it often helps to be fluent in abbreviations and acronyms.

Instructions

Presented on the next page is a list of common accounting acronyms. Identify the term for which each acronym stands, and provide a brief definition of each term.

(a) FEI	(g) FAF	(m) CPA
(b) IMA	(h) FASAC	(n) FASB
(c) AICPA	(i) FRR	(o) GASB
(d) CAP	(j) IRS	(p) SEC
(e) ARB	(k) SOP	(q) AAA
(f) APB	(l) GAAP	(r) IASC

C1-12 (Accounting Organizations and Documents Issued) Presented below are a number of accounting organizations and type of documents they have issued. Match the appropriate document to the organization involved. Note that more than one document may be issued by the same organization. If no document is provided for an organization, write in "0."

Organization
1. ____ Securities and Exchange Commission
2. ____ Accounting Standards Executive Committee
3. ____ Accounting Principles Board
4. ____ Committee on Accounting Procedure
5. ____ Financial Accounting Standards Board

Document
(a) Opinions
(b) Practice Bulletins
(c) Accounting Research Bulletins
(d) Financial Reporting Releases
(e) Financial Accounting Standards
(f) Statements of Position
(g) Technical Bulletins

C1-13 (Accounting Pronouncements) A number of authoritative pronouncements have been issued by standard-setting bodies during the last 50 years. A list is provided on the left with a description of these pronouncements on the right. Match the description to the pronouncements.

____ Technical Bulletin
____ Interpretations (of the Financial Accounting Standards Board)
____ Statement of Financial Accounting Standards
____ EITF Statements
____ Opinions
____ Statement of Financial Accounting Concepts

(a) Official pronouncements of the APB
(b) Sets forth fundamental objectives and concepts that will be used in developing future standards
(c) Primary document of the FASB that establishes GAAP
(d) Provides additional guidance on implementing or applying FASB Standards or Interpretations
(e) Provides guidance on how to account for new and unusual financial transactions that have the potential for creating diversity in financial reporting practices
(f) Represent extensions or modifications of existing standards

C1-14 (Issues Involving Standard Setting) There have been a number of articles on accounting matters in the financial press. Some of the comments made in these articles are presented below. Answer the related question for each comment.

1. "In its first formal action upon commencing operations the GASB unanimously approved GASB Statement No. 1, Authoritative Status of NCGA Pronouncements and AICPA Industry Audit Guide." What is the GASB and what role does it play in the standard-setting process?
2. Some people want the FASB to deal with emerging accounting issues more promptly. But prompt resolution of issues comes at the expense of some of the elaborate due process the FASB imposes on itself. If the FASB reduces that due process, it risks undermining the acceptance of accounting rules set by a nongovernmental standard-setting body. What is meant by "due process" and how is the profession attempting to handle the problem of providing timely guidance?
3. Recently the FASB has published what it considers to be the mission of the FASB. It noted that one concept it will follow will be to weigh carefully the views of its constituents in developing standards. Who are the FASB's major constituents and what role do they play in the standard-setting process?
4. "A Securities and Exchange Commission report to Congress on the accounting profession shows that the profession has taken significant strides in regulating itself." What might be some significant strides the profession has taken to regulate itself?

C1-15 (International Accounting Standards) Michael Sharpe, Deputy Chairman, International Accounting Standards Committee made the following comments before the FEI's 63rd Annual Conference: There is an irreversible movement towards the harmonization of financial reporting throughout the world. The international capital markets require an end to:

(a) The confusion caused by international companies announcing different results depending on the set of accounting standards applied. Recent announcements by Daimler Benz highlight the confusion that this causes.

(b) Companies in some countries obtaining unfair commercial advantages from the use of particular national accounting standards.

(c) The complications in negotiating commercial arrangements for international joint ventures caused by different accounting requirements.

(d) The inefficiency of international companies having to understand and use a myriad of different accounting standards depending on the countries in which they operate and the countries in which they raise capital and debt. Executive talent is wasted on keeping up to date with numerous sets of accounting standards and the never-ending changes to them.

(e) The inefficiency of investment managers, bankers and financial analysts as they seek to compare financial reporting drawn up in accordance with different sets of accounting standards.

(f) Failure of many stock exchanges and regulators to require companies subject to their jurisdiction to provide comparable, comprehensive and transparent financial reporting frameworks giving international comparability.

(g) Difficulty for developing countries and countries entering the free market economy such as China and Russia in accessing foreign capital markets because of the complexity of and differences between national standards.

(h) The restriction on the mobility of financial service providers across the world as a result of different accounting standards.

Clearly the elimination of these inefficiencies by having comparable high-quality financial reporting used across the world would benefit international businesses.

Instructions

(a) What is the International Accounting Standards Committee?

(b) What stakeholders might benefit from the use of International Accounting Standards?

(c) What do you believe are some of the major obstacles to harmonization?

C1-16 (Securities and Exchange Commission)   The U.S. Securities and Exchange Commission (SEC) was created in 1934 and consists of five commissioners and a large professional staff. The SEC professional staff is organized into five divisions and several principal offices. The primary objective of the SEC is to support fair securities markets. The SEC also strives to foster enlightened shareholder participation in corporate decisions of publicly traded companies. The SEC has a significant presence in financial markets, the development of accounting practices, and corporation-shareholder relations, and has the power to exert influence on entities whose actions lie within the scope of its authority.

Instructions

(a) Explain where the Securities and Exchange Commission receives its authority.

(b) Describe the official role of the Securities and Exchange Commission in the development of financial accounting theory and practices.

(c) Discuss the interrelationship between the Securities and Exchange Commission and Financial Accounting Standards Board with respect to the development and establishment of financial accounting theory and practices.

(CMA adapted)

C1-17 (Standard-Setting Process)   In 1973, the responsibility for developing and issuing rules on accounting practices was given to the Financial Accounting Foundation and, in particular, to an arm of the foundation called the Financial Accounting Standards Board (FASB). The generally accepted accounting principles established by the FASB are enunciated through a publication series entitled **Statements of Financial Accounting Standards**. These statements are issued periodically, and over 120 are currently in force. The statements have a significant influence on the way in which financial statements are prepared by U.S. corporations.

Instructions

(a) Describe the process by which a topic is selected or identified as appropriate for study by the Financial Accounting Standards Board (FASB).

(b) Once a topic is considered appropriate for consideration by the FASB, a series of steps are followed before a **Statement of Financial Accounting Standards** is issued. Describe the major steps in the process leading to the issuance of a standard.

(c) Identify at least three other organizations that influence the setting of generally accepted accounting principles (GAAP).

(CMA adapted)

❖ USING YOUR JUDGMENT ❖

❖ FINANCIAL REPORTING PROBLEM

Kate Jackson, a new staff accountant, is confused because of the complexities involving accounting standard setting. Specifically, she is confused by the number of bodies issuing financial reporting standards of one kind or another and the level of authoritative support that can be attached to these reporting standards. Kate decides that she must review the environment in which accounting standards are set, if she is to increase her understanding of the accounting profession.

Kate recalls that during her accounting education there was a chapter or two regarding the environment of financial accounting and the development of accounting standards. However, she remembers that little emphasis was placed on these chapters by her instructor.

Instructions
   (a) Help Kate by identifying key organizations involved in accounting standard setting.
   (b) In what ways is accounting involved in the environment as Kate refers to it? That is, what environmental factors influence accounting and how does accounting influence its environment?
   (c) Kate asks for guidance regarding authoritative support. Please assist her by explaining what is meant by authoritative support.
   (d) Give Kate a historical overview of how standard setting has evolved so that she will not feel that she is the only one to be confused.
   (e) What authority for compliance with GAAP has existed throughout the period of standard setting?

❖ RESEARCH CASES

Case 1

In 1994, the AICPA Special Committee on Financial Reporting issued *Improving Business Reporting—A Customer Focus* (the "Jenkins report"). The chapter includes a brief overview of the committee's findings.

Instructions
Obtain a copy of the report and use it to answer the following questions:

   (a) Identify three members of the committee and their professional backgrounds.
   (b) How is "business reporting" defined in the report?
   (c) In what ways did the committee investigate the information needs of financial statement users?
   (d) Identify two benefits and two costs of informative disclosure from the perspective of (1) the overall economy and (2) individual reporting entities and their owners.
   (e) The FASB has begun to address a number of the issues raised in the Jenkins report. Obtain a recent copy of the FASB's *Financial Accounting Series Status Report* which addresses an issue from the Jenkins report. Summarize the status of the FASB's investigation of the issue.

Case 2

In the *Journal of Corporate Accounting and Finance*/Autumn 1996, an article appeared entitled "The FAF Restructuring Controversy: What Happened, and How Will It Affect the FASB."

Instructions
Read the article and answer the following questions:

   (a) Explain the responsibility of the Financial Accounting Foundation.
   (b) What recommendations did the FEI's Committee on Corporate Reporting make regarding the Financial Accounting Standards Board?

(c) What was the reaction of the Securities and Exchange Commission to the recommendations of the FEI Committee on Corporate Reporting?

(d) What finally happened regarding the restructuring controversy?

(e) What does this controversy indicate about the standard setting process?

Case 3

In *The Wall Street Journal*, March 21, 1996, p. C1, an article appeared entitled "Can FASB Be Considered Antibusiness?"

Instructions

Read this article and answer the following questions:

(a) Why do certain parties believe the FASB is antibusiness?

(b) What is the author's conclusion?

Case 4

The following comments were made in a recent article that appeared in the *Financial Times Limited*.

Dennis Beresford, who stands 6 ft. 5 in. tall, says that he was 7 ft. when he started as chairman of the Financial Accounting Standards Board of the US 10 years ago. Later this year he is due to step down from the post. He may lose a few more inches before his successor is elected.

Beresford was in London last week to dampen expectations that international accounting is about to be transformed by a landmark agreement establishing a set of common core standards acceptable to the world's leading stock markets.

Cynics will see this as evidence that the Financial Accounting Standards Board considers global harmonisation as a threat to its own pre-eminent position in world financial reporting. More realistically, his remarks probably reflect fears that the bandwagon behind harmonisation may be in danger of getting out of control.

Instructions

(a) Identify five recent articles that have appeared on the subject of international accounting standards.

(b) What is FASB's, SEC's, and New York Stock Exchange's position on International Accounting Standards?

(c) What is supposed to happen in 1998 regarding international accounting standards?

❖ WRITING ASSIGNMENT

Beta Alpha Psi, your university's accounting society, has decided to publish a brief pamphlet for seniors in high school, detailing the various facets of the accountancy profession. As a junior accountancy major, you have been asked to contribute an article for this publication. Your topic is the evolution of accounting standard-setting organizations in the United States.

Instructions

Write a 1–1.5 page article on the historical development of the organizations responsible for giving us GAAP. (The most appropriate introduction would explain the increasing need for a more standardized approach to accounting for a company's assets.)

❖ GROUP ASSIGNMENT

Assume that your group is the investment department for a major corporation and that you have been charged with investing $1,000,000 of the company's idle cash as an intermediate-term investment (3–5 years). Further assume that you have been approached by an investment firm to either loan money to or purchase the common stock of one of the investment firm's clients. The investment firm is willing to meet with your department to answer questions about the client but would like a list of the questions prior to the meeting.

Your instructor will assign your group to explore either a debt investment or equity investment. Elect one member of your group to be the recorder and another member of the group to be the spokesperson. The spokesperson should be prepared to present the group's findings to the whole class.

Instructions

(a) Given the framework below, identify ten questions your group wishes to ask the investment firm about this company. Be sure the questions are pertinent to either the debt investment or the equity investment. State the reasons you want this information (what you hope to gain from this information) and identify a credible source for the information.

Question	Reason	Credible Source
1.		

(b) (1) Name three qualities that you require financial information to possess in order to be valuable to you for decision making. (2) Do you believe that generally accepted accounting principles provide these qualities for accounting information? Why or why not?

❖ ETHICS CASE

When the FASB issues new standards, the implementation date is usually 12 months from date of issuance, with early implementation encouraged. Paula Popovich, controller, discusses with her financial vice president the need for early implementation of a standard which would result in a fairer presentation of the company's financial condition and earnings. When the financial vice president determines that early implementation of the standard will adversely affect the reported net income for the year, he discourages Popovich from implementing the standard until it is required.

Instructions

Answer the following questions:

(a) What, if any, is the ethical issue involved in this case?
(b) Is the financial vice president acting improperly or immorally?
(c) What does Popovich have to gain by advocacy of early implementation?
(d) Which stakeholders might be affected by the decision against early implementation?

(CMA adapted)

A visit with
Arthur R. Wyatt

ARTHUR R. WYATT teaches financial reporting at the University of Illinois. In addition, he is an expert witness on litigation matters as well as a consultant to the Securities & Exchange Commission on matters relating to international accounting standards.

International Standard Setting

What are some recent developments in the international accounting arena? There've been some marked changes in the past two years. The primary change is in Germany. The German business community has come to recognize that their system was not really conducive to raising capital outside of Germany because their accounting standards were so different from elsewhere. Within the last year, they have agreed to support international accounting standards, and to urge their multinational companies to report in accordance with international accounting standards. Two years ago, Daimler-Benz, a German company, sought financing in the United States. To do so, it had to present financial statements in accordance with GAAP in the U.S. That shook up the German business community because no German company had ever done that.

What is so different about the German and U.S. accounting environments? In Germany, accounting is very much tied to the tax law, and it is much more legalistic than in the U.S. But the Germans have an "out" for consolidated financial statements. The law in Germany, as in most European countries, does not deal with consolidated statements. Instead, it deals with a given *entity's* financial statements. Multinational companies that report on a consolidated basis are urged to move towards international standards. The individual company reporting within Germany will continue to follow German standards. That gives you a two-track system, but it does put the multinationals into an arena that is more comparable with other companies reporting in Europe and around the world.

The capital markets are driving these changes. Historically, in Germany and Japan, most of the capital for corporations has been provided by a limited number of banks in each country. As a result, there wasn't a robust stock market in those countries. The stockholders were the big banks, not a lot of individual investors. In that environment, there was no motive for a company to report openly on its financial affairs. You had the banks knowing a great deal about what goes on in the large companies, but other shareholders not knowing very much.

What we have found in the U.S. and most other English-speaking countries is that the markets are much more efficient as more information is provided. Our system for the past 60 years has been premised on full disclosure. That is still not an acceptable notion in places like Germany and Japan where the disclosure that we have is viewed as benefiting competitors and not the company. For example, segment reporting is resisted, particularly if a company only has a few products and one or two major competitors.

What other international accounting standards are changing? German and Swiss companies used to tuck away reserves for rainy days. In a good year, they would make higher charges to a particular expense and credit a liability. The liability would be merged with other current or long-term liabilities rather than being displayed on its own. That would dampen that profit for the year, which wouldn't bother management since companies weren't beholden to a stock market. What they wanted to be able to do was smooth over bad years by reversing that entry—debiting the liability and crediting some kind of revenue or expense account to improve the current year's profits. That's not really a problem anymore.

The degree of disclosure is still a major issue around the world. For example, the Japanese don't want to disclose any significant information with regard to pension plans. Japanese pension plans are much more underfunded than U.S. pension plans. One of the reasons that U.S. pension plans are more funded is that we focus disclosure on pension plans, and that has forced companies, in order not to look bad in comparison to their peers, to improve their funding. It is directly related to the accountability that is required in the U.S.

Is there an international standard setting body? The International Accounting Standards Committee, based in London, has improved the quality of international standards over the past several years. A good many countries such as Malaysia, Singapore, and Zimbabwe have adopted these international standards as their own, and do not attempt to write their own standards. In other countries, the international standards are coming to be used more for cross-border financings, even though the individual countries will continue to have their own standard-setting body. A London bank might get loan applications from companies in 12 different countries. If each prepared their financial statements in accordance with the standards in their own countries, unless the banker understood all 12, he or she wouldn't be able to analyze those financial statements in a knowledgeable way. The international standards are viewed by some as a vehicle to get greater comparability.

One of the problems with the international standards as they currently exist is that they still contain a number of instances where alternatives are permitted, which really hampers comparability. A number of those alternatives have been eliminated over the past five years by the Committee, and they continue to reduce alternatives. They have a very ambitious mid-1998 date to issue new standards and consolidate alternatives.

Will the U.S. be willing to conform to an international set of standards? The big challenge for the SEC is to evaluate the body of international standards and decide that they're good enough for the U.S. capital markets. Right now, they're not good enough. If securities regulators in other countries start adopting the international standards, and the U.S. remained an outlier, then it could very well be a strong negative for the U.S. capital markets. At the current time, the SEC is monitoring very closely the work of the International Accounting Standards Committee, with an objective of at some point seeing international accounting standards be of sufficiently high quality that the SEC will be able to buy into them.

The biggest area of controversy is business combinations. Presently in the U.S., a combination is accounted for either as a purchase, in which the value paid to acquire is recognized, or as a pooling of interests, in which case the financial statements merely incorporate the existing book values and ignore the value of what was paid. International standards currently do not permit pooling of interests, except in extremely rare circumstances. The pooling of interests notion has been very popular in the U.S. because it has permitted companies to buy other companies and not record what they paid for it and to get the benefit of higher profits in future years. The current international standard would restrict that severely.

Of course, if you have fewer poolings of interests and more purchases, then you have to face accounting for often-significant amounts of goodwill. In the UK, they permit goodwill to be deducted directly from shareholders' equity. It never becomes a charge on the income statement. We had that policy back in the 1930s and 1940s, but more recently, we have rigorous requirements that goodwill be amortized over no more than 40 years. The international standards require goodwill to be amortized over 20 years. The SEC would be willing to move in that direction, but the UK wants to establish a policy that says no amortization for goodwill, with a periodic review to determine if the goodwill has been impaired. In the U.S., we would find that to be a big step backward.

CHAPTER 2

Conceptual Framework Underlying Financial Accounting

Are Marketing Costs an Asset or an Expense?

America Online (AOL) is an interactive on-line consumer service company that provides its subscribers access to many electronic databases. Started in 1992, AOL has more subscribers than any other on-line service, a result that should gladden the hearts and fatten the wallets of its owners. But AOL has a financial problem: On September 30, 1996, AOL took a charge to income of $335 million, an amount five times larger than its pretax income over the past five years. Many now question whether the company can ever be profitable in the future. How could a company that has reported profits every year suddenly say those profits were illusory?

To understand what happened, consider that AOL's largest expenditure is the cost of advertising and free trials to attract subscribers. These promotions are expensive: In its fiscal year ending June 30, 1996, subscription acquisition costs totaled $363 million. AOL booked only $126 million of that amount as an expense and recorded the remainder as an asset to be amortized over two years. The following two charts show how AOL's deferred subscriber acquisition costs overshadow the firm's profits.

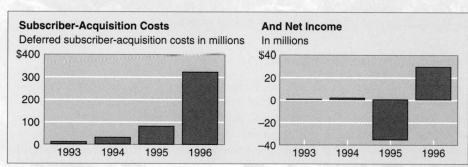

Should subscriber-acquisition costs be charged to revenue immediately, or are they an asset? AOL's biggest competitor, Compuserve, takes a more conservative approach by expensing these costs as incurred. Now that AOL has decided to do the same, it appears that AOL's accounting was too aggressive and misleading to the investment community.

As indicated in the opening story about America Online, users of financial statements need relevant and reliable information. To help develop this type of financial information, accountants use a conceptual framework that guides financial accounting and reporting. This chapter discusses the basic concepts underlying this conceptual framework. The content and organization of this chapter are as follows:

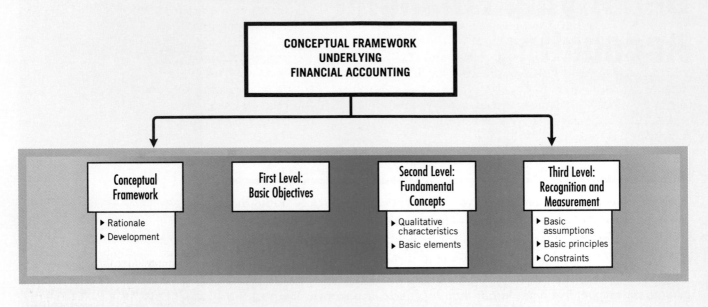

❖ CONCEPTUAL FRAMEWORK

A **conceptual framework** is like a **constitution**: It is "a coherent system of interrelated objectives and fundamentals that can lead to consistent standards and that prescribes the nature, function, and limits of financial accounting and financial statements."[1] Many have considered the Board's real contribution—and even its continued existence—to depend on the quality and utility of the conceptual framework.

Need for Conceptual Framework

Objective ❶

Describe the usefulness of a conceptual framework.

Why is a conceptual framework necessary? First, to be useful, standard setting should build on and relate to an established body of concepts and objectives. A soundly developed conceptual framework should enable the FASB to issue more useful and consistent standards in the future. **A coherent set of standards and rules should be the result**, because they would be built upon the same foundation. The framework should increase financial statement users' understanding of and confidence in financial reporting, and it should enhance comparability among companies' financial statements.

Second, new and emerging **practical problems should be more quickly solved by reference to an existing framework of basic theory**. To illustrate an emerging problem: Unique debt instruments were issued by companies in the early 1980s as a response to

---

[1]"Conceptual Framework for Financial Accounting and Reporting: Elements of Financial Statements and Their Measurement," *FASB Discussion Memorandum* (Stamford, Conn.: FASB, 1976), page 1 of the "Scope and Implications of the Conceptual Framework Project" section.

high interest and inflation rates. These included shared appreciation mortgages (debt in which the lender receives equity participation), zero coupon bonds (debt issued at a deep discount with no stated interest rate), and commodity-backed bonds (debt that may be repaid in a commodity). For example, Sunshine Mining (a silver mining company) sold two issues of bonds that it would redeem either with $1,000 in cash or with 50 ounces of silver, whichever was worth more at maturity. Both bond issues had a stated interest rate of 8.5%. At what amounts should the bonds have been recorded by Sunshine or the buyers of the bonds? What is the amount of the premium or discount on the bonds and how should it be amortized, if the bond redemption payments are to be made in silver (the future value of which was unknown at the date of issuance)?

It is difficult, if not impossible, for the FASB to prescribe the proper accounting treatment quickly for situations like this. Practicing accountants, however, must resolve such problems on a day-to-day basis. Through the exercise of good judgment and with the help of a universally accepted conceptual framework, it is hoped that practitioners will be able to dismiss certain alternatives quickly and then to focus upon a logical and acceptable treatment.

Development of Conceptual Framework

Over the years numerous organizations, committees, and interested individuals developed and published their own conceptual frameworks. But no single framework was universally accepted and relied on in practice. Perhaps the most successful was *Accounting Principles Board Statement No. 4*, "Basic Concepts and Accounting Principles Underlying Financial Statements of Business Enterprises," which described existing practice but did not prescribe what practice ought to be.[2] Recognizing the need for a generally accepted framework, the FASB in 1976 issued a massive three-part Discussion Memorandum entitled *Conceptual Framework for Financial Accounting and Reporting: Elements of Financial Statements and Their Measurement*. It set forth the major issues that must be addressed in establishing a conceptual framework that would be a basis for setting accounting standards and for resolving financial reporting controversies. Since the publication of that document, the FASB has issued five Statements of Financial Accounting Concepts that relate to financial reporting for business enterprises.[3] They are:

Objective ②

Describe the FASB's efforts to construct a conceptual framework.

❶ *SFAC No. 1*, "Objectives of Financial Reporting by Business Enterprises," presents the goals and purposes of accounting.

❷ *SFAC No. 2*, "Qualitative Characteristics of Accounting Information," examines the characteristics that make accounting information useful.

❸ *SFAC No. 3*, "Elements of Financial Statements of Business Enterprises," provides definitions of items in financial statements, such as assets, liabilities, revenues, and expenses.

❹ *SFAC No. 5*, "Recognition and Measurement in Financial Statements of Business Enterprises," sets forth fundamental recognition and measurement criteria and guidance on what information should be formally incorporated into financial statements and when.

❺ *SFAC No. 6*, "Elements of Financial Statements," replaces *SFAC No. 3* and expands its scope to include not-for-profit organizations.

INTERNATIONAL INSIGHT

The IASC has issued a conceptual framework that is broadly consistent with that of the U.S.

Illustration 2-1 provides an overview of the conceptual framework.[4] At the first level, the **objectives** identify the goals and purposes of accounting and are the building

---

[2]"Basic Concepts and Accounting Principles Underlying Financial Statements of Business Enterprises," *APB Statement No. 4* (New York: AICPA, 1970).

[3]The FASB has also issued a Statement of Financial Accounting Concepts that relates to nonbusiness organizations: *Statement of Financial Accounting Concepts No. 4*, "Objectives of Financial Reporting by Nonbusiness Organizations" (December 1980).

[4]Adapted from William C. Norby, *The Financial Analysts Journal* (March–April, 1982), p. 22.

ILLUSTRATION 2-1 A Conceptual Framework for Financial Reporting

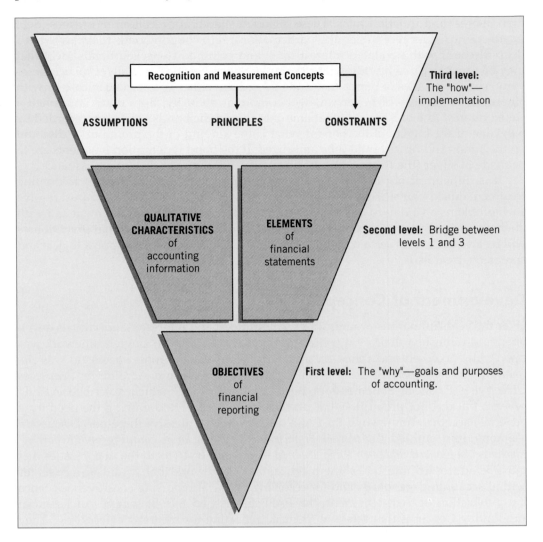

blocks for the conceptual framework. At the second level are the **qualitative characteristics** that make accounting information useful and the **elements** of financial statements (assets, liabilities, and so on). At the final or third level are the **measurement and recognition concepts** used in establishing and applying accounting standards. These concepts include assumptions, principles, and constraints that describe the present reporting environment.

Objective ❸

Understand the objectives of financial reporting.

🌐 **INTERNATIONAL INSIGHT**

In Sweden, the government often provides capital to businesses. Swedish financial reporting is more oriented toward helping government decision makers manage the economy.

❖ FIRST LEVEL: BASIC OBJECTIVES

As we discussed in Chapter 1, the objectives of financial reporting are to provide information that is: (1) useful to those making investment and credit decisions who have a reasonable understanding of business and economic activities; (2) helpful to present and potential investors, creditors, and other users in assessing the amounts, timing, and uncertainty of future cash flows; and (3) about economic resources, the claims to those resources, and the changes in them.

The objectives, therefore, begin with a broad concern about information that is useful to investor and creditor decisions. That concern narrows to the investors' and creditors' interest in the prospect of receiving cash from their investments in, or loans to, business enterprises. Finally, the objectives focus on the financial statements that provide information useful in the assessment of prospective cash flows to the business enterprise, cash flows upon which investors and creditors depend.

In providing information to users of financial statements, the accounting profession relies on general-purpose financial statements. The intent of such statements is to provide the most useful information possible at minimal cost to various user groups. Underlying these objectives is the notion that users need reasonable knowledge of business and financial accounting matters to understand the information contained in financial statements. This point is important: It means that in the preparation of financial statements a level of reasonable competence can be assumed; this has an impact on the way and the extent to which information is reported.

INTERNATIONAL INSIGHT

In Switzerland, Germany, Korea, and other nations, capital is provided to business primarily by large banks. Creditors have very close ties to firms and can obtain information directly from them. Creditors do not need to rely on publicly available information, and financial information is focused on creditor protection. This process of capital allocation, however, is starting to change.

❖ SECOND LEVEL: FUNDAMENTAL CONCEPTS

The objectives (first level) are concerned with the goals and purposes of accounting. Later, we will discuss the ways these goals and purposes are implemented (third level). Between these two levels it is necessary to provide certain conceptual building blocks that explain the qualitative characteristics of accounting information and define the elements of financial statements. These conceptual building blocks form a bridge between the **why** of accounting (the objectives) and the **how** of accounting (recognition and measurement).

Qualitative Characteristics of Accounting Information

How does one decide whether financial reports should provide information on how much a firm's assets cost to acquire (historical cost basis) or how much they are currently worth (current value basis)? Or how does one decide whether the three main segments that constitute PepsiCo—Beverages (Pepsi, Diet Pepsi, Mountain Dew), Snack Foods (Frito-Lay), and Restaurants (Pizza Hut, Taco Bell, Kentucky Fried Chicken)—should be combined and shown as one company or disaggregated and reported as three separate segments for financial reporting purposes?

Choosing an acceptable accounting method, the amount and types of information to be disclosed, and the format in which information should be presented involves determining **which alternative provides the most useful information for decision making purposes (decision usefulness)**. The FASB has identified the qualitative characteristics of accounting information that distinguish better (more useful) information from inferior (less useful) information for decision making purposes.[5] In addition, the FASB has identified certain constraints (cost-benefit and materiality) as part of the conceptual framework; these are discussed later in the chapter. The characteristics may be viewed as a hierarchy, as shown in Illustration 2-2 on the next page.

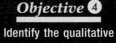

Objective ❹

Identify the qualitative characteristics of accounting information.

Decision Makers (Users) and Understandability

Decision makers vary widely in the types of decisions they make, the methods of decision making they employ, the information they already possess or can obtain from other sources, and their ability to process the information. For information to be useful, there must be a connection (linkage) between these users and the decisions they make. This link, understandability, is the quality of information that permits reasonably informed users to perceive its significance. To illustrate the importance of this linkage, assume that IBM Corp. issues a three-months' earnings report (interim report) that shows interim earnings way down. This report provides relevant and reliable information for decision making purposes. Some users, upon reading the report, decide to sell their stock. Other users do not understand the report's content and significance. They are surprised when IBM declares a smaller year-end dividend and the value of the stock declines. Thus, although the information presented was highly relevant and reliable, it was useless to users who did not understand it.

---

[5]"Qualitative Characteristics of Accounting Information," *Statement of Financial Accounting Concepts No. 2* (Stamford, Conn.: FASB, May 1980).

ILLUSTRATION 2-2 A Hierarchy of Accounting Qualities

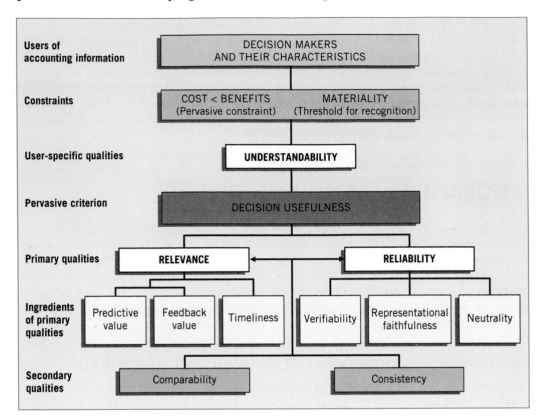

Primary Qualities: Relevance and Reliability

Relevance and reliability **are the two primary qualities that make accounting information useful for decision making**. As stated in FASB *Concepts Statement No. 2*, "the qualities that distinguish 'better' (more useful) information from 'inferior' (less useful) information are primarily the qualities of relevance and reliability, with some other characteristics that those qualities imply."[6]

Relevance. To be relevant, accounting information must be capable of making a difference in a decision.[7] If certain information has no bearing on a decision, it is irrelevant to that decision. Relevant information helps users make predictions about the ultimate outcome of past, present, and future events; that is, it has predictive value. Relevant information also helps users confirm or correct prior expectations; it has feedback value. For example, when IBM Corp. issues an interim report, this information is considered relevant because it provides a basis for forecasting annual earnings and provides feedback on past performance. For information to be relevant, it must also be available to decision makers before it loses its capacity to influence their decisions. Thus timeliness is a primary ingredient. If IBM Corp. did not report its interim results until six months after the end of the period, the information would be much less useful for decision making purposes. **For information to be relevant, it should have predictive or feedback value, and it must be presented on a timely basis.**

Reliability. Accounting information is reliable to the extent that **it is verifiable, is a faithful representation, and is reasonably free of error and bias.** Reliability is a necessity for individuals who have neither the time nor the expertise to evaluate the factual content of the information.

Verifiability is demonstrated when independent measurers, using the same measurement methods, obtain similar results. For example, would several independent auditors come to the same conclusion about a set of financial statements? If outside parties

---

[6]Ibid., par. 15.

[7]Ibid., par. 47.

using the same measurement methods arrive at different conclusions, then the statements are not verifiable. Auditors could not render an opinion on such statements.

Representational faithfulness means that the numbers and descriptions represent what really existed or happened. The accounting numbers and descriptions agree with the resources or events that these numbers and descriptions purport to represent. If General Motors income statement reports sales of $150 billion when it had sales of $138.2 billion, then the statements are not a faithful representation.

Neutrality means that information cannot be selected to favor one set of interested parties over another. Factual, truthful, unbiased information must be the overriding consideration. For example, ValuJet, Inc. should not be permitted to suppress information in the notes to its financial statements about the numerous lawsuits that have been filed against it because of airline safety issues—even though such disclosure is embarrassing and damaging to the company.

Neutrality in standard setting has come under increasing attack. Some argue that standards should not be issued if they cause undesirable economic effects on an industry or company. We disagree. Standards must be free from bias or we will no longer have credible financial statements. Without credible financial statements, individuals will no longer use this information. An analogy demonstrates the point: In the United States, we have both boxing and wrestling matches. Many individuals bet on boxing matches because such contests are assumed not to be fixed. But nobody bets on wrestling matches. Why? Because the public assumes that wrestling matches are rigged. If financial information is biased (rigged), the public will lose confidence and no longer use this information.

Secondary Qualities: Comparability and Consistency

Information about an enterprise is more useful if it can be compared with similar information about another enterprise (**comparability**) and with similar information about the same enterprise at other points in time (**consistency**).[8]

Comparability. Information that has been measured and reported in a similar manner for different enterprises is considered comparable. Comparability enables users to identify the real similarities and differences in economic phenomena because these differences and similarities have not been obscured by the use of noncomparable accounting methods. For example, as indicated in the opening story, if America Online capitalizes its marketing costs, but Compuserve expenses these costs, it is more difficult to compare and evaluate the financial results of these two companies. Also, resource allocation decisions involve evaluations of alternatives; a valid evaluation can be made only if comparable information is available.

Consistency. When an entity applies the same accounting treatment to similar events, from period to period, the entity is considered to be consistent in its use of accounting standards. It does not mean that companies cannot switch from one method of accounting to another. Companies can change methods, but the changes are restricted to situations in which it can be demonstrated that the newly adopted method is preferable to the old. Then the nature and effect of the accounting change, as well as the justification for it, must be disclosed in the financial statements for the period in which the change is made.[9]

---

[8]As indicated in Chapter 1, the environment of accounting is continually changing; comparability and consistency are thereby made more difficult to achieve. Tax laws change, new industries (e.g., computer software) grow dramatically, new financial instruments (e.g., financial futures, collateral mortgage obligations, zero-coupon convertible bonds) are created, and mergers and divestitures occur frequently.

[9]The AICPA Special Committee on Financial Reporting noted that users highly value consistency. They note that a change tends to destroy the comparability of data before and after the change. Some companies take the time to assist users to understand the pre- and post-change data. Generally, however, users say they lose the ability to analyze over time.

When there has been a change in accounting principles, the auditor refers to it in an explanatory paragraph of the audit report. This paragraph identifies the nature of the change and refers the reader to the note in the financial statements that discusses the change in detail.[10]

In summary, accounting reports for any given year are more useful if they can be compared with reports from other companies and with prior reports of the same entity. For example, if IBM is the only enterprise that prepares interim reports, the information is less useful because the user cannot relate it to interim reports for any other enterprise; that is, there is no comparability. Similarly, if the measurement methods used to prepare IBM's interim report change from one interim period to another, the information is considered less useful because the user cannot relate it to previous interim periods; that is, it lacks consistency.

Basic Elements

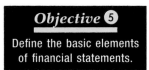

An important aspect of developing any theoretical structure is the body of **basic elements** or definitions to be included in the structure. At present, accounting uses many terms that have peculiar and specific meanings. These terms constitute the language of business or the jargon of accounting.

One such term is **asset**. Is it something we own? If the answer is yes, can we assume that any leased asset would not be shown on the balance sheet? Is an asset something we have the right to use, or is it anything of value used by the enterprise to generate revenues? If the answer is yes, then why should the management of the enterprise not be considered an asset? It seems necessary, therefore, to develop basic definitions for the elements of financial statements. *Concepts Statement No. 6* defines the ten interrelated elements that are most directly related to measuring the performance and financial status of an enterprise. We list them here for review and information purposes; you need not memorize these definitions at this point. Each of these elements will be explained and examined in more detail in subsequent chapters.

❖ ELEMENTS OF FINANCIAL STATEMENTS ❖

ASSETS. Probable future economic benefits obtained or controlled by a particular entity as a result of past transactions or events.

LIABILITIES. Probable future sacrifices of economic benefits arising from present obligations of a particular entity to transfer assets or provide services to other entities in the future as a result of past transactions or events.

EQUITY. Residual interest in the assets of an entity that remains after deducting its liabilities. In a business enterprise, the equity is the ownership interest.

INVESTMENTS BY OWNERS. Increases in net assets of a particular enterprise resulting from transfers to it from other entities of something of value to obtain or increase ownership interests (or equity) in it. Assets are most commonly received as investments by owners, but that which is received may also include services or satisfaction or conversion of liabilities of the enterprise.

DISTRIBUTIONS TO OWNERS. Decreases in net assets of a particular enterprise resulting from transferring assets, rendering services, or incurring liabilities by the enterprise to owners. Distributions to owners decrease ownership interests (or equity) in an enterprise.

COMPREHENSIVE INCOME. Change in equity (net assets) of an entity during a period from transactions and other events and circumstances from nonowner sources. It includes all changes in equity during a period except those resulting from investments by owners and distributions to owners.

---

[10]"Reports on Audited Financial Statements," *Statement on Auditing Standards No. 58* (New York: AICPA, April 1988), par. 34.

REVENUES. Inflows or other enhancements of assets of an entity or settlement of its liabilities (or a combination of both) during a period from delivering or producing goods, rendering services, or other activities that constitute the entity's ongoing major or central operations.

EXPENSES. Outflows or other using up of assets or incurrences of liabilities (or a combination of both) during a period from delivering or producing goods, rendering services, or carrying out other activities that constitute the entity's ongoing major or central operations.

GAINS. Increases in equity (net assets) from peripheral or incidental transactions of an entity and from all other transactions and other events and circumstances affecting the entity during a period except those that result from revenues or investments by owners.

LOSSES. Decreases in equity (net assets) from peripheral or incidental transactions of an entity and from all other transactions and other events and circumstances affecting the entity during a period except those that result from expenses or distributions to owners.[11]

Two important points should be noted about these definitions. First, the term **comprehensive income** represents a new concept. Comprehensive income is more inclusive than the traditional notion of net income. It includes net income and all other changes in equity exclusive of owners' investments and distributions. For example, unrealized holding gains and losses on available-for-sale securities, which are currently excluded from net income, are included under comprehensive income. The reporting of comprehensive income is discussed in Chapter 4.

Second, the FASB classifies the elements into two distinct groups. The first group of three elements—assets, liabilities, and equity—describes amounts of resources and claims to resources at a **moment in time**. The other seven elements (comprehensive income and its components—revenues, expenses, gains, and losses—as well as investments by owners and distributions to owners) describe transactions, events, and circumstances that affect an enterprise during a **period of time**. The first class—assets, liabilities, and equity—is changed by elements of the second class and at any time is the cumulative result of all changes. This interaction is referred to as "articulation." That is, key figures in one statement correspond to balances in another.

❖ THIRD LEVEL: RECOGNITION AND MEASUREMENT CONCEPTS

The third level of the framework consists of concepts that implement the basic objectives of level one. These concepts explain which, when, and how financial elements and events should be recognized, measured, and reported by the accounting system. Most of them are set forth in FASB *Statement of Financial Accounting Concepts No. 5*, "Recognition and Measurement in Financial Statements of Business Enterprises." According to *SFAC No. 5*, to be recognized, an item (event or transaction) must meet the definition of an "element of financial statements" as defined in *SFAC No. 6* and must be measurable. Most aspects of current practice are consistent with this recognition and measurement concept.

The accounting profession continues to use the concepts in *SFAC No. 5* as operational guidelines. For discussion purposes, we have chosen to identify the concepts as basic assumptions, principles, and constraints. Not everyone uses this classification system, so it is best to focus your attention more on **understanding the concepts** than on how they are classified and organized. These concepts serve as guidelines in devel-

---

[11]"Elements of Financial Statements," *Statement of Financial Accounting Concepts No. 6* (Stamford, Conn.: FASB, December 1985), pp. ix and x.

oping rational responses to controversial financial reporting issues. They have evolved over time and are fundamental to the specific accounting principles issued by the FASB and its predecessor organizations.

Basic Assumptions

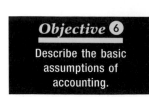

Objective ❻

Describe the basic assumptions of accounting.

Four basic assumptions underlie the financial accounting structure: (1) **economic entity,** (2) **going concern,** (3) **monetary unit,** and (4) **periodicity.**

Economic Entity Assumption

The economic entity assumption **means that economic activity can be identified with a particular unit of accountability.** In other words, the activity of a business enterprise can be kept separate and distinct from its owners and any other business unit. For example, if the activities and elements of General Motors could not be distinguished from those of Ford or Chrysler, then it would be impossible to know which company financially outperformed the other two in recent years. If there were no meaningful way to separate all of the economic events that occur, no basis for accounting would exist.

The entity concept does not apply solely to the segregation of activities among given business enterprises. An individual, a department or division, or an entire industry could be considered a separate entity if we chose to define the unit in such a manner. Thus, **the entity concept does not necessarily refer to a legal entity**. A parent and its subsidiaries are separate **legal** entities, but merging their activities for accounting and reporting purposes does not violate the **economic entity** assumption.[12]

Going Concern Assumption

Most accounting methods are based on the going concern assumption—**that the business enterprise will have a long life**. Experience indicates that, in spite of numerous business failures, companies have a fairly high continuance rate. Although accountants do not believe that business firms will last indefinitely, they do expect them to last long enough to fulfill their objectives and commitments.

The implications of this assumption are profound. The historical cost principle would be of limited usefulness if eventual liquidation were assumed. Under a liquidation approach, for example, asset values are better stated at net realizable value (sales price less costs of disposal) than at acquisition cost. **Depreciation and amortization policies are justifiable and appropriate only if we assume some permanence to the enterprise.** If a liquidation approach were adopted, the current-noncurrent classification of assets and liabilities would lose much of its significance. Labeling anything a fixed or long-term asset would be difficult to justify. Indeed, listing liabilities on the basis of priority in liquidation would be more reasonable.

The going concern assumption applies in most business situations. **Only where liquidation appears imminent is the assumption inapplicable.** In these cases a total revaluation of assets and liabilities can provide information that closely approximates the entity's net realizable value. Accounting problems related to an enterprise in liquidation are presented in advanced accounting courses.

Monetary Unit Assumption

The monetary unit assumption means that money is the common denominator of economic activity and provides an appropriate basis for accounting measurement and

---

[12]The concept of the entity is changing. For example, it is now harder to define the outer edges of companies. There are public companies with multiple public subsidiaries, each with joint ventures, licensing arrangements, and other affiliations. Increasingly, loose affiliations of enterprises in joint ventures or customer-supplier relationships are formed and dissolved in a matter of months or weeks. These "virtual companies" raise accounting issues about how to account for the entity. See Steven H. Wallman, "The Future of Accounting and Disclosure in an Evolving World: The Need for Dramatic Change," *Accounting Horizons*, September 1995.

analysis. This assumption implies that the monetary unit is the most effective means of expressing to interested parties changes in capital and exchanges of goods and services. **The monetary unit is relevant, simple, universally available, understandable, and useful.** Application of this assumption depends on the even more basic assumption that quantitative data are useful in communicating economic information and in making rational economic decisions.

In the United States, accountants have chosen generally to ignore the phenomenon of price-level change (inflation and deflation) by assuming that **the unit of measure— the dollar—remains reasonably stable.** This assumption about the monetary unit has been used to justify adding 1970 dollars to 1998 dollars without any adjustment. The FASB in *SFAC No. 5* indicated that it expects the dollar, unadjusted for inflation or deflation, to continue to be used to measure items recognized in financial statements. Only if circumstances change dramatically (such as if the United States were to experience high inflation similar to that in many South American countries) will the Board again consider "inflation accounting." Chapter 25 discusses the accounting problems and benefits of reporting price-level adjusted information.

INTERNATIONAL INSIGHT

Due to their experiences with persistent inflation, several South American countries produce "constant currency" financial reports. Typically, a general price level index is used to adjust for the effects of inflation.

Periodicity Assumption

The most accurate way to measure the results of enterprise activity would be to measure them at the time of the enterprise's eventual liquidation. Business, government, investors, and various other user groups, however, cannot wait that long for such information. Users need to be apprised of performance and economic status on a timely basis so that they can evaluate and compare firms. Therefore, information must be reported periodically.

The periodicity (or time period) assumption implies that **the economic activities of an enterprise can be divided into artificial time periods**. These time periods vary, but the most common are monthly, quarterly, and yearly.

The shorter the time period, the more difficult it becomes to determine the proper net income for the period. A month's results are usually less reliable than a quarter's results, and a quarter's results are likely to be less reliable than a year's results. Investors desire and demand that information be quickly processed and disseminated; yet the quicker the information is released, the more it is subject to error. This phenomenon provides an interesting example of the trade-off between relevance and reliability in preparing financial data.

This problem of defining the time period is becoming more serious because product cycles are shorter and products become obsolete more quickly. Many believe that, given technology advances, more on-line, real-time financial information needs to be provided to ensure that relevant information is available.

Basic Principles of Accounting

Four basic principles of accounting are used to record transactions: (1) **historical cost,** (2) **revenue recognition,** (3) **matching,** and (4) **full disclosure.**

Objective ❼

Explain the application of the basic principles of accounting.

Historical Cost Principle

GAAP requires that most assets and liabilities be accounted for and reported on the basis of acquisition price. This is often referred to as the historical cost principle

Cost has an important advantage over other valuations: it is reliable. To illustrate the importance of this advantage, consider the problems that would arise if we adopted some other basis for keeping records. If we were to select current selling price, for instance, we might have a difficult time in attempting to establish a sales value for a given item without selling it. Every member of the accounting department might have a different opinion regarding an asset's value, and management might desire still another figure. And how often would it be necessary to establish sales value? All companies close their accounts at least annually, and some compute their net income every month. These companies would find it necessary to place a sales value on every asset each time they wished to determine income—a laborious task and one that would result in a figure of net income materially affected by opinion. Similar objections have been leveled against current cost (replacement cost, present value of future cash flows) and any other basis of valuation *except cost*.

What about liabilities? Are they accounted for on a cost basis? Yes, they are. **If we convert the term "cost" to "exchange price," we find that it applies to liabilities as well.** Liabilities, such as bonds, notes, and accounts payable, are issued by a business enterprise in exchange for assets, or perhaps services, upon which an agreed price has usually been placed. This price, established by the exchange transaction, is the "cost" of the liability and provides the figure at which it should be recorded in the accounts and reported in financial statements.

A recent survey of users by the AICPA's Special Committee on Financial Reporting appears to support the historical cost principle in most situations. Users indicated that historical cost provides them with a stable and consistent benchmark that they can rely on to establish historical trends. They are concerned about the subjectivity and potential volatility in reported results of a model based on some type of current value.

Users also reported that they found fair value information useful for particular types of assets and liabilities and in certain types of industries. This result is not surprising because certain assets and liabilities are already reported at current values either in the financial statements or related notes. For example, most investments in debt and equity securities are currently reported at fair value, receivables are reported at net realizable value, and inventories are reported at the lower of cost or market (usually replacement cost). At this time, certain industries, such as brokerage houses and mutual funds, prepare their basic financial statements on a fair value basis.

As indicated from the above discussion, we presently have a "mixed attribute" system that permits the use of historical cost, fair value, lower of cost or market, and other valuation bases. Although the historical cost principle continues to be the primary basis of valuation, recording and reporting of fair value information is increasing. Most debt and equity security investments are now reported at fair value. And the FASB requires the disclosure of the fair value of most financial instruments. It appears this trend will continue.

Revenue Recognition Principle

A crucial question for many enterprises is when revenue should be recognized. Revenue is generally recognized when (1) **realized** or **realizable** and (2) **earned**. This approach has often been referred to as the revenue recognition principle. Revenues are realized when products (goods or services), merchandise, or other assets are exchanged for cash or claims to cash. Revenues are realizable when assets received or held are readily convertible into cash or claims to cash. Assets are readily convertible when they are salable or interchangeable in an active market at readily determinable prices without significant additional cost.

In addition to the first test (realized or realizable), revenues are not recognized until earned. And revenues are considered earned when the entity has substantially accomplished what it must do to be entitled to the benefits represented by the revenues.[13]

Generally, an objective test—confirmation by a sale to independent interests—is used to indicate the point at which revenue is recognized. Usually, only at the date of sale is there an objective and verifiable measure of revenue—the sales price. Any basis for revenue recognition short of actual sale opens the door to wide variations in practice. To give accounting reports uniform meaning, a rule of revenue recognition comparable to the cost rule for asset valuation is essential. **Recognition at the time of sale provides a uniform and reasonable test.**

There are, however, exceptions to the rule, and at times the basic rule is difficult to apply.

---

[13]"Recognition and Measurement in Financial Statements of Business Enterprises," *Statement of Financial Accounting Concepts No. 5* (Stamford, Conn.: FASB, December 1984), par. 83(a) and (b).

During Production. **Recognition of revenue is allowed before the contract is completed in certain long-term construction contracts.** The main feature of this method is that revenue is recognized periodically based on the percentage that the job has been completed instead of waiting until the entire job has been finished. Although technically a transfer of ownership has not occurred, the earning process is considered substantially completed at various stages as construction progresses. Naturally, if it is not possible to obtain dependable estimates of cost and progress, then revenue recognition is delayed until the job is completed.

End of Production. At times, **revenue might be recognized after the production cycle has ended but before the sale takes place**. This is the case where the selling price is certain as well as the amount. For instance, if products or other assets are salable in an active market at readily determinable prices without significant additional cost, then revenue can be recognized at the completion of production. An example would be the mining of certain minerals for which, once the mineral is mined, a ready market at a standard price exists. The same holds true for some artificial price supports set by the government in establishing agricultural prices.

Receipt of Cash. **Receipt of cash is another basis for revenue recognition.** The cash basis approach should be used only when it is impossible to establish the revenue figure at the time of sale because of the uncertainty of collection. One form of the cash basis is the installment sales method where payment is required in periodic installments over a long period of time. Its most common use is in the retail field. Farm and home equipment and furnishings are typically sold on an installment basis. The installment method is frequently justified on the basis that the risk of not collecting an account receivable is so great that the sale is not sufficient evidence for recognition to take place. In some instances, this reasoning may be valid. Generally, though, if a sale has been completed, it should be recognized; if bad debts are expected, they should be recorded as separate estimates.

Revenue, then, is recorded in the period when realized or realizable and earned. Normally, this is the date of sale. But circumstances may dictate application of the percentage-of-completion approach, the end-of-production approach, or the receipt-of-cash approach.

Conceptually, the proper accounting treatment for revenue recognition should be apparent and should fit nicely into one of the conditions mentioned above, but often it does not. For example, how should motion picture companies such as Metro-Goldwyn-Mayer, Inc., Warner Bros., and United Artists account for the sale of rights to show motion picture films on ABC, CBS, or NBC? Should the revenue from the sale of the rights be reported when the contract is signed, when the motion picture film is delivered to the network, when the cash payment is received by the motion picture company, or when the film is shown on television? The question of revenue recognition is complicated further since the TV networks are often restricted to the number of times the film may be shown and over what period of time.

For example, Metro-Goldwyn-Mayer Film Co. (MGM) sold CBS the rights to show *Gone With the Wind* for $35 million. CBS received the right to show this classic movie 20 times over a 20-year period. MGM argued that the right to show *Gone With the Wind* 20 times over a 20-year period was a significant contract restriction and, therefore, revenue recognition should coincide with the showings. The accounting profession on the other hand argued that when (1) the sales price and cost of each film are known, (2) collectibility is assured, and (3) the film is available and accepted by the network, revenue recognition should occur immediately. The restriction that *Gone With the Wind* be shown only once a year for 20 years was not considered significant enough or appropriate justification for deferring revenue recognition. It is interesting to note that MGM, in the appropriate first quarter, reported essentially the entire $35 million in revenue in one period as the following headline in *The Wall Street Journal* reported, ''MGM's Net Tripled in the First Quarter that Ended Nov. 30.''

As you can see, timing revenue recognition is no simple matter. The most straight-forward approach is to recognize revenue at the point of sale. Most uncertainties have usually been resolved by that time. And verifiable evidence, obtained through an exchange transaction, is available.

Matching Principle

In recognizing expenses, accountants attempt to follow the approach of "let the expense follow the revenues." Expenses are recognized not when wages are paid, or when the work is performed, or when a product is produced, but when the work (service) or the product actually makes its contribution to revenue. Thus, expense recognition is tied to revenue recognition. This practice is referred to as the matching principle because it dictates that **efforts (expenses) be matched with accomplishment (revenues) whenever it is reasonable and practicable to do so.**

For those costs for which it is difficult to adopt some type of rational association with revenue, some other approach must be developed. Often, a "rational and systematic" allocation policy is used that will approximate the matching principle. This type of expense recognition pattern involves assumptions about the benefits that are being received as well as the cost associated with those benefits. The cost of a long-lived asset, for example, must be allocated over all of the accounting periods during which the asset is used because the asset contributes to the generation of revenue throughout its useful life.

Some costs are charged to the current period as expenses (or losses) simply because no connection with revenue can be determined. Examples of these types of costs are officers' salaries and other administrative expenses.

Summarizing, we might say that costs are analyzed to determine whether a relationship exists with revenue. Where this association holds, the costs are expensed and matched against the revenue in the period when the revenue is recognized. If no connection appears between costs and revenues, an allocation of cost on some systematic and rational basis might be appropriate. Where this method does not seem desirable, the cost may be expensed immediately.

Costs are generally classified into two groups: **product costs and period costs**. **Product costs** such as material, labor, and overhead attach to the product and are carried into future periods if the revenue from the product is recognized in subsequent periods. **Period costs** such as officers' salaries and other administrative expenses are charged off immediately, even though benefits associated with these costs occur in the future, because no direct relationship between cost and revenue can be determined.

The problem of expense recognition is as complex as that of revenue recognition. For example, at one time a large oil company spent a considerable amount of money in an introductory advertising campaign in Hawaii. The company obviously hoped that this advertising campaign would attract new customers and develop brand loyalty. Over how many years, if any, should this outlay be expensed?

For another example, Stars To Go, a major video rental company, writes off the cost of its video tapes over 3 years, 36% the first year, 36% the second, and 28% the third. Other video rental companies take a more conservative approach. They note that Class A titles (hits such as *Mission Impossible* or *Toy Story*) average 28 rentals the first 3 months, 12 rentals the next 3 months, 12 more in the next 6 months, and 18 over the next year. As a result, they charge off these tapes in one year, or perhaps 2 years at most. As an executive of one of the major video rental companies noted, "If you ask 12 different people the useful life of a video tape, you get 12 different answers."

The conceptual validity of the matching principle has been a subject of debate. A major concern is that matching permits certain costs to be deferred and treated as assets on the balance sheet when in fact these costs may not have future benefits. If abused, this principle permits the balance sheet to become a "dumping ground" for unmatched costs. In addition, there appears to be no objective definition of "systematic and rational." For example, Hartwig, Inc. purchased an asset for $100,000 that will last 5 years. Various depreciation methods (all considered systematic and rational) might be used to allocate this cost over the 5-year period. What objective criteria should be used in determining what portion of the cost of the asset should be written off each period?[14]

Full Disclosure Principle

In deciding what information to report, the general practice of providing information that is of sufficient importance to influence the judgment and decisions of an informed user is followed. Often referred to as the full disclosure principle, it recognizes that the nature and amount of information included in financial reports reflects a series of judgmental trade-offs. These trade-offs strive for (1) sufficient detail to disclose matters that **make a difference** to users, yet (2) sufficient condensation to make the **information understandable**, keeping in mind costs of preparing and using it. Information about financial position, income, cash flows, and investments can be found in one of three places: (1) within the main body of financial statements, (2) in the notes to those statements, or (3) as supplementary information.

The financial statements are a formalized, structured means of communicating financial information. To be recognized in the main body of financial statements, **an item should meet the definition of a basic element, be measurable with sufficient certainty, and be relevant and reliable.**[15]

Disclosure is not a substitute for proper accounting. As the chief accountant of the SEC recently noted: Good disclosure does not cure bad accounting any more than an adjective or adverb can be used without—or in place of—a noun or verb. Thus, for example, cash basis accounting for cost of goods sold is misleading, even if accrual basis amounts were disclosed in the notes to the financial statements.

The notes to financial statements generally amplify or explain the items presented in the main body of the statements. If the information in the main body of the financial statements gives an incomplete picture of the performance and position of the enterprise, additional information that is needed to complete the picture should be included in the notes. Information in the notes does not have to be quantifiable, nor does it need to qualify as an element. Notes can be partially or totally narrative. Examples of notes are: descriptions of the accounting policies and methods used in measuring the elements reported in the statements; explanations of uncertainties and contingencies; and statistics and details too voluminous for inclusion in the statements. The notes are not only helpful but also essential to understanding the enterprise's performance and position.

Supplementary information may include details or amounts that present a different perspective from that adopted in the financial statements. It may be quantifiable information that is high in relevance but low in reliability, or information that is helpful but not essential. One example of supplementary information is the data and schedules provided by oil and gas companies: Typically they provide information on proven reserves as well as the related discounted cash flows.

Supplementary information may also include management's explanation of the financial information and its discussion of the significance of that information. For example, during the past decade many business combinations have produced innumerable conglomerate-type business organizations and financing arrangements that demand new and peculiar accounting and reporting practices and principles. In each of these situations, the same problem must be faced: making sure that enough information is presented to ensure that the **reasonably prudent investor** will not be misled.

A classic illustration of the problem of determining adequate disclosure guidelines is the recent question on what banks should disclose about loans made for highly lev-

---

[14]Some would suggest that even that procedure is nearly impossible, given that the revenue flow from any given asset is interrelated with the remaining asset structure of the enterprise. For example, see Arthur L. Thomas, "The Allocation Problem in Financial Accounting Theory," *Studies in Accounting Research No. 3* (Evanston, Ill.: American Accounting Association, 1969), and "The Allocation Problem: Part Two," *Studies in Accounting Research No. 9* (Sarasota, Fla.: American Accounting Association, 1974).

[15]*SFAC No. 5,* par. 63.

eraged transactions such as leveraged buyouts. Investors want to know the percentage of a bank's loans that are of this risky type. The problem is what do we mean by "leveraged"? As one regulator noted: "If it looks leveraged, it probably is leveraged, but most of us would be hard-pressed to come up with a definition." Is a loan to a company with a debt to equity ratio of 4 to 1 highly leveraged? Or is 8 to 1 or 10 to 1 high leverage? The problem is complicated because some highly leveraged companies have cash flows that cover interest payments; therefore, they are not as risky as they might appear. In short, providing the appropriate disclosure to help investors and regulators differentiate risky from safe is difficult.

The content, arrangement, and display of financial statements, along with other facets of full disclosure, are discussed in Chapters 4, 5, 24, and 25.

Constraints

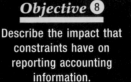

Objective 8

Describe the impact that constraints have on reporting accounting information.

In providing information with the qualitative characteristics that make it useful, two overriding **constraints** must be considered: (1) the **cost-benefit relationship** and (2) **materiality**. Two other less dominant yet important constraints that are part of the reporting environment are **industry practices** and **conservatism**.

Cost-Benefit Relationship

Too often, users assume that information is a cost-free commodity. But preparers and providers of accounting information know that it is not. Therefore, the **cost-benefit relationship** must be considered: The costs of providing the information must be weighed against the benefits that can be derived from using the information. Obviously the benefits should exceed the costs. Practicing accountants have traditionally applied this constraint through the notions of "expediency" ("it is or is not expedient") or "practicality" ("it is or is not practical"), but only recently have standard setting bodies and governmental agencies resorted to cost-benefit analysis before making their informational requirements final. In order to justify requiring a particular measurement or disclosure, the benefits perceived to be derived from it must exceed the costs perceived to be associated with it.

The following remark, made by a corporate executive about a proposed standard, was addressed to the FASB: "In all my years in the financial arena, I have never seen such an absolutely ridiculous proposal. . . . To dignify these 'actuarial' estimates by recording them as assets and liabilities would be virtually unthinkable except for the fact that the FASB has done equally stupid things in the past. . . . For God's sake, use common sense just this once."[16] Although this remark is extreme, it does indicate the frustration expressed by members of the business community about standard setting and whether the benefits of a given standard exceed the costs.

The difficulty in cost-benefit analysis is that the costs and especially the benefits are not always evident or measurable. The costs are of several kinds, including costs of collecting and processing, costs of disseminating, costs of auditing, costs of potential litigation, costs of disclosure to competitors, and costs of analysis and interpretation. Benefits accrue to preparers (in terms of greater management control and access to capital) and to users (in terms of allocation of resources, tax assessment, and rate regulation). But benefits are generally more difficult to quantify than are costs.

The FASB has attempted to address this issue. Included in its recent standard on Employers' Accounting for Postretirement Benefits Other Than Pensions is a section justifying the new rules on a cost-benefit basis. This special section was provided in response to criticisms received from the business community. As an FASB representative noted: "We may very well include such cost-benefit sections in future statements [rules], but we want to be sure they aren't just boilerplate and address each rule's specific costs and benefits."

Most recently, the AICPA Special Committee on Financial Reporting submitted the following **constraints to limit the costs of reporting**:

---

[16]"Decision-Usefulness: The Overriding Objective," *FASB Viewpoints*, October 19, 1983, p. 4.

a. Business reporting should exclude information outside of management's expertise or for which management is not the best source, such as information about competitors.

b. Management should not be required to report information that would significantly harm the company's competitive position.

c. Management should not be required to provide forecasted financial statements. Rather, management should provide information that helps users forecast for themselves the company's financial future.

d. Other than for financial statements, management need only report the information it knows. That is, management should be under no obligation to gather information it does not have, or need, to manage the business.

e. Certain elements of business reporting should be presented only if users and management agree they should be reported—a concept of flexible reporting.

f. Companies should not have to expand reporting of forward-looking information until there are more effective deterrents to unwarranted litigation that discourages companies from doing so.

Materiality

The constraint of **materiality** relates to an item's impact on a firm's overall financial operations. An item is material if its inclusion or omission would influence or change the judgment of a reasonable person.[17] It is immaterial and, therefore, irrelevant if it would have no impact on a decision maker. In short, **it must make a difference** or it need not be disclosed. The point involved here is one of **relative size and importance**. If the amount involved is significant when compared with the other revenues and expenses, assets and liabilities, or net income of the entity, sound and acceptable standards should be followed. If the amount is so small that it is quite unimportant when compared with other items, application of a particular standard may be considered of less importance. It is difficult to provide firm guides in judging when a given item is or is not material because materiality varies both with relative amount and with relative importance. For example, the two sets of numbers presented below illustrate relative size.

	Company A	Company B
Sales	$10,000,000	$100,000
Costs and expenses	9,000,000	90,000
Income from operations	$ 1,000,000	$ 10,000
Unusual gain	$ 20,000	$ 5,000

ILLUSTRATION 2-3
Materiality Comparison

During the period in question, the revenues and expenses and, therefore, the net incomes of Company A and Company B have been proportional. Each has had an unusual gain. In looking at the abbreviated income figures for Company A, it does not appear significant whether the amount of the unusual gain is set out separately or merged with the regular operating income. It is only 2% of the net income and, if merged, would not seriously distort the net income figure. Company B has had an unusual gain of only $5,000, but it is relatively much more significant than the larger gain realized by A. For Company B, an item of $5,000 amounts to 50% of its net income. Obviously, the inclusion of such an item in ordinary operating income would affect the amount of that income materially. Thus we see the importance of the **relative size** of an item in determining its materiality.

---

[17]*SFAC No. 2* (par. 132) sets forth the essence of materiality: "The omission or misstatement of an item in a financial report is material if, in the light of surrounding circumstances, the magnitude of the item is such that it is probable that the judgement of a reasonable person relying upon the report would have been changed or influenced by the inclusion or correction of the item." This same concept of materiality has been adopted by the auditing profession. See "Audit Risk and Materiality in Conducting an Audit," *Statement on Auditing Standards No. 47* (New York: AICPA, 1983), par. 6.

The **nature of the item may also be important**. For example, if a company is involved in a violation of a statute (Foreign Corrupt Practices Act or one of the antitrust laws), the amounts involved should be separately disclosed. Or, a $100,000 misclassification within the noncurrent section may not be considered material; but a $100,000 misclassification if it affects the current section instead of the noncurrent section may be material.

The application of the materiality constraint can be controversial. As an example, General Dynamics disclosed that at one time its Resources Group had improved its earnings by $5.8 million at the same time that its Stromberg Datagraphix subsidiary had taken write-offs of $6.7 million. Although both numbers were far larger than the $2.5 million that General Dynamics as a whole earned for the year, neither was disclosed as an unusual or nonrecurring item in the annual report; apparently the net effect on net income was not considered material. It seems clear that General Dynamics should have disclosed each item separately since the Stromberg write-off appeared to be a onetime charge, whereas the improvement in its Resources Group may have been ongoing.

In another case, GAC's first quarter earnings rose from 76 cents to 77 cents a share. Nowhere did the annual report disclose that a favorable tax carryforward of 4 cents a share prevented GAC's earnings from sliding to 73 cents a share. The company took the position that this carryforward should not be shown as an extraordinary item because it was not material (6%). As one executive noted, "You know that accountants have a rule of thumb which says that anything under 10% is not material." Of course, the executive's statement seems ill-advised. The firm should have considered it significant that the direction of the company's earnings was completely altered—even though 4 cents is a small amount. This information would have been of considerable importance to investors.

Materiality is a factor in a great many internal accounting decisions, too. The amount of classification required in a subsidiary expense ledger, the degree of accuracy required in prorating expenses among the departments of a business, and the extent to which adjustments should be made for accrued and deferred items, are examples of judgments that should finally be determined on a basis of reasonableness and practicability, which is the materiality constraint sensibly applied. Only by **the exercise of good judgment and professional expertise** can reasonable and appropriate answers be found.[18]

Industry Practices

INTERNATIONAL INSIGHT

In Japan, capital is also provided by very large banks. Assets are often undervalued and liabilities overvalued. These practices reduce the demand for dividends and protect creditors in event of a default.

Another practical consideration is industry practices. **The peculiar nature of some industries and business concerns** sometimes requires departure from basic theory. In the public utility industry, noncurrent assets are reported first on the balance sheet to highlight the industry's capital-intensive nature. Agricultural crops are often reported at market value because it is costly to develop accurate cost figures on individual crops. Such variations from basic theory are not many, yet they do exist. Whenever we find what appears to be a violation of basic accounting theory, we should determine whether it is explained by some peculiar feature of the type of business involved before we criticize the procedures followed.

---

[18]A search for a definition of materiality based upon interpretations by the courts in cases under the securities laws reveals differing concepts of materiality; see Kenneth R. Jeffries, "Materiality as Defined by the Courts," *The CPA Journal* (October 1981), pp. 13–17. The point was reinforced in a Supreme Court ruling on the question of whether a company has to disclose merger talks prior to the completion of the talks (*Combustion Engineering* v. *Basic Research*). Justice Blackmun noted that materiality depends on the significance the reasonable investor would place on the withheld or misrepresented information. When the event is uncertain, such as a pending merger, materiality depends on both the importance of the event if it does transpire and the probability that the deal will be completed.

Conservatism

Few conventions in accounting are as misunderstood as the constraint of conservatism. Conservatism means **when in doubt choose the solution that will be least likely to overstate assets and income**. Note that there is nothing in the conservatism convention urging that net assets or net income be *understated*. Unfortunately it has been interpreted by some to mean just that. All that conservatism does, properly applied, is provide a very reasonable guide in difficult situations: refrain from overstatement of net income and net assets. Examples of conservatism in accounting are the use of the lower of cost or market approach in valuing inventories and the rule that accrued net losses should be recognized on firm purchase commitments for goods for inventory. If the issue is in doubt, it is better to understate than overstate net income and net assets. Of course, if there is no doubt, there is no need to apply this constraint.

Summary of the Structure

Illustration 2-4 presents the conceptual framework discussed in this chapter. It is similar to Illustration 2-1, except that it provides additional information for each level. We cannot overemphasize the usefulness of this conceptual framework in helping to understand many of the problem areas that are examined in subsequent chapters.

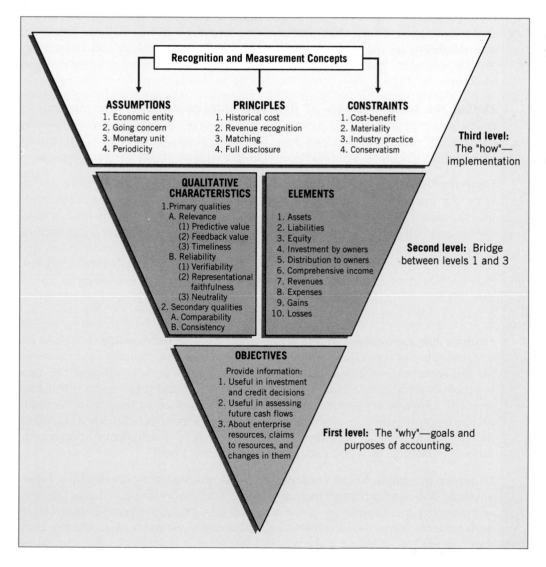

ILLUSTRATION 2-4
Conceptual Framework
for Financial Reporting

SUMMARY OF LEARNING OBJECTIVES

① **Describe the usefulness of a conceptual framework.** A conceptual framework is needed to (1) build on and relate to an established body of concepts and objectives, (2) provide a framework for solving new and emerging practical problems, (3) increase financial statement users' understanding of and confidence in financial reporting, and (4) enhance comparability among companies' financial statements.

② **Describe the FASB's efforts to construct a conceptual framework.** The FASB has issued five Statements of Financial Accounting Concepts that relate to financial reporting for business enterprises. These concept statements provide the framework for the conceptual framework and include objectives, qualitative characteristics, and elements. In addition, measurement and recognition concepts are developed.

③ **Understand the objectives of financial reporting.** The objectives of financial reporting are to provide information that is (1) useful to those making investment and credit decisions who have a reasonable understanding of business activities; (2) helpful to present and potential investors, creditors, and others in assessing future cash flows; and (3) about economic resources and the claims to and changes in them.

④ **Identify the qualitative characteristics of accounting information.** The overriding criterion by which accounting choices can be judged is decision usefulness; that is, providing information that is most useful for decision making. Relevance and reliability are the two primary qualities and comparability and consistency are the secondary qualities that make accounting information useful for decision making.

⑤ **Define the basic elements of financial statements.** The basic elements of financial statements are: (1) assets, (2) liabilities, (3) equity, (4) investments by owners, (5) distributions to owners, (6) comprehensive income, (7) revenues, (8) expenses, (9) gains, and (10) losses. These ten elements are defined on page 40.

⑥ **Describe the basic assumptions of accounting.** Four basic assumptions underlying the financial accounting structure are: (1) *Economic entity:* the assumption that the activity of a business enterprise can be kept separate and distinct from its owners and any other business unit. (2) *Going concern:* the assumption that the business enterprise will have a long life. (3) *Monetary unit:* the assumption that money is the common denominator by which economic activity is conducted, and that the monetary unit provides an appropriate basis for measurement and analysis. (4) *Periodicity:* the assumption that the economic activities of an enterprise can be divided into artificial time periods.

⑦ **Explain the application of the basic principles of accounting.** (1) *Historical cost principle:* Existing GAAP requires that most assets and liabilities be accounted for and reported on the basis of acquisition price. (2) *Revenue recognition:* Revenue is generally recognized when (a) realized or realizable and (b) earned. (3) *Matching principle:* Expenses are recognized when the work (service) or the product actually makes its contribution to revenue. (4) *Full disclosure principle:* Accountants follow the general practice of providing information that is of sufficient importance to influence the judgment and decisions of an informed user.

⑧ **Describe the impact that constraints have on reporting accounting information.** The constraints and their impact are: (1) *Cost-benefit relationship:* The costs of providing the information must be weighed against the benefits that can be derived from using the information. (2) *Materiality:* Sound and acceptable standards should be followed if the amount involved is significant when compared with the other revenues and expenses, assets and liabilities, or net income of the entity. (3) *Industry practices:* Follow the general practices in the firm's industry, which sometimes requires departure from basic theory. (4) *Conservatism:* When in doubt, choose the solution that will be least likely to overstate net assets and net income.

❖ QUESTIONS ❖

1 What is a conceptual framework? Why is a conceptual framework necessary in financial accounting?

2 What are the primary objectives of financial reporting as indicated in *Statement of Financial Accounting Concepts No. 1*?

3 What is meant by the term "qualitative characteristics of accounting information"?

4 Briefly describe the two primary qualities of useful accounting information.

5 What is the distinction between comparability and consistency?

6 Discuss whether the changes described in each of the cases below require recognition in the CPA's report as to consistency (assume that the amounts are material).
(a) After 3 years of computing depreciation under an accelerated method for income tax purposes and under the straight-line method for reporting purposes, the company adopted an accelerated method for reporting purposes.
(b) The company disposed of one of the two subsidiaries that had been included in its consolidated statements for prior years.
(c) The estimated remaining useful life of plant property was reduced because of obsolescence.
(d) The company is using an inventory valuation method that is different from all those used by other companies in its industry.

7 Why is it necessary to develop a definitional framework for the basic elements of accounting?

8 Expenses, losses, and distributions to owners are all decreases in net assets. What are the distinctions among them?

9 Revenues, gains, and investments by owners are all increases in net assets. What are the distinctions among them?

10 What are the four basic assumptions that underlie the financial accounting structure?

11 If the going concern assumption is not made in accounting, what difference does it make in the amounts shown in the financial statements for the following items?
(a) Land.
(b) Unamortized bond premium.
(c) Depreciation expense on equipment.
(d) Merchandise inventory.
(e) Prepaid insurance.

12 The life of a business is divided into specific time periods, usually a year, to measure results of operations for each such time period and to portray financial conditions at the end of each period.
(a) This practice is based on the accounting assumption that the life of the business consists of a series of time periods and that it is possible to measure accurately the results of operations for each period. Comment on the validity and necessity of this assumption.
(b) What has been the effect of this practice on accounting? What is its relation to the accrual system? What influence has it had on accounting entries and methodology?

13 What is the basic accounting problem created by the monetary unit assumption when there is significant inflation? What appears to be the FASB position on a stable monetary unit?

14 The chairman of the board of directors of the company for which you are chief accountant has told you that he is entirely out of sympathy with accounting figures based on cost. He believes that replacement values are of far more significance to the board of directors than "out-of-date costs." Present some arguments to convince him that accounting data should still be based on cost.

15 Develop an argument supporting the adjustment of cost figures in financial statements for general price-level changes, or at least, the preparation of supplementary statements adjusted for changes in the general price level.

16 When is revenue generally recognized? Why has the date of sale been chosen as the point at which to recognize the revenue resulting from the entire producing and selling process?

17 What is the difference between realized and realizable? Give an example of where the concept of realizable is used to recognize revenue.

18 What is the justification for the following deviations from recognizing revenue at the time of sale?
(a) Installment sales method of recognizing revenue.
(b) Recognition of revenue at completion of production for certain agricultural products.
(c) The percentage-of-completion basis in long-term construction contracts.

⑲ What accounting assumption, principle, or modifying convention does Accra Co. use in each of the situations below?

(a) Accra Co. uses the lower of cost or market basis to value inventories.

(b) Accra was involved in litigation with Kinshasa Co. over a product malfunction. This litigation is disclosed in the financial statements.

(c) Accra allocates the cost of its depreciable assets over the life it expects to receive revenue from these assets.

(d) Accra records the purchase of a new IBM PC at its cash equivalent price.

⑳ Jane Hull Company paid $135,000 for a machine in 1998. The Accumulated Depreciation account has a balance of $46,500 at the present time. The company could sell the machine today for $150,000. The company president believes that the company has a "right to this gain." What does the president mean by this statement? Do you agree?

㉑ Three expense recognition methods (associating cause and effect, systematic and rational allocation, and immediate recognition) were discussed in the text under the matching principle. Indicate the basic nature of each of these types of expenses and give two examples of each.

㉒ Explain how you would decide whether to record each of the following expenditures as an asset or an expense. Assume all items are material.

(a) Legal fees paid in connection with the purchase of land are $1,500.

(b) Benjamin Bratt, Inc. paves the driveway leading to the office building at a cost of $21,000.

(c) A meat market purchases a meat-grinding machine at a cost of $345.

(d) On June 30, Alan and Alda, medical doctors, pay six months' office rent to cover the month of June and the next five months.

(e) Tim Taylor's Hardware Company pays $9,000 in wages to laborers for construction on a building to be used in the business.

(f) Nancy Kwan's Florists pays wages of $2,100 for November to an employee who serves as driver of their delivery truck.

㉓ *Statement of Financial Accounting Concepts No. 5* identifies four characteristics that an item must have before it is recognized in the financial statements. What are these four characteristics?

㉔ Briefly describe the types of information concerning financial position, income, and cash flows that might be pro-

vided: (a) within the main body of the financial statements, (b) in the notes to the financial statements, or (c) as supplementary information.

㉕ In January 1998, Alan Jackson Inc. doubled the amount of its outstanding stock by selling on the market an additional 10,000 shares to finance an expansion of the business. You propose that this information be shown by a footnote on the balance sheet as of December 31, 1997. The president objects, claiming that this sale took place after December 31, 1997, and, therefore, should not be shown. Explain your position.

㉖ Describe the two major constraints inherent in the presentation of accounting information.

㉗ What are some of the costs of providing accounting information? What are some of the benefits of accounting information? Describe the cost/benefit factors that should be considered when new accounting standards are being proposed.

㉘ How are materiality (and immateriality) related to the proper presentation of financial statements? What factors and measures should the CPA consider in assessing the materiality of a misstatement in the presentation of a financial statement?

㉙ The treasurer of Joan Osborne Co. has heard that conservatism is a doctrine that is followed in accounting and, therefore, proposes that several policies be followed that are conservative in nature. State your opinion with respect to each of the policies listed below.

(a) The company gives a 2-year warranty to its customers on all products sold. The estimated warranty costs incurred from this year's sales should be entered as an expense this year instead of an expense in the period in the future when the warranty is made good.

(b) When sales are made on account, there is always uncertainty about whether the accounts are collectible. Therefore, the treasurer recommends recording the sale when the cash is received from the customers.

(c) A personal liability lawsuit is pending against the company. The treasurer believes that there is an even chance that the company will lose the suit and have to pay damages of $200,000 to $300,000. The treasurer recommends that a loss be recorded and a liability created in the amount of $300,000.

(d) The inventory should be valued at "cost or market whichever is lower" because the losses from price declines should be recognized in the accounts in the period in which the price decline takes place.

❖ BRIEF EXERCISES ❖

BE2-1 Identify which qualitative characteristic of accounting information is best described in each item below. (Do not use relevance and reliability.)

a. The annual reports of Garbo Corp. are audited by certified public accountants.

b. Klamoth Corp and Kutenai, Inc. both use the FIFO cost flow assumption.

   c. Claudio Abbado Corp. has used straight-line depreciation since they began operations.
   d. Augusta Corp. issues its quarterly reports immediately after each quarter ends.

BE2-2 For each item below, indicate to which category of elements of financial statements it belongs.

a. Retained earnings	**d.** Inventory	**h.** Dividends
b. Sales	**e.** Depreciation	**i.** Gain on sale of investment
c. Total increase in net assets from nonowner sources	**f.** Loss on sale of equipment	**j.** Issuance of common stock
	g. Interest payable	

BE2-3 Identify which basic assumption of accounting is best described in each item below.

   a. The economic activities of Kristi Thomas Corp. are divided into 12-month periods for the purpose of issuing annual reports.
   b. Watson Brewer, Inc. does not adjust amounts in its financial statements for the effects of inflation.
   c. Jessi Ramsey Company reports current and noncurrent classifications in its balance sheet.
   d. The economic activities of Mallory Pike Corporation and its subsidiaries are merged for accounting and reporting purposes.

BE2-4 Identify which basic principle of accounting is best described in each item below.

   a. New Hampshire Corporation reports revenue in its income statement when it earned instead of when the cash is collected.
   b. Vermont Enterprise recognizes depreciation expense for a machine over the five-year period during which that machine helps the company earn revenue.
   c. Massachusetts, Inc. reports information about pending lawsuits in the notes to its financial statements.
   d. Rhode Island Farms reports land on its balance sheet at the amount paid to acquire it, even though the estimated fair market value is greater.

BE2-5 Which constraints on accounting information are illustrated by the items below?

   a. Zip's Farms, Inc. reports agricultural crops on its balance sheet at market value.
   b. Crimson Tide Corporation does not accrue a contingent lawsuit gain of $650,000.
   c. Wildcat Company does not disclose any information in the notes to the financial statements unless the value of the information to financial statement users exceeds the expense of gathering it.
   d. Sun Devil Corporation expenses the cost of wastebaskets in the year they are acquired.

❖ EXERCISES ❖

E2-1 (Qualitative Characteristics) *SFAC No. 2* identifies the qualitative characteristics that make accounting information useful. Presented below are a number of questions related to these qualitative characteristics and underlying constraints.

   1. What is the quality of information that enables users to confirm or correct prior expectations?
   2. Identify the two overall or pervasive constraints developed in *SFAC No. 2.*
   3. The chairman of the SEC at one time noted that "if it becomes accepted or expected that accounting principles are determined or modified in order to secure purposes other than economic measurement—we assume a grave risk that confidence in the credibility of our financial information system will be undermined." Which qualitative characteristic of accounting information should ensure that such a situation will not occur? (Do not use reliability.)
   4. Billy Owens Corp. switches from FIFO to average cost to FIFO over a 2-year period. Which qualitative characteristic of accounting information is not followed?
   5. Assume that the profession permits the savings and loan industry to defer losses on investments it sells, because immediate recognition of the loss may have adverse economic consequences on the industry. Which qualitative characteristic of accounting information is not followed? (Do not use relevance or reliability.)
   6. What are the two primary qualities that make accounting information useful for decision making?
   7. Rex Chapman, Inc. does not issue its first-quarter report until after the second quarter's results are reported. Which qualitative characteristic of accounting is not followed? (Do not use relevance.)
   8. Predictive value is an ingredient of which of the two primary qualities that make accounting information useful for decision making purposes?
   9. Ronald Coles, Inc. is the only company in its industry to depreciate its plant assets on a straight-line basis. Which qualitative characteristic of accounting information may not be followed? (Do not use industry practices.)

10. Jeff Malone Company has attempted to determine the replacement cost of its inventory. Three different appraisers arrive at substantially different amounts for this value. The president, nevertheless, decides to report the middle value for external reporting purposes. Which qualitative characteristic of information is lacking in these data? (Do not use reliability or representational faithfulness.)

E2-2 (Qualitative Characteristics) The qualitative characteristics that make accounting information useful for decision-making purposes are as follows:

Relevance	Timeliness	Representational faithfulness
Reliability	Verifiability	Comparability
Predictive value	Neutrality	Consistency
Feedback value		

Instructions
Identify the appropriate qualitative characteristic(s) to be used given the information provided below.

1. Qualitative characteristic being employed when companies in the same industry are using the same accounting principles.
2. Quality of information that confirms users' earlier expectations.
3. Imperative for providing comparisons of a firm from period to period.
4. Ignores the economic consequences of a standard or rule.
5. Requires a high degree of consensus among individuals on a given measurement.
6. Predictive value is an ingredient of this primary quality of information.
7. Two qualitative characteristics that are related to both relevance and reliability.
8. Neutrality is an ingredient of this primary quality of accounting information.
9. Two primary qualities that make accounting information useful for decision-making purposes.
10. Issuance of interim reports is an example of this secondary quality of financial information.

E2-3 (Elements of Financial Statements) Ten interrelated elements that are most directly related to measuring the performance and financial status of an enterprise are provided below:

Assets	Distributions to owners	Expenses
Liabilities	Comprehensive income	Gains
Equity	Revenues	Losses
Investments by owners		

Instructions
For each of the phrases provided below, identify the element or elements associated with the 12 items below.

1. Arises from peripheral or incidental transactions.
2. Obligation to transfer resources arising from past transaction.
3. Increases ownership interest.
4. Declares and pays cash dividends to owners.
5. Increases in net assets in a period from nonowner sources.
6. Items characterized by service potential or future economic benefit.
7. Equals increase in assets less liabilities during the year, after adding disinvestments by owners and subtracting investments by owners.
8. Arises from income statement activities that constitute the entity's ongoing major or central operations.
9. Residual interest in the assets of the enterprise after deducting its liabilities.
10. Increases assets during a period through sale of product.
11. Decreases assets during the period by purchasing the company's own stock.
12. Includes all changes in equity during the period, except those resulting from investments by owners and distributions to owners.

E2-4 (Assumptions, Principles, and Constraints) Presented below are the assumptions, principles, and constraints used in this chapter:

a. Economic entity assumption	e. Historical cost principle	i. Materiality
b. Going concern assumption	f. Matching principle	j. Industry practices
c. Monetary unit assumption	g. Full disclosure principle	k. Conservatism
d. Periodicity assumption	h. Cost-benefit relationship	

Instructions

Identify by letter the accounting assumption, principle, or constraint that describes each situation below. Do not use a letter more than once.

1. Allocates expenses to revenues in the proper period.
2. Indicates that market value changes subsequent to purchase are not recorded in the accounts. (Do not use revenue recognition principle.)
3. Ensures that all relevant financial information is reported.
4. Rationale why plant assets are not reported at liquidation value. (Do not use historical cost principle.)
5. Anticipates all losses, but reports no gains.
6. Indicates that personal and business record keeping should be separately maintained.
7. Separates financial information into time periods for reporting purposes.
8. Permits the use of market value valuation in certain specific situations.
9. Requires that information significant enough to affect the decision of reasonably informed users should be disclosed. (Do not use full disclosure principle.)
10. Assumes that the dollar is the "measuring stick" used to report on financial performance.

E2-5 (Assumptions, Principles, and Constraints) Presented below are a number of operational guidelines and practices that have developed over time.

1. Price-level changes are not recognized in the accounting records.
2. Lower of cost or market is used to value inventories.
3. Financial information is presented so that reasonably prudent investors will not be misled.
4. Intangibles are capitalized and amortized over periods benefited.
5. Repair tools are expensed when purchased.
6. Brokerage firms use market value for purposes of valuation of all marketable securities.
7. Each enterprise is kept as a unit distinct from its owner or owners.
8. All significant postbalance sheet events are reported.
9. Revenue is recorded at point of sale.
10. All important aspects of bond indentures are presented in financial statements.
11. Rationale for accrual accounting is stated.
12. The use of consolidated statements is justified.
13. Reporting must be done at defined time intervals.
14. An allowance for doubtful accounts is established.
15. All payments out of petty cash are charged to Miscellaneous Expense. (Do not use conservatism.)
16. Goodwill is recorded only at time of purchase.
17. No profits are anticipated and all possible losses are recognized.
18. A company charges its sales commission costs to expense.

Instructions

Select the assumption, principle, or constraint that most appropriately justifies these procedures and practices. (Do not use qualitative characteristics.)

E2-6 (Assumptions, Principles, and Constraints) A number of operational guidelines used by accountants are described below.

1. The treasurer of Erik Kramer Co. wishes to prepare financial statements only during downturns in their wine production, which occur periodically when the rhubarb crop fails. He states that it is at such times that the statements could be most easily prepared. In no event would more than 30 months pass without statements being prepared.
2. The Chicago Power & Light Company has purchased a large amount of property, plant, and equipment over a number of years. They have decided that because the general price level has changed materially over the years, they will issue only price-level adjusted financial statements.
3. Robert Smith Manufacturing Co. decided to manufacture its own widgets because it would be cheaper to do so than to buy them from an outside supplier. In an attempt to make their statements more comparable with those of their competitors, Robert Smith charged its inventory account for what they felt the widgets would have cost if they had been purchased from an outside supplier. (Do not use the revenue recognition principle.)
4. Flanagan's Discount Centers buys its merchandise by the truck and train-carload. Flanagan does not defer any transportation costs in computing the cost of its ending inventory. Such costs, although varying from period to period, are always material in amount.
5. Grab & Run, Inc., a fast-food company, sells franchises for $100,000, accepting a $5,000 down payment and a 50-year note for the remainder. Grab & Run promises for 3 years to assist in site selection,

building, and management training. Grab & Run records the $100,000 franchise fee as revenue in the period in which the contract is signed.

6. Curtis Conway Company "faces possible expropriation (i.e., takeover) of foreign facilities and possible losses on sums owed by various customers on the verge of bankruptcy." The company president has decided that these possibilities should not be noted on the financial statements because Conway still hopes that these events will not take place.

7. Bryan Cox, manager of College Bookstore, Inc., bought a computer for his own use. He paid for the computer by writing a check on the bookstore checking account and charged the "Office Equipment" account.

8. Raashan Salaam, Inc. recently completed a new 120-story office building that houses their home offices and many other tenants. All the office equipment for the building that had a per item or per unit cost of $1,000 or less was expensed as immaterial, even though the office equipment has an average life of 10 years. The total cost of such office equipment was approximately $26 million. (Do not use the matching principle.)

9. The AICPA, in an accounting guide for brokers and other dealers in securities, stated that "the trading and investment accounts . . . should be valued at market or fair value for financial reporting purposes. . . ." The brokerage firm of James and Williams, Inc. continues to value its trading and investment accounts at cost or market, whichever is lower.

10. A large lawsuit has been filed against Big Cat Corp. by Perry Co. Big Cat has recorded a loss and related estimated liability equal to the maximum possible amount it feels it might lose. Big Cat is confident, however, that either it will win the suit or it will owe a much smaller amount.

Instructions

For each of the foregoing, list the assumption, principle, or constraint that has been violated. List only one term for each case.

❖ CONCEPTUAL CASES ❖

C2-1 (Conceptual Framework—General)   Roger Morgan has some questions regarding the theoretical framework in which standards are set. He knows that the FASB and other predecessor organizations have attempted to develop a conceptual framework for accounting theory formulation. Yet, Roger's supervisors have indicated that these theoretical frameworks have little value in the practical sense (i.e., in the real world). Roger did notice that accounting standards seem to be established after the fact rather than before. He thought this indicated a lack of theory structure but never really questioned the process at school because he was too busy doing the homework.

Roger feels that some of his anxiety about accounting theory and accounting semantics could be alleviated by identifying the basic concepts and definitions accepted by the profession and considering them in light of his current work. By doing this, he hopes to develop an appropriate connection between theory and practice.

Instructions

(a) Help Roger recognize the purpose of and benefit of a conceptual framework.

(b) Identify any *Statements of Financial Accounting Concepts* issued by FASB that may be helpful to Roger in developing his theoretical background.

C2-2 (Conceptual Framework—General)   The Financial Accounting Standards Board (FASB) has been working on a conceptual framework for financial accounting and reporting. The FASB has issued six *Statements of Financial Accounting Concepts*. These statements are intended to set forth objectives and fundamentals that will be the basis for developing financial accounting and reporting standards. The objectives identify the goals and purposes of financial reporting. The fundamentals are the underlying concepts of financial accounting—concepts that guide the selection of transactions, events, and circumstances to be accounted for; their recognition and measurement; and the means of summarizing and communicating them to interested parties.

The purpose of *Statement of Financial Accounting Concepts No. 2*, "Qualitative Characteristics of Accounting Information," is to examine the characteristics that make accounting information useful. The characteristics or qualities of information discussed in *SFAC No. 2* are the ingredients that make information useful and the qualities to be sought when accounting choices are made.

Instructions

(a) Identify and discuss the benefits that can be expected to be derived from the FASB's conceptual framework study.

(b) What is the most important quality for accounting information as identified in *Statement of Financial Accounting Concepts No. 2?* Explain why it is the most important.

(c) *Statement of Financial Accounting Concepts No. 2* describes a number of key characteristics or qualities for accounting information. Briefly discuss the importance of any three of these qualities for financial reporting purposes.

(CMA adapted)

C2-3 (Objectives of Financial Reporting) Regis Gordon and Kathy Medford are discussing various aspects of the FASB's pronouncement, *Statement of Financial Accounting Concepts No. 1,* "Objectives of Financial Reporting by Business Enterprises." Regis indicates that this pronouncement provides little, if any, guidance to the practicing professional in resolving accounting controversies. He believes that the statement provides such broad guidelines that it would be impossible to apply the objectives to present-day reporting problems. Kathy concedes this point but indicates that objectives are still needed to provide a starting point for the FASB in helping to improve financial reporting.

Instructions

(a) Indicate the basic objectives established in *Statement of Financial Accounting Concepts No. 1.*

(b) What do you think is the meaning of Kathy's statement that the FASB needs a starting point to resolve accounting controversies?

C2-4 (Qualitative Characteristics) Accounting information provides useful information about business transactions and events. Those who provide and use financial reports must often select and evaluate accounting alternatives. *FASB Statement of Financial Accounting Concepts No. 2,* "Qualitative Characteristics of Accounting Information," examines the characteristics of accounting information that make it useful for decision making. It also points out that various limitations inherent in the measurement and reporting process may necessitate trade-offs or sacrifices among the characteristics of useful information.

Instructions

(a) Describe briefly the following characteristics of useful accounting information:

1. Relevance.   4. Comparability.
2. Reliability.   5. Consistency.
3. Understandability.

(b) For each of the following pairs of information characteristics, give an example of a situation in which one of the characteristics may be sacrificed in return for a gain in the other:

1. Relevance and reliability.   3. Comparability and consistency.
2. Relevance and consistency.   4. Relevance and understandability.

(c) What criterion should be used to evaluate trade-offs between information characteristics?

C2-5 (Assumptions, Principles, and Constraints) You are engaged to review the accounting records of Jeremy Roenick Corporation prior to the closing of the revenue and expense accounts as of December 31, the end of the current fiscal year. The following information comes to your attention.

1. During the current year, Jeremy Roenick Corporation changed its policy in regard to expensing purchases of small tools. In the past, these purchases had always been expensed because they amounted to less than 2% of net income, but the president has decided that capitalization and subsequent depreciation should now be followed. It is expected that purchases of small tools will not fluctuate greatly from year to year.

2. Jeremy Roenick Corporation constructed a warehouse at a cost of $1,000,000. The company had been depreciating the asset on a straight-line basis over 10 years. In the current year, the controller doubled depreciation expense because the replacement cost of the warehouse had increased significantly.

3. The company decided in October of the current fiscal year to start a massive advertising campaign to enhance the marketability of their product. In November, the company paid $800,000 for advertising time on a major television network to advertise their product during the next 12 months. The controller expensed the $800,000 in the current year on the basis that "once the money is spent, it can never be recovered from the television network."

4. When the balance sheet was prepared, detailed information as to the amount of cash on deposit in each of several banks was omitted. Only the total amount of cash under a caption "Cash in banks" was presented.

5. On July 15 of the current year, Jeremy Roenick Corporation purchased an undeveloped tract of land at a cost of $320,000. The company spent $80,000 in subdividing the land and getting it ready for sale. An appraisal of the property at the end of the year indicated that the land was now worth $500,000. Although none of the lots were sold, the company recognized revenue of $180,000, less related expenses of $80,000, for a net income on the project of $100,000.

6. For a number of years the company used the FIFO method for inventory valuation purposes. During the current year, the president noted that all the other companies in their industry had switched to the LIFO method. The company decided not to switch to LIFO because net income would decrease $830,000.

Instructions
State whether or not you agree with the decisions made by Jeremy Roenick Corporation. Support your answers with reference, whenever possible, to the generally accepted principles, assumptions, and constraints applicable in the circumstances.

C2-6 (Revenue Recognition and Matching Principle)   After the presentation of your report on the examination of the financial statements to the board of directors of Bones Publishing Company, one of the new directors expresses surprise that the income statement assumes that an equal proportion of the revenue is earned with the publication of every issue of the company's magazine. She feels that the "crucial event" in the process of earning revenue in the magazine business is the cash sale of the subscription. She says that she does not understand why most of the revenue cannot be "recognized" in the period of the sale.

Instructions
(a) List the various accepted times for recognizing revenue in the accounts and explain when the methods are appropriate.
(b) Discuss the propriety of timing the recognition of revenue in Bones Publishing Company's account with:
   1. The cash sale of the magazine subscription.
   2. The publication of the magazine every month.
   3. Both events, by recognizing a portion of the revenue with cash sale of the magazine subscription and a portion of the revenue with the publication of the magazine every month.

C2-7 (Revenue Recognition and Matching Principle)   On June 5, 1998, McCoy Corporation signed a contract with Sulu Associates under which Sulu agreed (1) to construct an office building on land owned by McCoy, (2) to accept responsibility for procuring financing for the project and finding tenants, and (3) to manage the property for 35 years. The annual net income from the project, after debt service, was to be divided equally between McCoy Corporation and Sulu Associates. Sulu was to accept its share of future net income as full payment for its services in construction, obtaining finances and tenants, and management of the project.

By May 31, 1999, the project was nearly completed and tenants had signed leases to occupy 90% of the available space at annual rentals aggregating $4,000,000. It is estimated that, after operating expenses and debt service, the annual net income will amount to $1,500,000. The management of Sulu Associates believed that (a) the economic benefit derived from the contract with McCoy should be reflected on its financial statements for the fiscal year ended May 31, 1999, and directed that revenue be accrued in an amount equal to the commercial value of the services Sulu had rendered during the year, (b) this amount be carried in contracts receivable, and (c) all related expenditures be charged against the revenue.

Instructions
(a) Explain the main difference between the economic concept of business income as reflected by Sulu's management and the measurement of income under generally accepted accounting principles.
(b) Discuss the factors to be considered in determining when revenue should be recognized for the purpose of accounting measurement of periodic income.
(c) Is the belief of Sulu's management in accord with generally accepted accounting principles for the measurement of revenue and expense for the year ended May 31, 1999? Support your opinion by discussing the application to this case of the factors to be considered for asset measurement and revenue and expense recognition.

(AICPA adapted)

C2-8 (Matching Principle)   An accountant must be familiar with the concepts involved in determining earnings of a business entity. The amount of earnings reported for a business entity is dependent on the proper recognition, in general, of revenue and expense for a given time period. In some situations, costs are recognized as expenses at the time of product sale; in other situations, guidelines have been developed for recognizing costs as expenses or losses by other criteria.

Instructions

(a) Explain the rationale for recognizing costs as expenses at the time of product sale.

(b) What is the rationale underlying the appropriateness of treating costs as expenses of a period instead of assigning the costs to an asset? Explain.

(c) In what general circumstances would it be appropriate to treat a cost as an asset instead of as an expense? Explain.

(d) Some expenses are assigned to specific accounting periods on the basis of systematic and rational allocation of asset cost. Explain the underlying rationale for recognizing expenses on the basis of systematic and rational allocation of asset cost.

(e) Identify the conditions in which it would be appropriate to treat a cost as a loss.

(AICPA adapted)

C2-9 (Matching Principle) Accountants try to prepare income statements that are as accurate as possible. A basic requirement in preparing accurate income statements is to match costs against revenues properly. Proper matching of costs against revenues requires that costs resulting from typical business operations be recognized in the period in which they expired.

Instructions

(a) List three criteria that can be used to determine whether such costs should appear as charges in the income statement for the current period.

(b) As generally presented in financial statements, the following items or procedures have been criticized as improperly matching costs with revenues. Briefly discuss each item from the viewpoint of matching costs with revenues and suggest corrective or alternative means of presenting the financial information.

1. Receiving and handling costs.
2. Valuation of inventories at the lower of cost or market.
3. Cash discounts on purchases.

C2-10 (Matching Principle) Carlos Rodriguez sells and erects shell houses, that is, frame structures that are completely finished on the outside but are unfinished on the inside except for flooring, partition studding, and ceiling joists. Shell houses are sold chiefly to customers who are handy with tools and who have time to do the interior wiring, plumbing, wall completion and finishing, and other work necessary to make the shell houses livable dwellings.

Rodriguez buys shell houses from a manufacturer in unassembled packages consisting of all lumber, roofing, doors, windows, and similar materials necessary to complete a shell house. Upon commencing operations in a new area, Rodriguez buys or leases land as a site for its local warehouse, field office, and display houses. Sample display houses are erected at a total cost of $20,000 to $29,000 including the cost of the unassembled packages. The chief element of cost of the display houses is the unassembled packages, inasmuch as erection is a short, low-cost operation. Old sample models are torn down or altered into new models every 3 to 7 years. Sample display houses have little salvage value because dismantling and moving costs amount to nearly as much as the cost of an unassembled package.

Instructions

(a) A choice must be made between (1) expensing the costs of sample display houses in the periods in which the expenditure is made and (2) spreading the costs over more than one period. Discuss the advantages of each method.

(b) Would it be preferable to amortize the cost of display houses on the basis of (1) the passage of time or (2) the number of shell houses sold? Explain.

(AICPA adapted)

C2-11 (Full Disclosure Principle) Presented below are a number of facts related to R. Kelly, Inc. Assume that no mention of these facts was made in the financial statements and the related notes.

(a) The company decided that, for the sake of conciseness, only net income should be reported on the income statement. Details as to revenues, cost of goods sold, and expenses were omitted.

(b) Equipment purchases of $170,000 were partly financed during the year through the issuance of a $110,000 notes payable. The company offset the equipment against the notes payable and reported plant assets at $60,000.

(c) During the year, an assistant controller for the company embezzled $15,000. R. Kelly's net income for the year was $2,300,000. Neither the assistant controller nor the money have been found.

(d) R. Kelly has reported its ending inventory at $2,100,000 in the financial statements. No other information related to inventories is presented in the financial statements and related notes.

(e) The company changed its method of depreciating equipment from the double-declining balance to the straight-line method. No mention of this change was made in the financial statements.

Instructions
Assume that you are the auditor of R. Kelly, Inc. and that you have been asked to explain the appropriate accounting and related disclosure necessary for each of these items.

C2-12 (Accounting Principles—Comprehensive) Presented below are a number of business transactions that occurred during the current year for Fresh Horses, Inc.

1. The president of Fresh Horses, Inc. used his expense account to purchase a new Camaro solely for personal use. The following entry was made:

Miscellaneous Expense	29,000	
Cash		29,000

2. Merchandise inventory that cost $620,000 is reported on the balance sheet at $690,000, the expected selling price less estimated selling costs. The following entry was made to record this increase in value:

Merchandise Inventory	70,000	
Income		70,000

3. The company is being sued for $500,000 by a customer who claims damages for personal injury apparently caused by a defective product. Company attorneys feel extremely confident that the company will have no liability for damages resulting from the situation. Nevertheless, the company decides to make the following entry:

Loss from Lawsuit	500,000	
Liability for Lawsuit		500,000

4. Because the general level of prices increased during the current year, Fresh Horses, Inc. determined that there was a $16,000 understatement of depreciation expense on its equipment and decided to record it in its accounts. The following entry was made:

Depreciation Expense	16,000	
Accumulated Depreciation		16,000

5. Fresh Horses, Inc. has been concerned about whether intangible assets could generate cash in case of liquidation. As a consequence, goodwill arising from a purchase transaction during the current year and recorded at $800,000 was written off as follows:

Retained Earnings	800,000	
Goodwill		800,000

6. Because of a "fire sale," equipment obviously worth $200,000 was acquired at a cost of $155,000. The following entry was made:

Equipment	200,000	
Cash		155,000
Income		45,000

Instructions
In each of the situations above, discuss the appropriateness of the journal entries in terms of generally accepted accounting principles.

C2-13 (Accounting Principles—Comprehensive) Presented below is information related to Garth Brooks, Inc.

(a) Depreciation expense on the building for the year was $60,000. Because the building was increasing in value during the year, the controller decided to charge the depreciation expense to retained earnings instead of to net income. The following entry is recorded.

Retained Earnings	60,000	
Accumulated Depreciation—Buildings		60,000

(b) Materials were purchased on January 1, 1998 for $120,000 and this amount was entered in the Materials account. On December 31, 1998, the materials would have cost $141,000, so the following entry is made.

Inventory	21,000	
Gain on Inventories		21,000

(c) During the year, the company purchased equipment through the issuance of common stock. The stock had a par value of $135,000 and a fair market value of $450,000. The fair market value of the equipment was not easily determinable. The company recorded this transaction as follows:

Equipment	135,000	
Common Stock		135,000

(d) During the year, the company sold certain equipment for $285,000, recognizing a gain of $69,000. Because the controller believed that new equipment would be needed in the near future, the controller decided to defer the gain and amortize it over the life of any new equipment purchased.

(e) An order for $61,500 has been received from a customer for products on hand. This order was shipped on January 9, 1999. The company made the following entry in 1998.

Accounts Receivable	61,500	
Sales		61,500

Instructions

Comment on the appropriateness of the accounting procedures followed by Garth Brooks, Inc.

❖ FINANCIAL REPORTING PROBLEM—INTEL CORPORATION

The financial statements of Intel are presented in Appendix 5B. Refer to these financial statements and the accompanying notes to answer the following questions.

Instructions:

(a) Using the notes to the consolidated financial statements, determine Intel's revenue recognition policies regarding sales to distributors under agreements allowing price protection and/or right of return on merchandise unsold by distributors. Comment on whether Intel uses a conservative method for reporting revenue in this area.

(b) Give two examples of where historical cost information is reported on Intel's financial statements and related notes. Give two examples of the use of fair value information reported in either the financial statements or related notes.

(c) How can we determine that the accounting principles used by Intel are prepared on a basis consistent with those of last year?

(d) What is Intel's accounting policy related to advertising? What accounting principle does Intel follow regarding accounting for advertising?

❖ FINANCIAL STATEMENT ANALYSIS CASE

Weyerhaeuser Company

Presented below is a statement that appeared about Weyerhaeuser Company in a financial magazine.

The land and timber holdings are now carried on the company's books at a mere $422 million. The value of the timber alone is variously estimated at $3 billion to $7 billion and is rising all the time. "The understatement of the company is pretty severe," conceded Charles W. Bingham, a senior vice-president. Adds Robert L. Schuyler, another senior vice-president: "We have a whole stream of profit nobody sees and there is no way to show it on our books."

Instructions

(a) What does Schuyler mean when he says that "we have a whole stream of profit nobody sees and there is no way to show it on our books"?

(b) If the understatement of the company's assets is severe, why does accounting not report this information?

❖ COMPARATIVE ANALYSIS CASE

The Coca-Cola Company versus PepsiCo Inc.

Instructions

Go to our Web site. Answer the following questions related to The Coca-Cola Company and PepsiCo Inc.

(a) What are the primary lines of business of these two companies as shown in their notes to the financial statements?

(b) Which company has the dominant position in beverage sales?

(c) How are inventories for these two companies valued? What cost allocation method is used to report inventory? How does their accounting for inventories affect comparability between the two companies?

(d) Which company changed its accounting policies during 1995 which affected the consistency of the financial results from the previous year? What were these changes?

❖ RESEARCH CASES

Case 1 (Retrieval of Information on Public Company)

There are several commonly-available indexes which enable individuals to locate articles previously included in numerous business publications and periodicals. Articles can generally be searched by company or by subject matter. Four common indexes are *The Wall Street Journal Index*, *Business Abstracts* (formerly the *Business Periodical Index*), *Predicasts F&S Index*, and *ABI/Inform*.

Instructions

Use one of these resources to find an article about the company you selected in the case from the previous chapter. Read the article and answer the following questions. (*Note:* Your library may have hard copy or CD-ROM versions of these indexes.)

(a) What is the article about?
(b) What company-specific information is included in the article?
(c) Is the article somehow related to the article you read from the previous chapter?
(d) Identify any accounting-related issues discussed in the article.

Case 2 (Concepts and Quantitative Guidelines)

Obtain copies of the FASB's *Statements of Financial Accounting Concepts* (SFACs) from the library and use them to answer the following questions.

(a) The textbook indicates that it is "difficult to provide firm guides in judging when a given item is or is not material." SFAC No. 2 identifies a number of examples in which specific quantitative guidelines are provided to firms. Identify two of these examples. Do you think that materiality guidelines should be quantified? Why or why not?
(b) SFAC No. 3 discusses the concept of "articulation" between financial statement elements. Briefly summarize the meaning of this term and how it relates to an entity's financial statements.

❖ WRITING ASSIGNMENT

Recently, your Uncle Waldo Ralph, who knows that you always have your eye out for a profitable investment, has discussed the possibility of you purchasing some corporate bonds. He suggests that you may wish to get in on the "ground floor" of this deal. The bonds being issued by the Cricket Corp. are 10-year debentures which promise a 40 percent rate of return. Cricket manufactures novelty/party items.

You have told Waldo that, unless you can take a look at Cricket's financial statements, you would not feel comfortable about such an investment. Knowing that this is the chance of a lifetime, Uncle Waldo has procured a copy of Cricket's most recent, unaudited financial statements which are a year old. These statements were prepared by Mrs. John Cricket. You peruse these statements, and they are quite impressive. The balance sheet showed a debt-to-equity ratio of .10 and, for the year shown, the company reported net income of $2,424,240.

The financial statements are not shown in comparison with amounts from other years. In addition, no significant note disclosures about inventory valuation, depreciation methods, loan agreements, etc. are available.

Instructions

Write a letter to Uncle Waldo explaining why it would be unwise to base an investment decision on the financial statements which he has provided to you. Be sure to explain why these financial statements are neither relevant nor reliable.

❖ GROUP ASSIGNMENT

Assume that the FASB has decided to address the problem of information overload. It has agreed to eliminate one of the principles, assumptions, constraints, or qualitative characteristics listed below. This concept will be deleted from all textbooks and will no longer be considered important literature.

With the class divided into groups, each group will be assigned one or more of the following:

Relevance	Monetary unit	Full disclosure
Reliability	Time period	Cost
Comparability and consistency	Revenue recognition	Materiality
Economic entity	Matching	Conservatism

Instructions

(a) Discuss within your group why your specific concept(s) should *not* be eliminated.

(b) Pick a group leader who will present to the class the group's reasons why the FASB should not delete the group's concept(s).

(c) At the end of all presentations, the class should vote on which concept to delete.

❖ETHICS CASE

Hinckley Nuclear Power Plant will be "mothballed" at the end of its useful life (approximately 20 years) at great expense. The matching principle requires that expenses be matched to revenue. Accountants Jana Kingston and Pete Henning argue whether it is better to allocate the expense of mothballing over the next 20 years or ignore it until mothballing occurs.

Instructions

Answer the following questions.

(a) What stakeholders should be considered?

(b) What ethical issue, if any, underlies the dispute?

(c) What alternatives should be considered?

(d) Assess the consequences of the alternatives.

(e) What decision would you recommend?

CHAPTER 3

The Accounting Information System

Needed: A Reliable Information System

Maintaining a set of accounting records is not optional. The Internal Revenue Service requires that businesses prepare and retain a set of records and documents that can be audited. The Foreign Corrupt Practices Act (federal legislation) requires public companies to ''. . . make and keep books, records, and accounts, which, in reasonable detail, accurately and fairly reflect the transactions and dispositions of the assets. . . .'' But beyond these two reasons, a company that does not keep an accurate record of its business transactions may lose revenue and is more likely to operate inefficiently.

Some companies are inefficient partly because of poor accounting systems. Consider, for example, the Long Island Railroad, once one of the nation's busiest commuter lines. The LIRR lost money because its cash position was unknown; large amounts of money owed the railroad had not been billed; some payables were erroneously paid twice; and redemptions of bonds were not recorded. Also, consider Gould Inc., an electronics conglomerate, where accounting and record keeping became so chaotic that results from operations had to be restated for 5 of 7 years.

Similarly, when the International Gold Bullion Exchange (IGBE), one of the largest gold and silver retailers, was forced to declare bankruptcy, its records were in such shambles that it was difficult to determine how much money it lost. The company had failed to keep track of its revenues and had written checks on uncollected funds. IGBE had even allowed its employee health insurance to lapse while continuing to collect premiums from workers. Although these situations are not common in large enterprises, they illustrate our point: accounts and detailed records must be kept by every business enterprise.

Even the use of computers is no assurance of accuracy and efficiency. ''The conversion to a new system called MasterNet fouled up data processing records to the extent that BankAmerica is frequently unable to produce or deliver customer statements on a timely basis,'' said an executive at one of the country's largest banks.

LEARNING OBJECTIVES

After studying this chapter, you should be able to:

1. Understand basic accounting terminology.
2. Explain double-entry rules.
3. Identify steps in the accounting cycle.
4. Record transactions in journals, post to ledger accounts, and prepare a trial balance.
5. Explain the reasons for preparing adjusting entries.
6. Explain how inventory accounts are adjusted at year-end.
7. Prepare closing entries.
8. Identify adjusting entries that may be reversed.
9. Prepare a 10-column work sheet.

As the opening story indicates, a reliable information system is a necessity for all companies. The purpose of this chapter is to explain and illustrate the features of an accounting information system. The content and organization of this chapter are as follows:

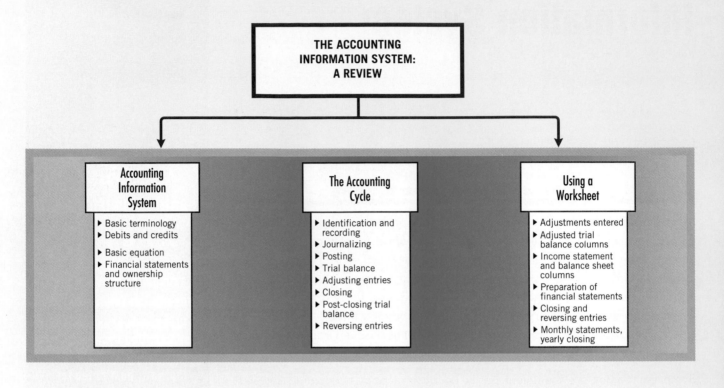

❖ ACCOUNTING INFORMATION SYSTEM

The system of collecting and processing transaction data and disseminating financial information to interested parties is known as the accounting information system. Accounting information systems vary widely from one business to another. Factors that shape these systems are the **nature of the business** and the transactions in which it engages, the **size of the firm**, the **volume of data** to be handled, and the **informational demands** that management and others place on the system.

A good accounting information system helps management answer such questions as:

How much and what kind of debt is outstanding?

Were our sales higher this period than last?

What assets do we have?

What were our cash inflows and outflows?

Did we make a profit last period?

Are any of our product lines or divisions operating at a loss?

Can we safely increase our dividends to stockholders?

Is our rate of return on net assets increasing?

Many other questions can be answered when there is an efficient accounting system to provide the data. A well-devised accounting information system is beneficial for every business enterprise.

Basic Terminology

Financial accounting rests on a set of concepts (discussed in Chapters 1 and 2) for identifying, recording, classifying, and interpreting transactions and other events relating to enterprises. It is important to understand the **basic terminology employed in collecting accounting data**.

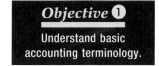

Objective ❶
Understand basic accounting terminology.

❖ BASIC TERMINOLOGY ❖

EVENT.   A happening of consequence. An event generally is the source or cause of changes in assets, liabilities, and equity. Events may be external or internal.

TRANSACTION.   An **external event** involving a transfer or exchange between two or more entities.

ACCOUNT.   A systematic arrangement that shows the effect of transactions and other events on a specific asset or equity. A separate account is kept for each asset, liability, revenue, expense, and for capital (owners' equity).

REAL AND NOMINAL ACCOUNTS.   Real (permanent) accounts are asset, liability, and equity accounts; they appear on the balance sheet. Nominal (temporary) accounts are revenue, expense, and dividend accounts; except for dividends, they appear on the income statement. Nominal accounts are periodically closed; real accounts are not.

LEDGER.   The book (or computer printouts) containing the accounts. Each account usually has a separate page. A **general ledger** is a collection of all the asset, liability, owners' equity, revenue, and expense accounts. A **subsidiary ledger** contains the details related to a given general ledger account.

JOURNAL.   The book of original entry where transactions and selected other events are initially recorded. Various amounts are transferred to the ledger from the book of original entry, the journal.

POSTING.   The process of transferring the essential facts and figures from the book of original entry to the ledger accounts.

TRIAL BALANCE.   A list of all open accounts in the ledger and their balances. A trial balance taken immediately after all adjustments have been posted is called an adjusted trial balance. A trial balance taken immediately after closing entries have been posted is designated as a post-closing or after-closing trial balance. A trial balance may be prepared at any time.

ADJUSTING ENTRIES.   Entries made at the end of an accounting period to bring all accounts up to date on an accrual accounting basis so that correct financial statements can be prepared.

FINANCIAL STATEMENTS.   Statements that reflect the collection, tabulation, and final summarization of the accounting data. Four statements are involved: (1) the balance sheet, which shows the financial condition of the enterprise at the end of a period, (2) the income statement, which measures the results of operations during the period, (3) the statement of cash flows, which reports the cash provided and used by operating, investing, and financing activities during the period, and (4) the statement of retained earnings, which reconciles the balance of the retained earnings account from the beginning to the end of the period.

CLOSING ENTRIES.   The formal process by which all nominal accounts are reduced to zero and the net income or net loss is determined and transferred to an owners' equity account, also known as "closing the ledger," "closing the books," or merely "closing."

Debits and Credits

Objective ❷
Explain double-entry rules.

The terms **debit** and **credit** mean left and right, respectively. They are commonly abbreviated as Dr. for debit and Cr. for credit. These terms do not mean increase or decrease. The terms debit and credit are used repeatedly in the recording process. For example, the act of entering an amount on the left side of an account is called **debiting** the account, and making an entry on the right side is **crediting** the account. When the totals of the two sides are compared, an account will have a **debit balance** if the total of the debit amounts exceeds the credits. Conversely, an account will have a **credit balance** if the credit amounts exceed the debits.

The procedure of having debits on the left and credits on the right is an accounting custom or rule. We could function just as well if debits and credits were reversed. However, the custom of having debits on the left side of an account and credits on the right side (like the custom of driving on the right-hand side of the road) has been adopted in the United States. **This rule applies to all accounts**.

The equality of debits and credits provides the basis for the double-entry system of recording transactions (sometimes referred to as double-entry bookkeeping). Under the universally used **double-entry accounting system**, the dual (two-sided) effect of each transaction is recorded in appropriate accounts. This system provides a logical method for recording transactions. It also offers a means of proving the accuracy of the recorded amounts. If every transaction is recorded with equal debits and credits, then the sum of all the debits to the accounts must equal the sum of all the credits.

All asset and expense accounts are increased on the left (or debit side) and decreased on the right (or credit side). Conversely, all liability and revenue accounts are increased on the right (or credit side) and decreased on the left (or debit side). Stockholders' equity accounts, like Common Stock and Retained Earnings, are increased on the credit side, whereas Dividends is increased on the debit side. The basic guidelines for an accounting system are presented in Illustration 3-1.

ILLUSTRATION 3-1
Double-entry (Debit and Credit) Accounting System

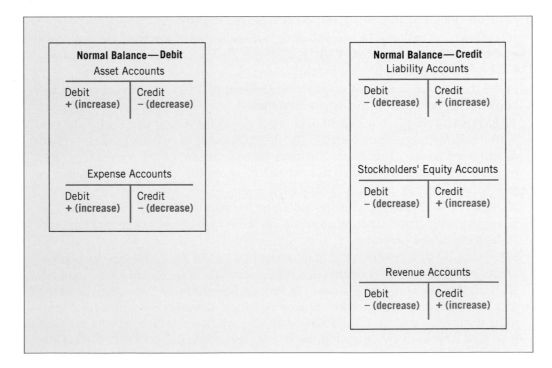

Basic Equation

In a double-entry system, for every debit there must be a credit and vice-versa. This leads us, then, to the basic equation in accounting (Illustration 3-2).

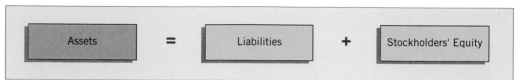

ILLUSTRATION 3-2
The Basic Accounting
Equation

Illustration 3-3 expands this equation to show the accounts that comprise stockholders' equity. In addition, the debit/credit rules and effects on each type of account are illustrated. Study this diagram carefully. It will help you understand the fundamentals of the double-entry system. Like the basic equation, the expanded basic equation must be in balance (total debits equal total credits).

ILLUSTRATION 3-3
Expanded Basic Equation
and Debit/Credit Rules
and Effects

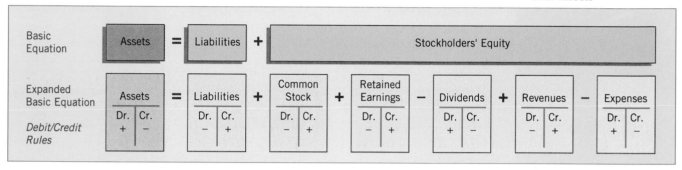

Every time a transaction occurs, the elements of the equation change, but the basic equality remains. To illustrate, here are eight different transactions for Perez Inc.

❶ Owners invest $40,000 in exchange for common stock:

❷ Disburse $600 cash for secretarial wages:

❸ Purchase office equipment priced at $5,200, giving a 10% promissory note in exchange:

4 Receive $4,000 cash for services rendered:

5 Pay off a short-term liability of $7,000:

6 Declare a cash dividend of $5,000:

7 Convert a long-term liability of $80,000 into common stock:

8 Pay cash of $16,000 for a delivery van:

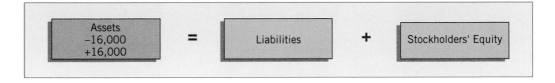

Financial Statements and Ownership Structure

Common stock and retained earnings are reported in the stockholders' equity section of the balance sheet. Dividends are reported on the statement of retained earnings. Revenues and expenses are reported on the income statement. Dividends, revenues, and expenses are eventually transferred to retained earnings at the end of the period. As a result, a change in any one of these three items affects stockholders' equity. The relationships related to stockholders' equity are shown in Illustration 3-4.

The type of ownership structure employed by a business enterprise dictates the types of accounts that are part of or affect the equity section. In a corporation, **Common Stock, Additional Paid-in Capital, Dividends**, and **Retained Earnings** are accounts commonly used. In a proprietorship or partnership, a Capital account is used to indicate the owner's or owners' investment in the company. A Drawing account is used to indicate withdrawals by the owner(s).

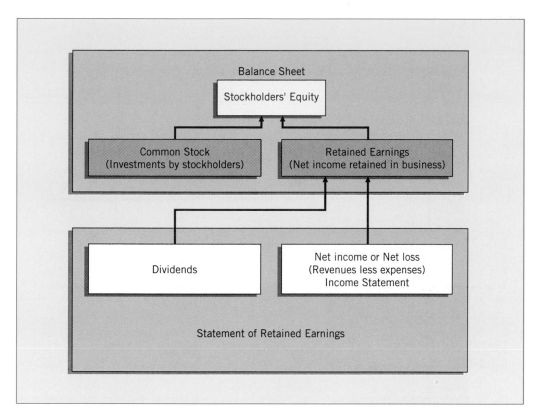

ILLUSTRATION 3-4
Financial Statements and
Ownership Structure

Illustration 3-5 summarizes and relates the transactions affecting owners' equity to the nominal (temporary) and real (permanent) classifications and to the types of business ownership.

ILLUSTRATION 3-5
Effects of Transactions on
Owners' Equity Accounts

| | | Ownership Structure | | | |
| | | Proprietorships and Partnerships | | Corporations | |
Transactions Affecting Owners' Equity	Impact on Owners' Equity	Nominal (Temporary) Accounts	Real (Permanent) Accounts	Nominal (Temporary) Accounts	Real (Permanent) Accounts
Investment by owner(s)	Increase		Capital		Common Stock and related accounts
Revenues earned	Increase	Revenue ⎫		Revenue ⎫	
Expenses incurred	Decrease	Expense ⎬	Capital	Expense ⎬	Retained Earnings
Withdrawal by owner(s)	Decrease	Drawing ⎭		Dividends ⎭	

❖ THE ACCOUNTING CYCLE

Illustration 3-6 flowcharts the steps in the **accounting cycle**. These are the accounting procedures normally used by enterprises to record transactions and prepare financial statements.

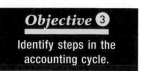

Objective ❸
Identify steps in the accounting cycle.

Identifying and Recording Transactions and Other Events

The first step in the accounting cycle is analysis of transactions and selected other events. The problem is to determine **what to record**. No simple rules exist that state whether an event should be recorded. Most agree that changes in personnel,

ILLUSTRATION 3-6
The Accounting Cycle

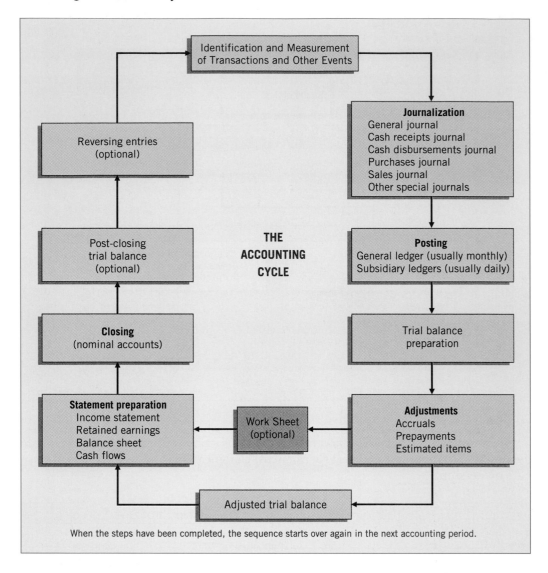

THE
ACCOUNTING
CYCLE

**Identification and Measurement
of Transactions and Other Events**

Journalization
General journal
Cash receipts journal
Cash disbursements journal
Purchases journal
Sales journal
Other special journals

Reversing entries
(optional)

Posting
General ledger (usually monthly)
Subsidiary ledgers (usually daily)

Post-closing
trial balance
(optional)

Trial balance
preparation

Closing
(nominal accounts)

Statement preparation
Income statement
Retained earnings
Balance sheet
Cash flows

Work Sheet
(optional)

Adjustments
Accruals
Prepayments
Estimated items

Adjusted trial balance

When the steps have been completed, the sequence starts over again in the next accounting period.

changes in managerial policies, and the value of human resources, though important, should not be recorded in the accounts. On the other hand, when the company makes a cash sale or purchase—no matter how small—it should be recorded.

The treatment relates to the accounting concepts presented in Chapter 2. **An item should be recognized in the financial statements if it is an element, is measurable, and is relevant and reliable.** Consider human resources. R. G. Barry & Co. at one time reported as supplemental data total assets of $14,055,926, including $986,094 for "net investments in human resources." AT&T and Mobil Oil Company have also experimented with human resource accounting. Should we value employees for balance sheet and income statement purposes? Certainly skilled employees are an important asset (highly relevant), but the problems of **determining their value and measuring it reliably have not yet been solved**. Consequently, human resources are not recorded. Perhaps when measurement techniques become more sophisticated and accepted, such information will be presented, if only in supplemental form.

---

[1]"Elements of Financial Statements of Business Enterprises," *Statement of Financial Accounting Concepts No. 6* (Stamford, Conn.: FASB, 1985), pp. 259–60.

The phrase "transactions and other events and circumstances that affect a business enterprise" is used to describe the sources or causes of changes in an entity's assets, liabilities, and equity.[1] **Events** are of two types: (1) **External events** involve interaction between an entity and its environment, such as a transaction with another entity, a change in the price of a good or service that an entity buys or sells, a flood or earthquake, or an improvement in technology by a competitor. (2) **Internal events** occur within an entity, such as using buildings and machinery in its operations or transferring or consuming raw materials in production processes.

Many events have both external and internal elements. For example, acquiring the services of employees or others involves exchange transactions, which are external events; using those services (labor), often simultaneously with their acquisition, is part of production, which is internal. Events may be initiated and controlled by an entity, such as the purchase of merchandise or the use of a machine, or they may be beyond its control, such as an interest rate change, a theft or vandalism, or the imposition of taxes.

Transactions, as particular kinds of external events, may be an exchange in which each entity both receives and sacrifices value, such as purchases and sales of goods or services. Or transactions may be transfers in one direction in which an entity incurs a liability or transfers an asset to another entity without directly receiving (or giving) value in exchange. Examples include investments by owners, distributions to owners, payment of taxes, gifts, charitable contributions, casualty losses, and thefts.

In short, accountants record as many events as possible that affect the **financial position** of the enterprise. Some events are omitted because of tradition and others because the problems of measuring them are too complex. The accounting profession in recent years has shown signs of breaking with age-old traditions and is more receptive than ever to accepting the challenge of measuring and reporting events and phenomena previously viewed as too complex and immeasurable.

Journalizing

Differing effects on the basic business elements (assets, liabilities, and equities) are categorized and collected in **accounts**. The **general ledger** is a collection of all the asset, liability, stockholders' equity, revenue, and expense accounts. A "T" account (as shown in Illustration 3-8) is a convenient method of illustrating the effect of transactions on particular asset, liability, equity, revenue, and expense items.

In practice, transactions and selected other events are not recorded originally in the ledger because a transaction affects two or more accounts, each of which is on a different page in the ledger. To circumvent this deficiency and to have a complete record of each transaction or other event in one place, a **journal** (the book of original entry) is employed. The simplest journal form is a chronological listing of transactions and other events expressed in terms of debits and credits to particular accounts. This is called a **general journal**. It is illustrated on the next page for the following transactions.

Objective ❹

Record transactions in journals, post to ledger accounts, and prepare a trial balance.

Nov. 1 Buys a new delivery truck on account from Auto Sales Co., $22,400.

3 Receives an invoice from the *Evening Graphic* for advertising, $280.

4 Returns merchandise to Yankee Supply for credit, $175.

16 Receives a $95 debit memo from Confederate Co., indicating that freight on a purchase from Confederate Co. was prepaid but is our obligation.

Each **general journal entry** consists of four parts: (1) the accounts and amounts to be debited (Dr.), (2) the accounts and amounts to be credited (Cr.), (3) a date, and (4) an explanation. Debits are entered first, followed by the credits, which are slightly indented. The explanation is begun below the name of the last account to be credited and may take one or more lines. The "Ref." column is completed at the time the accounts are posted.

ILLUSTRATION 3-7
General Journal with
Sample Entries

GENERAL JOURNAL				Page 12
Date 1999	Account Title and Explanation	Ref.	Amount Debit	Credit
Nov. 1	Delivery Equipment	8	22,400	
	Accounts Payable	34		22,400
	(Purchased delivery truck on account from Auto Sales Co.)			
3	Advertising Expense	65	280	
	Accounts Payable	34		280
	(Received invoice for advertising from *Evening Graphic*)			
4	Accounts Payable	34	175	
	Purchase Returns	53		175
	(Returned merchandise for credit to Yankee Supply)			
16	Transportation-In	55	95	
	Accounts Payable	34		95
	(Received debit memo for freight on merchandise purchased from Confederate Co.)			

Most businesses use **special journals** in addition to the general journal. Appendix 3B at the end of this chapter discusses and illustrates the following special journals:

> Cash receipts journal
>
> Sales journal
>
> Purchases journal (voucher register)
>
> Cash payments journal (check register)

Special journals summarize transactions possessing a common characteristic, thereby reducing the time necessary to accomplish the various bookkeeping tasks.

Posting

The items entered in a general journal must be transferred to the general ledger. This procedure, **posting**, is part of the summarizing and classifying process.

For example, the November 1 entry in the general journal in Illustration 3-7 showed a debit to Delivery Equipment of $22,400 and a credit to Accounts Payable of $22,400. The amount in the debit column is posted from the journal to the debit side of the ledger account (Delivery Equipment). The amount in the credit column is posted from the journal to the credit side of the ledger account (Accounts Payable).

The numbers in the "Ref." column of the general journal refer to the accounts in the ledger to which the respective items are posted. For example, the "34" placed in the column to the right of "Accounts Payable" indicates that this $22,400 item was posted to Account No. 34 in the ledger.

The posting of the general journal is completed when all of the posting reference numbers have been recorded opposite the account titles in the journal. Thus the number in the posting reference column serves two purposes: (1) to indicate the ledger account number of the account involved, and (2) to indicate that the posting has been completed for the particular item. Each business enterprise selects its own numbering system for its ledger accounts. One practice is to begin numbering with asset accounts and to follow with liabilities, owners' equity, revenue, and expense accounts, in that order.

The various ledger accounts in Illustration 3-8 are after the posting process is completed. The source of the data transferred to the ledger account is indicated by the reference GJ 12 (General Journal, page 12).

Delivery Equipment			No. 8
Nov. 1	GJ 12	22,400	

Accounts Payable					No. 34
Nov. 4	GJ 12	175	Nov. 1	GJ 12	22,400
			3	GJ 12	280
			16	GJ 12	95

Returned Purchases					No. 53
			Nov. 4	GJ 12	175

Transportation-In			No. 55
Nov. 16	GJ 12	95	

Advertising Expense			No. 65
Nov. 3	GJ 12	280	

ILLUSTRATION 3-8
Ledger Accounts, in T-Account Format

Trial Balance

A trial balance is a list of accounts and their balances at a given time. Customarily, a trial balance is prepared at the end of an accounting period. The accounts are listed in the order in which they appear in the ledger, with debit balances listed in the left column and credit balances in the right column. The totals of the two columns must be in agreement.

The primary purpose of a trial balance is to prove the mathematical equality of debits and credits after posting. Under the double-entry system this equality will occur when the sum of the debit account balances equals the sum of the credit account balances. **A trial balance also uncovers errors in journalizing and posting. In addition, it is useful in the preparation of financial statements**, as will be explained in the next two chapters. The procedures for preparing a trial balance consist of:

1 Listing the account titles and their balances.
2 Totaling the debit and credit columns.
3 Proving the equality of the two columns.

The trial balance prepared from the ledger of Pioneer Advertising Agency Inc. is presented below:

PIONEER ADVERTISING AGENCY INC.
Trial Balance
October 31, 1999

	Debit	Credit
Cash	$80,000	
Accounts Receivable	72,000	
Advertising Supplies	25,000	
Prepaid Insurance	6,000	
Office Equipment	50,000	
Notes Payable		$50,000
Accounts Payable		25,000
Unearned Fees		12,000
Common Stock		100,000
Dividends	5,000	
Fees Earned		100,000
Salaries Expense	40,000	
Rent Expense	9,000	
	$287,000	$287,000

ILLUSTRATION 3-9
Trial Balance (Unadjusted)

Note that the total debits $287,000 equal the total credits $287,000. Some accountants also show account numbers to the left of the account titles in the trial balance.

A trial balance does not prove that all transactions have been recorded or that the ledger is correct. Numerous errors may exist even though the trial balance columns agree. For example, the trial balance may balance even when (1) a transaction is not journalized, (2) a correct journal entry is not posted, (3) a journal entry is posted twice, (4) incorrect accounts are used in journalizing or posting, or (5) offsetting errors are made in recording the amount of a transaction. In other words, as long as equal debit and credits are posted, even to the wrong account or in the wrong amount, the total debits will equal the total credits.

Adjusting Entries

Objective 5

Explain the reasons for preparing adjusting entries.

In order for revenues to be recorded in the period in which they are earned, and for expenses to be recognized in the period in which they are incurred, **adjusting entries** are made at the end of the accounting period. In short, **adjustments are needed to ensure that the revenue recognition and matching principles are followed**.

The use of adjusting entries makes it possible to report on the balance sheet the appropriate assets, liabilities, and owners' equity at the statement date and to report on the income statement the proper net income (or loss) for the period. However, the trial balance—the first pulling together of the transaction data—may not contain up-to-date and complete data. This is true for the following reasons:

❶ Some events are not journalized daily because it is inexpedient to do so. Examples are the consumption of supplies and the earning of wages by employees.

❷ Some costs are not journalized during the accounting period because these costs expire with the passage of time rather than as a result of recurring daily transactions. Examples of such costs are building and equipment deterioration and rent and insurance.

❸ Some items may be unrecorded. An example is a utility service bill that will not be received until the next accounting period.

Adjusting entries are required every time financial statements are prepared. An essential starting point is an analysis of each account in the trial balance to determine whether it is complete and up-to-date for financial statement purposes. The analysis requires a thorough understanding of the company's operations and the interrelationship of accounts. The preparation of adjusting entries is often an involved process that requires the services of a skilled professional. In accumulating the adjustment data, the company may need to make inventory counts of supplies and repair parts. Also it may be desirable to prepare supporting schedules of insurance policies, rental agreements, and other contractual commitments. Adjustments are often prepared after the balance sheet date. However, the entries are dated as of the balance sheet date.

Types of Adjusting Entries

Adjusting entries can be classified as either prepayments or accruals. Each of these classes has two subcategories as shown below:

Prepayments	Accruals
1. Prepaid Expenses. Expenses paid in cash and recorded as assets before they are used or consumed.	3. Accrued Revenues. Revenues earned but not yet received in cash or recorded.
2. Unearned Revenues. Revenues received in cash and recorded as liabilities before they are earned.	4. Accrued Expenses. Expenses incurred but not yet paid in cash or recorded.

Specific examples and explanations of each type of adjustment are given in subsequent sections. Each example is based on the October 31 trial balance of Pioneer Advertising Agency Inc. (Illustration 3-9). We assume that Pioneer Advertising uses an accounting period of one month. Thus, monthly adjusting entries will be made. The entries will be dated October 31.

Adjusting Entries for Prepayments

As indicated earlier, prepayments are either prepaid expenses or unearned revenues. Adjusting entries for prepayments are required at the statement date to record the portion of the prepayment that represents the **expense incurred or the revenue earned** in the current accounting period. Assuming an adjustment is needed for both types of prepayments, the asset and liability are overstated and the related expense and revenue are understated. For example, in the trial balance, the balance in the asset, Supplies, shows only supplies purchased. This balance is overstated; the related expense account, Supplies Expense, is understated because the cost of supplies used has not been recognized. Thus the adjusting entry for prepayments will decrease a balance sheet account and increase an income statement account. The effects of adjusting entries for prepayments are graphically depicted in Illustration 3-10.

Prepaid Expenses. As stated on page 78, expenses paid in cash and recorded as assets before they are used or consumed are identified as prepaid expenses. When a cost is incurred, an asset account is debited to show the service or benefit that will be received in the future. Prepayments often occur in regard to insurance, supplies, advertising, and rent. In addition, prepayments are made when buildings and equipment are purchased.

Prepaid expenses expire either with the passage of time (e.g., rent and insurance) or through use and consumption (e.g., supplies). The expiration of these costs does not require daily recurring entries, which would be unnecessary and impractical. Accordingly, it is customary to postpone the recognition of such cost expirations until financial statements are prepared. At each statement date, adjusting entries are made

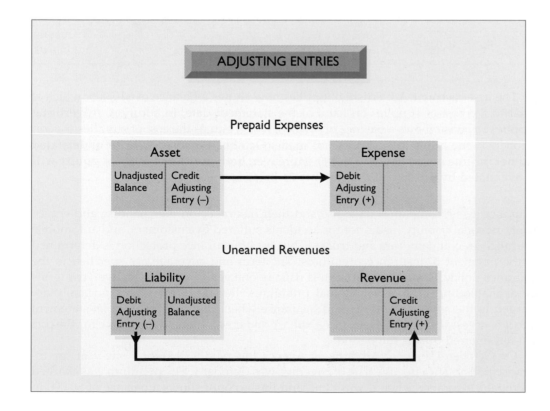

ILLUSTRATION 3-10
Adjusting Entries for Prepayments

to record the expenses that apply to the current accounting period and to show the unexpired costs in the asset accounts.

An asset-expense relationship exists with prepaid expenses. Prior to adjustment, assets are overstated and expenses are understated. **Thus, the prepaid expense adjusting entry results in a debit to an expense account and a credit to an asset account.**

Supplies

Oct. 5

Supplies purchased;
record asset

Oct. 31

Supplies used;
record supplies expense

Supplies. Several different types of supplies are used in a business enterprise. For example, a CPA firm will have **office supplies** such as stationery, envelopes, and accounting paper. In contrast, an advertising firm will have **advertising supplies** such as graph paper, video film, and poster paper. Supplies are generally debited to an asset account when they are acquired. During the course of operations, supplies are depleted or entirely consumed. However, recognition of supplies used is deferred until the adjustment process when a physical inventory (count) of supplies is taken. The difference between the balance in the Supplies (asset) account and the cost of supplies on hand represents the supplies used (expense) for the period.

Pioneer Advertising Agency (See Illustration 3-9) purchased advertising supplies costing $25,000 on October 5. The debit was made to the asset Advertising Supplies, and this account shows a balance of $25,000 in the October 31 trial balance. An inventory count at the close of business on October 31 reveals that $10,000 of supplies are still on hand. Thus, the cost of supplies used is $15,000 ($25,000 − $10,000), and the following adjusting entry is made:

Oct. 31

Advertising Supplies Expense	15,000	
Advertising Supplies		15,000
(To record supplies used)		

After the adjusting entry is posted, the two supplies accounts in T-account form show:

ILLUSTRATION 3-11
Supplies Accounts after Adjustment

Advertising Supplies				Advertising Supplies Expense	
10/5	25,000	10/31 Adj.	15,000	10/31 Adj. 15,000	
10/31 Bal.	10,000				

Insurance

Oct. 4

Insurance purchased;
record asset

Insurance Policy			
Oct	Nov	Dec	Jan
$500	$500	$500	$500
Feb	March	April	May
$500	$500	$500	$500
June	July	Aug	Sept
$500	$500	$500	$500
1 YEAR $6,000			

Oct. 31

Insurance expired;
record insurance expense

The asset account Advertising Supplies now shows a balance of $10,000, which is equal to the cost of supplies on hand at the statement date. In addition, Advertising Supplies Expense shows a balance of $15,000, which equals the cost of supplies used in October. **If the adjusting entry is not made, October expenses will be understated and net income overstated by $15,000. Moreover, both assets and owners' equity will be overstated by $15,000 on the October 31 balance sheet.**

Insurance. Most companies have fire and theft insurance on merchandise and equipment, personal liability insurance for accidents suffered by customers, and automobile insurance on company cars and trucks. The cost of insurance protection is determined by the payment of insurance premiums. The term and coverage are specified in the insurance policy. The minimum term is usually one year, but three- to five-year terms are available and offer lower annual premiums. Insurance premiums normally are charged to the asset account Prepaid Insurance when paid. At the financial statement date it is necessary to debit Insurance Expense and credit Prepaid Insurance for the cost that has expired during the period.

On October 4, Pioneer Advertising Agency Inc. paid $6,000 for a one-year fire insurance policy. The effective date of coverage was October 1. The premium was charged to Prepaid Insurance when it was paid, and this account shows a balance of $6,000 in the October 31 trial balance. An analysis of the policy reveals that $500 ($6,000 ÷ 12) of insurance expires each month. Thus, the following adjusting entry is made:

Oct. 31

Insurance Expense	500	
Prepaid Insurance		500
(To record insurance expired)		

After the adjusting entry is posted, the accounts show:

Prepaid Insurance				Insurance Expense		
10/4	6,000	10/31 Adj.	500	10/31 Adj.	500	
10/31 Bal.	5,500					

ILLUSTRATION 3-12
Insurance Accounts after Adjustment

The asset Prepaid Insurance shows a balance of $5,500, which represents the unexpired cost applicable to the remaining 11 months of coverage. At the same time, the balance in Insurance Expense is equal to the insurance cost that has expired in October. **If this adjustment is not made, October expenses will be understated by $500 and net income overstated by $500. Moreover, both assets and owners' equity also will be overstated by $500 on the October 31 balance sheet.**

Depreciation. A business enterprise typically owns a variety of productive facilities such as buildings, equipment, and motor vehicles. These assets provide a service for a number of years. The term of service is commonly referred to as the **useful life** of the asset. Because an asset such as a building is expected to provide service for many years, it is recorded as an asset, rather than an expense, in the year it is acquired. Such assets are recorded at cost, as required by the cost principle.

According to the matching principle, a portion of the cost of a long-lived asset should be reported as an expense during each period of the asset's useful life. **Depreciation** is the process of allocating the cost of an asset to expense over its useful life in a rational and systematic manner.

Need for depreciation adjustment. From an accounting standpoint, the acquisition of productive facilities is viewed essentially as a long-term prepayment for services. The need for making periodic adjusting entries for depreciation is, therefore, the same as described before for other prepaid expenses; that is, to recognize the cost that has expired (expense) during the period and to report the unexpired cost (asset) at the end of the period.

In determining the useful life of a productive facility, the primary causes of depreciation are actual use, deterioration due to the elements, and obsolescence. At the time an asset is acquired, the effects of these factors cannot be known with certainty, so they must be estimated. Thus, you should recognize that depreciation is an estimate rather than a factual measurement of the cost that has expired. A common procedure in computing depreciation expense is to divide the cost of the asset by its useful life. For example, if cost is $10,000 and useful life is expected to be 10 years, annual depreciation is $1,000.

For Pioneer Advertising, depreciation on the office equipment is estimated to be $4,800 a year, or $400 per month. Accordingly, depreciation for October is recognized by the following adjusting entry:

Oct. 31

Depreciation Expense	400	
Accumulated Depreciation—Office Equipment		400
(To record monthly depreciation)		

Depreciation

Oct. I

Office equipment purchased; record asset ($50,000)

Office Equipment			
Oct	Nov	Dec	Jan
$400	$400	$400	$400
Feb	March	April	May
$400	$400	$400	$400
June	July	Aug	Sept
$400	$400	$400	$400
Depreciation = $4,800/year			

Oct. 31
Depreciation recognized; record depreciation expense

After the adjusting entry is posted, the accounts show:

ILLUSTRATION 3-13
Accounts after
Adjustment for
Depreciation

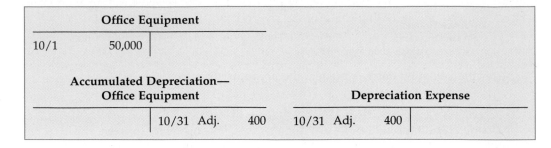

The balance in the accumulated depreciation account will increase $400 each month. Therefore, after journalizing and posting the adjusting entry at November 30, the balance will be $800.

Statement presentation. Accumulated Depreciation—Office Equipment is a contra asset account. A **contra asset account** is an account that is offset against an asset account on the balance sheet. This means that the accumulated depreciation account is offset against Office Equipment on the balance sheet and that its normal balance is a credit. This account is used instead of crediting Office Equipment in order to permit disclosure of **both the original cost** of the equipment **and the total cost that has expired to date**. In the balance sheet, Accumulated Depreciation—Office Equipment is deducted from the related asset account as follows:

ILLUSTRATION 3-14
Balance Sheet
Presentation of
Accumulated
Depreciation

Office equipment	$50,000	
Less: Accumulated depreciation—office equipment	400	$49,600

The difference between the cost of any depreciable asset and its related accumulated depreciation is referred to as the book value of that asset. In Illustration 3-14, the book value of the equipment at the balance sheet date is $49,600. It is important to realize that the book value and the market value of the asset are generally two different values. The reason the two are different is that depreciation is not a matter of valuation but rather a means of cost allocation.

Note also that depreciation expense identifies that portion of the asset's cost that has expired in October. As in the case of other prepaid adjustments, the omission of this adjusting entry would cause total assets, total owner's equity, and net income to be overstated and depreciation expense to be understated.

If additional equipment is involved, such as delivery or store equipment, or if the company has buildings, depreciation expense is recorded on each of these items. Related accumulated depreciation accounts also are established. These accumulated depreciation accounts would be described in the ledger as follows: Accumulated Depreciation—Delivery Equipment; Accumulated Depreciation—Store Equipment; and Accumulated Depreciation—Buildings.

Unearned Revenues. As stated on page 78, revenues received in cash and recorded as liabilities before they are earned are called **unearned revenues**. Such items as rent, magazine subscriptions, and customer deposits for future service may result in unearned revenues. Airlines such as United, American, and Delta treat receipts from the sale of tickets as unearned revenue until the flight service is provided. Similarly, tuition received prior to the start of a semester is considered to be unearned revenue. Unearned revenues are the opposite of prepaid expenses. Indeed, unearned revenue on the books of one company is likely to be a prepayment on the books of the company that has made the advance payment. For example, if identical accounting periods are assumed, a landlord will have unearned rent revenue when a tenant has prepaid rent.

When the payment is received for services to be provided in a future accounting period, an unearned revenue (a liability) account should be credited to recognize the obligation that exists. Unearned revenues are subsequently earned through rendering service to a customer. During the accounting period it may not be practical to make daily recurring entries as the revenue is earned. In such cases, the recognition of earned revenue is delayed until the adjustment process. Then an adjusting entry is made to record the revenue that has been earned and to show the liability that remains. **A liability–revenue account relationship therefore exists with unearned revenues.** In the typical case, liabilities are overstated and revenues are understated prior to adjustment. Thus, **the adjusting entry for unearned revenues results in a debit (decrease) to a liability account and a credit (increase) to a revenue account**.

Pioneer Advertising Agency received $12,000 on October 2 from R. Knox for advertising services expected to be completed by December 31. The payment was credited to Unearned Fees, and this account shows a balance of $12,000 in the October 31 trial balance. When analysis reveals that $4,000 of those fees has been earned in October, the following adjusting entry is made:

Unearned Revenues

Oct. 2

Thank you in advance for your work

I will finish by Dec. 31

~$12,000

Cash is received in advance; liability is recorded

Oct. 31
Service is provided; revenue is recorded

Oct. 31

Unearned Fees	4,000	
Fees Earned		4,000
(To record fees earned)		

After the adjusting entry is posted, the accounts show:

Unearned Fees			Fees Earned		
10/31 Adj. 4,000	10/2	12,000		10/31 Bal.	100,000
	10/31 Bal.	8,000		31 Adj.	4,000

ILLUSTRATION 3-15
Fees Accounts after Prepayments Adjustment

The liability Unearned Fees now shows a balance of $8,000, which represents the remaining advertising services expected to be performed in the future. At the same time, Fees Earned shows total revenue earned in October of $104,000. **If this adjustment is not made, revenues and net income will be understated by $4,000 in the income statement. Moreover, liabilities will be overstated and owners' equity will be understated by $4,000 on the October 31 balance sheet.**

Adjusting Entries for Accruals

The second category of adjusting entries is **accruals**. Adjusting entries for accruals are required to record revenues earned and expenses incurred in the current accounting period that have not been recognized through daily entries. If an accrual adjustment is needed, the revenue account (and the related asset account) and/or the expense account (and the related liability account) is understated. Thus, the adjusting entry for accruals will **increase both a balance sheet and an income statement account**. Adjusting entries for accruals are graphically depicted in Illustration 3-16.

Accrued Revenues. As explained on page 78, revenues earned but not yet received in cash or recorded at the statement date are **accrued revenues**. Accrued revenues may accumulate (accrue) with the passing of time, as in the case of interest revenue and rent revenue. Or they may result from services that have been performed but neither billed nor collected, as in the case of commissions and fees. The former are unrecorded because the earning of interest and rent does not involve daily transactions; the latter may be unrecorded because only a portion of the total service has been provided.

An adjusting entry is required to show the receivable that exists at the balance sheet date and to record the revenue that has been earned during the period. **An asset-revenue account relationship exists with accrued revenues.** Prior to adjustment both assets and revenues are understated. Accordingly, **an adjusting entry for accrued rev-**

ILLUSTRATION 3-16
Adjusting Entries for
Accruals

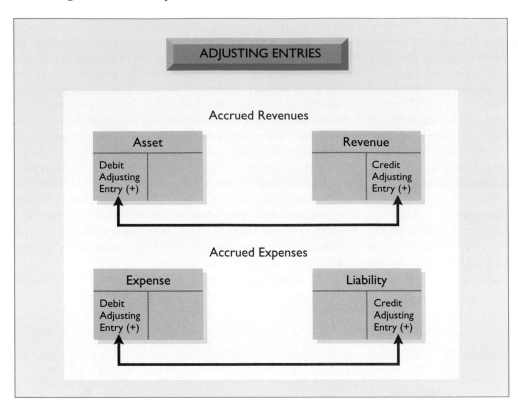

Accrued Revenues

Oct. 31

Service is provided;
revenue and receivable
are recorded

Nov.
Cash is received;
receivable is reduced

enues results in a debit (increase) to an asset account and a credit (increase) to a
revenue account.

In October Pioneer Advertising Agency earned $2,000 in fees for advertising serv-
ices that were not billed to clients before October 31. Because these services have not
been billed, they have not been recorded. Thus, the following adjusting entry is made:

Oct. 31

Accounts Receivable	2,000	
Fees Earned		2,000
(To accrue fees earned but not billed or collected)		

After the adjusting entry is posted, the accounts show:

ILLUSTRATION 3-17
Receivable and Revenue
Accounts after Accrual
Adjustment

Accounts Receivable				Fees Earned		
10/31	72,000				10/31	100,000
31 Adj.	2,000				31	4,000
					31 Adj.	2,000
					10/31 Bal.	106,000

The asset Accounts Receivable shows that $74,000 is owed by clients at the balance
sheet date. The balance of $106,000 in Fees Earned represents the total fees earned
during the month ($100,000 + $4,000 + $2,000). **If the adjusting entry is not made,
assets and owners' equity on the balance sheet, and revenues and net income on the
income statement, will all be understated.**

Accrued Expenses. As indicated on page 78, expenses incurred but not yet paid or
recorded at the statement date are called **accrued expenses**. Interest, rent, taxes, and
salaries can be accrued expenses. Accrued expenses result from the same causes as

accrued revenues. In fact, an accrued expense on the books of one company is an accrued revenue to another company. For example, the $2,000 accrual of fees by Pioneer is an accrued expense to the client that received the service.

Adjustments for accrued expenses are necessary to record the obligations that exist at the balance sheet date and to recognize the expenses that apply to the current accounting period. **A liability–expense relationship exists with accrued expenses.** Prior to adjustment both liabilities and expenses are understated. Therefore, **the adjusting entry for accrued expenses results in a debit (increase) to an expense account and a credit (increase) to a liability account.**

Accrued Interest. Pioneer Advertising Agency signed a 3-month note payable in the amount of $50,000 on October 1. The note requires interest at an annual rate of 12%. The amount of the interest accumulation is determined by three factors: (1) the face value of the note, (2) the interest rate, which is always expressed as an annual rate, and (3) the length of time the note is outstanding. In this instance, the total interest due on the $50,000 note at its due date 3 months hence is $1,500 ($50,000 × 12% × 3/12), or $500 for one month. The formula for computing interest and its application to Pioneer Advertising Agency for the month of October are shown in Illustration 3-18.

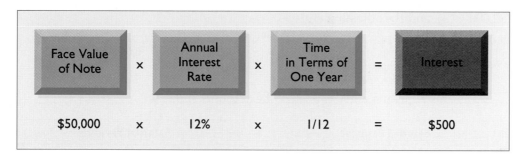

ILLUSTRATION 3-18
Formula for Computing Interest

Note that the time period is expressed as a fraction of a year. The accrued expense adjusting entry at October 31 is as follows:

Oct. 31

Interest Expense	500	
Interest Payable		500
(To accrue interest on notes payable)		

After this adjusting entry is posted, the accounts show:

Interest Expense		Interest Payable	
10/31 500			10/31 500

ILLUSTRATION 3-19
Interest Accounts after Adjustment

Interest Expense shows the interest charges applicable to the month of October. The amount of interest owed at the statement date is shown in Interest Payable. It will not be paid until the note comes due at the end of three months. The Interest Payable account is used instead of crediting Notes Payable to disclose the two types of obligations (interest and principal) in the accounts and statements. **If this adjusting entry is not made, liabilities and interest expense will be understated, and net income and owners' equity will be overstated.**

Accrued Salaries. Some types of expenses, such as employee salaries and commissions, are paid for after the services have been performed. At Pioneer Advertising, salaries were last paid on October 26; the next payment of salaries will not occur until November

9. As shown in the calendar below, three working days remain in October (October 29–31).

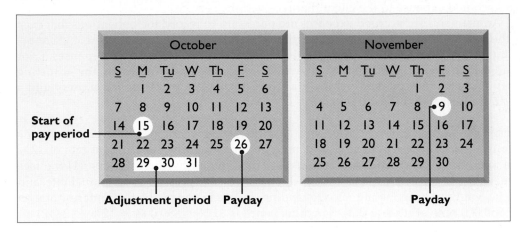

At October 31, the salaries for these days represent an accrued expense and a related liability to Pioneer Advertising. The employees receive total salaries of $10,000 for a five-day work week, or $2,000 per day. Thus, accrued salaries at October 31 are $6,000 ($2,000 × 3), and the adjusting entry is:

Oct. 31

Salaries Expense	6,000	
Salaries Payable		6,000
(To record accrued salaries)		

After this adjusting entry is posted, the accounts show:

ILLUSTRATION 3-20
Salary Accounts after Adjustment

Salaries Expense		Salaries Payable	
10/26 40,000			10/31 Adj. 6,000
31 Adj. 6,000			
10/31 Bal. 46,000			

After this adjustment, the balance in Salaries Expense of $46,000 (23 days × $2,000) is the actual salary expense for October. The balance in Salaries Payable of $6,000 is the amount of the liability for salaries owed as of October 31. **If the $6,000 adjustment for salaries is not recorded, Pioneer's expenses will be understated $6,000, and its liabilities will be understated $6,000.**

At Pioneer Advertising, salaries are payable every two weeks. Consequently, the next payday is November 9, when total salaries of $20,000 will again be paid. The payment consists of $6,000 of salaries payable at October 31 plus $14,000 of salaries expense for November (7 working days as shown in the November calendar × $2,000). Therefore, the following entry is made on November 9:

Nov. 9

Salaries Payable	6,000	
Salaries Expense	14,000	
Cash		20,000
(To record November 9 payroll)		

This entry eliminates the liability for Salaries Payable that was recorded in the October 31 adjusting entry and records the proper amount of Salaries Expense for the period between November 1 and November 9.

Bad Debts. Proper matching of revenues and expenses dictates recording bad debts as an expense of the period in which revenue is earned instead of the period in which the accounts or notes are written off. The proper valuation of the receivable balance also requires recognition of uncollectible, worthless receivables. Proper matching and valuation require an adjusting entry.

At the end of each period an estimate is made of the amount of current period revenue on account that will later prove to be uncollectible. The estimate is based on the amount of bad debts experienced in past years, general economic conditions, the age of the receivables, and other factors that indicate the element of uncollectibility. Usually it is expressed as a percent of the revenue on account for the period. Or it may be computed by adjusting the Allowance for Doubtful Accounts to a certain percent of the trade accounts receivable and trade notes receivable at the end of the period.

To illustrate, assume that experience indicates a reasonable estimate for bad debt expense for the month is $1,600. The adjusting entry for bad debts is:

Oct. 31

Bad Debt Expense	1,600	
Allowance for Doubtful Accounts		1,600
(To record monthly bad debt expense)		

After the adjusting entry is posted, the accounts show:

Accounts Receivable		
10/1	72,000	
31 Adj.	2,000	

Allowance for Doubtful Accounts		**Bad Debt Expense**	
10/31 Adj.	1,600	10/31 Adj. 1,600	

Adjusted Trial Balance

After all adjusting entries have been journalized and posted, another trial balance is prepared from the ledger accounts. This trial balance is called an adjusted trial balance. It shows the balance of all accounts, including those that have been adjusted, at the end of the accounting period. The purpose of an adjusted trial balance is to show the effects of all financial events that have occurred during the accounting period.

ILLUSTRATION 3-21
Trial Balance (Adjusted)

PIONEER ADVERTISING AGENCY, INC. Adjusted Trial Balance October 31, 1999		
	Debit	**Credit**
Cash	$80,000	
Accounts Receivable	74,000	
Allowance for Doubtful Accounts		$1,600
Advertising Supplies	10,000	
Prepaid Insurance	5,500	
Office Equipment	50,000	
Accumulated Depreciation— Office Equipment		400
Notes Payable		50,000
Accounts Payable		25,000
Interest Payable		500
Unearned Fees		8,000
Salaries Payable		6,000
Common Stock		100,000
Dividends	5,000	
Fees Earned		106,000
Salaries Expense	46,000	
Advertising Supplies Expense	15,000	
Rent Expense	9,000	
Insurance Expense	500	
Interest Expense	500	
Depreciation Expense	400	
Bad Debt Expense	1,600	
	$297,500	$297,500

Closing

Inventory and Related Accounts

End-of-period procedures for inventory depend on what inventory system is in use. With a **perpetual inventory system**, purchases and sales are recorded directly in the inventory account as the purchases and sales occur. Therefore, the balance in the Inventory account should represent the ending inventory amount, and no adjusting entries are needed. To ensure this accuracy, a physical count of the items in the inventory is generally made annually. No Purchases account is used because the purchases are debited directly to the Inventory account. However, a Cost of Goods Sold account is used to accumulate the issuances from inventory. That is, when inventory items are sold, the cost of the sold goods is credited to Inventory and debited to Cost of Goods Sold.

With a **periodic inventory system**, a Purchases account is used and the Inventory account is unchanged during the period. The Inventory account represents the beginning inventory amount throughout the period. At the end of the accounting period the Inventory account must be adjusted by **closing out the beginning inventory** amount and **recording the ending inventory** amount. The ending inventory is determined by physically counting the items on hand and valuing them at cost or at the lower of cost or market. Under the periodic inventory system, cost of goods sold is, therefore, determined by adding the beginning inventory together with net purchases and deducting the ending inventory.

Cost of goods sold is determined as part of the closing process. It transfers the various merchandise accounts under a periodic inventory system into the Cost of Goods Sold account by use of a closing entry. To illustrate, Collegiate Apparel Shop has a beginning inventory of $30,000; Purchases $200,000; Transportation-In $6,000; Purchase Returns $1,200; Purchase Allowances $800; Purchase Discounts $2,000; and the ending inventory is $26,000.

Objective 6

Explain how inventory accounts are adjusted at year-end.

Closing Entry

Inventory (ending)	26,000	
Purchase Discounts	2,000	
Purchase Allowances	800	
Purchase Returns	1,200	
Cost of Goods Sold	206,000	
Inventory (beginning)		30,000
Purchases		200,000
Transportation-In		6,000
(To transfer beginning inventory and net purchases to Cost of Goods Sold and to record the ending inventory)		

After the foregoing entry, only the Cost of Goods Sold account remains to be closed.[2] Illustration 3-22 illustrates in T-account form the process of determining cost of goods sold and closing the related nominal accounts.

Other Accounts

Objective 7

Prepare closing entries.

The procedure generally followed to reduce the balance of nominal (temporary) accounts to zero in order to prepare the accounts for the next period's transactions is known as the **closing process**. In the closing process all of the revenue and expense account balances (income statement items) are transferred to a clearing or suspense account called Income Summary, which is used only at the end of each accounting period (yearly). Revenues and expenses are matched in the Income Summary account and the net result of this matching, which represents the net income or net loss for the

---

[2]The change between the beginning and ending inventory balances may be made through adjusting entries rather than through closing entries. Some favor this method because they believe that changes in merchandise inventory should receive the same accounting treatment as changes in the cost of supplies on hand between two points in time. The adjusting entry method is just as acceptable as the closing entry method.

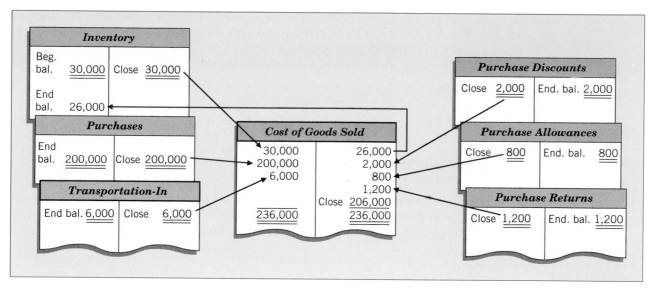

ILLUSTRATION 3-22
Determining Cost of Goods Sold and Closing Related Accounts (Periodic)

period, is then transferred to an owners' equity account (retained earnings for a corporation and capital accounts normally for proprietorships and partnerships). All closing entries are posted to the appropriate general ledger accounts.

For example, assume that revenue accounts of Collegiate Apparel Shop have the following balances, after adjustments, at the end of the year:

Revenue from Sales	$280,000
Rental Revenue	27,000
Interest Revenue	5,000

These **revenue accounts** would be closed and the balances transferred by the following closing journal entry:

Revenue from Sales	280,000	
Rental Revenue	27,000	
Interest Revenue	5,000	
Income Summary		312,000
(To close revenue accounts to Income Summary)		

Assume that the expense accounts, including Cost of Goods Sold, have the following balances, after adjustments, at the end of the year:

Cost of Goods Sold	$206,000
Selling Expenses	25,000
General and Adm. Expenses	40,600
Interest Expense	4,400
Income Tax Expense	13,000

These **expense accounts** would be closed and the balances transferred through the following closing journal entry:

Income Summary	289,000	
Cost of Goods Sold		206,000
Selling Expenses		25,000
General and Adm. Expenses		40,600
Interest Expense		4,400
Income Tax Expense		13,000
(To close expense accounts to Income Summary)		

The Income Summary account now has a credit balance of $23,000 which is net income. The **net income is transferred to owners' equity** by closing the Income Summary account to Retained Earnings as follows:

Income Summary	23,000	
Retained Earnings		23,000
(To close Income Summary to Retained Earnings)		

Assuming that dividends of $7,000 were declared and distributed during the year, the Dividends account is closed directly to Retained Earnings as follows:

Retained Earnings	7,000	
Dividends		7,000

After the closing process is completed, each income statement (i.e., nominal) account is balanced out to zero and is ready for use in the next accounting period. Illustration 3-23 shows the closing process in T-account form.

ILLUSTRATION 3-23
The Closing Process

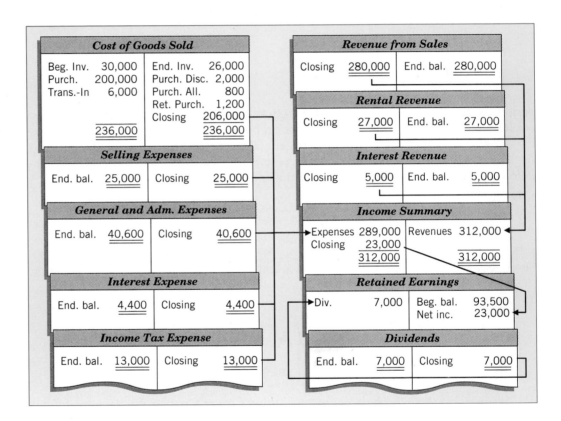

Post-Closing Trial Balance

We already mentioned that a trial balance is taken after the regular transactions of the period have been entered and that a second trial balance (the adjusted trial balance) is taken after the adjusting entries have been posted. A third trial balance may be taken after posting the closing entries. The trial balance after closing, often called the **post-closing trial balance**, shows that equal debits and credits have been posted to the Income Summary account. The post-closing trial balance consists only of asset, liability, and owners' equity (the real) accounts.

Reversing Entries

After the financial statements have been prepared and the books have been closed, it is often helpful to reverse some of the adjusting entries before recording the regular transactions of the next period. Such entries are called reversing entries. **A reversing** entry **is made at the beginning of the next accounting period and is the exact opposite of the related adjusting entry made in the previous period.** The recording of reversing entries is an **optional** step in the accounting cycle that may be performed at the beginning of the next accounting period.

The purpose of reversing entries is to simplify the recording of transactions in the next accounting period. The use of reversing entries does not change the amounts reported in the financial statements for the previous period.

Illustration of Reversing Entries—Accruals

Reversing entries are most often used to reverse two types of adjusting entries: accrued revenues and accrued expenses. To illustrate the optional use of reversing entries for accrued expenses, we will use the following transaction and adjustment data:

❶ October 24 (initial salary entry): $4,000 of salaries incurred between October 1 and October 24 are paid.

❷ October 31 (adjusting entry): Salaries incurred between October 25 and October 31 are $1,200. These will be paid in the November 8 payroll.

❸ November 8 (subsequent salary entry): Salaries paid are $2,500. Of this amount, $1,200 applied to accrued wages payable at October 31 and $1,300 was incurred between November 1 and November 8.

The comparative entries are shown in Illustration 3-24.

ILLUSTRATION 3-24
Comparison of Entries for Accruals, with and without Reversing Entries

Reversing Entries Not Used				Reversing Entries Used		
Initial Salary Entry						
Oct. 24	Salaries Expense	4,000		Oct. 24	Salaries Expense	4,000
	Cash		4,000		Cash		4,000
Adjusting Entry						
Oct. 31	Salaries Expense	1,200		Oct. 31	Salaries Expense	1,200
	Salaries Payable		1,200		Salaries Payable		1,200
Closing Entry						
Oct. 31	Income Summary	5,200		Oct. 31	Income Summary	5,200
	Salaries Expense		5,200		Salaries Expense		5,200
Reversing Entry						
Nov. 1	No entry is made.			Nov. 1	Salaries Payable	1,200
					Salaries Expense		1,200
Subsequent Salary Entry						
Nov. 8	Salaries Payable	1,200		Nov. 8	Salaries Expense	2,500
	Salaries Expense	1,300			Cash		2,500
	Cash		2,500				

The comparative entries show that the first three entries are the same whether or not reversing entries are used. The last two entries, however, are different. The November 1 reversing entry eliminates the $1,200 balance in Salaries Payable that was created by the October 31 adjusting entry. The reversing entry also creates a $1,200 credit balance in the Salaries Expense account. As you know, it is unusual for an expense account to have a credit balance. The balance is correct in this instance, though, because it anticipates that the entire amount of the first salary payment in the new accounting period will be debited to Salaries Expense. This debit will eliminate the credit balance, and the resulting debit balance in the expense account will equal the salaries expense incurred in the new accounting period ($1,300 in this example).

When reversing entries are made, all cash payments of expenses can be debited to the expense account. This means that on November 8 (and every payday) Salaries

Expense can be debited for the amount paid without regard to the existence of any accrued salaries payable. Being able to make the same entry each time simplifies the recording process in an accounting system.

Illustration of Reversing Entries—Prepayments

Prepayments may also be reversed if the initial entry to record the transaction is made to an expense or revenue account. To illustrate the use of reversing entries for prepaid expenses, we will use the following transaction and adjustment data:

❶ December 10 (initial entry): $20,000 of office supplies are purchased with cash.
❷ December 31 (adjusting entry): $5,000 of office supplies on hand.

The comparative entries are shown in Illustration 3-25.

Reversing Entries Not Used				Reversing Entries Used			
Initial Purchase of Supplies Entry							
Dec. 10	Office Supplies	20,000		Dec. 10	Office Supplies Expense	20,000	
	Cash		20,000		Cash		20,000
Adjusting Entry							
Dec. 31	Office Supplies Expense	15,000		Dec. 31	Office Supplies	5,000	
	Office Supplies		15,000		Office Supplies Expense		5,000
Closing Entry							
Dec. 31	Income Summary	15,000		Dec. 31	Income Summary	15,000	
	Office Supplies Expense		15,000		Office Supplies Expense		15,000
Reversing Entry							
Jan. 1	No entry			Jan. 1	Office Supplies Expense	5,000	
					Office Supplies		5,000

ILLUSTRATION 3-25
Comparison of Entries for Prepayments, with and without Reversing Entries

After the adjusting entry on December 31 (regardless of whether reversing entries are used), the asset account, Office Supplies, shows a balance of $5,000 and Office Supplies Expense a balance of $15,000. If Office Supplies Expense initially was debited when the supplies were purchased, a reversing entry is made to return to the expense account the cost of unconsumed supplies. The company then continues to debit Office Supplies Expense for additional purchases of office supplies during the next period.

With respect to prepaid items, why are all such items not entered originally into real accounts (assets and liabilities), thus making reversing entries unnecessary? Sometimes this practice is followed. It is particularly advantageous for items that need to be apportioned over several periods (e.g., supplies and parts inventories). However, items that do not follow this regular pattern and that may or may not involve two or more periods are ordinarily entered initially in revenue or expense accounts. The revenue and expense accounts may not require adjusting and are systematically closed to Income Summary. Using the nominal accounts adds consistency to the accounting system and makes the recording more efficient, particularly when a large number of such transactions occur during the year. For example, the bookkeeper knows that when an invoice is received for other than a capital asset acquisition, the amount is expensed. The bookkeeper need not worry at the time the invoice is received whether or not the item will result in a prepaid expense at the end of the period, because adjustments will be made at the end of the period.

Summary of Reversing Entries

A summary of guidelines for reversing entries is as follows:

❶ All accrued items should be reversed.

❷ All prepaid items for which the original cash transaction was debited or credited to an expense or revenue account should be reversed.

❸ Adjusting entries for depreciation and bad debts are not reversed.

Recognize that reversing entries do not have to be used; therefore, some accountants avoid them entirely.

The Accounting Cycle Summarized

A summary of the steps in the accounting cycle shows a logical sequence of the accounting procedures used during a fiscal period:

❶ Enter the transactions of the period in appropriate journals.
❷ Post from the journals to the ledger (or ledgers).
❸ Take an unadjusted trial balance (trial balance).
❹ Prepare adjusting journal entries and post to the ledger(s).
❺ Take a trial balance after adjusting (adjusted trial balance).
❻ Prepare the financial statements from the second trial balance.
❼ Prepare closing journal entries and post to the ledger(s).
❽ Take a trial balance after closing (post-closing trial balance).
❾ Prepare reversing entries (optional) and post to the ledger(s).

This list of procedures constitutes a complete accounting cycle that is normally performed in every fiscal period.

❖ USING A WORK SHEET

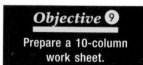

Objective ❾

Prepare a 10-column work sheet.

To facilitate the end-of-period (monthly, quarterly, or annually) accounting and reporting process, a work sheet is often used. A **work sheet** is a columnar sheet of paper used to adjust the account balances and prepare the financial statements. Use of a work sheet helps the accountant prepare the financial statements on a more timely basis. It is not necessary to delay preparation of the financial statements until the adjusting and closing entries are journalized and posted. The **10-column work sheet** illustrated in this chapter (Illustration 3-26) provides columns for the first trial balance, adjustments, adjusted trial balance, income statement, and balance sheet.

The work sheet does not replace the financial statements. Instead, it is an informal device for accumulating and sorting information needed for the financial statements. Completing the work sheet provides considerable assurance that all of the details related to the end-of-period accounting and statement preparation have been properly brought together.

Adjustments Entered on the Work Sheet

Items (a) through (f) below serve as the basis for the adjusting entries made in the work sheet shown in Illustration 3-26.

(a) Furniture and equipment is depreciated at the rate of 10% per year based on original cost of $67,000.
(b) Estimated bad debts, one-quarter of 1% of sales ($400,000).
(c) Insurance expired during the year, $360.
(d) Interest accrued on notes receivable as of December 31, $800.
(e) The Rent Expense account contains $500 rent paid in advance, which is applicable to next year.
(f) Property taxes accrued December 31, $2,000.

The adjusting entries shown on the December 31, 1999, work sheet are as follows:

(a)		
Depreciation Expense—Furniture and Equipment	6,700	
Accumulated Depreciation—Furniture and Equipment		6,700
(b)		
Bad Debts Expense	1,000	
Allowance for Doubtful Accounts		1,000
(c)		
Insurance Expense	360	
Prepaid Insurance		360
(d)		
Interest Receivable	800	
Interest Revenue		800
(e)		
Prepaid Rent Expense	500	
Rent Expense		500
(f)		
Property Tax Expense	2,000	
Property Tax Payable		2,000

These adjusting entries are transferred to the Adjustments columns of the work sheet, and each may be designated by letter. The accounts that are set up as a result of the adjusting entries and that are not already in the trial balance are listed below the totals of the trial balance, as illustrated on the work sheet. The Adjustments columns are then totaled and balanced.

The illustration does not include in the Adjustments columns the adjustments for cost of goods sold. Although these adjustments are sometimes included in these columns on a 10-column work sheet, this illustration assumes that these entries will be made during the closing process.

Adjusted Trial Balance Columns

The amounts shown in the Trial Balance columns are combined with the Adjustments columns and are extended to the Adjusted Trial Balance columns. For example, the $2,000 shown opposite the Allowance for Doubtful Accounts in the Trial Balance Cr. column is added to the $1,000 in the Adjustments Cr. column. The $3,000 total is then extended to the Adjusted Trial Balance Cr. column. Similarly, the $900 debit opposite Unexpired Insurance is reduced by the $360 credit in the Adjustments column. The result, $540, is shown in the Adjusted Trial Balance Dr. column. The Adjusted Trial Balance debit and credit columns are then totaled and determined to be in balance.

Income Statement and Balance Sheet Columns

All the debit items in the Adjusted Trial Balance columns are extended into the balance sheet or income statement columns to the right. All the credit items in the Adjusted Trial Balance columns are similarly extended.

Note that the January 1 inventory is extended to the Income Statement Dr. column, because beginning inventory will appear as an addition in the cost of goods sold section of the income statement.

Ending Inventory

The December 31 inventory, $40,000, is not in either of the trial balances but is listed as a separate item *below* the accounts already shown. It is listed in the Balance Sheet Dr. column because it is an asset at the end of the year, and in the Income Statement Cr. column because it will be used as a deduction in the cost of goods sold section of the income statement.

Uptown Cabinet Corp.
TEN-COLUMN WORK SHEET
For the Year Ended December 31, 1999

Accounts	Trial Balance Dr.	Cr.	Adjustments Dr.	Cr.	Adjusted Trial Balance Dr.	Cr.	Income Statement Dr.	Cr.	Balance Sheet Dr.	Cr.
Cash	1,200				1,200				1,200	
Notes receivable	16,000				16,000				16,000	
Accounts receivable	41,000				41,000				41,000	
Allowance for doubtful accounts		2,000		(b) 1,000		3,000				3,000
Inventory, Jan. 1, 1999	36,000				36,000		36,000			
Prepaid insurance	900			(c) 360	540				540	
Furniture and equipment	67,000				67,000				67,000	
Accumulated depreciation— furniture and equipment		12,000		(a) 6,700		18,700				18,700
Notes payable		20,000				20,000				20,000
Accounts payable		13,500				13,500				13,500
Bonds payable		30,000				30,000				30,000
Common stock		50,000				50,000				50,000
Retained earnings, Jan. 1, 1999		14,200				14,200				14,200
Sales		400,000				400,000		400,000		
Purchases	320,000				320,000		320,000			
Sales salaries expense	20,000				20,000		20,000			
Advertising expense	2,200				2,200		2,200			
Traveling expense	8,000				8,000		8,000			
Salaries, office and general	19,000				19,000		19,000			
Telephone and telegraph expense	600				600		600			
Rent expense	4,800			(e) 500	4,300		4,300			
Property tax expense	3,300		(f) 2,000		5,300		5,300			
Interest expense	1,700				1,700		1,700			
Totals	541,700	541,700								
Depreciation expense— furniture and equipment			(a) 6,700		6,700		6,700			
Bad debts expense			(b) 1,000		1,000		1,000			
Insurance expense			(c) 360		360		360			
Interest receivable			(d) 800		800				800	
Interest revenue				(d) 800		800		800		
Prepaid rent expense			(e) 500		500				500	
Property tax payable				(f) 2,000		2,000				2,000
Totals			11,360	11,360	552,200	552,200				
Inventory, Dec. 31, 1999								40,000	40,000	
Totals							425,160	440,800		
Income before income taxes							15,640			
Totals							440,800	440,800		
Income before income taxes								15,640		
Income tax expense			(g) 3,440				3,440			
Income tax payable				(g) 3,440						3,440
Net income							12,200			12,200
Totals							15,640	15,640	167,040	167,040

ILLUSTRATION 3-26
Use of a Work Sheet

Income Taxes and Net Income

The next step is to total the Income Statement columns; the figure necessary to balance the debit and credit columns is the pretax income or loss for the period. The income before income taxes of $15,640 is shown in the Income Statement Dr. column because the revenues exceeded expenses by that amount.

The federal and state income tax expense and related tax liability are then computed. The company applies an effective rate of 22% to arrive at $3,440. Because the Adjustments columns have been balanced, this adjustment is entered in the Income Statement Dr. column as Income Tax Expense and in the Balance Sheet Cr. column as Income Tax Payable. The following adjusting journal entry is recorded on December 31, 1999, and posted to the general ledger as well as entered on the work sheet.

(g)

Income Tax Expense	3,440	
Income Tax Payable		3,440

Next the Income Statement columns are balanced with the income taxes included. The $12,200 difference between the debit and credit columns in this illustration represents net income. The net income of $12,200 is entered in the Income Statement Dr. column to achieve equality and in the Balance Sheet Cr. column as the increase in retained earnings.

Preparing Financial Statements from a Work Sheet

The work sheet provides the information needed for preparation of the financial statements without reference to the ledger or other records. In addition, the data have been sorted into appropriate columns, which facilitates the preparation of the statements.

The financial statements prepared from the 10-column work sheet illustrated are:

Income Statement for the Year Ended December 31, 1999 (Illustration 3-27).

ILLUSTRATION 3-27
An Income Statement

Uptown Cabinet Corp. INCOME STATEMENT For the Year Ended December 31, 1999			
Net sales			$400,000
Cost of goods sold			
Inventory, Jan. 1, 1999		$ 36,000	
Purchases		320,000	
Cost of goods available for sale		356,000	
Deduct inventory, Dec. 31, 1999		40,000	
Cost of goods sold			316,000
Gross profit on sales			84,000
Selling expenses			
Sales salaries expense		20,000	
Advertising expense		2,200	
Traveling expense		8,000	
Total selling expenses		30,200	
Administrative expenses			
Salaries, office and general	$19,000		
Telephone and telegraph expense	600		
Rent expense	4,300		
Property tax expense	5,300		
Depreciation expense—furniture and equipment	6,700		
Bad debts expense	1,000		
Insurance expense	360		
Total administrative expenses		37,260	
Total selling and administrative expenses			67,460
Income from operations			16,540
Other revenues and gains			
Interest revenue			800
			17,340
Other expenses and losses			
Interest expense			1,700
Income before income taxes			15,640
Income taxes			3,440
Net income			$ 12,200
Earnings per share			$1.22

Statement of Retained Earnings for the Year Ended December 31, 1999 (Illustration 3-28).

ILLUSTRATION 3-28
A Statement of Retained Earnings

Uptown Cabinet Corp. STATEMENT OF RETAINED EARNINGS For the Year Ended December 31, 1999	
Retained earnings, Jan. 1, 1999	$14,200
Add net income for 1999	12,200
Retained earnings, Dec. 31, 1999	$26,400

Balance Sheet as of December 31, 1999 (Illustration 3-29).

ILLUSTRATION 3-29
A Balance Sheet

Uptown Cabinet Corp.
BALANCE SHEET
As of December 31, 1999

Assets

Current assets			
Cash			$ 1,200
Notes receivable	$16,000		
Accounts receivable	41,000		
Interest receivable	800	$57,800	
Less allowance for doubtful accounts		3,000	54,800
Merchandise inventory on hand			40,000
Prepaid insurance			540
Prepaid rent			500
Total current assets			97,040
Property, plant, and equipment			
Furniture and equipment		67,000	
Less accumulated depreciation		18,700	
Total property, plant, and equipment			48,300
Total assets			$145,340

Liabilities and Stockholders' Equity

Current liabilities			
Notes payable			$ 20,000
Accounts payable			13,500
Property tax payable			2,000
Income taxes payable			3,440
Total current liabilities			38,940
Long-term liabilities			
Bonds payable, due June 30, 2004			30,000
Total liabilities			68,940
Stockholders' equity			
Common stock, $5.00 par value, issued and outstanding, 10,000 shares		$50,000	
Retained earnings		26,400	
Total stockholders' equity			76,400
Total liabilities and stockholders' equity			$145,340

Income Statement

The income statement presented is that of a trading or merchandising concern; if a manufacturing concern were illustrated, three inventory accounts would be involved: raw materials, work in process, and finished goods. When these accounts are used, a supplementary statement entitled Cost of Goods Manufactured must be prepared.

Statement of Retained Earnings

The net income earned by a corporation may be retained in the business or it may be distributed to stockholders by payment of dividends. In the illustration the net income earned during the year was added to the balance of retained earnings on January 1, thereby increasing the balance of retained earnings to $26,400 on December 31. No dividends were declared during the year.

Balance Sheet

The balance sheet prepared from the 10-column work sheet contains new items resulting from year-end adjusting entries. Interest receivable, unexpired insurance, and prepaid rent expense are included as current assets. These assets are considered current because they will be converted into cash or consumed in the ordinary routine of the business within a relatively short period of time. The amount of Allowance for Doubtful Accounts is deducted from the total of accounts, notes, and interest receivable because it is estimated that only $54,800 of $57,800 will be collected in cash.

In the property, plant, and equipment section the accumulated depreciation is deducted from the cost of the furniture and equipment; the difference represents the book or carrying value of the furniture and equipment.

Property tax payable is shown as a current liability because it is an obligation that is payable within a year. Other short-term accrued liabilities would also be shown as current liabilities.

The bonds payable, due in 2004, are long-term liabilities and are shown in a separate section. (Interest on the bonds was paid on December 31.)

Because Uptown Cabinet Corp. is a corporation, the capital section of the balance sheet, called the stockholders' equity section in the illustration, is somewhat different from the capital section for a proprietorship. Total stockholders' equity consists of the common stock, which is the original investment by stockholders, and the earnings retained in the business.

Closing and Reversing Entries

The entries for the closing process are as follows:

General Journal
December 31, 1999

Inventory (December 31)	40,000	
Cost of Goods Sold	316,000	
Inventory (January 1)		36,000
Purchases		320,000
(To record ending inventory balance and to determine cost of goods sold)		
Interest Revenue	800	
Sales	400,000	
Cost of Goods Sold		316,000
Sales Salaries Expense		20,000
Advertising Expense		2,200
Traveling Expense		8,000
Salaries, Office and General		19,000
Telephone and Telegraph Expense		600
Rent Expense		4,300
Property Tax Expense		5,300
Depreciation Expense—Furniture and Equipment		6,700
Bad Debts Expense		1,000
Insurance Expense		360
Interest Expense		1,700
Income Tax Expense		3,440
Income Summary		12,200
(To close revenues and expenses to Income Summary)		
Income Summary	12,200	
Retained Earnings		12,200
(To close Income Summary to Retained Earnings)		

After the financial statements have been prepared, the enterprise may use reversing entries to simplify the accounting next period. The following reversing entries would be made if a reversing system were used.

January 1, 2000

(1)

Interest Revenue	800	
Interest Receivable		800

(2)

Rent Expense	500	
Prepaid Rent Expense		500

(3)

Property Tax Payable	2,000	
Property Tax Expense		2,000

Reversing entries would not appear on the 10-column work sheet because they are recorded in the next year (2000). The main object of the work sheet is to obtain the correct balances at the end of the year for financial statement presentation for the current year (1999).

Monthly Statements, Yearly Closing

The use of a work sheet at the end of each month or quarter permits the preparation of interim financial statements even though the books are closed only at the end of each year. For example, assume that a business closes its books on December 31 but that monthly financial statements are desired. At the end of January a work sheet similar to the one illustrated in this chapter can be prepared to supply the information needed for statements for January. At the end of February a work sheet can be used again. Note that because the accounts were not closed at the end of January, the income statement taken from the work sheet on February 28 will present the net income for two months. If an income statement for only the month of February is wanted, it can be obtained by subtracting the items in the January income statement from the corresponding items in the income statement for the two months of January and February.

A statement of retained earnings for February only also may be obtained by subtracting the January items. The balance sheet prepared from the February work sheet, however, shows assets, liabilities, and stockholders' equity as of February 28, the specific date for which a balance sheet is desired.

The March work sheet would show the revenues and expenses for three months, and the subtraction of the revenues and expenses for the first two months could be made to supply the amounts needed for an income statement for the month of March only, and so on throughout the year.

SUMMARY OF LEARNING OBJECTIVES

❶ *Understand basic accounting terminology.* An understanding of the following eleven terms is important: (1) Event. (2) Transaction. (3) Account. (4) Real and nominal accounts. (5) Ledger. (6) Journal. (7) Posting. (8) Trial balance. (9) Adjusting entries. (10) Financial statements. (11) Closing entries.

❷ *Explain double-entry rules.* The left side of any account is the debit side; the right side is the the credit side. All asset and expense accounts are increased on the left or debit side and decreased on the right or credit side. Conversely, all liability and revenue accounts are increased on the right or credit side and decreased on the left or debit side. Stockholders' equity accounts, Common Stock and Retained Earnings, are increased on the credit side, whereas Dividends is increased on the debit side.

③ *Identify steps in the accounting cycle.* The basic steps in the accounting cycle are (1) identification and measurement of transactions and other events; (2) journalization; (3) posting; (4) unadjusted trial balance; (5) adjustments; (6) adjusted trial balance; (7) statement presentation; and (8) closing.

④ *Record transactions in journals, post to ledger accounts, and prepare a trial balance.* The simplest journal form is a chronological listing of transactions and events expressed in terms of debits and credits to particular accounts. The items entered in a general journal must be transferred (posted) to the general ledger. An unadjusted trial balance should be prepared at the end of a given period after the entries have been recorded in the journal and posted to the ledger.

⑤ *Explain the reasons for preparing adjusting entries.* Adjustments are necessary to achieve a proper matching of revenues and expenses so as to determine net income for the current period and to achieve an accurate statement of end-of-the-period balances in assets, liabilities, and owners' equity accounts.

⑥ *Explain how inventory accounts are adjusted at year-end.* When the inventory records are maintained in a periodic inventory system, a Purchases account is used; the Inventory account is unchanged during the period. The Inventory account represents the beginning inventory amount throughout the period. At the end of the accounting period the inventory account must be adjusted by closing out the beginning inventory amount and recording the ending inventory amount. Under a perpetual inventory system the balance in the Inventory account should represent the ending inventory amount, and no adjusting entries are needed.

⑦ *Prepare closing entries.* In the closing process all of the revenue and expense account balances (income statement items) are transferred to a clearing account called Income Summary, which is used only at the end of each fiscal year. Revenues and expenses are matched in the Income Summary account. The net result of this matching, which represents the net income or net loss for the period, is then transferred to an owners' equity account (retained earnings for a corporation and capital accounts for proprietorships and partnerships).

⑧ *Identify adjusting entries that may be reversed.* Reversing entries are most often used to reverse two types of adjusting entries: accrued revenues and accrued expenses. Prepayments may also be reversed if the initial entry to record the transaction is made to an expense or revenue account.

⑨ *Prepare a 10-column work sheet.* The 10-column work sheet provides columns for the first trial balance, adjustments, adjusted trial balance, income statement, and balance sheet. The work sheet does not replace the financial statements. Instead, it is the accountant's informal device for accumulating and sorting information needed for the financial statements.

Appendix 3A

Cash Basis Accounting versus Accrual Basis Accounting

Most companies use the **accrual basis of accounting**, recognizing revenue when it is earned and recognizing expenses in the period incurred, without regard to the time of receipt or payment of cash. Some small enterprises and the average individual taxpayer, however, use a strict or modified cash basis approach. Under the **strict cash basis of accounting**, revenue is recorded only when the cash is received and expenses are recorded only when the cash is paid. The determination of income on the cash basis rests upon the collection of revenue and the payment of expenses, and the revenue recognition and the matching principle are ignored. Consequently, cash basis financial statements are not in conformity with generally accepted accounting principles.

Objective 10

After studying Appendix 3A, you should be able to: Differentiate the cash basis of accounting from the accrual basis of accounting.

To illustrate and contrast accrual basis accounting and cash basis accounting, assume that Quality Contractor signs an agreement to construct a garage for $22,000. In January, Quality Contractor begins construction, incurs costs of $18,000 on credit, and by the end of January delivers a finished garage to the buyer. In February, Quality Contractor collects $22,000 cash from the customer. In March, Quality pays the $18,000 due the creditors. The net incomes for each month under cash basis accounting and accrual basis accounting are as follows:

Quality Contractor—Cash Basis Accounting INCOME STATEMENT For the Month of				
	January	February	March	Total
Cash receipts	$ –0–	$22,000	$ –0–	$22,000
Cash payments	–0–	–0–	18,000	18,000
Net income (loss)	$ –0–	$22,000	$(18,000)	$ 4,000

ILLUSTRATION 3A-1
Income Statement—
Cash Basis

Quality Contractor—Accrual Basis Accounting INCOME STATEMENT For the Month of				
	January	February	March	Total
Revenues	$22,000	$ –0–	$ –0–	$22,000
Expenses	18,000	–0–	–0–	18,000
Net income (loss)	$ 4,000	$ –0–	$ –0–	$ 4,000

ILLUSTRATION 3A-2
Income Statement—
Accrual Basis

For the three months combined, total net income is the same under both cash basis accounting and accrual basis accounting; the difference is in the **timing** of net income.

The balance sheet is also affected by the basis of accounting. For instance, if cash basis accounting were used, Quality Contractor's balance sheets at each month-end would appear as follows:

ILLUSTRATION 3A-3
Balance Sheets—
Cash Basis

Quality Contractor—Cash Basis Accounting BALANCE SHEETS As of			
	January 31	February 28	March 31
Assets			
Cash	$ –0–	$22,000	$4,000
Total assets	$ –0–	$22,000	$4,000
Liabilities and Owners' Equity			
Owners' equity	$ –0–	$22,000	$4,000
Total liabilities and owners' equity	$ –0–	$22,000	$4,000

If accrual basis accounting were used, Quality Contractor's balance sheets at each month-end would appear as follows:

ILLUSTRATION 3A-4
Balance Sheets—
Accrual Basis

Quality Contractor—Accrual Basis Accounting BALANCE SHEETS As of			
	January 31	February 28	March 31
Assets			
Cash	$ –0–	$22,000	$4,000
Accounts receivable	22,000	–0–	–0–
Total assets	$22,000	$22,000	$4,000
Liabilities and Owners' Equity			
Accounts payable	$18,000	$18,000	$-0-
Owners' equity	4,000	4,000	4,000
Total liabilities and owners' equity	$22,000	$22,000	$4,000

An analysis of the preceding income statements and balance sheets shows the ways in which cash basis accounting is inconsistent with basic accounting theory:

❶ The cash basis understates revenues and assets from the construction and delivery of the garage in January. It ignores the $22,000 accounts receivable, representing a near-term future cash inflow.

❷ The cash basis understates expenses incurred with the construction of the garage and the liability outstanding at the end of January. It ignores the $18,000 accounts payable, representing a near-term future cash outflow.

❸ The cash basis understates owners' equity in January by not recognizing the revenues and the asset until February, and it overstates owners' equity in February by not recognizing the expenses and the liability until March.

In short, cash basis accounting violates the theory underlying the elements of financial statements.

The **modified cash basis**, a mixture of cash basis and accrual basis, is the method followed by service enterprises, such as lawyers, doctors, architects, advertising agencies, and public accountants. Expenditures having an economic life of more than one year are capitalized as assets and depreciated or amortized over future years. Prepaid expenses and accrued expenses are not treated in a consistent manner: Prepayments of expenses are deferred and deducted only in the year to which they apply, but expenses paid after the year of incurrence (accrued expenses) are deducted only in the year paid. Revenue is reported in the year of receipt.[1]

❖ CONVERSION FROM CASH BASIS TO ACCRUAL BASIS

Not infrequently an accountant is required to convert a cash basis set of financial statements to the accrual basis for presentation and interpretation to a banker or for audit by an independent CPA. Illustration 3A-5 illustrates how cash basis financial data are converted to the accrual basis through various adjusting items.

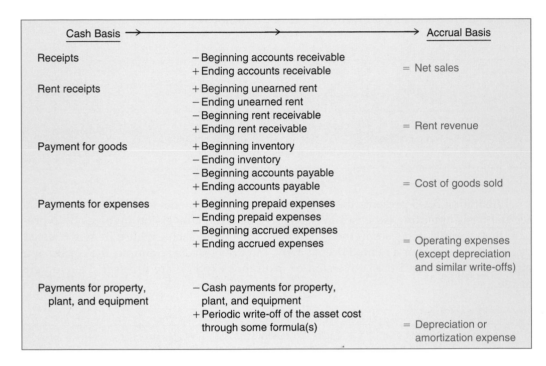

ILLUSTRATION 3A-5
Conversion of Cash Basis to Accrual Basis

In Illustration 3A-5, cash receipts are converted to **net sales** by subtracting beginning accounts receivable and adding ending accounts receivable. This procedure takes into account any accounts receivable written off during the period. By expanding the formula to include all of the accounts related to sales, cash receipts can be converted to **gross sales**, as shown in Illustration 3A-6.

Cash receipts from customers		xxx
Plus: Cash discounts	xx	
Sales returns and allowances	xx	
Accounts written off	xx	
Ending accounts receivable	xx	xx
		xxx
Less: Beginning accounts receivable		xx
Gross sales		xxx

ILLUSTRATION 3A-6
Conversion of Cash Receipts to Gross Sales

---

[1]For tax purposes individuals and personal service businesses may use modified cash basis accounting but its use by corporations (other than personal service corporations and S corporations) is prohibited if those corporations have average annual gross receipts over a 3-year period of more than $5 million. And any business in which inventory is a significant factor must use accrual accounting in reporting revenue from sales and cost of goods sold.

Cash receipts from customers can also be converted to net sales merely by adding or subtracting the change in the balance of accounts receivable from the beginning to the end of year, as shown below.

ILLUSTRATION 3A-7
Conversion of Cash
Receipts to Net Sales

$$\text{Cash receipts from customers} \begin{cases} + \text{ increase in accounts receivable} \\ \text{or} \\ - \text{ decrease in accounts receivable} \end{cases} = \text{Net sales}$$

Similarly, cash payments for goods can be converted to cost of goods sold by adding or deducting the change from the beginning to the end of the year in the accounts payable balance and in the inventory balance as follows:

ILLUSTRATION 3A-8
Conversion of Payments
for Goods to Cost of
Goods Sold

$$\text{Payments for goods} \begin{cases} + \text{ increase in accounts payable} \\ \text{or} \\ - \text{ decrease in accounts payable} \end{cases} = \text{Net purchases}$$

$$\text{Net purchases} \begin{cases} + \text{ decrease in inventory} \\ \text{or} \\ - \text{ increase in inventory} \end{cases} = \text{Cost of goods sold}$$

Illustration 3A-5 presents the conversion of cash payments for **all expenses** to the accrual basis operating expenses in the aggregate. That conversion involves both prepaid and accrued expenses in the conversion. Generally, each expense item is affected by a related accrual or a related prepayment, but not both. For example, the conversion of wages expense and the conversion of insurance expense are illustrated separately below.

ILLUSTRATION 3A-9
Conversion of Wages
Paid to Wages Expense

$$\text{Wages paid during the year} \begin{cases} + \text{ Ending accrued wages} \\ - \text{ Beginning accrued wages} \end{cases} = \text{Wages expense for the year}$$

ILLUSTRATION 3A-10
Conversion of Insurance
Paid to Insurance
Expense

$$\text{Insurance premiums paid during the year} \begin{cases} - \text{ Ending prepaid insurance} \\ + \text{ Beginning prepaid insurance} \end{cases} = \text{Insurance expense for the year}$$

Nonoperating items such as selling capital stock or paying off long-term debt are increases and decreases in cash, but they are not revenues or expenses under either the cash basis or the accrual basis.

Illustration. Diana Windsor, D.D.S., keeps her accounting records on a cash basis. During 1999, Dr. Windsor collected $80,000 from her patients and paid $30,000 for operating expenses, resulting in a cash basis net income of $50,000. At January 1 and December 31, 1999, she has accounts receivable, unearned revenue, accrued expenses, and prepaid expenses as follows:

	January 1, 1999	December 31, 1999
Accounts receivable	$12,000	$5,000
Unearned revenue	–0–	1,000
Accrued expenses (liabilities)	3,800	6,800
Prepaid expenses (assets)	2,000	3,000

One approach to restatement of Diana Windsor's income statement data is presented in work sheet form below.

Diana Windsor, D.D.S.
Conversion of Income Statement Data from Cash Basis to Accrual Basis
For the Year 1999

	Cash Basis	Adjustments Add	Adjustments Deduct	Accrual Basis
Receipts for fees:	$80,000			
− Accounts receivable, Jan. 1			$12,000	
+ Accounts receivable, Dec. 31		$5,000		
− Unearned revenue, Dec. 31			1,000	
Revenue from fees				$72,000
Disbursements for expenses:	30,000			
− Accrued expenses, Jan. 1			3,800	
+ Accrued expenses, Dec. 31		6,800		
+ Prepaid expenses, Jan. 1		2,000		
− Prepaid expenses, Dec. 31			3,000	
Operating expenses				32,000
Excess of receipts over disbursements— cash basis	**$50,000**			
Net income—accrual basis				**$40,000**

ILLUSTRATION 3A-11
Conversion of Statement of Cash Receipts and Disbursements to Income Statement

Another approach to converting from the cash basis statement of receipts and disbursements to the accrual basis income statement is illustrated below.

Diana Windsor, D.D.S.
Conversion of Income Statement Data from Cash Basis to Accrual Basis
For the Year 1999

Excess of receipts over disbursements	**$50,000**
− Decrease in accounts receivable ($12,000 to $5,000)	(7,000)
− Increase in unearned revenue ($–0– to $1,000)	(1,000)
− Increase in accrued expenses ($3,800 to $6,800)	(3,000)
+ Increase in prepaid expenses ($2,000 to $3,000)	1,000
Net income on an accrual basis	**$40,000**

ILLUSTRATION 3A-12
Alternative Conversion of Excess of Cash Receipts over Disbursements to Net Income

Under the first approach, receipts and disbursements on a cash basis are adjusted to revenues and expenses on an accrual basis, along with net income. Under the second approach, only the excess of receipts over disbursements is restated to net income.

❖ THEORETICAL WEAKNESSES OF THE CASH BASIS

The cash basis does report exactly when cash is received and when cash is disbursed. To many people that information represents something solid, something concrete. Isn't cash what it is all about? Does it make sense to invent something, design it, produce it, market and sell it, if you aren't going to get cash for it in the end? It is frequently said, "Cash is the real bottom line." It is also said, "Cash is the oil that lubricates the economy." If so, then what is the merit of accrual accounting?

Today's economy is considerably more lubricated by credit than by cash. And the accrual basis, not the cash basis, recognizes all aspects of the credit phenomenon. Investors, creditors, and other decision makers seek timely information about an enterprise's future cash flows. Accrual basis accounting provides this information by reporting the cash inflows and outflows associated with earnings activities as soon as these cash flows can be estimated with an acceptable degree of certainty. Receivables and payables are forecasters of future cash inflows and outflows. In other words, accrual basis accounting aids in predicting future cash flows by reporting transactions and other events with cash consequences at the time the transactions and events occur, rather than when the cash is received and paid.

<table>
<tr><td>

KEY TERMS

accrual basis, *101*
modified cash basis, *102*
strict cash basis, *101*

</td><td>

SUMMARY OF LEARNING OBJECTIVE FOR APPENDIX 3A

⑩ *Differentiate the cash basis of accounting from the accrual basis of accounting.* Accrual basis accounting provides information about cash inflows and outflows associated with earnings activities as soon as these cash flows can be estimated with an acceptable degree of certainty. That is, accrual basis accounting aids in predicting future cash flows by reporting transactions and events with cash consequences at the time the transactions and events occur, rather than when the cash is received and paid.

</td></tr>
</table>

Appendix 3B

Specialized Journals and Methods of Processing Accounting Data

Objective ⑪

After studying Appendix 3B, you should be able to: Identify (a) the use and types of subsidiary ledgers and (b) the use and types of special journals.

A business constantly needs detailed information about its dealings with individual customers and creditors. Imagine a business with several thousand charge (credit) customers and the transactions with these customers are shown in only one account, Accounts Receivable, in the general ledger. It would be virtually impossible to determine the balance owed by an individual customer at a specific time. Similarly, details of transactions affecting a single creditor are needed from time to time, and a single Accounts Payable account in the general ledger cannot make this information available.

❖ EXPANSION OF THE LEDGER—SUBSIDIARY LEDGERS

To provide this information, companies use a subsidiary ledger to keep track of individual balances. A subsidiary ledger is a group of accounts with a common characteristic, e.g., all are customer accounts, that is, all are accounts receivable. The subsidiary ledger facilitates the recording process by freeing the general ledger from the details of individual balances. Thus, a typical merchandising enterprise has subsidiary ledgers containing accounts with customers (accounts receivable or customers' ledger) and creditors (accounts payable or creditors' ledger). The enterprise maintains an account in the general ledger that summarizes the details in the accounts receivable and accounts payable ledgers. This summary account in the general ledger is called a control account, because the summary account controls the subsidiary ledger. **The general ledger control account balance must equal the composite balance of the individual accounts in the subsidiary ledger.**

As indicated, two common subsidiary ledgers are: (1) the accounts receivable ledger or customers' ledger, controlled by the general ledger account, Accounts Receivable; and (2) the accounts payable ledger or creditors' ledger, controlled by the general ledger account, Accounts Payable. In subsidiary ledgers, the individual accounts are usually arranged in alphabetical order.

An example of a control account and subsidiary ledger for accounts receivable is provided in Illustration 3B-1.

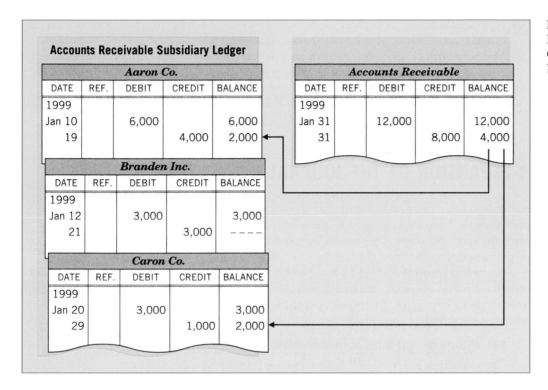

ILLUSTRATION 3B-1
Relationship between General and Subsidiary Ledgers

Illustration 3B-1 is based on the following transactions:

Sales and Collection Transactions

Credit Sales			Collections on Account		
Jan. 10	Aaron Co.	$ 6,000	Jan. 19	Aaron Co.	$ 4,000
12	Branden Inc.	3,000	21	Branden Inc.	3,000
20	Caron Co.	3,000	29	Caron Co.	1,000
		$12,000			$ 8,000

The total debits and credits in Accounts Receivable in the general ledger are reconcilable to the detailed debits and credits in the subsidiary accounts. The balance of $4,000 in the Accounts Receivable control account agrees with the total of the balances in the individual accounts receivable accounts ($2,000 + $0 + $2,000) in the subsidiary ledger.

Postings are made to the control accounts in the general ledger **monthly** for the purpose of preparing monthly financial statements. Postings to the individual accounts in the subsidiary ledger are made **daily**. The rationale for posting daily is to ensure that current account information can be used as a basis for monitoring credit limits, for billing customers, and also to answer inquiries from customers about their account balances.

Note also in this example that postings to the control account are made in total at the end of the month, whereas each of the individual transactions is posted daily to the subsidiary ledger. Procedures used for posting entries to the subsidiary ledger and to the general ledger control account generally involve the use of special journals, discussed in the next section.

In summary, the advantages of using subsidiary ledgers are that they:

❶ Show transactions affecting one customer or one creditor in a single account, thus providing necessary up-to-date information on specific account balances.

❷ Free the general ledger of excessive details relating to accounts receivable and accounts payable. As a result, a trial balance of the general ledger does not contain vast numbers of individual account balances.

❸ Help locate errors in individual accounts by reducing the number of accounts combined in one ledger and by using control accounts.

❹ Make possible a division of labor in posting by having one employee post to the general ledger and a different employee(s) post to the subsidiary ledgers.

Note that a business may also use control accounts and subsidiary ledgers for other accounts such as inventory, equipment, and selling and administrative expenses.

❖ EXPANSION OF THE JOURNAL—SPECIAL JOURNALS

So far you have learned to journalize transactions in a two-column general journal and post these entries individually to the general ledger. This procedure is satisfactory in only the very smallest companies. To expedite journalizing and posting transactions, most companies use special journals in addition to the general journal.

A **special journal** is used to group similar types of transactions, such as all sales of merchandise on account, or all cash receipts. The types of special journals an enterprise uses depend largely on the types of transactions that occur frequently in its business. Most merchandising enterprises use the following journals to record transactions daily:

Sales journal—all sales of merchandise on account.

Cash receipts journal—all cash received (including cash sales).

Purchases journal—all purchases of merchandise on account.

Cash payments journal—all cash paid (including cash purchases).

If the transaction cannot be recorded in a special journal, it is recorded in the general journal. For example, if you had special journals for only the four types of transactions listed, purchase returns and allowances or sales returns and allowances would be recorded in the general journal. Similarly, correcting, adjusting, and closing entries are recorded in the general journal. Other types of special journals may be used in some situations. For example, where purchase returns and allowances or sales returns and allowances are frequent, special journals may be employed to record these transactions.

The journalization and posting process is illustrated using the sales journal and the cash receipts journal. The same procedures apply to all special journals with only the column and account names being different.

Sales Journal

The **sales journal** is used to record sales of merchandise on account. Cash sales of merchandise are entered in the cash receipts journal. Similarly, credit sales of assets other than merchandise are entered in the general journal.

Journalizing Credit Sales

Each entry in the sales journal used here results in a debit to Accounts Receivable and a credit to Sales. Since each sale on account involves a debit to Accounts Receivable and a credit of equal amount to Sales, only one line is used to record the transaction. Postings from the sales journal are made **daily** to the individual accounts receivable in the subsidiary ledger and **monthly** to the general ledger.

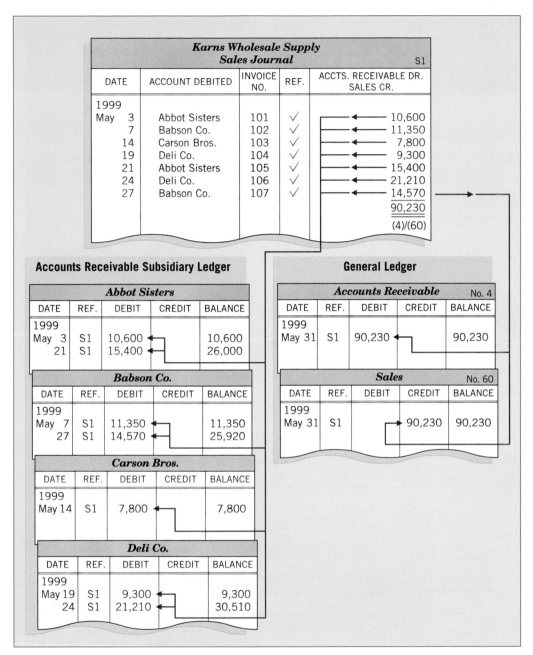

A check mark (√) is inserted in the reference posting column instead of an account number to indicate that the daily posting to the customer's account has been made. A check mark (√) is used when subsidiary ledger accounts are not numbered. A typical sales journal with related accounts is illustrated in Illustration 3B-2.

At the end of the month, the column total of the sales journal is posted to the general ledger—as a debit to Accounts Receivable (account No. 4) and as a credit to Sales (account No. 60). The insertion of the respective account numbers below the column total in the sales journal indicates that the postings have been made. In both the general ledger and subsidiary ledger accounts, the reference S1 indicates that the posting came from page 1 of the sales journal.

Cash Receipts Journal

All receipts of cash are recorded in the **cash receipts journal**. The most common types of cash receipts are cash sales of merchandise and collections of accounts receivable. Many other possibilities exist, however, such as receipt of money from bank loans and cash proceeds from disposals of equipment, buildings, or land. As a result, a one-column cash receipts journal is not sufficient to accommodate all possible cash receipts transactions; therefore, a multiple-column cash receipts journal is used. Generally, a cash receipts journal includes debit columns for cash and sales discounts and credit columns for accounts receivable, sales, and "other" accounts. The other accounts cate-

ILLUSTRATION 3B-3
Journalizing and Posting
Cash Receipts Journal

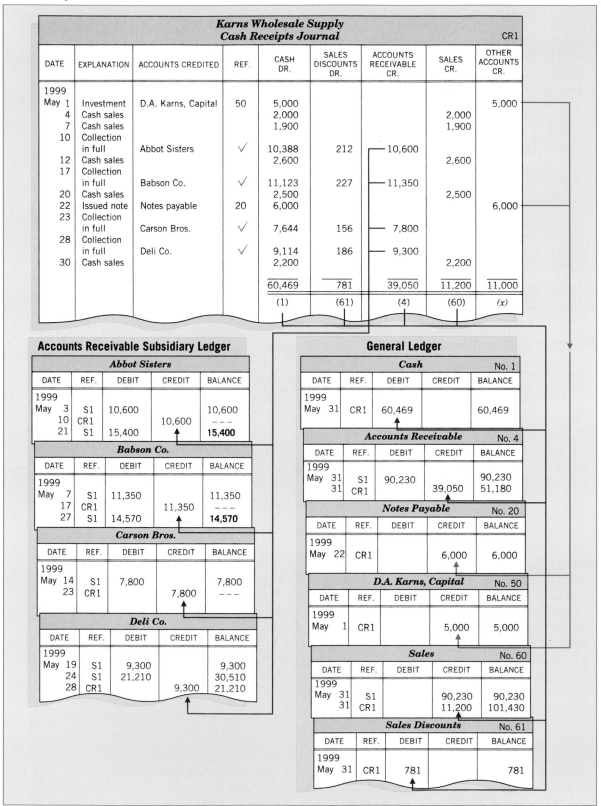

Karns Wholesale Supply
Cash Receipts Journal   CR1

DATE	EXPLANATION	ACCOUNTS CREDITED	REF.	CASH DR.	SALES DISCOUNTS DR.	ACCOUNTS RECEIVABLE CR.	SALES CR.	OTHER ACCOUNTS CR.
1999								
May 1	Investment	D.A. Karns, Capital	50	5,000				5,000
4	Cash sales			2,000			2,000	
7	Cash sales			1,900			1,900	
10	Collection in full	Abbot Sisters	✓	10,388	212	10,600		
12	Cash sales			2,600			2,600	
17	Collection in full	Babson Co.	✓	11,123	227	11,350		
20	Cash sales			2,500			2,500	
22	Issued note	Notes payable	20	6,000				6,000
23	Collection in full	Carson Bros.	✓	7,644	156	7,800		
28	Collection in full	Deli Co.	✓	9,114	186	9,300		
30	Cash sales			2,200			2,200	
				60,469	781	39,050	11,200	11,000
				(1)	(61)	(4)	(60)	(x)

Accounts Receivable Subsidiary Ledger

Abbot Sisters

DATE	REF.	DEBIT	CREDIT	BALANCE
1999				
May 3	S1	10,600		10,600
10	CR1		10,600	– – –
21	S1	15,400		**15,400**

Babson Co.

DATE	REF.	DEBIT	CREDIT	BALANCE
1999				
May 7	S1	11,350		11,350
17	CR1		11,350	– – –
27	S1	14,570		**14,570**

Carson Bros.

DATE	REF.	DEBIT	CREDIT	BALANCE
1999				
May 14	S1	7,800		7,800
23	CR1		7,800	– – –

Deli Co.

DATE	REF.	DEBIT	CREDIT	BALANCE
1999				
May 19	S1	9,300		9,300
24	S1	21,210		30,510
28	CR1		9,300	21,210

General Ledger

Cash   No. 1

DATE	REF.	DEBIT	CREDIT	BALANCE
1999				
May 31	CR1	60,469		60,469

Accounts Receivable   No. 4

DATE	REF.	DEBIT	CREDIT	BALANCE
1999				
May 31	S1	90,230		90,230
31	CR1		39,050	51,180

Notes Payable   No. 20

DATE	REF.	DEBIT	CREDIT	BALANCE
1999				
May 22	CR1		6,000	6,000

D.A. Karns, Capital   No. 50

DATE	REF.	DEBIT	CREDIT	BALANCE
1999				
May 1	CR1		5,000	5,000

Sales   No. 60

DATE	REF.	DEBIT	CREDIT	BALANCE
1999				
May 31	S1		90,230	90,230
31	CR1		11,200	101,430

Sales Discounts   No. 61

DATE	REF.	DEBIT	CREDIT	BALANCE
1999				
May 31	CR1	781		781

gory is used when the cash receipt does not involve a cash sale or a collection of accounts receivable. A five-column cash receipts journal is shown in Illustration 3B-3. When a special journal has more than one column it is often referred to as a **columnar journal**.

Additional credit columns may be used if they significantly reduce postings to a specific account. For example, the cash receipts of a loan company, such as Household Finance, include thousands of collections from customers that are credited to Loans Receivable and Interest Revenue. A significant saving in posting would result from using separate credit columns for Loans Receivable and Interest Revenue. In contrast, a retailer that has only one interest collection a month would not reduce its postings by using a separate column for interest revenue.

In a columnar journal, as in a single-column journal, only one line is needed for each entry. However, in contrast to a single-column journal, **an explanation is given for each entry**, and there must be equal debit and credit amounts for each line. When the collection from Abbot Sisters on May 10 is journalized, for example, three amounts are indicated. Note also that the Accounts Credited column is used to identify both general ledger and subsidiary ledger account titles. The former is illustrated in the May 1 entry for Karns' investment; the latter is illustrated in the May 10 entry for the collection in full from Abbot Sisters.

Posting the Cash Receipts Journal

Posting a columnar journal involves the following procedures:

❶ All column totals except the total for the Other Accounts column are posted once at the end of the month to the account title specified in the column heading, such as Cash or Accounts Receivable.

❷ The total of the Other Accounts column is not posted. Instead, the individual amounts comprising the total are posted separately to the general ledger accounts specified in the Accounts Credited column. See, for example, the credit posting to D. A. Karns, Capital. The symbol (X) is inserted below the total of this column to indicate that the amount is not posted.

❸ The individual amounts in a column, posted in total to a control account (Accounts Receivable, in this case), are posted daily to the subsidiary ledger account specified in the Accounts Credited column. See, for example, the credit posting of $10,600 to Abbot Sisters.

Therefore, cash is posted to account No. 1, accounts receivable to account No. 4, sales to account No. 60, and sales discounts to account No. 61. The symbol CR is used in the ledgers to identify postings from the cash receipts journal.

Format of Purchases Journal and Cash Payments Journal

The column headings that might be used in a typical single-column purchases journal and a multiple-column cash payments journal are shown in Illustration 3B-4.

Purchases Journal

P1

Date	Account Credited	Terms	Ref.	Purchases Dr. Accounts Payable Cr.

Cash Payments Journal

CP1

Date	Ck. No.	Explanation	Accounts Debited	Ref.	Other Accounts Dr.	Accounts Payable Dr.	Store Supplies Dr.	Purchase Discounts Cr.	Cash Cr.

ILLUSTRATION 3B-4
Purchases Journal and Cash Payments Journal

❖ METHODS OF PROCESSING ACCOUNTING DATA

The principles of recording, classifying, and summarizing large quantities of accounting data described in this appendix are those applicable to a situation where sophisticated types of accounting machinery are not needed. In most business enterprises, the mass of data is so great that it is simply too time-consuming to post journal entries manually, add the columns, update the files, and summarize the information. For this reason, computer systems are used.

The computer has revolutionized data processing not only because of its speed and accuracy in processing data, but also because it can be programmed to process the data in almost any manner desired by management. One of the more interesting developments in the computer area has been the development of **on-line computer systems.** In this system, the transaction is recorded in the computer as it occurs without the use of any basic source document. The advantages of a computer are that it can take different courses of action depending on the results of data collected previously and can process data more quickly and efficiently than other types of business equipment.

Nearly every medium- or large-sized business owns or rents a computer, but until recently a computer was too expensive for a small business to own or rent. Small businesses generally avoided investing large sums of money yet gained the use of computers through **EDP service centers** or through **time-sharing arrangements.** However, with the widespread availability of inexpensive **micro-** and **mini-computers,** most small businesses now own computers and obtain the operating and record keeping efficiencies they provide.

The growth in computers is nothing short of phenomenal. From the beginning of time through 1980, there were approximately 1 million computer systems of all types. In the early 1990s, it is estimated that there were 120 million personal computers alone. This is not surprising, given the level of technological change in this area. As one executive noted, "The amount of raw computing power available at a given price has been improving 25% a year. That which cost $1,000,000 in 1970 costs less than $10,000 in 1995." The following chart shows that in 1990, around 8 million individuals used the Internet. By the year 2000, that number is expected to increase over 100 times, to 1 billion! As one commentator recently noted, "Washington isn't pushing the National Information Infrastructure just because Al Gore likes to play with computers."

ILLUSTRATION 3B-5
The Growth of the Information Economy: Estimated Number of Internet Users, 1983–2001

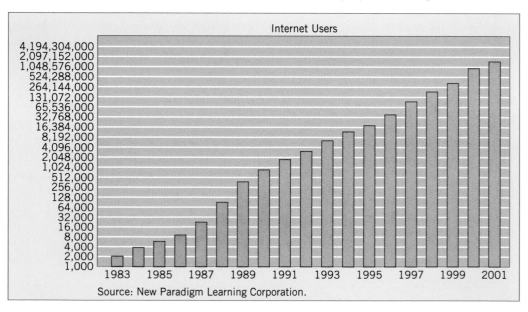

The effect this growth in home, office, and small-business computers has had on accounting is startling. Because computers are efficient and accurate at handling data, it is safe to say that most (if not all) record keeping will be performed on and by computers. Present and future accountants and auditors need to develop their computer competencies and skills in order to meet the challenges this growth brings.

SUMMARY OF LEARNING OBJECTIVES FOR APPENDIX 3B

⑪ *Identify (a) the use and types of subsidiary ledgers and (b) the use and types of special journals.* Subsidiary ledgers facilitate the recording process by freeing the general ledger from the details of individual entries and balances. Subsidiary ledgers group accounts with common characteristics (e.g., customers' accounts, creditors' accounts, inventory accounts, and equipment accounts).

Special journals expedite the journalizing and posting processes for frequently occurring transactions. The most common special journals are: sales journal, purchases journal, cash receipts journal, and cash payments journal.

KEY TERMS

accounts payable
(creditors') ledger, *106*
accounts receivable
(customers')
ledger, *106*
cash payments
journal, *108*
cash receipts journal, *108*
control account, *106*
purchases journal, *108*
sales journal, *108*
special journal, *108*
subsidiary ledger, *106*

Note: All **asterisked** Questions, Exercises, Problems, and Cases relate to material contained in an appendix to each chapter.

❖ QUESTIONS ❖

❶ Give an example of a transaction that results in
(a) A decrease in an asset and a decrease in a liability.
(b) A decrease in one asset and an increase in another asset.
(c) A decrease in one liability and an increase in another liability.

❷ Do the following events represent business transactions? Explain your answer in each case.
(a) A computer is purchased on account.
(b) A customer returns merchandise and is given credit on account.
(c) A prospective employee is interviewed.
(d) The owner of the business withdraws cash from the business for personal use.
(e) Merchandise is ordered for delivery next month.

❸ Name the accounts debited and credited for each of the following transactions:
(a) Billing a customer for work done.
(b) Receipt of cash from customer on account.
(c) Purchase of office supplies on account.
(d) Purchase of 15 gallons of gasoline for the delivery truck.

❹ Why are revenue and expense accounts called temporary or nominal accounts?

❺ What are the advantages of using the journal in the recording process?

❻ Is it necessary that a trial balance be taken periodically? What purpose does it serve?

❼ Indicate whether each of the items below is a real or nominal account and whether it appears in the balance sheet or the income statement.

(a) Prepaid Rent.
(b) Salaries and Wages Payable.
(c) Merchandise Inventory.
(d) Accumulated Depreciation.
(e) Office Equipment.
(f) Income from Services.
(g) Office Salaries Expense.
(h) Supplies on Hand.

❽ Employees are paid every Saturday for the preceding work week. If a balance sheet is prepared on Wednesday, December 31, what does the amount of wages earned during the first three days of the week (12/29, 12/30, 12/31) represent? Explain.

❾ Why is the Purchases account debited both when merchandise is purchased for cash and when it is purchased on account? Why is the inventory amount as determined at the end of the fiscal period under a periodic inventory system deducted from the cost of goods available for sale?

❿ What is the purpose of the Cost of Goods Sold account (assume a periodic inventory system)?

⑪ Under a periodic system is the amount shown for Inventory the same in a trial balance taken before closing as it is in a trial balance taken after closing? Why?

⑫ If the cost of a new microcomputer and printer ($3,900) purchased for office use were recorded as a debit to Purchases, what would be the effect of the error on the balance sheet and income statement in the period in which the error was made?

⑬ What differences are there between the trial balance before closing and the trial balance after closing with respect to the following?
(a) Accounts Payable.   (d) Retained Earnings account.
(b) Expense accounts.   (e) Cash.
(c) Revenue accounts.

14 What are "adjusting entries" and why are they necessary?

15 What are "closing entries" and why are they necessary?

16 What are "reversing entries" and why are they necessary?

17 Paul Molitor, maintenance supervisor for Blue Jay Insurance Co., has purchased a riding lawnmower and accessories to be used in maintaining the grounds around corporate headquarters. He has sent the following information to the accounting department:

Cost of mower and		Date purchased	7/1/98
accessories	$3,400	Monthly salary of	
Estimated useful life	5 yrs	groundskeeper	$1,100
Estimated salvage		Estimated annual	
value	$400	fuel cost	$150

Compute the amount of depreciation expense (related to the mower and accessories) that should be reported on Blue Jay's December 31, 1998 income statement. Assume straight-line depreciation.

18 Selanne Enterprises made the following entry on December 31, 1998.

Dec. 31, 1998	Interest Expense	10,000	
	Interest Payable		10,000
	(To record accrued interest expense due on loan from Anaheim National Bank.)		

What entry would Anaheim National Bank make regarding its outstanding loan to Selanne Enterprises? Explain why this must be the case.

***19** Distinguish between cash basis accounting and accrual basis accounting. Why for most business enterprises is accrual basis accounting acceptable and the cash basis unacceptable in the preparation of an income statement and a balance sheet?

***20** Why are beginning accrued wages subtracted from, and ending accrued wages added to, wages paid during the year when wages expense for the year is computed?

***21** List two types of transactions that would receive different accounting treatment using (a) strict cash basis accounting and (b) a modified cash basis.

***22** Why would a company use several journals instead of only a general journal? How would the company determine which special journals it should use?

***23** When the special journals illustrated in this chapter are used, how many monthly postings are made to the Cash account? Why?

***24** For each of the following transactions name the book of original entry and the accounts to be debited and credited, assuming that the five journals discussed in this chapter are used:
(a) Sale of merchandise for cash.
(b) Purchase of office equipment on account.
(c) Payment of cash to a creditor, no discount.
(d) Receipt of cash from customer on account.
(e) Loan from bank on a promissory note; interest payable at maturity date.
(f) Purchase of merchandise on account (periodic inventory system).
(g) Return of damaged merchandise to a supplier.

***25** What is a controlling account? What is its relationship to a subsidiary ledger?

***26** How does the use of controlling accounts and subsidiary ledgers affect (a) the taking of a trial balance, (b) the appearance of the trial balance, and (c) the equality of debits and credits in the trial balance?

❖ BRIEF EXERCISES ❖

BE3-1 Brett Favre Repair Shop had the following transactions during the first month of business. Journalize the transactions.

August 2	Invested $12,000 cash and $2,500 of equipment in the business.
7	Purchased supplies on account for $400.
12	Performed services for clients, for which $1,300 was collected in cash and $670 was billed to the clients.
15	Paid August rent, $600.
19	Counted supplies and determined that only $270 of the supplies purchased on August 7 are still on hand.

BE3-2 On August 1, George Bell Company paid $8,400 in advance for two years' insurance coverage. Prepare Bell's August 1 journal entry and the annual adjusting entry on December 31.

BE3-3 Mogilny Corporation owns a warehouse. On November 1, they rented storage space to a lessee (tenant) for three months for a total cash payment of $2,700 received in advance. Prepare Mogilny's November 1 journal entry and the December 31 annual adjusting entry.

BE3-4 Catherine Janeway Company's weekly payroll, paid on Fridays, totals $6,000. Employees work a five-day week. Prepare Janeway's adjusting entry on Wednesday, December 31 and the journal entry to record the $6,000 cash payment on Friday, January 2.

BE3-5 Included in Martinez Company's December 31 trial balance is a note receivable of $10,000. The note is a 4-month, 12% note dated October 1. Prepare Martinez's December 31 adjusting entry to record $300 of accrued interest, and the February journal entry to record receipt of $10,400 from the borrower.

BE3-6 At December 31, Tigerlily Company had account balances before adjustment of Sales, $1,000,000; Sales Returns and Allowances, $40,000; Accounts Receivable, $420,000; and Allowance for Doubtful Accounts, $4,100. Prepare the annual adjusting entry to record bad debts expense under the following two assumptions:

(a) Bad debts expense is 3% of net sales.
(b) Uncollectible accounts are 8% of accounts receivable.

BE3-7 Natalie Merchant Company purchased a computer on January 2 for $19,000. The computer is expected to be used for 4 years and then sold for $5,000. Prepare the December 31 entry to record depreciation for the first year.

BE3-8 Willis Corporation has beginning inventory, $81,000; Purchases, $540,000; Freight-in, $16,200; Purchase Returns, $5,800; Purchase Discounts, $5,000; and ending inventory, $70,200. Prepare the closing entry to record Cost of Goods Sold and ending inventory.

BE3-9 Karen Sepaniak has year-end account balances of Sales, $828,900; Interest Revenue, $13,500; Cost of Goods Sold, $556,200; Operating Expenses, $189,000; Income Tax Expense, $35,100; and Dividends, $18,900. Prepare the year-end closing entries.

BE3-10 Pelican Company made a December 31 adjusting entry to debit Salaries Expense and credit Salaries Payable for $3,600. On January 2, Pelican paid the weekly payroll of $6,000. Prepare Pelican's (a) January 1 reversing entry, (b) January 2 entry (assuming the reversing entry was prepared), and (c) January 2 entry (assuming the reversing entry was not prepared).

*BE3-11 Smith Company had cash receipts from customers in 1999 of $152,000. Cash payments for goods were $97,000. Smith has determined that at January 1, accounts receivable was $13,000, inventory was $17,500, and accounts payable was $9,000. At December 31, accounts receivable was $18,600, inventory was $23,200, and accounts payable was $10,100. Compute (a) net sales, and (b) cost of goods sold.

*BE3-12 Alomar Company had the following results during its first month of operations:

Credit Sales		Cash Collections		Sales Returns	
Wade	$4,000	Wade	$3,000	Boggs	$300
Boggs	$3,200	Boggs	$2,900		
Justice	$7,500	Justice	$5,000		
Boggs	$5,100				

Determine the balances in the customers' ledger and the accounts receivable control account at month end.

*BE3-13 Identify the special journal in which the following column headings would most likely appear.

(a) Purchases Dr./Accounts Payable Cr.   **(e)** Accounts Payable Dr.
(b) Cash Dr.   **(f)** Purchase Discounts Cr.
(c) Accts Receivable Dr./Sales Cr.   **(g)** Cash Cr.
(d) Accts Receivable Cr.   **(h)** Sales Cr.

❖ EXERCISES ❖

E3-1 (Transaction Analysis—Service Company) Beverly Crusher is a licensed CPA. During the first month of operations of her business, the following events and transactions occurred.

April 1 Invested $32,000 cash and equipment valued at $14,000 in the business.
2 Hired a secretary-receptionist at a salary of $290 per week payable monthly.
3 Purchased supplies on account $700 (debit an asset account).
7 Paid office rent of $600 for the month.
11 Completed a tax assignment and billed client $1,100 for services rendered. (Use professional fees account.)
12 Received $3,200 advance on a management consulting engagement.
15 Purchased a new computer for $6,100 with personal funds. (The computer will be used exclusively for business purposes.)
17 Received cash of $2,300 for services completed for Ferengi Co.
21 Paid insurance expense $110.
30 Paid secretary-receptionist $1,160 for the month.
30 A count of supplies indicated that $120 of supplies had been used.

Instructions

Journalize the transactions in the general journal (omit explanations).

E3-2 (Transaction Analysis—Merchandising Company) The Armando Benitez Hardware Store completed the following merchandising transactions in the month of May. On May 1, the company had a cash balance of $5,000.

May 1 Purchased merchandise on account from Mikiso Hane Wholesale Supply $6,100, terms 2/10, n/30.
  2 Sold merchandise on account $5,000, terms 2/10, n/30.
  5 Received credit from Mikiso Hane Wholesale Supply for merchandise returned $100.
  9 Received collections in full, less discounts, from customers billed for $2,000 of sales on May 2.
  10 Paid Mikiso Hane Wholesale Supply in full, less discount.
  12 Purchased merchandise for cash $2,400.
  15 Received refund for poor quality merchandise from supplier on cash purchase $230.
  17 Purchased merchandise from Irene Raczynski Distributors $1,900, FOB shipping point, terms 3/10, n/30.
  19 Paid freight on May 17 purchase $330.
  24 Sold merchandise for cash $6,400.
  25 Purchased merchandise for cash $600.
  27 Paid Irene Raczynski Distributors in full, less discount.
  29 Made refunds to cash customers for defective merchandise $80.
  31 Sold merchandise on account $2,100, terms n/30.

Armando Benitez Hardware's chart of accounts includes the following: Cash, Accounts Receivable, Merchandise Inventory, Accounts Payable, Sales, Sales Returns and Allowances, Sales Discounts, Purchases, Purchase Returns and Allowances, Purchase Discounts, Freight-in.

Instructions

(a) Journalize the transactions.
(b) Prepare an income statement through gross profit for the month of May 1999, assuming ending inventory is $2,400, and no beginning inventory.

E3-3 (Corrected Trial Balance) The trial balance of Wanda Landowska Company shown below does not balance. Your review of the ledger reveals the following: (a) each account had a normal balance, (b) the debit footings in Prepaid Insurance, Accounts Payable, and Property Tax Expense were each understated $100, (c) transposition errors were made in Accounts Receivable and Fees Earned; the correct balances are $2,750 and $6,690, respectively, (d) a debit posting to Advertising Expense of $300 was omitted, and (e) a $1,500 cash drawing by the owner was debited to Wanda Landowska, Capital, and credited to Cash.

Wanda Landowska Company
TRIAL BALANCE
April 30, 1998

	Debit	Credit
Cash	$ 4,800	
Accounts Receivable	2,570	
Prepaid Insurance	700	
Equipment		$ 8,000
Accounts Payable		4,500
Property Tax Payable	560	
Wanda Landowska, Capital		11,200
Fees Earned	6,960	
Salaries Expense	4,200	
Advertising Expense	1,100	
Property Tax Expense		800
	$20,890	$24,500

Instructions

Prepare a correct trial balance.

E3-4 (Corrected Trial Balance) The trial balance of Blues Traveler Corporation does not balance.

Blues Traveler Corporation
TRIAL BALANCE
April 30

Cash	$ 5,912	
Accounts Receivable	5,240	
Supplies on Hand	2,967	
Furniture and Equipment	6,100	
Accounts Payable		$ 7,044
Common Stock		8,000
Retained Earnings		2,000
Revenue from Fees		5,200
Office Expense	4,320	
	$24,539	$22,244

An examination of the ledger shows these errors.

1. Cash received from a customer on account was recorded (both debit and credit) as $1,380 instead of $1,830.
2. The purchase on account of a computer costing $3,200 was recorded as a debit to Office Expense and a credit to Accounts Payable.
3. Services were performed on account for a client, $2,250, for which Accounts Receivable was debited $2,250 and Revenue from Fees was credited $225.
4. A payment of $95 for telephone charges was entered as a debit to Office Expenses and a debit to Cash.
5. The Revenue from Fees account was totaled at $5,200 instead of $5,280.

Instructions
From this information prepare a corrected trial balance.

E3-5 (Corrected Trial Balance) The trial balance of Antoine Watteau Co. shown below does not balance.

Antoine Watteau Co.
TRIAL BALANCE
June 30, 1999

	Debit	Credit
Cash		$ 2,870
Fees Receivable	$ 3,231	
Supplies	800	
Equipment	3,800	
Accounts Payable		2,666
Unearned Fees	1,200	
Common Stock		6,000
Retained Earnings		3,000
Fees Earned		2,380
Wages Expense	3,400	
Office Expense	940	
	$13,371	$16,916

Each of the listed accounts has a normal balance per the general ledger. An examination of the ledger and journal reveals the following errors.

1. Cash received from a customer on account was debited for $570 and Fees Receivable was credited for the same amount. The actual collection was for $750.
2. The purchase of a computer printer on account for $500 was recorded as a debit to Supplies for $500 and a credit to Accounts Payable for $500.

3. Services were performed on account for a client for $890. Fees Receivable was debited for $890 and Fees Earned was credited for $89.
4. A payment of $65 for telephone charges was recorded as a debit to Office Expense for $65 and a debit to Cash for $65.
5. When the Unearned Fees account was reviewed, it was found that $325 of the balance was earned prior to June 30.
6. A debit posting to Wages Expense of $670 was omitted.
7. A payment on account for $206 was credited to Cash for $206 and credited to Accounts Payable for $260.
8. A dividend of $575 was debited to Wages Expense for $575 and credited to Cash for $575.

Instructions

Prepare a correct trial balance. (Note: It may be necessary to add one or more accounts to the trial balance.)

E3-6 (Adjusting Entries) Bjorn Borg is the new owner of Ace Computer Services. At the end of August 1998, his first month of ownership, Bjorn is trying to prepare monthly financial statements. Below is some information related to unrecorded expenses that the business incurred during August.

1. At August 31, Mr. Borg owed his employees $1,900 in wages that would be paid on September 1.
2. At the end of the month he had not yet received the month's utility bill. Based on past experience, he estimated the bill would be approximately $600.
3. On August 1, Mr. Borg borrowed $30,000 from a local bank on a 15-year mortgage. The annual interest rate is 8%.
4. A telephone bill in the amount of $117 covering August charges is unpaid at August 31.

Instructions

Prepare the adjusting journal entries as of August 31, 1998, suggested by the information above.

E3-7 (Adjusting Entries) Selected accounts of Urdu Company are shown below.

Supplies				Fees Receivable		
Beg. Bal.	800	10/31	470	10/17	2,400	
				10/31	1,650	

Salaries Expense			Salaries Payable		
10/15	800			10/31	600
10/31	600				

Unearned Fees				Supplies Expense	
10/31	400	10/20	650	10/31	470

Fees Earned		
	10/17	2,400
	10/31	1,650
	10/31	400

Instructions

From an analysis of the T-accounts, reconstruct (a) the October transaction entries, and (b) the adjusting journal entries that were made on October 31, 1998.

E3-8 (Adjusting Entries) The ledger of Rossini, Inc., on March 31 of the current year includes the following selected accounts before adjusting entries have been prepared.

	Debit	Credit
Prepaid Insurance	$ 3,600	
Supplies	2,800	
Delivery Equipment	25,000	
Accumulated Depreciation		$ 8,400
Notes Payable		20,000
Unearned Rent		9,600
Rent Revenue		60,000
Interest Expense	–0–	
Wages Expense	14,000	

An analysis of the accounts shows the following:

1. The delivery equipment depreciates $600 per month.
2. One-third of the unearned rent was earned during the quarter.

3. Accrued wages at March 31 total $2,300.
4. Interest of $400 is accrued on the notes payable.
5. Supplies on hand total $650.
6. Insurance expires at the rate of $200 per month.

Instructions

Prepare the adjusting entries at March 31, assuming that adjusting entries are made quarterly. Additional accounts are: Depreciation Expense, Insurance Expense, Interest Payable, Supplies Expense, and Wages Payable.

E3-9 (Adjusting Entries) Greco Resort opened for business on June 1 with eight air-conditioned units. Its trial balance on August 31 is as follows:

Greco Resort
TRIAL BALANCE
August 31, 1998

	Debit	Credit
Cash	$ 19,600	
Prepaid Insurance	4,500	
Supplies	2,600	
Land	20,000	
Cottages	120,000	
Furniture	16,000	
Accounts Payable		$ 4,500
Advanced Rentals		4,600
Mortgage Payable		60,000
Greco, Capital		100,000
Greco, Drawing	5,000	
Rent Revenue		76,200
Salaries Expense	44,800	
Utilities Expense	9,200	
Repair Expense	3,600	
	$245,300	$245,300

Other data:

1. The balance in prepaid insurance is a 1-year premium paid on June 1, 1998.
2. An inventory count on August 31 shows $450 of supplies on hand.
3. Annual depreciation rates are cottages (4%) and furniture (10%). Salvage value is estimated to be 10% of cost.
4. Advanced rentals of $3,800 were earned prior to August 31.
5. Salaries of $375 were unpaid at August 31.
6. Rentals of $800 were due from tenants at August 31.
7. The mortgage interest rate is 8% per year.

Instructions

(a) Journalize the adjusting entries on August 31 for the 3-month period June 1–August 31.
(b) Prepare an adjusted trial balance on August 31.

E3-10 (Adjusting Entries) The following trial balance and additional information is provided to you for Arthur Wyatt Company.

Arthur Wyatt Company
Worksheet
For the year ended December 31, 1999

	Trial Balance	
	Debit	Credit
Cash	$ 10,500	
Notes Receivable	15,000	
Accounts Receivable	35,600	
Allowance for Doubtful Accounts	100	
Merchandise Inventory	23,500	

Prepaid Insurance	5,490	
Equipment	50,000	
Accumulated Depreciation—Equipment		$ 14,000
Building	180,000	
Accumulated Depreciation—Building		9,000
Land	96,000	
Accounts Payable		25,800
Unearned Revenue		18,000
Long-Term Notes Payable		150,000
Capital Stock—$2 par		50,000
Paid-in Capital in excess of par		130,000
Retained Earnings		28,440
Sales		325,000
Sales Returns and Allowances	10,000	
Sales Discounts	6,000	
Purchases	170,000	
Purchase Returns		8,000
Freight In	3,000	
Advertising Expense	3,800	
Other Selling & Adm. Expenses	138,000	
Interest Expense	11,250	
	$758,240	$758,240

Additional Information

1. The Note Receivable was a 12% 90-day note received from a customer from the sale of $15,000 of merchandise. The note was received on November 1.
2. It was recently discovered that the inventory on December 31, 1998 (and January 1, 1999) was overstated by $5,000 due to a pricing error. Ignore income taxes and adjust through retained earnings.
3. The insurance policies consist of the following:
    Policy 1—a 24-month policy purchased on April 1, 1998—premium $5,520
    Policy 2—a 6-month policy purchased on October 31, 1999—premium $2,040
4. Depreciation should be computed as follows:
    EQUIPMENT—Purchased on 7-1-97, DDB with a $5,000 salvage value and 10-year life
    BUILDING—Purchased 1-1-96, SL with a $60,000 salvage value and 40-year life
5. Salaries of $4,000 have been earned but remain unpaid.
6. The Long-Term Note Payable is at 9% and requires semi-annual interest payments each May and November 1.
7. Unearned revenue consists of rent received on a section of the building. This $18,000 covers an annual lease from August 1, 1999 to July 31, 2000.
8. Uncollectible accounts are estimated at 5% of accounts receivable.

Instructions
Prepare the adjusting entries needed. (You may need to use additional accounts not on the trial balance.)

E3-11 (Adjusting and Reversing Entries)   When the accounts of Daniel Barenboim Inc. are examined, the adjusting data listed below are uncovered on December 31, the end of an annual fiscal period.

1. The unexpired insurance account shows a debit of $5,280, representing the cost of a 2-year fire insurance policy dated August 1 of the current year.
2. On November 1, Rental Income was credited for $1,800, representing income from a subrental for a 3-month period beginning on that date.
3. Purchase of advertising materials for $800 during the year was recorded in the Advertising Expense account. On December 31, advertising materials of $290 are on hand.
4. Interest of $770 has accrued on notes payable.

Instructions
Prepare in general journal form: (a) the adjusting entry for each item; (b) the reversing entry for each item where appropriate.

E3-12 (Find Missing Amounts—Gross Profit)   Financial information is presented below for four different companies.

	Pamela's Cosmetics	Dean's Grocery	Anderson Wholesalers	Baywatch Supply Co.
Sales	$78,000	c	$144,000	$100,000
Sales returns	a	$ 5,000	12,000	9,000
Net sales	74,000	94,000	132,000	g
Beginning inventory	16,000	d	44,000	24,000
Purchases	88,000	100,000	e	85,000
Purchase returns	6,000	10,000	8,000	h
Ending inventory	b	48,000	30,000	28,000
Cost of goods sold	64,000	72,000	f	72,000
Gross profit	10,000	22,000	18,000	i

Instructions

Determine the missing amounts (a–i). Show all computations.

E3-13 (Prepare Cost of Goods Sold Section) Information concerning the first month of operations of Victoria Principal Women's Wear is presented below. (The periodic inventory system is used.)

Transportation-in	$ 760
Total purchases on account	22,200
Purchase returns on account	700
Transportation-out	810
Total recorded as cash purchases	9,140
Purchase allowances on account	1,350
Inventory at the end of the month	4,800
Sales discounts	750
Refunds for defective items purchased for cash	400
Error made by bookkeeper debiting Supplies Expense, when in reality the item was a cash purchase of merchandise	790

Instructions

(a) Compute the correct amount of cost of goods sold.
(b) Prepare the cost of goods sold section of the income statement.
(c) Indicate in which section of the income statement items not used in the cost of goods sold section of this exercise should appear.

E3-14 (Prepare Cost of Goods Sold Section and Closing Entries) The trial balance of the Neville Mariner Company at the end of its fiscal year, August 31, 1999 includes the following accounts: Merchandise Inventory $17,500, Purchases $149,400, Sales $200,000, Freight-in $4,000, Sales Returns and Allowances $4,000, Freight-out $1,000, and Purchase Returns and Allowances $2,000. The ending merchandise inventory is $25,000.

Instructions

(a) Prepare a cost of goods sold section for the year ending August 31.
(b) Prepare the closing entries for the above accounts. Assume Neville Mariner Company is a corporation.

E3-15 (Prepare Adjusting and Reversing Entries) On December 31, adjusting information for James Lyman Corporation is as follows:

1. Estimated depreciation on equipment $1,100.
2. Personal property taxes amounting to $525 have accrued but are unrecorded and unpaid.
3. Employees' wages earned but unpaid and unrecorded $1,200.
4. Unearned Fees balance includes $1,500 that has been earned.
5. Interest of $250 on a $25,000 note receivable has accrued.

Instructions

(a) Prepare adjusting journal entries.
(b) Prepare reversing journal entries.

E3-16 (Closing and Reversing Entries) On December 31, the adjusted trial balance of Cree Co., Inc. shows the following selected data:

Commissions Receivable	$4,300	Commissions Earned	$96,000
Interest Expense	7,800	Interest Payable	2,400

Analysis shows that adjusting entries were made for (a) $4,300 of commissions earned but not billed, and (b) $2,400 of accrued but unpaid interest.

Instructions

(a) Prepare the closing entries for the temporary accounts at December 31.
(b) Prepare the reversing entries on January 1.
(c) Enter the adjusted trial balance data in the four accounts. Post the entries in (a) and (b) and rule and balance the accounts. (Use T accounts.)
(d) Prepare the entries to record (1) the collection of the accrued commissions on January 10, and (2) the payment of all interest due ($3,000) on January 15.
(e) Post the entries in (d) to the temporary accounts.

E3-17 (Closing Entries for a Corporation) Presented below are selected account balances for Homer Winslow Co. as of December 31, 1999.

Merchandise inventory 1/1/99	$ 40,000	Purchases	$250,000
Common stock	75,000	Purchase returns and	8,000
Retained earnings	45,000	allowances	
Dividends	18,000	Purchase discounts	4,000
Sales returns and allowances	12,000	Transportation-in	7,700
Sales discounts	15,000	Selling expenses	16,000
Sales	410,000	Administrative expenses	38,000
		Income tax expense	30,000

Instructions

Prepare closing entries for Homer Winslow Co. on December 31, 1999. Merchandise inventory was $60,000 on December 31, 1999.

 E3-18 (Work Sheet Preparation) The trial balance of R.L. Stein Roofing at March 31, 1999 is as follows:

R.L. Stein Roofing
TRIAL BALANCE
March 31, 1999

	Debit	Credit
Cash	$ 2,300	
Fees Receivable	2,600	
Roofing Supplies	1,100	
Equipment	6,000	
Accumulated Depreciation—Equipment		$ 1,200
Accounts Payable		1,100
Unearned Fees		300
Common Stock		6,400
Retained Earnings		600
Fees Earned		3,000
Salaries Expense	500	
Miscellaneous Expense	100	
	$12,600	$12,600

Other data:

1. A physical count reveals only $520 of roofing supplies on hand.
2. Equipment is depreciated at a rate of $120 per month.
3. Unearned fees amounted to $100 on March 31.
4. Accrued salaries are $850.

Instructions

Enter the trial balance on a work sheet and complete the work sheet, assuming that the adjustments relate only to the month of March (ignore income taxes).

E3-19 (Work Sheet and Balance Sheet Presentation) The adjusted trial balance of Ed Bradley Co. work sheet for the month ended April 30, 1998, contains the following:

Ed Bradley Co.
WORK SHEET (PARTIAL)
For the Month Ended April 30, 1998

Account Titles	Adjusted Trial Balance Dr.	Adjusted Trial Balance Cr.	Income Statement Dr.	Income Statement Cr.	Balance Sheet Dr.	Balance Sheet Cr.
Cash	$10,480					
Marketable Securities	8,992					
Accounts Receivable	6,920					
Prepaid Rent	2,280					
Equipment	18,050					
Accumulated Depreciation		$ 4,895				
Notes Payable		5,700				
Accounts Payable		5,472				
Bradley, Capital		34,960				
Bradley, Drawing	6,650					
Fees Earned		11,590				
Salaries Expense	6,840					
Rent Expense	2,260					
Depreciation Expense	145					
Interest Expense	83					
Interest Payable		83				

Instructions

Complete the work sheet and prepare a balance sheet as illustrated in this chapter.

E3-20 (Partial Work Sheet Preparation) Jurassic Park Co. prepares monthly financial statements from a work sheet. Selected portions of the January work sheet showed the following data:

Jurassic Park Co.
WORK SHEET (PARTIAL)
For Month Ended January 31, 1999

Account Title	Trial Balance Dr.	Trial Balance Cr.	Adjustments Dr.	Adjustments Cr.	Adjusted Trial Balance Dr.	Adjusted Trial Balance Cr.
Supplies	3,256			(a) 1,500	1,756	
Accumulated Depreciation		6,682		(b) 257		6,939
Interest Payable		100		(c) 50		150
Supplies Expense			(a) 1,500		1,500	
Depreciation Expense			(b) 257		257	
Interest Expense			(c) 50		50	

During February no events occurred that affected these accounts but at the end of February the following information was available:

(a)	Supplies on hand	$715
(b)	Monthly depreciation	$257
(c)	Accrued interest	$ 50

Instructions

Reproduce the data that would appear in the February work sheet and indicate the amounts that would be shown in the February income statement.

E3-21 (Transactions of a Corporation Including Investment and Dividend) Scratch Miniature Golf and Driving Range Inc. was opened on March 1 by Scott Verplank. The following selected events and transactions occurred during March:

Mar. 1 Invested $50,000 cash in the business in exchange for common stock.
    3 Purchased Lee Janzen's Golf Land for $38,000 cash. The price consists of land, $10,000; building, $22,000; and equipment, $6,000. (Make one compound entry.)
    5 Advertised the opening of the driving range and miniature golf course, paying advertising expenses of $1,600.
    6 Paid cash $1,480 for a one-year insurance policy.
   10 Purchased golf clubs and other equipment for $2,500 from Sluman Company payable in 30 days.
   18 Received golf fees of $1,200 in cash.

19 Sold 100 coupon books for $15.00 each. Each book contains 10 coupons that enable the holder to one round of miniature golf or to hit one bucket of golf balls.

25 Declared and paid a $500 cash dividend.

30 Paid wages of $900.

30 Paid Sluman Company in full.

31 Received $750 of fees in cash.

Scott Verplank uses the following accounts: Cash; Prepaid Insurance; Land; Buildings; Equipment; Accounts Payable; Unearned Golf Fees; Common Stock; Dividends; Golf Fees Earned; Advertising Expense; and Wages Expense.

Instructions
Journalize the March transactions.

*E3-22 (Cash and Accrual Basis) Robin Williams Company maintains its books on the accrual basis. The company reported insurance expense of $19,450 in its 1998 income statement. Prepaid insurance at December 31, 1998, amounted to $5,740; cash paid for insurance during the year 1998 totaled $24,100. There was no accrued insurance expense either at the beginning or at the end of 1998.

Instructions
What was the amount, if any, of prepaid insurance at January 1, 1998? Show computations.

*E3-23 (Cash to Accrual Basis) Jill Accardo, M.D., maintains the accounting records of Accardo Clinic on a cash basis. During 1998, Dr. Accardo collected $142,600 from her patients and paid $55,470 in expenses. At January 1, 1998, and December 31, 1998, she had fees receivable, unearned fees, accrued expenses, and prepaid expenses as follows (all long-lived assets are rented):

	January 1, 1998	December 31, 1998
Fees receivable	$9,250	$15,927
Unearned fees	2,840	4,111
Accrued expenses	3,435	2,108
Prepaid expenses	1,917	3,232

Instructions
Prepare a schedule that converts Dr. Accardo's "excess of cash collected over cash disbursed" for the year 1998 to net income on an accrual basis for the year 1998.

*E3-24 (Cash and Accrual Basis) Presented below are three independent situations:

1. Stoneybrook Co. had cash purchases of $470,000 during the past year. In addition, it had an increase in trade accounts payable of $9,000 and a decrease in merchandise inventory of $18,000. Determine purchases on an accrual basis.
2. Dawn Schafer, M.D., collected $125,000 in fees during 1999. At December 31, 1998, Dr. Schafer had accounts receivable of $15,000. At December 31, 1999, Dr. Schafer had accounts receivable of $31,000 and unearned fees of $5,200. Determine Dr. Schafer's fee income on an accrual basis for 1999.
3. Bart Taylor Company reported revenue of $1,400,000 in its accrual basis income statement for the year ended December 31, 1999. Additional information was as follows:

Accounts receivable December 31, 1998	$410,000
Accounts receivable December 31, 1999	520,000
Accounts written off during the year	41,000

Under the cash basis of accounting, determine how much revenue Bart Taylor should report.

*E3-25 (Cash and Accrual Basis) Wayne Rogers Corp. maintains its financial records on the cash basis of accounting. Interested in securing a long-term loan from its regular bank, Wayne Rogers Corp. requests you as its independent CPA to convert its cash basis income statement data to the accrual basis. You are provided with the following summarized data covering 1996, 1997, and 1998.

	1996	1997	1998
Cash receipts from sales:			
On 1996 sales	$295,000	$160,000	$ 30,000
On 1997 sales	–0–	355,000	90,000
On 1998 sales			408,000
Cash payments for expenses:			
On 1996 expenses	185,000	67,000	25,000
On 1997 expenses	40,000[a]	160,000	55,000
On 1998 expenses		45,000[b]	218,000

[a]Prepayments of 1997 expense.
[b]Prepayments of 1998 expense.

Instructions

(a) Using the data above, prepare abbreviated income statements for the years 1996 and 1997 on the cash basis.

(b) Using the data above, prepare abbreviated income statements for the years 1996 and 1997 on the accrual basis.

*E3-26 (Subsidiary Ledgers and Special Journals)** Kris Kross Company uses both special journals and a general journal as described in this chapter. On April 30, after all monthly postings had been completed, the Accounts Receivable controlling account in the general ledger had a debit balance of $350,000 and the Accounts Payable controlling account had a credit balance of $95,000.

The May transactions recorded in the special journals are summarized below. No entries affecting accounts receivable and accounts payable were recorded in the general journal for May.

Sales journal	Total sales, $162,000
Purchases journal	Total purchases, $61,350
Cash receipts journal	Accounts Receivable column total, $143,500
Cash payments journal	Accounts Payable column total, $55,000

Instructions

(a) What is the balance of the Accounts Receivable control account after the monthly postings on May 31?

(b) What is the balance of the Accounts Payable control account after the monthly postings on May 31?

(c) What posting would be made of the column total of $162,000 in the sales journal?

(d) What posting would be made of the accounts receivable column total of $143,500 in the cash receipts journal?

*E3-27 (Subsidiary Ledgers and Special Journals)** On September 1 the balance of the Accounts Payable controlling account in the general ledger of Rick Mahorn Company was $5,760. The creditors' subsidiary ledger contained account balances as follows: Khalid Reeves, $1,270; Kendall Gill, $970; Ed O'Bannon, $1,850; Yinka Dare, $1,670. At the end of September the various journals contained the following information:

Purchases journal: Purchases from Khalid Reeves, $1,500; from Kendall Gill, $1,350; from Ed O'Bannon, $1,080; from Yinka Dare, $1,150; from Armon Gilliam, $1,365.

Cash payments journal: Cash paid to Ed O'Bannon, $1,500; to Yinka Dare, $1,070; to Khalid Reeves, $2,746. (Khalid Reeves allowed Rick Mahorn a $24 discount.)

General journal: An allowance from Armon Gilliam, $45; a return of merchandise to Kendall Gill, $80; and an entry to correct a $30 overcharge that Yinka Dare made on an invoice.

Instructions

(a) Set up control and subsidiary accounts, and enter the beginning balances. Do not construct the journals.

(b) Post the various journals. Post the items as individual items or as totals, whichever would be the appropriate procedure in the usual posting process.

(c) Prepare a list of creditors and prove the agreement of the controlling account with the subsidiary ledger.

*E3-28 (Special Journals)** The Marty Carter Company uses the columnar cash journals illustrated in the text. In May, the following selected cash transactions occurred:

May 1 Paid cash for office equipment.
2 Received collection from customer within the 2% discount period.
3 Received cash refund from supplier for merchandise returned.
4 Made cash sales.
5 Received an advance from a customer on June sales.
6 Made cash purchases.
7 Paid a creditor within the 2% discount period.
8 Paid freight on merchandise purchased.
9 Paid dividends.
10 Made a refund to a customer for the return of damaged goods.
11 Received cash due on a non-interest-bearing note receivable.
12 Received collection from customer after the 2% discount period had expired.

Instructions

Indicate (a) the journal, and (b) the columns in the journal that should be used in recording each transaction.

*E3-29 (Special Journals) Below are some typical transactions incurred by the Bob Hamelin Company.

1. Sales of merchandise on account.
2. Payment of creditors on account.
3. Payment of employee wages.
4. Depreciation on building.
5. Purchase of office supplies for cash.
6. Return of merchandise purchased.
7. Sales discount given on goods sold.
8. Return of merchandise sold for credit.
9. Collection on account from customers.
10. Payment to building contractor of balance due on completed office building.
11. Sold land for cash.
12. Close income summary to owner's capital.
13. Sales of merchandise for cash.
14. Depreciation on machinery.
15. Purchase of merchandise on account.

Instructions
For each transaction, indicate whether it would normally be recorded in a cash receipts journal, cash payments journal, single-column sales journal, single-column purchases journal, or general journal.

❖ PROBLEMS ❖

P3-1 (Transactions, Financial Statements—Service Company) Listed below are the transactions of Isao Aoki, D.D.S., for the month of September:

Sept. 1 Isao Aoki begins practice as a dentist and invests $20,000 cash.
2 Purchases furniture and dental equipment on account from Green Jacket Co. for $17,280.
4 Pays rent for office space, $680 for the month.
4 Employs a receptionist, Michael Bradley.
5 Purchases dental supplies for cash, $942.
8 Receives cash of $1,690 from patients for services performed.
10 Pays miscellaneous office expenses, $430.
14 Bills patients $5,120 for services performed.
18 Pays Green Jacket Co. on account, $3,600.
19 Withdraws $3,000 cash from the business for personal use.
20 Receives $980 from patients on account.
25 Bills patients $2,110 for services performed.
30 Pays the following expenses in cash: office salaries, $1,400; miscellaneous office expenses, $85.
30 Dental supplies used during September, $330.

Instructions
(a) Enter the transactions shown above in appropriate general ledger accounts. Allow 10 lines for the Cash account and 5 lines for each of the other accounts needed. Record depreciation using a 5-year life on the furniture and equipment, the straight-line method, and no salvage value. Do not use a drawing account.
(b) Prepare a trial balance.
(c) Prepare an income statement, a balance sheet, and a statement of owner's equity.
(d) Close the ledger.
(e) Prepare a post-closing trial balance.

P3-2 (Transactions, Financial Statements—Merchandising Company) The balance sheet of Verbeek Company as of December 31, 1998, is presented below.

Verbeek Company
BALANCE SHEET
As of December 31, 1998

Assets		Liabilities and Stockholders' Equity		
Cash	$ 3,900	Accounts payable		$ 2,985
Accounts receivable	4,985	Notes payable		4,000
Inventory	3,300	Total liabilities		6,985
Office equipment	4,800			
Accum. depr.	(1,440)	Common stock	$10,000	
Furniture and fixtures	6,600	Retained earnings	2,960	12,960
Accum. depr.	(2,200)	Total liabilities and		
Total assets	$19,945	stockholders' equity		$19,945

The following transactions occur during the month of January 1999.

Jan. 2 Receives payment of $1,230 on accounts receivable.
3 Purchases merchandise on account from Weight Co. for $2,184, 2/30, n/60 f.o.b. shipping point (record at gross amount).
4 Receives an invoice from *Ranger*, a trade magazine, for advertising, $75.
4 Sells merchandise on account to Sandstrom Co. for $1,534, 2/10, n/30 f.o.b. shipping point.
4 Makes a cash sale to Kariya Inc., for $1,786.
6 Sends a letter to Weight Co., regarding a slight defect in one item of merchandise received.
9 Purchases merchandise on account from Fleury's Novelty Company, $651.
11 Pays freight on merchandise received from Weight Co., $76.
11 Receives a credit memo from Weight Co. granting an allowance of $34 on defective merchandise (see transaction of January 6).
15 Receives $600 on account from Sandstrom Co.
19 Sells merchandise on account to Brett Hull, $812, 2/10, n/30.
21 Pays display clerk's salary of $552.
25 Sells merchandise for cash, $2,350.
27 Purchases office equipment on account, $879 (begin depreciating in February).
29 Pays Weight Co. in full of account.
30 Receives a note from Brett Hull in full of account.
31 A count of the inventory on hand reveals $2,640 of salable merchandise.

Instructions

(a) Open ledger accounts at January 1, 1999.
(b) Enter the transactions into ledger accounts.
(c) Prepare a trial balance after adjusting for depreciation; use 8-year life, straight-line method, and no salvage for all long-term assets. Interest at 12% on the note payable is due every December 31.
(d) Prepare a balance sheet and income statement. (Ignore income taxes)
(e) Close the ledger.
(f) Take a post-closing trial balance.

P3-3 (Adjusting Entries) The accounts listed below appeared in the December 31 trial balance of the Jane Alexander Theater.

	Debit	Credit
Equipment	$192,000	
Accumulated Depreciation of Equipment		$ 60,000
Notes Payable		90,000
Admissions Revenue		380,000
Concessions Revenue		36,000
Advertising Expense	13,680	
Salaries Expense	57,600	
Interest Expense	1,400	

Instructions

(a) From the account balances listed above and the information given below prepare the annual adjusting entries necessary on December 31.
1. The equipment has an estimated life of 16 years and a trade-in value of $40,000 at the end of that time. (Use straight-line method.)
2. The note payable is a 90-day note given to the bank October 20 and bearing interest at 10%. (Use 360 days for denominator.)
3. In December 2,000 coupon admission books were sold at $25 each; they could be used for admission any time after January 1.
4. The concession stand is operated by a concessionaire who pays 10% of gross receipts for the privilege of selling popcorn, candy, and soft drinks in the lobby. Sales for December were $34,700, and the 10% due for December has not yet been received or entered.
5. Advertising expense paid in advance and included in Advertising Expense, $1,100.
6. Salaries accrued but unpaid, $4,700.
(b) What amounts should be shown for each of the following on the income statement for the year?
1. Interest expense.
2. Admissions revenue.
3. Concessions revenue.
4. Advertising expense.
5. Salaries expense.

P3-4 (Adjusting Entries and Financial Statements) Presented below are the trial balance and the other information related to Muhammad Ali, a consulting engineer.

Muhammad Ali, Consulting Engineer
TRIAL BALANCE
December 31, 1998

Cash	$ 31,500	
Accounts Receivable	49,600	
Allowance for Doubtful Accounts		$ 750
Engineering Supplies Inventory	1,960	
Unexpired Insurance	1,100	
Furniture and Equipment	25,000	
Accumulated Depreciation of Furniture and Equipment		6,250
Notes Payable		7,200
Muhammad Ali, Capital		35,010
Revenue from Consulting Fees		100,000
Rent Expense	9,750	
Office Salaries	28,500	
Heat, Light, and Water Expense	1,080	
Miscellaneous Office Expense	720	
	$149,210	$149,210

1. Fees received in advance from clients, $6,900.
2. Services performed for clients that were not recorded by December 31, $4,900.
3. The Allowance for Doubtful Accounts account should be adjusted to 4% of the corrected accounts receivable balance.
4. Insurance expired during the year, $480.
5. Furniture and equipment is being depreciated at 12½% per year.
6. Muhammad Ali gave the bank a 90-day, 10% note for $7,200 on December 1, 1998.
7. Rent of the building is $750 per month. The rent for 1998 has been paid, as has that for January 1999.
8. Office salaries earned but unpaid December 31, 1998, $2,510.

Instructions

(a) From the trial balance and other information given, prepare annual adjusting entries as of December 31, 1998.

(b) Prepare an income statement for 1998, a balance sheet, and a statement of owner's equity. Muhammad Ali withdrew $17,000 cash for personal use during the year.

P3-5 (Adjusting Entries and Financial Statements) The Ana Alicia Advertising Corporation was founded by Ana Alicia in January of 1995. Presented below are both the adjusted and unadjusted trial balances as of December 31, 1999.

Ana Alicia Advertising Corporation
TRIAL BALANCE
December 31, 1999

	Unadjusted		Adjusted	
	Dr.	Cr.	Dr.	Cr.
Cash	$ 7,000		$ 7,000	
Fees Receivable	19,000		22,000	
Art Supplies	8,500		5,500	
Prepaid Insurance	3,250		2,500	
Printing Equipment	60,000		60,000	
Accumulated Depreciation		$ 27,000		$ 33,750
Accounts Payable		5,000		5,000
Interest Payable		0		150
Notes Payable		5,000		5,000
Unearned Advertising Fees		7,000		5,600
Salaries Payable		0		1,500
Common Stock		10,000		10,000
Retained earnings		4,500		4,500
Advertising Fees		58,600		63,000

Salaries Expense	10,000	11,500	
Insurance Expense		750	
Interest Expense	350	500	
Depreciation Expense		6,750	
Art Supplies Expense	5,000	8,000	
Rent Expense	4,000	4,000	
	$117,100	$128,500	
	$117,100	$128,500	

Instructions

(a) Journalize the annual adjusting entries that were made.

(b) Prepare an income statement and a statement of retained earnings for the year ending December 31, 1999, and a balance sheet at December 31.

(c) Answer the following questions:

    (1) If the useful life of equipment is 8 years, what is the expected salvage value?

    (2) If the note has been outstanding three months, what is the annual interest rate on that note?

    (3) If the company paid $12,500 in salaries in 1999, what was the balance in Salaries Payable on December 31, 1998?

P3-6 (Adjusting and Reversing Entries) Presented below is information related to Jillian Anderson, Realtor, at the close of the fiscal year ending December 31.

    1. Jillian had paid the local newspaper $335 for an advertisement to be run in January of the next year, charging it to Advertising Expense.

    2. On November 1 Jillian borrowed $9,000 from Yorkville Bank issuing a 90-day, 10% note.

    3. Salaries and wages due and unpaid December 31: sales, $1,420; office clerks, $1,060.

    4. Interest accrued to date on Grant Muldaur's note, which Jillian holds, $500.

    5. Estimated loss on bad debts, $1,210 for the period.

    6. Stamps and stationery on hand, $110, charged to Stationery and Postage Expense account when purchased.

    7. Jillian has not yet paid the December rent on the building her business occupies, $1,000.

    8. Insurance paid November 1 for one year, $930, charged to Unexpired Insurance when paid.

    9. Property taxes accrued, $1,670.

    10. On December 1 Jillian gave Laura Palmer her (Jillian's) 60-day, 12% note for $6,000 on account.

    11. On October 31 Jillian received $2,580 from Douglas Raines in payment of 6 months' rent for office space occupied by him in the building and credited Unearned Rent.

    12. On September 1 she paid 6 months' rent in advance on a warehouse, $6,600, and debited the asset account Prepaid Rent.

    13. The bill from the Twin Peaks Light & Power Company for December has been received but not yet entered or paid, $510.

    14. Estimated depreciation on furniture and equipment, $1,400.

Instructions

(a) Prepare annual adjusting entries as of December 31.

(b) List the numbers of the entries that would be reversed.

P3-7 (Adjusting, Closing, Reversing) Following is the trial balance of the Platteville Golf Club, Inc. as of December 31. The books are closed annually on December 31.

Platteville Golf Club, Inc.
TRIAL BALANCE
December 31

Cash	$ 15,000	
Dues Receivable	13,000	
Allowance for Doubtful Accounts		$ 1,100
Land	350,000	
Buildings	120,000	
Accumulated Depreciation of Buildings		38,400
Equipment	150,000	
Accumulated Depreciation of Equipment		70,000
Unexpired Insurance	9,000	
Common Stock		400,000
Retained Earnings		82,000
Revenue from Dues		200,000

Revenue from Greens Fees		8,100
Rental Revenue		15,400
Utilities Expense	54,000	
Salaries Expense	80,000	
Maintenance	24,000	
	$815,000	$815,000

Instructions

(a) Enter the balances in ledger accounts. Allow five lines for each account.

(b) From the trial balance and the information given, prepare annual adjusting entries and post to the ledger accounts.

  1. The buildings have an estimated life of 25 years with no salvage value (straight-line method).
  2. The equipment is depreciated at 10% per year.
  3. Insurance expired during the year, $3,500.
  4. The rental revenue represents the amount received for 11 months for dining facilities. The December rent has not yet been received.
  5. It is estimated that 15% of the dues receivable will be uncollectible.
  6. Salaries earned but not paid by December 31, $3,600.
  7. Dues paid in advance by members, $8,900.

(c) Prepare an adjusted trial balance.

(d) Prepare closing entries and post.

(e) Prepare reversing entries and post.

(f) Prepare a trial balance after posting reversing entries.

P3-8 (Adjusting and Closing)   Presented below is the December 31 trial balance of Nancy Drew Boutique.

Nancy Drew Boutique
TRIAL BALANCE
December 31

Cash	$ 18,500	
Accounts Receivable	42,000	
Allowance for Doubtful Accounts		$ 700
Inventory, January 1	78,000	
Furniture and Equipment	84,000	
Accumulated Depreciation of Furniture and Equipment		35,000
Prepaid Insurance	5,100	
Notes Payable		28,000
Drew, Capital		90,600
Sales		600,000
Purchases	400,000	
Sales Salaries	50,000	
Advertising Expense	6,700	
Administrative Salaries	65,000	
Office Expense	5,000	
	$754,300	$754,300

Instructions

(a) Construct T-accounts and enter the balances shown.

(b) Prepare adjusting journal entries for the following and post to the T-accounts. Open additional T-accounts as necessary. (The books are closed yearly on December 31.)

  1. Adjust the Allowance for Doubtful Accounts to 5% of the accounts receivable.
  2. Furniture and equipment is depreciated based on a 6-year life (no salvage).
  3. Insurance expired during the year, $2,550.
  4. Interest accrued on notes payable, $3,360.
  5. Sales salaries earned but not paid, $2,400.
  6. Advertising paid in advance, $700.
  7. Office supplies on hand, $1,500, charged to Office Expense when purchased.

(c) Prepare closing entries and post to the accounts. The inventory on December 31 was $80,000.

P3-9 (Adjusting, Closing, Financial Statements) The balance sheet of Jane Addams Company as of December 31, 1998 is presented below:

Assets		Liabilities and Capital	
Cash	$ 4,000	Accounts payable	$ 5,000
Accounts receivable	7,500	Notes payable	6,000
Inventory	5,200	Total liabilities	11,000
Office equipment	7,400		
Accumulated depreciation	(2,220)	Jane Addams, capital	17,880
Furniture and fixtures	10,000		
Accumulated depreciation	(3,000)		
Total	$28,880	Total	$28,880

The following summary transactions occurred during January 1999.

Jan. 1 Sells merchandise on account, $2,800.
  2 Collects $3,210 on accounts receivable of $3,250. Sales discounts totaled $40.
  3 Sells merchandise for cash, $7,000.
  4 Receives a $1,300 note from a customer on payment of account.
  5 Purchases merchandise on account, $4,525.
  6 Pays freight on merchandise purchased, $100.
  7 Pays $3,470 on accounts payable of $3,500. Purchase discounts totaled $30.
  10 Purchases office equipment on account, $1,250.
  28 Pays expenses: advertising, $55; salaries, $840; rent, $400.

At January 31, the following information is available.

a. Interest on the note payable is paid every December 31. Accrued interest for January is $75. Principal is payable December 31, 1999.
b. Accrued interest on the note receivable for January is $15.
c. Accrued salaries at January 31 are $125.
d. Depreciation expense for January is $75 on office equipment and $100 on furniture and fixtures.
e. Ending inventory is $4,225.

Instructions
(a) Prepare journal entries in general journal form for the January transactions.
(b) Open ledger accounts, enter the December 31 balances, and post the journal entries from (a).
(c) Prepare a trial balance.
(d) Prepare adjusting entries at January 31 and post.
(e) Prepare an adjusted trial balance.
(f) Prepare an income statement for January and a balance sheet at January 31.
(g) Prepare closing entries at January 31 and post.
(h) Prepare a post-closing trial balance.

P3-10 (Adjusting, Reversing) The following list of accounts and their balances represents the unadjusted trial balance of Omar Uresti Corp. at December 31, 1999:

	Dr.	Cr.
Cash	$ 6,000	
Accounts Receivable	49,000	
Allowance for Doubtful Accounts		$ 750
Inventory	58,000	
Prepaid Insurance	2,940	
Prepaid Rent	13,200	
Investment in Corey Pavin Corp. Bonds	18,000	
Land	10,000	
Plant and Equipment	104,000	
Accumulated Depreciation		18,000
Accounts Payable		9,310
Bonds Payable		50,000
Discount on Bonds Payable	1,500	
Capital Stock		100,000
Retained Earnings		80,660
Sales		213,310
Rental Revenue		10,200
Purchases	170,000	
Purchase Discounts		2,400

Transportation-Out	9,000	
Transportation-In	3,500	
Salaries and Wages	35,000	
Interest Expense	3,600	
Miscellaneous Expense	890	
	$484,630	$484,630

Additional data:

1. On November 1, 1999, Omar Uresti received $10,200 rent from its lessee for a 6-month lease beginning on that date, crediting Rental Revenue.
2. Omar Uresti estimates that 5% of the Accounts Receivable balances on December 31, 1999, will become uncollectible. On December 28, 1999, the bookkeeper incorrectly credited Sales for a receipt on account in the amount of $2,000. This error had not yet been corrected on December 31.
3. Per a physical inventory, inventory on hand at December 31, 1999, was $67,000. Record the adjusting entry for inventory by using a Cost of Goods Sold account.
4. Prepaid insurance contains the premium costs of two policies: Policy A, cost of $1,320, 2-year term, taken out on September 1, 1999; Policy B, cost of $1,620, 3-year term, taken out on April 1, 1999.
5. The regular rate of depreciation is 10% per year. Acquisitions and retirements during a year are depreciated at half this rate. There were no retirements during the year. On December 31, 1998, the balance of Plant and Equipment was $88,000.
6. On April 1, 1999, Omar Uresti issued 50 $1,000, 11% bonds, maturing on April 1, 2009, at 97% of par value. Interest payment dates are April 1 and October 1.
7. On August 1, 1999, Omar Uresti purchased 18 $1,000, 13% Corey Pavin Corp. bonds, maturing on July 31, 2001, at par value. Interest payment dates are July 31 and January 31.
8. On May 30, 1999, Omar Uresti rented a warehouse for $1,650 per month, paying $13,200 in advance, debiting Prepaid Rent.

Instructions

(a) Prepare the year-end adjusting and correcting entries in general journal form using the information above.

(b) Indicate the adjusting entries that would be reversed.

P3-11 (Work Sheet and Financial Statement Preparation) Brunhilda Company closes its books only once a year, on December 31, but prepares monthly financial statements by estimating month-end inventories and by using work sheets. The company's trial balance on January 31, 1998, is presented below. Selling Expenses and Administrative Expenses are controlling accounts.

Brunhilda Company
TRIAL BALANCE
January 31, 1998

Cash	$ 11,000	
Accounts Receivable	23,000	
Notes Receivable	3,000	
Allowance for Doubtful Accounts		$ 720
Inventory, Jan. 1, 1998	24,000	
Furniture and Fixtures	30,000	
Accumulated Depreciation of Furniture and Fixtures		7,500
Unexpired Insurance	600	
Supplies on Hand	1,050	
Accounts Payable		6,000
Notes Payable		5,000
Common Stock		20,000
Retained Earnings		27,005
Sales		130,000
Sales Returns and Allowances	1,500	
Purchases	80,000	
Transportation-In	2,000	
Selling Expenses	11,000	
Administrative Expenses	9,000	
Interest Revenue		125
Interest Expense	200	
	$196,350	$196,350

Instructions

(a) Copy the trial balance in the first two columns of an eight-column work sheet. (Do not use adjusted trial balance columns.)

(b) Prepare adjusting entries in journal form (administrative expenses includes bad debts, depreciation, insurance, supplies, and office salaries).
   1. Estimated bad debts, 1% of net sales.
   2. Depreciation of furniture and fixtures, 10% per year.
   3. Insurance expired in January, $80.
   4. Supplies used in January, $210.
   5. Office salaries accrued, $500.
   6. Interest accrued on notes payable, $200.
   7. Interest unearned on notes receivable, $94.

(c) Transfer the adjusting entries to the work sheet.

(d) Estimate the January 31 inventory and enter it on the work sheet. The average gross profit earned by the company is 30% of net sales.

(e) Complete the work sheet.

(f) Prepare a balance sheet, an income statement, and a statement of retained earnings. Dividends of $4,000 were paid on the common stock during the month.

P3-12 (Work Sheet, Adjusting, Financial Statements) Presented below is the trial balance for Nancy Kerrigan, proprietor.

Nancy Kerrigan
TRIAL BALANCE
December 31, 1999

Cash	$ 13,600	
Accounts Receivable	64,800	
Allowance for Doubtful Accounts		$ 2,000
Inventory, January 1	74,000	
Land	40,000	
Building	90,000	
Accumulated Depreciation of Building		14,400
Furniture and Fixtures	22,000	
Accumulated Depreciation of Furniture and Fixtures		6,600
Unexpired Insurance	7,800	
Accounts Payable		34,200
Notes Payable		30,000
Mortgage Payable		40,000
Nancy Kerrigan, Capital		124,730
Sales		720,000
Sales Returns and Allowances	2,800	
Purchases	540,000	
Purchase Returns and Allowances		9,500
Transportation-In	14,800	
Sales Salaries	54,000	
Advertising Expense	9,400	
Salaries, Office and General	31,000	
Heat, Light, and Water Expense	15,100	
Telephone and Telex Expense	1,700	
Miscellaneous Office Expenses	2,000	
Purchase Discounts		9,600
Sales Discounts	5,900	
Interest Expense	2,130	
	$991,030	$991,030

Instructions

(a) Copy the trial balance above in the first two columns of a 10-column work sheet.

(b) Prepare adjusting entries in journal form from the following information. (The fiscal year ends December 31.)

    1. Estimated bad debts, .5% of sales less returns and allowances.
    2. Depreciation on building, 4% per year; on furniture and fixtures, 10% per year.
    3. Insurance expired during the year, $3,900.
    4. Interest at 12% is payable on the mortgage on January 1 of each year.
    5. Sales salaries accrued, December 31, $4,000.
    6. Advertising expense paid in advance, $740.
    7. Office supplies on hand December 31, $1,600. (Charged to Miscellaneous Office Expenses when purchased.)
    8. Interest accrued on notes payable December 31, $1,500.

  (c) Transfer the adjusting entries to the work sheet and complete it. Merchandise inventory on hand December 31, $76,000.
  (d) Prepare an income statement, a balance sheet, and a statement of owner's equity.
  (e) Prepare closing journal entries.
  (f) Indicate the adjusting entries that would be reversed.

P3-13 (Journalize, Post to Ledger, and Prepare Trial Balance)   Ana Linares and other student investors opened Campus Laundromat Inc. on September 1. During the first month of operations the following transactions occurred:

Sept.   1   Stockholders invested $20,000 cash in the business.
        2   Paid $1,000 cash for store rent for the month of September.
        3   Purchased washers and dryers for $24,000 paying $9,000 in cash and signing a $15,000, six-month, 14% note payable.
        4   Paid $1,080 for one-year accident insurance policy.
      10   Received bill from the *Daily News* for advertising the opening of the laundromat, $300.
      20   Declared and paid a cash dividend of $700 to stockholders.
      30   Determined the cash receipts for laundry fees for the month were $6,400.

The chart of accounts for the company is No. 1 Cash, No. 10 Prepaid Insurance, No. 15 Laundry Equipment, No. 25 Notes Payable, No. 26 Accounts Payable, No. 40 Common Stock, No. 42 Dividends, No. 50 Fees Earned, No. 61 Advertising Expense, No. 62 Rent Expense.

Instructions

  (a) Journalize the September transactions. (Use J1 for the journal page number.)
  (b) Open ledger accounts and post the September transactions.
  (c) Prepare a trial balance at September 30, 1999.

*P3-14 (Cash and Accrual Basis)   On January 1, 1999, Jill Monroe and Jenni Meno formed a computer sales and service enterprise in Soapsville, Arkansas by investing $90,000 cash. The new company, Razorback Sales and Service, has the following transactions during January:

    1. Pays $6,000 in advance for three months' rent of office, showroom, and repair space.
    2. Purchases 40 personal computers at a cost of $1,500 each, 6 graphic computers at a cost of $3,000 each, and 25 printers at a cost of $450 each, paying cash upon delivery.
    3. Sales, repair, and office employees earn $12,600 in salaries during January, of which $3,000 was still payable at the end of January.
    4. Sells 30 personal computers at $2,550 each, 4 graphic computers for $4,500 each, and 15 printers for $750 each; $75,000 is received in cash in January and $30,750 is sold on a deferred payment basis.
    5. Other operating expenses of $8,400 are incurred and paid for during January; $2,000 of incurred expenses are payable at January 31.

Instructions

  (a) Using the transaction data above, prepare (1) a cash basis income statement and (2) an accrual basis income statement for the month of January.
  (b) Using the transaction data above, prepare (1) a cash basis balance sheet and (2) an accrual basis balance sheet as of January 31, 1999.
  (c) Identify the items in the cash basis financial statements that make cash basis accounting inconsistent with the theory underlying the elements of financial statements.

*P3-15 (Cash to Accrual Basis)   Presented below is information pertaining to Strug Specialty Shops, a calendar-year sole proprietorship, maintaining its books on the cash basis during the year. At year-end, however, Kerri Strug's accountant adjusts the books to the accrual basis only for sales, purchases, and cost of sales, and records depreciation to more clearly reflect the business income for income tax purposes.

Strug Specialty Shops
TRIAL BALANCE (Cash Basis)
December 31, 1999

	Dr.	Cr.
Cash	$ 18,500	
Accounts receivable, 12/31/98	4,500	
Inventory, 12/31/98	20,000	
Equipment	35,000	
Accumulated depreciation, 12/13/98		$ 9,000
Accounts payable, 12/31/98		$ 4,800
Payroll taxes withheld		850
Kerri Strug, drawings	24,000	
Kerri Strug, capital, 12/31/98		33,650
Sales		187,000
Purchases	82,700	
Salaries	29,500	
Payroll taxes	2,900	
Rent	8,400	
Miscellaneous expense	3,900	
Insurance	2,400	
Utilities	3,500	
	$235,300	$235,300

During 1999 Strug signed a new 8-year lease for the store premises and is in the process of negotiating a loan for remodeling. The bank requires Strug to present financial statements for 1999 prepared on the accrual basis. During the course of compiling information, Strug's accountant obtained the following additional information:

1. Amounts due from customers totaled $7,400 at December 31, 1999.
2. A review of the receivables at December 31, 1999, disclosed that an allowance for doubtful accounts of $600 should be provided. Strug had no bad debt losses from inception of the business through December 31, 1999.
3. The inventory amounted to $24,000 at December 31, 1999, based on physical counts of goods priced at cost. No reduction to market was required.
4. On signing the new lease on October 1, 1999, Strug paid $8,400, representing one year's rent in advance for the lease year ending October 1, 2000. The $7,500 annual rent under the old lease was paid on October 1, 1998, for the lease year ended October 1, 1999.
5. On April 1, 1999, Strug paid $2,400 to renew the comprehensive insurance coverage for one year. The premium was $2,160 on the old policy which expired on April 1, 1999.
6. Depreciation on equipment was computed at $5,250 for 1999.
7. Unpaid vendors' invoices for purchases totaled $7,800 at December 31, 1999.
8. Accrued expenses at December 31, 1998, and December 31, 1999, were as follows:

	12/31/98	12/31/99
Payroll taxes	$250	$400
Salaries	375	510
Utilities	275	450

Instructions

(a) Prepare a work sheet to convert the trial balance of Strug Specialty Shops to the accrual basis for the year ended December 31, 1999. Journal entries are not required to support your adjustments. Use the following work sheet columns:

Cash Basis		Adjustments		Accrual Basis	
Dr.	Cr.	Dr.	Cr.	Dr.	Cr.

(b) Prepare the statement of owner's equity for the year ended December 31, 1999.

(AICPA adapted)

*P3-16 (Cash to Accrual Basis) On January 2, 1998, Logan, Inc., was organized with two stockholders, Lorna Michael and Frank Yerby. Michael purchased 500 shares of $100 par value common stock for $50,000 cash; Yerby received 600 shares of common stock in exchange for the assets and liabilities of a men's clothing shop that he had operated as a sole proprietorship. The trial balance immediately after incorporation appears on the work sheet.

No formal books have been kept during 1998. The following information has been gathered from the checkbooks, deposit slips, and other sources:

1. Most balance sheet account balances at December 31, 1998, have been determined and recorded on the work sheet.
2. Cash receipts for the year are summarized as follows:

Advances from customers	$ 1,500
Cash sales and collections on accounts receivable (after sales discounts of $1,600 and sales returns and allowances of $2,300)	133,700
Sale of equipment costing $6,000 on which $1,000 of depreciation had accumulated	5,800
	$141,000

3. During 1998, the depreciation expense on the building was $1,600; the depreciation expense on the equipment was $2,400.
4. Cash disbursements for the year are summarized as follows:

Insurance premiums	$ 1,400
Purchase of equipment	10,000
Addition to building	11,000
Cash purchases and payments on accounts payable (after purchase discounts of $2,200 and purchase returns and allowances of $1,800)	109,000
Salaries paid to employees	38,600
Utilities	3,200
Total cash disbursements	$173,200

5. Bad debts are estimated to be 1.5% of total sales for the year. The ending accounts receivable balance of $30,000 has been reduced by $760 for specific accounts that were written off as uncollectible.

Instructions

Complete the work sheet for the preparation of accrual basis financial statements. Formal financial statements and journal entries are not required. (Prepare your own work sheet because you will need additional accounts.)

(AICPA adapted)

Logan, Inc.
WORK SHEET FOR PREPARATION OF ACCRUAL BASIS FINANCIAL STATEMENTS
For the Year 1998

	Trial Balance January 2, 1998		Adjustments		Income Statement 1998		Balance Sheet December 31, 1998	
	Debit	Credit	Debit	Credit	Debit	Credit	Debit	Credit
Cash	55,000		___	___	___	___	___	___
Accounts receivable	12,000		___	___	___	___	30,000	___
Merchandise inventory	31,000		___	___	___	___	51,500	___
Unexpired insurance	800		___	___	___	___	900	___
Land	20,000		___	___	___	___	20,000	___
Buildings	30,000		___	___	___	___	___	___
Accumulated depreciation—buildings		8,000	___	___	___	___	___	___
Equipment	12,000		___	___	___	___	___	___
Accumulated depreciation—equipment		3,000	___	___	___	___	___	___
Accounts payable		36,600	___	___	___	___	___	25,600
Advances from customers		1,100	___	___	___	___	___	1,700
Salaries payable		2,100	___	___	___	___	___	4,600
Capital stock		110,000	___	___	___	___	___	110,000
	160,800	160,800						

P3-17 (Special Journals) Presented below is information related to Concord Company.

Journals

Sales journal	Page 17
Purchases journal	Page 8
Cash receipts journal	Page 43
Cash payments journal	Page 44
General journal	Page 12

Ledger Accounts

Title	Balance July 1	Acct. No.
Cash	$4,000	2
Accounts Receivable	9,000	5
Delivery Equipment	8,000	8
Sales Equipment	3,000	21
Accounts Payable	7,000	35
Advertising Expense	–0–	65
Purchases	–0–	52
Purchase Returns	–0–	53
Sales	–0–	69
Transportation-In	–0–	70

The following transactions occurred during the month of July.

July 1 Sells merchandise for cash, $9,500.
3 Buys a new delivery truck on account from Montpelier Motors, $23,000.
3 Receives an invoice from the *Daily Tattler* for a full-page advertisement, $700, which appeared in the paper on July 2.
5 Receives a purchase requisition for display equipment from the sales manager; the equipment sells for $1,320.
6 Returns merchandise for credit of $180 on a cash purchase.
7 Sells merchandise on account to Bob Boston, $19,000.
8 Purchases merchandise on account from Providence Co., $13,500, f.o.b. shipping point.
10 Receives cash of $180 for merchandise returned July 6.
11 Receives a debit memo for $140 from Providence Co., indicating that the merchandise purchased July 8 was shipped with freight prepaid.
13 Purchases display equipment for $1,320; the invoice is paid immediately. (See July 5 information.)
17 Sells merchandise on account to John Hartford, $3,000.
20 Pays Providence Co. in full of account.
24 Purchases merchandise on account from Albany Corp., $3,500.
28 Pays the *Daily Tattler*.
31 Receives full payment from Bob Boston.

Instructions
Complete the following:

(a) Open ledger accounts and enter the July 1 balances.
(b) Record the July transactions in appropriate journals.
(c) Post from the journals to the ledger with posting references in good form (omit subsidiary ledger postings).

❖ FINANCIAL REPORTING PROBLEM—Intel Corporation

The financial statements of Intel are presented in Appendix 5B. Refer to these financial statements and the accompanying notes to answer the following questions.

Instructions

(a) What were Intel's total assets at December 30, 1995? At December 31, 1994?

(b) How much cash (and cash equivalents) did Intel have on December 30, 1995?

(c) What were Intel's research and development costs in 1993? In 1995?

(d) What were Intel's net revenues in 1993? In 1995?

(e) Using Intel's financial statements and related notes, identify items that may result in adjusting entries for prepayments and accruals.

(f) What were the amounts of Intel's depreciation expense in 1993, 1994, and 1995?

❖ FINANCIAL STATEMENT ANALYSIS CASE

Kellogg Company

Kellogg Company has its headquarters in Battle Creek, Michigan. The company manufactures and sells ready-to-eat breakfast cereals and convenience foods including toaster pastries and cereal bars.

Selected data from Kellogg Company's 1994 annual report follows: (dollar amounts and share data in millions)

	1994	1993	1992
Net sales	$6,562.0	$6,295.4	$6,190.6
Cost of goods sold	2,950.7	2,989.0	2,987.7
Selling and administrative expense	2,448.7	2,237.5	2,140.1
Net income	705.4	680.7	431.2

In its 1994 annual report, Kellogg Company outlined its plans for the future, which it described as its six "global strategies." A brief description of these plans follows.

1. Focus on the cereal and convenience food markets that are considered to be core businesses. The company has already divested seven businesses in the past three years that it considered non-core, such as the Mrs. Smith's pie business. In the coming year, Kellogg Company plans to invest more heavily in advertising in order to build brand recognition in the U.S. cereal market.

2. Continue to launch more new products.

3. Continue to be the first to introduce ready-to-eat cereals in countries around the world. Kellogg Company achieved this goal in India and the Soviet Union, and plans to achieve the goal in China.

4. Maintain or reduce present levels of capital expenditures. Kellogg Company plans to achieve this goal by using value-based management and value engineering.

5. Reduce operating costs. This measure is made necessary because of the limited ability to increase sales prices. Kellogg Company reported that cost of goods sold per kilo was virtually flat in 1994.

6. Repurchase shares of its own stock aggressively. This is done partly to improve earnings per share.

Instructions

(a) For each of the six global strategies, describe how gross profit and net income are likely to be affected.

(b) Compute the percentage change in sales, gross profit, operating costs (cost of goods sold plus selling and administrative expenses), and net income from year to year for each of the three years shown. Evaluate Kellogg Company's performance. Which trend seems to be least favorable? Do you think the global strategies described will improve that trend? Explain.

❖ COMPARATIVE ANALYSIS CASE

The Coca-Cola Company versus PepsiCo, Inc.

Go to our Web site and answer the following questions regarding The Coca-Cola Company and PepsiCo, Inc.

Instructions

    (a) Which company had the greatest percentage increase in total assets from 1994 to 1995?

    (b) Using the Selected Financial Data section of these two companies, determine their 5-year compound growth rates related to net sales and net income.

    (c) What company had the most depreciation and amortization expense for 1995? Provide a rationale as to why there is a difference in these amounts between the two companies.

    (d) Which company was most profitable in 1995? Explain.

❖ RESEARCH CASES

Case 1

The Enterprise Standard Industrial Classification (SIC) coding scheme, a published classification of firms into separate industries, is commonly used in practice. SIC codes permit identification of company activities on three levels of detail. Two-digit codes designate a "major group," three-digit codes designate an "industry group," while four-digit codes identify a specific "industry."

Instructions

Use the *Standard Industrial Classification Manual* (published by the U.S. Government's Office of Management and Budget in 1987) to answer the following questions.

    (a) On what basis are SIC codes assigned to companies?

    (b) Identify the major group/industry group/industry represented by the following codes: 12, 271, 3571, 7033, 75, and 872.

    (c) Identify the SIC code for the following industries:

        1. Golfing equipment—manufacturing

        2. Worm farms

        3. Felt tip markers—manufacturing

        4. Household appliance stores, electric or gas—retail

        5. Advertising agencies

    (d) You are interested in examining several companies in the passenger airline industry. Determine the appropriate two-, three-, and four-digit SIC codes. Use *Wards Business Directory of U.S. Private and Public Companies (Vol. 5)* to compile a list of the five largest parent companies (by total sales) in the industry. *Note*: If Wards is not available, alternative sources include *Standard & Poor's Register of Corporations, Directors, and Executives, Standard & Poor's Industry Surveys*, and the Dun & Bradstreet *Million Dollar Directory*.

Case 2

The March 1995 issue of *Management Review* includes an article by Barbara Ettorre, entitled "How Motorola Closes Its Books in Two Days."

Instructions

Read the article and answer the following questions.

    (a) How often does Motorola close its books? How long did the process used to take?

    (b) What was the major change Motorola initiated to shorten the closing process?

    (c) What incentive does Motorola offer to ensure accurate and timely information?

    (d) In a given year, how many journal entry lines does Motorola process?

    (e) Provide an example of an external force that prevents Motorola from closing faster than a day-and-a-half.

    (f) According to Motorola's corporate vice president and controller, how do external financial statement users perceive companies that release information early?

❖ WRITING ASSIGNMENT

Dr. John Gleason, M.D., maintains the accounting records of Bones Clinic on a cash basis. During 1998, Dr. Gleason collected $146,000 from his patients and paid $55,470 in expenses. At January 1, 1998, and December 31, 1998, he had fees receivable, unearned fees, accrued expenses, and prepaid expenses as follows (all long-lived assets are rented):

	January 1, 1998	December 31, 1998
Fees receivable	$9,250	$16,100
Unearned fees	2,840	1,620
Accrued expenses	3,435	2,200
Prepaid expenses	2,000	1,775

Instructions
Last week, Dr. Gleason asked you, his CPA, to help him determine his income on the accrual basis. Write a letter to him explaining what you did to calculate net income on the accrual basis. Be sure to state net income on the accrual basis and to include a schedule of your calculations.

❖ GROUP ASSIGNMENT

Assume your group is performing the accounting services for Denise Rode, a consulting engineer. Ms. Rode has provided the following trial balance and other information for your task.

Denise Rode, Consulting Engineer
TRIAL BALANCE
December 31, 1998

Cash	$ 31,500	
Accounts Receivable	49,600	
Allowance for Doubtful Accounts		$ 1,750
Engineering Supplies Inventory	1,960	
Unexpired Insurance	1,100	
Furniture and Equipment	25,000	
Accumulated Depreciation of Furniture and Equipment		5,000
Notes Payable		7,200
Denise Rode, Capital		35,260
Revenue from Consulting Fees		100,000
Rent Expense	9,750	
Office Salaries Expense	28,500	
Heat, Light, and Water Expense	1,080	
Miscellaneous Office Expense	720	
	$149,210	$149,210

1. Fees received in advance from clients, $7,000.
2. Services performed for clients that were not recorded by December 31, $5,500.
3. The Allowance for Doubtful Accounts account should be adjusted to 6% of the corrected accounts receivable balance.
4. Insurance expired during the year, $600.
5. Furniture and equipment is being depreciated at 10% per year.
6. Denise Rode gave the bank a 90-day, 12% note for $7,200 on December 1, 1998.
7. Rent of the building is $750 per month. The rent for 1998 has been paid, as has that for January 1999.
8. Office salaries earned but unpaid December 31, 1998, $2,600.

Instructions
Your instructor will identify one member to serve as "keeper of the trial balance" and another member to prepare financial statements; the remaining members will serve as transaction analyzers. Divide the information items among the analyzers so that each has at least one item to analyze.

(a) From the trial balance and the other information for each item, the analyzers should prepare the entries needed for their items and report them to the keeper of the trial balance. He or she will update the trial balance for these adjusting entries as of December 31, 1998.

(b) The "preparer" member should prepare (with the help of other members) an income statement for 1998, a balance sheet, and a statement of owner's equity. Note that Ms. Rode withdrew $14,740 cash during the year for personal use. The group should be prepared to report its results to the class.

❖ ETHICS CASE

Ernest Banks is the manager and accountant for a small company privately owned by three individuals. Banks always has given the owners cash-based financial statements. The owners are not accountants and do not understand how financial statements are prepared. Recently, the business has experienced strong growth, and inventory, accounts receivable, and fixed assets have become more significant company assets. Banks understands generally accepted accounting principles and knows that net income would be lower if he prepared accrual-based financial statements. He is afraid that if he gave the owners financial statements prepared on an accrual basis, they would think he is not managing the business well; they might even decide to fire him.

Instructions
Answer the following questions.

(a) What are the ethical issues involved?
(b) What should Banks do?

A visit with
Penelope Flugger

PENELOPE FLUGGER is a Managing Director of J.P. Morgan & Co. She joined the company in 1975 as an assistant comptroller, assuming responsibility for the audit department in 1982. In 1994, she assumed responsibility for control and quality initiatives in Morgan's technology and operations group. Before joining Morgan, she was an audit manager with Price Waterhouse. She holds a bachelor's degree in accounting from the University of Illinois and an MBA from Baruch College, CUNY.

Investment Banking Accounting

There weren't very many women in the accounting profession when you started, were there? When I was a student at the University of Illinois in the early 1960s, there were very few women students. But I had some great professors who were very encouraging and gave me the confidence to go into public accounting. When I graduated, there were only two "Big Eight" firms in Chicago who would hire women. I went to work for Price Waterhouse in New York in 1964 on the audit staff. That summer, 225 people started at Price Waterhouse in New York. There was only one other woman.

Why did you leave public accounting? I had some very good clients, some of the top clients of the firm, so I was lucky in that respect. After a few years, I started to specialize in the brokerage industry, which I found very interesting. I was PW's banking industry specialist and was involved in the AICPA banking committee. But I decided that I wasn't cut out for public accounting, particularly the salesmanship aspect, and decided that I wanted to work for one of the three big banks in New York City—Citicorp, Morgan, or Chase. Luckily, I got job offers from all three, and took the one from Morgan.

Describe some highlights of your career at J.P. Morgan. Initially, I was in charge of the bank's accounting policy and procedures department as well as being in charge of SEC reporting. After a few years, I moved into areas such as international banking and consolidations. From there, I got involved in systems development, because I was very interested in how to make financial reporting easier. After about seven years, the firm asked if I would take over the internal audit department, where I spent about ten years, changing the approach to internal auditing and developing a training program so that we could use it as an entry-level recruiting tool.

What suggestions have you had in the teaching of accounting and auditing? I met the authors of your book when I was a member of the Accounting Education Change Commission. Part of my interest was that changes in accounting education weren't keeping up with what we needed. When I was in auditing, I was complaining that I was hiring from colleges but had to completely retrain these new graduates because they just didn't understand the business. Because internal auditing was so hard to recruit for, I spent time with professors at the schools where we were recruiting. The students were taught discrete things about accounting, marketing, etc. without any idea about how to put it together. They couldn't figure out how things would flow through an organization. I would see people who would pass the CPA exam but couldn't relate it to business.

What has been your role as chairman of the Financial Executives Institute? The FEI is an organization of 14,000 financial executives of major corporations. We represent our members with regulatory bodies such as the FASB, AICPA, etc. In financial accounting, the major issue is how to make sure that accounting reflects business reality. For instance, we'll mark an asset to market, but in a hedge transaction we don't mark the liability to market, so there often seems to be a disconnect between accounting principles and the business reality. You try to keep a balance so that you don't fix one side and create a bigger problem. We also have committees dealing with taxation, pension fund investment, employee benefits, etc. We try to get our voice heard on issues such as the balanced budget, tax reduction, and other initiatives that we think are important.

What are some major issues currently facing you at J.P. Morgan? With the current focus on business process re-engineering and quality, we're spending a lot of time trying to identify our fixed and variable costs. In an investment banking firm you've got to adjust your costs quickly as the markets go up and down. If you don't have a handle on what's fixed and what's variable, your profits get adversely affected, and the market doesn't wait to give you time to fix that. If you build a fixed-cost system that accommodates 20,000 trades a day, and all of a sudden you're trading only 5,000 transactions in that particular instrument, then you have quadrupled the cost to process those transactions.

What are some advantages of industry vs. public accounting for new graduates? If you know what industry you want to go into, then I think you have a leg up in industry. Industry has changed the way it treats entry-level people. Training is much better now than it used to be. And there are more options. If you like consulting work like you would get in public accounting, then we also have a track that allows you to do consulting work. My advice to students is that when they take a job, they should be having fun. If you don't enjoy the job but you have to do it for 40 more years, then that can be a horrible life sentence. Most students take their first job based on who they interview with and where they think the glamour is. That's unfortunate, because the person they interview with is probably not who they're going to work with.

CHAPTER 4

Income Statement and Related Information

Thumbs Up or Thumbs Down?

As a famous politician once remarked, "The American people will forgive you anything as long as you apologize for it." Corporate America apparently has applied these words to its own operations. In recent years, many companies have taken write-downs—reductions in the stated value of company assets—to acknowledge their financial problems and try to come to terms with them. Interestingly, investors have given a "thumbs up" to these write-downs: In a number of cases, a company's stock price has risen, not fallen, after the write-down because investors seem to believe that the worst is over and that the company's financial health is on the mend. The following companies saw a positive effect on their stock price after a large write-down:

Company	Pretax Write-Down (in $ millions)	Reason for Write-Down	Market Price at Time of Write-Down	Market Price 2 Weeks Later
IBM	$8,900	Work-force reduction and elimination of impaired assets	42⅜	43¼
Philip Morris	741	Work-force reduction of 8% and closing of 40 manufacturing facilities	54⅞	56
Xerox	700	Work-force reduction and consolidation of facilities	80¾	89½
Upjohn	255	Work-force reduction and plant closings	31⅝	32¼

Not all companies have experienced postive reactions to write-downs, however. For example, GTE, Kmart, Borden, and Food Lion all had a negative effect on their stock price after a write-down.

Because the market response to a write-down is unpredictable, few companies are eager to take this step. However, the increasing pace of technology, globalization, and the need for enhanced efficiency virtually ensure that companies will face the need to restructure, thus mandating future write-downs for some. And these write-downs raise difficult questions about how to account for and how to report restructurings on the income statement and in related notes. For example, a fundamental issue is whether write-downs are considered a part of ordinary operations, a discontinued operation, or an extraordinary item, or whether they should simply be reported in a new section called restructurings?

LEARNING OBJECTIVES

After studying this chapter, you should be able to:

1. Identify the uses and limitations of an income statement.

2. Prepare a single-step income statement.

3. Prepare a multiple-step income statement.

4. Explain how irregular items are reported.

5. Explain intraperiod tax allocation.

6. Explain where earnings per share information is reported.

7. Prepare a retained earnings statement.

8. Explain how other comprehensive income is reported.

As shown in the opening story, many well-known companies such as IBM, Philip Morris, and Xerox have reported significant write-downs which have affected net income and stockholders' equity. The purpose of this chapter is to examine the many different types of revenues, expenses, gains, and losses that affect the income statement and related information. The content and organization of this chapter are as follows:

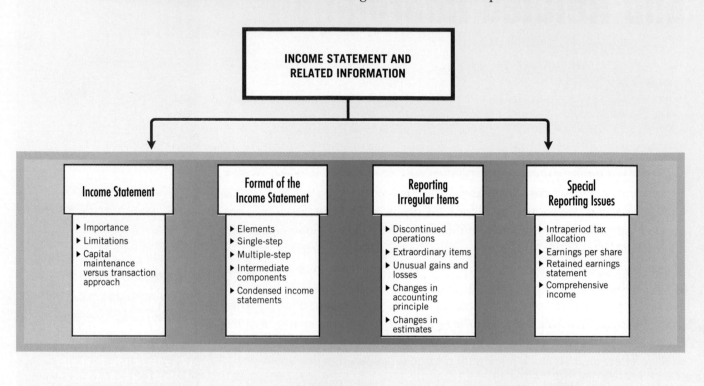

INCOME STATEMENT AND RELATED INFORMATION

Income Statement	Format of the Income Statement	Reporting Irregular Items	Special Reporting Issues
► Importance	► Elements	► Discontinued operations	► Intraperiod tax allocation
► Limitations	► Single-step	► Extraordinary items	► Earnings per share
► Capital maintenance versus transaction approach	► Multiple-step	► Unusual gains and losses	► Retained earnings statement
	► Intermediate components	► Changes in accounting principle	► Comprehensive income
	► Condensed income statements	► Changes in estimates	

UNDERLYING CONCEPTS

The measurement of income is a reflection of the many established assumptions and principles (standards) in accounting, such as the periodicity assumption, the revenue recognition principle, and the matching principle.

❖ INCOME STATEMENT

The **income statement**, often called the statement of income or statement of earnings,[1] is the report that measures the success of enterprise operations for a given period of time. The business and investment community uses this report to determine profitability, investment value, and credit worthiness. It provides investors and creditors with information that helps them predict the **amounts, timing, and uncertainty of future cash flows.**

Importance of the Income Statement

The income statement helps users of the financial statements predict future cash flows in a number of different ways. First, investors and creditors can use the information on the income statement **to evaluate the past performance of the enterprise**. Although success in the past does not necessarily mean success in the future, some important trends may be determined. It follows that if a reasonable correlation between past and future performance can be assumed, then predictions of future cash flows can be made with some confidence.

---

[1]*Accounting Trends and Techniques—1996* (New York: AICPA) indicates that for the 600 companies surveyed the term *income* was employed in the title of 298 income statements. The term *operations* was second in acceptance with 167, while the term *earnings* was used by 127 companies.

Second, the income statement helps users **determine the risk (level of uncertainty) of not achieving particular cash flows**. Information on the various components of income—revenues, expenses, gains, and losses—highlights the relationship among them. With such information one can, for example, assess better the effect of a change in demand for a company's product on revenues and expenses (and therefore income). Similarly, segregating operating performance from other aspects of performance can provide useful insights. Because operations are usually the major means by which revenues and ultimately cash are generated, results from regular continuing operations usually have greater significance than results from nonrecurring activities and events.

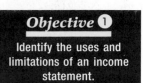

Objective ❶

Identify the uses and limitations of an income statement.

Sometimes, though, even "continuing operations" can mislead investors. Consider the case of National Patent Development, a company that specializes in soft contact lenses. It reported $18.6 million in income from continuing operations before taxes. A closer examination of this income, however, revealed that (1) $7.5 million of income came from a gain on the sale of stock by a subsidiary; (2) $2.4 million represented a gain on the exchange of stock; (3) $3.6 million came from a gain on the sale of stock in its investment portfolio; and, (4) $3.2 million came from settlement of lawsuits related to patent infringements. In addition, its largest revenue source, $9.9 million from royalties on its soft contact lenses, might not continue: a note indicates the company's patent on this process was about to expire. Our point here is that income, "the bottom line," doesn't tell the whole story.

Whether existing confidence in the income statement is well founded is a matter of conjecture. Because the derived income is at best a rough estimate, the reader of the statement should take care not to give it more significance than it deserves. However, taken in its entirety the income statement does, nonetheless, provide information on the nature of income and the likelihood that it will continue in the future.

Limitations of the Income Statement

Economists have often criticized accountants for their definition of income because accountants **do not include many items** that contribute to general growth and well-being of an enterprise. Economist J. R. Hicks defined income as the maximum value an entity can consume during a period and still be as well-off at the end as at the beginning.[2] Any effort to measure how well-off an entity is at any point in time, however, will prove fruitless unless certain restrictive assumptions are developed and applied.

What was your net income for last year? Let us suppose that you worked during the summer and earned $4,200. Because you paid taxes and incurred tuition and living expenses for school, your income statement may show a loss for the year, if measured in terms of straight dollar value. But have you sustained a loss? How do you value the education obtained during this one year? One interpretation of Hicks's definition states that you would measure not only monetary income but also psychic income ("well-offness"). Psychic income is defined as a measure of increase in net wealth arising from qualitative factors—in this case, the value of your educational experience.

Accountants know that the recognition of such experiences might be useful, but the problem of measurement has not been solved. So, items that cannot be quantified with any degree of reliability have been discarded in determining income.

That's not to say that income totals are uniform and precise. **Income numbers are often affected by the accounting methods employed.**[3] For example, one company may

[2]J. R. Hicks, *Value and Capital* (Oxford: Clarendon Press, 1946), p. 172.

[3]Experiences with Hollywood's movie producers illustrate the necessity to define net income, where possible, in advance. Numerous actors, writers, and producers signed "net profit contracts" on highly successful projects but never received a share of the profits. With the big studios' ability to allocate overhead costs creatively, "net profits" failed to materialize. Large-grossing productions like *Forrest Gump, Batman, J.F.K., Alien, Ghostbusters,* and *Coming to America* "never broke into net profit." Thus, several stars have brought lawsuits against the movie studios in an attempt to uncover the creative measurement of "net loss." (See *Forbes*, "Profits? What Profits?" February 19, 1990, pp. 38–40.)

choose to depreciate its plant assets on an accelerated basis; another may choose a straight-line basis. Assuming all other factors are equal, the income of the first company will be lower than that of the second even though the companies are essentially the same. Thus the **quality of earnings** of a given enterprise is important. Companies that use liberal (aggressive) accounting policies report higher income numbers in the short run. In such cases, we say that the quality of the earnings is low.

Other companies generate income in the short run as a result of a nonoperating or nonrecurring event that is not sustainable over a period of time. At one time Beatrice Cos. reported earnings of $4.77 per share, supposedly a 20% increase over the prior year's $3.99 per share earnings. However, $2.20 per share was earned from the sales of certain lines of business. Another $0.17 per share resulted from a nonoperating tax forgiveness granted to encourage exports. And an additional $0.19 per share of income resulted from a complicated nonrecurring exchange for its preferred stock. How real was the 20% increase? How sustainable was the reported $4.77 per share? It should not have been a surprise when Beatrice reported earnings of $2.09 per share the subsequent year, down 56%.

Capital Maintenance Approach versus Transaction Approach

People are sometimes surprised to learn that there are two ways to calculate net income. The first is represented by Hicks's definition of income. He subtracted beginning net assets (assets minus liabilities) from ending net assets and adjusted for any additional investments and any distributions (dividends declared or drawings made) during the period. This is the capital maintenance approach (sometimes referred to as the **change in equity** approach). It takes the net assets or "capital values" based on some valuation (e.g., historical cost, discounted cash flows, current cost, or fair market value) and measures income by the difference in capital values at two points in time.[4]

Suppose that a corporation had beginning net assets of $10,000 and end-of-the-year net assets of $18,000. During this same period additional owners' investments of $5,000 were made, and $1,000 of dividends were declared. Calculation of the net income for the period, employing the capital maintenance approach, is shown in Illustration 4-1.

ILLUSTRATION 4-1
Capital Maintenance Approach to Measuring Net Income

Net assets, December 31, 1999	$18,000
Net assets, January 1, 1999	10,000
Increase in net assets	8,000
Add:	
Dividends declared during the year	1,000
Deduct:	
Owners' investments during the year	(5,000)
Net income for 1999	$ 4,000

The calculation is relatively straightforward. But there is one important drawback to the capital maintenance approach: Detailed information concerning the composition of the income is not evident because the revenue and expense amounts are not presented to the financial statement reader.

The alternative procedure measures the basic income-related transactions that occur during a period and summarizes them in an income statement. This method is called the transaction approach and is the method with which you are familiar. This approach focuses on the activities that have occurred during a given period; instead of presenting only a net change, it discloses the components of the change. Income may be classified by customer, product line, or function; by operating and nonoperating, continuing and

---

[4]The Internal Revenue Service uses the capital maintenance approach to identify unreported income and refers to its approach as a "net worth check."

discontinued, and regular and irregular.[5] The transaction approach to income measurement is superior to the capital maintenance approach because it provides information on the elements of income.

❖ FORMAT OF THE INCOME STATEMENT

Elements of the Income Statement

The transaction approach to income measurement requires the use of revenue, expense, loss, and gain accounts, without which an income statement cannot be prepared. As indicated in Chapter 2, the major elements of the income statement are as follows:

❖ ELEMENTS OF THE INCOME STATEMENT ❖

REVENUES. Inflows or other enhancements of assets of an entity or settlements of its liabilities during a period from delivering or producing goods, rendering services, or other activities that constitute the entity's ongoing major or central operations.

EXPENSES. Outflows or other using-up of assets or incurrences of liabilities during a period from delivering or producing goods, rendering services, or carrying out other activities that constitute the entity's ongoing major or central operations.

GAINS. Increases in equity (net assets) from peripheral or incidental transactions of an entity except those that result from revenues or investments by owners.

LOSSES. Decreases in equity (net assets) from peripheral or incidental transactions of an entity except those that result from expenses or distributions to owners.[6]

Revenues take many forms, such as sales, fees, interest, dividends, and rents. Expenses also take many forms, such as cost of goods sold, depreciation, interest, rent, salaries and wages, and taxes. Gains and losses also are of many types, resulting from the sale of investments, sale of plant assets, settlement of liabilities, write-offs of assets due to obsolescence or casualty, and theft.

The distinction between revenues and gains and the distinction between expenses and losses depend to a great extent on the typical activities of the enterprise. For example, the sales price of investments sold by an insurance company such as Mutual of Omaha would generally be classified as revenue, whereas the sales price less book value on the sale of an investment by a manufacturing enterprise (such as Inland Steel Co.) would be classified as a gain or loss. The different treatment results because the sale of investments by an insurance company is part of its regular operations, whereas in a manufacturing enterprise it is not.

The importance of reporting these elements should not be underestimated. For most decision makers, the parts of a financial statement will often be more useful than the whole. As indicated earlier, investors and creditors are interested in predicting the amounts, timing, and uncertainty of future income and cash flows. Having income statement elements shown in some detail and in comparison form with prior years' data, decision makers are better able to assess future income and cash flows.

INTERNATIONAL INSIGHT

Nations that were previously part of the Soviet bloc are undergoing dramatic economic changes. One of the difficulties they face is creating terms for concepts such as "revenues," "expenses," "profits," and other basics of capitalist economies.

INTERNATIONAL INSIGHT

In many nations financial reporting is prepared on the same bases as tax returns. In such cases, companies have incentives to minimize reported income.

---

[5]Irregular encompasses transactions and other events that are derived from developments outside the normal operations of the business.

[6]"Elements of Financial Statements," *Statement of Financial Accounting Concepts No. 6* (Stamford, Conn.: FASB, 1985), pars. 78–89.

Single-Step Income Statements

Objective ❷

Prepare a single-step income statement.

In reporting revenues, gains, expenses, and losses, a format known as the **single-step income statement** is often used. In the single-step statement, just two groupings exist: revenues and expenses. Expenses are deducted from revenues to arrive at net income or loss. The expression "single-step" is derived from the single subtraction necessary to arrive at net income. Frequently income tax is reported separately as the last item before net income to indicate their relationship to income before income tax.

For example, Illustration 4-2 shows the single-step income statement of Dan Deines Company.

ILLUSTRATION 4-2
Single-step Income
Statement

Dan Deines Company INCOME STATEMENT For the Year Ended December 31, 1999	
Revenues	
Net sales	$2,972,413
Dividend revenue	98,500
Rental revenue	72,910
Total revenues	3,143,823
Expenses	
Cost of goods sold	1,982,541
Selling expenses	453,028
Administrative expenses	350,771
Interest expense	126,060
Income tax expense	66,934
Total expenses	2,979,334
Net income	$ 164,489
Earnings per common share	$1.74

The single-step form of income statement is widely used in financial reporting, although in recent years, the multiple-step form described below has regained its former popularity.[7]

The primary advantage of the single-step format lies in the simplicity of presentation and the absence of any implication that one type of revenue or expense item has priority over another. Potential classification problems are thus eliminated.

Multiple-Step Income Statements

Objective ❸

Prepare a multiple-step income statement.

Some contend that including other important revenue and expense data makes the income statement more informative and more useful. These further classifications include:

❶ A separation of operating and nonoperating activities of the company. For example, enterprises often present an income from operations figure and then sections entitled "other revenues and gains" and "other expenses and losses." These other categories include interest revenue and expense, gains or losses from sales of miscellaneous items, and dividends received.

❷ A classification of expenses by functions, such as merchandising or manufacturing (cost of goods sold), selling, and administration. This permits immediate comparison with costs of previous years and with the cost of other departments during the same year.

---

[7]*Accounting Trends and Techniques—1996.* Of the 600 companies surveyed by the AICPA, 411 employed the multiple-step form and 189 employed the single-step income statement format. This is a reversal from 1983, when 314 used the single-step form and 286 used the multiple-step form.

A **multiple-step income statement** is used to recognize these additional relationships. This statement recognizes a separation of operating transactions from nonoperating transactions and matches costs and expenses with related revenues. It highlights certain intermediate components of income that are used for the computation of ratios used to assess the performance of the enterprise.

To illustrate, Dan Deines Company's multiple-step statement of income is presented in Illustration 4-3. Note, for example, that in arriving at net income, three subtotals are

<table>
<tr><td colspan="4">**Dan Deines Company**
INCOME STATEMENT
For the Year Ended December 31, 1999</td></tr>
<tr><td>Sales Revenue</td><td></td><td></td><td></td></tr>
<tr><td> Sales</td><td></td><td></td><td>$3,053,081</td></tr>
<tr><td> Less: Sales discounts</td><td></td><td>$ 24,241</td><td></td></tr>
<tr><td>   Sales returns and allowances</td><td></td><td>56,427</td><td>80,668</td></tr>
<tr><td> Net sales revenue</td><td></td><td></td><td>2,972,413</td></tr>
<tr><td>Cost of Goods Sold</td><td></td><td></td><td></td></tr>
<tr><td> Merchandise inventory, Jan. 1, 1999</td><td></td><td>461,219</td><td></td></tr>
<tr><td> Purchases</td><td>$1,989,693</td><td></td><td></td></tr>
<tr><td> Less purchase discounts</td><td>19,270</td><td></td><td></td></tr>
<tr><td> Net purchases</td><td>1,970,423</td><td></td><td></td></tr>
<tr><td> Freight and transportation-in</td><td>40,612</td><td>2,011,035</td><td></td></tr>
<tr><td> Total merchandise available for sale</td><td></td><td>2,472,254</td><td></td></tr>
<tr><td> Less merchandise inventory, Dec. 31, 1999</td><td></td><td>489,713</td><td></td></tr>
<tr><td>   Cost of goods sold</td><td></td><td></td><td>1,982,541</td></tr>
<tr><td> Gross profit on sales</td><td></td><td></td><td>989,872</td></tr>
<tr><td>Operating Expenses</td><td></td><td></td><td></td></tr>
<tr><td> Selling expenses</td><td></td><td></td><td></td></tr>
<tr><td>   Sales salaries and commissions</td><td>202,644</td><td></td><td></td></tr>
<tr><td>   Sales office salaries</td><td>59,200</td><td></td><td></td></tr>
<tr><td>   Travel and entertainment</td><td>48,940</td><td></td><td></td></tr>
<tr><td>   Advertising expense</td><td>38,315</td><td></td><td></td></tr>
<tr><td>   Freight and transportation-out</td><td>41,209</td><td></td><td></td></tr>
<tr><td>   Shipping supplies and expense</td><td>24,712</td><td></td><td></td></tr>
<tr><td>   Postage and stationery</td><td>16,788</td><td></td><td></td></tr>
<tr><td>   Depreciation of sales equipment</td><td>9,005</td><td></td><td></td></tr>
<tr><td>   Telephone and telegraph</td><td>12,215</td><td>453,028</td><td></td></tr>
<tr><td> Administrative expenses</td><td></td><td></td><td></td></tr>
<tr><td>   Officers' salaries</td><td>186,000</td><td></td><td></td></tr>
<tr><td>   Office salaries</td><td>61,200</td><td></td><td></td></tr>
<tr><td>   Legal and professional services</td><td>23,721</td><td></td><td></td></tr>
<tr><td>   Utilities expense</td><td>23,275</td><td></td><td></td></tr>
<tr><td>   Insurance expense</td><td>17,029</td><td></td><td></td></tr>
<tr><td>   Depreciation of building</td><td>18,059</td><td></td><td></td></tr>
<tr><td>   Depreciation of office equipment</td><td>16,000</td><td></td><td></td></tr>
<tr><td>   Stationery, supplies, and postage</td><td>2,875</td><td></td><td></td></tr>
<tr><td>   Miscellaneous office expenses</td><td>2,612</td><td>350,771</td><td>803,799</td></tr>
<tr><td>Income from operations</td><td></td><td></td><td>186,073</td></tr>
<tr><td>Other Revenues and Gains</td><td></td><td></td><td></td></tr>
<tr><td> Dividend revenue</td><td></td><td>98,500</td><td></td></tr>
<tr><td> Rental revenue</td><td></td><td>72,910</td><td>171,410</td></tr>
<tr><td></td><td></td><td></td><td>357,483</td></tr>
<tr><td>Other Expenses and Losses</td><td></td><td></td><td></td></tr>
<tr><td> Interest on bonds and notes</td><td></td><td></td><td>126,060</td></tr>
<tr><td>Income before income tax</td><td></td><td></td><td>231,423</td></tr>
<tr><td> Income tax</td><td></td><td></td><td>66,934</td></tr>
<tr><td>Net income for the year</td><td></td><td></td><td>$ 164,489</td></tr>
<tr><td>Earnings per common share</td><td></td><td></td><td>$1.74</td></tr>
</table>

ILLUSTRATION 4-3
Multiple-step Income Statement

presented: net sales revenue, gross profit, and income from operations. The disclosure of net sales revenues is useful because regular revenues are reported as a separate item. Irregular or incidental revenues are disclosed elsewhere in the income statement. As a result, trends in revenue from continuing operations should be easier to understand and analyze. Similarly, the reporting of gross profit provides a useful number for evaluating performance and assessing future earnings. A study of the trend in gross profits may show how successfully a company uses its resources; it may also be a basis for understanding how profit margins have changed as a result of competitive pressure.

Finally, disclosing income from operations highlights the difference between regular and irregular or incidental activities. This disclosure helps users recognize that incidental or irregular activities are unlikely to continue at the same level. Furthermore, disclosure of operating earnings may assist in comparing different companies and assessing operating efficiencies.

Intermediate Components of the Income Statement

When a multiple-step income statement is used, some or all of the following sections or subsections may be prepared:

❖ INCOME STATEMENT SECTIONS ❖

1 Operating Section. A report of the revenues and expenses of the company's principal operations.

  (a) Sales or Revenue Section. A subsection presenting sales, discounts, allowances, returns, and other related information. Its purpose is to arrive at the net amount of sales revenue.

  (b) Cost of Goods Sold Section. A subsection that shows the cost of goods that were sold to produce the sales.

  (c) Selling Expenses. A subsection that lists expenses resulting from the company's efforts to make sales.

  (d) Administrative or General Expenses. A subsection reporting expenses of general administration.

2 Nonoperating Section. A report of revenues and expenses resulting from secondary or auxiliary activities of the company. In addition, special gains and losses that are infrequent or unusual, but not both, are normally reported in this section. Generally these items break down into two main subsections:

  (a) Other Revenues and Gains. A list of the revenues earned or gains incurred, generally net of related expenses, from nonoperating transactions.

  (b) Other Expenses and Losses. A list of the expenses or losses incurred, generally net of any related incomes, from nonoperating transactions.

3 Income Tax. A short section reporting federal and state taxes levied on income from continuing operations.

4 Discontinued Operations. Material gains or losses resulting from the disposition of a segment of the business.

5 Extraordinary Items. Unusual and infrequent material gains and losses.

6 Cumulative Effect of a Change in Accounting Principle.

7 Earnings Per Share.[8]

Items 1, 2, 3, and 7 above are shown in the Dan Deines Company income statement in Illustration 4-3.

---

[8]Earnings per share or net loss per share is required to be included on the face of the income statement.

Although the content of the operating section is always the same, the organization of the material need not be as described above. The breakdown above uses a **natural expense classification** and is commonly used for manufacturing concerns and for merchandising companies in the wholesale trade. Another classification of operating expenses recommended for retail stores uses a **functional expense classification** of administrative, occupancy, publicity, buying, and selling expenses.

Usually, financial statements that are provided to external users have less detail than internal management reports. The latter tend to have more expense categories—usually grouped along lines of responsibility. This detail allows top management to judge staff performance.

Whether a single-step or a multiple-step income statement is used, irregular transactions such as discontinued operations, extraordinary items, and cumulative effect of changes in accounting principles should be reported separately following income from continuing operations.

Condensed Income Statements

In some cases it is impossible to present in a single income statement of convenient size all the desired expense detail. This problem is solved by including only the totals of expense groups in the statement of income and preparing supplementary schedules of expenses to support the totals. With this format, the income statement itself may be reduced to a few lines on a single sheet. For this reason, readers who wish to study all the reported data on operations must give their attention to the supporting schedules. The income statement shown in Illustration 4-4 for Dan Deines Company is a condensed version of the more detailed multiple-step statement presented earlier and is more representative of the type found in practice.

Dan Deines Company
INCOME STATEMENT
For the Year Ended December 31, 1999

Net sales		$2,972,413
Cost of goods sold		1,982,541
Gross profit		989,872
Selling expense (see Note D)	$453,028	
Administrative expense	350,771	803,799
Income from operations		186,073
Other revenues and gains		171,410
		357,483
Other expenses and losses		126,060
Income before income tax		231,423
Income tax		66,934
Net income for the year		$ 164,489
Earnings per share		$1.74

ILLUSTRATION 4-4
Condensed Income Statement

An example of a supporting schedule, cross-referenced as Note D and detailing the selling expenses, is shown below in Illustration 4-5.

Note D: Selling expenses	
Sales salaries and commissions	$202,644
Sales office salaries	59,200
Travel and entertainment	48,940
Advertising expense	38,315
Freight and transportation-out	41,209
Shipping supplies and expense	24,712
Postage and stationery	16,788
Depreciation of sales equipment	9,005
Telephone and telegraph	12,215
Total selling expenses	$453,028

ILLUSTRATION 4-5
Sample Supporting Schedule

How much detail to include in the income statement is always a problem. On the one hand, we want to present a simple, summarized statement so that a reader can readily discover important facts. On the other hand, we want to disclose the results of all activities and to provide more than just a skeleton report.[9] Certain basic elements are always included, but as we'll see they can be presented in various formats.

❖ REPORTING IRREGULAR ITEMS

Objective ❹

Explain how irregular items are reported.

Either the single-step or the multiple-step income statement may be used for financial reporting purposes: Flexibility in the presentation of the components of income is thereby permitted. In two important areas, however, specific guidelines have been developed. These two areas relate to what is included in income and how certain unusual or irregular items are reported.

What should be included in net income has been a controversy for many years. For example, should irregular gains and losses and corrections of revenues and expenses of prior years be closed directly to Retained Earnings and therefore not be reported in the income statement? Or should they first be presented in the income statement and then carried to Retained Earnings along with the net income or loss for the period?

Advocates of the former—the **current operating performance concept**—argue that the net income figure should show only the regular, recurring earnings of the business. Irregular gains and losses do not reflect an enterprise's future earning power. Therefore, these items should not be included in computing net income but should be carried directly to Retained Earnings as special items. In addition many readers are not trained to differentiate between regular and irregular items and, therefore, would be confused if such items were included in computing net income.

Advocates of the second approach—the **all-inclusive concept**—insist that irregular items be included in net income. Any gain or loss experienced by the concern, whether directly or indirectly related to operations, contributes to its long-run profitability. Irregular gains and losses can be separated from the results of regular operations to arrive at income from operations, but net income for the year should include all transactions. Advocates believe that when judgment is allowed to determine irregular items, differences develop in treatment of questionable items and, as a result, a danger of manipulating income data arises. For example, at one time American Standard wrote off directly to Retained Earnings $17.9 million in losses from discontinued operations. This enabled the company to report earnings per share of $1.01; if the write-off had been charged to expense, American Standard would have reported a loss of 78 cents per share. As the example shows, it could be to the advantage of a corporation to run one-time losses through Retained Earnings, but gains through income. Supporters of the all-inclusive concept argue that this flexibility should not be allowed because it leads to poor financial reporting practices. In other words, Gresham's law applies; poor accounting practices drive out good ones.[10]

🌐 INTERNATIONAL INSIGHT

In many countries the "modified all-inclusive" income statement approach does not parallel that of the U.S. For example, some gains and losses are not reported on the income statement. Rather, they are taken directly to owners' equity accounts.

---

[9]As discussed later in this chapter, the FASB has issued a statement of concepts that offers some guidance on this topic—"Recognition and Measurement in Financial Statements of Business Enterprises," *Statement of Financial Accounting Concepts No. 5* (Stamford, Conn.: FASB, 1984).

[10]A recent study noted that even within the income statement, problems exist. For example, this study noted that users believe that management sometimes reports unusual losses as non-recurring but reports unusual gains as part of regular income. Although users do not believe, in general, that managements intentionally present misleading information, they believe that much of the information that companies disseminate is too promotional and that troubled companies take great pains to convey the impression that they are not seriously troubled. AICPA Special Committee on Financial Reporting, "The Information Needs of Investors and Creditors," November 1993, p. 13.

So, what to do? *APB Opinion No. 9* **adopted a modified all-inclusive concept and requires application of this approach in practice.** A number of subsequent pronouncements require **irregular items** to be highlighted so that the reader of financial statements can better determine the long-run earning power of the enterprise. These items fall into five general categories:

❶ Discontinued operations.   **❹** Changes in accounting principle.
❷ Extraordinary items.   **❺** Changes in estimates.
❸ Unusual gains and losses.

Discontinued Operations

One of the most common types of irregular items is the disposal of a business or a product line. Because of the increasing importance of this type of event, *APB Opinion No. 30* developed a set of classification and disclosure requirements.[11]

A separate income statement category for the gain or loss from **disposal of a segment of a business** must be provided. In addition, the **results of operations of a segment that has been or will be disposed of** is reported in conjunction with the gain or loss on disposal—separately from continuing operations. The effects of discontinued operations are shown net of tax as a separate category, after continuing operations but before extraordinary items.

To illustrate, Multiplex Products, Inc., a highly diversified company, decides to discontinue its electronics division. During the current year, the electronics division lost $300,000 (net of tax) and was sold at the end of the year at a loss of $500,000 (net of tax). The information is shown on the current year's income statement as follows:

Income from continuing operations		$20,000,000
Discontinued operations		
Loss from operation of discontinued electronics		
division (net of tax)	$300,000	
Loss from disposal of electronics division (net of tax)	500,000	800,000
Net income		$19,200,000

ILLUSTRATION 4-6
Income Statement Presentation of Discontinued Operations

Further complications of measuring and reporting discontinued operations are addressed in Appendix 4A. Note that the phrase **"Income from continuing operations"** is only used when gains or losses on discontinued operations occur.

To qualify as discontinued operations, the assets, results of operations, and activities of a segment of a business must be clearly distinguishable, physically and operationally, from the other assets, results of operations, and activities of the entity.

Disposal of assets incidental to the evolution of the entity's business is not considered to be disposal of a segment of the business. **Disposals of assets that do *not* qualify as disposals of a segment** of a business include the following:

❶ Disposal of *part* of a line of business.
❷ Shifting production or marketing activities for a particular line of business from one location to another.
❸ Phasing out of a product line or class of service.
❹ Other changes due to a technological improvement.

Examples that would qualify as a disposal of a segment of a business are: (1) sale by a meat-packing company of a 53% interest in a professional football team, or (2) sale by a communications company of all of its radio stations but none of its television stations or publishing houses.

---

[11]The reporting requirements for discontinued operations are complex. These complexities are discussed more fully in the appendix to this chapter. Our purpose here is to illustrate the basic presentation of this information on the income statement.

Conversely, examples that would not qualify are (1) discontinuance by a children's wear manufacturer of its operations in Italy but not elsewhere, or (2) sale by a diversified company of one furniture-manufacturing subsidiary but not all furniture-manufacturing subsidiaries. Judgment must be exercised in defining a disposal of a segment of a business because the criteria are difficult to apply in some cases.

Extraordinary Items

Extraordinary items are defined as nonrecurring **material** items that differ significantly from the entity's typical business activities. *APB Opinion No. 30* cites the following criteria for extraordinary items:

> Extraordinary items are events and transactions that are distinguished by their unusual nature **and** by the infrequency of their occurrence. **Both** of the following criteria must be met to classify an event or transaction as an extraordinary item:
>
> (a) **Unusual Nature.** The underlying event or transaction should possess a high degree of abnormality and be of a type clearly unrelated to, or only incidentally related to, the ordinary and typical activities of the entity, taking into account the environment in which the entity operates.
>
> (b) **Infrequency of Occurrence.** The underlying event or transaction should be of a type that would not reasonably be expected to recur in the foreseeable future, taking into account the environment in which the entity operates.[12]

For further clarification, the APB specified that the following gains and losses are **not** extraordinary items:

> (a) Writedown or writeoff of receivables, inventories, equipment leased to others, deferred research and development costs, or other intangible assets.
>
> (b) Gains or losses from exchange or translation of foreign currencies, including those relating to major devaluations and revaluations.
>
> (c) Gains or losses on disposal of a segment of a business.
>
> (d) Other gains or losses from sale or abandonment of property, plant, or equipment used in the business.
>
> (e) Effects of a strike, including those against competitors and major suppliers.
>
> (f) Adjustment of accruals on long-term contracts.[13]

The items listed above are not considered extraordinary "because they are usual in nature and may be expected to recur as a consequence of customary and continuing business activities."

Only rarely does an event or transaction clearly meet the criteria specified in *APB Opinion 30*.[14] For example, gains or losses such as (a) and (d) above would be classified as extraordinary if they are a **direct result of a major casualty** (such as an earthquake), **an expropriation**, or **a prohibition under a newly enacted law or regulation**. Such circumstances would clearly meet the criteria of unusual and infrequent. A good example of an extraordinary item is the approximately $36 million loss incurred by Weyerhaeuser Company (forest and lumber) as a result of volcanic activity at Mount St. Helens. Standing timber, logs, buildings, equipment, and transportation systems covering 68,000 acres were destroyed by the volcanic eruption.

---

[12]"Reporting the Results of Operations," *Opinions of the Accounting Principles Board No. 30* (New York: AICPA, 1973), par. 20.

[13]Ibid., par. 23.

[14]Some contend that the criteria for an extraordinary item are so restrictive that only such items as a single chemist who knew the secret formula for an enterprise's mixing solution but was eaten by a tiger on a big game hunt or a plant facility that was smashed by a meteor would qualify for extraordinary item treatment.

In determining whether an item is extraordinary, **the environment in which the entity operates is of primary importance**. The environment includes such factors as industry characteristics, geographic location, and the nature and extent of governmental regulations. Thus, extraordinary item treatment is accorded the loss from hail damages to a tobacco grower's crops because severe damage from hailstorms in its locality is rare. On the other hand, frost damage to a citrus grower's crop in Florida does not qualify as extraordinary because frost damage is normally experienced every 3 or 4 years. In this environment, the criterion of infrequency is not met.

Similarly, when a company sells the only significant security investment it has ever owned, the gain or loss meets the criteria of an extraordinary item. Another company, however, that has a portfolio of securities acquired for investment purposes would not have an extraordinary item. Sale of such securities would be considered part of its ordinary and typical activities.

There are **exceptions** to the general rules provided above. The disposal of a business segment at a gain or loss [item (c) above], which is not an extraordinary item, requires special accounting treatment. In addition, **material gains and losses from extinguishment of debt** should be reported as an extraordinary item even though these gains or losses do not meet the normal criteria mentioned above for extraordinary items.[15] The rationale for this position will be discussed in Chapter 14.

Unfortunately, it is often difficult to determine what is extraordinary. Firm guidelines for judging when an item is or is not material have not been established. Some companies have shown as extraordinary gains or losses items that accounted for less than 1% of income.[16] In making the materiality judgment, extraordinary items should be considered individually, and not in the aggregate.[17]

In addition, considerable judgment must be exercised in determining whether an item should be reported as extraordinary. For example, some paper companies have had their forest lands condemned by the government for state or national parks or forests. Is such an event extraordinary, or is it part of normal operations? Such determination is not easy; much depends on the frequency of previous condemnations, the expectation of future condemnations, materiality, and the like.

Extraordinary items are to be shown net of taxes in a separate section in the income statement, usually just before net income. After listing the usual revenues, costs and expenses, and income taxes, the remainder of the statement shows:

Income before extraordinary items
Extraordinary items (less applicable income tax of $_____)
Net income

ILLUSTRATION 4-7
Income Statement Placement of Extraordinary Items

For example, Keystone Consolidated Industries, Inc. presented its extraordinary loss in this manner:

Keystone Consolidated Industries, Inc.

Income before extraordinary item	$11,638,000
Extraordinary item—flood loss (Note E)	1,216,000
Net income	$10,422,000

Note E: Extraordinary Item. The Keystone Steel and Wire Division's Steel Works experienced a flash flood on June 22. The extraordinary item represents the estimated cost, net of related income taxes of $1,279,000, to restore the steel works to full operation.

ILLUSTRATION 4-8
Income Statement Presentation of Extraordinary Items

[15]"Reporting Gains and Losses from Extinguishment of Debt," *Statement of Financial Accounting Standards No. 4* (Stamford, Conn.: FASB, 1975), par. 8.

[16]Another problem deals with what is referred to as the "big-bath" approach. Many companies, if they see that a large loss is inevitable, write off as much as possible on the theory that investors do not make that great a distinction between a small loss and a larger one. Future statements are also relieved of these charges and provide a company with a quick earnings injection.

[17]"Reporting the Results of Operations," op. cit., par. 24.

Unusual Gains and Losses

Because of the restrictive criteria for extraordinary items, financial statement users must carefully examine the financial statements for items that are **unusual or infrequent but not both**. As indicated earlier, items such as write-downs of inventories and gains and losses from fluctuation of foreign exchange are not considered extraordinary items. Thus, these items are sometimes shown with the normal, recurring revenues, costs, and expenses. If they are not material in amount, they are combined with other items in the income statement. If they are material, they must be disclosed separately, but are shown **above** "income (loss) before extraordinary items."

For example, Meredith Corporation presented an unusual charge in the following manner in a single-step income statement:[18]

ILLUSTRATION 4-9
Income Statement
Presentation of Unusual
Charges

Meredith Corporation	
Total revenues	$718,236,000
Operating costs and expenses	
Production, distribution and editorial	334,476,000
Selling, general and administrative	343,615,000
Depreciation and amortization	17,545,000
Unusual items (Note 6)	26,383,000
Total operating costs and expenses	722,019,000
Loss from operations	$ (3,783,000)

Note 6: Unusual Items.   In the fourth quarter, unusual items of $26,383,000 were charged to operations. These items included $12,983,000 in restructuring charges related to the Company's special voluntary early retirement program and selective job eliminations; a $10,000,000 write-off in the Book Group, due to repositioning and downsizing its direct mail operations, of inventory and deferred promotion costs; and $3,400,000 for other corporate charges.

In recent years there has been a tendency to **report unusual items in a separate section just above income from operations before income taxes and extraordinary items**, especially when there are multiple unusual items. For example, when General Electric Company experienced multiple unusual items in one year, it reported them in a separate "Unusual items" section of the income statement below "Income before unusual items and income taxes." When a multiple-step income statement is being prepared for homework purposes, unusual gains and losses should be reported in the other revenues and gains or other expenses and losses section unless you are instructed to prepare a separate unusual items section.[19]

---

[18]Hardly a day goes by that *The Wall Street Journal* does not announce that a well-known company has taken a restructuring charge. A restructuring charge relates to a major reorganization of company affairs, such as costs associated with employee layoffs, plant closing costs, write-offs of assets, and so on. A restructuring charge should not be reported as an extraordinary item, because these write-offs are considered part of a company's ordinary and typical activities.

Research in this area questions whether the "big bath" works. See, for example, Don Fried, Michael Schiff, and Ashwenpaul C. Sondhi, *Impairments and Writeoffs of Long-Lived Assets* (Montvale, NJ: NAA) and John A. Elliot and Wayne Shaw, "Write-offs as Accounting Procedures to Manage Perceptions," *Journal of Accounting Research* (Supplement—1988).

[19]As indicated in the opening story, many companies are reporting writedowns related to restructurings. A difficult question is whether these writedowns should be considered part of operating earnings. For example, some companies have taken restructuring charges practically every year. Citicorp took restructuring charges six years in a row, between 1988 and 1993. Eastman Kodak Co. did so five out of six years in 1989–1994. And Westinghouse Electric did so in seven out of the 10 years from 1985–1994. As one skeptic noted, "If you whip open your Webster's and look at the definition of 'nonrecurring' and it becomes an annual event, you take out the 'non'."

In dealing with events that are either unusual or nonrecurring but not both, the profession attempted to prevent a practice that many believed was misleading. Companies often reported such transactions on a net-of-tax basis and prominently displayed the earnings per share effect of these items. Although not captioned extraordinary items, they were presented in the same manner. Some had referred to these as "first cousins" to extraordinary items. As a consequence, the Board specifically **prohibited a net-of-tax treatment for such items** to ensure that users of financial statements can easily differentiate extraordinary items—which are reported net of tax—from material items that are unusual or infrequent, but not both.

Changes in Accounting Principle

Changes in accounting occur frequently in practice, because important events or conditions may be in dispute or uncertain at the statement date. One type of accounting change, therefore, comprises the normal recurring corrections and adjustments that are made by every business enterprise. Another accounting change results when an accounting principle is adopted that is different from the one previously used. Changes in accounting principle would include a change in the method of inventory pricing from FIFO to average cost or a change in depreciation from the double-declining to the straight-line method.[20]

Changes in accounting principle are recognized by including the cumulative effect net of tax in the current year's income statement. This amount is based on a retroactive computation of changing to a new accounting principle. **The effect on net income of adopting the new accounting principle should be disclosed as a separate item following extraordinary items in the income statement.**

To illustrate, Gaubert Inc. decided at the beginning of 1999 to change from the sum-of-the-years'-digits method of computing depreciation on its plant assets to the straight-line method. The assets originally cost $100,000 in 1997 and have a service life of 4 years. The data assumed for this illustration and the manner of reporting the change are as shown in Illustration 4-10.

Year	Sum-of-the-Years'-Digits Depreciation	Straight-Line Depreciation	Excess of Sum-of-the-Years'-Digits over Straight-Line Method
1997	$40,000	$25,000	$15,000
1998	30,000	25,000	5,000
Total			$20,000

ILLUSTRATION 4-10
Calculation of a Change in Accounting Principle

The information presented in the 1999 financial statements is shown in Illustration 4-11. (The tax rate was 30%.)

Income before extraordinary item and cumulative effect of a change in accounting principle	$120,000
Extraordinary item—casualty loss (net of $12,000 tax)	(28,000)
Cumulative effect on prior years of retroactive application of new depreciation method (net of $6,000 tax)	14,000
Net income	$106,000

ILLUSTRATION 4-11
Income Statement Presentation of a Change in Accounting Principle

---

[20]"Accounting Changes," *Opinions of the Accounting Principles Board No. 20* (New York: AICPA, 1971), par. 18. Chapter 23 examines in greater detail the problems related to accounting changes; our purpose now is to provide general guidance for the major types of transactions affecting the income statement.

Changes in Estimates

Estimates are inherent in the accounting process. Estimates are made, for example, of useful lives and salvage values of depreciable assets, of uncollectible receivables, of inventory obsolescence, and of the number of periods expected to benefit from a particular expenditure. Not infrequently, as time passes, as circumstances change, or as additional information is obtained, even estimates originally made in good faith must be changed. Such **changes in estimates** are accounted for in the period of change if they affect only that period, or in the period of change and future periods if the change affects both.

To illustrate a change in estimate that affects only the period of change, assume that DuPage Materials Corp. has consistently estimated its bad debt expense at 1% of credit sales. In 1998, however, DuPage's controller determines that the estimate of bad debts for the current year's credit sales must be revised upward to 2%, or double the prior years' percentage. Using 2% results in a bad debt charge of $240,000 or double the amount using the 1% estimate for prior years. The 2% rate is necessary to reduce accounts receivable to net realizable value. The provision is recorded at December 31, 1998, as follows:

Bad Debt Expense	240,000	
Allowance for Doubtful Accounts		240,000

The entire change in estimate is included in 1998 income because no future periods are affected by the change. **Changes in estimate are not handled retroactively**, that is, carried back to adjust prior years. Changes in estimate that affect both the current period and future periods are examined in greater detail in Chapter 23. **Changes in estimate are not considered errors (prior period adjustments) or extraordinary items.**

Summary of Irregular Items

UNDERLYING CONCEPTS

The AICPA Special Committee on Financial Reporting indicates a company's core activities—usual and recurring events—provide the best historical data from which users determine trends and relationships and make their predictions about the future. Therefore, the effects of core and non-core activities should be separately displayed.

The public accounting profession now tends to accept a modified all-inclusive income concept instead of the current operating performance concept. Except for a couple of items (discussed later in this chapter) that are charged or credited directly to retained earnings, all other irregular gains or losses or nonrecurring items are closed to Income Summary and are included in the income statement. Of these, **discontinued operations of a segment** of a business is classified as a separate item in the income statement after continuing operations. The **unusual, material, nonrecurring items** that are significantly different from the typical or customary business activities are shown in a separate section for **"extraordinary items"** below discontinued operations. Other items of a material amount that are of an **unusual or nonrecurring** nature and are **not considered extraordinary** are separately disclosed. In addition, the cumulative adjustment that occurs when a change in accounting principles develops is disclosed as a separate item just before net income.

Because of the numerous intermediate income figures that are created by the reporting of these irregular items, careful evaluation of information reported by the financial press is needed. For example, at one time when RCA reported its first-quarter results, *The Wall Street Journal* reported that "RCA earnings climbed by 47% in the first quarter" as compared with the first quarter of last year. Conversely, *The New York Times* reported the following regarding the same first-quarter results, "RCA Slides 46%." Which article was correct? Both articles were factually correct. The difference arose because the *Times* article, in making its comparison with the quarter of the previous year, included the unusual nonrecurring gains in the income of the earlier quarter, whereas *The Wall Street Journal* did not. Such an illustration demonstrates the importance of understanding the intermediate components of net income.

Illustration 4-12 summarizes the basic concepts previously discussed. Although the chart is simplified, it provides a useful framework for determining the proper treatment of special items affecting the income statement.

ILLUSTRATION 4-12
Summary of Irregular
Items in the Income
Statement

Type of Situation[a]	Criteria	Examples	Placement on Financial Statements
Discontinued operations	Disposal of a segment of a business constituting a separate line of business or class of customer.	Sale by diversified company of major division that represents only activities in electronics industry. Food distributor that sells wholesale to supermarket chains and through fast-food restaurants decides to discontinue the division that sells to one of two classes of customers.	Shown in separate section of the income statement after continuing operations but before extraordinary items. (Shown net of tax.)
Extraordinary items	Material, and both unusual and infrequent (nonrecurring).	Gains or losses resulting from casualties, an expropriation, or a prohibition under a new law.[b]	Separate section in the income statement entitled extraordinary items. (Shown net of tax.)
Unusual gains or losses, not considered extraordinary	Material; character typical of the customary business activities; unusual or infrequent but not both.	Write-downs of receivables, inventories; adjustments of accrued contract prices; gains or losses from fluctuations of foreign exchange; gains or losses from sales of assets used in business.	Separate section in income statement above income before extraordinary items. Often reported in other revenues and gains or other expenses and losses section. (Not shown net of tax.)
Changes in principle[c]	Change from one generally accepted principle to another.	Changing the basis of inventory pricing from FIFO to average cost; change in the method of depreciation from accelerated to straight-line.	Cumulative effect of the change is reflected in the income statement between the captions extraordinary items and net income. (Shown net of tax.)
Changes in estimates	Normal, recurring corrections and adjustments.	Changes in the realizability of receivables and inventories; changes in estimated lives of equipment, intangible assets; changes in estimated liability for warranty costs, income taxes, and salary payments.	Change in income statement only in the account affected. (Not shown net of tax.)

[a]This summary provides only the general rules to be followed in accounting for the various situations described above. Exceptions do exist in some of these situations.
[b]Material gains and losses from extinguishment of debt are considered extraordinary, even though criteria for extraordinary items may not be met.
[c]The general rule per *APB Opinion No. 20* is to use the cumulative effect approach. However, all the recent FASB pronouncements require or permit the retroactive method whenever a new standard is adopted for the first time.

❖ SPECIAL REPORTING ISSUES

Intraperiod Tax Allocation

We noted that certain irregular items are shown on the income statement net of tax. Many believe that the resulting income tax effect should be directly associated with that event or item. In other words, the tax expense for the year should be related, where possible, to **specific** items on the income statement to provide a more informative disclosure to statement users. This procedure is called **intraperiod tax allocation**, that is, allocation within a period. Its main purpose is to relate the income tax expense of the fiscal period to the items that affect the amount of the tax provisions. Intraperiod tax allocation is used for the following items: (1) income from continuing operations, (2) discontinued operations, (3) extraordinary items, and (4) changes in accounting principle. The general concept is **"let the tax follow the income."**

Objective ❺
Explain intraperiod tax allocation.

The income tax expense attributable to "income from continuing operations" is computed by finding the income tax expense related to revenue and to expense transactions used in determining this income. In this tax computation, no effect is given to the tax consequences of the items excluded from the determination of "income from continuing operations." A separate tax effect is then associated with each irregular item.

Extraordinary Gains

In applying the concept of intraperiod tax allocation, assume that Schindler Co. has income before tax and extraordinary item of $250,000 and an extraordinary gain from the sale of a single stock investment of $100,000. If the income tax rate is assumed to be 30%, the following information is presented on the income statement:

ILLUSTRATION 4-13
Intraperiod Tax
Allocation,
Extraordinary Gain

Income before income tax and extraordinary item		$250,000
Income tax		75,000
Income before extraordinary item		175,000
Extraordinary gain—sale of investment	$100,000	
Less applicable income tax	30,000	70,000
Net income		$245,000

The income tax of $75,000 ($250,000 × 30%) attributable to "income before income tax and extraordinary item" is determined from revenue and expense transactions related to this income. In this income tax computation, the tax consequences of items excluded from the determination of "income before income tax and extraordinary item" are not considered. The "extraordinary gain—sale of investment" then shows a separate tax effect of $30,000.

Extraordinary Losses

To illustrate the reporting of an extraordinary loss, assume that Schindler Co. has income before income tax and extraordinary item of $250,000 and an extraordinary loss from a major casualty of $100,000. Assuming a 30% tax rate, the presentation of income tax on the income statement would be as follows:

ILLUSTRATION 4-14
Intraperiod Tax
Allocation,
Extraordinary Loss

Income before income tax and extraordinary item		$250,000
Income tax		75,000
Income before extraordinary item		175,000
Extraordinary item-loss from casualty	$100,000	
Less applicable income tax reduction	30,000	70,000
Net income		$105,000

In this case, the loss provides a positive tax benefit of $30,000 and, therefore, is subtracted from the $100,000 loss.

An extraordinary item may be reported "net of tax" with note disclosure as illustrated below:

ILLUSTRATION 4-15
Note Disclosure of
Intraperiod Tax
Allocation

Income before income tax and extraordinary item	$250,000
Income tax	75,000
Income before extraordinary item	175,000
Extraordinary item, less applicable income	
tax reduction (Note 1)	70,000
Net income	$105,000

Note 1: During the year the Company suffered a major casualty loss of $70,000, net of applicable income tax reduction of $30,000.

Earnings per Share

The results of a company's operations are customarily summed up in one important figure: net income. As if this condensation were not enough of a simplification, the financial world has widely accepted an even more distilled and compact figure as its most significant business indicator—**earnings per share**.

The computation of earnings per share is usually straightforward. **Net income minus preferred dividends (income available to common stockholders) is divided by the weighted average of common shares outstanding to arrive at earnings per share.**[21] To illustrate, assume that Lancer, Inc. reports net income of $350,000 and declares and pays preferred dividends of $50,000 for the year. The weighted average number of common shares outstanding during the year is 100,000 shares. Earnings per share is $3.00, as computed in Illustration 4-16.

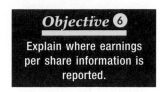

Objective **6**

Explain where earnings per share information is reported.

$$\frac{\text{Net Income} - \text{Preferred Dividends}}{\text{Weighted Average of Common Shares Outstanding}} = \text{Earnings per Share}$$

$$\frac{\$350,000 - \$50,000}{100,000} = \$3.00$$

ILLUSTRATION 4-16
Equation Illustrating Computation of Earnings per Share

Note that the EPS figure measures the number of dollars earned by each share of common stock—but not the dollar amount paid to stockholders in the form of dividends.

"Net income per share" or "earnings per share" is a ratio commonly used in prospectuses, proxy material, and annual reports to stockholders. It is also highlighted in the financial press, by statistical services like Standard & Poor's, and by Wall Street securities analysts. Because of its importance, **earnings per share is required to be disclosed on the face of the income statement**. A company that reports a discontinued operation, an extraordinary item, or the cumulative effect of a change in accounting principle, must report per share amounts for these line items either on the face of the income statement or in the notes to the financial statements.[22]

To illustrate both the income statement order of presentation and the earnings per share data, we present an income statement for Poquito Industries, Inc. in Illustration 4-17. Notice the order in which data are shown. In addition, per share information is shown at the bottom. Assume that the company had 100,000 shares outstanding for the entire year. The Poquito Industries Inc. income statement, in Illustration 4-17, is highly condensed. Items such as the "Unusual Charge," "Discontinued Operations," "Extraordinary Item," and the "Change in Accounting Principle" would have to be described fully and appropriately in the statement or related notes.

Many corporations have simple capital structures that include only common stock. For these companies, a presentation such as "earnings per common share" is appropriate on the income statement. In many instances, however, companies' earnings per share are subject to dilution (reduction) in the future because existing contingencies permit the issuance of additional common shares.[23]

In summary, the simplicity and availability of figures for per share earnings lead inevitably to their widespread use. Because of the undue importance that the public, even the well-informed public, attaches to earnings per share, the earnings per share figure must be made as meaningful as possible.

---

[21]In the calculation of earnings per share, preferred dividends are deducted from net income if declared or if cumulative though not declared.

[22]"Earnings Per Share," *Statement of Financial Accounting Standards No. 128* (Norwalk, Conn.: FASB, 1996).

[23]Ibid. The computational problems involved in accounting for these dilutive securities in earnings per share computations are discussed in Chapter 17.

ILLUSTRATION 4-17
Comprehensive Income
Statement

Poquito Industries, Inc. INCOME STATEMENT For the Year Ended December 31, 1998		
Sales revenue		$1,480,000
Cost of goods sold		600,000
Gross profit		880,000
Selling and administrative expenses		320,000
Income from operations		560,000
Other revenues and gains		
Interest revenue		10,000
Other expenses and losses		
Loss on disposal of part of Textile Division	$ (5,000)	
Unusual charge—loss on sale of investments	(45,000)	(50,000)
Income from continuing operations before income tax		520,000
Income tax		208,000
Income from continuing operations		312,000
Discontinued operations		
Income from operations of Pizza Division, less applicable income tax of $24,800	54,000	
Loss on disposal of Pizza Division, less applicable income tax of $41,000	(90,000)	(36,000)
Income before extraordinary item and cumulative effect of accounting change		276,000
Extraordinary item—loss from earthquake, less applicable income tax of $23,000		(45,000)
Cumulative effect in prior years of retroactive application of new depreciation method, less applicable income tax of $30,900		(60,000)
Net income		$ 171,000
Per share of common stock		
Income from continuing operations		$3.12
Income from operations of discontinued division, net of tax		.54
Loss on disposal of discontinued operation, net of tax		(.90)
Income before extraordinary item and cumulative effect		2.76
Extraordinary loss, net of tax		(.45)
Cumulative effect of change in accounting principle, net of tax		(.60)
Net income		$1.71

Retained Earnings Statement

Objective 7

Prepare a retained
earnings statement.

Net income increases retained earnings and a net loss decreases retained earnings. Both cash and stock dividends decrease retained earnings. Prior period adjustments may either increase or decrease retained earnings. A prior period adjustment is a correction of an error in the financial statements of a prior period. Prior period adjustments (net of tax) are charged or credited to the opening balance of retained earnings, and thus excluded from the determination of net income for the current period.

Information related to retained earnings may be shown in different ways. For example, some companies prepare a separate retained earnings statement, as shown in Illustration 4-18 on the next page. The reconciliation of the beginning to the ending balance in retained earnings provides information about why net assets increased or decreased during the year. The association of dividend distributions with net income for the period indicates what management is doing with earnings: It may be "plowing back" into the business part or all of the earnings, distributing all current income, or distributing current income plus the accumulated earnings of prior years.

Appropriations of Retained Earnings

Retained earnings is often restricted—**appropriated**—in accordance with contractual requirements, board of directors' policy, or the apparent necessity of the moment. The amounts of retained earnings appropriated are transferred to Appropriated Retained

ILLUSTRATION 4-18
Retained Earnings
Statement

TIGER WOODS INC. Retained Earnings Statement For the Year Ended December 31, 1999		
Balance, January 1, as reported		$1,050,000
Correction for understatement of net income in prior period (inventory error)		50,000
Balance, January 1, as adjusted		1,100,000
Add: Net income		360,000
		1,460,000
Less: Cash dividends	$100,000	
Stock dividends	200,000	300,000
Balance, December 31		$1,160,000

Earnings. The retained earnings section may therefore report two separate amounts— (1) retained earnings free (unrestricted) and (2) retained earnings appropriated (restricted). The total of these two amounts equals the total retained earnings.

Combined Income and Retained Earnings Statement

The income statement and retained earnings statement are sometimes combined into one report. The principal advantage of a combined statement is that all items affecting income, including operating items and prior period adjustments, appear in one report. On the other hand, net income for the year is "buried" in the body of the statement, a feature that some find objectionable. There once was a definite trend toward this method of presentation, but it is no longer gaining in favor.

When a combined statement is prepared, the income statement is presented as if it were to be issued as an independent report. But, instead of ending that statement with net income, the reconciliation of retained earnings is shown beneath it (as shown in Illustration 4-19).

ILLUSTRATION 4-19
Reconciliation of
Retained Earnings with
Income Statement

The Magnavox Company COMBINED INCOME AND RETAINED EARNINGS STATEMENT (lower portion only)	
Net income for the year	42,290,385
Retained earnings at beginning of year	106,734,310
	149,024,695
Cash dividends declared and paid	15,764,250
Retained earnings at end of year	$133,260,445

Comprehensive Income

As indicated earlier, the all-inclusive income concept is used in determining financial performance for a period of time. Under this concept, all revenues, expenses, and gains and losses recognized during the period are included in income. However, over time, specific exceptions to this general concept have developed so that certain items now bypass income and are reported directly in equity. An example of one of these items is unrealized gains and losses on available-for-sale securities.[24]

---

[24]Available-for-sale securities are further discussed in Chapter 18. Examples of other comprehensive items are translation gains and losses on foreign currency and excess of additional pension liability over unrecognized prior service cost.

Why are these gains and losses on available-for-sale securities excluded from net income? Because disclosing them separately (1) reduces the volatility of net income due to fluctuations in fair value, yet (2) informs the financial statement user of the gain or loss that would be incurred if the securities were sold at fair value.

Items that bypass the income statement are included under the concept of comprehensive income. **Comprehensive income** includes all changes in equity during a period except those resulting from investments by owners and distributions to owners. Comprehensive income, therefore, includes all revenues and gains, expenses and losses reported in net income, and, in addition it includes gains and losses that bypass net income but affect stockholders' equity. These items that bypass the income statement are referred to as **other comprehensive income**.

The users of financial statements have expressed concern over the increasing number of items that are being reported as other comprehensive income (adjustments to stockholders' equity). As one set of writers noted, equity is becoming a dumpster for an amorphous and growing mass of important information. As more and different types of items are reported as adjustments to stockholders' equity, many argue that a separate new statement is needed to report the information in an organized way.

Recently, the FASB evaluated several approaches to providing more information about other comprehensive income items. It decided that the components of other comprehensive income must be displayed in one of three ways: (1) a second separate income statement; (2) a combined income statement of comprehensive income; or (3) as a part of the statement of stockholders' equity.[25]

Regardless of the format used, net income must be added to other comprehensive income to arrive at comprehensive income. Earnings per share information related to comprehensive income is not required. To illustrate these three presentation formats, assume that V. Gill Inc. reports the following information for 1999: sales revenue $800,000, cost of goods sold $600,000, operating expenses $90,000, and an unrealized holding gain on available-for-sale securities of $30,000, net of tax.[26]

Second Income Statement

The two income statement format is shown below:

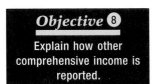

Objective 8

Explain how other comprehensive income is reported.

ILLUSTRATION 4-20
Two Statement Format:
Comprehensive Income

V. Gill Inc. Income Statement For the Year Ended December 31, 1999	
Sales revenue	$800,000
Cost of goods sold	600,000
Gross profit	200,000
Operating expenses	90,000
Net income	$110,000

V. Gill Inc. Comprehensive Income Statement For the Year Ended December 31, 1999	
Net income	$110,000
Other comprehensive income	
Unrealized holding gain, net of tax	30,000
Comprehensive income	$140,000

---

[25]"Reporting Comprehensive Income," *Statement of Financial Accounting Standards No. 130* (Norwalk, Conn: FASB, June 1997)

[26]A company is required to display the components of other comprehensive income either (1) net of related tax effects or (2) before related tax effects with one amount shown for the aggregate amount of tax related to the total amount of other comprehensive income. Under either alternative, each component of other comprehensive income must be shown, net of related taxes either in the face of the statement or in the notes.

Reporting comprehensive income in a separate statement indicates that the gains and losses identified as other comprehensive income have the same status as traditional gains and losses. In addition, the relationship of the traditional income statement to the comprehensive income statement is apparent because net income is the starting point in the comprehensive income statement.

Combined Income Statement

The second approach provides a combined statement in which the traditional net income would be a subtotal, with total comprehensive income shown as a final total. A combined statement of comprehensive income is shown in Illustration 4-21 below:

V. Gill Inc. Combined Statement of Comprehensive Income For the Year Ended December 31, 1999	
Sales revenue	$800,000
Cost of goods sold	600,000
Gross profit	200,000
Operating expenses	90,000
Net income	110,000
Unrealized holding gain, net of tax	30,000
Comprehensive income	$140,000

ILLUSTRATION 4-21
Combined Income
Statement Format:
Comprehensive Income

As shown, comprehensive income is $140,000 and net income is $110,000; the difference is due to the unrealized holding gain of $30,000. The combined statement has the advantage of not requiring the creation of a new financial statement. However, burying net income in a subtotal on the statement is a disadvantage.

Statement of Stockholders' Equity

A third approach is to report other comprehensive income items in a **statement of stockholders' equity** (often referred to as statement of changes in stockholders' equity). This statement reports the changes in each stockholder's equity account and in total stockholders' equity during the year. The statement of stockholders' equity is often **prepared in columnar form** with columns for each account and for total stockholders' equity.

To illustrate its presentation, assume the same information above related to V. Gill Inc. and that the company had the following stockholder equity account balances at the beginning of 1999: Common Stock $300,000; Retained Earnings $50,000; and Accumulated Other Comprehensive Income $60,000. No changes in the Common Stock account occurred during the year. A statement of stockholders' equity for V. Gill Inc. is shown below.

V. Gill Inc. Statement of Stockholders' Equity For the Year Ended December 31, 1999					
	Total	Comprehensive Income	Retained Earnings	Accumulated Other Comprehensive Income	Common Stock
Beginning balance	$410,000		$ 50,000	$60,000	$300,000
Comprehensive Income					
Net income	110,000	$110,000	110,000		
Other comprehensive income					
Unrealized holding gain net of tax	30,000	30,000		30,000	
Comprehensive income		$140,000			
Ending balance	$550,000		$160,000	$90,000	$300,000

ILLUSTRATION 4-22
Presentation of
Comprehensive Income
Items in Stockholders'
Equity Statement

Most companies will probably use the statement of stockholders' equity approach to provide information related to the components of other comprehensive income. Many companies already provide a statement of stockholders' equity; adding additional columns to display information related to comprehensive income is not costly.

Balance Sheet Presentation

Regardless of the display format used, the **accumulated other comprehensive income** of $90,000 is reported in the stockholders' equity section of the balance sheet of V. Gill Inc. as follows:

V. Gill Inc. Balance Sheet As of December 31, 1999 (Stockholders' Equity Section)	
Stockholders' Equity	
Common stock	300,000
Retained earnings	160,000
Accumulated other comprehensive income	90,000
Total stockholders' equity	550,000

By providing information on the components of comprehensive income as well as total accumulated other comprehensive income, the firm communicates information about all changes in net assets.[27] With this information, users will be better able to understand the quality of the company's earnings. This information should help users predict the amount, timing, and uncertainty of future cash flows.

Observations on Comprehensive Income

The FASB encourages, but does not require, that the term comprehensive income be used. The reason is that many oppose the use of the term comprehensive income because they believe this amount is neither "comprehensive" nor is it "income." Therefore, many companies will undoubtedly use terms such as "total nonowner changes in equity" instead of comprehensive income.

As indicated earlier, it is also likely that most companies will not report the components of comprehensive income using an income statement approach. Rather, the information related to comprehensive income will be reported in the statement of stockholders' equity. If companies choose to report the components of other comprehensive income in a statement of stockholders' equity, that statement must be displayed as a primary financial statement.[28]

SUMMARY OF LEARNING OBJECTIVES

❶ ***Identify the uses and limitations of an income statement.*** The income statement provides investors and creditors with information that helps them predict the amounts, timing, and uncertainty of future cash flows. Also, the income statement helps users determine the risk (level of uncertainty) of not achieving particular cash flows. The limitations of an income statement are: (1) the statement does not include many items that contribute to general growth and well-being of an

---

[27]Note that prior period adjustments and the cumulative effect of changes in accounting principle are not considerded other comprehensive income items.

[28]Some companies such as General Motors have provided a statement of stockholders' equity only in the notes to the financial statements. If it chooses to report its comprehensive income information in the statement of stockholders' equity, it will now have to give it equal prominence with the balance sheet, income statement and statement of cash flows.

enterprise; and (2) income numbers are often affected by the accounting methods used.

The *capital maintenance approach* takes the net assets or "capital values" based on some valuation and measures income by the difference in capital values at two points in time. The *transaction approach* focuses on the activities that have occurred during a given period; instead of presenting only a net change, it discloses the components of the change. The transaction approach to income measurement requires the use of revenue, expense, loss, and gain accounts.

② ***Prepare a single-step income statement.*** In a single-step income statement, just two groupings exist: revenues and expenses. Expenses are deducted from revenues to arrive at net income or loss—a single subtraction. Frequently, income tax is reported separately as the last item before net income to indicate its relationship to income before income tax.

③ ***Prepare a multiple-step income statement.*** A multiple-step income statement shows two further classifications: (1) a separation of operating results from those obtained through the subordinate or nonoperating activities of the company; and (2) a classification of expenses by functions, such as merchandising or manufacturing, selling, and administration.

④ ***Explain how irregular items are reported.*** Irregular gains or losses or nonrecurring items are generally closed to Income Summary and are included in the income statement. These are treated in the income statement as follows: (1) Discontinued operation of a segment of a business is classified as a separate item, after continuing operations. (2) The unusual, material, nonrecurring items that are significantly different from the customary business activities are shown in a separate section for "extraordinary items," below discontinued operations. (3) Other items of a material amount that are of an unusual or nonrecurring nature and are not considered extraordinary are separately disclosed. (4) The cumulative adjustment that occurs when a change in accounting principles develops is disclosed as a separate item, just before net income.

⑤ ***Explain intraperiod tax allocation.*** The tax expense for the year should be related, where possible, to specific items on the income statement, to provide a more informative disclosure to statement users. This procedure is called intraperiod tax allocation, that is, allocation within a period. Its main purpose is to relate the income tax expense for the fiscal period to the following items that affect the amount of the tax provisions: (1) income from continuing operations, (2) discontinued operations, (3) extraordinary items, and (4) changes in accounting principle.

⑥ ***Explain where earnings per share information is reported.*** Because of the inherent dangers of focusing attention solely on earnings per share, the profession concluded that earnings per share must be disclosed on the face of the income statement. A company that reports a discontinued operation, an extraordinary item, or the cumulative effect of a change in accounting principle, must report per share amounts for these line items either on the face of the income statement or in the notes to the financial statements.

⑦ ***Prepare a retained earnings statement.*** The retained earnings statement should disclose net income (loss), dividends, prior period adjustments, and transfers to and from retained earnings (appropriations).

⑧ ***Explain how other comprehensive income is reported.*** The components of other comprehensive income are reported in a second income statement, a combined income statement of comprehensive income, or in a statement of stockholders' equity.

Appendix 4A

Accounting for Discontinued Operations

Objective ❾

After studying Appendix 4A, you should be able to: Measure and report gains and losses from discontinued operations.

The chapter discussed how and where gains and losses related to discontinued operations are reported on the income statement. This appendix discusses the more technical aspects of how such a gain or loss is computed, along with related reporting issues.

Recall that the assets, results of operations, and activities of a **business segment** must be clearly distinguishable, physically and operationally, to qualify for discontinued operations treatment. Recall, too, that in the income statement, discontinued operations are classified as a separate item, net of tax, after continuing operations.

❖ FIRST ILLUSTRATION—NO PHASE-OUT PERIOD

To illustrate the accounting for a discontinued operation, assume that the Board of Directors of Heartland Inc. decided on October 1, 1997, to sell a division of their company called Record Phonograph. Record Phonograph had provided phonograph records for Heartland's 15 retail stores. Heartland's management could see that the compact disc was revolutionizing the stereo industry and would soon render its phonograph division unprofitable. Fortunately, a buyer was available immediately and the division was sold on October 1, 1997.

Heartland Inc. had income of $2,000,000 for the year 1997, not including a $150,000 loss from operations of Record Phonograph from January 1 to October 1, 1997. Heartland Inc. was able to sell the division at a gain of $400,000. Its tax rate on all items was 30%.

Heartland's accountants first must decide whether to treat the sale as a discontinued operation. The assets and operations of Record Phonograph can be easily identified, and the record business is distinct from Heartland's other lines of business. Accordingly, **the disposal of Record Phonograph does constitute the disposal of a segment of the business.**

For the period up to the time management commits itself to sell the division, the revenues and expenses of the discontinued operations are aggregated and reported as income or loss on discontinued operations, net of tax. The date at which time management formally commits itself to a formal plan to dispose of a segment of the business is referred to as the **measurement date**. In this case, it is October 1, 1997. The plan of disposal should include, as a minimum:

❶ Identification of the major assets to be disposed of.
❷ The expected method of disposal.
❸ The period expected to be required for completion of the disposal.
❹ An active program to find a buyer if disposal is to be by sale.
❺ Estimated results of operations of the segment from the measurement date to the disposal date.
❻ Estimated proceeds or salvage to be realized by disposal.

Because the segment has actually been sold on October 1, 1997, a gain or loss on disposal is computed. This date is referred to as the **disposal date**. Because the measurement date and the disposal date are the same, no unusual complications occur. The following diagram illustrates Heartland's situation:

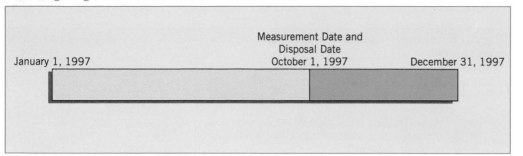

January 1, 1997

Measurement Date and
Disposal Date
October 1, 1997

December 31, 1997

ILLUSTRATION 4A-1
Example of Discontinued
Operations with No
Phase-Out Period

The condensed income statement presentation for Heartland Inc. for 1997 is as follows:

Income from continuing operations before income taxes		$2,000,000
Income taxes		600,000
Income from continuing operations		1,400,000
Discontinued operations:		
Loss from operation of Record Phonograph, less applicable income taxes of $45,000	$(105,000)	
Gain on disposal of Record Phonograph, less applicable income taxes of $120,000	280,000	175,000
Net income		$1,575,000

ILLUSTRATION 4A-2
Presentation of Discontinued Operations, No
Phase-Out Period

❖ SECOND ILLUSTRATION—PHASE-OUT PERIOD

In practice the measurement date and the disposal date are rarely the same. Normally, the disposal date would be later than the measurement date. Thus, **the gain or loss on disposal would be the sum of**:

❶ Income (loss) from the measurement date to the disposal date (called the phase-out period).
❷ Gain (loss) on the disposal of the net assets.

The reason for aggregating the above two items to compute the gain (loss) on disposal is that the selling company needs a reasonable period to phase out its discontinued operations. The income (loss) from operations of the discontinued segment is part of the computation of the gain (loss) on disposal because the phase-out period often enables the seller to obtain a better selling price.

To illustrate the combination of these two components, assume that Heartland's sale of Record Phonograph does not occur until December 1, 1997, at which time it is sold at a gain of $350,000. During the period October 1, 1997, to December 1, 1997, the Record Phonograph division suffered a loss of $50,000 from operations. The following diagram illustrates Heartland's situation.

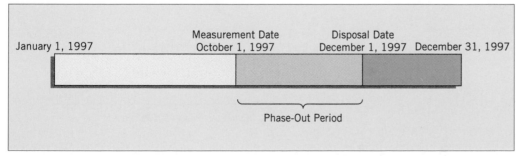

January 1, 1997

Measurement Date
October 1, 1997

Disposal Date
December 1, 1997   December 31, 1997

Phase-Out Period

ILLUSTRATION 4A-3
Example of Discontinued
Operations with Phase-
Out Period

The condensed income statement presentation for Heartland Inc. for 1997 is as follows:

ILLUSTRATION 4A-4
Presentation of Discontinued Operations with
Phase-Out Period

Income from continuing operations before income taxes		$2,000,000
Income taxes		600,000
Income from continuing operations		1,400,000
Discontinued operations:		
Loss from operation of Record Phonograph, less applicable income taxes of $45,000	$(105,000)	
Gain on disposal of Record Phonograph, including operating loss of $50,000 and gain on disposal of $350,000, less applicable income taxes of $90,000	210,000	105,000
Net income		$1,505,000

❖ THIRD ILLUSTRATION—EXTENDED PHASE-OUT PERIOD

In the preceding illustration, the disposal of the discontinued operation occurred in the same accounting period as the measurement date. As a result, determining the proper gain or loss on the disposal of Record Phonograph at the end of year was straightforward. However, the phase-out period often extends into another year. In this case, *APB Opinion No. 30* states that **if a loss is expected on disposal, the estimated loss should be reported at the measurement date. If a gain on disposal is expected, it should be recognized when realized, which is ordinarily the disposal date.** In other words, the profession has taken a conservative position by recognizing losses immediately but deferring gains until realized.

Implementing these general rules can be troublesome. In order to determine the gain or loss on disposal of the segment, the income (loss) from operations must be estimated and then combined with the estimated gain (loss) on sale. If a net loss results, then it is recognized at the measurement date. If a net gain arises, it generally is recognized at the date of disposal. **The major exception is when realized gains exceed estimated unrealized and realized net losses. In that special case, realized gains can be recognized in the period of the measurement date.**

Net Loss

To illustrate, assume that Heartland Inc. expects to sell its Record Phonograph division on May 1, 1998, at a gain of $350,000. In addition, from October 1, 1997, to December 31, 1997, it realized a loss of $400,000 on operations for this segment and expects to lose an additional $200,000 on it from January 1, 1998, to May 1, 1998. The following diagram illustrates Heartland's situation.

ILLUSTRATION 4A-5
Example of Discontinued
Operations with
Extended Phase-Out
Period

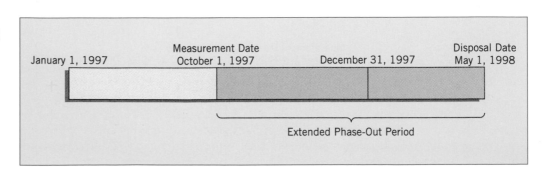

The computation of the net gain or loss on disposal is shown in Illustration 4A-6.

Realized loss on operations October 1–December 31, 1997	$(400,000)
Expected loss on operations January 1–May 1, 1998	(200,000)
Expected gain on sale of assets on May 1, 1998	350,000
Net loss on disposal	$(250,000)

ILLUSTRATION 4A-6
Computation of the Net
Loss on Disposal

Given that a net loss on disposal is expected, the loss on disposal is recognized in the period of the measurement date. The condensed income statement presentation for Heartland Inc. for 1997 is therefore reported as shown in Illustration 4A-7.

Income from continuing operations before income taxes		$2,000,000
Income taxes		600,000
Income from continuing operations		1,400,000
Discontinued operations:		
Loss from operation of Record Phonograph, net of applicable income taxes of $45,000	$(105,000)	
Loss on disposal of Record Phonograph, including provision for losses during phase-out period, $600,000, and estimated gain on sale of assets, $350,000, net of applicable income taxes of $75,000	(175,000)	(280,000)
Net income		$1,120,000

ILLUSTRATION 4A-7
Presentation of Expected
Loss from Discontinued
Operations

If the estimated amounts of any of the items later prove to be incorrect, the correction should be reported in the later period when the estimate is determined to be incorrect. Prior periods should not be restated.

Net Gain

To illustrate recognition of a realized gain and deferral of an unrealized gain in the same discontinued operation, assume that Heartland Inc. expects to sell its Record Phonograph division on May 1, 1998, at a gain of $350,000. In addition, from October 1, 1997, to December 31, 1997, it realized income of $200,000 on operations for this segment and expects to earn an additional $100,000 of profit on it from January 1, 1998, to May 1, 1998. The computation of the net gain or loss on disposal is as follows:

Realized income on operations October 1–December 31, 1997	$200,000
Expected income on operations January 1–May 1, 1998	100,000
Expected gain on sale of assets on May 1, 1998	350,000
Net gain on disposal	$650,000

ILLUSTRATION 4A-8
Computation of Net Gain
on Disposal

When a net gain on disposal is expected, the gain should be analyzed and classified into realized and unrealized amounts. In this situation, $200,000 of realized income is recognized in 1997 from the October 1–December 31 operations and $450,000 ($100,000 + $350,000) of unrealized gain is deferred to 1998. Assuming that the phonograph division, as before, suffers a loss of $150,000 from operations between January 1 and October 1, 1997, the discontinued operations section of the income statements for 1997 and 1998 would appear as follows:

ILLUSTRATION 4A-9
Presentation of Gain
from Discontinued
Operations

	1997	
Discontinued operations		
Loss from operations of Record Phonograph,		
less applicable income taxes of $45,000	$(105,000)	
Gain on disposal of Record Phonograph,		
less applicable income taxes of $60,000	140,000	35,000
	1998	
Discontinued operations		
Gain on disposal of Record Phonograph,		
less applicable income taxes of $135,000		$315,000

If a net unrealized loss of $150,000 had been expected during the 1998 portion of the extended phase-out period, instead of the $450,000 unrealized gain noted above, a net realized gain on disposal of $50,000 ($200,000 − $150,000) before income taxes would be recognized in 1997.

Summary

All realized and estimated unrealized gains and losses related to the extended phase-out period are netted as one "event" after the measurement date. To determine the amount to be reported on the "gain or loss from disposal of a segment" line (the second line of the discontinued operations section), the following simple algorithm may be used: If an overall loss is computed for the extended phase-out period, the amount reported is the overall loss; if an overall gain is computed, the amount reported is the lesser of the overall gain or the realized gain.

❖ EXTENDED PHASE-OUT—ADDITIONAL EXAMPLES

Provided in Illustration 4A-10 are some additional cases to help you understand how the gain (loss) on disposal of a segment of a business is reported for an extended phase-out period. We will use the same measurement and disposal dates as in the previous situation. All situations are reported on a pretax basis.

In Case 2, all three components related to the gain (loss) on disposal were losses; therefore **a net loss of $1,400,000 is reported at the measurement date.**

In Case 3, the loss of $600,000 on the sale of the segment assets is greater than the realized $100,000 and expected $400,000 income from operations; therefore **a net loss of $100,000 is reported at the measurement date.**

In Case 4, the gain of $900,000 on the sale of the segment assets is greater than the realized $500,000 and expected $300,000 losses from operations; therefore **a net gain of $100,000 is reported at the disposal date.**

In Case 5, both components of operations report income, and a gain is expected on the sale of the segment assets. As a result, the **realized income from operations of $400,000 can be reported at the date of measurement** because there are no realized or estimated losses. **The remaining estimated gain of $550,000 ($300,000 + $250,000) is deferred and recognized at the disposal date.**

In Case 6, the realized income from operations of $600,000 exceeds the estimated losses from operations $200,000 and sale $300,000. As a result, **a realized gain of $100,000 is reported at the end of 1997, because the net gain is realized.**

In Case 7, the net gain on disposal is expected to be $450,000, of which $400,000 is realized and $50,000 is unrealized. **The realized $400,000 is recognized in 1997 and the net unrealized gain of $50,000** (the net of a $300,000 expected loss from operations in 1998 and a $350,000 expected gain from disposal in 1998) is recognized in 1998.

ILLUSTRATION 4A-10
Gains or Losses Involving
Extended Phase-Out of
Discontinued Operations

Disposals of Segments Involving Extended Phase-Out of Discontinued Operations				
	Realized Income (Loss) on Operations October 1, 1997– December 31, 1997	Expected Income (Loss) on Operations January 1, 1998– May 1, 1998	Expected Gain (Loss) on Sale of Assets	Gain (Loss) on Disposal of Segment
Case 1	$(400,000)	$(200,000)	$350,000	1997 $ (250,000) 1998 0
Case 2	(300,000)	(600,000)	(500,000)	1997 $(1,400,000) 1998 0
Case 3	100,000	400,000	(600,000)	1997 $ (100,000) 1998 0
Case 4	(500,000)	(300,000)	900,000	1997 0 1998 $ 100,000
Case 5	400,000	300,000	250,000	1997 $ 400,000 1998 $ 550,000
Case 6	600,000	(200,000)	(300,000)	1997 $ 100,000 1998 0
Case 7	400,000	(300,000)	350,000	1997 $ 400,000 1998 $ 50,000
Case 8	400,000	(350,000)	300,000	1997 $ 350,000 1998 0

In Case 8, the net gain on disposal is expected to be $350,000, all of which is realized and, therefore, recognized in 1997. **The $400,000 of realized income from operations is reduced by the net expected unrealized loss of $50,000** from 1998 (the expected loss from operations of $350,000 less the expected gain on sale of $300,000).

❖ DISCLOSURE REQUIREMENTS

Amounts of income taxes applicable to the results of discontinued operations and the gain or loss from disposal of the segment should be disclosed on the face of the income statement or related notes. Revenues applicable to the discontinued operations should be separately disclosed in the related notes.

In addition to the amounts that should be reported in the financial statements, the notes to the financial statements for the period encompassing the measurement date should disclose:

1 The identity of the segment of the business that has been or will be discontinued.
2 The expected disposal date, if known.
3 The expected manner of disposition.
4 A description of the remaining assets and liabilities of the segment at the balance sheet date.
5 The income or loss from operations and any proceeds from disposal of the segment during the period from the measurement date to the date of the balance sheet.

An example of the income statement and the note disclosure taken from the annual report of Fluor Corporation is shown in Illustration 4A-11.

Companies frequently segregate the assets and liabilities of the segment on the balance sheet into net current and net noncurrent amounts, identifying these elements as related to discontinued operations.

ILLUSTRATION 4A-11
Note Disclosure of
Discontinued Operations

Go to our Web site for additional
examples of this disclosure.

Fluor Corporation		
Income from continuing operations before income taxes		$171,800,000
Income taxes		91,100,000
Income from continuing operations		80,700,000
Discontinued operations—Note G:		
Loss from operation of Distribution Group (net of income tax benefit of $22,952,000)	$(27,000,000)	
Loss on disposal of Distribution Group, including provision for estimated operating losses during phase-out period (net of income tax benefit of $15,538,000)	(26,000,000)	(53,000,000)
Net income		$27,700,000

Note G: Discontinued Operations. During the fourth quarter of the current year, the company adopted a plan to dispose of the Distribution Group through sale or liquidation. Negotiations for the sale of two of the companies are currently being conducted with the respective management groups. At October 31, the net assets of discontinued operations, consisting primarily of inventories, trade receivables, and warehouse facilities have been reclassified as current assets at estimated net realizable value.

Revenues from discontinued operations, including the Goldston Transportation Group which was sold during the year, were $368,551,000. Included in the loss on disposal is a pretax provision of $2,115,000 for estimated operating losses during the phase-out period.

As previously stated, if the estimates on income or losses from operations during the phase-out period and on gains or losses on the sale of assets prove to be incorrect, the correction should be reported in the period when the estimate is determined to be incorrect; prior periods are not restated. An example of such a correction is disclosed in a note to the financial statements of BMC Industries Inc.

ILLUSTRATION 4A-12
Example of Note
Explaining Correction to
Financial Statement

BMC Industries Inc.
Note 3:   Discontinued Operations.   In the prior year, the Company estimated a loss on the disposal of the discontinued operations of $60,000,000, which included a provision of approximately $8,000,000 for operating losses through the anticipated disposal periods. Actual operating losses exceeded the estimate by approximately $10,000,000, and the loss on the disposal of discontinued operations is expected to be approximately $5,000,000 less than the original estimate. Accordingly, the accompanying Consolidated Statement of Operations for the current year includes an additional provision for loss on disposal of $5,000,000.

Note that the amount of the correction—in the case of BMC Industries, $5,000,000—is reported net of tax in the discontinued operations section of the income statement.

SUMMARY OF LEARNING OBJECTIVE FOR APPENDIX 4A

(9) *Measure and report gains and losses from discontinued operations.* The accountant may be required to report gains and losses from discontinued operations (sale of a segment of the business) under three different situations: (1) no phase-out period, (2) a phase-out period, and (3) an extended phase-out period. The gain or loss on disposal of a segment involves the sum of: (1) income or loss from operations to the measurement date, and (2) the gain or loss on the disposal of the business segment (operating incomes or losses during the phase-out period and the gain or loss on the sale of the net assets). These two items are reported separately net of tax among the irregular items in the income statement.

KEY TERMS

disposal date, 170
measurement date, 170
phase-out period, 171

Note: All **asterisked** Questions, Exercises, Problems, and Conceptual Cases relate to material contained in the appendix to each chapter.

❖ QUESTIONS ❖

1 What is the importance of the income statement? What are its major limitations?

2 Why should caution be exercised in the use of the income figure derived in an income statement? What are the objectives of generally accepted accounting principles in their application to the income statement?

3 A *Wall Street Journal* article noted that if Canon Inc. had written off film costs in the first quarter as fast as some of its competitors, Canon would have had a loss instead of a profit. One analyst noted therefore that Canon's quality of earnings was low. What does the term "quality of earnings" mean?

4 What is the difference between the capital maintenance approach to income measurement and the transaction approach? Is the final income figure the same under both approaches?

5 What is the major distinction (a) between revenues and gains and (b) between expenses and losses?

6 What are the advantages and disadvantages of the "single-step" income statement?

7 What are the advantages and disadvantages of a combined income and retained earnings statement? What is the basis for distinguishing between operating and nonoperating items?

8 Distinguish between the "all-inclusive" income statement and the "current operating performance" income statement. According to present generally accepted accounting principles, which is recommended? Explain.

9 What is the significance of the materiality of an item in deciding the proper placement of a nonrecurring item in the retained earnings statement or in the income statement? Explain.

10 How should prior period adjustments be reported in the financial statements? Give an example of a prior period adjustment.

11 Discuss the appropriate treatment in the financial statements of each of the following:
(a) An amount of $113,000 realized in excess of the cash surrender value of an insurance policy on the life of one of the founders of the company who died during the year.
(b) A profit-sharing bonus to employees computed as a percentage of net income.
(c) Additional depreciation on factory machinery because of an error in computing depreciation for the previous year.

(d) Rent received from subletting a portion of the office space.
(e) A patent infringement suit, brought two years ago against the company by another company, was settled this year by a cash payment of $725,000.
(f) A reduction in the Allowance for Doubtful Accounts balance, because the account appears to be considerably in excess of the probable loss from uncollectible receivables.

12 Indicate where the following items would ordinarily appear on the financial statements of Allepo, Inc. for the year 1998:
(a) The service life of certain equipment was changed from 8 to 5 years. If a 5-year life had been used previously, additional depreciation of $425,000 would have been charged.
(b) In 1998 a flood destroyed a warehouse that had a book value of $1,600,000. Floods are rare in this locality.
(c) In 1998 the company wrote off $1,000,000 of inventory that was considered obsolete.
(d) An income tax refund related to the 1995 tax year was received.
(e) In 1995, a supply warehouse with an expected useful life of 7 years was erroneously expensed.
(f) Allepo, Inc. changed its depreciation from double-declining to straight-line on machinery in 1998. The cumulative effect of the change was $925,000 (net of tax).

13 Give the section of a multiple-step income statement in which each of the following is shown.
(a) Loss on inventory write-down.
(b) Loss from strike.
(c) Bad debt expense.
(d) Loss on disposal of a segment of the business.
(e) Gain on sale of machinery.
(f) Interest revenue.
(g) Depreciation expense.
(h) Material write-offs of notes receivable.

14 Barry Bonds Land Development, Inc. purchased land for $70,000 and spent $30,000 developing it. It then sold the land for $160,000. Tom Glavine Manufacturing purchased land for a future plant site for $100,000. Due to a change in plans, they later sold the land for $160,000. Should these two companies report the land sales, both at gains of $60,000, in a similar manner?

15 You run into Bart Simpson at a party and begin discussing financial statements. Bart says "I prefer the single-step income statement because the multiple-step format generally overstates income." How should you respond to Bart?

16 Federov Corporation has eight expense accounts in its general ledger which could be classified as selling expenses. Should Federov report these eight expenses separately in its income statement or simply report one total amount for selling expenses?

17 Jose DeLeon Investments reported an unusual gain from the sale of certain assets in its 1998 income statement. How does intraperiod tax allocation affect the reporting of this unusual gain?

18 What effect does intraperiod tax allocation have on reported net income?

19 Jane Pauley Company computed earnings per share as follows:

$$\frac{\text{Net Income}}{\text{Common Shares Outstanding at Year End}}$$

Jane Pauley has a simple capital structure. What possible errors might the company have made in the computation? Explain.

20 Maria Shriver Corporation reported 1998 earnings per share of $7.21. In 1999, Maria Shriver reported earnings per share as follows:

On income before extraordinary item	$6.40
On extraordinary item	1.88
On net income	$8.28

Is the increase in earnings per share from $7.21 to $8.28 a favorable trend?

21 What is meant by "tax allocation within a period"? What is the justification for such practice?

22 When does tax allocation within a period become necessary? How should this allocation be handled?

23 During 1998, Natsume Sozeki Company earned income of $1,000,000 before federal income taxes and realized a gain of $450,000 on a government-forced condemnation sale of a division plant facility. The income is subject to federal income taxation at the rate of 34%; the gain on the sale of the plant is taxed at 30%. Proper accounting suggests that the unusual gain be reported as an extraordinary item. Il-

lustrate an appropriate presentation of these items in the income statement.

24 On January 30, 1998, a suit was filed against Pierogi Corporation under the Environmental Protection Act. On August 6, 1999, Pierogi Corporation agreed to settle the action and pay $920,000 in damages to certain current and former employees. How should this settlement be reported in the 1999 financial statements? Discuss.

25 Tiger Paper Company decided to close two small pulp mills in Conway, New Hampshire, and Corvallis, Oregon. Would these closings be reported in a separate section entitled Discontinued Operations after Income from Continuing Operations? Discuss.

26 What major types of items are reported in the retained earnings statement?

27 The controller for Pierre Corneille, Inc. is discussing the possibility of presenting a combined income and retained earnings statement for the current year. Indicate a possible advantage and disadvantage of this presentation format.

28 Generally accepted accounting principles usually require the use of accrual accounting to "fairly present" income. If the cash receipts and disbursements method of accounting will "clearly reflect" taxable income, why does this method not usually also "fairly present" income?

29 State some of the more serious problems encountered in seeking to achieve the ideal measurement of periodic net income. Explain what accountants do as a practical alternative.

30 What is meant by the terms "components," "elements," and "items" as they relate to the income statement? Why might items have to be disclosed in the income statement?

31 What are the three ways that other comprehensive income may be displayed (reported)?

*32 How are the measurement and disposal dates defined for a disposal of a segment of a business?

*33 How are gains or losses on disposal of a segment of a business determined?

*34 How should the disposal of a segment of a business be disclosed in the income statement?

❖ BRIEF EXERCISES ❖

BE4-1 Karen Allen Company had net assets of $450,000 at December 31, 1999, and $250,000 at January 1, 1999. During 1999, Allen made owner investments of $125,000 and withdrew $35,000 from the business. (a) Compute Allen's 1999 net income. (b) If Allen's 1999 revenues and gains total $300,000, what are their total expenses and losses?

BE4-2 Kirstie Alley Corporation had net sales of $1,780,000 and investment revenue of $103,000 in 1999. Their 1999 expenses were: cost of goods sold, $1,190,000; selling expenses, $272,000; administrative expenses, $211,000; interest expense, $76,000; and income tax expense, $40,000. Prepare a single-step income statement for Kirstie Alley Corporation, which has 10,000 shares of stock outstanding.

BE4-3 Use the information provided in BE4-2 for Kirstie Alley Corporation to prepare a multiple-step income statement.

BE4-4 Green Day Corporation had income from continuing operations of $12,600,000 in 1999. During 1999, they disposed of their restaurant division at an after-tax loss of $189,000. Prior to disposal, the division operated at a loss of $315,000 (net of tax) in 1999. Green Day had 10,000,000 shares of common stock outstanding during 1999. Prepare a partial income statement for Green Day beginning with income from continuing operations.

BE4-5 Boyz II Men Corporation had income before income taxes for 1999 of $7,300,000. In addition, they suffered an unusual and infrequent pretax loss from a volcano eruption of $770,000. The corporation's tax rate is 30%. Prepare a partial income statement for Boyz II Men beginning with income before income taxes. The corporation had 5,000,000 shares of common stock outstanding during 1999.

BE4-6 Shawn Bradley Company changed from straight-line depreciation to double-declining balance depreciation at the beginning of 1999. The plant assets originally cost $1,500,000 in 1997. Using straight-line depreciation, depreciation expense is $60,000 per year. Under the double-declining balance method, depreciation expense would be $120,000; $110,400; and $101,568 for 1997, 1998, and 1999. If Bradley's tax rate is 30%, by what amount would the cumulative effect of a change in accounting principle increase or decrease 1999 net income?

BE4-7 Jana Kingston Company has recorded bad debts expense in the past at a rate of 1½% of net sales. In 1999, Irvin decides to increase its estimate to 2%. If the new rate had been used in prior years, cumulative bad debt expense would have been $380,000 instead of $285,000. In 1999, bad debt expense will be $120,000 instead of $90,000. If Kingston's tax rate is 30%, what amount should they report as the cumulative effect of changing estimated bad debt rate?

BE4-8 In 1999, Kirby Puckett Corporation reported net income of $1,200,000. It declared and paid preferred stock dividends of $250,000. During 1999, Puckett had a weighted average of 190,000 common shares outstanding. Compute Puckett's 1999 earnings per share.

BE4-9 Turgeon Corporation had retained earnings of $529,000 at January 1, 1999. Net income in 1999 was $1,496,000, and cash dividends of $650,000 were declared and paid. Prepare a 1999 retained earnings statement for Turgeon Corporation.

BE4-10 Use the information provided in BE4-9 to prepare a retained earnings statement for Turgeon Corporation, assuming that in 1999 Turgeon discovered that it had overstated 1997 depreciation by $125,000 (net of tax).

BE4-11 On January 1, 1998, Creative Works Inc. had cash and common stock of $60,000. At that date the company had no other asset, liability or equity balances. On January 2, 1998, it purchased for cash $20,000 of equity securities that it classified as available-for-sale. It received cash dividends of $3,000 during the year on these securities. In addition, it has an unrealized holding gain on these securities of $5,000 net of tax. Determine the following amounts for 1998: (a) net income; (b) comprehensive income; (c) other comprehensive income; and (d) accumulated other comprehensive income (end of 1998).

*BE4-12 Garok Company decided on Sept. 1, 1999, to dispose of its Cardassian Division. The Cardassian Division operated at a loss of $190,000 during the first eight months of 1999 and a loss of $114,000 during the last four months of the year. Garok estimates the division will incur a loss of $130,000 in 2000 before it is sold at a gain of $85,000. Garok's tax rate is 30%. Prepare the discontinued operations section of Garok's 1999 income statement.

❖ EXERCISES ❖

E4-1 (Computation of Net Income) Presented below are changes in all the account balances of Fritz Reiner Furniture Co. during the current year, except for retained earnings.

	Increase (Decrease)		Increase (Decrease)
Cash	$ 79,000	Accounts payable	$(51,000)
Accounts receivable (net)	45,000	Bonds payable	82,000
Inventory	127,000	Common stock	125,000
Investments	(47,000)	Additional paid-in capital	13,000

Instructions
Compute the net income for the current year, assuming that there were no entries in the Retained Earnings account except for net income and a dividend declaration of $19,000 which was paid in the current year.

E4-2 (Capital Maintenance Approach)   Presented below is selected information pertaining to the Video-hound Video Company:

Cash balance, January 1, 1999	$ 13,000
Accounts receivable, January 1, 1999	19,000
Collections from customers in 1999	210,000
Capital account balance, January 1, 1999	38,000
Total assets, January 1, 1999	75,000
Cash investment added, July 1, 1999	5,000
Total assets, December 31, 1999	101,000
Cash balance, December 31, 1999	20,000
Accounts receivable, December 31, 1999	36,000
Merchandise taken for personal use during 1999	11,000
Total liabilities, December 31, 1999	41,000

Instructions
Compute the net income for 1999.

E4-3 (Income Statement Items)   Presented below are certain account balances of Paczki Products Co.

Ending inventory	$ 48,000	Sales returns	$ 12,400
Rental revenue	6,500	Sales discounts	7,800
Interest expense	12,700	Selling expenses	99,400
Purchase returns and allowances	10,500	Sales	390,000
Beginning retained earnings	114,400	Income tax	31,000
Ending retained earnings	134,000	Beginning inventory	45,300
Freight-in	10,100	Purchases	190,000
Dividends earned	71,000	Purchase discounts	2,500
		Administrative expenses	82,500

Instructions
From the foregoing, compute the following: (a) total net revenue; (b) cost of goods sold; (c) net income; (d) dividends declared during the current year.

E4-4 (Single-step Income Statement)   The financial records of LeRoi Jones Inc., were destroyed by fire at the end of 1999. Fortunately the controller had kept certain statistical data related to the income statement as presented below.

1. The beginning merchandise inventory was $92,000 and decreased 20% during the current year.
2. Sales discounts amount to $17,000.
3. 20,000 shares of common stock were outstanding for the entire year.
4. Interest expense was $20,000.
5. The income tax rate is 30%.
6. Cost of goods sold amounts to $500,000.
7. Administrative expenses are 20% of cost of goods sold but only 8% of gross sales.
8. Four-fifths of the operating expenses relate to sales activities.

Instructions
From the foregoing information prepare an income statement for the year 1999 in single-step form.

E4-5 (Multiple-step and Single-step)   Two accountants for the firm of Elwes and Wright are arguing about the merits of presenting an income statement in a multiple-step versus a single-step format. The discussion involves the following 1999 information related to P. Bride Company ($000 omitted).

Administrative expense	
Officers' salaries	$ 4,900
Depreciation of office furniture and equipment	3,960
Purchase returns	5,810
Purchases	64,800
Rental revenue	17,230
Selling expense	
Transportation-out	2,690
Sales commissions	7,980
Depreciation of sales equipment	6,480
Merchandise inventory, beginning inventory	15,400
Merchandise inventory, ending inventory	16,600
Sales	96,500
Transportation-in	2,780
Income tax	9,070
Interest expense on bonds payable	1,860

Instructions

    (a) Prepare an income statement for the year 1999 using the multiple-step form. Common shares outstanding for 1999 total $40,550 ($000 omitted).

    (b) Prepare an income statement for the year 1999 using the single-step form.

    (c) Which one do you prefer? Discuss.

E4-6 (Multiple-step and Extraordinary Items) The following balances were taken from the books of the Maria Conchita Alonzo Corp. on December 31, 1999:

Interest revenue	$ 86,000	Accumulated depreciation—equipment	40,000
Cash	51,000	Purchases returns and allowances	125,000
Sales	1,380,000	Accumulated depreciation—building	28,000
Accounts receivable	150,000	Purchase discounts	59,000
Prepaid insurance	20,000	Notes receivable	155,000
Sales returns and allowances	150,000	Selling expenses	194,000
Allowance for doubtful accounts	7,000	Accounts payable	170,000
Sales discounts	45,000	Bonds payable	100,000
Land	100,000	Administrative and general expenses	97,000
Inventory January 1, 1999	246,000	Accrued liabilities	32,000
Equipment	200,000	Interest expense	60,000
Inventory December 31, 1999	331,000	Notes payable	100,000
Building	140,000	Loss from earthquake damage (extraordinary item)	150,000
Purchases	890,000	Common stock	500,000
		Retained earnings	21,000

    Assume the total effective tax rate on all items is 34%.

Instructions

Prepare a multiple-step income statement; 100,000 shares of common stock were outstanding during the year.

E4-7 (Multiple-step and Single-step) The accountant of Whitney Houston Shoe Co. has compiled the following information from the company's records as a basis for an income statement for the year ended 12/31/99.

Rental revenue	$ 29,000
Interest on notes payable	18,000
Market appreciation on land above cost	31,000
Merchandise purchases	459,000
Transportation-in	37,000
Wages and salaries—sales	114,800
Materials and supplies—sales	17,600
Common stock outstanding (no. of shares)	20,000[a]
Income tax	37,400
Wages and salaries—administrative	135,900
Other administrative expense	51,700
Merchandise inventory, January 1, 1999	92,000
Merchandise inventory, December 31, 1999	81,000
Purchase returns and allowances	11,000
Net sales	980,000
Depreciation on plant assets (70% selling, 30% administrative)	65,000
Dividends declared	16,000

[a]Remained unchanged all year.

Instructions

    (a) Prepare a multiple-step income statement.

    (b) Prepare a single-step income statement.

    (c) Which format do you prefer? Discuss.

E4-8 (Multiple-step and Single-step) Presented below is income statement information related to Klingon Corporation for the year 1999.

Administrative expenses:		Transportation-in	14,000
Officers' salaries	$ 39,000	Purchase discounts	10,000
Depreciation expense—building	28,500	Inventory (beginning)	120,000
Office supplies expense	9,500	Sales returns and allowances	15,000
Inventory (ending)	137,000	Selling expenses:	
Flood damage (pretax extraordinary item)	50,000	Sales salaries	71,000
Purchases	600,000	Depreciation expense—store equipment	18,000
Sales	930,000	Store supplies expense	9,000

In addition, the corporation has other revenue from dividends received of $20,000 and other expense of interest on notes payable of $9,000. There are 20,000 shares of common stock outstanding for the year. The total effective tax rate on all income is 34%.

Instructions

(a) Prepare a multiple-step income statement for 1999.
(b) Prepare a single-step income statement for 1999.
(c) Discuss the relative merits of the two income statements.

E4-9 (Combined Statement) During 1999 John Ross Co. had pretax earnings of $500,000 exclusive of a realized and tax deductible loss of $130,000 from the condemnation of properties (extraordinary item). In addition, the company discovered that depreciation expense was overstated by $80,000 in 1997. Retained earnings at January 1, 1997, before error correction was $670,000; dividends of $150,000 were declared on common stock during 1999. Fifty thousand shares of common stock were outstanding during 1999. Assume that the income tax rate on income is 34% for both 1997 and 1999.

Instructions

Prepare a combined income and retained earnings statement beginning with income before income tax and extraordinary item.

E4-10 (Combined Single-step) The following information was taken from the records of Roland Carlson Inc. for the year 1999. Income tax applicable to income from continuing operations, $187,000; income tax applicable to loss on discontinued operations, $25,500; income tax applicable to extraordinary gain, $32,300; income tax applicable to extraordinary loss, $20,400.

Extraordinary gain	$ 95,000	Cash dividends declared	150,000
Loss on discontinued operations	75,000	Retained earnings January 1, 1999	600,000
Administrative expenses	240,000	Cost of goods sold	850,000
Rent revenue	40,000	Selling expenses	300,000
Extraordinary loss	60,000	Sales	1,900,000

Shares outstanding during 1999 were 100,000.

Instructions

(a) Prepare a single-step income statement for 1999. Include per share data.
(b) Prepare a combined single-step income and retained earnings statement.
(c) Which one do you prefer? Discuss.

E4-11 (Multiple-step Statement with Retained Earnings) Presented below is information related to Ivan Calderon Corp., for the year 1999.

Net sales	$1,300,000	Writeoff of inventory due to obsolescence	80,000
Cost of goods sold	780,000	Depreciation expense omitted by accident in 1998	55,000
Selling expenses	65,000	Casualty loss (extraordinary item) before taxes	50,000
Administrative expenses	48,000	Dividends declared	45,000
Dividend revenue	20,000	Retained earnings at December 31, 1998	980,000
Interest revenue	7,000	Federal tax rate of 34% on all items	

Instructions

(a) Prepare a multiple-step income statement for 1999. Assume that 60,000 shares of common stock are outstanding.
(b) Prepare a separate retained earnings statement for 1999.

E4-12 (Earnings Per Share) The stockholders' equity section of Tkachuk Corporation appears below as of December 31, 1999:

8% cumulative preferred stock, $50 par value, authorized		
100,000 shares, outstanding 90,000 shares		$ 4,500,000
Common stock, $1.00 par, authorized and issued		
10 million shares		10,000,000
Additional paid-in capital		20,500,000
Retained earnings Dec. 31, 1998	$134,000,000	
Net income for 1999	33,000,000	167,000,000
		$202,000,000

Net income for 1999 reflects a total effective tax rate of 34%. Included in the net income figure is a loss of $18,000,000 (before tax) as a result of a major casualty.

Instructions
Compute earnings per share data as it should appear on the financial statements of Tkachuk Corporation.

E4-13 (Condensed Income Statement) Presented below are selected ledger accounts of Spock Corporation at December 31, 1999:

Cash	185,000	Travel and entertainment	69,000
Merchandise inventory	535,000	Accounting and legal services	33,000
Sales	4,275,000	Insurance expense	24,000
Advances from customers	117,000	Advertising	54,000
Purchases	2,786,000	Transportation-out	93,000
Sales discounts	34,000	Depreciation of office	48,000
Purchase discounts	27,000	Depreciation of sales equipment	36,000
Sales salaries	284,000	Telephone—sales	17,000
Office salaries	346,000	Utilities—office	32,000
Purchase returns	15,000	Miscellaneous office expenses	8,000
Sales returns	79,000	Rental revenue	240,000
Transportation-in	72,000	Extraordinary loss (before tax)	70,000
Accounts receivable	142,500	Interest expense	176,000
Sales commissions	83,000	Common stock ($10 par)	900,000

Spock's effective tax rate on all items is 34%. A physical inventory indicates that the ending inventory is $686,000.

Instructions
Prepare a condensed 1999 income statement for Spock Corporation.

E4-14 (Retained Earnings Statement) Eddie Zambrano Corporation began operations on January 1, 1996. During its first 3 years of operations, Zambrano reported net income and declared dividends as follows:

	Net income	Dividends declared
1996	$ 40,000	$ –0–
1997	125,000	50,000
1998	160,000	50,000

The following information relates to 1999:

Income before income tax	$240,000
Prior period adjustment: understatement of 1997 depreciation expense (before taxes)	25,000
Cumulative decrease in income from change in inventory methods (before taxes)	35,000
Dividends declared (of this amount, $25,000 will be paid on Jan. 15, 2000)	100,000
Effective tax rate	40%

Instructions
(a) Prepare a 1999 retained earnings statement for Eddie Zambrano Corporation.
(b) Assume Eddie Zambrano Corp. appropriated retained earnings in the amount of $70,000 on December 31, 1999. After this action, what would Zambrano report as total retained earnings in its December 31, 1999 balance sheet?

E4-15 (Earnings Per Share) At December 31, 1998, Shiga Naoya Corporation had the following stock outstanding:

10% cumulative preferred stock, $100 par, 107,500 shares	$10,750,000
Common stock, $5 par, 4,000,000 shares	20,000,000

During 1999, Shiga Naoya's only stock transaction was the issuance of 400,000 shares of common on April 1. During 1999, the following also occurred:

Income from continuing operations before taxes	$23,650,000
Discontinued operations (loss before taxes)	$ 3,225,000
Preferred dividends declared	$ 1,075,000
Common dividends declared	2,200,000
Effective tax rate	35%

Instructions
Compute earnings per share data as it should appear in the 1999 income statement of Shiga Naoya Corporation.

E4-16 (Comprehensive Income) C. Reither Co. reports the following information for 1999: sales revenue, $700,000; cost of goods sold, $500,000; operating expenses, $80,000; and an unrealized holding loss on available-for-sale securities for 1999 of $60,000. It declared and paid a cash dividend of $10,000 in 1999.

Instructions
(a) Show how comprehensive income is reported using the separate income statement format.
(b) Show how comprehensive income is reported using the combined income statement format.

E4-17 (Comprehensive Income) C. Reither Co. has January 1, 1999, balances in common stock, $350,000; accumulated other comprehensive income, $80,000; and retained earnings, $90,000. It issued no stock during 1999.

Instructions
Using the information from Exercise 4-16, prepare a statement of stockholders' equity.

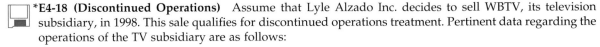 ***E4-18 (Discontinued Operations)** Assume that Lyle Alzado Inc. decides to sell WBTV, its television subsidiary, in 1998. This sale qualifies for discontinued operations treatment. Pertinent data regarding the operations of the TV subsidiary are as follows:

Loss from operations from beginning of year to measurement date, $1,000,000 (net of tax).

Realized loss from operations from measurement date to end of 1998, $700,000 (net of tax).

Estimated income from operations from end of year to disposal date of June 1, 1999, $400,000 (net of tax).

Estimated gain on sale of net assets on June 1, 1999, $150,000 (net of tax).

Instructions
(a) What is the gain (loss) on the disposal of the segment reported in 1998? In 1999?
(b) Prepare the discontinued operations section of the income statement for the year ended 1998.
(c) If the amount reported in 1998 as gain or loss from disposal of a segment by Lyle Alzado Inc. proves to be materially incorrect, when and how is the correction reported, if at all?
(d) If the TV subsidiary had a realized income of $100,000 (net of tax) instead of a realized loss from the measurement date to the end of 1998, what is the gain or loss on disposal of the segment reported in 1998? In 1999?

***E4-19 (Discontinued Operations)** On October 5, 1999, Blues Inc.'s board of directors decided to dispose of the Jake and Elwood Division. Blues is a real estate firm with approximately 25% of its income from management of apartment complexes. The Jake and Elwood Division contracts to clean apartments after tenants move out in the Blues complexes and several others. The board decided to dispose of the division because of unfavorable operating results.

Net income for Blues was $91,000 after tax (assume a 30% rate) for the fiscal year ended December 31, 1999. The Jake and Elwood Division accounted for only $4,200 (after tax) of this amount and only $1,050 (after tax) in the fourth quarter. Jake and Elwood accounted for $50,000 in revenues, of which $8,000 were earned in the last quarter. The average number of common shares outstanding was 20,000 for the year.

Because of the unfavorable results and the extreme competition, the board believes selling the business intact is impossible. Their final decision is to complete all current contracts, the last of which expires on May 3, 2001, and then auction off the cleaning equipment on May 10, 2001. This, the only asset of the division, will have a depreciated value of $25,000 at the disposal date. The board believes the sale proceeds will approximate $5,000 after the auction expenses and estimates Jake and Elwood earnings in fiscal year 2000 as $3,800 (before tax), with a loss of $3,000 (before tax) in fiscal year 2001.

Instructions
Prepare the income statement and the appropriate footnotes that relate to the Jake and Elwood Division for 1999. The income statement should begin with income from continuing operations before income taxes. Earnings per share computations are not required.

❖ PROBLEMS ❖

P4-1 (Combined Multiple-step) Presented below is information related to American Horse Company for 1999.

Retained earnings balance, January 1, 1999	$ 980,000
Sales for the year	25,000,000
Cost of goods sold	17,000,000

Interest revenue	70,000
Selling and administrative expenses	4,700,000
Write-off of goodwill (not tax deductible)	520,000
Federal income taxes for 1999	905,000
Assessment for additional 1996 income taxes (normal recurring)	300,000
Gain on the sale of investments (normal recurring)	110,000
Loss due to flood damage—extraordinary item (net of tax)	390,000
Loss on the disposition of the wholesale division (net of tax)	440,000
Loss on operations of the wholesale division (net of tax)	90,000
Dividends declared on common stock	250,000
Dividends declared on preferred stock	70,000

Instructions

Prepare a combined income and retained earnings statement using the multiple-step form. American Horse Company decided to discontinue its entire wholesale operations and to retain its manufacturing operations. On September 15, American Horse sold the wholesale operations to Rogers Company. During 1999, there were 300,000 shares of common stock outstanding all year.

P4-2 (Combined Single-step) Presented below is the trial balance of Mary J. Blige Corporation at December 31, 1999.

Mary J. Blige Corporation
TRIAL BALANCE
Year Ended December 31, 1999

	Debits	Credits
Purchase discounts		$ 10,000
Cash	$ 205,100	
Accounts receivable	105,000	
Rent revenue		18,000
Retained earnings		260,000
Salaries payable		18,000
Sales		1,000,000
Notes receivable	110,000	
Accounts payable		49,000
Accumulated depreciation—equipment		28,000
Sales discounts	14,500	
Sales returns	17,500	
Notes payable		70,000
Selling expenses	232,000	
Administrative expenses	99,000	
Common stock		300,000
Income tax expense	38,500	
Cash dividends	45,000	
Allowance for doubtful accounts		5,000
Supplies	14,000	
Freight-in	20,000	
Land	70,000	
Equipment	140,000	
Bonds payable		100,000
Gain on sale of land		30,000
Accumulated depreciation—building		19,600
Merchandise inventory	89,000	
Building	98,000	
Purchases	610,000	
Totals	$1,907,600	$1,907,600

A physical count of inventory on December 31 resulted in an inventory amount of $124,000.

Instructions

Prepare a combined income and retained earnings statement using the single-step form. Assume that the only changes in the retained earnings during the current year were from net income and dividends. Thirty thousand shares of common stock were outstanding the entire year.

P4-3 (Irregular Items)   Tony Rich, Inc., reported income from continuing operations before taxes during 1999 of $790,000. Additional transactions occurring in 1999 but not considered in the $790,000 are as follows:

1. The corporation experienced an uninsured flood loss (extraordinary) in the amount of $80,000 during the year. The tax rate on this item is 46%.
2. At the beginning of 1997, the corporation purchased a machine for $54,000 (salvage value of $9,000) that had a useful life of six years. The bookkeeper used straight-line depreciation for 1997, 1998, and 1999 but failed to deduct the salvage value in computing the depreciation base.
3. Sale of securities held as a part of its portfolio resulted in a loss of $57,000 (pretax).
4. When its president died, the corporation realized $110,000 from an insurance policy. The cash surrender value of this policy had been carried on the books as an investment in the amount of $46,000 (the gain is nontaxable).
5. The corporation disposed of its recreational division at a loss of $115,000 before taxes. Assume that this transaction meets the criteria for discontinued operations.
6. The corporation decided to change its method of inventory pricing from average cost to the FIFO method. The effect of this change on prior years is to increase 1997 income by $60,000 and decrease 1998 income by $20,000 before taxes. The FIFO method has been used for 1999. The tax rate on these items is 40%.

Instructions

Prepare an income statement for the year 1999 starting with income from continuing operations before taxes. Compute earnings per share as it should be shown on the face of the income statement. Common shares outstanding for the year are 80,000 shares. (Assume a tax rate of 30% on all items, unless indicated otherwise.)

P4-4 (Combined Statement, Multiple- and Single-step)   The following account balances were included in the trial balance of J.R. Reid Corporation at June 30, 1999.

Sales	$1,678,500	Depreciation of office furniture	
Sales discounts	31,150	and equipment	7,250
Purchases	910,000	Real estate and other local	
Freight-in	31,600	taxes	7,320
Purchase returns	5,150	Bad debt expense—selling	4,850
Purchase discounts	21,580	Building expense—prorated to	
Sales salaries	56,260	administration	9,130
Sales commissions	97,600	Miscellaneous office expenses	6,000
Travel expense—salespersons	28,930	Sales returns	62,300
Freight-out	21,400	Dividends received	38,000
Entertainment expense	14,820	Bond interest expense	18,000
Telephone and		Income taxes	133,000
telegraph—sales	9,030	Depreciation understatement	
Depreciation of sales equipment	4,980	due to error—1996 (net of	
Building expense—prorated to		tax)	17,700
sales	6,200	Dividends declared on	
Miscellaneous selling		preferred stock	9,000
expenses	4,715	Dividends declared on	
Office supplies used	3,450	common stock	32,000
Telephone and		Merchandise inventory—July	
telegraph—administration	2,820	1, 1998	250,000

The merchandise inventory at June 30, 1999, amounted to $268,100. The Unappropriated Retained Earnings account had a balance of $287,000 at June 30, 1999, before closing; the only entry in that account during the year was a debit of $50,000 to establish an Appropriation for Bonded Indebtedness. There are 80,000 shares of common stock outstanding.

Instructions

(a) Using the multiple-step form, prepare a combined income and unappropriated retained earnings statement for the year ended June 30, 1999.
(b) Using the single-step form, prepare a combined income and unappropriated retained earnings statement for the year ended June 30, 1999.

P4-5 (Irregular Items)   Presented below is a combined single-step income and retained earnings statement for Sandy Freewalt Company for 1998.

	(000 omitted)
Net sales	$640,000
Cost and expenses:	
Cost of goods sold	500,000
Selling, general, and administrative expenses	66,000
Other, net	17,000
	583,000
Income before income tax	57,000
Income tax	19,400
Net income	37,600
Retained earnings at beginning of period, as previously reported — 141,000	
Adjustment required for correction of error — (7,000)	
Retained earnings at beginning of period, as restated	134,000
Dividends on common stock	(12,200)
Retained earnings at end of period	$159,400

Additional facts are as follows:

1. "Selling, general, and administrative expenses" for 1998 included a usual but infrequently occurring charge of $10,500,000.
2. "Other, net" for 1998 included an extraordinary item (charge) of $9,000,000. If the extraordinary item (charge) had not occurred, income taxes for 1998 would have been $22,400,000 instead of $19,400,000.
3. "Adjustment required for correction of an error" was a result of a change in estimate (useful life of certain assets reduced to 8 years and a catch-up adjustment made).
4. Sandy Freewalt Company disclosed earnings per common share for net income in the notes to the financial statements.

Instructions

Determine from these additional facts whether the presentation of the facts in the Sandy Freewalt Company income and retained earnings statement is appropriate. If the presentation is not appropriate, describe the appropriate presentation and discuss its theoretical rationale (do not prepare a revised statement).

P4-6 (Retained Earnings Statement, Prior Period Adjustment) Below is the Retained Earnings account for the year 1999 for LeClair Corp.

Retained earnings, January 1, 1999		$257,600
Add:		
Gain on sale of investments (net of tax)	$41,200	
Net income	84,500	
Refund on litigation with government, related to the year 1996 (net of tax)	21,600	
Recognition of income earned in 1998, but omitted from income statement in that year (net of tax)	25,400	172,700
		430,300
Deduct		
Loss on discontinued operations (net of tax)	25,000	
Write-off of goodwill	60,000	
Cumulative effect on income in changing from straight-line depreciation to accelerated depreciation in 1999 (net of tax)	18,200	
Cash dividends declared	32,000	135,200
Retained earnings, December 31, 1999		$295,100

Instructions

(a) Prepare a corrected retained earnings statement. LeClair Corp. normally sells investments of the type mentioned above.
(b) State where the items that do not appear in the corrected retained earnings statement should be shown.

P4-7 (Income Statement and Irregular Items) The Rufino Tamayo Corporation commenced business on January 1, 1996. Recently the corporation has had several unusual accounting problems related to the presentation of their income statement for financial reporting purposes.

You have been the CPA for Rufino Tamayo Corporation for several years and have been asked to examine the following data.

Rufino Tamayo Corporation
INCOME STATEMENT
For the Year Ended December 31, 1999

Sales	$9,500,000
Cost of goods sold	5,900,000
Gross profit	3,600,000
Selling and administrative expense	1,300,000
Income before income tax	2,300,000
Income tax (30%)	690,000
Net income	$1,610,000

In addition, this information was provided:

1. The controller mentioned that the corporation has had difficulty in collecting on several of their receivables. For this reason, the bad debt write-off was increased from 1% to 2% of sales. The controller estimates that if this rate had been used in past periods, an additional $83,000 worth of expense would have been charged. The bad debt expense for the current period was calculated using the new rate and is part of selling and administrative expense.

2. Common shares outstanding at the end of 1999 totaled 400,000. No additional shares were purchased or sold during 1999.

3. Rufino Tamayo noted also that the following items were not included in the income statement.
   (a) Inventory in the amount of $72,000 was obsolete.
   (b) The major casualty loss suffered by the corporation was partially uninsured and cost $127,000, net of tax (extraordinary item).

4. Retained earnings as of January 1, 1999, was $2,800,000. Cash dividends of $700,000 were paid in 1999.

5. In January, 1999, Rufino Tamayo Corporation changed its method of accounting for plant assets from the straight-line method to the accelerated method (double-declining balance). The controller has prepared a schedule indicating what depreciation expense would have been in previous periods if the double-declining method had been used. (The effective tax rate for 1996, 1997, and 1998 was 30%.)

	Depreciation Expense under Straight-Line	Depreciation Expense under Double-Declining	Difference
1996	$ 75,000	$150,000	$ 75,000
1997	75,000	112,500	37,500
1998	75,000	84,375	9,375
	$225,000	$346,875	$121,875

6. In 1999, Rufino Tamayo discovered that two errors were made in previous years. First, when it took a physical inventory at the end of 1996, one of the count sheets was apparently lost. The ending inventory for 1996 was therefore understated by $95,000. The inventory was correctly taken in 1997, 1998, and 1999. Also, the corporation found that in 1998 it had failed to record $40,000 as an expense for sales commissions. The effective tax rate for 1996, 1997, and 1998 was 30%. The sales commissions for 1998 are included in 1999 expenses.

Instructions
Prepare the income statement for Rufino Tamayo Corporation in accordance with professional pronouncements. Do not prepare footnotes.

*P4-8 **(Discontinued Operations)**   Bill Campbell Corporation management formally decided to discontinue operation of its Rocketeer Division on November 1, 1997. Campbell is a successful corporation with earnings in excess of $38.5 million before taxes for each of the past 5 years. The Rocketeer Division is being discontinued because it has not contributed to this profitable performance.

The principal assets of this division are the land, plant, and equipment used to manufacture engine components. The land, plant, and equipment had a net book value of $56 million on November 1, 1997.

Campbell's management has entered into negotiations for a cash sale of the facility for $39 million. The expected date of the sale and final disposal of the segment is July 1, 1998.

Campbell Corporation has a fiscal year ending May 31. The results of operations for the Rocketeer Division for the 1997–98 fiscal year and the estimated results for June 1998 are presented below. The before-tax losses after October 31, 1997, are computed without depreciation on the plant and equipment because the net book value as of November 1, 1997, is being used as a basis of negotiation for the sale.

Period	Before-tax Income (Loss)
June 1, 1997—October 31, 1997	$(4,100,000)
November 1, 1997—May 31, 1998	$(5,900,000)
June 1–30, 1998 (estimated)	$(750,000)

The Rocketeer Division will be accounted for as a discontinued operation on Campbell's 1997–98 fiscal year financial statements. Campbell is subject to a 30% tax rate (federal and state income taxes) on operating income and all gains and losses.

Instructions

(a) Explain how the Rocketeer Division's assets would be reported on Bill Campbell Corporation's balance sheet as of May 31, 1998.

(b) Explain how the discontinued operations and pending sale of the Rocketeer Division would be reported on Bill Campbell Corporation's income statement for the year ended May 31, 1998.

(c) Explain what information ordinarily should be disclosed in the notes to the financial statements regarding discontinued operations.

(CMA adapted)

❖ CONCEPTUAL CASES ❖

C4-1 (Identification of Income Statement Deficiencies) John Amos Corporation was incorporated and began business on January 1, 1998. It has been successful and now requires a bank loan for additional working capital to finance expansion. The bank has requested an audited income statement for the year 1998. The accountant for John Amos Corporation provides you with the following income statement which John Amos plans to submit to the bank:

INCOME STATEMENT

Sales		$850,000
Dividends		32,300
Gain on recovery of insurance proceeds from earthquake loss (extraordinary)		38,500
		920,800
Less:		
Selling expenses	$101,100	
Cost of goods sold	510,000	
Advertising expense	13,700	
Loss on obsolescence of inventories	34,000	
Loss on discontinued operations	48,600	
Administrative expense	73,400	780,800
Income before income tax		140,000
Income tax		56,000
Net income		$ 84,000

Instructions

Indicate the deficiencies in the income statement presented above. Assume that the corporation desires a single-step income statement.

C4-2 (All-inclusive vs. Current Operating) Information concerning the operations of a corporation is presented in an income statement or in a combined "income and retained earnings statement." Income statements are prepared on a "current operating performance" basis ("earning power concept") or an "all-inclusive" basis ("historical concept"). Proponents of the two types of income statements do not agree upon the proper treatment of material nonrecurring charges and credits.

Instructions

(a) Define "current operating performance" and "all-inclusive" as used above.

(b) Explain the differences in content and organization of a "current operating performance" income statement and an "all-inclusive" income statement. Include a discussion of the proper treatment of material nonrecurring charges and credits.

(c) Give the principal arguments for the use of each of the three statements, "all-inclusive" income statement, "current operating performance" income statement, and a combined "income and retained earnings statement."

(AICPA adapted)

C4-3 (Extraordinary Items) Jeff Foxworthy, vice-president of finance for Red Neck Company, has recently been asked to discuss with the company's division controllers the proper accounting for extraordinary items. Jeff Foxworthy prepared the factual situations presented below as a basis for discussion.

1. An earthquake destroys one of the oil refineries owned by a large multinational oil company. Earthquakes are rare in this geographical location.

2. A publicly held company has incurred a substantial loss in the unsuccessful registration of a bond issue.

3. A large portion of a cigarette manufacturer's tobacco crops are destroyed by a hailstorm. Severe damage from hailstorms is rare in this locality.

4. A large diversified company sells a block of shares from its portfolio of securities acquired for investment purposes.

5. A company sells a block of common stock of a publicly traded company. The block of shares, which represents less than 10% of the publicly held company, is the only security investment the company has ever owned.

6. A company that operates a chain of warehouses sells the excess land surrounding one of its warehouses. When the company buys property to establish a new warehouse, it usually buys more land than it expects to use for the warehouse with the expectation that the land will appreciate in value. Twice during the past 5 years the company sold excess land.

7. A textile manufacturer with only one plant moves to another location and sustains relocation costs of $725,000.

8. A company experiences a material loss in the repurchase of a large bond issue that has been outstanding for 3 years. The company regularly repurchases bonds of this nature.

9. A railroad experiences an unusual flood loss to part of its track system. Flood losses normally occur every 3 or 4 years.

10. A machine tool company sells the only land it owns. The land was acquired 10 years ago for future expansion, but shortly thereafter the company abandoned all plans for expansion but decided to hold the land for appreciation.

Instructions

Determine whether the foregoing items should be classified as extraordinary items. Present a rationale for your position.

C4-4 (Income Reporting Items) Woody Allen Corp. is an entertainment firm that derives approximately 30% of its income from the Casino Royale Division, which manages gambling facilities. As auditor for Woody Allen Corp., you have recently overheard the following discussion between the controller and financial vice-president.

VICE-PRESIDENT: If we sell the Casino Royale Division, it seems ridiculous to segregate the results of the sale in the income statement. Separate categories tend to be absurd and confusing to the stockholders. I believe that we should simply report the gain on the sale as other income or expense without detail.

CONTROLLER: Professional pronouncements would require that we disclose this information separately in the income statement. If a sale of this type is considered unusual and infrequent, it must be reported as an extraordinary item.

VICE-PRESIDENT: What about the walkout we had last month when our employees were upset about their commission income? Would this situation not also be an extraordinary item?

CONTROLLER: I am not sure whether this item would be reported as extraordinary or not.

VICE-PRESIDENT: Oh well, it doesn't make any difference because the net effect of all these items is immaterial, so no disclosure is necessary.

Instructions

(a) On the basis of the foregoing discussion, answer the following questions: Who is correct about handling the sale? What would be the income statement presentation for the sale of the Casino Royale Division?

(b) How should the walkout by the employees be reported?

(c) What do you think about the vice-president's observation on materiality?

(d) What are the earnings per share implications of these topics?

C4-5 (Identification of Extraordinary Items) Loni Anderson Company is a major manufacturer of food-stuffs whose products are sold in grocery and convenience stores throughout the United States. The company's name is well known and respected because its products have been marketed nationally for over 50 years.

In April 1998 the company was forced to recall one of its major products. A total of 35 persons in Oshkosh were treated for severe intestinal pain, and eventually 3 people died from complications. All of the people had consumed Anderson's product.

The product causing the problem was traced to one specific lot. Anderson keeps samples from all lots of foodstuffs. After thorough testing, Anderson and the legal authorities confirmed that the product had been tampered with after it had left the company's plant and was no longer under the company's control.

All of the product was recalled from the market—the only time an Anderson product has been recalled nationally and the only time for tampering. Persons who still had the product in their homes, even though it was not from the affected lot, were encouraged to return the product for credit or refund. A media campaign was designed and implemented by the company to explain what had happened and what the company was doing to minimize any chance of recurrence. Anderson decided to continue the product with the same trade name and same wholesale price. However, the packaging was redesigned completely to be tamper resistant and safety sealed. This required the purchase and installation of new equipment.

The corporate accounting staff recommended that the costs associated with the tampered product be treated as an extraordinary charge on the 1998 financial statements. Corporate accounting was asked to identify the various costs that could be associated with the tampered product and related recall. These costs ($000 omitted) are as follows.

1.	Credits and refunds to stores and consumers	$30,000
2.	Insurance to cover lost sales and idle plant costs for possible future recalls	5,000
3.	Transportation costs and off-site warehousing of returned product	2,000
4.	Future security measures for other Anderson products	4,000
5.	Testing of returned product and inventory	900
6.	Destroying returned product and inventory	2,400
7.	Public relations program to reestablish brand credibility	4,200
8.	Communication program to inform customers, answer inquiries, prepare press releases, etc.	1,600
9.	Higher cost arising from new packaging	800
10.	Investigation of possible involvement of employees, former employees, competitors, etc.	500
11.	Packaging redesign and testing	2,000
12.	Purchase and installation of new packaging equipment	6,000
13.	Legal costs for defense against liability suits	750
14.	Lost sales revenue due to recall	32,000

Anderson's estimated earnings before income taxes and before consideration of any of the above items for the year ending December 31, 1998, are $225 million.

Instructions

(a) Loni Anderson Company plans to recognize the costs associated with the product tampering and recall as an extraordinary charge.

   1. Explain why Anderson could classify this occurrence as an extraordinary charge.

   2. Describe the placement and terminology used to present the extraordinary charge in the 1998 income statement.

(b) Refer to the 14 cost items identified by the corporate accounting staff of Anderson Company.

   1. Identify the cost items by number that should be included in the extraordinary charge for 1998.

   2. For any item that is not included in the extraordinary charge, explain why it would not be included in the extraordinary charge.

(CMA adapted)

C4-6 (All-inclusive vs. Current Operating) Aaron Neville, controller for Tatooed Heart Inc., has recently prepared an income statement for 1999. Mr. Neville admits that he has not examined any recent professional pronouncements, but believes that the following presentation presents fairly the financial progress of this company during the current period.

Tatooed Heart Inc.
INCOME STATEMENT
For the Year Ended December 31, 1999

Sales			$377,852
Less: sales returns and allowances			16,320
Net sales			361,532
Cost of goods sold:			
Inventory, January 1, 1999		$ 50,235	
Purchases	$192,143		
Less: purchase discounts	3,142	189,001	
Cost of goods available for sale		239,236	
Inventory, December 31, 1999		41,124	
Cost of goods sold			198,112
Gross profit			163,420
Selling expenses		41,850	
Administrative expenses		32,142	73,992
Income before income tax			89,428
Other revenues and gains			
Dividends received			40,000
			129,428
Income tax			43,900
Net income			$ 85,528

Tatooed Heart Inc.
RETAINED EARNINGS STATEMENT
For the Year Ended December 31, 1999

Retained earnings, January 1, 1999			$216,000
Add			
Net income for 1999	$85,528		
Gain from casualty (net of tax)	10,000		
Gain on sale of plant assets	21,400	$116,928	
Deduct			
Loss on expropriation (net of tax)	13,000		
Cash dividends declared on common stock	30,000		
Correction of mathematical error in depreciating plant assets in 1997 (net of tax)	17,186	(60,186)	56,742
Retained earnings, December 31, 1999			$272,742

Instructions

(a) Determine whether these statements are prepared under the "current operating" or "all-inclusive" concept of income. Cite specific details.

(b) Which method do you favor and why?

(c) Which method must be used, and how should the information be presented? Common shares outstanding for the year are 50,000 shares.

For questionable items, use the classification that ordinarily would be appropriate.

C4-7 (Identification of Income Statement Weaknesses) The following financial statement was prepared by employees of Cynthia Taylor Corporation.

Cynthia Taylor Corporation
INCOME AND RETAINED EARNINGS STATEMENT
Year Ended December 31, 1999

Revenues	
Gross sales, including sales taxes	$1,044,300
Less returns, allowances, and cash discounts	56,200
Net sales	988,100
Dividends, interest, and purchase discounts	30,250
Recoveries of accounts written off in prior years	13,850
Total revenues	1,032,200
Costs and expenses	
Cost of goods sold, including sales taxes	465,900
Salaries and related payroll expenses	60,500
Rent	19,100
Freight-in and freight-out	3,400
Bad debt expense	24,000
Addition to reserve for possible inventory losses	3,800
Total costs and expenses	576,700
Income before extraordinary items	455,500
Extraordinary items	
Loss on discontinued styles (Note 1)	37,000
Loss on sale of marketable securities (Note 2)	39,050
Loss on sale of warehouse (Note 3)	86,350
Retroactive settlement of federal income taxes for 1998 and 1997 (Note 4)	34,500
Total extraordinary items	196,900
Net income	258,600
Retained earnings at beginning of year	310,700
Total	569,300
Less: Federal income taxes	87,924
Cash dividends on common stock	21,900
Total	109,824
Retained earnings at end of year	$ 459,476
Net income per share of common stock	$2.30

Note 1: New styles and rapidly changing consumer preferences resulted in a $37,000 loss on the disposal of discontinued styles and related accessories.

Note 2: The corporation sold an investment in marketable securities at a loss of $39,050. The corporation normally sells securities of this nature.

Note 3: The corporation sold one of its warehouses at an $86,350 loss.

Note 4: The corporation was charged $34,500 retroactively for additional income taxes resulting from a settlement in 1996. Of this amount, $17,000 was applicable to 1998, and the balance was applicable to 1997. Litigation of this nature is recurring for this company.

Instructions

Identify and discuss the weaknesses in classification and disclosure in the single-step Income and Retained Earnings Statement above. You should explain why these treatments are weaknesses and what the proper presentation of the items would be in accordance with recent professional pronouncements.

C4-8 (Classification of Income Statement Items) As audit partner for Noriyuki and Morita, you are in charge of reviewing the classification of unusual items that have occurred during the current year. The following items have come to your attention:

1. A merchandising company incorrectly overstated its ending inventory 2 years ago by a material amount. Inventory for all other periods is correctly computed.
2. An automobile dealer sells for $137,000 an extremely rare 1930 S type Invicta which it purchased for $21,000 10 years ago. The Invicta is the only such display item the dealer owns.
3. A drilling company during the current year extended the estimated useful life of certain drilling equipment from 9 to 15 years. As a result, depreciation for the current year was materially lowered.

4. A retail outlet changed its computation for bad debt expense from 1% to ½ of 1% of sales because of changes in its customer clientele.

5. A mining concern sells a foreign subsidiary engaged in uranium mining, although it (the seller) continues to engage in uranium mining in other countries.

6. A steel company changes from straight-line depreciation to accelerated depreciation in accounting for its plant assets.

7. A construction company, at great expense, prepares a major proposal for a government loan. The loan is not approved.

8. A water pump manufacturer has had large losses resulting from a strike by its employees early in the year.

9. Depreciation for a prior period was incorrectly understated by $950,000. The error was discovered in the current year.

10. A large sheep rancher suffered a major loss because the state required that all sheep in the state be killed to halt the spread of a rare disease. Such a situation has not occurred in the state for 20 years.

11. A food distributor that sells wholesale to supermarket chains and to fast-food restaurants (two major classes of customers) decides to discontinue the division that sells to one of the two classes of customers.

Instructions

From the foregoing information, indicate in what section of the income statement or retained earnings statement these items should be classified. Provide a brief rationale for your position.

C4-9 (Capital Maintenance vs. Transaction Approach)   In early 1984 the Andre Giant Company was formed when it issued 10,000 shares of common stock at $20 per share. A few years later, 3,000 additional shares were issued at $37 per share. No other common stock transactions occurred until the company was liquidated in 1998. At that time, corporate assets were sold for $1,180,000 and $100,000 of corporate liabilities were paid off. The remaining cash was distributed to stockholders. During the corporation's life, it paid total dividends of $200,000.

Instructions

(a) Discuss the two approaches to calculating income.

(b) If only the facts given above are available, which approach must be used to compute income?

(c) Compute the income of Andre Giant Company over its 15-year life.

*C4-10 (Discontinued Operations)**   You're the engagement partner on a multi-divisional, calendar year-end client with annual sales of $90 million. The company primarily sells electronic transistors to small customers and has one division that deals in acoustic transmitters for Navy submarines. The Red October Division has approximately $18 million in sales.

It's an evening in February, 1998, and the audit work is complete. You're working in the client's office on the report, when you overhear a conversation between the financial vice-president, the treasurer, and the controller. They're discussing the sale of the Red October Division, expected to take place in June of this year, and the related reporting problems.

The vice-president thinks no segregation of the sale is necessary in the income statement because separate categories tend to be abused and confuse the stockholders. The treasurer disagrees. He feels that if an item is unusual or infrequent, it should be classified as an extraordinary item, including the sale of the Red October Division. The controller says an item should be both infrequent and unusual to be extraordinary. He feels the sale of the Red October Division should be shown separately, but not as an extraordinary item.

The sale is not new to you because you read about it in the minutes of the December 16, 1997, board of directors meeting. The minutes indicated plans to sell the transmitter plant and equipment by June 30, 1998, to its major competitor, who seems interested. The board estimates that net income and sales will remain constant until the sale, on which the company expects a $700,000 profit.

You also hear the controller disagree with the vice-president that the results of the strike last year and the sale of the old transistor ovens, formerly used in manufacturing, would also be extraordinary items. In addition, the treasurer thinks the government regulation issued last month, which made much of their inventory of raw material useless, would be extraordinary. The regulations set beta emission standards at levels lower than those in the raw materials supply, and there's no alternative use for the materials. Finally, the controller claims the discussion is academic. Since the net effect of all three items is immaterial, no disclosure is required.

Instructions

(a) Does the Red October Division qualify as a segment of a business in more than one way? If so, why?

(b) Does the Red October Division qualify as a discontinued operation? Why?

(c) Do the minutes indicate that a formal plan has been established? If not, why?

(d) When should the gain be recognized? What if a loss were anticipated?

(e) Who is correct about reporting the sale? What would the income statement presentation be for the next fiscal year?

(f) Who is right about whether the strike, the sale of fixed assets and the imposition of a new government regulation constitute extraordinary items?

(g) What do you think about the controller's observation on materiality?

(h) What facts can you give the group about the earnings per share ramifications of these topics?

❖ FINANCIAL REPORTING PROBLEM — INTEL CORPORATION

The financial statements of Intel and accompanying notes, as presented in the Company's 1995 Annual Report, are in Appendix 5B.

Instructions
Refer to this information and answer the following questions:

1. What type of income statement format does Intel use? Indicate why this format might be used to present income statement information.
2. What are Intel's primary revenue sources?
3. Compute Intel's gross profit for each of the years 1993–1995. Explain why cost of sales has increased over these years.
4. Why does Intel make a distinction between operating and nonoperating revenue? Explain what happened to Intel's nonoperating revenue in 1995.
5. What financial ratios did Intel choose to report in its "Facts and Figures" section covering the years 1986–1995?

❖ FINANCIAL STATEMENT ANALYSIS CASES

Case 1 (Comptronix Corporation)

Comptronix Corporation manufactures circuit boards and other electronic parts used in computers, computer peripherals, medical devices, and testing equipment. During 1995, the company ceased operations in two locations. A manufacturing facility in San Jose, California, was sold and one in Colorado Springs, Colorado, was closed. The products that had been manufactured in both locations were similar to those manufactured in the remaining plants.

The sale of the San Jose facility was completed in 1995. Suppose that the operating loss from this facility was $400,000, net of applicable tax benefit of $103,000, and that the sale of the assets resulted in a $4.7 million loss based on a book value of $7.2 million.

Instructions
(a) Should Comptronix account for this as a discontinued segment? Why or why not?
(b) Describe how the sale of the San Jose facility should be shown on the income statement of Comptronix if the company determined that it should be shown as a discontinued segment.
(c) Describe how the sale of the San Jose facility should be shown on the income statement of Comptronix if the company determined that it should *not* be shown as a discontinued segment.

Case 2 (Dresser Industries)

Dresser Industries provides products and services to oil and natural gas exploration, production, transmission and processing companies. The company's 1992 income statement is reproduced below. Dollar amounts are in millions.

Sales	$2,697.0
Service revenues	1,933.9
Share of earnings of unconsolidated affiliates	92.4
Total revenues	4,723.3
Cost of sales	1,722.7
Cost of services	1,799.9
Total costs of sales and services	3,522.6
Gross earnings	1,200.7
Selling, engineering, administrative and general expenses	(919.8)
Special charges	(70.0)

Other income (deductions)	
Interest expense	(47.4)
Interest earned	19.1
Other, net	4.8
Earnings before income taxes and other items below	187.4
Income taxes	(79.4)
Minority interest	(10.3)
Earnings from continuing operations	97.7
Discontinued operations	(35.3)
Earnings before extraordinary items and accounting changes	62.4
Extraordinary items	(6.3)
Cumulative effect of accounting changes	(393.8)
Net earnings (loss)	$(337.7)

Instructions

Assume that 177,636,000,000 shares of stock were issued and outstanding. Prepare the per-share portion of the income statement. Remember to begin with Income from Continuing Operations.

❖ COMPARATIVE ANALYSIS CASE

The Coca-Cola Company versus PepsiCo Inc.

Instructions

Go to our Web site and answer the following questions.

1. What type of income format(s) is used by these two companies? Indentify any differences in income statement format between these two companies.
2. What are the gross profits, operating profit, and net income for these two companies over the three-year period 1993–1995? Which company has had better financial results over this period of time?
3. Identify the irregular items reported by these two companies in their income statements over the three-year period 1993–1995. Do these irregular items appear to be significant?
4. In PepsiCo's Management Analysis section under results of operation, examine the company's presentation of "Operating Profit" and "Income and Income Per Share Before Cumulative Effect of Accounting Changes." Why do you believe PepsiCo reports information on both a "reported" and "ongoing" basis?

www.wiley.com/college/kieso

❖ RESEARCH CASES

Case 1

Most libraries maintain the annual reports of large companies on file or on microfiche.

Instructions

Obtain the 1995 annual reports for UAL Corp. and NIKE, Inc. and answer the following questions concerning their income statements. (*Note:* Larger libraries may have CD-ROM products such as *Laser Disclosure* or *Compact Disclosure*.)

(a) Describe the major differences between the income statement formats.
(b) Identify any irregular items on either of the income statements.
(c) UAL includes a separate line for depreciation expense, while NIKE does not. Why is this the case? Does NIKE's depreciation expense appear on another financial statement?
(d) UAL's income statement includes significantly more detail than NIKE's. Which presentation do you prefer? Why?

Case 2

The April 1996 issue of the *Journal of Accountancy* includes an article by Dennis R. Beresford, L. Todd Johnson, and Cheri L. Reither, entitled "Is a Second Income Statement Needed?"

Instructions

Read the article and answer the following questions.

(a) On what basis would the "second income statement" be prepared? Briefly describe this basis.

(b) Why is there a perceived need for a second income statement?

(c) Identify three alternatives for reporting the proposed measure of income.

❖ WRITING ASSIGNMENT

As a practicing CPA, you have just received the following letter from your client, Buy-Rite Corp., a parent corporation with a number of subsidiaries. All amounts are shown net of tax.

December 21, 1997

Dear Student Accountant:

In April of 1998, Buy-Rite is planning a bond issue to raise $3,000,000 which will allow us to expand our overseas operations. However, we have encountered two situations which may dramatically affect 1997 net income and, consequently, our ability to sell the bonds.

The first problem is that, on July 3, 1997, our Board of Directors voted unanimously to dispose of Bailey's Inns, our Southern restaurant chain (a business segment), which has become increasingly unprofitable. From January 1, 1997 until that date, Bailey's lost $400,000. With only ten days left in 1997, Bailey's has realized an additional $250,000 loss. The bright side is that we have arranged to sell Bailey's on April 1, 1998 for a gain of $400,000. We also estimate that Bailey's will bring in net operating income of $100,000 from January 1, 1998 to the date of disposal (the first quarter, peak season, being its usual profitable one).

Our greatest concern is that we must claim the entire loss of $650,000 on our 1997 income statement, deferring the recognition of the $400,000 gain and $100,000 of net operating income until the 1998 income statement. This loss may adversely affect our 1998 bond issue.

In itself, this loss would not appear so problematic if it did not also coincide with an extraordinary loss that our company took on translation of foreign currency. Last April when the Yen was very weak, Buy-Rite made several transactions with Japanese companies. Because the Yen was so weak, we did not bother to hedge. Unexpectedly, the Yen became very strong, so by the time our Japanese payables came due, we incurred a $300,000 loss.

Please explain to us how we can present these items in such a way that investors will not be reluctant to purchase our bonds.

Sincerely,

Jack O. Lantern, Chief Accountant

Instructions
Draft a letter to Mr. Lantern, explaining how Buy-Rite must account for the disposition of the segment, including what amounts will be reported in both 1997 and 1998. In addition, address the issue of the loss on translation of foreign currency.

❖ GROUP ASSIGNMENT

Rap Corp. has 100,000 shares of common stock outstanding. In 1999, the company reports income from continuing operations before taxes of $1,210,000. Additional transactions not considered in the $1,210,000 are as follows:

1. In 1999, Rap Corp. sold equipment for $40,000. The machine had originally cost $80,000 and had accumulated depreciation of $36,000. The gain or loss is considered ordinary.

2. The company discontinued operations of one of its subsidiaries during the current year at a loss of $190,000 before taxes. Assume that this transaction meets the criteria for discontinued operations. The loss on operations of the discontinued subsidiary was $90,000 before taxes; the loss from disposal of the subsidiary was $100,000 before taxes.

3. The sum of $100,000, applicable to a breached 1995 contract, was received as a result of a lawsuit. Prior to the award, legal counsel was uncertain about the outcome of the suit and had not established a receivable.

4. In 1999 the company reviewed its accounts receivable and determined that $26,000 of accounts receivable that had been carried for years appeared unlikely to be collected.

5. An internal audit discovered that amortization of intangible assets was understated by $35,000 (net of tax) in a prior period. The amount was charged against retained earnings.
6. The company sold its only investment in common stock during the year at a gain of $145,000. The gain is taxed at a total effective rate of 40%. Assume that the transaction meets the requirements of an extraordinary item.

Instructions

Your instructor will identify one member of the group to serve as a recorder and one member to serve as spokesperson. As a group, analyze the above information so that the recorder can prepare an income statement for the year 1999 starting with income from continuing operations before income taxes. Compute earnings per share as it should be shown on the face of the income statement. (Assume a total effective tax rate of 38% on all items, unless otherwise indicated.)

❖ ETHICS CASES

Case 1

The following represents the *entire* 1997 Income Statement for the Boeing Company:

Sales	$21,924,000,000
Costs and Expenses	20,773,000,000
Earnings from Operations	1,151,000,000
Other Income	122,000,000
Interest and Debt Expense	(130,000,000)
Earnings before Income Taxes	1,143,000,000
Income Taxes	(287,000,000)
Net Earnings	$ 856,000,000

It includes only *five* separate numbers (two of which are in billions of dollars), *two* subtotals, and the net earnings figure.

Instructions

Is it ethical to provide this level of disclosure?

Case 2

Ferguson Arthur, Jr., controller for the Jenkins Corporation, is preparing the company's income statement at year-end. He notes that the company lost a considerable sum on the sale of some equipment it had decided to replace. Since the company has sold equipment routinely in the past, Arthur knows the losses cannot be reported as extraordinary. He also does not want to highlight it as a material loss since he feels that will reflect poorly on him and the company. He reasons that if the company had recorded more depreciation during the assets' lives the losses would not be so great. Since depreciation is included among the company's operating expenses, he wants to report the losses along with the company's expenses, where he hopes it will not be noticed.

Instructions

(a) What are the ethical issues involved?
(b) What should Arthur do?

Accounting Ethics

A visit with
Robert Sack

ROBERT SACK teaches accounting and ethics at the Darden Graduate School of Business at the University of Virginia. Prior to joining academia, Mr. Sack was chief accountant in the enforcement division of the Securities & Exchange Commission, as well as a partner with what is now Deloitte & Touche.

How has the discussion of ethics evolved over the years? If we had been discussing ethics many years ago, we'd have been concerned about the conflicts between auditing and consulting, about how much of an investment a CPA could have with his or her client, and whether or not a CPA could keep the books for the client and also audit their financial statements. That was the scope of the discussion. Today, we've moved well beyond that which is in the AICPA code of ethics.

What are some of today's difficult ethical questions? When you do an audit for a client who has been with your firm for many years, you'll be looking at work that either you or your peers at the firm did last year. That's a supreme ethics question, because you have to say, "If I find something wrong that we did last year, or I see something that we overlooked, don't I have an obligation to my firm, to the client, to my peers, to come forward to say something? And yet, the cost of fixing it will be very high, for me and the firm. Don't I have an obligation to my firm, and my family, to try to avoid that cost unless it is absolutely necessary?" We have seen examples of people who confronted that question but stepped up to it and brought the problem out into the open. In each case, it cost the firm a great deal of money, and yet it was the right thing to do. In the last several years, the SEC has brought enforcement actions against individual members of an audit team, acknowledging that the primary responsibility rests with the signing partner, but also arguing that the staff people have a professional responsibility to keep the firm from making a mistake. In one case, the manager on the job had been fighting with the client over some accounting adjustments. The client didn't want to make them, but the manager thought they had to be made. Then the manager was called out of town to work on another job. The partner came in to close out the first job and agreed with the client on some of the debates. When the manager came back and found out that the job was done and that the partner had agreed to amounts that the manager didn't agree to, he was confronted with a very difficult ethical choice. To whom did he owe loyalty? To the partner, who after all had the final responsibility? Or to the readers of the financial statements? In the end, the manager signed off on the papers. Someone else on the audit team alerted the national office, which after a thorough review recalled the audit report and admitted that the partner and manager had made a mistake.

The FASB received an enormous amount of pressure on the stock options issue. Is there a conflict of interest between the CFO's corporate responsibility and his or her true opinion on accounting principles? I took a poll of my second-year MBA class, and 98% of the people said they thought stock options represent a cost which should be on the income statement. But what would you do if you were the CFO of a high-tech firm and you were paying your people a lot of money with stock options? Would you go to the FASB and say that you thought the Board is doing the right thing, even if it cut your earnings in half? That discussion helped my students see that it is easy to answer accounting questions in the abstract, but more difficult to deal with questions that have a more personal impact. Suddenly, those abstract theoretical questions become ethical questions.

The issue of independence is still relevant, isn't it? Yes, but in a broader context. Today, accountants are part of the management team. They're expected to think about the world from a business standpoint. As the sales team hones in on a lead, they often send the CEO, the sales person, the chief operations person, and the chief accountant. Their presentation includes how they're going to structure this transaction, why the product is terrific, and why the financing that the chief accountant has been able to come up with will save the customer a lot of money. This is a classic case of a teamwork approach to an opportunity. When that closing team wins the sale, they will be very excited and everyone will celebrate. But the next morning, the accountant will be forced to evaluate that transaction, to be sure that it qualifies for revenue recognition in accordance with GAAP. But let's assume that there are some serious contingencies in the customer's acceptance of the deal. Can the accountant be independent of his or her work, and independent of the peer team members? Can the accountant be independent enough to tell the team that their hard fought victory doesn't count? That would be a difficult discussion, at best, but it has to happen for the good of the firm. The dual role we expect management accountants to play, working as a part of line management but also acting as the primary gatekeeper for financial reporting, requires a great deal of personal independence.

Does the accountant have an ethical responsibility to be concerned about the social implications of downsizing? When the subject of cost control comes up, everyone turns to the accountant. Cost management is a current hot button in management circles. But costs are only part of the profitability equation. An accountant who thinks that the only function of a business is to make money for the stockholders is going to hurt the stockholders in the end. An accountant can't say that costs are the only thing that matter. He or she has to be concerned with the people, the products, the quality of the relationships in the town, and all of the other factors which go into the long-term success of the firm. Accountants must lead the way in helping their managements see that the company is more than cash and costs and so forth, and see that the company's success depends on its people. Where downsizing hurts the cadre of people who make the business succeed, it is bad business. Where downsizing breaks the faith with people who have given heavily to the firm, it is immoral. And accountants need to help their companies keep that faith because it is good business and it is the right thing to do.

CPA firms have been trying to accommodate women in their childbearing years. Do they have an ethical obligation to allow professional women to work part-time once they become mothers? Of course you have an obligation to these employees. Once again, it is a matter of keeping the faith. But you also have an obligation to the rest of the staff. Let's say you have five people working on a team, and only one has a family. Is it fair to say to the other four that they have to work 12 hours a day but Joan has to work only six? How do you evaluate those people? Can you honestly say that you will give a fair evaluation to that person who by necessity goes home in the middle of the afternoon? It's a terribly tough question. The reason that it's an ethical question is that it requires the manager to balance the conflicting interests of so many people, all of whom are entitled to expect fair treatment.

CHAPTER 5

Balance Sheet and Statement of Cash Flows

Warning Signs!

Commodore International reported earnings of $4.66 per share in one year, up approximately 63% over the prior year. Yet, its stock price dropped from a high of 60⅝ to less than 30 over this one-year period. Why? The balance sheet indicated that accounts receivable increased substantially and the composition of the inventory changed dramatically. The substantial receivable buildup indicated that the receivable collection was a problem. Furthermore, while inventory overall remained stable, finished goods inventory increased 50%. In other words, goods were piling up because sales were lagging. Savvy investors, who saw the trouble signs in the financial statements, began selling their stock. In the following year, Commodore reported a fourth quarter loss of $124 million caused by substantial inventory write-offs.

Earnings declines at Commodore could have been predicted, given the deteriorating financial information provided in the balance sheet and statement of cash flows. And just as these deteriorating financial statements warned of trouble, improving balance sheet and related cash flow quality often foreshadows long-term improvements in earnings.

LEARNING OBJECTIVES

After studying this chapter, you should be able to:

1 Identify the uses and limitations of a balance sheet.

2 Identify the major classifications of the balance sheet.

3 Prepare a classified balance sheet using the report and account formats.

4 Identify balance sheet information requiring supplemental disclosure.

5 Identify major disclosure techniques for the balance sheet.

6 Indicate the purpose of the statement of cash flows.

7 Identify the content of the statement of cash flows.

8 Prepare a statement of cash flows.

9 Understand the usefulness of the statement of cash flows.

Preview of Chapter 5

Until recently, the balance sheet was skimmed and the cash flow statement all but ignored. However, these financial statements offer important information. For example, as shown in the opening story involving Commodore International, surprises in earnings per share could have been anticipated if these financial statements had not been overlooked. The purpose of this chapter is to examine the many different types of assets, liabilities, and stockholders' equity items that affect the balance sheet and the statement of cash flows. The content and organization of this chapter are as follows:

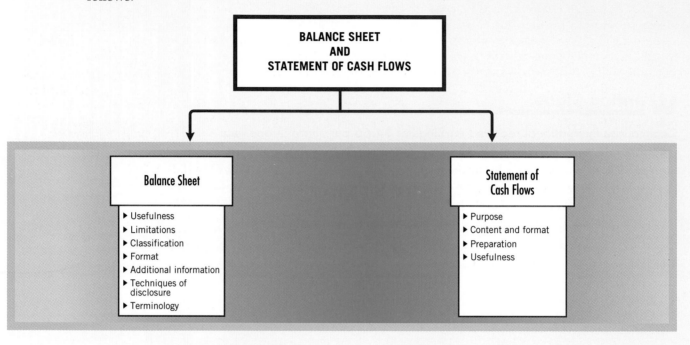

SECTION 1 — *BALANCE SHEET*

The balance sheet, sometimes referred to as the statement of financial position, reports the assets, liabilities, and stockholders' equity of a business enterprise at a specific date. This financial statement provides information about the nature and amounts of investments in enterprise resources, obligations to creditors, and the owners' equity in net resources.[1] It therefore helps in predicting the amounts, timing, and uncertainty of future cash flows.

---

[1]*Accounting Trends and Techniques—1996* indicates that approximately 94% of the companies surveyed used the term "balance sheet." The term "statement of financial position" is used infrequently, although it is conceptually appealing.

❖ USEFULNESS OF THE BALANCE SHEET

The balance sheet provides a basis for (1) computing rates of return, (2) evaluating the capital structure of the enterprise, and (3) assessing its liquidity and financial flexibility. In order to judge enterprise risk[2] and assess future cash flows, the balance sheet is analyzed for enterprise liquidity and financial flexibility.

Liquidity describes "the amount of time that is expected to elapse until an asset is realized or otherwise converted into cash or until a liability has to be paid."[3] Both short-term and long-term credit grantors are interested in such short-term ratios as cash or near cash to current liabilities. Such ratios measure the enterprise's ability to meet current and maturing obligations. Similarly, present and prospective equity holders study liquidity to gauge future cash dividends or the possibility of expanded operations. Generally, the greater the liquidity, the lower the risk of enterprise failure.

Financial flexibility is the "ability of an enterprise to take effective actions to alter the amounts and timing of cash flows so it can respond to unexpected needs and opportunities."[4] For example, a company may become so loaded with debt—so financially inflexible—that its sources of cash to finance expansion or to pay off maturing debt are limited or nonexistent. An enterprise with a high degree of financial flexibility is better able to survive bad times, to recover from unexpected setbacks, and to take advantage of profitable and unexpected investment opportunities. Generally, the greater the financial flexibility, the lower the risk of enterprise failure.

Lack of liquidity and inadequate financial flexibility seriously affected the U.S. airline industry in the 1980s and again in the early 1990s. American, Eastern, United, and TWA all reported quarterly operating losses that stemmed primarily from high interest costs, increased fuel costs, and price cutting resulting from deregulation. Because of operating losses and lowered liquidity, some airlines asked their employees to sign labor contracts that provided no wage increases. Other airlines, already heavily in debt and lacking financial flexibility and liquidity, had to cancel orders for new, more efficient aircraft. TWA had to sell routes and planes to raise cash. Some of the major airlines (such as Braniff, Continental, Eastern, Midway, and America West) have even declared bankruptcy. All of this was no secret. The airlines' balance sheets clearly revealed their financial inflexibility and low liquidity.

> **Objective ❶**
>
> Identify the uses and limitations of a balance sheet.

> ✦ **UNDERLYING CONCEPTS**
>
> The presentation of balance sheet information meets one of the objectives of financial reporting—to provide information about enterprise resources, claims to resources, and changes in them.

❖ LIMITATIONS OF THE BALANCE SHEET

As indicated in earlier chapters, historical cost is used in valuing and reporting most assets and liabilities. Thus, the balance sheet **does not reflect the current value** of many items. When a balance sheet is prepared in accordance with generally accepted accounting principles, most assets are stated at cost; exceptions are receivables and most investment securities.

Many believe that all assets should be restated in terms of current values; there are, however, widely differing opinions about the type of valuation basis to be employed. Some contend that **historical cost statements** should be adjusted for constant dollars (general price-level changes) when inflation is significant; others believe that a **current cost concept** (specific price-level changes) is more useful; still others believe that a **net realizable value** concept or some variant should be adopted. Regardless of the method favored, all are significantly different from the historical cost approach. Each approach

> ✦ **UNDERLYING CONCEPTS**
>
> This section, Limitations of the Balance Sheet, demonstrates the trade-off between relevance and reliability. On the one hand, the historical cost principle and the monetary unit assumption ensure that the information is reliable; unfortunately application of these concepts may lead to less relevant reporting because current values are not reported and significant non-quantitative information is excluded.

---

[2]Risk is an expression of the unpredictability of future events, transactions, circumstances, and results of the enterprise.

[3]"Reporting Income, Cash Flows, and Financial Position of Business Enterprises," *Proposed Statement of Financial Accounting Concepts* (Stamford, Conn.: FASB, 1981), par. 29.

[4]Ibid., par. 25.

has this advantage over the historical cost basis: Each presents a more accurate assessment of the current value of the enterprise, although the question of whether reliable valuations can be obtained is still unresolved.

Another basic limitation of the balance sheet is that **judgments and estimates must be used**. The collectibility of receivables, the salability of inventory, and the useful life of long-term tangible and intangible assets are difficult to determine. Although the process of depreciating long-term assets is a generally accepted practice, the recognition of an increase in asset value is generally ignored.

In addition, the balance sheet necessarily **omits many items that are of financial value to the business** but cannot be recorded objectively. The value of a company's human resources (employee workforce) is certainly significant, but it is omitted because such assets are difficult to quantify. Other items of value not reported are customer base, managerial skills, research superiority, and reputation. Such omissions are understandable. But many items that could and should appear on the balance sheet (most are liabilities) are reported in an "off-balance-sheet" manner, if reported at all.[5] Several of these omitted items (such as leases, through-put arrangements, take-or-pay contracts, and pensions) are discussed in later chapters.

One of the most significant challenges facing the accounting profession is the limitations of financial statements. As indicated in Chapter 1, the AICPA has recently concluded a study examining the information needs of investors and creditors. Some major observations are related to the balance sheet: Users oppose replacing the current historical-cost–based accounting model with a fair value accounting model. However, they view fair value information as useful for particular types of assets and liabilities and in certain types of industries. Also users want companies to disclose information about the estimates and assumptions used to determine material asset and liability amounts. Finally, they want more qualitative and quantitative information about the risks associated with financial instruments and off-balance-sheet financing arrangements.[6]

❖ CLASSIFICATION IN THE BALANCE SHEET

Objective ❷

Identify the major classifications of the balance sheet.

Balance sheet accounts are **classified** so that similar items are grouped together to arrive at significant subtotals. Furthermore, the material is arranged so that important relationships are shown.

The FASB has often noted that the parts and subsections of financial statements can be more informative than the whole. Therefore, as one would expect, the reporting of summary accounts (total assets, net assets, total liabilities, etc.) alone is discouraged. Individual items should be separately reported and classified in sufficient detail to permit users to assess the amounts, timing, and uncertainty of future cash flows, as well as the evaluation of liquidity and financial flexibility, profitability, and risk.

Classification in financial statements helps analysts by grouping items with similar characteristics and separating items with different characteristics:[7]

❶ Assets that differ in their **type or expected function** in the central operations or other activities of the enterprise should be reported as separate items; for example, merchandise inventories should be reported separately from property, plant, and equipment.

---

[5]For a discussion of various methods that businesses have devised to remove debt from the balance sheet, read: "Get It Off the Balance Sheet," Richard Dieter and Arthur R. Wyatt, *Financial Executive* (Vol. 48, January 1980).

[6]"Meeting the Information Needs of Investors and Creditors," The AICPA Special Committee on Financial Reporting (Supplement to the *Journal of Accountancy*), September 1994.

[7]"Reporting Income, Cash Flows, and Financial Positions of Business Enterprises," *Proposed Statement of Financial Accounting Concepts* (Stamford, Conn.: FASB, 1981), par. 51.

❷ Assets and liabilities with **different implications for the financial flexibility** of the enterprise should be reported as separate items; for example, assets used in operations should be reported separately from assets held for investment, and assets subject to restrictions such as leased equipment.

❸ Assets and liabilities with **different general liquidity characteristics** should be reported as separate items. For example, cash should be reported separately from inventories.

The three general classes of items included in the balance sheet are assets, liabilities, and equity. Here is how we defined them in Chapter 2:

❖ ELEMENTS OF THE BALANCE SHEET ❖

❶ *Assets.* Probable future economic benefits obtained or controlled by a particular entity as a result of past transactions or events.

❷ *Liabilities.* Probable future sacrifices of economic benefits arising from present obligations of a particular entity to transfer assets or provide services to other entities in the future as a result of past transactions or events.

❸ *Equity.* Residual interest in the assets of an entity that remains after deducting its liabilities. In a business enterprise, the equity is the ownership interest.[8]

These items are then divided into several subclassifications. Illustration 5-1 indicates the general format of balance sheet presentation.

Assets	Liabilities and Owners' Equity
Current assets	Current liabilities
Long-term investments	Long-term debt
Property, plant, and equipment	Owners' equity
Intangible assets	Capital stock
Other assets	Additional paid-in capital
	Retained earnings

ILLUSTRATION 5-1
Balance Sheet Classifications

The balance sheet may be classified in some other manner, but there is very little departure from these major subdivisions in practice. If a proprietorship or partnership is involved, the classifications within the owners' equity section are presented a little differently, as will be shown later in the chapter.

Current Assets

Current assets **are cash and other assets expected to be converted into cash, sold, or consumed either in one year or in the operating cycle, whichever is longer.** The operating cycle is the average time between the acquisition of materials and supplies and the realization of cash through sales of the product for which the materials and supplies were acquired. The cycle operates from cash through inventory, production, and receivables back to cash. When there are several operating cycles within one year, the one-year period is used. If the operating cycle is more than one year, the longer period is used.

---

[8]"Elements of Financial Statements of Business Enterprises," *Statement of Financial Accounting Concepts No. 6* (Stamford, Conn.: FASB, 1985), paras. 25, 35 and 49.

Current assets are presented in the balance sheet in order of liquidity. The five major items found in the current asset section are cash, short-term investments, receivables, inventories, and prepayments. **Cash** is included at its stated value; **short-term investments** are generally valued at fair value; **accounts receivable** are stated at the estimated amount collectible; **inventories** generally are included at cost or the lower of cost or market; and **prepaid items** are valued at cost.

The above items are not considered current assets if they are not expected to be realized in one year or in the operating cycle, whichever is longer. For example, cash restricted for purposes other than payment of current obligations or for use in current operations is excluded from the current asset section. **Generally, the rule is that if an asset is to be turned into cash or is to be used to pay a current liability within a year or the operating cycle, whichever is longer, it is classified as current.** This requirement is subject to exceptions. An investment in common stock is classified as either a current asset or a noncurrent asset depending on management's intent. When a company has small holdings of common stocks or bonds that are going to be held long-term, they should not be classified as current.

Although a current asset is well defined, certain theoretical problems develop. One problem is justifying the inclusion of prepaid expense in the current asset section. The normal justification is that if these items had not been paid in advance, they would require the use of current assets during the operating cycle. If we follow this logic to its ultimate conclusion, however, any asset purchased previously saves the use of current assets during the operating cycle and would be considered current.

Another problem occurs in the current asset definition when fixed assets are consumed during the operating cycle. A literal interpretation of the accounting profession's position on this matter would indicate that an amount equal to the current depreciation and amortization charges on the noncurrent assets should be placed in the current asset section at the beginning of the year, because they will be consumed in the next operating cycle. This conceptual problem is ignored, which illustrates that the formal distinction made between current and noncurrent assets is somewhat arbitrary.[9]

Cash

Any restrictions on the general availability of cash or any commitments on its probable disposition must be disclosed. An example of such a presentation is excerpted from the Annual Report of Owens-Corning Fiberglas Corp. below:

ILLUSTRATION 5-2
Balance Sheet
Presentation of Restricted
Cash

Owens-Corning Fiberglas Corp.

Current assets	
Cash	$ 3,927,000
Restricted cash (Note 22)	85,043,000

Note 22: Restricted Funds. The Company has 222,885,000 Brazilian cruzados (approximately $15,000,000) of restricted funds deposited in a Brazilian bank account representing a recent dividend payment from a Brazilian subsidiary. Those funds are expected to be available to the Company in the next year.

The Company also has 116,707,000 Swiss Francs (approximately $70,000,000) in trust and restricted for payment of the Company's maturing bonds payable in Swiss Francs.

In the example above, cash was restricted to meet an obligation due currently and, therefore, was included under current assets. If cash is restricted for purposes other

---

[9]For an interesting discussion of the shortcomings of the current and noncurrent classification framework, see Loyd Heath, "Financial Reporting and the Evaluation of Solvency," *Accounting Research Monograph No. 3* (New York: AICPA, 1978), pp. 43–69. The principal recommendation is that the current and noncurrent classification be abolished, and that assets and liabilities simply be listed without classification in their present order. This approach is justified on the basis that any classification scheme is arbitrary and that users of the financial statements can assemble the data in the manner they believe most appropriate.

than current obligations, it is excluded from current assets. An example of a noncurrent presentation is excerpted from the Annual Report of The Penn Traffic Company below:

ILLUSTRATION 5-3
Balance Sheet
Presentation of
Noncurrent Restricted
Cash

The Penn Traffic Company	
Current assets	
Cash and short-term investments	$9,123,000
Other assets	
Restricted funds (Note 1)	8,101,000

Note 1: Restricted Funds. During the current year, the Company entered into a long-term debt agreement for construction of a new perishables distribution center. The principal amount has been included in long-term debt, and the unexpended cash proceeds at year end have been reported as restricted funds.

Short-Term Investments

Investments in debt and equity securities are grouped into three separate portfolios for valuation and reporting purposes. These portfolios are categorized as follows:

Held-to-maturity: Debt securities that the enterprise has the positive intent and ability to hold to maturity.

Trading: Debt and equity securities bought and held primarily for sale in the near term to generate income on short-term price differences.

Available-for-sale: Debt and equity securities not classified as held-to-maturity or trading securities.

Trading securities (whether debt or equity) should be reported as current assets. Individual held-to-maturity and available-for-sale securities are classified as current or noncurrent depending upon the circumstances. All trading and available-for-sale securities are to be reported at fair value.[10]

The example below is excerpted from the Annual Report of Anchor BanCorp Wisconsin Inc.

ILLUSTRATION 5-4
Balance Sheet
Presentation of
Investment in Securities

Anchor BanCorp Wisconsin Inc. (in thousands)	
Assets	
Cash and cash equivalents	$ 45,784
Securities available for sale:	
Investment securities	10,284
Mortgage-related securities	51,814
Securities held to maturity:	
Mortgage-related securities (fair value of $134.2 million and $223.7 million, respectively)	135,896
Loans receivable, net	
Held for sale	16,542
Held for investment	1,066,945
Foreclosed properties and repossessed assets, net	5,294

Receivables

Any anticipated loss due to uncollectibles, the amount and nature of any nontrade receivables, and any receivables designated or pledged as collateral should be clearly identified. Mack Trucks, Inc. reported its receivables as follows:

---

[10]"Accounting for Certain Investments in Debt and Equity Securities," *Statement of Financial Accounting Standards No. 115* (Norwalk, Conn.: FASB, 1993).

ILLUSTRATION 5-5
Balance Sheet
Presentation of
Receivables

Mack Trucks, Inc.		
Current assets		
Trade receivables:		
Accounts receivable	$102,212,000	
Affiliated companies	1,157,000	
Installment notes and contracts	625,000	
Total	103,994,000	
Less allowance for uncollectible accounts	8,194,000	
Trade receivables—net	95,800,000	
Receivable from unconsolidated financial subsidiaries	22,106,000	

UNDERLYING CONCEPTS

The lower of cost or market valuation is an example of the use of conservatism in accounting.

Inventories

For a proper presentation of inventories, the basis of valuation (i.e., lower of cost or market), and the method of pricing (FIFO or LIFO) are disclosed. For a manufacturing concern (like General Signal Corporation, shown below), the stage of completion of the inventories is also indicated.

ILLUSTRATION 5-6
Balance Sheet
Presentation of
Inventories, Showing
Stage of Completion

General Signal Corporation		
Current assets		
Inventories—at the lower of cost (determined by the first-in, first-out method) or market		
Finished goods	$103,405,000	
Work in process	126,667,000	
Raw materials and purchased parts	167,972,000	$398,044,000

Weyerhaeuser Company, a forestry company and lumber manufacturer with several finished goods product lines, reported its inventory as follows:

ILLUSTRATION 5-7
Balance Sheet
Presentation of
Inventories, Showing
Product Lines

Weyerhaeuser Company		
Current assets		
Inventories—at FIFO lower of cost or market		
Logs and chips	$ 68,471,000	
Lumber, plywood and panels	86,741,000	
Pulp, newsprint and paper	47,377,000	
Containerboard, paperboard, containers and cartons	59,682,000	
Other products	161,717,000	
Total product inventories	423,988,000	
Materials and supplies	175,540,000	

Prepaid Expenses

Prepaid expenses included in current assets are expenditures already made for benefits (usually services) to be received within one year or the operating cycle, whichever is longer.[11] These items are current assets because if they had not already been paid, they would require the use of cash during the next year or the operating cycle. A common example is the payment in advance for an insurance policy. It is classified as a prepaid expense at the time of the expenditure because the payment precedes the receipt of the benefit of coverage. Prepaid expenses are reported at the amount of the unexpired or unconsumed cost. Other common prepaid expenses include prepaid rent, advertising,

---

[11]*Accounting Trends and Techniques—1996* in its survey of 600 annual reports identified 357 companies that reported prepaid expenses.

taxes, and office or operating supplies. Munsingwear, Inc., for example, listed its prepaid expenses in current assets as follows:

Munsingwear, Inc.	
Current assets	
Inventories	$18,013,000
Prepaid expenses	1,492,000
Net assets related to discontinued operations	5,162,000

ILLUSTRATION 5-8
Balance Sheet
Presentation of Prepaid
Expenses

Companies often include insurance and other prepayments for 2 or 3 years in current assets even though part of the advance payment applies to periods beyond one year or the current operating cycle.

Long-Term Investments

Long-term investments, often referred to simply as investments, normally consist of one of four types:

❶ Investments in securities, such as bonds, common stock, or long-term notes.
❷ Investments in tangible fixed assets not currently used in operations, such as land held for speculation.
❸ Investments set aside in special funds such as a sinking fund, pension fund, or plant expansion fund. The cash surrender value of life insurance is included here.
❹ Investments in nonconsolidated subsidiaries or affiliated companies.

Long-term investments are to be held for many years. They are not acquired with the intention of disposing of them in the near future. They are usually presented on the balance sheet just below Current Assets in a separate section called Investments. Many securities that are properly shown among long-term investments are, in fact, readily marketable. But they are not included as current assets unless the intent is to convert them to cash in the short-term—within a year or in the operating cycle, whichever is longer. Securities classified as available-for-sale should be reported at fair value. Securities classified as held-to-maturity are reported at amortized cost.

Alco Standard Corporation reported its investments section between Current Assets and Property, Plant, and Equipment in the following manner:

Alco Standard Corporation	
Investments	
Investment in Alco Health Services Corporation	$ 62,255,000
Other investments	37,533,000
Long-term receivables	22,191,000
Total investments	121,979,000

ILLUSTRATION 5-9
Balance Sheet
Presentation of Long-
Term Investments

Property, Plant, and Equipment

Property, plant, and equipment are properties of a durable nature used in the regular operations of the business. These assets consist of physical property such as land, buildings, machinery, furniture, tools, and wasting resources (timberland, minerals). With the exception of land, most assets are either depreciable (such as buildings) or consumable (such as timberlands).

Mattel, Inc., a manufacturer of toys and games, presented its property, plant, and equipment in its balance sheet as follows:

Mattel, Inc.	
Property, plant, and equipment	
Land	$ 5,812,000
Buildings	46,490,000
Machinery and equipment	72,513,000
Capitalized leases	39,425,000
Leasehold improvements	19,068,000
	183,308,000
Less: Accumulated depreciation	55,496,000
	127,812,000
Tools, dies and molds, less amortization	37,053,000
Property, plant, and equipment, net	164,865,000

The basis of valuing the property, plant, and equipment, any liens against the properties, and accumulated depreciation should be disclosed—usually in notes to the statements.

Intangible Assets

Intangible assets lack physical substance and usually have a high degree of uncertainty concerning their future benefits. They include patents, copyrights, franchises, goodwill, trademarks, trade names, secret processes, and organization costs. Generally, all of these intangibles are written off (amortized) to expense over 5 to 40 years. Intangibles can represent significant economic resources, yet financial analysts often ignore them, and accountants write them down or off arbitrarily because valuation is difficult.

Unipack Corporation reported intangible assets in its balance sheet as follows:

ILLUSTRATION 5-11
Balance Sheet
Presentation of Intangible
Assets

Unipack Corporation	
Intangible assets	
Goodwill less $57,827 accumulated amortization	$145,617
Patents, licenses, and trademarks less $198,026 accumulated amortization	371,005
Software development costs less $46,280 accumulated amortization	120,214
Total intangibles	636,836

Other Assets

The items included in the section "Other Assets" vary widely in practice. Some of the items commonly included are deferred charges (long-term prepaid expenses), noncurrent receivables, intangible assets, assets in special funds, deferred income taxes, property held for sale, and advances to subsidiaries. Such a section unfortunately is too general a classification. Instead, it should be restricted to unusual items sufficiently different from assets included in specific categories. Some deferred costs such as organization costs incurred during the early life of the business are commonly classified here. Even these costs, however, are more properly placed in the intangible asset section.

Current Liabilities

Current liabilities are the obligations that are reasonably expected to be liquidated either through the use of current assets or the creation of other current liabilities. This concept includes:

❶ Payables resulting from the acquisition of goods and services: accounts payable, wages payable, taxes payable, and so on.

❷ Collections received in advance for the delivery of goods or performance of services such as unearned rent revenue or unearned subscriptions revenue.

❸ Other liabilities whose liquidation will take place within the operating cycle such as the portion of long-term bonds to be paid in the current period, or short-term obligations arising from purchase of equipment.

At times, a liability payable next year is not included in the current liability section. This occurs either when the debt is expected to be refinanced through another long-term issue,[12] or when the debt is retired out of noncurrent assets. This approach is used because liquidation does not result from the use of current assets or the creation of other current liabilities.

Current liabilities are not reported in any consistent order. The items most commonly listed first are notes payable, accounts payable, or "short-term debt"; income taxes payable, current maturities of long-term debt, or "other current liabilities" are commonly listed last. An example of Dresser Industries' current liabilities section is shown below.

Dresser Industries, Inc.	
Current liabilities	
Short-term debt	$ 22,500,000
Accounts payable—public	240,400,000
Accounts payable to unconsolidated affiliates	18,200,000
Advances from customers on contracts	161,100,000
Accrued compensation and benefits	169,400,000
Accrued warranty costs	34,100,000
Accrued taxes other than income taxes	21,900,000
Accrued interest	28,300,000
Other accrued liabilities	151,000,000
Income taxes payable	112,200,000
Current portion of long-term debt	12,400,000
Total current liabilities	971,500,000

ILLUSTRATION 5-12
Balance Sheet
Presentation of Current
Liabilities

Current liabilities include such items as trade and nontrade notes and accounts payable, advances received from customers, and current maturities of long-term debt. Income taxes and other accrued items are classified separately, if material. Any secured liability—for example, stock held as collateral on notes payable—is fully described in the notes so that the assets providing the security can be identified.

The excess of total current assets over total current liabilities is referred to as **working capital** (sometimes called net working capital). Working capital represents the net amount of a company's relatively liquid resources. That is, it is the liquid buffer available to meet the financial demands of the operating cycle. Working capital as an amount is seldom disclosed on the balance sheet, but it is computed by bankers and other creditors as an indicator of the short-run liquidity of a company. In order to determine the actual liquidity and availability of working capital to meet current obligations, however, one must analyze the composition of the current assets and their nearness to cash.[13]

Long-Term Liabilities

Long-term liabilities are obligations that are not reasonably expected to be liquidated within the normal operating cycle but, instead, are payable at some date beyond that

---

[12]A detailed discussion of accounting for debt expected to be refinanced is found in Chapter 13 and in "Classification of Short-term Obligations Expected to Be Refinanced," *Statement of Financial Accounting Standards No. 6* (Stamford, Conn.: FASB, 1975).

[13]The FASB in a discussion memorandum has suggested alternative classifications of assets that might help financial statement users assess the nature, amounts, and liquidity of available resources. See "Reporting Funds Flows, Liquidity, and Financial Flexibility," *FASB Discussion Memorandum* (Stamford, Conn.: FASB, 1980), Chapters 8 and 9.

time. Bonds payable, notes payable, deferred income taxes, lease obligations, and pension obligations are the most common examples. Generally, a great deal of supplementary disclosure is needed for this section, because most long-term debt is subject to various covenants and restrictions for the protection of lenders.[14] Long-term liabilities that mature within the current operating cycle are classified as current liabilities if their liquidation requires the use of current assets.

Generally, long-term liabilities are of three types:

❶ Obligations arising from specific financing situations, such as the issuance of bonds, long-term lease obligations, and long-term notes payable.

❷ Obligations arising from the ordinary operations of the enterprise, such as pension obligations and deferred income tax liabilities.

❸ Obligations that are dependent upon the occurrence or nonoccurrence of one or more future events to confirm the amount payable, or the payee, or the date payable, such as service or product warranties and other contingencies.

It is desirable to report any premium or discount separately as an addition to or subtraction from the bonds payable. The terms of all long-term liability agreements (including maturity date or dates, rates of interest, nature of obligation, and any security pledged to support the debt) are frequently described in notes to the financial statements. An example of the financial statement and accompanying note presentation is shown below in the excerpt from The Great Atlantic & Pacific Tea Company's financials.

ILLUSTRATION 5-13
Balance Sheet
Presentation of Long-
Term Debt

The Great Atlantic & Pacific Tea Company, Inc.	
Total current liabilities	$978,109,000
Long-term debt (See note)	254,312,000
Obligations under capital leases	252,618,000
Deferred income taxes	57,167,000
Other non-current liabilities	127,321,000
Note: Indebtedness. Debt consists of:	
9.5% Senior notes, due in annual installments of $10,000,000	$ 40,000,000
Mortgages and other notes due through 2011 (average interest rate of 9.9%)	107,604,000
Bank borrowings at 9.7%	67,225,000
Commercial paper at 9.4%	100,102,000
	314,931,000
Less current portion	(60,619,000)
Total long-term debt	$254,312,000

Owners' Equity

The **owners' equity** (stockholders' equity) section is one of the most difficult sections to prepare and understand. This is due to the complexity of capital stock agreements and the various restrictions on residual equity imposed by state corporation laws, liability agreements, and boards of directors. The section is usually divided into three parts:

---

[14]The pertinent rights and privileges of the various securities (both debt and equity) outstanding are usually explained in the notes to the financial statements. Examples of information that should be disclosed are dividend and liquidation preferences, participation rights, call prices and dates, conversion or exercise prices or rates and pertinent dates, sinking fund requirements, unusual voting rights, and significant terms of contracts to issue additional shares. "Disclosure of Information about Capital Structure," *Statement of Financial Accounting Standards No. 129* (Norwalk: FASB, 1997), par. 4.

❖ STOCKHOLDERS' EQUITY SECTION ❖

❶ *Capital Stock.* The par or stated value of the shares issued.

❷ *Additional Paid-In Capital.* The excess of amounts paid in over the par or stated value.

❸ *Retained Earnings.* The corporation's undistributed earnings.

The major disclosure requirements for capital stock are the authorized, issued, and outstanding par value amounts. The additional paid-in capital is usually presented in one amount, although subtotals are informative if the sources of additional capital are varied and material. The retained earnings section may be divided between the unappropriated (the amount that is usually available for dividend distribution) and any amounts that are restricted (e.g., by bond indentures or other loan agreements). In addition, any capital stock reacquired (treasury stock) is shown as a reduction of stockholders' equity. As indicated in Chapter 4, accumulated other comprehensive income (loss) is shown as an addition (reduction) to stockholders' equity, if applicable.

The ownership or stockholders' equity accounts in a corporation are considerably different from those in a partnership or proprietorship. Partners' permanent capital accounts and the balance in their temporary accounts (drawing accounts) are shown separately. Proprietorships ordinarily use a single capital account that handles all of the owners' equity transactions.

Presented below is an example of the stockholders' equity section from Quanex Corporation.

ILLUSTRATION 5-14
Balance Sheet
Presentation of
Stockholders' Equity

Quanex Corporation	
	($000)
Stockholders' equity (Note 12):	
Preferred stock, no par value, 1,000,000 shares authorized; 345,000 in 1992 and none in 1991 issued and outstanding	$ 86,250
Common stock, $.50 par value, 25,000,000 shares authorized; 13,638,005 shares in 1992 and 11,735,166 shares in 1991 issued and outstanding	6,819
Additional paid-in capital	87,260
Retained earnings	57,263
	$237,592

❖ BALANCE SHEET FORMAT

One common arrangement followed in the presentation of a classified balance sheet is called the **account form**. It lists assets by sections on the left side and liabilities and stockholders' equity by sections on the right side. The main disadvantage is the need for two facing pages. To avoid the use of facing pages, the **report form**, shown in Illustration 5-15, lists liabilities and stockholders' equity directly below assets on the same page.[15] (Also see Intel's balance sheet on page 238 for the report form.)

Other balance sheet formats are used infrequently. For example, current liabilities are sometimes deducted from current assets to arrive at working capital, or all liabilities are deducted from all assets. Caterpillar, for instance, is one of the few large companies to prepare its balance sheet in this latter unorthodox format, referred to as the **financial position form**.

Objective **❸**

Prepare a classified balance sheet using the report and account formats.

---

[15]*Accounting Trends and Techniques—1996* indicates that all of the 600 companies surveyed use either the "report form" (436) or the "account form" (164), sometimes collectively referred to as the "customary form."

ILLUSTRATION 5-15
Classified Report Form
Balance Sheet

Scientific Products, Inc.
BALANCE SHEET
December 31, 1998

Assets

Current assets

Cash		$ 42,485	
Available-for-sale securities—at fair value		28,250	
Accounts receivable	$165,824		
Less allowance for doubtful accounts	1,850	163,974	
Notes receivable		23,000	
Inventories—at average cost		489,713	
Supplies on hand		9,780	
Prepaid expenses		16,252	
Total current assets			$ 773,454

Long-term investments

Investments in Warren Co.			87,500

Property, plant, and equipment

Land—at cost		125,000	
Buildings—at cost	975,800		
Less accumulated depreciation	341,200	634,600	
Total property, plant, and equipment			759,600

Intangible assets

Goodwill			100,000
Total assets			$1,720,554

Liabilities and Stockholders' Equity

Current liabilities

Notes payable to banks		$ 50,000	
Accounts payable		197,532	
Accrued interest on notes payable		500	
Income taxes payable		62,520	
Accrued salaries, wages, and other liabilities		9,500	
Deposits received from customers		420	
Total current liabilities			$ 320,472

Long-term debt

Twenty-year 12% debentures, due January 1, 2008			500,000
Total liabilities			820,472

Stockholders' equity

Paid in on capital stock			
Preferred, 7%, cumulative			
Authorized, issued, and outstanding,			
30,000 shares of $10 par value	$300,000		
Common—			
Authorized, 500,000 shares of $1.00 par value;			
issued and outstanding, 400,000 shares	400,000		
Additional paid-in capital	37,500	737,500	
Earnings retained in the business		162,582	
Total stockholders' equity			900,082
Total liabilities and stockholders' equity			$1,720,554

UNDERLYING CONCEPTS

The basis for inclusion of additional information should meet the full disclosure principle; that is, the information should be of sufficient importance to influence the judgment of an informed user.

❖ ADDITIONAL INFORMATION REPORTED

The balance sheet is not complete simply because the assets, liabilities, and owners' equity accounts have been listed. Great importance is given to supplemental information. It may be information not presented elsewhere in the statement, or it may be an elaboration or qualification of items in the balance sheet. There are normally four types of information that are supplemental to account titles and amounts presented in the balance sheet:

❖ **SUPPLEMENTAL BALANCE SHEET INFORMATION** ❖

❶ *Contingencies.* Material events that have an uncertain outcome.

❷ *Accounting Policies.* Explanations of the valuation methods used or the basic assumptions made concerning inventory valuations, depreciation methods, investments in subsidiaries, etc.

❸ *Contractual Situations.* Explanations of certain restrictions or covenants attached to specific assets or, more likely, to liabilities.

❹ *Post-Balance Sheet Disclosures.* Disclosures of certain events that have occurred after the balance sheet date but before the financial statements have been issued.

Objective ❹
Identify balance sheet information requiring supplemental disclosure.

Contingencies

A **contingency** is defined as an existing situation involving uncertainty as to possible gain (gain contingency) or loss (loss contingency) that will ultimately be resolved when one or more future events occur or fail to occur. In short, they are material events that have an uncertain future. Examples of gain contingencies are tax operating loss carryforwards or company litigation against another party. Typical loss contingencies relate to litigation, environmental issues, possible tax assessments, or government investigation. The accounting and reporting requirements involving contingencies are examined fully in Chapter 13, and, therefore, additional discussion is not provided here.

Accounting Policies

APB Opinion No. 22 recommends disclosure for all significant accounting principles and methods that involve selection from among alternatives or those that are peculiar to a given industry[16] For instance, inventories can be computed under several cost flow assumptions (such as LIFO and FIFO); plant and equipment can be depreciated under several accepted methods of cost allocation (such as double-declining balance and straight-line); and investments can be carried at different valuations (such as cost, equity, and fair value). Sophisticated users of financial statements know of these possibilities and examine the statements closely to determine the methods used.

Companies are also required to disclose information about the nature of their operations, the use of estimates in preparing financial statements, certain significant estimates, and vulnerabilities due to certain concentrations.[17] An example of such a disclosure is provided below.

Chesapeake Corporation

Risks and Uncertainties: Chesapeake operates in three business segments which offer a diversity of products over a broad geographic base. The Company is not dependent on any single customer, group of customers, market, geographic area or supplier of materials, labor or services. Financial statements include, where necessary, amounts based on the judgments and estimates of management. These estimates include allowances for bad debts, accruals for landfill closing costs, environmental remediation costs, loss contingencies for litigation, self-insured medical and workers' compensation insurance and income taxes and determinations of discount and other rate assumptions for pensions and postretirement benefit expenses.

ILLUSTRATION 5-16
Balance Sheet Disclosure of Significant Risks and Uncertainties

---

[16]"Disclosure of Accounting Policies," *Opinions of the Accounting Principles Board No. 22* (New York: AICPA, 1972).

[17]"Disclosure of Certain Significant Risks and Uncertainties," *Statement of Position 94-6* (New York: AICPA, 1994).

Disclosure of significant accounting principles and methods and of risks and uncertainties is particularly useful if given in a separate **Summary of Significant Accounting Policies** preceding the notes to the financial statements or as the initial note.

Contractual Situations

In addition to contingencies and different methods of valuation, contractual situations of significance should be disclosed in the notes to the financial statements. It is mandatory, for example, that the essential provisions of lease contracts, pension obligations, and stock option plans be clearly stated in the notes. The analyst who examines a set of financial statements wants to know not only the amount of the liabilities, but also how the different contractual provisions affect the company at present and in the future.

Commitments related to obligations to maintain working capital, to limit the payment of dividends, to restrict the use of assets, and to require the maintenance of certain financial ratios must all be disclosed if material. Considerable judgment is necessary to determine whether omission of such information is misleading. The axiom in this situation is, "When in doubt, disclose." It is better to disclose a little too much information than not enough.

The accountant's judgment should reflect ethical considerations, because the manner of disclosing the accounting principles, methods, and other items that have important effects on the enterprise may subtly represent the interests of a particular stakeholder (at the expense of others). A reader, for example, may benefit by the highlighting of information in comprehensive notes, whereas the company—not wishing to emphasize certain information—may choose to provide limited (rather than comprehensive) note information.

Post-Balance Sheet Events (Subsequent Events)

Notes to the financial statements should explain any significant financial events that took place after the formal balance sheet date, but before it is finally issued. These events are referred to as post-balance sheet events, events subsequent to the balance sheet date, or just plain **subsequent events**. The subsequent events period is time-diagrammed as shown in Illustration 5-17.

ILLUSTRATION 5-17
Time Periods for
Subsequent Events

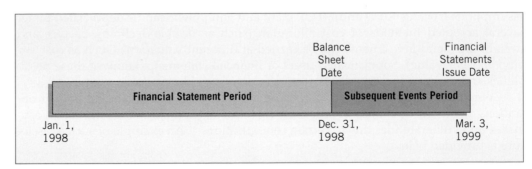

A period of several weeks, and sometimes months, may elapse after the end of the year before the financial statements are issued. Taking and pricing the inventory, reconciling subsidiary ledgers with controlling accounts, preparing necessary adjusting entries, assuring that all transactions for the period have been entered, obtaining an audit of the financial statements by independent certified public accountants, and printing the annual report all take time. During the period between the balance sheet date and its distribution to stockholders and creditors, important transactions or other events may occur that materially affect the company's financial position or operating situation.

Many who read a recent balance sheet believe the balance sheet condition is constant and project it into the future. However, readers must be told if the company has sold one of its plants, acquired a subsidiary, suffered extraordinary losses, settled significant litigation, or experienced any other important event in the post-balance sheet period. Without an explanation in a note, the reader might be misled and draw inappropriate conclusions.

Two types of events or transactions occurring after the balance sheet date may have a material effect on the financial statements or may need to be considered to interpret these statements accurately:

❶ **Events that provide additional evidence about conditions that existed at the balance sheet date, affect the estimates used in preparing financial statements, and, therefore, result in needed adjustments:** All information available prior to the issuance of the financial statements is used to evaluate estimates previously made. To ignore these subsequent events is to pass up an opportunity to improve the accuracy of the financial statements. This first type encompasses information that would have been recorded in the accounts had it been known at the balance sheet date.

For example, if a loss on an account receivable results from a customer's bankruptcy subsequent to the balance sheet date, the financial statements are adjusted before their issuance. The bankruptcy stems from the customer's poor financial health existing at the balance sheet date.

The same criterion applies to settlements of litigation. The financial statements must be adjusted if the events that gave rise to the litigation, such as personal injury or patent infringement, took place prior to the balance sheet date. If the event giving rise to the claim took place subsequent to the balance sheet date, no adjustment is necessary but disclosure is. To illustrate, a loss resulting from a customer's fire or flood after the balance sheet date is not indicative of conditions existing at that date. Thus, adjustment of the financial statements is not necessary.

❷ **Events that provide evidence about conditions that did not exist at the balance sheet date but arise subsequent to that date and do not require adjustment of the financial statements:** Some of these events may have to be disclosed to keep the financial statements from being misleading. These disclosures take the form of notes, supplemental schedules, or even pro forma "as if" financial data prepared as if the event had occurred on the balance sheet date. Below are examples of such events that require disclosure (but do not result in adjustment):

(a) Sale of bonds or capital stock; stock splits or stock dividends.
(b) Business combination pending or effected.
(c) Settlement of litigation when the event giving rise to the claim took place subsequent to the balance sheet date.
(d) Loss of plant or inventories from fire or flood.
(e) Losses on receivables resulting from conditions (such as customer's major casualty) arising subsequent to the balance sheet date.
(f) Gains or losses on certain marketable securities.[18]

Chrysler Corporation

Note 21: Subsequent Events. On February 10, 1993, the Company completed a public offering of 52 million shares of newly issued common stock for proceeds of approximately $1.95 billion, net of expenses. Chrysler plans to contribute approximately $1.1 billion of the net proceeds to its pension fund.

On February 1, 1993, the final stage of the sale of substantially all of the net assets of the consumer and inventory financing businesses of Chrysler First was completed for aggregate cash proceeds of $2.2 billion. On February 1, 1993, CFC also sold certain assets of its commercial leasing and lending subsidiary, Chrysler Capital Corporation, for $116 million. Proceeds from these sales approximated the net carrying value of the assets sold, and were used to reduce CFC's outstanding indebtedness.

As of February 3, 1993, the scheduled reductions of $1.35 billion under CFC's New Bank Facility and $855 million under CFC's U.S. receivable sale agreement were accomplished.

ILLUSTRATION 5-18
Balance Sheet Disclosure of Subsequent Events

---

[18]"Subsequent Events," *Statement on Auditing Standards No. 1* (New York: AICPA, 1973), pp. 123–124. *Accounting Trends and Techniques—1996* listed the following types of subsequent events and their frequency of occurrence among the 600 companies surveyed: debt incurred, reduced, or refinanced, 66; business combinations pending or effected, 72; discontinued operations, 39; litigation, 36; capital stock issued or repurchased, 11; employee benefit plans, 14; stock splits or dividends, 17.

An example of subsequent events disclosure, excerpted from Chrysler's Annual Report, is presented in Illustration 5-18 on the previous page.

Many subsequent events or developments are not likely to require either adjustment of or disclosure in the financial statements. Typically, these are nonaccounting events or conditions that managements normally communicate by other means. These events include legislation, product changes, management changes, strikes, unionization, marketing agreements, and loss of important customers.

❖ TECHNIQUES OF DISCLOSURE

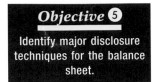

Objective 5

Identify major disclosure techniques for the balance sheet.

The effect of various contingencies on financial condition, the methods of valuing assets, and the companies' contracts and agreements should be disclosed as completely and as intelligently as possible. These methods of disclosing pertinent information are available: parenthetical explanations, notes, cross reference and contra items, and supporting schedules.

Parenthetical Explanations

Additional information is often provided by parenthetical explanations following the item. For example, investments in available-for-sale securities are shown on the balance sheet under Investments as follows:

Investments in Available-for-Sale Securities (cost, $330,586)—at fair value	$401,500

UNDERLYING CONCEPTS

The user-specific quality of understandability requires accountants to be careful in describing transactions and events.

This device permits disclosure of additional pertinent balance sheet information that adds clarity and completeness. It has an advantage over a note because it brings the additional information into the body of the statement where it is less likely to be overlooked. Of course, lengthy parenthetical explanations that might distract the reader from the balance sheet information must be used with care.

Notes

Notes are used if additional explanations cannot be shown conveniently as parenthetical explanations. For example, inventory costing methods are reported in The Quaker Oats Company's accompanying notes as follows:

ILLUSTRATION 5-19
Notes Disclosure

The Quaker Oats Company

Inventories (Note 1)

Finished goods	$326,000,000
Grain and raw materials	114,100,000
Packaging materials and supplies	39,000,000
Total inventories	479,100,000

Note 1: Inventories. Inventories are valued at the lower of cost or market, using various cost methods, and include the cost of raw materials, labor, and overhead. The percentage of year-end inventories valued using each of the methods is as follows:

Average quarterly cost	21%
Last-in, first-out (LIFO)	65%
First-in, first-out (FIFO)	14%

If the LIFO method of valuing certain inventories was not used, total inventories would have been $60,100,000 higher than reported.

Notes are commonly used to disclose the existence and amount of any preferred stock dividends in arrears, the terms of or obligations imposed by purchase commitments, special financial arrangements and instruments, depreciation policies, any changes in the application of accounting principles, and the existence of contingencies.

The following notes illustrate a common method of presenting such information:

ILLUSTRATION 5-19
(continued)

Consolidated Papers, Inc.

Note 7: Commitments. The company had capital expenditure purchase commitments outstanding of approximately $17 million.

Alberto-Culver Company

Note 3: Long-Term Debt. Various borrowing arrangements impose restrictions on such items as total debt, working capital, dividend payments, treasury stock purchases and interest expense. The company was in compliance with these arrangements and $68 million of consolidated retained earnings was not restricted as to the payment of dividends and purchases of treasury stock.

Ampco-Pittsburgh Corporation

Note 11: Change in Accounting Estimate. The Corporation revised its estimate of the useful lives of certain machinery and equipment. Previously, all machinery and equipment, whether new when placed in use or not, were in one class and depreciated over 15 years. The change principally applies to assets purchased new when placed in use. Those lives are now extended to 20 years. These changes were made to better reflect the estimated periods during which such assets will remain in service. The change had the effect of reducing depreciation expense and increasing net income by approximately $991,000 ($.10 per share).

The notes must present all essential facts as completely and succinctly as possible. Careless wording may mislead rather than aid readers. Notes should add to the total information made available in the financial statements, not raise unanswered questions or contradict other portions of the statements.

Cross Reference and Contra Items

A direct relationship between an asset and a liability is "cross referenced" on the balance sheet. For example, on December 31, 1998, among the current assets this might be shown:

Cash on deposit with sinking fund trustee for redemption of bonds payable—see current liabilities	$800,000

Included among the current liabilities is the amount of bonds payable to be redeemed within one year:

Bonds payable to be redeemed in 1999—see current assets	$2,300,000

This cross reference points out that $2,300,000 of bonds payable are to be redeemed currently, for which only $800,000 in cash has been set aside. Therefore, the additional cash needed must come from unrestricted cash, from sales of investments, from profits, or from some other source. The same information can be shown parenthetically, if this technique is preferred.

Another common procedure is to establish contra or adjunct accounts. A **contra account** on a balance sheet is an item that reduces either an asset, liability, or owners' equity account. Examples include Accumulated Depreciation and Discount on Bonds Payable. Contra accounts provide some flexibility in presenting the financial information. With the use of the Accumulated Depreciation account, for example, a reader of the statement can see the original cost of the asset as well as the depreciation to date.

An **adjunct account**, on the other hand, increases either an asset, liability, or owners' equity account. An example is Premium on Bonds Payable, which, when added to the Bonds Payable account, describes the total liability of the enterprise.

Supporting Schedules

Often a separate schedule is needed to present more detailed information about certain assets or liabilities, because the balance sheet provides just a single summary item.

ILLUSTRATION 5-20
Disclosure through Use
of Supporting Schedules

Property, plant, and equipment	
Land, buildings, equipment, and other fixed assets—net (see Schedule 3)	$643,300

A separate schedule then might be presented as follows:

Schedule 3
LAND, BUILDINGS, EQUIPMENT, AND OTHER FIXED ASSETS

	Total	Land	Buildings	Equip.	Other Fixed Assets
Balance January 1, 1999	$740,000	$46,000	$358,000	$260,000	$76,000
Additions in 1999	161,200		120,000	38,000	3,200
	901,200	46,000	478,000	298,000	79,200
Assets retired or sold in 1999	31,700			27,000	4,700
Balance December 31, 1999	869,500	46,000	478,000	271,000	74,500
Depreciation taken to January 1, 1999	196,000		102,000	78,000	16,000
Depreciation taken in 1999	56,000		28,000	24,000	4,000
	252,000		130,000	102,000	20,000
Depreciation on assets retired in 1999	25,800			22,000	3,800
Depreciation accumulated December 31, 1999	226,200		130,000	80,000	16,200
Book value of assets	$643,300	$46,000	$348,000	$191,000	$58,300

❖ TERMINOLOGY

INTERNATIONAL INSIGHT

Internationally, accounting terminology is problematic. Confusing differences arise even between nations that share a language. For example, American investors normally think of "stock" as "equity" or "ownership," but the British refer to inventory as "stocks." In the U.S. "fixed assets" generally refers to "property, plant, and equipment," while in Britain the category includes more items.

The account titles in the general ledger do not necessarily represent the best terminology for balance sheet purposes. Account titles are often brief and include technical terms that are understood only by accountants. But balance sheets are examined by many persons who are not acquainted with the technical vocabulary of accounting. Thus, they should contain descriptions that will be generally understood and not be subject to misinterpretation.

The profession has recommended that the word **reserve** be used only to describe an appropriation of retained earnings. This term had been used in several ways: to describe amounts deducted from assets (contra accounts such as accumulated depreciation and allowance for doubtful accounts), and as a part of the title of contingent or estimated liabilities. Because of the different meanings attached to this term, misinterpretation often resulted from its use. The use of "reserve" only to describe appropriated retained earnings has resulted in a better understanding of its significance when it appears in a balance sheet. However, the term "appropriated" appears more logical, and its use should be encouraged.

For years the profession has recommended that the use of the word **surplus** be discontinued in balance sheet presentations of owners' equity. The use of the terms capital surplus, paid-in surplus, and earned surplus is confusing. Although condemned by the profession, these terms appear all too frequently in current financial statements.

STATEMENT OF CASH FLOWS	SECTION 2

In Chapter 2, "assessing the amounts, timing, and uncertainty of cash flows" was presented as one of the three basic objectives of financial reporting. The balance sheet, the income statement, and the statement of stockholders' equity each present, to a limited extent and in a fragmented manner, information about the cash flows of an enterprise during a period. For instance, comparative balance sheets might show what new assets have been acquired or disposed of and what liabilities have been incurred or liquidated. The income statement provides information about resources, but not exactly cash, provided by operations. The statement of stockholders' equity shows the amount of cash used to pay dividends or purchase treasury stock. But none of these statements presents a detailed summary of all the cash inflows and outflows, or the sources and uses of cash during the period. To fill this need, the FASB requires the statement of cash flows (also called the cash flow statement).[19]

**UNDERLYING
CONCEPTS**

The statement of cash flows meets one of the objectives of financial reporting—to help assess the amounts, timing, and uncertainty of future cash flows.

❖ PURPOSE OF THE STATEMENT OF CASH FLOWS

The primary purpose of a statement of cash flows is to provide relevant information about the cash receipts and cash payments of an enterprise during a period. To achieve this purpose, the statement of cash flows reports (1) the cash effects of operations during a period, (2) investing transactions, (3) financing transactions, and (4) the net increase or decrease in cash during the period.[20]

Reporting the sources, uses, and net increase or decrease in cash helps investors, creditors, and others know what is happening to a company's most liquid resource. Because most individuals maintain their checkbook and prepare their tax return on a cash basis, they can relate to the statement of cash flows and comprehend the causes and effects of cash inflows and outflows and the net increase or decrease in cash. The statement of cash flows provides answers to the following simple but important questions:

❶ Where did the cash come from during the period?
❷ What was the cash used for during the period?
❸ What was the change in the cash balance during the period?

Objective **❻**

Indicate the purpose of the statement of cash flows.

❖ CONTENT AND FORMAT OF
   THE STATEMENT OF CASH FLOWS

Cash receipts and cash payments during a period are classified in the statement of cash flows into three different activities—operating, investing, and financing activities. These classifications are defined as follows:

❶ **Operating activities** involve the cash effects of transactions that enter into the determination of net income.
❷ **Investing activities** include making and collecting loans and acquiring and disposing of investments (both debt and equity) and property, plant, and equipment.

Objective **❼**

Identify the content of the statement of cash flows.

---

[19]"Statement of Cash Flows," *Statement of Financial Accounting Standards No. 95* (Stamford, Conn.: FASB, 1987).

[20]The basis recommended by the FASB is actually "cash and cash equivalents." Cash equivalents are short-term, highly liquid investments such as treasury bills, commercial paper, and money market funds purchased with cash that is in excess of immediate needs.

❸ **Financing activities** involve liability and owners' equity items. They include (a) obtaining resources from owners and providing them with a return on (and a return of) their investment and (b) borrowing money from creditors and repaying the amounts borrowed.

With cash flows classified into those three categories, the statement of cash flows has assumed the following basic format:

ILLUSTRATION 5-21
Basic Format of Cash
Flow Statement

Cash flows from operating activities	$XXX
Cash flows from investing activities	XXX
Cash flows from financing activities	XXX
Net increase (decrease) in cash	XXX
Cash at beginning of year	XXX
Cash at end of year	$XXX

The inflows and outflows of cash classified by activity are shown in Illustration 5-22.

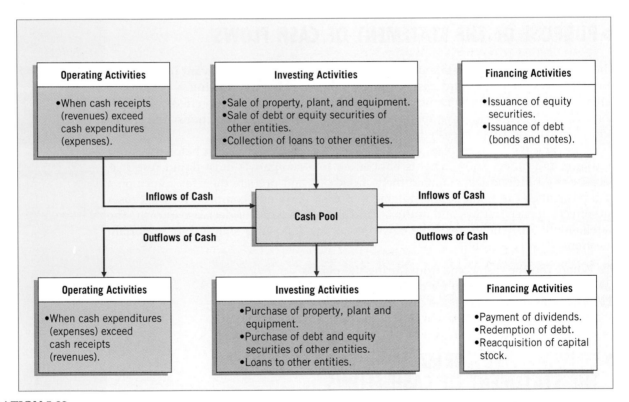

ILLUSTRATION 5-22
Cash Inflows and
Outflows

The statement's value is that it helps users evaluate liquidity, solvency, and financial flexibility. Liquidity refers to the "nearness to cash" of assets and liabilities. **Solvency** refers to the firm's ability to pay its debts as they mature. And **financial flexibility** refers to a firm's ability to respond and adapt to financial adversity and unexpected needs and opportunities.

We have devoted Chapter 24 entirely to the preparation and content of the statement of cash flows. Our comprehensive coverage of this topic has been deferred to that later chapter so that we can cover in the intervening chapters several elements and complex topics that make up the content of a typical statement of cash flows. The presentation in this chapter is introductory, a reminder of the existence of the statement of cash flows and its usefulness.

❖ PREPARATION OF THE STATEMENT OF CASH FLOWS

The information to prepare the statement of cash flows usually comes from (1) comparative balance sheets, (2) the current income statement, and (3) selected transaction data. Preparing the statement of cash flows from these sources involves the following steps:

❶ Determine the cash provided by operations.
❷ Determine the cash provided by or used in investing and financing activities.
❸ Determine the change (increase or decrease) in cash during the period.
❹ Reconcile the change in cash with the beginning and the ending cash balances.

The following simple illustration demonstrates how these steps are applied in the preparation of a statement of cash flows.

Telemarketing Inc. in its first year of operations issued on January 1, 1999, 50,000 shares of $1.00 par value common stock for $50,000 cash. The company rented its office space, furniture, and telecommunications equipment and performed surveys and marketing services throughout the first year. The comparative balance sheets at the beginning and end of the year 1999 are shown in Illustration 5-23.

Objective ❽

Prepare a statement of cash flows.

🌐 **INTERNATIONAL INSIGHT**

Statements of cash flows are not widely required. Some nations require a statement reporting sources and applications of "funds" (often defined as working capital); others have no requirement for either cash or funds flow statements.

ILLUSTRATION 5-23
Comparative Balance Sheets

Telemarketing Inc. BALANCE SHEETS			
Assets	Dec. 31, 1999	Jan. 1, 1999	Increase/Decrease
Cash	$46,000	$ –0–	$46,000 Increase
Accounts receivable	41,000	–0–	41,000 Increase
Total	$87,000	$ –0–	
Liabilities and Stockholders' Equity			
Accounts payable	$12,000	$ –0–	12,000 Increase
Common stock	50,000	–0–	50,000 Increase
Retained earnings	25,000	–0–	25,000 Increase
Total	$87,000	$ –0–	

The income statement and additional information for Telemarketing Inc. are as follows:

ILLUSTRATION 5-24
Income Statement Data

Telemarketing Inc. INCOME STATEMENT For the Year Ended December 31, 1999	
Revenues	$172,000
Operating expenses	120,000
Income before income taxes	52,000
Income tax expense	13,000
Net income	$ 39,000

Additional information:
Dividends of $14,000 were paid during the year.

Cash provided by operations (the excess of cash receipts over cash payments) is determined by converting net income on an accrual basis to a cash basis. This is accomplished by adding to or deducting from net income those items in the income statement not affecting cash. This procedure requires an analysis not only of the current year's income statement but also of the comparative balance sheets and selected transaction data.

Analysis of Telemarketing's comparative balance sheets reveals two items that give rise to noncash credits or charges to the income statement: (1) the increase in accounts receivable reflects a noncash credit of $41,000 to revenues, and (2) the increase in accounts payable reflects a noncash charge of $12,000 to expenses. **To arrive at cash provided by operations, the increase in accounts receivable must be deducted from net income, and the increase in accounts payable must be added back to net income.**

As a result of the accounts receivable and accounts payable adjustments, cash provided by operations is determined to be $10,000, computed as follows:

ILLUSTRATION 5-25
Computation of Net Cash
Provided by Operations

Net income		$39,000
Adjustments to reconcile net income		
to net cash provided by operating activities:		
Increase in accounts receivable	$(41,000)	
Increase in accounts payable	12,000	(29,000)
Net cash provided by operating activities		$10,000

The increase of $50,000 in common stock resulting from the issuance of 50,000 shares for cash, is classified as a financing activity. Likewise, the payment of $14,000 cash in dividends is a financing activity. Telemarketing Inc. did not engage in any investing activities during the year. The statement of cash flows for Telemarketing Inc. for 1999 is as follows:

ILLUSTRATION 5-26
Statement of Cash Flows

Telemarketing Inc. STATEMENT OF CASH FLOWS For the Year Ended December 31, 1999		
Cash flows from operating activities		
Net income		$39,000
Adjustments to reconcile net income to		
net cash provided by operating activities:		
Increase in accounts receivable	$(41,000)	
Increase in accounts payable	12,000	(29,000)
Net cash provided by operating activities		10,000
Cash flows from financing activities		
Issuance of common stock	50,000	
Payment of cash dividends	(14,000)	
Net cash provided by financing activities		36,000
Net increase in cash		46,000
Cash at beginning of year		–0–
Cash at end of year		$46,000

 **INTERNATIONAL INSIGHT**

International Accounting Standard 7 requires a statement of cash flows. Both international standards and U.S. GAAP specify that the cash flows must be classified as operating, investing, or financing.

The increase in cash of $46,000 reported in the statement of cash flows agrees with the increase of $46,000 in the Cash account calculated from the comparative balance sheets.

An illustration of a more comprehensive statement of cash flows is presented in Illustration 5-27.

❖ USEFULNESS OF THE STATEMENT OF CASH FLOWS

Objective 9
Understand the usefulness of the statement of cash flows.

"Happiness is a positive cash flow" is certainly true. Although net income provides a long-term measure of a company's success or failure, cash is the lifeblood of a company. Without cash, a company will not survive. For small and newly developing companies, cash flow is the single most important element of survival. In a recent survey of over 60,000 companies that failed, over 60 percent blamed their failure on factors linked to cash flows. Even medium and large companies indicate a major concern in controlling cash flow.

Creditors examine the cash flow statement carefully because they are concerned about being paid. A good starting point in their examination is to find net cash provided by operating activities. A high amount of net cash provided by operating activities indicates that a company is able to generate sufficient cash internally from operations

ILLUSTRATION 5-27
Comprehensive
Statement of Cash Flows

Nestor Company
STATEMENT OF CASH FLOWS
For the Year Ended December 31, 1999

Cash flows from operating activities		
Net income		$320,750
Adjustments to reconcile net income to net		
cash provided by operating activities:		
Depreciation expense	$88,400	
Amortization of intangibles	16,300	
Gain on sale of plant assets	(8,700)	
Increase in accounts receivable (net)	(11,000)	
Decrease in inventory	15,500	
Decrease in accounts payable	(9,500)	91,000
Net cash provided by operating activities		411,750
Cash flows from investing activities		
Sale of plant assets	90,500	
Purchase of equipment	(182,500)	
Purchase of land	(70,000)	
Net cash used by investing activities		(162,000)
Cash flows from financing activities		
Payment of cash dividend	(19,800)	
Issuance of common stock	100,000	
Redemption of bonds	(50,000)	
Net cash provided by financing activities		30,200
Net increase in cash		279,950
Cash at beginning of year		135,000
Cash at end of year		$414,950

to pay its bills without further borrowing. Conversely, a low or negative amount of net cash provided by operating activities indicates that a company cannot generate enough cash internally from its operations and, therefore, must borrow or issue equity securities to acquire additional cash. Consequently, creditors look for answers to the following questions in the company's cash flow statements:

❶ How successful is the company in generating net cash provided by operating activities?

❷ What are the trends in net cash flow provided by operating activities over time?

❸ What are the major reasons for the positive or negative net cash provided by operating activities?

You should recognize that companies can fail even though they are profitable. The difference between net income and net cash provided by operating activities can be substantial. Companies such as W.T. Grant Company and Prime Motor Inn, for example, reported high net income numbers but negative net cash provided by operating activities. Eventually both these companies filed for bankruptcy.

In many cases the reasons for the difference between a positive net income and a negative net cash provided by operating activities are substantial increases in receivables and/or inventory. To illustrate, Ho Inc. in its first year of operations reported a net income of $80,000. Its net cash provided by operating activities, however, was a negative $95,000, as shown in Illustration 5-28 on the next page.

Note that the negative net cash provided by operating activities occurred for Ho even though it reported a positive net income. Ho could easily experience a "cash crunch" because it has tied up its cash in receivables and inventory. If problems in collecting receivables occur or inventory is slow moving or becomes obsolete, the creditors of Ho may have difficulty collecting on their loans.

ILLUSTRATION 5-28
Negative Net Cash
Provided by Operating
Activities

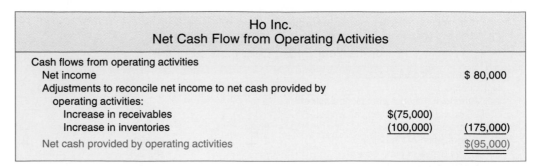

Ho Inc. Net Cash Flow from Operating Activities		
Cash flows from operating activities		
Net income		$ 80,000
Adjustments to reconcile net income to net cash provided by operating activities:		
Increase in receivables	$(75,000)	
Increase in inventories	(100,000)	(175,000)
Net cash provided by operating activities		$(95,000)

Financial Liquidity

One relationship (ratio) that is often used to assess liquidity is the **current cash debt coverage ratio.** It indicates whether the company can pay off its current liabilities in a given year from its operations. The formula for this ratio is:

ILLUSTRATION 5-29
Formula for Current
Cash Debt Coverage
Ratio

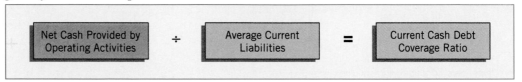

The higher this ratio, the less likely a company will have liquidity problems. For example, a ratio near 1:1 is good because it indicates that the company can meet all of its current obligations from internally generated cash flow.

Financial Flexibility

A more long-run measure which provides information on financial flexibility is the **cash debt coverage ratio.** This ratio indicates a company's ability to repay its liabilities from net cash provided by operating activities, without having to liquidate the assets employed in its operations. The formula for this ratio is:

ILLUSTRATION 5-30
Formula for Cash Debt
Coverage Ratio

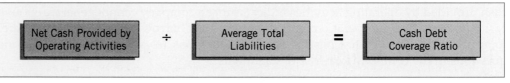

The higher this ratio, the less likely the company will experience difficulty in meeting its obligations as they come due. As a result, it signals whether the company can pay its debts and survive if external sources of funds become limited or too expensive.

Free Cash Flow

A more sophisticated way to examine a company's financial flexibility is to develop a free cash flow analysis. This analysis starts with net cash provided by operating activities and ends with free cash flow, which is calculated as net cash provided by operating activities less capital expenditures and dividends.[21] Free cash flow is the amount of discretionary cash flow a company has for purchasing additional investments, retiring its debt, purchasing treasury stock, or simply adding to its liquidity. This measure indicates a company's level of financial flexibility. Questions that a free cash flow analysis answers are:

❶ Is the company able to pay its dividends without resorting to external financing?
❷ If business operations decline, will the company be able to maintain its needed capital investment?

---

[21]In determining free cash flows, some companies do not subtract dividends because they believe these expenditures to be discretionary.

❸ What is the free cash flow that can be used for additional investment, retirement of debt, purchase of treasury stock, or addition to liquidity?

Presented below is a free cash flow analysis using the cash flow statement for Nestor Company shown in Illustration 5-27 (page 227):

ILLUSTRATION 5-31
Free Cash Flow
Computation

Free Cash Flow Analysis Nestor Company	
Net cash provided by operating activities	$411,750
Less: Capital expenditures	(252,500)
Dividends	(19,800)
Free cash flow	$139,450

This analysis shows that Nestor has a positive, and substantial, net cash provided by operating activities of $411,750. Nestor reports on its statement of cash flows that it purchased equipment of $182,500 and land of $70,000 for total capital spending of $252,500. This amount is subtracted from net cash provided by operating activities because without continued efforts to maintain and expand facilities it is unlikely that Nestor can continue to maintain its competitive position. Capital spending is deducted first on the free cash flow statement to indicate it is the least discretionary expenditure a company generally makes. Dividends are then deducted, to arrive at free cash flow. Although a company can cut its dividend, it will usually do so only in a financial emergency. Nestor has more than sufficient cash flow to meet its dividend payment and therefore has satisfactory financial flexibility.

Nestor used its free cash flow to redeem bonds and add to its liquidity. If it finds additional investments that are profitable, it can increase its spending without putting its dividend or basic capital spending in jeopardy. Companies that have strong financial flexibility can take advantage of profitable investments even in tough times. In addition, strong financial flexibility frees companies from worry about survival in poor economic times. In fact, those with strong financial flexibility often fare better in poor economic times because they can take advantage of opportunities that other companies cannot.

SUMMARY OF LEARNING OBJECTIVES

❶ *Identify the uses and limitations of a balance sheet.* The balance sheet provides information about the nature and amounts of investments in enterprise resources, obligations to creditors, and the owners' equity in net resources. The balance sheet contributes to financial reporting by providing a basis for (1) computing rates of return, (2) evaluating the capital structure of the enterprise, and (3) assessing the liquidity and financial flexibility of the enterprise. The limitations of a balance sheet are: (1) The balance sheet does not reflect current value because accountants have adopted a historical cost basis in valuing and reporting assets and liabilities. (2) Judgments and estimates must be used in preparing a balance sheet. The collectibility of receivables, the salability of inventory, and the useful life of long-term tangible and intangible assets are difficult to determine. (3) The balance sheet omits many items that are of financial value to the business but cannot be recorded objectively, such as human resources, customer base, and reputation.

❷ *Identify the major classifications of the balance sheet.* The general elements of the balance sheet are assets, liabilities, and equity. The major classifications within the balance sheet on the asset side are current assets; long-term investments; property, plant, and equipment; intangible assets; and other assets. The major classifications of liabilities are current and long-term liabilities. In a corporation, owners' equity is generally classified as capital stock, additional paid-in capital, and retained earnings.

(3) ***Prepare a classified balance sheet using the report and account formats.*** The report form lists liabilities and stockholders' equity directly below assets on the same page. The account form lists assets by sections on the left side and liabilities and stockholders' equity by sections on the right side.

(4) ***Identify balance sheet information requiring supplemental disclosure.*** Four types of information normally are supplemental to account titles and amounts presented in the balance sheet: (1) *Contingencies:* Material events that have an uncertain outcome. (2) *Accounting policies:* Explanations of the valuation methods used or the basic assumptions made concerning inventory valuation, depreciation methods, investments in subsidiaries, etc. (3) *Contractual situations:* Explanations of certain restrictions or covenants attached to specific assets or, more likely, to liabilities. (4) *Post-balance sheet disclosures:* Disclosures of certain events that have occurred after the balance sheet date but before the financial statements have been issued.

(5) ***Identify major disclosure techniques for the balance sheet.*** There are four methods of disclosing pertinent information in the balance sheet: (1) *Parenthetical explanations:* Additional information or description is often provided by parenthetical explanations following the item. (2) *Notes:* Notes are used if additional explanations or descriptions cannot be shown conveniently as parenthetical explanations. (3) *Cross reference and contra items:* A direct relationship between an asset and a liability is "cross referenced" on the balance sheet. (4) *Supporting schedules:* Often a separate schedule is needed to present more detailed information about certain assets or liabilities, because the balance sheet provides just a single summary item.

(6) ***Indicate the purpose of the statement of cash flows.*** The primary purpose of a statement of cash flows is to provide relevant information about the cash receipts and cash payments of an enterprise during a period. Reporting the sources, uses, and net increase or decrease in cash enables investors, creditors, and others to know what is happening to a company's most liquid resource.

(7) ***Identify the content of the statement of cash flows.*** Cash receipts and cash payments during a period are classified in the statement of cash flows into three different activities: (1) *Operating activities:* Involve the cash effects of transactions that enter into the determination of net income. (2) *Investing activities:* Include making and collecting loans and acquiring and disposing of investments (both debt and equity) and property, plant, and equipment. (3) *Financing activities:* Involve liability and owners' equity items and include (a) obtaining capital from owners and providing them with a return on their investment and (b) borrowing money from creditors and repaying the amounts borrowed.

(8) ***Prepare a statement of cash flows.*** The information to prepare the statement of cash flows usually comes from (1) comparative balance sheets, (2) the current income statement, and (3) selected transaction data. Preparing the statement of cash flows from these sources involves the following steps: (1) determine the cash provided by operations; (2) determine the cash provided by or used in investing and financing activities; (3) determine the change (increase or decrease) in cash during the period; and (4) reconcile the change in cash with the beginning and the ending cash balances.

(9) ***Understand the usefulness of the statement of cash flows.*** Creditors examine the cash flow statement carefully because they are concerned about being paid. The amount and trend of net cash flow provided by operating activities in relation to the company's liabilities is helpful in making this assessment. In addition, measures such as a free cash flow analysis provide creditors and stockholders with a better picture of the company's financial flexibility.

SABINA ZAMAN is in her second year of auditing at Coopers & Lybrand in Chicago. She holds a master's degree in accounting from the University of Illinois. She also holds master's and bachelor's degrees in economics from Carleton College in Ottawa, Canada. The daughter of a diplomat, Ms. Zaman, born in Bangladesh, has lived in many countries of the world.

What kinds of clients have you been auditing?
Quite a number, ranging from manufacturing, financial services, retail, and also some not-for-profit organizations. I've audited large companies such as Hyatt and Harris Bank, as well as some smaller clients too.

Did your studies in Intermediate Accounting relate to what you're doing now? The issues that the student is exposed to in Intermediate Accounting really come up frequently in real life, especially if you decide to go into manufacturing. For example, one client I was working on had a lot of debt. At times I had to refer back to the textbook just to refresh my memory on all those issues related to gains and losses and the early extinguishment of debt. Also, the statement of cash flows is important to understand because of its use in gauging a company's ability to meet its obligations with current assets. If you are very conversant in reading a statement of cash flows, it helps you to understand where the company is headed and what implications may arise from the ratios that you use in the analysis. There have been instances where I actually had to prepare a statement of cash flows for a client because they didn't have the necessary accounting support staff.

What has surprised you the most about your professional career? I didn't realize how much of the accounting/auditing process is really about communicating and interacting with people and the ability to manage clients and deal with different situations.

Interpersonal/communications skills are very critical to your success in this field. There are still people who view accountants in the traditional manner—"the accountants are coming in and they're going to find fault with us"—but I think now the trend is to move more toward a business advisory role, where you go in and you assess the client's operation and you try to add value to their operation in more of a teamwork framework. When I do an audit, I try to learn the business, because I think that once you have a good handle on the business, then it's easier to provide input about internal controls. Yes, you will meet clients who are very difficult and very resistant. You're coming in as an outsider with relatively little experience in that industry—there is a hurdle that you have to overcome, but it is possible if you have the ability to communicate and project your recommendations in a positive way. Practice makes perfect—the more you do, the easier it gets when you enter the workforce. I've had numerous occasions to give presentations and communicate with professors. I think those skills have helped me in my work life in terms of dealing with clients.

Do you have any advice for accounting students?
You have to know your accounting and auditing material and procedures. If you have substance, then your clients will rely on the judgments that you render. But the second set of skills are the soft skills that you have to cultivate during school. With that combination, you're quite a powerhouse.

Appendix 5A

Ratio Analysis—A Reference

❖ USING RATIOS TO ANALYZE FINANCIAL PERFORMANCE

Objective ⑩

After studying Appendix 5A, you should be able to: Identify the major types of financial ratios and what they measure.

Qualitative information from financial statements can be gathered by examining relationships between items on the statements and identifying trends in these relationships. A useful starting point in developing this information is the application of ratio analysis.

A **ratio** expresses the mathematical relationship between one quantity and another. Ratio analysis expresses the relationship among selected financial statement data. The relationship is expressed in terms of either a percentage, a rate, or a simple proportion. To illustrate, recently IBM Corporation had current assets of $41,338 million and current liabilities of $29,226 million. The relationship is determined by dividing current assets by current liabilities. The alternative means of expression are:

Percentage: Current assets are 141% of current liabilities.
Rate: Current assets are 1.41 times greater than current liabilities.
Proportion: The relationship of current assets to liabilities is 1.41:1.

For analysis of financial statements, ratios can be classified into four types, as follows:

❖ MAJOR TYPES OF RATIOS ❖

Liquidity Ratios. Measures of the enterprise's short-run ability to pay its maturing obligations.
Activity Ratios. Measures of how effectively the enterprise is using the assets employed.
Profitability Ratios. Measures of the degree of success or failure of a given enterprise or division for a given period of time.
Coverage Ratios. Measures of the degree of protection for long-term creditors and investors.

In Chapter 5 two ratios related to the statement of cash flows were discussed. Throughout the remainder of the textbook, ratios are provided to help you understand and interpret the information presented. In an Appendix to Chapter 25, an extensive discussion of financial statement analysis, of which ratio analysis is one part, is presented. In Illustration 5A-1 are the ratios that will be used throughout the text. You should find this chart helpful as you examine these ratios in more detail in the following chapters.

SUMMARY OF LEARNING OBJECTIVE FOR APPENDIX 5A

⑩ *Identify the major types of financial ratios and what they measure.* Ratios express the mathematical relationship between one quantity and another, in terms of either a percentage, a rate, or a proportion. Liquidity ratios measure the short-run ability to pay maturing obligations. Activity ratios measure the effectiveness of asset usage. Profitability ratios measure the success or failure of an enterprise. Coverage ratios measure the degree of protection for long-term creditors and investors.

KEY TERMS

activity ratios, 232
coverage ratios, 232
liquidity ratios, 232
profitability ratios, 232
ratio analysis, 232

Ratio	Formula	Purpose or Use
I. Liquidity		
1. Current ratio	$\dfrac{\text{Current assets}}{\text{Current liabilities}}$	Measures short-term debt-paying ability
2. Quick or acid-test ratio	$\dfrac{\text{Cash, marketable securities, and receivables (net)}}{\text{Current liabilities}}$	Measures immediate short-term liquidity
3. Current cash debt coverage ratio	$\dfrac{\text{Net cash provided by operating activities}}{\text{Average current liabilities}}$	Measures a company's ability to pay off its current liabilities in a given year from its operations
II. Activity		
4. Receivable turnover	$\dfrac{\text{Net sales}}{\text{Average trade receivables (net)}}$	Measures liquidity of receivables
5. Inventory turnover	$\dfrac{\text{Cost of goods sold}}{\text{Average inventory}}$	Measures liquidity of inventory
6. Asset turnover	$\dfrac{\text{Net sales}}{\text{Average total assets}}$	Measures how efficiently assets are used to generate sales
III. Profitability		
7. Profit margin on sales	$\dfrac{\text{Net income}}{\text{Net sales}}$	Measures net income generated by each dollar of sales
8. Rate of return on assets	$\dfrac{\text{Net income}}{\text{Average total assets}}$	Measures overall profitability of assets
9. Rate of return on common stock equity	$\dfrac{\text{Net income minus preferred dividends}}{\text{Average common stockholders' equity}}$	Measures profitability of owners' investment
10. Earnings per share	$\dfrac{\text{Net income minus preferred dividends}}{\text{Weighted shares outstanding}}$	Measures net income earned on each share of common stock
11. Price earnings ratio	$\dfrac{\text{Market price of stock}}{\text{Earnings per share}}$	Measures the ratio of the market price per share to earnings per share
12. Payout ratio	$\dfrac{\text{Cash dividends}}{\text{Net income}}$	Measures percentage of earnings distributed in the form of cash dividends
IV. Coverage		
13. Debt to total assets	$\dfrac{\text{Total debt}}{\text{Total assets or equities}}$	Measures the percentage of total assets provided by creditors
14. Times interest earned	$\dfrac{\text{Income before interest charges and taxes}}{\text{Interest charges}}$	Measures ability to meet interest payments as they come due
15. Cash debt coverage ratio	$\dfrac{\text{Net cash provided by operating activities}}{\text{Average total liabilities}}$	Measures a company's ability to repay its total liabilities in a given year from its operations
16. Book value per share	$\dfrac{\text{Common stockholders' equity}}{\text{Outstanding shares}}$	Measures the amount each share would receive if the company were liquidated at the amounts reported on the balance sheet

ILLUSTRATION 5A-1
A Summary of
Financial Ratios

To the Student:

The following 19 pages contain the financial statements and accompanying notes to the world's leading manufacturer of microprocessors and semiconductors and one of the largest and most profitable U.S. companies in the fast-growing, ever-changing computer industry. Because of its size, worldwide scope, and diversity of operations, Intel's accounting and reporting practices are affected by most of the accounting topics covered in this textbook and by nearly every facet of generally accepted accounting principles. Of all U.S. industrial companies in 1995, Intel was 56th largest in sales ($16.2 billion), 7th most profitable (net income of $3.6 billion), 130th in terms of assets ($17.5 billion), and 4th in net profit margin (22%). Intel employs 42,000 workers and in 1996 was named by *Fortune* magazine as the fifth most admired company in America.

We do not expect that you will comprehend Intel's financial statements and the accompanying notes in their entirety at your first reading. But we expect that by the time you complete the coverage of the material in this text, your level of understanding and interpretive ability will have grown enormously.

At this point we recommend that you take 20 to 30 minutes to scan the statements and notes, to familiarize yourself with the contents and accounting elements. Throughout the following twenty-one chapters when you are asked to refer to specific parts of Intel's financials, do so! Then, when you have completed reading this book, we challenge you to reread Intel's financials to see how much greater and more sophisticated is your understanding of them.

❖ INTEL CORPORATION ❖

FINANCIAL INFORMATION BY QUARTER
1995 ANNUAL REPORT

(In millions—except per share data)

1995 for quarter ended		December 30	September 30	July 1	April 1
Net revenues		$4,580	$4,171	$3,894	$3,557
Cost of sales		$2,389	$2,008	$1,805	$1,609
Net income		$ 867	$ 931	$ 879	$ 889
Earnings per share		$ .98	$ 1.05	$ .99	$ 1.02
Dividends per share	Declared	$ .04	$ .04	$ .04	$ .03
	Paid	$ .04	$ .04	$ .03	$ .03
Market price range Common Stock	High	$72.88	$76.44	$65.63	$44.25
	Low	$56.75	$58.63	$42.75	$31.81
Market price range Step-Up Warrants	High	$39.00	$43.63	$31.88	$11.91
	Low	$26.75	$30.44	$11.31	$ 6.97

We are happy to report our sixth consecutive year of both record revenues and earnings per share.

Revenues totaled $16.2 billion, up 41 percent from $11.5 billion in 1994. Earnings per share rose 54 percent over last year, to $4.03.

Our strong performance in 1995 was rooted in growing demand for PCs based on our Pentium® processors. The PC market continued its remarkable growth, with approximately 60 million PCs sold worldwide this year, up about 25 percent from 1994.

We were pleased to see the increased popularity of the Internet and other communications applications this year. In particular, we are very excited by the opportunities represented by the booming World Wide Web. With more than 180 million units in use worldwide, PCs are the predominant gateway to the World Wide Web. We believe that this easy-to-use, graphically based Internet interface will continue to attract new users and investments in the PC communications world, helping to expand the PC's role as a consumer communications device and driving future PC sales.

At Intel, our most important job is to make high-performance microprocessors for the computing industry. To do this, we follow four basic strategies:

1. Develop products quickly. We try to bring new technology to the market as quickly as possible. In 1995, we introduced the new high-end Pentium® Pro processor. This came less than three years after the introduction of the Pentium processor, which is now the processor of choice in the mainstream PC market. Together, these products provide computer buyers with a wide spectrum of computing choices.

2. Invest in manufacturing. We believe Intel's state-of-the-art chip manufacturing facilities are the best in the industry. We spent $3.6 billion on capital in 1995, up 45 percent from 1994. These heavy investments are paying off: in 1995, we were able to bring our new 0.35-micron manufacturing process into production months earlier than originally planned. Our newest facility, the most advanced in the microprocessor industry, makes our highest speed Pentium and Pentium Pro processors. In the end, these investments benefit PC buyers directly in the form of more powerful, less expensive computing options.

3. Remove barriers to technology flow. We believe that if computers work better, do more and are easier to use, more PCs will be sold and more Intel processors will be needed. We therefore work with other industry leaders to develop new PC technologies, such as the PCI "bus," which has been widely adopted. This technology removes bottlenecks to provide greatly enhanced graphics capabilities. We incorporate our chips into PCI building blocks, such as PC motherboards, to help computer manufacturers bring their products to market faster. We also work closely with software developers to help create rich applications, such as PC video conferencing and animated 3D Web sites, that make the most of the power of Intel processors.

4. Promote the Intel brand. We continue to invest in education and marketing programs that describe the benefits of genuine Intel technology. Our Intel Inside® program expanded in 1995 to include broadcast advertising. Hundreds of OEMs worldwide are participating to let users know that there are genuine Intel microprocessors inside their PCs.

Beyond our primary task of making microprocessors, we invest in a range of computing and communications applications that support our core business. Our supercomputer and network server efforts take advantage of the flexibility and power of the Intel architecture, while our flash memory business supports booming communications applications such as cellular phones. These product areas are detailed on the following pages.

Overall, our focused strategies have kept us on the right track. Of course, we continue to attract competition, both from makers of software-compatible microprocessors and from makers of alternative-architecture chips. We will try to stay nimble to maintain our position in the industry.

This is a particularly exciting time to be in the computing industry. New applications like the Internet are driving increased demand for computers, and emerging markets around the world are quickly adopting the latest computer technology. We look forward to meeting the challenges of this business as the computer's role continues to expand.

GORDON E. MOORE
Chairman

ANDREW S. GROVE
President and
Chief Executive Officer

CRAIG R. BARRETT
Executive Vice President and
Chief Operating Officer

235

Driven by strong sales of the Pentium® processor, Intel's 1995 revenues and earnings set new Company records.

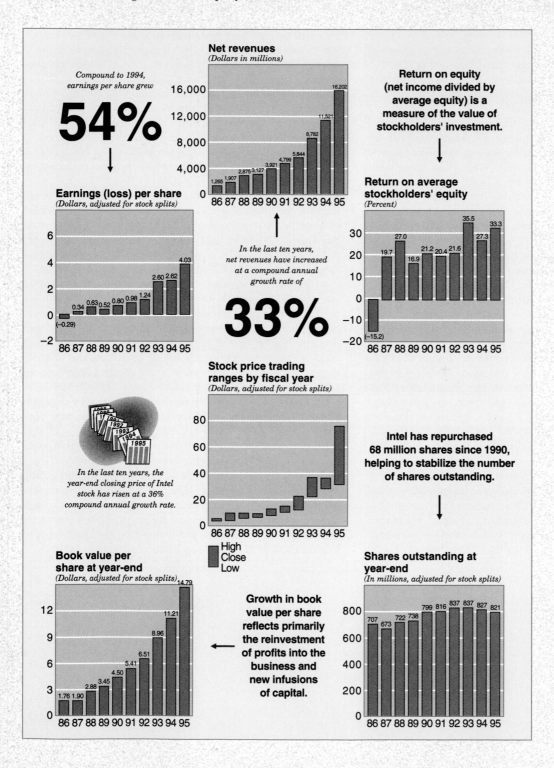

Compound to 1994, earnings per share grew

54%

Earnings (loss) per share
(Dollars, adjusted for stock splits)

Net revenues
(Dollars in millions)

In the last ten years, net revenues have increased at a compound annual growth rate of

33%

Return on equity (net income divided by average equity) is a measure of the value of stockholders' investment.

Return on average stockholders' equity
(Percent)

Stock price trading ranges by fiscal year
(Dollars, adjusted for stock splits)

High
Close
Low

In the last ten years, the year-end closing price of Intel stock has risen at a 36% compound annual growth rate.

Intel has repurchased 68 million shares since 1990, helping to stabilize the number of shares outstanding.

Book value per share at year-end
(Dollars, adjusted for stock splits)

Growth in book value per share reflects primarily the reinvestment of profits into the business and new infusions of capital.

Shares outstanding at year-end
(In millions, adjusted for stock splits)

The Board of Directors and Stockholders, Intel Corporation

We have audited the accompanying consolidated balance sheets of Intel Corporation as of December 30, 1995 and December 31, 1994, and the related consolidated statements of income, stockholders' equity, and cash flows for each of the three years in the period ended December 30, 1995. These financial statements are the responsibility of the Company's management. Our responsibility is to express an opinion on these financial statements based on our audits.

We conducted our audits in accordance with generally accepted auditing standards. Those standards require that we plan and perform the audit to obtain reasonable assurance about whether the financial statements are free of material misstatement. An audit includes examining, on a test basis, evidence supporting the amounts and disclosures in the financial statements. An audit also includes assessing the accounting principles used and significant estimates made by management, as well as evaluating the overall financial statement presentation. We believe that our audits provide a reasonable basis for our opinion.

In our opinion, the consolidated financial statements referred to above present fairly, in all material respects, the consolidated financial position of Intel Corporation at December 30, 1995 and December 31, 1994, and the consolidated results of its operations and its cash flows for each of the three years in the period ended December 30, 1995, in conformity with generally accepted accounting principles.

Ernst + Young LLP

San Jose, California
January 15, 1996

CONSOLIDATED STATEMENTS OF INCOME | Intel Corporation

Three years ended December 30, 1995

(In millions—except per share amounts)	1995	1994	1993
Net revenues	**$16,202**	**$11,521**	**$8,782**
Cost of sales	7,811	5,576	3,252
Research and development	1,296	1,111	970
Marketing, general and administrative	1,843	1,447	1,168
Operating costs and expenses	10,950	8,134	5,390
Operating income	**5,252**	**3,387**	**3,392**
Interest expense	(29)	(57)	(50)
Interest income and other, net	415	273	188
Income before taxes	**5,638**	**3,603**	**3,530**
Provision for taxes	2,072	1,315	1,235
Net income	**$ 3,566**	**$ 2,288**	**$2,295**
Earnings per common and common equivalent share	**$ 4.03**	**$ 2.62**	**$ 2.60**
Weighted average common and common equivalent shares outstanding	884	874	882

See accompanying notes.

December 30, 1995 and December 31, 1994

(In millions—except per share amounts)

	1995	1994
Assets		
Current assets:		
Cash and cash equivalents	$ 1,463	$ 1,180
Short-term investments	995	1,230
Accounts receivable, net of allowance for doubtful accounts of $57 ($32 in 1994)	3,116	1,978
Inventories	2,004	1,169
Deferred tax assets	408	552
Other current assets	111	58
Total current assets	**8,097**	**6,167**
Property, plant and equipment:		
Land and buildings	3,145	2,292
Machinery and equipment	7,099	5,374
Construction in progress	1,548	850
	11,792	8,516
Less accumulated depreciation	4,321	3,149
Property, plant and equipment, net	**7,471**	**5,367**
Long-term investments	**1,653**	**2,127**
Other assets	**283**	**155**
Total assets	**$17,504**	**$13,816**
Liabilities and stockholders' equity		
Current liabilities:		
Short-term debt	$ 346	$ 517
Accounts payable	864	575
Deferred income on shipments to distributors	304	269
Accrued compensation and benefits	758	588
Accrued advertising	218	108
Other accrued liabilities	328	538
Income taxes payable	801	429
Total current liabilities	**3,619**	**3,024**
Long-term debt	**400**	**392**
Deferred tax liabilities	**620**	**389**
Put warrants	**725**	**744**
Commitments and contingencies		
Stockholders' equity:		
Preferred Stock, $.001 par value, 50 shares authorized; none issued	—	—
Common Stock, $.001 par value, 1,400 shares authorized; 821 issued and outstanding in 1995 (827 in 1994) and capital in excess of par value	2,583	2,306
Retained earnings	9,557	6,961
Total stockholders' equity	**12,140**	**9,267**
Total liabilities and stockholders' equity	**$17,504**	**$13,816**

See accompanying notes.

Three years ended December 30, 1995

(In millions)	1995	1994	1993
Cash and cash equivalents, beginning of year	**$1,180**	**$1,659**	**$1,843**
Cash flows provided by (used for) operating activities:			
Net income	3,566	2,288	2,295
Adjustments to reconcile net income to net cash provided by (used for) operating activities:			
Depreciation	1,371	1,028	717
Net loss on retirements of property, plant and equipment	75	42	36
Amortization of debt discount	8	19	17
Change in deferred tax assets and liabilities	346	(150)	12
Changes in assets and liabilities:			
(Increase) in accounts receivable	(1,138)	(530)	(379)
(Increase) in inventories	(835)	(331)	(303)
(Increase) in other assets	(241)	(13)	(68)
Increase in accounts payable	289	148	146
Tax benefit from employee stock plans	116	61	68
Increase in income taxes payable	372	38	32
Increase in accrued compensation and benefits	170	44	109
(Decrease) increase in other liabilities	(73)	337	119
Total adjustments	460	693	506
Net cash provided by operating activities	**4,026**	**2,981**	**2,801**
Cash flows provided by (used for) investing activities:			
Additions to property, plant and equipment	(3,550)	(2,441)	(1,933)
Purchases of long-term, available-for-sale investments	(129)	(975)	(1,165)
Sales of long-term, available-for-sale investments	114	10	5
Maturities and other changes in available-for-sale investments, net	878	503	(244)
Net cash (used for) investing activities	**(2,687)**	**(2,903)**	**(3,337)**
Cash flows provided by (used for) financing activities:			
(Decrease) increase in short-term debt, net	(179)	(63)	197
Additions to long-term debt	—	128	148
Retirement of long-term debt	(4)	(98)	—
Proceeds from sales of shares through employee stock plans and other	192	150	133
Proceeds from sale of Step-Up Warrants, net	—	—	287
Proceeds from sales of put warrants, net of repurchases	85	76	62
Repurchase and retirement of Common Stock	(1,034)	(658)	(391)
Payment of dividends to stockholders	(116)	(92)	(84)
Net cash (used for) provided by financing activities	**(1,056)**	**(557)**	**352**
Net increase (decrease) in cash and cash equivalents	**283**	**(479)**	**(184)**
Cash and cash equivalents, end of year	**$1,463**	**$1,180**	**$1,659**
Supplemental disclosures of cash flow information:			
Cash paid during the year for:			
Interest	$ 182	$ 76	$ 39
Income taxes	$1,209	$1,366	$1,123

Cash paid for interest in 1995 includes approximately $108 million of accumulated interest on Zero Coupon Notes that matured in 1995.

See accompanying notes.

239

Three years ended December 30, 1995

(In millions)	Common Stock and capital in excess of par value		Retained earnings	Total
	Number of shares	Amount		
Balance at December 26, 1992	837	$1,776	$3,669	$ 5,445
Proceeds from sales of shares through employee stock plans, tax benefit of $68 and other	14	201	—	201
Proceeds from sales of put warrants	—	62	—	62
Reclassification of put warrant obligation, net	—	(37)	(278)	(315)
Proceeds from sale of Step-Up Warrants	—	287	—	287
Repurchase and retirement of Common Stock	(14)	(95)	(296)	(391)
Cash dividends declared ($.10 per share)	—	—	(84)	(84)
Net income	—	—	2,295	2,295
Balance at December 25, 1993	837	2,194	5,306	7,500
Proceeds from sales of shares through employee stock plans, tax benefit of $61 and other	12	215	—	215
Proceeds from sales of put warrants	—	76	—	76
Reclassification of put warrant obligation, net	—	(15)	(106)	(121)
Repurchase and retirement of Common Stock	(22)	(164)	(429)	(593)
Redemption of Common Stock Purchase Rights	—	—	(2)	(2)
Cash dividends declared ($.115 per share)	—	—	(96)	(96)
Net income	—	—	2,288	2,288
Balance at December 31, 1994	827	2,306	6,961	9,267
Proceeds from sales of shares through employee stock plans, tax benefit of $116 and other	13	310	—	310
Proceeds from sales of put warrants	—	85	—	85
Reclassification of put warrant obligation, net	—	61	(42)	19
Repurchase and retirement of Common Stock	(19)	(179)	(855)	(1,034)
Cash dividends declared ($.15 per share)	—	—	(124)	(124)
Unrealized gain on available-for-sale investments, net	—	—	51	51
Net income	—	—	3,566	3,566
Balance at December 30, 1995	821	$2,583	$9,557	$12,140

See accompanying notes.

Accounting Policies

Fiscal year. Intel Corporation ("Intel" or "the Company") has a fiscal year that ends the last Saturday in December. Fiscal years 1995 and 1993, each 52-week years, ended on December 30 and 25, respectively. Fiscal 1994 was a 53-week year and ended on December 31, 1994. The next 53-week year will end on December 30, 2000.

Basis of presentation. The consolidated financial statements include the accounts of Intel and its wholly owned subsidiaries. Significant intercompany accounts and transactions have been eliminated. Accounts denominated in foreign currencies have been remeasured into the functional currency in accordance with Statement of Financial Accounting Standards (SFAS) No. 52, "Foreign Currency Translation," using the U.S. dollar as the functional currency.

The preparation of financial statements in conformity with generally accepted accounting principles requires management to make estimates and assumptions that affect the amounts reported in the financial statements and accompanying notes. Actual results could differ from those estimates.

Investments. Highly liquid investments with insignificant interest rate risk and with original maturities of three months or less are classified as cash and cash equivalents. Investments with maturities greater than three months and less than one year are classified as short-term investments. Investments with maturities greater than one year are classified as long-term investments.

The Company accounts for investments in accordance with SFAS No. 115, "Accounting for Certain Investments in Debt and Equity Securities," effective as of the beginning of fiscal 1994. The Company's policy is to protect the value of its investment portfolio and to minimize principal risk by earning returns based on current interest rates. All of the Company's marketable investments are classified as available-for-sale as of the balance sheet date and are reported at fair value, with unrealized gains and losses, net of tax, recorded in stockholders' equity. The cost of securities sold is based on the specific identification method. Realized gains or losses and declines in value, if any, judged to be other than temporary on available-for-sale securities are reported in other income or expense. Investments in non-marketable instruments are recorded at the lower of cost or market and included in other assets.

Fair values of financial instruments. Fair values of cash and cash equivalents, short-term investments and short-term debt approximate cost due to the short period of time to maturity. Fair values of long-term investments, long-term debt, non-marketable instruments, swaps, currency forward contracts, currency options and options hedging non-marketable

instruments are based on quoted market prices or pricing models using current market rates.

Derivative financial instruments. The Company utilizes derivative financial instruments to reduce financial market risks. These instruments are used to hedge foreign currency, equity and interest rate market exposures of underlying assets, liabilities and other obligations. The Company does not use derivative financial instruments for speculative or trading purposes. The Company's accounting policies for these instruments are based on the Company's designation of such instruments as hedging transactions. The criteria the Company uses for designating an instrument as a hedge include its effectiveness in risk reduction and one-to-one matching of derivative instruments to underlying transactions. Gains and losses on currency forward contracts, and options that are designated and effective as hedges of anticipated transactions, for which a firm commitment has been attained, are deferred and recognized in income in the same period that the underlying transactions are settled. Gains and losses on currency forward contracts, options and swaps that are designated and effective as hedges of existing transactions are recognized in income in the same period as losses and gains on the underlying transactions are recognized and generally offset. Gains and losses on options hedging investments in non-marketable instruments are deferred and recognized in income in the same period as the hedges mature or when the underlying transaction is sold, whichever comes first. Income or expense on swaps is accrued as an adjustment to the yield of the related investments or debt they hedge.

Inventories. Inventories are stated at the lower of cost or market. Cost is computed on a currently adjusted standard basis (which approximates actual cost on a current average or first-in, first-out basis). Inventories at fiscal year-ends were as follows:

(In millions)	1995	1994
Materials and purchased parts	$ 674	$ 345
Work in process	707	528
Finished goods	623	296
Total	**$2,004**	**$1,169**

Property, plant and equipment. Property, plant and equipment are stated at cost. Depreciation is computed for financial reporting purposes principally by use of the straight-line method over the following estimated useful lives: machinery and equipment, 2–4 years; land and buildings, 4–45 years.

The Company adopted SFAS No. 121, "Accounting for the Impairment of Long-Lived Assets and for Long-Lived Assets to Be Disposed Of," effective as of the beginning of fiscal 1995. This adoption had no material effect on the Company's financial statements.

Deferred income on shipments to distributors. Certain of the Company's sales are made to distributors under agreements allowing price protection and/or right of return on merchandise unsold by the distributors. Because of frequent sales price reductions and rapid technological obsolescence in the industry, Intel defers recognition of such sales until the merchandise is sold by the distributors.

Advertising. Cooperative advertising obligations are accrued and the costs expensed at the same time the related revenue is recognized. All other advertising costs are expensed as incurred. The Company does not incur any direct-response advertising costs. Advertising expense was $654 million, $459 million and $325 million in 1995, 1994 and 1993, respectively.

Interest. Interest as well as gains and losses related to contractual agreements to hedge certain investment positions and debt (see "Derivative financial instruments") are recorded as net interest income or expense on a monthly basis. Interest expense capitalized as a component of construction costs was $46 million, $27 million and $8 million for 1995, 1994 and 1993, respectively.

Earnings per common and common equivalent share. Earnings per common and common equivalent share are computed using the weighted average number of outstanding common and dilutive common equivalent shares outstanding. Fully diluted earnings per share have not been presented as part of the consolidated statements of income because the differences are insignificant.

Stock distribution. On June 16, 1995, the Company effected a stock distribution in the form of a two-for-one stock split to stockholders of record as of May 19, 1995. Share, per share, Common Stock, capital in excess of par value, stock option and warrant amounts herein have been restated to reflect the effect of this split.

Common Stock

1998 Step-Up Warrants. In 1993, the Company issued 40 million 1998 Step-Up Warrants to purchase 40 million shares of Common Stock. This transaction resulted in an increase of $287 million in Common Stock and capital in excess of par value, representing net proceeds from the offering. The Warrants became exercisable in May 1993 at an effective price of $35.75 per share of Common Stock, subject to annual increases to a maximum price of $41.75 per share effective in March 1997. As of December 30, 1995, approximately 40 million Warrants were exercisable at a price of $38.75 and expire on March 14, 1998 if not previously exercised. For 1995, the Warrants had a dilutive effect on earnings per share and represented approximately 11 million common equivalent shares. The Warrants did not have a dilutive effect on earnings per share in 1994 or 1993.

Stock repurchase program. In 1990, the Board of Directors authorized the repurchase of up to 80 million shares of Intel's Common Stock in open market or negotiated transactions. The Board increased this authorization to a maximum of 110 million shares in July 1994. As of December 30, 1995, the Company had repurchased and retired approximately 68 million shares for the program to date at a cost of $2.19 billion. As of December 30, 1995, after reserving shares to cover outstanding put warrants, 29.9 million shares remained available under the repurchase authorization.

Put Warrants

In a series of private placements from 1991 through 1995, the Company sold put warrants that entitle the holder of each warrant to sell one share of Common Stock to the Company at a specified price. Activity during the past three years is summarized as follows:

(In millions)	Cumulative premium received	Number of warrants	Potential obligation
December 26, 1992	$ 56	28.0	$373
Sales	62	21.6	561
Expirations	—	(20.0)	(246)
December 25, 1993	118	29.6	688
Sales	76	25.0	744
Exercises	—	(2.0)	(65)
Expirations	—	(27.6)	(623)
December 31, 1994	194	25.0	744
Sales	85	17.5	925
Repurchases	—	(5.5)	(201)
Expirations	—	(25.0)	(743)
December 30, 1995	$279	12.0	$725

The amount related to Intel's potential repurchase obligation has been reclassified from stockholders' equity to put warrants. The 12 million put warrants outstanding at December 30, 1995 expire on various dates between February 1996 and November 1996 and have exercise prices ranging from $38 to $68 per share, with an average exercise price of $60 per share. There is no significant dilutive effect on earnings per share for the periods presented.

Borrowings

Short-term debt. Short-term debt and weighted average interest rates at fiscal year-ends were as follows:

(In millions)	1995 Balance	1995 Weighted average interest rate	1994 Balance	1994 Weighted average interest rate
Borrowed under lines of credit	$ 57	3.2%	$ 68	3.2%
Reverse repurchase agreements payable in non-U.S. currencies	124	9.2%	99	8.0%
Notes payable	2	4.7%	5	4.7%
Short-term portion of long-term debt	—	—	179	11.8%
Drafts payable	163	N/A	166	N/A
Total	**$346**		**$517**	

At December 30, 1995, the Company had established foreign and domestic lines of credit of approximately $1.16 billion. The Company generally renegotiates these lines annually. Compensating balance requirements are not material.

The Company also borrows under commercial paper programs. Maximum borrowings reached $700 million during both 1995 and 1994. This debt is rated A1+ by Standard and Poor's and P1 by Moody's. Proceeds are used to fund short-term working capital needs.

Long-term debt. Long-term debt at fiscal year-ends was as follows:

(In millions)	1995	1994
Payable in U.S. dollars:		
AFICA Bonds due 2013 at 4%	$110	$110
Zero Coupon Notes due 1995 at 11.8%, net of		
unamortized discount of $8 in 1994	—	179
Other U.S. dollar debt	4	4
Payable in other currencies:		
Irish punt due 2008–2024 at 6%–12%	240	228
Greek drachma due 2001	46	46
Other foreign currency debt	—	4
(Less short-term portion)	—	(179)
Total	**$400**	**$392**

The Company has guaranteed repayment of principal and interest on the AFICA Bonds issued by the Puerto Rico Industrial, Medical and Environmental Pollution Control Facilities Financing Authority (AFICA). The bonds are adjustable and redeemable at the option of either the Company or the bondholder every five years through 2013 and are next adjustable and redeemable in 1998. The Zero Coupon Notes matured during 1995. The Irish punt borrowings were made in connection with the financing of a factory in Ireland, and Intel has invested the proceeds in Irish punt denominated instruments of similar maturity to hedge foreign currency and interest rate exposures. The Greek drachma borrowings were made under a tax incentive program in Ireland, and the proceeds and cash flows have been swapped to U.S. dollars.

In 1994, the Company filed a shelf registration statement with the Securities and Exchange Commission (SEC) that became effective in 1995. When combined with previous shelf registration statements, this filing gave Intel the authority to issue up to $3.3 billion in the aggregate of Common Stock, Preferred Stock, depositary shares, debt securities and warrants to purchase the Company's or other issuers' Common Stock, Preferred Stock and debt securities, and, subject to certain limits, stock index warrants and foreign currency exchange units. In 1993, Intel completed an offering of Step-Up Warrants (see "1998 Step-Up Warrants"). The Company may issue up to $1.4 billion in additional securities under effective registration statements.

As of December 30, 1995, aggregate debt maturities were as follows: 1996—none; 1997—none; 1998—$110 million; 1999—none; 2000—none; and thereafter—$290 million.

Investments

The stated return on a majority of the Company's marketable investments in long-term fixed rate debt and equity securities are swapped to U.S. dollar LIBOR-based returns. The currency risks of investments denominated in foreign currencies are hedged with foreign currency borrowings, currency forward contracts or currency interest rate swaps (see "Derivative financial instruments" under "Accounting policies").

Investments with maturities of greater than six months consist primarily of A and A2 or better rated financial instruments and counterparties. Investments with maturities of up to six months consist primarily of A1/P1 or better rated financial instruments and counterparties. Foreign government regulations imposed upon investment alternatives of foreign subsidiaries, or the absence of A and A2 rated counterparties in certain countries, result in some minor exceptions. Intel's practice is to obtain and secure available collateral from counterparties against obligations whenever Intel deems appropriate. At December 30, 1995, investments were placed with approximately 100 different counterparties.

Investments at December 30, 1995 were as follows:

(In millions)	Cost	Gross unrealized gains	Gross unrealized losses	Estimated fair value
Commercial paper	$ 576	$ —	$ —	$ 576
Repurchase agreements	474	—	—	474
Securities of foreign governments	456	1	(1)	456
Corporate bonds	375	5	—	380
Bank time deposits	360	—	—	360
Loan participations	278	—	—	278
Floating rate notes	224	—	—	224
Fixed rate notes	159	1	(1)	159
Collateralized mortgage obligations	129	—	(1)	128
Other debt securities	119	—	(1)	118
Total debt securities	3,150	7	(4)	3,153
Hedged equity	431	45	—	476
Preferred stock and other equity	309	91	(11)	389
Total equity securities	740	136	(11)	865
Swaps hedging investments in debt securities	—	2	(9)	(7)
Swaps hedging investments in equity securities	—	5	(47)	(42)
Currency forward contracts hedging investments in debt securities	—	3	—	3
Total available-for-sale securities	3,890	153	(71)	3,972
Less amounts classified as cash equivalents	(1,324)	—	—	(1,324)
Total investments	**$2,566**	**$153**	**$(71)**	**$2,648**

Investments at December 31, 1994 were as follows:

(In millions)	Cost	Gross unrealized gains	Gross unrealized losses	Estimated fair value
Commercial paper	$ 544	$ —	$ —	$ 544
Repurchase agreements	194	—	—	194
Securities of foreign governments	518	2	(7)	513
Corporate bonds	440	12	(14)	438
Bank time deposits	406	—	—	406
Loan participations	266	6	(2)	270
Fixed rate notes	167	1	(2)	166
Collateralized mortgage obligations	170	—	(4)	166
Floating rate notes	488	1	(1)	488
Other debt securities	293	—	(5)	288
Total debt securities	3,486	22	(35)	3,473
Hedged equity	431	—	(58)	373
Preferred stock and other equity	368	20	(16)	372
Total equity securities	799	20	(74)	745
Swaps hedging investments in debt securities	—	22	(14)	8
Swaps hedging investments in equity securities	—	60	—	60
Currency forward contracts hedging investments in debt securities	—	1	—	1
Total available-for-sale securities	4,285	125	(123)	4,287
Less amounts classified as cash equivalents	(930)	—	—	(930)
Total investments	$3,355	$125	$(123)	$3,357

Note: Certain 1994 amounts have been restated to conform to the 1995 presentation.

During the year ended December 30, 1995, debt and marketable securities with a fair value at the date of sale of $114 million were sold. The gross realized gains on such sales totaled $60 million. There were no material proceeds or gross realized gains or losses from sales of securities during 1994.

The amortized cost and estimated fair value of investments in debt securities at December 30, 1995, by contractual maturity, were as follows:

(In millions)	Cost	Estimated fair value
Due in 1 year or less	$2,172	$2,172
Due in 1–2 years	486	489
Due in 2–5 years	214	214
Due after 5 years	278	278
Total investments in debt securities	$3,150	$3,153

Derivative Financial Instruments

Outstanding notional amounts for derivative financial instruments at fiscal year-ends were as follows:

(In millions)	1995	1994
Swaps hedging investments in debt securities	$ 824	$1,080
Swaps hedging investments in equity securities	$ 567	$ 567
Swaps hedging debt	$ 156	$ 156
Currency forward contracts	$1,310	$ 784
Currency options	$ 28	$ 10
Options hedging investments in non-marketable instruments	$ 82	$ —

While the contract or notional amounts provide one measure of the volume of these transactions, they do not represent the amount of the Company's exposure to credit risk. The amounts potentially subject to credit risk (arising from the possible inability of counterparties to meet the terms of their contracts) are generally limited to the amounts, if any, by which the counterparties' obligations exceed the obligations of the Company. The Company controls credit risk through credit approvals, limits and monitoring procedures. Credit rating criteria for off-balance-sheet transactions are similar to those for investments.

Swap agreements. The Company utilizes swap agreements to exchange the foreign currency, equity, and interest rate returns of its investment and debt portfolios for a floating U.S. dollar interest rate based return. The floating rates on swaps are based primarily on U.S. dollar LIBOR and reset on a monthly, quarterly or semiannual basis.

Weighted average pay and receive rates, average maturities and range of maturities on swaps at December 30, 1995 were as follows:

	Weighted average pay rate	Weighted average receive rate	Weighted average maturity	Range of maturities
Swaps hedging investments in U.S. dollar debt securities	6.5%	6.2%	1.1 years	0–3 years
Swaps hedging investments in foreign currency debt securities	10.4%	9.1%	1.1 years	0–3 years
Swaps hedging investments in equity securities	N/A	5.4%	1.2 years	0–2 years
Swaps hedging debt	5.9%	5.2%	3.6 years	3–6 years

Note: Pay and receive rates are based on the reset rates that were in effect at December 30, 1995.

Pay rates on swaps hedging investments in debt securities generally match the yields on the underlying investments they hedge. Payments on swaps hedging investments in equity securities generally match the equity returns on the underlying investments they hedge. Receive rates on swaps hedging debt generally match the expense on the underlying debt they hedge. Maturity dates of swaps generally match those of the underlying investment or the debt they hedge.

There is approximately a one-to-one matching of investments and debt to swaps. Swap agreements generally remain in effect until expiration. Income or expense on swaps is accrued as an adjustment to the yield of the related investments or debt they hedge.

Other foreign currency instruments. Intel transacts business in various foreign currencies, primarily Japanese yen and certain European currencies. The maturities on most of these foreign currency instruments are less than 12 months. Deferred gains or losses attributable to foreign currency instruments are not material.

Fair Values of Financial Instruments

The estimated fair values of financial instruments outstanding at fiscal year-ends were as follows:

(In millions)	1995 Carrying amount	1995 Estimated fair value	1994 Carrying amount	1994 Estimated fair value
Cash and cash equivalents	$1,463	$1,463	$1,180	$1,180
Short-term investments	$ 995	$ 995	$1,230	$1,230
Long-term investments	$1,699	$1,699	$2,058	$2,058
Non-marketable instruments	$ 239	$ 259	$ 59	$ 144
Swaps hedging investments in debt securities	$ (7)	$ (7)	$ 8	$ 8
Swaps hedging investments in equity securities	$ (42)	$ (42)	$ 60	$ 60
Options hedging investments in non-marketable instruments	$ (9)	$ (13)	$ —	$ —
Short-term debt	$ (346)	$ (346)	$ (517)	$ (517)
Long-term debt	$ (400)	$ (399)	$ (392)	$ (384)
Swaps hedging debt	$ —	$ (1)	$ —	$ (12)
Currency forward contracts	$ 3	$ 4	$ 1	$ 5
Currency options	$ —	$ —	$ —	$ —

Concentrations of Credit Risk

Financial instruments that potentially subject the Company to concentrations of credit risk consist principally of investments and trade receivables. Intel places its investments with high-credit-quality counterparties and, by policy, limits the amount of credit exposure to any one counterparty. A substantial majority of the Company's trade receivables are derived from sales to manufacturers of microcomputer systems, with the remainder spread across various other industries.

During 1995, the Company experienced an increase in its concentration of credit risk due to increasing trade receivables from sales to manufacturers of microcomputer systems. The Company's five largest customers accounted for approximately 33% of net revenues for 1995. At December 30, 1995, these customers accounted for approximately 34% of net accounts receivable. A portion of the receivable balance from one of the Company's five largest customers has been converted into a loan. The total amount receivable from this customer was approximately $400 million at December 30, 1995.

The Company endeavors to keep pace with the evolving computer industry and has adopted credit policies and standards intended to accommodate industry growth and inherent risk. Management believes that credit risks are moderated by the diversity of its end customers and geographic sales areas. Intel performs ongoing credit evaluations of its customers' financial condition and requires collateral as deemed necessary.

Interest Income and Other

(In millions)	1995	1994	1993
Interest income	$272	$235	$155
Foreign currency gains	29	15	—
Other income	114	23	33
Total	**$415**	**$273**	**$188**

Other income for 1995 included approximately $58 million from the settlement of ongoing litigation and $60 million from sales of a portion of the Company's investment in marketable equity securities. Other income for 1994 included non-recurring gains from the settlement of various insurance claims. Other income for 1993 included non-recurring gains from the sale of certain benefits related to the Company's Irish expansion and dividend income earned on equity investments.

Provision for Taxes

The provision for taxes consisted of the following:

(In millions)	1995	1994	1993
Income before taxes:			
U.S.	$3,427	$2,460	$2,587
Foreign	2,211	1,143	943
Total income before taxes	**$5,638**	**$3,603**	**$3,530**
Provision for taxes:			
Federal:			
Current	$1,169	$1,169	$ 946
Deferred	307	(178)	35
	1,476	991	981
State:			
Current	203	162	150
Foreign:			
Current	354	134	127
Deferred	39	28	(23)
	393	162	104
Total provision for taxes	**$2,072**	**$1,315**	**$1,235**
Effective tax rate	**36.8%**	**36.5%**	**35.0%**

The tax benefit associated with dispositions from employee stock plans reduced taxes currently payable for 1995 by $116 million ($61 million and $68 million for 1994 and 1993, respectively).

The provision for taxes reconciled to the amount computed by applying the statutory federal rate of 35% to income before taxes as follows:

(In millions)	1995	1994	1993
Computed expected tax	$1,973	$1,261	$1,235
State taxes, net of federal benefits	132	105	98
Other	(33)	(51)	(98)
Provision for taxes	**$2,072**	**$1,315**	**$1,235**

Deferred income taxes reflect the net tax effects of temporary differences between the carrying amount of assets and liabilities for financial reporting purposes and the amounts used for income tax purposes.

Significant components of the Company's deferred tax assets and liabilities at fiscal year-ends were as follows:

(In millions)	1995	1994
Deferred tax assets		
Accrued compensation and benefits	$ 61	$ 49
Deferred income	127	127
Inventory valuation and related reserves	104	255
Interest and taxes	61	54
Other, net	55	67
	408	552
Deferred tax liabilities		
Depreciation	(475)	(338)
Unremitted earnings of certain subsidiaries	(116)	(51)
Other, net	(29)	—
	(620)	(389)
Net deferred tax (liability) asset	**$(212)**	**$ 163**

U.S. income taxes were not provided for on a cumulative total of approximately $615 million of undistributed earnings for certain non-U.S. subsidiaries. The Company intends to reinvest these earnings indefinitely in operations outside the United States.

The Company's U.S. income tax returns for the years 1978 through 1987 have been examined by the Internal Revenue Service (IRS). In 1989, the Company received a notice of proposed deficiencies from the IRS totaling $36 million, exclusive of penalties and interest, for the years 1978 through 1982. These proposed deficiencies relate primarily to operations in Puerto Rico. In 1989, the Company filed a petition in the U.S. Tax Court contesting these proposed deficiencies and subsequently reached settlement of certain issues with the IRS. In 1993, the U.S. Tax Court ruled in favor of the Company on an export source issue and for the IRS on another, smaller issue. The IRS appealed the decision to the United States Court of Appeals for the Ninth Circuit, and the Company filed a cross-appeal of the decision. In 1995, the Court of Appeals affirmed the decision of the Tax Court. The IRS has subsequently requested a re-hearing.

The Company has also received an examination report for the years 1983 through 1987. Intel has lodged a protest, which relates solely to the export source issue referenced above, to the IRS Appeals Office, but no decisions have been reached.

The Company's U.S. income tax returns for the years 1988 through 1990 are presently under examination by the IRS. Final proposed adjustments have not yet been received for these years. Management believes that adequate amounts of tax and related interest and penalties, if any, have been provided for any adjustments that may result from unsettled portions of the 1978–1987 cases or the years now under examination.

Employee Benefit Plans

Stock option plans. Intel has a stock option plan (hereafter referred to as the EOP Plan) under which officers, key employees and non-employee directors may be granted options to purchase shares of the Company's authorized but unissued Common Stock. The Company also has an Executive Long-Term Stock Option Plan (ELTSOP) under which certain key executive officers may be granted options to purchase shares of the Company's authorized but unissued Common Stock. Under all plans, the option purchase price is not less than fair market value at the date of grant. The Company accounts for stock options in accordance with APB Opinion No. 25, "Accounting for Stock Issued to Employees." In accordance with SFAS No. 123, "Accounting for Stock-Based Compensation," the Company intends to continue to apply APB No. 25 for purposes of determining net income and to adopt the pro forma disclosure requirements for fiscal 1996.

Options currently expire no later than ten years from the grant date. Proceeds received by the Company from exercises are credited to Common Stock and capital in excess of par value. Additional information with respect to EOP Plan activity was as follows:

(In millions)	Shares available for options	Number of shares	Aggregate price
December 26, 1992	65.4	73.6	$ 669
Grants	(15.2)	15.2	357
Exercises	—	(9.0)	(56)
Cancellations	1.8	(1.8)	(24)
December 25, 1993	52.0	78.0	946
Grants	(12.0)	12.0	397
Exercises	—	(8.2)	(54)
Cancellations	1.6	(1.6)	(33)
December 31, 1994	41.6	80.2	1,256
Grants	(13.5)	13.5	645
Exercises	—	(9.8)	(81)
Cancellations	3.0	(3.0)	(77)
December 30, 1995	31.1	80.9	$1,743
Options exercisable at:			
December 25, 1993		20.4	$ 135
December 31, 1994		26.2	$ 198
December 30, 1995		25.3	$ 236

The range of exercise prices for options outstanding under the EOP Plan at December 30, 1995 was $3.13 to $69.43. These options will expire if not exercised at specific dates ranging from January 1996 to December 2005. Prices for options exercised during the three-year period ended December 30, 1995 ranged from $3.04 to $36.13.

Activity for the ELTSOP Plan is summarized below:

(In millions)	Shares available for options	Outstanding options	
		Number of shares	Aggregate price
December 26, 1992	**13.2**	**6.0**	**$44**
Grants	(0.4)	0.4	11
Exercises	—	(0.8)	(6)
December 25, 1993	**12.8**	**5.6**	**49**
Exercises	—	(0.6)	(4)
December 31, 1994	**12.8**	**5.0**	**45**
Grants	(0.5)	0.5	30
Exercises	—	(0.9)	(6)
December 30, 1995	**12.3**	**4.6**	**$69**
Options exercisable at:			
December 25, 1993		1.4	$11
December 31, 1994		2.6	$19
December 30, 1995		3.8	$29

The range of exercise prices for options outstanding under the ELTSOP Plan at December 30, 1995 was $7.31 to $60.48.

These options will expire if not exercised at specific dates ranging from April 1999 to September 2005. Prices for options exercised during the three-year period ended December 30, 1995 ranged from $7.31 to $7.34.

Stock participation plan. Under this plan, eligible employees may purchase shares of Intel's Common Stock at 85% of fair market value at specific, predetermined dates. Of the 59.0 million shares authorized to be issued under the plan, 11.9 million shares were available for issuance at December 30, 1995. Employees purchased 3.5 million shares in 1995 (4.0 million and 4.4 million in 1994 and 1993, respectively) for $110 million ($94 million and $71 million in 1994 and 1993, respectively).

Retirement plans. The Company provides tax-qualified profit-sharing retirement plans (the "Qualified Plans") for the benefit of eligible employees in the U.S. and Puerto Rico. The plans are designed to provide employees with an accumulation of funds for retirement on a tax-deferred basis and provide for annual discretionary contributions to trust funds.

The Company also provides a non-qualified profit-sharing retirement plan (the "Non-Qualified Plan") for the benefit of eligible employees in the U.S. This plan is designed to permit certain discretionary employer contributions in excess of the tax limits applicable to the Qualified Plans and to permit employee deferrals in excess of certain tax limits. This plan is unfunded.

The Company accrued $188 million for the Qualified Plans and the Non-Qualified Plan in 1995 ($152 million in 1994 and $103 million in 1993). Of the $188 million accrued in 1995, the Company expects to fund approximately $145 million for the 1995 contribution to the Qualified Plans and to allocate approximately $6 million for the Non-Qualified Plan. The remainder, plus approximately $140 million carried forward from prior years, is expected to be contributed to these plans when allowable under IRS regulations and plan rules.

Contributions made by the Company vest based on the employee's years of service. Vesting begins after three years of service in 20% annual increments until the employee is 100% vested after seven years.

The Company provides tax-qualified defined-benefit pension plans for the benefit of eligible employees in the U.S. and Puerto Rico. Each plan provides for minimum pension benefits that are determined by a participant's years of service, final average compensation (taking into account the participant's social security wage base) and the value of the Company's contributions, plus earnings, in the Qualified Plan. If the balance in the participant's Qualified Plan exceeds the pension guarantee, the participant will receive benefits from the Qualified Plan only. Intel's funding policy is consistent with the funding requirements of federal laws and regulations.

Pension expense for 1995, 1994 and 1993 for the U.S. and Puerto Rico plans was less than $1 million per year, and no component of expense exceeded $2 million.

The funded status of these plans as of December 30, 1995 and December 31, 1994 was as follows:

(In millions)	1995	1994
Vested benefit obligation	**$(3)**	**$(3)**
Accumulated benefit obligation	**$(4)**	**$(3)**
Projected benefit obligation	$(6)	$(5)
Fair market value of plan assets	8	6
Projected benefit obligation less than plan assets	2	1
Unrecognized net (gain)	(12)	(12)
Unrecognized prior service cost	3	4
Accrued pension costs	**$(7)**	**$(7)**

At fiscal year-ends, the weighted average discount rates and long-term rates for compensation increases used for estimating the benefit obligations and the expected return on plan assets were as follows:

	1995	1994	1993
Discount rate	7.0%	8.5%	7.0%
Rate of increase in compensation levels	5.0%	5.5%	5.0%
Expected long-term return on assets	8.5%	8.5%	8.5%

Plan assets of the U.S. and Puerto Rico plans consist primarily of listed stocks and bonds, repurchase agreements, money market securities, U.S. government securities and stock index derivatives.

The Company provides defined-benefit pension plans in certain foreign countries where required by statute. The Company's funding policy for foreign defined-benefit plans is consistent with the local requirements in each country. Pension expense for 1995, 1994 and 1993 for the foreign plans included the following:

(In millions)	1995	1994	1993
Service cost-benefits earned during the year	$9	$5	$5
Interest cost of projected benefit obligation	6	5	6
Actual investment (return) on plan assets	(4)	(8)	(7)
Net amortization and deferral	(2)	3	2
Net pension expense	**$9**	**$5**	**$6**

The funded status of the foreign defined-benefit plans as of December 30, 1995 and December 31, 1994 is summarized below:

1995 (In millions)	Assets exceed accumulated benefits	Accumulated benefits exceed assets
Vested benefit obligation	**$(44)**	**$ (8)**
Accumulated benefit obligation	**$(46)**	**$(14)**
Projected benefit obligation	$(62)	$(22)
Fair market value of plan assets	67	4
Projected benefit obligation less than (in excess of) plan assets	5	(18)
Unrecognized net loss	4	5
Unrecognized net transition obligation	2	—
Prepaid (accrued) pension costs	**$ 11**	**$(13)**

1994 (In millions)	Assets exceed accumulated benefits	Accumulated benefits exceed assets
Vested benefit obligation	**$(32)**	**$ (4)**
Accumulated benefit obligation	**$(34)**	**$ (9)**
Projected benefit obligation	$(49)	$(16)
Fair market value of plan assets	51	3
Projected benefit obligation less than (in excess of) plan assets	2	(13)
Unrecognized net loss	2	2
Unrecognized net transition obligation	—	1
Prepaid (accrued) pension costs	**$ 4**	**$(10)**

At fiscal year-ends, the weighted average discount rates and long-term rates for compensation increases used for estimating the benefit obligations and the expected return on plan assets were as follows:

	1995	1994	1993
Discount rate	5.5%–14%	5.5%–14%	5.5%–14%
Rate of increase in compensation levels	4.5%–11%	4.5%–11%	4.5%–11%
Expected long-term return on assets	5.5%–14%	5.5%–14%	5.5%–14%

Plan assets of the foreign plans consist primarily of listed stocks, bonds and cash surrender value life insurance policies.

Other postemployment benefits. The Company has adopted SFAS No. 106, "Employers' Accounting for Postretirement Benefits Other Than Pensions," and SFAS No. 112, "Employers' Accounting for Postemployment Benefits." There was no material impact on the Company's financial statements for the periods presented.

Commitments

The Company leases a portion of its capital equipment and certain of its facilities under operating leases that expire at various dates through 2011. Rental expense was $38 million in 1995, $38 million in 1994 and $35 million in 1993. Minimum rental commitments under all non-cancelable leases with an initial term in excess of one year are payable as follows: 1996—$25 million; 1997—$20 million; 1998—$15 million; 1999—$12 million; 2000—$10 million; 2001 and beyond—$23 million. Commitments for construction or purchase of property, plant and equipment approximated $1.47 billion at December 30, 1995. In connection with certain manufacturing arrangements, Intel had minimum purchase commitments of approximately $1.12 billion at December 30, 1995 for flash memories and other memory components and for production capacity of board-level products.

Contingencies

On March, 29, 1995, Thorn EMI North America Inc. brought suit in Federal Court in Delaware against Intel and Advanced Micro Devices, Inc. (AMD) alleging infringement of a U.S. patent relating to processes for manufacturing semiconductors, certain of which processes are utilized in the manufacture of the Company's Pentium® and Pentium® Pro microprocessors. The plaintiff is seeking injunctive relief and unspecified damages. On September 8, 1995, Intel was granted a motion to sever its case from the AMD case. Trial of the plaintiff's claims against Intel is presently set for June 1996. The Company believes this lawsuit to be without merit and intends to defend the lawsuit vigorously. Although the ultimate outcome of this lawsuit cannot be determined at this time, management, including internal counsel, does not believe that the outcome of this litigation will have a material adverse effect on the Company's financial position or overall trends in results of operations.

Intel has been named to the California and U.S. Superfund lists for three of its sites and has completed, along with two other companies, a Remedial Investigation/Feasibility study with the U.S. Environmental Protection Agency (EPA) to evaluate the groundwater in areas adjacent to one of its former sites. The EPA has issued a Record of Decision with respect to a groundwater cleanup plan at that site, including expected costs to complete. Under the California and U.S. Superfund statutes, liability for cleanup of this site and the adjacent area is joint and several. The Company, however, has reached agreement with those same two companies which significantly limits the Company's liabilities under the proposed cleanup plan. Also, the Company has completed extensive studies at its other sites and is engaged in cleanup at several of these sites. In the opinion of management, including internal counsel, the potential losses to the Company in excess of amounts already accrued arising out of these matters will not have a material adverse effect on the Company's financial position or overall trends in results of operations, even if joint and several liability were to be assessed.

The Company is party to various other legal proceedings. In the opinion of management, including internal counsel, these proceedings will not have a material adverse effect on the financial position or overall trends in results of operations of the Company.

The estimate of the potential impact on the Company's financial position or overall results of operations for the above legal proceedings could change in the future.

Industry Segment Reporting

The Company operates predominantly in one industry segment. The Company designs, develops, manufactures and markets microcomputer components and related products at various levels of integration. The Company sells its products directly to original equipment manufacturers (OEMs) and also to a network of industrial and retail distributors throughout the world. The Company's principal markets are in the United States, Europe, Asia-Pacific and Japan, with the U.S. and Europe being the largest based on revenues. The Company's major products include microprocessors and related board-level products, chipsets, embedded processors and microcontrollers, flash memory chips, and network and communications products. Microprocessors and related board-level products account for a substantial majority of the Company's net revenues. No customer exceeded 10% of revenues in 1995 or 1994. One significant customer accounted for 10% of revenues in 1993. Summary balance sheet information for operations outside the United States at fiscal year-ends is as follows:

(In millions)	1995	1994
Total assets	$4,404	$2,940
Total liabilities	$1,661	$ 962
Net property, plant and equipment	$1,414	$1,238

Geographic information for the three years ended December 30, 1995 is presented in the following table. Transfers between geographic areas are accounted for at amounts that are generally above cost and consistent with rules and regulations of governing tax authorities. Such transfers are eliminated in the consolidated financial statements. Operating income by geographic segment does not include an allocation of general corporate expenses. Identifiable assets are those that can be directly associated with a particular geographic area. Corporate assets include cash and cash equivalents, short-term investments, deferred tax assets, other current assets, long-term investments and certain other assets.

(In millions)	Sales to unaffiliated customers	Transfers between geographic areas	Net revenues	Operating income	Identifiable assets
1995					
United States	$ 7,922	$6,339	$14,261	$3,315	$12,603
Europe	4,560	1,190	5,750	1,383	2,517
Japan	1,737	28	1,765	353	665
Asia-Pacific	1,983	1,566	3,549	271	893
Other	—	684	684	410	329
Eliminations	—	(9,807)	(9,807)	124	(3,651)
Corporate	—	—	—	(604)	4,148
Consolidated	$16,202	$ —	$16,202	$5,252	$17,504
1994					
United States	$ 5,826	$4,561	$10,387	$2,742	$ 7,771
Europe	3,158	380	3,538	418	1,733
Japan	944	61	1,005	125	343
Asia-Pacific	1,593	1,021	2,614	154	540
Other	—	639	639	378	324
Eliminations	—	(6,662)	(6,662)	179	(1,878)
Corporate	—	—	—	(609)	4,983
Consolidated	$11,521	$ —	$11,521	$3,387	$13,816
1993					
United States	$ 4,416	$3,406	$ 7,822	$2,896	$ 5,379
Europe	2,476	51	2,527	309	1,214
Japan	678	119	797	108	351
Asia-Pacific	1,212	745	1,957	132	420
Other	—	566	566	348	207
Eliminations	—	(4,887)	(4,887)	85	(1,123)
Corporate	—	—	—	(486)	4,896
Consolidated	$ 8,782	$ —	$ 8,782	$3,392	$11,344

Supplemental Information (unaudited)

Quarterly information for the two years ended December 30, 1995 is presented on page 234.

Results of operations. Intel posted record net revenues in 1995, for the ninth consecutive year, rising by 41% from 1994 to 1995 and by 31% from 1993 to 1994. Higher volumes of the rapidly ramping Pentium® microprocessor family, partially offset by lower prices, and increased sales of related board-level products were responsible for most of the growth in revenues in 1994 and 1995. Revenues from the Intel486™ microprocessor family declined substantially in 1995 due to a shift in market demand toward the Company's Pentium microprocessors and lower Intel486 microprocessor prices.

Higher volumes of flash memory and chipset products also contributed toward the increase in revenues from 1993 to 1995 and also helped enable the successful Pentium microprocessor ramp. Sales of system platforms, embedded control products, and networking and communications products also grew.

Cost of sales increased by 40% from 1994 to 1995 and by 71% from 1993 to 1994. The growth in cost of sales from 1993 to 1995 was driven by Pentium microprocessor and board-level unit volume growth, new factories coming into production, shifts in process and product mix, and in the fourth quarter of 1995, by costs associated with unusually high reserves related to inventories of certain purchased components. Gross margin for the fourth quarter of 1994 included the impact of a $475 million charge, primarily to cost of sales, to cover replacement costs, replacement material and an inventory writedown related to a divide problem in the floating point unit of the Pentium microprocessor. As a result of the above factors, the gross margin percentage was 52% in 1995 and 1994, compared to 63% in 1993.

Quarterly unit shipments of the Pentium microprocessor family surpassed those of the Intel486 microprocessor family during the third quarter of 1995. The Company helped accelerate this transition by offering chipsets and motherboards to enable computer manufacturers to bring their products to market faster. Sales of the Pentium microprocessor family comprised a majority of the Company's revenues and a substantial majority of its gross margin during 1995. During 1995, the Intel486 microprocessor family represented a significant but rapidly declining portion of the Company's revenues and gross margins. The Intel486 microprocessor family comprised a majority of the Company's revenues and a substantial majority of its gross margin during 1993 and 1994.

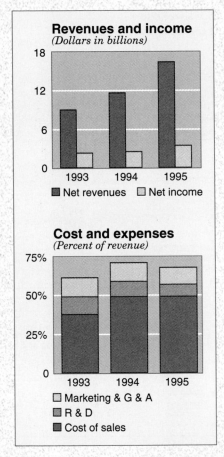

Revenues and income
(Dollars in billions)

■ Net revenues ☐ Net income

Cost and expenses
(Percent of revenue)

☐ Marketing & G & A
▨ R & D
■ Cost of sales

Research and development spending grew by 17% from 1994 to 1995, as the Company continued to invest in strategic programs, particularly for the internal development of microprocessor products and related manufacturing technology. Increased spending for marketing programs, including media merchandising and the Company's Intel Inside® cooperative advertising program, drove the 27% increase in marketing, general and administrative expenses from 1994 to 1995.

The $28 million decrease in interest expense from 1994 to 1995 was mainly due to lower average borrowing balances in addition to higher interest capitalization resulting from increased facility construction programs. The increase in interest expense from 1993 to 1994 was primarily due to higher average interest rates on borrowings, partially offset by higher interest capitalization.

Interest and other income increased by $142 million from 1994 to 1995, primarily due to higher average interest rates on investments in 1995, gains of $58 million related to the settlement of litigation and gains of $60 million from the sale of a portion of the Company's investment in marketable equity securities. Interest and other income increased by $85 million from 1993 to 1994, mainly due to higher average interest rates on investments in 1994, gains related to the settlement of various insurance claims in 1994, and higher foreign exchange gains and investment balances in 1994. Interest and other income in 1993 included gains of $27 million from the sale of certain foreign benefits related to a plant expansion in Ireland during 1993.

The Company utilizes investments and corresponding interest rate swaps to preserve principal while enhancing the yield on its investment portfolio without significantly increasing risk, and uses forward contracts, options and swaps to hedge currency, market and interest rate exposures. Gains and losses on these instruments are generally offset by those on the underlying hedged transactions; as a result, there was no material net impact on the Company's financial results during the 1993–1995 period.

The Company's effective income tax rate increased to 36.8% in 1995 compared to 36.5% and 35.0% in 1994 and 1993, respectively. The increases in rate from 1993 to 1995 resulted from the fact that tax credits have not grown as rapidly as overall pretax income.

Financial condition. The Company's financial condition remains very strong. As of December 30, 1995, total cash and short- and long-term investments totaled $4.11 billion, down from $4.54 billion at December 31, 1994. Cash generated from operating activities rose to $4.03 billion in 1995, compared to $2.98 billion and $2.80 billion in 1994 and 1993, respectively.

Investing activities consumed $2.69 billion in cash during 1995, compared to $2.90 billion during 1994 and $3.34 billion during 1993. Capital expenditures increased substantially in both 1994 and 1995, as the Company continued to invest in the property, plant and equipment needed for future business requirements, including manufacturing capacity. The Company expects to spend approximately $4.1 billion for capital additions in 1996 and had committed approximately $1.47 billion for the construction or purchase of property, plant and equipment as of December 30, 1995.

Inventory levels, particularly raw materials and finished goods, increased significantly in 1995. This increase was primarily attributable to the increased level of business and, to a lesser extent, to an unusually low level of inventory at the end of 1994 because of a writedown of inventories in the fourth quarter of 1994 in connection with the divide problem in the floating point unit of the Pentium processor. The increase in accounts receivable in 1995 was mainly due to revenue growth, including the growth of non-domestic sales that have longer payment terms. During 1995, the Company experienced an increase in its concentration of credit risk due to increasing trade receivables from sales to manufacturers of microcomputer systems. The Company's five largest customers accounted for approximately 33% of net revenues for 1995. At December 30, 1995, these customers accounted for approximately 34% of net accounts receivable. A portion of the receivable balance from one of its five largest customers has been converted into a loan. The total amount receivable from this customer was approximately $400 million at December 30, 1995.

The Company used $1.06 billion and $557 million for financing activities in 1995 and 1994, respectively, while $352 million was provided in 1993. The major financing application of cash in 1995 was for stock repurchases totaling $1.03 billion. Financing applications of cash in 1994 included stock repurchases of $658 million and the early retirement of the Company's 8⅛% debt. Sources of financing in 1993 included the Company's public offering of the 1998 Step-Up Warrants, which resulted in proceeds of $287 million.

As part of its authorized stock repurchase program, the Company had outstanding put warrants at the end of 1995, with the potential obligation to buy back 12 million shares of its Common Stock at an aggregate price of $725 million. The exercise price of these warrants ranges from $38 to $68

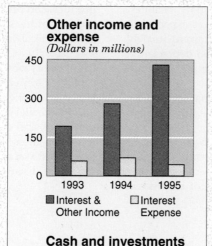

Other income and expense
(Dollars in millions)

■ Interest & Other Income □ Interest Expense

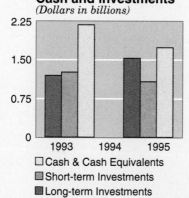

Cash and investments
(Dollars in billions)

□ Cash & Cash Equivalents
■ Short-term Investments
■ Long-term Investments

per share, with an average exercise price of $60 per share.

Other sources of liquidity include combined credit lines and authorized commercial paper borrowings of $1.86 billion, $57 million of which was outstanding at December 30, 1995. The Company also maintains the ability to issue an aggregate of approximately $1.4 billion in debt, equity and other securities under Securities and Exchange Commission (SEC) shelf registration statements. The Company believes that it has the financial resources needed to meet business requirements in the foreseeable future, including capital expenditures for the recently announced expansion of international manufacturing sites, working capital requirements, the potential put warrant obligation and the dividend program.

Outlook. The statements contained in this Outlook are based on current expectations. These statements are forward looking, and actual results may differ materially.

Intel expects that the total number of personal computers using Intel's Pentium microprocessors and other semiconductor components sold worldwide will continue to grow in 1996. Intel has expanded manufacturing capacity over the last few years and continues to expand capacity to be able to meet the potential increase in demand. Intel's financial results are to a large extent dependent on this market segment. Revenue is also a function of the distribution of microprocessor speed and performance levels, which is difficult to forecast. Because of the large price difference between components for the highest and lowest performance computers, this distribution affects the average price Intel will realize and has a large impact on Intel's revenues.

Intel's strategy has been, and continues to be, to introduce ever higher performance microprocessors and work with the software industry to develop compelling applications that can take advantage of this higher performance, thus driving demand toward the newer products. Capacity has been planned based on the assumed continued success of the Company's strategy. In line with this strategy, the Company has recently announced higher speed members of the Pentium® Pro microprocessor family. If the market demand does not continue to grow and move rapidly toward higher performance products, revenue growth may be impacted, the manufacturing capacity installed might be under-utilized and capital spending may be slowed. The Company may continue to reduce microprocessor prices aggressively and systematically to bring its technology to market.

The Company's gross margin percentage is a sensitive function of the product mix sold in any period. Because the percentage of motherboards that Intel's customers purchase changes with maturity of the product cycle, and motherboards generally have lower gross margin percentages than microprocessors, Intel's gross margin percentage varies depending on the mix of microprocessors and related motherboards within a product family. Various other factors, including unit volumes and costs and yield issues associated with initiating production at new factories or on new processes, also will continue to affect the amount of cost of sales and the variability of gross margin percentages in future quarters. From time to time the Company may forecast a range of gross margin percentages for the coming quarter. Actual results may differ. Longer term gross margin percentages are even more difficult to predict.

To implement its strategy, Intel continues to build capacity to produce high-performance microprocessors and other products. The Company expects that capital spending will increase to approximately $4.1 billion in 1996. This spending plan is dependent upon delivery times of various machines and construction schedules for new facilities. Based on this forecast, depreciation for 1996 is expected to be approximately $1.9 billion, an increase of approximately $500 million from 1995. Most of this increased depreciation will be included in cost of sales and research and development spending.

The industry in which Intel operates is characterized by very short product life cycles. Intel considers it imperative to maintain a strong research and development program to continue to succeed. Accordingly, research and development spending is expected to grow in 1996 to approximately $1.6 billion. The Company will also continue spending to promote its products and to increase the value of its product brands. Based on current forecasts, spending for marketing and general and administrative expenses is expected to increase in 1996.

The Company expects its tax rate to decrease to 36.5% for 1996. This estimate is based on current tax law and is subject to change.

The Company's future results of operations and the other forward looking statements contained in this Outlook, in particular the statements regarding growth in the personal computer industry, capital spending, depreciation, research and development, and marketing and general and administrative expenses, involve a number of risks and uncertainties. In addition to the factors discussed above, among the other factors that could cause actual results to differ materially are the following: business conditions and the general economy; competitive factors, such as rival chip architectures, competing software compatible microprocessors, acceptance of new products and price pressures; availability of third-party component products at reasonable prices; risk of nonpayment of accounts receivable or customer loans; manufacturing ramp and capacity; risks associated with foreign operations; risk of inventory obsolescence due to shifts in market demand; timing of software industry product introductions; and litigation involving intellectual property and consumer issues.

Intel believes that it has the product offerings, facilities, personnel, and competitive and financial resources for continued business success, but future revenues, costs, margins, product mix and profits are all influenced by a number of factors, as discussed above.

Ten Years Ended December 30, 1995

(In millions)	Net investment in property, plant & equip.	Total assets	Long-term debt & put warrants	Stockholders' equity	Additions to property, plant & equipment
1995	**$7,471**	**$17,504**	**$1,125**	**$12,140**	**$3,550**
1994	$5,367	$13,816	$1,136	$ 9,267	$2,441
1993	$3,996	$11,344	$1,114	$ 7,500	$1,933
1992	$2,816	$ 8,089	$ 622	$ 5,445	$1,228
1991	$2,163	$ 6,292	$ 503	$ 4,418	$ 948
1990	$1,658	$ 5,376	$ 345	$ 3,592	$ 680
1989	$1,284	$ 3,994	$ 412	$ 2,549	$ 422
1988	$1,122	$ 3,550	$ 479	$ 2,080	$ 477
1987	$ 891	$ 2,499	$ 298	$ 1,276	$ 302
1986	$ 779	$ 1,977	$ 287	$ 1,245	$ 155

(In millions—except per share amounts)	Net revenues	Cost of sales	Research & development	Operating income (loss)	Net income (loss)	Earnings (loss) per share	Dividends declared per share
1995	**$16,202**	**$7,811**	**$1,296**	**$5,252**	**$3,566**	**$ 4.03**	**$0.15**
1994	$11,521	$5,576	$1,111	$3,387	$2,288	$ 2.62	$0.115
1993	$ 8,782	$3,252	$ 970	$3,392	$2,295	$ 2.60	$0.10
1992	$ 5,844	$2,557	$ 780	$1,490	$1,067	$ 1.24	$0.05
1991	$ 4,779	$2,316	$ 618	$1,080	$ 819	$ 0.98	—
1990	$ 3,921	$1,930	$ 517	$ 858	$ 650	$ 0.80	—
1989	$ 3,127	$1,721	$ 365	$ 557	$ 391	$ 0.52	—
1988	$ 2,875	$1,506	$ 318	$ 594	$ 453	$ 0.63	—
1987	$ 1,907	$1,044	$ 260	$ 246	$ 248	$ 0.34	—
1986	$ 1,265	$ 861	$ 228	$ (195)	$ (203)	$(0.29)	—

In 1971, Intel introduced the world's first microprocessor, which sparked a computer revolution that has changed the world. About 75 percent of the personal computers in use around the world today are based on Intel-architecture microprocessors. Today, Intel supplies the personal computing industry with the chips, boards, systems and software that are the "ingredients" of the most popular computing architecture. These products help create advanced computing systems for personal computer users.

❖ QUESTIONS ❖

1 How does information from the balance sheet help users of the financial statements?

2 A recent financial magazine indicated that a drug company had good financial flexibility. What is meant by financial flexibility and why is it important?

3 What is meant by liquidity? Rank the following assets from one to five in order of liquidity.
(a) Goodwill
(b) Inventories
(c) Buildings
(d) Short-term investments
(e) Accounts receivable

4 What are the major limitations of the balance sheet as a source of information?

5 In its December 31, 1999 balance sheet Oakley Corporation reported as an asset "Net Notes and Accounts Receivable, $7,100,000." What other disclosures are necessary?

6 Should available-for-sale securities always be reported as a current asset? Explain.

7 A stock analyst recently noted that a balance sheet is more critical than the income statement. He stated, "You can show beautiful profits by burying inventories." Explain the analyst's comments.

8 What is the relationship between current assets and current liabilities?

9 The New York Knicks, Inc. sold 10,000 season tickets at $1,000 each. By December 31, 1999, 18 of the 40 home games had been played. What amount should be reported as a current liability at December 31, 1999?

10 What is working capital? How does working capital relate to the operating cycle?

11 In what section of the balance sheet should the following items appear, and what balance sheet terminology would you use?
(a) Treasury stock (recorded at cost, which is below par).
(b) Checking account at bank.
(c) Land (held as an investment).
(d) Reserve for sinking fund.
(e) Unamortized premium on bonds payable.
(f) Investment in copyrights.
(g) Employees' pension fund (consisting of cash and securities).
(h) Premium on capital stock.
(i) Long-term investments (pledged against bank loans payable).

12 Where should the following items be shown on the balance sheet, if shown at all?
(a) Allowance for doubtful accounts receivable.
(b) Merchandise held on consignment.
(c) Advances received on sales contract.
(d) Cash surrender value of life insurance.
(e) Land.
(f) Merchandise out on consignment.

(g) Pension fund on deposit with a trustee (under a trust revocable at depositor's option).
(h) Franchises.
(i) Accumulated depreciation of plant and equipment.
(j) Materials in transit—purchased f.o.b. destination.

13 State the generally accepted accounting principle (standard) applicable to the balance sheet valuation of each of the following assets.
(a) Trade accounts receivable.
(b) Land.
(c) Inventories.
(d) Trading securities (common stock of other companies).
(e) Prepaid expenses.

14 Refer to the definition of assets on page 207. Discuss how a leased building might qualify as an asset of the lessee under this definition.

15 Christine Agazzi says, "Retained earnings should be reported as an asset, since it is earnings which are reinvested in the business." How would you respond to Agazzi?

16 The president of your company has recently read an article that disturbs her greatly. The author of this article stated that "although the balance sheet and income statement balance to the penny, they are full of estimates and subject to material error." Indicate items found in these statements that are based on estimates and explain why you must resort to "guessing" these amounts.

17 The creditors of Nick Anderson Company agree to accept promissory notes for the amount of its indebtedness with a proviso that two-thirds of the annual profits must be applied to their liquidation. How should these notes be reported on the balance sheet of the issuing company? Give a reason for your answer.

18 What are the major types of subsequent events? Indicate how each of the following "subsequent events" would be reported.
(a) Collection of a note written off in a prior period.
(b) Issuance of a large preferred stock offering.
(c) Acquisition of a company in a different industry.
(d) Destruction of a major plant in a flood.
(e) Death of the company's chief executive officer (CEO).
(f) Settlement of a four-week strike at additional wage costs.
(g) Settlement of a federal income tax case at considerably more tax than anticipated at year-end.
(h) Change in the product mix from consumer goods to industrial goods.

19 What are some of the techniques of disclosure for the balance sheet?

20 What is the difference between the report form and the account form for the purpose of balance sheet presentation?

㉑ What is a "Summary of Significant Accounting Policies"?

㉒ What types of contractual obligations must be disclosed in great detail in the notes to the balance sheet? Why do you think these detailed provisions should be disclosed?

㉓ What is the profession's recommendation in regard to the use of the term "surplus"? Explain.

㉔ What is the purpose of a statement of cash flows? How does it differ from a balance sheet and an income statement?

㉕ The net income for the year for Won Long, Inc. is $750,000, but the statement of cash flows reports that the cash provided by operating activities is $970,000. What might account for the difference?

㉖ Differentiate between operating activities, investing activities, and financing activities.

㉗ Each of the following items must be considered in preparing a statement of cash flows. Indicate where each item is to be reported in the statement, if at all. Assume that net income is reported as $90,000.
(a) Accounts receivable increased from $32,000 to $39,000 from the beginning to the end of the year.
(b) During the year, 10,000 shares of preferred stock with a par value of $100 a share were issued at $115 per share.
(c) Depreciation expense amounted to $14,000 and bond premium amortization amounted to $5,000.

㉘ Marker Co. has net cash provided by operating activities of $900,000. Its average current liabilities for the period are $1,000,000 and its average total liabilities are $1,500,000. Comment on the company's liquidity and financial flexibility, given this information.

㉙ What is the purpose of a free cash flow analysis?

❖ BRIEF EXERCISES ❖

BE5-1 La Bouche Corporation has the following accounts included in its 12/31/99 trial balance: Accounts Receivable, $110,000; Inventories, $290,000; Allowance for Doubtful Accounts, $8,000; Patents, $72,000; Prepaid Insurance, $9,500; Accounts Payable, $77,000; Cash $27,000. Prepare the current asset section of the balance sheet listing the accounts in proper sequence.

BE5-2 Included in Goo Goo Dolls Company's 12/31/99 trial balance are the following accounts: Prepaid Rent, $5,200; Held-to-Maturity Securities, $61,000; Unearned Fees, $17,000; Land held for Investment, $39,000; Long-term Receivables, $42,000. Prepare the long-term investments section of the balance sheet.

BE5-3 Adam Ant Company's 12/31/99 trial balance includes the following accounts: Inventories, $120,000; Buildings, $207,000; Accumulated Depreciation–Equipment, $19,000; Equipment, $190,000; Land held for Investment, $46,000; Accumulated Depreciation–Buildings, $45,000; Land, $61,000; Capital Leases, $70,000. Prepare the property, plant, and equipment section of the balance sheet.

BE5-4 Mason Corporation has the following accounts included in its 12/31/99 trial balance: Trading Securities, $21,000; Goodwill, $150,000; Prepaid Insurance, $12,000; Patents, $220,000; Franchises, $110,000. Prepare the intangible asset section of the balance sheet.

BE5-5 Included in Ewing Company's 12/31/99 trial balance are the following accounts: Accounts Payable, $240,000; Obligations under Capital Leases, $375,000; Discount on Bonds Payable, $24,000; Advances from Customers, $41,000; Bonds Payable, $400,000; Wages Payable, $27,000; Interest Payable, $12,000; Income Taxes Payable, $29,000. Prepare the current liability section of the balance sheet.

BE5-6 Use the information presented in BE5-5 for Ewing Company to prepare the long-term liability section of the balance sheet.

BE5-7 Young Company's 12/31/99 trial balance includes the following accounts: Investment in Common Stock, $70,000; Retained Earnings, $114,000; Trademarks, $31,000; Preferred Stock, $172,000; Common Stock, $55,000; Deferred Income Taxes, $88,000; Additional Paid-in Capital, $174,000. Prepare the stockholders' equity section of the balance sheet.

BE5-8 Linden Corporation is preparing its December 31, 1999, financial statements. Two events which occurred between 12/31/99 and 3/10/00, when the statements were issued, are described below.

1. A liability, estimated at $150,000 at 12/31/99, was settled on 2/26/00 at $170,000.
2. A flood loss of $80,000 occurred on 3/1/00.

What effect do these subsequent events have on 1999 net income?

BE5-9 Kes Company reported 1999 net income of $151,000. During 1999, accounts receivable increased by $13,000 and accounts payable increased by $9,500. Depreciation expense was $39,000. Prepare the cash flows from operating activities section of the statement of cash flows.

BE5-10 Yorkis Perez Corporation engaged in the following cash transactions during 1999:

Sale of land and building	$181,000
Purchase of treasury stock	40,000
Purchase of land	37,000
Payment of cash dividend	85,000
Purchase of equipment	53,000
Issuance of common stock	147,000
Retirement of bonds	100,000

Compute the net cash provided (used) by investing activities.

BE5-11 Use the information presented in BE5-10 for Yorkis Perez Corporation to compute the net cash used (provided) by financing activities.

BE5-12 Using the information in BE-10, determine Yorkis Perez's free cash flow, assuming that it reported net cash provided by operating activities of $400,000.

❖ EXERCISES ❖

E5-1 (Balance Sheet Classifications)   Presented below are a number of balance sheet accounts of Deep Blue Something, Inc.:

1. Investment in Preferred Stock
2. Treasury Stock
3. Common Stock Distributable
4. Cash Dividends Payable
5. Accumulated Depreciation
6. Warehouse in Process of Construction
7. Petty Cash

8. Accrued Interest on Notes Payable
9. Deficit
10. Trading Securities
11. Income Taxes Payable
12. Unearned Subscriptions
13. Work in Process
14. Accrued Vacation Pay

Instructions
For each of the accounts above, indicate the proper balance sheet classification. In the case of borderline items, indicate the additional information that would be required to determine the proper classification.

E5-2 (Classification of Balance Sheet Accounts)   Presented below are the captions of Faulk Company's balance sheet:

A. Current Assets
B. Investments
C. Property, Plant, and Equipment
D. Intangible Assets
E. Other Assets

F. Current Liabilities
G. Noncurrent Liabilities
H. Capital Stock
I. Additional Paid-in Capital
J. Retained Earnings

Instructions
Indicate by letter where each of the following items would be classified:

1. Preferred stock
2. Goodwill
3. Wages payable
4. Trade accounts payable
5. Buildings
6. Trading securities
7. Current portion of long-term debt
8. Premium on bonds payable
9. Allowance for doubtful accounts
10. Accounts receivable

11. Cash surrender value of life insurance
12. Notes payable (due next year)
13. Office supplies
14. Common stock
15. Land
16. Bond sinking fund
17. Merchandise inventory
18. Prepaid insurance
19. Bonds payable
20. Taxes payable

E5-3 (Classification of Balance Sheet Accounts) Assume that Fielder Enterprises uses the following headings on its balance sheet:

A. Current Assets
B. Investments
C. Property, Plant, and Equipment
D. Intangible Assets
E. Other Assets

F. Current Liabilities
G. Long-term Liabilities
H. Capital Stock
I. Paid-in Capital in Excess of Par
J. Retained Earnings

Instructions

Indicate by letter how each of the following usually should be classified. If an item should appear in a note to the financial statements, use the letter "N" to indicate this fact. If an item need not be reported at all on the balance sheet, use the letter "X."

1. Unexpired insurance.
2. Stock owned in affiliated companies.
3. Unearned subscriptions.
4. Advances to suppliers.
5. Unearned rent.
6. Treasury stock.
7. Premium on preferred stock.
8. Copyrights.
9. Petty cash fund.
10. Sale of large issue of common stock 15 days after balance sheet date.
11. Accrued interest on notes receivable.
12. Twenty-year issue of bonds payable which will mature within the next year. (No sinking fund exists and refunding is not planned.)
13. Machinery retired from use and held for sale.
14. Fully depreciated machine still in use.
15. Organization costs.
16. Accrued interest on bonds payable.
17. Salaries that company budget shows will be paid to employees within the next year.
18. Discount on bonds payable. (Assume related to bonds payable in No. 12.)
19. Accumulated depreciation.

E5-4 (Preparation of a Classified Balance Sheet) Assume that Denis Savard Inc. has the following accounts at the end of the current year.

1. Common Stock
2. Discount on Bonds Payable
3. Treasury Stock (at cost)
4. Common Stock Subscribed
5. Raw Materials
6. Preferred Stock Investments—Long-term
7. Unearned Rent
8. Work in Process
9. Copyrights
10. Buildings
11. Notes Receivable (short-term)
12. Cash
13. Accrued Salaries Payable
14. Accumulated Depreciation—Buildings
15. Cash Restricted for Plant Expansion
16. Land Held for Future Plant Site
17. Allowance for Doubtful Accounts—Accounts Receivable
18. Retained Earnings—Unappropriated
19. Premium on Common Stock
20. Unearned Subscriptions
21. Receivables—Officers (due in one year)
22. Finished Goods
23. Accounts Receivable
24. Bonds Payable (due in 4 years)
25. Stock Subscriptions Receivable

Instructions

Prepare a classified balance sheet in good form (no monetary amounts are necessary).

E5-5 (Preparation of a Corrected Balance Sheet) Uhura Company has decided to expand their operations. The bookkeeper recently completed the balance sheet presented below in order to obtain additional funds for expansion.

Uhura Company
BALANCE SHEET
For the Year Ended 1999

Current assets	
Cash (net of bank overdraft of $30,000)	$200,000
Accounts receivable (net)	340,000
Inventories at lower of average cost or market	401,000
Trading securities—at cost (fair value $120,000)	140,000
Property, plant, and equipment	
Building (net)	570,000
Office equipment (net)	160,000
Land held for future use	175,000

Intangible assets		
Goodwill		80,000
Cash surrender value of life insurance		90,000
Prepaid expenses		12,000
Current liabilities		
Accounts payable		105,000
Notes payable (due next year)		125,000
Pension obligation		82,000
Rent payable		49,000
Premium on bonds payable		53,000
Long-term liabilities		
Bonds payable		500,000
Stockholders' equity		
Common stock, $1.00 par, authorized		
400,000 shares, issued 290,000		290,000
Additional paid-in capital		160,000
Retained earnings		?

Instructions

Prepare a revised balance sheet given the available information. Assume that the accumulated depreciation balance for the buildings is $160,000 and for the office equipment, $105,000. The allowance for doubtful accounts has a balance of $17,000. The pension obligation is considered a long-term liability.

E5-6 (Corrections of a Balance Sheet)   The bookkeeper for Geronimo Company has prepared the following balance sheet as of July 31, 1999:

Geronimo Company
BALANCE SHEET
As of July 31, 1999

Cash	$ 69,000	Notes and accounts payable	$ 44,000
Accounts receivable (net)	40,500	Long-term liabilities	75,000
Inventories	60,000	Stockholders' equity	155,500
Equipment (net)	84,000		
Patents	21,000		
	$274,500		$274,500

The following additional information is provided:

1. Cash includes $1,200 in a petty cash fund and $15,000 in a bond sinking fund.
2. The net accounts receivable balance comprises the following three items: (a) accounts receivable—debit balances $52,000; (b) accounts receivable—credit balances $8,000; (c) allowance for doubtful accounts $3,500.
3. Merchandise inventory costing $5,300 was shipped out on consignment on July 31, 1999. The ending inventory balance does not include the consigned goods. Receivables in the amount of $5,300 were recognized on these consigned goods.
4. Equipment had a cost of $112,000 and an accumulated depreciation balance of $28,000.
5. Taxes payable of $6,000 were accrued on July 31. Geronimo Company, however, had set up a cash fund to meet this obligation. This cash fund was not included in the cash balance, but was offset against the taxes payable amount.

Instructions

Prepare a corrected classified balance sheet as of July 31, 1999 from the available information, adjusting the account balances using the additional information.

E5-7 (Current Asset Section of the Balance Sheet)   Presented below are selected accounts of Yasunari Kawabata Company at 12/31/99:

Finished goods	$ 52,000	Cost of goods sold	2,100,000
Revenue received in advance	90,000	Notes receivable	40,000
Bank overdraft	8,000	Accounts receivable	161,000
Equipment	253,000	Raw materials	207,000
Work-in-process	34,000	Supplies expense	60,000
Cash	37,000	Allowance for doubtful accounts	12,000
Short-term investments in stock	31,000	Licenses	18,000
Customer advances	36,000	Additional paid-in capital	88,000
Cash restricted for plant expansion	50,000	Treasury stock	22,000

The following additional information is available:

1. Inventories are valued at lower of cost or market using LIFO.
2. Equipment is recorded at cost. Accumulated depreciation, computed on a straight-line basis, is $50,600.
3. The short-term investments have a fair value of $29,000 (assume they are trading securities).
4. The notes receivable are due April 30, 2001, with interest receivable every April 30. The notes bear interest at 12% (Hint: accrue interest due on 12/31/99).
5. The allowance for doubtful accounts applies to the accounts receivable. Accounts receivable of $50,000 are pledged as collateral on a bank loan.
6. Licenses are recorded net of accumulated amortization of $14,000.
7. Treasury stock is recorded at cost.

Instructions
Prepare the current asset section of Yasunari Kawabata Company's December 31, 1999, balance sheet, with appropriate disclosures.

E5-8 (Current vs. Long-term Liabilities) Frederic Chopin Corporation is preparing its December 31, 1999, balance sheet. The following items may be reported as either a current or long-term liability.

1. On December 15, 1999, Chopin declared a cash dividend of $2.50 per share to stockholders of record on December 31. The dividend is payable on January 15, 2000. Chopin has issued 1,000,000 shares of common stock, of which 50,000 shares are held in treasury.
2. Also on December 31, Chopin declared a 10% stock dividend to stockholders of record on January 15, 2000. The dividend will be distributed on January 31, 2000. Chopin's common stock has a par value of $10 per share and a market value of $38 per share.
3. At December 31, bonds payable of $100,000,000 are outstanding. The bonds pay 12% interest every September 30 and mature in installments of $25,000,000 every September 30, beginning September 30, 2000.
4. At December 31, 1998, customer advances were $12,000,000. During 1999, Chopin collected $30,000,000 of customer advances, and advances of $25,000,000 were earned.
5. At December 31, 1999, retained earnings appropriated for future inventory losses is $15,000,000.

Instructions
For each item above indicate the dollar amounts to be reported as a current liability and as a long-term liability, if any.

E5-9 (Post-Balance Sheet Events) Madrasah Corporation issued its financial statements for the year ended December 31, 1999, on March 10, 2000. The following events took place early in 2000.

1. On January 10, 10,000 shares of $5 par value common stock were issued at $66 per share.
2. On March 1, Madrasah determined after negotiations with the Internal Revenue Service that income taxes payable for 1999 should be $1,270,000. At December 31, 1999, income taxes payable were recorded at $1,100,000.

Instructions
Discuss how the preceding post-balance sheet events should be reflected in the 1999 financial statements.

E5-10 (Current Assets and Current Liabilities) The current asset and liability sections of the balance sheet of Allessandro Scarlatti Company appear as follows:

Allessandro Scarlatti Company
PARTIAL BALANCE SHEET
December 31, 1999

Cash		$ 40,000	Accounts payable	$61,000
Accounts receivable	$89,000		Notes payable	67,000
Less allowance for doubtful accounts	7,000	82,000		
Inventories		171,000		
Prepaid expenses		9,000		
		$302,000		$128,000

The following errors in the corporation's accounting have been discovered:

1. January 2000 cash disbursements entered as of December 1999 included payments of accounts payable in the amount of $39,000, on which a cash discount of 2% was taken.
2. The inventory included $27,000 of merchandise that had been received at December 31 but for which no purchase invoices had been received or entered. Of this amount, $12,000 had been received on consignment; the remainder was purchased f.o.b. destination, terms 2/10, n/30.
3. Sales for the first four days in January 2000 in the amount of $30,000 were entered in the sales book as of December 31, 1999. Of these, $21,500 were sales on account and the remainder were cash sales.
4. Cash, not including cash sales, collected in January 2000 and entered as of December 31, 1999, totaled $35,324. Of this amount, $23,324 was received on account after cash discounts of 2% had been deducted; the remainder represented the proceeds of a bank loan.

Instructions

(a) Restate the current asset and liability sections of the balance sheet in accordance with good accounting practice. (Assume that both accounts receivable and accounts payable are recorded gross.)

(b) State the net effect of your adjustments on Allesandro Scarlatti Company's retained earnings balance.

E5-11 (Post-Balance Sheet Events) For each of the following subsequent (post-balance sheet) events, indicate whether a company should (a) adjust the financial statements, (b) disclose in notes to the financial statements, or (c) neither adjust nor disclose.

1. Settlement of federal tax case at a cost considerably in excess of the amount expected at year-end.
2. Introduction of a new product line.
3. Loss of assembly plant due to fire.
4. Sale of a significant portion of the company's assets.
5. Retirement of the company president.
6. Prolonged employee strike.
7. Loss of a significant customer.
8. Issuance of a significant number of shares of common stock.
9. Material loss on a year-end receivable because of a customer's bankruptcy.
10. Hiring of a new president.
11. Settlement of prior year's litigation against the company.
12. Merger with another company of comparable size.

E5-12 (Statement of Cash Flows—Classifications) The major classifications of activities reported in the statement of cash flows are operating, investing, and financing. Classify each of the transactions listed below as:

1. Operating activity—add to net income.
2. Operating activity—deduct from net income.
3. Investing activity.
4. Financing activity.
5. Not reported as a cash flow.

The transactions are as follows:

(a) Issuance of capital stock.
(b) Purchase of land and building.
(c) Redemption of bonds.
(d) Sale of equipment.
(e) Depreciation of machinery.
(f) Amortization of patent.
(g) Issuance of bonds for plant assets.

(h) Payment of cash dividends.
(i) Exchange of furniture for office equipment.
(j) Purchase of treasury stock.
(k) Loss on sale of equipment.
(l) Increase in accounts receivable during the year.
(m) Decrease in accounts payable during the year.

E5-13 (Preparation of a Statement of Cash Flows) The comparative balance sheets of Constantine Cavamanlis Inc. at the beginning and the end of the year 1999 appear below.

Constantine Cavamanlis Inc.
BALANCE SHEETS

Assets	Dec. 31, 1999	Jan. 1, 1999	Inc./Dec.
Cash	$ 45,000	$ 13,000	$32,000 Inc.
Accounts receivable	91,000	88,000	3,000 Inc.
Equipment	39,000	22,000	17,000 Inc.
Less accumulated depreciation	(17,000)	(11,000)	6,000 Inc.
Total	$158,000	$112,000	

Liabilities and Stockholders' Equity

Accounts payable	$ 20,000	$ 15,000	5,000 Inc.
Common stock	100,000	80,000	20,000 Inc.
Retained earnings	38,000	17,000	21,000 Inc.
Total	$158,000	$112,000	

Net income of $44,000 was reported and dividends of $23,000 were paid in 1999. New equipment was purchased and none was sold.

Instructions
Prepare a statement of cash flows for the year 1999.

E5-14 (Preparation of a Statement of Cash Flows) Presented below is a condensed version of the comparative balance sheets for Zubin Metha Corporation for the last two years at December 31:

	1999	1998
Cash	$177,000	$ 78,000
Accounts receivable	180,000	185,000
Investments	52,000	74,000
Equipment	298,000	240,000
Less accumulated depreciation	(106,000)	(89,000)
Current liabilities	134,000	151,000
Capital stock	160,000	160,000
Retained earnings	307,000	177,000

Additional information:
Investments were sold at a loss (not extraordinary) of $10,000; no equipment was sold; cash dividends paid were $30,000; and net income was $160,000.

Instructions
(a) Prepare a statement of cash flows for 1999 for Zubin Metha Corporation.
(b) Determine Zubin Metha Corporation's free cash flow.

E5-15 (Preparation of a Statement of Cash Flows) A comparative balance sheet for Shabbona Corporation is presented below.

	December 31	
Assets	1999	1998
Cash	$ 73,000	$ 22,000
Accounts receivable	82,000	66,000
Inventories	180,000	189,000
Land	71,000	110,000
Equipment	260,000	200,000
Accumulated depreciation—equipment	(69,000)	(42,000)
Total	$597,000	$545,000
Liabilities and Stockholders' Equity		
Accounts payable	$ 34,000	$ 47,000
Bonds payable	150,000	200,000
Common stock ($1 par)	214,000	164,000
Retained earnings	199,000	134,000
Total	$597,000	$545,000

Additional information:

1. Net income for 1999 was $125,000.
2. Cash dividends of $60,000 were declared and paid.
3. Bonds payable amounting to $50,000 were retired through issuance of common stock.

Instructions
(a) Prepare a statement of cash flows for 1999 for Shabbona Corporation.
(b) Determine Shabbona Corporation's current cash debt ratio, cash debt coverage ratio, and free cash flow. Comment on its liquidity and financial flexibility.

E5-16 (Preparation of a Balance Sheet)   Presented below is the trial balance of William Melvin Kelly Corporation at December 31, 1999.

	Debits	Credits
Cash	$ 197,000	
Sales		$ 8,100,000
Trading securities (at cost, $145,000)	153,000	
Cost of goods sold	4,800,000	
Long-term investments in bonds	299,000	
Long-term investments in stocks	277,000	
Short-term notes payable		90,000
Accounts payable		455,000
Selling expenses	2,000,000	
Investment revenue		63,000
Land	260,000	
Buildings	1,040,000	
Dividends payable		136,000
Accrued liabilities		96,000
Accounts receivable	435,000	
Accumulated depreciation—buildings		152,000
Allowance for doubtful accounts		25,000
Administrative expenses	900,000	
Interest expense	211,000	
Inventories	597,000	
Extraordinary gain		80,000
Prior period adjustment—depr. error	140,000	
Long-term notes payable		900,000
Equipment	600,000	
Bonds payable		1,000,000
Accumulated depreciation—equipment		60,000
Franchise (net of $80,000 amort.)	160,000	
Common stock ($5 par)		1,000,000
Treasury stock	191,000	
Patent (net of $30,000 amort.)	195,000	
Retained earnings		218,000
Additional paid-in capital		80,000
Totals	$12,455,000	$12,455,000

Instructions
Prepare a balance sheet at December 31, 1999, for William Melvin Kelly Corporation. Ignore income taxes.

E5-17 (Preparation of a Statement of Cash Flows and a Balance Sheet)   Grant Wood Corporation's balance sheet at the end of 1998 included the following items:

Current assets	$235,000	Current liabilities	$150,000
Land	30,000	Bonds payable	100,000
Building	120,000	Common stock	180,000
Equipment	90,000	Retained earnings	44,000
Accum. depr.—build.	(30,000)		
Accum. depr.—equip.	(11,000)		
Patents	40,000		
Total	$474,000	Total	$474,000

The following information is available for 1999.

1. Net income was $55,000.
2. Equipment (cost, $20,000 and accumulated depreciation, $8,000) was sold for $10,000.
3. Depreciation expense was $4,000 on the building and $9,000 on equipment.
4. Patent amortization was $2,500.
5. Current assets other than cash increased by $29,000. Current liabilities increased by $13,000.
6. An addition to the building was completed at a cost of $27,000.
7. A long-term investment in stock was purchased for $16,000.
8. Bonds payable of $50,000 were issued.
9. Cash dividends of $30,000 were declared and paid.
10. Treasury stock was purchased at a cost of $11,000.

Instructions
(a) Prepare a statement of cash flows for 1999.
(b) Prepare a balance sheet at December 31, 1999.

❖ PROBLEMS ❖

P5-1 (Preparation of a Classified Balance Sheet) Presented below is a list of accounts in alphabetical order.

Accounts Receivable	Inventory—Ending
Accrued Wages	Land
Accumulated Depreciation—Buildings	Land for Future Plant Site
Accumulated Depreciation—Equipment	Loss from Flood
Advances to Employees	Notes Payable
Advertising Expense	Patent (net of amortization)
Allowance for Doubtful Accounts	Pension Obligations
Bond Sinking Fund	Petty Cash
Bonds Payable	Preferred Stock
Buildings	Premium on Bonds Payable
Cash in Bank	Premium on Preferred Stock
Cash on Hand	Prepaid Rent
Cash Surrender Value of Life Insurance	Purchases
Commission Expense	Purchase Returns and Allowances
Common Stock	Retained Earnings
Copyright (net of amortization)	Sales
Dividends Payable	Sales Discounts
Equipment	Sales Salaries
FICA Taxes Payable	Trading Securities
Gain on Sale of Equipment	Transportation-in
Interest Receivable	Treasury Stock (at cost)
Inventory—Beginning	Unearned Subscriptions

Instructions
Prepare a classified balance sheet in good form (no monetary amounts are to be shown).

P5-2 (Balance Sheet Preparation) Presented below are a number of balance sheet items for Jay Leno, Inc., for the current year, 1999.

Goodwill	$ 125,000	Accumulated depreciation—equipment	$ 292,000
Payroll taxes payable	177,591	Inventories	239,800
Bonds payable	300,000	Rent payable—short-term	45,000
Discount on bonds payable	15,000	Taxes payable	98,362
Cash	360,000	Long-term rental obligations	480,000
Land	480,000	Common stock, $1 par value	200,000
Notes receivable	545,700	Preferred stock, $10 par value	150,000
Notes payable to banks	265,000	Prepaid expenses	87,920
Accounts payable	590,000	Equipment	1,470,000
Retained earnings	?	Trading securities	121,000
Refundable federal and state income taxes	97,630	Accumulated depreciation—building	170,200
Unsecured notes payable (long-term)	1,600,000	Building	1,640,000

Instructions
Prepare a classified balance sheet in good form. Common stock authorized was 400,000 shares and preferred stock authorized was 20,000 shares. Assume that notes receivable and notes payable are short-term, unless stated otherwise. Cost and fair value of marketable securities are the same.

P5-3 (Balance Sheet Adjustment and Preparation)   The trial balance of Side Kicks Company and other related information for the year 1999 is presented below.

Side Kicks Company
TRIAL BALANCE
December 31, 1999

Cash	$ 41,000	
Accounts Receivable	163,500	
Allowance for Doubtful Accounts		$ 8,700
Prepaid Insurance	5,900	
Inventory	308,500	
Long-term Investments	339,000	
Land	85,000	
Construction Work in Progress	124,000	
Patents	36,000	
Equipment	400,000	
Accumulated Depreciation of Equipment		140,000
Unamortized Discount on Bonds Payable	20,000	
Accounts Payable		148,000
Accrued Expenses		49,200
Notes Payable		94,000
Bonds Payable		400,000
Capital Stock		500,000
Premium on Capital Stock		45,000
Retained Earnings		138,000
	$1,522,900	$1,522,900

Additional information:

1. The inventory has a replacement market value of $353,000. The LIFO method of inventory value is used.
2. The cost and fair value of the long-term investments that consist of stocks and bonds is the same.
3. The amount of the Construction Work in Progress account represents the costs expended to date on a building in the process of construction. (The company rents factory space at the present time.) The land on which the building is being constructed cost $85,000, as shown in the trial balance.
4. The patents were purchased by the company at a cost of $36,000 and are being amortized on a straight-line basis.
5. Of the unamortized discount on bonds payable, $2,000 will be amortized in 2000.
6. The notes payable represent bank loans that are secured by long-term investments carried at $120,000. These bank loans are due in 2000.
7. The bonds payable bear interest at 11% payable every December 31 and are due January 1, 2010.
8. Six hundred thousand shares of common stock of a par value of $1 were authorized, of which 500,000 shares were issued and are outstanding.

Instructions
Prepare a balance sheet as of December 31, 1999 so that all important information is fully disclosed.

P5-4 (Preparation of a Corrected Balance Sheet)   Presented below is the balance sheet of Tom Cruise Corporation as of December 31, 1999:

Tom Cruise
BALANCE SHEET
December 31, 1999

Assets

Goodwill (Note 2)	$ 120,000
Building (Note 1)	1,640,000
Inventories	312,100
Land	750,000
Accounts receivable	170,000
Treasury stock (50,000 shares, no par)	87,000
Cash on hand	175,900

Assets allocated to trustee for plant expansion

Cash in bank	70,000
U.S. Treasury notes, at cost and fair value	$ 138,000
	$3,463,000

Equities

Notes payable (Note 3)	$ 600,000
Common stock, authorized and issued, 1,000,000 shares, no par	1,150,000
Retained earnings	658,000
Appreciation capital (Note 1)	570,000
Federal income taxes payable	75,000
Reserve for depreciation of building	410,000
	$3,463,000

Note 1: Buildings are stated at cost, except for one building that was recorded at appraised value. The excess of appraisal value over cost was $570,000. Depreciation has been recorded based on cost.
Note 2: Goodwill in the amount of $120,000 was recognized because the company believed that book value was not an accurate representation of the fair market value of the company. The gain of $120,000 was credited to Retained Earnings.
Note 3: Notes payable are long-term except for the current installment due of $100,000.

Instructions

Prepare a corrected classified balance sheet in good form. The notes above are for information only.

P5-5 (Balance Sheet Adjustment and Preparation) Presented below is the balance sheet of Stephen King Corporation for the current year, 1999.

Stephen King Corporation
BALANCE SHEET
December 31, 1999

Current assets	$ 435,000	Current liabilities	$ 330,000
Investments	640,000	Long-term liabilities	1,000,000
Property, plant, and equipment	1,720,000	Stockholders' equity	1,770,000
Intangible assets	305,000		
	$3,100,000		$3,100,000

The following information is presented:

1. The current asset section includes: cash $100,000, accounts receivable $170,000 less $10,000 for allowance for doubtful accounts, inventories $180,000, and prepaid revenue $5,000. The cash balance is composed of $114,000, less a bank overdraft of $14,000. Inventories are stated on the lower of FIFO cost or market.
2. The investments section includes the cash surrender value of a life insurance contract $40,000; investments in common stock, short-term (trading) $80,000 and long-term (available-for-sale) $140,000; bond sinking fund $250,000; and organization costs $130,000. The cost and fair value of investments in common stock are the same.
3. Property, plant, and equipment includes buildings $1,040,000 less accumulated depreciation $360,000; equipment $450,000 less accumulated depreciation $180,000; land $500,000; and land held for future use $270,000.
4. Intangible assets include a franchise $165,000, goodwill $100,000, and discount on bonds payable $40,000.
5. Current liabilities include accounts payable $90,000, notes payable—short-term $80,000 and long-term $120,000, and taxes payable $40,000.
6. Long-term liabilities are composed solely of 10% bonds payable due 2007.
7. Stockholders' equity has preferred stock, no par value, authorized 200,000 shares, issued 70,000 shares for $450,000, and common stock, $1.00 par value, authorized 400,000 shares, issued 100,000 shares at an average price of $10. In addition, the corporation has retained earnings of $320,000.

Instructions

Prepare a balance sheet in good form, adjusting the amounts in each balance sheet classification as affected by the "information" given above.

P5-6 **(Preparation of a Statement of Cash Flows and a Balance Sheet)** Alistair Cooke Inc. had the following balance sheet at the end of operations for 1998:

Alistair Cooke Inc.
BALANCE SHEET
December 31, 1998

Cash	$ 20,000	Accounts payable	$ 30,000
Accounts receivable	21,200	Long-term notes payable	41,000
Investments	32,000	Capital stock	100,000
Plant assets (net)	81,000	Retained earnings	23,200
Land	40,000		
	$194,200		$194,200

During 1999 the following occurred:

1. Alistair Cooke Inc. sold part of its investment portfolio for $17,000. This transaction resulted in a gain of $3,400 for the firm. The company often sells and buys securities of this nature.
2. A tract of land was purchased for $18,000 cash.
3. Long-term notes payable in the amount of $16,000 were retired before maturity by paying $16,000 cash.
4. An additional $24,000 in capital stock was issued at par.
5. Dividends totalling $8,200 were declared and paid to stockholders.
6. Net income for 1999 was $32,000 after allowing for depreciation of $12,000.
7. Land was purchased through the issuance of $30,000 in bonds.
8. At December 31, 1999, Cash was $39,000, Accounts Receivable was $41,600, and Accounts Payable remained at $30,000.

Instructions

(a) Prepare a statement of cash flows for 1999.
(b) Prepare the balance sheet as it would appear at December 31, 1999.
(c) How might the statement of cash flows help the user of the financial statements? Compute two cash flow ratios.

P5-7 (Income Statement and Balance Sheet Preparation) Mary Anne Spier has prepared baked goods for resale since 1991. She started a baking business in her home and has been operating in a rented building with a storefront since 1996. Spier incorporated the business as MAS Inc. on January 1, 1999, with an initial stock issue of 1,000 shares of common stock at a par value of $2.50 per share. Mary Anne Spier is the principal stockholder of MAS Inc.

Sales have increased 30 percent annually since operations began at the present location, and additional equipment is needed to accommodate expected continued growth. Spier wishes to purchase some additional baking equipment and to finance the equipment through a long-term note from a commercial bank. Wisconsin State Bank & Trust has asked Spier to submit an income statement for MAS Inc. for the first five months of 1999 and a balance sheet as of May 31, 1999.

Spier assembled the following information from the cash basis records of the corporation for use in preparing the financial statements requested by the bank.

1. The check register showed the following 1999 deposits through May 31.

Sale of common stock	$ 2,500
Cash sales	22,770
Rebates from purchases	130
Collections on credit sales	5,320
Bank loan proceeds	2,880
	$33,600

2. The following amounts were disbursed through May 31, 1999.

Baking materials	$14,400
Rent	1,800
Salaries and wages	5,500
Maintenance	110
Utilities	4,000
Insurance premium	1,920
Equipment	3,000
Principal and interest payment on bank loan	312
Advertising	424
	$31,466

3. Unpaid invoices at May 31, 1999, were as follows.

Baking materials	$256
Utilities	270
	$526

4. Customer records showed uncollected sales of $4,226 at May 31, 1999.

5. Baking materials costing $1,840 were on hand at May 31, 1999. There were no materials in process or finished goods on hand at that date. No materials were on hand or in process and no finished goods were on hand at January 1, 1999.

6. The note evidencing the 3-year bank loan is dated January 1, 1999, and states a simple interest rate of 10%. The loan requires quarterly payments on April 1, July 1, October 1, and January 1 consisting of equal principal payments plus accrued interest since the last payment.

7. Mary Anne Spier receives a salary of $750 on the last day of each month. The other employees had been paid through Friday, May 25, 1999, and were due an additional $240 on May 31, 1999.

8. New display cases and equipment costing $3,000 were purchased on January 2, 1999, and have an estimated useful life of 5 years. These are the only fixed assets currently used in the business. Straight-line depreciation is to be used for book purposes.

9. Rent was paid for six months in advance on January 2, 1999.

10. A one-year insurance policy was purchased on January 2, 1999.

11. MAS Inc. is subject to an income tax rate of 20%.

12. Payments and collections pertaining to the unincorporated business through December 31, 1998, were not included in the records of the corporation, and no cash was transferred from the unincorporated business to the corporation.

Instructions

Using the accrual basis of accounting, prepare for MAS Inc.:
  (a) An income statement for the five months ended May 31, 1999.
  (b) A balance sheet as of May 31, 1999.

(CMA adapted)

❖ CONCEPTUAL CASES ❖

C5-1 (Post-Balance Sheet Events) At December 31, 1998, Joni Brandt Corp. has assets of $10,000,000, liabilities of $6,000,000, common stock of $2,000,000 (representing 2,000,000 shares of $1.00 par common stock), and retained earnings of $2,000,000. Net sales for the year 1998 were $18,000,000 and net income was $800,000. As auditors of this company, you are making a review of subsequent events on February 13, 1999, and find the following.

1. On February 3, 1999, one of Brandt's customers declared bankruptcy. At December 31, 1998, this company owed Brandt $300,000, of which $40,000 was paid in January, 1999.

2. On January 18, 1999, one of the three major plants of the client burned.

3. On January 23, 1999, a strike was called at one of Brandt's largest plants, which halted 30% of its production. As of today (February 13) the strike has not been settled.

4. A major electronics enterprise has introduced a line of products that would compete directly with Brandt's primary line, now being produced in a specially designed new plant. Because of manufacturing innovations, the competitor has been able to achieve quality similar to that of Brandt's products, but at a price 50% lower. Brandt officials say they will meet the lower prices, which are high enough to cover variable manufacturing and selling costs but which permit recovery of only a portion of fixed costs.

5. Merchandise traded in the open market is recorded in the company's records at $1.40 per unit on December 31, 1998. This price had prevailed for two weeks, after release of an official market report that predicted vastly enlarged supplies; however, no purchases were made at $1.40. The price throughout the preceding year had been about $2.00, which was the level experienced over several years. On January 18, 1999, the price returned to $2.00, after public disclosure of an error in the official calculations of the prior December, correction of which destroyed the expectations of excessive supplies. Inventory at December 31, 1998, was on a lower of cost or market basis.

6. On February 1, 1999, the board of directors adopted a resolution accepting the offer of an investment banker to guarantee the marketing of $1,200,000 of preferred stock.

Instructions

State in each case how the 1998 financial statements would be affected, if at all.

C5-2 (Reporting the Financial Effects of Varied Transactions)   In an examination of Juan Acevedo Corporation as of December 31, 1999, you have learned that the following situations exist. No entries have been made in the accounting records for these items.

1. The corporation erected its present factory building in 1984. Depreciation was calculated by the straight-line method, using an estimated life of 35 years. Early in 1999, the board of directors conducted a careful survey and estimated that the factory building had a remaining useful life of 25 years as of January 1, 1999.
2. An additional assessment of 1998 income taxes was levied and paid in 1999.
3. When calculating the accrual for officers' salaries at December 31, 1999, it was discovered that the accrual for officers' salaries for December 31, 1998, had been overstated.
4. On December 15, 1999, Acevedo Corporation declared a 1% common stock dividend on its common stock outstanding, payable February 1, 2000, to the common stockholders of record December 31, 1999.
5. Acevedo Corporation, which is on a calendar-year basis, changed its inventory method as of January 1, 1999. The inventory for December 31, 1998, was costed by the average method, and the inventory for December 31, 1999, was costed by the FIFO method.

Instructions

Describe fully how each of the items above should be reported in the financial statements of Acevedo Corporation for the year 1999.

C5-3 (Current Asset and Liability Classification)   Below are the account titles of a number of debit and credit accounts as they might appear on the balance sheet of Ethan Allen Corporation as of October 31, 1999.

Debits	Credits
Interest accrued on U.S. government securities	Capital stock—preferred
Notes receivable	11% first mortgage bonds due in 2006
Petty cash fund	Preferred cash dividend, payable Nov. 1, 1999
U.S. government securities	Allowance for doubtful accounts receivable
Treasury stock	Federal income taxes payable
Unamortized bond discount	Customers' advances (on contracts to be completed next year)
Cash in bank	Premium on bonds redeemable in 1999
Land	Officers' 1999 bonus accrued
Inventory of operating parts and supplies	Accrued payroll
Inventory of raw materials	Notes payable
Patents	Accrued interest on bonds
Cash and U.S. government bonds set aside for property additions	Accumulated depreciation
Investment in subsidiary	Accounts payable
Accounts receivable	Capital in excess of par
U.S. government contracts	Accrued interest on notes payable
Regular	8% first mortgage bonds to be redeemed in 1999 out of current assets
Installments—due next year	
Installments—due after next year	
Goodwill	
Inventory of finished goods	
Inventory of work in process	
Deficit	

Instructions

Select the current asset and current liability items from among these debits and credits. If there appear to be certain borderline cases that you are unable to classify without further information, mention them and explain your difficulty, or give your reasons for making questionable classifications, if any.

(AICPA adapted)

C5-4 (Identifying Balance Sheet Deficiencies) The assets of LaShon Johnson Corporation are presented below (000s omitted):

LaShon Johnson Corporation
BALANCE SHEET (Partial)
December 31, 1999

Assets

Current assets		
Cash		$ 100,000
Unclaimed payroll checks		27,500
Marketable securities (cost $30,000) at fair value		37,000
Accounts receivable (less bad debt reserve)		75,000
Inventories—at lower of cost (determined by the next-in, first-out method) or market		240,000
Total current assets		479,500
Tangible assets		
Land (less accumulated depreciation)		80,000
Buildings and equipment	$800,000	
Less accumulated depreciation	250,000	550,000
Net tangible assets		630,000
Long-term investments		
Stocks and bonds		100,000
Treasury stock		70,000
Total long-term investments		170,000
Other assets		
Discount on bonds payable		19,400
Sinking fund		975,000
Total other assets		994,400
Total assets		$2,273,900

Instructions

Indicate the deficiencies, if any, in the foregoing presentation of LaShon Johnson Corporation's assets. Marketable securities are considered trading securities.

C5-5 (Critique of Balance Sheet Format and Content) Presented below is the balance sheet of Bellemy Brothers Corporation (000s omitted):

Bellemy Brothers Corporation
BALANCE SHEET
December 31, 1999

Assets

Current assets		
Cash	$26,000	
Marketable securities	18,000	
Accounts receivable	25,000	
Merchandise inventory	20,000	
Supplies inventory	4,000	
Stock investment in Subsidiary Company	20,000	$113,000
Investments		
Treasury stock		25,000
Property, plant, and equipment		
Buildings and land	91,000	
Less: Reserve for depreciation	31,000	60,000
Other assets		
Cash surrender value of life insurance		19,000
		$217,000

Liabilities and Capital

Current liabilities		
Accounts payable	$22,000	
Reserve for income taxes	15,000	
Customers' accounts with credit balances	1	$ 37,001
Deferred credits		
Unamortized premium on bonds payable		2,000
Long-term liabilities		
Bonds payable		60,000
Total liabilities		99,001
Capital stock		
Capital stock, par $5	85,000	
Earned surplus	24,999	
Cash dividends declared	8,000	117,999
		$217,000

Instructions

Criticize the balance sheet presented. State briefly the proper treatment of the item criticized.

C5-6 (Identifying Balance Sheet Deficiencies)   The financial statement below was prepared by employees of your client, Walt Whitman Co. The statement is unaccompanied by notes.

Walt Whitman Co.
BALANCE SHEET
As of November 30, 1999

Current assets			
Cash		$ 100,000	
Accounts receivable (less allowance of $30,000 for doubtful accounts)		419,900	
Inventories		1,954,000	$2,473,900
Less current liabilities			
Accounts payable		306,400	
Accrued payroll		28,260	
Accrued interest on mortgage note		12,000	
Estimated taxes payable		66,000	412,660
Net working capital			2,061,240

Property, plant, and equipment (at cost)

	Cost	Depreciation	Value	
Land and buildings	$ 983,300	$410,000	573,300	
Machinery and equipment	1,135,700	568,699	567,001	
	$2,119,000	$978,699		1,140,301

Deferred charges			
Prepaid taxes and other expenses		23,700	
Unamortized discount on mortgage note		10,800	34,500
Total net working capital and noncurrent assets			3,236,041
Less deferred liabilities			
Mortgage note payable		300,000	
Unearned revenue		1,808,000	2,108,000
Total net assets			$1,128,041
Stockholders' equity			
10% Preferred stock at par value			$ 300,000
Common stock at par value			397,000
Paid-in surplus			210,000
Retained earnings			265,641
Treasury stock at cost (400 shares)			(44,600)
Total stockholders' equity			$1,128,041

Instructions

Indicate the deficiencies, if any, in the balance sheet above in regard to form, terminology, descriptions, content, and the like.

❖ USING YOUR JUDGMENT ❖

❖ FINANCIAL REPORTING PROBLEM—INTEL CORPORATION

The financial statements of Intel Corporation appear in Appendix 5B.

Instructions

Refer to those financial statements and the accompanying notes to answer the following questions.

(a) What alternative formats could Intel have adopted for its balance sheet? Which format did it adopt?

(b) Identify the various techniques of disclosure Intel might have used to disclose additional pertinent financial information. Which technique does it use in its financials?

(c) Why are certain investments included in Intel's short-term investments? Long-term investments? What valuation basis does Intel use to report its investments? How much working capital did Intel have on December 30, 1995? December 31, 1994?

(d) What were Intel's cash flows from its operating, investing, and financing activities for 1995? What were its trends in net cash provided by operating activities over the period 1993–1995? Explain why an increase in accounts payable is added to net income to arrive at net cash provided by operating activities.

(e) Compute Intel's (a) current cash debt coverage ratio, (b) cash debt coverage ratio, and (c) free cash flow for 1995. What do these ratios indicate about the financial condition of Intel?

❖ FINANCIAL STATEMENT ANALYSIS CASES

Case 1 (Uniroyal Technology Corporation)

Uniroyal Technology Corporation (UTC), with corporate offices in Sarasota, Florida, is organized into three operating segments. The high performance plastics segment is responsible for research, development, and manufacture of a wide variety of products, including orthopedic braces, graffiti-resistant seats for buses and airplanes, and a static-resistant plastic used in the central processing units of microcomputers. The coated fabrics segment manufactures products such as automobile seating, door and instrument panels, and specialty items such as waterproof seats for personal watercraft and stain-resistant, easy cleaning upholstery fabrics. The foams and adhesives segment develops and manufactures products used in commercial roofing applications.

The following items relate to fiscal 1995 (UTC's fiscal year ends on the Sunday following the last Friday in September—thus the 1995 fiscal year began October 3, 1994, and ended October 1, 1995.):

a. Serious pressure was placed on profitability by sharply increasing raw material prices. Some raw materials increased in price 50% during 1995. Cost containment programs were instituted and product prices were increased wherever possible, which resulted in profit margins actually improving over the course of the year.

b. The company entered into a revolving credit agreement, under which UTC may borrow the lesser of $15,000,000 or 80% of eligible accounts receivable. At the end of the year, approximately $4,000,000 was outstanding under this agreement. The company plans to use this line of credit in the upcoming year to finance operations and expansion.

Instructions

(a) Should investors be informed of raw materials price increases, such as described in item a? Does the fact that the company successfully met the challenge of higher prices affect the answer? Explain.

(b) How should the information in item b be presented in the financial statements of UTC?

Case 2 (Sherwin-Williams Company)

Sherwin-Williams, based in Cleveland, Ohio, manufactures a wide variety of paint and other coatings, which are marketed through its specialty stores and in other retail outlets. The company also manufactures paint for automobiles. The Automotive Division has had financial difficulty. During 1994, five branch locations of the Automotive Division were closed, and new management was put in place for the branches remaining.

The following account titles were taken from Sherwin-Williams' 1994 balance sheet.

Accounts payable	Long-term debt
Accounts receivable, less allowance	Machinery and equipment
Accrued taxes	Other accruals
Buildings	Other capital
Cash and cash equivalents	Other current assets
Common stock	Other long-term liabilities
Construction in progress	Postretirement benefits other than pensions
Deferred pension assets	Retained earnings
Employee compensation payable	Short-term investments
Finished goods inventories	Taxes withheld
Intangibles and other assets	Work in process and raw materials inventories
Land	

Instructions

(a) Organize the accounts in the general order in which they would have been presented in a classified balance sheet.

(b) When several of the branch locations of the Automotive Division were closed, what balance sheet accounts were most likely affected? Did the balance in those accounts decrease or increase?

❖ COMPARATIVE ANALYSIS CASE

The Coca-Cola Company versus PepsiCo Inc.

Instructions

Go to our Web site and answer the following questions.

(a) What format(s) did these companies use to present their balance sheet?

(b) How much working capital did each of these companies have at the end of 1995? Speculate as to their rationale for the amount of working capital they maintain.

(c) What is the most significant difference in the asset structure of the two companies? What causes this difference?

(d) What are the companies' annual, five-year, and 10-year growth rates in total assets and total debt?

(e) What were these two companies' trends in net cash provided by operating activities over the period 1993–1995?

(f) Compute both company's (a) current cash debt coverage ratio, (b) cash debt coverage ratio, and (c) free cash flow. What do these ratios indicate about the financial condition of these two companies?

(g) What ratios do each of these companies use in their management's discussion and analysis section to explain their financial condition related to debt financing?

❖ RESEARCH CASES

Case 1

Publicly-owned companies registered with the Securities and Exchange Commission electronically file required reports via the EDGAR (Electronic Data Gathering, Analysis, and Retrieval) system.

EDGAR can easily be accessed via the Internet (http://www.sec.gov) using the following steps:

1. Select "EDGAR Database of Corporate Information" from the home page.
2. Select "Search the EDGAR Database."
3. Select "CIK (Central Index Key) and Ticker Symbol Lookup" and enter the name(s) of the company(ies) you are investigating. Write down the CIK number(s) and return to the previous page.
4. To examine filings, click on "Search the EDGAR Archives" and enter the appropriate CIK number (including all zeroes). When the list of filings appears, click on the desired filing under the "Company name" column.

Instructions

(a) Determine the CIK numbers for the following companies: Ford Motor Company, Wisconsin Electric Power Company, and Orion Pictures.

(b) Examine the balance sheet formats included in the following filings: (1) Ford Motor Co. Form 10-K filed 3/19/96, (2) Wisconsin Electric Power Co. annual report to shareholders (ARS) filed 4/26/96, and (3) Orion Pictures Form 10-K filed 4/14/95. Do you notice anything "unusual" about the balance sheet formats? Why do you think the balance sheets are presented in this manner?

Case 2

The January 1995 issue of *The CPA Journal* includes an article by John D. Gould, entitled "A Second Opinion on International Accounting Standards."

Instructions

Read the article and answer the following questions.

(a) With regard to compliance with U.S. GAAP, what are the two alternatives for foreign issuers desiring to register securities with the U.S. Securities and Exchange Commission?

(b) In general, how do German accounting principles differ from U.S. GAAP?

(c) What does the author assert regarding the costs to German companies of complying with U.S. GAAP versus International Accounting Standards?

(d) According to the author, what are the advantages of the proposed SEC rule changes for filings by foreign companies?

(e) While the author predicts that international accounting standards are "unlikely to be accepted in practice," what useful purpose has the International Accounting Standards Committee served?

❖ WRITING ASSIGNMENT

The partner in charge of the James Spencer Corporation audit comes by your desk and leaves a letter he has started to the CEO and a copy of the cash flow statement for the year ended December 31, 1998. Because he must leave on an emergency, he asks you to finish the letter by explaining: (1) the disparity between net income and cash flow; (2) the importance of operating cash flow; (3) the renewable source(s) of cash flow; and (4) possible suggestions to improve the cash position.

James Spencer Corporation
STATEMENT OF CASH FLOWS
For the Year Ended December 31, 1998

Cash flows from operating activities:		
Net income		$ 100,000
Adjustments to reconcile net income to net cash provided by operating activities:		
Depreciation expense	$ 10,000	
Amortization expense	1,000	
Loss on sale of fixed assets	5,000	
Increase in accounts receivable (net)	(40,000)	
Increase in inventory	(35,000)	
Decrease in accounts payable	(41,000)	(100,000)
Net cash provided by operating activities		–0–
Cash flows from investing activities:		
Sale of plant assets	$ 25,000)	
Purchase of equipment	(100,000)	
Purchase of land	(200,000)	
Net cash used by investing activities		(275,000)
Cash flows from financing activities:		
Payment of dividends	$ (10,000)	
Redemption of bonds	(100,000)	
Net Cash used by financing activities		(110,000)
Net decrease in cash		(385,000)
Cash balance, January 1, 1998		400,000
Cash balance, December 31, 1998		$ 15,000

Date

James Spencer, III, CEO
James Spencer Corporation
125 Wall Street
Middleton, Kansas 67458

Dear Mr. Spencer:

I have good news and bad news about the financial statements for the year ended December 31, 1998. The good news is that net income of $100,000 is close to what we predicted in the strategic plan last year indicating strong performance this year. The bad news is that the cash balance is seriously low. Enclosed is the Statement of Cash Flows, which best illustrates how both of these situations occurred simultaneously. . . .

Instructions
Complete the letter to the CEO including the four components requested by your boss.

❖ GROUP ASSIGNMENT

Your group has been engaged to examine the financial statements of Sabrina Corporation for the year 1999. The bookkeeper who maintains the financial records has prepared all the unaudited financial statements for the corporation since its organization on January 2, 1993. The client provides you with the information below.

Sabrina Corporation
BALANCE SHEET
As of December 31, 1999

Assets		Liabilities	
Current assets	$1,881,100	Current liabilities	$ 962,400
Other assets	5,171,400	Long-term liabilities	1,439,500
		Capital	4,650,600
	$7,052,500		$7,052,500

An analysis of current assets discloses the following:

Cash (restricted in the amount of $400,000 for plant expansion)	$ 571,000
Investments in land	185,000
Accounts receivable less allowance of $30,000	480,000
Inventories (LIFO flow assumption)	645,000
	$1,881,100

Other assets include:

Prepaid expenses	$ 47,400
Plant and equipment less accumulated depreciation of $1,430,000	4,130,000
Cash surrender value of life insurance policy	84,000
Unamortized bond discount	49,500
Notes receivable (short term)	162,300
Goodwill, at cost less amortization of $63,000	252,000
Land	446,200
	$5,171,400

Current liabilities include:

Accounts payable	$ 510,000
Notes payable (due 2001)	157,400
Estimated income taxes payable	145,000
Premium on common stock	150,000
	$ 962,400

Long-term liabilities include:

Unearned revenue	$ 489,500
Dividends payable (cash)	200,000
8% bonds payable (due May 1, 2004)	750,000
	$1,439,500

Capital includes:	
Retained earnings	$2,810,600
Capital stock, par value $10; authorized 200,000 shares, 184,000 shares issued	1,840,000
	$4,650,600

The supplementary information below is also provided.

1. On May 1, 1999, the corporation issued at 93.4, $750,000 of bonds to finance plant expansion. The long-term bond agreement provided for the annual payment of interest every May 1. The existing plant was pledged as security for the loan. Use straight-line method for discount amortization.
2. The bookkeeper made the following mistakes:
   (a) In 1997, the ending inventory was overstated by $183,000. The ending inventories for 1998 and 1999 were correctly computed.
   (b) In 1999, accrued wages in the amount of $275,000 were omitted from the balance sheet and these expenses were not charged on the income statement.
   (c) In 1999, a gain of $175,000 (net of tax) on the sale of certain plant assets was credited directly to retained earnings.
3. A major competitor has introduced a line of products that will compete directly with Sabrina's primary line, now being produced in a specially designed new plant. Because of manufacturing innovations, the competitor's line will be of comparable quality but priced 50% below the client's line. The competitor announced its new line on January 14, 2000. The client indicates that the company will meet the lower prices that are high enough to cover variable manufacturing and selling expenses, but permit recovery of only a portion of fixed costs.
4. You learned on January 28, 2000, prior to completion of the audit, of heavy damage because of a recent fire to one of the client's two plants; the loss will not be reimbursed by insurance. The newspapers described the event in detail.

Instructions

Your instructor will identify one member of the group to serve as a recorder and one member to serve as a spokesperson. As a group, analyze the above information so that the recorder can prepare a corrected balance sheet for Sabrina in accordance with proper accounting and reporting principles. Prepare a description of any notes that might need to be prepared (to be reported to the class). The books are closed and adjustments to income are to be made through retained earnings.

❖ ETHICS CASES

Case 1

In June 1998, the board of directors for Holtzman Enterprises Inc. authorized the sale of $10,000,000 of corporate bonds. Michelle Collins, treasurer for Holtzman Enterprises Inc., is concerned about the date when the bonds are issued. The company really needs the cash, but she is worried that if the bonds are issued before the company's year-end (December 31, 1998) the additional liability will have an adverse effect on a number of important ratios. In July, she explains to company president Kenneth Holtzman that if they delay issuing the bonds until after December 31 the bonds will not affect the ratios until December 31, 1999. They will have to report the issuance as a subsequent event which requires only footnote disclosure. Collins expects that with expected improved financial performance in 1999 ratios should be better.

Instructions

Answer the following questions:

(a) What are the ethical issues involved?
(b) Should Holtzman agree to the delay?

Case 2

Andrea Pafko, corporate comptroller for Nicholson Industries, is trying to decide how to present "Property, plant, and equipment" in the balance sheet. She realizes that the statement of cash flows will show that the company made a significant investment in purchasing new equipment this year, but overall she knows the company's plant assets are rather old. She feels that she can disclose one figure titled "Property, plant, and equipment, net of depreciation," and the result will be a low figure. However, it will not disclose the age of the assets. If she chooses to show the cost less accumulated depreciation, the age of the assets will be apparent. She proposes the following:

Property, plant, and equipment, net of depreciation	$10,000,000
rather than	
Property, plant and equipment	$50,000,000
Less: Accumulated depreciation	(40,000,000)
Net book value	$10,000,000

Instructions

Answer the following questions:

(a) What are the ethical issues involved?
(b) What should Pafko do?

CHAPTER 6

Accounting and the Time Value of Money

The Magic of Interest

Sidney Homer (author of *A History of Interest Rates*) wrote, "$1,000 invested at a mere 8% for 400 years would grow to $23 quadrillion—$5 million for every human on earth. But the first 100 years are the hardest."

This startling quote highlights the power of time and compounding interest on money. Equally significant, although not mentioned in the quote, is the fact that a small difference in the interest rate makes a big difference in the amount of monies accumulated over time. Taking a more realistic example, assume that you had $20,000 in a tax-free retirement account. Half the money is in stocks returning 12% and the other half in bonds earning 8%. Assuming reinvested profits and quarterly compounding, your bonds would be worth $22,080 after ten years, a doubling of their value. But your stocks, returning 4% more, would be worth $32,620, or triple your initial value. The following chart shows this impact.

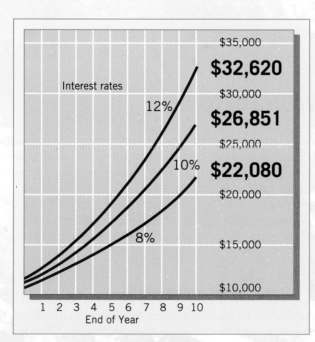

Money tomorrow is not the same as money today. Business people are acutely aware of this timing factor, and they invest and borrow only after carefully analyzing the relative values of the cash flows.

As indicated from the opening story, the timing of the returns on investments has an important effect on the worth of the investment (asset), and the timing of debt repayments has a similarly important effect on the value of the debt commitment (liability). As a financial expert, you will be expected to make present and future value measurements and to understand their implications. The purpose of this chapter is to present the tools and techniques that will help you measure the present value of future cash inflows and outflows. The content and organization of the chapter are as follows:

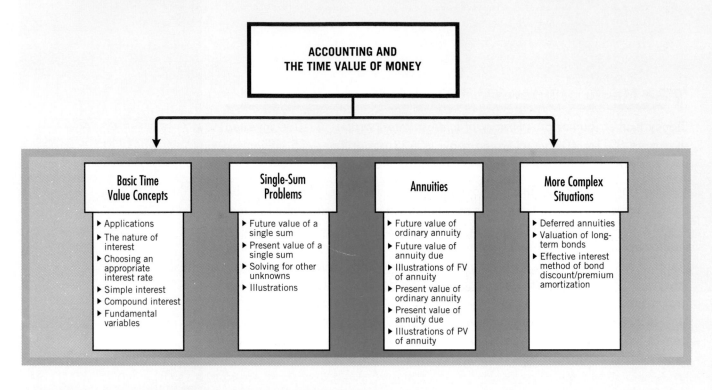

❖ BASIC TIME VALUE CONCEPTS

In accounting (and finance), the term time value of money is used to indicate a relationship between time and money—that a dollar received today is worth more than a dollar promised at some time in the future. Why? Because of the opportunity to invest today's dollar and receive interest on the investment. Yet, when you have to decide among various investment or borrowing alternatives, it is essential to be able to compare today's dollar and tomorrow's dollar on the same footing—to "compare apples to apples." We do that by using the concept of **present value**, which has many applications in accounting.

Applications of Time Value Concepts

Financial reporting uses different measurements in different situations. Present value is one of these measurements, and its usage has been increasing.[1] Recognizing that fact,

---

[1]Many of the recent standards, such as FASB Statements No. 106, 107, 109, 113, 114, 116, 118, 121, and 122, addressed the issue of present value somewhere in the pronouncement or related basis for conclusions.

the FASB has embarked upon a project to develop a framework for applying these measurements.[2]

Some of the applications of present value-based measurements to accounting topics are listed below, several of which are required in succeeding chapters of this textbook:

Objective ❶

Identify accounting topics where the time value of money is relevant.

❖ PRESENT VALUE-BASED ACCOUNTING MEASUREMENTS ❖

❶ *Notes.* Valuing noncurrent receivables and payables that carry no stated interest rate or a lower than market interest rate.

❷ *Leases.* Valuing assets and obligations to be capitalized under long-term leases and measuring the amount of the lease payments and annual leasehold amortization.

❸ *Amortization of Premiums and Discounts.* Measuring amortization of premium or discount on both bond investments and bonds payable.

❹ *Pensions and Other Postretirement Benefits.* Measuring service cost components of employers' postretirement benefits expense and postretirement benefits obligation.

❺ *Long-Term Assets.* Evaluating alternative long-term investments by discounting future cash flows. Determining the value of assets acquired under deferred payment contracts. Measuring impairments of assets.

❻ *Sinking Funds.* Determining the contributions necessary to accumulate a fund for debt retirements.

❼ *Business Combinations.* Determining the value of receivables, payables, liabilities, accruals, and commitments acquired or assumed in a "purchase."

❽ *Disclosures.* Measuring the value of future cash flows from oil and gas reserves for disclosure in supplementary information.

❾ *Installment Contracts.* Measuring periodic payments on long-term purchase contracts.[3]

In addition to accounting and business applications, compound interest, annuity, and present value concepts apply to personal finance and investment decisions. In purchasing a home or car, planning for retirement, and evaluating alternative investments, you will need to understand time value of money concepts.

The Nature of Interest

Interest is payment for the use of money. It is the excess cash received or repaid over and above the amount lent or borrowed (**principal**). For example, if the Corner Bank lends you $1,000 with the understanding that you will repay $1,150, then the excess over $1,000, or $150, represents interest expense. Or if you lend your roommate $100 and then collect $110 in full payment, the $10 excess represents interest revenue.

The amount of interest to be paid is generally stated as a rate over a specific period of time. For example, if you used $1,000 for one year before repaying $1,150, the rate of interest is 15% per year ($150 ÷ $1,000). The custom of expressing interest as a rate

---

[2]See, for example, Wayne S. Upton, "The FASB Project on Present Value Based Measurement, an Analysis of Deliberations and Techniques, Special Report" (Norwalk, Conn.: FASB, February 1996).

[3]A complete list of where GAAP specifically forbids and requires discounting is presented in an article by Roman L. Weil, "Role of the Time Value of Money in Financial Reporting," *Accounting Horizons* (December 1990), pp. 47–67.

is an established business practice.[4] In fact, business managers make investing and borrowing decisions on the basis of the rate of interest involved rather than on the actual dollar amount of interest to be received or paid.

How is the interest rate determined? One of the most important factors is the level of credit risk (risk of nonpayment) involved. Other factors being equal, the higher the credit risk, the higher the interest rate. Low-risk borrowers like Microsoft or Intel can probably obtain a loan at or slightly below the going market rate of interest. You or the neighborhood delicatessen, on the other hand, would probably be charged several percentage points above the market rate, if you can get a loan at all!

The amount of interest involved in any financing transaction is a function of three variables:

❖ VARIABLES IN INTEREST COMPUTATION ❖

❶ Principal. The amount borrowed or invested.
❷ Interest Rate. A percentage of the outstanding principal.
❸ Time. The number of years or fractional portion of a year that the principal is outstanding.

The larger the principal amount, or the higher the interest rate, or the longer the time period, the larger the dollar amount of interest.

Choosing an Appropriate Interest Rate

A perplexing problem is the selection of an appropriate interest rate to measure assets and liabilities. Consider the following debates that have taken place in practice.

❶ In oil and gas accounting, the Securities and Exchange Commission at one time recommended that the fair value of oil and gas reserves in the ground be computed at the present value of the future revenues discounted at a flat 10% rate. The SEC argued that the use of one rate leads to comparability and that a rate of this magnitude provides a reasonable representation of the present value of future oil and gas reserves. Others disagreed, noting that a 10% rate was unrealistic for two reasons. First, it ignores the current level of interest rate benchmarks such as the prime rate. Second, not all companies and situations deserve the same rate because of differences in risk.

❷ In trying to resolve the problem of capitalizing interest cost incurred (recording as an asset) during construction, the profession encountered support for two different measurement bases. Some accountants favored capitalizing the interest cost associated with the specific borrowing. Others disagreed, arguing that a weighted average is preferable because the borrowing on any specific project affects the borrowing costs of the entire company as it relates to other projects.

How then should we select an interest rate for purposes of present value computations? In the past, interest rates have often been selected on the basis of expediency (availability), regulatory stipulations, and ease of auditability. No consistent approach has been adopted. This is not surprising, given the wide variety of rates from which to choose, such as the general borrowing rate (prime rate), a specific borrowing rate for a given company, opportunity cost rate, investment rate of return, cost-of-capital rate on a weighted-average basis, and so on.

---

[4]Federal law requires the disclosure of interest rates on an **annual basis** in all contracts. That is, instead of stating the rate as "1% per month," it must be stated as "12% per year" if it is simple interest or "12.68% per year" if it is compounded monthly.

An interest rate has three components:

❖ THREE COMPONENTS OF INTEREST ❖

① *Pure Rate of Interest* (2%–4%). This would be the amount a lender would charge if there were no possibilities of default and no expectation of inflation.

② *Credit Risk Rate of Interest* (0%–5%). The government has little or no credit risk (i.e., risk of nonpayment) when it issues bonds; a business enterprise, however, depending upon its financial stability, profitability, etc., can have a low or a high credit risk.

③ *Expected Inflation Rate of Interest* (0%–?). Lenders recognize that in an inflationary economy, they are being paid back with less valuable dollars. As a result, they increase their interest rate to compensate for this loss in purchasing power. When inflationary expectations are high, interest rates are high.

Identifying and mixing these three components in the appropriate ratio for any given company or investor at any given moment is not easy. Yet, the relevance and reliability of accounting information depend on the selection of appropriate interest rates.

Throughout the remainder of this chapter, we will focus on the mechanics of computing present values and future values. In most cases, interest rates will be provided. Occasionally, a problem will ask you to solve for the interest rate as the only unknown variable.

Simple Interest

Simple interest is computed on the amount of the principal only. It is the return on (or growth of) the principal for one time period. Simple interest is commonly expressed as follows:[5]

Objective ②

Distinguish between simple and compound interest.

$$\text{Interest} = p \times i \times n$$

where

$$p = \text{principal}$$
$$i = \text{rate of interest for a single period}$$
$$n = \text{number of periods.}$$

To illustrate, if you borrow $1,000 for 3 years with a simple interest rate of 15% per year, the total interest you will pay is $450, computed as follows:

$$\text{Interest} = (p)(i)(n)$$
$$(\$1,000)(.15)(3)$$
$$\$450$$

If you borrow $1,000 for 3 months at 15%, the interest is $37.50, computed as follows:

$$\text{Interest} = (\$1,000)(.15)(.25)$$
$$= \$37.50$$

---

[5]Simple interest is traditionally expressed in textbooks in business mathematics or business finance as: *I*(interest) = *P*(principal) × *R*(rate) × *T*(time).

Compound Interest

John Maynard Keynes, the legendary English economist, supposedly called it magic. Mayer Rothschild, the founder of the famous European banking firm, is said to have proclaimed it the eighth wonder of the world. Today people continue to extol its wonder and its power. The object of their affection is compound interest.

Compound interest is computed on principal **and** on any interest earned that has not been paid or withdrawn. It is the return on (or growth of) the principal for two or more time periods. Compounding computes interest not only on the principal but also on the interest earned to date on that principal, assuming the interest is left on deposit.[6]

To illustrate the difference between simple and compound interest, assume that you deposit $1,000 in the Last National Bank, where it will earn simple interest of 9% per year, and you deposit another $1,000 in the First State Bank, where it will earn compound interest of 9% per year compounded annually. Also assume that in both cases you will not withdraw any interest until 3 years from the date of deposit. The computation of interest to be received and the accumulated year-end balance are indicated in Illustration 6-1.

ILLUSTRATION 6-1
Simple vs. Compound Interest

Last National Bank				First State Bank		
Simple Interest Calculation	Simple Interest	Accumulated Year-end Balance		Compound Interest Calculation	Compound Interest	Accumulated Year-end Balance
Year 1 $1,000.00 × 9%	$ 90.00	$1,090.00		Year 1 $1,000.00 × 9%	$ 90.00	$1,090.00
Year 2 $1,000.00 × 9%	90.00	$1,180.00		Year 2 $1,090.00 × 9%	98.10	$1,188.10
Year 3 $1,000.00 × 9%	90.00	$1,270.00		Year 3 $1,188.10 × 9%	106.93	$1,295.03
	$270.00				$295.03	

$25.03 Difference

Note in the illustration above that simple interest uses the initial principal of $1,000 to compute the interest in all 3 years. Compound interest uses the accumulated balance (principal plus interest to date) at each year-end to compute interest in the succeeding year—which explains why your compound interest account is larger.

Obviously if you had a choice between investing your money at simple interest or at compound interest, you would choose compound interest, all other things—especially risk—being equal. In the example, compounding provides $25.03 of additional interest revenue. For practical purposes compounding assumes that unpaid interest earned becomes a part of the principal, and the accumulated balance at the end of each year becomes the new principal sum on which interest is earned during the next year.

Compound interest is the typical interest computation applied in business situations, particularly in our economy where large amounts of long-lived assets are used productively and financed over long periods of time. Financial managers view and evaluate their investment opportunities in terms of a series of periodic returns, each of which can be reinvested to yield additional returns. Simple interest is usually applicable only to short-term investments and debts that involve a time span of one year or less.

---

[6]Here is an illustration of the power of *time* and *compounding* interest on money. In 1626, Peter Minuit bought Manhattan Island from the Manhattoe Indians for $24 worth of trinkets and beads. If the Indians had taken a boat to Holland, invested the $24 in Dutch securities returning just 6% per year, and kept the money and interest invested at 6%, by 1971 they would have had $13 billion, enough to buy back Manhattan and still have a couple of billion dollars left for doodads (*Forbes*, June 1, 1971). By 1997, 365 years after the trade, the $24 would have grown to approximately $58 billion—or to $57 trillion had the money compounded at 8%.

Compound Interest Tables (see pages 320–329)

Five different types of compound interest tables are presented at the end of this chapter. These tables should help you study this chapter as well as solve later problems involving interest.[7] The titles of these five tables and their contents are:

Objective ③

Learn how to use appropriate compound interest tables.

❖ INTEREST TABLES AND CONTENTS ❖

❶ *Future Value of 1* table. Contains the amounts to which 1 will accumulate if deposited now at a specified rate and left for a specified number of periods. (Table 6-1)

❷ *Present Value of 1* table. Contains the amounts that must be deposited now at a specified rate of interest to equal 1 at the end of a specified number of periods. (Table 6-2)

❸ *Future Value of an Ordinary Annuity of 1* table. Contains the amounts to which periodic rents of 1 will accumulate if the payments (rents) are invested at the **end** of each period at a specified rate of interest for a specified number of periods. (Table 6-3)

❹ *Present Value of an Ordinary Annuity of 1* table. Contains the amounts that must be deposited now at a specified rate of interest to permit withdrawals of 1 at the **end** of regular periodic intervals for the specified number of periods. (Table 6-4)

❺ *Present Value of an Annuity Due of 1* table. Contains the amounts that must be deposited now at a specified rate of interest to permit withdrawals of 1 at the **beginning** of regular periodic intervals for the specified number of periods. (Table 6-5)

The excerpt below illustrates the general format and content of these tables. This excerpt from Table 6-1 indicates how much principal plus interest a dollar accumulates to at the end of each of five periods at three different rates of compound interest.

FUTURE VALUE OF 1 AT COMPOUND INTEREST (Excerpt from Table 6-1, page 321)			
Period	9%	10%	11%
1	1.09000	1.10000	1.11000
2	1.18810	1.21000	1.23210
3	1.29503	1.33100	1.36763
4	1.41158	1.46410	1.51807
5	1.53862	1.61051	1.68506

ILLUSTRATION 6-2
Excerpt from Table 6-1

The compound tables are computed using basic formulas. For example, the formula to determine the future value factor (FVF) for 1 is:

$$FVF_{n,i} = (1 + i)^n$$

where

$FVF_{n,i}$ = future value factor for n periods at i interest

n = number of periods

i = rate of interest for a single period

---

[7]Compound interest tables make no allowance for inflation or deflation. If you need to consider the changes in the purchasing power of the dollar, you have to do so outside the framework of these tables or by adjusting the interest rate to reflect inflation.

To illustrate, assuming an interest rate of 9%, the future value to which 1 accumulates (the future value factor) is shown below.

ILLUSTRATION 6-3
Accumulation of
Compound Amounts

Period	Beginning-of-Period Amount	×	Multiplier (1 + i)	=	End-of-Period Amount*	Formula $(1 + i)^n$
1	1.00000		1.09		1.09000	$(1.09)^1$
2	1.09000		1.09		1.18810	$(1.09)^2$
3	1.18810		1.09		1.29503	$(1.09)^3$

*Note that these amounts appear in Table 6-1 in the 9% column.

Throughout the discussion of compound interest tables the use of the term **periods** instead of **years** is intentional. Interest is generally expressed in terms of an annual rate but in many business circumstances the compounding period is less than one year. In such circumstances the annual interest rate must be converted to correspond to the length of the period. The process is to convert the "annual interest rate" into the "compounding period interest rate" by **dividing the annual rate by the number of compounding periods per year**.

In addition, the number of periods is determined by **multiplying the number of years involved by the number of compounding periods per year**. To illustrate, assume that $1.00 is invested for 6 years at 8% annual interest compounded **quarterly**. Using Table 6-1, page 320, we can determine the amount to which this $1.00 will accumulate: read the factor that appears in the 2% column on the 24th row—6 years × 4 compounding periods per year, namely 1.60844, or approximately $1.61. Thus, the term **periods**, not **years**, is used in all compound interest tables to express the quantity of *n*.

The following schedule shows how to determine (1) the interest rate per compounding period and (2) the number of compounding periods in four situations of differing compounding frequency.[8]

ILLUSTRATION 6-4
Frequency of
Compounding

12% Annual Interest Rate over 5 Years Compounded	Interest Rate per Compounding Period	Number of Compounding Periods
Annually (1)	.12 ÷ 1 = .12	5 years × 1 compounding per year = 5 periods
Semiannually (2)	.12 ÷ 2 = .06	5 years × 2 compoundings per year = 10 periods
Quarterly (4)	.12 ÷ 4 = .03	5 years × 4 compoundings per year = 20 periods
Monthly (12)	.12 ÷ 12 = .01	5 years × 12 compoundings per year = 60 periods

How often interest is compounded can make a substantial difference in the rate of return. For example, a 9% annual interest compounded **daily** provides a 9.42% yield, or a difference of .42%. The 9.42% is referred to as the **effective yield**.[9] The annual

---

[8]Because interest is theoretically earned (accruing) every second of every day, it is possible to calculate interest that is **compounded continuously**. Computations involving continuous compounding are facilitated through the use of the natural, or Napierian, system of logarithms. As a practical matter, however, most business transactions assume interest to be compounded no more frequently than daily.

[9]The formula for calculating the **effective rate** in situations where the compounding frequency (*n*) is greater than once a year is as follows:

$$\text{Effective rate} = (1 + i)^n - 1$$

To illustrate, if the stated annual rate is 8% compounded quarterly (or 2% per quarter), the effective annual rate is:

$$\text{Effective rate} = (1 + .02)^4 - 1$$
$$= (1.02)^4 - 1$$
$$= 1.0824 - 1$$
$$= .0824$$
$$= 8.24\%$$

interest rate (9%) is called the **stated**, **nominal**, or **face rate**. When the compounding frequency is greater than once a year, the effective interest rate will always be greater than the stated rate.

The schedule below shows how compounding for five different time periods affects the effective yield and the amount earned by an investment of $10,000 for one year.

ILLUSTRATION 6-5
Comparison of Different
Compounding Periods

Interest Rate	Compounding Periods				
	Annually	Semiannually	Quarterly	Monthly	Daily
8%	8.00% $800	8.16% $816	8.24% $824	8.30% $830	8.33% $833
9%	9.00% $900	9.20% $920	9.31% $931	9.38% $938	9.42% $942
10%	10.00% $1,000	10.25% $1,025	10.38% $1,038	10.47% $1,047	10.52% $1,052

Fundamental Variables

The following four variables are fundamental to all compound interest problems:

Objective 4

Identify variables
fundamental to solving
interest problems.

❖ FUNDAMENTAL VARIABLES ❖

❶ *Rate of Interest.* This rate, unless otherwise stated, is an annual rate that must be adjusted to reflect the length of the compounding period if less than a year.

❷ *Number of Time Periods.* This is the number of compounding periods (a period may be equal to or less than a year).

❸ *Future Value.* The value at a future date of a given sum or sums invested assuming compound interest.

❹ *Present Value.* The value now (present time) of a future sum or sums discounted assuming compound interest.

The relationship of these four fundamental variables is depicted in the following **time diagram**:

ILLUSTRATION 6-6
Basic Time Diagram

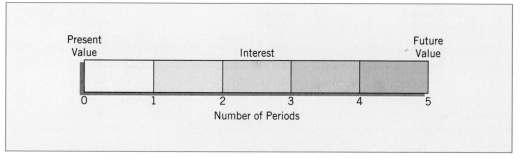

In some cases all four of these variables are known, but in many business situations at least one variable is unknown. As an aid to better understanding the problems and to finding solutions, we encourage you to sketch compound interest problems in the form of the preceding time diagram.

❖ SINGLE-SUM PROBLEMS

Many business and investment decisions involve a single amount of money that either exists now or will in the future. Single sum problems can generally be classified into one of the following two categories:

Objective ❺

Solve future and present value of 1 problems.

❶ Computing the **unknown future value** of a known single sum of money that is invested now for a certain number of periods at a certain interest rate.

❷ Computing the **unknown present value** of a known single sum of money in the future that is discounted for a certain number of periods at a certain interest rate.

When analyzing the information provided, you determine first whether it is a future value problem or a present value problem. **If you are solving for a future value**, all cash flows must be *accumulated* to a future point. In this instance, the effect of interest is to increase the amounts or values over time so that the future value is greater than the present value. However, **if you are solving for a present value**, all cash flows must be *discounted* from the future to the present. In this case, the **discounting** reduces the amounts or values so that the present value is less than the future amount.

Preparation of time diagrams aids in identifying the unknown as an item in the future or the present. Sometimes it is neither a future value nor a present value that is to be determined but, rather, the interest or discount rate or the number of compounding or discounting periods.

Future Value of a Single Sum

To determine the **future value** of a single sum, multiply the future value factor by its present value (principal), as follows:

$$FV = PV\ (FVF_{n,i})$$

where

$$FV = \text{future value}$$

$$PV = \text{present value (principal or single sum)}$$

$$FVF_{n,i} = \text{future value factor for } n \text{ periods at } i \text{ interest}$$

To illustrate, what is the future value of $50,000 invested for 5 years compounded annually at an interest rate of 11%? In time-diagram form, this investment situation would appear as follows:

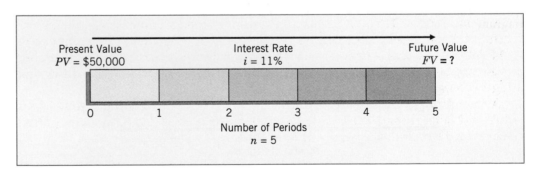

Using the formula, this investment problem is solved as follows:

$$\text{Future value} = PV\ (FVF_{n,i})$$

$$= \$50{,}000\ (FVF_{5,11\%})$$

$$= \$50{,}000\ (1 + .11)^5$$

$$= \$50{,}000\ (1.68506)$$

$$= \$84{,}253$$

To determine the future value factor of 1.68506 in the formula above, use a financial calculator or read the appropriate table, in this case Table 6-1 (11% column and the 5-period row).

This time diagram and formula approach can be applied to a routine business situation. To illustrate, Commonwealth Edison Company deposited $250 million in an escrow account with the Northern Trust Company at the beginning of 1997 as a commitment toward a power plant to be completed December 31, 2000. How much will be on deposit at the end of 4 years if interest is 10%, compounded semiannually?

With a known present value of $250 million, a total of 8 compounding periods (4 × 2), and an interest rate of 5% per compounding period (.10 ÷ 2), this problem can be time diagrammed and the future value determined as follows:

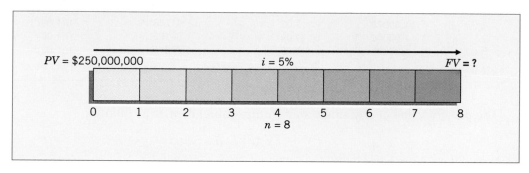

$$\text{Future value} = \$250{,}000{,}000 \; (FVF_{8,5\%})$$

$$= \$250{,}000{,}000 \; (1 + .05)^8$$

$$= \$250{,}000{,}000 \; (1.47746)$$

$$= \$369{,}365{,}000$$

Using a future value factor found in Table 6-1 (5% column, 8-period row), we find that the deposit of $250 million will accumulate to $369,365,000 by December 31, 2000.

Present Value of a Single Sum

The example on page 286 showed that $50,000 invested at an annually compounded interest rate of 11% will be worth $84,253 at the end of 5 years. It follows, then, that $84,253, 5 years in the future is worth $50,000 now; that is, $50,000 is the present value of $84,253. The **present value** is the amount that must be invested now to produce the known future value. **The present value is always a smaller amount than the known future value because interest will be earned and accumulated on the present value to the future date.** In determining the future value we move forward in time using a process of **accumulation**; in determining present value, we move backward in time using a process of **discounting**.

As indicated earlier, a "present value of 1 table" appears at the end of this chapter as Table 6-2. Illustration 6-7 demonstrates the nature of such a table. It shows the present value of 1 for five different periods at three different rates of interest.

PRESENT VALUE OF 1 AT COMPOUND INTEREST (Excerpt from Table 6-2, page 323)			
Period	9%	10%	11%
1	0.91743	0.90909	0.90090
2	0.84168	0.82645	0.81162
3	0.77218	0.75132	0.73119
4	0.70843	0.68301	0.65873
5	0.64993	0.62092	0.59345

ILLUSTRATION 6-7
Excerpt from Table 6-2

The present value of 1 (present value factor) may be expressed as a formula:

$$PVF_{n,i} = \frac{1}{(1 + i)^n}$$

where

$$PVF_{n,i} = \text{present value factor for } n \text{ periods at } i \text{ interest}$$

To illustrate, assuming an interest rate of 9%, the present value of 1 discounted for three different periods is as follows:

ILLUSTRATION 6-8
Present Value of $1
Discounted at 9% for
Three Periods

Discount Periods	1	÷	$(1 + i)^n$	=	**Present Value***	Formula $1/(1 + i)^n$
1	1.00000		1.09		.91743	$1/(1.09)^1$
2	1.00000		$(1.09)^2$		.84168	$1/(1.09)^2$
3	1.00000		$(1.09)^3$		.77218	$1/(1.09)^3$

*Note that these amounts appear in Table 6-2 in the 9% column.

The present value of any single sum (future value) then, is as follows:

$$PV = FV\ (PVF_{n,i})$$

where

$$PV = \text{present value}$$

$$FV = \text{future value}$$

$$PVF_{n,i} = \text{present value factor for } n \text{ periods at } i \text{ interest}$$

To illustrate, what is the present value of $84,253 to be received or paid in 5 years discounted at 11% compounded annually? In time-diagram form, this problem is drawn as follows:

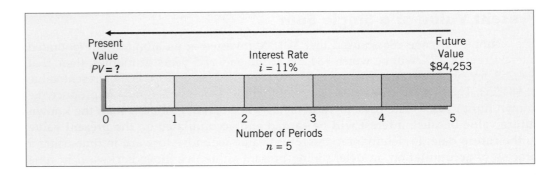

Using the formula, this problem is solved as follows:

$$\text{Present value} = FV\ (PVF_{n,i})$$

$$= \$84{,}253\ (PVF_{5,11\%})$$

$$= \$84{,}253 \left(\frac{1}{(1 + .11)^5}\right)$$

$$= \$84{,}253\ (.59345)$$

$$= \$50{,}000$$

To determine the present value factor of .59345, use a financial calculator or read the present value of a single sum in Table 6-2 (11% column, 5-period row).

The time diagram and formula approach can be applied in a variety of situations. For example, assume that your rich uncle proposes to give you $2,000 for a trip to Europe when you graduate from college 3 years from now. He proposes to finance the trip by investing a sum of money now at 8% compound interest that will provide you with $2,000 upon your graduation. The only conditions are that you graduate and that you tell him how much to invest now.

To impress your uncle, you might set up the following time diagram and solve this problem as follows:

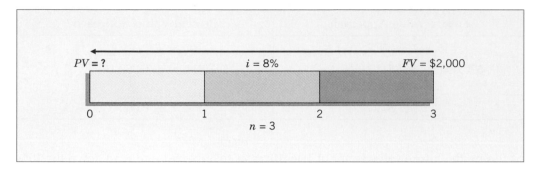

$$\text{Present value} = \$2,000 \ (PVF_{3,8\%})$$

$$= \$2,000 \left(\frac{1}{(1 + .08)^3} \right)$$

$$= \$2,000 \ (.79383)$$

$$= \$1,587.66$$

Advise your uncle to invest $1,587.66 now to provide you with $2,000 upon graduation. To satisfy your uncle's other condition, you must pass this course and many more.

Solving for Other Unknowns in Single-Sum Problems

In computing either the future value or the present value in the previous single-sum illustrations, both the number of periods and the interest rate were known. In many business situations, both the future value and the present value are known, but the number of periods or the interest rate is unknown. The following two illustrations are single-sum problems (future value and present value) with either an unknown number of periods (n) or an unknown interest rate (i). These illustrations and the accompanying solutions demonstrate that if any three of the four values (future value, *FV*; present value, *PV*; number of periods, *n*; interest rate, *i*) are known, the remaining unknown variable can be derived.

Illustration—Computation of the Number of Periods

The Village of Somonauk wants to accumulate $70,000 for the construction of a veterans monument in the town square. If at the beginning of the current year the Village deposited $47,811 in a memorial fund that earns 10% interest compounded annually, how many years will it take to accumulate $70,000 in the memorial fund?

In this illustration, both the present value ($47,811) and the future value ($70,000) are known along with the interest rate of 10%. A time diagram of this investment problem is as follows:

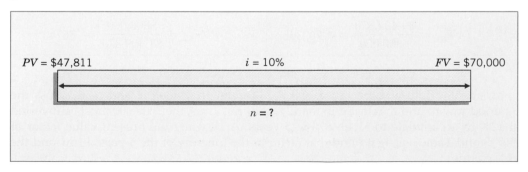

Because both the present value and the future value are known, we can solve for the unknown number of periods using either the future value or the present value formulas as shown below:

Future Value Approach	Present Value Approach
$FV = PV (FVF_{n,10\%})$	$PV = FV (PVF_{n,10\%})$
$\$70{,}000 = \$47{,}811 (FVF_{n,10\%})$	$\$47{,}811 = \$70{,}000 (PVF_{n,10\%})$
$FVF_{n,10\%} = \dfrac{\$70{,}000}{\$47{,}811} = 1.46410$	$PVF_{n,10\%} = \dfrac{\$47{,}811}{\$70{,}000} = .68301$

Using the future value factor of 1.46410, refer to Table 6-1 and read down the 10% column to find that factor in the 4-period row. Thus, it will take 4 years for the $47,811 to accumulate to $70,000 if invested at 10% interest compounded annually. Using the present value factor of .68301, refer to Table 6-2 and read down the 10% column to find again that factor in the 4-period row.

Illustration—Computation of the Interest Rate

Advanced Design, Inc. wishes to have $1,409,870 for basic research 5 years from now. The firm currently has $800,000 to invest for that purpose. At what rate of interest must the $800,000 be invested to fund basic research projects of $1,409,870, 5 years from now?

A time diagram of this investment situation is as follows:

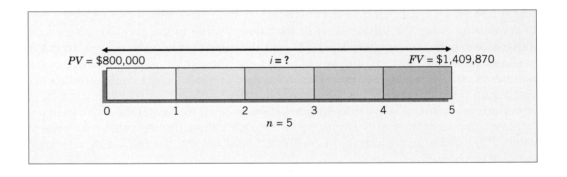

The unknown interest rate may be determined from either the future value approach or the present value approach as shown below:

Future Value Approach	Present Value Approach
$FV = PV (FVF_{5,i})$	$PV = FV (PVF_{5,i})$
$\$1{,}409{,}870 = \$800{,}000 (FVF_{5,i})$	$\$800{,}000 = \$1{,}409{,}870 (PVF_{5,i})$
$FVF_{5,i} = \dfrac{\$1{,}409{,}870}{\$800{,}000} = 1.76234$	$PVF_{5,i} = \dfrac{\$800{,}000}{\$1{,}409{,}870} = .56743$

Using the future value factor of 1.76234, refer to Table 6-1 and read across the 5-period row to find that factor in the 12% column. Thus, the $800,000 must be invested at 12% to accumulate to $1,409,870 in 5 years. And, using the present value factor of .56743 and Table 6-2, again find that factor at the juncture of the 5-period row and the 12% column.

❖ ANNUITIES

The preceding discussion involved only the accumulation or discounting of a single principal sum. Individuals frequently encounter situations in which a series of dollar amounts are to be paid or received periodically, such as loans or sales to be repaid in installments, invested funds that will be partially recovered at regular intervals, or cost savings that are realized repeatedly. A life insurance contract is probably the most common and most familiar type of transaction involving a series of equal payments made at equal intervals of time. Such a process of periodic saving represents the accumulation of a sum of money through an annuity. An annuity by definition requires that (1) the periodic payments or receipts (called **rents**) always be the same amount, (2) the **interval** between such rents always be the same, and (3) the **interest be compounded** once each interval. The **future value of an annuity** is the sum of all the rents plus the accumulated compound interest on them.

It should be noted that the rents may occur at either the beginning or the end of the periods. To distinguish annuities under these two alternatives, an annuity is classified as an ordinary annuity if the rents occur at the end of each period, and as an annuity due if the rents occur at the beginning of each period.

Future Value of an Ordinary Annuity

One approach to the problem of determining the future value to which an annuity will accumulate is to compute the value to which **each** of the rents in the series will accumulate and then total their individual future values. For example, assume that $1 is deposited at the **end** of each of 5 years (an ordinary annuity) and earns 12% interest compounded annually. The future value can be computed as follows using the "future value of 1" table (Table 6-1) for each of the five $1 rents:

Objective ⑥

Solve future value of ordinary and annuity due problems.

END OF PERIOD IN WHICH $1.00 IS TO BE INVESTED	Value at End of Year 5
Present 1 2 3 4 5	
|--------$1.00 ————————————————————————|	$1.57352
|----------------$1.00 ——————————————————|	1.40493
|---------------------------$1.00 ——————————|	1.25440
|----------------------------------$1.00 ———|	1.12000
|-- $1.00	1.00000
Total (future value of an ordinary annuity of $1.00 for 5 periods at 12%)	$6.35285

ILLUSTRATION 6-11
Solving for the Future Value of an Ordinary Annuity

Because the rents that compose an ordinary annuity are deposited at the end of the period, they can earn no interest during the period in which they are originally deposited. For example, the third rent earns interest for only two periods (periods four and five). Obviously the third rent earns no interest for the first two periods since it is not deposited until the third period; furthermore, it can earn no interest for the third period since it is not deposited until the end of the third period. Any time the future value of an ordinary annuity is computed, the number of compounding periods will always be **one less than the number of rents**.

Although the foregoing procedure for computing the future value of an ordinary annuity will always produce the correct answer, it can become cumbersome if the number of rents is large. A more efficient way of expressing the future value of an ordinary annuity of 1 is in a formula that is a summation of the individual rents plus the compound interest:

$$FVF\text{-}OA_{n,i} = \frac{(1 + i)^n - 1}{i}$$

where

$$FVF\text{-}OA_{n,i} = \text{future value factor of an ordinary annuity}$$

$$i = \text{rate of interest per period}$$

$$n = \text{number of compounding periods}$$

For example, $FVF\text{-}OA_{5,12\%}$ refers to the value to which an ordinary annuity of 1 will accumulate in 5 periods at 12% interest.

Using the formula above, tables have been developed similar to those used for the "future value of 1" and the "present value of 1" for both an ordinary annuity and an annuity due. The table in Illustration 6-12 is an excerpt from the "future value of an ordinary annuity of 1" table.

ILLUSTRATION 6-12
Excerpt from Table 6-3

FUTURE VALUE OF AN ORDINARY ANNUITY OF 1
(Excerpt from Table 6-3, page 325)

Period	10%	11%	12%
1	1.00000	1.00000	1.00000
2	2.10000	2.11000	2.12000
3	3.31000	3.34210	3.37440
4	4.64100	4.70973	4.77933
5	6.10510	6.22780	6.35285*

*Note that this annuity table factor is the same as the sum of the future values of 1 factors shown in Illustration 6-11.

Interpreting the table, if $1.00 is invested at the end of each year for 4 years at 11% interest compounded annually, the value of the annuity at the end of the fourth year will be $4.71 (4.70973 × $1.00). Multiply the factor from the appropriate line and column of the table by the dollar amount of **one rent** involved in an ordinary annuity. The result: the accumulated sum of the rents and the compound interest to the date of the last rent.

The future value of an ordinary annuity is computed as follows:

$$\text{Future value of an ordinary annuity} = R\ (FVF\text{-}OA_{n,i})$$

where

$$R = \text{periodic rent}$$

$$FVF\text{-}OA_{n,i} = \text{future value of an ordinary annuity factor}$$
$$\text{for } n \text{ periods at } i \text{ interest}$$

To illustrate, what is the future value of five $5,000 deposits made at the end of each of the next 5 years, earning interest of 12%? In time-diagram form, this problem is drawn as follows:

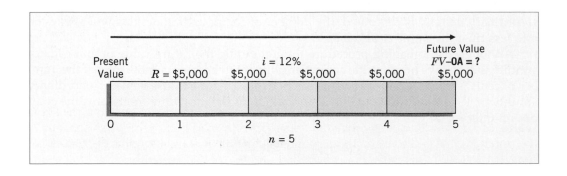

Using the formula, this investment problem is solved as follows:

$$\text{Future value of an ordinary annuity} = R \; (FVF\text{-}OA_{n,i})$$

$$= \$5,000 \; (FVF\text{-}OA_{5,12\%})$$

$$= \$5,000 \left(\frac{(1 + .12)^5 - 1}{.12} \right)$$

$$= \$5,000 \; (6.35285)$$

$$= \$31,764.25$$

Determine the future value of an ordinary annuity factor of 6.35285 in the formula above using a financial calculator or by reading the appropriate table, in this case Table 6-3 (12% column and the 5-period row).

To illustrate these computations in a business situation, assume that Hightown Electronics decides to deposit $75,000 at the end of each 6-month period for the next 3 years for the purpose of accumulating enough money to meet debts that mature in 3 years. What is the future value that will be on deposit at the end of 3 years if the annual interest rate is 10%?

The time diagram and formula solution are as follows:

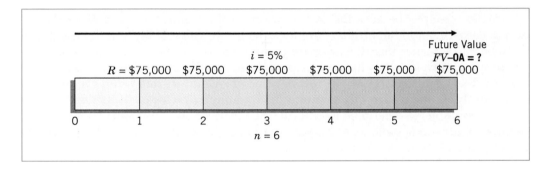

$$\text{Future value of an ordinary annuity} = R \; (FVF\text{-}OA_{n,i})$$

$$= \$75,000 \; (FVF\text{-}OA_{6,5\%})$$

$$= \$75,000 \left(\frac{(1 + .05)^6 - 1}{.05} \right)$$

$$= \$75,000 \; (6.80191)$$

$$= \$510,143.25$$

Thus, six 6-month deposits of $75,000 earning 5% per period will grow to $510,143.25.

Future Value of an Annuity Due

The preceding analysis of an ordinary annuity was based on the assumption that the periodic rents occur at the **end** of each period. An annuity due assumes periodic rents occur at the **beginning** of each period. This means an annuity due will accumulate interest during the first period, whereas an ordinary annuity rent will earn no interest during the first period because the rent is not received or paid until the end of the period. In other words, the significant difference between the two types of annuities is in the number of interest accumulation periods involved.

If rents occur at the end of a period (ordinary annuity), in determining the **future value of an annuity** there will be one less interest period than if the rents occur at the beginning of the period (annuity due). The distinction is shown graphically on the next page.

ILLUSTRATION 6-13
Comparison of the
Future Value of an
Ordinary Annuity with
an Annuity Due

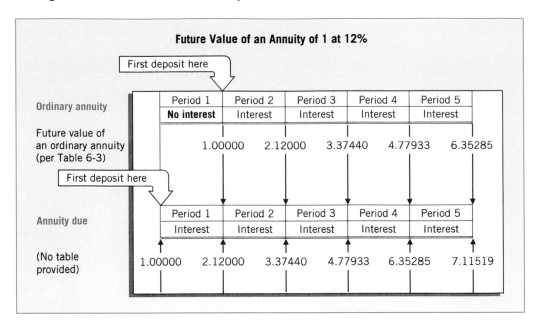

Future Value of an Annuity of 1 at 12%

In this example, because the cash flows from the annuity due come exactly one period earlier than for an ordinary annuity, the future value of the annuity due factor is exactly 12% higher than the ordinary annuity factor. For example, the value of an ordinary annuity factor at the end of period one at 12% is 1.00000, whereas for an annuity due it is 1.12000. **Thus, the future value of an annuity due factor can be found by multiplying the future value of an ordinary annuity factor by 1 plus the interest rate.** For example, to determine the future value of an annuity due interest factor for 5 periods at 12% compound interest, simply multiply the future value of an ordinary annuity interest factor for 5 periods (6.35285) by one plus the interest rate (1 + .12), to arrive at 7.11519 (6.35285 × 1.12).

To illustrate the use of the ordinary annuity tables in converting to an annuity due, assume that Sue Lotadough plans to deposit $800 a year on each birthday of her son Howard, starting today, his tenth birthday, at 12% interest compounded annually. Sue wants to know the amount she will have accumulated for college expenses by her son's eighteenth birthday. If the first deposit is made on Howard's tenth birthday, Sue will make a total of 8 deposits over the life of the annuity (assume no deposit on the eighteenth birthday). Because all the deposits will be made at the beginning of the periods, they represent an annuity due.

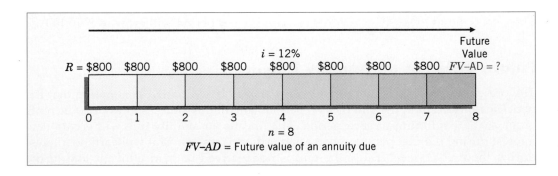

Referring to the "future value of an ordinary annuity of 1" table for 8 periods at 12%, we find a factor of 12.29969. This factor is then multiplied by (1 + .12) to arrive at the future value of an annuity due factor. As a result, the accumulated value on Howard's eighteenth birthday is computed as follows:

1. Future value of an ordinary annuity of 1 for 8 periods at 12% (Table 6-3)	12.29969
2. Factor (1 + .12)	× 1.12
3. Future value of an annuity due of 1 for 8 periods at 12%	13.77565
4. Periodic deposit (rent)	× $800
5. Accumulated value on son's eighteenth birthday	$11,020.52

ILLUSTRATION 6-14
Computation of
Accumulated Value of
Annuity Due

Depending on the college he chooses, Howard may have only enough to finance his first year of school.

Illustrations of Future Value of Annuity Problems

In the foregoing annuity examples three values were known—amount of each rent, interest rate, and number of periods. They were used to determine the fourth value, future value, which was unknown. The first two future value problems presented illustrate the computations of (1) the amount of the rents and (2) the number of rents. The third problem illustrates the computation of the future value of an annuity due.

Computation of Rent

Assume that you wish to accumulate $14,000 for a down payment on a condominium apartment 5 years from now; for the next 5 years you can earn an annual return of 8% compounded semiannually. How much should you deposit at the end of each 6-month period?

The $14,000 is the future value of 10 (5 × 2) semiannual end-of-period payments of an unknown amount, at an interest rate of 4% (8% ÷ 2). This problem appears in the form of a time diagram as follows:

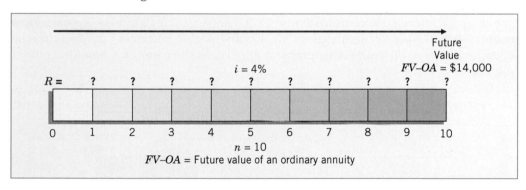

Using the formula for the future value of an ordinary annuity, the amount of each rent is determined as follows:

$$\text{Future value of an ordinary annuity} = R\ (FVF\text{-}OA_{n,i})$$

$$\$14,000 = R\ (FVF\text{-}OA_{10,4\%})$$

$$\$14,000 = R(12.00611)$$

$$\frac{\$14,000}{12.00611} = R$$

$$R = \$1,166.07$$

Thus, you must make 10 semiannual deposits of $1,166.07 each in order to accumulate $14,000 for your down payment.

Computation of the Number of Periodic Rents

Suppose that your company wishes to accumulate $117,332 by making periodic deposits of $20,000 at the end of each year that will earn 8% compounded annually while accumulating. How many deposits must be made?

The $117,332 represents the future value of $n(?)$ $20,000 deposits, at an 8% annual rate of interest. This problem appears in the form of a time diagram as follows:

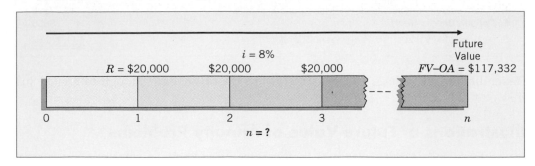

Using the future value of an ordinary annuity formula, we obtain the following factor:

$$\text{Future value of an ordinary annuity} = R \ (FVF\text{-}OA_{n,i})$$

$$\$117,332 = \$20,000 \ (FVF\text{-}OA_{n,8\%})$$

$$FVF\text{-}OA_{n,8\%} = \frac{\$117,332}{\$20,000} = 5.86660$$

Using Table 6-3 and reading down the 8% column, we find 5.86660 in the 5-period row. Thus, five deposits of $20,000 each must be made.

Computation of the Future Value

Walter Goodwrench, a mechanic, has taken on weekend work in the hope of creating his own retirement fund. Mr. Goodwrench deposits $2,500 today in a savings account that earns 9% interest. He plans to deposit $2,500 every year for a total of 30 years. How much cash will have accumulated in Mr. Goodwrench's retirement savings account when he retires in 30 years? This problem appears in the form of a time diagram as follows:

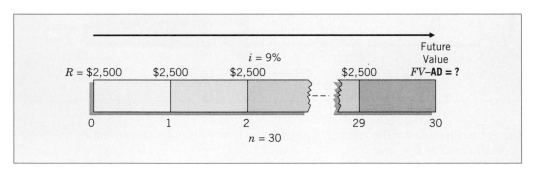

Using the "future value of an ordinary annuity of 1" table, the solution is computed as follows:

ILLUSTRATION 6-15
Computation of
Accumulated Value of an
Annuity Due

1. Future value of an ordinary annuity of 1 for 30 periods at 9%	136.30754
2. Factor (1 + .09)	× 1.09
3. Future value of an annuity due of 1 for 30 periods at 9%	148.57522
4. Periodic rent	× $2,500
5. Accumulated value at end of 30 years	$371,438

Objective **7**

Solve present value of
ordinary and annuity due
problems.

Present Value of an Ordinary Annuity

The present value of an annuity is **the single sum** that, if invested at compound interest now, would provide for an annuity (a series of withdrawals) for a certain number of future periods. In other words, the present value of an ordinary annuity is the present value of a series of equal rents to be withdrawn at equal intervals.

One approach is to determine the present value of each of the rents in the series and then total their individual present values. For example, an annuity of $1.00 to be received at the **end** of each of 5 periods may be viewed as separate amounts; the present value of each is computed from the table of present values (see pages 322–323), assuming an interest rate of 12%.

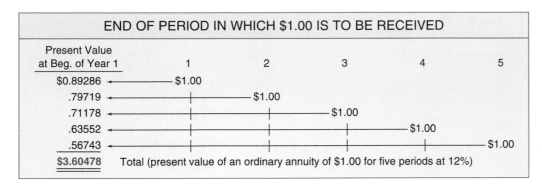

ILLUSTRATION 6-16
Solving for the Present Value of an Ordinary Annuity

This computation tells us that if we invest the single sum of $3.60 today at 12% interest for 5 periods, we will be able to withdraw $1.00 at the end of each period for 5 periods. This cumbersome procedure can be summarized by:

$$PVF\text{-}OA_{n,i} = \frac{1 - \dfrac{1}{(1 + i)^n}}{i}$$

The expression $PVF\text{-}OA_{n,i}$ refers to the present value of an ordinary annuity of 1 factor for n periods at i interest. Using this formula, present value of ordinary annuity tables are prepared. An excerpt from such a table is shown below:

PRESENT VALUE OF AN ORDINARY ANNUITY OF 1
(Excerpt from Table 6-4, page 327)

Period	10%	11%	12%
1	0.90909	0.90090	0.89286
2	1.73554	1.71252	1.69005
3	2.48685	2.44371	2.40183
4	3.16986	3.10245	3.03735
5	3.79079	3.69590	3.60478*

*Note that this annuity table factor is equal to the sum of the present value of 1 factors shown in Illustration 6-16.

ILLUSTRATION 6-17
Excerpt from Table 6-4

The general formula for the present value of any ordinary annuity is as follows:

Present value of an ordinary annuity = R $(PVF\text{-}OA_{n,i})$

where

R = periodic rent (ordinary annuity)

$PVF\text{-}OA_{n,i}$ = present value of an ordinary annuity of 1 for n periods at i interest

To illustrate, what is the present value of rental receipts of $6,000 each to be received at the end of each of the next 5 years when discounted at 12%? This problem may be time-diagrammed and solved as follows:

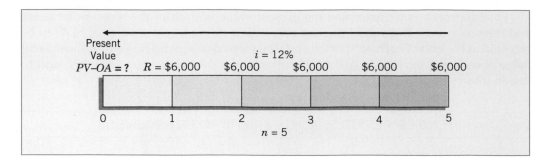

$$\text{Present value of an ordinary annuity} = R\ (PVF\text{-}OA_{n,i})$$

$$= \$6{,}000\ (PVF\text{-}OA_{5,12\%})$$

$$= \$6{,}000\ (3.60478)$$

$$= \$21{,}628.68$$

The present value of the 5 ordinary annuity rental receipts of $6,000 each is $21,628.68. Determining the present value of the ordinary annuity factor 3.60478 can be accomplished using a financial calculator or by reading the appropriate table, in this case Table 6-4 (12% column and 5-period row).

Present Value of an Annuity Due

In the discussion of the present value of an ordinary annuity, the final rent was discounted back the same number of periods that there were rents. In determining the present value of an annuity due, there is always one fewer discount period. This distinction is shown graphically below:

ILLUSTRATION 6-18
Comparison of Present Value of an Ordinary Annuity with an Annuity Due

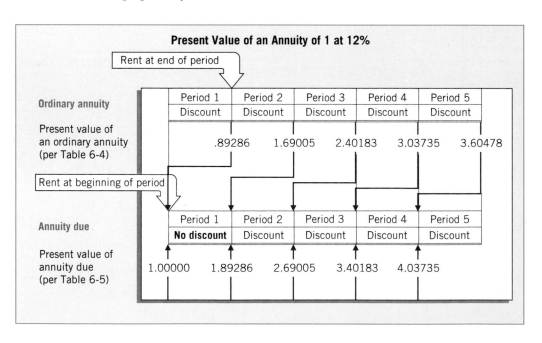

Because each cash flow comes exactly one period sooner in the present value of the annuity due, the present value of the cash flows is exactly 12% higher than the present value of an ordinary annuity. Thus, **the present value of an annuity due factor can be found by multiplying the present value of an ordinary annuity factor by 1 plus the interest rate.**

To determine the present value of an annuity due interest factor for 5 periods at 12% interest, take the present value of an ordinary annuity for 5 periods at 12% interest

(3.60478) and multiply it by 1.12 to arrive at the present value of an annuity due, 4.03735 (3.60478 × 1.12). Because the payment and receipt of rentals at the beginning of periods (such as leases, insurance, and subscriptions) are as common as those at the end of the periods (referred to as "in arrears"), we have provided present value annuity due factors in the form of Table 6-5.

Space Odyssey, Inc., rents a communications satellite for 4 years with annual rental payments of $4.8 million to be made at the beginning of each year. If the relevant annual interest rate is 11%, what is the present value of the rental obligations?

This problem is time-diagrammed as follows:

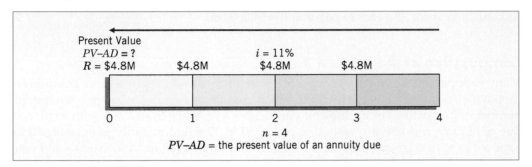

This problem is solved in the following manner.

1. Present value of an ordinary annuity of 1 for 4 periods at 11% (Table 6-4)		3.10245
2. Factor (1 + .11)	×	1.11
3. Present value of an annuity due of 1 for 4 periods at 11%		3.44372
4. Periodic deposit (rent)		× $4,800,000
5. Present value of payments		$16,529,856

ILLUSTRATION 6-19
Computation of Present
Value of an Annuity Due

Since we have Table 6-5 for present value of an annuity due problems, we can also locate the desired factor 3.44372 and compute the present value of the lease payments to be $16,529,856.

Illustrations of Present Value of Annuity Problems

The following three illustrations demonstrate the computation of (1) the present value, (2) the interest rate, and (3) the amount of each rent.

Computation of the Present Value of an Ordinary Annuity

You have just won a lottery totaling $4,000,000 and learned that you will be paid the money by receiving a check in the amount of $200,000 at the end of each of the next 20 years. What amount have you really won? That is, what is the present value of the $200,000 checks you will receive over the next 20 years? A time diagram of this enviable situation is as follows (assuming an appropriate interest rate of 10%):

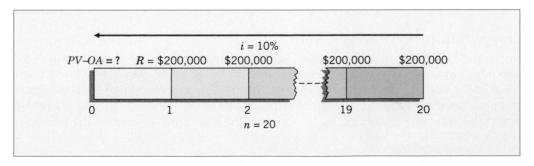

The present value is determined as follows:

$$\text{Present value of an ordinary annuity} = R\,(PVF\text{-}OA_{n,i})$$

$$= \$200{,}000\,(PVF\text{-}OA_{20,10\%})$$

$$= \$200{,}000\,(8.51356)$$

$$= \$1{,}702{,}712$$

As a result, if the state deposits \$1,702,712 now and earns 10% interest, it can withdraw \$200,000 a year for 20 years to pay you the \$4,000,000.

Computation of the Interest Rate

Many shoppers make purchases by using a credit card. When you receive the invoice for payment you may pay the total amount due or you may pay the balance in a certain number of payments. For example, if you receive an invoice from VISA with a balance due of \$528.77 and you are invited to pay it off in 12 equal monthly payments of \$50 each with the first payment due one month from now, what rate of interest would you be paying?

The \$528.77 represents the present value of the 12 payments of \$50 each at an unknown rate of interest. This situation in the form of a time diagram appears as follows:

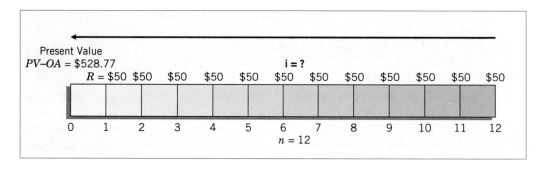

The rate is determined as follows:

$$\text{Present value of an ordinary annuity} = R\,(PVF\text{-}OA_{n,i})$$

$$\$528.77 = \$50\,(PVF\text{-}OA_{12,i})$$

$$(PVF\text{-}OA_{12,i}) = \frac{\$528.77}{\$50} = 10.57540$$

Referring to Table 6-4 and reading across the 12-period row, we find 10.57534 in the 2% column. Since 2% is a monthly rate, the nominal annual rate of interest is 24% (12 × 2%) and the effective annual rate is 26.82413% [$(1 + .02)^{12} - 1$]. Obviously, you're better off paying the entire bill now if you possibly can.

Computation of a Periodic Rent

Norm and Jackie Remmers have saved \$18,000 to finance their daughter Dawna's college education. The money has been deposited in the Bloomington Savings and Loan Association and is earning 10% interest compounded semiannually. What equal amounts can their daughter withdraw at the end of every 6 months during the next 4 years while she attends college, without exhausting the fund? This is time-diagrammed as follows:

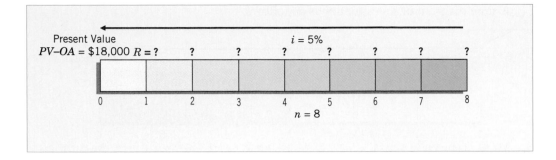

The answer is not determined simply by dividing $18,000 by 8 withdrawals because that would ignore the interest earned on the money remaining on deposit. Taking into consideration that interest is compounded semiannually at 5% (10% ÷ 2) for 8 periods (4 years × 2), and using the same present value of an ordinary annuity formula, we determine the amount of each withdrawal that she can make as follows:

$$\text{Present value of an ordinary annuity} = R\ (\text{PVF-OA}_{n,i})$$

$$\$18,000 = R\ (\text{PVF-OA}_{8,5\%})$$

$$\$18,000 = R\ (6.46321)$$

$$R = \$2,784.99$$

❖ MORE COMPLEX SITUATIONS

Often it is necessary to use more than one table to solve time value problems. The business problem encountered may require that computations of both present value of a single sum and present value of an annuity be made. Two common situations are:

❶ Deferred annuities.
❷ Bond problems.

Deferred Annuities

A deferred annuity is an annuity in which the rents begin after a specified number of periods. A deferred annuity does not begin to produce rents until 2 or more periods have expired. For example, "an **ordinary annuity** of six annual rents deferred 4 years" means that no rents will occur during the first 4 years, and that the first of the six rents will occur at the end of the fifth year. "An **annuity due** of six annual rents deferred 4 years" means that no rents will occur during the first 4 years, and that the first of six rents will occur at the beginning of the fifth year.

Future Value of a Deferred Annuity

In the case of the future value of a deferred annuity the computations are relatively straightforward. Because there is no accumulation or investment on which interest may accrue, the future value of a deferred annuity is the same as the future value of an annuity not deferred. That is, the deferral period is ignored in computing the future value.

To illustrate, assume that Sutton Corporation plans to purchase a land site in 6 years for the construction of its new corporate headquarters. Because of cash flow problems, Sutton is able to budget deposits of $80,000 that are expected to earn 12% annually only at the end of the fourth, fifth, and sixth periods. What future value will Sutton have accumulated at the end of the sixth year?

A time diagram of this situation is as follows:

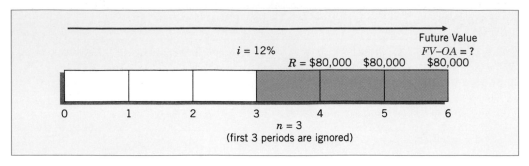

The value accumulated is determined by using the standard formula for the future value of an ordinary annuity:

$$\text{Future value of an ordinary annuity} = R\ (FVF\text{-}OA_{n,i})$$

$$= \$80,000\ (FVF\text{-}OA_{3,12\%})$$

$$= \$80,000\ (3.37440)$$

$$= \$269,952$$

Present Value of a Deferred Annuity

In computing the present value of a deferred annuity, the interest that accrues on the original investment during the deferral period must be recognized.

To compute the present value of a deferred annuity, we compute the present value of an ordinary annuity of 1 as if the rents had occurred for the entire period, and then subtract the present value of rents which were not received during the deferral period. We are left with the present value of the rents actually received subsequent to the deferral period.

To illustrate, Tom Bytehead has developed and copyrighted a software computer program that is a tutorial for students in advanced accounting. He agrees to sell the copyright to Campus Micro Systems for six annual payments of $5,000 each. The payments are to begin 5 years from today. Given an annual interest rate of 8%, what is the present value of the six payments?

This situation is an ordinary annuity of six payments deferred four periods. The following time diagram helps to visualize this sales agreement:

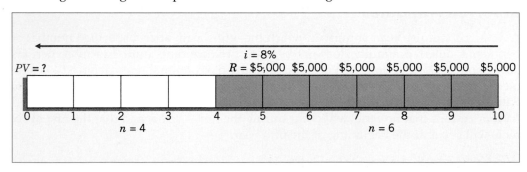

Two options are available to solve this problem. The first is to use only Table 6-4 as follows:

ILLUSTRATION 6-20
Computation of the
Present Value of a
Deferred Annuity

1. Each periodic rent		$5,000
2. Present value of an ordinary annuity of 1 for total periods (10) [number of rents (6) plus number of deferred periods (4)] at 8%	6.71008	
3. Less: Present value of an ordinary annuity of 1 for the number of deferred periods (4) at 8%	−3.31213	
4. Difference		× 3.39795
5. Present value of six rents of $5,000 deferred 4 periods		$16,989.75

The subtraction of the present value of an annuity of 1 for the deferred periods eliminates the nonexistent rents during the deferral period and converts the present value of an ordinary annuity of $1.00 for 10 periods to the present value of 6 rents of $1.00, deferred 4 periods.

Alternatively, the present value of the 6 rents could be computed using both Table 6-2 and Table 6-4. One can first discount the annuity 6 periods, but because the annuity is deferred 4 periods, the present value of the annuity must then be treated as a future amount to be discounted another 4 periods. A time diagram illustrates this two-step process as follows:

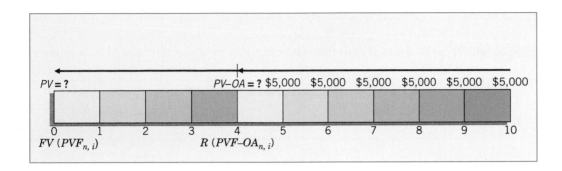

Step 1: Present value of
an ordinary annuity $= R\ (PVF\text{-}OA_{n,i})$

$= \$5,000\ (PVF\text{-}OA_{6,8\%})$

$= \$5,000\ (4.62288)$
(Table 6-4 Present value of an ordinary annuity)

$= \$23,114.40$

Step 2: Present value $= FV\ (PVF_{n,i})$

$= \$23,114.40\ (PVF_{4,8\%})$

$= \$23,114.40\ (.73503)$
(Table 6-2 Present value of a single sum)

$= \mathbf{\$16,989.78}$

The present value of $16,989.78 computed above is the same result although computed differently from the first illustration.

Valuation of Long-Term Bonds

A long-term bond produces two cash flows: (1) periodic interest payments during the life of the bond, and (2) the principal (face value) paid at maturity. At the date of issue, bond buyers determine the present value of these two cash flows using the market rate of interest.

The periodic interest payments represent an annuity and the principal represents a single sum problem. The current market value of the bonds is the combined present values of the interest annuity and the principal amount.

To illustrate, Alltech Corporation on January 1, 1998, issues $100,000 of 9% bonds due in 5 years with interest payable annually at year-end. The current market rate of interest for bonds of similar risk is 11%. What will the buyers pay for this bond issue?

The time diagram depicting both cash flows is shown below:

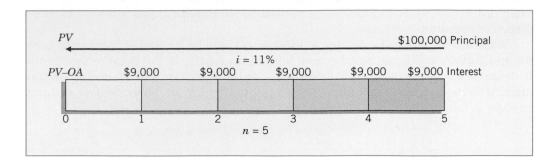

The present value of the two cash flows is computed by discounting at 11% as follows:

ILLUSTRATION 6-21
Computation of the
Present Value of an
Interest-Bearing Bond

1. Present value of the principal: $FV\ (PVF_{5,11\%})$ = $100,000 (.59345)	$59,345.00
2. Present value of the interest payments: $R\ (PVF\text{-}OA_{5,11\%})$ = $9,000 (3.69590)	33,263.10
3. Combined present value (market price)—carrying value of bonds	**$92,608.10**

By paying $92,608.10 at date of issue, the buyers of the bonds will realize an effective yield of 11% over the 5-year term of the bonds. This is true because the cash flows were discounted at 11%.

Effective Interest Method of Amortization of Bond Discount or Premium

In the Alltech Corporation bond issue, Illustration 6-21, the bonds were issued at a discount computed as follows:

Maturity value (face amount) of bonds		$100,000.00
Present value of the principal	$59,345.00	
Present value of the interest	33,263.10	
Proceeds (present value and cash received)		92,608.10
Discount on bonds issued		$ 7,391.90

This discount of $7,391.90 under acceptable accrual accounting is amortized (written off) over the life of the bond issue to interest expense.

The profession's preferred procedure for amortization of a discount or premium is the **effective interest method** (also called **present value amortization**). Under the effective interest method:

❶ Bond interest expense is computed first by multiplying the carrying value of the bonds at the beginning of the period by the effective interest rate.

❷ The bond discount or premium amortization is then determined by comparing the bond interest expense with the interest to be paid.

The computation of the amortization is depicted graphically as follows:

ILLUSTRATION 6-22
Amortization
Computation

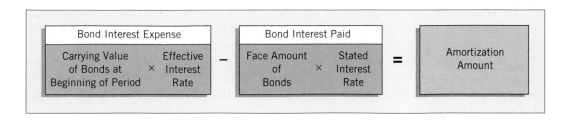

The effective interest method produces a periodic interest expense equal to **a constant percentage of the carrying value of the bonds**. Since the percentage used is the effective rate of interest incurred by the borrower at the time of issuance, the effective interest method results in matching expenses with revenues.

The effective interest method of amortization can be illustrated using the data from the Alltech Corporation example, where $100,000 face value of bonds were issued at a discount of $7,391.90 resulting in a carrying value of $92,608.10. The effective interest amortization schedule is shown in Illustration 6-23:

ILLUSTRATION 6-23
Effective Interest
Amortization Schedule

	Cash Interest Paid	Interest Expense	Bond Discount Amortization	Carrying Value of Bonds
Date				
1/1/98				$ 92,608.10
12/31/98	$9,000[a]	$10,186.89[b]	$1,186.89[c]	93,794.99[d]
12/31/99	9,000	10,317.45	1,317.45	95,112.44
12/31/00	9,000	10,462.37	1,462.37	96,574.81
12/31/01	9,000	10,623.23	1,623.23	98,198.04
12/31/02	9,000	10,801.96	1,801.96	100,000.00
	$45,000	$52,391.90	$7,391.90	

Schedule of Bond Discount Amortization
5-Year, 9% Bonds Sold to Yield 11%

[a]$100,000 × .09 = $9,000
[b]$92,608.10 × .11 = $10,186.89
[c]$10,186.89 − $9,000 = $1,186.89
[d]$92,608.10 + $1,186.89 = $93,794.99

The amortization schedule illustrated above is used for note and bond transactions in Chapters 7 and 14.

SUMMARY OF LEARNING OBJECTIVES

① *Identify accounting topics where the time value of money is relevant.* Some of the applications of present value–based measurements to accounting topics are: (1) notes, (2) leases, (3) amortization of premiums and discounts, (4) pensions and other postretirement benefits, (5) long-term assets, (6) sinking funds, (7) business combinations, (8) disclosures, and (9) installment contracts.

② *Distinguish between simple and compound interest.* See Fundamental Concepts following this Summary.

③ *Learn how to use appropriate compound interest tables.* In order to identify the appropriate compound interest table to use of the five given, you must identify whether you are solving for (1) the future value of a single sum, (2) the present value of a single sum, (3) the future value of a series of sums (an annuity), or (4) the present value of a series of sums (an annuity). In addition, when a series of sums (an annuity) is involved, you must identify whether these sums are received or paid (1) at the beginning of each period (annuity due) or (2) at the end of each period (ordinary annuity).

④ *Identify variables fundamental to solving interest problems.* The following four variables are fundamental to all compound interest problems: (1) *Rate of interest:* unless otherwise stated, an annual rate that must be adjusted to reflect the length of the compounding period if less than a year. (2) *Number of time periods:* the number of compounding periods (a period may be equal to or less than a year). (3) *Future value:* the value at a future date of a given sum or sums invested assuming compound interest. (4) *Present value:* the value now (present time) of a future sum or sums discounted assuming compound interest.

KEY TERMS

annuity, *291*
annuity due, *291*
compound interest, *282*
deferred annuity, *301*
discounting, *286*
effective yield, *284*
face rate, *285*
future value, *286*
interest, *279*
nominal rate, *285*
ordinary annuity, *291*
present value, *287*
principal, *279*
simple interest, *281*
stated rate, *285*
time value of money, *278*

⑤ *Solve future and present value of 1 problems.* See Fundamental Concepts following this Summary, items 5(a) and 6(a).

⑥ *Solve future value of ordinary and annuity due problems.* See Fundamental Concepts following this Summary, item 5(b).

⑦ *Solve present values of ordinary and annuity due problems.* See Fundamental Concepts following this Summary, item 6(b).

❖ FUNDAMENTAL CONCEPTS ❖

❶ *Simple Interest.* Interest on principal only, regardless of interest that may have accrued in the past.

❷ *Compound Interest.* Interest accrues on the unpaid interest of past periods as well as on the principal.

❸ *Rate of Interest.* Interest is usually expressed as an annual rate, but when the interest period is shorter than one year, the interest rate for the shorter period must be determined.

❹ *Annuity.* A series of payments or receipts (called rents) that occur at equal intervals of time.
Types of annuities:
(a) *Ordinary Annuity.* Each rent is payable (receivable) at the end of the period.
(b) *Annuity Due.* Each rent is payable (receivable) at the beginning of the period.

❺ *Future Value.* Value at a later date of a single sum that is invested at compound interest.
(a) *Future Value of 1* (or value of a single sum). The future value of $1.00 (or a single given sum), *FV*, at the end of *n* periods at *i* compound interest rate (Table 6-1).
(b) *Future Value of an Annuity.* The future value of a series of rents invested at compound interest; in other words, the accumulated total that results from a series of equal deposits at regular intervals invested at compound interest. Both deposits and interest increase the accumulation.
(1) *Future Value of an Ordinary Annuity.* The future value on the date of the last rent.
(2) *Future Value of an Annuity Due.* The future value one period after the date of the last rent. When an annuity due table is not available, use Table 6-3 with the following formula:

$$\begin{array}{c} \text{Value of annuity due of 1} \\ \text{for } n \text{ rents} \end{array} = \begin{array}{c} \text{(Value of ordinary annuity for} \\ n \text{ rents)} \times (1 + \text{interest rate).} \end{array}$$

❻ *Present Value.* The value at an earlier date (usually now) of a given future sum discounted at compound interest.
(a) *Present Value of 1* (or present value of a single sum). The present value (worth) of $1.00 (or a given sum), due *n* periods hence, discounted at *i* compound interest (Table 6-2).
(b) *Present Value of an Annuity.* The present value (worth) of a series of rents discounted at compound interest; in other words, it is the sum when invested at compound interest that will permit a series of equal withdrawals at regular intervals.
(1) *Present Value of an Ordinary Annuity.* The value now of $1.00 to be received or paid at the end of each period (rents) for *n* periods, discounted at *i* compound interest (Table 6-4).

> **(2) *Present Value of an Annuity Due.*** The value now of $1.00 to be received or paid at the beginning of each period (rents) for the n periods, discounted at i compound interest (Table 6-5). To use Table 6-4 for an annuity due, apply this formula:
>
> $$\text{Present value of annuity due of 1 for } n \text{ rents} = (\text{Present value of an ordinary annuity of } n \text{ rents}) \times (1 + \text{interest rate}).$$

❖ QUESTIONS ❖

1 What is the time value of money? Why should accountants have an understanding of compound interest, annuities, and present value concepts?

2 What is the nature of interest? Distinguish between "simple interest" and "compound interest."

3 What are the components of an interest rate? Why is it important for accountants to understand these components?

4 Presented are a number of values taken from compound interest tables involving the same number of periods and the same rate of interest. Indicate what each of these four values represent.

(a) 6.71008   (c) .46319
(b) 2.15892   (d) 14.48656

5 Brenda Starr deposited $18,000 in a money market certificate that provides interest of 10% compounded quarterly if the amount is maintained for 3 years. How much will Brenda Starr have at the end of 3 years?

6 Charlie Brown will receive $50,000 on December 31, 2003 (5 years from now) from a trust fund established by his father. Assuming the appropriate interest rate for discounting is 12% (compounded semiannually), what is the present value of this amount today?

7 What are the primary characteristics of an annuity? Differentiate between an "ordinary annuity" and an "annuity due."

8 Linus, Inc. owes $30,000 to Peanuts Company. How much would Linus have to pay each year if the debt is retired through four equal payments (made at the end of the year), given an interest rate on the debt of 12%? (Round to two decimal places.)

9 The Lockhorns are planning for a retirement home. They estimate they will need $160,000, 4 years from now to purchase this home. Assuming an interest rate of 10%, what amount must be deposited at the end of each of the 4 years to fund the home price? (Round to two decimal places.)

10 Assume the same situation as in Question 9, except that the four equal amounts are deposited at the beginning of the period rather than at the end. In this case, what amount must be deposited at the beginning of each period? (Round to two decimals.)

11 Explain how the future value of an ordinary annuity interest table is converted to the future value of an annuity due table.

12 Explain how the present value of an ordinary annuity interest table is converted to the present value of an annuity due interest table.

13 In a book named *Treasure*, the reader has to figure out where a 2.2 pound, 24 kt gold horse has been buried. If the horse is found, a prize of $25,000 a year for 20 years is provided. The actual cost of the publisher to purchase an annuity to pay for the prize is $210,000. What interest rate (to the nearest percent) was used to determine the amount of the annuity? (Assume end-of-year payments.)

14 Greg Norman Enterprises leases property to Tiger Woods, Inc. Because Tiger Woods, Inc. is experiencing financial difficulty, Norman agrees to receive five rents of $10,000 at the end of each year, with the rents deferred 3 years. What is the present value of the five rents discounted at 12%?

15 Answer the following questions:

(a) On May 1, 1998, Liselotte Neumann Company sold some machinery to Tee-off Company on an installment contract basis. The contract required five equal annual payments, with the first payment due on May 1, 1998. What present value concept is appropriate for this situation?

(b) On June 1, 1998, Mike Brisky Inc. purchased a new machine that it does not have to pay for until May 1, 2000. The total payment on May 1, 2000 will include both principal and interest. Assuming interest at a 12% rate, the cost of the machine would be the total payment multiplied by what time value of money concept?

(c) Kelly Gibson Inc. wishes to know how much money it will have available in 5 years if five equal amounts of $35,000 are invested, with the first amount invested immediately. What interest table is appropriate for this situation?

(d) Patty Sheehan invests in a "jumbo" $200,000, 3-year certificate of deposit at First Wisconsin. What table would be used to determine the amount accumulated at the end of 3 years?

16 Recently Vickie Maher was interested in purchasing a Honda Acura. The salesperson indicated that the price of the car was either $27,000 cash or $6,900 at the end of each of 5 years. Compute the effective interest rate to the nearest percent that Vickie would pay if she chooses to make the five annual payments.

17 Recently, property/casualty insurance companies have been criticized because they reserve for the total loss as much as 5 years before it may happen. Recently the IRS has joined the debate because they say the full reserve is unfair from a taxation viewpoint. What do you believe is the IRS position?

❖ BRIEF EXERCISES ❖

BE6-1 Steve Allen invested $10,000 today in a fund that earns 8% compounded annually. To what amount will the investment grow in 3 years? To what amount would the investment grow in 3 years if the fund earns 8% annual interest compounded semiannually?

BE6-2 Itzak Perlman needs $20,000 in 4 years. What amount must he invest today if his investment earns 12% compounded annually? What amount must he invest if his investment earns 12% annual interest compounded quarterly?

BE6-3 Janet Jackson will invest $30,000 today. She needs $222,000 in 21 years. What annual interest rate must she earn?

BE6-4 Dan Webster will invest $10,000 today in a fund that earns 5% annual interest. How many years will it take for the fund to grow to $13,400?

BE6-5 Anne Boleyn will invest $5,000 a year for 20 years in a fund that will earn 12% annual interest. If the first payment into the fund occurs today, what amount will be in the fund in 20 years? If the first payment occurs at year-end, what amount will be in the fund in 20 years?

BE6-6 William Cullen Bryant needs $200,000 in 10 years. How much must he invest at the end of each year, at 11% interest, to meet his needs?

BE6-7 Luther Vandross is investing $12,961 at the end of each year in a fund that earns 10% interest. In how many years will the fund be at $100,000?

BE6-8 Grupo Rana wants to withdraw $20,000 each year for 10 years from a fund that earns 8% interest. How much must he invest today if the first withdrawal is at year-end? How much must he invest today if the first withdrawal takes place immediately?

BE6-9 Mark Twain's VISA balance is $1,124.40. He may pay it off in 18 equal end-of-month payments of $75 each. What interest rate is Mark paying?

BE6-10 Corinne Dunbar is investing $200,000 in a fund that earns 8% interest compounded annually. What equal amounts can Corinne withdraw at the end of each of the next 20 years?

BE6-11 Bayou Inc. will deposit $20,000 in a 12% fund at the end of each year for 8 years beginning December 31, 2002. What amount will be in the fund immediately after the last deposit?

BE6-12 Hollis Stacy wants to create a fund today that will enable her to withdraw $20,000 per year for 8 years, with the first withdrawal to take place 5 years from today. If the fund earns 8% interest, how much must Hollis invest today?

BE6-13 Acadian Inc. issues $1,000,000 of 7% bonds due in 10 years with interest payable at year-end. The current market rate of interest for bonds of similar risk is 8%. What amount will Acadian receive when it issues the bonds?

❖ EXERCISES ❖

(Interest rates are per annum unless otherwise indicated.)

E6-1 (Using Interest Tables) For each of the following cases, indicate (a) to what rate columns and (b) to what number of periods you would refer in looking up the interest factor.

1. In a future value of 1 table

	Annual Rate	Number of Years Invested	Compounded
a.	9%	9	Annually
b.	12%	5	Quarterly
c.	10%	15	Semiannually

2. In a present value of an annuity of 1 table

Annual Rate	Number of Years Involved	Number of Rents Involved	Frequency of Rents
a. 9%	25	25	Annually
b. 10%	15	30	Semiannually
c. 12%	7	28	Quarterly

E6-2 (Simple and Compound Interest Computations) Alan Jackson invests $20,000 at 8% annual interest, leaving the money invested without withdrawing any of the interest for 8 years. At the end of the 8 years, Alan withdrew the accumulated amount of money.

Instructions

(a) Compute the amount Alan would withdraw assuming the investment earns simple interest.

(b) Compute the amount Alan would withdraw assuming the investment earns interest compounded annually.

(c) Compute the amount Alan would withdraw assuming the investment earns interest compounded semiannually.

E6-3 (Computation of Future Values and Present Values) Using the appropriate interest table, answer each of the following questions (each case is independent of the others).

(a) What is the future value of $7,000 at the end of 5 periods at 8% compounded interest?

(b) What is the present value of $7,000 due 8 periods hence, discounted at 11%?

(c) What is the future value of 15 periodic payments of $7,000 each made at the end of each period and compounded at 10%?

(d) What is the present value of $7,000 to be received at the end of each of 20 periods, discounted at 5% compound interest?

E6-4 (Computation of Future Values and Present Values) Using the appropriate interest table, answer the following questions (each case is independent of the others).

(a) What is the future value of 20 periodic payments of $4,000 each made at the beginning of each period and compounded at 8%?

(b) What is the present value of $2,500 to be received at the beginning of each of 30 periods, discounted at 10% compound interest?

(c) What is the future value of 15 deposits of $2,000 each made at the beginning of each period and compounded at 10%? (Future value as of the end of the fifteenth period.)

(d) What is the present value of six receipts of $1,000 each received at the beginning of each period, discounted at 9% compounded interest?

E6-5 (Computation of Present Value) Using the appropriate interest table, compute the present values of the following periodic amounts due at the end of the designated periods.

(a) $30,000 receivable at the end of each period for 8 periods compounded at 12%.

(b) $30,000 payments to be made at the end of each period for 16 periods at 9%.

(c) $30,000 payable at the end of the seventh, eighth, ninth, and tenth periods at 12%.

E6-6 (Future Value and Present Value Problems) Presented below are three unrelated situations:

(a) Horace Grant Company recently signed a lease for a new office building, for a lease period of 10 years. Under the lease agreement, a security deposit of $12,000 is made, with the deposit to be returned at the expiration of the lease, with interest compounded at 10% per year. What amount will the company receive at the time the lease expires?

(b) Sharone Wright Corporation, having recently issued a $20 million, 15-year bond issue, is committed to make annual sinking fund deposits of $600,000. The deposits are made on the last day of each year, and yield a return of 10%. Will the fund at the end of 15 years be sufficient to retire the bonds? If not, what will the deficiency be?

(c) Under the terms of his salary agreement, president Rex Walters has an option of receiving either an immediate bonus of $40,000, or a deferred bonus of $70,000, payable in 10 years. Ignoring tax considerations, and assuming a relevant interest rate of 8%, which form of settlement should Walters accept?

E6-7 (Computation of Bond Prices) What would you pay for a $50,000 debenture bond that matures in 15 years and pays $5,000 a year in interest if you wanted to earn a yield of:

(a) 8%?   (b) 10%?   (c) 12%?

E6-8 (Computations for a Retirement Fund) Clarence Weatherspoon, a super salesman contemplating retirement on his fifty-fifth birthday, decides to create a fund on an 8% basis that will enable him to withdraw $20,000 per year on June 30, beginning in 2003, and continuing through 2006. To develop this fund, Clarence intends to make equal contributions on June 30 of each of the years 1999–2002.

Instructions

    (a) How much must the balance of the fund equal on June 30, 2002, in order for Clarence Weatherspoon to satisfy his objective?

    (b) What are each of Clarence's contributions to the fund?

E6-9 (Unknown Periods and Unknown Interest Rate)   **(a)** Jerry Stackhouse wishes to become a millionaire. His money market fund has a balance of $92,296 and has a guaranteed interest of 10%.

Instructions

How many years must Jerry leave that balance in the fund in order to get his deserved $1,000,000?

    (b) Assume that Russell Maryland desires to accumulate $1 million in 15 years using his money market fund balance of $182,696.

Instructions

At what interest rate must Russell's investment compound annually?

E6-10 (Analysis of Alternatives)   The Black Knights Inc., a manufacturer of high-sugar, low-sodium, low-cholesterol TV dinners, would like to increase its market share in the Sunbelt. In order to do so, Black Knights has decided to locate a new factory in the Panama City area. Black Knights will either buy or lease a site depending upon which is more advantageous. The site location committee has narrowed down the available sites to the following three buildings.

Building A: Purchase for a cash price of $600,000, useful life 25 years.

Building B: Lease for 25 years with annual lease payments of $69,000 being made at the beginning of the year.

Building C: Purchase for $650,000 cash. This building is larger than needed; however, the excess space can be sublet for 25 years at a net annual rental of $7,000. Rental payments will be received at the end of each year. The Black Knights Inc. has no aversion to being a landlord.

Instructions

In which building would you recommend that The Black Knights Inc. locate assuming a 12% cost of funds?

E6-11 (Amount in Trust)   Tim Salmon intends to invest $10,000 in a trust on January 10 of every year, 1999 through 2013. He anticipates that interest rates will change during that period of time as follows:

1/10/99–1/10/02	10%
1/11/02–1/10/09	11%
1/11/09–1/10/13	12%

How much will Tim have in trust on January 10, 2013?

E6-12 (Amount Needed to Retire Stock)   Alexandra Inc. is a computer software development company. In recent years, the company has experienced significant growth in sales. As a result, the board of directors has decided to raise funds by issuing redeemable preferred stock to meet the need for expansion. On January 1, 1997, the company issued 100,000 shares of 12% redeemable preferred stock with the intent to redeem this preferred stock on January 1, 2007. The redemption price per share of preferred stock will be $25.

    As the controller of the company, Al Iskan is asked to set up a plan to accumulate the funds that will be needed to retire the redeemable preferred stock on January 1, 2007. He expects that the company will have a surplus of funds of $125,000 each year for the next 10 years and decides to set up a sinking fund for these funds. Beginning January 1, 1998, the company will deposit $125,000 into the sinking fund annually for 10 years. The sinking fund is expected to generate 10% interest and compound annually. However, the sinking fund will not be sufficient for the redemption of preferred stock. Therefore, Al plans to deposit on January 1, 2002, a single amount of money into a savings account which is expected to earn 9% interest.

Instructions

Help Al Iskan to determine the amount to be deposited on January 1, 2002.

E6-13 (Computation of Bond Liability)   Katarina Witt, Inc. manufactures skating equipment. Recently the Vice President of Operations of the company has requested construction of a new plant to meet the increasing needs for the company's skates. After a careful evaluation of the request, the board of directors has decided to raise funds for the new plant by issuing $2,000,000 of 11% term corporate bonds on March 1, 1997, due on March 1, 2012, with interest payable each March 1 and September 1. At the time of issuance, the market interest rate for similar financial instruments is 10%.

Instructions

As the controller of the company, determine the selling price of the bonds.

E6-14 (Computation of Pension Liability) Nerwin, Inc. is a furniture manufacturing company with 50 employees. Recently, after a long negotiation with the local labor union, the company decided to initiate a pension plan as a part of its compensation plan. The plan will start on January 1, 1998. Each employee covered by the plan is entitled to a pension payment each year after retirement. As required by accounting standards, the controller of the company needs to report the pension obligation (liability). On the basis of a discussion with the supervisor of the Personnel Department and an actuary from an insurance company, the controller develops the following information related to the pension plan:

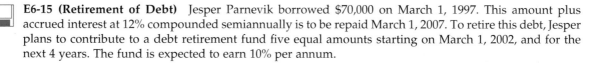

Average length of time to retirement	15 years
Expected life duration after retirement	10 years
Total pension payment expected each year after retirement for all employees. Payment made at the end of the year.	$700,000 per year

The interest rate to be used is 8%.

Instructions

On the basis of the information above, determine the present value of the pension obligation (liability).

E6-15 (Retirement of Debt) Jesper Parnevik borrowed $70,000 on March 1, 1997. This amount plus accrued interest at 12% compounded semiannually is to be repaid March 1, 2007. To retire this debt, Jesper plans to contribute to a debt retirement fund five equal amounts starting on March 1, 2002, and for the next 4 years. The fund is expected to earn 10% per annum.

Instructions

How much must be contributed each year by Jesper Parnevik to provide a fund sufficient to retire the debt on March 1, 2007?

E6-16 (Computation of Bond Liability) Your client, Faith Hill, Inc., has acquired Tracy Lawrence Manufacturing Company in a business combination that is to be accounted for as a purchase transaction (at fair market value). Along with the assets and business of Tracy Lawrence, Faith Hill assumed an outstanding debenture bond issue having a principal amount of $8,000,000 with interest payable semiannually at a stated rate of 8%. Tracy Lawrence received $7,300,000 in proceeds from the issuance 5 years ago. The bonds are currently 20 years from maturity. Equivalent securities command a 12% rate of interest, interest paid semiannually.

Instructions

Your client requests your advice regarding the amount to record for the acquired bond issue.

E6-17 (Computation of Amount of Rentals) Your client, Vince Gill Leasing Company, is preparing a contract to lease a machine to Souvenirs Corporation for a period of 25 years. Gill has an investment cost of $365,755 in the machine, which has a useful life of 25 years and no salvage value at the end of that time. Your client is interested in earning an 11% return on its investment and has agreed to accept 25 equal rental payments at the end of each of the next 25 years.

Instructions

You are requested to provide Gill with the amount of each of the 25 rentals that will yield an 11% return on investment.

E6-18 (Least Costly Payoff) Sonic Hedgehog Corporation has outstanding a contractual debt. The corporation has available two means of settlement: It can either make immediate payment of $2,600,000, or it can make annual payments of $300,000 for 15 years, each payment due on the last day of the year.

Instructions

Which method of payment do you recommend, assuming an expected effective interest rate of 8% during the future period?

E6-19 (Least Costly Payoff) Assuming the same facts as those in Exercise 6–18 except that the payments must begin now and be made on the first day of each of the 15 years, what payment method would you recommend?

(To solve Exercises 6-20, 6-21, and 6-22, a calculator is needed.)

E6-20 (Determine Interest Rate) Reba McEntire wishes to invest $19,000 on July 1, 1998, and have it accumulate to $49,000 by July 1, 2008.

Instructions

At what exact annual rate of interest must Reba invest the $19,000?

E6-21 (Determine Interest Rate) On July 17, 1997, Tim McGraw borrowed $42,000 from his grandfather to open a clothing store. Starting July 17, 1998, Tim has to make ten equal annual payments of $6,500 each to repay the loan.

Instructions

What interest rate is Tim paying?

E6-22 (Determine Interest Rate) As the purchaser of a new house, Patty Loveless has signed a mortgage note to pay the Memphis National Bank and Trust Co. $14,000 every 6 months for 20 years, at the end of which time she will own the house. At the date the mortgage is signed the purchase price was $198,000, and a down payment of $20,000 was made. The first payment will be made 6 months after the date the mortgage is signed.

Instructions

Compute the exact rate of interest earned on the mortgage by the bank.

❖ PROBLEMS ❖

(Interest rates are per annum unless otherwise indicated.)

P6-1 (Computation of Present Value) Answer each of these unrelated questions.

1. On January 1, 1998, Rather Corporation sold a building that cost $250,000 and that had accumulated depreciation of $100,000 on the date of sale. Rather received as consideration a $275,000 noninterest-bearing note due on January 1, 2001. There was no established exchange price for the building, and the note had no ready market. The prevailing rate of interest for a note of this type on January 1, 1998, was 9%. At what amount should the gain from the sale of the building be reported?

2. On January 1, 1998, Rather Corporation purchased 200 of the $1,000 face value, 9%, 10-year bonds of Walters Inc. The bonds mature on January 1, 2008, and pay interest annually beginning January 1, 1999. Rather Corporation purchased the bonds to yield 11%. How much did Rather pay for the bonds?

3. Rather Corporation bought a new machine and agreed to pay for it in equal annual installments of $4,000 at the end of each of the next 10 years. Assuming that a prevailing interest rate of 8% applies to this contract, how much should Rather record as the cost of the machine?

4. Rather Corporation purchased a special tractor on December 31, 1998. The purchase agreement stipulated that Rather should pay $20,000 at the time of purchase and $5,000 at the end of each of the next 8 years. The tractor should be recorded on December 31, 1998, at what amount, assuming an appropriate interest rate of 12%?

5. Rather Corporation wants to withdraw $100,000 (including principal) from an investment fund at the end of each year for 9 years. What should be the required initial investment at the beginning of the first year if the fund earns 11%?

P6-2 (Computation of Unknown Interest Factors) Using the appropriate interest table, provide the solution to each of the following four questions by computing the unknowns.

(a) What is the amount of the payments that Tom Brokaw must make at the end of each of 8 years to accumulate a fund of $70,000 by the end of the eighth year, if the fund earns 8% interest, compounded annually?

(b) Peter Jennings is 40 years old today and he wishes to accumulate $500,000 by his sixty-fifth birthday so he can retire to his summer place on Lake Hopatcong. He wishes to accumulate this amount by making equal deposits on his fortieth through his sixty-fourth birthdays. What annual deposit must Peter make if the fund will earn 12% interest compounded annually?

(c) Jane Pauley has $20,000 to invest today at 9% to pay a debt of $56,253. How many years will it take her to accumulate enough to liquidate the debt?

(d) Maria Shriver has a $27,600 debt that she wishes to repay 4 years from today; she has $18,181 that she intends to invest for the 4 years. What rate of interest will she need to earn annually in order to accumulate enough to pay the debt?

P6-3 (Future Values of Annuities Due) Mack Aroni, a bank robber, is worried about his retirement. He decides to start a savings account. Mack deposits annually his net share of the "loot," which consists of $75,000 per year, for 3 years beginning January 1, 1994. Mack is arrested on January 4, 1996, (after making the third deposit) and spends the rest of 1996 and most of 1997 in jail. He escapes in September of 1997. He resumes his savings plan with semiannual deposits of $30,000 each beginning January 1, 1998. Assume that the bank's interest rate was 9% compounded annually from January 1, 1994, through January 1, 1997, and 12% annual rate compounded semiannually thereafter.

Instructions

When Mack retires on January 1, 2001 (6 months after his last deposit), what is the balance in his savings account?

P6-4 (Analysis of Alternatives) Derrick Coleman Inc., has decided to surface and maintain for 10 years a vacant lot next to one of its discount-retail outlets to serve as a parking lot for customers. Management is considering the following bids involving two different qualities of surfacing for a parking area of 12,000 square yards:

Bid A: A surface that costs $5.25 per square yard to install. This surface will have to be replaced at the end of 5 years. The annual maintenance cost on this surface is estimated at 20 cents per square yard for each year but the last year of its service. The replacement surface will be similar to the initial surface.

Bid B: A surface that costs $9.50 per square yard to install. This surface has a probable useful life of 10 years and will require annual maintenance in each year except the last year, at an estimated cost of 9 cents per square yard.

Instructions

Prepare computations showing which bid should be accepted by Derrick Coleman Inc. You may assume that the cost of capital is 9%, that the annual maintenance expenditures are incurred at the end of each year, and that prices are not expected to change during the next 10 years.

P6-5 (Computation of Unknown Interest Factors) Solve for the unknowns in each of the following three situations using the interest tables.

    (a) Mr. and Mrs. Scott Williams have decided to provide for their handicapped son by investing $187,400 today in an annuity at 8% interest, compounded annually. They feel their son should receive approximately $20,000 per year beginning one year from today. The investment of the $187,400 will provide approximately $20,000 per year for how many years before being depleted?

    (b) Chris Webber wishes to invest $150,000 today to ensure $18,610 payments to his son at the end of each year for the next 15 years. At what approximate interest rate must the $150,000 be invested?

    (c) On June 1, 1998, Cheryl Miller purchases 20 acres of farmland from her neighbor, Juwann Howard, and agrees to pay the purchase price in five payments of $21,000 each, the first payment to be payable June 1, 2002 (Assume interest compounded annually at the rate of 9% is implicit in the payments.) What is the purchase price of the 20 acres?

P6-6 (Analysis of Alternatives) Sally Brown died, leaving to her husband Linus an insurance policy contract that provides that the beneficiary (Linus) can choose any one of the following four options.

    (a) $55,000 immediate cash.

    (b) $3,700 every 3 months payable at the end of each quarter for 5 years.

    (c) $18,000 immediate cash and $1,600 every 3 months for 10 years, payable at the beginning of each 3-month period.

    (d) $4,000 every 3 months for 3 years and $1,200 each quarter for the following 25 quarters, all payments payable at the end of each quarter.

Instructions

If money is worth 2½% per quarter, compounded quarterly, which option would you recommend that Linus exercise?

P6-7 (Computation of Unknown Payments) Provide a solution to each of the following situations by computing the unknowns (use the interest tables).

    (a) Laura Davies invests in a $180,000 annuity insurance policy at 9% compounded annually on February 8, 1999. The first of 20 receipts from the annuity is payable to Laura 10 years after the annuity is purchased, or on February 8, 2009. What will be the amount of each of the 20 equal annual receipts?

    (b) Jim Harbaugh owes a debt of $30,000 from the purchase of his new sports car. The debt bears interest of 8% payable annually. Jim wishes to pay the debt and interest in eight annual installments, beginning one year hence. What equal annual installments will pay the debt and interest?

    (c) On January 1, 1999, Neil O'Donnel offers to buy Scott Mitchell's used combine for $45,000, payable in 10 equal installments, which are to include 9% interest on the unpaid balance and a portion of the principal with the first payment to be made on January 1, 1999. How much will each payment be?

P6-8 (Purchase Price of a Business (Deferred Annuities)) During the past year, Nicole Bobek planted a new vineyard on 150 acres of land that she leases for $27,000 a year. She has asked you as her accountant to assist her in determining the value of her vineyard operation.

The vineyard will bear no grapes for the first 5 years (1–5). In the next 5 years (6–10), Nicole estimates that the vines will bear grapes that can be sold for $60,000 each year. For the next 20 years (11–30) she expects the harvest will provide annual revenues of $100,000. But during the last 10 years (31–40) of the vineyard's life she estimates that revenues will decline to $80,000 per year.

During the first 5 years the annual cost of pruning, fertilizing, and caring for the vineyard is estimated at $9,000; during the years of production, 6–40, these costs will rise to $10,000 per year. The relevant market rate of interest for the entire period is 12%. Assume that all receipts and payments are made at the end of each year.

Instructions

Dick Button has offered to buy Nicole's vineyard business by assuming the 40-year lease. On the basis of the current value of the business what is the minimum price Nicole should accept?

P6-9 (Annuity with Varying Interest Rates) Mrs. Paul plans to establish an annuity arrangement whereby her four children would each receive $3,700 on December 25 of the years 2001 to 2015, inclusive. Variations in the interest rates during that period of time are estimated as follows:

12/26/00–12/25/05	12%
12/26/05–12/25/11	11%
12/26/11–12/25/15	9%

Instructions

Compute the amount that Mrs. Paul must invest on December 26, 2000, to assure these annual payments to her children.

P6-10 (Time Value Concepts Applied to Solve Business Problems) Answer the following questions related to Mark Grace Inc.

1. Mark Grace Inc. has $572,000 to invest. The company is trying to decide between two alternative uses of the funds. One alternative provides $80,000 at the end of each year for 12 years, and the other is to receive a single lump sum payment of $1,900,000 at the end of the 12 years. Which alternative should Grace select? Assume the interest rate is constant over the entire investment.
2. Mark Grace Inc. has completed the purchase of a new IBM computer. The fair market value of the equipment is $824,150. The purchase agreement specifies an immediate down payment of $200,000 and semiannual payments of $76,952 beginning at the end of 6 months for 5 years. What is the interest rate, to the nearest percent, used in discounting this purchase transaction?
3. Mark Grace Inc. loans money to John Kruk Corporation in the amount of $600,000. Grace accepts an 8% note due in 7 years with interest payable semiannually. After 2 years (and receipt of interest for 2 years), Grace needs money and therefore sells the note to Chicago National Bank, which demands interest on the note of 10% compounded semiannually. What is the amount Grace will receive on the sale of the note?
4. Mark Grace Inc. wishes to accumulate $1,300,000 by December 31, 2008, to retire bonds outstanding. The company deposits $300,000 on December 31, 1998, which will earn interest at 10% compounded quarterly, to help in the retirement of this debt. In addition, the company wants to know how much should be deposited at the end of each quarter for 10 years to ensure that $1,300,000 is available at the end of 2008. (The quarterly deposits will also earn at a rate of 10%, compounded quarterly.) Round to even dollars.

P6-11 (Analysis of Alternatives) Homer Simpson Inc., a manufacturer of steel school lockers, plans to purchase a new punch press for use in its manufacturing process. After contacting the appropriate vendors, the purchasing department received differing terms and options from each vendor. The Engineering Department has determined that each vendor's punch press is substantially identical and each has a useful life of 20 years. In addition, Engineering has estimated that required year-end maintenance costs will be $1,000 per year for the first 5 years, $2,000 per year for the next 10 years, and $3,000 per year for the last 5 years. Following is each vendor's sale package.

Vendor A: $45,000 cash at time of delivery and 10 year-end payments of $15,000 each. Vendor A offers all its customers the right to purchase at the time of sale a separate 20-year maintenance service contract under which Vendor A will perform all year-end maintenance at a one-time initial cost of $10,000.

Vendor B: Forty semiannual payments of $8,000 each with the first installment due upon delivery. Vendor B will perform all year-end maintenance for the next 20 years at no extra charge.

Vendor C: Full cash price of $125,000 will be due upon delivery.

Instructions

Assuming that both Vendor A and B will be able to perform the required year-end maintenance, that Simpson's cost of funds is 10%, and the machine will be purchased on January 1, from which vendor should the press be purchased?

P6-12 (Analysis of Business Problems)   Jean-Luc is a financial executive with Starship Enterprises. Although Jean-Luc has not had any formal training in finance or accounting, he has a "good sense" for numbers and has helped the company grow from a very small company ($500,000 sales) to a large operation ($45 million in sales). With the business growing steadily, however, the company needs to make a number of difficult financial decisions in which Jean-Luc feels a little "over his head." He therefore has decided to hire a new employee with facility in "numbers" to help him. As a basis for determining whom to employ, he has decided to ask each prospective employee to prepare answers to questions relating to the following situations he has encountered recently. Here are the questions.

1. In 1996, Starship Enterprises negotiated and closed a long-term lease contract for newly constructed truck terminals and freight storage facilities. The buildings were constructed on land owned by the company. On January 1, 1997, Starship took possession of the leased property. The 20-year lease is effective for the period January 1, 1997, through December 31, 2016. Advance rental payments of $800,000 are payable to the lessor (owner of facilities) on January 1 of each of the first 10 years of the lease term. Advance payments of $300,000 are due on January 1 for each of the last 10 years of the lease term. Starship has an option to purchase all the leased facilities for $1.00 on December 31, 2016. At the time the lease was negotiated, the fair market value of the truck terminals and freight storage facilities was approximately $7,200,000. If the company had borrowed the money to purchase the facilities, it would have to pay 10% interest. Should the company have purchased rather than leased the facilities?

2. Last year the company exchanged a piece of land for a noninterest-bearing note. The note is to be paid at the rate of $12,000 per year for 9 years, beginning one year from the date of disposal of the land. An appropriate rate of interest for the note was 11%. At the time the land was originally purchased, it cost $90,000. What is the fair value of the note?

3. The company has always followed the policy to take any cash discounts on goods purchased. Recently the company purchased a large amount of raw materials at a price of $800,000 with terms 2/10, n/30 on which it took the discount. Starship has recently estimated its cost of funds at 10%. Should Starship continue this policy of always taking the cash discount?

P6-13 (Analysis of Various Business Problems)   Bela Koroly has had a difficult year as controller for Pommel Inc. The company lost a considerable amount of money this year, and now the Board of Directors has decided to hire a management consulting team to review the major financial decisions made over the last 3 years. As controller, Koroly has been asked by the board to highlight the three major financial decisions over the last 2 years, and indicate what decisions the company made.

1. During this period, the company had to decide to replace its old equipment in the plant with automated equipment. A schedule relating to pertinent information about the old equipment and automated equipment is as follows:

	Old Equipment	Automated Equipment
Original cost (new)	$2,800,000	$2,000,000
Accumulated depreciation to date	100,000	—
Current salvage value	50,000	—
Estimated cost savings each year over old equipment (Assume that cost savings occur at the end of each year.)	—	500,000
Remaining useful life	6 years	6 years
Salvage value at end of 6 years	—	—

Pommel Inc. decided to continue using the old equipment. Its cost of funds was 10%.

2. During this period, the company had $25,000,000 to invest. The company had two principal alternatives for the use of investment funds. These alternatives are provided below.

	Project I Investment	Project II Investment
Required investment	$25,000,000	$25,000,000
Annual cash inflows (Assume they will be received at the end of each year.)	9,000,000	
Cash inflows at the end of the 9th year		90,000,000
Life of the project	9 years	9 years

Pommel decided to invest its funds in Project I. The cost of funds is 10%.

3. Pommel has 400 employees. At the end of each year, it has given a bonus to its employees based on their productivity. The total bonus in a year is approximately $1 million. A number of the employees indicated that they would prefer a pension plan rather than a bonus payment each year because they have a tendency to spend the bonus immediately. Pertinent data related to a bonus plan versus

a pension plan are provided below:

	Bonus Plan	Pension Plan
Number of employees	400	400
Length of time to retirement	15 years	15 years
Expected life duration after retirement	—	12 years
Bonus payment expected until retirement (paid at end of year)	$1,000,000/year	—
Pension payment expected at retirement (to be paid at the beginning of each year, starting at the beginning of the 16th year)	—	$3,200,000/year

The cost of funds in this case is assumed to be 10%. The company decided to go with the pension plan.

Instructions

Assuming that you are one of the management consultants working for the board of directors, would you agree with these decisions?

P6-14 (Analysis of Lease vs. Purchase)   Jose Rijo Inc. owns and operates a number of hardware stores in the New England region. Recently the company has decided to locate another store in a rapidly growing area of Maryland; the company is trying to decide whether to purchase or lease the building and related facilities.

Purchase: The company can purchase the site, construct the building, and purchase all store fixtures. The cost would be $1,650,000. An immediate down payment of $400,000 is required, and the remaining $1,250,000 would be paid off over 5 years at $300,000 per year (including interest). The property is expected to have a useful life of 12 years and then it will be sold for $500,000. As the owner of the property, the company will have the following out-of-pocket expenses each period:

Property taxes (to be paid at the end of each year)	$40,000
Insurance (to be paid at the beginning of each year)	27,000
Other (primarily maintenance which occurs at the end of each year)	16,000
	$83,000

Lease: First National Bank has agreed to purchase the site, construct the building, and install the appropriate fixtures for Rijo Inc. if Rijo will lease the completed facility for 12 years. The annual costs for the lease would be $240,000. Rijo would have no responsibility related to the facility over the 12 years. The terms of the lease are that Rijo would be required to make 12 annual payments (the first payment to be made at the time the store opens and then each following year). In addition, a deposit of $100,000 is required when the store is opened which will be returned at the end of the twelfth year, assuming no unusual damage to the building structure or fixtures.

Currently the cost of funds for Rijo Inc. is 10%.

Instructions

Which of the two approaches should Rijo Inc. follow?

P6-15 (Business Problems)   Presented below are a series of time value of money problems. Solve each of them.

(a) Your client, Kate Janeway, wishes to provide for the payment of an obligation of $250,000 due on July 1, 2004. Kate plans to deposit $20,000 in a special fund each July 1 for 8 years, starting July 1, 1997. She also wishes to make a deposit on July 1, 1996, of an amount which, with its accumulated interest, will bring the fund up to $250,000 at the maturity of the obligation. She expects that the fund will earn interest at the rate of 4% compounded annually. Compute the amount to be deposited on July 1, 1996.

(b) Many employers establish pension plans for their employees. Accountants are often required to determine the present value of pension obligations for financial reporting. To illustrate, assume that on January 1, 1996, Tuvok Corporation initiated a pension plan under which each of its employees would receive a pension annuity of $10,000 per year beginning one year after retirement and continuing until death. Employee A will retire at the end of 2002 and, according to mortality tables, is expected to live long enough to receive eight pension payments. What is the present value of Tuvok Corporation's pension obligation for employee A at the beginning of 1996 if the interest rate is 10%?

(c) Neelix Company purchases bonds from Ocampa Corporation in the amount of $500,000. The bonds are 10-year, 12% bonds that pay interest semiannually. After 3 years (and receipt of interest for 3 years), Neelix needs money and, therefore, sells the bonds to Nystrum Company, which demands interest at 16% compounded semiannually. What is the amount that Neelix will receive on the sale of the bonds?

❖ **USING YOUR JUDGMENT** ❖

❖ FINANCIAL REPORTING PROBLEM—INTEL CORPORATION

The financial statements and accompanying notes of Intel Corp. are presented in Appendix 5B.

Instructions

1. Examining each item in Intel's balance sheet, identify those items that require present value, discounting, or interest computations in establishing the amount reported. (The accompanying notes are an additional source for this information.)
2. What interest rates are disclosed by Intel as being used to compute interest and present values? Why are there so many different interest rates applied to Intel's financial statement elements (assets, liabilities, revenues, and expenses)?

❖ FINANCIAL STATEMENT ANALYSIS CASE

Consolidated Natural Gas Company

Consolidated Natural Gas Company (CNG), with corporate headquarters in Pittsburgh, Pennsylvania, is one of the largest producers, transporters, distributors, and marketers of natural gas in North America.

During 1996, the company experienced a decrease in the value of its gas and oil producing properties, and a special charge to income was recorded in order to reduce the carrying value of those assets. The company also wrote down the cost of its undeveloped coal properties to their estimated value.

In addition, special charges were incurred for severance pay and early retirement incentives as CNG reduced its workforce.

Assume the following information: In 1995, CNG estimated the cash inflows from its oil and gas producing properties to be $350,000 per year. During 1996, the write-downs described above caused the estimate to be decreased to $275,000 per year. Production costs (cash outflows) associated with all these properties were estimated to be $125,000 per year in 1995, but this amount was revised to $175,000 per year in 1996.

Instructions

(Assume that all cash flows occur at the end of the year.)

(a) Calculate the present value of net cash flows for 1995–1997 (three years) using the 1995 estimates, and a 10% discount factor.
(b) Calculate the present value of net cash flows for 1996–1998 (three years) using the 1996 estimates, and a 10% discount factor.
(c) Compare the results using the two estimates. Is information on future cash flows from oil and gas producing properties useful, considering that the estimates must be revised each year? Explain.

❖ RESEARCH CASES

Case 1

To access the Internet and EDGAR, follow the steps outlined in Research Case 1 on page 272.

Firms registered with the U.S. Securities and Exchange Commission (SEC) are required to file an annual report on Form 10-K within 90 days of their fiscal year end. The Form 10-K includes certain information not provided in a firm's annual report to shareholders.

Instructions

Examine the most recent Form 10-K of a company of your choice and answer the following questions.

(a) Each 10-K is required to include information regarding several aspects of a firm, referenced by item numbers. Identify the 14 items included in the 10-K.

(b) Each 10-K must include the firm's financial statements. Does the 10-K you examined include the firm's financial statements? If not, how did the firm comply with the financial statement requirement?

(c) What financial statement schedules are included with the 10-K you examined?

Case 2

The May 1996 issue of the *Journal of Accountancy* includes an article by Paul Miller and Paul Bahnson entitled "Four Steps to Useful Present Values."

Instructions

Read the article and answer the following questions.

(a) Present value techniques are designed to understand the relationship between what two observed facts?

(b) According to the authors, present value measurements for financial reporting are useful only if they follow four steps. Identify these four steps.

(c) What are the authors' recommendations regarding present value measurements?

❖ WRITING ASSIGNMENT

Assume that you are the chief financial officer of the Orlando Magic basketball organization. You have been involved in contracting to sign Anfernee "Penny" Hardaway. You have devised the following 13-year guaranteed contract which Hardaway is willing to sign.

Salary: To accommodate salary-cap rules, Hardaway will get $1.24 million in the slot vacated by traded Brian Williams this year. In fact, Hardaway received the payment in lump sum upon signing. The salary will increase the maximum 30% a year under NBA rules for the next 12 years.

Line of credit: He can borrow $2 million this year from the Magic. In following years, he can borrow 36% more a year up to a total of $20 million. He must repay the money at the end of the contract.

Floating option: After any year in which he reaches one of 12 personal and/or team goals, he can become a restricted free agent.

A year-by-year breakdown:

Year	Salary +30%	Credit +36%	Total[1]
1993–94	$ 1.244	$ 2.000	$ 3.244
1994–95	1.617	2.720	4.337
1995–96	1.990	3.440	5.430
1996–97	2.363	4.160	6.523
1997–98	2.736	4.880	7.616
1998–99	3.109	2.800	5.909
'99–2000	3.483	—	3.483
2000–01	3.856	—	3.856
2001–02	4.229	—	4.229
2002–03	4.602	—	4.602
2003–04	4.975	—	4.975
2004–05	5.348	—	5.348
2005–06	5.722	—	5.722
Total	**$45.274**	**$20.000**	**$65.274**

[1]Figures in millions (rounded to nearest thousand)

Instructions

The newspapers are reporting that the cost to the Magic is approximately $65 million. Some Board members are wondering where the club is getting $65 million to sign Hardaway.

Write a letter to members of the Board of Directors of the Orlando Magic explaining the financial arrangement and details of the contract. In your letter, be sure to include what you believe to be the real cost to the club for this contract.

❖ GROUP ASSIGNMENT

Your group has been hired as benefit consultants by Maugarite Alomar, the owner of Attic Angels. She wants to establish a retirement plan for herself and her three employees. Maugarite has provided the following information:

> The retirement plan is to be based upon annual salary for the last year before retirement and is to provide 50% of Maugarite's last year annual salary and 40% of the last year annual salary for each employee. The plan will make annual payments at the beginning of each year for 20 years from the date of retirement. Maugarite wishes to fund the plan by making 15 annual deposits beginning January 1, 1998. Invested funds will earn 12% compounded annually. Information about plan participants as of January 1, 1998, is as follows:

> Maugarite Alomar, owner, current annual salary of $40,000, estimated retirement date January 1, 2023.

> Kenny Rogers, flower arranger, current annual salary of $30,000, estimated retirement date January 1, 2028.

> Anita Baker, sales clerk, current annual salary of $15,000, estimated retirement date January 1, 2018.

> Willie Nelson, part-time bookkeeper, current annual salary of $15,000, estimated retirement date January 1, 2013.

> In the past, Maugarite has given herself and each employee a year-end salary increase of 4%. Maugarite plans to continue this policy in the future.

Instructions
Your instructor will identify one member of the group to serve as a recorder and one member to serve as spokesperson. As a group, provide the information for the recorder to prepare responses to the following three requirements. Upon completion of each requirement and before moving on to the next part, the spokesperson will report the group findings to the class.

(a) Based upon the above information, what will be the annual retirement benefit for each plan participant? (Round to the nearest dollar.) (Hint: Maugarite will receive raises for 24 years.)

(b) What amount must be on deposit at the end of 15 years to ensure that all benefits will be paid? (Round to the nearest dollar.)

(c) What is the amount of each annual deposit Maugarite must make to the retirement plan?

❖ ETHICS CASE

James Qualls, newly appointed controller of KBS, is considering ways to reduce his company's expenditures on annual pension costs. One way to do this is to switch KBS's pension fund assets from First Security to NET Life. KBS is a very well-respected computer manufacturer that recently has experienced a sharp decline in its financial performance for the first time in its 25-year history. Despite financial problems, KBS still is committed to providing its employees with good pension and postretirement health benefits.

   Under its present plan with First Security, KBS is obligated to pay $43 million to meet the expected value of future pension benefits that are payable to employees as an annuity upon their retirement from the company. On the other hand, NET Life requires KBS to pay only $35 million for identical future pension benefits. First Security is one of the oldest and most reputable insurance companies in North America. NET Life has a much weaker reputation in the insurance industry. In pondering the significant difference in annual pension costs, Qualls asks himself, "Is this too good to be true?"

Instructions
Answer the followimg questions:

(a) Why might NET Life's pension cost requirement be $8 million less than First Security's requirement for the same future value?

(b) What ethical issues should James Qualls consider before switching KBS's pension fund assets?

(c) Who are the stakeholders that could be affected by Qualls's decision?

TABLE 6-1   FUTURE VALUE OF 1 (FUTURE VALUE OF A SINGLE SUM)

$$FVF_{n,i} = (1 + i)^n$$

(n) Periods	2%	2½%	3%	4%	5%	6%
1	1.02000	1.02500	1.03000	1.04000	1.05000	1.06000
2	1.04040	1.05063	1.06090	1.08160	1.10250	1.12360
3	1.06121	1.07689	1.09273	1.12486	1.15763	1.19102
4	1.08243	1.10381	1.12551	1.16986	1.21551	1.26248
5	1.10408	1.13141	1.15927	1.21665	1.27628	1.33823
6	1.12616	1.15969	1.19405	1.26532	1.34010	1.41852
7	1.14869	1.18869	1.22987	1.31593	1.40710	1.50363
8	1.17166	1.21840	1.26677	1.36857	1.47746	1.59385
9	1.19509	1.24886	1.30477	1.42331	1.55133	1.68948
10	1.21899	1.28008	1.34392	1.48024	1.62889	1.79085
11	1.24337	1.31209	1.38423	1.53945	1.71034	1.89830
12	1.26824	1.34489	1.42576	1.60103	1.79586	2.01220
13	1.29361	1.37851	1.46853	1.66507	1.88565	2.13293
14	1.31948	1.41297	1.51259	1.73168	1.97993	2.26090
15	1.34587	1.44830	1.55797	1.80094	2.07893	2.39656
16	1.37279	1.48451	1.60471	1.87298	2.18287	2.54035
17	1.40024	1.52162	1.65285	1.94790	2.29202	2.69277
18	1.42825	1.55966	1.70243	2.02582	2.40662	2.85434
19	1.45681	1.59865	1.75351	2.10685	2.52695	3.02560
20	1.48595	1.63862	1.80611	2.19112	2.65330	3.20714
21	1.51567	1.67958	1.86029	2.27877	2.78596	3.39956
22	1.54598	1.72157	1.91610	2.36992	2.92526	3.60354
23	1.57690	1.76461	1.97359	2.46472	3.07152	3.81975
24	1.60844	1.80873	2.03279	2.56330	3.22510	4.04893
25	1.64061	1.85394	2.09378	2.66584	3.38635	4.29187
26	1.67342	1.90029	2.15659	2.77247	3.55567	4.54938
27	1.70689	1.94780	2.22129	2.88337	3.73346	4.82235
28	1.74102	1.99650	2.28793	2.99870	3.92013	5.11169
29	1.77584	2.04641	2.35657	3.11865	4.11614	5.41839
30	1.81136	2.09757	2.42726	3.24340	4.32194	5.74349
31	1.84759	2.15001	2.50008	3.37313	4.53804	6.08810
32	1.88454	2.20376	2.57508	3.50806	4.76494	6.45339
33	1.92223	2.25885	2.65234	3.64838	5.00319	6.84059
34	1.96068	2.31532	2.73191	3.79432	5.25335	7.25103
35	1.99989	2.37321	2.81386	3.94609	5.51602	7.68609
36	2.03989	2.43254	2.89828	4.10393	5.79182	8.14725
37	2.08069	2.49335	2.98523	4.26809	6.08141	8.63609
38	2.12230	2.55568	3.07478	4.43881	6.38548	9.15425
39	2.16474	2.61957	3.16703	4.61637	6.70475	9.70351
40	2.20804	2.68506	3.26204	4.80102	7.03999	10.28572

TABLE 6-1 FUTURE VALUE OF 1

8%	9%	10%	11%	12%	15%	(n) Periods
1.08000	1.09000	1.10000	1.11000	1.12000	1.15000	1
1.16640	1.18810	1.21000	1.23210	1.25440	1.32250	2
1.25971	1.29503	1.33100	1.36763	1.40493	1.52088	3
1.36049	1.41158	1.46410	1.51807	1.57352	1.74901	4
1.46933	1.53862	1.61051	1.68506	1.76234	2.01136	5
1.58687	1.67710	1.77156	1.87041	1.97382	2.31306	6
1.71382	1.82804	1.94872	2.07616	2.21068	2.66002	7
1.85093	1.99256	2.14359	2.30454	2.47596	3.05902	8
1.99900	2.17189	2.35795	2.55803	2.77308	3.51788	9
2.15892	2.36736	2.59374	2.83942	3.10585	4.04556	10
2.33164	2.58043	2.85312	3.15176	3.47855	4.65239	11
2.51817	2.81267	3.13843	3.49845	3.89598	5.35025	12
2.71962	3.06581	3.45227	3.88328	4.36349	6.15279	13
2.93719	3.34173	3.79750	4.31044	4.88711	7.07571	14
3.17217	3.64248	4.17725	4.78459	5.47357	8.13706	15
3.42594	3.97031	4.59497	5.31089	6.13039	9.35762	16
3.70002	4.32763	5.05447	5.89509	6.86604	10.76126	17
3.99602	4.71712	5.55992	6.54355	7.68997	12.37545	18
4.31570	5.14166	6.11591	7.26334	8.61276	14.23177	19
4.66096	5.60441	6.72750	8.06231	9.64629	16.36654	20
5.03383	6.10881	7.40025	8.94917	10.80385	18.82152	21
5.43654	6.65860	8.14028	9.93357	12.10031	21.64475	22
5.87146	7.25787	8.95430	11.02627	13.55235	24.89146	23
6.34118	7.91108	9.84973	12.23916	15.17863	28.62518	24
6.84847	8.62308	10.83471	13.58546	17.00000	32.91895	25
7.39635	9.39916	11.91818	15.07986	19.04007	37.85680	26
7.98806	10.24508	13.10999	16.73865	21.32488	43.53532	27
8.62711	11.16714	14.42099	18.57990	23.88387	50.06561	28
9.31727	12.17218	15.86309	20.62369	26.74993	57.57545	29
10.06266	13.26768	17.44940	22.89230	29.95992	66.21177	30
10.86767	14.46177	19.19434	25.41045	33.55511	76.14354	31
11.73708	15.76333	21.11378	28.20560	37.58173	87.56507	32
12.67605	17.18203	23.22515	31.30821	42.09153	100.69983	33
13.69013	18.72841	25.54767	34.75212	47.14252	115.80480	34
14.78534	20.41397	28.10244	38.57485	52.79962	133.17552	35
15.96817	22.25123	30.91268	42.81808	59.13557	153.15185	36
17.24563	24.25384	34.00395	47.52807	66.23184	176.12463	37
18.62528	26.43668	37.40434	52.75616	74.17966	202.54332	38
20.11530	28.81598	41.14479	58.55934	83.08122	232.92482	39
21.72452	31.40942	45.25926	65.00087	93.05097	267.86355	40

TABLE 6-2   PRESENT VALUE OF 1 (PRESENT VALUE OF A SINGLE SUM)

$$PVF_{n,i} = \frac{1}{(1 + i)^n} = (1 + i)^{-n}$$

(n) Periods	2%	2½%	3%	4%	5%	6%
1	.98039	.97561	.97087	.96154	.95238	.94340
2	.96117	.95181	.94260	.92456	.90703	.89000
3	.94232	.92860	.91514	.88900	.86384	.83962
4	.92385	.90595	.88849	.85480	.82270	.79209
5	.90573	.88385	.86261	.82193	.78353	.74726
6	.88797	.86230	.83748	.79031	.74622	.70496
7	.87056	.84127	.81309	.75992	.71068	.66506
8	.85349	.82075	.78941	.73069	.67684	.62741
9	.83676	.80073	.76642	.70259	.64461	.59190
10	.82035	.78120	.74409	.67556	.61391	.55839
11	.80426	.76214	.72242	.64958	.58468	.52679
12	.78849	.74356	.70138	.62460	.55684	.49697
13	.77303	.72542	.68095	.60057	.53032	.46884
14	.75788	.70773	.66112	.57748	.50507	.44230
15	.74301	.69047	.64186	.55526	.48102	.41727
16	.72845	.67362	.62317	.53391	.45811	.39365
17	.71416	.65720	.60502	.51337	.43630	.37136
18	.70016	.64117	.58739	.49363	.41552	.35034
19	.68643	.62553	.57029	.47464	.39573	.33051
20	.67297	.61027	.55368	.45639	.37689	.31180
21	.65978	.59539	.53755	.43883	.35894	.29416
22	.64684	.58086	.52189	.42196	.34185	.27751
23	.63416	.56670	.50669	.40573	.32557	.26180
24	.62172	.55288	.49193	.39012	.31007	.24698
25	.60953	.53939	.47761	.37512	.29530	.23300
26	.59758	.52623	.46369	.36069	.28124	.21981
27	.58586	.51340	.45019	.34682	.26785	.20737
28	.57437	.50088	.43708	.33348	.25509	.19563
29	.56311	.48866	.42435	.32065	.24295	.18456
30	.55207	.47674	.41199	.30832	.23138	.17411
31	.54125	.46511	.39999	.29646	.22036	.16425
32	.53063	.45377	.38834	.28506	.20987	.15496
33	.52023	.44270	.37703	.27409	.19987	.14619
34	.51003	.43191	.36604	.26355	.19035	.13791
35	.50003	.42137	.35538	.25342	.18129	.13011
36	.49022	.41109	.34503	.24367	.17266	.12274
37	.48061	.40107	.33498	.23430	.16444	.11579
38	.47119	.39128	.32523	.22529	.15661	.10924
39	.46195	.38174	.31575	.21662	.14915	.10306
40	.45289	.37243	.30656	.20829	.14205	.09722

TABLE 6-2 PRESENT VALUE OF 1

8%	9%	10%	11%	12%	15%	(n) Periods
.92593	.91743	.90909	.90090	.89286	.86957	1
.85734	.84168	.82645	.81162	.79719	.75614	2
.79383	.77218	.75132	.73119	.71178	.65752	3
.73503	.70843	.68301	.65873	.63552	.57175	4
.68058	.64993	.62092	.59345	.56743	.49718	5
.63017	.59627	.56447	.53464	.50663	.43233	6
.58349	.54703	.51316	.48166	.45235	.37594	7
.54027	.50187	.46651	.43393	.40388	.32690	8
.50025	.46043	.42410	.39092	.36061	.28426	9
.46319	.42241	.38554	.35218	.32197	.24719	10
.42888	.38753	.35049	.31728	.28748	.21494	11
.39711	.35554	.31863	.28584	.25668	.18691	12
.36770	.32618	.28966	.25751	.22917	.16253	13
.34046	.29925	.26333	.23199	.20462	.14133	14
.31524	.27454	.23939	.20900	.18270	.12289	15
.29189	.25187	.21763	.18829	.16312	.10687	16
.27027	.23107	.19785	.16963	.14564	.09293	17
.25025	.21199	.17986	.15282	.13004	.08081	18
.23171	.19449	.16351	.13768	.11611	.07027	19
.21455	.17843	.14864	.12403	.10367	.06110	20
.19866	.16370	.13513	.11174	.09256	.05313	21
.18394	.15018	.12285	.10067	.08264	.04620	22
.17032	.13778	.11168	.09069	.07379	.04017	23
.15770	.12641	.10153	.08170	.06588	.03493	24
.14602	.11597	.09230	.07361	.05882	.03038	25
.13520	.10639	.08391	.06631	.05252	.02642	26
.12519	.09761	.07628	.05974	.04689	.02297	27
.11591	.08955	.06934	.05382	.04187	.01997	28
.10733	.08216	.06304	.04849	.03738	.01737	29
.09938	.07537	.05731	.04368	.03338	.01510	30
.09202	.06915	.05210	.03935	.02980	.01313	31
.08520	.06344	.04736	.03545	.02661	.01142	32
.07889	.05820	.04306	.03194	.02376	.00993	33
.07305	.05340	.03914	.02878	.02121	.00864	34
.06763	.04899	.03558	.02592	.01894	.00751	35
.06262	.04494	.03235	.02335	.01601	.00653	36
.05799	.04123	.02941	.02104	.01510	.00568	37
.05369	.03783	.02674	.01896	.01348	.00494	38
.04971	.03470	.02430	.01708	.01204	.00429	39
.04603	.03184	.02210	.01538	.01075	.00373	40

TABLE 6-3   FUTURE VALUE OF AN ORDINARY ANNUITY OF 1

$$\text{FVF-OA}_{n,i} = \frac{(1 + i)^n - 1}{i}$$

(n) Periods	2%	2½%	3%	4%	5%	6%
1	1.00000	1.00000	1.00000	1.00000	1.00000	1.00000
2	2.02000	2.02500	2.03000	2.04000	2.05000	2.06000
3	3.06040	3.07563	3.09090	3.12160	3.15250	3.18360
4	4.12161	4.15252	4.18363	4.24646	4.31013	4.37462
5	5.20404	5.25633	5.30914	5.41632	5.52563	5.63709
6	6.30812	6.38774	6.46841	6.63298	6.80191	6.97532
7	7.43428	7.54743	7.66246	7.89829	8.14201	8.39384
8	8.58297	8.73612	8.89234	9.21423	9.54911	9.89747
9	9.75463	9.95452	10.15911	10.58280	11.02656	11.49132
10	10.94972	11.20338	11.46338	12.00611	12.57789	13.18079
11	12.16872	12.48347	12.80780	13.48635	14.20679	14.97164
12	13.41209	13.79555	14.19203	15.02581	15.91713	16.86994
13	14.68033	15.14044	15.61779	16.62684	17.71298	18.88214
14	15.97394	16.51895	17.08632	18.29191	19.59863	21.01507
15	17.29342	17.93193	18.59891	20.02359	21.57856	23.27597
16	18.63929	19.38022	20.15688	21.82453	23.65749	25.67253
17	20.01207	20.86473	21.76159	23.69751	25.84037	28.21288
18	21.41231	22.38635	23.41444	25.64541	28.13238	30.90565
19	22.84056	23.94601	25.11687	27.67123	30.53900	33.75999
20	24.29737	25.54466	26.87037	29.77808	33.06595	36.78559
21	25.78332	27.18327	28.67649	31.96920	35.71925	39.99273
22	27.29898	28.86286	30.53678	34.24797	38.50521	43.39229
23	28.84496	30.58443	32.45288	36.61789	41.43048	46.99583
24	30.42186	32.34904	34.42647	39.08260	44.50200	50.81558
25	32.03030	34.15776	36.45926	41.64591	47.72710	54.86451
26	33.67091	36.01171	38.55304	44.31174	51.11345	59.15638
27	35.34432	37.91200	40.70963	47.08421	54.66913	63.70577
28	37.05121	39.85980	42.93092	49.96758	58.40258	68.52811
29	38.79223	41.85630	45.21885	52.96629	62.32271	73.63980
30	40.56808	43.90270	47.57542	56.08494	66.43885	79.05819
31	42.37944	46.00027	50.00268	59.32834	70.76079	84.80168
32	44.22703	48.15028	52.50276	62.70147	75.29883	90.88978
33	46.11157	50.35403	55.07784	66.20953	80.06377	97.34316
34	48.03380	52.61289	57.73018	69.85791	85.06696	104.18376
35	49.99448	54.92821	60.46208	73.65222	90.32031	111.43478
36	51.99437	57.30141	63.27594	77.59831	95.83632	119.12087
37	54.03425	59.73395	66.17422	81.70225	101.62814	127.26812
38	56.11494	62.22730	69.15945	85.97034	107.70955	135.90421
39	58.23724	64.78298	72.23423	90.40915	114.09502	145.05846
40	60.40198	67.40255	75.40126	95.02552	120.79977	154.76197

TABLE 6-3   FUTURE VALUE OF AN ORDINARY ANNUITY OF 1

8%	9%	10%	11%	12%	15%	(n) Periods
1.00000	1.00000	1.00000	1.00000	1.00000	1.00000	1
2.08000	2.09000	2.10000	2.11000	2.12000	2.15000	2
3.24640	3.27810	3.31000	3.34210	3.37440	3.47250	3
4.50611	4.57313	4.64100	4.70973	4.77933	4.99338	4
5.86660	5.98471	6.10510	6.22780	6.35285	6.74238	5
7.33592	7.52334	7.71561	7.91286	8.11519	8.75374	6
8.92280	9.20044	9.48717	9.78327	10.08901	11.06680	7
10.63663	11.02847	11.43589	11.85943	12.29969	13.72682	8
12.48756	13.02104	13.57948	14.16397	14.77566	16.78584	9
14.48656	15.19293	15.93743	16.72201	17.54874	20.30372	10
16.64549	17.56029	18.53117	19.56143	20.65458	24.34928	11
18.97713	20.14072	21.38428	22.71319	24.13313	29.00167	12
21.49530	22.95339	24.52271	26.21164	28.02911	34.35192	13
24.21492	26.01919	27.97498	30.09492	32.39260	40.50471	14
27.15211	29.36092	31.77248	34.40536	37.27972	47.58041	15
30.32428	33.00340	35.94973	39.18995	42.75328	55.71747	16
33.75023	36.97371	40.54470	44.50084	48.88367	65.07509	17
37.45024	41.30134	45.59917	50.39593	55.74972	75.83636	18
41.44626	46.01846	51.15909	56.93949	63.43968	88.21181	19
45.76196	51.16012	57.27500	64.20283	72.05244	102.44358	20
50.42292	56.76453	64.00250	72.26514	81.69874	118.81012	21
55.45676	62.87334	71.40275	81.21431	92.50258	137.63164	22
60.89330	69.53194	79.54302	91.14788	104.60289	159.27638	23
66.76476	76.78981	88.49733	102.17415	118.15524	184.16784	24
73.10594	84.70090	98.34706	114.41331	133.33387	212.79302	25
79.95442	93.32398	109.18177	127.99877	150.33393	245.71197	26
87.35077	102.72314	121.09994	143.07864	169.37401	283.56877	27
95.33883	112.96822	134.20994	159.81729	190.69889	327.10408	28
103.96594	124.13536	148.63093	178.39719	214.58275	377.16969	29
113.28321	136.30754	164.49402	199.02088	241.33268	434.74515	30
123.34587	149.57522	181.94343	221.91317	271.29261	500.95692	31
134.21354	164.03699	201.13777	247.32362	304.84772	577.10046	32
145.95062	179.80032	222.25154	275.52922	342.42945	644.66553	33
158.62667	196.98234	245.47670	306.83744	384.52098	765.36535	34
172.31680	215.71076	271.02437	341.58955	431.66350	881.17016	35
187.10215	230.12472	299.12681	380.16441	484.46312	1014.34568	36
203.07032	258.37595	330.03949	422.98249	543.59869	1167.49753	37
220.31595	282.62978	364.04343	470.51056	609.83053	1343.62216	38
238.94122	309.06646	401.44778	523.26673	684.01020	1546.16549	39
259.05652	337.88245	442.59256	581.82607	767.09142	1779.09031	40

Payments at end of year

TABLE 6-4   PRESENT VALUE OF AN ORDINARY ANNUITY OF 1

$$PVF\text{-}OA_{n,i} = \frac{1 - \dfrac{1}{(1 + i)^n}}{i}$$

(n) Periods	2%	2½%	3%	4%	5%	6%
1	.98039	.97561	.97087	.96154	.95238	.94340
2	1.94156	1.92742	1.91347	1.88609	1.85941	1.83339
3	2.88388	2.85602	2.82861	2.77509	2.72325	2.67301
4	3.80773	3.76197	3.71710	3.62990	3.54595	3.46511
5	4.71346	4.64583	4.57971	4.45182	4.32948	4.21236
6	5.60143	5.50813	5.41719	5.24214	5.07569	4.91732
7	6.47199	6.34939	6.23028	6.00205	5.78637	5.58238
8	7.32548	7.17014	7.01969	6.73274	6.46321	6.20979
9	8.16224	7.97087	7.78611	7.43533	7.10782	6.80169
10	8.98259	8.75206	8.53020	8.11090	7.72173	7.36009
11	9.78685	9.51421	9.25262	8.76048	8.30641	7.88687
12	10.57534	10.25776	9.95400	9.38507	8.86325	8.38384
13	11.34837	10.98319	10.63496	9.98565	9.39357	8.85268
14	12.10625	11.69091	11.29607	10.56312	9.89864	9.29498
15	12.84926	12.38138	11.93794	11.11839	10.37966	9.71225
16	13.57771	13.05500	12.56110	11.65230	10.83777	10.10590
17	14.29187	13.71220	13.16612	12.16567	11.27407	10.47726
18	14.99203	14.35336	13.75351	12.65930	11.68959	10.82760
19	15.67846	14.97889	14.32380	13.13394	12.08532	11.15812
20	16.35143	15.58916	14.87747	13.59033	12.46221	11.46992
21	17.01121	16.18455	15.41502	14.02916	12.82115	11.76408
22	17.65805	16.76541	15.93692	14.45112	13.16300	12.04158
23	18.29220	17.33211	16.44361	14.85684	13.48857	12.30338
24	18.91393	17.88499	16.93554	15.24696	13.79864	12.55036
25	19.52346	18.42438	17.41315	15.62208	14.09394	12.78336
26	20.12104	18.95061	17.87684	15.98277	14.37519	13.00317
27	20.70690	19.46401	18.32703	16.32959	14.64303	13.21053
28	21.28127	19.96489	18.76411	16.66306	14.89813	13.40616
29	21.84438	20.45355	19.18845	16.98371	15.14107	13.59072
30	22.39646	20.93029	19.60044	17.29203	15.37245	13.76483
31	22.93770	21.39541	20.00043	17.58849	15.59281	13.92909
32	23.46833	21.84918	20.38877	17.87355	15.80268	14.08404
33	23.98856	22.29188	20.76579	18.14765	16.00255	14.23023
34	24.49859	22.72379	21.13184	18.41120	16.19290	14.36814
35	24.99862	23.14516	21.48722	18.66461	16.37419	14.49825
36	25.48884	23.55625	21.83225	18.90828	16.54685	14.62099
37	25.96945	23.95732	22.16724	19.14258	16.71129	14.73678
38	26.44064	24.34860	22.49246	19.36786	16.86789	14.84602
39	26.90259	24.73034	22.80822	19.58448	17.01704	14.94907
40	27.35548	25.10278	23.11477	19.79277	17.15909	15.04630

TABLE 6-4   PRESENT VALUE OF AN ORDINARY ANNUITY OF 1

8%	9%	10%	11%	12%	15%	(n) Periods
.92593	.91743	.90909	.90090	.89286	.86957	1
1.78326	1.75911	1.73554	1.71252	1.69005	1.62571	2
2.57710	2.53130	2.48685	2.44371	2.40183	2.28323	3
3.31213	3.23972	3.16986	3.10245	3.03735	2.85498	4
3.99271	3.88965	3.79079	3.69590	3.60478	3.35216	5
4.62288	4.48592	4.35526	4.23054	4.11141	3.78448	6
5.20637	5.03295	4.86842	4.71220	4.56376	4.16042	7
5.74664	5.53482	5.33493	5.14612	4.96764	4.48732	8
6.24689	5.99525	5.75902	5.53705	5.32825	4.77158	9
6.71008	6.41766	6.14457	5.88923	5.65022	5.01877	10
7.13896	6.80519	6.49506	6.20652	5.93770	5.23371	11
7.53608	7.16073	6.81369	6.49236	6.19437	5.42062	12
7.90378	7.48690	7.10336	6.74987	6.42355	5.58315	13
8.24424	7.78615	7.36669	6.98187	6.62817	5.72448	14
8.55948	8.06069	7.60608	7.19087	6.81086	5.84737	15
8.85137	8.31256	7.82371	7.37916	6.97399	5.95424	16
9.12164	8.54363	8.02155	7.54879	7.11963	6.04716	17
9.37189	8.75563	8.20141	7.70162	7.24967	6.12797	18
9.60360	8.95012	8.36492	7.83929	7.36578	6.19823	19
9.81815	9.12855	8.51356	7.96333	7.46944	6.25933	20
10.01680	9.29224	8.64869	8.07507	7.56200	6.31246	21
10.20074	9.44243	8.77154	8.17574	7.64465	6.35866	22
10.37106	9.58021	8.88322	8.26643	7.71843	6.39884	23
10.52876	9.70661	8.98474	8.34814	7.78432	6.43377	24
10.67478	9.82258	9.07704	8.42174	7.84314	6.46415	25
10.80998	9.92897	9.16095	8.48806	7.89566	6.49056	26
10.93516	10.02658	9.23722	8.54780	7.94255	6.51353	27
11.05108	10.11613	9.30657	8.60162	7.98442	6.53351	28
11.15841	10.19828	9.36961	8.65011	8.02181	6.55088	29
11.25778	10.27365	9.42691	8.69379	8.05518	6.56598	30
11.34980	10.34280	9.47901	8.73315	8.08499	6.57911	31
11.43500	10.40624	9.52638	8.76860	8.11159	6.59053	32
11.51389	10.46444	9.56943	8.80054	8.13535	6.60046	33
11.58693	10.51784	9.60858	8.82932	8.15656	6.60910	34
11.65457	10.56682	9.64416	8.85524	8.17550	6.61661	35
11.71719	10.61176	9.67651	8.87859	8.19241	6.62314	36
11.77518	10.65299	9.70592	8.89963	8.20751	6.62882	37
11.82887	10.69082	9.73265	8.91859	8.22099	6.63375	38
11.87858	10.72552	9.75697	8.93567	8.23303	6.63805	39
11.92461	10.75736	9.77905	8.95105	8.24378	6.64178	40

Due at beginning of year

TABLE 6-5   PRESENT VALUE OF AN ANNUITY DUE OF 1

$$PVF\text{-}AD_{n,i} = 1 + \frac{1 - \dfrac{1}{(1 + i)^{n-1}}}{i}$$

(n) Periods	2%	2½%	3%	4%	5%	6%
1	1.00000	1.00000	1.00000	1.00000	1.00000	1.00000
2	1.98039	1.97561	1.97087	1.96154	1.95238	1.94340
3	2.94156	2.92742	2.91347	2.88609	2.85941	2.83339
4	3.88388	3.85602	3.82861	3.77509	3.72325	3.67301
5	4.80773	4.76197	4.71710	4.62990	4.54595	4.46511
6	5.71346	5.64583	5.57971	5.45182	5.32948	5.21236
7	6.60143	6.50813	6.41719	6.24214	6.07569	5.91732
8	7.47199	7.34939	7.23028	7.00205	6.78637	6.58238
9	8.32548	8.17014	8.01969	7.73274	7.46321	7.20979
10	9.16224	8.97087	8.78611	8.43533	8.10782	7.80169
11	9.98259	9.75206	9.53020	9.11090	8.72173	8.36009
12	10.78685	10.51421	10.25262	9.76048	9.30641	8.88687
13	11.57534	11.25776	10.95400	10.38507	9.86325	9.38384
14	12.34837	11.98319	11.63496	10.98565	10.39357	9.85268
15	13.10625	12.69091	12.29607	11.56312	10.89864	10.29498
16	13.84926	13.38138	12.93794	12.11839	11.37966	10.71225
17	14.57771	14.05500	13.56110	12.65230	11.83777	11.10590
18	15.29187	14.71220	14.16612	13.16567	12.27407	11.47726
19	15.99203	15.35336	14.75351	13.65930	12.68959	11.82760
20	16.67846	15.97889	15.32380	14.13394	13.08532	12.15812
21	17.35143	16.58916	15.87747	14.59033	13.46221	12.46992
22	18.01121	17.18455	16.41502	15.02916	13.82115	12.76408
23	18.65805	17.76541	16.93692	15.45112	14.16300	13.04158
24	19.29220	18.33211	17.44361	15.85684	14.48857	13.30338
25	19.91393	18.88499	17.93554	16.24696	14.79864	13.55036
26	20.52346	19.42438	18.41315	16.62208	15.09394	13.78336
27	21.12104	19.95061	18.87684	16.98277	15.37519	14.00317
28	21.70690	20.46401	19.32703	17.32959	15.64303	14.21053
29	22.28127	20.96489	19.76411	17.66306	15.89813	14.40616
30	22.84438	21.45355	20.18845	17.98371	16.14107	14.59072
31	23.39646	21.93029	20.60044	18.29203	16.37245	14.76483
32	23.93770	22.39541	21.00043	18.58849	16.59281	14.92909
33	24.46833	22.84918	21.38877	18.87355	16.80268	15.08404
34	24.98856	23.29188	21.76579	19.14765	17.00255	15.23023
35	25.49859	23.72379	22.13184	19.41120	17.19290	15.36814
36	25.99862	24.14516	22.48722	19.66461	17.37419	15.49825
37	26.48884	24.55625	22.83225	19.90828	17.54685	15.62099
38	26.96945	24.95732	23.16724	20.14258	17.71129	15.73678
39	27.44064	25.34860	23.49246	20.36786	17.86789	15.84602
40	27.90259	25.73034	23.80822	20.58448	18.01704	15.94907

TABLE 6-5 PRESENT VALUE OF AN ANNUITY DUE OF 1

8%	9%	10%	11%	12%	15%	(n) Periods
1.00000	1.00000	1.00000	1.00000	1.00000	1.00000	1
1.92593	1.91743	1.90909	1.90090	1.89286	1.86957	2
2.78326	2.75911	2.73554	2.71252	2.69005	2.62571	3
3.57710	3.53130	3.48685	3.44371	3.40183	3.28323	4
4.31213	4.23972	4.16986	4.10245	4.03735	3.85498	5
4.99271	4.88965	4.79079	4.69590	4.60478	4.35216	6
5.62288	5.48592	5.35526	5.23054	5.11141	4.78448	7
6.20637	6.03295	5.86842	5.71220	5.56376	5.16042	8
6.74664	6.53482	6.33493	6.14612	5.96764	5.48732	9
7.24689	6.99525	6.75902	6.53705	6.32825	5.77158	10
7.71008	7.41766	7.14457	6.88923	6.65022	6.01877	11
8.13896	7.80519	7.49506	7.20652	6.93770	6.23371	12
8.53608	8.16073	7.81369	7.49236	7.19437	6.42062	13
8.90378	8.48690	8.10336	7.74987	7.42355	6.58315	14
9.24424	8.78615	8.36669	7.98187	7.62817	6.72448	15
9.55948	9.06069	8.60608	8.19087	7.81086	6.84737	16
9.85137	9.31256	8.82371	8.37916	7.97399	6.95424	17
10.12164	9.54363	9.02155	8.54879	8.11963	7.04716	18
10.37189	9.75563	9.20141	8.70162	8.24967	7.12797	19
10.60360	9.95012	9.36492	8.83929	8.36578	7.19823	20
10.81815	10.12855	9.51356	8.96333	8.46944	7.25933	21
11.01680	10.29224	9.64869	9.07507	8.56200	7.31246	22
11.20074	10.44243	9.77154	9.17574	8.64465	7.35866	23
11.37106	10.58021	9.88322	9.26643	8.71843	7.39884	24
11.52876	10.70661	9.98474	9.34814	8.78432	7.43377	25
11.67478	10.82258	10.07704	9.42174	8.84314	7.46415	26
11.80998	10.92897	10.16095	9.48806	8.89566	7.49056	27
11.93518	11.02658	10.23722	9.54780	8.94255	7.51353	28
12.05108	11.11613	10.30657	9.60162	8.98442	7.53351	29
12.15841	11.19828	10.36961	9.65011	9.02181	7.55088	30
12.25778	11.27365	10.42691	9.69379	9.05518	7.56598	31
12.34980	11.34280	10.47901	9.73315	9.08499	7.57911	32
12.43500	11.40624	10.52638	9.76860	9.11159	7.59053	33
12.51389	11.46444	10.56943	9.80054	9.13535	7.60046	34
12.58693	11.51784	10.60858	9.82932	9.15656	7.60910	35
12.65457	11.56682	10.64416	9.85524	9.17550	7.61661	36
12.71719	11.61176	10.67651	9.87859	9.19241	7.62314	37
12.77518	11.65299	10.70592	9.89963	9.20751	7.62882	38
12.82887	11.69082	10.73265	9.91859	9.22099	7.63375	39
12.87858	11.72552	10.75697	9.93567	9.23303	7.63805	40

CHAPTER 7

Cash and Receivables

Due Diligence

Henry Burkhardt III was exuberant about Kendall Square Research, the super-computer company he started in 1986. Enthusiasm came naturally to the 49-year-old president and chief executive, who first made his name as cofounder of Data General. His reassuring manner proved valuable when dealing with Wall Street's restless stock analysts and investors. One day in August 1993, Burkhardt didn't have to do the selling—Wall Street analysts were doing it for him. The analysts predicted that Kendall Square's earnings would rise to 45–50 cents a share in the next year, eclipsing last year's loss of $1.22 a share.

Was Burkhardt comfortable with these estimates? A *Wall Street Journal* reporter asked him that question after the predictions were made. "Quite comfortable," Burkhardt replied. The next day, Kendall Square's stock spiked up 75 cents a share, to $19.75. However, around the time of the interview Burkhardt's actions belied his public persona: He sold $1 million dollars worth of his stock in Kendall Square Research—not what you'd expect from someone who expected his stock price to soar.

If investors had done some research and looked at Kendall Square's financial statements for the quarter ended June 30, they might have found Burkhardt's motivation to sell his stock. Some disquieting news could be found on one line on the balance sheet, the line that read "Accounts Receivable."

In the case of Kendall Square Research, the dollar amount of the company's accounts receivable had jumped 57% in the first six months of the year. Also the company was sending out bills to its credit customers and then waiting an average of 154 days before payment was received.

What happened to Kendall Square Research's stock price? The company's stock continued to rise for two months after Burkhardt's comments to the financial press, to a high of $24.25 a share. Then shareholders discovered that Burkhardt had sold the $1 million stake in the company. The share price dropped sharply and continued downward to $2.88 a share as of the following April. At that point Burkhardt departed from the company.[1]

---

[1]Adapted from Jonathan Burton, "Due Diligence," *Worth*, June 1994.

LEARNING OBJECTIVES

After studying this chapter, you should be able to:

1 Identify items considered cash.

2 Indicate how cash and related items are reported.

3 Define receivables and identify the different types of receivables.

4 Explain accounting issues related to recognition of accounts receivable.

5 Explain accounting issues related to valuation of accounts receivable.

6 Explain accounting issues related to recognition of notes receivable.

7 Explain accounting issues related to valuation of notes receivable.

8 Explain accounting issues related to disposition of accounts and notes receivable.

9 Explain how receivables are reported and analyzed.

As the opening story indicates, the growth of accounts receivable and their slow collection were major contributors to the declining health of Kendall Square Research. Kendall Square's story illustrates that collection on accounts is one of the most significant challenges facing businesses that rely on credit sales. The purpose of this chapter is to discuss the two assets of importance at Kendall Square Research—cash and receivables. The content and organization of the chapter are as follows:

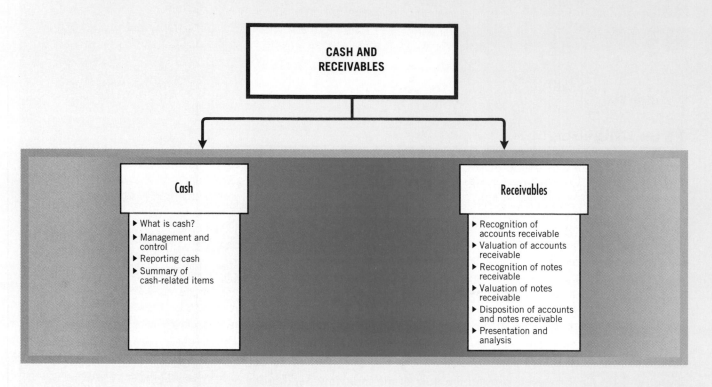

CASH AND RECEIVABLES

Cash
- What is cash?
- Management and control
- Reporting cash
- Summary of cash-related items

Receivables
- Recognition of accounts receivable
- Valuation of accounts receivable
- Recognition of notes receivable
- Valuation of notes receivable
- Disposition of accounts and notes receivable
- Presentation and analysis

SECTION 1   *CASH*

❖ WHAT IS CASH?

Objective ❶

Identify items considered cash.

Cash, the most liquid of assets, is the standard medium of exchange and the basis for measuring and accounting for all other items. It is generally classified as a current asset. To be reported as cash, it must be readily available for the payment of current obligations, and it must be free from any contractual restriction that limits its use in satisfying debts.

Cash consists of coin, currency, and available funds on deposit at the bank. Negotiable instruments such as money orders, certified checks, cashier's checks, personal checks, and bank drafts are also viewed as cash. Savings accounts are usually classified as cash, although the bank has the legal right to demand notice before withdrawal. But, because prior notice is rarely demanded by banks, savings accounts are considered cash.

Money market funds, money market savings certificates, certificates of deposit

(CDs), and similar types of deposits and "short-term paper"[2] that provide small investors with an opportunity to earn high rates of interest are more appropriately classified as temporary investments than as cash. The reason is that these securities usually contain restrictions or penalties on their conversion to cash. Money market funds that provide checking account privileges, however, are usually classified as cash.

Certain items present classification problems: **Postdated checks and I.O.U.s** are treated as receivables. **Travel advances** are properly treated as receivables if the advances are to be collected from the employees or deducted from their salaries. Otherwise, classification of the travel advance as a prepaid expense is more appropriate. **Postage stamps on hand** are classified as part of office supplies inventory or as a prepaid expense. **Petty cash funds and change funds** are included in current assets as cash because these funds are used to meet current operating expenses and to liquidate current liabilities.

❖ MANAGEMENT AND CONTROL OF CASH

Cash is the asset most susceptible to improper diversion and use. Two problems of accounting for cash transactions face management: (1) Proper controls must be established to ensure that no unauthorized transactions are entered into by officers or employees; and (2) information necessary to the proper management of cash on hand and cash transactions must be provided. Yet even with sophisticated control devices errors can and do happen. *The Wall Street Journal* ran a story entitled "A $7.8 Million Error Has a Happy Ending for a Horrified Bank," which described how Manufacturers Hanover Trust Co. mailed about $7.8 million too much in cash dividends to its stockholders. As implied in the headline, most of the monies were subsequently returned.

To safeguard cash and to ensure the accuracy of the accounting records for cash, effective **internal control** over cash is imperative. And control may become even more difficult in the age of digital cash. Already, most paychecks are handled electronically. Banks are offering checklike debit cards, and we now have cards that store digital cash. And we have many companies that are starting to transact business over the Internet. All this will lead to changes in consumer behavior patterns and new types of frauds. However, we have survived credit cards, so we should be able to handle these changes as well. The appendix to this chapter discusses some of the basic control procedures used to ensure that cash is reported correctly.

❖ REPORTING CASH

Although the reporting of cash is relatively straightforward, there are a number of issues that merit special attention. These issues relate to the reporting of:

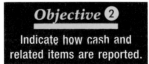

Objective ②
Indicate how cash and related items are reported.

❶ Restricted cash.
❷ Bank overdrafts.
❸ Cash equivalents.

---

[2]A variety of "short-term paper" is available for investment. For example, **certificates of deposit** (CDs) represent formal evidence of indebtedness, issued by a bank, subject to withdrawal under the specific terms of the instrument. Issued in $10,000 and $100,000 denominations, they mature in 30 to 360 days and generally pay interest at the short-term interest rate in effect at date of issuance. **Money market savings certificates** are issued by banks and savings and loan associations in denominations of $10,000 or more for 6-month periods (6 to 48 months). The interest rate is tied to the 26-week Treasury bill rate. In **money market funds**, a relatively recent variation of the mutual fund, the yield is determined by the mix of Treasury bills and commercial paper making up the fund's portfolio. Most money market funds require an initial minimum investment of $5,000; many allow withdrawal by check or wire transfer. **Treasury bills** are U.S. government obligations generally having 91- and 182-day maturities; they are sold in $10,000 denominations at weekly government auctions. **Commercial paper** is a short-term note (30 to 270 days) issued by corporations with good credit ratings. Issued in $5,000 and $10,000 denominations, these notes generally yield a higher rate than Treasury bills.

Restricted Cash

Compensating Balances

Banks and other lending institutions often require customers to whom they lend money to maintain minimum cash balances in checking or savings accounts. These minimum balances, called compensating balances, are defined by the SEC as: "that portion of any demand deposit (or any time deposit or certificate of deposit) maintained by a corporation which constitutes support for existing borrowing arrangements of the corporation with a lending institution. Such arrangements would include both outstanding borrowings and the assurance of future credit availability."[3]

Compensating balances may be payment for bank services rendered to the company for which there is no direct fee, for example, check processing and lockbox management. By requiring a compensating balance, the bank achieves an effective interest rate on a loan that is higher than the stated rate because it has use of the restricted amount that must remain on deposit.

To illustrate, assume that on January 1, 1999, Biddle Co. borrowed $10,000,000 for one year from First Union Bank at an interest rate of 10%. In addition, Biddle is required to keep a compensatory balance of $2,000,000 on deposit at First Union, which will earn 6%. Normally, Biddle would deposit $1,000,000 at the bank for transaction purposes. The effective interest that Biddle pays on this loan is 10.4% computed as follows:

ILLUSTRATION 7-1
Computation of Interest
Cost

$10,000,000 × 10%	$1,000,000
($2,000,000 − $1,000,000) × 4%	40,000
Total interest cost	$1,040,000

$$\frac{\text{Total interest cost}}{\text{Total principal}} = \frac{\$1,040,000}{\$10,000,000} = 10.4\%$$

Biddle pays $1,000,000 interest on the original loan of $10,000,000 and it is required to maintain an additional $1,000,000 cash balance on which it can earn only 6%. If it has to borrow this additional $1,000,000, it will be losing 4% (10% − 6%) on every dollar borrowed.

The need for the disclosure of compensating balances was highlighted in the 1970s when a number of companies were involved in a liquidity crisis. Many investors believed that the cash reported on the balance sheet was fully available to meet recurring obligations, but these funds were actually restricted because of the need for these companies to maintain minimum cash balances at various lending institutions.

The SEC recommends that **legally restricted deposits** held as compensating balances against **short-term** borrowing arrangements be stated separately among the "cash and cash equivalent items" in Current Assets. Restricted deposits held as compensating balances against **long-term** borrowing arrangements should be separately classified as noncurrent assets in either the Investments or Other Assets sections, using a caption such as "Cash on Deposit Maintained as Compensating Balance."

In cases where compensating balance arrangements exist without agreements that restrict the use of cash amounts shown on the balance sheet, the arrangements and the amounts involved should be described in the notes. Compensating balances that are maintained under an agreement to assure future credit availability also must be disclosed separately in the notes, together with the amount and duration of such agreement.

---

[3]*Accounting Series Release No. 148*, "Amendments to Regulations S-X and Related Interpretations and Guidelines Regarding the Disclosure of Compensating Balances and Short-Term Borrowing Arrangements," Securities and Exchange Commission (November 13, 1973). The SEC defines 15% of liquid assets (current cash balances, whether restricted or not, plus marketable securities) as being material.

Snap-On Tools reported the following note regarding compensating balances:

ILLUSTRATION 7-2
Disclosure of
Compensating Balances

Snap-On Tools

Note: Compensating Balances. At the end of the current year, the Company had total bank lines of credit available under short-term borrowing arrangements of $37.3 million. Of that amount, $35.0 million requires compensatory balances of 3% relative to these arrangements.

Other Types of Restrictions

Petty cash, payroll, and dividend funds are examples of cash set aside for a particular purpose. In most situations, these fund balances are not material and therefore are not segregated from cash when reported in the financial statements. When material in amount, restricted cash is segregated from "regular" cash for reporting purposes. The restricted cash is classified either in the Current Assets or in the Long-term Assets section, depending on the date of availability or disbursement. Classification in the current section is appropriate if the cash is to be used (within a year or the operating cycle, whichever is longer) for payment of existing or maturing obligations. On the other hand, if the cash is to be held for a longer period of time, the restricted cash is shown in the long-term section of the balance sheet.

INTERNATIONAL INSIGHT

Among other potential restrictions, companies need to determine whether any of the cash in accounts outside the U.S. is restricted by regulations against exportation of currency.

Cash classified in the long-term section is frequently set aside for plant expansion, retirement of long-term debt or, in the case of Par Pharmaceutical, for self-insurance:

ILLUSTRATION 7-3
Disclosure of Restricted
Cash

Par Pharmaceutical

Restricted cash and investments (See Note) $3,000,000

Note: Restricted Cash. As a result of escalating products liability insurance premiums and in view of Par's favorable products liability experience, the Company instituted a Products Liability Self-Insurance Program effective June of the current period. Pursuant to this Program, $3,000,000 has been deposited with a financial institution and its use restricted to costs arising from such product liability claims against the Company. Such funds are invested in income-producing securities, the income from which is available to the Company for general corporate purposes.

Go to Web site for additional disclosures of restricted cash.

Bank Overdrafts

Bank overdrafts occur when a check is written for more than the amount in the cash account. They should be reported in the current liabilities section and are usually added to the amount reported as accounts payable. If material, these items should be separately disclosed either on the face of the balance sheet or in the related notes.[4]

Bank overdrafts are generally not offset against the cash account. A major exception is when available cash is present in another account in the same bank on which the overdraft occurred. Offsetting in this case is required.

Cash Equivalents

A current classification that has become popular is "cash and cash equivalents."[5] **Cash equivalents** are short-term, highly liquid investments that are both (a) readily convertible to known amounts of cash, and (b) so near their maturity that they present insignificant risk of changes in interest rates. Generally only investments with original

---

[4]Bank overdrafts usually occur because of a simple oversight by the company writing the check. Banks often expect companies to have overdrafts from time to time and therefore negotiate a fee as payment for this possible occurrence. However, in the early 1980s, E. F. Hutton (a large brokerage firm) intentionally began overdrawing their accounts by astronomical amounts—on some days exceeding $1 billion—thus obtaining interest-free loans which it could invest. Because the amounts were so large and fees were not negotiated in advance, E. F. Hutton came under criminal investigation for its actions.

[5]*Accounting Trends and Techniques—1996*, indicates that approximately 11% of the companies surveyed use the caption "cash," 78% use "cash and cash equivalents," and 11% use a caption such as "cash and marketable securities" or similar terminology.

maturities of 3 months or less qualify under these definitions. Examples of cash equivalents are treasury bills, commercial paper, and money market funds. Some companies combine cash with temporary investments on the balance sheet. In these cases, the amount of the temporary investments is described either parenthetically or in the notes.

❖ SUMMARY OF CASH-RELATED ITEMS

Cash and cash equivalents includes the medium of exchange and most negotiable instruments. If the item cannot be converted to coin or currency on short notice, it is separately classified as an investment, as a receivable, or as a prepaid expense. Cash that is not available for payment of currently maturing liabilities is segregated and classified in the long-term assets section. Illustration 7-4 summarizes the classification of cash-related items.

ILLUSTRATION 7-4
Classification of Cash-Related Items

Classification of Cash, Cash Equivalent, and Noncash Items		
Item	Classification	Comment
Cash	Cash	If unrestricted, report as cash. If restricted, identify and classify as current and noncurrent assets.
Petty cash and change funds	Cash	Report as cash.
Short-term paper	Cash equivalents	Investments with maturity of less than three months, often combined with cash.
Short-term paper	Temporary investments	Investments with maturity of 3 to 12 months.
Postdated checks and IOU's	Receivables	Assumed to be collectible.
Travel advances	Receivables	Assumed to be collected from employees or deducted from their salaries.
Postage on hand (as stamps or in postage meters)	Prepaid expenses	May also be classified as office supplies inventory.
Bank overdrafts	Current liability	If right of offset exists, reduce cash.
Compensating balances		
1. Legally restricted	Cash separately classified as a deposit maintained as compensating balance	Classify as current or noncurrent in the balance sheet.
2. Arrangement without legal restriction	Cash with note disclosure	Disclose separately in notes details of the arrangement.

SECTION 2   *RECEIVABLES*

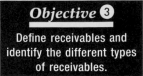

Objective ❸

Define receivables and identify the different types of receivables.

Receivables are claims held against customers and others for money, goods, or services. For financial statement purposes, receivables are classified as either **current** (short-term) or **noncurrent** (long-term). **Current receivables** are expected to be collected within a year or during the current operating cycle, whichever is longer. All other receivables are classified as **noncurrent**. Receivables are further classified in the balance sheet as either trade or nontrade receivables.

Trade receivables are amounts owed by customers for goods sold and services rendered as part of normal business operations. Trade receivables, usually the most significant an enterprise possesses, may be subclassified into accounts receivable and notes receivable. **Accounts receivable** are oral promises of the purchaser to pay for goods and services sold. They are normally collectible within 30 to 60 days and represent "open accounts" resulting from short-term extensions of credit. **Notes receivable** are written promises to pay a certain sum of money on a specified future date. They may arise from sales, financing, or other transactions. Notes may be short-term or long-term.

Nontrade receivables arise from a variety of transactions and can be written promises either to pay or to deliver. Some examples of nontrade receivables are:

❶ Advances to officers and employees.
❷ Advances to subsidiaries.
❸ Deposits to cover potential damages or losses.
❹ Deposits as a guarantee of performance or payment.
❺ Dividends and interest receivable.
❻ Claims against:
   (a) Insurance companies for casualties sustained.
   (b) Defendants under suit.
   (c) Governmental bodies for tax refunds.
   (d) Common carriers for damaged or lost goods.
   (e) Creditors for returned, damaged, or lost goods.
   (f) Customers for returnable items (crates, containers, etc.).

Because of the peculiar nature of nontrade receivables, they are generally classified and reported as separate items in the balance sheet.

The basic issues in accounting for accounts and notes receivable are the same: **recognition**, **valuation**, and **disposition**. We will discuss these basic issues of accounts and notes receivable in the following sequence:

❶ Recognition and valuation of accounts receivable.
❷ Recognition and valuation of notes receivable.
❸ Disposition of accounts and notes receivable.

❖ RECOGNITION OF ACCOUNTS RECEIVABLE

In most receivables transactions, the amount to be recognized is the exchange price between the two parties. **The exchange price is the amount due from the debtor** (a customer or a borrower) and is generally evidenced by some type of business document, often an invoice. Two factors that may complicate the measurement of the exchange price are (1) the availability of discounts (trade and cash discounts) and (2) the length of time between the sale and the due date of payments (the interest element).

Objective ❹

Explain accounting issues related to recognition of accounts receivable.

Trade Discounts

Customers are often quoted prices on the basis of list or catalog prices that may be subject to a trade or quantity discount. Such **trade discounts** are used to avoid frequent changes in catalogs, to quote different prices for different quantities purchased, or to hide the true invoice price from competitors.

Trade discounts are commonly quoted in percentages. For example, if your textbook has a list price of $60.00 and the publisher sells it to college bookstores for list less a 30% trade discount, the receivable recorded by the publisher is $42.00 per textbook. The normal practice is simply to deduct the trade discount from the list price and bill the customer net.

As another example, Maxwell House at one time sold a 10 oz. jar of its instant coffee listing at $4.65 to supermarkets for $3.90, a trade discount of approximately 16%. The supermarkets in turn sold the instant coffee for $3.99 per jar. Maxwell House records the receivable and related sales revenue at $3.90 per jar, not $4.65.

Cash Discounts (Sales Discounts)

Cash discounts (sales discounts) are offered as an inducement for prompt payment. They are communicated in terms that read, for example, 2/10, n/30 (2% if paid within 10 days, gross amount due in 30 days), or 2/10, E.O.M. (2% if paid within 10 days of the end of the month).

Companies that fail to take sales discounts are usually not employing their money advantageously. An enterprise that receives a 1% reduction in the sales price for payment within 10 days, total payment due within 30 days, is effectively earning 18.25% (.01 ÷ [20/365]), or at least avoiding that rate of interest cost. For this reason, companies usually take the discount unless their cash is severely limited.

The easiest and most commonly used method of recording sales and related sales discount transactions is to enter the receivable and sale at the gross amount. Under this method, sales discounts are recognized in the accounts only when payment is received within the discount period. Sales discounts would then be shown in the income statement as a deduction from sales to arrive at net sales.

Some contend that sales discounts not taken reflect penalties added to an established price to encourage prompt payment. That is, the seller offers sales on account at a slightly higher price than if selling for cash, and the increase is offset by the cash discount offered. Thus, customers who pay within the discount period purchase at the cash price; those who pay after expiration of the discount period are penalized because they must pay an amount in excess of the cash price. If this reasoning is used, sales and receivables are recorded net, and any discounts not taken are subsequently debited to Accounts Receivable and credited to Sales Discounts Forfeited. The following entries illustrate the difference between the gross and net methods.

ILLUSTRATION 7-5
Entries under Gross and Net Methods of Recording Cash (Sales) Discounts

Gross Method			Net Method		
Sale of $10,000, terms 2/10, n/30:					
Accounts Receivable	10,000		Accounts Receivable	9,800	
Sales		10,000	Sales		9,800
Payment of $4,000 received within discount period:					
Cash	3,920		Cash	3,920	
Sales Discounts	80		Accounts Receivable		3,920
Accounts Receivable		4,000			
Payment of $6,000 received after discount period:					
Cash	6,000		Accounts Receivable	120	
Accounts Receivable		6,000	Sales Discounts		
			Forfeited		120
			Cash	6,000	
			Accounts Receivable		6,000

If the gross method is employed, sales discounts are reported as a deduction from sales in the income statement. Proper matching would dictate that a reasonable estimate of material amounts of expected discounts to be taken also should be charged against sales. If the net method is used, Sales Discounts Forfeited are considered as an other revenue item.

Theoretically, the recognition of Sales Discounts Forfeited is correct because the receivable is stated closer to its realizable value and the net sale figure measures the revenue earned from the sale. As a practical matter, however, the net method is seldom used because it requires additional analysis and bookkeeping. For one thing, the net method requires adjusting entries to record sales discounts forfeited on accounts receivable that have passed the discount period.

Nonrecognition of Interest Element

Ideally, receivables should be measured in terms of their present value, that is, the discounted value of the cash to be received in the future. When expected cash receipts require a waiting period, the receivable face amount is not worth the amount that is ultimately received.

To illustrate, assume that a company makes a sale on account for $1,000 with payment due in 4 months. The applicable annual rate of interest is 12% and payment is made at the end of 4 months. The present value of that receivable is not $1,000 but $961.54 ($1,000 × .96154, Table 6–2; $n = 1, i = 4\%$). In other words, $1,000 to be received 4 months from now is not the same as $1,000 received today.

Theoretically, any revenue after the period of sale is interest revenue. In practice, interest revenue related to accounts receivable is ignored because the amount of the discount is not usually material in relation to the net income for the period. The profession specifically excludes from the present value considerations "receivables arising from transactions with customers in the normal course of business which are due in customary trade terms not exceeding approximately one year."[6]

UNDERLYING CONCEPTS

Materiality means it must make a difference to a decision maker. The FASB believes that present value concepts can be ignored for short-term notes.

❖ VALUATION OF ACCOUNTS RECEIVABLE

Having recorded receivables at their face value (the amount due), the problem of financial statement presentation then occurs. Reporting of receivables involves (1) classification and (2) valuation on the balance sheet.

Classification, as already discussed, involves a determination of the length of time each receivable will be outstanding. Receivables intended to be collected within a year or the operating cycle, whichever is longer, are classified as current; all other receivables are classified as long-term.

The valuation of receivables is slightly more complex. **Short-term receivables are valued and reported at** net realizable value—**the net amount expected to be received in cash**, which is not necessarily the amount legally receivable. Determining net realizable value requires an estimation of both uncollectible receivables and any returns or allowances to be granted.

Objective ⑤

Explain accounting issues related to valuation of accounts receivable.

Uncollectible Accounts Receivable

As one accountant so aptly noted, the credit manager's idea of heaven probably would be a place where everyone (eventually) paid his or her debts.[7] Unfortunately, as Illustration 7-6 indicates, a number of companies are experiencing increased credit losses as borrowings increase.

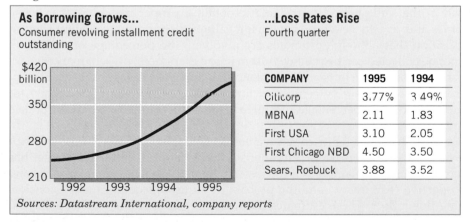

As Borrowing Grows...
Consumer revolving installment credit outstanding

...Loss Rates Rise
Fourth quarter

COMPANY	1995	1994
Citicorp	3.77%	3.49%
MBNA	2.11	1.83
First USA	3.10	2.05
First Chicago NBD	4.50	3.50
Sears, Roebuck	3.88	3.52

Sources: Datastream International, company reports

ILLUSTRATION 7-6
Losses Escalate

---

[6]"Interest on Receivables and Payables," *Opinions of the Accounting Principles Board No. 21* (New York: AICPA, 1971), par. 3(a). According to *APB Opinion No. 21*, all receivables are subject to present value measurement techniques and interest imputation, if necessary, except for the following specifically excluded types:
1. Normal accounts receivable due within one year.
2. Security deposits, retainages, advances, or progress payments.
3. Transactions between parent and subsidiary.
4. Receivables due at some indeterminable future date.

[7]William J. Vatter, *Managerial Accounting* (Englewood Cliffs, N.J.: Prentice-Hall, 1950), p. 60.

Sales on any basis other than for cash make possible the subsequent failure to collect the account. An uncollectible account receivable is a loss of revenue that requires, through proper entry in the accounts, a decrease in the asset accounts receivable and a related decrease in income and stockholders' equity. The loss in revenue and the decrease in income are recognized by recording bad debt expense.

The chief problem in recording uncollectible accounts receivable is establishing the time at which to record the loss. Two general procedures are in use:

❖ METHODS FOR RECORDING UNCOLLECTIBLES ❖

1 *Direct Write-Off Method.* No entry is made until a specific account has definitely been established as uncollectible. Then the loss is recorded by crediting Accounts Receivable and debiting Bad Debt Expense.

2 *Allowance Method.* An estimate is made of the expected uncollectible accounts from all sales made on account or from the total of outstanding receivables. This estimate is entered as an expense and an indirect reduction in accounts receivable (via an increase in the allowance account) in the period in which the sale is recorded.

The direct write-off method records the bad debt in the year it is determined that a specific receivable cannot be collected. The allowance method enters the expense on an estimated basis in the accounting period in which the sales on account are made.

Supporters of the **direct write-off method** contend that facts, not estimates, are recorded. It assumes that a good account receivable resulted from each sale, and that later events proved certain accounts to be uncollectible and worthless. From a practical standpoint this method is simple and convenient to apply, although receivables do not generally become worthless at an identifiable moment of time. The direct write-off method is theoretically deficient because it usually does not match costs with revenues of the period, nor does it result in receivables being stated at estimated realizable value on the balance sheet. **As a result, its use is not considered appropriate, except when the amount uncollectible is immaterial.**

INTERNATIONAL INSIGHT

The "allowance for doubtful accounts" is actually a "reserve" against the possibility of noncollectibility. Although, in general, the use of "reserves" is not acceptable in U.S. accounting, this is one instance where such a reserve is often mandatory. Full disclosure is, of course, also required.

Advocates of the **allowance method** believe that bad debt expense should be recorded in the same period as the sale to obtain a proper matching of expenses and revenues and to achieve a proper carrying value for accounts receivable. They support the position that although estimates are involved, the percentage of receivables that will not be collected can be predicted from past experiences, present market conditions, and an analysis of the outstanding balances. Many companies set their credit policies to provide for a certain percentage of uncollectible accounts. (In fact, many feel that failure to reach that percentage means that sales are being lost by credit policies that are too restrictive.)

Because the collectibility of receivables is considered a loss contingency, the allowance method is appropriate in situations where it is probable that an asset has been impaired and that the amount of the loss can be reasonably estimated.[8] A receivable is a prospective cash inflow, and the probability of its collection must be considered in valuing this inflow. These estimates normally are made either on (1) the basis of percentage of sales or (2) the basis of outstanding receivables.

Percentage-of-Sales (Income Statement) Approach

If there is a fairly stable relationship between previous years' charge sales and bad debts, then that relationship can be turned into a percentage and used to determine this year's bad debt expense.

---

[8]"Accounting for Contingencies," *Statement of Financial Accounting Standards No. 5* (Stamford, Conn.: FASB, 1975), par. 8.

The **percentage-of-sales approach** matches costs with revenues because it relates the charge to the period in which the sale is recorded. To illustrate, assume that Chad Shumway Corp. estimates from past experience that about 2% of charge sales become uncollectible. If Shumway Corp. has charge sales of $400,000 in 1998, the entry to record bad debt expense using the percentage-of-sales method is as follows:

Bad Debt Expense	8,000	
Allowance for Doubtful Accounts		8,000

The Allowance for Doubtful Accounts is a valuation account (i.e., a contra asset) and is subtracted from trade receivables on the balance sheet.[9] The amount of bad debt expense and the related credit to the allowance account are unaffected by any balance currently existing in the allowance account. Because the bad debt expense estimate is related to a nominal account (Sales), and any balance in the allowance is ignored, this method is frequently referred to as the **income statement approach**. A proper matching of cost and revenues is therefore achieved.

Percentage-of-Receivables (Balance Sheet) Approach

Using past experience, a company can estimate the percentage of its outstanding receivables that will become uncollectible, without identifying specific accounts. This procedure provides a reasonably accurate estimate of the receivables' realizable value, but does not fit the concept of matching cost and revenues. Rather, its objective is to report receivables in the balance sheet at net realizable values; hence it is referred to as the **percentage-of-receivables** or **balance sheet approach**.

The percentage of receivables may be applied using one **composite rate** that reflects an estimate of the uncollectible receivables. Another approach that is more sensitive to the actual status of the accounts receivable sets up an **aging schedule** and applies a different percentage based on past experience to the various age categories. An aging schedule is frequently used in practice. It indicates which accounts require special attention by providing the age of such accounts receivable. The following schedule of Wilson & Co. is an example.

ILLUSTRATION 7-7
Accounts Receivable Aging Schedule

Wilson & Co.
AGING SCHEDULE

Name of Customer	Balance Dec. 31	Under 60 days	61–90 days	91–120 days	Over 120 days
Western Stainless Steel Corp.	$ 98,000	$ 80,000	$18,000		
Brockway Steel Company	320,000	320,000			
Freeport Sheet & Tube Co.	55,000				$55,000
Allegheny Iron Works	74,000	60,000		$14,000	
	$547,000	$460,000	$18,000	$14,000	$55,000

Summary

Age	Amount	Percentage Estimated to be Uncollectible	Required Balance in Allowance
Under 60 days old	$460,000	4%	$18,400
61–90 days old	18,000	15%	2,700
91–120 days old	14,000	20%	2,800
Over 120 days	55,000	25%	13,750
Year-end balance of allowance for doubtful accounts			$37,650

The amount $37,650 would be the bad debt expense to be reported for this year, assuming that no balance existed in the allowance account.

---

[9]The account description employed for the allowance account is usually Allowance for Doubtful Accounts or simply Allowance. *Accounting Trends and Techniques—1996*, for example, indicates that approximately 78% of the companies surveyed used "allowance" in their description.

To change the illustration slightly, **assume that the allowance account had a credit balance of $800 before adjustment**. In this case, the amount to be added to the allowance account is $36,850 ($37,650 − $800), and the following entry is made.

Bad Debt Expense	36,850	
Allowance for Doubtful Accounts		36,850

The balance in the Allowance account is therefore stated at $37,650. **If the Allowance balance before adjustment had a debit balance of $200**, then the amount to be recorded for bad debt expense would be $37,850 ($37,650 desired balance + $200 debit balance). In the percentage-of-receivables method, the balance in the allowance account **cannot be ignored** because the percentage is related to a real account (Accounts Receivable).

An aging schedule is usually not prepared to determine the bad debt expense. Rather, it is prepared as a control device to determine the composition of receivables and to identify delinquent accounts. The estimated loss percentage developed for each category is based on previous loss experience and the advice of credit department personnel. Regardless of whether a composite rate or an aging schedule is employed, the primary objective of the percentage of outstanding receivables method for financial statement purposes is to report receivables in the balance sheet at net realizable value. However, it is deficient in that it may not match the bad debt expense to the period in which the sale takes place.

The allowance for doubtful accounts as a percentage of receivables will vary, depending upon the industry and the economic climate. Companies such as Eastman Kodak, General Electric, and Monsanto have recorded allowances ranging from $3.00 to $6.00 per $100 of accounts receivable. Others such as CPC International ($1.48), Texaco ($1.23), and U.S. Steel ($0.78) are examples of large enterprises that have had bad debt allowances of less than $1.50 per $100. At the other extreme are hospitals that allow for $15.00 to $20.00 per $100.00 of accounts receivable.[10]

In summary, the percentage-of-receivables method results in a more accurate valuation of receivables on the balance sheet. From a matching viewpoint, the percentage-of-sales approach provides the better results. The following diagram relates these methods to the basic theory:

ILLUSTRATION 7-8
Comparison of Methods
for Estimating
Uncollectibles

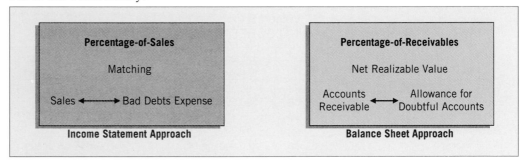

The account title employed for the allowance account is usually Allowance for Doubtful Accounts or simply Allowance.

Collection of Accounts Receivable Written Off

When a particular account receivable is determined to be uncollectible, the balance is removed from the books by debiting Allowance for Doubtful Accounts and crediting

---

[10]A U.S. Department of Commerce study indicated, as a general rule, the following relationships between the age of accounts receivable and their uncollectibility:

30 days or less	4% uncollectible
31–60 days	10% uncollectible
61–90 days	17% uncollectible
91–120 days	26% uncollectible

After 120 days, an approximate 3–4% increase in uncollectibles for every 30 days outstanding occurs for the remainder of the first year.

Accounts Receivable. If a collection is made on a receivable that was previously written off, the procedure is first to reestablish the receivable by debiting Accounts Receivable and crediting Allowance for Doubtful Accounts. An entry is then made to debit Cash and credit the customer's account for the amount received.

If the direct write-off approach is employed, the amount collected is debited to Cash and credited to a revenue account entitled Uncollectible Amounts Recovered, with proper notation in the customer's account.

Special Allowance Accounts

To properly match expenses to sales revenues, it is sometimes necessary to establish additional allowance accounts. These allowance accounts are reported as contra accounts to accounts receivable, and they establish the receivables at net realizable value. The most common allowances are:

❶ Allowance for sales returns and allowances.
❷ Allowance for collection expenses.

Sales Returns and Allowances

Many question the soundness of recording returns and allowances in the current period when they are derived from sales made in the preceding period. Normally, however, the amount of mismatched returns and allowances is not material, if such items are handled consistently from year to year. Yet, if a company completes a few special orders involving large amounts near the end of the accounting period, sales returns and allowances should be anticipated in the period of the sale to avoid distorting the income statement of the current period. And, there are some companies that by their nature have significant returns and customarily establish an allowance for sales returns.

As an example, Astro Turf Corporation recognizes that approximately 5% of its $1,000,000 trade receivables outstanding are returned or some adjustment made to the sale price. Omission of a $50,000 charge could have a material effect on net income for the period. The entry to reflect anticipated sales returns and allowances is:

Sales Returns and Allowances	50,000	
Allowance for Sales Returns and Allowances		50,000

Sales returns and allowances are reported as an offset to sales revenue in the income statement. Returns and allowances are accumulated separately instead of debited directly to the Sales account simply to let the business manager and the statement reader know their magnitude. The allowance is an asset valuation account (contra asset) and is deducted from total accounts receivable.

In most cases, the inclusion in the income statement of all returns and allowances made during the period, whether or not they resulted from the current period's sales, is an acceptable accounting procedure justified by practicality and immateriality.[11]

Collection Expense

A similar concept holds true for collection expense. If a significant handling and service charge is incurred to collect the open accounts receivable at the end of the year, an allowance for collection expenses should be recorded. For example, Sears, Roebuck and Co. reports its receivables net, with an attached schedule indicating the types of receivables outstanding. Sears' contra account is entitled "Allowance for Collection Expenses

---

[11]An interesting sidelight to the entire problem of returns and allowances is determining when a sale is a sale. In certain circumstances the seller is exposed to such a high risk of ownership through possible return of the property that the entire transaction is nullified and the sale not recognized. Such situations have developed particularly in sales to related parties. This subject is discussed in more detail in Chapters 8 and 19.

and Losses on Customer Accounts" as shown below:

Sears, Roebuck and Co.	
Receivables	
Customer installment accounts receivable	
Easy payment accounts	$2,221,017,167
Revolving charge accounts	1,372,874,725
	3,593,891,892
Other customer accounts	101,904,882
Miscellaneous accounts and notes receivable	96,446,334
	3,792,243,108
Less allowance for collection expenses and losses on customer accounts	236,826,866
	$3,555,416,242

❖ RECOGNITION OF NOTES RECEIVABLE

A note receivable is supported by a formal **promissory note**, a written promise to pay a certain sum of money at a specific future date. Such a note is a negotiable instrument that is signed by a **maker** in favor of a designated **payee** who may legally and readily sell or otherwise transfer the note to others. Although notes contain an interest element because of the time value of money, notes are classified as interest-bearing or noninterest-bearing. **Interest-bearing notes** have a stated rate of interest, whereas **zero-interest-bearing notes** (noninterest-bearing) include interest as part of their face amount instead of stating it explicitly. Notes receivable are considered fairly liquid, even if long-term, because they may be easily converted to cash.

Notes receivable are frequently accepted from customers who need to extend the payment period of an outstanding receivable. Notes are also sometimes required of high-risk or new customers. In addition, notes are often used in loans to employees and subsidiaries and in the sales of property, plant, and equipment. In some industries (e.g., the pleasure and sport boat industry) all credit sales are supported by notes. The majority of notes, however, originate from lending transactions. The basic issues in accounting for notes receivable are the same as those for accounts receivable: recognition, valuation, and disposition.

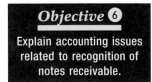

Objective ❻

Explain accounting issues related to recognition of notes receivable.

Short-term notes are generally recorded at face value (less allowances) because the interest implicit in the maturity value is immaterial. A general rule is that notes treated as cash equivalents (maturities of 3 months or less) are not subject to premium or discount amortization. Long-term notes receivable, however, should be recorded and reported at the **present value of the cash expected to be collected**. When the interest stated on an interest-bearing note is equal to the effective (market) rate of interest, the note sells at face value.[12] When the stated rate is different from the market rate, the cash exchanged (present value) is different from the face value of the note. The difference between the face value and the cash exchanged, either a discount or a premium, is then recorded and amortized over the life of a note to approximate the effective (market) interest rate.

Note Issued at Face Value

To illustrate the discounting of a note issued at face value, assume that Bigelow Corp. lends Scandinavian Imports $10,000 in exchange for a $10,000, 3-year note bearing in-

---

[12]The **stated interest rate**, also referred to as the face rate or the coupon rate, is the rate contracted as part of the note. The **effective interest rate**, also referred to as the market rate or the effective yield, is the rate used in the market to determine the value of the note—that is, the discount rate used to determine present value.

terest at 10% annually. The market rate of interest for a note of similar risk is also 10%. This time diagram depicting both cash flows is shown below:

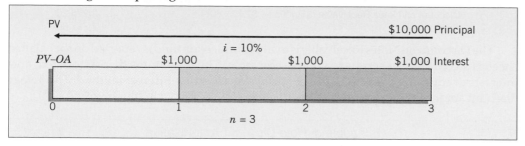

The present value or exchange price of the note is computed as follows:

Face value of the note		$10,000
Present value of the principal:		
$10,000 ($PVF_{3,10\%}$) = $10,000 (.75132)	$7,513	
Present value of the interest:		
$1,000 ($PVF\text{-}OA_{3,10\%}$) = $1,000 (2.48685)	2,487	
Present value of the note		10,000
Difference		$ –0–

ILLUSTRATION 7-9
Present Value of Note—
Stated and Market Rates
the Same

In this case, the present value of the note and its face value are the same, that is, $10,000 because the effective and stated rates of interest are also the same. The receipt of the note is recorded by Bigelow Corp. as follows:

Notes Receivable	10,000	
Cash		10,000

Bigelow Corp. would recognize the interest earned each year as follows:

Cash	1,000	
Interest Revenue		1,000

Note Not Issued at Face Value

Zero-Interest-Bearing Notes

If a zero-interest-bearing note is received solely for cash, its present value is the cash paid to the issuer. Because both the future amount and the present value of the note are known, the interest rate can be computed, i.e., it is implied. The **implicit interest rate** is the rate that equates the cash paid with the amounts receivable in the future. The difference between the future (face) amount and the present value (cash paid) is recorded as a discount and amortized to interest revenue over the life of the note.

To illustrate, Jeremiah Company receives a 3-year, $10,000 zero-interest-bearing note, the present value of which is $7,721.80. The implicit rate that equates the total cash to be received ($10,000 at maturity) to the present value of the future cash flows ($7,721.80) is 9% (the present value of $1 for 3 periods at 9% is $.77218). The time diagram depicting the one cash flow is shown below.

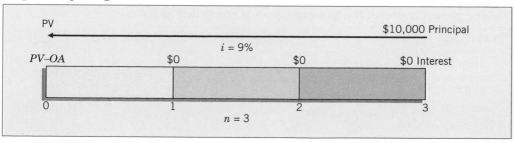

The entry to record the transaction is as follows:

Notes Receivable	10,000.00	
Discount on Notes Receivable ($10,000 − $7,721.80)		2,278.20
Cash		7,721.80

The Discount on Notes Receivable is a valuation account and is reported on the balance sheet as a contra-asset account to notes receivable. The discount is then amortized, and interest revenue is recognized annually using the **effective interest method**. The 3-year discount amortization and interest revenue schedule is shown in Illustration 7-10.

ILLUSTRATION 7-10
Discount Amortization
Schedule—Effective
Interest Method

Schedule of Note Discount Amortization
Effective Interest Method
0% Note Discounted at 9%

	Cash Received	Interest Revenue	Discount Amortized	Carrying Amount of Note
Date of issue				$ 7,721.80
End of year 1	$-0-	$ 694.96[a]	$ 694.96[b]	8,416.76[c]
End of year 2	-0-	757.51	757.51	9,174.27
End of year 3	-0-	825.73[d]	825.73	10,000.00
	$-0-	$2,278.20	$2,278.20	

[a]$7,721.80 × .09 = $694.96
[b]$694.96 − 0 = $694.96
[c]$7,721.80 + $694.96 = $8,416.76
[d]5¢ adjustment to compensate for rounding

Interest revenue at the end of the first year using the effective interest method is recorded as follows:

Discount on Notes Receivable	694.96	
Interest Revenue ($7,721.80 × 9%)		694.96

The amount of the discount, $2,278.20 in this case, represents the interest revenue to be received from the note over the three years.

Interest-Bearing Notes

Often the stated rate and the effective rate are different. The zero-interest-bearing case above is one example of such a situation.

To illustrate a more common situation, assume that Morgan Corp. made a loan to Marie Co. and received in exchange a 3-year, $10,000 note bearing interest at 10% annually. The market rate of interest for a note of similar risk is 12%. The time diagram depicting both cash flows is shown below:

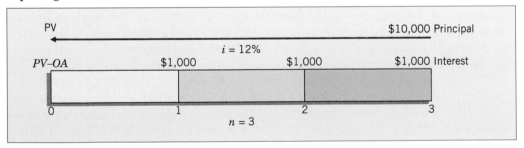

The present value of the two cash flows is computed as follows:

ILLUSTRATION 7-11
Computation of Present
Value—Effective Rate
Different from Stated
Rate

Face value of the note		$10,000
Present value of the principal:		
$10,000 ($PVF_{3,12\%}$) = $10,000 (.71178)	$7,118	
Present value of the interest:		
$1,000 ($PVF\text{-}OA_{3,12\%}$) = $1,000 (2.40183)	2,402	
Present value of the note		9,520
Difference (Discount)		$ 480

In this case, because the effective rate of interest (12%) is greater than the stated rate (10%), the present value of the note is less than the face value; that is, the note was exchanged at a **discount**. The receipt of the note at a discount is recorded by Morgan as follows:

Notes Receivable	10,000	
Discount on Notes Receivable		480
Cash		9,520

The discount is then amortized and interest revenue is recognized annually using the **effective interest method**. The 3-year discount amortization and interest revenue schedule is shown below:

ILLUSTRATION 7-12
Discount Amortization Schedule—Effective Interest Method

Schedule of Note Discount Amortization Effective Interest Method 10% Note Discounted at 12%			
	Cash Received	Interest Revenue	Discount Amortized	Carrying Amount of Note
Date of issue				$ 9,520
End of year 1	$1,000[a]	$1,142[b]	$142[c]	9,662[d]
End of year 2	1,000	1,159	159	9,821
End of year 3	1,000	1,179	179	10,000
	$3,000	$3,480	$480	

[a]$10,000 × 10% = $1,000
[b]$9,520 × 12% = $1,142
[c]$1,142 − $1,000 = $142
[d]$9,520 + $142 = $9,662

On the date of issue, the note has a present value of $9,520. Its unamortized discount—additional interest revenue to be spread over the 3-year life of the note—is $480.

At the end of year 1, Morgan receives $1,000 in cash. But its interest revenue is $1,142 ($9,520 × 12%). The difference between $1,000 and $1,142 is the amortized discount, $142. The carrying amount of the note is now $9,662 ($9,520 + $142). This process is repeated until the end of year 3.

Receipt of the annual interest and amortization of the discount for the first year are recorded by Morgan as follows (amounts per amortization schedule):

Cash	1,000	
Discount on Notes Receivable	142	
Interest Revenue		1,142

When the present value exceeds the face value, the note is exchanged at a premium. The premium on a note receivable is recorded as a debit and amortized using the effective interest method over the life of the note as annual reductions in the amount of interest revenue recognized.

Special Situations

The note transactions just discussed are the common types of situations encountered in practice. Special situations are as follows:

1. Notes received for cash and other rights.
2. Notes received for property, goods, or services.
3. Imputed interest.

Notes Received for Cash and Other Rights

The lender may also accept a **note in exchange for cash and other rights and privileges**. For example, Ideal Equipment Co. accepts a 5-year, $100,000, zero-interest-bearing note from Outland Steel Corp. plus the right to purchase 10,000 tons of steel at a bargain price in exchange for $100,000 in cash. Assume that the current rate of interest that would be charged on another note without the right to purchase at a bargain is 10%. The acceptance of the note is recorded and the present value of the note is computed as follows:

Notes Receivable	100,000	
Prepaid Purchases	37,908	
Discount on Notes Receivable		37,908*
Cash		100,000

*Present value = $100,000 \times (PVF_{5,10\%}) = \$100,000 \times .62092 = \$62,092;$
Discount = $\$100,000 - \$62,092 = \$37,908.$

The difference between the $62,092 present value of the note and its maturity value of $100,000 represents implicit interest of $37,908. It is amortized to interest revenue over the 5-year life of the note using the effective interest method. The excess of the $100,000 over the $62,092 represents an asset, Prepaid Purchases. Prepaid Purchases is allocated to purchases or inventory in proportion to the number of tons of steel purchased each year relative to the total 10,000 tons for which a bargain price is available. For example, if 3,000 tons of steel were purchased during the first year of the 5-year bargain period, the following entry would be recorded by Ideal Equipment:

Purchases (Inventory)	11,372	
Prepaid Purchases		11,372
(3,000/10,000 $\times$ $37,908)		

Note that although prepaid purchases and the discount on notes receivable are both recorded initially at the same amount, $37,908, they are written off differently. Prepaid purchases are written off in the ratio of tons purchased, whereas the discount is amortized using the effective interest method. The value of the right or privilege, in this case the price reduction, aids in determining the interest implicit in the transaction.

Notes Received for Property, Goods, or Services

When a **note is received in exchange for property, goods, or services** in a bargained transaction entered into at arm's length, the stated interest rate is presumed to be fair unless:

❶ No interest rate is stated, or
❷ The stated interest rate is unreasonable, or
❸ The face amount of the note is materially different from the current cash sales price for the same or similar items or from the current market value of the debt instrument.[13]

In these circumstances, the present value of the note is measured by the fair value of the property, goods, or services or by an amount that reasonably approximates the market value of the note.

To illustrate, Oasis Development Co. sold a corner lot to Rusty Pelican as a restaurant site and accepted in exchange a 5-year note having a maturity value of $35,247 and no stated interest rate. The land originally cost Oasis $14,000 and at the date of sale had an appraised fair value of $20,000. Given the criterion above, it is acceptable to use the fair market value of the land, $20,000, as the present value of the note. The entry to record the sale therefore is:

Notes Receivable	35,247	
Discount on Notes Receivable ($35,247 − $20,000)		15,247
Land		14,000
Gain on Sale of Land ($20,000 − $14,000)		6,000

The discount is amortized to interest revenue over the 5-year life of the note using the effective interest method.

---

[13]"Interest on Receivables and Payables," *Opinions of the Accounting Principles Board No. 21* (New York: AICPA, 1971), par. 12.

Imputed Interest

In note transactions, the effective or real interest rate is either evident or determinable by other factors involved in the exchange, such as the fair market value of what is given or received. But, if the fair value of the property, goods, services, or other rights is not determinable and if the note has no ready market, the problem of determining the present value of the note is more difficult. To estimate the present value of a note under such circumstances, an applicable interest rate that may differ from the stated interest rate must be approximated. This process of interest-rate approximation is called **imputation**, and the resulting interest rate is called an imputed interest rate. The imputed interest rate is used to establish the present value of the note by discounting, at that rate, all future receipts (interest and principal) on the note.

> The objective for computing the appropriate interest rate is to approximate the rate which would have resulted if an independent borrower and an independent lender had negotiated a similar transaction under comparable terms and conditions with the option to pay the cash price upon purchase or to give a note for the amount of the purchase which bears the prevailing rate of interest to maturity. The rate used for valuation purposes will normally be at least equal to the rate at which the debtor can obtain financing of a similar nature from other sources at the date of the transaction.[14]

The choice of a rate is affected by the prevailing rates for similar instruments of issuers with similar credit ratings. It is also affected specifically by restrictive covenants, collateral, payment schedule, the existing prime interest rate, etc. Determination of the imputed interest rate is made when the note is received; any subsequent changes in prevailing interest rates are ignored.

To illustrate, assume that on December 31, 1998, Brown Interiors Company rendered architectural services and accepted in exchange a long-term promissory note with a face value of $550,000, a due date of December 31, 2003, and a stated interest rate of 2%, interest receivable at the end of each year. The fair value of the services is not readily determinable, and the note is not readily marketable. Given the circumstances—the maker's credit rating, the absence of collateral, the prime rate, and the prevailing interest rate on the maker's outstanding debt—an 8% interest rate is determined to be appropriate. The time diagram depicting both cash flows is shown below:

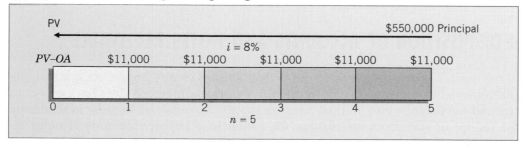

The present value of the note and the imputed fair value of the architectural services are computed as follows:

Face value of the note		$550,000
Present value of $550,000 due in 5 years		
at 8%—$550,000 ($PVF_{5,8\%}$) = $550,000 × .68058	$374,319	
Present value of $11,000 ($550,000 × .02) payable		
annually for 5 years at 8%—		
$11,000 ($PVF\text{-}OA_{5,8\%}$) = $11,000 × 3.99271	43,920	
Present value of the note		418,239
Discount		$131,761

ILLUSTRATION 7-13
Computation of Present Value—Imputed Interest Rate

---

[14]Ibid., par. 13.

The value of the services is thus determined to be $418,239, the current value of the note. The receipt of the note in exchange for the services is recorded as follows:

December 31, 1998

Notes Receivable	550,000	
Discount on Notes Receivable		131,761
Revenue from Services		418,239

An amortization schedule similar to Illustration 7-12 is then prepared to help record transactions in future periods.

❖ VALUATION OF NOTES RECEIVABLE

Objective 7

Explain accounting issues related to valuation of notes receivable.

Like accounts receivable, short-term notes receivable are recorded and reported at their net realizable value; that is, at their face amount less all necessary allowances. The primary notes receivable allowance account is Allowance for Doubtful Accounts. The computations and estimations involved in valuing short-term notes receivable and in recording bad debt expense and the related allowance are **exactly the same as for trade accounts receivable**. Either a percentage of sales revenue or an analysis of the receivables can be used to estimate the amount of uncollectibles.

Long-term notes receivable, however, pose additional estimation problems. We need only look at the problems our financial institutions, most notably money-center banks, have had in collecting receivables from energy loans, real estate loans, and loans to less-developed countries.[15]

A note receivable is considered **impaired** when it is probable that the creditor will be unable to collect all amounts due (both principal and interest) according to the contractual terms of the loan. In that case, the present value of the expected future cash flows is determined by discounting those flows at the historical effective rate. This present value amount is deducted from the carrying amount of the receivable to measure the loss. Impairments, as well as restructurings, of receivables and debts are discussed and illustrated in considerable detail in Chapter 14, Appendix A.

❖ DISPOSITION OF ACCOUNTS AND NOTES RECEIVABLE

Objective 8

Explain accounting issues related to disposition of accounts and notes receivable.

In the normal course of events, accounts and notes receivable are collected when due and removed from the books. However, as credit sales and receivables have grown in size and significance, this "normal course of events" has evolved. **In order to accelerate the receipt of cash from receivables, the owner may transfer accounts or notes receivables to another company for cash.**

There are various reasons for this early transfer. First, for competitive reasons, providing sales financing for customers is virtually mandatory in many industries. In the sale of durable goods, such as automobiles, trucks, industrial and farm equipment, computers, and appliances, a large majority of sales are on an installment contract basis. Many major companies in these industries have created wholly-owned subsidiaries specializing in receivables financing. General Motors Corp. has General Motors Acceptance Corp. (GMAC), Sears has Sears Roebuck Acceptance Corp. (SRAC), and Chrysler Corporation has Chrysler Finance Corporation (CFC).

Second, the **holder** may sell receivables because money is tight and access to normal credit is not available or is prohibitively expensive. Also, a firm may have to sell its receivables, instead of borrowing, to avoid violating existing lending agreements.

---

[15]A wise person once said that a bank lending money to a Third World country is like lending money to one's children: you should never expect to get the interest, let alone the principal.

Finally, billing and collection of receivables are often time-consuming and costly. Credit card companies such as MasterCard, VISA, American Express, Diners Club, and others provide merchants with immediate cash.

Conversely, some **purchasers** of receivables buy them to obtain the legal protection of ownership rights afforded a purchaser of assets versus the lesser rights afforded a secured creditor. In addition, banks and other lending institutions may be forced to purchase receivables because of legal lending limits; that is, they cannot make any additional loans but they can buy receivables and charge a fee for this service.

The transfer of receivables to a third party for cash is accomplished in one of two ways:

❶ Secured borrowing.
❷ Sales of receivables.

Secured Borrowing

Receivables are often used as collateral in a borrowing transaction. A creditor often requires that the debtor designate (assign) or pledge[16] receivables as security for the loan. If the loan is not paid when due, the creditor has the right to convert the collateral to cash—that is, to collect the receivables.

To illustrate, on March 1, 1998, Howat Mills, Inc., provides (assigns) $700,000 of its accounts receivable to Citizens Bank as collateral for a $500,000 note. Howat Mills will continue to collect the accounts receivable; the account debtors are not notified of the arrangement. Citizens Bank assesses a finance charge of 1% of the accounts receivable and interest on the note of 12%. Settlement by Howat Mills to the bank is made monthly for all cash collected on the receivables.

ILLUSTRATION 7-14
Entries for Transfer of Receivables—Secured Borrowing

Howat Mills, Inc.			Citizens Bank		
Transfer of accounts receivable and issuance of note on March 1, 1998:					
Cash	493,000		Notes Receivable	500,000	
Finance Charge	7,000*		Finance Revenue		7,000*
Notes Payable		500,000	Cash		493,000
			*(1% × $700,000)		
Collection in March of $440,000 of accounts less cash discounts of $6,000. In addition, sales returns of $14,000 were received:					
Cash	434,000				
Sales Discounts	6,000				
Sales Returns	14,000		(No entry)		
Accounts Receivable		454,000			
($440,000 + $14,000 = $454,000)					
Remitted March collections plus accrued interest to the bank on April 1:					
Interest Expense	5,000*		Cash	439,000	
Notes Payable	434,000		Interest Revenue		5,000*
Cash		439,000	Notes Receivable		434,000
*($500,000 × .12 × 1/12)					
Collection in April of the balance of accounts less $2,000 written off as uncollectible:					
Cash	244,000				
Allow. for Doubtful Accts.	2,000		(No entry)		
Accounts Receivable		246,000*			
*($700,000 − $454,000)					
Remitted the balance due of $66,000 ($500,000 − $434,000) on the note plus interest on May 1:					
Interest Expense	660*		Cash	66,660	
Notes Payable	66,000		Interest Revenue		660*
Cash		66,660	Notes Receivable		66,000
*($66,000 × .12 × 1/12)					

---

[16]If the receivables are transferred to the transferee for custodial purposes, the custodial arrangement is often referred to as a **pledge**.

In addition to recording the collection of receivables, all discounts, returns and allowances, and bad debts must be recognized. Each month the proceeds from the collection of the accounts receivable are used to retire the note obligation. In addition, interest on the note is paid.[17]

Sales of Receivables

Sales of receivables have increased substantially in recent years. A common type is a sale to a factor. **Factors** are finance companies or banks that buy receivables from businesses for a fee and then collect the remittances directly from the customers. **Factoring receivables** is traditionally associated with the textile, apparel, footwear, furniture, and home furnishing industries.[18]

An illustration of a factoring arrangement is shown below.

ILLUSTRATION 7-15
Basic Procedures in
Factoring

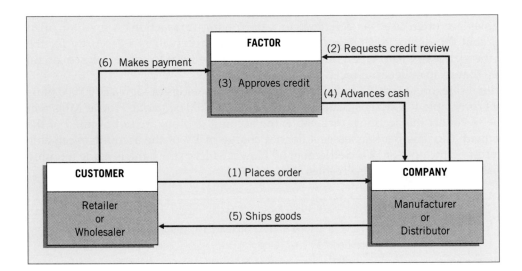

A recent phenomenon in the sale (transfer) of receivables is "securitization." **Securitization** takes a pool of assets such as credit card receivables, mortgage receivables, or car loan receivables and sells shares in these pools of interest and principal payments (in effect, creating securities backed by these pools of assets). Virtually every asset with a payment stream and a long-term payment history is a candidate for securitization.

The differences between factoring and securitization are that factoring usually involves sale to only one company, fees are high, the quality of the receivables is low, and the seller afterward does not service the receivables. In a securitization, many investors are involved, margins are tight, the receivables are of high quality, and the seller usually continues to service the receivables.

---

[17]What happens if Citizens Bank collected the transferred accounts receivable rather than Howat Mills? In that case, Citizens Bank would simply remit the cash proceeds to Howat Mills, and Howat Mills would make the same entries shown in Illustration 7-14. As a result, the receivables used as collateral are reported as an asset on the transferors' balance sheet. In some cases, if the transferee can sell or pledge the receivables received from the transferor, the transferee may be required to report an additional asset and related liability.

[18]Credit cards like MasterCard and VISA are a type of factoring arrangement. Typically the purchaser of the receivable charges a ¾% to 1½% commission of the receivables purchased (the commission is 4–5% for credit card factoring).

In either a factoring or a securitization transaction, receivables are sold on either a **without recourse** or a **with recourse** basis.[19]

Sale without Recourse

When receivables are sold **without recourse**, the purchaser assumes the risk of collectibility and absorbs any credit losses. The transfer of accounts receivable in a nonrecourse transaction is an outright sale of the receivables both in form (transfer of title) and substance (transfer of control). In nonrecourse transactions, as in any sale of assets, Cash is debited for the proceeds. Accounts Receivable is credited for the face value of the receivables. The difference, reduced by any provision for probable adjustments (discounts, returns, allowances, etc.), is recognized as a Loss on the Sale of Receivables. The seller uses a Due from Factor account (reported as a receivable) to account for the proceeds retained by the factor to cover probable sales discounts, sales returns, and sales allowances.

To illustrate, Crest Textiles, Inc. factors $500,000 of accounts receivable with Commercial Factors, Inc., on a **without recourse** basis. The receivable records are transferred to Commercial Factors, Inc., which will receive the collections. Commercial Factors assesses a finance charge of 3% of the amount of accounts receivable and retains an amount equal to 5% of the accounts receivable. The journal entries for both Crest Textiles and Commercial Factors for the receivables transferred without recourse are as follows:

Go to Web Site for a comprehensive illustration of sale without recourse

Crest Textiles, Inc.				Commercial Factors, Inc.		
Cash	460,000			Accounts (Notes) Receivable	500,000	
Due from Factor	25,000*			Due to Crest Textiles		25,000
Loss on Sale of Receivables	15,000**			Financing Revenue		15,000
Accounts (Notes) Receivable		500,000		Cash		460,000
*(5% × $500,000)						
**(3% × $500,000)						

ILLUSTRATION 7-16
Entries for Sale of Receivables Without Recourse

In recognition of the sale of receivables, Crest Textiles records a loss of $15,000. The factor's net income will be the difference between the financing revenue of $15,000 and the amount of any uncollectible receivables.

Sale with Recourse

If receivables are sold **with recourse**, the seller guarantees payment to the purchaser in the event the debtor fails to pay. To record this type of transaction, a **financial components approach** is used, because the seller has a continuing involvement with the receivable.[20] In this approach, each party to the sale recognizes the assets and liabilities

---

[19]**Recourse** is the right of a transferee of receivables to receive payment from the transferor of those receivables for (1) failure of the debtors to pay when due, (2) the effects of prepayments, or (3) adjustments resulting from defects in the eligibility of the transferred receivables. See "Accounting for Transfers and Servicing of Financial Assets and Extinguishments of Liabilities," *Statement of Financial Accounting Standards No. 125* (Stamford, Conn.: FASB, 1996), pp. 3–4.

[20]Previous accounting standards generally required that the transferor account for financial assets transferred as an inseparable unit that had been entirely sold or entirely retained. Those standards were difficult to apply and produced inconsistent and arbitrary results. Values are now assigned to such components as the recourse provision, servicing rights, and agreement to reacquire.

that it controls after the sale and no longer recognizes the assets and liabilities that were sold or extinguished.

To illustrate, assume the same information as in Illustration 7-16 for Crest Textiles and for Commercial Factors except that the receivables are sold on a with recourse basis. It is determined that this recourse obligation has a fair value of $6,000. To determine the loss on the sale of the receivables by Crest Textiles, the net proceeds from the sale are computed:

ILLUSTRATION 7-17
Net Proceeds
Computation

Cash received	$460,000	
Due from factor	25,000	$485,000
Less: Recourse obligation		6,000
Net proceeds		$479,000

Net proceeds are cash or other assets received in a sale less any liabilities incurred. The loss is then computed as follows:

ILLUSTRATION 7-18
Loss on Sale
Computation

Carrying (book) value	$500,000
Net proceeds	479,000
Loss on sale of receivables	$ 21,000

The journal entries for both Crest Textiles and Commercial Factors for the receivables sold with recourse are as follows:

ILLUSTRATION 7-19
Entries for Sale of
Receivables with
Recourse

Crest Textiles, Inc.			Commercial Factors, Inc.		
Cash	460,000		Accounts Receivable	500,000	
Due from Factor	25,000		Due to Crest Textiles		25,000
Loss on Sale of Receivables	21,000		Financing Revenue		15,000
Accounts (Notes) Receivable		500,000	Cash		460,000
Recourse Liability		6,000			

In this case, Crest Textiles recognizes a loss of $21,000. In addition, a liability of $6,000 is recorded to indicate the probable payment to Commercial Factors for uncollectible receivables. If all the receivables are collected, Crest Textiles would eliminate its recourse liability and increase income. Commercial Factors' net income is the financing revenue of $15,000 because it will have no bad debts related to these receivables.

Secured Borrowing versus Sale

The FASB concluded that a sale occurs only if the seller surrenders control of the receivables to the buyer. The following three conditions must be met before a sale can be recorded:

a. The transferred asset has been isolated from the transferor (put beyond reach of the transferor and its creditors).
b. The transferees have obtained the right to pledge or exchange either the transferred assets or beneficial interests in the transferred assets.
c. The transferor does not maintain effective control over the transferred assets through an agreement to repurchase or redeem them before their maturity.

If the three conditions are met, a sale occurs. Otherwise, the transferor should record the transfer as a secured borrowing. If sale accounting is appropriate, it is still necessary to consider assets obtained and liabilities incurred in the transaction. The rules of accounting for transfers of receivables are shown in Illustration 7-20.

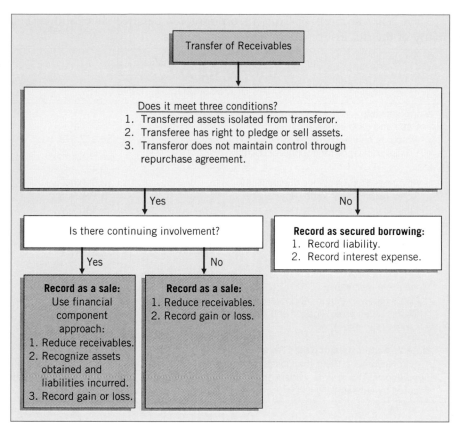

ILLUSTRATION 7-20
Accounting for Transfers
of Receivables

As shown in Illustration 7-20, if there is continuing involvement in a sale transaction, the assets obtained and liabilities incurred must be recorded at fair value.

Objective **9**

Explain how receivables are reported and analyzed.

❖ PRESENTATION AND ANALYSIS

Presentation of Receivables

The general rules in classifying receivables are: (1) segregate the different types of receivables that an enterprise possesses, if material; (2) insure that the valuation accounts are appropriately offset against the proper receivable accounts; (3) determine that receivables classified in the current assets section will be converted into cash within the year or the operating cycle, whichever is longer; (4) disclose any loss contingencies that exist on the receivables; (5) disclose any receivables designated or pledged as collateral; (6) disclose all significant concentrations of credit risk arising from receivables.[21]

---

[21]Concentrations of credit risk exist when receivables have common characteristics that may affect their collection. These common characteristics might be companies in the same industry or same region of the country. For example, financial statements users want to know if a substantial amount of receivables are with defense contractors or with companies in the Middle East. No numerical guidelines are provided as to what is meant by a "concentration of credit risk." When a concentration is identified, three items should be disclosed: (1) information on the characteristic that determines the concentration should be identified, (2) the amount of loss that could occur upon nonperformance, and (3) information on any collateral related to the receivable. "Disclosure of Information About Financial Instruments with Off-Balance-Sheet Risk and Financial Instruments with Concentrations of Credit Risk," *Statement of Financial Accounting Standards No. 105* (Norwalk, CT: FASB, 1990).

The asset sections of Colton Corporation's balance sheet shown below illustrate many of the disclosures required for receivables:

ILLUSTRATION 7-21
Disclosure of Receivables

Go to Web Site for additional disclosures of receivables

INTERNATIONAL INSIGHT

Holding receivables that will be paid in a foreign currency represents risk that the exchange rate may move against the company, causing a decrease in the amount collected in terms of U.S. dollars. Companies engaged in cross-border transactions often "hedge" these receivables by buying contracts to exchange currencies at specified amounts at future dates.

Colton Corporation
PARTIAL BALANCE SHEET
As of December 31, 1998

Current assets		
Cash and cash equivalents		$ 1,870,250
Accounts receivable (Note 2)	$8,977,673	
Less allowance for doubtful accounts	500,226	
	8,477,447	
Advances to subsidiaries due 9/30/99	2,090,000	
Notes receivable—trade (Note 2)	1,532,000	
Federal income taxes refundable	146,704	
Dividends and interest receivable	75,500	
Other receivables and claims (including debit balances in accounts payable)	174,620	12,496,271
Total current assets		14,366,521
Noncurrent receivables		
Notes receivable from officers and key employees		376,090
Claims receivable (litigation settlement to be collected over four years)		585,000

Note 2: Accounts and Notes Receivable
In November 1998, the Company arranged with a finance company to refinance a part of its indebtedness. The loan is evidenced by a 12% note payable. The note is payable on demand and is secured by substantially all the accounts receivable.

Analysis of Receivables

Financial ratios are frequently computed to evaluate the liquidity of a company's accounts receivable. The ratio used to assess the liquidity of the receivables is the **receivables turnover ratio**. This ratio measures the number of times, on average, receivables are collected during the period. The ratio is computed by dividing net sales by average receivables (net) outstanding during the year. Theoretically, the numerator should include only net credit sales. This information is frequently not available, however, and if the relative amounts of charge and cash sales remain fairly constant, the trend indicated by the ratio will still be valid. Unless seasonal factors are significant, average receivables outstanding can be computed from the beginning and ending balances of net trade receivables.

To illustrate, Apple Computer reported 1996 net sales of $9,833 million, its beginning and ending accounts receivable balances were $1,931 million and $1,496 million, respectively. Its accounts receivables turnover ratio is computed as follows:

ILLUSTRATION 7-22
Computation of Accounts Receivable Turnover

$$\text{Accounts Receivable Turnover} = \frac{\text{Net sales}}{\text{Average trade receivables (net)}}$$

$$= \frac{\$9,833}{\dfrac{\$1,931 + \$1,496}{2}}$$

$$= 5.74 \text{ times, or every 64 days (365 days} \div 5.74)^{22}$$

---

[22]Often the receivables turnover is transformed to **days to collect accounts receivable** or days outstanding—an average collection period. In this case, 5.74 is divided into 365 days to obtain 64 days. Several figures other than 365 could be used here; a most common alternative is 360 days because it is divisible by 30 (days) and 12 (months). Use 365 days in any homework computations.

This information provides some indication of the quality of the receivables, and also an idea of how successful the firm is in collecting its outstanding receivables. If possible, an aging schedule should also be prepared to determine how long receivables have been outsanding. It is possible that a satisfactory receivables turnover may have resulted because certain receivables were collected quickly though others have been outstanding for a relatively long period. An aging schedule would reveal such patterns.

UNDERLYING CONCEPTS

Providing information that will help users assess an enterprises's current liquidity and prospective cash flows is a primary objective of accounting.

SUMMARY OF LEARNING OBJECTIVES

❶ *Identify items considered cash.* To be reported as "cash," an asset must be readily available for the payment of current obligations and free from contractual restrictions that limit its use in satisfying debts. Cash consists of coin, currency, and available funds on deposit at the bank. Negotiable instruments such as money orders, certified checks, cashier's checks, personal checks, and bank drafts are also viewed as cash. Savings accounts are usually classified as cash.

❷ *Indicate how cash and related items are reported.* Cash is reported as a current asset in the balance sheet. The reporting of other related items are: (1) *Restricted cash:* The SEC recommends that legally restricted deposits held as compensating balances against short-term borrowing be stated separately among the "cash and cash equivalent items" in Current Assets. Restricted deposits held against long-term borrowing arrangements should be separately classified as noncurrent assets in either the Investments or Other Assets sections. (2) *Bank overdrafts:* They should be reported in the current liabilities section and are usually added to the amount reported as accounts payable. If material, these items should be separately disclosed either on the face of the balance sheet or in the related notes. (3) *Cash equivalents:* This item is often reported together with cash as "cash and cash equivalents."

❸ *Define receivables and identify the different types of receivables.* Receivables are claims held against customers and others for money, goods, or services. The receivables are classified into three types: (1) current or noncurrent; (2) trade or nontrade; (3) accounts receivable or notes receivable.

❹ *Explain accounting issues related to recognition of accounts receivable.* Two issues that may complicate the measurement of accounts receivable are: (1) The availability of discounts (trade and cash discounts) and (2) the length of time between the sale and the payment due dates (the interest element).

Ideally, receivables should be measured in terms of their present value—that is, the discounted value of the cash to be received in the future. The profession specifically excludes from the present value considerations receivables arising from normal business transactions that are due in customary trade terms within approximately one year.

❺ *Explain accounting issues related to valuation of accounts receivable.* Short-term receivables are valued and reported at net realizable value—the net amount expected to be received in cash, which is not necessarily the amount legally receivable. Determining net realizable value requires an estimation of both uncollectible receivables and any returns or allowances.

❻ *Explain accounting issues related to recognition of notes receivable.* Short-term notes are recorded at face value. Long-term notes receivable are recorded at the present value of the cash expected to be collected. When the interest stated on an interest-bearing note is equal to the effective (market) rate of interest, the note sells at face value. When the stated rate is different from the effective rate, either a discount or premium is recorded.

KEY TERMS

accounts receivable, *337*
aging schedule, *341*
allowance method, *340*
bank overdrafts, *335*
cash, *332*
cash discounts, *338*
cash equivalents, *335*
compensating balances, *334*
direct write-off method, *340*
factoring receivables, *352*
financial components approach, *353*
imputed interest rate, *349*
net realizable value, *339*
nontrade receivables, *337*
notes receivable, *337*
percentage-of-receivables approach, *341*
percentage-of-sales approach, *341*
promissory note, *344*
receivables, *336*
receivables turnover ratio, *356*
restricted cash, *335*
sales discounts, *338*
sales returns and allowances, *343*
securitization, *352*
trade discounts, *337*
trade receivables, *336*
with recourse, *353*
without recourse, *353*
zero-interest-bearing notes, *344*

⑦ ***Explain accounting issues related to valuation of notes receivable.*** Like accounts receivable, short-term notes receivable are recorded and reported at their net realizable value. The same is also true of long-term receivables. Special issues relate to impairments and notes receivable past due.

⑧ ***Explain accounting issues related to disposition of accounts and notes receivable.*** To accelerate the receipt of cash from receivables, the owner may transfer the receivables to another company for cash. The transfer of receivables to a third party for cash may be accomplished in one of two ways: (1) *Secured borrowing:* A creditor often requires that the debtor designate or pledge receivables as security for the loan. (2) *Sales (factoring) of receivables:* Factors are finance companies or banks that buy receivables from businesses and then collect the remittances directly from the customers. In many cases, transferors may have some continuing involvement with the receivable sold. A financial components approach is used to record this type of transaction.

⑨ ***Explain how receivables are reported and analyzed.*** Disclosure of receivables requires valuation accounts be appropriately offset against receivables, receivables be appropriately classified as current or noncurrent, pledged or designated receivables be identified, and concentrations of risks arising from receivables be identified. Receivables may be analyzed relative to turnover and the days outstanding.

Appendix **7A**

Cash Controls

After studying Appendix 7A, you should be able to: Explain common techniques employed to control cash.

As indicated in Chapter 7, cash creates many management and control problems. The purpose of this appendix is to discuss some of the basic control issues related to cash.

❖ USING BANK ACCOUNTS

INTERNATIONAL INSIGHT

Multinational corporations often have cash accounts in more than one currency. For financial statement purposes these currencies are typically translated into U.S. dollars using the exchange rate in effect at the balance sheet date.

A company can vary the number and location of banks and the types of bank accounts to obtain desired control objectives. For large companies operating in multiple locations, the location of bank accounts can be important. Establishing collection accounts in strategic locations can accelerate the flow of cash into the company by shortening the time between a customer's mailing of a payment and the company's use of the cash. Multiple collection centers generally are used to reduce the size of a company's **collection float**, which is the difference between the amount on deposit according to the company's records and the amount of collected cash according to the bank record.

The **general checking account** is the principal bank account in most companies and frequently the only bank account in small businesses. Cash is deposited in and disbursed from this account as all transactions are cycled through it. Deposits from and disbursements to all other bank accounts are made through the general checking account.

Imprest bank accounts are used to make a specific amount of cash available for a limited purpose. The account acts as a clearing account for a large volume of checks or for a specific type of check. The specific and intended amount to be cleared through the imprest account is deposited by transferring that amount from the general checking account or other source. Imprest bank accounts are often used for disbursing payroll checks, dividends, commissions, bonuses, confidential expenses (e.g., officers' salaries), and travel expenses.

Lockbox accounts are frequently used by large, multilocation companies to make collections in cities within areas of heaviest customer billing. The company rents a local post office box and authorizes a local bank to pick up the remittances mailed to that box number. The bank empties the box at least once a day and immediately credits the company's account for collections. The greatest advantage of a lockbox is that it accelerates the availability of collected cash. Generally, in a lockbox arrangement the bank microfilms the checks for record purposes and provides the company with a deposit slip, a list of collections, and any customer correspondence. If the control over cash is improved and if the income generated from accelerating the receipt of funds exceeds the cost of the lockbox system, then it is considered a worthwhile undertaking.

❖ THE IMPREST PETTY CASH SYSTEM

Almost every company finds it necessary to pay small amounts for a great many things such as employees' lunches, taxi fares, minor office supplies, and other miscellaneous expenses. It is frequently impractical to require that such disbursements be made by check, yet some control over them is important. A simple method of obtaining reasonable control, while adhering to the rule of disbursement by check, is the **imprest system for petty cash** disbursements.

This is how the system works:

❶ Someone is designated petty cash custodian and given a small amount of currency from which to make small payments. The transfer of funds to petty cash is recorded as:

Petty Cash	300	
Cash		300

❷ As disbursements are made, the petty cash custodian obtains signed receipts from each individual to whom cash is paid. If possible, evidence of the disbursement should be attached to the petty cash receipt.

Petty cash transactions are not recorded until the fund is reimbursed and then such entries are recorded by someone other than the petty cash custodian.

❸ When the supply of cash runs low, the custodian presents to the general cashier a request for reimbursement supported by the petty cash receipts and other disbursement evidence. The custodian receives a company check to replenish the fund. At this point, transactions are recorded based on petty cash receipts:

Office Supplies Expense	42	
Postage Expense	53	
Entertainment Expense	76	
Cash Over and Short	2	
Cash		173

❹ If it is decided that the amount of cash in the petty cash fund is excessive, an adjustment may be made as follows (lowering the fund balance from $300 to $250):

Cash	50	
Petty Cash		50

Entries are made to the Petty Cash account only to increase or decrease the size of the fund.

A **Cash Over and Short** account is used when the petty cash fund fails to prove out. When this occurs, it is usually due to an error (failure to provide correct change, overpayment of expense, lost receipt, etc.). If cash proves out **short** (i.e., the sum of the receipts and cash in the fund is less than the imprest amount), the shortage is debited to the Cash Over and Short account. If it proves out **over**, the overage is credited to Cash Over and Short. This account is left open until the end of the year, when it is closed and generally shown on the income statement as an other expense or revenue.

There are usually expense items in the fund except immediately after reimbursement; therefore, if accurate financial statements are desired, the funds must be reimbursed at the end of each accounting period and also when nearly depleted.

Under the imprest system the petty cash custodian is responsible at all times for the amount of the fund on hand either as cash or in the form of signed receipts. These receipts provide the evidence required by the disbursing officer to issue a reimbursement check. Two additional procedures are followed to obtain more complete control over the petty cash fund:

❶ Surprise counts of the fund are made from time to time by a superior of the petty cash custodian to determine that the fund is being accounted for satisfactorily.

❷ Petty cash receipts are canceled or mutilated after they have been submitted for reimbursement, so that they cannot be used to secure a second reimbursement.

❖ PHYSICAL PROTECTION OF CASH BALANCES

Not only must cash receipts and cash disbursements be safeguarded through internal control measures, but also the cash on hand and in banks must be protected. Because receipts become cash on hand and disbursements are made from cash in banks, adequate control of receipts and disbursements is a part of the protection of cash balances. Certain other procedures, however, should be given some consideration.

Physical protection of cash is so elementary a necessity that it requires little discussion. Every effort should be made to minimize the cash on hand in the office. A petty cash fund, the current day's receipts, and perhaps funds for making change should be all that is on hand at any one time. Insofar as possible, these funds should be kept in a vault, safe, or locked cash drawer. Each day's receipts should be transmitted intact to the bank as soon as practicable. Accurately stating the amount of available cash both in internal management reports and in external financial statements is also extremely important.

Every company has a record of cash received, disbursed, and the balance. Because of the many cash transactions, however, errors or omissions may be made in keeping this record. Therefore, it is necessary periodically to prove the balance shown in the general ledger. Cash actually present in the office—petty cash, change funds, and undeposited receipts—can be counted, for comparison with the company records. Cash on deposit is not available for count and is proved by preparing a bank reconciliation— a reconciliation of the company's record and the bank's record of the company's cash.

❖ RECONCILIATION OF BANK BALANCES

At the end of each calendar month the bank supplies each customer with a **bank statement** (a copy of the bank's account with the customer) together with the customer's checks that have been paid by the bank during the month. If no errors were made by the bank or the customer, if all deposits made and all checks drawn by the customer reached the bank within the same month, and if no unusual transactions occurred that affected either the company's or the bank's record of cash, the balance of cash reported by the bank to the customer would be the same as that shown in the customer's own records. This condition seldom occurs for one or more of the following reasons:

❖RECONCILING ITEMS ❖

❶ *Deposits in Transit.* End-of-month deposits of cash recorded on the depositor's books in one month are received and recorded by the bank in the following month.

❷ *Outstanding Checks.* Checks written by the depositor are recorded when written but may not be recorded by—or "clear"—the bank until the next month.

❸ *Bank Charges.* Charges recorded by the bank against the depositor's balance for such items as bank services, printing checks, **not-sufficient-funds (NSF) checks**, and safe-deposit box rentals. The depositor may not be aware of these charges until the receipt of the bank statement.

❹ *Bank Credits.* Collections or deposits by the bank for the benefit of the depositor that may be unknown to the depositor until receipt of the bank statement. Examples are note collection for the depositor and interest earned on interest-bearing checking accounts.

❺ *Bank or Depositor Errors.* Errors on either the part of the bank or the part of the depositor cause the bank balance to disagree with the depositor's book balance.

Hence, differences between the depositor's record of cash and the bank's record are usual and expected. Therefore, the two must be reconciled to determine the nature of the differences between the two amounts.

A **bank reconciliation** is a schedule explaining any differences between the bank's and the company's records of cash. If the difference results only from transactions not yet recorded by the bank, the company's record of cash is considered correct. But, if some part of the difference arises from other items, the bank's records or the company's records must be adjusted.

Two forms of bank reconciliation may be prepared. One form reconciles from the bank statement balance to the book balance or vice versa. The other form reconciles both the bank balance and the book balance to a correct cash balance. This latter form is more widely used. A sample of that form and its common reconciling items are shown in Illustration 7A-1.

Balance per bank statement (end of period)		$$$
Add: Deposits in transit	$$	
Undeposited receipts (cash on hand)	$$	
Bank errors that understate the bank statement balance	$$	$$
Deduct: Outstanding checks	$$	$$$
Bank errors that overstate the bank statement balance	$$	$$
Correct cash balance		$$$
Balance per depositor's books		$$$
Add: Bank credits and collections not yet recorded in the books	$$	
Book errors that understate the book balance	$$	$$
		$$$
Deduct: Bank charges not yet recorded in the books	$$	
Book errors that overstate the book balance	$$	$$
Correct cash balance		$$$

ILLUSTRATION 7A-1
Bank Reconciliation Form and Content

This form of reconciliation consists of two sections: (1) "Balance per bank statement" and (2) "Balance per depositor's books." Both sections end with the same "correct cash balance." The correct cash balance is the amount to which the books must be adjusted and is the amount reported on the balance sheet. Adjusting journal entries are prepared for all the addition and deduction items appearing in the "Balance per depositor's books" section. Any errors attributable to the bank should be called to the bank's attention immediately.

To illustrate, Nugget Mining Company's books show a cash balance at the Denver National Bank on November 30, 1998, of $20,502. The bank statement covering the month of November shows an ending balance of $22,190. An examination of Nugget's accounting records and November bank statement identified the following reconciling items:

❶ A deposit of $3,680 was mailed November 30 but does not appear on the bank statement.

❷ Checks written in November but not charged to the November bank statement are:

Check #7327	$ 150
#7348	4,820
#7349	31

❸ Nugget has not yet recorded the $600 of interest collected by the bank Nov. 20 on Sequoia Co. bonds held by the bank for Nugget.

❹ Bank service charges of $18 are not yet recorded on Nugget's books.

❺ One of Nugget's customer's checks for $220 was returned with the bank statement and marked "NSF." The bank treated this bad check as a disbursement.

❻ Nugget discovered that check #7322, written in November for $131 in payment of an account payable; had been incorrectly recorded in their books as $311.

❼ A check for Nugent Oil Co. in the amount of $175 accompanied the bank statement that had been incorrectly charged to Nugget Mining.

The reconciliation of bank and book balances to the correct cash balance of $21,044 would appear as follows:

ILLUSTRATION 7A-2
Sample Bank
Reconciliation

Nugget Mining Company
Bank Reconciliation
Denver National Bank, November 30, 1998

Balance per bank statement (end of period)			$22,190
Add: Deposit in transit	(1)	$3,680	
Bank error—incorrect check charged to account by bank	(7)	175	3,855
			26,045
Deduct: Outstanding checks	(2)		5,001
Correct cash balance			$21,044
Balance per books			$20,502
Add: Interest collected by the bank	(3)	$ 600	
Error in recording check #7322	(6)	180	780
			21,282
Deduct: Bank service charges	(4)	18	
NSF check returned	(5)	220	238
Correct cash balance			$21,044

The journal entries required to adjust and correct Nugget Mining's books in early December 1998 are taken from the items in the "Balance per books" section and are as follows:

Cash	600	
Interest Revenue		600
(To record interest on Sequoia Co. bonds, collected by bank)		
Cash	180	
Accounts Payable		180
(To correct error in recording amount of check #7322)		
Office Expense—Bank Charges	18	
Cash		18
(To record bank service charges for November)		

| Accounts Receivable | 220 | |
| Cash | | 220 |

(To record customer's check returned NSF)

When the entries are posted, Nugget's cash account will have a balance of $21,044. Nugget should return the Nugent Oil Co. check to Denver National Bank, informing the bank of the error.

Another widely used form of bank reconciliation is the **four-column reconciliation** ("proof of cash"), which is discussed and illustrated in Appendix 7B.

SUMMARY OF LEARNING OBJECTIVE FOR APPENDIX 7A

(10) ***Explain common techniques employed to control cash.*** The common techniques employed to control cash are: (1) *Using bank accounts:* a company can vary the number and location of banks and the types of accounts to obtain desired control objectives. (2) *The imprest petty cash system:* It may be impractical to require small amounts of various expenses be paid by check, yet some control over them is important. (3) *Physical protection of cash balances:* Adequate control of receipts and disbursements is a part of the protection of cash balances. Every effort should be made to minimize the cash on hand in the office. (4) *Reconciliation of bank balances:* Cash on deposit is not available for count and is proved by preparing a bank reconciliation.

KEY TERMS

bank reconciliation, *361*
imprest system for petty cash, *359*
not-sufficient-funds (NSF) checks, *361*

Appendix 7B

Four-Column Bank Reconciliation

❖ RECONCILIATION OF RECEIPTS AND DISBURSEMENTS

In addition to the form presented in Appendix 7A, another form of reconciliation is frequently used by auditors (and typically illustrated in auditing textbooks). That is the so-called **proof of cash** or **four-column bank reconciliation**. It is an expanded version of the bank reconciliation shown in Illustration 7A-2.

The proof-of-cash form of reconciliation is actually four reconciliations in one (see Illustration 7B-1):

❶ Reconciliation of the **beginning-of-the-period cash balances** per the bank statement and the books (first column).
❷ Reconciliation of the **current period cash receipts** (deposits) per the bank statement to receipts recorded in the books (second column).
❸ Reconciliation of the **current period cash disbursements** per the bank statement to disbursements recorded in the books (third column).
❹ Reconciliation of the **end-of-the-period cash balances** per the bank statement and the books (fourth column).

Objective **⑪**

After studying Appendix 7B, you should be able to: Prepare a proof of cash (four-column bank reconciliation).

The top row ("Per bank statement") is a summary of transactions for the period as taken from the bank statement. The beginning and ending bank balances are shown on the bank statement as are the bank receipts (as shown in the "deposits" column) and the bank disbursements (as shown in the "charges" or "checks cashed" column).

The "Per books" line is a summary of the cash transactions as recorded in the books. These totals should be taken directly from the books, preferably from the Cash account itself, which should, of course, show receipts and disbursements as debit and credit entries and the beginning and ending cash balances.

The left-hand and right-hand columns are simply **end-of-the-prior-period** and **end-of-the-current-period** reconciliations, the preparation of which was illustrated on page 362. The two center columns, receipts and disbursements, tie the left-hand column and right-hand column reconciliations together. With few exceptions, the amounts needed to complete these center columns may be found in the figures included in either the top or bottom rows or in the left- and right-hand columns; no new data need be added.[1]

The four-column proof of cash is preferred by auditors as a means of identifying all differences between the books and the bank statement during the period covered by the reconciliation. It is generally prepared by auditors when a company has weak internal control over cash; it assists in identifying unauthorized and unrecorded transfers of cash.

To illustrate the four-column reconciliation, the data provided for the Nugget Mining Company at November 30 in Illustration 7A-2 will be used, along with the following information:

❶ The cash balance as of October 31, 1998, per the bank statement (the beginning of November balance) was $17,520.

❷ The cash balance as of October 31, 1998, per Nugget's books was $18,020.

ILLUSTRATION 7B-1
Four-column Bank Reconciliation—Bank and Book Balance to Corrected Balance Form

Nugget Mining Company
Proof of Cash for November 1998
Denver National Bank—Checking Account

	Balance October 31	November Receipts	November Disbursements	Balance November 30
Per bank statement	$17,520	$96,450	$91,780	$22,190
Deposits in transit				
at October 31	4,200	(4,200)		
at November 30		3,680		3,680
Outstanding checks				
at October 31	(3,700)		(3,700)	
at November 30			5,001	(5,001)
Bank error—incorrect check				
charged by bank			(175)	175
Correct amounts	$18,020	$95,930	$92,906	$21,044
Per books	$18,020	$95,330	$92,848	$20,502
Interest collected by bank		600		600
Error in recording check #7322			(180)	180
Unrecorded service charges				
at November 30			18	(18)
NSF check returned			220	(220)
Correct amounts	$18,020	$95,930	$92,906	$21,044

---

[1]An exception would be a customer's check deposited, returned NSF, and redeposited without entry in the same period. In this situation, receipts and disbursements per bank would be higher than the receipts and disbursements per books. Deposits would have been reported twice in the bank statement but only recorded once for books' purposes. Also, the bank would have shown a disbursement when the check bounced. No disbursement has been recorded in the accounting records.

3 The total cash receipts (deposits) per the November bank statement are $96,450. These receipts include a deposit in transit of $4,200 at October 31.

4 The total cash receipts per Nugget's books during November are $95,330.

5 The total cash disbursements per the bank statement for November are $91,780. These disbursements include $3,700 of checks outstanding at October 31.

6 The total cash disbursements per the books during November are $92,848.

The completed reconciliation, reconciling to the corrected balance, is shown in Illustration 7B-1.

An alternative procedure for preparing a proof-of-cash reconciliation involves reconciling from the bank balance to the book balance rather than reconciling both amounts to a correct cash balance. This alternative is shown in Illustration 7B-2.

	Balance October 31	November Receipts	November Disbursements	Balance November 30
Nugget Mining Company Proof of Cash for November 1998 Denver National Bank—Checking Account				
Per bank statement	$17,520	$96,450	$91,780	$22,190
Deposits in transit				
at October 31	4,200	(4,200)		
at November 30		3,680		3,680
Outstanding checks				
at October 31	(3,700)		(3,700)	
at November 30			5,001	(5,001)
Bank error—incorrect check			(175)	175
Interest collected by bank		(600)		(600)
Error per books—check #7322			180	(180)
Unrecorded service charges				
at November 30			(18)	18
NSF check returned by bank			(220)	220
Per books	$18,020	$95,330	$92,848	$20,502

ILLUSTRATION 7B-2
Four-column Bank Reconciliation—Bank to Book Form

The "bank to book" reconciliation form in Illustration 7B-2 is generally illustrated in auditing textbooks. Auditors frequently use this form because their main objective is to identify all of the items that make up the difference between the bank's records and the depositor's records. Preparation of the adjusting entries is secondary. This form is usually more difficult to prepare because each of the reconciling items must be analyzed carefully to determine whether an addition or subtraction from the top of the column "Per bank" amount is the correct reconciliation treatment.

SUMMARY OF LEARNING OBJECTIVE FOR APPENDIX 7B

11 *Prepare a proof of cash (four-column bank reconciliation).* The proof of cash reconciles four items per the bank statement to four items per the company's books: (1) the beginning-of-the-period cash balances, (2) the current period cash receipts, (3) the current period cash disbursements, and (4) the end-of-the-period cash balances.

KEY TERM

proof of cash, *363*

Note: All **asterisked** Questions, Brief Exercises, Exercises, Problems, and Conceptual Cases relate to material covered in the appendix to each Chapter.

❖ QUESTIONS ❖

1 What may be included under the heading of "cash"?

2 In what accounts should the following items be classified?
(a) Coins and currency.
(b) U.S. Treasury (Government) bonds.
(c) Certificate of deposit.
(d) Cash in a bank that is in receivership.
(e) NSF check (returned with bank statement).
(f) Deposit in foreign bank (exchangeability limited).
(g) Postdated checks.
(h) Cash (to be used for retirement of long-term bonds).
(i) Deposits in transit.
(j) 100 shares of America Online stock (intention is to sell in one year or less).
(k) Savings and checking accounts.
(l) Petty cash.
(m) Stamps.
(n) Travel advances.

3 Define a "compensating balance." How should a compensating balance be reported?

4 Michael Tilsen Thomas Inc. reported in a recent annual report "Restricted cash for debt redemption." What section of the balance sheet would report this item?

5 What are the reasons that a company gives trade discounts? Why are trade discounts not recorded in the accounts like cash discounts?

6 What are two methods of recording accounts receivable transactions when a cash discount situation is involved? Which is the most theoretically correct? Which is used in practice most of the time? Why?

7 What are the basic problems that occur in the valuation of accounts receivable?

8 Why is the account "Allowance for Sales Returns and Allowances" sometimes used? What other type of allowance account (similar to Allowance for Sales Returns and Allowances) is employed? What is its purpose?

9 What is the theoretical justification of the allowance method as contrasted with the direct write-off method of accounting for bad debts?

10 Indicate how well the percentage-of-sales method and the aging method accomplish the objectives of the allowance method of accounting for bad debts.

11 Of what merit is the contention that the allowance method lacks the objectivity of the direct write-off method? Discuss in terms of accounting's measurement function.

12 Because of calamitous earthquake losses, Kishwaukee Company, one of your client's oldest and largest customers, suddenly and unexpectedly became bankrupt. Approximately 30% of your client's total sales have been made to Kishwaukee Company during each of the past several years. The amount due from Kishwaukee Company—none of which is collectible—equals 22% of total accounts receivable, an amount that is considerably in excess of what was determined to be an adequate provision for doubtful accounts at the close of the preceding year. How would your client record the write-off of the Kishwaukee Company receivable if it is using the allowance method of accounting for bad debts? Justify your suggested treatment.

13 What is the normal procedure for handling the collection of accounts receivable previously written off using the direct write-off method? The allowance method?

14 On January 1, 1998, John Singer Co. sells property for which it had paid $690,000 to Sargent Company receiving in return Sargent's zero-interest-bearing note for $1,000,000 payable in 5 years. What entry would John Singer make to record the sale, assuming that John Singer frequently sells similar items of property for a cash sales price of $620,000?

15 What is "imputed interest"? In what situations is it necessary to impute an interest rate for notes receivable? What are the considerations in imputing an appropriate interest rate?

16 Indicate three reasons why a company might sell its receivables to another company.

17 When is the financial components approach to recording the transfers of receivables used? When should a transfer of receivables be recorded as a sale?

18 The Morley Safer Company includes in its trial balance for December 31 an item for "Accounts Receivable, $769,000." This balance consists of the following items:

Due from regular customers	$523,000
Refund receivable on prior year's income taxes (an established claim)	15,500
Loans to officers	22,000
Loan to wholly owned subsidiary	45,500
Advances to creditors for goods ordered	61,000
Accounts receivable assigned as security for loans payable	75,000
Notes receivable past due plus interest on these notes	27,000
Total	$769,000

Illustrate how these items should be shown in the balance sheet as of December 31.

19 What is the accounts receivable turnover ratio and what type of information does it provide?

20 Distinguish among the following: (1) a general checking account, (2) an imprest bank account, and (3) a lockbox account.

❖ BRIEF EXERCISES ❖

BE7-1 Stowe Enterprises owns the following assets at December 31, 1999:

Cash in bank—savings account	63,000	Checking account balance	17,000
Cash on hand	9,300	Postdated checks	750
Cash refund due from IRS	31,400	Certificates of deposit (180 day)	90,000

What amount should be reported as cash?

BE7-2 Hawthorne Corporation on July 1, 1998, obtained a $4,000,000, 6-month loan at an annual rate of 11% from Salem Bank. As part of the loan agreement, Hawthorne is required to maintain a $500,000 compensating balance in a checking account at Salem Bank. Normally Hawthorne would maintain only a balance of $200,000 in this checking account. The checking account pays 4% interest. Determine the effective interest rate paid by Hawthorne for this loan.

BE7-3 Saturn Company made sales of $25,000 with terms 1/10, n/30. Within the discount period it received payment from customers owing $15,000; after the discount period it received payment from customers owing $10,000. If Saturn uses the gross method of recording sales, prepare journal entries for the transactions described above.

BE7-4 Use the information presented for Saturn Company in BE7-3. If Saturn uses the net method of recording sales, prepare journal entries for the transactions described.

BE7-5 Battle Tank, Incorporated, had net sales in 1998 of $1,200,000. At December 31, 1998, before adjusting entries, the balances in selected accounts were: Accounts Receivable, $250,000 debit, and Allowance for Doubtful Accounts, $2,100 credit. If Battle Tank estimates that 2% of its net sales will prove to be uncollectible, prepare the December 31, 1998, journal entry to record bad debt expense.

BE7-6 Use the information presented for Battle Tank, Incorporated, in BE7-5.

(a) Instead of estimating the uncollectibles at 2% of net sales, assume that 10% of accounts receivable will prove to be uncollectible. Prepare the entry to record bad debts expense.

(b) Instead of estimating uncollectibles at 2% of net sales, assume Battle Tank prepares an aging schedule that estimates total uncollectible accounts at $24,600. Prepare the entry to record bad debts expense.

BE7-7 Addams Family Importers sold goods to Acme Decorators for $20,000 on November 1, 1998, accepting Acme's $20,000, 6-month, 12% note. Prepare Addams' November 1 entry, December 31 annual adjusting entry, and May 1 entry for the collection of the note and interest.

BE7-8 Aero Acrobats lent $15,944 to Afterburner, Inc., accepting Afterburner's 2-year, $20,000, zero-interest-bearing note. The implied interest is 12%. Prepare Aero's journal entries for the initial transaction, recognition of interest each year, and the collection of $20,000 at maturity.

BE7-9 On October 1, 1998, Akira, Inc., assigns $1,000,000 of its accounts receivable to Alisia National Bank as collateral for a $700,000 note. The bank assesses a finance charge of 2% of the receivables assigned and interest on the note of 13%. Prepare the October 1 journal entries for both Akira and Alisia.

BE7-10 Landstalker Enterprises sold $400,000 of accounts receivable to Leander Factors, Inc., on a without recourse basis. Leander Factors assesses a finance charge of 4% of the amount of accounts receivable and retains an amount equal to 5% of accounts receivable. Prepare journal entries for both Landstalker and Leander.

BE7-11 Use the information presented for Landstalker Enterprises in BE7-10. Assume the receivables are sold with recourse. Prepare the journal entry for Landstalker to record the sale, assuming the recourse obligation has a fair value of $6,000.

BE7-12 The financial statements of General Mills, Inc. report net sales of $5,416,000,000. Accounts receivable are $277,300,000 at the beginning of the year and $337,800,000 at the end of the year. Compute General Mill's accounts receivable turnover ratio. Compute General Mill's average collection period for accounts receivable in days.

***BE7-13** Genesis Company designated Alex Kidd as petty cash custodian and established a petty cash fund of $200. The fund is reimbursed when the cash in the fund is at $17. Petty cash receipts indicate funds were disbursed for office supplies, $94, and miscellaneous expense, $87. Prepare journal entries for the establishment of the fund and the reimbursement.

*BE7-14 Jaguar Corporation is preparing a bank reconciliation and has identified the following potential reconciling items. For each item, indicate if it is (1) added to balance per bank statement, (2) deducted from balance per bank statement, (3) added to balance per books, or (4) deducted from balance per books.

(a) Deposit in transit, $5,500.
(b) Interest credited to Jaguar's account, $31.
(c) Bank service charges, $25.
(d) Outstanding checks, $7,422.
(e) NSF check returned, $377.

*BE7-15 Use the information presented for Jaguar Corporation in BE7-14. Prepare any entries necessary to make Jaguar's accounting records correct and complete.

*BE7-16 Indicate how the following items would be entered in Mustafa Company's October 31, 1998, proof of cash (reconciling from bank to books).

(a) October 31, deposit-in-transit.
(b) September 30 outstanding checks.
(c) October bank service charge.
(d) NSF check returned by bank with September bank statement.

❖ EXERCISES ❖

E7-1 (Determining Cash Balance)   The controller for Clint Eastwood Co. is attempting to determine the amount of cash to be reported on its December 31, 1998, balance sheet. The following information is provided:

1. Commercial savings account of $600,000 and a commercial checking account balance of $900,000 are held at First National Bank of Yojimbo.
2. Money market fund account held at Volonte Co. (a mutual fund organization) that permits Eastwood to write checks on this balance, $5,000,000.
3. Travel advances of $180,000 for executive travel for the first quarter of next year (employee to reimburse through salary reduction).
4. A separate cash fund in the amount of $1,500,000 is restricted for the retirement of long-term debt.
5. Petty cash fund of $1,000.
6. An I.O.U. from Marianne Koch, a company officer, in the amount of $190,000.
7. A bank overdraft of $110,000 has occurred at one of the banks the company uses to deposit its cash receipts. At the present time, the company has no deposits at this bank.
8. The company has two certificates of deposit, each totaling $500,000. These certificates of deposit have a maturity of 120 days.
9. Eastwood has received a check that is dated January 12, 1999, in the amount of $125,000.
10. Eastwood has agreed to maintain a cash balance of $500,000 at all times at First National Bank of Yojimbo to insure future credit availability.
11. Eastwood has purchased $2,100,000 of commercial paper of Sergio Leone Co. which is due in 60 days.
12. Currency and coin on hand amounted to $7,700.

Instructions

(a) Compute the amount of cash to be reported on Eastwood Co.'s balance sheet at December 31, 1998.
(b) Indicate the proper reporting for items that are not reported as cash on the December 31, 1998, balance sheet.

E7-2 (Determine Cash Balance)   Presented below are a number of independent situations. For each individual situation, determine the amount that should be reported as cash. If the item(s) is not reported as cash, explain the rationale.

1. Checking account balance $925,000; certificate of deposit $1,400,000; cash advance to subsidiary of $980,000; utility deposit paid to gas company $180.
2. Checking account balance $600,000; an overdraft in special checking account at same bank as normal checking account of $17,000; cash held in a bond sinking fund $200,000; petty cash fund $300; coins and currency on hand $1,350.
3. Checking account balance $590,000; postdated check from customer $11,000; cash restricted due to maintaining compensating balance requirement of $100,000; certified check from customer $9,800; postage stamps on hand $620.
4. Checking account balance at bank $37,000; money market balance at mutual fund (has checking privileges) $48,000; NSF check received from customer $800.

5. Checking account balance $700,000; cash restricted for future plant expansion $500,000; short-term treasury bills $180,000; cash advance received from customer $900 (not included in checking account balance); cash advance of $7,000 to company executive, payable on demand; refundable deposit of $26,000 paid to federal government to guarantee performance on construction contract.

E7-3 (Financial Statement Presentation of Receivables) Jack Gleason Company shows a balance of $181,140 in the Accounts Receivable account on December 31, 1998. The balance consists of the following:

Installment accounts due in 1999	$23,000
Installment accounts due after 1999	34,000
Overpayments to creditors	2,640
Due from regular customers, of which $40,000 represents accounts pledged as security for a bank loan	79,000
Advances to employees	1,500
Advance to subsidiary company (made in 1993)	81,000

Instructions

Illustrate how the information above should be shown on the balance sheet of Jack Gleason Company on December 31, 1998.

 E7-4 (Determine Ending Accounts Receivable) Your accounts receivable clerk, Ms. Mitra Adams, to whom you pay a salary of $1,500 per month, has just purchased a new Cadillac. You decided to test the accuracy of the accounts receivable balance of $82,000 as shown in the ledger.

The following information is available for your *first year* in business:

(1) Collections from customers	$198,000
(2) Merchandise purchased	320,000
(3) Ending merchandise inventory	90,000
(4) Goods are marked to sell at 40% above cost	

Instructions

Compute an estimate of the ending balance of accounts receivable from customers that should appear in the ledger and any apparent shortages. Assume that all sales are made on account.

E7-5 (Record Sales Gross and Net) On June 3, Benedict Arnold Company sold to Chester Arthur merchandise having a sale price of $3,000 with terms of 2/10, n/60, f.o.b. shipping point. An invoice totaling $90, terms n/30, was received by Chester on June 8 from the John Booth Transport Service for the freight cost. On receipt of the goods, June 5, Chester notified the Benedict Arnold Company that merchandise costing $500 contained flaws that rendered it worthless; the same day Benedict Arnold Company issued a credit memo covering the worthless merchandise and asked that it be returned at company expense. The freight on the returned merchandise was $25, paid by Benedict Arnold Company on June 7. On June 12, the company received a check for the balance due from Chester Arthur.

Instructions

(a) Prepare journal entries on the Benedict Arnold Company books to record all the events noted above under each of the following bases:
1. Sales and receivables are entered at gross selling price.
2. Sales and receivables are entered at net of cash discounts.
(b) Prepare the journal entry under basis 2, assuming that Chester Arthur did not remit payment until July 29.

E7-6 (Computing Bad Debts) At January 1, 1999, the credit balance in the Allowance for Doubtful Accounts of the Van Amos Company was $400,000. For 1999, the provision for doubtful accounts is based on a percentage of net sales. Net sales for 1999 were $70,000,000. On the basis of the latest available facts, the 1999 provision for doubtful accounts is estimated to be 0.8% of net sales. During 1999, uncollectible receivables amounting to $500,000 were written off against the allowance for doubtful accounts.

Instructions

Prepare a schedule computing the balance in Van Amos' Allowance for Doubtful Accounts at December 31, 1999.

E7-7 (Computing Bad Debts and Preparing Journal Entries) The trial balance before adjustment of Patsy Cline Inc. shows the following balances:

	Dr.	Cr.
Accounts Receivable	$90,000	
Allowance for Doubtful Accounts	1,750	
Sales (all on credit)		$680,000
Sales Returns and Allowances	30,000	

Instructions

Give the entry for estimated bad debts assuming that the allowance is to provide for doubtful accounts on the basis of (a) 4% of gross accounts receivable and (b) 1% of net sales.

E7-8 (Bad Debt Reporting) The chief accountant for Emily Dickinson Corporation provides you with the following list of accounts receivable written off in the current year.

Date	Customer	Amount
March 31	E. L. Masters Company	$7,800
June 30	Stephen Crane Associates	6,700
September 30	Amy Lowell's Dress Shop	7,000
December 31	R. Frost, Inc.	9,830

Emily Dickinson Corporation follows the policy of debiting Bad Debt Expense as accounts are written off. The chief accountant maintains that this procedure is appropriate for financial statement purposes because the Internal Revenue Service will not accept other methods for recognizing bad debts.

All of Emily Dickinson Corporation's sales are on a 30-day credit basis. Sales for the current year total $2,200,000 and research has determined that bad debt losses approximate 2% of sales.

Instructions

(a) Do you agree or disagree with Emily Dickinson Corporation policy concerning recognition of bad debt expense? Why or why not?

(b) By what amount would net income differ if bad debt expense was computed using the percentage-of-sales approach?

E7-9 (Bad Debts—Aging) Gerard Manley, Inc. includes the following account among its trade receivables.

Hopkins Co.

Date	Description	Amount	Date	Description	Amount
1/1	Balance forward	700	1/28	Cash (#1710)	1,100
1/20	Invoice #1710	1,100	4/2	Cash (#2116)	1,350
3/14	Invoice #2116	1,350	4/10	Cash (1/1 Balance)	155
4/12	Invoice #2412	1,710	4/30	Cash (#2412)	1,000
9/5	Invoice #3614	490	9/20	Cash (#3614 and	
10/17	Invoice #4912	860		part of #2412)	790
11/18	Invoice #5681	2,000	10/31	Cash (#4912)	860
12/20	Invoice #6347	800	12/1	Cash (#5681)	1,250
			12/29	Cash (#6347)	800

Instructions

Age the balance and specify any items that apparently require particular attention at year-end.

E7-10 (Journalizing Various Receivable Transactions) Presented below is information related to James Garfield Corp.

July 1 James Garfield Corp. sold to Warren Harding Co. merchandise having a sales price of $8,000 with terms 2/10, net/60. Garfield records its sales and receivables net.

3 Warren Harding Co. returned merchandise having a sales price of $700 that was defective.

5 Accounts receivable of $9,000 (gross) are factored with Andrew Jackson Credit Corp. without recourse at a financing charge of 9%. Cash is received for the proceeds; collections are handled by the finance company. (These accounts were all past the discount period.)

9 Specific accounts receivable of $9,000 (gross) are pledged to Alf Landon Credit Corp. as security for a loan of $6,000 at a finance charge of 6% of the amount of the loan. The finance company will make the collections. (All the accounts receivable are past the discount period.)

Dec. 29 Warren Harding Co. notifies Garfield that it is bankrupt and will pay only 10% of its account. Give the entry to write off the uncollectible balance using the allowance method. (Note: First record the increase in the receivable on July 11 when the discount period passed.)

Instructions

Prepare all necessary entries in general journal form for Garfield Corp.

E7-11 (Assigned Accounts Receivable) Presented below is information related to A. E. Housman Co.

1. Customers' accounts in the amount of $40,000 are assigned (designated) to the W. B. Yeats Finance Company as security for a loan of $30,000. The finance charge is 4% of the amount borrowed.
2. Cash collections on assigned accounts amount to $18,000.
3. Collections on assigned accounts to date, plus a $300 check for interest on the loan, are forwarded to W. B. Yeats Finance Company.

4. Additional collections on assigned accounts amount to $16,200.
5. The loan is paid in full plus additional interest of $120.

Instructions
Prepare entries in journal form for A. E. Housman Co.

E7-12 (Journalizing Various Receivable Transactions) The trial balance before adjustment for Judy Collins Company shows the following balances:

	Dr.	Cr.
Accounts Receivable	$82,000	
Allowance for Doubtful Accounts	2,120	
Sales		$430,000
Sales Returns and Allowances	7,600	

Instructions
Using the data above, give the journal entries required to record each of the following cases (each situation is independent):

1. To obtain additional cash, Collins factors, without recourse, $25,000 of accounts receivable with Stills Finance. The finance charge is 10% of the amount factored.
2. To obtain a one-year loan of $55,000, Collins assigns $65,000 of specific receivable accounts to Crosby Financial. The finance charge is 8% of the loan; the cash is received and the accounts turned over to Crosby Financial.
3. The company wants to maintain the Allowance for Doubtful Accounts at 5% of gross accounts receivable.
4. The company wishes to increase the allowance by 1½% of net sales.

E7-13 (Transfer of Receivables with Recourse) Ames Quartet Inc. factors receivables with a carrying amount of $200,000 to Joffrey Company for $160,000 on a with recourse basis.

Instructions
The recourse provision has a fair value of $1,000. This transaction should be recorded as a sale. Prepare the appropriate journal entry to record this transaction on the books of Ames Quartet Inc.

E7-14 (Transfer of Receivables with Recourse) Whitney Houston Corporation factors $175,000 of accounts receivable with Kathleen Battle Financing, Inc. on a with recourse basis. Kathleen Battle Financing will collect the receivables. The receivable records are transferred to Kathleen Battle Financing on August 15, 1998. Kathleen Battle Financing assesses a finance charge of 2% of the amount of accounts receivable and also reserves an amount equal to 4% of accounts receivable to cover probable adjustments.

Instructions
(a) What conditions must be met for a transfer of receivables with recourse to be accounted for as a sale?
(b) Assume the conditions from part (a) are met. Prepare the journal entry on August 15, 1998, for Whitney Houston to record the sale of receivables, assuming the recourse obligation has a fair value of $2,000.

E7-15 (Transfer of Receivables Without Recourse) JFK Corp. factors $300,000 of accounts receivable with LBJ Finance Corporation on a without recourse basis on July 1, 1998. The receivable records are transferred to LBJ Finance, which will receive the collections. LBJ Finance assesses a finance charge of 1½% of the amount of accounts receivable and retains an amount equal to 4% of accounts receivable to cover sales discounts, returns, and allowances. The transaction is to be recorded as a sale.

Instructions
(a) Prepare the journal entry on July 1, 1998, for JFK Corp. to record the sale of receivables without recourse.
(b) Prepare the journal entry on July 1, 1998, for LBJ Finance Corporation to record the purchase of receivables without recourse.

E7-16 (Note Transactions at Unrealistic Interest Rates) On July 1, 1999, Agincourt Inc. made two sales:

1. It sold land having a fair market value of $700,000 in exchange for a 4-year noninterest-bearing promissory note in the face amount of $1,101,460. The land is carried on Agincourt's books at a cost of $590,000.

2. It rendered services in exchange for a 3%, 8-year promissory note having a face value of $400,000 (interest payable annually).

Agincourt Inc. recently had to pay 8% interest for money that it borrowed from British National Bank. The customers in these two transactions have credit ratings that require them to borrow money at 12% interest.

Instructions

Record the two journal entries that should be recorded by Agincourt Inc. for the sales transactions above that took place on July 1, 1999.

E7-17 (Note Receivable at Unrealistic Interest Rates)   On December 31, 1999, James Fenimore Company sold some of its product to Cooper Company, accepting a $340,000 noninterest-bearing note, receivable in full on December 31, 2002. James Fenimore Company enjoys a high credit rating and, therefore, borrows funds from its several lines of credit at 9%. Cooper Company, however, pays 12% for its borrowed funds. The product sold is carried on the books of James Fenimore Company at a manufactured cost of $180,000. Assume that the effective interest method is used for discount amortization.

Instructions

   (a) Prepare the journal entry to record the sale on December 31, 1999, by James Fenimore Company. Assume that a perpetual inventory system is used.
   (b) Prepare the journal entries on the books of James Fenimore Company for the year 2000 that are necessitated by the sales transaction of December 31, 1999. Preparation of an amortization schedule may be of assistance.
   (c) Prepare the journal entries on the books of James Fenimore Company for the year 2001 that are necessitated by the sale on December 31, 1999.

*E7-18 (Petty Cash)   Carolyn Keene, Inc. decided to establish a petty cash fund to help insure internal control over its small cash expenditures. The following information is available for the month of April.

   1. On April 1, it established a petty cash fund in the amount of $200.
   2. A summary of the petty cash expenditures made by the petty cash custodian as of April 10, is as follows:

Delivery charges paid on merchandise purchased	$60.00
Supplies purchased and used	25.00
Postage expense	33.00
I.O.U. from employees	17.00
Miscellaneous expense	36.00

The petty cash fund was replenished on April 10. The balance in the fund was $27.
   3. The petty cash fund balance was increased $100 to $300 on April 20.

Instructions

Prepare the journal entries to record transactions related to petty cash for the month of April.

*E7-19 (Petty Cash)   The petty cash fund of Fonzarelli's Auto Repair Service, a sole proprietorship, contains the following:

1. Coins and currency		$ 15.20
2. Postage stamps		2.90
3. An I.O.U. from Richie Cunningham, an employee, for cash advance		40.00
4. Check payable to Fonzarelli's Auto Repair from		
Pottsie Weber, an employee, marked NSF		34.00
5. Vouchers for the following:		
Stamps	$ 20.00	
Two Rose Bowl tickets for Nick Fonzarelli	170.00	
Printer cartridge	14.35	204.35
		$296.45

The general ledger account Petty Cash has a balance of $300.00.

Instructions

Prepare the journal entry to record the reimbursement of the petty cash fund.

*E7-20 (Bank Reconciliation and Adjusting Entries)   Angela Lansbury Company deposits all receipts and makes all payments by check. The following information is available from the cash records.

June 30 Bank Reconciliation

Balance per bank	$7,000
Add: Deposits in transit	1,540
Deduct: Outstanding checks	(2,000)
Balance per books	$6,540

Month of July Results

	Per Bank	Per Books
Balance July 31	$8,650	$9,250
July deposits	5,000	5,810
July checks	4,000	3,100
July note collected (not included in July deposits)	1,000	—
July bank service charge	15	—
July NSF check of a customer returned by the bank (recorded by bank as a charge)	335	—

Instructions

(a) Prepare a bank reconciliation going from balance per bank and balance per book to correct cash balance.

(b) Prepare the general journal entry or entries to correct the Cash account.

*E7-21 (Bank Reconciliation and Adjusting Entries) Logan Bruno Company has just received the August 31, 1998, bank statement, which is summarized below:

County National Bank	Disbursements	Receipts	Balance
Balance, August 1			$ 9,369
Deposits during August		$32,200	41,569
Note collected for depositor, including $40 interest		1,040	42,609
Checks cleared during August	$34,500		8,109
Bank service charges	20		8,089
Balance, August 31			8,089

The general ledger Cash account contained the following entries for the month of August:

Cash			
Balance, August 1	10,050	Disbursements in August	34,903
Receipts during August	35,000		

Deposits in transit at August 31 are $3,800 and checks outstanding at August 31 are determined to total $1,050. Cash on hand at August 31 is $310. The bookkeeper improperly entered one check in the books at $146.50 which was written for $164.50 for supplies (expense); it cleared the bank during the month of August.

Instructions

(a) Prepare a bank reconciliation dated August 31, 1998, proceeding to a correct balance.

(b) Prepare any entries necessary to make the books correct and complete.

(c) What amount of cash should be reported in the August 31 balance sheet?

*E7-22 (Proof of Cash) Following is the general format of a four-column bank reconciliation with the various categories and operations numbered (1) through (8):

	Balance 10/31	November Receipts	November Disbursements	Balance 11/30
Per Bank Statement	$XXXXX	$XXXXX	$XXXXX	$XXXXX
Items to be *added:*	(1)	(3)	(5)	(7)
Items to be *deducted:*	(2)	(4)	(6)	(8)
Per Books	$XXXXX	$XXXXX	$XXXXX	$XXXXX

Instructions

(a) For each of the following items indicate in which columns the reconciling items would appear. Question 1 is answered as an example.

   6   7   **1.** November service charge of $25 is included on bank statement.

   ___ , ___   **2.** The bank collected a $1,000 note receivable for the firm in November plus $40 interest. The firm has not yet recorded this receipt.

       ____ ____ **3.** An "NSF" check in the amount of $357 was returned with the November bank statement. This check will be redeposited in December. The firm has not yet made an entry for this "NSF" check.

       ____ ____ **4.** All $9,200 of checks written in October, which had not cleared the bank at October 31, cleared the bank in November.

       ____ ____ **5.** October service charge of $23 is included in book disbursements for November.

       ____ ____ **6.** A $5,100 deposit in transit is included in book receipts for November.

       ____ ____ **7.** The bank, in error, credited the firm's account for $420 in November for another firm's deposit.

       ____ ____ **8.** A check written in November for $670 was written in the check register in error in the amount of $760. This check cleared the bank in November for $670. Both the debit to Rent Expense and the credit were overstated as a result of this error in the books.

       ____ ____ **9.** The initial $4,700 deposit shown on the November bank statement was included in October's book receipts.

       ____ ____ **10.** $8,220 of checks written in November have not cleared the bank by November 30.

    (b) Prepare the entries that should be recorded to make the books complete and accurate at November 30.

❖ PROBLEMS ❖

P7-1 (Determine Proper Cash Balance)   Dumaine Equipment Co. closes its books regularly on December 31, but at the end of 1998 it held its cash book open so that a more favorable balance sheet could be prepared for credit purposes. Cash receipts and disbursements for the first 10 days of January were recorded as December transactions. The following information is given.

    1. January cash receipts recorded in the December cash book totaled $39,640, of which $22,000 represents cash sales and $17,640 represents collections on account for which cash discounts of $360 were given.

    2. January cash disbursements recorded in the December check register liquidated accounts payable of $26,450 on which discounts of $250 were taken.

    3. The ledger has not been closed for 1998.

    4. The amount shown as inventory was determined by physical count on December 31, 1998.

Instructions

    (a) Prepare any entries you consider necessary to correct Dumaine's accounts at December 31.

    (b) To what extent was Dumaine Equipment Co. able to show a more favorable balance sheet at December 31 by holding its cash book open (use ratio analysis)? Assume that the balance sheet that was prepared by the company showed the following amounts:

	Dr.	Cr.
Cash	$39,000	
Receivables	42,000	
Inventories	67,000	
Accounts payable		$45,000
Other current liabilities		14,200

P7-2 (Bad Debt Reporting)   Presented below are a series of unrelated situations.

    1. Spock Company's unadjusted trial balance at December 31, 1998, included the following accounts:

	Debit	Credit
Allowance for doubtful accounts	$ 4,000	
Sales		$1,500,000
Sales returns and allowances	70,000	

Spock Company estimates its bad debt expense to be 1½% of net sales. Determine its bad debt expense for 1998.

2. An analysis and aging of Scotty Corp. accounts receivable at December 31, 1998, disclosed the following:

Amounts estimated to be uncollectible	$ 180,000
Accounts receivable	1,750,000
Allowance for doubtful accounts (per books)	125,000

What is the net realizable value of Scotty's receivables at December 31, 1998?

3. Uhura Co. provides for doubtful accounts based on 3% of credit sales. The following data are available for 1998.

Credit sales during 1998	$2,100,000
Allowance for doubtful accounts 1/1/98	17,000
Collection of accounts written off in prior years (customer credit was reestablished)	8,000
Customer accounts written off as uncollectible during 1998	30,000

What is the balance in the Allowance for Doubtful Accounts at December 31, 1998?

4. At the end of its first year of operations, December 31, 1998, Chekov Inc. reported the following information:

Accounts receivable, net of allowance for doubtful accounts	$950,000
Customer accounts written off as uncollectible during 1998	24,000
Bad debt expense for 1998	84,000

What should be the balance in accounts receivable at December 31, 1998, before subtracting the allowance for doubtful accounts?

5. The following accounts were taken from Chappel Inc.'s balance sheet at December 31, 1998.

	Debit	Credit
Net credit sales		$750,000
Allowance for doubtful accounts	$ 14,000	
Accounts receivable	410,000	

If doubtful accounts are 3% of accounts receivable, determine the bad debt expense to be reported for 1998.

Instructions

Answer the questions relating to each of the five independent situations as requested.

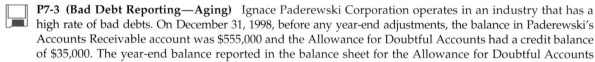

P7-3 (Bad Debt Reporting—Aging) Ignace Paderewski Corporation operates in an industry that has a high rate of bad debts. On December 31, 1998, before any year-end adjustments, the balance in Paderewski's Accounts Receivable account was $555,000 and the Allowance for Doubtful Accounts had a credit balance of $35,000. The year-end balance reported in the balance sheet for the Allowance for Doubtful Accounts will be based on the aging schedule shown below.

Days Account Outstanding	Amount	Probability of Collection
Less than 16 days	$300,000	.98
Between 16 and 30 days	100,000	.90
Between 31 and 45 days	80,000	.85
Between 46 and 60 days	40,000	.75
Between 61 and 75 days	20,000	.40
Over 75 days	15,000	.00

Instructions

(a) What is the appropriate balance for the Allowance for Doubtful Accounts on December 31, 1998?

(b) Show how accounts receivable would be presented on the balance sheet prepared on December 31, 1998.

(c) What is the dollar effect of the year-end bad debt adjustment on the before-tax income for 1998?

(CMA adapted)

P7-4 (Bad Debt Reporting) From inception of operations to December 31, 1999, Blaise Pascal Corporation provided for uncollectible accounts receivable under the allowance method: provisions were made monthly at 2% of credit sales; bad debts written off were charged to the Allowance account; recoveries of bad debts previously written off were credited to the allowance account; and no year-end adjustments to the allowance account were made. Pascal's usual credit terms are net 30 days.

The balance in the Allowance for Doubtful Accounts was $154,000 at January 1, 1999. During 1999 credit sales totaled $9,000,000, interim provisions for doubtful accounts were made at 2% of credit sales, $95,000 of bad debts were written off, and recoveries of accounts previously written off amounted to $15,000. Pascal installed a computer facility in November 1999 and an aging of accounts receivable was prepared for the first time as of December 31, 1999. A summary of the aging is as follows:

Classification by Month of Sale	Balance in Each Category	Estimated % Uncollectible
November–December 1999	$1,080,000	2%
July–October	650,000	10%
January–June	420,000	25%
Prior to 1/1/99	150,000	70%
	$2,300,000	

Based on the review of collectibility of the account balances in the "prior to 1/1/99" aging category, additional receivables totaling $60,000 were written off as of December 31, 1999. The 70% uncollectible estimate applies to the remaining $90,000 in the category. Effective with the year ended December 31, 1999, Pascal adopted a new accounting method for estimating the allowance for doubtful accounts at the amount indicated by the year-end aging analysis of accounts receivable.

Instructions

(a) Prepare a schedule analyzing the changes in the Allowance for Doubtful Accounts for the year ended December 31, 1999. Show supporting computations in good form. (*Hint:* In computing the 12/31/99 allowance, subtract the $60,000 write-off.)

(b) Prepare the journal entry for the year-end adjustment to the Allowance for Doubtful Accounts balance as of December 31, 1999.

(AICPA adapted)

P7-5 (Bad Debt Reporting) Presented below is information related to the Accounts Receivable accounts of Gulistan Inc. during the current year 1999.

1. An aging schedule of the accounts receivable as of December 31, 1999, is as follows:

Age	Net Debit Balance	% to Be Applied after Correction Made
Under 60 days	$172,342	1%
61–90 days	136,490	3%
91–120 days	39,924*	6%
Over 120 days	23,644	$4,200 definitely uncollectible; estimated remainder uncollectible is 25%
	$372,400	

*The $2,740 write-off of receivables is related to the 91-to-120 day category.

2. The Accounts Receivable control account has a debit balance of $372,400 on December 31, 1999.
3. Two entries were made in the Bad Debt Expense account during the year: (1) a debit on December 31 for the amount credited to Allowance for Doubtful Accounts, and (2) a credit for $2,740 on November 3, 1999, and a debit to Allowance for Doubtful Accounts because of a bankruptcy.
4. The Allowance for Doubtful Accounts is as follows for 1999:

	Allowance for Doubtful Accounts				
Nov. 3	Uncollectible accounts written off	2,740	Jan. 1	Beginning balance	8,750
			Dec. 31	5% of $372,400	18,620

5. A credit balance exists in the Accounts Receivable (61–90 days) of $4,840, which represents an advance on a sales contract.

Instructions

Assuming that the books have not been closed for 1999, make the necessary correcting entries.

P7-6 (Journalize Various Account and Notes Receivable Transactions) The balance sheet of Antonio Vivaldi Company at December 31, 1998, includes the following:

Notes receivable	$ 36,000	
Accounts receivable	182,100	
Less: Allowance for doubtful accounts	17,300	200,800

Transactions in 1999 include the following:

1. Accounts receivable of $138,000 were collected including accounts of $40,000 on which 2% sales discounts were allowed.
2. $6,300 was received in payment of an account which was written off the books as worthless in 1997. (*Hint:* Reestablish the receivable account.)
3. Customer accounts of $17,500 were written off during the year.
4. At year-end the Allowance for Doubtful Accounts was estimated to need a balance of $20,000. This estimate is based on an analysis of aged accounts receivable.

Instructions

Prepare all journal entries necessary to reflect the transactions above.

P7-7 (Assigned Accounts Receivable—Journal Entries) Nikos Company finances some of its current operations by assigning accounts receivable to a finance company. On July 1, 1999, it assigned, under guarantee, specific accounts amounting to $100,000, the finance company advancing to Nikos 80% of the accounts assigned (20% of the total to be withheld until the finance company has made its full recovery), less a finance charge of ½% of the total accounts assigned.

On July 31, Nikos Company received a statement that the finance company had collected $55,000 of these accounts, and had made an additional charge of ½% of the total accounts outstanding as of July 31, this charge to be deducted at the time of the first remittance due Nikos Company from the finance company. (Hint: Make entries at this time.) On August 31, 1999, Nikos Company received a second statement from the finance company, together with a check for the amount due. The statement indicated that the finance company had collected an additional $30,000 and had made a further charge of ½% of the balance outstanding as of August 31.

Instructions

Make all entries on the books of Nikos Company that are involved in the transactions above.

(AICPA adapted)

P7-8 (Notes Receivable Journal Entries) Heinrich Boll Sports Company produces soccer, football, and track shoes. The treasurer has recently completed negotiations in which Heinrich Boll Sports agrees to loan Max Frisch Company, a leather supplier, $500,000. Max Frisch Company will issue a noninterest-bearing note due in five years (a 12% interest rate is appropriate), and has agreed to furnish Heinrich Boll Sports with leather at prices that are 10% lower than those usually charged.

Instructions

(a) Prepare the accounting entry to record this transaction on Heinrich Boll Sports Company's books.
(b) Determine the balances at the end of each year the note is outstanding for the following accounts for Heinrich Boll Sports Company: Notes receivable, Unamortized discount, Interest revenue.

P7-9 (Notes Receivable Journal Entries) On December 31, 1999, Menachem Inc. rendered services to Begin Corporation at an agreed price of $91,844.10, accepting $36,000 down and agreeing to accept the balance in four equal installments of $18,000 receivable each December 31. An assumed interest rate of 11% is imputed.

Instructions

Prepare the entries that would be recorded by Menachem Inc. for the sale and for the receipts and interest on the following dates (assume that the effective interest method is used for amortization purposes):

(a) December 31, 1999.   (c) December 31, 2001.   (e) December 31, 2003.
(b) December 31, 2000.   (d) December 31, 2002.

P7-10 (Comprehensive Accounts Receivable) Jair Lynch Supply produces paints and related products for sale to the construction industry throughout the southwest United States. While sales have remained relatively stable despite a decline in the amount of new construction, there has been a noticeable change in the timeliness with which Lynch's customers are paying their bills.

Lynch sells its products on payment terms of 2/10, n/30. In the past, over 75 percent of the credit customers have taken advantage of the discount by paying within ten days of the invoice date. During the fiscal year ended November 30, 1998, the number of customers taking the full 30 days to pay has increased. Current indications are that less than 60 percent of the customers are now taking the discount. Uncollectible accounts as a percentage of total credit sales have risen from the 1.5 percent provided in past years to 4.0 percent in the current year.

In response to a request for more information on the deterioration of accounts receivable collections, Lynch's controller has prepared the following report.

Jair Lynch Supply
Accounts Receivable Collections
November 30, 1998

The fact that some credit accounts will prove uncollectible is normal, and annual bad debt write-offs had been 1.5 percent of total credit sales for many years. However, during the 1997–98 fiscal year, this percentage increased to 4.0 percent. The current accounts receivable balance is $1,500,000, and the condition of this balance in terms of age and probability of collection is shown below.

Proportion of Total	Age Categories	Probability of Collection
64.0%	1 to 10 days	99.0%
18.0	11 to 30 days	97.5
8.0	Past due 31 to 60 days	95.0
5.0	Past due 61 to 120 days	80.0
3.0	Past due 121 to 180 days	65.0
2.0	Past due over 180 days	20.0

At the beginning of the fiscal year, December 1, 1997, the Allowance for Doubtful Accounts had a credit balance of $27,300. Lynch has provided for a monthly bad debt expense accrual during the fiscal year just ended based on the assumption that four percent of total credit sales will be uncollectible. Total credit sales for the 1997–98 fiscal year amounted to $8,000,000, and write-offs of uncollectible accounts during the year totaled $292,500.

Instructions

(a) Prepare an accounts receivable aging schedule at November 30, 1998, for Jair Lynch Supply using the age categories identified in the controller's report showing
   1. the amount of accounts receivable outstanding for each age category and in total.
   2. the estimated amount that is uncollectible for each category and in total.
(b) Compute the amount of the year-end adjustment necessary to bring Jair Lynch Supply's Allowance for Doubtful Accounts to the balance indicated by the aging analysis.
(c) Calculate the net realizable value of Jair Lynch Supply's accounts receivable at November 30, 1998. Ignore any discounts that may be applicable to the accounts not yet due.
(d) Describe the accounting to be performed for subsequent collections of previously written-off accounts receivable.

(CMA adapted)

P7-11 (Comprehensive Receivables Problem) Connecticut Inc. had the following long-term receivable account balances at December 31, 1998:

Note receivable from sale of division	$1,800,000
Note receivable from officer	400,000

Transactions during 1999 and other information relating to Connecticut's long-term receivables were as follows:

1. The $1,800,000 note receivable is dated May 1, 1998, bears interest at 9%, and represents the balance of the consideration received from the sale of Connecticut's electronics division to New York Company. Principal payments of $600,000 plus appropriate interest are due on May 1, 1999, 2000, and 2001. The first principal and interest payment was made on May 1, 1999. Collection of the note installments is reasonably assured.
2. The $400,000 note receivable is dated December 31, 1998, bears interest at 8%, and is due on December 31, 2001. The note is due from Marcus Camby, president of Connecticut Inc. and is collateralized by 10,000 shares of Connecticut's common stock. Interest is payable annually on December 31 and all interest payments were paid on their due dates through December 31, 1999. The quoted market price of Connecticut's common stock was $45 per share on December 31, 1999.
3. On April 1, 1999, Connecticut sold a patent to Pennsylvania Company in exchange for a $200,000 noninterest-bearing note due on April 1, 2001. There was no established exchange price for the patent, and the note had no ready market. The prevailing rate of interest for a note of this type at April 1, 1999, was 12%. The present value of $1 for two periods at 12% is 0.797 (use this factor). The patent had a carrying value of $40,000 at January 1, 1999, and the amortization for the year ended December 31, 1999, would have been $8,000. The collection of the note receivable from Pennsylvania is reasonably assured.

4. On July 1, 1999, Connecticut sold a parcel of land to Harrisburg Company for $200,000 under an installment sale contract. Harrisburg made a $60,000 cash down payment on July 1, 1999, and signed a 4-year 11% note for the $140,000 balance. The equal annual payments of principal and interest on the note will be $45,125 payable on July 1, 2000, through July 1, 2003. The land could have been sold at an established cash price of $200,000. The cost of the land to Connecticut was $150,000. Circumstances are such that the collection of the installments on the note is reasonably assured.

Instructions

(a) Prepare the long-term receivables section of Connecticut's balance sheet at December 31, 1999.

(b) Prepare a schedule showing the current portion of the long-term receivables and accrued interest receivable that would appear in Connecticut's balance sheet at December 31, 1999.

(c) Prepare a schedule showing interest revenue from the long-term receivables that would appear on Connecticut's income statement for the year ended December 31, 1999.

*P7-12 (Bank Reconciliation and Adjusting Entries) The cash account of Jose Orozco Co. showed a ledger balance of $3,969.85 on June 30, 1998. The bank statement as of that date showed a balance of $4,150. Upon comparing the statement with the cash records, the following facts were determined:

1. There were bank service charges for June of $25.00.

2. A bank memo stated that Bao Dai's note for $900 and interest of $36 had been collected on June 29, and the bank had made a charge of $5.50 on the collection. (No entry had been made on Orozco's books when Bao Dai's note was sent to the bank for collection.)

3. Receipts for June 30 for $2,890 were not deposited until July 2.

4. Checks outstanding on June 30 totaled $2,136.05.

5. The bank had charged the Orozco Co.'s account for a customer's uncollectible check amounting to $453.20 on June 29.

6. A customer's check for $90 had been entered as $60 in the cash receipts journal by Orozco on June 15.

7. Check no. 742 in the amount of $491 had been entered in the cashbook as $419, and check no. 747 in the amount of $58.20 had been entered as $582. Both checks had been issued to pay for purchases of equipment.

Instructions

(a) Prepare a bank reconciliation dated June 30, 1998, proceeding to a correct cash balance.

(b) Prepare any entries necessary to make the books correct and complete.

*P7-13 (Bank Reconciliation and Adjusting Entries) Presented below is information related to Tanizaki Inc.

Balance per books at October 31, $41,847.85; receipts, $173,523.91; disbursements, $166,193.54. Balance per bank statement November 30, $56,274.20.

The following checks were outstanding at November 30:

1224	$1,635.29
1230	2,468.30
1232	3,625.15
1233	482.17

Included with the November bank statement and not recorded by the company were a bank debit memo for $27.40 covering bank charges for the month, a debit memo for $572.13 for a customer's check returned and marked NSF, and a credit memo for $1,400 representing bond interest collected by the bank in the name of Tanizaki Inc. Cash on hand at November 30 recorded and awaiting deposit amounted to $1,915.40.

Instructions

(a) Prepare a bank reconciliation (to the correct balance) at November 30, 1998, for Tanizaki Inc. from the information above.

(b) Prepare any journal entries required to adjust the cash account at November 30.

P7-14 (Bank Reconciliation)   Presented below is information related to Junichiro Industries.

Junichiro Industries
BANK RECONCILIATION
May 31, 1998

Balance per bank statement		$30,928.46
Less outstanding checks		
No. 6124	$2,125.00	
No. 6138	932.65	
No. 6139	960.57	
No. 6140	1,420.00	5,438.22
		25,490.24
Add deposit in transit		4,710.56
Balance per books (correct balance)		$30,200.80

CHECK REGISTER—JUNE

Date	Payee	No.	V. Pay	Discount	Cash
June 1	Ren Mfg.	6141	$ 237.50		$ 237.50
1	Stimpy Mfg.	6142	915.00	$ 9.15	905.85
8	Rugrats Co., Inc.	6143	122.90	2.45	120.45
9	Ren Mfg.	6144	306.40		306.40
10	Petty Cash	6145	89.93		89.93
17	Muppet Babies Photo	6146	706.00	14.12	691.88
22	Hey Dude Publishing	6147	447.50		447.50
23	Payroll Account	6148	4,130.00		4,130.00
25	Dragnet Tools, Inc.	6149	390.75	3.91	386.84
28	Double Dare Insurance Agency	6150	1,050.00		1,050.00
28	Get Smart Construction	6151	2,250.00		2,250.00
29	MMT, Inc.	6152	750.00		750.00
30	Lassie Co.	6153	400.00	8.00	392.00
			$11,795.98	$37.63	$11,758.35

STATEMENT
Nickelodeon State Bank
General Checking Account of Junichiro Industries—June 1998

Debits			Date	Credits	Balance
					$30,928.46
$2,125.00	$ 237.50	$ 905.85	June 1	$4,710.56	32,370.67
932.65	120.45		12	1,507.06	32,824.63
1,420.00	447.50	306.40	23	1,458.55	32,109.28
4,130.00		11.05 (BC)	26		27,968.23
89.93	2,250.00	1,050.00	28	4,157.48	28,735.78

Cash received June 29 and 30 and deposited in the mail for the general checking account June 30 amounted to $4,607.96. Because the cash account balance at June 30 is not given, it must be calculated from other information in the problem.

Instructions
From the information above, prepare a bank reconciliation (to the correct balance) as of June 30, 1998, for Junichiro Industries.

P7-15 (Proof of Cash)   You have been hired as the new assistant controller of Falcons Inc. and assigned the task of proving the cash account balance. As of December 31, 1998, you have obtained the following information relative to the December cash operations:

1. Balance per bank

	11/30/98	$138,300
	12/31/98	115,716

2. Balance per books

	11/30/98	101,162
	12/31/98	105,046

3. Receipts for the month of December 1998

	per bank	714,330
	per books	742,415

4. Outstanding checks

	11/30/98	37,958
	12/31/98	45,297

5. Dishonored checks returned by the bank and recorded by Falcons Inc. amounted to $3,125 during the month of December 1998; according to the books $2,500 was redeposited. Dishonored checks, recorded on the bank statement but not on the books until the following months, amounted to $820 at November 30, 1998, and $1,150 at December 31, 1998.

6. On December 31, 1998, a $1,162 check of the Cougars Company was charged to Falcons Inc. account by the bank in error.

7. Proceeds of a note of Golden Bears Company collected by the bank for Falcons on December 10, 1998, were not entered on the books:

Principal	$2,000
Interest	80
	2,080
Less: Collection charge	15
	$2,065

8. Interest on a bank loan for the month of December charged by the bank but not recorded on the books amounted to $4,230.

9. Deposit in transit:

12/31/98	$30,150

Instructions

Prepare bank reconciliations as of November 30, 1998, and December 31, 1998, using a four-column "proof of cash" with the following column headings for amounts:

11/30/98 Beginning Reconciliation	Receipts	Disbursements	12/31/98 Ending Reconciliation

Proceed from "balance per bank statement" to "balance per books."

*P7-16 (Proof of Cash) Using the data given in Problem 7–16, prepare (a) a four-column bank reconciliation proceeding from "balance per bank statement" to "correct balance" and "balance per books" to "correct balance," and (b) accompanying entries to adjust the books at December 31.

*P7-17 (Proof of Cash) You have been hired by Algiers Manufacturing Company as an internal auditor. One of your first assignments is to reconcile the bank account for the Dresden Division.

The bank statement shows the following:

Beginning Balance, August 1, 1999	$ 90,425
Deposits—(20)	915,176
Checks—(64) plus debit memos	(851,715)
Service charges—new checks	(44)
Ending Balance, August 31, 1999	$ 153,842

The cash account on the books of the Dresden Division is as follows:

	Cash		
July 1	64,192	July 31—Cash Disbursements	665,441
July 31—Cash Receipts	682,429	August 1—Bank Reconciliation	375
August 31—Cash Receipts	919,872	August 31—Cash Disbursements	856,446

Your review of last month's bank reconciliation and the current bank statement reveals the following:

1. Outstanding checks

July 31, 1999	$26,042
August 31, 1999	33,561

2. Deposits in transit

July 31, 1996	16,422
August 31, 1996	21,118

3. Check #216 for office furniture was written for $695 but recorded in the cash disbursements journal as $965. The bank deducted the check as $695.
4. A check written on the account of Algiers Manufacturing Co. for $583 was deducted by the bank from the Dresden Division account.
5. Included with the bank statement was a debit memorandum dated August 31 for $2,475 for interest on a note taken out by the Dresden Division on July 30.
6. The service charge for new checks has not been recorded.
7. The July 31, 1999, bank reconciliation showed as reconciling items a service charge of $26 and an NSF check for $349.

Instructions

(a) Prepare a four-column proof of cash reconciling the balance per bank to the balance per book.
(b) Prepare a four-column proof of cash reconciling balance per bank to the "correct balance" and balance per books to the "correct balance."
(c) Prepare any adjusting journal entries necessary to correct the cash account per the books of the Dresden Division.

For additional coverage of sales of receivables including a comprehensive illustration of journal entries by the seller and the factor in a without recourse transaction (accompanied with assignment material), refer to our Web site.

❖ CONCEPTUAL CASES ❖

C7-1 (Bad Debt Accounting) Ariel Company has significant amounts of trade accounts receivable. Ariel uses the allowance method to estimate bad debts instead of the direct writeoff method. During the year, some specific accounts were written off as uncollectible, and some that were previously written off as uncollectible were collected.

Instructions

(a) What are the deficiencies of the direct writeoff method?
(b) What are the two basic allowance methods used to estimate bad debts, and what is the theoretical justification for each?
(c) How should Ariel account for the collection of the specific accounts previously written off as uncollectible?

C7-2 (Various Receivable Accounting Issues) Anne Archer Company uses the net method of accounting for sales discounts. Anne Archer also offers trade discounts to various groups of buyers.

On August 1, 1998, Archer sold some accounts receivable on a without recourse basis. Archer incurred a finance charge.

Archer also has some notes receivable bearing an appropriate rate of interest. The principal and total interest are due at maturity. The notes were received on October 1, 1998, and mature on September 30, 2000. Archer's operating cycle is less than one year.

Instructions

(a) 1. Using the net method, how should Archer account for the sales discounts at the date of sale? What is the rationale for the amount recorded as sales under the net method?

2. Using the net method, what is the effect on Archer's sales revenues and net income when customers do not take the sales discounts?

(b) What is the effect of trade discounts on sales revenues and accounts receivable? Why?

(c) How should Archer account for the accounts receivable factored on August 1, 1998? Why?

(d) How should Archer account for the note receivable and the related interest on December 31, 1998? Why?

C7-3 (Bad Debt Reporting Issues) Ben Gazarra conducts a wholesale merchandising business that sells approximately 5,000 items per month with a total monthly average sales value of $250,000. Its annual bad debt ratio has been approximately 1½% of sales. In recent discussions with his bookkeeper, Mr. Gazarra has become confused by all the alternatives apparently available in handling the Allowance for Doubtful Accounts balance. The following information has been shown.

1. An allowance can be set up (a) on the basis of a percentage of sales or (b) on the basis of a valuation of all past due or otherwise questionable accounts receivable—those considered uncollectible being charged to such allowance at the close of the accounting period or specific items charged off directly against (1) Gross Sales, or to (2) Bad Debt Expense in the year in which they are determined to be uncollectible.

2. Collection agency and legal fees, and so on, incurred in connection with the attempted recovery of bad debts can be charged to (a) Bad Debt Expense, (b) Allowance for Doubtful Accounts, (c) Legal Expense, or (d) General Expense.

3. Debts previously written off in whole or in part but currently recovered can be credited to (a) other revenue, (b) bad debt expense, or (c) allowance for doubtful accounts.

Instructions

Which of the foregoing methods would you recommend to Mr. Gazarra in regard to (1) allowances and charge-offs, (2) collection expenses, and (3) recoveries? State briefly and clearly the reasons supporting your recommendations.

C7-4 (Basic Note and Accounts Receivable Transactions)

Part 1

On July 1, 1999, Eve Arden Company, a calendar-year company, sold special-order merchandise on credit and received in return an interest-bearing note receivable from the customer. Eve Arden Company will receive interest at the prevailing rate for a note of this type. Both the principal and interest are due in one lump sum on June 30, 2000.

Instructions

When should Eve Arden Company report interest income from the note receivable? Discuss the rationale for your answer.

Part 2

On December 31, 1999, Eve Arden Company had significant amounts of accounts receivable as a result of credit sales to its customers. Eve Arden Company uses the allowance method based on credit sales to estimate bad debts. Past experience indicates that 2% of credit sales normally will not be collected. This pattern is expected to continue.

Instructions

(a) Discuss the rationale for using the allowance method based on credit sales to estimate bad debts. Contrast this method with the allowance method based on the balance in the trade receivables accounts.

(b) How should Eve Arden Company report the allowance for bad debts account on its balance sheet at December 31, 1999? Also, describe the alternatives, if any, for presentation of bad debt expense in Eve Arden Company's 1999 income statement.

(AICPA adapted)

C7-5 (Bad Debt Reporting Issues) The Rosita Arenas Company sells office equipment and supplies to many organizations in the city and surrounding area on contract terms of 2/10, n/30. In the past, over 75% of the credit customers have taken advantage of the discount by paying within 10 days of the invoice date.

The number of customers taking the full 30 days to pay has increased within the last year. Current indications are that less than 60% of the customers are now taking the discount. Bad debts as a percentage of gross credit sales have risen from the 1.5% provided in past years to about 4% in the current year.

The controller has responded to a request for more information on the deterioration in collections of accounts receivable with the report reproduced below.

The Rosita Arenas Company
Finance Committee Report—Accounts Receivable Collections
May 31, 1999

The fact that some credit accounts will prove uncollectible is normal. Annual bad debt write-offs have been 1.5% of gross credit sales over the past five years. During the last fiscal year, this percentage increased to slightly less than 4%. The current Accounts Receivable balance is $1,600,000. The condition of this balance in terms of age and probability of collection is as follows:

Proportion of Total	Age Categories	Probability of Collection
68%	not yet due	99%
15%	less than 30 days past due	96½%
8%	30 to 60 days past due	95%
5%	61 to 120 days past due	91%
2½%	121 to 180 days past due	70%
1½%	over 180 days past due	20%

The Allowance for Doubtful Accounts had a credit balance of $43,300 on June 1, 1998. The Rosita Arenas Company has provided for a monthly bad debts expense accrual during the current fiscal year based on the assumption that 4% of gross credit sales will be uncollectible. Total gross credit sales for the 1998–99 fiscal year amounted to $4,000,000. Write-offs of bad accounts during the year totaled $145,000.

Instructions

(a) Prepare an accounts receivable aging schedule for The Rosita Arenas Company using the age categories identified in the controller's report to the Finance Committee showing:

1. The amount of accounts receivable outstanding for each age category and in total.
2. The estimated amount that is uncollectible for each category and in total.

(b) Compute the amount of the year-end adjustment necessary to bring Allowance for Doubtful Accounts to the balance indicated by the age analysis. Then prepare the necessary journal entry to adjust the accounting records.

(c) In a recessionary environment with tight credit and high interest rates:

1. Identify steps The Rosita Arenas Company might consider to improve the accounts receivable situation.
2. Then evaluate each step identified in terms of the risks and costs involved. (CMA adapted)

C7-6 (Sale of Notes Receivable) Sergey Luzov Wholesalers Co. sells industrial equipment for a standard three-year note receivable. Revenue is recognized at time of sale. Each note is secured by a lien on the equipment and has a face amount equal to the equipment's list price. Each note's stated interest rate is below the customer's market rate at date of sale. All notes are to be collected in three equal annual installments beginning one year after sale. Some of the notes are subsequently sold to a bank with recourse, some are subsequently sold without recourse, and some are retained by Luzov. At year end, Luzov evaluates all outstanding notes receivable and provides for estimated losses arising from defaults.

Instructions

(a) What is the appropriate valuation basis for Luzov's notes receivable at the date it sells equipment?

(b) How should Luzov account for the sale, without recourse, of a February 1, 1998, note receivable sold on May 1, 1998? Why is it appropriate to account for it in this way?

(c) At December 31, 1998, how should Luzov measure and account for the impact of estimated losses resulting from notes receivable that it

1. Retained and did **not** sell?
2. Sold to bank with recourse? (AICPA adapted)

C7-7 (Noninterest-Bearing Note Receivable) On September 30, 1998, Tiger Machinery Co. sold a machine and accepted the customer's noninterest-bearing note. Tiger normally makes sales on a cash basis. Since the machine was unique, its sales price was not determinable using Tiger's normal pricing practices.

After receiving the first of two equal annual installments on September 30, 1999, Tiger immediately sold the note with recourse. On October 9, 2000, Tiger received notice that the note was dishonored, and it paid all amounts due. At all times prior to default, the note was reasonably expected to be paid in full.

Instructions
- (a) 1. How should Tiger determine the sales price of the machine?
  2. How should Tiger report the effects of the noninterest-bearing note on its income statement for the year ended December 31, 1998? Why is this accounting presentation appropriate?
- (b) What are the effects of the sale of the note receivable with recourse on Tiger's income statement for the year ended December 31, 1999, and its balance sheet at December 31, 1999?
- (c) How should Tiger account for the effects of the note being dishonored?

C7-8 (Reporting of Notes Receivable, Interest, and Sale of Receivables) On July 1, 1999, Gale Sondergaard Company sold special-order merchandise on credit and received in return an interest-bearing note receivable from the customer. Sondergaard will receive interest at the prevailing rate for a note of this type. Both the principal and interest are due in one lump sum on June 30, 2000.

On September 1, 1999, Sondergaard sold special-order merchandise on credit and received in return a noninterest-bearing note receivable from the customer. The prevailing rate of interest for a note of this type is determinable. The note receivable is due in one lump sum on August 31, 2001.

Sondergaard also has significant amounts of trade accounts receivable as a result of credit sales to its customers. On October 1, 1999, some trade accounts receivable were assigned to Irene Dunne Finance Company on a non-notification (Sondergaard handles collections) basis for an advance of 75% of their amount at an interest charge of 12% on the balance outstanding.

On November 1, 1999, other trade accounts receivable were sold on a without recourse basis. The factor withheld 5% of the trade accounts receivable factored as protection against sales returns and allowances and charged a finance charge of 3%.

Instructions
- (a) How should Sondergaard determine the interest income for 1999 on the:
  1. Interest-bearing note receivable? Why?
  2. Noninterest-bearing note receivable? Why?
- (b) How should Sondergaard report the interest-bearing note receivable and the noninterest-bearing note receivable on its balance sheet at December 31, 1999?
- (c) How should Sondergaard account for subsequent collections on the trade accounts receivable assigned on October 1, 1999, and the payments to Irene Dunne Finance? Why?
- (d) How should Sondergaard account for the trade accounts receivable factored on November 1, 1999? Why?

(AICPA adapted)

C7-9 (Accounting for Non-interest-Bearing Note) Soon after beginning the year-end audit work on March 10 at Alan Arkin Company, the auditor has the following conversation with the controller.

CONTROLLER: The year ended March 31st should be our most profitable in history and, as a consequence, the Board of Directors has just awarded the officers generous bonuses.

AUDITOR: I thought profits were down this year in the industry, according to your latest interim report.

CONTROLLER: Well, they were down but 10 days ago we closed a deal that will give us a substantial increase for the year.

AUDITOR: Oh, what was it?

CONTROLLER: Well, you remember a few years ago our former president bought stock in Rocketeer Enterprises because he had those grandiose ideas about becoming a conglomerate. For 6 years we have not been able to sell this stock, which cost us $3,000,000 and has not paid a nickel in dividends. Thursday we sold this stock to Campbell Inc. for $4,000,000. So, we will have a gain of $700,000 ($1,000,000 pretax) which will increase our net income for the year to $4,000,000, compared with last year's $3,800,000. As far as I know, we'll be the only company in the industry to register an increase in net income this year. That should help the market value of the stock!

AUDITOR: Do you expect to receive the $4,000,000 in cash by March 31st, your fiscal year-end?

CONTROLLER: No. Although Campbell Inc. is an excellent company, they are a little tight for cash because of their rapid growth. Consequently, they are going to give us a $4,000,000 noninterest-bearing note due $400,000 per year for the next 10 years. The first payment is due on March 31 of next year.

AUDITOR: Why is the note noninterest-bearing?

CONTROLLER: Because that's what everybody agreed to. Since we don't have any interest-bearing debt, the funds invested in the note do not cost us anything and besides, we were not getting any dividends on the Rocketeer Enterprises stock.

Instructions

Do you agree with the way the controller has accounted for the transaction? If not, how should the transaction be accounted for?

❖ FINANCIAL REPORTING PROBLEM—INTEL CORPORATION

The financial statements of Intel Corporation appear in Appendix 5B.

Instructions
Refer to these financial statements and the accompanying notes to answer the following questions.

(a) What criteria does Intel use to differentiate among (1) "cash and cash equivalents," (2) "short-term investments," and (3) "long-term investments" as reported in its balance sheet?

(b) As of December 31, 1995, Intel has $1,463 million in cash and cash equivalents and $995 million in short-term investments. Why does Intel have such a large amount in highly liquid assets?

(c) During 1995 Intel's accounts receivable increased significantly from $1,978 million to $3,116 million. What explanation does Intel give for this increase?

(d) In recent years the accounting profession has encouraged companies to disclose any concentration of risk not apparent in their financial statements. What risks relative to accounts receivable does Intel disclose in its discussion and analysis section?

❖ FINANCIAL STATEMENT ANALYSIS CASE

Occidental Petroleum Corporation

Occidental Petroleum Corporation reported the following information in its 1996 Annual Report:

Occidental Petroleum Corporation CONSOLIDATED BALANCE SHEETS (in millions)		
Assets at December 31,	**1996**	1995
Current assets		
Cash and cash equivalents (Note 1)	$ 279	$520
Trade receivables, net of reserves of $24 in 1996 and $19 in 1995	635	643
Receivables from joint ventures, partnerships and other	236	248
Inventories (Notes 1 and 6)	633	647
Prepaid expenses and other (Note 12)	407	461
Total current assets	2,190	2,519
Long-term receivables, net	152	158

Notes to Consolidated Financial Statements

Cash and Cash Equivalents. Cash equivalents consist of highly liquid money-market mutual funds and bank deposits with initial maturities of three months or less. Cash equivalents totaled approximately $206 million and $620 million at December 31, 1996, and 1995, respectively.

Trade Receivables. In 1992, Occidental entered into an agreement to sell, under a revolving sale program, an undivided percentage ownership interest in a designated pool of domestic trade receivables, with limited recourse. Under this program, Occidental serves as the collection agent with respect to the receivables sold. An interest in new receivables is sold as collections are made from customers. As of December 31, 1996, Occidental had received cash proceeds totaling $600 million, of which $100 million was received in the fourth quarter of 1996 and the remainder in 1993 and 1992. Fees and expenses under this program are included in Selling, general and administrative and other operating expenses. During the years ended December 31, 1996, 1995 and 1994, the cost of this program amounted to approximately 5.8 percent, 6.3 percent and 4.8 percent, respectively, of the weighted average amount of proceeds received.

Instructions

(a) What items other than coin and currency may be included in "cash"?

(b) What items may be included in "cash equivalents"?

(c) What are compensating balance arrangements and how should they be reported in financial statements?

(d) What are the possible differences between cash equivalents and short-term (temporary) investments?

(e) Why is petty cash not reported in the financial statements?

(f) What is the difference between a demand deposit and a time deposit?

(g) What types of arrangements, events, or situations result in restricted cash?

❖ COMPARATIVE ANALYSIS CASE

The Coca-Cola Company versus PepsiCo Inc.

Instructions

Go to our Web site and answer the following questions.

1. What were the cash and cash equivalents reported by Coca-Cola and PepsiCo at the end of 1995? What does each company classify as cash equivalents?

2. What were the accounts receivable (net) for Coca-Cola and PepsiCo at the end of 1995? Which company reports the greater allowance for doubtful accounts receivable (amount and percentage of gross receivable) at the end of 1995?

3. Assuming that all "net operating revenues" (Coca-Cola) and all "net sales" (PepsiCo) were net *credit* sales, compute the receivables turnover ratio for 1995 for Coca-Cola and PepsiCo; also compute the days outstanding for receivables. What is your evaluation of the difference?

❖ RESEARCH CASES

Case 1

Accounting Trends and Techniques, published annually by the American Institute of Certified Public Accountants, is a survey of 600 annual reports to stockholders. The survey covers selected industrial, merchandising, and service companies.

Instructions

Examine the section regarding the use of receivables for financing and answer the following questions.

(a) For the most recent year, how many of the companies surveyed disclosed (i) sales of receivables to finance subsidiaries, (ii) sales of receivables to independent entities, and (iii) receivables used as collateral?

(b) Examine the disclosure provided by a company that sold receivables and a company that used its receivables as collateral. Summarize the major terms of the transactions.

Case 2

The May 6, 1996 issue of *Forbes* includes an article by Matthew Schifrin and Howard Rudnitsky, entitled "Rx for receivables."

Instructions

Read the article and answer the following questions.

(a) Why has the pharmacy business moved from a cash-based business to a receivables-based business?

(b) What is the economic motivation for pharmacists to sell their receivables?

(c) What is the economic motivation for the Pharmacy Fund to purchase the receivables?

❖ WRITING ASSIGNMENT

As the manager of the accounts receivable department for Vicki Maher Leather Goods, Ltd., you recently noticed that Percy Shelley, your accounts receivable clerk who is paid $1,200 per month, has been wearing unusually tasteful and expensive clothing. (This is Vicki Maher's first year in business.) This morning, Shelley drove up to work in a brand new Cadillac.

Naturally suspicious by nature, you decide to test the accuracy of the accounts receivable balance of $132,000 as shown in the ledger. The following information is available for your first year (precisely nine months ended September 30, 1998) in business:

(1)	Collections from customers	$198,000
(2)	Merchandise purchased	360,000
(3)	Ending merchandise inventory	90,000
(4)	Goods are marked to sell at 40% above cost.	

Instructions
Assuming all sales were made on account, compute the ending accounts receivable balance that should appear in the ledger, noting any apparent shortage. Then, draft a memo dated October 3, 1998, to John Castle, the branch manager, explaining the facts in this situation. Remember that this problem is serious, and you do not want to make hasty accusations.

❖ GROUP ASSIGNMENT

Radisson Company requires additional cash for its business. Radisson has decided to use its accounts receivable to raise the additional cash and has asked your group to determine the income statement effects of the following contemplated transactions.

1. On July 1, 1998, Radisson assigned $400,000 of accounts receivable to Stickum Finance Company. Radisson received an advance from Stickum of 85% of the assigned accounts receivable less a commission on the advance of 3%. Prior to December 31, 1998, Radisson collected $220,000 on the assigned accounts receivable, and remitted $232,720 to Stickum, $12,720 of which represented interest on the advance from Stickum.
2. On December 1, 1998, Radisson sold $300,000 of net accounts receivable to Wunsch Company for $250,000. The receivables were sold outright on a without recourse basis.
3. On December 31, 1998, an advance of $120,000 was received from the First Bank by pledging $160,000 of Radisson's accounts receivable. Radisson's first payment to First Bank is due on January 30, 1999.

Instructions
Your instructor will identify one member of the group to serve as a recorder and one member to serve as spokesperson. Work within your group to provide information for the recorder to prepare a schedule showing the income statement effect for the year ended December 31, 1998, as a result of the above facts. The spokesperson will report the group findings to the class and be prepared to show supporting computations.

❖ ETHICS CASES

Case 1
Rudolph Company is a subsidiary of Hundley Corp. The controller believes that the yearly allowance for doubtful accounts for Rudolph should be 2% of net credit sales. The president, nervous that the parent company might expect the subsidiary to sustain its 10% growth rate, suggests that the controller increase the allowance for doubtful accounts to 3% yearly. The supervisor thinks that the lower net income, which reflects a 6% growth rate, will be a more sustainable rate for Rudolph Company.

Instructions
Answer the following questions:
(a) Should the controller be concerned with Rudolph Company's growth rate in estimating the allowance? Explain your answer.
(b) Does the president's request pose an ethical dilemma for the controller? Give your reasons.

Case 2
Heath Corporation has several current notes receivable on its year-end balance sheet. While collection seems certain, it may be delayed beyond one year. Because of this, the controller wants to re-classify these notes as non-current. Heath's treasurer also thinks that collection will be delayed but does not favor reclassification because this will reduce the current ratio from 1.5:1 to .8:1. This reduction in current ratio is detrimental to company prospects for securing a major loan.

Instructions
Answer the following questions:
(a) Should the controller re-classify the notes? Give your reasons.
(b) Does the treasurer's position pose an ethical dilemma for the controller? Explain your answer.

CORPORATE BACKGROUND

Whitepeak Company, located in Denver, Colorado, opened its doors on January 1, 1944. Whitepeak began its operations as one retail store in downtown Denver, specializing in merchandise for the ski industry in Colorado. Through the years Whitepeak has grown and diversified to become an enormous conglomerate and a major player in the world's ski industry.

At the end of most chapters, look for the mountain logo (shown above) for a brief description of the issue or problem Whitepeak is facing in developing its year-end financial statements. Then print out the narrative question from your Whitepeak disk and apply your expertise to the issues presented. Throughout, assume that Whitepeak operates on a calendar-year basis, with a 360-day year. You will be making your entries as of December 31, 1999.

MODULE 1

Section 1.1 Accounts Receivable Disposition

Factoring of accounts receivable is growing more popular as a means for firms to expedite receipt of cash without borrowing. On November 1, 1997, Whitepeak factored an account receivable to R.A. Factoring and recorded the transaction by increasing Accounts Receivable—Factored and decreasing Accounts Receivable. Specifics of the agreement involve a 1% finance charge and a 5% retainer deposit on the balance of receivables transferred. The receivable is sold without recourse.

Instructions Correct the error in the recording of this event.

Section 1.2 Notes Receivable

On December 1, 1997, Whitepeak made a $50,000 sale in exchange for a 6-month, non-interest-bearing note. The sale was recorded by increasing Notes Receivable and Sales by $50,000.

Instructions Correct this mistake and provide the necessary entries for the sale and subsequent interest adjustment. ∎

A visit with
Tom Mulflur

TOM MULFLUR is president of Mt. Hood Chemical Corporation, a manufacturer of cleaning compounds based in Portland, Oregon. His initial position with Mt. Hood Chemical was corporate controller, but over the years his role broadened to include sales and operations. Mr. Mulflur is a graduate of the University of Oregon with a bachelor's degree in accounting.

Describe your first job from college. After graduation, I went to work for what is now Deloitte & Touche and spent three years in the Portland office. I was in the audit department, with an emphasis on small-business clients. I enjoyed auditing these clients because I could see that one manager could have a big impact on a small business. You could develop a plan for a company and it might benefit from that plan for years to come. In about 20 minutes, you could look at their financials and understand a whole lot about their business. And then you could go to lunch with the owner and you can ask him or her questions to get to the heart of the business in no time. You can put your arms around the whole thing, whereas in a large audit, you don't get to go to lunch with the boss, let alone ask any questions.

How did you find out about Mt. Hood Chemical? You get exposed to many small businesses through your work with a CPA firm. Plus, you start networking like you would in any other situation—people you play golf or tennis with, people you go to the health club with, or people you work with. I met the owner of Mt. Hood Chemical playing tennis. He was in need of a financial guy at the time. We had two or three discussions. He thought it was a fit, I thought it was a fit, and we went for it.

What were your main duties when you started back in 1980? When I came here, they had a controller position. A controller controls the accounting functions of a business, making sure that the people who do the payables, the receivables, and the payroll do it correctly. Your job is also to make sure the financial statements and management reports are done properly and come out on a timely basis. In a lot of cases, that's where a controller's position stops. I came in with the attitude that I wanted to take care of the controller duties, but if I was done early, then I would dive into whatever else needed to be done.

How did you broaden your role at the company? In a manufacturing company such as ours, the most natural transfer from pure accounting is to go into purchasing. I remember looking at four or five items we were purchasing, grabbing the file, and seeing if it made any sense. And it didn't make any sense the way we were buying some items. We could save a lot of money buying certain items by the truckload every five weeks instead of buying one fifth every week. And the owner said, "You're right, let's go do it." And then you start gaining his confidence. That's the key to moving from the controller's spot to what I would call operations. We significantly improved our margins based upon better purchasing and analysis of what we were doing.

Besides purchasing, where else did you make an impact? For instance, we had a piece of machinery out in the plant that was sitting around gathering dust. When we hired a new purchasing agent, I asked him to make that piece of equipment work. That piece of equipment has saved us over $100,000 over five years, which is a lot of money in our business. I also got involved in labor negotiations out in the plant. We had a bad situation where we had to endure a strike, but afterwards, we put in an incentive program that was fair for both sides. I installed a computer system that gave us the ability to analyze our margins on a real-time basis so that we could make better pricing decisions. I also got involved in real estate investment decisions and lease versus buy decisions on vehicles, equipment, and building facilities. Not every owner encourages the controller to expand into other areas. But as soon as you show ways to improve the bottom line, you usually get the owner's attention very fast.

What advice would you give to students interested in a career in small business? If you have a chance, you work for a CPA firm for two to three years. That gives you an overall understanding of businesses. Then you get into a smaller company and you'll probably start at the controller slot. As soon as you can, you become operational—getting into things that affect the bottom line of the business. That's the way you gain stature and responsibility in a firm. That last thing you do if you want to make the big leap from an operational person to a top manager is to become proficient in selling. There are very few people in a president/CEO position who don't sell. Sooner or later, you have to address that issue. Many people trained in accounting don't focus on sales. It's a mindset—Oh, I'm in this box called accounting and it doesn't include sales. If you really want to make that last step, then you've got to make a conscious decision at some point that yes, I am going to get myself into the selling side of this business. One way to get started is to begin relationships with the sales managers and the vice-presidents of marketing. It's just like if you were working for a CPA firm and you were going to bring in an account, then you would socialize with them.

What are your current duties? I'm the president and CEO of a superregional detergent company which makes me responsible for 75 employees, with at least 50 involved in sales. I'm responsible for all aspects of the business with an emphasis on sales, where I spend about half my time. In a lot of cases, the people we do business with want to see the president of the company. Having the accounting knowledge makes me be able to walk into a prospective account and enables me to analyze the numbers much quicker than my competition and much more thoroughly. I'm dealing with people who are very cost conscious, and they know I have an accounting background and that's a plus.

CHAPTER 8

Valuation of Inventories: A Cost Basis Approach

Where's My Inventory?

Recent cases of fraudulent financial reporting have emphasized the importance of inventory. According to *The Wall Street Journal*, "Creating phantom inventory instantly benefits a company's bottom line."[1] For example, it is alleged that Phar-Mor Inc., a deep-discount store chain, overstated its profits by $50 million by keeping in its inventory records items that had already been sold, maintaining secret inventory records, and creating phantom inventory.

Similarly, Crazy Eddie Inc.'s new management alleged that previous management had created phantom inventory and profits. The company, known in the New York area for its wacky TV commercials, said its former management inflated the inventory count by $10 million by drafting phony count sheets and improperly including merchandise that was being returned to suppliers. The total shortfall for the consumer electronics retailer was later determined to be $65 million.[2] In short, Crazy Eddie went crazy.

At Kurzweil Applied Intelligence Inc. millions of dollars in phony inventory sales were booked during a two-year period that straddled two audits and an initial public stock offering. Employees dummied up phony shipping documents and logbooks to support bogus sales transactions. High-tech equipment was shipped all right, but not to customers. Instead, the goods were shipped to a public warehouse for "temporary" storage; Kurzweil still had ownership. Some "sold" equipment sat in storage for 17 months. To foil auditors' attempts to verify the existence of the "sold" inventory, Kurzweil employees moved the goods from warehouse to warehouse. To cover the fraudulently recorded sales transactions, as auditors closed in, the still-hidden goods were brought back under the pretense that they were returned by customers. When the fraud was finally exposed in mid-1994, the bottom dropped out of Kurzweil's stock.[3]

---

[1]"Inventory Chicanery Tempts More Firms, Fools More Auditors," *The Wall Street Journal*, December 12, 1992, p. A1. Overstatement of ending inventory reduces cost of sales and thus increases profits.

[2]"Short Circuit: How Mounting Woes at Crazy Eddie Sank a Turnaround Effort," *The Wall Street Journal*, July 10, 1989, p. A1. "Peat Settles Crazy Eddie Case," *Accounting Today*, April 19, 1993, p. 37.

[3]"Anatomy of a Fraud," *Business Week*, September 16, 1996, pp. 90–94.

LEARNING OBJECTIVES

After studying this chapter, you should be able to:

1. Identify major classifications of inventory.
2. Distinguish between perpetual and periodic inventory systems.
3. Identify the effects of inventory errors on the financial statements.
4. Identify the items that should be included as inventory cost.
5. Describe and compare the flow assumptions used in accounting for inventories.
6. Explain the significance and use of a LIFO reserve.
7. Explain the effect of LIFO liquidations.
8. Explain the dollar-value LIFO method.
9. Identify the major advantages and disadvantages of LIFO.
10. Identify the reasons why a given inventory method is selected.

As indicated in the opening story, inventories are often a significant portion of a company's total assets. As a result, improper accounting and reporting for this asset can materially affect the financial statements. The purpose of this chapter is to discuss the basic issues related to accounting and reporting for the costs of inventory. The content and organization of the chapter are as follows:

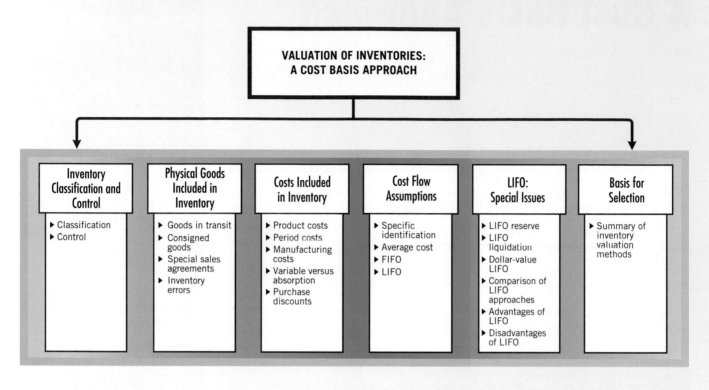

VALUATION OF INVENTORIES: A COST BASIS APPROACH					
Inventory Classification and Control	**Physical Goods Included in Inventory**	**Costs Included in Inventory**	**Cost Flow Assumptions**	**LIFO: Special Issues**	**Basis for Selection**
▸ Classification ▸ Control	▸ Goods in transit ▸ Consigned goods ▸ Special sales agreements ▸ Inventory errors	▸ Product costs ▸ Period costs ▸ Manufacturing costs ▸ Variable versus absorption ▸ Purchase discounts	▸ Specific identification ▸ Average cost ▸ FIFO ▸ LIFO	▸ LIFO reserve ▸ LIFO liquidation ▸ Dollar-value LIFO ▸ Comparison of LIFO approaches ▸ Advantages of LIFO ▸ Disadvantages of LIFO	▸ Summary of inventory valuation methods

❖ INVENTORY CLASSIFICATION AND CONTROL

Classification

Inventories are asset items held for sale in the ordinary course of business or goods that will be used or consumed in the production of goods to be sold. The description and measurement of inventory require careful attention because the investment in inventories is frequently the largest current asset of merchandising (retail) and manufacturing businesses.

A **merchandising concern**, such as Wal-Mart, ordinarily purchases its merchandise in a form ready for sale. It reports the cost assigned to unsold units left on hand as merchandise inventory. Only one inventory account, Merchandise Inventory, appears in the financial statements. **Manufacturing concerns,** on the other hand, produce goods to be sold to the merchandising firms. Many of the largest U.S. businesses are manufacturers—Boeing, IBM, Exxon, Procter and Gamble, Ford, Motorola, to name only a few. Although the products they produce may be quite different, manufacturers normally have three inventory accounts—Raw Materials, Work in Process, and Finished Goods.

Objective ❶

Identify major classifications of inventory.

The cost assigned to goods and materials on hand but not yet placed into production is reported as raw materials inventory. Raw materials include the wood to make a baseball bat or the steel to make a car. These materials ultimately can be traced directly to the end product.

At any point in a continuous production process some units are not completely processed. The cost of the raw material on which production has been started but not completed, plus the direct labor cost applied specifically to this material and a ratable share of manufacturing overhead costs, constitute the work in process inventory.

The costs identified with the completed but unsold units on hand at the end of the fiscal period are reported as finished goods inventory. The current asset sections presented in Illustration 8-1 contrast the financial statement presentation of inventories of a merchandising company and those of a manufacturing company. The remainder of the balance sheet is essentially similar for the two types of companies.

Go to our Web site for additional inventory disclosures

ILLUSTRATION 8-1
Comparison of Current Asset Presentation for Merchandising and Manufacturing Companies

Merchandising Company BALANCE SHEET December 31, 1999			Manufacturing Company BALANCE SHEET December 31, 1999		
Current assets			Current assets		
Cash		$100,000	Cash		$180,000
Receivables (net)		210,000	Receivables (net)		210,000
Merchandise inventory		400,000	Inventories:		
Prepaid expenses		22,000	Finished goods	$ 80,000	
Total		$732,000	Work in process	95,000	
			Raw materials	160,000	335,000
			Prepaid expenses		18,000
			Total		$743,000

A manufacturing company also might include a **manufacturing or factory supplies inventory** account. In it would be items such as machine oils, nails, cleaning materials, and the like that are used in production but are not the primary materials being processed. The flow of costs through a merchandising company is different from that of a manufacturing company, as shown in Illustration 8-2.

Control

For various reasons, management is vitally interested in inventory planning and control. An accurate accounting system with up-to-date records is essential. If unsalable items have accumulated in the inventory, a potential loss exists. Sales and customers may be lost if products ordered by customers are not available in the desired style, quality, and quantity. Also, businesses must monitor inventory levels carefully to limit the financing costs of carrying large inventories. In recent years, with the introduction and use of "just-in-time" (JIT) inventory order systems and better supplier relationships, inventory levels have become leaner for many enterprises.[4]

Perpetual System

As indicated in Chapter 3, inventory records may be maintained on a perpetual or periodic basis. Under a perpetual inventory system, a continuous record of changes in inventory is maintained in the Inventory account. That is, all purchases and sales (issues) of goods are recorded directly in the Inventory account as they occur. The ac-

Objective ❷
Distinguish between perpetual and periodic inventory systems.

---

[4]On the other hand, Lands' End, a catalogue clothier, flouts just-in-time—it builds inventory. The reason: a complete inventory is vital to cementing customer loyalty.

ILLUSTRATION 8-2
Flow of Costs through
Manufacturing and
Merchandising
Companies

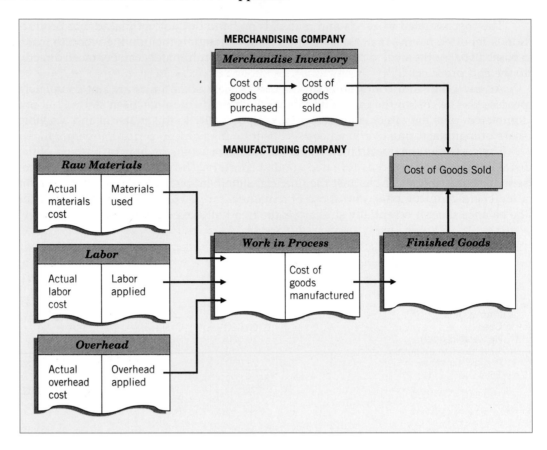

counting features of a perpetual inventory system are:

❶ Purchases of merchandise for resale or raw materials for production are debited to Inventory rather than to Purchases.

❷ Freight-in, purchase returns and allowances, and purchase discounts are recorded in Inventory rather than in separate accounts.

❸ Cost of goods sold is recognized for each sale by debiting the account, Cost of Goods Sold, and crediting Inventory.

❹ Inventory is a control account that is supported by a subsidiary ledger of individual inventory records. The subsidiary records show the quantity and cost of each type of inventory on hand.

The perpetual inventory system provides a continuous record of the balances in both the Inventory account and the Cost of Goods Sold account.

Under a computerized recordkeeping system, additions to and issuances from inventory can be recorded nearly instantaneously. The popularity and affordability of computerized accounting software have made the perpetual system cost-effective for many kinds of businesses. Recording sales with optical scanners at the cash register has been incorporated into perpetual inventory systems at many retail stores.

Periodic System

Under a periodic inventory system, the quantity of inventory on hand is determined, as its name implies, only periodically. All acquisitions of inventory during the accounting period are recorded by debits to a Purchases account. The total in the Purchases account at the end of the accounting period is added to the cost of the inventory on hand at the beginning of the period to determine the total cost of the goods available for sale during the period. Ending inventory is subtracted from the cost of goods available for sale to compute the cost of goods sold. Note that under a periodic inventory system, the cost of goods sold is a residual amount that is dependent upon a physically counted ending inventory.

The **physical inventory count** required by a periodic system is taken once a year at the end of the year.[5] However, most companies need more current information regarding their inventory levels to protect against stockouts or overpurchasing and to aid in the preparation of monthly or quarterly financial data. As a consequence, many companies use a **modified perpetual inventory system** in which increases and decreases in quantities only—not dollar amounts—are kept in a detailed inventory record. It is merely a memorandum device outside the double-entry system which helps in determining the level of inventory at any point in time.

Whether a company maintains a perpetual inventory in quantities and dollars, quantities only, or has no perpetual inventory record at all, it probably takes a physical inventory once a year. No matter what type of inventory records are in use or how well organized the procedures for recording purchases and requisitions, the danger of loss and error is always present. Waste, breakage, theft, improper entry, failure to prepare or record requisitions, and any number of similar possibilities may cause the inventory records to differ from the actual inventory on hand. This requires periodic verification of the inventory records by actual count, weight, or measurement. These counts are compared with the detailed inventory records. The records are corrected to agree with the quantities actually on hand.

Insofar as possible, the physical inventory should be taken near the end of a company's fiscal year so that correct inventory quantities are available for use in preparing annual accounting reports and statements. Because this is not always possible, however, physical inventories taken within two or three months of the year's end are satisfactory, if the detailed inventory records are maintained with a fair degree of accuracy.

To illustrate the difference between a perpetual and a periodic system, assume that Fesmire Company had the following transactions during the current year:

Beginning inventory	100 units at $ 6 = $ 600
Purchases	900 units at $ 6 = $5,400
Sales	600 units at $12 = $7,200
Ending inventory	400 units at $ 6 = $2,400

The entries to record these transactions during the current year are shown in Illustration 8-3.

Perpetual Inventory System			Periodic Inventory System		
1. Beginning inventory, 100 units at $6:					
The inventory account shows the inventory on hand at $600.			The inventory account shows the inventory on hand at $600.		
2. Purchase 900 units at $6:					
Inventory	5,400		Purchases	5,400	
Accounts Payable		5,400	Accounts Payable		5,400
3. Sale of 600 units at $12:					
Accounts Receivable	7,200		Accounts Receivable	7,200	
Sales		7,200	Sales		7,200
Cost of Goods Sold	3,600			(No entry)	
(600 at $6)					
Inventory		3,600			
4. End-of-period entries for inventory accounts, 400 units at $6:					
No entry necessary.			Inventory (ending, by count)	2,400	
The account, Inventory, shows the ending			Cost of Goods Sold	3,600	
balance of $2,400			Purchases		5,400
($600 + $5,400 − $3,600).			Inventory (beginning)		600

ILLUSTRATION 8-3
Comparative Entries—
Perpetual vs. Periodic

---

[5]In recent years, some companies have developed methods of determining inventories, including statistical sampling, that are sufficiently reliable to make unnecessary an annual physical count of each item of inventory.

When a perpetual inventory system is used and a difference exists between the perpetual inventory balance and the physical inventory count, a separate entry is needed to adjust the perpetual inventory account. To illustrate, assume that at the end of the reporting period, the perpetual inventory account reported an inventory balance of $4,000, but a physical count indicated $3,800 was actually on hand. The entry to record the necessary writedown is as follows:

Inventory Over and Short	200	
Inventory		200

Perpetual inventory overages and shortages generally represent a misstatement of cost of goods sold. The difference is a result of normal and expected shrinkage, breakage, shoplifting, incorrect record keeping, and the like. Inventory Over and Short would therefore be an adjustment of cost of goods sold. In practice, the account Inventory Over and Short is sometimes reported in the other revenues and gains or other expenses and losses section, depending on its balance. Note that in a periodic inventory system the account Inventory Over and Short does not arise because there are no accounting records available against which to compare the physical count. Thus, inventory overages and shortages are buried in cost of goods sold.

❖ BASIC ISSUES IN INVENTORY VALUATION

Because the goods sold or used during an accounting period seldom correspond exactly to the goods bought or produced during that period, the physical inventory either increases or decreases. The cost of all the goods available for sale or use should be allocated between the goods that were sold or used and those that are still on hand. The **cost of goods available for sale or use** is the sum of (1) the cost of the goods on hand at the beginning of the period and (2) the cost of the goods acquired or produced during the period. The **cost of goods sold** is the difference between the cost of goods available for sale during the period and the cost of goods on hand at the end of the period.

ILLUSTRATION 8-4
Computation of Cost of
Goods Sold

Beginning inventory, Jan. 1	$100,000
Cost of goods acquired or produced during the year	800,000
Total cost of goods available for sale	900,000
Ending inventory, Dec. 31	200,000
Cost of goods sold during the year	$700,000

The valuation of inventories can be a complex process that requires determination of:

❶ **The physical goods to be included in inventory** (who owns the goods?—goods in transit, consigned goods, special sales agreements).
❷ **The costs to be included in inventory** (product vs. period costs, variable costing vs. absorption costing).
❸ **The cost flow assumption to be adopted** (specific identification, average cost, FIFO, LIFO, retail, etc.).

We will explore these basic issues in the next three sections of the chapter.

❖ PHYSICAL GOODS INCLUDED IN INVENTORY

Technically, purchases should be recorded when legal title to the goods passes to the buyer. General practice, however, is to record acquisitions when the goods are received, because it is difficult for the buyer to determine the exact time of legal passage of title for every purchase. In addition, no material error is likely to result from such a practice if it is consistently applied.

Goods in Transit

Sometimes purchased merchandise is in transit—not yet received—at the end of a fiscal period. The accounting for these shipped goods depends on who owns them. That can be determined by application of the "passage of title" rule. If the goods are shipped **f.o.b. shipping point**, title passes to the buyer when the seller delivers the goods to the common carrier, who acts as an agent for the buyer. (The abbreviation f.o.b. stands for free on board.) If the goods are shipped **f.o.b. destination**, title does not pass until the buyer receives the goods from the common carrier. "Shipping point" and "destination" are often designated by a particular location, for example, f.o.b. Denver.

The accounting rule is that goods to which legal title has passed should be recorded as purchases of the fiscal period. Goods shipped f.o.b. shipping point that are in transit at the end of the period belong to the buyer and should be shown in the buyer's records. Legal title to these goods passed to the buyer when the goods were shipped. To disregard such purchases would result in an understatement of inventories and accounts payable in the balance sheet and an understatement of purchases and ending inventories in the income statement.

Consigned Goods

A specialized method of marketing certain products uses a device known as a **consignment** shipment. Under this arrangement, one party (the consignor) ships merchandise to another (the consignee), who acts as the consignor's agent in selling the consigned goods. The consignee agrees to accept the goods without any liability, except to exercise due care and reasonable protection from loss or damage, until the goods are sold to a third party. When the consignee sells the goods, the revenue less a selling commission and expenses incurred in accomplishing the sale is remitted to the consignor.

Goods out on consignment remain the property of the consignor and are included in the consignor's inventory at purchase price or production cost. Occasionally, the inventory out on consignment is shown as a separate item, but unless the amount is large there is little need for this. Sometimes the inventory on consignment is reported in the notes to the financial statements. For example, Eagle Clothes, Inc. reported the following related to consigned goods: "Inventories consist of finished goods shipped on consignment to customers of the Company's subsidiary April-Marcus, Inc."

The consignee makes no entry to the inventory account for goods received because they are the property of the consignor. The consignee should be extremely careful *not* to include any of the goods consigned as a part of inventory.

Special Sale Agreements

As indicated earlier, transfer of legal title is the general guideline used to determine whether an item should be included in inventory. Unfortunately, transfer of legal title and the underlying substance of the transaction often do not match. For example, it is possible that legal title has passed to the purchaser but the seller of the goods retains the risks of ownership. Conversely, transfer of legal title may not occur, but the economic substance of the transaction is such that the seller no longer retains the risks of ownership. Three special sale situations are illustrated here to indicate the types of problems encountered in practice. These are:

❶ Sales with buyback agreement.
❷ Sales with high rates of return.
❸ Sales on installment.

Sales with Buyback Agreement

Sometimes an enterprise finances its inventory without reporting either the liability or the inventory on its balance sheet. Such an approach—often referred to as a **product financing arrangement**—usually involves a "sale" with either an implicit or explicit "buyback" agreement. To illustrate, Hill Enterprises transfers ("sells") inventory to

Chase, Inc. and simultaneously agrees to repurchase this merchandise at a specified price over a specified period of time. Chase then uses the inventory as collateral and borrows against it. Chase uses the loan proceeds to pay Hill. Hill repurchases the inventory in the future, and Chase employs the proceeds from repayment to meet its loan obligation.

The essence of this transaction is that Hill Enterprises is financing its inventory—and retaining risk of ownership—even though technical legal title to the merchandise was transferred to Chase. The advantage to Hill Enterprises for structuring a transaction in this manner is the avoidance of personal property taxes in certain states, the removal of the current liability from its balance sheet, and the ability to manipulate income. The advantages to Chase are that the purchase of the goods may solve a LIFO liquidation problem (discussed later), or that Chase may be interested in a reciprocal agreement at a later date.

These arrangements are often described as "**parking transactions**" in practice, because the seller simply parks the inventory on another enterprise's balance sheet for a short period of time. When a repurchase agreement exists at a set price and this price covers all costs of the inventory plus related holding costs, the accounting profession now requires that the inventory and related liability remain on the seller's books.[6]

Sales with High Rates of Return

Formal or informal agreements often exist in industries such as publishing, music, and toys and sporting goods that permit inventory to be returned for a full or partial refund. To illustrate, Quality Publishing Company sells textbooks to Campus Bookstores with an agreement that any books not sold may be returned for full credit. In the past, approximately 25% of the textbooks sold to Campus Bookstores were returned. How should Quality Publishing report its sales transactions? One alternative is to record the sale at the full amount and establish an estimated sales returns and allowances account. A second possibility is to not record any sale until circumstances indicate the amount of inventory the buyer will return. The key question is: Under what circumstances should the inventory be considered sold and removed from Quality's inventory? The answer is that when the amount of returns can be reasonably estimated, the goods should be considered sold. Conversely, if returns are unpredictable, removal of these goods from the inventory of the seller is inappropriate.[7]

Sales on Installment

"Goods sold on installment" describes any type of sale in which payment is required in periodic installments over an extended period of time. Because the risk of loss from uncollectibles is higher in installment sale situations than in other sales transactions, the seller often withholds legal title to the merchandise until all the payments have been made. The question is whether the inventory should be considered sold, even though legal title has not passed. The answer is that **the goods should be excluded from the seller's inventory if the percentage of bad debts can be reasonably estimated.** Installment sales are discussed here to show that in some cases, the goods should be removed from inventory, although legal title may not have passed.

Effect of Inventory Errors

As related in the opening stories about Phar-Mor Inc., Crazy Eddie Inc., and Kurzweil Applied Intelligence Inc., items incorrectly included or excluded in determining cost of goods sold by inventory misstatements will result in errors in the financial statements. Let's look at two cases:

---

[6]"Accounting for Product Financing Arrangements," *Statement of Financial Accounting Standards No. 49* (Stamford, Conn.: FASB, 1981).

[7]"Revenue Recognition When Right of Return Exists," *Statement of Financial Accounting Standards No. 48* (Stamford, Conn.: FASB, 1981).

Ending Inventory Misstated

What would happen if the beginning inventory and purchases are recorded correctly, but some items are not included in ending inventory? In this situation, we would have the following effect on the financial statements at the end of the period:

Balance Sheet		Income Statement	
Inventory	Understated	Cost of goods sold	Overstated
Retained earnings	Understated		
Working capital	Understated	Net income	Understated
(current assets less current liabilities)			
Current ratio	Understated		
(current assets divided by current liabilities)			

ILLUSTRATION 8-5
Financial Statement Effects of Misstated Ending Inventory

Working capital and the current ratio are understated because ending inventory is understated; net income is understated because cost of goods sold is overstated.

To illustrate the effect on net income over a 2-year period, assume that the ending inventory of Jay Weiseman Corp. is understated by $10,000 and that all other items are correctly stated. The effect of this error will be to decrease net income in the current year and to increase net income in the following year. The error will be counterbalanced (offset) in the next period because beginning inventory will be understated and net income will be overstated. Both net income figures are misstated, but the total for the two years is correct as shown in Illustration 8-6.

UNDERLYING CONCEPTS

When inventory is misstated, its presentation lacks representational faithfulness.

ILLUSTRATION 8-6
Effect of Ending Inventory Error on Two Periods

		Jay Weiseman Corp. (All figures assumed)		
	Incorrect Recording		Correct Recording	
	1998	1999	1998	1999
Revenues	$100,000	$100,000	$100,000	$100,000
Cost of goods sold				
Beginning inventory	25,000	20,000	25,000	30,000
Purchased or produced	45,000	60,000	45,000	60,000
Goods available for sale	70,000	80,000	70,000	90,000
Less: Ending inventory	20,000*	40,000	30,000	40,000
Cost of goods sold	50,000	40,000	40,000	50,000
Gross profit	50,000	60,000	60,000	50,000
Administrative and selling expenses	40,000	40,000	40,000	40,000
Net income	$ 10,000	$ 20,000	$ 20,000	$ 10,000
	Total income for two years = $30,000		Total income for two years = $30,000	

*Ending inventory understated by $10,000 in 1998.

If ending inventory is *overstated*, the reverse effect occurs. Inventory, working capital, current ratio, and net income are overstated and cost of goods sold is understated. The effect of the error on net income will be counterbalanced in the next year, but both years' net income figures will be misstated.

Purchases and Inventory Misstated

Suppose that certain goods that the company owns are not recorded as a purchase and are not counted in ending inventory. The effect on the financial statements (assuming this is a purchase on account) is as follows:

ILLUSTRATION 8-7
Financial Statement
Effects of Misstated
Purchases and Inventory

Balance Sheet		Income Statement	
Inventory	Understated	Purchases	Understated
Retained earnings	No effect	Cost of goods sold	No effect
Accounts payable	Understated	Net income	No effect
Working capital	No effect	Inventory (ending)	Understated
Current ratio	Overstated		

To omit goods from purchases and inventory results in an understatement of inventory and accounts payable in the balance sheet and an understatement of purchases and ending inventory in the income statement. Net income for the period is not affected by the omission of such goods because purchases and ending inventory are both understated by the same amount—the error thereby offsetting itself in cost of goods sold. Total working capital is unchanged, but the **current ratio** is overstated because of the omission of equal amounts from inventory and accounts payable.

To illustrate the effect on the current ratio, assume that Larry Mall Company understated accounts payable and ending inventory by $40,000. The understated and correct data are shown below.

ILLUSTRATION 8-8
Effects of Purchases and
Ending Inventory Errors

Purchases and Ending Inventory Understated		Purchases and Ending Inventory Correct	
Current assets	$120,000	Current assets	$160,000
Current liabilities	$ 40,000	Current liabilities	$ 80,000
Current ratio	3 to 1	Current ratio	2 to 1

The correct ratio is 2 to 1 rather than 3 to 1. Thus, understatement of accounts payable and ending inventory can lead to a "window dressing" of the current ratio (make it appear better than it is).

If both purchases (on account) and ending inventory are overstated, then the effects on the balance sheet are exactly the reverse. Inventory and accounts payable are overstated and the current ratio is understated; working capital is not affected. Cost of goods sold and net income are not affected because the errors offset one another.

We cannot overemphasize the importance of a proper inventory computation in presenting accurate financial statements. For example, Leslie Fay, a women's apparel maker, had accounting irregularities that wiped out 1992 net income and caused a restatement of 1991's earnings. One reason, it inflated inventory and deflated cost of goods sold. Or remember Phar-Mor Inc. mentioned earlier. Or, Anixter Bros. Inc. had to restate its income by $1.7 million because an accountant in the antenna manufacturing division overstated the ending inventory, thereby reducing its cost of sales. Similarly, AM International allegedly recorded as sold products that were only being rented. As a result, inaccurate inventory figures added $7.9 million to pretax income.

❖ COSTS INCLUDED IN INVENTORY

Objective ❹

Identify the items that should be included as inventory cost.

One of the most important problems in dealing with inventories concerns the amount at which the inventory should be carried in the accounts. **The acquisition of inventories, like other assets, is generally accounted for on a basis of cost.** (Other bases are discussed in Chapter 9.)

Product Costs

Product costs are those costs that "attach" to the inventory and are recorded in the inventory account. These costs are directly connected with the bringing of goods to the place of business of the buyer and converting such goods to a salable condition. Such charges would include freight charges on goods purchased, other direct costs of acquisition, and labor and other production costs incurred in processing the goods up to the time of sale.

It would seem proper also to allocate to inventories a share of any buying costs or expenses of a purchasing department, storage costs, and other costs incurred in storing or handling the goods before they are sold. Because of the practical difficulties involved in allocating such costs and expenses, however, these items are not ordinarily included in valuing inventories.

Period Costs

Selling expenses and, under ordinary circumstances, **general and administrative expenses** are not considered to be directly related to the acquisition or production of goods and, therefore, are not considered to be a part of inventories. Such costs are period costs.

Conceptually, these expenses are as much a cost of the product as the initial purchase price and related freight charges attached to the product. Why then are these costs not considered inventoriable items? Selling expenses are generally considered as more directly related to the cost of goods sold than to the unsold inventory. In most cases, though, the costs, especially administrative expenses, are so unrelated or indirectly related to the immediate production process that any allocation is purely arbitrary.

Interest costs associated with getting inventories ready for sale usually are expensed as incurred. A major argument for this approach is that interest costs are really a cost of financing. Others have argued, however, that interest costs incurred to finance activities associated with bringing inventories to a condition and place ready for sale are as much a cost of the asset as materials, labor, and overhead and, therefore, should be capitalized.[8] **The FASB has ruled that interest costs related to assets constructed for internal use or assets produced as discrete projects (such as ships or real estate projects) for sale or lease should be capitalized.**[9] The FASB emphasized that these discrete projects should take considerable time, entail substantial expenditures, and be likely to involve significant amounts of interest cost. Interest costs should not be capitalized for inventories that are routinely manufactured or otherwise produced in large quantities on a repetitive basis because the informational benefit does not justify the cost.

Manufacturing Costs

As previously indicated, a business that manufactures goods utilizes three inventory accounts—Raw Materials, Work in Process, and Finished Goods. Work in process and finished goods include materials, direct labor, and manufacturing overhead costs. Manufacturing overhead costs include indirect material, indirect labor, and such items as depreciation, taxes, insurance, heat, and electricity incurred in the manufacturing process.

Variable Costing versus Absorption Costing

In a variable costing system (frequently called a direct costing system), all costs must be classified as variable or fixed. Variable costs are those that fluctuate in direct proportion to changes in output, and fixed costs are those that remain constant in spite of changes in output. Under variable costing only costs that vary directly with the pro-

[8]The reporting rules related to interest cost capitalization have their greatest impact in accounting for long-term assets and, therefore, are discussed in detail in Chapter 10.

[9]"Capitalization of Interest Cost," *Statement of Financial Accounting Standards No. 34* (Stamford, Conn.: FASB, 1979).

Components of inventory differ internationally. In determining the cost of inventories, U.S. practice requires the inclusion not only of direct material and labor but also of variable and fixed manufacturing overhead. In other nations (India and Chile, for example) only direct materials and labor are included.

duction volume are charged to products as manufacturing takes place. Because variable costing is so useful to management in decision making, cost control, and budget preparation, it is widely used internally. However, it is not acceptable for tax purposes or for use in published financial reports (external reporting) because it understates the company's investment in inventories.

Under absorption costing (often referred to as full costing), all manufacturing costs, variable and fixed, direct and indirect, that are incurred in the factory or production process attach to the product and are included in the cost of inventory. Absorption costing (full costing) is required by GAAP as the basis of inventory valuation for financial statements. A modified version of absorption costing is required for tax purposes too.[10]

Treatment of Purchase Discounts

The use of a Purchase Discounts account indicates that the company is reporting its purchases and accounts payable at the gross amount. Another approach is to record the purchases and accounts payable at an amount **net** of the cash discounts. This treatment is considered to be better because (1) it provides a correct reporting of the cost of the asset and related liability and (2) it presents the opportunity to measure inefficiency of management if the discount is not taken. In the net approach, the failure to take a purchase discount within the discount period is recorded in a Purchase Discounts Lost account (for which someone, probably the treasurer, is held responsible). To illustrate the difference between the gross and net method, assume the following transactions:

ILLUSTRATION 8-9
Entries under Gross and Net Methods

Gross Method			Net Method		
Purchase cost $10,000, terms 2/10, net 30:					
Purchases	10,000		Purchases	9,800	
Accounts Payable		10,000	Accounts Payable		9,800
Invoices of $4,000 are paid within discount period:					
Accounts Payable	4,000		Accounts Payable	3,920	
Purchase Discounts		80	Cash		3,920
Cash		3,920			
Invoices of $6,000 are paid after discount period:					
Accounts Payable	6,000		Accounts Payable	5,880	
Cash		6,000	Purchase Discounts Lost	120	
			Cash		6,000

Not using the net method because of resultant difficulties is an example of the application of the cost-benefit constraint.

If the gross method is employed, purchase discounts should be reported as a deduction from purchases on the income statement. If the net method is used, purchase discounts lost should be considered a financial expense and reported in the other expense and loss section of the income statement. Many believe that the difficulty involved in using the somewhat more complicated net method is not justified considering the resulting benefits. This could account for the widespread use of the less logical but simpler gross method. In addition, some contend that management is reluctant to report the amount of purchase discounts lost in the financial statements.

---

[10]The Tax Reform Act of 1986 requires that all manufacturers and most wholesalers and retailers replace the previously existing full absorption costing provisions with the following new rules related to costs to be capitalized as inventory. **The new tax rules require that in addition to direct material and direct labor, indirect costs that directly benefit or are incurred by reason of the performance of a production or resale activity must be capitalized.**

In December 1986, the FASB's Emerging Issues Task Force concluded that the fact that a cost (such as bidding, warehousing, purchasing, officer salaries, and administrative and selling expenses) is capitalizable for tax purposes does not, in itself, indicate that capitalizing the cost for financial reporting is preferable—or even appropriate. Task Force members, however, indicated that certain of the additional costs that now have to be capitalized for tax purposes **may be** capitalizable for financial reporting purposes, but only after the individual facts and circumstances have been analyzed.

❖ WHAT COST FLOW ASSUMPTION SHOULD BE ADOPTED?

During any given fiscal period it is very likely that merchandise will be purchased at several different prices. If inventories are to be priced at cost and numerous purchases have been made at different unit costs, which of the various cost prices should be used? Conceptually, a specific identification of the given items sold and unsold seems optimal, but this measure is often not only expensive but impossible to achieve. Consequently, one of several systematic inventory cost flow assumptions is used. Indeed, the actual physical flow of goods and the cost flow assumption are often quite different. **There is no requirement that the cost flow assumption adopted be consistent with the physical movement of goods.** The major objective in selecting a method should be to choose the one which, under the circumstances, most clearly reflects periodic income.[11]

> **Objective 5**
> Describe and compare the flow assumptions used in accounting for inventories.

To illustrate, assume that Call-Mart Inc. had the following transactions in its first month of operations.

Date	Purchases	Sold or Issued	Balance
March 2	2,000 @ $4.00		2,000 units
March 15	6,000 @ $4.40		8,000 units
March 19		4,000 units	4,000 units
March 30	2,000 @ $4.75		6,000 units

From this information, we can compute the ending inventory of 6,000 units and the cost of goods available for sale (beginning inventory + purchases) of $43,900 [(2,000 @ $4.00) + (6,000 @ $4.40) + (2,000 @ $4.75)]. The question is, which price or prices should be assigned to the 6,000 units of ending inventory? The answer depends on which cost flow assumption is employed.

Specific Identification

Specific identification calls for identifying each item sold and each item in inventory. The costs of the specific items sold are included in the cost of goods sold, and the costs of the specific items on hand are included in the inventory. This method may be used only in instances where it is practical to separate physically the different purchases made. It can be successfully applied in situations where a relatively small number of costly, easily distinguishable items are handled. In the retail trade this includes some types of jewelry, fur coats, automobiles, and some furniture. In manufacturing it includes special orders and many products manufactured under a job cost system.

To illustrate the specific identification method, assume that Call-Mart Inc.'s 6,000 units of inventory is composed of 1,000 units from the March 2 purchase, 3,000 from the March 15 purchase, and 2,000 from the March 30 purchase. The ending inventory and cost of goods sold would be computed as shown in Illustration 8-10.

Date	No. of Units	Unit Cost	Total Cost
March 2	1,000	$4.00	$ 4,000
March 15	3,000	4.40	13,200
March 30	2,000	4.75	9,500
Ending inventory	6,000		$26,700
Cost of goods available for sale (computed in previous section)		$43,900	
Deduct ending inventory		26,700	
Cost of goods sold		$17,200	

ILLUSTRATION 8-10
Specific Identification
Method

---

[11]"Restatement and Revision of Accounting Research Bulletins," *Accounting Research Bulletin No. 43* (New York: AICPA, 1953), Ch. 4, Statement 4.

Conceptually, this method appears ideal because actual costs are matched against actual revenue, and ending inventory is reported at actual cost. In other words, under specific identification the cost flow matches the physical flow of the goods. On closer observation, however, this method has certain deficiencies.

One argument against specific identification is that it makes it possible to manipulate net income. For example, assume that a wholesaler purchases otherwise identical plywood early in the year at three different prices. When the plywood is sold, the wholesaler can select either the lowest or the highest price to charge to expense simply by selecting the plywood from a specific lot for delivery to the customer. A business manager, therefore, can manipulate net income simply by delivering to the customer the higher- or lower-priced item, depending on whether higher or lower reported earnings is desired for the period.

Another problem relates to the arbitrary allocation of costs that sometimes occurs with specific inventory items. In certain circumstances, it is difficult to relate adequately, for example, shipping charges, storage costs, and discounts directly to a given inventory item. The alternative, then, is to allocate these costs somewhat arbitrarily, which leads to a "breakdown" in the precision of the specific identification method.[12]

Average Cost

As the name implies, the average cost method prices items in the inventory on the basis of the average cost of all similar goods available during the period. To illustrate, assuming that Call-Mart Inc. used the periodic inventory method, the ending inventory and cost of goods sold would be computed as follows using a weighted-average method:

ILLUSTRATION 8-11
Weighted-Average
Method—Periodic
Inventory

Date of Invoice	No. Units	Unit Cost	Total Cost
March 2	2,000	$4.00	$ 8,000
March 15	6,000	4.40	26,400
March 30	2,000	4.75	9,500
Total goods available	10,000		$43,900

Weighted-average cost per unit $\dfrac{\$43,900}{10,000} = \$4.39$

Inventory in units   6,000 units

Ending inventory   6,000 × $4.39 = $26,340

Cost of goods available for sale	$43,900
Deduct ending inventory	26,340
Cost of goods sold	$17,560

If the company has a beginning inventory, it is included both in the total units available and in the total cost of goods available in computing the average cost per unit.

Another average cost method is the moving-average method, which is used with perpetual inventory records. The application of the average cost method for perpetual records is shown in Illustration 8-12.

ILLUSTRATION 8-12
Moving-Average
Method—Perpetual
Inventory

Date	Purchased		Sold or Issued		Balance	
March 2	(2,000 @ $4.00)	$ 8,000			(2,000 @ $4.00)	$ 8,000
March 15	(6,000 @ 4.40)	26,400			(8,000 @ 4.30)	34,400
March 19			(4,000 @ $4.30)	$17,200	(4,000 @ 4.30)	17,200
March 30	(2,000 @ 4.75)	9,500			(6,000 @ 4.45)	26,700

---

[12]A good illustration of the cost allocation problem arises in the motion picture industry. Often actors and actresses receive a percentage of net income for a given movie or television program. Some actors such as James Garner and Fess Parker, who had these arrangements, have alleged that their programs have been extremely profitable to the motion picture studios but they have received little in the way of profit sharing. Actors contend that the studios allocate additional costs to successful projects to ensure that there will be no profits to share.

In this method, a new average unit cost is computed each time a purchase is made. On March 15, after 6,000 units are purchased for $26,400, 8,000 units costing $34,400 ($8,000 plus $26,400) are on hand. The average unit cost is $34,400 divided by 8,000, or $4.30. This unit cost is used in costing withdrawals until another purchase is made, when a new average unit cost is computed. Accordingly, the cost of the 4,000 units withdrawn on March 19 is shown at $4.30, a total cost of goods sold of $17,200. On March 30, following the purchase of 2,000 units for $9,500, a new unit cost of $4.45 is determined for an ending inventory of $26,700.

The use of the average cost methods is usually justified on the basis of practical rather than conceptual reasons. These methods are simple to apply, objective, and not as subject to income manipulation as some of the other inventory pricing methods. In addition, proponents of the average cost methods argue that it is often impossible to measure a specific physical flow of inventory and therefore it is better to cost items on an average price basis. This argument is particularly persuasive when the inventory involved is relatively homogeneous in nature.

First-In, First-Out (FIFO)

The FIFO method assumes that goods are used in the order in which they are purchased. In other words, it assumes that **the first goods purchased are the first used** (in a manufacturing concern) **or sold** (in a merchandising concern). The inventory remaining must therefore represent the most recent purchases.

To illustrate, assume that Call-Mart Inc. uses the periodic inventory system (amount of inventory computed only at the end of the month). The cost of the ending inventory is computed by taking the cost of the most recent purchase and working back until all units in the inventory are accounted for. The ending inventory and cost of goods sold are determined as shown in Illustration 8-13.

Date	No. Units	Unit Cost	Total Cost
March 30	2,000	$4.75	$ 9,500
March 15	4,000	4.40	17,600
Ending inventory	6,000		$27,100

Cost of goods available for sale	$43,900	
Deduct ending inventory	27,100	
Cost of goods sold	$16,800	

ILLUSTRATION 8-13
FIFO Method—Periodic Inventory

If a perpetual inventory system in quantities and dollars is used, a cost figure is attached to each withdrawal. Then the cost of the 4,000 units removed on March 19 would be made up of the items purchased on March 2 and March 15. The inventory on a FIFO basis perpetual system for Call-Mart Inc. is shown in Illustration 8-14.

Date	Purchased	Sold or Issued	Balance
March 2	(2,000 @ $4.00) $ 8,000		2,000 @ $4.00 $ 8,000
March 15	(6,000 @ 4.40) 26,400		2,000 @ 4.00 ⎱ 34,400 6,000 @ 4.40 ⎰
March 19		2,000 @ $4.00 ⎱ 2,000 @ 4.40 ⎰ ($16,800)	4,000 @ 4.40 17,600
March 30	(2,000 @ 4.75) 9,500		4,000 @ 4.40 ⎱ 27,100 2,000 @ 4.75 ⎰

ILLUSTRATION 8-14
FIFO Method—Perpetual Inventory

The ending inventory in this situation is $27,100, and the cost of goods sold is $16,800 [(2,000 @ 4.00) + (2,000 @ $4.40)].

Notice that in these two FIFO examples, the cost of goods sold and ending inventory are the same. **In all cases where FIFO is used, the inventory and cost of goods sold would be the same at the end of the month whether a perpetual or periodic system**

is used. This is true because the same costs will always be first in and, therefore, first out whether cost of goods sold is computed as goods are sold throughout the accounting period (the perpetual system) or as a residual at the end of the accounting period (the periodic system).

One objective of FIFO is to approximate the physical flow of goods. When the physical flow of goods is actually first-in, first-out, the FIFO method closely approximates specific identification. At the same time, it does not permit manipulation of income because the enterprise is not free to pick a certain cost item to be charged to expense.

Another **advantage** of the FIFO method is that the ending inventory is close to current cost. Because the first goods in are the first goods out, the ending inventory amount will be composed of the most recent purchases. This is particularly true where the inventory turnover is rapid. This approach generally provides a reasonable approximation of replacement cost on the balance sheet when price changes have not occurred since the most recent purchases.

The basic **disadvantage** of the FIFO method is that current costs are not matched against current revenues on the income statement. The oldest costs are charged against the more current revenue, which can lead to distortions in gross profit and net income.

Last-In, First-Out (LIFO)

The **LIFO method** first matches the cost of the last goods purchased against revenue. If a periodic inventory is used, then it would be assumed that **the cost of the total quantity sold or issued during the month would have come from the most recent purchases.** The ending inventory would be priced by using the total units as a basis of computation and disregarding the exact dates involved. The example below assumes that the cost of the 4,000 units withdrawn absorbed the 2,000 units purchased on March 30 and 2,000 of the 6,000 units purchased on March 15. The inventory and related cost of goods sold would then be computed as shown in Illustration 8-15.

INTERNATIONAL INSIGHT

Until recently, LIFO was typically used only in the United States. However, LIFO is acceptable under the Directives of the European Union, and its use has now spread in some degree to other countries. Nonetheless, LIFO is still used primarily in the United States and is still prohibited in several nations, including, for example, Australia, Hong Kong, and the United Kingdom.

ILLUSTRATION 8-15
LIFO Method—Periodic Inventory

Date of Invoice	No. Units	Unit Cost	Total Cost
March 2	2,000	$4.00	$ 8,000
March 15	4,000	4.40	17,600
Ending inventory	6,000		$25,600
	Goods available for sale	$43,900	
	Deduct ending inventory	25,600	
	Cost of goods sold	$18,300	

If a perpetual inventory record is kept in quantities and dollars, application of the last-in, first-out method will result in **different ending inventory and cost of goods sold amounts,** as shown in Illustration 8-16.

ILLUSTRATION 8-16
LIFO Method—Perpetual Inventory

Date	Purchased		Sold or Issued	Balance	
March 2	(2,000 @ $4.00)	$ 8,000		2,000 @ $4.00	$ 8,000
March 15	(6,000 @ 4.40)	26,400		2,000 @ 4.00 ⎱ 6,000 @ 4.40 ⎰	34,400
March 19			(4,000 @ $4.40) $17,600	2,000 @ 4.00 ⎱ 2,000 @ 4.40 ⎰	16,800
March 30	(2,000 @ 4.75)	9,500		2,000 @ 4.00 ⎱ 2,000 @ 4.40 ⎬ 2,000 @ 4.75 ⎰	26,300

The month-end periodic inventory computation presented in Illustration 8-15 (inventory $25,600 and cost of goods sold $18,300) shows a different amount from the perpetual inventory computation (inventory $26,300 and cost of goods sold $17,600).

This is because the periodic system matches the total withdrawals for the month with the total purchases for the month in applying the last-in, first-out method, whereas the perpetual system matches each withdrawal with the immediately preceding purchases. In effect, the first computation assumed that the cost of the goods that were purchased on March 30 were included in the sale or issue on March 19.

❖ SPECIAL ISSUES RELATED TO LIFO

LIFO Reserve

Many companies use LIFO for tax and external reporting purposes, but maintain a FIFO, average cost, or standard cost system for internal reporting purposes. There are several reasons to do so: (1) Companies often base their pricing decisions on a FIFO, average, or standard cost assumption, rather than on a LIFO basis. (2) Record keeping on some other basis is easier because the LIFO assumption usually does not approximate the physical flow of the product. (3) Profit-sharing and other bonus arrangements are often not based on a LIFO inventory assumption. Finally, (4) the use of a pure LIFO system is troublesome for interim periods, for which estimates must be made of year-end quantities and prices.

Objective ⑥

Explain the significance and use of a LIFO reserve.

The difference between the inventory method used for internal reporting purposes and LIFO is referred to as the Allowance to Reduce Inventory to LIFO or the **LIFO reserve**. The change in the allowance balance from one period to the next is called the **LIFO effect**. The LIFO effect is the adjustment that must be made to the accounting records in a given year. To illustrate, assume that Acme Boot Company uses the FIFO method for internal reporting purposes and LIFO for external reporting purposes. At January 1, 1999, the Allowance to Reduce Inventory to LIFO balance was $20,000 and the ending balance should be $50,000. The LIFO effect is, therefore, $30,000 and the following entry is made at year-end:

| Cost of Goods Sold | 30,000 | |
| Allowance to Reduce Inventory to LIFO | | 30,000 |

The Allowance to Reduce Inventory to LIFO would be deducted from inventory to ensure that the inventory is stated on a LIFO basis at year-end.

The AICPA Task Force on LIFO Inventory Problems concluded that either the LIFO reserve or the replacement cost of the inventory should be disclosed.[13] Two types of this kind of disclosure are shown below.

American Maize-Products Company

Inventories (Note 3) $80,320,000

Note 3: Inventories. At December 31, $31,516,000 of inventories were valued using the LIFO method. This amount is less than the corresponding replacement value by $3,765,000.

Brown Group, Inc.

Inventories, net of adjustment to last-in,
first-out cost of $68,736,000 (Note D) $309,426,000

Note D: Inventories. Inventories are valued at the lower of cost or market determined principally by the last-in, first-out (LIFO) method. If the first-in, first-out (FIFO) cost method had been used, inventories would have been $68,736,000 higher.

ILLUSTRATION 8-17
Note Disclosures of LIFO Reserve

Go to our Web site for additional LIFO reserve disclosures

---

[13]The AICPA Task Force on LIFO Inventory Problems defined **LIFO reserve** for its purposes as "the difference between (a) inventory at the lower of LIFO cost or market and (b) inventory at replacement cost or at the lower of cost determined by some acceptable inventory accounting method (such as FIFO or average cost) or market." *Issues Paper* (New York: AICPA, November 30, 1984), par. 2–24.

LIFO Liquidation

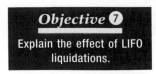

Objective ❼

Explain the effect of LIFO liquidations.

Up to this point, we have emphasized a **specific goods approach** to costing LIFO inventories (also called traditional LIFO or unit LIFO). This approach is often unrealistic for two reasons:

❶ When a company has many different inventory items, the accounting cost of keeping track of each inventory item is expensive.

❷ Erosion of the LIFO inventory can easily occur (referred to as **LIFO liquidation**). This often leads to distortions of net income and substantial tax payments.

To understand the LIFO liquidation problem, assume that Basler Co. has 30,000 pounds of steel in its inventory on December 31, 1999, costed on a specific goods LIFO approach.

	Ending Inventory (1999)		
	Pounds	Unit Cost	LIFO Cost
1996	8,000	$ 4	$ 32,000
1997	10,000	6	60,000
1998	7,000	9	63,000
1999	5,000	10	50,000
	30,000		$205,000

As indicated, the ending 1999 inventory for Basler Co. comprises costs from past periods. These costs are called layers (increases from period to period), with the first layer identified as the base layer. An illustration of the layers for Basler is as follows:

ILLUSTRATION 8-18
Layers of LIFO Inventory

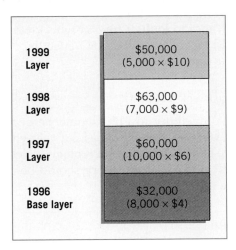

1999 Layer — $50,000 (5,000 × $10)

1998 Layer — $63,000 (7,000 × $9)

1997 Layer — $60,000 (10,000 × $6)

1996 Base layer — $32,000 (8,000 × $4)

The price of steel has increased over the 4-year period. In 2000, Basler Co. experienced metal shortages and had to liquidate much of its inventory (a LIFO liquidation). At the end of 2000, only 6,000 pounds of steel remained in inventory. Because the company is using LIFO, the most recent layer, 1999, is liquidated first, followed by the 1998 layer, and so on. The result: costs from preceding periods are matched against sales revenues reported in current dollars; this leads to a distortion in net income and a substantial tax bill in the current period. These effects are shown in Illustration 8-19. Unfortunately LIFO liquidations can occur frequently when a specific goods LIFO approach is employed.

To alleviate the LIFO liquidation problems and to simplify the accounting, goods can be combined into pools. A **pool** is defined as a group of items of a similar nature. Thus, instead of only identical units, a number of similar units or products are combined and accounted for together. This method is referred to as the **specific goods pooled LIFO approach**. Using the specific goods pooled LIFO approach, LIFO liquidations are less likely to happen because the reduction of one quantity in the pool may be offset by an increase in another.

ILLUSTRATION 8-19
LIFO Liquidation

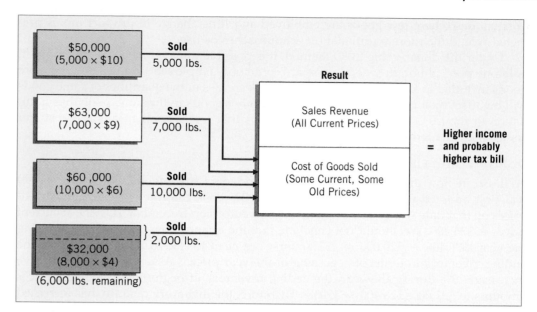

The specific goods pooled LIFO approach eliminates some of the disadvantages of the specific goods (traditional) accounting for LIFO inventories. This pooled approach, using quantities as its measurement basis, however, creates other problems.

First, most companies are continually changing the mix of their products, materials, and production methods. A business once engaged in manufacturing train locomotives may now be involved in the automobile or aircraft business. A business that had used cotton fabric in its clothing now uses synthetic fabric (dacron, nylon, etc.). If a pooled approach using quantities is employed, it means that the pools must be continually redefined; this can be time consuming and costly.

Second, even when such an approach is practical, an erosion ("LIFO liquidation") of the layers often results, and much of the LIFO costing benefit is lost. An erosion of the layers results because a specific good or material in the pool may be replaced by another good or material either temporarily or permanently. This replacement may occur for competitive reasons or simply because a shortage of a certain material exists. Whatever the reason, the new item may not be similar enough to be treated as part of the old pool. Therefore any inflationary profit deferred on the old goods may have to be recognized as the old goods are replaced.

Dollar-Value LIFO

To overcome the problems of redefining pools and eroding layers, the dollar-value LIFO method was developed. **An important feature of the dollar-value LIFO method is that increases and decreases in a pool are determined and measured in terms of total dollar value, not the physical quantity of the goods in the inventory pool.**

Objective 8

Explain the dollar-value LIFO method.

Such an approach has two important advantages over the specific goods pooled approach. First, a broader range of goods may be included in a dollar-value LIFO pool. Second, in a dollar-value LIFO pool, replacement is permitted if it is a similar material, or similar in use, or interchangeable. (In contrast, in a specific goods LIFO pool, an item may be replaced only with an item that is substantially identical.)

Thus, dollar-value LIFO techniques help protect LIFO layers from erosion. Because of this advantage, the dollar-value LIFO method is frequently used in practice.[14] Only

---

[14]A study by James M. Reeve and Keith G. Stanga disclosed that the vast majority of respondent companies applying LIFO use the dollar-value method or the dollar-value retail method (explained in Chapter 9) to apply LIFO. Only a small minority of companies use the specific goods (unit LIFO) approach or the specific goods pooling approach. See "The LIFO Pooling Decision," *Accounting Horizons* (June 1987), p. 27.

in situations where few goods are employed and little change in product mix is predicted would the more traditional LIFO approaches be used.

Under the dollar-value LIFO method, it is possible to have the entire inventory in only one pool, although several pools are commonly employed.[15] In general, the more goods included in a pool, the more likely that decreases in the quantities of some goods will be offset by increases in the quantities of other goods in the same pool; thus liquidation of the LIFO layers is avoided. It follows that fewer pools means less cost and less chance of a reduction of a LIFO layer.[16]

Dollar-Value LIFO Illustration

To illustrate how the dollar-value LIFO method works, assume that dollar-value LIFO was first adopted (base period) on December 31, 1998, that the inventory at current prices on that date was $20,000, and that the inventory on December 31, 1999, at current prices is $26,400. We should not conclude that the quantity has increased 32% during the year ($26,400 ÷ $20,000 = 132%). First, we need to ask: What is the value of the ending inventory in terms of beginning-of-the-year prices? Assuming that prices have increased 20% during the year, the ending inventory at beginning-of-the-year prices amounts to $22,000 ($26,400 ÷ 120%). Therefore, the inventory quantity has increased 10%, or from $20,000 to $22,000 in terms of beginning-of-the-year prices.

The next step is to price this real dollar quantity increase. This real dollar quantity increase of $2,000 valued at year-end prices is $2,400 (120% × $2,000). This increment (layer) of $2,400, when added to the beginning inventory of $20,000, gives a total of $22,400 for the December 31, 1999, inventory, as shown below:

First layer—(beginning inventory) in terms of 100	$20,000
Second layer—(1999 increase) in terms of 120	2,400
Dollar-value LIFO inventory, December 31, 1999	$22,400

It should be emphasized that **a layer is formed only when the ending inventory at base-year prices exceeds the beginning inventory at base-year prices**. And only when a new layer is formed must a new index be computed.

Comprehensive Dollar-Value LIFO Illustration

To illustrate the use of the dollar-value LIFO method in a more complex situation, assume that Bismark Company develops the following information:

December 31	Inventory at End-of-Year Prices	÷	Price Index (percentage)	=	End-of-Year Inventory at Base-Year Prices
(Base year) 1996	$200,000		100		$200,000
1997	299,000		115		260,000
1998	300,000		120		250,000
1999	351,000		130		270,000

---

[15]The Reeve and Stanga study (ibid.,) reports that most companies have only a few pools (the median is six for retailers and three for nonretailers), but the distributions are highly skewed; some companies have 100 or more pools. Retailers that use LIFO have significantly more pools than nonretailers. About a third of the nonretailers (mostly manufacturers) use a single pool for their entire LIFO inventory.

[16]In a later study, William R. Coon and Randall B. Hayes point out that when quantities are increasing, multiple pools over a period of time may produce (under rather general conditions) significantly higher cost of goods sold deductions than a single pool approach. When a stock-out occurs, a single pool approach may lessen the layer liquidation for that year, but it may not erase the cumulative cost of goods sold advantage accruing to the use of multiple pools built up over the preceding years. See "The Dollar Value LIFO Pooling Decision: The Conventional Wisdom Is Too General," *Accounting Horizons* (December 1989), pp. 57–70.

At December 31, 1996, the ending inventory under dollar-value LIFO is simply the $200,000 computed as shown in Illustration 8-20.

Ending Inventory at Base-Year Prices	Layer at Base-Year Prices		Price Index (percentage)		Ending Inventory at LIFO Cost
$200,000	$200,000	×	100	=	$200,000

ILLUSTRATION 8-20
Computation of 1996
Inventory at LIFO Cost

At December 31, 1997, a comparison of the ending inventory at base-year prices ($260,000) with the beginning inventory at base-year prices ($200,000), indicates that the quantity of goods has increased $60,000 ($260,000 − $200,000). This increment (layer) is then priced at the 1997 index of 115% to arrive at a new layer of $69,000. Ending inventory for 1997 is $269,000, composed of the beginning inventory of $200,000 and the new layer of $69,000. These computations are shown in Illustration 8-21.

Ending Inventory at Base-Year Prices	Layers at Base-Year Prices			Price Index (percentage)		Ending Inventory at LIFO Cost
$260,000	1996	$200,000	×	100	=	$200,000
	1997	60,000	×	115	=	69,000
		$260,000				$269,000

ILLUSTRATION 8-21
Computation of 1997
Inventory at LIFO Cost

At December 31, 1998, a comparison of the ending inventory at base-year prices ($250,000) with the beginning inventory at base-year prices ($260,000) indicates that the quantity of goods has decreased $10,000 ($250,000 − $260,000). If the ending inventory at base-year prices is less than the beginning inventory at base-year prices, **the decrease must be subtracted from the most recently added layer. When a decrease occurs, previous layers must be "peeled off" at the prices in existence when the layers were added.** In Bismark Company's situation, this means that $10,000 in base-year prices must be removed from the 1997 layer of $60,000 at base-year prices. The balance of $50,000 ($60,000 − $10,000) at base-year prices must be valued at the 1997 price index of 115% so that this 1997 layer now is valued at $57,500 ($50,000 × 115%). The ending inventory is therefore computed at $257,500, consisting of the beginning inventory of $200,000 and the second layer, $57,500. The computations for 1998 are shown in Illustration 8-22.

Ending Inventory at Base-Year Prices	Layers at Base-Year Prices			Price Index (percentage)		Ending Inventory at LIFO Cost
$250,000	1996	$200,000	×	100	=	$200,000
	1997	50,000	×	115	=	57,500
		$250,000				$257,500

ILLUSTRATION 8-22
Computation of 1998
Inventory at LIFO Cost

Note that if a layer or base (or portion thereof) has been eliminated, it cannot be rebuilt in future periods. That is, it is gone forever.

At December 31, 1999, a comparison of the ending inventory at base-year prices ($270,000) with the beginning inventory at base-year prices ($250,000) indicates that the dollar quantity of goods has increased $20,000 ($270,000 − $250,000) in terms of base-year prices. After converting the $20,000 increase to the 1999 price index, the ending inventory is $283,500, composed of the beginning layer of $200,000, a 1997 layer of $57,500, and a 1999 layer of $26,000 ($20,000 × 130%). This computation is shown in Illustration 8-23.

ILLUSTRATION 8-23
Computation of 1999
Inventory at LIFO Cost

Ending Inventory at Base-Year Prices	Layers at Base-Year Prices		Price Index (percentage)		Ending Inventory at LIFO Cost
	1996	$200,000	× 100	=	$200,000
$270,000	1997	50,000	× 115	=	57,500
	1999	20,000	× 130	=	26,000
		$270,000			$283,500

The ending inventory at base-year prices must always equal the total of the layers at base-year prices; checking that this situation exists will help to ensure that the dollar-value computation is made correctly.

Selecting a Price Index

Obviously, price changes are critical in dollar-value LIFO. How are the price indexes determined? Many companies use the general price-level index prepared and published monthly by the federal government; the most popular general external price-level index is the Consumers Price Index for Urban Consumers (CPI-U).[17] Specific external price indexes are also widely used. For instance, specific indexes are computed and published daily for most commodities (gold, silver, other metals, corn, wheat, and other farm products). Many trade associations prepare indexes for specific product lines or industries. Any of these indexes may be used for dollar-value LIFO purposes.

When a specific external price index is not readily available or relevant, a company may compute its own specific internal price index. The desired approach is to price ending inventory at the most current cost. Current cost is ordinarily determined by referring to the actual cost of those goods most recently purchased. The price index provides a measure of the change in price or cost levels between the base year and the current year. An index is computed for each year after the base year. The general formula for computing the index is as follows:

ILLUSTRATION 8-24
Formula for Computing a
Price Index

$$\frac{\text{Ending Inventory for the Period at Current Cost}}{\text{Ending Inventory for the Period at Base-Year Cost}} = \text{Price Index for Current Year}$$

This approach is generally referred to as the double-extension method because the value of the units in inventory is extended at both base-year prices and current-year prices. To illustrate this computation, assume that Toledo Company's base-year inventory (January 1, 1999) was composed of the following:

Items	Quantity	Cost per Unit	Total Cost
A	1,000	$ 6	$ 6,000
B	2,000	20	40,000
(January 1, 1999, inventory at base-year costs)			$46,000

Examination of the ending inventory indicates that 3,000 units of Item A and 6,000 units of Item B are held on December 31, 1999. The most recent actual purchases related to these items were as follows:

Items	Purchase Date	Quantity Purchased	Cost per Unit
A	December 1, 1999	4,000	$ 7
B	December 15, 1999	5,000	25
B	November 16, 1999	1,000	22

---

[17]Indexes may be **general** (composed of several commodities, goods, or services) or **specific** (for one commodity, good, or service) and **external** (computed by an outside party, such as the government, commodity exchange, or trade association) or **internal** (computed by the enterprise for its own product or service).

We double-extend the inventory as shown in Illustration 8-25.

	12/31/99 Inventory at Base-Year Costs			12/31/99 Inventory at Current-Year Costs		
Items	Units	Base-Year Cost per Unit	Total	Units	Current-Year Cost per Unit	Total
A	3,000	$ 6	$ 18,000	3,000	$ 7	$ 21,000
B	6,000	20	120,000	5,000	25	125,000
B				1,000	22	22,000
			$138,000			$168,000

ILLUSTRATION 8-25
Double-Extension
Method of Selecting
a Price Index

After the inventories are double-extended, the formula above is used to develop the index for the current year (1999) as shown in Illustration 8-26.

$$\frac{\text{Ending Inventory for the Period at Current Cost}}{\text{Ending Inventory for the Period at Base-Year Cost}} = \frac{\$168,000}{\$138,000} = 121.74\%$$

ILLUSTRATION 8-26
Computation of 1999
Index

This index (121.74%) is then applied to the layer added in 1999. Note in this illustration that Toledo Company used the most recent actual purchases to determine current cost; other approaches such as FIFO and average cost may also be used. Whichever flow assumption is adopted, consistent use from one period to another is required.[18]

Use of the double-extension method is time consuming and difficult where substantial technological change has occurred or where a large number of items is involved. That is, as time passes, a new base-year cost must be determined for new products and a base-year cost must be kept for each inventory item.[19]

Comparison of LIFO Approaches

Three different approaches to computing LIFO inventories are presented in this chapter—specific goods LIFO, specific goods pooled LIFO, and dollar-value LIFO. As indicated earlier, the use of the specific goods LIFO is unrealistic because most enterprises have numerous goods in inventory at the end of a period, and costing (pricing) them on a unit basis is extremely expensive and time consuming.

The specific goods pooled LIFO approach is better in that it reduces record keeping and clerical costs. In addition, it is more difficult to erode the layers because the reduction of one quantity in the pool may be offset by an increase in another. Nonetheless,

---

[18]Another approach to finding an index is the **link-chain method**. Under the link-chain method the base cost of ending inventory is determined by applying a cumulative index to the dollar value of the ending inventory. The cumulative index is the relationship of the current-year prices to those of the prior year (based on either double-extension or an index) multiplied by the prior year's cumulative index. Thus each year's index may be characterized as a link in a chain of indexes back to the base year. It is not illustrated here because it is permitted only in limited circumstances.

[19]Another approach, which was initially sanctioned by the Internal Revenue Service for tax purposes, may be used to simplify the analysis. Under this method, an index is obtained by reference to an outside source or by double-extending only a sample portion of the inventory. For example, all companies are allowed to use 80% of the inflation rate reported by the appropriate consumer or producer price indexes prepared by the Bureau of Labor Statistics (BLS) as their inflation rate for a LIFO pool. Small companies (less than $2 million in sales) can use 100% of the inflation rate reported by such indexes as their inflation rate. Once the index is obtained, the ending inventory at current cost is divided by the index to find the base-year cost. Using generally available external indexes greatly simplifies LIFO computations as internal indexes need not be computed. Although this approach was initially established for reporting taxable income, it is permissible to use this method for financial reporting as well.

the pooled approach using quantities as its measurement basis can lead to untimely LIFO liquidations.

As a result, **dollar-value LIFO is the method employed by most companies that currently use a LIFO system**. Although the approach appears complex, the logic and the computations are actually quite simple, once an appropriate index is determined.

This is not to suggest that problems do not exist with the dollar-value LIFO method. The selection of the items to be put in a pool can be subjective.[20] Such a determination, however, is extremely important because manipulation of the items in a pool without conceptual justification can affect reported net income. For example, the SEC noted that some companies have set up pools that are easy to liquidate. As a result, when the company wants to increase its income, it decreases inventory, thereby matching low-cost inventory items to current revenues.

To curb this practice, the SEC has taken a much harder line on the number of pools that companies may establish. In the well-publicized Stauffer Chemical Company case, Stauffer had increased the number of LIFO pools from eight to 280, boosting its net income by $16,515,000 or approximately 13%.[21] Stauffer justified the change in its Annual Report on the basis of "achieving a better matching of cost and revenue." The SEC required Stauffer to reduce the number of its inventory pools, contending that some pools were inappropriate and alleging income manipulation.

Major Advantages of LIFO Approaches

Objective 9

Identify the major advantages and disadvantages of LIFO.

One obvious advantage of LIFO approaches is that in certain situations the LIFO cost flow actually approximates the physical flow of the goods in and out of inventory. For instance, in the case of a coal pile, the last coal in is the first coal out because it is on the top of the pile. The coal remover is not going to take the coal from the bottom of the pile! The coal that is going to be taken first is the coal that was placed on the pile last.

However, the coal pile situation is one of only a few situations where the actual physical flow corresponds to LIFO. Therefore most adherents of LIFO use other arguments for its widespread employment, as follows:

Matching

In LIFO, the more recent costs are matched against current revenues to provide a better measure of current earnings. During periods of inflation, many challenge the quality of non-LIFO earnings, noting that by failing to match current costs against current revenues, **transitory or "paper" profits ("inventory profits") are created**. Inventory profits occur when the inventory costs matched against sales are less than the inventory replacement cost. The cost of goods sold therefore is understated and profit is overstated. Using LIFO (rather than a method such as FIFO), current costs are matched against revenues and inventory profits are thereby reduced.

 **INTERNATIONAL INSIGHT**

LIFO tends to be found in financial statements in countries where it is allowed for tax purposes, such as Belgium, Germany, Japan, South Korea, and Taiwan.

Tax Benefits

Tax benefits are the major reason why LIFO has become popular. As long as the price level increases and inventory quantities do not decrease, a deferral of income tax occurs, because the items most recently purchased at the higher price level are matched against revenues. For example, when Fuqua Industries decided to switch to LIFO, it had a resultant tax savings of about $4 million. Even if the price level decreases later, the

---

[20]It is suggested that companies analyze how inventory purchases are affected by price changes, how goods are stocked, how goods are used, and if future liquidations are likely. See William R. Cron and Randall Hayes, "The Dollar Value LIFO Pooling Decision: The Conventional Wisdom is Too General," *Accounting Horizons* (December 1989), p. 57.

[21]Commerce Clearing House, *SEC Accounting Rules* (Chicago: CCH, 1983), par. 4035.

company has been given a temporary deferral of its income taxes.[22] The tax law requires that if a company uses LIFO for tax purposes, it must also use LIFO for financial accounting purposes[23] (although neither tax law nor GAAP requires a company to pool its inventories in the same manner for book and tax purposes). This requirement is often referred to as the **LIFO conformity rule**. Other inventory valuation methods do not have this requirement. Unfortunately, the general attitude too frequently is: "Whatever is good for tax is good for financial reporting."

Improved Cash Flow

Improved cash flow is related to the tax benefits, because taxes must be paid in cash. As a consequence, some companies not receiving LIFO tax benefits are forced to borrow to finance replacement of existing inventory levels, and interest costs can be staggering. Fuqua Industries expected to save approximately $400,000 in interest costs by switching to LIFO. Even if the company has plenty of cash to pay its taxes, LIFO permits management to invest these funds and earn a return unavailable to those using FIFO.[24]

Future Earnings Hedge

With LIFO, a company's future reported earnings will not be affected substantially by future price declines. LIFO eliminates or substantially minimizes write-downs to market as a result of price decreases. The reason: since the most recent inventory is sold first, there isn't much ending inventory sitting around at high prices vulnerable to a price decline. In contrast, inventory costed under FIFO is more vulnerable to price declines, which can reduce net income substantially.

Major Disadvantages of LIFO Approaches

Despite its advantages, LIFO has the following drawbacks:

Reduced Earnings

Many corporate managers view the lower profits reported under the LIFO method in inflationary times as a distinct disadvantage and would rather have higher reported profits than lower taxes. Some fear that an accounting change to LIFO may be misunderstood by investors and that, as a result of the lower profits, the price of the company's stock will fall. In fact, though, there is some evidence to refute this contention. Non-LIFO earnings are now highly suspect and may be severely penalized by Wall Street.

Inventory Understated

LIFO may have a distorting effect on a company's balance sheet. The inventory valuation is normally outdated because the oldest costs remain in inventory. This understatement makes the working capital position of the company appear worse than it really is.

---

[22]In periods of rising prices, the use of fewer pools will translate into greater income tax benefits through the use of LIFO. The use of fewer pools allows inventory reductions of some items to be offset by inventory increases in others. In contrast, the use of more pools increases the likelihood that old, low-cost inventory layers will be liquidated and tax consequences will be negative. See Reeve and Stanga, *Accounting Horizons*, pp. 28–29.

[23]Management often selects an accounting procedure because a lower tax results from its use, instead of an accounting method that is conceptually more appealing. Throughout this textbook, an effort has been made to identify accounting procedures that provide income tax benefits to the user.

[24]Note that, even though some would receive substantial tax benefits if they switched to LIFO, they have chosen not to. Some of the reasons for not changing to LIFO are presented in Gary C. Biddle, "Accounting Methods and Management Decisions: The Case of Inventory Costing and Inventory Policy," *The Journal of Accounting Research*, Supplement 1980.

The magnitude and direction of this variation between the carrying amount of inventory and its current price depend on the degree and direction of the price changes and the amount of inventory turnover.[25] The combined effect of rising product prices and avoidance of inventory liquidations increases the difference between the inventory carrying value at LIFO and current prices of that inventory, thereby magnifying the balance sheet distortion attributed to the use of LIFO.[26]

Physical Flow

LIFO does not approximate the physical flow of the items except in peculiar situations (such as the coal pile). Originally LIFO could be used only in certain circumstances. This situation has changed over the years to the point where physical flow characteristics no longer play an important role in determining whether LIFO may be employed.

Current Cost Income Not Measured

LIFO falls short of measuring current cost (replacement cost) income though not as far as FIFO. When measuring current cost income, the cost of goods sold should consist not of the most recently incurred costs but rather of the cost that will be incurred to replace the goods that have been sold. Using replacement cost is referred to as the next-in, first-out method, which is not currently acceptable for purposes of inventory valuation.

Involuntary Liquidation

If the base or layers of old costs are eliminated, strange results can occur because old, irrelevant costs can be matched against current revenues. A distortion in reported income for a given period may result, as well as consequences that are detrimental from an income tax point of view.[27]

For example, Allied Corporation reported net earnings of $.09 per share in a year in which its inventory reductions resulted in liquidations of LIFO inventory quantities. The effect of the inventory reduction was to increase income by $13 million or $.17 per share. The income tax problem is particularly severe when the involuntary liquidation results from a strike or a shortage of materials. In these situations, companies may incur high tax bills when they can least afford to pay taxes.

Poor Buying Habits

Because of the liquidation problem, LIFO may cause poor buying habits. A company may simply purchase more goods and match these goods against revenue to ensure that the old costs are not charged to expense. Furthermore, the possibility always exists with LIFO that a company will attempt to manipulate its net income at the end of the year simply by altering its pattern of purchases.[28]

---

[25]In 1986, the Accounting Standards Executive Committee (AcSEC) of the AICPA considered but voted down (by 8 to 6) a draft issues paper that explored an intriguing alternative to the way some companies report inventories in their financial statements. Under the suggested method, dubbed LIFO/FIFO, a company would use LIFO to measure cost of goods sold in its income statement and FIFO to report inventories in its balance sheet. See M. P. Bohan and S. Rubin, "LIFO/FIFO: How Would It Work?" *Journal of Accountancy* (September 1986), p. 106.

[26]This position is supported by the findings of James M. Reeve and Keith G. Stanga, "Balance Sheet Impact of Using LIFO: An Empirical Study," *Accounting Horizons* (September 1987), pp. 9–15.

[27]The AICPA Task Force on LIFO Inventory Problems recommends that the effects on income of LIFO inventory liquidations be disclosed in the notes to the financial statements but that the effects not receive special treatment in the income statement, *Issues Paper* (New York: AICPA, 1984), pp. 36–37.

[28]For example, one reason why General Tire and Rubber at one time accelerated raw material purchases at the end of the year was to minimize the book profit from a liquidation of LIFO inventories and to minimize income taxes for the year.

Because price rises have been the way of life in the U.S. economy during the last four decades, LIFO has provided a tax advantage over FIFO. During periods of price decreases, this tax advantage could become a disadvantage. And during periods of stable prices, FIFO and LIFO methods of inventory costing would generally produce identical results.

One survey uncovered the following reasons why companies reject LIFO:[29]

Reasons to Reject LIFO	Number	% of Total*
No expected tax benefits		
No required tax payment	34	16%
Declining prices	31	15
Rapid inventory turnover	30	14
Immaterial inventory	26	12
Miscellaneous tax related	38	17
	159	74%
Regulatory or other restrictions	26	12%
Excessive cost		
High administrative costs	29	14
LIFO liquidation–related costs	12	6
	41	20%
Other adverse consequences		
Lower reported earnings	18	8
Bad accounting	7	3
	25	11%

*Percentage totals more than 100% as some companies offered more than one explanation.

ILLUSTRATION 8-27
Why Do Companies Reject LIFO? Summary of Responses

INTERNATIONAL INSIGHT

Despite an effort to eliminate it, LIFO remains acceptable under international accounting standards.

❖ BASIS FOR SELECTION OF INVENTORY METHOD

How does one choose among the various inventory methods? Although no absolute rules can be stated, preferability for LIFO can ordinarily be established in either of the following circumstances: (1) if selling prices and revenues have been increasing faster than costs, thereby distorting income, and (2) in situations where LIFO has been traditional, such as department stores and industries where a fairly constant "base stock" is present such as refining, chemicals, and glass.

Conversely, LIFO would probably not be appropriate: (1) where prices tend to lag behind costs; (2) in situations where specific identification is traditional, such as in the sale of automobiles, farm equipment, art, and antique jewelry; or (3) where unit costs tend to decrease as production increases, thereby nullifying the tax benefit that LIFO might provide.[30]

Tax consequences are another consideration. Switching from FIFO to LIFO usually results in an immediate tax benefit. However, switching from LIFO to FIFO can result in a substantial tax burden. For example, when Chrysler changed from LIFO to FIFO, it became responsible for an additional $53 million in taxes that had been deferred over 14 years of LIFO inventory valuation. Why, then, would Chrysler, and other companies, change to FIFO? The major reason was the profit crunch of that era. Although Chrysler showed a loss of $7.6 million dollars after the switch, the loss would have been $20 million *more* if the company had not changed its inventory valuation back to FIFO from LIFO.

Objective ❿
Identify the reasons why a given inventory method is selected.

---

[29]Michael H. Granof and Daniel Short, "Why Do Companies Reject LIFO," *Journal of Accounting, Auditing, and Finance* (Summer 1984), pp. 323–333, Table 1, p. 327.

[30]See Barry E. Cushing and Marc J. LeClere, "Evidence on the Determinants of Inventory Accounting Policy Choice," *The Accounting Review* (April 1992), pp. 355–366, Table 4, p. 363, for a list of factors hypothesized to affect FIFO–LIFO choices.

It is questionable whether companies should switch from LIFO to FIFO for the sole purpose of increasing reported earnings.[31] Intuitively one would assume that companies with higher reported earnings would have a higher share (common stock price) valuation. Some studies have indicated, however, that the users of financial data exhibit a much higher sophistication than might be expected. Share prices are the same and, in some cases, even higher under LIFO in spite of lower reported earnings.[32]

The concern about reduced income resulting from adoption of LIFO has even less substance now because the IRS has relaxed the LIFO conformity rule which required a company that employed LIFO for tax purposes to use it for book purposes as well. The IRS has relaxed restrictions against providing non-LIFO income numbers as supplementary information. As a result, the profession now permits supplemental non-LIFO disclosures but not on the face of the income statement. The supplemental disclosure, while not intended to override the basic LIFO method adopted for financial reporting, may be useful in comparing operating income and working capital with companies not on LIFO.

For example, J. C. Penney, Inc. (a LIFO user) in its Annual Report presented the following information.

ILLUSTRATION 8-28
Supplemental Non-LIFO
Disclosure

J. C. Penney, Inc.

Some companies in the retail industry use the FIFO method in valuing part or all of their inventories. Had J. C. Penney used the FIFO method and made no other assumptions with respect to changes in income resulting therefrom, income and income per share from continuing operations would have been:

Income from continuing operations (in millions)	$ 325
Income from continuing operations per share	$4.63

Another user of LIFO, Weyerhaeuser Company, made the following disclosure in its Annual Report relative to product inventories carried in its balance sheet at $423,988,000 (current period) and $379,399,000 (prior period):

ILLUSTRATION 8-29
Supplemental Non-LIFO
Disclosure

Weyerhaeuser Company

Had the FIFO method been used to cost all inventories, the amounts at which product inventories are stated would have been $178,122,000 and $183,001,000 greater during the current and prior period, respectively.

Relaxation of the LIFO conformity rule has led more companies to select LIFO as their inventory valuation method because they will be able to disclose FIFO income numbers in the financial reports if they so desire.[33]

---

[31]*Accounting Trends and Techniques—1996* reports that of 983 inventory method disclosures, 347 used LIFO, 411 used FIFO, 185 used average cost, and 40 used other methods.

[32]See, for example, Shyam Sunder, "Relationship Between Accounting Changes and Stock Prices: Problems of Measurement and Some Empirical Evidence," *Empirical Research in Accounting: Selected Studies, 1973* (Chicago: University of Chicago), pp. 1–40; but see Robert Moren Brown, "Short-Range Market Reaction to Changes to LIFO Accounting Using Preliminary Earnings Announcement Dates," *The Journal of Accounting Research* (Spring 1980), which found that companies that do change to LIFO suffer a short-run decline in the price of their stock; see also William E. Ricks, "Market's Response to the 1974 LIFO Adoptions," *The Journal of Accounting Research* (Autumn 1982), pp. 367–387.

[33]Note that a company can use one variation of LIFO for financial reporting purposes and another for tax without violating the LIFO conformity rule. Such a relaxation has caused many problems because the general approach to accounting for LIFO has been "whatever is good for tax is good for financial reporting." The AICPA published a useful paper on this subject entitled "Identification and Discussion of Certain Financial Accounting and Reporting Issues Concerning LIFO Inventories," (New York: AICPA, November 30, 1984).

Often the inventory methods are used in combination with other methods. For example, most companies never use LIFO totally, but rather use it in combination with other valuation approaches. One reason is that certain product lines can be highly susceptible to deflation instead of inflation. In addition, if the level of inventory is unstable, unwanted involuntary liquidations may result in certain product lines if LIFO is used. Finally, where inventory turnover in certain product lines is high, the additional recordkeeping and expense are not justified by LIFO. Average cost is often used in such cases because it is easy to compute.[34]

This variety of inventory methods has been devised to assist in accurate computation of net income rather than to permit manipulation of reported income. Hence, it is recommended that the pricing method most suitable to a company be selected and, once selected, be applied consistently thereafter. If conditions indicate that the inventory pricing method in use is unsuitable, serious consideration should be given to all other possibilities before selecting another method. Any change should be clearly explained and its effect disclosed in the financial statements.

Inventory Valuation Methods—Summary Analysis

A number of inventory valuation methods are described in the preceding sections of this chapter. A brief summary of the three major inventory methods, assuming periodic inventory procedures, is presented below to show the differing effects these valuation methods have on the financial statements. The first schedule provides selected data for the comparison as follows:

<table>
<tr><td colspan="3" align="center">**Selected Data**</td></tr>
<tr><td colspan="3">Given</td></tr>
<tr><td>Beginning cash balance</td><td></td><td>$ 7,000</td></tr>
<tr><td>Beginning retained earnings</td><td></td><td>$10,000</td></tr>
<tr><td>Beginning inventory</td><td>4,000 units @ $3</td><td>$12,000</td></tr>
<tr><td>Purchases</td><td>6,000 units @ $4</td><td>$24,000</td></tr>
<tr><td>Sales</td><td>5,000 units @ $12</td><td>$60,000</td></tr>
<tr><td>Operating expenses</td><td></td><td>$10,000</td></tr>
<tr><td>Income tax rate</td><td></td><td>40%</td></tr>
</table>

The comparative results of using average cost, FIFO, and LIFO on net income are computed as shown in Illustration 8-30.

	Average Cost	FIFO	LIFO
Sales	$60,000	$60,000	$60,000
Cost of goods sold	18,000[a]	16,000[b]	20,000[c]
Gross profit	42,000	44,000	40,000
Operating expenses	10,000	10,000	10,000
Income before taxes	32,000	34,000	30,000
Income taxes (40%)	12,800	13,600	12,000
Net income	$19,200	$20,400	$18,000

[a]4,000 @ $3 = $12,000
6,000 @ $4 = 24,000
$36,000

$36,000 ÷ 10,000 = $3.60
$3.60 × 5,000 = $18,000

[b]4,000 @ $3 = $12,000
1,000 @ $4 = 4,000
$16,000

[c]5,000 = $4 = $20,000

ILLUSTRATION 8-30
Comparative Results of Average Cost, FIFO, and LIFO Methods

[34]For an interesting discussion of the reasons for and against the use of FIFO and average cost, see Michael H. Granof and Daniel G. Short ''For Some Companies, FIFO Accounting Makes Sense,'' *The Wall Street Journal* (August 30, 1982) and the subsequent rebuttal by Gary C. Biddle ''Taking Stock of Inventory Accounting Choices,'' *The Wall Street Journal* (September 15, 1982).

Notice that gross profit and net income are lowest under LIFO, highest under FIFO and somewhere in the middle under Average Cost.

The table below then shows the final balances of selected items at the end of the period:

ILLUSTRATION 8-31
Balances of Selected Items Under Alternative Inventory Valuation Methods

	Inventory	Gross Profit	Taxes	Net Income	Retained Earnings	Cash
Average Cost	$18,000 (5,000 × $3.60)	$42,000	$12,800	$19,200	$29,200 ($10,000 + $19,200)	$20,200[a]
FIFO	$20,000 (5,000 × $4)	$44,000	$13,600	$20,400	$30,400 ($10,000 + $20,400)	$19,400[a]
LIFO	$16,000 (4,000 × $3) (1,000 × $4)	$40,000	$12,000	$18,000	$28,000 ($10,000 + $18,000)	$21,000[a]

			Beg. balance	+	sales	−	purchases	−	operating expenses	−	taxes
[a]Cash at year-end											
Average cost—$20,200	=		$7,000	+	$60,000	−	$24,000	−	$10,000	−	$12,800
FIFO—$19,400	=		$7,000	+	$60,000	−	$24,000	−	$10,000	−	$13,600
LIFO—$21,000	=		$7,000	+	$60,000	−	$24,000	−	$10,000	−	$12,000

LIFO results in the highest cash balance at year-end because taxes are lower. This example assumes prices are rising; the opposite result occurs if prices are declining.

KEY TERMS

absorption costing, *404*

average cost method, *406*

consigned goods, *399*

cost flow assumptions, *405*

current ratio, *402*

dollar-value LIFO, *411*

double-extension method, *414*

finished goods inventory, *395*

first-in, first-out (FIFO) method, *407*

fixed costs, *403*

f.o.b. destination, *399*

f.o.b. shipping point, *399*

gross method, *404*

inventories, *394*

last-in, first-out (LIFO) method, *408*

LIFO effect, *409*

LIFO liquidation, *410*

LIFO reserve, *409*

merchandise inventory, *394*

moving-average method, *406*

net method, *404*

period costs, *403*

periodic inventory system, *396*

SUMMARY OF LEARNING OBJECTIVES

❶ *Identify major classifications of inventory.* Only one inventory account, Merchandise Inventory, appears in the financial statements of a merchandising concern. A manufacturer normally has three inventory accounts: Raw Materials, Work in Process, and Finished Goods. The cost assigned to goods and materials on hand but not yet placed into production is reported as raw materials inventory. The cost of the raw materials on which production has been started but not completed, plus the direct labor cost applied specifically to this material and a ratable share of manufacturing overhead costs, constitute the work in process inventory. The costs identified with the completed but unsold units on hand at the end of the fiscal period are reported as finished goods inventory.

❷ *Distinguish between perpetual and periodic inventory systems.* Under a perpetual inventory system, a continuous record of changes in inventory is maintained in the Inventory account. That is, all purchases and sales (issues) of goods are recorded directly in the Inventory account as they occur. Under a periodic inventory system, the quantity of inventory on hand is determined only periodically. The Inventory account remains the same and a Purchases account is debited. Cost of goods sold is determined at the end of the period using a formula. Ending inventory is ascertained by physical count.

❸ *Identify the effects of inventory errors on the financial statements.* *If the ending inventory is misstated,* (1) the inventory, retained earnings, working capital, and current ratio in the balance sheet will be misstated, and (2) the cost of goods sold and net income in the income statement will be misstated. *If purchases and inventory are misstated,* (1) the inventory, accounts payable, and current ratio will be misstated, and (2) purchases, and ending inventory in the income statement will be misstated.

❹ *Identify the items that should be included as inventory cost.* Product costs are directly connected with the bringing of goods to the place of business of the buyer and converting such goods to a salable condition. Such charges would include freight charges on goods purchased, other direct costs of acquisition, and labor and other production costs incurred in processing the goods up to the time of sale. Manufacturing overhead costs that include indirect material, indirect labor, and such items as depreciation, taxes, insurance, heat, and electricity incurred in the manufacturing process are also allocated to inventory.

⑤ Describe and compare the flow assumptions used in accounting for inventories. (1) *Average cost* prices items in the inventory on the basis of the average cost of all similar goods available during the period. (2) *First-in, first-out (FIFO)* assumes that goods are used in the order in which they are purchased. The inventory remaining must therefore represent the most recent purchases. (3) *Last-in, first-out (LIFO)* matches the cost of the last goods purchased against revenue.

⑥ Explain the significance and use of a LIFO reserve. The difference between the inventory method used for internal reporting purposes and LIFO is referred to as the Allowance to Reduce Inventory to LIFO. Either the LIFO reserve or the replacement cost of the inventory should be disclosed.

⑦ Explain the effect of LIFO liquidations. The effect of LIFO liquidations is that costs from preceding periods are matched against sales revenues reported in current dollars. This leads to a distortion in net income and a substantial tax bill in the current period. LIFO liquidations can occur frequently when a specific goods LIFO approach is employed.

⑧ Explain the dollar-value LIFO method. An important feature of the dollar-value LIFO method is that increases and decreases in a pool are determined and measured in terms of total dollar value, not the physical quantity of the goods in the inventory pool.

⑨ Identify the major advantages and disadvantages of LIFO. The major advantages of LIFO are: (1) recent costs are matched against current revenues to provide a better measure of current earnings; (2) as long as the price level increases and inventory quantities do not decrease, a deferral of income tax occurs in LIFO; (3) because of the deferral of income tax, there is improvement of cash flow; (4) a company's future reported earnings will not be affected substantially by future price declines (future earnings hedge). Major disadvantages are: (1) reduced earnings, (2) understated inventory, and (3) no approximated physical flow of the items except in peculiar situations.

⑩ Identify the reasons why a given inventory method is selected. Preferability for LIFO can ordinarily be established if: (1) selling prices and revenues have been increasing faster than costs, and (2) LIFO has been traditional, such as department stores and industries like refining, chemicals, and glass where a fairly constant "base stock" is present. Conversely, LIFO would probably not be appropriate: (1) where prices tend to lag behind costs; (2) in situations where specific identification is traditional, such as in the sales of automobiles, farm equipment, art, and antique jewelry; and (3) where unit costs tend to decrease as production increases, thereby nullifying the tax benefit that LIFO might provide.

❖ QUESTIONS ❖

❶ In what ways are the inventory accounts of a retailing concern different from those of a manufacturing enterprise?

❷ Why should inventories be included in (a) a statement of financial position and (b) the computation of net income?

❸ What is the difference between a perpetual inventory and a physical inventory? If a company maintains a perpetual inventory, should its physical inventory at any date be equal to the amount indicated by the perpetual inventory records? Why?

❹ Mariah Carey, Inc. indicated in a recent annual report that approximately $8 million of merchandise was received on consignment. Should Mariah Carey, Inc. report this amount on their balance sheet? Explain.

5 What is a product financing arrangement? How should product financing arrangements be reported in the financial statements?

6 Where, if at all, should the following items be classified on a balance sheet?
(a) Goods out on approval to customers.
(b) Goods in transit that were recently purchased f.o.b. destination.
(c) Land held by a realty firm for sale.
(d) Raw materials.
(e) Goods received on consignment.
(f) Manufacturing supplies.

7 At the balance sheet date Paula Abdul Company held title to goods in transit amounting to $214,000. This amount was omitted from the purchases figure for the year and also from the ending inventory. What is the effect of this omission on the net income for the year as calculated when the books are closed? On the company's financial position as shown in its balance sheet? Is materiality a factor in determining whether an adjustment for this item should be made?

8 Define "cost" as applied to the valuation of inventories.

9 What is the difference between variable costing and conventional absorption costing? Is variable costing acceptable for external financial reporting and for income tax purposes? Why?

10 Dana Barros Corp. is considering alternate methods of accounting for the cash discounts it takes when paying suppliers promptly. One method suggested was to report these discounts as financial income when payments are made. Comment on the propriety of this approach.

11 Harold Baines Inc. purchases 300 units of an item at an invoice cost of $30,000. What is the cost per unit? If the goods are shipped f.o.b. shipping point and the freight bill was $1,500, what is the cost per unit if Baines Inc. pays the freight charges? If these items were bought on 2/10, n/30 terms and the invoice and the freight bill were paid within the 10-day period, what would be the cost per unit?

12 Specific identification is sometimes said to be the ideal method of assigning cost to inventory and to cost of goods sold. Briefly indicate the arguments for and against this method of inventory valuation.

13 First-in, first-out; weighted average; and last-in, first-out methods are often used instead of specific identification for inventory valuation purposes. Compare these methods with the specific identification method, discussing the theoretical propriety of each method in the determination of income and asset valuation.

14 How might a company obtain a price index in order to apply dollar-value LIFO?

15 Describe the LIFO double-extension method. Using the following information, compute the index at December 31, 1999, applying the double-extension method to a LIFO pool consisting of 25,500 units of product A and 10,350 units of product B: the base-year cost of product A is $10.20 and of product B is $37.00; the price at December 31, 1999, for product A is $19.00 and for product B is $45.60.

16 As compared with the FIFO method of costing inventories, does the LIFO method result in a larger or smaller net income in a period of rising prices? What is the comparative effect on net income in a period of falling prices?

17 What is the dollar-value method of LIFO inventory valuation? What advantage does the dollar-value method have over the specific goods approach of LIFO inventory valuation? Why will the traditional LIFO inventory costing method and the dollar-value LIFO inventory costing method produce different inventory valuations if the composition of the inventory base changes?

18 What is the LIFO conformity rule? How has the LIFO conformity rule been relaxed?

19 On December 31, 1998, the inventory of Mario Lemieux Company amounts to $800,000. During 1999, the company decides to use the dollar-value LIFO method of costing inventories. On December 31, 1999, the inventory is $1,026,000 at December 31, 1999, prices. Using the December 31, 1998, price level of 100 and the December 31, 1999, price level of 108, compute the inventory value at December 31, 1999, under the dollar-value LIFO method.

20 In an article that appeared in *The Wall Street Journal*, the phrases "phantom (paper) profits" and "high LIFO profits" through involuntary liquidation were used. Explain these phrases.

❖ BRIEF EXERCISES ❖

BE8-1 Included in the December 31 trial balance of Billie Joel Company are the following assets:

Cash	$ 190,000	Work in process	$200,000
Equipment (net)	1,100,000	Receivables (net)	400,000
Prepaid insurance	41,000	Patents	110,000
Raw materials	335,000	Finished goods	150,000

Prepare the current assets section of the December 31 balance sheet.

BE8-2 Alanis Morrissette Company uses a perpetual inventory system. Its beginning inventory consists of 50 units which cost $30 each. During June, the company purchased 150 units at $30 each, returned 6 units for credit, and sold 125 units at $50 each. Journalize the June transactions.

BE8-3 Mayberry Company took a physical inventory on December 31 and determined that goods costing $200,000 were on hand. Not included in the physical count were $15,000 of goods purchased from Taylor Corporation, f.o.b. shipping point; and $22,000 of goods sold to Mount Pilot Company for $30,000, f.o.b. destination. Both the Taylor purchase and the Mount Pilot sale were in transit at year-end. What amount should Mayberry report as its December 31 inventory?

BE8-4 Gavin Bryars Enterprises reported cost of goods sold for 1999 of $1,400,000 and retained earnings of $5,200,000 at December 31, 1999. Gavin Bryars later discovered that its ending inventories at December 31, 1998 and 1999 were overstated by $110,000 and $45,000, respectively. Determine the corrected amounts for 1999 cost of goods sold and December 31, 1999, retained earnings.

BE8-5 Jose Zorilla Company uses a periodic inventory system. For April, when the company sold 700 units, the following information is available:

	Units	Unit Cost	Total Cost
April 1 inventory	250	$10	$ 2,500
April 15 purchase	400	12	4,800
April 23 purchase	350	13	4,550
	1,000		$11,850

Compute the April 30 inventory and the April cost of goods sold using the average cost method.

BE8-6 Data for Jose Zorilla Company are presented in BE8-5. Compute the April 30 inventory and the April cost of goods sold using the FIFO method.

BE8-7 Data for Jose Zorilla Company are presented in BE8-5. Compute the April 30 inventory and the April cost of goods sold using the LIFO method.

BE8-8 Easy-E Company had ending inventory at end-of-year prices of $100,000 at 12/31/97; $123,200 at 12/31/98; and $134,560 at 12/31/99. The year-end price indexes were 100 at 12/31/97, 110 at 12/31/98, and 116 at 12/31/99. Compute the ending inventory for Easy-E Company for 1997 through 1999 using the dollar-value LIFO method.

❖ EXERCISES ❖

E8-1 (Inventoriable Costs) Presented below is a list of items that may or may not be reported as inventory in a company's December 31 balance sheet.

1. Goods out on consignment at another company's store.
2. Goods sold on an installment basis.
3. Goods purchased f.o.b. shipping point that are in transit at December 31.
4. Goods purchased f.o.b. destination that are in transit at December 31.
5. Goods sold to another company, for which our company has signed an agreement to repurchase at a set price that covers all costs related to the inventory.
6. Goods sold where large returns are predictable.
7. Goods sold f.o.b. shipping point that are in transit at December 31.
8. Freight charges on goods purchased.
9. Factory labor costs incurred on goods still unsold.
10. Interest costs incurred for inventories that are routinely manufactured.
11. Costs incurred to advertise goods held for resale.
12. Materials on hand not yet placed into production by a manufacturing firm.
13. Office supplies.
14. Raw materials on which a manufacturing firm has started production, but which are not completely processed.
15. Factory supplies.
16. Goods held on consignment from another company.
17. Costs identified with units completed by a manufacturing firm, but not yet sold.
18. Goods sold f.o.b. destination that are in transit at December 31.
19. Temporary investments in stocks and bonds that will be resold in the near future.

Instructions
Indicate which of these items would typically be reported as inventory in the financial statements. If an item should **not** be reported as inventory, indicate how it should be reported in the financial statements.

E8-2 (Inventoriable Costs) In your audit of the Jose Oliva Company, you find that a physical inventory on December 31, 1997, showed merchandise with a cost of $441,000 was on hand at that date. You also discover the following items were all excluded from the $441,000.

1. Merchandise of $61,000 which is held by Oliva on consignment. The consignor is the Max Suzuki Company.
2. Merchandise costing $38,000 which was shipped by Oliva f.o.b. destination to a customer on December 31, 1997. The customer was expected to receive the merchandise on January 6, 1998.
3. Merchandise costing $46,000 which was shipped by Oliva f.o.b. shipping point to a customer on December 29, 1997. The customer was scheduled to receive the merchandise on January 2, 1998.
4. Merchandise costing $83,000 shipped by a vendor f.o.b. destination on December 30, 1997, and received by Oliva on January 4, 1998.
5. Merchandise costing $51,000 shipped by a vendor f.o.b. seller on December 31, 1997, and received by Oliva on January 5, 1998.

Instructions
Based on the above information, calculate the amount that should appear on Oliva's balance sheet at December 31, 1997, for inventory.

E8-3 (Inventoriable Costs) In an annual audit of Jan Matejko Company at December 31, 1999, you find the following transactions near the closing date.

1. A special machine, fabricated to order for a customer, was finished and specifically segregated in the back part of the shipping room on December 31, 1999. The customer was billed on that date and the machine excluded from inventory although it was shipped on January 4, 2000.
2. Merchandise costing $2,800 was received on January 3, 2000, and the related purchase invoice recorded January 5. The invoice showed the shipment was made on December 29, 1999, f.o.b. destination.
3. A packing case containing a product costing $3,400 was standing in the shipping room when the physical inventory was taken. It was not included in the inventory because it was marked "Hold for shipping instructions." Your investigation revealed that the customer's order was dated December 18, 1999, but that the case was shipped and the customer billed on January 10, 2000. The product was a stock item of your client.
4. Merchandise received on January 6, 2000, costing $680 was entered in the purchase journal on January 7, 2000. The invoice showed shipment was made f.o.b. supplier's warehouse on December 31, 1999. Because it was not on hand at December 31, it was not included in inventory.
5. Merchandise costing $720 was received on December 28, 1999, and the invoice was not recorded. You located it in the hands of the purchasing agent; it was marked on consignment.

Instructions
Assuming that each of the amounts is material, state whether the merchandise should be included in the client's inventory and give your reason for your decision on each item.

E8-4 (Inventoriable Costs) Colin Davis Machine Company maintains a general ledger account for each class of inventory, debiting such accounts for increases during the period and crediting them for decreases. The transactions below relate to the Raw Materials inventory account, which is debited for materials purchased and credited for materials requisitioned for use.

1. An invoice for $8,100, terms f.o.b. destination, was received and entered January 2, 1999. The receiving report shows that the materials were received December 28, 1998.
2. Materials costing $28,000, shipped f.o.b. destination, were not entered by December 31, 1998, "because they were in a railroad car on the company's siding on that date and had not been unloaded."
3. Materials costing $7,300 were returned on December 29, 1998, to the creditor, and were shipped f.o.b. shipping point. The return was entered on that date, even though the materials are not expected to reach the creditor's place of business until January 6, 1999.
4. An invoice for $7,500, terms f.o.b. shipping point, was received and entered December 30, 1998. The receiving report shows that the materials were received January 4, 1999, and the bill of lading shows that they were shipped January 2, 1999.
5. Materials costing $19,800 were received December 30, 1998, but no entry was made for them because "they were ordered with a specified delivery of no earlier than January 10, 1999."

Instructions
Prepare correcting general journal entries required at December 31, 1998, assuming that the books have not been closed.

E8-5 (Inventoriable Costs—Error Adjustments) The following purchase transactions occurred during the last few days of Paul Dunbar Company's business year, which ends October 31, or in the first few days after that date. A periodic inventory system is used.

1. An invoice for $6,000, terms f.o.b. shipping point, was received and entered November 1. The invoice shows that the material was shipped October 29, but the receiving report indicates receipt of goods on November 3.
2. An invoice for $2,700, terms f.o.b. destination, was received and entered November 2. The receiving report indicates that the goods were received October 29.
3. An invoice for $3,150, terms f.o.b. shipping point, was received October 15 but never entered. Attached to it is a receiving report indicating that the goods were received October 18. Across the face of the receiving report is the following notation: "Merchandise not of same quality as ordered—returned for credit October 19."
4. An invoice for $3,600, terms f.o.b. shipping point, was received and entered October 27. The receiving report attached to the invoice indicates that the shipment was received October 27 in satisfactory condition.
5. An invoice for $4,800, terms f.o.b. destination, was received and entered October 28. The receiving report indicates that the merchandise was received November 2.

Before preparing financial statements for the year, you are instructed to review these transactions and to determine whether any correcting entries are required and whether the inventory of $77,500 determined by physical count on October 31 should be changed.

Instructions

Complete the following schedule, and state the correct inventory at October 31. Assume that the books have not been closed.

Transaction	Purchase and Related Payable Should Be Recognized in (month)	Purchase and Related Payable Were Recognized in (month)	Correcting Journal Entries Needed	Should Inventory Be Included in October Ending Inventory?	Was Inventory Included in October Ending Inventory?	Dollar Adjustments Needed to October Ending Inventory

E8-6 (Determining Merchandise Amounts) Two or more items are omitted in each of the following tabulations of income statement data. Fill in the amounts that are missing.

	1997	1998	1999
Sales	$290,000	$_____	$410,000
Sales Returns	11,000	13,000	_____
Net Sales	_____	347,000	_____
Beginning Inventory	20,000	32,000	_____
Ending Inventory	_____	_____	_____
Purchases	_____	260,000	298,000
Purchase Returns and Allowances	5,000	8,000	10,000
Transportation-in	8,000	9,000	12,000
Cost of Goods Sold	233,000	_____	293,000
Gross Profit on Sales	46,000	91,000	97,000

E8-7 (Financial Statement Presentation of Manufacturing Amounts) Navajo Company is a manufacturing firm. Presented below is selected information from their 1998 accounting records.

Raw materials inventory, 1/1/98	$ 30,800	Transportation-out	8,000
Raw materials inventory, 12/31/98	37,400	Selling expenses	300,000
Work in process inventory, 1/1/98	72,600	Administrative expenses	180,000
Work in process inventory, 12/31/98	61,600	Purchase discounts	10,640
Finished goods inventory, 1/1/98	35,200	Purchase returns and allowances	6,460
Finished goods inventory, 12/31/98	22,000	Interest expense	15,000
Purchases	278,600	Direct labor	440,000
Transportation-in	6,600	Manufacturing overhead	330,000

Instructions

(a) Compute raw materials used.
(b) Compute the cost of goods manufactured.
(c) Compute cost of goods sold.
(d) Indicate how inventories would be reported in the 12/31/98 balance sheet.

E8-8 (Manufacturing Closing Entries)   The following accounts, among others, appear on the trial balance of Gilbert Stuart Corporation at the end of the year 1999:

Raw Materials Inventory 1/1/99	$ 31,000
Goods in Process Inventory 1/1/99	50,000
Finished Goods Inventory 1/1/99	60,000
Raw Materials Purchased	75,000
Direct Labor	87,000
Manufacturing Overhead	98,000
Sales	410,000
General and Administrative Expense	65,000

Instructions

Assuming that no other nominal accounts existed, give the closing entries that would be made at the end of the year. Inventories on December 31, 1999, are: raw materials, $36,000; goods in process, $65,000; finished goods, $80,000. Ignore income tax effects.

E8-9 (Purchases Recorded Net)   Presented below are transactions related to Tom Brokaw, Inc.

May 10   Purchased goods billed at $15,000 subject to cash discount terms of 2/10, n/60.
    11   Purchased goods billed at $13,200 subject to terms of 1/15, n/30.
    19   Paid invoice of May 10.
    24   Purchased goods billed at $11,500 subject to cash discount terms of 2/10, n/30.

Instructions

(a) Prepare general journal entries for the transactions above under the assumption that purchases are to be recorded at net amounts after cash discounts and that discounts lost are to be treated as financial expense.

(b) Assuming no purchase or payment transactions other than those given above, prepare the adjusting entry required on May 31 if financial statements are to be prepared as of that date.

E8-10 (Periodic versus Perpetual Entries)   The Fong Sai-Yuk Company sells one product. Presented below is information for January for the Fong Sai-Yuk Company.

Jan. 1	Inventory	100 units at $5 each
4	Sale	80 units at $8 each
11	Purchase	150 units at $6 each
13	Sale	120 units at $8.75 each
20	Purchase	160 units at $7 each
27	Sale	100 units at $9 each

Fong Sai-Yuk uses the FIFO cost flow assumption. All purchases and sales are on account.

Instructions

(a) Assume Fong Sai-Yuk uses a periodic system. Prepare all necessary journal entries, including the end-of-month closing entry to record cost of goods sold. A physical count indicates that the ending inventory for January is 110 units.

(b) Compute gross profit using the periodic system.

(c) Assume Fong Sai-Yuk uses a perpetual system. Prepare all necessary journal entries.

(d) Compute gross profit using the perpetual system.

E8-11 (Inventory Errors)   Ann M. Martin Company makes the following errors during the current year.

1. Ending inventory is overstated, but purchases are recorded correctly.
2. Both ending inventory and purchases on account are understated (assume this purchase was recorded in the following year).
3. Ending inventory is correct, but a purchase on account was not recorded (assume this purchase was recorded in the following year).

Instructions

Indicate the effect of each of these errors on working capital, current ratio (assume that the current ratio is greater than 1), retained earnings, and net income for the current year and the subsequent year.

E8-12 (Inventory Errors)   Marcy Walker Company has a calendar-year accounting period. The following errors have been discovered in 1999.

1. The December 31, 1997, merchandise inventory had been understated by $21,000.
2. Merchandise purchased on account during 1998 was recorded on the books for the first time in February 1999, when the original invoice for the correct amount of $5,430 arrived. The merchandise had arrived December 28, 1998, and was included in the December 31, 1998, merchandise inventory. The invoice arrived late because of a mixup on the wholesaler's part.

3. Accrued interest of $1,300 at December 31, 1998, on notes receivable had not been recorded until the cash for the interest was received in March 1999.

Instructions
(a) Compute the effect each error had on the 1998 net income.
(b) Compute the effect, if any, each error had on the related December 31, 1998, balance sheet items.

E8-13 (Inventory Errors) At December 31, 1998, Stacy McGill Corporation reported current assets of $370,000 and current liabilities of $200,000. The following items may have been recorded incorrectly.

1. Goods purchased costing $22,000 were shipped f.o.b. shipping point by a supplier on December 28. McGill received and recorded the invoice on December 29, but the goods were not included in McGill's physical count of inventory because they were not received until January 4.
2. Goods purchased costing $15,000 were shipped f.o.b. destination by a supplier on December 26. McGill received and recorded the invoice on December 31, but the goods were not included in McGill's physical count of inventory because they were not received until January 2.
3. Goods held on consignment from Claudia Kishi Company were included in McGill's physical count of inventory at $13,000.
4. Freight-in of $3,000 was debited to advertising expense on December 28.

Instructions
(a) Compute the current ratio based on McGill's balance sheet.
(b) Recompute the current ratio after corrections are made.
(c) By what amount will income (before taxes) be adjusted up or down as a result of the corrections?

E8-14 (Inventory Errors) The net income per books of Linda Dizburg Company was determined without knowledge of the errors indicated.

Year	Net Income per Books	Error in Ending Inventory	
1994	$50,000	Overstated	$ 3,000
1995	52,000	Overstated	9,000
1996	54,000	Understated	11,000
1997	56,000	No error	
1998	58,000	Understated	2,000
1999	60,000	Overstated	8,000

Instructions
Prepare a work sheet to show the adjusted net income figure for each of the 6 years after taking into account the inventory errors.

E8-15 (FIFO and LIFO—Periodic and Perpetual) Inventory information for Part 311 of Monique Aaron Corp. discloses the following information for the month of June:

June 1:	Balance	300 units @ $10	June 10:	Sold	200 units @ $24
11:	Purchased	800 units @ $12	15:	Sold	500 units @ $25
20:	Purchased	500 units @ $13	27:	Sold	300 units @ $27

Instructions
(a) Assuming that the periodic inventory method is used, compute the cost of goods sold and ending inventory under (1) LIFO; (2) FIFO.
(b) Assuming that the perpetual inventory record is kept in dollars, and costs are computed at the time of each withdrawal, what is the value of the ending inventory at LIFO?
(c) Assuming that the perpetual inventory record is kept in dollars, and costs are computed at the time of each withdrawal, what is the gross profit if the inventory is valued at FIFO?
(d) Why is it stated that LIFO usually produces a lower gross profit than FIFO?

E8-16 (FIFO, LIFO and Average Cost Determination) John Adams Company's record of transactions for the month of April was as follows:

Purchases			Sales		
April 1 (balance on hand)	600 @ $6.00		April 3	500 @ $10.00	
4	1,500 @ 6.08		9	1,400 @ 10.00	
8	800 @ 6.40		11	600 @ 11.00	
13	1,200 @ 6.50		23	1,200 @ 11.00	
21	700 @ 6.60		27	900 @ 12.00	
29	500 @ 6.79			4,600	
	5,300				

Instructions

(a) Assuming that perpetual inventory records are kept in units only, compute the inventory at April 30 using (1) LIFO; (2) average cost.

(b) Assuming that perpetual inventory records are kept in dollars, determine the inventory using (1) FIFO; (2) LIFO.

(c) Compute cost of goods sold assuming periodic inventory procedures and inventory priced at FIFO.

(d) In an inflationary period, which of the following inventory methods (FIFO, LIFO, average cost) will show the highest net income?

E8-17 (FIFO, LIFO, Average Cost Inventory) Shania Twain Company was formed on December 1, 1997. The following information is available from Twain's inventory records for Product BAP:

	Units	Unit Cost
January 1, 1998 (beginning inventory)	600	$ 8.00
Purchases:		
January 5, 1998	1,200	$ 9.00
January 25, 1998	1,300	$10.00
February 16, 1998	800	$11.00
March 26, 1998	600	$12.00

A physical inventory on March 31, 1998, shows 1,600 units on hand.

Instructions

Prepare schedules to compute the ending inventory at March 31, 1998, under each of the following inventory methods:

(a) FIFO.   (b) LIFO.   (c) Weighted average.

(AICPA adapted)

E8-18 (Compute FIFO, LIFO, Average Cost—Periodic) Presented below is information related to Blowfish radios for the Hootie Company for the month of July:

Date	Transaction	Units In	Unit Cost	Total	Units Sold	Selling Price	Total
July 1	Balance	100	$4.10	$ 410			
6	Purchase	800	4.20	3,360			
7	Sale				300	$7.00	$ 2,100
10	Sale				300	$7.30	2,190
12	Purchase	400	4.50	1,800			
15	Sale				200	7.40	1,480
18	Purchase	300	4.60	1,380			
22	Sale				400	7.40	2,960
25	Purchase	500	4.58	2,290			
30	Sale				200	7.50	1,500
	Totals	2,100		$9,240	1,400		$10,230

Instructions

(a) Assuming that the periodic inventory method is used, compute the inventory cost at July 31 under each of the following cost flow assumptions:

1. FIFO.

2. LIFO.

3. Weighted-average (round the weighted-average unit cost to the nearest one-tenth of one cent).

(b) Answer the following questions:

1. Which of the methods used above will yield the lowest figure for gross profit for the income statement? Explain why.

2. Which of the methods used above will yield the lowest figure for ending inventory for the balance sheet? Explain why.

E8-19 (FIFO and LIFO; Periodic and Perpetual) The following is a record of Pervis Ellison Company's transactions for Boston teapots for the month of May 1999:

May 1	Balance 400 units @ $20	May 10	Sale 300 units @ $38
12	Purchase 600 units @ $25	20	Sale 540 units @ $38
28	Purchase 400 units @ $30		

Instructions

(a) Assuming that perpetual inventories are **not** maintained and that a physical count at the end of the month shows 560 units on hand, what is the cost of the ending inventory using (1) FIFO? and (2) LIFO?

(b) Assuming that perpetual records are maintained and they tie into the general ledger, calculate the ending inventory using (1) FIFO; (2) LIFO.

E8-20 (FIFO and LIFO; Income Statement Presentation) The board of directors of Deion Sanders Corporation is considering whether or not it should instruct the accounting department to shift from a first-in, first-out (FIFO) basis of pricing inventories to a last-in, first-out (LIFO) basis. The following information is available.

Sales	21,000 units @ $50
Inventory January 1	6,000 units @ 20
Purchases	6,000 units @ 22
	10,000 units @ 25
	7,000 units @ 30
Inventory December 31	8,000 units @ ?
Operating expenses	$200,000

Instructions
Prepare a condensed income statement for the year on both bases for comparative purposes.

E8-21 (FIFO and LIFO Effects) You are the vice-president of finance of Sandy Alomar Corporation, a retail company that prepared two different schedules of gross margin for the first quarter ended March 31, 1999. These schedules appear below.

	Sales ($5 per unit)	Cost of Goods Sold	Gross Margin
Schedule 1	$150,000	$124,900	$25,100
Schedule 2	150,000	129,400	20,600

The computation of cost of goods sold in each schedule is based on the following data:

	Units	Cost per Unit	Total Cost
Beginning inventory, January 1	10,000	$4.00	$40,000
Purchase, January 10	8,000	4.20	33,600
Purchase, January 30	6,000	4.25	25,500
Purchase, February 11	9,000	4.30	38,700
Purchase, March 17	11,000	4.40	48,400

Jane Torville, the president of the corporation, cannot understand how two different gross margins can be computed from the same set of data. As the vice-president of finance you have explained to Ms. Torville that the two schedules are based on different assumptions concerning the flow of inventory costs, i.e., first-in, first-out; and last-in, first-out. Schedules 1 and 2 were not necessarily prepared in this sequence of cost flow assumptions.

Instructions
Prepare two separate schedules computing cost of goods sold and supporting schedules showing the composition of the ending inventory under both cost flow assumptions.

E8-22 (FIFO and LIFO—Periodic) Howie Long Shop began operations on January 1, 1999. The following stock record card for footballs was taken from the records at the end of the year.

Date	Voucher	Terms	Units Received	Unit Invoice Cost	Gross Invoice Amount
1/15	10624	Net 30	50	$20.00	$1,000.00
3/15	11437	1/5, net 30	65	16.00	1,040.00
6/20	21332	1/10, net 30	90	15.00	1,350.00
9/12	27644	1/10, net 30	84	12.00	1,008.00
11/24	31269	1/10, net 30	76	11.00	836.00
	Totals		365		$5,234.00

A physical inventory on December 31, 1999, reveals that 100 footballs were in stock. The bookkeeper informs you that all the discounts were taken. Assume that Howie Long Shop uses the invoice price less discount for recording purchases.

Instructions
(a) Compute the 12/31/99 inventory using the FIFO method.
(b) Compute the 1999 cost of goods sold using the LIFO method.
(c) What method would you recommend to the owner to minimize income taxes in 1999, using the inventory information for footballs as a guide?

E8-23 (Specific Goods and Specific Goods Pooled LIFO Contrasted) Presented below is inventory, purchases and sales data for Brooke Adams Inc. for 1999.

	Material X		Material Y	
	Units	Price	Units	Price
Inventory, January 1	100	$4	400	$2
Purchases	1,000	6	600	5
Sales	900		700	

Brooke Adams Inc. uses the periodic method of inventory valuation.

Instructions
(a) Determine the ending inventory of these two products using specific goods LIFO.
(b) Determine the ending inventory of these two products using specific goods pooled LIFO; that is, assume that Material X and Material Y are one pool.
(c) Determine which of these two methods will result in Adams Inc. reporting higher net income in 1999. Provide an explanation for this result.

E8-24 (Alternative Inventory Methods—Comprehensive) Tori Amos Corporation began operations on December 1, 1998. The only inventory transaction in 1998 was the purchase of inventory on December 10, 1998, at a cost of $20 per unit. None of this inventory was sold in 1998. Relevant information is as follows:

Ending inventory units		
December 31, 1998		100
December 31, 1999, by purchase date		
December 2, 1999	100	
July 20, 1999	50	150

During the year the following purchases and sales were made:

Purchases		Sales	
March 15	300 units at $24	April 10	200
July 20	300 units at $25	August 20	300
September 4	200 units at $28	November 18	150
December 2	100 units at $30	Dec. 12	200

The company uses the periodic inventory method.

Instructions
(a) Determine ending inventory under (1) specific identification, (2) FIFO, (3) LIFO periodic, and (4) average cost.
(b) Determine ending inventory using dollar-value LIFO. Assume that the December 2, 1999 purchase cost is the current cost of inventory (Hint: The beginning inventory is the base layer priced at $20 per unit).

E8-25 (Dollar-Value LIFO) Oasis Company has used the dollar-value LIFO method for inventory cost determination for many years. The following data were extracted from Oasis' records:

Date	Price Index	Ending Inventory at Base Prices	Ending Inventory at Dollar-value LIFO
December 31, 1997	105	$92,000	$92,600
December 31, 1998	?	97,000	98,350

Instructions
Calculate the index used for 1998 which yielded the above results.

E8-26 (Dollar-Value LIFO) The dollar-value LIFO method was adopted by Enya Corp. on January 1, 1999. Its inventory on that date was $160,000. On December 31, 1999, the inventory at prices existing on that date amounted to $140,000. The price level at January 1, 1999, was 100, and the price level at December 31, 1999, was 112.

Instructions
(a) Compute the amount of the inventory at December 31, 1999, under the dollar-value LIFO method.
(b) On December 31, 2000, the inventory at prices existing on that date was $172,500, and the price level was 115. Compute the inventory on that date under the dollar-value LIFO method.

E8-27 (Dollar-Value LIFO)   Presented below is information related to Dino Radja Company.

Date	Ending Inventory (End-of-Year Prices)	Price Index
December 31, 1996	$ 80,000	100
December 31, 1997	115,500	105
December 31, 1998	108,000	120
December 31, 1999	122,200	130
December 31, 2000	154,000	140
December 31, 2001	176,900	145

Instructions

Compute the ending inventory for Dino Radja Company for 1996 through 2001 using the dollar-value LIFO method.

E8-28 (Dollar-Value LIFO)   The following information relates to the Jimmy Johnson Company.

Date	Ending Inventory (End-of-Year Prices)	Price Index
December 31, 1995	$ 70,000	100
December 31, 1996	90,300	105
December 31, 1997	95,120	116
December 31, 1998	105,600	120
December 31, 1999	100,000	125

Instructions

Use the dollar-value LIFO method to compute the ending inventory for Johnson Company for 1995 through 1999.

❖ PROBLEMS ❖

P8-1 (Various Inventory Issues)   The following independent situations relate to inventory accounting.

1. Jagr Co. purchased goods with a list price of $150,000, subject to trade discounts of 20% and 10%, with no cash discounts allowable. How much should Jagr Co. record as the cost of these goods?

2. Francis Company's inventory of $1,100,000 at December 31, 1998, was based on a physical count of goods priced at cost and before any year-end adjustments relating to the following items:
   a. Goods shipped f.o.b. shipping point on December 24, 1998, from a vendor at an invoice cost of $69,000 to Francis Company were received on January 4, 1999.
   b. The physical count included $29,000 of goods billed to Sakic Corp. f.o.b. shipping point on December 31, 1998. The carrier picked up these goods on January 3, 1999.
   What amount should Francis report as inventory on its balance sheet?

3. Mark Messier Corp. had 1,500 units of Part M.O. on hand May 1, 1998, costing $21 each. Purchases of Part M.O. during May were as follows:

	Units	Unit Cost
May 9	2,000	$22.00
17	3,500	23.00
26	1,000	24.00

A physical count on May 31, 1998, shows 2,100 units of Part M.O. on hand. Using the FIFO method, what is the cost of Part M.O. inventory at May 31, 1998? Using the LIFO method, what is the inventory cost? Using the average cost method, what is the inventory cost?

4. Forsberg Company adopted the dollar-value LIFO method on January 1, 1998 (using internal price indexes and multiple pools). The following data are available for Inventory Pool A for the 2 years following adoption of LIFO:

Inventory	At Base-Year Cost	At Current-Year Cost
1/1/98	$200,000	$200,000
12/31/98	240,000	252,000
12/31/99	256,000	286,720

Computing an internal price index and using the dollar-value LIFO method, at what amount should the inventory be reported at December 31, 1999?

5. Eric Lindros Inc., a retail store chain, had the following information in its general ledger for the year 1999:

Merchandise purchased for resale	$909,400
Interest on notes payable to vendors	8,700
Purchase returns	16,500
Freight-in	22,000
Freight-out	17,100
Cash discounts on purchases	6,800

What is Lindros' inventoriable cost for 1999?

Instructions

Answer each of the questions above about inventories and explain your answer.

P8-2 (Inventory Adjustments)   James T. Kirk Company, a manufacturer of small tools, provided the following information from its accounting records for the year ended December 31, 1999:

Inventory at December 31, 1999 (based on physical count of goods in Kirk's plant at cost on December 31, 1999)	$1,520,000
Accounts payable at December 31, 1999	1,200,000
Net sales (sales less sales returns)	8,150,000

Additional information is as follows:

1. Included in the physical count were tools billed to a customer f.o.b. shipping point on December 31, 1999. These tools had a cost of $31,000 and were billed at $40,000. The shipment was on Kirk's loading dock waiting to be picked up by the common carrier.
2. Goods were in transit from a vendor to Kirk on December 31, 1999. The invoice cost was $71,000, and the goods were shipped f.o.b. shipping point on December 29, 1999.
3. Work in process inventory costing $30,000 was sent to an outside processor for plating on December 30, 1999.
4. Tools returned by customers and held pending inspection in the returned goods area on December 31, 1999, were not included in the physical count. On January 8, 2000, the tools costing $32,000 were inspected and returned to inventory. Credit memos totaling $47,000 were issued to the customers on the same date.
5. Tools shipped to a customer f.o.b. destination on December 26, 1999, were in transit at December 31, 1999, and had a cost of $21,000. Upon notification of receipt by the customer on January 2, 2000, Kirk issued a sales invoice for $42,000.
6. Goods, with an invoice cost of $27,000, received from a vendor at 5:00 p.m. on December 31, 1999, were recorded on a receiving report dated January 2, 2000. The goods were not included in the physical count, but the invoice was included in accounts payable at December 31, 1999.
7. Goods received from a vendor on December 26, 1999, were included in the physical count. However, the related $56,000 vendor invoice was not included in accounts payable at December 31, 1999, because the accounts payable copy of the receiving report was lost.
8. On January 3, 2000, a monthly freight bill in the amount of $6,000 was received. The bill specifically related to merchandise purchased in December 1999, one-half of which was still in the inventory at December 31, 1999. The freight charges were not included in either the inventory or in accounts payable at December 31, 1999.

Instructions

Using the format shown below, prepare a schedule of adjustments as of December 31, 1999, to the initial amounts per Kirk's accounting records. Show separately the effect, if any, of each of the eight transactions on the December 31, 1999 amounts. If the transactions would have no effect on the initial amount shown, state NONE.

	Inventory	Accounts Payable	Net Sales
Initial amounts	$1,520,000	$1,200,000	$8,150,000
Adjustments—increase (decrease)			
1			
2			
3			
4			
5			
6			
7			
8			
Total adjustments			
Adjusted amounts	$	$	$

(AICPA adapted)

P8-3 (Purchases Recorded Gross and Net) Some of the transactions of William Dubois Company during August are listed below. Dubois uses the periodic inventory method.

August 10 Purchased merchandise on account, $9,000, terms 2/10, n/30.
       13 Returned part of the purchase of August 10, $1,200, and received credit on account.
       15 Purchased merchandise on account, $12,000, terms 1/10, n/60.
       25 Purchased merchandise on account, $15,000, terms 2/10, n/30.
       28 Paid invoice of August 15 in full.

Instructions

(a) Assuming that purchases are recorded at gross amounts and that discounts are to be recorded when taken:
    1. Prepare general journal entries to record the transactions.
    2. Describe how the various items would be shown in the financial statements.
(b) Assuming that purchases are recorded at net amounts and that discounts lost are treated as financial expenses:
    1. Prepare general journal entries to enter the transactions.
    2. Prepare the adjusting entry necessary on August 31 if financial statements are to be prepared at that time.
    3. Describe how the various items would be shown in the financial statements.
(c) Which of the two methods do you prefer and why?

P8-4 (Compute FIFO, LIFO, and Average Cost—Periodic and Perpetual) Taos Company's record of transactions concerning Part X for the month of April was as follows:

Purchases		Sales	
April 1 (balance on hand)	100 @ $5.00	April 5	300
April 4	400 @ 5.10	April 12	200
April 11	300 @ 5.30	April 27	800
April 18	200 @ 5.35	April 28	100
April 26	500 @ 5.60		
April 30	200 @ 5.80		

Instructions

(a) Compute the inventory at April 30 on each of the following bases. Assume that perpetual inventory records are kept in units only. Carry unit costs to the nearest cent.
    1. First-in, first-out (FIFO).
    2. Last-in, first-out (LIFO).
    3. Average cost.
(b) If the perpetual inventory record is kept in dollars, and costs are computed at the time of each withdrawal, what amount would be shown as ending inventory in 1, 2, and 3 above? Carry average unit costs to four decimal places.

P8-5 (Compute FIFO, LIFO and Average Cost—Periodic and Perpetual) Some of the information found on a detail inventory card for David Letterman Inc., for the first month of operations is as follows:

	Received		Issued,	Balance,
Date	No. of Units	Unit Cost	No. of Units	No. of Units
January 2	1,200	$3.00		1,200
7			700	500
10	600	3.20		1,100
13			500	600
18	1,000	3.30	300	1,300
20			1,100	200
23	1,300	3.40		1,500
26			800	700
28	1,500	3.60		2,200
31			1,300	900

Instructions

(a) From these data compute the ending inventory on each of the following bases. (Assume that perpetual inventory records are kept in units only; carry unit costs to the nearest cent and ending inventory to the nearest dollar.)
    1. First-in, first-out (FIFO).
    2. Last-in, first-out (LIFO).
    3. Average cost.

(b) If the perpetual inventory record is kept in dollars, and costs are computed at the time of each withdrawal, would the amounts shown as ending inventory in 1, 2, and 3 above be the same? Explain and compute.

P8-6 (Compute FIFO, LIFO, Average Cost—Periodic and Perpetual) Iowa Company is a multi-product firm. Presented below is information concerning one of their products, the Hawkeye:

Date	Transaction	Quantity	Price/Cost
1/1	Beginning inventory	1,000	$12
2/4	Purchase	2,000	18
2/20	Sale	2,500	30
4/2	Purchase	3,000	23
11/4	Sale	2,000	33

Instructions

Compute cost of goods sold, assuming Iowa uses:

(a) Periodic system, FIFO cost flow.

(b) Perpetual system, FIFO cost flow.

(c) Periodic system, LIFO cost flow.

(d) Perpetual system, LIFO cost flow.

(e) Periodic system, weighted-average cost flow.

(f) Perpetual system, moving-average cost flow.

P8-7 (Financial Statement Effects of FIFO and LIFO) The management of Maine Company has asked its accounting department to describe the effect upon the company's financial position and its income statements of accounting for inventories on the LIFO rather than the FIFO basis during 1999 and 2000. The accounting department is to assume that the change to LIFO would have been effective on January 1, 1999, and that the initial LIFO base would have been the inventory value on December 31, 1998. Presented below are the company's financial statements and other data for the years 1999 and 2000 when the FIFO method was in fact employed.

Financial Position as of	12/31/98	12/31/99	12/31/00
Cash	$ 90,000	$130,000	$ 141,600
Accounts receivable	80,000	100,000	120,000
Inventory	120,000	140,000	180,000
Other assets	160,000	170,000	200,000
Total assets	$450,000	$540,000	$ 641,600
Accounts payable	$ 40,000	$ 60,000	$ 80,000
Other liabilities	70,000	80,000	110,000
Common stock	200,000	200,000	200,000
Retained earnings	140,000	200,000	251,600
Total equities	$450,000	$540,000	$ 641,600

Income for Years Ended	12/31/97	12/31/98
Sales	$900,000	$1,350,000
Less: Cost of goods sold	505,000	770,000
Other expenses	205,000	304,000
	710,000	1,074,000
Net income before income taxes	190,000	276,000
Income taxes (40%)	76,000	110,400
Net income	$114,000	$ 165,600

Other data:

1. Inventory on hand at 12/31/98 consisted of 40,000 units valued at $3.00 each.
2. Sales (all units sold at the same price in a given year):

   1999—150,000 units @ $6.00 each   2000—180,000 units @ $7.50 each

3. Purchases (all units purchased at the same price in given year):

   1999—150,000 units @ $3.50 each   2000—180,000 units @ $4.50 each

4. Income taxes at the effective rate of 40% are paid on December 31 each year.

Instructions

Name the account(s) presented in the financial statement that would have different amounts for 2000 if LIFO rather than FIFO had been used and state the new amount for each account that is named. Show computations.

(CMA adapted)

P8-8 (Dollar-Value LIFO) Falcon's Televisions produces television sets in three categories: portable, midsize, and console. On January 1, 1998, Falcon adopted dollar-value LIFO and decided to use a single inventory pool. The company's January 1 inventory consists of:

Category	Quantity	Cost per Unit	Total Cost
Portable	6,000	$100	$ 600,000
Midsize	8,000	250	2,000,000
Console	3,000	400	1,200,000
	17,000		$3,800,000

During 1998, the company had the following purchases and sales:

Category	Quantity Purchased	Cost per Unit	Quantity Sold	Selling Price per Unit
Portable	15,000	$120	14,000	$150
Midsize	20,000	300	24,000	$405
Console	10,000	460	6,000	$600
	45,000		44,000	

Instructions
(Round to four decimals)
  (a) Compute ending inventory, cost of goods sold, and gross profit.
  (b) Assume the company uses three inventory pools instead of one. Repeat instruction (a).

P8-9 (LIFO Effect on Income) Kristi Yamaguchi Inc. sells two products: figure skates and speed skates. At December 31, 1999, Yamaguchi used the first-in, first-out (FIFO) inventory method. Effective January 1, 2000, Yamaguchi changed to the last-in, first-out (LIFO) inventory method. The cumulative effect of this change is not determinable and, as a result, the ending inventory of 1999 for which the FIFO method was used is also the beginning inventory for 2000 for the LIFO method. Any layers added during 2000 should be costed by reference to the first acquisitions of 2000 and any layers liquidated during 2000 should be considered a permanent liquidation.

The following information was available from Yamaguchi's inventory records for the 2 most recent years:

	Figure Skates		Speed Skates	
	Units	Unit Cost	Units	Unit Cost
1999 purchases				
January 7	7,000	$40.00	22,000	$20.00
April 16	12,000	45.00		
November 8	17,000	54.00	18,500	34.00
December 13	9,000	62.00		
2000 purchases				
February 11	3,000	66.00	23,000	36.00
May 20	8,000	75.00		
October 15	20,000	81.00		
December 23			15,500	42.00
Units on hand				
December 31, 1999	15,100		15,000	
December 31, 2000	18,000		13,200	

Instructions
Compute the effect on income before income taxes for the year ended December 31, 2000, resulting from the change from the FIFO to the LIFO inventory method.

(AICPA adapted)

P8-10 (Internal Indexes—Dollar-Value LIFO) On January 1, 1998, Addis Abeba Wholesalers Inc. adopted the dollar-value LIFO inventory method for income tax and external financial reporting purposes. However, Abeba continued to use the FIFO inventory method for internal accounting and management purposes. In applying the LIFO method, Abeba uses internal conversion price indexes and the multiple pools approach under which substantially identical inventory items are grouped into LIFO inventory pools. The following data were available for Inventory Pool No. 1, which comprises products A and B, for the two years following the adoption of LIFO:

| | | FIFO Basis per Records | | |
		Units	Unit Cost	Total Cost
Inventory, 1/1/98				
	Product A	10,000	$30	$300,000
	Product B	9,000	25	225,000
				$525,000
Inventory, 12/31/98				
	Product A	17,000	35	$595,000
	Product B	9,000	26	234,000
				$829,000
Inventory, 12/31/99				
	Product A	13,000	40	$520,000
	Product B	10,000	32	320,000
				$840,000

Instructions

(a) Prepare a schedule to compute the internal conversion price indexes for 1998 and 1999. Round indexes to two decimal places.

(b) Prepare a schedule to compute the inventory amounts at December 31, 1998 and 1999, using the dollar-value LIFO inventory method.

(AICPA adapted)

P8-11 (Internal Indexes—Dollar-Value LIFO)   Presented below is information related to Mellon Collie Corporation for the last three years:

Item	Quantities in Ending Inventories	Base-Year Cost		Current-Year Cost	
		Unit Cost	Amount	Unit Cost	Amount
December 31, 1997					
A	9,000	$2.00	$18,000	$2.40	$21,600
B	6,000	3.00	18,000	3.55	21,300
C	4,000	5.00	20,000	5.40	21,600
		Totals	$56,000		$64,500
December 31, 1998					
A	9,000	$2.00	$18,000	$2.60	$23,400
B	6,800	3.00	20,400	3.75	25,500
C	6,000	5.00	30,000	6.40	38,400
		Totals	$68,400		$87,300
December 31, 1999					
A	8,000	$2.00	$16,000	$2.70	$21,600
B	8,000	3.00	24,000	4.00	32,000
C	6,000	5.00	30,000	6.20	37,200
		Totals	$70,000		$90,800

Instructions

Compute the ending inventories under the dollar-value method for 1997, 1998, and 1999. The base period is January 1, 1997, and the beginning inventory cost at that date was $45,000. Compute indexes to two decimal places.

Additional Chapter 8 assignment materials—problems and cases—are available on our Web site.

❖ CONCEPTUAL CASES ❖

C8-1 (Inventoriable Costs) You are asked to travel to Milwaukee to observe and verify the inventory of the Milwaukee branch of one of your clients. You arrive on Thursday, December 30, and find that the inventory procedures have just been started. You spot a railway car on the sidetrack at the unloading door and ask the warehouse superintendent Predrag Danilovic how he plans to inventory the contents of the car. He responds: "We are not going to include the contents in the inventory."

Later in the day, you ask the bookkeeper for the invoice on the carload and the related freight bill. The invoice lists the various items, prices, and extensions of the goods in the car. You note that the carload was shipped December 24 from Albuquerque f.o.b. Albuquerque, and that the total invoice price of the goods in the car was $35,300. The freight bill called for a payment of $1,500. Terms were net 30 days. The bookkeeper affirms the fact that this invoice is to be held for recording in January.

Instructions
  (a) Does your client have a liability that should be recorded at December 31? Discuss.
  (b) Prepare a journal entry(ies), if required, to reflect any accounting adjustment required.
  (c) For what possible reason(s) might your client wish to postpone recording the transaction?

C8-2 (Inventoriable Costs) Alonzo Spellman, an inventory control specialist, is interested in better understanding the accounting for inventories. Although Alonzo understands the more sophisticated computer inventory control systems, he has little knowledge of how inventory cost is determined. In studying the records of Ditka Enterprises, which sells normal brand-name goods from its own store and on consignment through Wannstedt Inc., he asks you to answer the following questions.

Instructions
  (a) Should Ditka Enterprises include in its inventory normal brand-name goods purchased from its suppliers but not yet received if the terms of purchase are f.o.b. shipping point (manufacturer's plant)? Why?
  (b) Should Ditka Enterprises include freight-in expenditures as an inventory cost? Why?
  (c) If Ditka Enterprises purchases its goods on terms 2/10, net 30, should the purchases be recorded gross or net? Why?
  (d) What are products on consignment? How should they be reported in the financial statements?

(AICPA adapted)

C8-3 (Inventoriable Costs—Complex) Jack McDowell, the controller for McDowell Lumber Company, has recently hired you as assistant controller. He wishes to determine your expertise in the area of inventory accounting and therefore asks you to answer the following unrelated questions:
  (a) A company is involved in the wholesaling and retailing of automobile tires for foreign cars. Most of the inventory is imported, and it is valued on the company's records at the actual inventory cost plus freight-in. At year-end, the warehousing costs are prorated over cost of goods sold and ending inventory. Are warehousing costs considered a product cost or a period cost?
  (b) A certain portion of a company's "inventory" is composed of obsolete items. Should obsolete items that are not currently consumed in the production of "goods or services to be available for sale" be classified as part of inventory?
  (c) A company purchases airplanes for sale to others. However, until they are sold, the company charters and services the planes. What is the proper way to report these airplanes in the company's financial statements?
  (d) A company wants to buy coal deposits but does not want the financing for the purchase to be reported on its financial statements. The company therefore establishes a trust to acquire the coal deposits. The company agrees to buy the coal over a certain period of time at specified prices. The trust is able to finance the coal purchase and pay off the loan as it is paid by the company for the minerals. How should this transaction be reported?

C8-4 (Accounting Treatment of Purchase Discounts) Wayne Gretzky Corp., a household appliances dealer, purchases its inventories from various suppliers. Gretzky has consistently stated its inventories at the lower of cost (FIFO) or market.

Instructions
Gretzky is considering alternate methods of accounting for the cash discounts it takes when paying its suppliers promptly. From a theoretical standpoint, discuss the acceptability of each of the following methods:

  1. Financial income when payments are made.
  2. Reduction of cost of goods sold for period when payments are made.
  3. Direct reduction of purchase cost.

(AICPA adapted)

C8-5 (General Inventory Issues) In January 1999, Wesley Crusher Inc. requested and secured permission from the Commissioner of the Internal Revenue Service to compute inventories under the last-in, first-out (LIFO) method and elected to determine inventory cost under the dollar-value method. Crusher Inc. satisfied the Commissioner that cost could be accurately determined by use of an index number computed from a representative sample selected from the company's single inventory pool.

Instructions
(a) Why should inventories be included in (1) a balance sheet and (2) the computation of net income?
(b) The Internal Revenue Code allows some accountable events to be considered differently for income tax reporting purposes and financial accounting purposes, while other accountable events must be reported the same for both purposes. Discuss why it might be desirable to report some accountable events differently for financial accounting purposes than for income tax reporting purposes.
(c) Discuss the ways and conditions under which the FIFO and LIFO inventory costing methods produce different inventory valuations. Do not discuss procedures for computing inventory cost.

(AICPA adapted)

C8-6 (Variable Costing and Financial Statement Presentation) Akihito Co. is a manufacturing business with relatively heavy fixed costs and large inventories of finished goods. These inventories constitute a very material item on the balance sheet. The company has a departmental cost accounting system that assigns all manufacturing costs to the product each period.

Edward Gierek, controller of the company, has informed you that the management is giving serious consideration to the adoption of variable (direct) costing as a method of accounting for plant operations and inventory valuation. The management wishes to have your opinion of the effect, if any, that such a change would have on: (1) the year-end financial position, and (2) the net income for the year.

Instructions
State your reply to the request and the reasons for your conclusions.

(AICPA adapted)

C8-7 (LIFO Inventory Advantages) Jean Honore, president of Fragonard Co., recently read an article that claimed that at least 100 of the country's largest 500 companies were either adopting or considering adopting the last-in, first-out (LIFO) method for valuing inventories. The article stated that the firms were switching to LIFO to (1) neutralize the effect of inflation in their financial statements, (2) eliminate inventory profits, and (3) reduce income taxes. Ms. Honore wonders if the switch would benefit her company.

Fragonard currently uses the first-in, first-out (FIFO) method of inventory valuation in its periodic inventory system. The company has a high inventory turnover rate, and inventories represent a significant proportion of the assets.

In discussing this trend toward LIFO inventory with business friends, Ms. Honore has been told that the LIFO system is more costly to operate and will provide little benefit to companies with high turnover. She intends to use the inventory method that is best for the company in the long run rather than selecting a method just because it is the current fad.

Instructions
(a) Explain to Ms. Honore what "inventory profits" are and how the LIFO method of inventory valuation could reduce them.
(b) Explain to Ms. Honore the conditions that must exist for Fragonard Co. to receive tax benefits from a switch to the LIFO method.

C8-8 (Average Cost, FIFO, and LIFO) Presented below are three independent situations.
(a) Describe the cost flow assumptions used in average cost, FIFO, and LIFO methods of inventory valuation.
(b) Distinguish between weighted average cost and moving average cost for inventory costing purposes.
(c) Identify the effects on both the balance sheet and the income statement of using the LIFO method instead of the FIFO method for inventory costing purposes over a substantial time period when purchase prices of inventoriable items are rising. State why these effects take place.

C8-9 (LIFO Application and Advantages) The Neshki Corporation is a medium-sized manufacturing company with two divisions and three subsidiaries, all located in the United States. The Metallic Division manufactures metal castings for the automotive industry, and the Plastic Division produces small plastic items for electrical products and other uses. The three subsidiaries manufacture various products for other industrial users.

Neshki Corporation plans to change from the lower of first-in, first-out (FIFO) cost or market method of inventory valuation to the last-in, first-out (LIFO) method of inventory valuation to obtain tax benefits.

To make the method acceptable for tax purposes, the change also will be made for its annual financial statements.

Instructions

(a) Describe the establishment of and subsequent pricing procedures for each of the following LIFO inventory methods:
   1. LIFO applied to units of product when the periodic inventory system is used.
   2. Application of the dollar-value method to LIFO units of product.
(b) Discuss the specific advantages and disadvantages of using the dollar-value LIFO application as compared to specific goods LIFO (unit LIFO). Ignore income tax considerations.
(c) Discuss the general advantages and disadvantages claimed for LIFO methods.

C8-10 (Dollar-Value LIFO Issues) Maria Callas Co. is considering switching from the specific goods LIFO approach to the dollar value LIFO approach. Because the financial personnel at Callas know very little about dollar value LIFO, they ask you to answer the following questions.
   (a) What is a LIFO pool?
   (b) Is it possible to use a LIFO pool concept and not use dollar-value LIFO? Explain.
   (c) What is a LIFO liquidation?
   (d) How are price indexes used in the dollar-value LIFO method?
   (e) What are the advantages of dollar-value LIFO over specific goods LIFO?

C8-11 (FIFO and LIFO) Günter Grass Company is considering changing its inventory valuation method from FIFO to LIFO because of the potential tax savings. However, the management wishes to consider all of the effects on the company, including its reported performance, before making the final decision.

The inventory account, currently valued on the FIFO basis, consists of 1,000,000 units at $7 per unit on January 1, 1999. There are 1,000,000 shares of common stock outstanding as of January 1, 1999, and the cash balance is $400,000.

The company has made the following forecasts for the period 1999–2001.

	1999	2000	2001
Unit sales (in millions of units)	1.1	1.0	1.3
Sales price per unit	$11	$11	$13
Unit purchases (in millions of units)	1.0	1.1	1.2
Purchase price per unit	$7	$8	$9
Annual depreciation (in thousands of dollars)	$300	$300	$300
Cash dividends per share	$.15	$.15	$.15
Cash payments for additions to and replacement of plant and equipment (in thousands of dollars)	$350	$350	$350
Income tax rate	40%	40%	40%
Operating expense (exclusive of depreciation) as a percent of sales	15%	15%	15%
Common shares outstanding (in millions)	1	1	1

Instructions

(a) Prepare a schedule that illustrates and compares the following data for Günter Grass Company under the FIFO and the LIFO inventory method for 1999–2001. Assume the company would begin LIFO at the beginning of 1999.

   1. Year-end inventory balances. **3.** Earnings per share.
   2. Annual net income after taxes. **4.** Cash balance.

Assume all sales are collected in the year of sale and all purchases, operating expenses, and taxes are paid during the year incurred.

(b) Using the data above, your answer to (a), and any additional issues you believe need to be considered, prepare a report that recommends whether or not Günter Grass Company should change to the LIFO inventory method. Support your conclusions with appropriate arguments.

(CMA adapted)

❖USING YOUR JUDGMENT❖

❖FINANCIAL STATEMENT ANALYSIS CASES

T J International

T J International was founded in 1969 as Trus Joist International. The firm, a manufacturer of specialty building products, has its headquarters in Boise, Idaho. The company, through its partnership in the Trus Joist MacMillan joint venture, develops and manufactures engineered lumber. This product is a high-quality substitute for structural lumber, and uses lower-grade wood and materials formerly considered waste. The company also is majority owner of the Outlook Window Partnership, which is a consortium of three wood and vinyl window manufacturers.

Following is T J International's adapted income statement and information concerning inventories from the 1994 annual report.

Sales	$618,876,000
Cost of goods sold	475,476,000
Gross profit	143,400,000
Selling and administrative expenses	102,112,000
Income from operations	41,288,000
Other income (expense)	24,712,000
Income before income tax	16,576,000
Income taxes	7,728,000
Net income	$ 8,848,000

Inventories. Inventories are valued at the lower of cost or market and include material, labor, and production overhead costs. Inventories consisted of the following:

	December 31, 1994	December 31, 1993
Finished goods	$27,512,000	$23,830,000
Raw materials and work-in-progress	34,363,000	33,244,000
	61,875,000	57,074,000
Reduction to LIFO cost	(5,263,000)	(3,993,000)
	$56,612,000	$53,081,000

The last-in, first-out (LIFO) method is used for determining the cost of lumber, veneer, Microllam lumber, TJI joists, and open web joists. Approximately 35 percent of total inventories at the end of 1994 were valued using the LIFO method. The first-in, first-out (FIFO) method is used to determine the cost of all other inventories.

Instructions

(a) How much would income before taxes have been if FIFO costing had been used to value all inventories?

(b) If the income tax rate is 46.6%, what would income tax have been if FIFO costing had been used to value all inventories? In your opinion, is this difference in net income between the two methods material? Explain.

(c) Does the use of a different costing system for different types of inventory mean that there is a different physical flow of goods among the different types of inventory? Explain.

Noven Pharmaceuticals, Inc.

Noven Pharmaceuticals, Inc., headquartered in Miami, Florida, describes itself in its 1995 annual report as follows:

"Noven is a place of ideas—a company where scientific excellence and state-of-the-art manufacturing combine to create new answers to human needs. Our transdermal delivery systems speed drugs painlessly and effortlessly into the bloodstream by means of a simple skin patch. This technology has proven applications in estrogen replacement, but at Noven we are developing a variety of systems incorporating best-selling drugs that fight everything from asthma, anxiety and dental pain to cancer, heart disease and neurological illness. Our research portfolio also includes new technologies, such as iontophoresis, in which drugs are delivered through the skin by means of electrical currents, as well as products that could satisfy broad consumer needs, such as our anti-microbial mouthrinse."

Noven also reported in its 1995 annual report that its activities to date have consisted of product development efforts, some of which have been independent and some of which have been completed in conjunction with Rhone-Poulenc Rorer (RPR) and Ciba-Geigy. The revenues so far have consisted of money received from licensing fees, "milestone" payments (payments made under licensing agreements when certain stages of the development of a certain product have been completed), and interest on its investments. The company expects that it will have significant revenue in the upcoming fiscal year from the launch of its first product, a transdermal estrogen delivery system.

The current assets portion of Noven's balance sheet follows:

Cash and cash equivalents	$12,070,272
Securities held to maturity	23,445,070
Inventory of supplies	1,264,553
Prepaid and other current assets	825,159
Total current assets	$37,605,054

Inventory of supplies is recorded at the lower of cost (first-in, first-out) or net realizable value and consists mainly of supplies for research and development.

Instructions

(a) What would you expect the physical flow of goods for a pharmaceutical manufacturer to be most like: FIFO, LIFO, or random (flow of goods does not follow a set pattern)? Explain.

(b) What are some of the factors that Noven should consider as it selects an inventory measurement method?

(c) Suppose that Noven had $49,000 in an inventory of transdermal estrogen delivery patches. These patches are from an initial production run, and will be sold during the coming year. Why do you think that this amount is not shown in a separate inventory account? In which of the accounts shown is the inventory likely to be? At what point will the inventory be transferred to a separate inventory account?

❖ RESEARCH CASES

Case 1

As indicated in the chapter, the FIFO and LIFO inventory methods can result in significantly different income statement and balance sheet figures. However, it is possible to convert income for a LIFO firm to its FIFO-based equivalent. To assist financial statement users in this task, firms using LIFO are required to disclose in their footnotes the "LIFO reserve" (LR)—i.e., the difference between the inventory balance shown on the balance sheet and the amount that would have been reported had the firm used current cost (or FIFO). The following equation can be used to convert LIFO cost of goods sold (COGS) to FIFO COGS:

$$COGS_{FIFO} = COGS_{LIFO} - LIFO\ EFFECT,$$

where

$$LIFO\ EFFECT = [LR_{ending} - LR_{beginning}].$$

The following equation can be used to convert LIFO net income (NI) to FIFO NI:

$$NI_{FIFO} = NI_{LIFO} + (LIFO\ EFFECT)(1 - tax\ rate).$$

Instructions

Obtain the annual report of a firm which reports a LIFO reserve in its footnotes.

(a) Identify the LIFO reserve at the two most recent balance sheet dates.

(b) Determine the LIFO effect during the most recent year.

(c) By how much would cost of goods sold during the most recent year change if the firm used FIFO?

(d) By how much would net income during the most recent year change if the firm used FIFO? (*HINT:* To estimate the tax rate, divide income tax expense by income before taxes.)

Go to our Web site for examples of LIFO reserves.

Case 2

The "Fortune 500" issue of *Fortune* magazine can serve as a useful reference. This annual issue, generally appearing in late April or early May, contains a great deal of information regarding the largest U.S. industrial and service companies.

Instructions

Examine the most recent edition and answer the following questions.

(a) Identify the three largest U.S. corporations in terms of revenue, profit, assets, market value, and employees.

(b) Identify the largest corporation in your state (by total revenue).

❖ WRITING ASSIGNMENT

Warren Dunn Company cans a variety of vegetable-type soups. Recently, the company decided to value its inventories using dollar-value LIFO pools. The clerk who accounts for inventories does not understand how to value the inventory pools using this new method, so, as a private consultant, you have been asked to teach him how this new method works.

He has provided you with the following information about purchases made over a 6-year period:

Date	Ending Inventory (End-of-Year Prices)	Price Index
Dec. 31, 1993	$ 80,000	100
Dec. 31, 1994	115,500	105
Dec. 31, 1995	108,000	120
Dec. 31, 1996	131,300	130
Dec. 31, 1997	154,000	140
Dec. 31, 1998	174,000	145

You have already explained to him how this inventory method is maintained, but he would feel better about it if you were to leave him detailed instructions explaining how these calculations are done and why he needs to put all inventories at a base-year value.

Instructions

Compute the ending inventory for Warren Dunn Company for 1993 through 1998 using dollar-value LIFO. Using your computation schedules as your illustration, write a step-by-step set of instructions explaining how the calculations are done. Begin your explanation by briefly explaining the theory behind this inventory method, including the purpose of putting all amounts into base-year price levels.

❖ GROUP ASSIGNMENT

Presented below is information related to Product A of Stone Co. for the month of July:

Date	Transaction	Units In	Unit Cost	Total	Units Sold	Selling Price	Total
July 1	Balance	100	$4.10	$ 410			
6	Purchase	800	4.21	3,368			
7	Sale				300	$7.00	$ 2,100
10	Sale				300	7.30	2,190
12	Purchase	400	4.54	1,816			
15	Sale				200	7.40	1,480
18	Purchase	300	4.60	1,380			
22	Sale				400	7.40	2,960
25	Purchase	500	4.70	2,350			
29	Sale				200	7.50	1,500
	Totals	2,100		$9,324	1,400		$10,230

Instructions

Work within your group to address the following requirements related to the above data (you may want to divide the items among group members). Your instructor will assign one member to record your group responses and one member to serve as group spokesperson.

(a) Assuming that the periodic inventory method is used, compute the inventory cost at July 31 under each of the following cost flow assumptions:
  1. FIFO.
  2. LIFO.
  3. Weighted-average (round the weighted-average unit cost to the nearest one-tenth of one cent).

(b) Answer the following questions:
  1. Which of the methods used above will yield the lowest figure for gross profit for the income statement? Explain why.
  2. Which of the methods used above will yield the lowest figure for ending inventory for the balance sheet? Explain why.

(c) Discuss how use of a perpetual inventory system would change the responses to parts (a) and (b).

❖ ETHICS CASE

Gamble Company uses the LIFO method for inventory costing. In an effort to lower net income, company president Oscar Gamble tells the plant accountant to take the unusual step of recommending to the purchasing department a large purchase of inventory at year-end. The price of the item to be purchased has nearly doubled during the year, and the item represents a major portion of inventory value.

Instructions

Answer the following questions:

(a) Identify the major stakeholders. If the plant accountant recommends the purchase, what are the consequences?

(b) If Gamble Company had been using the FIFO method of inventory costing, would Oscar Gamble give the same order? Why or why not?

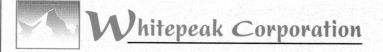 **W**hitepeak Corporation   **MODULE 2**

Section 2.1 Moving Average Inventory

Whitepeak has an inventory of cross-country skis for sale in its various retail outlets across the Western United States and Canada. These skis are accounted for under the moving-average method.

During 1997, numerous sales and purchases of Whitepeak's skis were made; detailed figures are provided on the Whitepeak disk. Fortunately, previous computations are correct.

Instructions Compute the cost of the ending inventory using the moving-average method. ∎

CHAPTER 9

Inventories: Additional Valuation Issues

LIFO to the Rescue If Inflation Revives

After five consecutive years of 3% or lower inflation, many managers and investors have built low inflation into their financial and earnings expectations. But what if inflation returns? What effect would inflation have on reported earnings? Although most investors and even some managers pay little attention to it, the choice of an inventory valuation method can have a considerable impact on the bottom line.

Are public companies' earnings and inventories protected by LIFO against inflation? The stock market bellweather Dow Jones Industrial Average is made up of 30 companies. Shown below is a tally of the inventory costing methods used by these companies:

Inventory Methods Used by 30 Dow Jones Companies[1]

AT&T	FIFO	DuPont	LIFO	Minnesota Mining	FIFO
Allied Chemical	LIFO	Exxon	LIFO	J P Morgan	NA
Alcoa Aluminum	LIFO	General Electric	LIFO	Philip Morris	LIFO
American Express	NA	General Motors	LIFO	Proctor & Gamble	LIFO
Bethlehem Steel	LIFO	Goodyear Tire	LIFO	Sears	LIFO
Boeing	Avg. Cost	IBM	Avg. Cost	Texaco	LIFO
Caterpillar	LIFO	International Paper	LIFO	Union Carbide	LIFO
Chevron	LIFO	Kodak	LIFO	United Technology	LIFO
Coca-Cola	Avg. Cost	McDonald's	FIFO	Westinghouse	Avg. Cost
Disney	Avg. Cost	Merck	LIFO	Woolworth	LIFO

Two-thirds of the DJIA companies use LIFO. The major reason is the opportunity LIFO provides to reduce income taxes during rising prices, enhancing cash flow. For example, the $11.5 billion that General Motors (GM) reported as inventories on December 31, 1995, would have been $2.4 billion greater under the FIFO method. Use of LIFO saved GM taxes and cash of nearly $720 million. It appears that from an inventory costing point of view, most Dow Jones Industrial Average companies are ready for inflation, should it revive.

---

[1]"Twin Towers," *Barron's*, July 15, 1996. Recently, four companies in the Dow Jones were replaced.

LEARNING OBJECTIVES

After studying this chapter, you should be able to:

1. Explain and apply the lower of cost or market rule.
2. Identify when inventories are valued at net realizable value.
3. Explain when the relative sales value method is used to value inventories.
4. Explain accounting issues related to purchase commitments.
5. Determine ending inventory by applying the gross profit method.
6. Determine ending inventory by applying the retail inventory method.
7. Explain how inventory is reported and analyzed.

As indicated in the opening story, most Dow Jones companies use the LIFO method for costing their inventories. However, irrespective of the costing method a company uses, it is sometimes necessary to adjust this cost because of changing circumstances. The purpose of this chapter is to discuss and illustrate some of the valuation and estimation concepts that are used to develop relevant inventory information. The content and organization of the chapter are as follows:

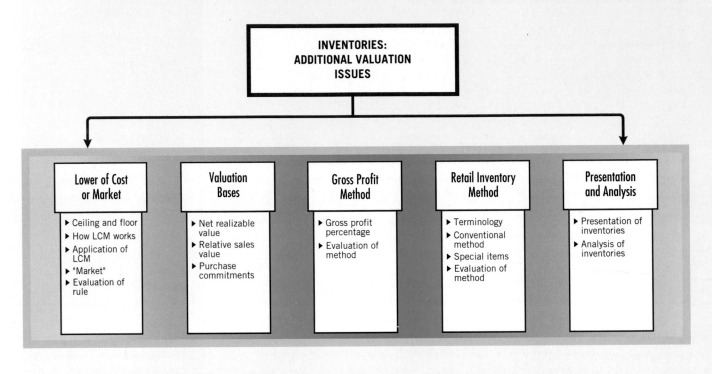

❖ LOWER OF COST OR MARKET

Objective ①

Explain and apply the lower of cost or market rule.

As noted in Chapter 8, inventories are recorded at their original cost. However, a major departure from the historical cost principle is made in the area of inventory valuation if inventory declines in value below its original cost. Whatever the reason for a decline—obsolescence, price-level changes, damaged goods, and so forth—the inventory should be written down to reflect this loss. **The general rule is that the historical cost principle is abandoned when the future utility (revenue-producing ability) of the asset is no longer as great as its original cost.**

Inventories that experience a decline in utility are valued therefore on the basis of the lower of cost or market, instead of on an original cost basis. **Cost** is the acquisition price of inventory computed using one of the historical cost-based methods—specific identification, average cost, FIFO, or LIFO. The term market in the phrase "the lower of cost or market" (LCM) generally means the cost to replace the item by purchase or reproduction. In a retailing business the term "market" refers to the market in which goods were purchased, not the market in which they are sold; in manufacturing, the term "market" refers to the cost to reproduce. Thus the rule really means that **goods are to be valued at cost or cost to replace, whichever is lower.** For example, a Casio calculator wristwatch that costs a retailer $30.00 when purchased, that can be sold for

$48.95, and that can be replaced for $25.00 should be valued at $25.00 for inventory purposes under the lower of cost or market rule. The lower of cost or market rule of valuation can be used after any of the cost flow methods discussed in Chapter 8 have been applied to determine the inventory cost.

A departure from cost is justified because **a loss of utility should be charged against revenues in the period in which the loss occurs**, not in the period in which it is sold. In addition, the lower of cost or market method is **a conservative approach to inventory valuation**. That is, when doubt exists about the value of an asset, it is preferable to undervalue rather than to overvalue it.

UNDERLYING CONCEPTS

The use of the lower of cost or market method is an excellent example of the conservatism constraint.

Lower of Cost or Market—Ceiling and Floor

Why use replacement cost to represent market value? The reason is that a decline in the replacement cost of an item usually reflects or predicts a decline in selling price. Using replacement cost allows a company to maintain a consistent rate of gross profit on sales (normal profit margin). Sometimes, however, a reduction in the replacement cost of an item does not indicate a corresponding reduction in its utility. Then, two additional valuation limitations are used to value ending inventory—net realizable value and net realizable value less a normal profit margin.

Net realizable value (NRV) is defined as the estimated selling price in the ordinary course of business less reasonably predictable costs of completion and disposal. A normal profit margin is subtracted from that amount to arrive at net realizable value less a normal profit margin.

To illustrate, assuming that Jerry Mander Corp. has unfinished inventory with a sales value of $1,000, estimated cost of completion of $300, and a normal profit margin of 10% of sales, the following can be determined:

Inventory—sales value	$1,000
Less: Estimated cost of completion and disposal	300
Net realizable value	700
Less: Allowance for normal profit margin (10% of sales)	100
Net realizable value less a normal profit margin	$ 600

ILLUSTRATION 9-1
Computation of Net Realizable Value

The general rule of lower of cost or market **is: inventory is valued at the lower of cost or market, with market limited to an amount that is not more than net realizable value or less than net realizable value less a normal profit margin.**[2]

What is the rationale for these two limitations? The upper (ceiling) and lower (floor) limits for the value of the inventory are intended to prevent the inventory from being reported at an amount in excess of the net selling price or at an amount less than the net selling price less a normal profit margin. The maximum limitation, **not to exceed the net realizable value (ceiling)**, covers obsolete, damaged, or shopworn material and prevents overstatement of inventories and understatement of the loss in the current period. That is, if the replacement cost of an item is greater than its net realizable value, inventory should not be reported at replacement cost because the company can only receive the selling price less cost of disposal. To report the inventory at replacement cost would result in an overstatement of inventory and an understated loss in the current period. To illustrate, assume that Computerland paid $2,500 for a laser printer that can now be replaced for $2,200 and whose net realizable value is $1,800. At what amount should the laser printer be reported in the financial statements? To report the replacement cost of $2,200 overstates the ending inventory and understates the loss for the period. The printer should, therefore, be reported at $1,800.

The minimum limitation, **not to be less than net realizable value reduced by an allowance for an approximately normal profit margin (floor)**, deters understatement of inventory and overstatement of the loss in the current period. It establishes a

UNDERLYING CONCEPTS

Setting a floor and a ceiling increases the relevancy of the inventory presentation. The inventory figure provides a better understanding of how much revenue the inventory will generate.

---

[2]"Restatement and Revision of Accounting Research Bulletins," *Accounting Research Bulletin No. 43* (New York: AICPA, 1953), Ch. 4, par. 8.

floor below which the inventory should not be priced regardless of replacement cost. It makes no sense to price inventory below net realizable value less a normal margin because this minimum amount (floor) measures what the company can receive for the inventory and still earn a normal profit. These guidelines are illustrated graphically in Illustration 9-2.

ILLUSTRATION 9-2
Inventory Valuation—
Lower of Cost or Market

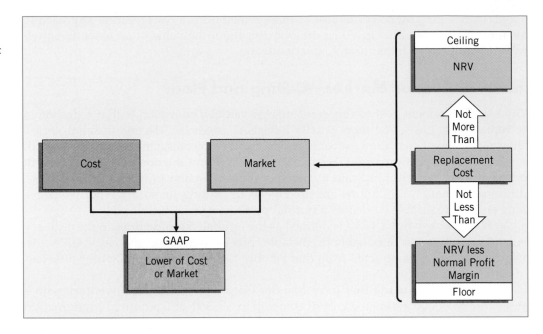

How Lower of Cost or Market Works

The amount that is compared to cost, often referred to as **designated market value**, is **always the middle value of three amounts**: replacement cost, net realizable value, and net realizable value less a normal profit margin. To illustrate how designated market value is computed, assume the following information relative to the inventory of Regner Foods, Inc.

ILLUSTRATION 9-3
Computation of
Designated Market Value

Food	Replacement Cost	Net Realizable Value (Ceiling)	Net Realizable Value Less a Normal Profit Margin (Floor)	Designated Market Value
Spinach	$ 88,000	$120,000	$104,000	$104,000
Carrots	90,000	100,000	70,000	90,000
Cut Beans	45,000	40,000	27,500	40,000
Peas	36,000	72,000	48,000	48,000
Mixed Vegetables	105,000	92,000	80,000	92,000

Designated Market Value Decision:

Spinach	Net realizable value less a normal profit margin is selected because it is the middle value.
Carrots	Replacement cost is selected because it is the middle value.
Cut Beans	Net realizable value is selected because it is the middle value.
Peas	Net realizable value less a normal profit margin is selected because it is the middle value.
Mixed Vegetables	Net realizable value is selected because it is the middle value.

Designated market value is then compared to cost to determine the lower of cost or market. To illustrate, the final inventory value for Regner Foods is determined as follows:

Food	Cost	Replacement Cost	Net Realizable Value (Ceiling)	Net Realizable Value Less a Normal Profit Margin (Floor)	Designated Market Value	Final Inventory Value
Spinach	$ 80,000	$ 88,000	$120,000	$104,000	$104,000	$ 80,000
Carrots	100,000	90,000	100,000	70,000	90,000	90,000
Cut Beans	50,000	45,000	40,000	27,500	40,000	40,000
Peas	90,000	36,000	72,000	48,000	48,000	48,000
Mixed Vegetables	95,000	105,000	92,000	80,000	92,000	92,000
						$350,000

Final Inventory Value:

Spinach	Cost ($80,000) is selected because it is lower than designated market value (net realizable value less a normal profit margin).
Carrots	Designated market value (replacement cost, $90,000) is selected because it is lower than cost.
Cut Beans	Designated market value (net realizable value, $40,000) is selected because it is lower than cost.
Peas	Designated market value (net realizable value less a normal profit margin, $48,000) is selected because it is lower than cost.
Mixed Vegetables	Designated market value (net realizable value, $92,000) is selected because it is lower than cost.

ILLUSTRATION 9-4
Determining Final
Inventory Value

The application of the lower of cost or market rule incorporates only losses in value that occur in the normal course of business from such causes as style changes, shift in demand, or regular shop wear. Damaged or deteriorated goods are reduced to net realizable value. When material, such goods may be carried in separate inventory accounts.

Methods of Applying Lower of Cost or Market

In the previous illustration for Regner Foods, we assumed that the lower of cost or market rule was applied to each individual type of food. However, the lower of cost or market rule may be "applied either directly to each item, to each category, or to the total of the inventory." Increases in market prices tend to offset decreases in market prices, if a major category or total inventory approach is followed in applying the lower of cost or market rule. To illustrate, assume that Regner Foods separates its food products into frozen and canned for purposes of designating major categories.

Regner Foods, Inc.			Lower of Cost or Market By:		
	Cost	Designated Market	Individual Items	Major Categories	Total Inventory
Frozen					
Spinach	$ 80,000	$104,000	$ 80,000		
Carrots	100,000	90,000	90,000		
Cut Beans	50,000	40,000	40,000		
Total frozen	230,000	234,000		$230,000	
Canned					
Peas	90,000	48,000	48,000		
Mixed Vegetables	95,000	92,000	92,000		
Total canned	185,000	140,000		140,000	
Total	$415,000	$374,000	$350,000	$370,000	$374,000

ILLUSTRATION 9-5
Alternative Applications
of Lower of Cost
or Market

If the lower of cost or market rule is applied to individual items, the amount of inventory is $350,000; if applied to major categories, it is $370,000; if applied to the total inventory, it is $374,000. The reason for the difference is that market values higher than cost are offset against market values lower than cost when the major categories or total inventory approach is adopted. For Regner Foods, the high market value for spinach is partially offset when the major categories approach is adopted and is totally offset when the total inventory approach is used.

The most common practice is to price the inventory on an item-by-item basis. For one thing, tax rules require that an individual item basis be used unless it involves practical difficulties. In addition, the individual item approach gives the most conservative valuation for balance sheet purposes.[3] Inventory is often priced on a total inventory basis when there is only one end product (comprised of many different raw materials) because the main concern is the pricing of the final inventory. If several end products are produced, a category approach might be used. The method selected should be the one that most clearly reflects income. **Whichever method is selected, it should be applied consistently from one period to another.**[4]

Recording "Market" Instead of Cost

Two methods are used for recording inventory at market. One method, referred to as the **direct method**, substitutes the market value figure for cost when valuing the inventory. As a result, no loss is reported in the income statement because the loss is buried in cost of goods sold. The second method, referred to as the **indirect method** or **allowance method**, does not change the cost amount, but establishes a separate contra asset account and a loss account to record the writeoff.

The following illustrations of entries under both methods are based on the following inventory data:

Inventory	At Cost	At Market
Beginning of the period	$65,000	$65,000
End of the period	82,000	70,000

The following entries assume the use of a **periodic** inventory system.

---

[3]If a company uses dollar-value LIFO, determining the LIFO cost of an individual item may be more difficult. The company might decide that it is more appropriate to apply the lower of cost or market rule to the total amount of each pool. The AICPA Task Force on LIFO Inventory Problems concluded that the most reasonable approach to applying the lower of cost or market provisions to LIFO inventories is to base the determination on reasonable groupings of items and that a pool constitutes a reasonable grouping. Both the Task Force and AcSEC, however, support the use of the item-by-item approach for identifying product obsolescence and product discontinuance writedowns and writeoffs.

[4]Inventory accounting for financial statement purposes can be different from income tax purposes. For example, the lower of cost or market rule cannot be used with LIFO for tax purposes. There is nothing, however, to prevent the use of the lower of cost or market and LIFO for financial accounting purposes. In addition, for financial accounting purposes, companies often write down slow-moving inventory because experience indicates that some of it will not be sold for many years, if at all. However, to be deductible for tax purposes a writedown in inventory value resulting from the application of lower of cost or market rule can be taken only in the year in which the actual decline in the sale price of the item occurs, and the writedown must be computed on an individual item basis rather than on classes of inventory or on the inventory as a whole.

Ending Inventory Recorded at Market (Direct Method)		Ending Inventory Recorded at Cost and Reduced to Market (Indirect or Allowance Method)	
To close beginning inventory:			
Cost of Goods Sold (or Income Summary) 65,000		Cost of Goods Sold (or Income Summary) 65,000	
Inventory	65,000	Inventory	65,000
To record ending inventory:			
Inventory 70,000		Inventory 82,000	
Cost of Goods Sold (or Income Summary)	70,000	Cost of Goods Sold (or Income Summary)	82,000
To write down inventory to market:			
No entry		Loss Due to Market Decline of Inventory 12,000	
		Allowance to Reduce Inventory to Market	12,000

ILLUSTRATION 9-6
Accounting for the Reduction of Inventory to Market—Periodic Inventory System

If the company had used a **perpetual** inventory system, the entries would be as follows:

(No inventory closing entries are necessary under the perpetual method; only the reduction to market is recorded.)

Direct Method		Indirect or Allowance Method	
To reduce inventory from cost to market:			
Cost of Goods Sold 12,000		Loss Due to Market Decline of Inventory 12,000	
Inventory	12,000	Allowance to Reduce Inventory to Market	12,000

ILLUSTRATION 9-7
Accounting for the Reduction of Inventory to Market—Perpetual Inventory System

The advantage of identifying the loss due to market decline is that it is shown separately from cost of goods sold in the income statement (not as an extraordinary item); the cost of goods sold for the year is not distorted. The data from the preceding illustration are used to contrast the differing amounts reported in the income statements below.

Direct Method		
Revenue from sales		$200,000
Cost of goods sold		
Inventory Jan. 1	$ 65,000	
Purchases	125,000	
Goods available	190,000	
Inventory Dec. 31 (at market which is lower than cost)	70,000	
Cost of goods sold		120,000
Gross profit on sales		$ 80,000
Indirect or Allowance Method		
Revenue from sales		$200,000
Cost of goods sold		
Inventory Jan. 1	$ 65,000	
Purchases	125,000	
Goods available	190,000	
Inventory Dec. 31 (at cost)	82,000	
Cost of goods sold		108,000
Gross profit on sales		92,000
Loss due to market decline of inventory		12,000
		$ 80,000

ILLUSTRATION 9-8
Income Statement Presentation—Direct and Indirect Methods of Reducing Inventory to Market

The second presentation is preferable, because it clearly discloses the loss resulting from the market decline of inventory prices. The first presentation buries the loss in the cost of goods sold. The Allowance to Reduce Inventory to Market would be reported on the balance sheet as a $12,000 deduction from the inventory. This deduction permits both the income statement and the balance sheet to show the ending inventory of $82,000, although the balance sheet shows a net amount of $70,000. It also keeps subsidiary inventory ledgers and records in correspondence with the control account without changing unit prices.

Although use of an allowance account permits balance sheet disclosure of the inventory at cost and the lower of cost or market, it raises the problem of how to dispose of the balance of the new account in the following period. If the merchandise in question is still on hand, the allowance account should be retained. Otherwise, beginning inventory and cost of goods are overstated. But if the goods have been sold, then the account should be closed. A "new allowance account" is then established for any decline in inventory value that has taken place in the current year.[5]

Some accountants leave this account on the books and merely adjust the balance at the next year-end to agree with the discrepancy between cost and the lower of cost or market at that balance sheet date. Thus, if prices are falling, a loss is recorded. If prices are rising, a loss recorded in prior years is recovered and a "gain" (which is not really a gain, but a recovery of a previously recognized loss) is recorded, as illustrated in the example below.

ILLUSTRATION 9-9
Effect on Net Income of Reducing Inventory to Market

Date	Inventory at Cost	Inventory at Market	Amount Required in Valuation Account	Adjustment of Valuation Account Balance	Effect on Net Income
Dec. 31, 1997	$188,000	$176,000	$12,000	$12,000 inc.	Loss
Dec. 31, 1998	194,000	187,000	7,000	5,000 dec.	Gain
Dec. 31, 1999	173,000	174,000	0	7,000 dec.	Gain
Dec. 31, 2000	182,000	180,000	2,000	2,000 inc.	Loss

This net "gain" can be thought of as the excess of the credit effect of closing the beginning allowance balance over the debit effect of setting up the current year-end allowance account. Recognition of gain or loss has the same effect on net income as closing the allowance balance to beginning inventory or to cost of goods sold. Recovery of the loss up to the original cost is permitted, **but it may not exceed original cost.**

Evaluation of the Lower of Cost or Market Rule

The lower of cost or market rule suffers some conceptual deficiencies:

❶ Decreases in the value of the asset and the charge to expense are recognized in the period in which the loss in utility occurs—not in the period of sale. On the other hand, increases in the value of the asset are recognized only at the point of sale. This treatment is inconsistent and can lead to distortions in income data.

❷ Application of the rule results in inconsistency because the inventory of a company may be valued at cost in one year and at market in the next year.

❸ Lower of cost or market values the inventory in the balance sheet conservatively, but its effect on the income statement may or may not be conservative. Net income for the year in which the loss is taken is definitely lower; net income of the subsequent period may be higher than normal if the expected reductions in sales price do not materialize.

---

[5]The AICPA Task Force on LIFO Inventory Problems concluded that for LIFO inventories the allowance from the prior year should be closed and that the allowance at the end of the year should be based on a new lower of cost or market computation. *Issues Paper* (New York: AICPA, November 30, 1984), pp. 50–55.

❹ Application of the lower of cost or market rule uses a "normal profit" in determining inventory values. Since "normal profit" is an estimated figure based upon past experience (and might not be attained in the future), it is not objective in nature and presents an opportunity for income manipulation.

Many financial statement users appreciate the lower of cost or market rule because they at least know that the inventory is not overstated. In addition, recognizing all losses but anticipating no gains generally results in lower income.

❖ VALUATION BASES

Valuation at Net Realizable Value

For the most part, inventory is recorded at cost or the lower of cost or market.[6] However, many believe that market should always be defined as net realizable value (rather than replacement cost) for purposes of applying the lower of cost or market rule. This argument is based on the fact that net realizable value is the amount that will be collected from this inventory in the future.[7] Under limited circumstances, support exists for **recording inventory at net realizable value (selling price less estimated costs to complete and sell)** even if that amount is above cost. This exception to the normal recognition rule is permitted where (1) there is a controlled market with a quoted price applicable to all quantities and (2) no significant costs of disposal are involved. Inventories of certain minerals (rare metals especially), are ordinarily reported at selling prices because there is often a controlled market without significant costs of disposal. A similar treatment is given agricultural products that are immediately marketable at quoted prices.

Another reason for allowing this method of valuation is that sometimes the cost figures are too difficult to obtain. In a manufacturing plant, various raw materials and purchased parts are put together to create a finished product. The various items in inventory, whether completely or partially finished, can be accounted for on a basis of cost because the cost of each individual component part is known. In a meat-packing house, however, a different situation prevails. The "raw material" consists of cattle, hogs, or sheep, each unit of which is purchased as a whole and then divided into parts that are the products. Instead of one product out of many raw materials or parts, many products are made from one "unit" of raw material. To allocate the cost of the animal "on the hoof" into the cost of ribs, chucks, and shoulders, for instance, is a practical

Objective ❷
Identify when inventories are valued at net realizable value.

 **INTERNATIONAL INSIGHT**

In the Netherlands, Canada, and the United Kingdom, inventory is valued at "lower of cost or market," but in contrast to the U.S., *market* in these nations is defined as "net realizable value." The U.S. is the only country that defines *market* as something other than net realizable value.

---

[6]Manufacturing companies frequently employ a **standardized cost system** that predetermines the unit costs for material, labor, and manufacturing overhead and values raw materials, work in process, and finished goods inventories at their standard costs. For financial reporting purposes the pricing of inventories at standard costs is acceptable if there is no significant difference between the actual costs and standard costs. If there is a significant difference, the inventory amounts should be adjusted to actual cost. In *Accounting Research and Terminology Bulletin, Final Edition* the profession notes that **"standard costs are acceptable if adjusted at reasonable intervals to reflect current conditions."** Burlington Industries, Syntex, Hewlett-Packard, and Westinghouse Electric are just a few of the many companies that use standard costs for valuing at least a portion of their inventory.

[7]*Accounting Research Study No. 13*, "The Accounting Basis of Inventories" (New York: AICPA, 1973) recommends that net realizable value be adopted. It also should be noted that a literal interpretation of the rules of lower of cost or market is frequently not applied in practice. For example, the lower limit, net realizable value less a normal markup, is rarely computed and applied because it results in an extremely conservative inventory valuation approach. In addition, inventory is often not reduced to market unless its disposition is expected to result in a loss. Furthermore, if the net realizable value of finished goods exceeds cost, it is usually assumed that both work in process and raw materials do as well. In practice, therefore, *ARB No. 43* is considered a guide, and professional judgment is often exercised in lieu of following this pronouncement literally.

impossibility. It is much easier and more useful to determine the market price of the various products and value them in the inventory at selling price less the various costs, such as shipping and handling, necessary to get them to market. Hence, because of a peculiarity of the meat-packing industry, **inventories are sometimes carried at sales price less distribution costs.**

Valuation Using Relative Sales Value

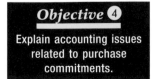

Objective ③
Explain when the relative sales value method is used to value inventories.

A special problem arises when a group of varying units is purchased at a single lump sum price, a so-called **basket purchase**. Assume that Woodland Developers purchases land for $1 million that can be subdivided in 400 lots. These lots are of different sizes and shapes but can be roughly sorted into three groups graded A, B, and C. As lots are sold, the purchase cost of $1 million is apportioned among the lots sold and the lots remaining on hand.

It is inappropriate to divide 400 lots into the total cost of $1 million to get a cost of $2,500 for each lot, because they vary in size, shape, and attractiveness. When such a situation is encountered—and it is not at all unusual—the common and most logical practice is to allocate the total cost among the various units on the basis of their relative sales value. For the example given, the allocation works out as follows:

ILLUSTRATION 9-10
Allocation of Costs, Using Relative Sales Value

Lots	Number of Lots	Sales Price Per Lot	Total Sales Price	Relative Sales Price	Total Cost	Cost Allocated to Lots	Cost Per Lot
A	100	$10,000	$1,000,000	100/250	$1,000,000	$ 400,000	$4,000
B	100	6,000	600,000	60/250	1,000,000	240,000	2,400
C	200	4,500	900,000	90/250	1,000,000	360,000	1,800
			$2,500,000			$1,000,000	

The cost of lots sold can be computed by using the amounts given in the column for "Cost Per Lot," and the gross profit is determined as follows:

ILLUSTRATION 9-11
Determination of Gross Profit, Using Relative Sales Value

Lots	Number of Lots Sold	Cost Per Lot	Cost of Lots Sold	Sales	Gross Profit
A	77	$4,000	$308,000	$ 770,000	$ 462,000
B	80	2,400	192,000	480,000	288,000
C	100	1,800	180,000	450,000	270,000
			$680,000	$1,700,000	$1,020,000

The ending inventory is therefore $320,000 ($1,000,000 − $680,000). This inventory amount can also be computed in another manner. The ratio of cost to selling price for all the lots is $1 million divided by $2,500,000, or 40%. Accordingly, if the total sales price of lots sold is, say $1,700,000, then the cost of these lots sold is 40% of $1,700,000, or $680,000. The inventory of lots on hand is then $1 million less $680,000, or $320,000.

The relative sales value method is used throughout the petroleum industry to value (at cost) the many products and by-products obtained from a barrel of crude oil.

Purchase Commitments—A Special Problem

Objective ④
Explain accounting issues related to purchase commitments.

In many lines of business, the survival and continued profitability of a firm depends on it having a sufficient stock of merchandise to meet all customer demands. Consequently, it is quite common for a company to agree to buy inventory weeks, months, or even years in advance. Such arrangements may be made on the basis of estimated or firm sales commitments by the company's customers. Generally, title to the merchandise or materials described in these purchase commitments has not passed to the buyer. Indeed, the goods may exist only as natural resources or, in the case of commodities, as unplanted seed, or in the case of a product, as work in process.

Usually it is neither necessary nor proper for the buyer to make any entries to reflect commitments for purchases of goods that have not been shipped by the seller. Ordinary orders, for which the prices are determined at the time of shipment and **which are subject to cancellation** by the buyer or seller, do not represent either an asset or a liability to the buyer. Therefore they need not be recorded in the books or reported in the financial statements.

Even with formal, noncancelable purchase contracts, no asset or liability is recognized at the date of inception, **because the contract is "executory" in nature:** neither party has fulfilled its part of the contract. However, if material, such contract details should be disclosed in the buyer's balance sheet in a note:

> **Note 1:** Contracts for the purchase of raw materials in 1999 have been executed in the amount of $600,000. The market price of such raw materials on December 31, 1998, is $640,000.

ILLUSTRATION 9-12
Disclosure of Purchase Commitment

In the foregoing illustration the contracted price was less than the market price at the balance sheet date. **If the contracted price is in excess of market and it is expected that losses will occur when the purchase is effected, losses should be recognized in the period during which such declines in market prices take place.**[8]

In the early 1980s, many Northwest forest product companies such as Boise Cascade, Georgia-Pacific, Weyerhaeuser, and St. Regis signed long-term timber-cutting contracts with the United States Forest Service. These contracts required that the companies pay $310 per thousand board feet for timber-cutting rights. Unfortunately, the market price for timber-cutting rights in late 1984 dropped to $80 per thousand board feet. As a result, a number of these companies had long-term contracts that, if fulfilled, projected substantial future losses.

To illustrate the accounting problem, assume that St. Regis Paper Co. signed timber-cutting contracts to be executed in 1999 at a firm price of $10,000,000 and that the market price of the timber cutting rights on December 31, 1998, dropped to $7,000,000. The following entry is made on December 31, 1998:

Estimated Loss on Purchase Commitments	3,000,000	
Estimated Liability on Purchase Commitments		3,000,000

UNDERLYING CONCEPTS

Reporting the loss is *conservative*. However, reporting the decline in market price is debatable because no asset is recorded. This area demonstrates the need for good definitions of assets and liabilities.

This loss would be reported in the income statement under Other Expenses and Losses. The Estimated Liability on Purchase Commitments is reported in the current liability section of the balance sheet because the contract is to be executed within the next fiscal year. When St. Regis cuts the timber at a cost of $10 million, the following entry would be made:

Purchases (Inventory)	7,000,000	
Estimated Liability on Purchase Commitments	3,000,000	
Cash		10,000,000

The company paid $10 million for a contract worth only $7 million. The loss was recorded in the previous period—when the price actually declined.

If the price is partially or fully recovered before the timber is cut, the Estimated Liability on Purchase Commitments is reduced. A resulting gain (Recovery of Loss) is then reported in the period of the price increase for the amount of the partial or full recovery. For example, Congress permitted some of these companies to buy out of their contracts at reduced prices in order to avoid some potential bankruptcies. To illustrate, assume that St. Regis is permitted to reduce its contract price and therefore its commitment by $1,000,000. The entry to record this transaction is as follows:

Estimated Liability on Purchase Commitments	1,000,000	
Recovery of Loss on Purchase Commitments		1,000,000

If the market price at the time the timber is cut is more than $2,000,000 below the contract price, St. Regis will have to recognize an additional loss in the period of cutting and record the purchase at the lower of cost or market.

---

[8]*Accounting Research Bulletin No. 43,* op. cit., par. 16.

The purchasers in purchase commitments can protect themselves against the possibility of market price declines of goods under contract by hedging. Hedging is accomplished through a futures contract in which the purchaser in the purchase commitment simultaneously contracts to a future sale of the same quantity of the same or similar goods at a fixed price. When a company holds a buy position in a purchase commitment and a sell position in a futures contract in the same commodity, it will be better off under one contract by approximately (maybe exactly) the same amount by which it is worse off under the other contract. That is, a loss on one will be offset by a gain on the other. For example, if St. Regis Paper Co. had hedged its purchase commitment contract by selling futures contracts for timber rights of the same amount, its loss of $3,000,000 on the purchase commitment would have been offset by a $3,000,000 gain on the futures contract.[9]

Accounting for purchase commitments (and, for that matter, all commitments) is unsettled and controversial. Some argue that these contracts should be reported as assets and liabilities at the time the contract is signed.[10] Others believe that the present recognition at the delivery date is more appropriate. *FASB Concepts Statement No. 6* states that "a purchase commitment involves both an item that might be recorded as an asset and an item that might be recorded as a liability. That is, it involves both a right to receive assets and an obligation to pay. . . . If both the right to receive assets and the obligation to pay were recorded at the time of the purchase commitment, the nature of the loss and the valuation account that records it when the price falls would be clearly seen." Although the discussion in *Concepts Statement No. 6* does not exclude the possibility of recording assets and liabilities for purchase commitments, it contains no conclusions or implications about whether they should be recorded.[11]

❖ THE GROSS PROFIT METHOD OF ESTIMATING INVENTORY

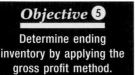

Objective ⑤

Determine ending inventory by applying the gross profit method.

Recall that the basic purpose of taking a physical inventory is to verify the accuracy of the perpetual inventory records or, if no records exist, to arrive at an inventory amount. Sometimes, taking a physical inventory is impractical. Then, substitute measures are used to approximate inventory on hand. One substitute method of verifying or determining the inventory amount is called the gross profit method (often called the gross margin method). This method is widely used by auditors in situations (e.g., interim reports) where only an estimate of the company's inventory is needed. It is also used where either inventory or inventory records have been destroyed by fire or other catastrophe.

The gross profit method is based on three assumptions: (1) the beginning inventory plus purchases equal total goods to be accounted for; (2) goods not sold must be on hand; and (3) if the sales, reduced to cost, are deducted from the sum of the opening inventory plus purchases, the result is the ending inventory.

---

[9]A complete discussion regarding hedging and the use of derivatives such as futures is provided in an appendix to Chapter 18.

[10]See, for example, Yuji Ijiri; *Recognition of Contractual Rights and Obligations*, Research Report (Stamford, Conn.: FASB, 1980), who argues that firm purchase commitments should be capitalized. "Firm" means that it is unlikely that performance under the contract can be avoided without a severe penalty.

Also, see Mahendra R. Gujarathi and Stanley F. Biggs, "Accounting for Purchase Commitments: Some Issues and Recommendations," *Accounting Horizons*, September 1988, pages 75–78, who conclude, "Recording an asset and liability on the date of inception for the noncancelable purchase commitments is suggested as the first significant step towards alleviating the accounting problems associated with the issue. At year-end, the potential gains and losses should be treated as contingencies under FASB 5 which provides a coherent structure for the accounting and informative disclosure for such gains and losses."

[11]"Elements of Financial Statements," *Statement of Financial Accounting Concepts No. 6* (Stamford, Conn.: FASB, 1985), pars. 251–253.

To illustrate, assume that Cetus Corp. has a beginning inventory of $60,000 and purchases of $200,000, both at cost. Sales at selling price amount to $280,000. The gross profit on selling price is 30%. The gross margin method is applied as follows:

Beginning inventory (at cost)		$ 60,000
Purchases (at cost)		200,000
Goods available (at cost)		260,000
Sales (at selling price)	$280,000	
Less gross profit (30% of $280,000)	84,000	
Sales (at cost)		196,000
Approximate inventory (at cost)		$ 64,000

ILLUSTRATION 9-13
Application of Gross
Profit Method

All the information needed to compute Cetus' inventory at cost, except for the gross profit percentage, is available in the current period's records. The gross profit percentage is determined by reviewing company policies or prior period records. In some cases, this percentage must be adjusted if prior periods are not considered representative of the current period.[12]

Computation of Gross Profit Percentage

In most situations, the gross profit percentage is given as a percentage of selling price. The previous illustration, for example, used a 30% gross profit on sales. Gross profit on selling price is the common method for quoting the profit for several reasons: (1) Most goods are stated on a retail basis, not a cost basis. (2) A profit quoted on selling price is lower than one based on cost, and this lower rate gives a favorable impression to the consumer. (3) The gross profit based on selling price can never exceed 100%.[13]

In the previous example, the gross profit was a given. But how was that figure derived? To see how a gross profit percentage is computed, assume that an article cost $15.00 and sells for $20.00, a gross profit of $5.00. This markup is ¼ or 25% of retail and ⅓ or 33⅓% of cost:

$$\frac{\text{Markup}}{\text{Retail}} = \frac{\$ 5.00}{\$20.00} = 25\% \text{ at retail} \qquad \frac{\text{Markup}}{\text{Cost}} = \frac{\$ 5.00}{\$15.00} = 33\tfrac{1}{3}\% \text{ on cost}$$

ILLUSTRATION 9-14
Computation of Gross
Profit Percentage

Although it is normal to compute the gross profit on the basis of selling price, you should understand the basic relationship between markup on cost and markup on selling price.

---

[12]An alternative method of estimating inventory using the gross profit percentage, considered by some to be less complicated than the traditional method illustrated above, uses the standard income statement format as follows (assume the same data as in the Cetus Corp. illustration above):

Sales		$280,000		$280,000	
Cost of sales					
Beginning inventory	$ 60,000		$ 60,000		
Purchases	200,000		200,000		
Goods available for sale	260,000		260,000		
Ending inventory	(3) ?		(3) **64,000** Est.		
Cost of goods sold		(2) ?		(2)**196,000** Est.	
Gross profit on sales (30%)		(1) ?		(1) **84,000** Est.	

Compute the unknowns as follows: first the gross profit amount, then cost of goods sold, and then the ending inventory.
(1) $280,000 × 30% = $84,000 (gross profit on sales).
(2) $280,000 − $84,000 = $196,000 (cost of goods sold).
(3) $260,000 − $196,000 = $64,000 (ending inventory).

[13]The terms "gross margin percentage," "rate of gross profit," and "percentage markup" are synonymous, although "markup" is more commonly used in reference to cost and "gross profit" in reference to sales.

For example, assume that you were told that the markup on cost for a given item is 25%. What, then, is the **gross profit on selling price**? To find the answer, assume that the sale price of the item is $1.00. In this case, the following formula applies:

$$\text{Cost} + \text{Gross profit} = \text{Selling price}$$
$$C + .25C = SP$$
$$(1 + .25)C = SP$$
$$1.25C = \$1.00$$
$$C = \$0.80$$

The gross profit equals $0.20 ($1.00 − $0.80), and the rate of gross profit on selling price is therefore 20% ($0.20/$1.00).

Conversely, assume that you were told that the gross profit on selling price is 20%. What is the **markup on cost**? To find the answer, again assume that the sales price is $1.00. Again, the same formula holds:

$$\text{Cost} + \text{Gross profit} = \text{Selling price}$$
$$C + .20SP = SP$$
$$C = (1 - .20)SP$$
$$C = .80SP$$
$$C = .80(\$1.00)$$
$$C = \$0.80$$

Here, as in the example above, the markup equals $0.20 ($1.00 − $0.80) and the markup on cost is 25% ($0.20/$0.80).

Retailers use the following formulas to express these relationships:

ILLUSTRATION 9-15
Formulas Relating
to Gross Profit

$$\textbf{1. } \text{Gross profit on selling price} = \frac{\text{Percentage markup on cost}}{100\% + \text{Percentage markup on cost}}$$

$$\textbf{2. } \text{Percentage markup on cost} = \frac{\text{Gross profit on selling price}}{100\% - \text{Gross profit on selling price}}$$

To understand how these formulas are employed, consider the following calculations:

ILLUSTRATION 9-16
Application of Gross
Profit Formulas

Gross Profit on Selling Price	Percentage Markup on Cost
Given: 20% $\longrightarrow$	$\dfrac{.20}{1.00 - .20} = 25\%$
Given: 25% $\longrightarrow$	$\dfrac{.25}{1.00 - .25} = 33\frac{1}{3}\%$
$\dfrac{.25}{1.00 + .25} = 20\%$ $\longleftarrow$	Given: 25%
$\dfrac{.50}{1.00 + .50} = 33\frac{1}{3}\%$ $\longleftarrow$	Given: 50%

Because selling price is greater than cost, and with the gross profit amount the same for both, **gross profit on selling price will always be less than the related percentage based on cost.** It should be emphasized that sales may not be multiplied by a cost-based markup percentage; the gross profit percentage must be converted to a percentage based on selling price.

Gross profits are closely followed by managements and analysts. A small change in the gross profit rate can have a significant effect on the bottom line. In 1993, Apple Computer suffered a textbook case of shrinking gross profits. In response to pricing wars in the personal computer market, Apple was forced to quickly reduce the price of its signature Macintosh computers—reducing prices more quickly than it could reduce its costs. As a result its gross profit rate fell from 44% in 1992 to 40% in 1993.

While the drop of 4% may appear small, its impact on the bottom line caused Apple's stock price to drop from $57 per share on June 1, 1993, to $27.50 by mid-July 1993. A similar effect (a 40% plummet in stock price) occurred when Woolworth Corp. disclosed a "correction of gross profits" due to a reporting of inaccurate gross profits in at least three of the company's quarterly reports during the fiscal year ended January 29, 1994.[14]

Evaluation of Gross Profit Method

The gross profit method is not normally acceptable for financial reporting purposes because it provides only an estimate. A physical inventory is needed as additional verification that the inventory indicated in the records is actually on hand. Nevertheless, the gross profit method is permitted to determine ending inventory for interim (generally quarterly) reporting purposes provided the use of this method is disclosed. Note that the gross profit method will follow closely the inventory method used (FIFO, LIFO, average cost) because it is based on historical records.

What are the major disadvantages of the gross profit method? One major disadvantage is that **it provides an estimate**; as a result, a physical inventory must be taken once a year to verify that the inventory is actually on hand. Second, the gross profit method **uses past percentages** in determining the markup. Although the past can often provide answers to the future, a current rate is more appropriate. It is important to emphasize that whenever significant fluctuations occur, the percentage should be adjusted as appropriate. Third, **care must be taken in applying a blanket gross profit rate**. Frequently, a store or department handles merchandise with widely varying rates of gross profit. In these situations, the gross profit method may have to be applied by subsections, lines of merchandise, or a similar basis that classifies merchandise according to their respective rates of gross profit.

❖ RETAIL INVENTORY METHOD

Accounting for inventory in a retail operation presents several challenges. Retailers with certain types of inventory may use the specific identification method to value their inventories. Such an approach makes sense when individual inventory units are significant, such as automobiles, pianos, or fur coats. However, imagine attempting to use such an approach at Kmart, True-Value Hardware, Sears, or Bloomingdales—high-volume retailers that have many different types of merchandise. It would be extremely difficult to determine the cost of each sale, to enter cost codes on the tickets, to change the codes to reflect declines in value of the merchandise, to allocate costs such as transportation, and so on.

Objective **6**

Determine ending inventory by applying the retail inventory method.

An alternative is to compile the inventories at retail prices. In most retail concerns, an observable pattern between cost and price exists. Retail prices can therefore be converted to cost through formula. This method, called the retail inventory method, **requires that a record be kept of (1) the total cost and retail value of goods purchased, (2) the total cost and retail value of the goods available for sale, and (3) the sales for the period**.

Here is how it works: The sales for the period are deducted from the retail value of the goods available for sale, to produce an estimated inventory (goods on hand) at retail. The ratio of cost to retail for all goods passing through a department or firm is then determined by dividing the total goods available for sale at cost by the total goods available at retail. The inventory valued at retail is converted to ending inventory at cost by applying the cost-to-retail ratio. Use of the retail inventory method is very common. Safeway and Giant supermarkets both use the retail inventory method as do the department store chains of Dayton Hudson Corp. and Marshall Field and Company.

---

[14]"Two Top Woolworth Officers Step Down Amid Probe of Accounting Irregularities," *The Wall Street Journal*, April 4, 1994, p. A3.

The retail inventory method is illustrated below for Jordan-Guess Inc.

ILLUSTRATION 9-17
Retail Inventory Method

Jordan-Guess Inc. (current period)	Cost	Retail
Beginning inventory	$14,000	$ 20,000
Purchases	63,000	90,000
Goods available for sale	$77,000	110,000
Deduct sales		85,000
Ending inventory, at retail		$ 25,000
Ratio of cost to retail ($77,000 ÷ $110,000)		70%
Ending inventory at cost (70% of $25,000)		$ 17,500

To avoid a potential overstatement of the inventory, periodic inventory counts are made, especially in retail operations where loss due to shoplifting and breakage is common.

There are different versions of the retail inventory method—the conventional (lower of average cost or market) method, the cost method, the LIFO retail method, and the dollar-value LIFO retail method. Regardless of which version is used, the retail inventory method is sanctioned by the IRS, various retail associations, and the accounting profession. One of its advantages is that the inventory balance **can be approximated without a physical count**.

The retail inventory method is particularly useful for any type of interim report, because a fairly quick and reliable measure of the inventory value is usually needed. Insurance adjusters often use this approach to estimate losses from fire, flood, or other type of casualty. This method also acts as a **control device** because any deviations from a physical count at the end of the year have to be explained. In addition, the retail method **expedites the physical inventory count** at the end of the year. The crew taking the physical inventory need record only the retail price of each item; there is no need to look up each item's invoice cost, thereby saving time and expense.

Retail Method Terminology

The amounts shown in the Retail column of Illustration 9-17 represent the original retail prices, assuming no price changes. Sales prices are frequently marked up or down. For retailers, the term markup means an additional markup of the original retail price. (In another context, such as the gross profit discussion on page 460, we often think of markup on the basis of cost.) Markup cancellations are decreases in prices of merchandise that had been marked up above the original retail price.

Markdowns below the original sale prices may be necessary because of a decrease in the general level of prices, special sales, soiled or damaged goods, overstocking, and competition. Markdowns are common in retailing these days. Markdown cancellations occur when the markdowns are later offset by increases in the prices of goods that had been marked down—such as after a one-day sale, for example. Neither a markup cancellation nor a markdown cancellation can exceed the original markup or markdown.

To illustrate these different concepts, assume that the Designer Clothing Store recently purchased 100 dress shirts from Marroway, Inc. The cost for these shirts was $1,500, or $15.00 a shirt. Designer Clothing established the selling price on these shirts at $30.00 a shirt. The manager noted that the shirts were selling quickly, so he added a markup of $5.00 per shirt. This markup made the price too high for customers and sales lagged. The manager then reduced the price to $32.00. At this point we would say that Designer Clothing has had a markup of $5.00 and a markup cancellation of $3.00. As soon as the major marketing season passed, the manager marked the remaining shirts down to a sales price of $23.00. At this point, an additional markup cancellation of $2.00 has taken place and a $7.00 markdown has occurred. If the shirts are later written up to $24.00, a markdown cancellation of $1.00 would occur.

Retail Inventory Method with Markups and Markdowns—Conventional Method

Retailers use markup and markdown concepts in developing the proper inventory valuation at the end of the accounting period. To obtain the appropriate inventory figures, proper treatment must be given to markups, markup cancellations, markdowns, and markdown cancellations.

To illustrate the different possibilities, consider the data for In-Fashion Stores Inc., shown in Illustration 9-18. In-Fashion's ending inventory at cost can be calculated under two assumptions, A and B (the reasons for the two will be explained later):

Assumption A: Computes a cost ratio after markups (and markup cancellations) but before markdowns.

Assumption B: Computes a cost ratio after both markups and markdowns (and cancellations).

ILLUSTRATION 9-18
Retail Inventory Method with Markups and Markdowns

	Cost	Retail
Beginning inventory	$ 500	$ 1,000
Purchases (net)	20,000	35,000
Markups		3,000
Markup cancellations		1,000
Markdowns		2,500
Markdown cancellations		2,000
Sales (net)		25,000

In-Fashion Stores Inc.

	Cost	Retail	
Beginning inventory	$ 500	$ 1,000	
Purchases (net)	20,000	35,000	
Merchandise available for sale	20,500	36,000	
Add:			
Markups	$3,000		
Less markup cancellations	(1,000)		
Net markups		2,000	
	20,500	38,000	
Cost-to-retail ratio $\frac{\$20,500}{\$38,000}$ = 53.9%...			(A)
Deduct:			
Markdowns		2,500	
Less markdown cancellations		(2,000)	
Net markdowns		500	
	$20,500	37,500	
Cost-to-retail ratio $\frac{\$20,500}{\$37,500}$ = 54.7%...			(B)
Deduct sales (net)		25,000	
Ending inventory at retail		$12,500	

The computations for In-Fashion Stores are:

> Ending inventory at retail × cost ratio = Value of ending inventory
> Assumption A: $12,500 × 53.9% = $6,737.50
> Assumption B: 12,500 × 54.7% = 6,837.50

The question becomes: Which assumption and which percentage should be employed to compute the ending inventory valuation?

The answer depends on the retail inventory method chosen. **The** conventional retail inventory method **uses assumption A only. It is designed to approximate the lower of average cost or market.** We will refer to this approach as the **lower of cost or**

market approach or **the conventional retail inventory method**. To understand why the markups but not the markdowns are considered in the cost percentage, we must understand how a retail outlet operates. Markup normally indicates that the market value of that item has increased. On the other hand, a markdown means that a decline in the utility of that item has occurred. Therefore, if we attempt to approximate the lower of cost or market, markdowns are considered a current loss and are not involved in the calculation of the cost-to-retail ratio. Thus, the cost-to-retail ratio is lower, which leads to an approximate lower of cost or market.

An example will make this clear. Two items were purchased for $5.00 apiece, and the original sales price was established at $10.00 each. One item was subsequently written down to $2.00. Assuming no sales for the period, **if markdowns are considered** in the cost-to-retail ratio (assumption B, above), we compute the ending inventory in the following manner:

ILLUSTRATION 9-19
Retail Inventory Method Including Markdowns— Cost Method

Markdowns Included in Cost-to-Retail Ratio		
	Cost	Retail
Purchases	$10.00	$20.00
Deduct markdowns		8.00
Ending inventory, at retail		$12.00
Cost-to-retail ratio $\dfrac{\$10.00}{\$12.00} = 83.3\%$		
Ending inventory at cost ($12.00 × .833) = $10.00		

This approach is the **cost method**. It reflects an average cost of the two items of the commodity without considering the loss on the one item.

If markdowns are not considered, the result is the lower of cost or market method (assumption A). The calculation is made as shown below.

ILLUSTRATION 9-20
Retail Inventory Method Excluding Markdowns— Conventional Method (LCM)

Markdowns Not Included in Cost-to-Retail Ratio		
	Cost	Retail
Purchases	$10.00	$20.00
Cost-to-retail ratio $\dfrac{\$10.00}{\$20.00} = 50\%$		
Deduct markdowns		8.00
Ending inventory, at retail		$12.00
Ending inventory, at cost ($12 × .50) = $6.00		

Under the conventional retail inventory method (when markdowns are **not** considered in computing the cost-to-retail ratio), the ratio would be 50% ($10.00/$20.00) and ending inventory would be $6.00 ($12.00 × .50).

The inventory valuation of $6.00 reflects two inventory items, one inventoried at $5.00, the other at $1.00. Basically, the sale price was reduced from $10.00 to $2.00 and the cost reduced from $5.00 to $1.00.[15] To approximate the lower of cost or market, therefore, the cost-to-retail ratio must be established by dividing the cost of goods available by the sum of the original retail price of these goods plus the net markups; the markdowns and markdown cancellations are excluded. The basic format for the retail inventory method using the lower of cost or market approach is shown in Illustration 9-21 using the In-Fashion Stores information.

---

[15]This figure is really not market (replacement cost), but is net realizable value less the normal margin that is allowed. In other words, the sale price of the goods written down is $2.00, but subtracting a normal margin of 50% ($5.00 cost, $10 price), the figure becomes $1.00.

ILLUSTRATION 9-21
Comprehensive
Conventional Retail
Inventory Method Format

In-Fashion Stores Inc.

	Cost		Retail
Beginning inventory	$ 500.00		$ 1,000.00
Purchases (net)	20,000.00		35,000.00
Totals	20,500.00		36,000.00
Add net markups—			
Markups		$3,000.00	
Markup cancellations		1,000.00	2,000.00
Totals	$20,500.00 ⟵	⟶	38,000.00
Deduct net markdowns—			
Markdowns		2,500.00	
Markdown cancellations		2,000.00	500.00
Sales price of goods available			37,500.00
Deduct sales (net)			25,000.00
Ending inventory, at retail			$12,500.00

$$\text{Cost-to-retail ratio} = \frac{\text{cost of goods available}}{\text{original retail price of goods available, plus net markups}}$$

$$= \frac{\$20,500}{\$38,000} = 53.9\%$$

Ending inventory at lower of cost or market (53.9% × $12,500.00)	$ 6,737.50

Because an averaging effect occurs, an exact lower of cost or market inventory valuation is ordinarily not obtained, but an adequate approximation can be achieved. In contrast, adding net markups **and** deducting net markdowns yields **approximate cost**.

Special Items Relating to Retail Method

The retail inventory method becomes more complicated when such items as freight-in, purchase returns and allowances, and purchase discounts are involved. **Freight costs** are treated as a part of the purchase cost; **purchase returns and allowances** are ordinarily considered both as a reduction of the price at cost and retail; and **purchase discounts** usually are considered as a reduction of the cost of purchases. When the purchase allowance is not reflected by a reduction in the selling price, no adjustment is made to the retail column. In short, the treatment for the items affecting the cost column of the retail inventory approach follows the computation for cost of goods available for sale.

Note also that **sales returns and allowances** are considered as proper adjustments to gross sales; **sales discounts**, however, are not recognized when sales are recorded gross. To adjust for the sales discount account in such a situation would provide an ending inventory figure at retail that would be overvalued.

In addition, a number of special items require careful analysis. **Transfers-in** from another department, for example, should be reported in the same way as purchases from an outside enterprise. **Normal shortages** (breakage, damage, theft, shrinkage) should reduce the retail column because these goods are no longer available for sale. Such costs are reflected in the selling price because a certain amount of shortage is considered normal in a retail enterprise. As a result, this amount is not considered in computing the cost to retail percentage. Rather, it is shown as a deduction similar to sales to arrive at ending inventory at retail. **Abnormal shortages** should be deducted from both the cost and retail columns and reported as a special inventory amount or as a loss. To do otherwise distorts the cost-to-retail ratio and overstates ending inventory. Finally, companies often provide their employees with special discounts to encourage loyalty, better performance, and so on. **Employee discounts** should be deducted from the retail column in the same way as sales. These discounts should not be considered in the cost-to-retail percentage because they do not reflect an overall change in the selling price.

Illustration 9-22 shows some of these concepts. The company, Feminine Executive Apparel, determines its inventory using the conventional retail inventory method.

ILLUSTRATION 9-22
Conventional Retail Inventory Method— Special Items Included

Feminine Executive Apparel		
	Cost	Retail
Beginning inventory	$ 1,000	$ 1,800
Purchases	30,000	60,000
Freight-in	600	—
Purchase returns	(1,500)	(3,000)
Totals	30,100	58,800
Net markups		9,000
Abnormal shortage	(1,200)	(2,000)
Totals	$28,900 ⟵————————⟶	65,800
Deduct:		
Net markdowns		1,400
Sales	$36,000	
Sales returns	(900)	35,100
Employee discounts		800
Normal shortage		1,300
		$27,200

$$\text{Cost-to-retail ratio} = \frac{\$28,900}{\$65,800} = 43.9\%$$

Ending inventory at lower of cost or market (43.9% × $27,200) = $11,940.80

Evaluation of Retail Inventory Method

The retail inventory method of computing inventory is used widely (1) to permit the computation of net income without a physical count of inventory, (2) as a control measure in determining inventory shortages, (3) in regulating quantities of merchandise on hand, and (4) for insurance information.

One characteristic of the retail inventory method is that it **has an averaging effect on varying rates of gross profit**. When applied to an entire business where rates of gross profit vary among departments, no allowance is made for possible distortion of results because of such differences. Some companies refine the retail method under such conditions by computing inventory separately by departments or by classes of merchandise with similar gross profits. In addition, the reliability of this method assumes that the distribution of items in inventory is similar to the "mix" in the total goods available for sale.

Objective ❼

Explain how inventory is reported and analyzed.

❖ PRESENTATION AND ANALYSIS

Presentation of Inventories

Accounting standards require financial statement disclosure of the composition of the inventory, inventory financing arrangements, and the inventory costing methods employed. The standards also require the consistent application of costing methods from one period to another.

Manufacturers should report the inventory composition either in the balance sheet or in a separate schedule in the notes. The relative mix of raw materials, work in process, and finished goods is important in assessing liquidity and in computing the stage of inventory completion.

Significant or unusual financing arrangements relating to inventories may require note disclosure. Examples are: transactions with related parties, product financing arrangements, firm purchase commitments, involuntary liquidation of LIFO inventories, and pledging of inventories as collateral. Inventories pledged as collateral for a loan should be presented in the Current Asset section rather than as an offset to the liability.

www.wiley.com/college/kieso

Go to our Web site for additional inventory disclosures.

The basis upon which inventory amounts are stated (lower of cost or market) and the method used in determining cost (LIFO, FIFO, average cost, etc.) should also be reported. For example, the annual report of Mumford of Wyoming contains the following disclosures:

ILLUSTRATION 9-23
Disclosure of Inventory
Methods

Mumford of Wyoming	
Note A: Significant Accounting Policies	
Live feeder cattle and feed—last-in, first-out (LIFO) cost, which is below approximate market	$854,800
Live range cattle—lower of principally identified cost or market	$1,240,500
Live sheep and supplies—lower of first-in, first-out (FIFO) cost or market	$674,000
Dressed meat and by-products—principally at market less allowances for distribution and selling expenses	$362,630

The preceding illustration shows that a company can use different pricing methods for different elements of its inventory. If Mumford changes the method of pricing any of its inventory elements, a change in accounting principle must be reported. For example, if Mumford changes its method of accounting for live sheep from FIFO to average cost, this change, along with the effect on income, should be separately reported in the financial statements. Changes in accounting principle require an explanatory paragraph in the auditor's report describing the change in method.

American Brands, Inc. reported its inventories in its Annual Report as follows (note the "trade practice" followed in classifying inventories among the current assets):

INTERNATIONAL INSIGHT

In Switzerland, inventory may be reported on the balance sheet at amounts substantially (one-third or more) below cost or market due to provisions of the tax code. Further, Swiss accounting principles do not require any specific disclosures related to inventories.

ILLUSTRATION 9-24
Disclosure of Trade
Practice in Valuing
Inventories

American Brands, Inc.	
Current assets	
Inventories (Note 2)	
Leaf tobacco	$ 563,424,000
Bulk whiskey	232,759,000
Other raw materials, supplies and work in process	238,906,000
Finished products	658,326,000
	1,693,415,000

Note 2: Inventories

Inventories are priced at the lower of cost (average; first-in, first-out; and minor amounts at last-in, first-out) or market. In accordance with generally recognized trade practice, the leaf tobacco and bulk whiskey inventories are classified as current assets, although part of such inventories due to the duration of the aging process, ordinarily will not be sold within one year.

The following inventory disclosures by Newmont Gold Company reveal the application of different bases of valuation, including market value, for different classifications of inventory.

ILLUSTRATION 9-25
Disclosure of Different
Bases of Valuation

Newmont Gold Company	
Current assets	
Inventories (Note 2)	$44,303,000
Noncurrent assets	
Inventories—ore in stockpiles (Note 2)	$5,250,000

Note 2: Inventories

Inventories included in current assets at December 31 were:

Ore and in-process inventory	$11,303,000
Gold bullion and gold precipitates	24,209,000
Materials and supplies	8,791,000
	$44,303,000

Ore and in-process inventory and materials and supplies are stated at the lower of average cost or net realizable value. Gold bullion and gold precipitates are stated at market value, less a provision for estimated refining and delivery charges. Expenditures capitalized as ore and in-process inventory include labor, material and other production costs.

Noncurrent inventories are stated at the lower of average cost or net realizable value and represent ore in stockpiles anticipated to be processed in future years.

Analysis of Inventories

The amount of inventory that a company carries can have significant economic consequences. As a result, inventories must be managed. But, inventory management is a double-edged sword that requires constant attention. On the one hand, management wants to have a great variety and quantity on hand so customers have the greatest selection and always find what they want in stock. However, such an inventory policy may incur excessive carrying costs (e.g., investment, storage, insurance, taxes, obsolescence, and damage). On the other hand, low inventory levels lead to stockouts, lost sales, and disgruntled customers. Financial ratios can be used to help chart a middle course between these two dangers. Common ratios used in the management and evaluation of inventory levels are inventory turnover and a related measure, average days to sell the inventory.

The inventory turnover ratio measures the number of times on average the inventory was sold during the period. Its purpose is to measure the liquidity of the inventory. A manager may extrapolate from past turnover experience how long the inventory now in stock will take to be sold. The inventory turnover is computed by dividing the cost of goods sold by the average inventory on hand during the period. Unless seasonal factors are significant, average inventory can be computed from the beginning and ending inventory balances. For example, in its 1996 annual report Campbell Soup Company reported a beginning inventory of $755,000,000, an ending inventory of $739,000,000, and cost of goods sold of $4,363,000,000 for the year. The inventory turnover formula and Campbell Soup's fiscal 1996 ratio computation are shown below:

ILLUSTRATION 9-26
Inventory Turnover Ratio

$$\text{Inventory Turnover} = \frac{\text{Cost of Goods Sold}}{\text{Average Inventory}}$$

$$= \frac{\$4,363,000,000}{\dfrac{\$755,000,000 + \$739,000,000}{2}} = 5.8 \text{ times}$$

A variant of the inventory turnover ratio is the average days to sell inventory, which represents the average number of days sales for which inventory is on hand. For example, the inventory turnover for Campbell Soup Company of 5.8 times divided into 365 is approximately 63 days.

There are typical levels of inventory in every industry. However, companies that are able to keep their inventory at lower levels with higher turnovers than those of their competitors, and still satisfy customer needs, are the most successful.

SUMMARY OF LEARNING OBJECTIVES

① *Explain and apply the lower of cost or market rule.* If inventory declines in value below its original cost for whatever reason, the inventory should be written down to reflect this loss. The general rule is that the historical cost principle is abandoned when the future utility (revenue-producing ability) of the asset is no longer as great as its original cost.

② *Identify when inventories are valued at net realizable value.* Inventories are valued at net realizable value when (1) there is a controlled market with a quoted price applicable to all quantities, (2) no significant costs of disposal are involved, and (3) the cost figures are too difficult to obtain.

③ *Explain when the relative sales value method is used to value inventories.* When a group of varying units is purchased at a single lump sum price, a so-called basket purchase, the total purchase price may be allocated to the individual items on the basis of relative sales value.

④ *Explain accounting issues related to purchase commitments.* Accounting for purchase commitments is controversial. Some argue that these contracts should be reported as assets and liabilities at the time the contract is signed; others believe that the present recognition at the delivery date is most appropriate. The FASB neither excludes nor recommends the recording of assets and liabilities for purchase commitments but notes that if they were recorded at the time of commitment, "the nature of the loss and the valuation account that records it when the price falls would be clearly seen."

(5) *Determine ending inventory by applying the gross profit method.* The steps to determine ending inventory by applying the gross profit method are as follows: (1) Compute the gross profit percentage on selling price; (2) compute gross profit by multiplying net sales by the gross profit percentage; (3) compute cost of goods sold by subtracting gross profit from net sales; (4) compute ending inventory by subtracting cost of goods sold from total goods available for sale.

(6) *Determine ending inventory by applying the retail inventory method.* The steps to determine ending inventory by applying the conventional retail method are: (1) the sales for the period are deducted from the retail value of the goods available for sale to produce an estimated inventory at retail; (2) the ratio of cost to retail for all goods passing through a department or firm is then determined by dividing the total goods available for sale at cost by the total goods available at retail; (3) the inventory valued at retail is converted to approximate cost by applying the cost-to-retail ratio.

(7) *Explain how inventory is reported and analyzed.* Accounting standards require financial statement disclosure of: (1) the composition of the inventory (in a balance sheet or a separate schedule in the notes); (2) significant or unusual inventory financing arrangements; and (3) inventory costing methods employed (which may differ for different elements of inventory). Accounting standards also require the consistent application of costing methods from one period to another. Common ratios used in the management and evaluation of inventory levels are inventory turnover and a related measure, average days to sell the inventory.

Appendix 9A

LIFO Retail Methods

Many argue that the conventional retail method follows a flow assumption that does not match current cost against current revenues. They suggest that a LIFO assumption be adopted to obtain a better matching of costs and revenues.

❖ LIFO RETAIL METHODS

Many retail establishments have changed from the more conventional treatment to the LIFO retail method for the tax advantages associated with valuing inventories on a LIFO basis.

The application of LIFO retail is made under two assumptions: (1) stable prices and (2) fluctuating prices.

Objective ❽

After studying Appendix 9A, you should be able to: Determine ending inventory by applying the LIFO retail methods.

Stable Prices—LIFO Retail Method

Computing the final inventory balance assuming a LIFO flow is much more complex than the calculation for the conventional retail method. Under the LIFO retail method, **both markups and markdowns are considered** in obtaining the proper cost-to-retail percentage. Furthermore, since the LIFO method is concerned only with the additional layer, or the amount that should be subtracted from the previous layer, the beginning inventory is excluded from the cost-to-retail percentage. **A major assumption of the LIFO retail method—one that is debatable—is that the markups and markdowns apply only to the goods purchased during the current period and not to the beginning inventory.** In addition, to simplify the accounting, we have assumed that the price level has remained unchanged. The concepts are presented in Illustration 9A-1.

ILLUSTRATION 9A-1
LIFO Retail Method—
Stable Prices

	Cost	Retail
Beginning inventory—1998	$ 27,000	$ 45,000
Net purchases during the period	346,500	480,000
Net markups		20,000
Net markdowns		(5,000)
Total (excluding beginning inventory)	346,500 ⟷	495,000
Total (including beginning inventory)	$373,500	540,000
Net sales during the period		(484,000)
Ending inventory at retail		$ 56,000
Establishment of cost-to-retail percentage under assumptions of LIFO retail ($346,500 ÷ $495,000)		70%

Illustration 9A-2 indicates that the inventory is composed of two layers: the beginning inventory and the additional increase that occurred in the inventory this period (1998). If we start the next period (1999), the beginning inventory will be composed of those two layers, and if an increase in inventory occurs again, an additional layer will be added.

ILLUSTRATION 9A-2
Ending Inventory at LIFO
Cost, 1998—Stable Prices

Ending Inventory at Retail Prices—1998	Layers at Retail Prices		Cost-to-Retail (Percentage)		Ending Inventory at LIFO Cost
$56,000	→1997 $45,000	×	60%[a]	=	$27,000
	→1998 11,000	×	70	=	7,700
	$56,000				$34,700

[a] $\frac{\$27,000}{\$45,000}$ (prior year's cost-to-retail)

However, if the final inventory figure is below the beginning inventory, it is necessary to reduce the beginning inventory starting with the most recent layer. For example, assume that the ending inventory for 1999 at retail is $50,000. The computation of the ending inventory at cost is shown below.

ILLUSTRATION 9A-3
Ending Inventory at LIFO
Cost, 1999—Stable Prices

Ending Inventory at Retail Prices—1999	Layers at Retail Prices		Cost-to-Retail (Percentage)		Ending Inventory at LIFO Cost
$50,000	→1997 $45,000	×	60%	=	$27,000
	→1998 5,000	×	70	=	3,500
	$50,000				$30,500

Notice that the 1998 layer is reduced from $11,000 to $5,000.

Fluctuating Prices—Dollar-Value LIFO Retail Method

The computation of the LIFO retail method was simplified in the previous illustration because changes in the selling price of the inventory were ignored. Let us now assume that a change in the price level of the inventories occurs (as is usual). If the price level does change, **the price change must be eliminated** because we are measuring the real increase in inventory, not the dollar increase.

To illustrate, assume that the beginning inventory had a retail market value of $10,000 and the ending inventory a retail market value of $15,000. If the price level has risen from 100 to 125, it is inappropriate to suggest that a real increase in inventory of $5,000 has occurred. Instead, the ending inventory at retail should be deflated as indicated by the computation shown below.

Ending inventory at retail (deflated) $15,000 ÷ 1.25*	$12,000	
Beginning inventory at retail	10,000	
Real increase in inventory at retail	$ 2,000	
Ending inventory at retail on LIFO basis:		
First layer	$10,000	
Second layer ($2,000 × 1.25)	2,500	$12,500
*1.25 = 125 ÷ 100		

ILLUSTRATION 9A-4
Ending Inventory at Retail—Deflated and Restated

This approach is essentially the dollar-value LIFO method previously discussed in Chapter 8. In computing the LIFO inventory under a dollar-value LIFO approach, the dollar increase in inventory is found and deflated to beginning-of-the-year prices to determine whether actual increases or decreases in quantity have occurred. If an increase in quantities occurs, this increase is priced at the new index to compute the value of the new layer. If a decrease in quantities happens, it is subtracted from the most recent layers to the extent necessary.

The following computations, taken from Illustration 9A-4, illustrate the differences between the dollar-value LIFO retail method and the regular LIFO retail approach. Assume that the current 1998 price index is 112 (prior year = 100) and that the inventory ($56,000) has remained unchanged. In comparing these two illustrations, note that the computations involved in finding the cost-to-retail percentage are exactly the same. However, the dollar-value method determines the increase that has occurred in the inventory in terms of base-year prices.

	Cost	Retail
Beginning inventory—1998	$ 27,000	$ 45,000
Net purchases during the period	346,500	480,000
Net markups		20,000
Net markdowns		(5,000)
Total (excluding beginning inventory)	346,500 ⟶	495,000
Total (including beginning inventory)	$373,500	540,000
Net sales during the period at retail		(484,000)
Ending inventory at retail		$ 56,000
Establishment of cost-to-retail percentage under assumptions of LIFO retail ($346,500 ÷ $495,000)	70%	
A. Ending inventory at retail prices deflated to base year prices		
$56,000 ÷ 112 =	$50,000	
B. Beginning inventory (retail) at base-year prices	45,000	
C. Inventory increase (retail) from beginning of period	$ 5,000	

ILLUSTRATION 9A-5
Dollar-Value LIFO Retail Method—Fluctuating Prices

From this information, we compute the inventory amount at cost:

Ending Inventory at Base-Year Retail Prices—1998	Layers at Base-Year Retail Prices		Price Index (percentage)		Cost-to-Retail (percentage)		Ending Inventory at LIFO Cost
$50,000 →	1997	$45,000	× 100%	×	60%	=	$27,000
→	1998	5,000	× 112	×	70	=	3,920
		$50,000					$30,920

As illustrated above, layers of a particular year must be restated to the prices in effect in the year when the layer was added before the conversion to cost takes place.

Note the difference between the LIFO approach (stable prices) and the dollar-value LIFO method as indicated below:

	LIFO (stable prices)	LIFO (fluctuating prices)
Beginning inventory	$27,000	$27,000
Increment	7,700	3,920
Ending inventory	$34,700	$30,920

The difference of $3,780 ($34,700 − $30,920) is a result of an increase in the price of goods, not of an increase in the quantity of goods.

Subsequent Adjustments under Dollar-Value LIFO Retail

The dollar-value LIFO retail method follows the same procedures in subsequent periods as the traditional dollar-value method discussed in Chapter 8. That is, when a real increase in inventory occurs, a new layer is added. Using the data from the previous illustration, assume that the retail value of the 1999 ending inventory at current prices is $64,800, the 1999 price index is 120% of base-year, and the cost-to-retail percentage is 75%. In base-year dollars, the ending inventory is therefore $54,000 ($64,800/120%). The computation of the ending inventory at LIFO cost is as follows:

Ending Inventory at Base-Year Retail Prices—1999	Layers at Base-Year Retail Prices		Price Index (percentage)		Cost-to-Retail (percentage)		Ending Inventory at LIFO Cost
$54,000 →	1997	$45,000	× 100%	×	60%	=	$27,000
→	1998	5,000	× 112	×	70	=	3,920
→	1999	4,000	× 120	×	75	=	3,600
		$54,000					$34,520

Conversely, when a real decrease in inventory develops, previous layers are "peeled off" at prices in existence when the layers were added. To illustrate, assume that in 1999 the ending inventory in base-year prices is $48,000. The computation of the LIFO inventory is as follows:

Ending Inventory at Base-Year Retail Prices—1999	Layers at Base-Year Retail Prices		Price Index (percentage)		Cost-to-Retail (percentage)		Ending Inventory at LIFO Cost
$48,000 →	1997	$45,000	× 100%	×	60%	=	$27,000
→	1998	3,000	× 112	×	70	=	2,352
		$48,000					$29,352

The advantages and disadvantages of the lower of cost or market method (conventional retail) versus LIFO retail are the same for retail as for nonretail operations. As a practical matter, the selection of the retail inventory method to be used often involves determining which method provides a lower taxable income. Although it might appear that retail LIFO will provide the lower taxable income in a period of rising prices, such is not always the case. LIFO will provide an approximate current cost matching, but the ending inventory is stated at cost. The conventional retail method may have a large write-off because of the use of the lower of cost or market approach which may offset the LIFO current cost matching.

❖ CHANGING FROM CONVENTIONAL RETAIL TO LIFO

When changing from the conventional retail method to LIFO retail, neither a cumulative adjustment nor a retroactive adjustment can be made easily. Because conventional retail is a lower of cost or market approach, the beginning inventory must be restated to a cost basis. The usual approach is to compute the cost basis from the purchases of the prior year, adjusted for both markups and markdowns.[1] To illustrate, assume that Clark Clothing Store employs the conventional retail method but wishes to change to the LIFO retail method beginning in 1999. The amounts shown by the firm's books are as follows:

	At Cost	At Retail
Inventory, January 1, 1998	$ 5,210	$ 15,000
Net purchases in 1998	47,250	100,000
Net markups in 1998		7,000
Net markdowns in 1998		2,000
Sales in 1998		95,000

Ending inventory under the conventional retail method for 1998 is computed as shown in Illustration 9A-10.

	Cost	Retail
Inventory January 1, 1998	$ 5,210	$ 15,000
Net purchases	47,250	100,000
Net additional markups		7,000
	$52,460	122,000
Net markdowns		(2,000)
Sales		(95,000)
Ending inventory at retail		$ 25,000
Establishment of cost-to-retail percentage ($52,460 ÷ $122,000)	43%	
December 31, 1998, inventory at cost		
Inventory at retail		$ 25,000
Cost-to-retail ratio		43%
Inventory at cost under conventional retail		$ 10,750

ILLUSTRATION 9A-10
Conventional Retail Inventory Method

The ending inventory for 1998 under the LIFO retail method can then be quickly approximated in the following way.

---

[1]A logical question to ask is, "Why are only the purchases from the prior period considered and not also the beginning inventory?" Apparently the IRS believes that "the purchases only approach" provides a more reasonable cost basis. The IRS position is debatable. However, for our purposes, it seems appropriate to use the purchases only approach.

ILLUSTRATION 9A-11
Conversion to LIFO
Retail Inventory Method

December 31, 1998 inventory at LIFO cost			
	Retail	Ratio	LIFO
Ending inventory	$25,000 ×	45%ᵃ =	$11,250

ᵃThe cost-to-retail ratio was computed as follows:

$$\frac{\text{Net purchases at cost}}{\text{Net purchases at retail plus markups less markdowns}} = \frac{\$47,250}{\$100,000 + \$7,000 - \$2,000} = 45\%$$

The difference of $500 ($11,250 − $10,750) between the LIFO retail method and the conventional retail method in the ending inventory for 1998 is the amount by which the beginning inventory for 1999 must be adjusted. The entry to adjust the inventory to a cost basis is as follows:

Inventory	500	
Adjustment to Record Inventory at Cost		500

KEY TERMS

SUMMARY OF LEARNING OBJECTIVE FOR APPENDIX 9A

(8) *Determine ending inventory by applying the LIFO retail methods.* The application of LIFO retail is made under two assumptions: stable prices and fluctuating prices. *Procedures under stable prices:* (a) Because the LIFO method is a cost method, both the markups and the markdowns must be considered in obtaining the proper cost-to-retail percentage. (b) Since the LIFO method is concerned only with the additional layer, or the amount that should be subtracted from the previous layer, the beginning inventory is excluded from the cost-to-retail percentage. (c) The markups and markdowns apply only to the goods purchased during the current period and not to the beginning inventory. *Procedures under fluctuating prices:* The steps are the same as for stable prices except that in computing the LIFO inventory under a dollar-value LIFO approach, the dollar increase in inventory is found and deflated to beginning-of-the-year prices to determine whether actual increases or decreases in quantity have occurred. If quantities increase, this increase is priced at the new index to compute the new layer. If quantities decrease, the decrease is subtracted from the most recent layers to the extent necessary.

DAVID MINIKEN is a staff auditor with Sweeney Conrad, a Seattle-based CPA firm. Prior to joining Sweeney Conrad, Mr. Miniken held several accounting positions with Boeing, the giant aircraft company. He holds a B.A. in accounting from the University of Washington and an M.B.A. from Seattle University.

How did you happen to start your career with Boeing? Boeing's employment needs are very cyclical. I happened to drop off my resume in their application basket at the same moment that somebody had canceled an interview, and I was on top of the pile when they were looking for a replacement. At the time, there was a lot of hiring. My initial job was to be a cost accountant on the B-2 Bomber program. Because we're spending taxpayers' money, there are many more cost accountants employed on the military programs than in commercial aviation. I was an estimator who would negotiate contracts for spare parts. After the end of the Cold War, a lot of military programs were canceled, so I became an internal auditor for the company. At that point, Boeing's labor force was shrinking, and people who were not let go were seeing that they would not achieve management until the next wave of hiring occurred, which could have been several years.

Was it difficult to get into public accounting at this point? Finding the right job in public accounting wasn't easy, but once I was hired by Sweeney Conrad, the transition was relatively smooth. I sent my resume to all the large and midsized CPA firms in the area, but I was applying during the summer when the firms aren't hiring. Then, I got a call from a friend of my wife's who was the controller for a client of Sweeney Conrad.

She heard they had an opening, and things clicked fast. I was hired on the audit staff. Even though I had six years of experience, I knew that I would have to swallow some pride. Once I was hired and working with people five years younger than me, I went out of my way not to wear my master's degree on my sleeve or to talk about my years of experience. Not all of my experience translated into public accounting. I had been auditing inventory and overhead but had never touched cash or receivables. At Boeing, I did have the experience of working with organizations as large as Westinghouse and as small as a 30-person machine shop. I also had the advantage of having business experience and the ability to communicate with clients.

What topics from Intermediate Accounting are relevant to you now? One of my clients is a commodities broker that also maintains an inventory of paper products. I had to go back to the textbook to look at inventory valuation to see which costs should be included in inventory. In this commodity, the rail cost from source to destination can be well over half the total cost. Recently, I went to the textbook to refresh my memory on accounting for income taxes. That's one of the more advanced topics that senior auditors need to understand.

Note: All **asterisked** Questions, Brief Exercises, Exercises, Problems, and Conceptual Cases relate to material contained in the appendix to each chapter.

❖ QUESTIONS ❖

1 Where there is evidence that the utility of inventory goods, as part of their disposal in the ordinary course of business, will be less than cost, what is the proper accounting treatment?

2 Why are inventories valued at the lower of cost or market? What are the arguments against the use of the lower of cost or market method of valuing inventories?

3 What approaches may the accountant employ in applying the lower of cost or market procedure? Which approach is normally used and why?

4 In some instances accounting principles require a departure from valuing inventories at cost alone. Determine the proper unit inventory price in the following cases:

	Cases				
	1	2	3	4	5
Cost	$15.90	$16.10	$15.90	$15.90	$15.90
Net realizable value	14.30	19.20	15.20	10.40	16.40
Net realizable value less normal profit	12.80	17.60	13.75	8.80	14.80
Market (replacement cost)	14.80	17.20	12.80	9.70	16.80

5 What method(s) might be used in the accounts to record a loss due to a price decline in the inventories? Discuss.

6 What factors might call for inventory valuation at sales prices (net realizable value or market price)?

7 Under what circumstances is relative sales value an appropriate basis for determining the price assigned to inventory?

8 At December 31, 1999, James Arness Co. has outstanding purchase commitments for purchase of 150,000 gallons, at $6.40 per gallon, of a raw material to be used in its manufacturing process. The company prices its raw material inventory at cost or market, whichever is lower. Assuming that the market price as of December 31, 1999, is $5.90, how would you treat this situation in the accounts?

9 What are the major uses of the gross profit method?

10 Distinguish between gross profit as a percentage of cost and gross profit as a percentage of sales price. Convert the following gross profit percentages based on cost to gross profit percentages based on sales price: 20% and 33⅓%. Convert the following gross profit percentages based on sales price to gross profit percentages based on cost: 33⅓% and 60%.

11 Carole Lombard Co. with annual net sales of $6 million maintains a markup of 25% based on cost. Lombard's expenses average 15% of net sales. What is Lombard's gross profit and net profit in dollars?

12 A fire destroys all of the merchandise of Rosanna Arquette Company on February 10, 1999. Presented below is information compiled up to the date of the fire.

Inventory January 1, 1999	$ 400,000
Sales to February 10, 1999	1,750,000
Purchases to February 10, 1999	1,140,000
Freight-in to February 10, 1999	60,000
Rate of gross profit on selling price	40%

What is the approximate inventory on February 10, 1999?

13 What conditions must exist for the retail inventory method to provide valid results?

14 The conventional retail inventory method yields results that are essentially the same as those yielded by the lower of cost or market method. Explain. Prepare an illustration of how the retail inventory method reduces inventory to market.

15 (a) Determine the ending inventory under the conventional retail method for the furniture department of Gin Blossoms Department Stores from the following data.

	Cost	Retail
Inventory Jan. 1	$ 149,000	$ 283,500
Purchases	1,400,000	2,160,000
Freight-in	70,000	
Markups, net		92,000
Markdowns, net		48,000
Sales		2,235,000

(b) If the results of a physical inventory indicated an inventory at retail of $240,000, what inferences would you draw?

16 Bodeans Company reported inventory in its balance sheet as follows:

Inventories $115,756,800

What additional disclosures might be necessary to present the inventory fairly?

17 Of what significance is inventory turnover to a retail store?

*✱**18** What modifications to the conventional retail method are necessary to approximate a LIFO retail flow?

❖ BRIEF EXERCISES ❖

BE9-1 Batman Company has unfinished inventory on hand that will cost $2,000 to complete, at which time it can be sold for $10,000. Batman's normal profit margin is 25% of sales. Compute net realizable value (ceiling) and net realizable value less a normal profit margin (floor).

BE9-2 Robin Corporation has the following four items in its ending inventory:

Item	Cost	Replacement Cost	Net Realizable Value (NRV)	NRV Less Normal Profit Margin
Jokers	$2,000	$1,900	$2,100	$1,600
Penguins	5,000	5,100	4,950	4,100
Riddlers	4,400	4,550	4,625	3,700
Scarecrows	3,200	2,990	3,830	3,070

Determine the final lower of cost of market inventory value for each item.

BE9-3 Battletoads Inc. uses a perpetual inventory system. At January 1, 1999, inventory was $214,000 at both cost and market value. At December 31, 1999, the inventory was $286,000 at cost and $269,000 at market value. Prepare the necessary December 31 entry under (a) the direct method and (b) the indirect method.

BE9-4 PC Plus buys 1,000 computer game CDs from a distributor who is discontinuing those games. The purchase price for the lot is $6,000. PC Plus will group the CDs into three price categories for resale, as indicated below:

Group	No. of CDs	Price per CD
1	100	$ 5.00
2	800	10.00
3	100	15.00

Determine the cost per CD for each group, using the relative sales value method.

BE9-5 Beavis Company signed a long-term noncancelable purchase commitment with a major supplier to purchase raw materials in 1999 at a cost of $1,000,000. At December 31, 1998, the raw materials to be purchased have a market value of $930,000. Prepare any necessary December 31 entry.

BE9-6 Use the information for Beavis Company from BE9-5. In 1999, Beavis paid $1,000,000 to obtain the raw materials which were worth $930,000. Prepare the entry to record the purchase.

BE9-7 Big Hurt Corporation's April 30 inventory was destroyed by fire. January 1 inventory was $150,000, and purchases for January through April totaled $500,000. Sales for the same period were $700,000. Big Hurt's normal gross profit percentage is 31%. Using the gross profit method, estimate Big Hurt's April 30 inventory that was destroyed by fire.

BE9-8 Bimini Inc. had beginning inventory of $12,000 at cost and $20,000 at retail. Net purchases were $120,000 at cost and $170,000 at retail. Net markups were $10,000; net markdowns were $7,000; and sales were $157,000. Compute ending inventory at cost using the conventional retail method.

BE9-9 In its 1995 Annual Report, Deere and Company reported inventory of $721 million on Oct. 31, 1995, and $698 million on Oct. 31, 1994, cost of goods sold of $6,922 million for fiscal year 1995, and net sales of $8,830 million. Compute Deere and Company's inventory turnover and the average days to sell inventory for the fiscal year 1995.

*BE9-10 Use the information for Bimini Inc. from BE9-8. Compute ending inventory at cost using the LIFO retail method.

*BE9-11 Use the information for Bimini Inc. from BE9-8, and assume the price level increased from 100 at the beginning of the year to 120 at year-end. Compute ending inventory at cost using the dollar-value LIFO retail method.

❖ EXERCISES ❖

E9-1 (Lower of Cost or Market) The inventory of 3T Company on December 31, 1999, consists of these items:

Part No.	Quantity	Cost per Unit	Cost to Replace per Unit
110	600	$ 90	$100
111	1,000	60	52
112	500	80	76
113	200	170	180
120	400	205	208
121ᵃ	1,600	16	14
122	300	240	235

ᵃPart No. 121 is obsolete and has a realizable value of $0.20 each as scrap.

Instructions

(a) Determine the inventory as of December 31, 1999, by the lower of cost or market method, applying this method directly to each item.

(b) Determine the inventory by the lower of cost or market method, applying the method to the total of the inventory.

E9-2 (Lower of Cost or Market) Smashing Pumpkins Company uses the lower of cost or market method, on an individual-item basis, in pricing its inventory items. The inventory at December 31, 1999, consists of products D, E, F, G, H, and I. Relevant per-unit data for these products appear below:

	Item D	Item E	Item F	Item G	Item H	Item I
Estimated selling price	$120	$110	$95	$90	$110	$90
Cost	75	80	80	80	50	36
Replacement cost	120	72	70	30	70	30
Estimated selling expense	30	30	30	25	30	30
Normal profit	20	20	20	20	20	20

Instructions

Using the lower of cost or market rule, determine the proper unit value for balance sheet reporting purposes at December 31, 1999, for each of the inventory items above.

E9-3 (Lower of Cost or Market) Michael Bolton Company follows the practice of pricing its inventory at the lower of cost or market, on an individual-item basis.

Item No.	Quantity	Cost per Unit	Cost to Replace	Estimated Selling Price	Cost of Completion and Disposal	Normal Profit
1320	1,200	$3.20	$3.00	$4.50	$.35	$1.25
1333	900	2.70	2.30	3.50	.50	.50
1426	800	4.50	3.70	5.00	.40	1.00
1437	1,000	3.60	3.10	3.20	.25	.90
1510	700	2.25	2.00	3.25	.80	.60
1522	500	3.00	2.70	3.80	.40	.50
1573	3,000	1.80	1.60	2.50	.75	.50
1626	1,000	4.70	5.20	6.00	.50	1.00

Instructions

From the information above, determine the amount of Bolton Company inventory.

E9-4 (Lower of Cost or Market—Journal Entries) Corrs Company determined its ending inventory at cost and at lower of cost or market at December 31, 1998, and December 31, 1999. This information is presented below:

	Cost	Lower of cost or market
12/31/98	$346,000	$327,000
12/31/99	410,000	395,000

Instructions

(a) Prepare the journal entries required at 12/31/98 and 12/31/99, assuming that the inventory is recorded at market, and a periodic inventory system (direct method) is used.

(b) Prepare journal entries required at 12/31/98 and 12/31/99, assuming that the inventory is recorded at cost and an allowance account is adjusted at each year-end under a periodic system.

(c) Which of the two methods above provides the higher net income in each year?

E9-5 (Lower of Cost or Market—Valuation Account) Presented below is information related to Candlebox Enterprises:

	Jan. 31	Feb. 28	Mar. 31	Apr. 30
Inventory at cost	$15,000	$15,100	$17,000	$13,000
Inventory at the lower of cost or market	14,500	12,600	15,600	12,300
Purchases for the month		20,000	24,000	26,500
Sales for the month		29,000	35,000	40,000

Instructions

(a) From the information prepare (as far as the data permit) monthly income statements in columnar form for February, March, and April. The inventory is to be shown in the statement at cost, the gain or loss due to market fluctuations is to be shown separately, and a valuation account is to be set up for the difference between cost and the lower of cost or market.

(b) Prepare the journal entry required to establish the valuation account at January 31 and entries to adjust it monthly thereafter.

E9-6 (Lower of Cost or Market——Error Effect) Winans Company uses the lower of cost or market method, on an individual-item basis, in pricing its inventory items. The inventory at December 31, 1998, included Product X. Relevant per-unit data for Product X appear below:

Estimated selling price	$45
Cost	40
Replacement cost	35
Estimated selling expense	14
Normal profit	9

There were 1,000 units of Product X on hand at December 31, 1998. Product X was incorrectly valued at $35 per unit for reporting purposes. All 1,000 units were sold in 1999.

Instructions

Compute the effect of this error on net income for 1998 and the effect on net income for 1999 and indicate the direction of the misstatement for each year.

 E9-7 (Relative Sales Value Method) Phil Collins Realty Corporation purchased a tract of unimproved land for $55,000. This land was improved and subdivided into building lots at an additional cost of $34,460. These building lots were all of the same size but owing to differences in location were offered for sale at different prices as follows:

Group	No. of Lots	Price per Lot
1	9	$3,000
2	15	4,000
3	17	2,400

Operating expenses for the year allocated to this project total $18,200. Lots unsold at the year-end were as follows:

Group 1	5 lots
Group 2	7 lots
Group 3	2 lots

Instructions

At the end of the fiscal year Phil Collins Realty Corporation instructs you to arrive at the net income realized on this operation to date.

E9-8 (Relative Sales Value Method) Pretenders Furniture Company purchases, during 1999, a carload of wicker chairs. The manufacturer sells the chairs to Pretenders for a lump sum of $59,850, because it is discontinuing manufacturing operations and wishes to dispose of its entire stock. Three types of chairs are included in the carload. The three types and the estimated selling price for each are listed below.

Type	No. of Chairs	Estimated Selling Price Each
Lounge chairs	400	$90
Armchairs	300	80
Straight chairs	700	50

During 1999, Pretenders sells 200 lounge chairs, 100 armchairs, and 120 straight chairs.

Instructions

What is the amount of gross profit realized during 1999? What is the amount of inventory of unsold wicker chairs on December 31, 1999?

E9-9 (Purchase Commitments)   Marvin Gaye Company has been having difficulty obtaining key raw materials for its manufacturing process. The company therefore signed a long-term noncancelable purchase commitment with its largest supplier of this raw material on November 30, 1999, at an agreed price of $400,000. At December 31, 1999, the raw material had declined in price to $365,000.

Instructions
What entry would you make on December 31, 1999, to recognize these facts?

E9-10 (Purchase Commitments)   At December 31, 1999, Indigo Girls Company has outstanding noncancelable purchase commitments for 36,000 gallons, at $3.00 per gallon, of raw material to be used in its manufacturing process. The company prices its raw material inventory at cost or market, whichever is lower.

Instructions
  (a) Assuming that the market price as of December 31, 1999, is $3.30, how would this matter be treated in the accounts and statements? Explain.
  (b) Assuming that the market price as of December 31, 1999, is $2.70, instead of $3.30, how would you treat this situation in the accounts and statements?
  (c) Give the entry in January 2000, when the 36,000-gallon shipment is received, assuming that the situation given in (b) above existed at December 31, 1999, and that the market price in January 2000 was $2.70 per gallon. Give an explanation of your treatment.

E9-11 (Gross Profit Method)   Each of the following gross profit percentages is expressed in terms of cost.

  1. 20%.   **3.** 33⅓%.
  2. 25%.   **4.** 50%.

Instructions
Indicate the gross profit percentage in terms of sales for each of the above.

E9-12 (Gross Profit Method)   Mark Price Company uses the gross profit method to estimate inventory for monthly reporting purposes. Presented below is information for the month of May:

Inventory, May 1	$ 160,000
Purchases (gross)	640,000
Freight-in	30,000
Sales	1,000,000
Sales returns	70,000
Purchase discounts	12,000

Instructions
  (a) Compute the estimated inventory at May 31, assuming that the gross profit is 30% of sales.
  (b) Compute the estimated inventory at May 31, assuming that the gross profit is 30% of cost.

E9-13 (Gross Profit Method)   Tim Legler requires an estimate of the cost of goods lost by fire on March 9. Merchandise on hand on January 1 was $38,000. Purchases since January 1 were $72,000; freight-in, $3,400; purchase returns and allowances, $2,400. Sales are made at 33⅓% above cost and totaled $100,000 to March 9. Goods costing $10,900 were left undamaged by the fire; remaining goods were destroyed.

Instructions
  (a) Compute the cost of goods destroyed.
  (b) Compute the cost of goods destroyed, assuming that the gross profit is 33⅓% of sales.

E9-14 (Gross Profit Method)   Rasheed Wallace Company lost most of its inventory in a fire in December just before the year-end physical inventory was taken. The corporation's books disclosed the following:

Beginning inventory	$170,000	Sales	$650,000
Purchases for the year	390,000	Sales returns	24,000
Purchase returns	30,000	Rate of gross margin on sales	40%

Merchandise with a selling price of $21,000 remained undamaged after the fire. Damaged merchandise with an original selling price of $15,000 had a net realizable value of $5,300.

Instructions
Compute the amount of the loss as a result of the fire, assuming that the corporation had no insurance coverage.

E9-15 (Gross Profit Method)   You are called by Calbert Cheany of Bullets Inc. on July 16 and asked to prepare a claim for insurance as a result of a theft that took place the night before. You suggest that an inventory be taken immediately. The following data are available:

Inventory, July 1	$ 38,000
Purchases—goods placed in stock July 1–15	85,000
Sales—goods delivered to customers (gross)	116,000
Sales returns—goods returned to stock	4,000

Your client reports that the goods on hand on July 16 cost $30,500, but you determine that this figure includes goods of $6,000 received on a consignment basis. Your past records show that sales are made at approximately 40% over cost.

Instructions
Compute the claim against the insurance company.

E9-16 (Gross Profit Method) Gheorghe Moresan Lumber Company handles three principal lines of merchandise with these varying rates of gross profit on cost:

Lumber	25%
Millwork	30%
Hardware and fittings	40%

On August 18, a fire destroyed the office, lumber shed, and a considerable portion of the lumber stacked in the yard. To file a report of loss for insurance purposes, the company must know what the inventories were immediately preceding the fire. No detail or perpetual inventory records of any kind were maintained. The only pertinent information you are able to obtain are the following facts from the general ledger, which was kept in a fireproof vault and thus escaped destruction.

	Lumber	Millwork	Hardware
Inventory, Jan. 1, 1999	$ 250,000	$ 90,000	$ 45,000
Purchases to Aug. 18, 1999	1,500,000	375,000	160,000
Sales to Aug. 18, 1999	2,080,000	533,000	210,000

Instructions
Submit your estimate of the inventory amounts immediately preceding the fire.

E9-17 (Gross Profit Method) Presented below is information related to Warren Moon Corporation for the current year:

Beginning inventory	$ 600,000	
Purchases	1,500,000	
Total goods available for sale		$2,100,000
Sales		2,500,000

Instructions
Compute the ending inventory, assuming that (1) gross profit is 45% of sales; (2) gross profit is 60% of cost; (3) gross profit is 35% of sales; and (4) gross profit is 25% of cost.

E9-18 (Retail Inventory Method) Presented below is information related to Bobby Engram Company:

	Cost	Retail
Beginning inventory	$ 58,000	$100,000
Purchases (net)	122,000	200,000
Net markups		10,345
Net markdowns		26,135
Sales		186,000

Instructions
(a) Compute the ending inventory at retail.
(b) Compute a cost-to-retail percentage (round to two decimals).
    1. Excluding both markups and markdowns.
    2. Excluding markups but including markdowns.
    3. Excluding markdowns but including markups.
    4. Including both markdowns and markups.
(c) Which of the methods in (b) above (1, 2, 3, or 4)
    1. Provides the most conservative estimate of ending inventory?
    2. Provides an approximation of lower of cost or market?
    3. Is used in the conventional retail method?
(d) Compute ending inventory at lower of cost or market (round to nearest dollar).
(e) Compute cost of goods sold based on (d).
(f) Compute gross margin based on (d).

E9-19 (Retail Inventory Method)   Presented below is information related to Ricky Henderson Company.

	Cost	Retail
Beginning inventory	$ 200,000	$ 280,000
Purchases	1,375,000	2,140,000
Markups		95,000
Markup cancellations		15,000
Markdowns		35,000
Markdown cancellations		5,000
Sales		2,200,000

Instructions
Compute the inventory by the conventional retail inventory method.

E9-20 (Retail Inventory Method)   The records of Ellen's Boutique report the following data for the month of April.

Sales	$99,000	Purchases (at cost)	$48,000
Sales returns	2,000	Purchases (at sales price)	88,000
Additional markups	10,000	Purchase returns (at cost)	2,000
Markup cancellations	1,500	Purchase returns (at sales price)	3,000
Markdowns	9,300	Beginning inventory (at cost)	30,000
Markdown cancellations	2,800	Beginning inventory (at sales price)	46,500
Freight on purchases	2,400		

Instructions
Compute the ending inventory by the conventional retail inventory method.

E9-21 (Analysis of Inventories)   The financial statements of General Mills, Inc's. 1996 Annual Report disclose the following information:

(in millions)	May 26, 1996	May 28, 1995	May 29, 1994
Inventories	$395.5	$372.0	$360.4

	Fiscal Year	
	1996	1995
Sales	$5,416.0	$5,026.7
Cost of goods sold	$2,241.0	$2,123.0
Net income	$476.4	$367.4

Instructions
Compute General Mills' (a) inventory turnover and (b) the average days to sell inventory for 1996 and 1995.

***E9-22 (Retail Inventory Method—Conventional and LIFO)**   Helen Keller Company began operations on January 1, 1997, adopting the conventional retail inventory system. None of its merchandise was marked down in 1997 and, because there was no beginning inventory, its ending inventory for 1997 of $38,100 would have been the same under either the conventional retail system or the LIFO retail system. On December 31, 1998, the store management considers adopting the LIFO retail system, and desires to know how the December 31, 1998, inventory would appear under both systems. All pertinent data regarding purchases, sales, markups, and markdowns are shown below. There has been no change in the price level.

	Cost	Retail
Inventory, Jan. 1, 1998	$ 38,100	$ 60,000
Markdowns (net)		13,000
Markups (net)		22,000
Purchases (net)	130,900	178,000
Sales (net)		167,000

Instructions
Determine the cost of the 1998 ending inventory under both (1) the conventional retail method and (2) the LIFO retail method.

***E9-23 (Retail Inventory Method—Conventional and LIFO)**   Leonard Bernstein Company began operations late in 1997 and adopted the conventional retail inventory method. Because there was no beginning inventory for 1997 and no markdowns during 1997, the ending inventory for 1997 was $14,000 under both the conventional retail method and the LIFO retail method. At the end of 1998, management wants to compare the results of applying the conventional and LIFO retail methods. There was no change in the price level during 1998. The following data are available for computations:

	Cost	Retail
Inventory, January 1, 1998	$14,000	$20,000
Sales		80,000
Net markups		9,000
Net markdowns		1,600
Purchases	58,800	81,000
Freight-in	7,500	
Estimated theft		2,000

Instructions
Compute the cost of the 1998 ending inventory under both (1) the conventional retail method and (2) the LIFO retail method.

*E9-24 (Dollar-Value LIFO Retail) You assemble the following information for Seneca Department Store, which computes its inventory under the dollar-value LIFO method.

	Cost	Retail
Inventory on January 1, 1999	$216,000	$300,000
Purchases	364,800	480,000
Increase in price level for year		9%

Instructions
Compute the cost of the inventory on December 31, 1999, assuming that the inventory at retail is (1) $294,300, (2) $365,150.

*E9-25 (Dollar-Value LIFO Retail) Presented below is information related to Langston Hughes Corporation:

	Price Index	LIFO Cost	Retail
Inventory on December 31, 1999, when dollar-value LIFO is adopted	100	$36,000	$74,500
Inventory, December 31, 2000	110	?	100,100

Instructions
Compute the ending inventory under the dollar-value LIFO method at December 31, 2000. The cost-to-retail ratio for 2000 was 60%.

*E9-26 (Conventional Retail and Dollar-Value LIFO Retail) Black Feet Corporation began operations on January 1, 1998, with a beginning inventory of $30,100 at cost and $50,000 at retail. The following information relates to 1998:

	Retail
Net purchases ($108,500 at cost)	$150,000
Net markups	10,000
Net markdowns	5,000
Sales	126,900

Instructions
(a) Assume Black Feet decided to adopt the conventional retail method. Compute the ending inventory to be reported in the balance sheet.
(b) Assume instead that Black Feet decides to adopt the dollar-value LIFO retail method. The appropriate price indexes are 100 at January 1 and 110 at December 31. Compute the ending inventory to be reported in the balance sheet.
(c) On the basis of the information in part (b), compute cost of goods sold.

*E9-27 (Dollar-Value LIFO Retail) The Connie Chung Corporation adopted the dollar-value LIFO retail inventory method on January 1, 1997. At that time the inventory had a cost of $54,000 and a retail price of $100,000. The following information is available:

	Year-End Inventory at Retail	Current Year Cost—Retail %	Year-End Price Index
1997	$118,720	57%	106
1998	138,750	60%	111
1999	125,350	61%	115
2000	162,500	58%	125

The price index at January 1, 1997, is 100.

Instructions

Compute the ending inventory at December 31 of the years 1997–2000. Round to the nearest dollar.

*E8-28 (Change to LIFO Retail) John Olerud Ltd., a local retailing concern in the Bronx, N.Y., has decided to change from the conventional retail inventory method to the LIFO retail method starting on January 1, 1999. The company recomputed its ending inventory for 1998 in accordance with the procedures necessary to switch to LIFO retail. The inventory computed was $212,600.

Instructions

Assuming that John Olerud Ltd.'s ending inventory for 1998 under the conventional retail inventory method was $205,000, prepare the appropriate journal entry on January 1, 1999.

❖ PROBLEMS ❖

P9-1 (Lower of Cost or Market) Grant Wood Company manufactures desks. Most of the company's desks are standard models and are sold on the basis of catalog prices. At December 31, 1999, the following finished desks appear in the company's inventory:

Finished desks	A	B	C	D
1999 catalog selling price	$450	$480	$900	$1,050
FIFO cost per inventory list 12/31/99	470	450	830	960
Estimated current cost to manufacture (at December 31, 1999, and early 2000)	460	440	610	1,000
Sales commissions and estimated other costs of disposal	45	60	90	130
2000 catalog selling price	500	540	900	1,200

The 1999 catalog was in effect through November 1999, and the 2000 catalog is effective as of December 1, 1999. All catalog prices are net of the usual discounts. Generally, the company attempts to obtain a 20% gross margin on selling price and has usually been successful in doing so.

Instructions

At what amount should each of the four desks appear in the company's December 31, 1999, inventory, assuming that the company has adopted a lower of FIFO cost or market approach for valuation of inventories on an individual-item basis?

P9-2 (Lower of Cost or Market) T. Allen Home Improvement Company installs replacement siding, windows, and louvered glass doors for single family homes and condominium complexes in northern New Jersey and southern New York. The company is in the process of preparing its annual financial statements for the fiscal year ended May 31, 1998, and Tim Taylor, controller for T. Allen, has gathered the following data concerning inventory.

At May 31, 1998, the balance in T. Allen's Raw Material Inventory account was $408,000, and the Allowance to Reduce Inventory to Market had a credit balance of $29,500. Taylor summarized the relevant inventory cost and market data at May 31, 1998, in the schedule below.

Taylor assigned Patricia Richardson, an intern from a local college, the task of calculating the amount that should appear on T. Allen's May 31, 1998, financial statements for inventory under the lower of cost or market rule as applied to each item in inventory. Richardson expressed concern over departing from the cost principle.

	Cost	Replacement Cost	Sales Price	Net Realizable Value	Normal Profit
Aluminum siding	$ 70,000	$ 62,500	$ 64,000	$ 56,000	$ 5,100
Cedar shake siding	86,000	79,400	94,000	84,800	7,400
Louvered glass doors	112,000	124,000	186,400	168,300	18,500
Thermal windows	140,000	122,000	154,800	140,000	15,400
Total	$408,000	$387,900	$499,200	$449,100	$46,400

Instructions

(a) 1. Determine the proper balance in the Allowance to Reduce Inventory to Market at May 31, 1998.
  2. For the fiscal year ended May 31, 1998, determine the amount of the gain or loss that would be recorded due to the change in the Allowance to Reduce Inventory to Market.
(b) Explain the rationale for the use of the lower of cost or market rule as it applies to inventories.

(CMA adapted)

P9-3 (Lower of Cost or Market) Jonathan Brandis Company is a food wholesaler that supplies independent grocery stores in the immediate region. The company has a perpetual inventory system for all of its food products. The first-in, first-out (FIFO) method of inventory valuation is used to determine the cost of the inventory at the end of each month. Transactions and other related information regarding two of the items (instant coffee and sugar) carried by Brandis are given below for October 1998, the last month of Brandis' fiscal year.

	Instant Coffee	Sugar
Standard unit of packaging:	Case containing 24, one-pound jars	Baler containing 12, five-pound bags
Inventory, 10/1/98:	1,000 cases @ $60.20 per case	500 balers @ $6.50 per baler
Purchases:	**1.** 10/10/98—1,600 cases @ $62.10 per case plus freight of $480.	**1.** 10/5/98—850 balers @ $5.76 per baler plus freight of $320.
	2. 10/20/98—2,400 cases @ $64.00 per case plus freight of $480.	**2.** 10/16/98—640 balers @ $6.00 per baler plus freight of $320.
		3. 10/24/98—600 balers @ $6.20 per baler plus freight of $360.
Purchase terms:	2/10, net/30, f.o.b. shipping point	Net 30 days, f.o.b. shipping point
October sales:	3,600 cases @ $76.00 per case	1,950 balers @ $8.00 per baler
Returns and allowances:	A customer returned 50 cases that had been shipped by error. The customer's account was credited for $3,800.	As the October 16 purchase was unloaded, 20 balers were discovered damaged. A representative of the trucking firm confirmed the damage and the balers were discarded. Credit of $120 for the merchandise and $10 for the freight was received by Brandis.
Inventory values 10/31/98:		
• Net realizable value	$66.00 per case	$6.60 per baler
• Net realizable value less a normal profit of 15%	$56.10 per case	$5.61 per baler

Brandis' sales terms are 1/10, net/30, f.o.b. shipping point. Brandis records all purchases net of purchase discounts and takes all purchase discounts. The most recent quoted price for coffee is $60 per case and for sugar $6.10 per baler before freight and purchase discounts.

Instructions

(a) Calculate the number of units in inventory and the FIFO unit cost for instant coffee and sugar as of October 31, 1998.

(b) Brandis Company applies the lower of cost or market rule in valuing its year-end inventory. Calculate the total dollar amount of the inventory for instant coffee and sugar applying the lower of cost or market rule on an individual-product basis.

(c) Could Brandis Company apply the lower of cost or market rule to groups of products or the inventory as a whole rather than on an individual product basis? Explain your answer.

(CMA adapted)

P9-4 (Entries for Lower of Cost or Market—Direct and Allowance) Mary Stuart Company determined its ending inventory at cost and at lower of cost or market at December 31, 1997, December 31, 1998, and December 31, 1999, as shown below:

	Cost	Lower of Cost or Market
12/31/97	$650,000	$650,000
12/31/98	780,000	722,000
12/31/99	900,000	830,000

Instructions

(a) Prepare the journal entries required at 12/31/98 and 12/31/99 assuming that a periodic inventory system and the direct method of adjusting to market is used.

(b) Prepare the journal entries required at 12/31/98 and 12/31/99 assuming that a periodic inventory is recorded at cost and reduced to market through the use of an allowance account (indirect method).

P9-5 (Gross Profit Method) David Hasselholf Company lost most of its inventory in a fire in December just before the year-end physical inventory was taken. Corporate records disclose the following:

Inventory (beginning)	$ 80,000	Sales	$415,000
Purchases	280,000	Sales returns	21,000
Purchase returns	28,000	Gross profit % based on selling price	34%

Merchandise with a selling price of $30,000 remained undamaged after the fire, and damaged merchandise has a salvage value of $7,150. The company does not carry fire insurance on its inventory.

Instructions
Prepare a formal labeled schedule computing the fire loss incurred. (Do not use the retail inventory method.)

P9-6 (Gross Profit Method)   On April 15, 1999, fire damaged the office and warehouse of John Kimmel Corporation. The only accounting record saved was the general ledger, from which the trial balance below was prepared.

John Kimmel Corporation
TRIAL BALANCE
March 31, 1999

Cash	$ 20,000	
Accounts receivable	40,000	
Inventory, December 31, 1998	75,000	
Land	35,000	
Building and equipment	110,000	
Accumulated depreciation		$ 41,300
Other assets	3,600	
Accounts payable		23,700
Other expense accruals		10,200
Capital stock		100,000
Retained earnings		52,000
Sales		135,000
Purchases	52,000	
Other expenses	26,600	
	$362,200	$362,200

The following data and information have been gathered:

1. The fiscal year of the corporation ends on December 31.
2. An examination of the April bank statement and canceled checks revealed that checks written during the period April 1–15 totaled $13,000: $5,700 paid to accounts payable as of March 31, $3,400 for April merchandise shipments, and $3,900 paid for other expenses. Deposits during the same period amounted to $12,950, which consisted of receipts on account from customers with the exception of a $950 refund from a vendor for merchandise returned in April.
3. Correspondence with suppliers revealed unrecorded obligations at April 15 of $10,600 for April merchandise shipments, including $2,300 for shipments in transit (FOB Shipping Point) on that date.
4. Customers acknowledged indebtedness of $36,000 at April 15, 1999. It was also estimated that customers owed another $8,000 that will never be acknowledged or recovered. Of the acknowledged indebtedness, $600 will probably be uncollectible.
5. The companies insuring the inventory agreed that the corporation's fire-loss claim should be based on the assumption that the overall gross profit ratio for the past 2 years was in effect during the current year. The corporation's audited financial statements disclosed this information:

	Year Ended December 31	
	1998	1997
Net sales	$530,000	$390,000
Net purchases	280,000	235,000
Beginning inventory	50,000	75,200
Ending inventory	75,000	50,000

6. Inventory with a cost of $7,000 was salvaged and sold for $3,500. The balance of the inventory was a total loss.

Instructions

Prepare a schedule computing the amount of inventory fire loss. The supporting schedule of the computation of the gross profit should be in good form.

(AICPA adapted)

P9-7 (Retail Inventory Method) The records for Clothing Department of Magdalena Aguilar's Discount Store are summarized below for the month of January.

Inventory; January 1:   at retail, $25,000; at cost, $17,000
Purchases in January: at retail, $137,000; at cost, $86,500
Freight-in: $7,000
Purchase returns: at retail, $3,000; at cost, $2,300
Purchase allowances: $2,200
Transfers in from suburb branch: at retail, $13,000; at cost, $9,200
Net markups: $8,000
Net markdowns: $4,000
Inventory losses due to normal breakage, etc.:   at retail, $400
Sales at retail: $85,000
Sales returns: $2,400

Instructions

Compute the inventory for this department as of January 31, at (1) retail and (2) lower of average cost or market.

P9-8 (Retail Inventory Method) Presented below is information related to Edward Braddock Inc.

	Cost	Retail
Inventory 12/31/1998	$250,000	$ 390,000
Purchases	914,500	1,460,000
Purchase returns	60,000	80,000
Purchase discounts	18,000	—
Gross sales (after employee discounts)	—	1,460,000
Sales returns	—	97,500
Markups	—	120,000
Markup cancellations	—	40,000
Markdowns	—	45,000
Markdown cancellations	—	20,000
Freight-in	79,000	—
Employee discounts granted	—	8,000
Loss from breakage (normal)	—	2,500

Instructions

Assuming that Edward Braddock Inc. uses the conventional retail inventory method, compute the cost of their ending inventory at December 31, 1999.

P9-9 (Retail Inventory Method) Jared Jones Inc. uses the retail inventory method to estimate ending inventory for its monthly financial statements. The following data pertain to a single department for the month of October 1999.

Inventory, October 1, 1999	
At cost	$ 52,000
At retail	78,000
Purchases (exclusive of freight and returns):	
At cost	262,000
At retail	423,000
Freight-in	16,600
Purchase returns	
At cost	5,600
At retail	8,000
Additional markups	9,000
Markup cancellations	2,000
Markdowns (net)	3,600
Normal spoilage and breakage	10,000
Sales	380,000

Instructions

(a) Using the conventional retail method, prepare a schedule computing estimated lower of cost or market inventory for October 31, 1999.

(b) A department store using the conventional retail inventory method estimates the cost of its ending inventory as $60,000. An accurate physical count reveals only $47,000 of inventory at lower of cost or market. List the factors that may have caused the difference between the computed inventory and the physical count.

P9-10 (Statement and Note Disclosure, LCM, and Purchase Commitment) Garth Brooks Specialty Company, a division of Fresh Horses Inc., manufactures three models of gear shift components for bicycles that are sold to bicycle manufacturers, retailers, and catalog outlets. Since beginning operations in 1969, Brooks has used normal absorption costing and has assumed a first-in, first-out cost flow in its perpetual inventory system. Except for overhead, manufacturing costs are accumulated using actual costs. Overhead is applied to production using predetermined overhead rates. The balances of the inventory accounts at the end of Brooks' fiscal year, November 30, 1998, are shown below. The inventories are stated at cost before any year-end adjustments.

Finished goods	$647,000
Work-in-process	112,500
Raw materials	240,000
Factory supplies	69,000

The following information relates to Brooks' inventory and operations.

1. The finished goods inventory consists of the items analyzed below.

	Cost	Market
Down tube shifter		
Standard model	$ 67,500	$67,000
Click adjustment model	94,500	87,000
Deluxe model	108,000	110,000
Total down tube shifters	270,000	264,000
Bar end shifter		
Standard model	83,000	90,050
Click adjustment model	99,000	97,550
Total bar end shifters	182,000	187,600
Head tube shifter		
Standard model	78,000	77,650
Click adjustment model	117,000	119,300
Total head tube shifters	195,000	196,950
Total finished goods	$647,000	$648,550

2. One-half of the head tube shifter finished goods inventory is held by catalog outlets on consignment.
3. Three-quarters of the bar end shifter finished goods inventory has been pledged as collateral for a bank loan.
4. One-half of the raw materials balance represents derailleurs acquired at a contracted price 20 percent above the current market price. The market value of the rest of the raw materials is $127,400.
5. The total market value of the work-in-process inventory is $108,700.
6. Included in the cost of factory supplies are obsolete items with an historical cost of $4,200. The market value of the remaining factory supplies is $65,900.
7. Brooks applies the lower of cost or market method to each of the three types of shifters in finished goods inventory. For each of the other three inventory accounts, Brooks applies the lower of cost or market method to the total of each inventory account.
8. Consider all amounts presented above to be material in relation to Brooks' financial statements taken as a whole.

Instructions
(a) Prepare the inventory section of Brooks' Statement of Financial Position as of November 30, 1998, including any required note(s).
(b) Without prejudice to your answer to requirement (a), assume that the market value of Brooks' inventories is less than cost. Explain how this decline would be presented in Brooks' income statement for the fiscal year ended November 30, 1998.
(c) Assume that Brooks has a firm purchase commitment for the same type of derailleur included in the raw materials inventory as of November 30, 1998, and that the purchase commitment is at a contracted price 15 percent greater than the current market price. These derailleurs are to be delivered to Brooks after November 30, 1998. Discuss the impact, if any, that this purchase commitment would have on Brooks' financial statements prepared for the fiscal year ended November 30, 1998.

(CMA adapted)

*P9-11 (Conventional and Dollar-Value LIFO Retail) As of January 1, 1999, Carl Sandburg Inc. installed the retail method of accounting for its merchandise inventory.

To prepare the store's financial statements at June 30, 1999, you obtain these data.

	Cost	Selling Price
Inventory, January 1	$ 30,000	$ 43,000
Markdowns		10,500
Markups		9,200
Markdown cancellations		6,500
Markup cancellations		3,200
Purchases	108,800	155,000
Sales		159,000
Purchase returns and allowances	2,800	4,000
Sales returns and allowances		8,000

Instructions

(a) Prepare a schedule to compute Sandburg's June 30, 1999, inventory under the conventional retail method of accounting for inventories.

(b) Without prejudice to your solution to part (a), assume that you computed the June 30, 1999, inventory to be $54,000 at retail and the ratio of cost to retail to be 70%. The general price level has increased from 100 at January 1, 1999, to 108 at June 30, 1999. Prepare a schedule to compute the June 30, 1999, inventory at the June 30 price level under the dollar-value LIFO retail method.

(AICPA adapted)

*P9-12 (Retail, LIFO Retail, and Inventory Shortage) Late in 1995, Sara Teasdale and four other investors took the chain of Sprint Department Stores private, and the company has just completed its third year of operations under the ownership of the investment group. Elinor Wylie, controller of Sprint Department Stores, is in the process of preparing the year-end financial statements. Based on the preliminary financial statements, Teasdale has expressed concern over inventory shortages, and she has asked Wylie to determine whether an abnormal amount of theft and breakage has occurred. The accounting records of Sprint Department Stores contain the following amounts on November 30, 1998, the end of the fiscal year.

	Cost	Retail
Beginning inventory	$ 68,000	$100,000
Purchases	248,200	400,000
Net markups		50,000
Net markdowns		110,000
Sales		330,000

According to the November 30, 1998, physical inventory, the actual inventory at retail is $107,000.

Instructions

(a) Describe the circumstances under which the retail inventory method would be applied, and the advantages of using the retail inventory method.

(b) Assuming that prices have been stable, calculate the value, at cost, of Sprint Department Stores' ending inventory using the last-in, first-out (LIFO) retail method. Be sure to furnish supporting calculations.

(c) Estimate the amount of shortage, at retail, that has occurred at Sprint Department Stores during the year ended November 30, 1998.

(d) Complications in the retail method can be caused by such items as (1) freight-in expense, (2) purchase returns and allowances, (3) sales returns and allowances, and (4) employee discounts. Explain how each of these four special items is handled in the retail inventory method.

(CMA adapted)

*P9-13 (Change to LIFO Retail) Ulysses Grant Stores Inc., which uses the conventional retail inventory method, wishes to change to the LIFO retail method beginning with the accounting year ending December 31, 1998.

Amounts as shown below appear on the store's books before adjustment:

	At Cost	At Retail
Inventory, January 1, 1998	$ 13,600	$ 24,000
Purchases in 1998	116,200	184,000
Markups in 1998		12,000
Markdowns in 1998		5,500
Sales in 1998		170,000

You are to assume that all markups and markdowns apply to 1998 purchases, and that it is appropriate to treat the entire inventory as a single department.

Instructions

Compute the inventory at December 31, 1998, under:

(a) Conventional retail method.

(b) Last-in, first-out retail method, effecting the change in method as of January 1, 1998. Assume that the cost-to-retail percentage for 1997 was recomputed correctly in accordance with procedures necessary to change to LIFO. This ratio was 57%.

(AICPA adapted)

*P9-14 (Change to LIFO Retail; Dollar-Value LIFO Retail) Rudyard Kipling Department Store converted from the conventional retail method to the LIFO retail method on January 1, 1997, and is now considering converting to the dollar-value LIFO inventory method. During your examination of the financial statements for the year ended December 31, 1998, management requested that you furnish a summary showing certain computations of inventory cost for the past 3 years.

Here is the available information.

1. The inventory at January 1, 1996, had a retail value of $56,000 and cost of $26,700 based on the conventional retail method.

2. Transactions during 1996 were as follows:

	Cost	Retail
Gross purchases	$311,000	$554,000
Purchase returns	5,200	10,000
Purchase discounts	6,000	
Gross sales (after employee discounts)		551,000
Sales returns		9,000
Employee discounts		3,000
Freight-in	17,600	
Net markups		20,000
Net markdowns		12,000

3. The retail value of the December 31, 1997, inventory was $73,500, the cost ratio for 1997 under the LIFO retail method was 61%, and the regional price index was 105% of the January 1, 1997, price level.

4. The retail value of the December 31, 1998, inventory was $65,880, the cost ratio for 1998 under the LIFO retail method was 60%, and the regional price index was 108% of the January 1, 1997, price level.

Instructions

(a) Prepare a schedule showing the computation of the cost of inventory on hand at December 31, 1996, based on the conventional retail method.

(b) Prepare a schedule showing the recomputation of the inventory to be reported on December 31, 1996, in accordance with procedures necessary to convert from the conventional retail method to the LIFO retail method beginning January 1, 1997. Assume that the retail value of the December 31, 1996, inventory was $63,000.

(c) Without prejudice to your solution to part (b), assume that you computed the December 31, 1996, inventory (retail value $63,000) under the LIFO retail method at a cost of $34,965. Prepare a schedule showing the computations of the cost of the store's 1997 and 1998 year-end inventories under the dollar-value LIFO method.

(AICPA adapted)

❖ CONCEPTUAL CASES ❖

C9-1 (Lower of Cost or Market) You have been asked by the financial vice-president to develop a short presentation on the lower of cost or market method for inventory purposes. The financial VP needs to explain this method to the president, because it appears that a portion of the company's inventory has declined in value.

Instructions

The financial VP asks you to answer the following questions.

1. What is the purpose of the lower of cost or market method?

2. What is meant by market? (Hint: discuss the ceiling and floor constraints.)

3. Do you apply the lower of cost or market method to each individual item, to a category, or to the total of the inventory? Explain.
4. What are the potential disadvantages of the lower of cost or market method?

C9-2 (Lower of Cost or Market) YoYoMa Inc. manufactures and sells four products, the inventories of which are priced at cost or market, whichever is lower. A normal profit margin rate of 30% is usually maintained on each of the four products.

The following information was compiled as of December 31, 1998.

Product	Original Cost	Cost to Replace	Estimated Cost to Dispose	Expected Selling Price[a]
A	$17.50	$14.00	$ 6.00	$ 30.00
B	48.00	78.00	26.00	100.00
C	35.00	42.00	15.00	80.00
D	47.50	45.00	20.50	95.00

[a]Normal margin is 30% of selling price.

Instructions
(a) Why are expected selling prices important in the application of the lower of cost or market rule?
(b) Prepare a schedule containing unit values (including "floor" and "ceiling") for determining the lower of cost or market on an individual-product basis. The last column of the schedule should contain for each product the unit value for the purpose of inventory valuation resulting from the application of the lower of cost or market rule.

C9-3 (Lower of Cost or Market) Lena Horne Corporation purchased a significant amount of raw materials inventory for a new product that it is manufacturing.

Horne uses the lower of cost or market rule for these raw materials. The replacement cost of the raw materials is above the net realizable value and both are below the original cost.

Horne uses the average cost inventory method for these raw materials. In the last 2 years, each purchase has been at a lower price than the previous purchase, and the ending inventory quantity for each period has been higher than the beginning inventory quantity for that period.

Instructions
(a) 1. At which amount should Horne's raw materials inventory be reported on the balance sheet? Why?
  2. In general, why is the lower of cost or market rule used to report inventory?
(b) What would have been the effect on ending inventory and cost of goods sold had Horne used the LIFO inventory method instead of the average cost inventory method for the raw materials? Why?

C9-4 (Retail Inventory Method) Aragon Company, your client, manufactures paint. The company's president, Ms. Catherine Aragon, has decided to open a retail store to sell Aragon paint as well as wallpaper and other supplies that would be purchased from other suppliers. She has asked you for information about the conventional retail method of pricing inventories at the retail store.

Instructions
Prepare a report to the president explaining the retail method of pricing inventories. Your report should include these points:
(a) Description and accounting features of the method.
(b) The conditions that may distort the results under the method.
(c) A comparison of the advantages of using the retail method with those of using cost methods of inventory pricing.
(d) The accounting theory underlying the treatment of net markdowns and net markups under the method.

(AICPA adapted)

C9-5 (Cost Determination, LCM, Retail Method) E. A. Poe Corporation, a retailer and wholesaler of national brand-name household lighting fixtures, purchases its inventories from various suppliers.

Instructions
(a) 1. What criteria should be used to determine which of Poe's costs are inventoriable?
  2. Are Poe's administrative costs inventoriable? Defend your answer.
(b) 1. Poe uses the lower of cost or market rule for its wholesale inventories. What are the theoretical arguments for that rule?

    2. The replacement cost of the inventories is below the net realizable value less a normal profit margin, which, in turn, is below the original cost. What amount should be used to value the inventories? Why?

(c) Poe calculates the estimated cost of its ending inventories held for sale at retail using the conventional retail inventory method. How would Poe treat the beginning inventories and net markdowns in calculating the cost ratio used to determine its ending inventories? Why?

(AICPA adapted)

*C9-6 (Retail Inventory Method and LIFO Retail)   Presented below are a number of items that may be encountered in computing the cost to retail percentage when using the conventional retail method or the LIFO retail method.

  1. Markdowns.
  2. Markdown cancellations.
  3. Cost of items transferred in from other departments.
  4. Retail value of items transferred in from other departments.
  5. Sales discounts.
  6. Purchases discounts (purchases recorded gross).
  7. Estimated retail value of goods broken or stolen.
  8. Cost of beginning inventory.
  9. Retail value of beginning inventory.
 10. Cost of purchases.
 11. Retail value of purchases.
 12. Markups.
 13. Markup cancellations.
 14. Employee discounts (sales recorded net).

Instructions

For each of the items listed above, indicate whether this item would be considered in the cost to retail percentage under (1) conventional retail, (2) LIFO retail.

❖FINANCIAL REPORTING PROBLEM—INTEL CORPORATION

The financial statements of Intel are presented in Appendix 5B

Instructions

Refer to these financial statements and the accompanying notes to answer the following questions.

(a) How does Intel value its inventories? Which inventory costing method does Intel use as a basis for reporting its inventories?

(b) How does Intel report its inventories in the balance sheet? In the notes to its financial statements, what three descriptions are used to classify its inventories?

(c) What was the dollar amount and percentage change in Intel's inventories from December 31, 1994, to December 31, 1995? What does Intel give as an explanation for this significant change in investment in inventories?

(d) What was Intel's inventory turnover ratio in 1995? What is its gross profit percentage? Evaluate Intel's inventory turnover ratio and gross profit percentage.

❖FINANCIAL STATEMENT ANALYSIS CASES

Case 1 (Prab Robots, Inc.)

Prab Robots, Inc., reported the following information regarding 1991–1992 inventory:

Prab Robots, Inc.

	1992	1991
Current Assets		
Cash	$ 153,010	$ 538,489
Accounts receivable, net of allowance for doubtful accounts of $46,000 in 1992 and $160,000 in 1991	1,627,980	2,596,291
Inventories (Note 2)	1,340,494	1,734,873
Other current assets	123,388	90,592
Assets of discontinued operations	—	32,815
Total current assets	3,244,872	4,993,060

Notes to Consolidated Financial Statements

Note 1:   (In Part): Nature of Business and Significant Accounting Policies

Inventories—Inventories are stated at the lower of cost or market. Cost is determined by the last-in, first-out (LIFO) method by the parent company and by the first-in, first-out (FIFO) method by its subsidiaries.

Note 2:   Inventories

Inventories consist of the following:

	1992	1991
Raw materials	$1,264,646	$2,321,178
Work in process	240,988	171,222
Finished goods and display units	129,406	711,252
Total inventories	1,635,040	3,203,652
Less amount classified as long-term	294,546	1,468,779
Current portion	$1,340,494	$1,734,873

Inventories are stated at the lower of cost determined by the LIFO method or market for Prab Robots, Inc. Inventories for the two wholly-owned subsidiaries, Prab Command, Inc. (U.S.) and Prab Limited (U.K.) are stated on the FIFO method which amounted to $566,000 at October 31, 1991. No inventory is stated on the FIFO method at October 31, 1992. Included in inventory stated at FIFO cost was $32,815 at October 31, 1991 of Prab Command inventory classified as an asset from discontinued operations (see Note 14). If the FIFO method had been used for the entire consolidated group, inventories after an adjustment to the lower of cost or market, would have been approximately $2,000,000 and $3,800,000 at October 31, 1992 and 1991, respectively.

Inventory has been written down to estimated net realizable value, and results of operations for 1992, 1991 and 1990 include a corresponding charge of approximately $868,000, $960,000, and $273,000, respectively, which represents the excess of LIFO cost over market.

Inventory of $294,546 and $1,468,779 at October 31, 1992 and 1991, respectively, shown on the balance sheet as a noncurrent asset represents that portion of the inventory that is not expected to be sold currently.

Reduction in inventory quantities during the years ended October 31, 1992, 1991 and 1990 resulted in liquidation of LIFO inventory quantities carried at a lower cost prevailing in prior years as compared with the cost of fiscal 1992 purchases. The effect of these reductions was to decrease the net loss by approximately $24,000, $157,000 and $90,000 at October 31, 1992, 1991 and 1990, respectively.

Instructions

(a) Why might Prab Robots, Inc., use two different methods for valuing inventory?

(b) Comment on why Prab Robots, Inc., might disclose how its LIFO inventories would be valued under FIFO.

(c) Why does the LIFO liquidation reduce operating costs?

(d) Comment on whether Prab Robots would report more or less income if it had been on a FIFO basis for all its inventory.

Case 2 (Barrick Gold Corporation)

Barrick Gold Corporation, with headquarters in Toronto, Canada, is the world's most profitable and largest gold mining company outside South Africa. Part of the key to Barrick's success has been due to its ability to maintain cash flow while improving production and increasing its reserves of gold-containing property. During 1995, Barrick achieved record growth in cash flow, production, and reserves.

The company maintains an aggressive policy of developing previously identified target areas that have the possibility of a large amount of gold ore, and that have not been previously developed. Barrick limits the riskiness of this development by choosing only properties that are located in politically stable regions, and by the company's use of internally generated funds, rather than debt, to finance growth.

Barrick's inventories are as follows:

INVENTORIES	
(in millions, US dollars)	**1995**
Current:	
Gold in process	$54.8
Mine operating supplies	53.1
	$107.9
Non-current (included in property,	
plant, and equipment)	
Ore in stockpiles	$60.5

Instructions

(a) Why do you think that there are no finished goods inventories? Why do you think the raw material, ore in stockpiles, is considered to be a non-current asset?

(b) Consider that Barrick has no finished goods inventories. What journal entries are made to record a sale?

(c) Suppose that gold bouillon that cost $1.8 million to produce was sold for $2.4 million. The journal entry was made to record the sale, but no entry was made to remove the gold from the gold in process inventory. How would this error affect the following?

Balance Sheet		Income Statement	
Inventory	?	Cost of goods sold	?
Retained earnings	?	Net income	?
Accounts payable	?		
Working capital	?		
Current ratio	?		

❖ COMPARATIVE ANALYSIS CASE

The Coca-Cola Company versus PepsiCo, Inc.

Instructions

Go to our Web site and, using The Coca-Cola Company and the PepsiCo, Inc. annual report information, answer the following questions.

1. What is the amount of inventory reported by Coca-Cola at December 31, 1995, and by PepsiCo at December 30, 1995? What percent of total assets is invested in inventory by each company?
2. What inventory costing methods are used by Coca-Cola and PepsiCo? How does each company value its inventories?
3. In the notes, what classifications (descriptions) are used by Coca-Cola and PepsiCo to categorize their inventories?
4. By how much would the reported inventory cost be different if PepsiCo used current cost instead of LIFO in 1995?
5. Compute and compare the inventory turnover ratios and days to sell inventory for 1995 for Coca-Cola and PepsiCo. Indicate why there might be a significant difference between the two companies.

❖ RESEARCH CASES

Case 1

Numerous companies have established home pages on the Internet, e.g., Boston Beer Company (http://www.samadams.com), Ford Motor Company (http://www.ford.com), and Kodak (http://www.kodak.com). You may have noticed company Internet addresses in television comercials or magazine advertisements.

Instructions

Examine the home pages of any two companies and answer the following questions.

(a) What type of information is available?
(b) Is any accounting-related information presented?
(c) Would you describe the home page as informative, promotional, or both? Why?

Case 2

The September 23, 1994, edition of *The Wall Street Journal* includes an article entitled "CompUSA Auctions Notebook Computers Through Bulk Sale."

Instructions

Read the article and answer the following questions.

(a) At what amount did CompUSA estimate the retail value of the computers? What was the estimate made by one of the bidders?
(b) What was wrong with the computers?
(c) What were the rules of the auction as specified by CompUSA?
(d) CompUSA had just recorded a $3 million inventory writedown in the preceding quarter. Based on the information in the article, does it appear that additional writedowns were called for?

❖ WRITING ASSIGNMENT

Fortner Co. follows the practice of valuing its inventory at the lower of cost or market. The following information is available from the company's inventory records as of December 31, 1997:

Item	Quantity	Unit Cost	Replacement Cost/Unit	Estimated Selling Price/Unit	Completion & Disposal Cost/Unit	Normal Profit Margin/Unit
A	1,100	$7.50	$8.40	$10.50	$1.50	$1.80
B	800	8.20	8.00	9.40	.90	1.20
C	1,000	5.60	5.40	7.20	1.10	.60
D	1,000	3.80	4.20	6.30	.80	1.50
E	1,400	6.40	6.30	6.80	.70	1.00

Instructions

Finn Berg is an accounting clerk in the accounting department of Fortner Co., and he cannot understand why the market value keeps changing from replacement cost to net realizable value to something that he cannot even figure out. Finn is very confused, and he is the one who records inventory purchases and calculates ending inventory.

You are the manager of the department and an accountant. Calculate the lower of cost or market using the "individual item" approach. Then write a memo to Finn explaining what designated market value is as well as how it is computed. Use your calculations to aid in your explanation. Finally, include the journal entry he will need to make in order to write down the ending inventory from cost to market.

❖GROUP ASSIGNMENT

(General Inventory Estimation Issues) Your group has been engaged as accountants for the accounting firm of Check and Doublecheck. The manager of the office is interested in your collective formal educations and describes the following factual situations that were recently encountered in their practice. Work within your group to analyze each situation and develop a group response for each item. Your instructor will assign one member of the group to serve as a recorder and one member to serve as spokesperson. The spokesperson will be asked to report your group findings to the class before moving on to the next situation.

Situation 1: In December 1998, one of our clients underwent a major management change and a new president was hired. After reviewing the various policies of the company, the president's opinion was that prior systems employed by the company did not allow for adequate testing of obsolescence (including discontinued products) and overstocks in inventories. Accordingly, the president changed the mechanics of the procedures of reviewing for obsolete and excess stock and determining the amount. These reviews resulted in a significant increase between years in the amount of inventory that was written off. You are satisfied that these procedures are accurate and provide reliable results. The amounts charged against operations for excess and obsolete stock for the last 3 years were: 1998—$500,000; 1997—$120,000; and 1996—$115,000. Net income for 1998 before adjustment for these additional obsolescence charges was $600,000.

Instructions

How should these charges be reported in the financial statements, if at all?

Situation 2: Another of our clients, Sunset Foods, was upset because we forced them to write down their inventory on an item-by-item basis. For example, our computation resulted in a write-down of approximately $380,000 as follows:

	Frozen	Cans
Spinach	$183,000	$ 8,000
Carrots	12,000	7,000
Cut beans	—	25,000
Peas	—	45,000
Mixed vegetables	75,000	25,000
	$270,000	$110,000

The company argued that the products are sold on a line basis (frozen or canned) with customers taking all varieties, and only rarely are sales made on an individual product basis. As a result, they argued that the application of the lower of cost or market rule to the total product line would result in the proper determination of income (loss). A pricing of the inventory on this basis would result in a $140,000 write-off.

Instructions

Why do you believe our accounting firm argued for the item-by-item approach? Which method should be used, given the information in this case?

Situation 3: One of our client's major business activities is the purchase and resale of used heavy mining and construction equipment, including trucks, cranes, shovels, conveyors, crushers, etc. The company was organized in 1981. In its earlier years it purchased individual items of heavy equipment and resold them to customers throughout the United States. In the late-1980s, the company began negotiating the "package" purchase of all the existing equipment at mine sites, concurrent with the closing down of several of the large iron mines in Minnesota and exhausted coal mines in Ohio. The mine operators preferred to liquidate their mine assets on that basis rather than holding auctions or leaving the mine site open until all of the equipment could be liquidated. As there were numerous pieces of equipment in these package purchases, the client found it difficult to assign costs to each individual item. As a result, the company followed the policy of valuing these "package" purchases by the cost recovery method. Under this method, the company recognized no income until the entire cost had been recovered through sales revenues. This produced a desirable tax answer by deferring income to later periods and represented, for financial reporting purposes, a "conservative" valuation of inventories in what was essentially a new field for the company.

Instructions

Comment on the propriety of this approach.

❖ ETHICS CASE

Case 1

The market value of Lake Corporation's inventory has declined below its cost. Vickie Maher, the controller, wants to use the allowance method to write down inventory because it more clearly discloses the decline in market value, and it does not distort the cost of goods sold. Her supervisor, financial vice-president Doug Brucki, prefers the direct method to write down inventory because it does not call attention to the decline in market value.

Instructions

Answer the following questions:

   (a) What, if any, is the ethical issue involved?
   (b) Is any stakeholder harmed if Brucki's preference is used?
   (c) What should Vickie Maher do?

Case 2

Vineland Company signed a long-term purchase contract to buy timber from The United States Forest Service at $300 per thousand board feet. Under these terms, Vineland must cut and pay $6,000,000 for this timber during the next year. Currently the market value is $250 per thousand board feet. At this rate, the market price is $5,000,000. Ruben Walker, the Controller, wants to recognize the loss in value on the year-end financial statements; but the Financial Vice-President, Billie Hands, argues that the loss is temporary and should be ignored. Walker notes that market value has remained near $250 for many months, and he sees no sign of significant change.

Instructions

Answer the following questions:

   (a) What are the ethical issues, if any?
   (b) Is any particular stakeholder harmed by the financial vice-president's decision?
   (c) What should the controller do?

 **W**hitepeak Corporation   **MODULE 3**

Section 3.1   Lower-of-Cost-or-Market Adjustment

Once Whitepeak determines the correct cost of cross-country skis (in Section 2.1, in Chapter 8), it needs to determine whether a lower of cost or market adjustment is necessary. A recent sharp drop in the current replacement cost of skis necessitates close scrutiny of the inventory for a possible write down.

Instructions Determine if a write down is necessary, and record one if appropriate.

Section 3.2   Dollar Value LIFO

The balance of Whitepeak's inventory is kept in a LIFO retail pool system. Unfortunately a small toaster oven started a fire in the records room during 1997, destroying the ending inventory listing. Whitepeak now needs an estimate of the balance of ending inventory.

From your Whitepeak disk you can generate detailed information regarding the cost/retail price structure for this inventory, going back to 1989. Fortunately good records were maintained and not destroyed in the fire.

Instructions Estimate the value of this inventory using the dollar-value LIFO retail estimation method. ■

CHAPTER 10

Acquisition and Disposition of Property, Plant, and Equipment

Landfill Accounting That SMELLS

In 1991, Chambers Development Co., the nation's fastest-growing developer and operator of landfills, based in Pittsburgh, reported that earnings rose 45 percent. Net sales approached $322 million, a ten-fold increase in just five years. This amazing growth, not uncommon for waste management firms in the 1980s, was powered by the acquisition and rapid development of new landfills. During 1991, its stock price rose from $16.13 to $37. Unfortunately, on March 17, 1992, in a tersely worded statement, Chambers revealed that its profit growth had been greatly overstated. The highly profitable company was not so profitable after all. In October 1992, Chambers restated income for 1991 and several prior years, wiping out $362 million in earnings and retained earnings. Not surprisingly, the next day, Chambers' stock plunged 63%—from $30.50 to $11.13 in one day!

What happened? As Chambers' stockholders would learn, the company had been deferring recognition of certain "indirect" landfill development expenses by capitalizing these costs and writing them off over the life of the landfills (3 to 10 years). The deferred expenses included executives' salaries and travel, legal and public relations costs, and security guard contracts, along with costs of initiating new trash hauling routes. These capitalized costs were tucked near the bottom of the balance sheet under the heading "other assets" on a line described "deferred costs." As one Wall Street analyst remarked, "Whenever you see an asset called 'deferred anything' hold on to your pocketbook."

While Chambers says it is now recognizing rather than deferring indirect costs, it is continuing to defer substantial interest costs that most firms capitalize. This concerns investors and analysts because it is consistent with Chambers' penchant for showing generous earnings growth through liberal accounting practices. As one observer noted, "What got them in trouble is that they'd led the world to believe they were using conservative accounting methods when they weren't."[1] Once a company gets this kind of dubious reputation, the investment community loses faith in the quality of its reported earnings for years to come.

[1]"Audit Report Shows How Far Chambers Would Go for Profits," *The Wall Street Journal*, October 21, 1992, p. A1.

LEARNING OBJECTIVES

After studying this chapter, you should be able to:

1 Describe the major characteristics of property, plant, and equipment.

2 Identify the costs included in the initial valuation of land, buildings, and equipment.

3 Describe the accounting problems associated with self-constructed assets.

4 Describe the accounting problems associated with interest capitalization.

5 Understand accounting issues related to acquiring and valuing plant assets.

6 Describe the accounting treatment for costs subsequent to acquisition.

7 Describe the accounting treatment for the disposal of property, plant, and equipment.

Preview of Chapter 10

As indicated in the opening story, Chambers Development Co. used questionable criteria to capitalize certain costs and report them as assets. The purpose of this chapter is to discuss (1) the proper accounting for costs related to property, plant, and equipment, and (2) the accounting methods used to record the retirement or disposal of these costs. Depreciation—allocating costs of property, plant, and equipment to accouting periods—is presented in Chapter 11. The content and organization of this chapter are as follows.

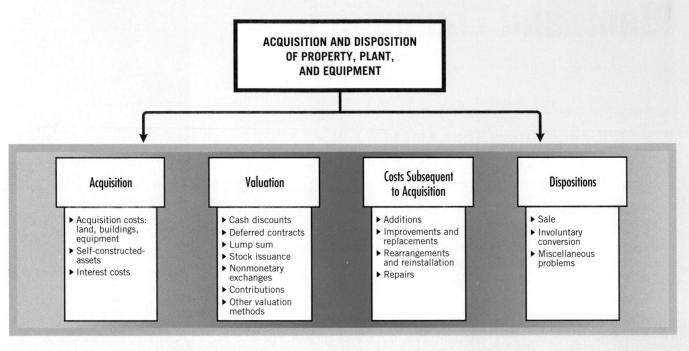

ACQUISITION AND DISPOSITION OF PROPERTY, PLANT, AND EQUIPMENT

Acquisition	Valuation	Costs Subsequent to Acquisition	Dispositions
▶ Acquisition costs: land, buildings, equipment ▶ Self-constructed-assets ▶ Interest costs	▶ Cash discounts ▶ Deferred contracts ▶ Lump sum ▶ Stock issuance ▶ Nonmonetary exchanges ▶ Contributions ▶ Other valuation methods	▶ Additions ▶ Improvements and replacements ▶ Rearrangements and reinstallation ▶ Repairs	▶ Sale ▶ Involuntary conversion ▶ Miscellaneous problems

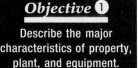

Objective ❶

Describe the major characteristics of property, plant, and equipment.

Almost every business enterprise of any size or activity uses assets of a durable nature. Such assets, commonly referred to as **property, plant, and equipment; plant assets**; or **fixed assets**, include land, building structures (offices, factories, warehouses), and equipment (machinery, furniture, tools). These terms are used interchangeably throughout this textbook. The major characteristics of property, plant, and equipment are:

❶ *They are acquired for use in operations and not for resale.* Only assets used in normal business operations should be classified as property, plant, and equipment. An idle building is more appropriately classified separately as an investment; land held by land developers or subdividers is classified as inventory.

❷ *They are long-term in nature and usually subject to depreciation.* Property, plant, and equipment yield services over a number of years. The investment in these assets is assigned to future periods through periodic depreciation charges. The exception is land, which is not depreciated unless a material decrease in value occurs, such as a loss in fertility of agricultural land because of poor crop rotation, drought, or soil erosion.

❸ *They possess physical substance.* Property, plant, and equipment are characterized by physical existence or substance and thus are differentiated from intangible assets, such as patents or goodwill. Unlike raw material, however, property, plant, and equipment do not physically become part of a product held for resale.

❖ ACQUISITION OF PROPERTY, PLANT, AND EQUIPMENT

Historical cost is the usual basis for valuing property, plant, and equipment. Historical cost **is measured by the cash or cash equivalent price of obtaining the asset and bringing it to the location and condition necessary for its intended use.** The purchase price, freight costs, sales taxes, and installation costs of a productive asset are considered part of the asset's cost. These costs are allocated to future periods through depreciation. Any related costs incurred **after the asset's acquisition,** such as additions, improvements, or replacements, are **added to the asset's cost if they provide future service potential.** Otherwise they are expensed immediately.

> **Objective ❷**
>
> Identify the costs included in the initial valuation of land, buildings, and equipment.

Cost should be the basis used at the acquisition date because the cash or cash equivalent price best measures the asset's value at that time. Disagreement does exist concerning differences between historical cost and other valuation methods (such as replacement cost or fair market value) arising after acquisition. *APB Opinion No. 6* states that "property, plant, and equipment should not be written up to reflect appraisal, market, or current values which are above cost." Although minor exceptions are noted, current standards indicate that departures from historical cost are rare.

The main reasons for this position are (1) at the date of acquisition, cost reflects fair value; (2) historical cost involves actual, not hypothetical transactions, and as a result is the most reliable; and (3) gains and losses should not be anticipated but should be recognized when the asset is sold.

Several other valuation methods have been considered, such as (1) constant dollar accounting (adjustments for general price-level changes), (2) current cost accounting (adjustments for specific price-level changes), (3) net realizable value, or (4) a combination of constant dollar accounting and current cost or net realizable value. These alternative valuation concepts are discussed in Chapter 25.

> **✳ UNDERLYING CONCEPTS**
>
> Market value is relevant to inventory but less so for property, plant, and equipment which, consistent with the going concern assumption, are held for use in the business, not for sale like inventory.

Cost of Land

All expenditures made to acquire land and to ready it for use are considered part of the land cost. Land costs typically include (1) the purchase price, (2) closing costs, such as title to the land, attorney's fees, and recording fees, (3) costs incurred in getting the land in condition for its intended use, such as grading, filling, draining, and clearing, (4) assumption of any liens, mortgages, or encumbrances on the property, and (5) any additional land improvements that have an indefinite life.

When land has been purchased for the purpose of constructing a building, all costs incurred up to the excavation for the new building are considered land costs. **Removal of old buildings—clearing, grading, and filling—are considered land costs because these costs are necessary to get the land in condition for its intended purpose.** Any proceeds obtained in the process of getting the land ready for its intended use, such as salvage receipts on the demolition of an old building or the sale of cleared timber are treated as **reductions in the price of the land.**

In some cases, the purchaser of land has to assume certain obligations on the land such as back taxes or liens. In such situations, the cost of the land is the cash paid for it, plus the encumbrances. In other words, if the purchase price of the land is $50,000 cash, but accrued property taxes of $5,000 and liens of $10,000 are assumed, the cost of the land is $65,000.

Special assessments for local improvements, such as pavements, street lights, sewers, and drainage systems, are usually charged to the Land account because they are relatively permanent in nature and are maintained and replaced by the local government body. In addition, permanent improvements made by the owner, such as landscaping, are properly chargeable to the Land account. **Improvements with limited lives**, such as private driveways, walks, fences, and parking lots, are recorded separately as Land Improvements so they can be depreciated over their estimated lives.

Generally, land is part of property, plant, and equipment. If the major purpose of acquiring and holding land is speculative, however, it is more appropriately classified

>  **INTERNATIONAL INSIGHT**
>
> In many nations, such as Great Britain and Brazil, companies are allowed to revalue their fixed assets at amounts above historical cost. These revaluations may be at appraisal values or at amounts linked to a specified index. Other nations, such as Japan and Germany, do not allow such revaluations.

as an investment. If the land is held by a real estate concern for resale, it should be classified as inventory.

In cases where land is held as an investment, what accounting treatment should be given taxes, insurance, and other direct costs incurred while holding the land? Many believe these costs should be capitalized because the revenue from the investment still has not been received. This approach is reasonable and seems justified except in cases where the asset is currently producing revenue (such as rental property).

Cost of Buildings

INTERNATIONAL INSIGHT

Under international accounting standards historical cost is the benchmark (preferred) treatment for property, plant, and equipment. However, it is also allowable to use revalued amounts. If revaluation is used, companies are required to revalue the class of assets regularly.

The cost of buildings should include all expenditures related directly to their acquisition or construction. These costs include (1) materials, labor, and overhead costs incurred during construction and (2) professional fees and building permits. Generally, companies contract to have their buildings constructed. All costs incurred, from excavation to completion, are considered part of the building costs.

One accounting problem is deciding what to do about an old building that is on the site of a newly proposed building. Is the cost of removal of the old building a cost of the land or a cost of the new building? The answer is that if land is purchased with an old building on it, then the cost of demolition less its salvage value is a cost of getting the land ready for its intended use and relates to the land rather than to the new building. As indicated earlier, all costs of getting an asset ready for its intended use are costs of that asset.

Cost of Equipment

The term "equipment" in accounting includes delivery equipment, office equipment, machinery, furniture and fixtures, furnishings, factory equipment, and similar fixed assets. The cost of such assets includes the purchase price, freight and handling charges incurred, insurance on the equipment while in transit, cost of special foundations if required, assembling and installation costs, and costs of conducting trial runs. Costs thus include all expenditures incurred in acquiring the equipment and preparing it for use.

Self-Constructed Assets

Objective ❸

Describe the accounting problems associated with self-constructed assets.

Occasionally companies (particularly in the railroad and utility industries) construct their own assets. Determining the cost of such machinery and other fixed assets can be a problem. Without a purchase price or contract price, the company must allocate costs and expenses to arrive at the cost of the self-constructed asset. Materials and direct labor used in construction pose no problem; these costs can be traced directly to work and material orders related to the fixed assets constructed.

However, the assignment of indirect costs of manufacturing creates special problems. These indirect costs, called overhead or burden, include power, heat, light, insurance, property taxes on factory buildings and equipment, factory supervisory labor, depreciation of fixed assets, and supplies.

These costs might be handled in one of three ways:

❶ *Assign No Fixed Overhead to the Cost of the Constructed Asset.* The major argument for this treatment is that indirect overhead is generally fixed in nature and does not increase as a result of constructing one's own plant or equipment. This approach assumes that the company will have the same costs regardless of whether the company constructs the asset or not, so to charge a portion of the overhead costs to the equipment will normally relieve current expenses and consequently overstate income of the current period. In contrast, variable overhead costs that increase as a result of the construction are assigned to the cost of the asset.

❷ *Assign a Portion of All Overhead to the Construction Process.* This approach, a full costing concept, is appropriate if one believes that costs attach to all products and assets manufactured or constructed. This procedure assigns overhead costs to construction as it would to normal production. Advocates say that failure to allocate overhead costs understates the initial cost of the asset and results in an inaccurate future allocation.

❸ *Allocate on the Basis of Lost Production.* A third alternative is to allocate to the construction project the cost of any curtailed production that occurs because the asset is built instead of purchased. This method is conceptually appealing, but is based on "what might have occurred"—an opportunity cost concept—which is difficult to measure.

A pro rata portion of the fixed overhead should be assigned to the asset to obtain its cost. This treatment is employed extensively because many believe a better matching of costs with revenues is obtained. If the allocated overhead results in recording construction costs in excess of the costs that would be charged by an outside independent producer, the excess overhead should be recorded as a period loss rather than be capitalized to avoid capitalizing the asset at more than its probable market value.

Interest Costs During Construction

The proper accounting for interest costs has been a long-standing controversy. Three approaches have been suggested to account for the interest incurred in financing the construction or acquisition of property, plant, and equipment:

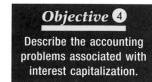

Objective ❹

Describe the accounting problems associated with interest capitalization.

❶ *Capitalize No Interest Charges During Construction.* Under this approach interest is considered a cost of financing and not a cost of construction. It is contended that if the company had used stock financing rather than debt financing, this expense would not have been incurred. The major argument against this approach is that an implicit interest cost is associated with the use of cash regardless of its source; if stock financing is employed, a real cost exists to the stockholders although a contractual claim does not take place.

❷ *Capitalize Only the Actual Interest Costs Incurred During Construction.* This approach relies on the historical cost concept that only actual transactions are recorded. It is argued that interest incurred is as much a cost of acquiring the asset as the cost of the materials, labor, and other resources used. As a result, a company that uses debt financing will have an asset of higher cost than an enterprise that uses stock financing. The results achieved by this approach are considered unsatisfactory by some because the cost of an asset should be the same whether cash, debt financing, or stock financing is employed.

❸ *Charge Construction with All Costs of Funds Employed, Whether Identifiable or Not.* This method maintains that one part of the cost of construction is the cost of financing, whether by debt, cash, or stock financing. An asset should be charged with all costs necessary to get it ready for its intended use. Interest, whether actual or imputed, is a cost of building, just as labor, materials, and overhead are costs. A major criticism of this approach is that imputation of a cost of equity capital is subjective and outside the framework of an historical cost system.

The profession generally adopts the second approach: **Actual interest (with modification) should be capitalized**, in accordance with the concept that the historical cost of acquiring an asset includes all costs (including interest) incurred to bring the asset to the condition and location necessary for its intended use. The rationale for this approach is that during construction the asset is not generating revenues, and therefore interest costs should be deferred (capitalized).[2] Once construction is completed, the asset is ready for its intended use and revenues can be earned. At this point interest should be reported as an expense and matched to these revenues. It follows that any interest cost incurred in purchasing an asset that is ready for its intended use should be expensed.

---

[2]"Capitalization of Interest Cost," *Statement of Financial Accounting Standards No. 34* (Stamford, Conn.: FASB, 1979).

To implement this general approach, three items must be considered:

❶ Qualifying assets.
❷ Capitalization period.
❸ Amount to capitalize.

Qualifying Assets

To qualify for interest capitalization, assets must require a period of time to get them ready for their intended use. Interest costs are capitalized starting with the first expenditure related to the asset, and capitalization continues until the asset is substantially completed and ready for its intended use.

Assets that qualify for interest cost capitalization include assets under construction for an enterprise's own use (including buildings, plants, and large machinery) and assets intended for sale or lease that are constructed or otherwise produced as discrete projects (e.g., ships or real estate developments).

Examples of assets that do not qualify for interest capitalization are (1) assets that are in use or ready for their intended use, and (2) assets that are not being used in the earnings activities of the enterprise and that are not undergoing the activities necessary to get them ready for use (such as land that is not being developed and assets not being used because of obsolescence, excess capacity, or need for repair).

Capitalization Period

**INTERNATIONAL
INSIGHT**

Under international accounting standards capitalization of interest is allowed, but it is not the preferred treatment. The benchmark treatment is to expense interest in the period incurred.

The **capitalization period** is the period of time during which interest must be capitalized. It begins when three conditions are present:

❶ Expenditures for the asset have been made.
❷ Activities that are necessary to get the asset ready for its intended use are in progress.
❸ Interest cost is being incurred.

Interest capitalization **continues as long as these three conditions are present**. The capitalization period ends when the asset is substantially complete and ready for its intended use.

Amount to Capitalize

**INTERNATIONAL
INSIGHT**

In Saudi Arabia, interest cannot be charged for the use of money as a result of a Moslem religious principle. Thus, there is no provision for the capitalization of interest.

The amount of interest to be capitalized is limited to the lower of actual interest cost incurred during the period or avoidable interest. **Avoidable interest** is the amount of interest cost during the period that theoretically could have been avoided if expenditures for the asset had not been made. If the actual interest cost for the period is $90,000 and the avoidable interest is $80,000, only $80,000 is capitalized. Or, if the actual interest cost is $80,000 and the avoidable interest is $90,000, only $80,000 is capitalized. In no situation should interest cost include a cost of capital charge for stockholders' equity. And, interest capitalization is required for a qualifying asset only if its effect, compared with the effect of expensing interest, is material.[3]

To apply the avoidable interest concept, the potential amount of interest that may be capitalized during an accounting period is determined by multiplying an interest rate(s) by the **weighted-average amount of accumulated expenditures** for qualifying assets during the period.

Weighted-Average Accumulated Expenditures. In computing the weighted-average accumulated expenditures, the construction expenditures are weighted by the amount of time (fraction of a year or accounting period) that interest cost could be incurred on the expenditure. To illustrate, assume a 17-month bridge construction project with current-year payments to the contractor of $240,000 on March 1, $480,000 on July 1, and $360,000 on November 1. The weighted-average accumulated expenditures for the year ended December 31 is computed as follows:

---

[3]Ibid., summary paragraph.

Expenditures			Capitalization		Weighted-Average	
Date	Amount	×	Period*	=	Accumulated Expenditures	
March 1	$ 240,000		10/12		$200,000	
July 1	480,000		6/12		240,000	
November 1	360,000		2/12		60,000	
	$1,080,000				$500,000	

*Months between date of expenditure and date interest capitalization stops or end of year, which-ever comes first (in this case December 31).

ILLUSTRATION 10-1
Computation of
Weighted-Average
Accumulated
Expenditures

To compute the weighted-average accumulated expenditures, we weight the expenditures by the amount of time that interest cost could be incurred on each one. For the March 1 expenditure a 10 months' interest cost can be associated with the expenditure, whereas for the expenditure on July 1, only 6 months' interest costs can be incurred, and for the expenditure made on November 1, only 2 months of interest cost is incurred.

Interest Rates. The principles to be used in selecting the appropriate interest rates to be applied to the weighted-average accumulated expenditures are:

❶ For the portion of weighted-average accumulated expenditures that is less than or equal to any amounts borrowed specifically to finance construction of the assets, **use the interest rate incurred on the specific borrowings.**

❷ For the portion of weighted-average accumulated expenditures that is greater than any debt incurred specifically to finance construction of the assets, **use a weighted average of interest rates incurred on all other outstanding debt during the period.**[4]

An illustration of the computation of a weighted-average interest rate for debt greater than the amount incurred specifically to finance construction of the assets is shown below:

	Principal	Interest
12%, 2-year note	$ 600,000	$ 72,000
9%, 10-year bonds	2,000,000	180,000
7.5%, 20-year bonds	5,000,000	375,000
	$7,600,000	$627,000

$$\text{Weighted-average interest rate} = \frac{\text{Total interest}}{\text{Total principal}} = \frac{\$627,000}{\$7,600,000} = 8.25\%$$

ILLUSTRATION 10-2
Computation of
Weighted-Average
Interest Rate

Comprehensive Illustration of Interest Capitalization

To illustrate the issues related to interest capitalization, assume that on November 1, 1997 Shalla Company contracted with Pfeifer Construction Co. to have a building constructed for $1,400,000 on land costing $100,000 (purchased from the contractor and included in the first payment). Shalla made the following payments to the construction company during 1998:

January 1	March 1	May 1	December 31	Total
$210,000	$300,000	$540,000	$450,000	$1,500,000

---

[4]The interest rate to be used may be based exclusively on an average rate of all the borrowings, if desired. For our purposes, we will use the specific borrowing rate followed by the average interest rate because we believe it to be more conceptually consistent. Either method can be used; *FASB Statement No. 34* does not provide explicit guidance on this measurement. For a discussion of this issue and others related to interest capitalization see Kathryn M. Means and Paul M. Kazenski, "SFAS 34: Receipt for Diversity," *Accounting Horizons*, September 1988; and, Wendy A. Duffy, "A Graphical Analysis of Interest Capitalization," *Journal of Accounting Education*, Fall 1990.

506 • *Chapter 10* **Acquisition and Disposition of Property, Plant, and Equipment**

Construction was completed and the building was ready for occupancy on December 31, 1998. Shalla Company had the following debt outstanding at December 31, 1998:

Specific Construction Debt

1. 15%, 3-year note to finance purchase of land and construction of the building, dated December 31, 1997, with interest payable annually on December 31 .... $750,000

Other Debt

2. 10%, 5-year note payable, dated December 31, 1994, with interest payable annually on December 31 .... $550,000
3. 12%, 10-year bonds issued December 31, 1993, with interest payable annually on December 31 .... $600,000

The weighted-average accumulated expenditures during 1998 are computed as follows:

ILLUSTRATION 10-3
Computation of
Weighted-Average
Accumulated
Expenditures

Expenditures			Current Year Capitalization		Weighted-Average
Date	Amount	×	Period	=	Accumulated Expenditures
January 1	$ 210,000		12/12		$210,000
March 1	300,000		10/12		250,000
May 1	540,000		8/12		360,000
December 31	450,000		0		0
	$1,500,000				$820,000

Note that the expenditure made on December 31, the last day of the year, does not have any interest cost.

The avoidable interest is computed as follows:

ILLUSTRATION 10-4
Computation of
Avoidable Interest

Weighted-Average Accumulated Expenditures	×	Interest Rate	=	Avoidable Interest
$750,000		.15 (construction note)		$112,500
70,000[a]		.1104 (weighted average of other debt)[b]		7,728
$820,000				$120,228

[a]The amount by which the weighted-average accumulated expenditures exceeds the specific construction loan.

[b]Weighted-average interest rate computation:

	Principal	Interest
10%, 5-year note	$ 550,000	$ 55,000
12%, 10-year bonds	600,000	72,000
	$1,150,000	$127,000

$$\text{Weighted-average interest rate} = \frac{\text{Total interest}}{\text{Total principal}} = \frac{\$127,000}{\$1,150,000} = 11.04\%$$

The actual interest cost, which represents the maximum amount of interest that may be capitalized during 1998, is computed as shown below.

ILLUSTRATION 10-5
Computation of Actual
Interest Cost

Construction note	$750,000 × .15	=	$112,500
5-year note	$550,000 × .10	=	55,000
10-year bonds	$600,000 × .12	=	72,000
Actual interest			$239,500

The interest cost to be capitalized is the lesser of $120,228 (avoidable interest) or $239,500 (actual interest), which is **$120,228**.

The journal entries to be made by Shalla Company during 1998 would be as follows:

January 1

Land	100,000	
Building (or Construction in Process)	110,000	
Cash		210,000

March 1

Building	300,000	
Cash		300,000

May 1

Building	540,000	
Cash		540,000

December 31

Building	450,000	
Cash		450,000

Building (Capitalized interest)	120,228	
Interest Expense ($239,500 − $120,228)	119,272	
Cash ($112,500 + $55,000 + $72,000)		239,500

Capitalized interest cost should be written off as part of depreciation over the useful life of the assets involved and not over the term of the debt. The total interest cost incurred during the period should be disclosed, with the portion charged to expense and the portion capitalized indicated.

At December 31, 1998, Shalla would disclose the amount of interest capitalized either as part of the nonoperating section of the income statement or in the notes accompanying the financial statements. Both forms of disclosure are illustrated below.

Income from operations		XXXX
Other expenses and losses:		
Interest expense	$239,500	
Less capitalized interest	120,228	119,272
Income before taxes on income		XXXX
Income taxes		XXX
Net income		XXXX

ILLUSTRATION 10-6
Capitalized Interest Reported in the Income Statement

Note 1:   Accounting Policies.   *Capitalized interest.* During 1998 total interest cost was $239,500, of which $120,228 was capitalized and $119,272 was charged to expense.

ILLUSTRATION 10-7
Capitalized Interest Disclosed in a Note

Special Issues Related to Interest Capitalization

Three issues related to interest capitalization merit special attention:

❶ Expenditures for land.
❷ Interest revenue.
❸ Significance of interest capitalization.

Expenditures for Land. When land is purchased with the intention of developing it for a particular use, interest costs associated with those expenditures qualify for interest capitalization. If land is purchased as a site for a structure (such as a plant site), interest costs capitalized during the period of construction are part of the cost of the plant, not the land. In the Shalla illustration where land was acquired for a structure, all interest costs capitalized (including those related to land expenditures) should be allocated to the cost of the building. Conversely, if land is being developed for lot sales, any capitalized interest cost should be part of the acquisition cost of the developed land. However, interest costs involved in purchasing land held **for speculation** should **not** be capitalized because the asset is ready for its intended use.

Interest Revenue. Companies frequently borrow money to finance construction of assets and temporarily invest the excess borrowed funds in interest-bearing securities until the funds are needed to pay for construction. During the early stages of construction, interest revenue earned may exceed the interest cost incurred on the borrowed funds.

The question is whether it is appropriate to offset interest revenue against interest cost when determining the amount of interest to be capitalized as a part of the construc-

Go to our Web site for expanded discussion of interest capitalization issues.

tion cost of assets. According to *FASB Statement No. 62* on capitalization of interest cost, **interest revenue should not be netted or offset against interest cost**, except in cases involving externally restricted tax exempt borrowings. Temporary or short-term investment decisions are not related to the interest incurred as part of the acquisition cost of assets. Therefore, the interest incurred on qualifying assets should be capitalized whether or not excess funds are temporarily invested in short-term securities. Some are critical of this accounting because a company can defer the interest cost but report the interest revenue in the current period.

Significance of Interest Capitalization. The requirement of interest capitalization can have a substantive impact on the financial statements of business enterprises. When Jim Walter Corporation's earnings dropped from $1.51 to $1.17 per share, the building manufacturer, looking for ways to regain its profitability, was able to pick up an additional 11 cents per share by capitalizing the interest on coal mining projects and several plants under construction.

Public utilities have been permitted to capitalize interest during construction (whether actual or imputed) for many years.[5] For example, at one time it was estimated that Duke Power's net income of $58.5 million would be reduced by more than 85% if capitalized interest costs were shown as an expense.

The interest capitalization requirement, while now universally adopted, is still debated. From a conceptual viewpoint, many believe that either no interest cost should be capitalized or all interest costs, actual or imputed, should be capitalized for the reasons mentioned earlier in this section.

❖ VALUATION

Objective 5

Understand accounting issues related to acquiring and valuing plant assets.

We have seen that **an asset should be recorded at the fair market value of what is given up or the fair value of the asset received, whichever is more clearly evident**. Fair market value, however, is sometimes obscured by the process through which the asset is acquired. As an example, assume that land and buildings are bought together for one price. How are separate values for the land and building determined? A number of accounting problems of this nature are examined in the following sections.

Cash Discount

When plant assets are purchased subject to cash discounts for prompt payment, how should the discount be reported? If the discount is taken, it should be considered a reduction in the purchase price of the asset. What is not clear, however, is whether a reduction in the asset cost should occur even if the discount is not taken.

Two points of view exist on this matter. Under one approach, the discount, whether taken or not, is considered a reduction in the cost of the asset. The rationale for this approach is that the real cost of the asset is the cash or cash equivalent price of the asset. In addition, some argue that the terms of cash discounts are so attractive that failure to take them indicates management error or inefficiency. Proponents of the other approach

---

[5]Nonutility companies traditionally had not capitalized any interest cost during construction, whether actual or imputed. In the early 1970s, however, a number of companies decided to do so. The reason for this switch was to prevent the decline in earnings that resulted when an enterprise expensed these interest costs. In 1974, the SEC in *ASR No. 163* declared a temporary moratorium on the capitalization of interest costs for most nonutility companies, indicating that these practices were leading to noncomparability of financial data. In 1979, the FASB finally standardized accounting for interest costs during construction.

Public utility companies are allowed to include in the costs of additions to plant and equipment an "allowance for funds used during construction" (AFUDC) in conformity with Federal Energy Regulatory Commission pronouncements. AFUDC includes not only interest on borrowed funds but also an **imputed interest on equity funds** used during construction.

argue that the discount should not always be considered a loss because the terms may be unfavorable or because it might not be prudent for the company to take the discount. At present, both methods are employed in practice. The former method is generally preferred.

Deferred Payment Contracts

Plant assets are purchased frequently on long-term credit contracts through the use of notes, mortgages, bonds, or equipment obligations. **To properly reflect cost, assets purchased on long-term credit contracts should be accounted for at the present value of the consideration exchanged between the contracting parties at the date of the transaction.** For example, an asset purchased today in exchange for a $10,000 zero-interest-bearing note payable 4 years from now should not be recorded at $10,000. The present value of the $10,000 note establishes the exchange price of the transaction (the purchase price of the asset). Assuming an appropriate interest rate of 12% at which to discount this single payment of $10,000 due 4 years from now, this asset should be recorded at $6,355.20 [$10,000 × .63552; see Table 6–2 for the present value of a single sum, $PV = $10,000 $(PVF_{4,12\%})$].

When no interest rate is stated, or if the specified rate is unreasonable, an appropriate interest rate must be imputed. The objective is to approximate the interest rate that the buyer and seller would negotiate at arm's length in a similar borrowing transaction. Factors to be considered in imputing an interest rate are the borrower's credit rating, the amount and maturity date of the note, and prevailing interest rates. If determinable, the cash exchange price of the asset acquired should be used as the basis for recording the asset and measuring the interest element.

To illustrate, Sutter Company purchases a specially built robot spray painter for its production line. The company issues a $100,000, 5-year, zero-interest-bearing note to Wrigley Robotics, Inc. for the new equipment when the prevailing market rate of interest for obligations of this nature is 10%. Sutter is to pay off the note in five $20,000 installments made at the end of each year. The fair market value of this specially built robot is not readily determinable and must therefore be approximated by establishing the market value (present value) of the note. Computation of the present value of the note and the date of purchase and dates of payment entries are as follows:

Date of Purchase

Equipment	75,816*	
Discount on Notes Payable	24,184	
Notes Payable		100,000

*Present value of note = $20,000 $(PVF\text{-}OA_{5,10\%})$
= $20,000 (3.79079) Table 6-4
= $75,816

End of First Year

Interest Expense	7,582	
Notes Payable	20,000	
Cash		20,000
Discount on Notes Payable		7,582

Interest expense in the first year under the effective interest approach is $7,582 [($100,000 − $24,184) × 10%]. The entry at the end of the second year to record interest and principal payment is as follows:

End of Second Year

Interest Expense	6,340	
Notes Payable	20,000	
Cash		20,000
Discount on Notes Payable		6,340

Interest expense in the second year under the effective interest approach is $6,340 [($100,000 − $24,184) − ($20,000 − $7,582)] × 10%.

If an interest rate were not imputed for such deferred payment contracts, the asset would be recorded at an amount greater than its fair value. In addition, interest expense reported in the income statement would be understated for all periods involved.

Lump Sum Purchase

A special problem of pricing fixed assets arises when a group of plant assets is purchased at a single lump sum price. When such a situation occurs, and it is not at all unusual, the practice is to allocate the total cost among the various assets on the basis of their relative fair market values. The assumption is that costs will vary in direct proportion to sales value. This is the same principle that is applied to allocate a lump sum cost among different inventory items.

To determine fair market value, any of the following might be used: an appraisal for insurance purposes, the assessed valuation for property taxes, or simply an independent appraisal by an engineer or other appraiser.

To illustrate, Norduct Homes, Inc. decides to purchase several assets of a small heating concern, Comfort Heating, for $80,000. Comfort Heating is in the process of liquidation, and its assets sold are:

	Book Value	Fair Market Value
Inventory	$30,000	$ 25,000
Land	20,000	25,000
Building	35,000	50,000
	$85,000	$100,000

The $80,000 purchase price would be allocated on the basis of the relative fair market values (assuming specific identification of costs is not practicable) in the following manner:

ILLUSTRATION 10-8
Allocation of Purchase Price—Relative Fair Market Value Basis

Inventory	$\dfrac{\$25,000}{\$100,000} \times \$80,000 = \$20,000$
Land	$\dfrac{\$25,000}{\$100,000} \times \$80,000 = \$20,000$
Building	$\dfrac{\$50,000}{\$100,000} \times \$80,000 = \$40,000$

Issuance of Stock

When property is acquired by issuance of securities, such as common stock, the cost of the property is not properly measured by the par or stated value of such stock. If the stock is being actively traded, **the market value of the stock issued is a fair indication of the cost of the property acquired because the stock is a good measure of the current cash equivalent price.**

For example, Upgrade Living Co. decides to purchase some adjacent land for expansion of its carpeting and cabinet operation. In lieu of paying cash for the land, the company issues to Deedland Company 5,000 shares of common stock (par value $10) that have a fair market value of $12 per share. Upgrade Living Co. would make the following entry.

Land (5,000 × $12)	60,000	
Common Stock		50,000
Additional Paid-In Capital		10,000

If the market value of the common stock exchanged is not determinable, the market value of the property should be established and used as the basis for recording the asset and issuance of the common stock.[6]

Exchanges of Nonmonetary Assets

The proper accounting for exchanges of nonmonetary assets (such as inventories and property, plant, and equipment) is controversial.[7] Some argue that the accounting for these types of exchanges should be based on the fair value of the asset given up or the fair value of the asset received with a gain or loss recognized. Others believe that the accounting should be based on the recorded amount (book value) of the asset given up, with no gain or loss recognized. Still others favor an approach that would recognize losses in all cases, but defer gains in special situations.

Ordinarily accounting for the exchange of nonmonetary assets should be based on **the fair value of the asset given up or the fair value of the asset received, whichever is clearly more evident**.[8] Thus, any gains or losses on the exchange **should be recognized immediately**. The rationale for such immediate recognition is that the earnings process related to these assets is completed and, therefore, a gain or loss should be recognized. This approach is always employed when the assets are **dissimilar** in nature, such as the exchange of land for a building, or the exchange of equipment for inventory. If the fair value of either asset is not reasonably determinable, the book value of the asset given up is usually used as the basis for recording the nonmonetary exchange.

The general rule of immediate recognition is modified when exchanges of **similar** nonmonetary assets occur for gain situations. For example, when a company exchanges its inventory items with inventory of another company because of color, size, etc. to facilitate sale to an outside customer, the earnings process is not considered completed and a **gain** should not be recognized. Likewise if a company trades **similar productive assets** such as land for land or equipment for equipment, the earnings process is not considered complete and, therefore, **a gain should not be recognized**. However, if the exchange transaction involving **similar assets** would result in a loss, **the loss is recognized immediately**.

In certain situations, gains on exchange of similar nonmonetary assets may be recognized where **monetary consideration (boot)** is received. When monetary consideration such as cash is received in addition to the nonmonetary asset, it is assumed that a portion of the earnings process is completed and, therefore, a partial gain is recognized (see footnote 9).[9]

In summary, losses on nonmonetary transactions are always recognized whether the exchange involves dissimilar or similar assets. Gains on nonmonetary transactions are recognized if the exchange involves dissimilar assets; gains are deferred if the exchange involves similar assets, unless cash or some other form of monetary consid-

---

[6]When the fair market value of the stock is used as the basis of valuation, careful consideration must be given to the effect that the issuance of additional shares will have on the existing market price. Where the effect on market price appears significant, an independent appraisal of the asset received should be made. This valuation should be employed as the basis for valuation of the asset as well as for the stock issued. In the unusual case where the fair market value of the stock or the fair market value of the asset cannot be determined objectively, the board of directors of the corporation may set the value.

[7]Nonmonetary assets are items whose price in terms of the monetary unit may change over time, whereas monetary assets—cash and short- or long-term accounts and notes receivable— are fixed in terms of units of currency by contract or otherwise.

[8]"Accounting for Nonmonetary Transactions," *Opinions of the Accounting Principles Board No. 29* (New York: AICPA, 1973), par. 18.

[9]When the monetary consideration is significant, i.e., **25% or more** of the fair value of the exchange, the transaction is considered a **monetary exchange** by both parties. In such "monetary" exchanges the fair values are used to measure the gains or losses that are recognized in their entirety. *EITF Issue No. 86-29*, "Nonmonetary Transactions: Magnitude of Boot and the Exception to the Use of Fair Value," *Emerging Issues Task Force Abstracts* (October 1, 1987).

eration is received, in which case a partial gain is recognized. Any gain or loss on disposal of nonmonetary assets is computed by comparing the book value with the fair value of the asset given up.

To illustrate the accounting for these different types of transactions, we will look at the following three situations:

❶ Accounting for dissimilar assets.
❷ Accounting for similar assets—loss situation.
❸ Accounting for similar assets—gain situation.

Dissimilar Assets

The cost of a nonmonetary asset acquired in exchange for a dissimilar nonmonetary asset is usually recorded at the **fair value of the asset given up**, and a gain or loss is recognized. The **fair value of the asset received** should be used only if it is more clearly evident than the fair value of the asset given up.

To illustrate, Interstate Transportation Company exchanged a number of used trucks plus cash for vacant land that might be used for a future plant site. The trucks have a combined book value of $42,000 (cost $64,000 less $22,000 accumulated depreciation). Interstate's purchasing agent, who has had previous dealings in the second-hand market, indicates that the trucks have a fair market value of $49,000. In addition to the trucks, Interstate must pay $17,000 cash for the land. The cost of the land to Interstate is $66,000 computed as follows:

ILLUSTRATION 10-9
Computation of Land Cost

Fair value of trucks exchanged	$49,000
Cash paid	17,000
Cost of land	$66,000

The journal entry to record the exchange transaction is:

Land	66,000	
Accumulated Depreciation—Trucks	22,000	
Trucks		64,000
Gain on Disposal of Trucks		7,000
Cash		17,000

The gain is the difference between the fair value of the trucks and their book value. It is verified as follows:

ILLUSTRATION 10-10
Computation of Gain on Disposal of Used Trucks

Fair value of trucks		$49,000
Cost of trucks	$64,000	
Less accumulated depreciation	22,000	
Book value of trucks		42,000
Gain on disposal of used trucks		$ 7,000

It follows that if the fair value of the trucks was $39,000 instead of $49,000, a loss on the exchange of $3,000 ($42,000 − $39,000) would be reported. In either case, as a result of the exchange of dissimilar assets, the earnings process on the used trucks has been completed and **a gain or loss should be recognized**.

Similar Assets—Loss Situation

Similar nonmonetary assets are those that are of the same general type, or that perform the same function, or that are employed in the same line of business. When similar nonmonetary assets are exchanged and a loss results, the loss should be recognized immediately. For example, Information Processing, Inc. trades its used accounting machine for a new model. The accounting machine given up has a book value of $8,000 (original cost $12,000 less $4,000 accumulated depreciation) and a fair value of $6,000. It is traded for a new model that has a list price of $16,000. In negotiations with the seller, a trade-in allowance of $9,000 is finally agreed on for the used machine. The cash payment that must be made for the new asset and the cost of the new machine are computed as follows:

List price of new machine	$16,000
Less trade-in allowance for used machine	9,000
Cash payment due	7,000
Fair value of used machine	6,000
Cost of new machine	$13,000

ILLUSTRATION 10-11
Computation of Cost of New Machine

The journal entry to record this transaction is:

Equipment	13,000	
Accumulated Depreciation—Equipment	4,000	
Loss on Disposal of Equipment	2,000	
Equipment		12,000
Cash		7,000

The loss on the disposal of the used machine can be verified as follows:

Fair value of used machine	$6,000
Book value of used machine	8,000
Loss on disposal of used machine	$2,000

ILLUSTRATION 10-12
Computation of Loss on Disposal of Used Machine

Why was the trade-in allowance or the book value of the old asset not used as a basis for the new equipment? The trade-in allowance is not used because it included a price concession (similar to a price discount) to the purchaser. Few individuals pay list price for a new car. Trade-in allowances on the used car are often inflated so that actual selling prices are below list prices. To record the car at list price would state it at an amount in excess of its cash equivalent price because the new car's list price is usually inflated. Use of book value in this situation would overstate the value of the new accounting machine by $2,000. Because assets should not be valued at more than their cash equivalent price, the loss should be recognized immediately rather than added to the cost of the newly acquired asset.

Similar Assets—Gain Situation, No Cash Received

The accounting treatment for exchanges of **similar** nonmonetary assets when a gain develops is more complex. If the exchange does not complete the earnings process, then any **gain should be deferred**.

The real estate industry provides a good example of why the accounting profession decided not to recognize gains on exchanges of similar nonmonetary assets. In this industry, it is common practice for companies to "swap" real estate holdings. Assume that Landmark Company and Hillfarm, Inc. each had undeveloped land on which they intended to build shopping centers. Appraisals indicated that the land of both companies had increased significantly in value. The companies decided to exchange (swap) their undeveloped land, record a gain, and report their new parcels of land at current fair values. But, should gains be recognized at this point? No: the earnings process is not completed because the companies remain in the same economic position after the swap as before. Therefore, the asset acquired should be recorded at book value with no gain recognized. In contrast, had book value exceeded fair value, a loss would be recognized immediately.

Davis Rent-A-Car has a rental fleet of automobiles consisting primarily of Ford Motor Company products. Davis' management is interested in increasing the variety of automobiles in its rental fleet by adding numerous General Motors models. Davis arranges with Nertz Rent-A-Car to exchange a group of Ford automobiles with a fair value of $160,000 and a book value of $135,000 (cost $150,000 less accumulated depreciation $15,000) for a number of Chevy and Pontiac models with a fair value of $170,000; Davis pays $10,000 in cash in addition to the Ford automobiles exchanged. The total gain to Davis Rent-A-Car is computed as shown in Illustration 10-13.

ILLUSTRATION 10-13
Computation of Gain
(Unrecognized)

Fair value of Ford automobiles exchanged	$160,000
Book value of Ford automobiles exchanged	135,000
Total gain (unrecognized)	$ 25,000

But the earnings process is not considered completed in this transaction. The company still has a fleet of cars, although different models. Therefore, the total gain is deferred and the basis of the General Motors automobiles is reduced via two different but acceptable computations as shown below:

ILLUSTRATION 10-14
Basis of New
Automobiles—Fair Value
vs. Book Value

Fair value of GM automobiles	$170,000		Book value of Ford automobiles	$135,000
Less gain deferred	(25,000)	OR	Cash paid	10,000
Basis of GM automobiles	$145,000		Basis of GM automobiles	$145,000

The entry by Davis to record this transaction is as follows:

Automobiles (GM)	145,000	
Accumulated Depreciation—Automobiles	15,000	
Automobiles (Ford)		150,000
Cash		10,000

The gain that reduced the basis of the new automobiles will be recognized when those automobiles are sold to an outside party. While these automobiles are held, depreciation charges will be lower and net income will be higher in subsequent periods because of the reduced basis.

Similar Assets—Gain Situation, Some Cash Received

The accounting issue of gain recognition becomes more difficult if monetary consideration such as cash is **received** in an exchange of similar nonmonetary assets. When cash is received, part of the nonmonetary asset is considered sold and part exchanged; therefore, only a portion of the gain is deferred. The general formula for gain recognition when some cash is received is as follows:

ILLUSTRATION 10-15
Formula for Gain
Recognition, Some Cash
Received

$$\frac{\text{Cash Received (Boot)}}{\text{Cash Received (Boot)} + \text{Fair Value of Other Assets Received}} \times \text{Total Gain} = \frac{\text{Recognized}}{\text{Gain}}$$

If the book value of Nertz's Chevy and Pontiac automobiles exchanged in the foregoing example is $136,000 (cost $200,000 less accumulated depreciation $64,000), then the total gain on the exchange to Nertz would be computed as follows:

ILLUSTRATION 10-16
Computation of
Total Gain

Fair value of GM automobiles exchanged	$170,000
Book value of GM automobiles exchanged	136,000
Total gain	$ 34,000

But, because Nertz received $10,000 in cash, the recognized gain on this transaction is computed as follows:

ILLUSTRATION 10-17
Computation of
Recognized Gain Based
on Ratio of Cash
Received

$$\frac{\$10,000}{\$10,000 + \$160,000} \times \$34,000 = \$2,000$$

The ratio of monetary assets ($10,000) to the total consideration received ($10,000 + $160,000) is the portion of the total gain ($34,000) to be recognized—that is, $2,000. Because only a gain of $2,000 is recognized on this transaction, the remaining $32,000 ($34,000 − $2,000) is deferred and reduces the basis (recorded cost) of the new automobiles. The computation of the basis is as follows:

Fair value of Ford automobiles	$160,000		Book value of GM automobiles	$136,000
Less gain deferred	(32,000)	OR	Portion of book value	
Basis of Ford automobiles	$128,000		presumed sold	(8,000)*
			Basis of Ford automobiles	$128,000

$$* \frac{\$10,000}{\$170,000} \times \$136,000 = \$8,000$$

ILLUSTRATION 10-18
Basis of New
Automobiles—Fair Value
vs. Book Value

The entry by Nertz to record this transaction is as follows:

Cash	10,000	
Automobiles (Ford)	128,000	
Accumulated Depreciation—Automobiles (GM)	64,000	
Automobiles (GM)		200,000
Gain on Disposal of GM Automobiles		2,000

The rationale for this treatment is as follows: Before the exchange, Nertz Rent-A-Car had an unrecognized gain of $34,000, as evidenced by the difference between the book value ($136,000) and the fair value ($170,000) of its GM automobiles. When the exchange occurred, a portion ($10,000/$170,000 or 1/17) of the fair value was converted to a more liquid asset. The ratio of this liquid asset ($10,000) to the total consideration received ($160,000 + $10,000) is the portion of the gain ($34,000) realized. Thus, a gain of $2,000 (1/17 × $34,000) is recognized and recorded.

Presented below in summary form are the accounting requirements for recognizing gains and losses on exchanges of nonmonetary assets.[10]

1. Compute the total gain or loss on the transaction, which is equal to the difference between the fair value of the asset given up and the book value of the asset given up.
2. If a loss is computed in 1, always recognize the entire loss.
3. If a gain is computed in 1,
   (a) and the earnings process is considered completed, the entire gain is recognized (dissimilar assets).
   (b) and the earnings process is not considered completed (similar assets),
       (1) and no cash is involved, no gain is recognized.
       (2) and some cash is given, no gain is recognized.
       (3) and some cash is received, the following portion of the gain is recognized:

$$\frac{\text{Cash Received (Boot)}}{\text{Cash Received (Boot)} + \text{Fair Value of Other Assets Received}} \times \text{Total Gain}$$

ILLUSTRATION 10-19
Summary of Gain and
Loss Recognition on
Exchanges of
Nonmonetary Assets

An enterprise that engages in one or more nonmonetary exchanges during a period should disclose in financial statements for the period the nature of the transactions, the method of accounting for the assets transferred, and gains or losses recognized on transfers.[11]

Accounting for Contributions

Companies sometimes receive or make contributions (donations or gifts). Such contributions are referred to as nonreciprocal transfers because they are transfers of assets in one direction. Contributions are often some type of asset (such as cash, securities, land, buildings, or use of facilities), but it also could be the forgiveness of a debt.

When assets are acquired as a donation, a strict cost concept dictates that the valuation of the asset should be zero. A departure from the cost principle seems justified, however, because the only costs incurred (legal fees and other relatively minor expenditures) do not constitute a reasonable basis of accounting for the assets acquired. To record nothing is to ignore the economic realities of an increase in wealth and assets.

---

[10]Adapted from an article by Robert Capettini and Thomas E. King, "Exchanges of Nonmonetary Assets: Some Changes," *The Accounting Review* (January 1976).

[11]"Accounting for Nonmonetary Transactions," op. cit., par. 28.

Therefore, **the fair value of the asset should be used to establish its value on the books**.

Two general approaches have been used to record the credit for the asset received. Some believe the credit should be to Donated Capital (an additional paid-in capital account). The increase in assets is viewed more as contributed capital than as earned revenue. Others argue that capital is contributed only by the owners of the business and that donations are benefits to the enterprise that should be reported as revenues from contributions. At issue is whether the revenue should be reported immediately or over the period that the asset is employed. To attract new industry a city may offer land, but the receiving enterprise may incur additional costs in the future (transportation, higher state income taxes, etc.) because the location is not the most desirable. As a consequence, some argue that the revenue should be deferred and recognized as the costs are incurred.

In a recent standard, the FASB has taken the position that, **in general, contributions received should be recognized as revenues in the period received**.[12] Contributions would be measured at the fair value of the assets received.[13] To illustrate, Max Wayer Meat Packing, Inc. has recently accepted a donation of land with a fair value of $150,000 from the Memphis Industrial Development Corp. in return for a promise to build a packing plant in Memphis. Max Wayer's entry is:

Land	150,000	
Contribution Revenue		150,000

When a nonmonetary asset is contributed, the amount of the donation should be recorded as an expense at the fair value of the donated asset. If a difference exists between the fair value of the asset and its book value, a gain or loss should be recognized. To illustrate, Kline Industries donates land that cost $80,000 and has a fair market value of $110,000 to the city of Los Angeles for a city park. The entry to record this donation would be:

Contribution Expense	110,000	
Land		80,000
Gain on Disposal of Land		30,000

In some cases, companies will promise to give (pledge) some type of asset in the future. The question is whether this promise should be recorded immediately or at the time the assets are given. If the promise is **unconditional** (depends only on the passage of time or on demand by the recipient for performance), the contribution expense and related payable should be reported. If the promise is **conditional**, the expense is recognized in the period benefited by the contribution, which is generally when the asset is transferred.

Other Asset Valuation Methods

As indicated above, an exception to the historical cost principle arises in the acquisition of plant assets through donation, which is based on fair value. Another approach that is sometimes allowed and not considered a violation of historical cost is a concept often referred to as prudent cost. This concept states that if for some reason you were ignorant about a certain price and paid too much for the asset originally, it is theoretically preferable to charge a loss immediately.

As an example, assume that a company constructs an asset at a cost substantially in excess of its present economic usefulness. In this case, it would be appropriate to

---

[12]"Accounting for Contributions Received and Contributions Made," *Statement of Financial Accounting Standards No. 116* (Norwalk, CT: FASB, 1993). Transfers of assets from governmental units to business enterprises are excluded from the scope of this standard. However, we believe that the basic requirements should hold also for these types of contributions and, therefore, all assets should be recorded at fair value and all credits should be recorded as revenue.

[13]"Accounting for Nonmonetary Transactions," op. cit., par. 18. Also, *FASB No. 116* indicates that expenses on contributions made should be recorded at the fair value of the assets given up.

charge these excess costs as a loss to the current period, rather than capitalize them as part of the cost of the asset. This problem seldom develops because at the outset individuals either use good reasoning in paying a given price or fail to recognize any such errors.

On the other hand, a purchase that is obtained at a bargain, or a piece of equipment internally constructed at a cost savings, should not result in immediate recognition of a gain under any circumstances. Although immediate recognition of a gain is conceptually appealing, the implications of such a treatment would be to change completely the entire basis of accounting.

❖ COSTS SUBSEQUENT TO ACQUISITION

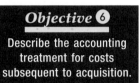

Objective ❻

Describe the accounting treatment for costs subsequent to acquisition.

After plant assets are installed and ready for use, additional costs are incurred that range from ordinary repair to significant additions. The major problem is allocating these costs to the proper time periods. **In general, costs incurred to achieve greater future benefits should be capitalized, whereas expenditures that simply maintain a given level of services should be expensed.** In order for costs to be capitalized, one of three conditions must be present:

❶ The useful life of the asset must be increased.
❷ The quantity of units produced from the asset must be increased.
❸ The quality of the units produced must be enhanced.

Expenditures that do not increase an asset's future benefits should be expensed. Ordinary repairs are expenditures that maintain the existing condition of the asset or restore it to normal operating efficiency and should be expensed immediately.

Most expenditures below an established arbitrary minimum amount are expensed rather than capitalized. Many enterprises have adopted the rule that expenditures below, say, $100 or $500, should always be expensed. Although conceptually this treatment may not be correct, expediency demands it. Otherwise, depreciation schedules would have to be set up for such items as wastepaper baskets and ash trays.

The distinction between a capital (asset) and revenue (expense) expenditure is not always clear-cut. Determining the **property unit** with which costs should be associated is critical. If a fully equipped steamship is considered a property unit, then replacement of the engine might be considered an expense. On the other hand, if the ship's engine is considered a property unit, then its replacement would be capitalized. AT&T at one time argued that it should be permitted to expense its station connectors (wires that connect your telephone to the outside wall). Previously, these wires had been capitalized and depreciated over an 8-year period. AT&T argued that continual home occupancy changes resulted in so much rewiring that expensing these wires was more appropriate. The Federal Communications Commission approved this request, and, the cost of wiring is now expensed. This decision is significant: it was at one time estimated that the cost of phone installation in Illinois would triple as a result of this accounting change. In most cases, **consistent application of a capital/expense policy** is justified as more important than attempting to provide general theoretical guidelines for each transaction.

Generally, four major types of expenditures are incurred relative to existing assets.

❖ MAJOR TYPES OF EXPENDITURES ❖

ADDITIONS. Increase or extension of existing assets.

IMPROVEMENTS AND REPLACEMENTS. Substitution of an improved asset for an existing one.

REARRANGEMENT AND REINSTALLATION. Movement of assets from one location to another.

REPAIRS. Expenditures that maintain assets in condition for operation.

Additions

Additions should present no major accounting problems. By definition, **any addition to plant assets is capitalized** because a new asset has been created. The addition of a wing to a hospital or the addition of an air conditioning system to an office, for example, increases the service potential of that facility. Such expenditures should be capitalized and matched against the revenues that will result in future periods.

The most difficult problem that develops in this area is accounting for any changes related to the existing structure as a result of the addition. Is the cost that is incurred to tear down an old wall to make room for the addition a cost of the addition or an expense or loss of the period? The answer is that it depends on the original intent. If the company had anticipated that an addition was going to be added later, then this cost of removal is a proper cost of the addition. But if the company had not anticipated this development, it should properly be reported as a loss in the current period on the basis that the company was inefficient in its planning. Normally, the carrying amount of the old wall remains in the accounts, although theoretically it should be removed.

Improvements and Replacements

Improvements (often referred to as betterments) and replacements are substitutions of one asset for another. What is the difference between an improvement and a replacement? An improvement is the substitution of a **better asset** for the one currently used (say, a concrete floor for a wooden floor). A replacement, on the other hand, is the substitution of a **similar asset** (a wooden floor for a wooden floor).

Many times improvements and replacements result from a general policy to modernize or rehabilitate an older building or piece of equipment. The problem is differentiating these types of expenditure from normal repairs. Does the expenditure increase the **future service potential** of the asset, or does it merely **maintain the existing level** of service? Frequently, the answer is not clear-cut, and good judgment must be used in order to classify these expenditures.

If it is determined that the expenditure increases the future service potential of the asset and, therefore, should be capitalized, the accounting is handled in one of three ways, depending on the circumstances.

❶ *Substitution Approach.* Conceptually, the substitution approach is the correct procedure if the carrying amount of the old asset is available. If the carrying amount of the old asset can be determined, it is a simple matter to remove the cost of the old asset and replace it with the cost of the new asset.

To illustrate, Instinct Enterprises decides to replace the pipes in its plumbing system. A plumber suggests that in place of the cast iron pipes and copper tubing, a newly developed plastic tubing be used. The old pipe and tubing have a book value of $15,000 (cost of $150,000 less accumulated depreciation of $135,000), and a scrap value of $1,000. The plastic tubing system has a cost of $125,000. Assuming that Instinct has to pay $124,000 for the new tubing after exchanging the old tubing, the entry is:

Plumbing System	125,000	
Accumulated Depreciation	135,000	
Loss on Disposal of Plant Assets	14,000	
Plumbing System		150,000
Cash ($125,000 − $1.000)		124,000

The problem is determining the book value of the old asset. Generally, the components of a given asset depreciate at different rates, but no separate accounting is made. As an example, the tires, motor, and body of a truck depreciate at different rates, but most concerns use only one depreciation rate for the entire truck. Separate depreciation rates could be set for each component, but it would be impractical. If the carrying amount of the old asset cannot be determined, one of two other approaches is adopted.

❷ *Capitalizing the New Cost.* The justification for capitalizing the cost of the improvement or replacement is that even though the carrying amount of the old asset is not removed from the accounts, sufficient depreciation was taken on the item to reduce the carrying amount almost to zero. Although this assumption may not be true in every case, the differences are not often significant. Improvements are usually handled in this manner.

❸ *Charging to Accumulated Depreciation.* There are times when the quantity or quality of the asset itself has not been improved, but its useful life has been extended. Replacements, particularly, may extend the useful life of the asset, yet may not improve its quality or quantity. In these circumstances, the expenditure may be debited to Accumulated Depreciation rather than to an asset account. The theory behind this approach is that the replacement extends the useful life of the asset and thereby recaptures some or all of the past depreciation. The net carrying amount of the asset is the same whether the asset is debited or the accumulated depreciation is debited.

Rearrangement and Reinstallation

Rearrangement and reinstallation costs, which are expenditures intended to benefit future periods, are different from additions, replacements, and improvements. An example is the rearrangement and reinstallation of a group of machines to facilitate future production. If the original installation cost and the accumulated depreciation taken to date can be determined or estimated, the rearrangement and reinstallation cost is handled as a replacement. If not, which is generally the case, the new costs (if material in amount) should be capitalized as an asset to be amortized over those future periods expected to benefit.[14] If these costs are not material, if they cannot be separated from other operating expenses, or if their future benefit is questionable, they should be immediately expensed.

Repairs

Ordinary repairs are expenditures made to maintain plant assets in operating condition; they are charged to an expense account in the period in which they are incurred on the basis that **it is the primary period benefited**. Replacement of minor parts, lubricating and adjusting of equipment, repainting, and cleaning are examples of maintenance charges that occur regularly and are treated as ordinary operating expenses.

It is often difficult to distinguish a repair from an improvement or replacement. The major consideration is whether the expenditure benefits more than one year or one operating cycle, whichever is longer. If a major repair, such as an overhaul, occurs, several periods will benefit and the cost should be handled as an addition, improvement, or replacement.

If income statements are prepared for short periods of time, say, monthly or quarterly, the same principles apply. Ordinary repairs and other regular maintenance charges for an annual period may benefit several quarters, and allocation of the cost among the periods concerned might be required. A concern will often find it advantageous to concentrate its repair program at a certain time of the year, perhaps during the period of least activity or when the plant is shut down for vacation. Short-term comparative statements might be misleading if such expenditures were shown as expenses of the quarter in which they were incurred. To give comparability to monthly or quarterly income statements, an account such as Allowance for Repairs might be used so that repair costs could be better assigned to periods benefited.

To illustrate, Cricket Tractor Company estimated that its total repair expense for the year would be $720,000. It decided to charge each quarter for a portion of the repair cost even though the total cost for the year would occur only in two quarters.

---

[14]Another cost of this nature is relocation costs. For example, when Shell Oil moved its headquarters from New York to Houston, it amortized the cost of relocating over 4 years. Conversely, estimated relocation costs of $15 million were charged to expense at GAF Corp. The point is that no definitive guidelines have been established in this area, and generally costs are deferred over some arbitrary period in the future. Some writers have argued that these costs should generally be expensed as incurred. See, for example, Charles W. Lamden, Dale L. Gerboth, and Thomas W. McRae, "Accounting for Depreciable Assets," *Accounting Research Monograph No. 1* (New York: AICPA, 1975), pp. 54–61.

End of First Quarter (zero repair costs incurred):

Repair Expense	180,000	
Allowance for Repairs (¼ × 720,000)		180,000

End of Second Quarter ($344,000 repair costs incurred):

Allowance for Repairs	344,000	
Cash, Wages Payable, Inventory, etc.		344,000
Repair Expense	180,000	
Allowance for Repairs (¼ × $720,000)		180,000

End of Third Quarter (zero repair costs incurred):

Repair Expense	180,000	
Allowance for Repairs (¼ × $720,000)		180,000

End of Fourth Quarter ($380,800 repair costs incurred):

Allowance for Repairs	380,800	
Cash, Wages Payable, Inventory, etc.		380,800
Repair Expense	184,800	
Allowance for Repairs		184,800
($344,000 + $380,800 − $180,000 − $180,000 − $180,000)		

Ordinarily, no balance in the Allowance for Repairs account should be carried over to the following year. The fourth quarter would normally absorb the variation from estimates. If balance sheets are prepared during the year, the Allowance account should be added to or subtracted from the property, plant, and equipment section to obtain a proper valuation.

Some advocate accruing estimated repair costs beyond one year on the assumption that depreciation does not take into consideration the incurrence of repair costs. For example, in aircraft overhaul and open hearth furnace rebuilding, an allowance for repairs is sometimes established because the amount of repairs can be estimated with a high degree of certainty. Although conceptually appealing, it is difficult to justify the Allowance for Repairs account as a liability because one might ask, To whom do you owe the liability? Placement in the stockholders' equity section is also illogical because no addition to the stockholders' investment has taken place. One possibility might be to treat allowance for repairs as an addition to or subtraction from the asset on the basis that the value has changed. In general, expenses should not be anticipated before they arise unless estimates of the future are reasonably predictable.

Summary of Costs Subsequent to Acquisition

The following schedule summarizes the accounting treatment for various costs incurred subsequent to the acquisition of capitalized assets.

ILLUSTRATION 10-20
Summary of Costs
Subsequent to
Acquisition of Property,
Plant, and Equipment

Type of Expenditure	Normal Accounting Treatment
Additions	Capitalize cost of addition to asset account.

Improvements and Replacements	(a) **Carrying value known:** Remove cost of and accumulated depreciation on old asset, recognizing any gain or loss. Capitalize cost of improvement/replacement.
	(b) **Carrying value unknown:**
	  1. If the asset's useful life is extended, debit accumulated depreciation for cost of improvement/replacement.
	  2. If the quantity or quality of the asset's productivity is increased, capitalized cost of improvement/replacement to asset account.

Rearrangement and Reinstallation	(a) If original installation cost is **known,** account for cost of rearrangement/reinstallation as a replacement (carrying value known). (b) If original installation cost is **unknown** and rearrangement/reinstallation cost is **material** in amount and benefits future periods, capitalize as an asset. (c) If original installation cost is **unknown** and rearrangement/reinstallation cost is **not material or future benefit is questionable,** expense the cost when incurred.
Repairs	(a) **Ordinary:** Expense cost of repairs when incurred. (b) **Major:** As appropriate, treat as an addition, improvement, or replacement.

❖ DISPOSITIONS OF PLANT ASSETS

Plant assets may be retired voluntarily or disposed of by sale, exchange, involuntary conversion, or abandonment. Regardless of the time of disposal, depreciation must be taken up to the date of disposition, and then all accounts related to the retired asset should be removed. Ideally, the book value of the specific plant asset would be equal to its disposal value. But this is generally not the case. As a result, a gain or loss develops. The reason: depreciation is an estimate of cost allocation and not a process of valuation. **The gain or loss is really a correction of net income** for the years during which the fixed asset was used. If it had been possible at the time of acquisition to forecast the exact date of disposal and the amount to be realized at disposition, then a more accurate estimate of depreciation could have been recorded and no gain or loss would be incurred.

Gains or losses on the retirement of plant assets should be shown in the income statement along with other items that arise from customary business activities. If, however, the "operations of a segment of a business" are sold, abandoned, spun off, or otherwise disposed of, then the results of "continuing operations" should be reported separately from "discontinued operations." Any gain or loss from disposal of a segment of a business should be reported with the related results of discontinued operations and not as an extraordinary item.

> ### Objective ❼
>
> Describe the accounting treatment for the disposal of property, plant, and equipment.

Sale of Plant Assets

Depreciation must be recorded for the period of time between the date of the last depreciation entry and the date of sale. To illustrate, assume that depreciation on a machine costing $18,000 has been recorded for nine years at the rate of $1,200 per year. If the machine is sold in the middle of the tenth year for $7,000, the entry to record depreciation to the date of sale is:

Depreciation Expense	600	
Accumulated Depreciation—Machinery		600

This separate entry ordinarily is not made because most companies enter all depreciation, including this amount, in one entry at the end of the year. In either case the entry for the sale of the asset is:

Cash	7,000	
Accumulated Depreciation—Machinery	11,400	
[($1,200 × 9) + $600]		
Machinery		18,000
Gain on Disposal of Machinery		400

The book value of the machinery at the time of the sale is $6,600 ($18,000 − $11,400); because it is sold for $7,000, the amount of the gain on the sale is $400.

Involuntary Conversion

Sometimes, an asset's service is terminated through some type of involuntary conversion such as fire, flood, theft, or condemnation. The gains or losses are treated no differently from those in any other type of disposition except that **they are often reported in the extraordinary items section of the income statement**.

To illustrate, Camel Transport Corp. was forced to sell a plant located on company property that stood directly in the path of an interstate highway. For a number of years the state had sought to purchase the land on which the plant stood, but the company resisted. The state ultimately exercised its right of eminent domain and was upheld by the courts. In settlement, Camel received $500,000, which was substantially in excess of the $200,000 book value of the plant and land (cost of $400,000 less accumulated depreciation of $200,000). The following entry was made:

Cash	500,000	
Accumulated Depreciation—Plant Assets	200,000	
Plant Assets		400,000
Gain on Disposal of Plant Assets		300,000

However, some object to the recognition of a gain or loss in certain involuntary conversions. For example, the federal government often condemns forests for national parks; as a result, the paper companies that owned these forests are required to report a gain or loss on the condemnation. However, companies such as Georgia-Pacific contend that because they must replace this condemned forest land immediately, they are in the same economic position as they were before and no gain or loss should be reported. The issue is whether the condemnation and subsequent purchase should be viewed as one or two transactions. *FASB Interpretation No. 30* rules against the companies by requiring "that gain or loss be recognized when a nonmonetary asset is involuntarily converted to monetary assets even though an enterprise reinvests or is obligated to reinvest the monetary assets in replacement nonmonetary assets."[15]

The gain or loss that develops on these types of unusual, nonrecurring transactions should be shown as an extraordinary item. Similar treatment is given to other types of involuntary conversions such as those resulting from a major casualty (such as an earthquake) or an expropriation, assuming that it meets other conditions for extraordinary item treatment. The difference between the amount recovered (condemnation award or insurance recovery), if any, and the asset's book value is reported as a gain or loss.

Miscellaneous Problems

If an asset is scrapped or abandoned without any cash recovery, a loss should be recognized equal to the asset's book value. If scrap value exists, the gain or loss that occurs is the difference between the asset's scrap value and its book value. If an asset still can be used even though it is fully depreciated, it may be kept on the books at historical cost less depreciation, or the asset may be carried at scrap value.

Disclosure of the amount of fully depreciated assets in service should be made in notes to the financial statements. For example, Petroleum Equipment Tools Inc. in its Annual Report disclosed: "The amount of fully depreciated assets included in property, plant, and equipment at December 31 amounted to approximately $98,900,000."

SUMMARY OF LEARNING OBJECTIVES

❶ Describe the major characteristics of property, plant, and equipment. The major characteristics of property, plant, and equipment are: (1) They are acquired for use in operations and not for resale; (2) they are long-term in nature and usually subject to depreciation; and (3) they possess physical substance.

❷ Identify the costs included in the initial valuation of land, buildings, and equipment. *Cost of land:* Includes all expenditures made to acquire land and to ready it for use. Land costs typically include (1) the purchase price; (2) closing costs, such as title to the land, attorney's fees, and recording fees; (3) costs incurred in getting the land in condition for its intended use, such as grading, filling, draining, and clearing; (4) assumption of any liens, mortgages, or encumbrances on the property; and (5) any additional land improvements that have an indefinite life.

Cost of buildings: Includes all expenditures related directly to their acquisition or construction. These costs include (1) materials, labor, and overhead costs incurred during construction and (2) professional fees and building permits.

Cost of equipment: Includes the purchase price, freight and handling charges incurred, insurance on the equipment while in transit, cost of special foundations if required, assembling and installation costs, and costs of conducting trial runs.

❸ Describe the accounting problems associated with self-constructed assets. The assignment of indirect costs of manufacturing creates special problems because these costs cannot be traced directly to work and material orders related to

KEY TERMS

additions, *518*
avoidable interest, *504*
betterments, *518*
capital expenditure, *517*
capitalization period, *504*
dissimilar nonmonetary asset, *512*
fixed assets, *500*
historical cost, *501*
improvements (betterments), *518*
involuntary conversion, *521*
lump sum price, *510*
major repairs, *519*
nonmonetary assets, *511*
nonreciprocal transfers, *515*
ordinary repairs, *519*
plant assets, *500*
property, plant, and equipment, *500*
prudent cost, *516*
rearrangement and reinstallation costs, *519*
replacements, *518*
revenue expenditure, *517*
self-constructed asset, *502*
similar nonmonetary assets, *512*
weighted-average accumulated expenditures, *504*

[15]"Accounting for Involuntary Conversions of Nonmonetary Assets to Monetary Assets," *FASB Interpretation No. 30* (Stamford, Conn.: FASB, 1979), summary paragraph.

the fixed assets constructed. These costs might be handled in one of three ways: (1) Assign no fixed overhead to the cost of the constructed asset, (2) assign a portion of all overhead to the construction process, or (3) allocate on the basis of lost production. The second method is used extensively in practice.

4 *Describe the accounting problems associated with interest capitalization.* Only actual interest (with modifications) should be capitalized. The rationale for this approach is that during construction, the asset is not generating revenue and therefore interest cost should be deferred (capitalized); once construction is completed, the asset is ready for its intended use and revenues can be earned. Any interest cost incurred in purchasing an asset that is ready for its intended use should be expensed.

5 *Understand accounting issues related to acquiring and valuing plant assets.* The following issues relate to acquiring and valuing plant assets: (1) *Cash discounts*: Whether taken or not, they are generally considered a reduction in the cost of the asset; the real cost of the asset is the cash or cash equivalent price of the asset. (2) *Assets purchased on long-term credit contracts*: Are accounted for at the present value of the consideration exchanged between the contracting parties. (3) *Lump sum purchase*: Allocate the total cost among the various assets on the basis of their relative fair market values. (4) *Issuance of stock*: If the stock is being actively traded, the market value of the stock issued is a fair indication of the cost of the property acquired; if the market value of the common stock exchanged is not determinable, the value of the property should be established and used as the basis for recording the asset and issuance of the common stock. (5) *Exchanges of property, plant, and equipment.* See Illustration 10-19 for a summary of how to account for exchanges. (6) *Contributions*: Should be recorded at the fair value of the asset received and a related credit should be made to revenue for the same amount.

6 *Describe the accounting treatment for costs subsequent to acquisition.* See Illustration 10-20 for a summary of how to account for costs subsequent to acquisition.

7 *Describe the accounting treatment for the disposal of property, plant, and equipment.* Regardless of the time of disposal, depreciation must be taken up to the date of disposition, and then all accounts related to the retired asset should be removed. Gains or losses on the retirement of plant assets should be shown in the income statement along with other items that arise from customary business activities. Gains or losses on involuntary conversions should be reported as extraordinary items. If an asset is scrapped or abandoned without any cash recovery, a loss should be recognized equal to the asset's book value. If scrap value exists, the gain or loss that occurs is the difference between the asset's scrap value and its book value.

❖ QUESTIONS ❖

1 What are the major characteristics of plant assets?

2 Esplanade Inc. owns land that it purchased on January 1, 1991, for $420,000. At December 31, 1998, its current value is $770,000 as determined by appraisal. At what amount should Esplanade report this asset on its December 31, 1998, balance sheet? Explain.

3 Name the items, in addition to the amount paid to the former owner or contractor, that may properly be included as part of the acquisition cost of the following plant assets:
(a) Land.
(b) Machinery and equipment.
(c) Buildings.

4 Indicate where the following items would be shown on a balance sheet.
(a) A lien that was attached to the land when purchased.
(b) Landscaping costs.

(c) Attorney's fees and recording fees related to purchasing land.

(d) Variable overhead related to construction of machinery.

(e) A parking lot servicing employees in the building.

(f) Cost of temporary building for workers during construction of building.

(g) Interest expense on bonds payable incurred during construction of a building.

(h) Assessments for sidewalks that are maintained by the city.

(i) The cost of demolishing an old building that was on the land when purchased.

5 Three positions have normally been taken with respect to the recording of fixed manufacturing overhead as an element of the cost of plant assets constructed by a company for its own use:

(a) It should be excluded completely.

(b) It should be included at the same rate as is charged to normal operations.

(c) It should be allocated on the basis of the lost production that occurs from normal operations.

What are the circumstances or rationale that support or deny the application of these methods?

6 The Buildings account of Diego Rivera Inc. includes the following items that were used in determining the basis for depreciating the cost of a building:

(a) Organization and promotion expenses.

(b) Architect's fees.

(c) Interest and taxes during construction.

(d) Commission paid on the sale of capital stock.

(e) Bond discount and expenses.

Do you agree with these charges? If not, how would you deal with each of the items above in the corporation's books and in its annual financial statements?

7 One financial accounting issue encountered when a company constructs its own plant is whether the interest cost on funds borrowed to finance construction should be capitalized and then amortized over the life of the assets constructed. What is a common accounting justification for capitalizing such interest?

8 What interest rates should be used in determining the amount of interest to be capitalized? How should the amount of interest to be capitalized be determined?

9 How should the amount of interest capitalized be disclosed in the footnotes to the financial statements? How should interest revenue from temporarily invested excess funds borrowed to finance the construction of assets be accounted for?

10 Discuss the basic accounting problem that arises in handling each of the following situations.

(a) Assets purchased by issuance of capital stock.

(b) Acquisition of plant assets by gift or donation.

(c) Purchase of a plant asset subject to a cash discount.

(d) Assets purchased on a long-term credit basis.

(e) A group of assets acquired for a lump sum.

(f) An asset traded in or exchanged for another asset.

11 Yukio Mishima Industries acquired equipment this year to be used in its operations. The equipment was delivered by the suppliers, installed by Mishima, and placed into operation. Some of it was purchased for cash with discounts available for prompt payment. Some of it was purchased under long-term payment plans for which the interest charges approximated prevailing rates. What costs should Mishima capitalize for the new equipment purchased this year? Explain.

12 Adam Mickiewicz Co. purchased for $2,200,00 property that included both land and a building to be used in operations. The seller's book value was $300,000 for the land and $900,000 for the building. By appraisal, the fair market value was estimated to be $500,000 for the land and $2,000,000 for the building. At what amount should Mickiewicz report the land and the building at the end of the year?

13 Jean Rousseau is studying for an accounting examination. She is having difficulty with the topic of exchanging plant assets. Explain to Jean what steps should be followed when accounting for an exchange of plant assets.

14 Saadi Company purchased a heavy-duty truck on July 1, 1995, for $30,000. It was estimated that it would have a useful life of 10 years and then would have a trade-in value of $6,000. It was traded on August 1, 1999, for a similar truck costing $39,000; $13,000 was allowed as trade-in value (also fair value) on the old truck and $26,000 was paid in cash. What is the entry to record the trade-in? The company uses the straight-line method.

15 Once equipment has been installed and placed in operation, subsequent expenditures relating to this equipment are frequently thought of as repairs or general maintenance and, hence, chargeable to operations in the period in which the expenditure is made. Actually, determination of whether such an expenditure should be charged to operations or capitalized involves a much more careful analysis of the character of the expenditure. What are the factors that should be considered in making such a decision? Discuss fully.

16 What accounting treatment is normally given to the following items in accounting for plant assets?

(a) Additions.

(b) Major repairs.

(c) Improvements and replacements.

17 New machinery, which replaced a number of employees, was installed and put in operation in the last month of the fiscal year. The employees had been dismissed after payment of an extra month's wages and this amount was added to the cost of the machinery. Discuss the propriety of the charge and, if it was improper, describe the proper treatment.

18 To what extent do you consider the following items to be proper costs of the fixed asset? Give reasons for your opinions.

(a) Overhead of a business that builds its own equipment.
(b) Cost of constructing new models of machinery.
(c) Cash discounts on purchases of equipment.
(d) Interest paid during construction of a building.
(e) Cost of a safety device installed on a machine.
(f) Freight on equipment returned before installation, for replacement by other equipment of greater capacity.
(g) Cost of moving machinery to a new location.
(h) Cost of plywood partitions erected as part of the remodeling of the office.
(i) Replastering of a section of the building.
(j) Cost of a new motor for one of the trucks.

19 Recently, Michelangelo Manufacturing Co. presented the account "Allowance for Repairs" in the long-term liability section. Evaluate this procedure.

20 Dimitri Enterprises has a number of fully depreciated assets that are still being used in the main operations of the business. Because the assets are fully depreciated, the president of the company decides not to show them on the balance sheet or disclose this information in the footnotes. Evaluate this procedure.

❖ BRIEF EXERCISES ❖

BE10-1 Bonanza Brothers Inc. purchased land at a price of $27,000. Closing costs were $1,400. An old building was removed at a cost of $12,200. What amount should be recorded as the cost of the land?

BE10-2 Brett Hull Company is constructing a building. Construction began on February 1 and was completed on December 31. Expenditures were $1,500,000 on March 1, $1,200,000 on June 1, and $3,000,000 on December 31. Compute Hull's weighted-average accumulated expenditures for interest capitalization purposes.

BE10-3 Brett Hull Company (See BE10-2) borrowed $1,000,000 on March 1 on a 5-year, 12% note to help finance construction of the building. In addition, the company had outstanding all year a 13%, 5-year, $2,000,000 note payable and a 15%, 4-year, $3,500,000 note payable. Compute the weighted-average interest rate used for interest capitalization purposes.

BE10-4 Use the information for Brett Hull Company from BE10-2 and BE10-3. Compute avoidable interest for Brett Hull Company.

BE10-5 Chavez Corporation purchased a truck by issuing an $80,000, 4-year, noninterest-bearing note to Equinox Inc. The market rate of interest for obligations of this nature is 12%. Prepare the journal entry to record the purchase of this truck.

BE10-6 Cool Spot Inc. purchased land, building and equipment from Pinball Wizard Corporation for a cash payment of $306,000. The estimated fair values of the assets are land $60,000; building $220,000; and equipment $80,000. At what amounts should each of the three assets be recorded?

BE10-7 Dark Wizard Company obtained land by issuing 2,000 shares of its $10 par value common stock. The land was recently appraised at $85,000. The common stock is actively traded at $41 per share. Prepare the journal entry to record the acquisition of the land.

BE10-8 Strider Corporation traded a used truck (cost $20,000, accumulated depreciation $18,000) for a small computer worth $3,700. Strider also paid $1,000 in the transaction. Prepare the journal entry to record the exchange.

BE10-9 Bubey Company traded a used truck for a new truck. The used truck cost $30,000 and has accumulated depreciation of $27,000. The new truck is worth $35,000. Bubey also made a cash payment of $33,000. Prepare Bubey's entry to record the exchange.

BE10-10 Buck Rogers Corporation traded a used truck for a new truck. The used truck cost $20,000 and has accumulated depreciation of $17,000. The new truck is worth $35,000. Rogers also made a cash payment of $33,000. Prepare Rogers' entry to record the exchange.

BE10-11 Indicate which of the following costs should be expensed when incurred.

(a) $13,000 paid to rearrange and reinstall machinery.
(b) $200 paid for tune-up and oil change on delivery truck.

(c) $200,000 paid for addition to building.
(d) $7,000 paid to replace a wooden floor with a concrete floor.
(e) $2,000 paid for a major overhaul on a truck, which extends useful life.
(f) $700,000 paid for relocation of company headquarters.

BE10-12 Sim City Corporation owns machinery that cost $20,000 when purchased on January 1, 1995. Depreciation has been recorded at a rate of $3,000 per year, resulting in a balance in accumulated depreciation of $9,000 at December 31, 1997. The machinery is sold on September 1, 1998, for $10,500. Prepare journal entries to (a) update depreciation for 1998 and (b) record the sale.

BE10-13 Use the information presented for Sim City Corporation in BE10-12, but assume the machinery is sold for $5,200 instead of $10,500. Prepare journal entries to (a) update depreciation for 1998 and (b) record the sale.

❖ EXERCISES ❖

E10-1 (Acquisition Costs of Realty) The following expenditures and receipts are related to land, land improvements, and buildings acquired for use in a business enterprise. The receipts are enclosed in parentheses.

(a)	Money borrowed to pay building contractor (signed a note)	$(275,000)
(b)	Payment for construction from note proceeds	275,000
(c)	Cost of land fill and clearing	8,000
(d)	Delinquent real estate taxes on property assumed by purchaser	7,000
(e)	Premium on six-month insurance policy during construction	6,000
(f)	Refund of one-month insurance premium because construction completed early	(1,000)
(g)	Architect's fee on building	22,000
(h)	Cost of real estate purchased as a plant site (land $200,000 and building $50,000)	250,000
(i)	Commission fee paid to real estate agency	9,000
(j)	Installation of fences around property	4,000
(k)	Cost of razing and removing building	11,000
(l)	Proceeds from salvage of demolished building	(5,000)
(m)	Interest paid during construction on money borrowed for construction	13,000
(n)	Cost of parking lots and driveways	19,000
(o)	Cost of trees and shrubbery planted (permanent in nature)	14,000
(p)	Excavation costs for new building	3,000

Instructions
Identify each item by letter and list the items in columnar form, as shown below. All receipt amounts should be reported in parentheses. For any amounts entered in the Other Accounts column also indicate the account title.

Item	Land	Land Improvements	Building	Other Accounts

E10-2 (Acquisition Costs of Realty) Martin Buber Co. purchased land as a factory site for $400,000. The process of tearing down two old buildings on the site and constructing the factory required 6 months.

The company paid $42,000 to raze the old buildings and sold salvaged lumber and brick for $6,300. Legal fees of $1,850 were paid for title investigation and drawing the purchase contract. Payment to an engineering firm was made for a land survey, $2,200, and for drawing the factory plans, $68,000. The land survey had to be made before definitive plans could be drawn. Title insurance on the property cost $1,500, and a liability insurance premium paid during construction was $900. The contractor's charge for construction was $2,740,000. The company paid the contractor in two installments: $1,200,000 at the end of 3 months and $1,540,000 upon completion. Interest costs of $170,000 were incurred to finance the construction.

Instructions
Determine the cost of the land and the cost of the building as they should be recorded on the books of Martin Buber Co. Assume that the land survey was for the building.

E10-3 (Acquisition Costs of Trucks) Alexei Urmanov Corporation operates a retail computer store. To improve delivery services to customers, the company purchases four new trucks on April 1, 1998. The terms of acquisition for each truck are described below:

1. Truck #1 has a list price of $15,000 and is acquired for a cash payment of $13,900.
2. Truck #2 has a list price of $16,000 and is acquired for a down payment of $2,000 cash and a noninterest-bearing note with a face amount of $14,000. The note is due April 1, 1999. Urmanov would normally have to pay interest at a rate of 10% for such a borrowing, and the dealership has an incremental borrowing rate of 8%.
3. Truck #3 has a list price of $16,000. It is acquired in exchange for a computer system that Urmanov carries in inventory. The computer system cost $12,000 and is normally sold by Urmanov for $15,200. Urmanov uses a perpetual inventory system.
4. Truck #4 has a list price of $14,000. It is acquired in exchange for 1,000 shares of common stock in Urmanov Corporation. The stock has a par value per share of $10 and a market value of $13 per share.

Instructions

Prepare the appropriate journal entries for the foregoing transactions for Urmanov Corporation.

E10-4 (Purchase and Self-Constructed Cost of Assets) Worf Co. both purchases and constructs various equipment it uses in its operations. The following items for two different types of equipment were recorded in random order during the calendar year 1999.

Purchase

Cash paid for equipment, including sales tax of $5,000	$105,000
Freight and insurance cost while in transit	2,000
Cost of moving equipment into place at factory	3,100
Wage cost for technicians to test equipment	4,000
Insurance premium paid during first year of operation on this equipment	1,500
Special plumbing fixtures required for new equipment	8,000
Repair cost incurred in first year of operations related to this equipment	1,300

Construction

Material and purchased parts (gross cost $200,000; failed to take 2% cash discount)	$200,000
Imputed interest on funds used during construction (stock financing)	14,000
Labor costs	190,000
Overhead costs (fixed—$20,000; variable—$30,000)	50,000
Profit on self-construction	30,000
Cost of installing equipment	4,400

Instructions

Compute the total cost for each of these two pieces of equipment. If an item is not capitalized as a cost of the equipment, indicate how it should be reported.

E10-5 (Treatment of Various Costs) Ben Sisko Supply Company, a newly formed corporation, incurred the following expenditures related to Land, to Buildings, and to Machinery and Equipment.

Abstract company's fee for title search		$ 520
Architect's fees		2,800
Cash paid for land and dilapidated building thereon		87,000
Removal of old building	$20,000	
Less salvage	5,500	14,500
Surveying before construction		370
Interest on short-term loans during construction		7,400
Excavation before construction for basement		19,000
Machinery purchased (subject to 2% cash discount, which was not taken)		55,000
Freight on machinery purchased		1,340
Storage charges on machinery, necessitated by noncompletion of building when machinery was delivered		2,180
New building constructed (building construction took 6 months from date of purchase of land and old building)		485,000
Assessment by city for drainage project		1,600
Hauling charges for delivery of machinery from storage to new building		620
Installation of machinery		2,000
Trees, shrubs, and other landscaping after completion of building (permanent in nature)		5,400

Instructions

Determine the amounts that should be debited to Land, to Buildings, and to Machinery and Equipment. Assume the benefits of capitalizing interest during construction exceed the cost of implementation. Indicate how any costs not debited to these accounts should be recorded.

E10-6 (Correction of Improper Cost Entries)   Plant acquisitions for selected companies are as follows:

1. Belanna Industries Inc. acquired land, buildings, and equipment from a bankrupt company, Torres Co., for a lump sum price of $700,000. At the time of purchase, Torres assets had the following book and appraisal values:

	Book Values	Appraisal Values
Land	$200,000	$150,000
Buildings	250,000	350,000
Equipment	300,000	300,000

To be conservative, the company decided to take the lower of the two values for each asset acquired. The following entry was made:

Land	150,000	
Buildings	250,000	
Equipment	300,000	
Cash		700,000

2. Harry Enterprises purchased store equipment by making a $2,000 cash down payment and signing a 1-year $23,000, 10% note payable. The purchase was recorded as follows:

Store Equipment	27,300	
Cash		2,000
Note Payable		23,000
Interest Payable		2,300

3. Kim Company purchased office equipment for $20,000, terms 2/10, n/30. Because the company intended to take the discount, it made no entry until it paid for the acquisition. The entry was:

Office Equipment	20,000	
Cash		19,600
Purchase Discounts		400

4. Kaisson Inc. recently received at zero cost land from the Village of Cardassia as an inducement to locate their business in the Village. The appraised value of the land is $27,000. The company made no entry to record the land because it had no cost basis.

5. Zimmerman Company built a warehouse for $600,000. It could have purchased the building for $740,000. The controller made the following entry:

Warehouse	740,000	
Cash		600,000
Profit on Construction		140,000

Instructions

Prepare the entry that should have been made at the date of each acquisition.

E10-7 (Capitalization of Interest)   Harrisburg Furniture Company started construction of a combination office and warehouse building for its own use at an estimated cost of $5,000,000 on January 1, 1998. Harrisburg expected to complete the building by December 31, 1998. Harrisburg has the following debt obligations outstanding during the construction period.

Construction loan—12% interest, payable semiannually, issued December 31, 1997	$2,000,000
Short-term loan—10% interest, payable monthly, and principal payable at maturity on May 30, 1999	1,400,000
Long-term loan—11% interest, payable on January 1 of each year. Principal payable on January 1, 2002	1,000,000

Instructions (Carry all computations to two decimal places.)

(a) Assume that Harrisburg completed the office and warehouse building on December 31, 1998, as planned at a total cost of $5,200,000 and the weighted average of accumulated expenditures was $3,600,000. Compute the avoidable interest on this project.

(b) Compute the depreciation expense for the year ended December 31, 1999. Harrisburg elected to depreciate the building on a straight-line basis and determined that the asset has a useful life of 30 years and a salvage value of $300,000.

E10-8 (Capitalization of Interest) On December 31, 1997, Alma-Ata Inc. borrowed $3,000,000 at 12% payable annually to finance the construction of a new building. In 1998, the company made the following expenditures related to this building: March 1, $360,000; June 1, $600,000; July 1, $1,500,000; December 1, $1,500,000. Additional information is provided as follows:

1. Other debt outstanding
   Ten-year, 13% bond, December 31, 1991, interest payable annually $4,000,000
   Six-year, 10% note, dated December 31, 1995, interest payable annually $1,600,000
2. March 1, 1998, expenditure included land costs of $150,000
3. Interest revenue earned in 1998 $49,000

Instructions
   (a) Determine the amount of interest to be capitalized in 1998 in relation to the construction of the building.
   (b) Prepare the journal entry to record the capitalization of interest and the recognition of interest expense, if any, at December 31, 1998.

E10-9 (Capitalization of Interest) On July 31, 1998, Amsterdam Company engaged Minsk Tooling Company to construct a special-purpose piece of factory machinery. Construction was begun immediately and was completed on November 1, 1998. To help finance construction, on July 31, Amsterdam issued a $300,000, 3-year, 12% note payable at Netherlands National Bank, on which interest is payable each July 31. $200,000 of the proceeds of the note was paid to Minsk on July 31. The remainder of the proceeds was temporarily invested in short-term marketable securities at 10% until November 1. On November 1, Amsterdam made a final $100,000 payment to Minsk. Other than the note to Netherlands, Amsterdam's only outstanding liability at December 31, 1998, is a $30,000, 8%, 6-year note payable, dated January 1, 1995, on which interest is payable each December 31.

Instructions
   (a) Calculate the interest revenue, weighted-average accumulated expenditures, avoidable interest, and total interest cost to be capitalized during 1998. Round all computations to the nearest dollar.
   (b) Prepare the journal entries needed on the books of Amsterdam Company at each of the following dates:
   1. July 31, 1998.
   2. November 1, 1998.
   3. December 31, 1998.

E10-10 (Capitalization of Interest) The following three situations involve the capitalization of interest:

Situation I

On January 1, 1998, Oksana Baiul, Inc. signed a fixed-price contract to have Builder Associates construct a major plant facility at a cost of $4,000,000. It was estimated that it would take 3 years to complete the project. Also on January 1, 1998, to finance the construction cost, Oksana Baiul borrowed $4,000,000 payable in 10 annual installments of $400,000, plus interest at the rate of 10%. During 1998, Oksana Baiul made deposit and progress payments totaling $1,500,000 under the contract; the weighted-average amount of accumulated expenditures was $800,000 for the year. The excess borrowed funds were invested in short-term securities, from which Oksana Baiul realized investment income of $250,000.

Instructions
What amount should Oksana Baiul report as capitalized interest at December 31, 1998?

Situation II

During 1998, Midori Ito Corporation constructed and manufactured certain assets and incurred the following interest costs in connection with those activities:

	Interest costs incurred
Warehouse constructed for Ito's own use	$30,000
Special-order machine for sale to unrelated customer, produced according to customer's specifications	9,000
Inventories routinely manufactured, produced on a repetitive basis	8,000

All of these assets required an extended period of time for completion.

Instructions
Assuming the effect of interest capitalization is material, what is the total amount of interest costs to be capitalized?

Situation III

Peggy Fleming, Inc. has a fiscal year ending April 30. On May 1, 1998, Peggy Fleming borrowed $10,000,000 at 11% to finance construction of its own building. Repayments of the loan are to commence the month following completion of the building. During the year ended April 30, 1999, expenditures for the partially completed structure totaled $7,000,000. These expenditures were incurred evenly throughout the year. Interest earned on the unexpended portion of the loan amounted to $650,000 for the year.

Instructions

How much should be shown as capitalized interest on Peggy Fleming's financial statements at April 30, 1999?

(CPA adapted)

E10-11 (Entries for Equipment Acquisitions) Jane Geddes Engineering Corporation purchased conveyor equipment with a list price of $10,000. The vendor's credit terms were 2/10, n/30. Presented below are three independent cases related to the equipment. Assume that the purchases of equipment are recorded gross. (Round to nearest dollar.)
  (a) Geddes paid cash for the equipment eight days after the purchase.
  (b) Geddes traded in equipment with a book value of $2,000 (initial cost $8,000), and paid $9,500 in cash one month after the purchase. The old equipment could have been sold for $400 at the date of trade (assume similar equipment).
  (c) Geddes gave the vendor a $10,800 noninterest-bearing note for the equipment on the date of purchase. The note was due in one year and was paid on time. Assume that the effective interest rate in the market was 9%.

Instructions

Prepare the general journal entries required to record the acquisition and payment in each of the independent cases above. Round to the nearest dollar.

E10-12 (Entries for Asset Acquisition, Including Self-Construction) Below are transactions related to Fred Couples Company.
  (a) The City of Pebble Beach gives the company 5 acres of land as a plant site. The market value of this land is determined to be $81,000.
  (b) 13,000 shares of common stock with a par value of $50 per share are issued in exchange for land and buildings. The property has been appraised at a fair market value of $810,000, of which $180,000 has been allocated to land and $630,000 to buildings. The stock of Fred Couples Company is not listed on any exchange, but a block of 100 shares was sold by a stockholder 12 months ago at $65 per share, and a block of 200 shares was sold by another stockholder 18 months ago at $58 per share.
  (c) No entry has been made to remove from the accounts for Materials, Direct Labor, and Overhead the amounts properly chargeable to plant asset accounts for machinery constructed during the year. The following information is given relative to costs of the machinery constructed.

Materials used	$12,500
Factory supplies used	900
Direct labor incurred	15,000
Additional overhead (over regular) caused by construction of machinery, excluding factory supplies used	2,700
Fixed overhead rate applied to regular manufacturing operations	60% of direct labor cost
Cost of similar machinery if it had been purchased from outside suppliers	44,000

Instructions

Prepare journal entries on the books of Fred Couples Company to record these transactions.

E10-13 (Entries for Acquisition of Assets) Presented below is information related to Zonker Company.

  1. On July 6 Zonker Company acquired the plant assets of Doonesbury Company, which had discontinued operations. The appraised value of the property is:

Land	$ 400,000
Building	1,200,000
Machinery and equipment	800,000
Total	$2,400,000

Zonker Company gave 12,500 shares of its $100 par value common stock in exchange. The stock had a market value of $168 per share on the date of the purchase of the property.

2. Zonker Company expended the following amounts in cash between July 6 and December 15, the date when it first occupied the building:

Repairs to building	$105,000
Construction of bases for machinery to be installed later	135,000
Driveways and parking lots	122,000
Remodeling of office space in building, including new partitions and walls	161,000
Special assessment by city on land	18,000

3. On December 20, the company paid cash for machinery, $260,000, subject to a 2% cash discount, and freight on machinery of $10,500.

Instructions
Prepare entries on the books of Zonker Company for these transactions.

E10-14 (Purchase of Equipment with Noninterest-Bearing Debt) Chippewas Inc. has decided to purchase equipment from Central Michigan Industries on January 2, 1998, to expand its production capacity to meet customers' demand for its product. Chippewas issues an $800,000, 5-year, noninterest-bearing note to Central Michigan for the new equipment when the prevailing market rate of interest for obligations of this nature is 12%. The company will pay off the note in five $160,000 installments due at the end of each year over the life of the note.

Instructions
(a) Prepare the journal entry(ies) at the date of purchase. (Round to nearest dollar in all computations.)
(b) Prepare the journal entry(ies) at the end of the first year to record the payment and interest, assuming that the company employs the effective interest method.
(c) Prepare the journal entry(ies) at the end of the second year to record the payment and interest.
(d) Assuming that the equipment had a 10-year life and no salvage value, prepare the journal entry necessary to record depreciation in the first year. (Straight-line depreciation is employed.)

E10-15 (Purchase of Computer with Noninterest-Bearing Debt) Cardinals Corporation purchased a computer on December 31, 1997, for $105,000, paying $30,000 down and agreeing to pay the balance in five equal installments of $15,000 payable each December 31 beginning in 1998. An assumed interest rate of 10% is implicit in the purchase price.

Instructions
(a) Prepare the journal entry(ies) at the date of purchase. (Round to two decimal places.)
(b) Prepare the journal entry(ies) at December 31, 1998, to record the payment and interest (effective interest method employed).
(c) Prepare the journal entry(ies) at December 31, 1999, to record the payment and interest (effective interest method employed).

E10-16 (Nonmonetary Exchange With Boot) Busytown Corporation, which manufactures shoes, hired a recent college graduate to work in their accounting department. On the first day of work, the accountant was assigned to total a batch of invoices with the use of an adding machine. Before long, the accountant, who had never before seen such a machine, managed to break the machine. Busytown Corporation gave the machine plus $340 to Dick Tracy Business Machine Company (dealer) in exchange for a new machine. Assume the following information about the machines:

	Busytown Corp. (Old Machine)	Dick Tracy Co. (New Machine)
Machine cost	$290	$270
Accumulated depreciation	140	–0–
Fair value	85	425

Instructions
For each company, prepare the necessary journal entry to record the exchange.

E10-17 (Nonmonetary Exchange with Boot) Cannondale Company purchased an electric wax melter on 4/30/99 by trading in their old gas model and paying the balance in cash. The following data relate to the purchase:

List price of new melter	$15,800
Cash paid	10,000
Cost of old melter (5-year life, $700 residual value)	11,200
Accumulated depreciation—old melter (straight-line)	6,300
Second-hand market value of old melter	5,200

Instructions

Prepare the journal entry(ies) necessary to record this exchange, assuming that the melters exchanged are (a) similar in nature; (b) dissimilar in nature. Cannondale's fiscal year ends on December 31, and depreciation has been recorded through December 31, 1998.

E10-18 (Nonmonetary Exchange with Boot)   Carlos Arruza Company exchanged equipment used in its manufacturing operations plus $3,000 in cash for similar equipment used in the operations of Tony LoBianco Company. The following information pertains to the exchange:

	Carlos Arruza Co.	Tony LoBianco Co.
Equipment (cost)	$28,000	$28,000
Accumulated depreciation	19,000	10,000
Fair value of equipment	12,500	15,500
Cash given up	3,000	

Instructions

Prepare the journal entries to record the exchange on the books of both companies.

E10-19 (Nonmonetary Exchange with Boot)   Dana Ashbrook Inc. has negotiated the purchase of a new piece of automatic equipment at a price of $8,000 plus trade-in, f.o.b. factory. Dana Ashbrook Inc. paid $8,000 cash and traded in used equipment. The used equipment had originally cost $62,000; it had a book value of $42,000 and a secondhand market value of $47,800, as indicated by recent transactions involving similar equipment. Freight and installation charges for the new equipment required a cash payment of $1,100.

Instructions

(a) Prepare the general journal entry to record this transaction, assuming that the assets Dana Ashbrook Inc. exchanged are similar in nature.

(b) Assuming the same facts as in (a) except that the assets exchanged are dissimilar in nature, prepare the general journal entry to record this transaction.

E10-20 (Analysis of Subsequent Expenditures)   King Donovan Resources Group has been in its plant facility for 15 years. Although the plant is quite functional, numerous repair costs are incurred to maintain it in sound working order. The company's plant asset book value is currently $800,000, as indicated below:

Original cost	$1,200,000
Accumulated depreciation	400,000
	$ 800,000

During the current year, the following expenditures were made to the plant facility:

(a) Because of increased demands for its product, the company increased its plant capacity by building a new addition at a cost of $270,000.

(b) The entire plant was repainted at a cost of $23,000.

(c) The roof was an asbestos cement slate; for safety purposes it was removed and replaced with a wood shingle roof at a cost of $61,000. Book value of the old roof was $41,000.

(d) The electrical system was completely updated at a cost of $22,000. The cost of the old electrical system was not known. It is estimated that the useful life of the building will not change as a result of this updating.

(e) A series of major repairs were made at a cost of $47,000, because parts of the wood structure were rotting. The cost of the old wood structure was not known. These extensive repairs are estimated to increase the useful life of the building.

Instructions

Indicate how each of these transactions would be recorded in the accounting records.

E10-21 (Analysis of Subsequent Expenditures)   The following transactions occurred during 1999. Assume that depreciation of 10% per year is charged on all machinery and 5% per year on buildings, on a straight-line basis, with no estimated salvage value. Depreciation is charged for a full year on all fixed assets acquired during the year, and no depreciation is charged on fixed assets disposed of during the year.

Jan. 30   A building that cost $132,000 in 1982 is torn down to make room for a new building. The wrecking contractor was paid $5,100 and was permitted to keep all materials salvaged.

Mar. 10   Machinery that was purchased in 1992 for $16,000 is sold for $2,900 cash, f.o.b. purchaser's plant. Freight of $300 is paid on this machinery.

Mar. 20   A gear breaks on a machine that cost $9,000 in 1994, and the gear is replaced at a cost of $385.

May 18   A special base installed for a machine in 1993 when the machine was purchased has to be replaced at a cost of $5,500 because of defective workmanship on the original base. The cost of the machinery was $14,200 in 1993; the cost of the base was $3,500, and this amount was charged to the Machinery account in 1993.

June 23   One of the buildings is repainted at a cost of $6,900. It had not been painted since it was constructed in 1995.

Instructions

Prepare general journal entries for the transactions. (Round to nearest dollar.)

E10-22 (Analysis of Subsequent Expenditures)   Plant assets often require expenditures subsequent to acquisition. It is important that they be accounted for properly. Any errors will affect both the balance sheets and income statements for a number of years.

Instructions

For each of the following items, indicate whether the expenditure should be capitalized (C) or expensed (E) in the period incurred.

_____   1. Improvement.
_____   2. Replacement of a minor broken part on a machine.
_____   3. Expenditure that increases the useful life of an existing asset.
_____   4. Expenditure that increases the efficiency and effectiveness of a productive asset but does not increase its salvage value.
_____   5. Expenditure that increases the efficiency and effectiveness of a productive asset and increases the asset's salvage value.
_____   6. Expenditure that increases the quality of the output of the productive asset.
_____   7. Improvement to a machine that increased its fair market value and its production capacity by 30% without extending the machine's useful life.
_____   8. Ordinary repairs.
_____   9. Improvement.
_____ 10. Interest on borrowing necessary to finance a major overhaul of machinery. The overhaul extended the life of the machinery.

E10-23 (Entries for Disposition of Assets)   On December 31, 1998, Travis Tritt Inc. has a machine with a book value of $940,000. The original cost and related accumulated depreciation at this date are as follows:

Machine	$1,300,000
Accumulated depreciation	360,000
	$ 940,000

Depreciation is computed at $60,000 per year on a straight-line basis.

Instructions

Presented below is a set of independent situations. For each independent situation, indicate the journal entry to be made to record the transaction. Make sure that depreciation entries are made to update the book value of the machine prior to its disposal.

(a) A fire completely destroys the machine on August 31, 1999. An insurance settlement of $430,000 was received for this casualty. Assume the settlement was received immediately.

(b) On April 1, 1999, Tritt sold the machine for $1,040,000 to Dwight Yoakam Company.

(c) On July 31, 1999, the company donated this machine to the Mountain King City Council. The fair market value of the machine at the time of the donation was estimated to be $1,100,000.

E10-24 (Disposition of Assets)   On April 1, 1998, Gloria Estefan Company received a condemnation award of $430,000 cash as compensation for the forced sale of the company's land and building, which stood in the path of a new state highway. The land and building cost $60,000 and $280,000, respectively, when they were acquired. At April 1, 1998, the accumulated depreciation relating to the building amounted to $160,000. On August 1, 1998, Estafan purchased a piece of replacement property for cash. The new land cost $90,000, and the new building cost $400,000.

Instructions

Prepare the journal entries to record the transactions on April 1 and August 1, 1998.

For additional interest capitalization coverage including a comprehensive illustration and accompanying assignment material, see our Web site.

❖ PROBLEMS ❖

P10-1 (Classification of Acquisition and Other Asset Costs) At December 31, 1997, certain accounts included in the property, plant, and equipment section of Craig Ehlo Company's balance sheet had the following balances:

Land	$230,000
Buildings	890,000
Leasehold improvements	660,000
Machinery and equipment	875,000

During 1998 the following transactions occurred:

Land site number 621 was acquired for $850,000. In addition, to acquire the land Ehlo paid a $51,000 commission to a real estate agent. Costs of $35,000 were incurred to clear the land. During the course of clearing the land, timber and gravel were recovered and sold for $13,000.

A second tract of land (site number 622) with a building was acquired for $420,000. The closing statement indicated that the land value was $300,000 and the building value was $120,000. Shortly after acquisition, the building was demolished at a cost of $41,000. A new building was constructed for $330,000 plus the following costs:

Excavation fees	$38,000
Architectural design fees	11,000
Building permit fee	2,500
Imputed interest on funds used during construction (stock financing)	8,500

The building was completed and occupied on September 30, 1998.

A third tract of land (site number 623) was acquired for $650,000 and was put on the market for resale.

During December 1998 costs of $89,000 were incurred to improve leased office space. The related lease will terminate on December 31, 2000, and is not expected to be renewed. (*Hint:* Leasehold improvements should be handled in the same manner as land improvements.)

A group of new machines was purchased under a royalty agreement that provides for payment of royalties based on units of production for the machines. The invoice price of the machines was $87,000, freight costs were $3,300, installation costs were $2,400, and royalty payments for 1998 were $17,500.

Instructions

(a) Prepare a detailed analysis of the changes in each of the following balance sheet accounts for 1998:

Land	Leasehold improvements
Buildings	Machinery and equipment

Disregard the related accumulated depreciation accounts.

(b) List the items in the situation that were not used to determine the answer to (a) above, and indicate where, or if, these items should be included in Ehlo's financial statements.

(AICPA adapted)

P10-2 (Classification of Acquisition Costs) Selected accounts included in the property, plant, and equipment section of Spud Webb Corporation's balance sheet at December 31, 1997, had the following balances:

Land	$ 300,000
Land improvements	140,000
Buildings	1,100,000
Machinery and equipment	960,000

During 1998 the following transactions occurred:

1. A tract of land was acquired for $150,000 as a potential future building site.
2. A plant facility consisting of land and building was acquired from Ken Norman Company in exchange for 20,000 shares of Webb's common stock. On the acquisition date, Webb's stock had a closing market price of $37 per share on a national stock exchange. The plant facility was carried on Norman's books at $110,000 for land and $320,000 for the building at the exchange date. Current appraised values for the land and building, respectively, are $230,000 and $690,000.
3. Items of machinery and equipment were purchased at a total cost of $400,000. Additional costs were incurred as follows:

Freight and unloading	$13,000
Sales taxes	20,000
Installation	26,000

4. Expenditures totaling $95,000 were made for new parking lots, streets, and sidewalks at the corporation's various plant locations. These expenditures had an estimated useful life of 15 years.
5. A machine costing $80,000 on January 1, 1990, was scrapped on June 30, 1998. Double-declining-balance depreciation has been recorded on the basis of a 10-year life.
6. A machine was sold for $20,000 on July 1, 1998. Original cost of the machine was $44,000 on January 1, 1995, and it was depreciated on the straight-line basis over an estimated useful life of 7 years and a salvage value of $2,000.

Instructions

(a) Prepare a detailed analysis of the changes in each of the following balance sheet accounts for 1998:

> Land
> Land improvements
> Buildings
> Machinery and equipment

(*Hint:* Disregard the related accumulated depreciation accounts.)

(b) List the items in the fact situation that were not used to determine the answer to (a), showing the pertinent amounts and supporting computations in good form for each item. In addition, indicate where, or if, these items should be included in Spud Webb's financial statements.

(AICPA adapted)

P10-3 (Classification of Land and Building Costs) Lenny Wilkins Company was incorporated on January 2, 1999, but was unable to begin manufacturing activities until July 1, 1999, because new factory facilities were not completed until that date.

The Land and Building account at December 31, 1999, was as follows:

January 31, 1999	Land and building	$160,000
February 28, 1999	Cost of removal of building	9,800
May 1, 1999	Partial payment of new construction	60,000
May 1, 1999	Legal fees paid	3,770
June 1, 1999	Second payment on new construction	40,000
June 1, 1999	Insurance premium	2,280
June 1, 1999	Special tax assessment	4,000
June 30, 1999	General expenses	36,300
July 1, 1999	Final payment on new construction	40,000
December 31, 1999	Asset write-up	43,800
		399,950
December 31, 1999	Depreciation—1999 at 1%	4,000
	Account balance	$395,950

The following additional information is to be considered:

1. To acquire land and building the company paid $80,000 cash and 800 shares of its 8% cumulative preferred stock, par value $100 per share. Fair market value of the stock is $107 per share.
2. Cost of removal of old buildings amounted to $9,800, and the demolition company retained all materials of the building.
3. Legal fees covered the following:

Cost of organization	$ 610
Examination of title covering purchase of land	1,300
Legal work in connection with construction contract	1,860
	$3,770

4. Insurance premium covered the building for a two-year term beginning May 1, 1999.
5. The special tax assessment covered street improvements that are permanent in nature.
6. General expenses covered the following for the period from January 2, 1999, to June 30, 1999.

President's salary	$32,100
Plant superintendent covering supervision of new building	4,200
	$36,300

7. Because of a general increase in construction costs after entering into the building contract, the Board of Directors increased the value of the building $43,800, believing that such an increase was justified to reflect the current market at the time the building was completed. Retained earnings was credited for this amount.

8. Estimated life of building—50 years.
Writeoff for 1999—1% of asset value (1% of $400,000, or $4,000).

Instructions

(a) Prepare entries to reflect correct land, building, and depreciation allowance accounts at December 31, 1999.

(b) Show the proper presentation of land, building, and depreciation on the balance sheet at December 31, 1999.

(AICPA adapted)

P10-4 (Dispositions, Including Condemnation, Demolition, and Trade-in) Presented below is a schedule of property dispositions for Frank Thomas Co.

SCHEDULE OF PROPERTY DISPOSITIONS

	Cost	Accumulated Depreciation	Cash Proceeds	Fair Market Value	Nature of Disposition
Land	$40,000	—	$31,000	$31,000	Condemnation
Building	15,000	—	3,600	—	Demolition
Warehouse	70,000	$11,000	74,000	74,000	Destruction by fire
Machine	8,000	3,200	900	7,200	Trade-in
Furniture	10,000	7,850	—	3,100	Contribution
Automobile	8,000	3,460	2,960	2,960	Sale

The following additional information is available:

Land

On February 15, a condemnation award was received as consideration for unimproved land held primarily as an investment, and on March 31, another parcel of unimproved land to be held as an investment was purchased at a cost of $35,000.

Building

On April 2, land and building were purchased at a total cost of $75,000, of which 20% was allocated to the building on the corporate books. The real estate was acquired with the intention of demolishing the building, and this was accomplished during the month of November. Cash proceeds received in November represent the net proceeds from demolition of the building.

Warehouse

On June 30, the warehouse was destroyed by fire. The warehouse was purchased January 2, 1985, and had depreciated $11,000. On December 27, the insurance proceeds and other funds were used to purchase a replacement warehouse at a cost of $90,000.

Machine

On December 26, the machine was exchanged for another machine having a fair market value of $6,300 and cash of $900 was received.

Furniture

On August 15, furniture was contributed to a qualified charitable organization. No other contributions were made or pledged during the year.

Automobile

On November 3, the automobile was sold to Ozzie Guillen, a stockholder.

Instructions

Indicate how these items would be reported on the income statement of Frank Thomas Co.

(AICPA adapted)

P10-5 (Classification of Costs and Interest Capitalization) On January 1, 1998, George Solti Corporation purchased a tract of land (site number 101) with a building for $600,000. Solti paid a real estate broker's commission of $36,000, legal fees of $6,000, and title guarantee insurance of $18,000. The closing statement indicated that the land value was $500,000 and the building value was $100,000. Shortly after acquisition, the building was razed at a cost of $54,000.

Solti entered into a $3,000,000 fixed-price contract with Slatkin Builders, Inc. on March 1, 1998, for the construction of an office building on land site number 101. The building was completed and occupied on September 30, 1999. Additional construction costs were incurred as follows:

Plans, specifications, and blueprints	$21,000
Architects' fees for design and supervision	82,000

The building is estimated to have a 40-year life from date of completion and will be depreciated using the 150% declining balance method.

To finance the construction cost, Solti borrowed $3,000,000 on March 1, 1998. The loan is payable in ten annual installments of $300,000 plus interest at the rate of 10%. Solti's weighted-average amounts of accumulated building construction expenditures were as follows:

For the period March 1 to December 31, 1998	$1,200,000
For the period January 1 to September 30, 1999	1,900,000

Instructions

(a) Prepare a schedule that discloses the individual costs making up the balance in the land account in respect of land site number 101 as of September 30, 1999.

(b) Prepare a schedule that discloses the individual costs that should be capitalized in the office building account as of September 30, 1999. Show supporting computations in good form.

(AICPA adapted)

P10-6 (Nonmonetary Exchanges with Boot) Susquehanna Corporation wishes to exchange a machine used in its operations. Susquehanna has received the following offers from other companies in the industry:

1. Choctaw Company offered to exchange a similar machine plus $23,000.
2. Powhatan Company offered to exchange a similar machine.
3. Shawnee Company offered to exchange a similar machine, but wanted $8,000 in addition to Susquehanna's machine.

In addition, Susquehanna contacted Seminole Corporation, a dealer in machines. To obtain a new machine, Susquehanna must pay $93,000 in addition to trading in its old machine.

	Susquehanna	Choctaw	Powhatan	Shawnee	Seminole
Machine cost	$160,000	$120,000	$147,000	$160,000	$130,000
Accumulated depreciation	50,000	45,000	71,000	75,000	–0–
Fair value	92,000	69,000	92,000	100,000	185,000

Instructions

For each of the four independent situations, prepare the journal entries to record the exchange on the books of each company. (Round to nearest dollar.)

P10-7 (Nonmonetary Exchanges with Boot) On August 1, 1999, Arna, Inc. exchanged productive assets with Bontemps, Inc. Arna's asset is referred to below as "Asset A" and Bontemps' is referred to as "Asset B." The following facts pertain to these assets:

	Asset A	Asset B
Original cost	$96,000	$110,000
Accumulated depreciation (to date of exchange)	45,000	52,000
Fair market value at date of exchange	60,000	75,000
Cash paid by Arna, Inc.	15,000	
Cash received by Bontemps, Inc.		15,000

Instructions

(a) Assume that Assets A and B are dissimilar, and record the exchange for both Arna, Inc. and Bontemps, Inc. in accordance with generally accepted accounting principles.

(b) Assume that Assets A and B are similar, and record the exchange for both Arna, Inc. and Bontemps, Inc. in accordance with generally accepted accounting principles.

P10-8 (Nonmonetary Exchanges with Boot) During the current year, Garrison Construction trades an old crane that has a book value of $80,000 (original cost $140,000 less accumulated depreciation $60,000) for a new crane from Keillor Manufacturing Co. The new crane cost Keillor $165,000 to manufacture and is classified as inventory. The following information is also available.

	Garrison Const.	Keillor Mfg. Co.
Fair market value of old crane	$ 72,000	
Fair market value of new crane		$190,000
Cash paid	118,000	
Cash received		118,000

Instructions

(a) Assume that this exchange is considered to involve dissimilar assets, and prepare the journal entries on the books of (1) Garrison Construction and (2) Keillor Manufacturing.

(b) Assume that this exchange is considered to involve similar assets and prepare the journal entries on the books of (1) Garrison Construction and (2) Keillor Manufacturing.

(c) Assuming the same facts as those in (a), except that the fair market value of the old crane is $98,000 and the cash paid $92,000, prepare the journal entries on the books of (1) Garrison Construction and (2) Keillor Manufacturing.

(d) Assuming the same facts as those in (b), except that the fair market value of the old crane is $87,000 and the cash paid $103,000, prepare the journal entries on the books of (1) Garrison Construction and (2) Keillor Manufacturing.

P10-9 (Costs of Self-Constructed Assets) George Fayne Mining Co. received a $760,000 low bid from a reputable manufacturer for the construction of special production equipment needed by Fayne in an expansion program. Because the company's own plant was not operating at capacity, Fayne decided to construct the equipment there and recorded the following production costs related to the construction:

Services of consulting engineer	$ 40,000
Work subcontracted	31,000
Materials	300,000
Plant labor normally assigned to production	114,000
Plant labor normally assigned to maintenance	160,000
Total	$645,000

Management prefers to record the cost of the equipment under the incremental cost method. Approximately 40% of the company's production is devoted to government supply contracts which are all based in some way on cost. The contracts require that any self-constructed equipment be allocated its full share of all costs related to the construction.

The following information is also available:

(a) The production labor was for partial fabrication of the equipment in the plant. Skilled personnel were required and were assigned from other projects. The maintenance labor would have been idle time of nonproduction plant employees who would have been retained on the payroll whether or not their services were utilized.

(b) Payroll taxes and employee fringe benefits are approximately 35% of labor cost and are included in manufacturing overhead cost. Total manufacturing overhead for the year was $6,084,000, including the $160,000 maintenance labor used to construct the equipment.

(c) Manufacturing overhead is approximately 60% variable and is applied on the basis of production labor cost. Production labor cost for the year for the corporation's normal products totaled $8,286,000.

(d) General and administrative expenses include $27,000 of allocated executive salary cost and $13,750 of postage, telephone, supplies, and miscellaneous expenses identifiable with this equipment construction.

Instructions

(a) Prepare a schedule computing the amount that should be reported as the full cost of the constructed equipment to meet the requirements of the government contracts. Any supporting computations should be in good form.

(b) Prepare a schedule computing the incremental cost of the constructed equipment.

(c) What is the greatest amount that should be capitalized as the cost of the equipment? Why?

(AICPA adapted)

P10-10 (Purchases by Deferred Payment, Lump-sum, and Nonmonetary Exchanges) Kent Adamson Company is a manufacturer of ballet shoes and is experiencing a period of sustained growth. In an effort to expand its production capacity to meet the increased demand for its product, the company recently made several acquisitions of plant and equipment. Tod Mullinger, newly hired in the position of fixed-asset accountant, requested that Watt Kaster, Adamson's controller, review the following transactions.

Transaction 1

On June 1, 1998, Adamson Company purchased equipment from Venghaus Corporation. Adamson issued a $20,000 four-year noninterest-bearing note to Venghaus for the new equipment. Adamson will pay off the note in four equal installments due at the end of each of the next 4 years. At the date of the transaction, the prevailing market rate of interest for obligations of this nature was 10 percent. Freight costs of $425 and installation costs of $500 were incurred in completing this transaction. The appropriate factors for the time value of money at a 10 percent rate of interest are given in the next column.

Future value of $1 for 4 periods	1.46
Future value of an ordinary annuity for 4 periods	4.64
Present value of $1 for 4 periods	0.68
Present value of an ordinary annuity for 4 periods	3.17

Transaction 2

On December 1, 1998, Adamson Company purchased several assets of Haukap Shoes Inc., a small shoe manufacturer whose owner was retiring. The purchase amounted to $210,000 and included the assets listed below. Adamson Company engaged the services of Tennyson Appraisal Inc., an independent appraiser, to determine the fair market values of the assets which are also presented below.

	Haukap Book Value	Fair Market Value
Inventory	$ 60,000	$ 50,000
Land	40,000	80,000
Building	70,000	120,000
	$170,000	$250,000

During its fiscal year ended May 31, 1999, Adamson incurred $8,000 for interest expense in connection with the financing of these assets.

Transaction 3

On March 1, 1999, Adamson Company exchanged a number of used trucks plus cash for vacant land adjacent to its plant site. Adamson intends to use the land for a parking lot. The trucks had a combined book value of $35,000, as Adamson had recorded $20,000 of accumulated depreciation against these assets. Adamson's purchasing agent, who has had previous dealings in the second-hand market, indicated that the trucks had a fair market value of $46,000 at the time of the transaction. In addition to the trucks, Adamson Company paid $19,000 cash for the land.

Instructions

(a) Plant assets such as land, buildings, and equipment receive special accounting treatment. Describe the major characteristics of these assets that differentiate them from other types of assets.

(b) For each of the three transactions described above, determine the value at which Adamson Company should record the acquired assets. Support your calculations with an explanation of the underlying rationale.

(c) The books of Adamson Company show the following additional transactions for the fiscal year ended May 31, 1998.

1. Acquisition of a building for speculative purposes.
2. Purchase of a two-year insurance policy covering plant equipment.
3. Purchase of the rights for the exclusive use of a process used in the manufacture of ballet shoes.

For each of these transactions, indicate whether the asset should be classified as a plant asset. If it is a plant asset, explain why it is. If it is not a plant asset, explain why not, and identify the proper classification.

(CMA adapted)

❖ CONCEPTUAL CASES ❖

C10-1 (Options to Purchase Property) Your client, Salvador Plastics Co., found three suitable sites, each having certain unique advantages, for a new plant facility. In order to thoroughly investigate the advantages and disadvantages of each site, 1-year options were purchased for an amount equal to 6% of the contract price of each site. The costs of the options cannot be applied against the contracts. Before the options expired, one of the sites was purchased at the contract price of $400,000. The option on this site had cost $24,000. The two options not exercised had cost $16,000 each.

Instructions

Present arguments in support of recording the cost of the land at each of the following amounts.

(a) $400,000
(b) $424,000
(c) $456,000.

(AICPA adapted)

C10-2 (Acquisition, Improvements, and Sale of Realty) William Bradford Company purchased land for use as its corporate headquarters. A small factory that was on the land when it was purchased was torn down before construction of the office building began. Furthermore, a substantial amount of rock blasting and removal had to be done to the site before construction of the building foundation began. Because the office building was set back on the land far from the public road, Bradford Company had the contractor construct a paved road that led from the public road to the parking lot of the office building.

Three years after the office building was occupied, Bradford Company added four stories to the office building. The four stories had an estimated useful life of 5 years more than the remaining estimated useful life of the original office building.

Ten years later the land and building were sold at an amount more than their net book value, and Bradford Company had a new office building constructed in another state for use as its new corporate headquarters.

Instructions

(a) Which of the expenditures above should be capitalized? How should each be depreciated or amortized? Discuss the rationale for your answers.

(b) How would the sale of the land and building be accounted for? Include in your answer an explanation of how to determine the net book value at the date of sale. Discuss the rationale for your answer.

C10-3 (Accounting for Self-Constructed Assets)   Shanette Medical Labs, Inc., began operations 5 years ago producing stetrics, a new type of instrument it hoped to sell to doctors, dentists, and hospitals. The demand for stetrics far exceeded initial expectations, and the company was unable to produce enough stetrics to meet demand.

The company was manufacturing its product on equipment that it built at the start of its operations. To meet demand, more efficient equipment was needed. The company decided to design and build the equipment, because the equipment currently available on the market was unsuitable for producing stetrics.

In 1998, a section of the plant was devoted to development of the new equipment and a special staff was hired. Within 6 months a machine developed at a cost of $714,000 increased production dramatically and reduced labor costs substantially. Elated by the success of the new machine, the company built three more machines of the same type at a cost of $441,000 each.

Instructions

(a) In general, what costs should be capitalized for self-constructed equipment?

(b) Discuss the propriety of including in the capitalized cost of self-constructed assets:
   1. The increase in overhead caused by the self-construction of fixed assets.
   2. A proportionate share of overhead on the same basis as that applied to goods manufactured for sale.

(c) Discuss the proper accounting treatment of the $273,000 ($714,000 − $441,000) by which the cost of the first machine exceeded the cost of the subsequent machines. This additional cost should not be considered research and development costs.

C10-4 (Capitalization of Interest)   Zucker Airline is converting from piston-type planes to jets. Delivery time for the jets is 3 years, during which substantial progress payments must be made. The multimillion-dollar cost of the planes cannot be financed from working capital; Zucker must borrow funds for the payments.

Because of high interest rates and the large sum to be borrowed, management estimates that interest costs in the second year of the period will be equal to one-third of income before interest and taxes, and one-half of such income in the third year.

After conversion, Zucker's passenger-carrying capacity will be doubled with no increase in the number of planes, although the investment in planes would be substantially increased. The jet planes have a 7-year service life.

Instructions

Give your recommendation concerning the proper accounting for interest during the conversion period. Support your recommendation with reasons and suggested accounting treatment. (Disregard income tax implications.)

(AICPA adapted)

C10-5 (Assets Acquired through Issuance of Stock)   You have been engaged to examine the financial statements of Richard Corporation for the year ending December 31, 1998. Richard was organized in January, 1998, by Messrs. Dean and Anderson, original owners of options to acquire oil leases on 5,000 acres of land for $1,200,000. They expected that (1) the oil leases would be acquired by the corporation and (2) subsequently 180,000 shares of the corporation's common stock would be sold to the public at $20 per share. In February 1999, they exchanged their options, $400,000 cash, and $200,000 of other assets for 75,000 shares of common stock of the corporation. The corporation's board of directors appraised the leases at $2,100,000, basing its appraisal on the price of other acreage recently leased in the same area. The options were, therefore, recorded at $900,000 ($2,100,000 − $1,200,000 option price).

The options were exercised by the corporation in March 1999, prior to the sale of common stock to the public in April 1999. Leases on approximately 500 acres of land were abandoned as worthless during the year.

Instructions

(a) Why is the valuation of assets acquired by a corporation in exchange for its own common stock sometimes difficult?

(b) 1. What reasoning might Richard Corporation use to support valuing the leases at $2,100,000, the amount of the appraisal by the board of directors?

    2. Assuming that the board's appraisal was sincere, what steps might Richard Corporation have taken to strengthen its position to use the $2,100,000 value and to provide additional information if questions were raised about possible overvaluation of the leases?

(c) Discuss the propriety of charging one-tenth of the recorded value of the leases to expense at December 31, 1999, because leases on 500 acres of land were abandoned during the year.

(AICPA adapted)

C10-6 (Costs of Acquisition) The invoice price of a machine is $40,000. Various other costs relating to the acquisition and installation of the machine including transportation, electrical wiring, special base, and so on amount to $7,500. The machine has an estimated life of 10 years, with no residual value at the end of that period.

The owner of the business suggests that the incidental costs of $7,500 be charged to expense immediately for the following reasons.

1. If the machine should be sold, these costs cannot be recovered in the sales price;

2. The inclusion of the $7,500 in the machinery account on the books will not necessarily result in a closer approximation of the market price of this asset over the years, because of the possibility of changing demand and supply levels; and

3. Charging the $7,500 to expense immediately will reduce federal income taxes.

Instructions

Discuss each of the points raised by the owner of the business.

(AICPA adapted)

❖ FINANCIAL STATEMENT ANALYSIS CASE

Johnson & Johnson

Johnson & Johnson, the world's leading and most diversified health care corporation, serves its customers through specialized worldwide franchises. Each of their franchises consists of a number of companies throughout the world that focus on a particular health care market, such as surgical sutures, consumer pharmaceuticals, or contact lenses. Information related to its property, plant, and equipment in its 1994 annual report is shown in the notes to the financial statements as follows:

> **Note 1: Depreciation of Property**
>
> The company utilizes the straight-line method of depreciation for financial statement purposes for all additions to property, plant and equipment placed in service after January 1, 1989. Property, plant and equipment placed in service prior to January 1, 1989, is generally depreciated using an accelerated method.
>
> **Note 3: Property, Plant and Equipment**
>
> At the end of 1994 and 1993, property, plant and equipment at cost and accumulated depreciation comprised:

(Dollars in Millions)	1994	1993
Land and land improvements	$ 300	$ 276
Buildings and building equipment	2,521	2,389
Machinery and equipment	4,102	3,454
Construction in progress	732	664
	7,655	6,783
Less accumulated depreciation	2,745	2,377
	$4,910	$4,406

The Company capitalizes interest expense as part of the cost of construction of facilities and equipment. Interest expense capitalized in 1994, 1993 and 1992 was $44, $48 and $53 million, respectively.

Upon retirement or other disposal of fixed assets, the cost and related amount of accumulated depreciation or amortization are eliminated from the asset and reserve accounts, respectively. The difference, if any, between the net asset value and the proceeds is adjusted to income.

In its cash flow statement, the following selected information is provided:

Net cash flows from operating activities	**$ 2,975**
Cash flows from investing activities	
Additions to property, plant and equipment	(937)
Proceeds from the disposal of assets	332
Acquisition of businesses, net of cash acquired (Note 18)	(1,932)
Other, principally marketable securities	(19)
Net cash used by investing activities	**(2,556)**
Cash flows from financing activities	
Dividends to stockholders	(727)
Repurchase of common stock	(185)
Proceeds from short-term debt	328
Retirement of short-term debt	(263)
Proceeds from long-term debt	960
Retirement of long-term debt	(363)
Proceeds from the exercise of stock options	62
Net cash used by financing activities	**$ (188)**
Supplemental cash flow data	
Cash paid during the year for:	
Interest, net of portion capitalized	$ 133
Income taxes	612

Instructions

(a) What was the cost of buildings and building equipment at the end of 1994?

(b) Does Johnson & Johnson use a conservative or liberal method to depreciate its property, plant and equipment?

(c) What was the actual interest expense incurred by the company in 1994?

(d) What is Johnson & Johnson's free cash flow? From the information provided, comment on Johnson & Johnson's financial flexibility.

❖ RESEARCH CASES

Case 1

All companies registered with the Securities and Exchange Commission whose net fixed assets exceed 25% of total net assets are required to file Schedules V and VI as part of their Form 10-K. Schedule V presents detailed information regarding the activity in the major fixed asset accounts, while Schedule VI reports activity in the associated accumulated depreciation accounts.

Instructions

Examine Schedules V and VI for the company of your choice and answer the following questions.

(a) What specific information is included in each of the schedules?

(b) Which fixed asset classifications are included in the schedules?

(c) Did the company have any sales or retirements of fixed assets in the period covered by the schedules? If so, determine the net book value of the assets sold or retired.

Case 2

The December 18, 1995, issue of *Forbes* includes an article by Rita Koselka, entitled "Tall Story."

Instructions

Read the article and answer the following questions.

(a) What is the biggest expense in running a video rental store?

(b) Over how long a period does Hollywood Entertainment Corp. depreciate its video tapes? How did the author arrive at this figure?

(c) The author asserts that, once a store is fully stocked, depreciation expense should be approximately equal to the cost of new tapes. Calculate and compare the ratio of depreciation expense to new purchases for Hollywood and Blockbuster.

(d) If Hollywood can open a new store for $400,000 or buy an existing store for $1.2 million, why might investors value Hollywood at an average of $3 million per store?

❖ WRITING ASSIGNMENT

Petri Magazine Company started construction of a warehouse building for its own use at an estimated cost of $6,000,000 on January 1, 1996, and completed the building on December 31, 1996. During the construction period, Petri has the following debt obligations outstanding:

Construction loan—12% interest, payable semiannually, issued December 31, 1995.	$2,000,000
Short-term loan—10% interest, payable monthly, and principal payable at maturity, on May 30, 1997.	1,400,000
Long-term loan—11% interest, payable on January 1 of each year. Principal payable on January 1, 1999.	2,000,000

Total cost amounted to $6,200,000 and the weighted average of accumulated expenditures was $4,000,000.

Dee Pettepiece, the president of the company, has been shown the costs associated with this construction project and capitalized on the balance sheet. She is bothered by the "avoidable interest" included in the cost. She argues that, first, all the interest is unavoidable—no one lends money without expecting to be compensated for it. Second, why can't the company use all the interest on all the loans when computing this avoidable interest? Finally, why can't her company capitalize all the annual interest which accrued over the period of construction?

Instructions

You are the manager of accounting for the company. In a memo, explain what avoidable interest is, how you computed it (being especially careful to explain why you used the interest rates which you did), and why the company cannot capitalize all its interest for the year. Attach a schedule supporting any computations which you use.

❖ GROUP ASSIGNMENT

Wordcrafters Inc. is a book distributor that had been operating in its original facility since 1973. The increase in certification programs and continuing education requirements in several professions has contributed to an annual growth rate of 15% for Wordcrafters since 1993. Wordcrafters' original facility became obsolete by early 1998 because of the increased sales volume and the fact that Wordcrafters now carries tapes and disks in addition to books.

On June 1, 1998, Wordcrafters contracted with Favre Construction to have a new building constructed for $5,000,000 on land owned by Wordcrafters. The payments made by Wordcrafters to Favre Construction are shown in the schedule below.

Date	Amount
July 30, 1998	$1,200,000
January 30, 1999	1,500,000
May 30, 1999	1,300,000
Total payments	$4,000,000

Construction was completed and the building was ready for occupancy on May 27, 1999. Wordcrafters had no new borrowings directly associated with the new building but had the following debt outstanding at May 31, 1999, the end of its fiscal year:

14½%, 5-year note payable of $2,000,000, dated April 1, 1995, with interest payable annually on April 1.

12%, 10-year bond issue of $3,000,000 sold at par on June 30, 1991, with interest payable annually on June 30.

The new building qualifies for interest capitalization. The effect of capitalizing the interest on the new building, compared with the effect of expensing the interest, is material.

Instructions

Work within your group to answer the following questions. Your instructor will assign one member of the group to serve as a recorder and one member to serve as spokesperson. Upon completion of each requirement, the spokesperson should be prepared to report the group findings to the class.

(a) Compute the weighted-average accumulated expenditures on Wordcrafters' new building during the capitalization period.

(b) Compute the avoidable interest on Wordcrafters' new building.

(c) Some interest cost of Wordcrafters Inc. is capitalized for the year ended May 31, 1999.

   1. Identify the items relating to interest cost that must be disclosed in Wordcrafters' financial statements.

   2. Compute the amount of each of the items that must be disclosed.

(CMA adapted)

❖ ETHICS CASE

Field Company purchased a warehouse in a downtown district where land values are rapidly increasing. Adolph Phillips, controller, and Wilma Smith, financial vice-president, are trying to allocate the cost of the purchase between the land and the building. Phillips, noting that depreciation can be taken only on the building, favors placing a very high proportion of the cost on the warehouse itself, thus reducing taxable income and income taxes. Smith, his supervisor, argues that the allocation should recognize the increasing value of the land, regardless of the depreciation potential of the warehouse. Besides, she says, net income is negatively impacted by additional depreciation and will cause the company's stock price to go down.

Instructions
Answer the following questions:

(a) What stakeholder interests are in conflict?

(b) What ethical issues does Phillips face?

(c) How should these costs be allocated?

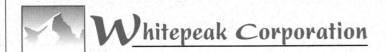 **W**hitepeak Corporation   **MODULE 4**

Sections 4.1 & 4.2   *Interest Capitalization*

Last year, on June 1, 1996, Whitepeak began a major construction project to build a $10,000,000 retail store in a Castle Rock, Colorado, outlet mall. While some existing loans were used to help fund the project, additional funds were obtained from new borrowings specifically to build the project. However, Whitepeak failed to capitalize appropriate interest in 1996, charging it instead to interest expense.

Instructions Analyze the situation and make corrections for 1996. Record interest entries for 1997 as well.

MODULE 5

Sections 5.1, 5.2, & 5.3   *Exchanges of Property and Equipment*

Whitepeak was involved in three transactions during 1997 that resulted in exchanges of nonmonetary assets. In one case Whitepeak exchanged real estate near the Great Sand Dunes Monument for a storage unit in Lakewood, Colorado. In another exchange, Whitepeak obtained some new Windows NT networked computers by paying cash and giving up some older computer equipment someone wanted for parts. In the third swap, Whitepeak acquired a new, high-altitude efficient delivery van and also received cash in exchange for a model purchased just 2 years ago that was not efficient. Whitepeak is confused, though, because the accounting rules are different for each of these exchanges.

Instructions Evaluate these three asset exchanges and complete the entries to record the exchanges in 1997. ∎

CHAPTER 11

Depreciation, Impairments, and Depletion

I s Nothing Sacred—Not Even Churches?

At the chancery of the Roman Catholic diocese in Brooklyn, New York, Monsignor Austin Bennett was going about his spiritual and worldly chores. He helped minority students get entry to the diocese's twenty-two schools. He helped a local church custodian from Central America apply for U.S. citizenship. He helped priests take care of their aging parents. Then he wrote a nasty letter to the Financial Accounting Standards Board.

Why was this affable, pipe-smoking churchman launching barbs against the chief rule-making body for accountants? "Because the Board is on the verge of causing more trouble for American churches than all the sinners in their congregations," says Monsignor Bennett, who also is the accounting practice chairman of the U.S. Catholic Conference. The FASB had proposed that not-for-profit organizations should depreciate, and deduct as an expense, the cost of houses of worship, monuments, and historical treasures.

Opponents argued that "depreciating cathedrals and churches is stupid. . . . It would be like trying to compare the cost per soul saved among the churches." Others argued that "depreciating churches would be like depreciating the Pyramids and the Sphinx of Egypt, and the Sistine Chapel of the Vatican. Figuring such depreciation is the acme of futility!" The FASB countered by noting that "the Parthenon may still be there but its roof has fallen in. Physical assets that are exhaustible should be depreciated."[1]

LEARNING OBJECTIVES

After studying this chapter, you should be able to:

1. Explain the concept of depreciation.
2. Identify the factors involved in the depreciation process.
3. Compare activity, straight-line, and decreasing charge methods of depreciation.
4. Explain special depreciation methods.
5. Identify reasons why depreciation methods are selected.
6. Explain the accounting issues related to asset impairment.
7. Explain the accounting procedures for depletion of natural resources.
8. Explain how property, plant, equipment, and natural resources are reported and analyzed.

---

[1]Adapted from *The Wall Street Journal*, Lee Baxton, April 10, 1987, pp. 1 and 10. Subsequently the FASB decided not to require the recognition of depreciation on historical works of art or historical treasures whose economic benefits diminish very slowly over long periods of time. "Recognition of Depreciation for Not-for-Profit Organizations," *Statement of Financial Accounting Standards No. 93* (Norwalk, Conn.: FASB, 1987).

In spite of Monsignor Bennett's concern, narrated in the opening story, accountants, engineers, appraisers, and economists—each of whom defines depreciation differently—all agree that most assets are on "an inevitable march to the rubbish heap." As a result, some type of write-off of cost is needed to indicate that the usefulness of an asset has declined. The purpose of this chapter is to examine the depreciation process and the methods of writing off the cost of tangible assets and natural resources. The content and organization of the chapter are as follows:

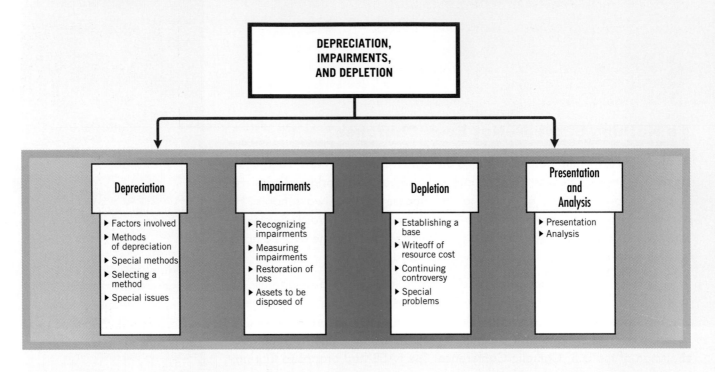

❖ DEPRECIATION—A METHOD OF COST ALLOCATION

Objective ①

Explain the concept of depreciation.

Most individuals at one time or another purchase and trade in an automobile. In discussions with the automobile dealer, depreciation is a consideration on two points. First, how much has the old car "depreciated"? That is, what is the trade-in value? Second, how fast will the new car depreciate? That is, what will its trade-in value be? In both cases depreciation is thought of as a loss in value.

To accountants, however, **depreciation is not a matter of valuation but a means of cost allocation.** Assets are not depreciated on the basis of a decline in their fair market value, but on the basis of systematic charges to expense. **Depreciation is defined as the accounting process of allocating the cost of tangible assets to expense in a systematic and rational manner to those periods expected to benefit from the use of the asset.**

This approach is employed because the value of the asset may fluctuate between the time the asset is purchased and the time it is sold or junked. Attempts to measure these interim value changes have not been well received by accountants because values are difficult to measure objectively. Therefore, the asset's cost is charged to depreciation expense over its estimated life, making no attempts to value the asset at fair market value between acquisition and disposition. The cost allocation approach is used because a matching of costs with revenues occurs and because fluctuations in market value are tenuous and difficult to measure.

When long-lived assets are written off, the term depreciation is most often used to indicate that tangible plant assets have declined in value. Where natural resources, such as timber, gravel, oil, and coal, are involved, the term depletion is employed. The expiration of intangible assets, such as patents or goodwill, is called amortization.

Factors Involved in the Depreciation Process

Before a pattern of charges to revenue can be established, three basic questions must be answered:

❶ What depreciable base is to be used for the asset?
❷ What is the asset's useful life?
❸ What method of cost apportionment is best for this asset?

Objective ❷
Identify the factors involved in the depreciation process.

The answers to these questions involve the distillation of several estimates into one single figure. The calculations on which depreciation is based assume perfect knowledge of the future, which is never attainable.

Depreciable Base for the Asset

The base established for depreciation is a function of two factors: the original cost and salvage or disposal value. We discussed historical cost in Chapter 10. Salvage value is the estimated amount that will be received at the time the asset is sold or removed from service. It is the amount to which the asset must be written down or depreciated during its useful life. To illustrate, if an asset has a cost of $10,000 and a salvage value of $1,000, its depreciation base is $9,000.

Original cost	$10,000
Less salvage value	1,000
Depreciation base	$ 9,000

ILLUSTRATION 11-1
Computation of
Depreciation Base

From a practical standpoint, salvage value is often considered to be zero because its valuation is small. Some long-lived assets, however, have substantial salvage values.

Companies also differ as to their estimate of salvage value. At one time Leasco, Greyhound Corp., and Boothe Computer all depreciated the same IBM computer equipment on a straight-line basis, but Leasco and Greyhound assumed a 10% salvage value, whereas Boothe assumed zero.

Estimation of Service Lives

The service life of an asset and its physical life are often not the same. A piece of machinery may be physically capable of producing a given product for many years beyond its service life, but the equipment is not used for all of those years because the cost of producing the product in later years may be too high. For example, the old Slater cotton mill in Pawtucket, Rhode Island is preserved in remarkable physical condition as an historic landmark in American industrial development, although its service life was terminated many years ago.[2]

Assets are retired for two reasons: **physical factors** (such as casualty or expiration of physical life) and **economic factors** (obsolescence). Physical factors are the wear and tear, decay, and casualties that make it difficult for the asset to perform indefinitely. These physical factors set the outside limit for the service life of an asset.

---

[2]Taken from J. D. Coughlan and W. K. Strand, *Depreciation Accounting, Taxes and Business Decisions* (New York: The Ronald Press, 1969), pp. 10–12.

The economic or functional factors can be classified into three categories: inadequacy, supersession, and obsolescence. **Inadequacy** results when an asset ceases to be useful to a given enterprise because the demands of the firm have increased. Example: the need for a larger building to handle increased production. Although the old building may still be sound, it may have become inadequate for that enterprise's purposes. **Supersession** is the replacement of one asset with another more efficient and economical asset. Example: the replacement of the mainframe computer with a PC network, or the replacement of the Boeing 767 with the Boeing 777. **Obsolescence** is the catchall for situations not involving inadequacy and supersession. Because the distinction between these categories appears artificial, it is probably best to consider economic factors totally instead of trying to make distinctions that are not clear-cut.

To illustrate the concepts of physical and economic factors, consider a new nuclear power plant. Which do you think would be more important in determining the useful life of a nuclear power plant—physical factors or economic factors? The limiting factors seem to be (1) ecological considerations, (2) competition from other power sources (nonnuclear), and (3) safety concerns. Physical life does not appear to be the primary factor affecting useful life. Although the plant's physical life may be far from over, the plant may become obsolete in 10 years.

For a house, physical factors undoubtedly are more important than the economic or functional factors relative to useful life. Whenever the physical nature of the asset is the primary determinant of useful life, maintenance plays an extremely vital role. The better the maintenance, the longer the life of the asset.[3]

In some cases, arbitrary service lives are selected; in others, sophisticated statistical methods are employed to establish a useful life for accounting purposes. In many cases, the primary basis for estimating the useful life of an asset is the enterprise's past experience with the same or similar assets. In a highly industrial economy such as that of the United States, where research and innovation are so prominent, technological factors have as much effect, if not more, on service lives of tangible plant assets as physical factors do.

Methods of Depreciation

The third factor involved in the depreciation process is the **method** of cost apportionment. The profession requires that the depreciation method employed be "systematic and rational."

A number of depreciation methods are used. They may be classified as follows.

❶ Activity method (units of use or production).
❷ Straight-line method.
❸ Decreasing charge methods (accelerated).
  (a) Sum-of-the-years'-digits.
  (b) Declining-balance method.
❹ Special depreciation methods.
  (a) Group and composite methods.
  (b) Hybrid or combination methods.[4]

---

[3]The airline industry also illustrates the type of problem involved in estimation. In the past, aircraft were assumed not to wear out—they just became obsolete. However, some jets have been in service as long as 20 years, and maintenance of these aircraft has become increasingly expensive. In addition, the public's concern about worn-out aircraft has been heightened by some recent air disasters. As a result, some airlines are finding it necessary to replace aircraft not because of obsolescence but because of physical deterioration.

[4]*Accounting Trends and Techniques—1996* reports that of its 600 surveyed companies various depreciation methods were used for financial reporting purposes: straight-line, 572; declining-balance, 27; sum-of-the-years'-digits, 12; accelerated method (not specified), 49; units of production, 38. No utility or transportation companies (the ones that use the "special depreciation methods") are included in the AICPA's survey.

To illustrate some of these depreciation methods, assume that Stanley Coal Mines recently purchased an additional crane for digging purposes. Pertinent data concerning the purchase of the crane are:

Cost of crane	$500,000
Estimated useful life	5 years
Estimated salvage value	$ 50,000
Productive life in hours	30,000 hours

ILLUSTRATION 11-2
Data Used to Illustrate
Depreciation Methods

Activity Method

The activity method (also called the variable charge approach) assumes that depreciation is **a function of use or productivity instead of the passage of time**. The life of the asset is considered in terms of either the **output** it provides (units it produces), or an **input** measure such as the number of hours it works. Conceptually, the proper cost association is established in terms of output instead of hours used, but often the output is not easily measurable. In such cases, an input measure such as machine hours is a more appropriate method of measuring the dollar amount of depreciation charges for a given accounting period.

Objective ❸

Compare activity, straight-line, and decreasing charge methods of depreciation.

The crane poses no particular problem because the usage (hours) is relatively easy to measure. If the crane is used 4,000 hours the first year, the depreciation charge is:

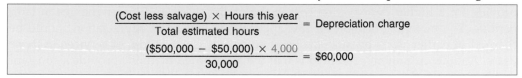

$$\frac{(\text{Cost less salvage}) \times \text{Hours this year}}{\text{Total estimated hours}} = \text{Depreciation charge}$$

$$\frac{(\$500,000 - \$50,000) \times 4,000}{30,000} = \$60,000$$

ILLUSTRATION 11-3
Depreciation Calculation,
Activity Method—Crane
Example

The major limitation of this method is that it is not appropriate in situations in which depreciation is a function of time instead of activity. For example, a building is subject to a great deal of steady deterioration from the elements (time) regardless of its use. In addition, where an asset is subject to economic or functional factors, independent of its use, the activity method loses much of its significance. For example, if a company is expanding rapidly, a particular building may soon become obsolete for its intended purposes. In both cases, activity is irrelevant. Another problem in using an activity method is that an estimate of units of output or service hours received is often difficult to determine.

Where loss of services is a result of activity or productivity, the activity method will best match costs and revenues. Companies that desire low depreciation during periods of low productivity and high depreciation during high productivity either adopt or switch to an activity method. In this way, a plant running at 40% of capacity generates 60% lower depreciation charges. Inland Steel, for example, switched to units-of-production depreciation at one time and reduced its losses by $43 million, or $1.20 per share.[5]

Straight-Line Method

The straight-line method considers depreciation a **function of time rather than a function of usage**. This method is widely employed in practice because of its simplicity. The straight-line procedure is often the most conceptually appropriate, too. When creeping obsolescence is the primary reason for a limited service life, a decline in usefulness may be constant from period to period. The depreciation charge for the crane is computed as follows:

UNDERLYING CONCEPTS

If those benefits flow on a "straight-line" basis, then justification exists for matching the cost of the asset on a straight-line basis with these benefits.

$$\frac{\text{Cost less salvage}}{\text{Estimated service life}} = \text{Depreciation charge}$$

$$\frac{\$500,000 - \$50,000}{5} = \$90,000$$

ILLUSTRATION 11-4
Depreciation Calculation,
Straight-Line Method—
Crane Example

---

[5]"Double Standard," *Forbes* (November 22, 1982), p. 178.

The major objection to the straight-line method is that it rests on two unrealistic assumptions: (1) the asset's economic usefulness is the same each year, and (2) the repair and maintenance expense is essentially the same each period.

One additional problem that occurs in using straight-line—as well as some others—is that distortions in the rate of return analysis (income/assets) develop. Illustration 11-5 indicates how the rate of return increases, given constant revenue flows, because the asset's book value decreases.

ILLUSTRATION 11-5
Depreciation and Rate of Return Analysis—Crane Example

Year	(1) Depreciation Expense	(2) Undepreciated Asset Balance (book value)	(3) Income (after depreciation expense)	(4) Rate of Return (income ÷ assets)
0		$500,000		
1	$90,000	410,000	$100,000	24.4%
2	90,000	320,000	100,000	31.2%
3	90,000	230,000	100,000	43.5%
4	90,000	140,000	100,000	71.4%
5	90,000	50,000	100,000	200.0%

Decreasing Charge Methods

The decreasing charge methods—often called accelerated depreciation methods—provide for a higher depreciation cost in the earlier years and lower charges in later periods. The main justification for this approach is that more depreciation should be charged in earlier years because the asset suffers its greatest loss of services in those years. Another argument presented is that the accelerated methods provide a constant cost because the depreciation charge is lower in the later periods, at the time when the repair and maintenance costs are often higher. Generally, one of two decreasing charge methods is employed: the sum-of-the-years'-digits method or the declining-balance method.

Sum-of-the-Years'-Digits. The sum-of-the-years'-digits method results in a decreasing depreciation charge based on a decreasing fraction of depreciable cost (original cost less salvage value). Each fraction uses the sum of the years as a denominator (5 + 4 + 3 + 2 + 1 = 15) and the number of years of estimated life remaining as of the beginning of the year as a numerator. In this method, the numerator decreases year by year and the denominator remains constant (5/15, 4/15, 3/15, 2/15, and 1/15). At the end of the asset's useful life, the balance remaining should be equal to the salvage value. This method of computation is shown in Illustration 11-6 below.[6]

ILLUSTRATION 11-6
Sum-of-the-Years'-Digits Depreciation Schedule—Crane Example

Year	Depreciation Base	Remaining Life in Years	Depreciation Fraction	Depreciation Expense	Book Value, End of Year
1	$450,000	5	5/15	$150,000	$350,000
2	450,000	4	4/15	120,000	230,000
3	450,000	3	3/15	90,000	140,000
4	450,000	2	2/15	60,000	80,000
5	450,000	1	1/15	30,000	50,000[a]
		15	15/15	$450,000	

[a]Salvage value.

Declining-Balance Method. Another decreasing charge method is the declining-balance method, which utilizes a depreciation rate (expressed as a percentage) that is some multiple of the straight-line method. For example, the double-declining rate for

---

[6]What happens if the estimated service life of the asset is, let us say, 51 years? How would you calculate the sum-of-the-years'-digits? Fortunately the mathematicians have developed a formula that permits easy computation as follows. It is:

$$\frac{n(n + 1)}{2} = \frac{51(51 + 1)}{2} = 1{,}326$$

a 10-year asset would be 20% (double the straight-line rate, which is 1/10 or 10%). The declining-balance rate remains constant and is applied to the reducing book value each year. Unlike other methods, in the declining-balance method the salvage value is not deducted in computing the depreciation base. The declining-balance rate is multiplied by the book value of the asset at the beginning of each period. Since the book value of the asset is reduced each period by the depreciation charge, the constant-declining-balance rate is applied to a successively lower book value which results in lower depreciation charges each year. This process continues until the book value of the asset is reduced to its estimated salvage value, at which time depreciation is discontinued.

As indicated above, various multiples are used in practice, such as twice (200%) the straight-line rate (**double-declining-balance method**) and 150% of the straight-line rate. Using the double-declining approach in the crane example, Stanley Coal Mines would have the depreciation charges shown in Illustration 11-7 below.

INTERNATIONAL INSIGHT

German companies depreciate their fixed assets at a much faster rate than U.S. companies because German tax laws permit accelerated depreciation of up to triple the straight-line rate.

Year	Book Value of Asset First of Year	Rate on Declining Balance[a]	Debit Depreciation Expense	Balance Accumulated Depreciation	Book Value, End of Year
1	$500,000	40%	$200,000	$200,000	$300,000
2	300,000	40%	120,000	320,000	180,000
3	180,000	40%	72,000	392,000	108,000
4	108,000	40%	43,200	435,200	64,800
5	64,800	40%	14,800[b]	450,000	50,000

[a]Based on twice the straight-line rate of 20% ($90,000/$450,000 = 20%; 20% × 2 = 40%).
[b]Limited to $14,800 because book value should not be less than salvage value.

ILLUSTRATION 11-7
Double-Declining Depreciation Schedule—Crane Example

Enterprises often switch from the declining-balance method to the sum-of-the-years'-digits or straight-line method near the end of the asset's useful life to ensure that the asset is depreciated only to its salvage value.[7]

Special Depreciation Methods

Sometimes an enterprise does not select one of the more popular depreciation methods because the assets involved have unique characteristics, or the nature of the industry dictates that a special depreciation method be adopted. Two of these special methods are discussed below:[8]

❶ Group and composite methods.
❷ Hybrid or combination methods.

Objective ❹

Explain special depreciation methods.

Group and Composite Methods

Depreciation methods are usually applied to a single asset. In certain circumstances, however, multiple-asset accounts are depreciated using one rate. For example, an en-

---

[7]A pure form of the declining-balance method (sometimes appropriately called the "fixed percentage of book value method") has also been suggested as a possibility. This approach finds a rate that depreciates the asset exactly to salvage value at the end of its expected useful life. The formula for determination of this rate is as follows:

$$\text{Depreciation rate} = 1 - \sqrt[n]{\frac{\text{Salvage value}}{\text{Acquisition cost}}}$$

The life in years is n. Once the depreciation rate is computed, it is applied on the declining book value of the asset from period to period, which means that depreciation expense will be successively lower. This method is not used extensively in practice because the computations are cumbersome and it is not permitted for tax purposes.

[8]Public utilities and railroads that own many similar units of small value (such as poles, ties, conductors, transformers, meters, and telephones) use the **retirement** and **replacement methods**. The purpose of these methods is to avoid elaborate depreciation schedules for individual assets. Under these methods, depreciation is recorded when retirement or replacement of the assets occurs (which is fairly constant), assuming either a FIFO cost flow (retirement method) or a LIFO cost flow (replacement methods).

terprise such as American Telephone and Telegraph Co. might depreciate telephone poles, microwave systems, or switchboards by groups.

Two methods of depreciating multiple-asset accounts are employed: the group method and the composite method. The term **"group" refers to a collection of assets that are similar in nature; "composite" refers to a collection of assets that are dissimilar in nature**. The group method is frequently used when the assets are fairly homogeneous and have approximately the same useful lives. The composite approach is used when the assets are heterogeneous and have different lives. The group method more closely approximates a single-unit cost procedure because the dispersion from the average is not as great. The method of computation for group or composite is essentially the same: find an average and depreciate on that basis.

To illustrate, Mooney Motors depreciates its fleet of cars, trucks, and campers on a composite basis. The depreciation rate is established in this manner:

ILLUSTRATION 11-8
Depreciation Calculation,
Composite Basis

Asset	Original Cost	Residual Value	Depreciable Cost	Estimated Life (yrs.)	Depreciation per Year (straight-line)
Cars	$145,000	$25,000	$120,000	3	$40,000
Trucks	44,000	4,000	40,000	4	10,000
Campers	35,000	5,000	30,000	5	6,000
	$224,000	$34,000	$190,000		$56,000

$$\text{Composite depreciation rate} = \frac{\$56,000}{\$224,000} = 25\%$$

Composite life = 3.39 years ($190,000 ÷ $56,000)

The composite depreciation rate is determined by dividing the depreciation per year by the total cost of the assets. If there are no changes in the asset account, the group of assets will be depreciated to the residual or salvage value at the rate of $56,000 ($224,000 $\times$ 25%) a year. As a result, it will take Mooney 3.39 years (composite life as indicated above) to depreciate these assets.

The differences between the group or composite method and the single-unit depreciation method become accentuated when we look at asset retirements. If an asset is retired before, or after, the average service life of the group is reached, the resulting gain or loss is buried in the Accumulated Depreciation account. This practice is justified because some assets will be retired before the average service life and others after the average life. For this reason, the debit to Accumulated Depreciation is the difference between original cost and cash received. No gain or loss on disposition is recorded. To illustrate, suppose that one of the campers with a cost of $5,000 was sold for $2,600 at the end of the third year. The entry is:

Accumulated Depreciation	2,400	
Cash	2,600	
Cars, Trucks, and Campers		5,000

If a new type of asset is purchased (mopeds, for example), a new depreciation rate must be computed and applied in subsequent periods.

A typical financial statement disclosure of the group depreciation method is shown for Ampco-Pittsburg Corporation as follows:

ILLUSTRATION 11-9
Disclosure of Group
Depreciation Method

Ampco-Pittsburg Corporation

Depreciation rates are based on estimated useful lives of the asset groups. Gains or losses on normal retirements or replacements of depreciable assets, subject to composite depreciation methods, are not recognized; the difference between the cost of the assets retired or replaced and the related salvage value is charged or credited to the accumulated depreciation.

The group or composite method simplifies the bookkeeping process and tends to average out errors caused by over- or underdepreciation. As a result, periodic income is not distorted by gains or losses on disposals of assets.

On the other hand, the unit method has several advantages over the group or composite methods: (1) it simplifies the computation mathematically; (2) it identifies gains and losses on disposal; (3) it isolates depreciation on idle equipment; and (4) it represents the best estimate of the depreciation of each asset, not the result of averaging the cost over a longer period of time. As a consequence, the unit method is generally used in practice and is generally assumed to be used in homework problems unless stated otherwise.

Hybrid or Combination Methods

In addition to the aforementioned depreciation methods, companies are free to develop their own special or tailor-made depreciation methods. GAAP requires only that the method result in the allocation of an asset's cost over the asset's life in a systematic and rational manner.

A hybrid depreciation method widely used in the steel industry is a combination straight-line/activity approach referred to as the **production variable method**. The following note from WHX Corporation's 1994 Annual Report explains one variation of this method:

WHX Corporation

The Company utilizes the modified units of production method of depreciation which recognizes that the depreciation of steelmaking machinery is related to the physical wear of the equipment as well as a time factor. The modified units of production method provides for straight-line depreciation charges modified (adjusted) by the level of raw steel production. In 1993 and 1994 depreciation under the modified units of production method was $2.9 million or 7.0% and $2.8 million or 6.1%, respectively, less than straight-line depreciation.

ILLUSTRATION 11-10
Disclosure of Hybrid Depreciation Method

Selecting a Depreciation Method

Which depreciation method should be selected? Many believe that the **method which best matches revenues and expenses** should be used. For example, if revenues generated by the asset are constant over the asset's useful life, straight-line depreciation is employed. On the other hand, if revenues are higher (or lower) at the beginning, some form of decreasing (or increasing) charge method of depreciation appears justified. Others argue that it is difficult in most cases to project future revenues and therefore **simplicity** (the straight-line method) should govern. Similarly, others argue that whatever is used for tax purposes should be used for book purposes because it **eliminates some record-keeping costs**.

Because it is difficult to defend one approach as more useful than another on a conceptual basis, the selection of the depreciation method is often made on more practical grounds. Many companies use the straight-line method for book purposes and adopt the accelerated depreciation method for tax purposes. This provides the best of both worlds—a **lower tax** and usually a **higher net income** for financial reporting purposes. At one time, U.S. Steel (now USX) changed its method of depreciation from an accelerated to a straight-line method for financial reporting purposes. Many observers note that the reason for the change was to report higher income so that it would be less susceptible to takeover by another enterprise. In effect, U.S. Steel wanted to report higher income so that the market value of its stock would rise.[9] In 1995 the giant chem-

Objective 5
Identify reasons why depreciation methods are selected.

INTERNATIONAL INSIGHT

In most non-Anglo Saxon nations, companies are not permitted to use one depreciation method for financial statements and a different method for tax returns. The financial statements must conform to the tax return.

---

[9]This assumption is highly tenuous. It is based on the belief that stock market analysts will not be able to recognize that the change in depreciation methods is purely cosmetic and therefore will give more value to the stock after the change. In fact, research in this area reports just the opposite. One study showed that companies that switched from accelerated to straight-line (which increased income) experienced declines in stock value after the change; see Robert J. Kaplan and Richard Roll, "Investor Evaluation of Accounting Information: Some Empirical Evidence," *The Journal of Business* (April 1972), pp. 225–257. Others have noted that switches to more liberal accounting policies (generating higher income numbers) have resulted in lower stock market performance. One rationale is that such changes signal that the company is in trouble and also leads to skepticism about management's attitudes and behavior.

ical company Du Pont switched from accelerated depreciation to straight-line for a $250 million drop in depreciation expense and a warning that the eventual impact on net income would depend "on the level of future capital spending" (averaging $3.5 billion annually from 1993 to 1995).

The real estate industry is frustrated with depreciation accounting because it argues that real estate often does not decline in value. In addition, because real estate is highly debt financed, most real estate concerns report losses in earlier years when the sum of depreciation and interest charges exceeds the revenues from the real estate project. The industry argues for some form of increasing charge method of depreciation (lower depreciation at the beginning and higher depreciation at the end), so that higher total assets and net income are reported in the earlier years of the project.

Tax policy also has an impact. In the 1980s railroads changed from a special-industry method of accounting for railroad tracks to a more traditional method of capitalizing these track costs and depreciating them. Although the railroads wished to use the traditional method for many years, they had been reluctant to switch because higher tax deductions were achieved through their special methods. The railroads feared that changing to a more traditional method of depreciating for financial reporting purposes might suggest to Congress that this method be used for tax purposes. Ultimately, Congress provided favorable tax legislation to the industry and the concern was alleviated. As a result, companies have changed to traditional methods of depreciation.

To summarize, the selection of a depreciation method involves factors such as the nature and uncertainty of revenue flows, matching costs and revenues, effect on income and asset book values, tax considerations, and record-keeping costs.

Special Depreciation Issues

Several special issues related to depreciation remain to be discussed. The major issues are:

❶ How should depreciation be computed for partial periods?
❷ Does depreciation provide for the replacement of assets?
❸ How are revisions in depreciation rates handled?
❹ How is depreciation computed for income tax purposes?

Depreciation and Partial Periods

Plant assets are seldom purchased on the first day of a fiscal period or disposed of on the last day of a fiscal period. A practical question is: How much depreciation should be charged for the partial periods involved? Assume, for example, that an automated drill machine with a 5-year life is purchased by Steeltex Company for $45,000 (no salvage value) on June 10, 1997. The company's fiscal year ends December 31 and depreciation is charged for 6⅔ months during that year. The total depreciation for a full year (assuming straight-line depreciation) is $9,000 ($45,000/5), and the depreciation for the first, partial year is:

$$\frac{6\tfrac{2}{3}}{12} \times \$9,000 = \$5,000$$

The partial-period calculation is relatively simple when straight-line depreciation is used. But how is partial period depreciation handled when an accelerated method such as sum-of-the-years'-digits or double-declining balance is used when partial periods are involved? As an illustration, assume that an asset was purchased for $10,000 on July 1, 1997, with an estimated useful life of 5 years; the depreciation figures for 1997, 1998, and 1999 are shown in Illustration 11-11.

In computing depreciation expense for partial periods, it is necessary to determine the depreciation expense for the full year and then to prorate this depreciation expense between the two periods involved. This process should continue throughout the useful life of the asset.

	Sum-of-the-Years'-Digits	Double-Declining Balance
1st full year	(5/15 × $10,000) = $3,333.33	(40% × $10,000) = $4,000
2nd full year	(4/15 × 10,000) = 2,666.67	(40% × 6,000) = 2,400
3rd full year	(3/15 × 10,000) = 2,000.00	(40% × 3,600) = 1,440

Depreciation from July 1, 1997 to December 31, 1997

6/12 × $3,333.33 =	$1,666.67	6/12 × $4,000 = $2,000

Depreciation for 1998

6/12 × $3,333.33 =	$1,666.67	6/12 × $4,000 =	$2,000
6/12 × 2,666.67 =	1,333.33	6/12 × 2,400 =	1,200
	$3,000.00		$3,200

or ($10,000 − $2,000) × 40% = $3,200

Depreciation for 1999

6/12 × $2,666.67 =	$1,333.33	6/12 × $2,400 =	$1,200
6/12 × 2,000.00 =	1,000.00	6/12 × 1,440 =	720
	$2,333.33		$1,920

or ($10,000 − $5,200) × 40% = $1,920

ILLUSTRATION 11-11
Calculation of Partial-Period Depreciation, Two Methods

Sometimes the process of allocating costs to a partial period is modified to handle acquisitions and disposals of plant assets more simply. Depreciation may be computed for the full period on the opening balance in the asset account and no depreciation is charged on acquisitions during the year. Other variations charge a full year's depreciation on assets used for a full year, charge one-half year's depreciation in the year of acquisition and in the year of disposal, or charge a full year in the year of acquisition and none in the year of disposal.

A company is at liberty to adopt any one of these several fractional-year policies in allocating cost to the first and last years of an asset's life so long as the method is applied consistently. However, **unless otherwise stipulated, depreciation is normally computed on the basis of the nearest full month**. The schedule below shows depreciation allocated under five different fractional-year policies using the straight-line method on the $45,000 automated drill machine purchased on June 10, 1997, by Steeltex Company discussed earlier.

ILLUSTRATION 11-12
Fractional-Year Depreciation Policies

Machine Cost = $45,000	Depreciation Allocated per Period Over 5-Year Life*					
Fractional-Year Policy	1997	1998	1999	2000	2001	2002
1. Nearest fraction of a year.	$5,000[a]	$9,000	$9,000	$9,000	$9,000	$4,000[b]
2. Nearest full month.	5,250[c]	9,000	9,000	9,000	9,000	3,750[d]
3. Half year in period of acquisition and disposal.	4,500	9,000	9,000	9,000	9,000	4,500
4. Full year in period of acquisition, none in period of disposal.	9,000	9,000	9,000	9,000	9,000	–0–
5. None in period of acquisition, full year in period of disposal.	–0–	9,000	9,000	9,000	9,000	9,000

[a]6.667/12 ($9,000) [b]5.333/12 ($9,000) [c]7/12 ($9,000) [d]5/12 ($9,000)
*(Rounded to nearest dollar)

Depreciation and Replacement of Fixed Assets

A common misconception about depreciation is that it provides funds for the replacement of fixed assets. Depreciation is similar to any other expense in that it reduces net income, but it differs in that **it does not involve a current cash outflow**.

To illustrate why depreciation does not provide funds for replacement of plant assets, assume that a business starts operating with plant assets of $500,000, which have a useful life of 5 years. The company's balance sheet at the beginning of the period is:

Plant Assets	$500,000	Owners' Equity	$500,000

Now if we assume that the enterprise earned no revenue over the 5 years, the income statements are:

	Year 1	Year 2	Year 3	Year 4	Year 5
Revenue	$ –0–	$ –0–	$ –0–	$ –0–	$ –0–
Depreciation	(100,000)	(100,000)	(100,000)	(100,000)	(100,000)
Loss	$(100,000)	$(100,000)	$(100,000)	$(100,000)	$(100,000)

The balance sheet at the end of the 5 years is:

Plant Assets	–0–	Owners' Equity	–0–

This extreme example illustrates that depreciation in no way provides funds for the replacement of assets. **The funds for the replacement of the assets come from the revenues**; without the revenues no income materializes and no cash inflow results. A separate decision must be made by management to set aside cash to accumulate asset replacement funds.

Revision of Depreciation Rates

When a plant asset is purchased, depreciation rates are carefully determined based on past experience with similar assets and other pertinent information. The provisions for depreciation are only estimates, however, and it may be necessary to revise them during the life of the asset. Unexpected physical deterioration or unforeseen obsolescence may make the useful life of the asset less than originally estimated. Improved maintenance procedures, revision of operating procedures, or similar developments may prolong the life of the asset beyond the expected period.[10]

For example, assume that machinery originally costing $90,000 is estimated to have a 20-year life with no salvage value. However, during year 11 it is estimated that the machine will be used an additional 20 years. Its total life, therefore, will be 30 years instead of 20. Depreciation has been recorded at the rate of 1/20 of $90,000, or $4,500 per year by the straight-line method. On the basis of a 30-year life, depreciation should have been 1/30 of $90,000, or $3,000 per year. Depreciation, therefore, has been over-estimated, and net income has been understated by $1,500 for each of the past 10 years, or a total amount of $15,000. The amount of the difference can be computed as shown below.

ILLUSTRATION 11-13
Computation of Accumulated Difference Due to Revisions

	Per Year	For 10 Years
Depreciation charged per books (1/20 × $90,000)	$4,500	$45,000
Depreciation based on a 30-year life (1/30 × $90,000)	3,000	30,000
Excess depreciation charged	$1,500	$15,000

Changes in estimate should be handled in the current and prospective periods. No changes should be made in previously reported results. Opening balances are not adjusted and no attempt is made to "catch up" for prior periods. The reason is that changes in estimates are a continual and inherent part of any estimation process, and continual restatement of prior periods would occur for revisions of estimates unless they are handled prospectively. Therefore, no entry is made at the time the change in

---

[10]As an example of a change in operating procedures, General Motors (GM) used to write off its tools—such as dies and equipment used to manufacture car bodies—over the life of the body type. Through this procedure, it expensed tools twice as fast as Ford and three times as fast as Chrysler. Now it has slowed the depreciation process on these tools and lengthened the lives on its plant and equipment. These revisions had the effect of reducing depreciation and amortization charges by approximately $1.23 billion, or $2.55 per share, in the year of the change.

estimate occurs, and charges for depreciation in subsequent periods (assuming use of the straight-line method) are based on **dividing the remaining book value less any salvage value by the remaining estimated life**:

Machinery	$90,000
Less: Accumulated depreciation	45,000
Book value of machinery at end of 10th year	$45,000
Depreciation (future periods) = $45,000 book value ÷ 20 years remaining life = $2,250	

ILLUSTRATION 11-14
Computing Depreciation after Revision of Estimated Life

The entry to record depreciation for each of the remaining 20 years is:

Depreciation Expense	2,250	
Accumulated Depreciation—Machinery		2,250

❖ IMPAIRMENTS

The general accounting standard of **lower of cost or market for inventories does not apply to property, plant, and equipment**. Even when property, plant, and equipment has suffered partial obsolescence, accountants have been reluctant to reduce the carrying amount of the asset. This reluctance occurs because, unlike inventories, it is difficult to arrive at a fair value for property, plant, and equipment that is not subjective and arbitrary. For example, Falconbridge Nickel Mines had to decide whether all or a part of its property, plant, and equipment in a nickel-mining operation in the Dominican Republic should be written off. The project had been incurring losses because nickel prices were low and operating costs were high. Only if nickel prices increased by approximately 33% would the project be reasonably profitable. Whether a write-off was appropriate depended on the future price of nickel. Even if the decision were made to write off the asset, another important question would be: How much should be written off?[11]

Objective **6**
Explain the accounting issues related to asset impairment.

Recognizing Impairments

Recognizing that guidance was needed in this area, "Accounting for Impairments of Long-Lived Assets" was issued by the FASB in 1995.[12] In this standard, an *impairment* occurs when the carrying amount of an asset is not recoverable and, therefore, a write-off is needed. Various events and changes in circumstances might lead to an impairment. Examples are:

a. A significant decrease in the market value of an asset.
b. A significant change in the extent or manner in which an asset is used.
c. A significant adverse change in legal factors or in the business climate that affects the value of an asset.
d. An accumulation of costs significantly in excess of the amount originally expected to acquire or construct an asset.
e. A projection or forecast that demonstrates continuing losses associated with an asset.

If these events or changes in circumstances indicate that the carrying amount of the asset may not be recoverable, a *recoverability test* is used to determine whether an impairment has occurred. To apply the first step of the recoverability test, you estimate

UNDERLYING CONCEPTS

The *going concern* concept assumes that the firm can recover the cost of the investment in its assets. Under GAAP the fair value of long-lived assets is not reported because a *going* concern does not plan to sell such assets. However, if the assumption of being able to recover the cost of the investment is not valid, then a reduction in value should be reported.

---

[11]Even given these difficult valuation problems, many companies during the earlier part of the 1990s, before issuance of the standard, took a number of large write-offs. One study, for example, noted that write-offs of long-lived assets during a recent 5-year period totaled over $50 billion. Also it has been estimated that over one-third of the largest companies in the United States in recent years have taken restructuring losses of some amount.

[12]"Accounting for Impairments of Long-Lived Assets," *Statement of Financial Accounting Standards No. 121* (Norwalk, Conn.: 1995).

the future net cash flows expected from the **use of that asset and its eventual disposition**. If the sum of the expected future net cash flows (undiscounted) is **less than the carrying amount** of the asset, the asset has been impaired. Conversely, if the sum of the expected future net cash flows (undiscounted) is **equal to or greater than the carrying amount** of the asset, no impairment has occurred.

The recoverability test is a screening device to determine whether an impairment has occurred. For example, if the expected future net cash flows from an asset are $400,000 and its carrying amount is $350,000, no impairment has occurred. However, if the expected future net cash flows are $300,000, an impairment has occurred. The rationale for the recoverability test is the basic presumption that a balance sheet should report long-lived assets at no more than the carrying amounts that are recoverable.

Measuring Impairments

If the recoverability test indicates that an impairment has occurred, a loss is computed. **The impairment loss is the amount by which the carrying amount of the asset exceeds its fair value.** The fair value of an asset is measured by its market value if an active market for it exists. If no active market exists, the **present value of expected future net cash flows** should be used. The company's market rate of interest should be used in discounting to present value. To summarize, the process of determining an impairment loss is as follows:

❶ Review events or changes in circumstances for possible impairment.
❷ If the review indicates impairment, apply the recoverability test. If the sum of the expected future net cash flows from the long-lived asset is less than the carrying amount of the asset, an impairment has occurred.
❸ Assuming an impairment, the impairment loss is the amount by which the carrying amount of the asset is greater than the fair value of the asset. The fair value is the market value or the present value.

Illustration One

M. Alou Inc. has an asset that, due to changes in its use, is reviewed for possible impairment. The asset's carrying amount is $600,000 ($800,000 cost less $200,000 accumulated depreciation). The expected future net cash flows (undiscounted) from the use of the asset and its eventual disposition are determined to be $650,000.

The recoverability test indicates that the $650,000 of expected future net cash flows from the asset's use exceed its carrying amount of $600,000. As a result, no impairment is assumed to have occurred. The undiscounted future net cash flows must be less than the carrying amount for an asset to be deemed impaired and for the impairment loss to be measured. M. Alou Inc. will thus not recognize an impairment loss in this case.

Illustration Two

Assume the same facts as Illustration One, except that the expected future net cash flows from Alou's equipment is $580,000 (instead of $650,000). The recoverability test indicates that the expected future net cash flows of $580,000 from the use of the asset are less than its carrying amount of $600,000. Therefore an impairment has occurred. The difference between the carrying amount of Alou's asset and its fair value is the impairment loss. This asset has a market value of $525,000. The computation of the loss is:

ILLUSTRATION 11-15
Computation of
Impairment Loss

Carrying amount of the equipment	$600,000
Fair value of equipment (market value)	525,000
Loss on impairment	$ 75,000

The entry to record the impairment loss is as follows:

Loss on Impairment	75,000	
Accumulated Depreciation		75,000

The impairment loss is reported as part of income from continuing operations, generally in the other expenses and losses section. This loss should **not be reported as an extraordinary item**. Costs associated with an impairment loss are the same costs that would flow through operations and be reported as part of continuing operations. These assets will continue to be used in operations and, therefore, the loss should not be reported below income from continuing operations.

A company that recognizes an impairment loss should disclose the asset(s) impaired, the events leading to the impairment, the amount of the loss, and how fair value was determined (disclosing the interest rate used, if appropriate).

U.S. oil companies are particularly affected by this new standard because for the first time they have to assess each of their producing fields on a case-by-case basis. In the past, oil fields were evaluated on a total company basis. Texaco, for instance, took a $640 million fourth-quarter charge in 1995 that swung a quarterly profit into a loss. Other 1995 oil company impairment charges were reported by Mobil ($487 million), Amoco ($380 million), Ashland Inc. ($90 million), and Phillips Petroleum ($49 million).

As disclosed in its Property, Plant, and Equipment note (page 241), Intel Corporation adopted *FASB Statement No. 121* effective as of the beginning of 1995. Intel reports that "this adoption had no material effect on the Company's financial statements."

Restoration of Impairment Loss

Once an impairment loss is recorded, the reduced carrying amount of an asset held for use becomes its new cost basis. As a result, the new cost basis is not changed except for depreciation in future periods or for additional impairments. To illustrate, assume that Ortiz Company at December 31, 1997, has equipment with a carrying amount of $500,000, which is impaired and is written down to its fair value of $400,000. At the end of 1998, assume that the fair value of this asset is $480,000. The carrying amount of the asset should not change in 1998 except for the depreciation taken in 1998. **The impairment loss may not be restored for an asset held for use.** The rationale for not writing the asset up in value is that the new cost basis puts the impaired asset on an equal basis with other assets that are not impaired.

 **INTERNATIONAL INSIGHT**

International accounting standards permit writeups for subsequent recoveries of impairment whereas U.S. GAAP prohibits those writeups, except for assets to be disposed of.

Assets to Be Disposed Of

What happens if the impaired asset is intended to be disposed of instead of held for use? In this case, the impaired asset is reported at the lower of cost or fair value less cost to sell (net realizable value). Because the asset is intended to be disposed of in a short period of time, net realizable value is used in order to provide a better measure of the net cash flows that will be received from this asset.

Assets that are being held for disposal are not depreciated during the period they are held. The rationale is that depreciation is inconsistent with the notion of assets to be disposed of and with the use of the lower of cost or net realizable value. In other words, **assets held for disposal are like inventory and should be reported at the lower of cost or net realizable value**.

Because assets held for disposal will be recovered through sale rather than through operations, they are continually revalued. Each period they are reported at the lower of cost or net realizable value. Thus **an asset held for disposal can be written up or down in future periods, as long as the write-up is never greater than the carrying amount of the asset before the impairment**. Losses or gains related to these impaired assets should be reported as part of **income from continuing operations**. The disclosure requirements for these assets are complex; we leave that issue for an advanced course. A summary of the key concepts in accounting for impairments is presented in Illustration 11-16.

ILLUSTRATION 11-16
Graphic of Accounting
for Impairments

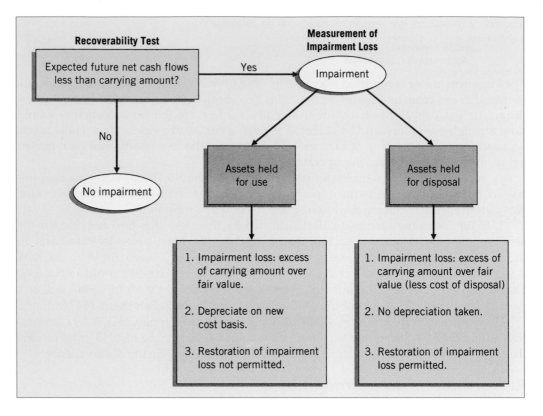

❖ DEPLETION

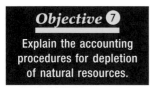

Objective ❼

Explain the accounting
procedures for depletion
of natural resources.

Natural resources, often called wasting assets, include petroleum, minerals, and timber. They are characterized by two main features: (1) the complete removal (consumption) of the asset, and (2) replacement of the asset only by an act of nature. Unlike plant and equipment, natural resources are consumed physically over the period of use and do not maintain their physical characteristics. Still, the accounting problems associated with natural resources are similar to those encountered with fixed assets. The questions to be answered are:

❶ How is the cost basis for write-off (depletion) established?
❷ What pattern of allocation should be employed?

Establishing a Depletion Base

How do we determine the depletion base for natural resources? Sizable expenditures are needed to find these natural resources, and for every successful discovery there are many "failures." Furthermore, long delays are encountered between the time the costs are incurred and the benefits are obtained from the extracted resources. As a result, a conservative policy frequently is adopted in accounting for the expenditures incurred in finding and extracting natural resources. The computation of the depletion base involves four factors: (1) acquisition cost of the deposit, (2) exploration costs, (3) development costs, and (4) restoration costs.

Acquisition Costs

Acquisition cost is the price paid to obtain the property right to search and find an undiscovered natural resource or the price paid for an already discovered resource. In some cases, property is leased and special royalty payments paid to the owner if a productive natural resource is found and is commercially profitable. Generally, the acquisition cost is placed in an account titled Undeveloped Property and assigned to the natural resource if exploration efforts are successful. If they are unsuccessful, the cost is written off as a loss.

Exploration Costs

As soon as a company has the right to use the property, exploration costs are often needed to find the resource. In most cases, these costs are expensed as incurred. When these costs are substantial and the risks of finding the resource uncertain (such as in the oil and gas industry), capitalization may occur. The unique issues related to the oil and gas industry are examined on page 562.

Development Costs

Development costs are divided into: (1) tangible equipment and (2) intangible development costs. Tangible equipment includes all of the transportation and other heavy equipment necessary to extract the resource and get it ready for production or shipment. Because the asset can be moved from one drilling or mining site to another, **tangible equipment costs are normally not considered in the depletion base**. Instead, separate depreciation charges are employed. Tangible assets that cannot be moved should be depreciated over their useful life or the life of the resource, whichever is shorter. **Intangible development costs, on the other hand, are considered part of the depletion base.** These costs are for such items as the drilling costs, tunnels, shafts, and wells, which have no tangible characteristics but are needed for the production of the natural resource.

Restoration Costs

Companies sometimes incur substantial costs to restore property to its natural state after extraction has occurred. These restoration costs should be added to the depletion base for purposes of computing the depletion cost per unit. It follows that any salvage value received on the property should be deducted from the depletion base.

Write-Off of Resource Cost

As soon as the depletion base is established, the next problem is determining how the cost of the natural resource should be allocated to accounting periods. Normally, depletion is computed on the units of production method (activity approach), which means that depletion is a function of the number of units withdrawn during the period. In adopting this approach, the total cost of the natural resource less salvage value is divided by the number of units estimated to be in the resource deposit, to obtain a cost per unit of product. This cost per unit is multiplied by the number of units extracted to compute depletion.

For example, MaClede Co. has acquired the right to use 1,000 acres of land in Alaska to mine for gold. The lease cost is $50,000; the related exploration costs on the property are $100,000; and intangible development costs incurred in opening the mine are $850,000. Total costs related to the mine before the first ounce of gold is extracted are, therefore, $1,000,000. MaClede estimates that the mine will provide approximately 100,000 ounces of gold. The depletion rate established is computed in the following manner:

$$\frac{\text{Total cost} - \text{Salvage value}}{\text{Total estimated units available}} = \text{Depletion cost per unit}$$

$$\frac{\$1,000,000}{100,000} = \$10.00 \text{ per ounce}$$

ILLUSTRATION 11-17 Computation of Depletion Rate

If 25,000 ounces are extracted in the first year, then the depletion for the year is $250,000 (25,000 ounces at $10.00). The entry to record the depletion is:

Inventory	250,000	
Accumulated Depletion		250,000

Inventory is first debited for the total depletion for the year, and then is credited for the cost of materials sold during the year. The amount not sold remains in inventory and is reported in the current asset section.

In some instances an Accumulated Depletion account is not used, and the credit goes directly to the natural resources asset account. The balance sheet presents the cost of the property and the amount of accumulated depletion entered to date as follows:

ILLUSTRATION 11-18
Balance Sheet
Presentation of
Natural Resource

Gold mine (at cost)	$1,000,000	
Less accumulated depletion	250,000	$750,000

In the income statement the depletion cost is part of the cost of goods sold.

The tangible equipment used in extracting the gold may also be depreciated on a units of production basis, especially if the estimated lives of the equipment can be directly assigned to one given resource deposit. If the equipment is used on more than one job, other cost allocation methods such as straight-line or accelerated depreciation methods would be more appropriate.

Continuing Controversy

A major controversy relates to the accounting for exploration costs in the oil and gas industry. Conceptually, the question is whether unsuccessful exploration costs are a cost of those that are successful. Some believe that unsuccessful ventures are a cost of those that are successful (**full cost concept**) because the cost of drilling a dry hole is a cost that is needed to find the commercially profitable wells. Those who believe that only the costs of successful projects should be capitalized (**successful efforts concept**) contend that an unsuccessful company will end up capitalizing many costs that will make it, over a short period of time, show no less income than does one that is successful.[13] In addition, the only relevant measure for a single property unit is the cost directly related to that unit. The remainder of the costs should be reported as period charges.

The FASB has attempted to narrow the available alternatives but has met with little success. Here is a brief history of the debate.

❶ **1977—The FASB issued** *Statement No. 19*, **which required oil and gas companies to follow successful efforts accounting.** However, after small oil and gas producers, voicing strong opposition, lobbied extensively in Congress, governmental agencies assessed the implications of this standard from a public interest perspective and reacted contrary to the FASB's position.[14]

❷ **1978—In response to criticisms of the FASB's actions, the SEC reexamined the issue and found both successful efforts and full cost accounting inadequate because neither reflects the economic substance of oil and gas exploration.** As a substitute, the SEC argued in favor of a yet-to-be developed method, **reserve recognition accounting (RRA)**, which it believed would provide more useful infor-

---

[13]Large international oil companies such as Exxon and Mobil use the successful efforts approach. Full-cost accounting is used by most of the smaller, exploration-oriented companies. The differences in net income figures under the two methods can be staggering. It was estimated that Texaco's full-cost accounting increased its reported profits by $500 million over a 10-year period.

[14]The Department of Energy indicated that companies now using the full-cost method would reduce their exploration activities because of the unfavorable earnings impact associated with successful efforts accounting. The Justice Department asked the SEC to postpone adoption of one uniform method of accounting in the oil and gas industry until the SEC could determine whether the information reported to investors would be enhanced and competition constrained by adoption of the successful efforts method.

mation. Under RRA, as soon as a company discovers oil, it reports the value of the oil on the balance sheet and in the income statement. Thus, RRA is a current value approach as opposed to full costing and successful efforts, which are historical cost approaches.[15]

❸ 1979–1981—As a result of the SEC's actions, the FASB had no choice but to issue another standard that suspended the requirement that companies follow successful efforts accounting. Therefore, full costing again became permissible. In attempting to implement RRA, however, the SEC encountered practical problems in estimating **(1) the amount of the reserves, (2) the future production costs, (3) the periods of expected disposal, (4) the discount rate, and (5) the selling price.** An estimate for each of these elements is necessary to arrive at an accurate valuation of the existing oil or gas reserve. If the oil or gas reserve is not to be extracted and sold for several years, estimating the future selling price, the appropriate discount rate, and the future costs of extraction and delivery can each be a formidable task.

❹ 1981—The SEC announced that it had abandoned RRA as a potential accounting method in the primary financial statements of oil and gas producers. Because of the inherent uncertainty of determining recoverable quantities of proved oil and gas reserves, the SEC indicated that RRA does not currently possess the required degree of reliability for use as a primary method of financial reporting. However, the SEC continued to stress that some form of value-based disclosure was needed for oil and gas reserves. As a result, the FASB issued *Statement No. 69,* "Disclosure about Oil and Gas Producing Activities," which requires current value disclosures.

❺ 1986—One requirement of full-cost accounting is that costs can only be capitalized up to a ceiling, the height of which is determined by the present value of company reserves. Capitalized costs above that ceiling have to be expensed. In 1986 the price of oil plummeted and as a result a number of companies faced massive write-offs of their reserves because capitalized costs exceeded the present value of the companies' reserves. Companies lobbied for leniency, but the SEC decided that the write-offs had to be taken. As a result, Mesa Limited Partnerships' $31 million profit was restated to a $169 million loss and Pacific Lighting's $44.5 million profit was changed to a $70.5 million loss.

Either the full-cost approach or the successful efforts approach is currently acceptable. It does seem ironic that Congress directed the FASB to develop one method of accounting for the oil and gas industry, and when the FASB did so, the government chose not to accept it. Subsequently, the government (SEC) attempted to develop a new approach, failed, and then urged the FASB to develop the disclosure requirements in this area. After all these changes, alternatives still exist in the oil and gas industry.

This controversy in the oil and gas industry provides a number of lessons to the student in accounting. First, it demonstrates the strong influence that the federal government has in financial reporting matters. Second, the concern for economic consequences places considerable pressure on the FASB to weigh the economic effects of any required standard. Third, the experience with RRA highlights the problems that are encountered when a change from an historical cost to a current value approach is proposed. Fourth, this controversy illustrates the difficulty of establishing standards when affected groups have differing viewpoints. And finally, it reinforces the need for a conceptual framework with carefully developed guidelines for recognition, measurement, and reporting, so that issues of this nature hopefully may be more easily resolved in the future.

UNDERLYING CONCEPTS

Failure to consider the economic consequences of accounting principles is a frequent criticism of the profession. However, the neutrality concept requires that the statements be free from bias. Freedom from bias requires that the statements reflect economic reality, even if undesirable effects occur.

---

[15]The use of RRA would make a substantial difference in the balance sheets and income statements of oil companies. For example, Atlantic Richfield Co. at one time reported net producing property of $2.6 billion. If RRA were adopted, the same properties would be valued at $11.8 billion. Similarly, Standard Oil of Ohio, which reported net producing properties of $1.7 billion, would have reported approximately $10.7 billion under RRA.

Special Problems in Depletion Accounting

Accounting for natural resources has some interesting problems that are uncommon to most other types of assets. For purposes of discussion we have divided these problems into four categories:

❶ Difficulty of estimating recoverable reserves.
❷ Problems of discovery value.
❸ Tax aspects of natural resources.
❹ Accounting for liquidating dividends.

Estimating Recoverable Reserves

Not infrequently the estimate of recoverable reserves has to be changed either because new information has become available or because production processes have become more sophisticated. Natural resources such as oil and gas deposits and some rare metals have recently provided the greatest challenges. Estimates of these reserves are in large measure "knowledgeable guesses."

This problem is the **same as accounting for changes in estimates of the useful lives of plant and equipment**. The procedure is to revise the depletion rate on a prospective basis by dividing the remaining cost by the estimate of the new recoverable reserves. This approach has much merit because the required estimates are so tenuous.

Discovery Value

Discovery value accounting and reserve recognition accounting are similar. RRA is specifically related to the oil and gas industry, whereas discovery value is a broader term associated with the whole natural resources area. As indicated earlier, accountants do not recognize discovery values. However, if discovery value were to be recorded, an asset account would be debited and an Unrealized Appreciation account would be credited. Unrealized Appreciation is part of stockholders' equity. Unrealized Appreciation would then be transferred to revenue as the natural resources are sold.

A similar issue arises with resources such as growing timber, aging liquor, and maturing livestock that increase in value over time. One method is to record the increase in value as the accretion occurs. Debit the asset account and credit revenue or an unrealized revenue account. These increases can be substantial. Boise Cascade's timber resources were at one time valued at $1.7 billion, whereas its book value was approximately $289 million. Accountants have been hesitant to record these increases because of the uncertainty regarding the final sales price and the problem of estimating the costs involved in getting the resources ready for sale.

Tax Aspects of Natural Resources

The tax aspects of accounting for most natural resources have comprised some of the most controversial provisions of the Internal Revenue Code (IRC). The tax law has long provided a deduction for the greater of **cost** or percentage depletion against revenue from oil, gas, and most minerals. The percentage or statutory depletion allows a write-off ranging from 5% to 22% (depending on the natural resource) of gross revenue received. As a result, the amount of depletion may exceed the cost assigned to a given natural resource. An asset's carrying amount may be zero, but a depletion deduction may still be taken if the enterprise has gross revenue. The significance of the percentage depletion allowance is now greatly reduced because it has been repealed for most oil and gas companies and is of only limited use in most other situations.

Liquidating Dividends

A company often owns as its only major asset a certain property from which it intends to extract natural resources. If the company does not expect to purchase additional properties, it may distribute gradually to stockholders their capital investments by paying dividends greater than the amount of accumulated net income. The major accounting problem is to distinguish between dividends that are a return of capital and those that are not. The company issuing a liquidating dividend should debit Paid-in Capital in Excess of Par for that portion related to the original investment instead of Retained Earnings, because the dividend is a return of part of the investor's original contribution.

To illustrate, at December 31, 1996, Callahan Mining had a retained earnings balance of $1,650,000, accumulated depletion on mineral properties of $2,100,000, and paid-in capital in excess of par of $5,435,493. Callahan's board declared a dividend of $3.00 a share on the 1,000,000 shares outstanding. The entry to record the $3,000,000 cash dividend is as follows:

Retained Earnings	1,650,000	
Paid-in Capital in Excess of Par	1,350,000	
Cash		3,000,000

Stockholders must be informed that each $3.00 dividend per share represents a $1.65 ($1,650,000 ÷ 1,000,000 shares) per share return on investment and a $1.35 ($1,350,000 ÷ 1,000,000 shares) per share liquidating dividend.

❖ PRESENTATION AND ANALYSIS

Presentation of Property, Plant, Equipment, and Natural Resources

The basis of valuation—usually historical cost—for property, plant, equipment, and natural resources should be disclosed along with pledges, liens, and other commitments related to these assets. Any liability secured by property, plant, equipment, and natural resources should not be offset against these assets, but should be reported in the liability section. Property, plant, equipment, and natural resources not currently employed as producing assets in the business (such as idle facilities or land held as an investment) should be segregated from assets used in operations.

Objective 8

Explain how property, plant, equipment, and natural resources are reported and analyzed.

When assets are depreciated, a valuation account normally called Accumulated Depreciation is credited. The employment of an Accumulated Depreciation account permits the user of the financial statements to see the original cost of the asset and the amount of depreciation that has been charged to expense in past years. When assets are depleted, some companies use an Accumulated Depletion account. Many companies, however, simply credit the natural resource account directly. The rationale for this approach is that the natural resources are physically consumed and, therefore, direct reduction of the cost of the natural resources is appropriate.

Because of the significant impact on the financial statements of the depreciation method(s) used, the following disclosures should be made:

a. Depreciation expense for the period.
b. Balances of major classes of depreciable assets, by nature and function.
c. Accumulated depreciation, either by major classes of depreciable assets or in total.
d. A general description of the method or methods used in computing depreciation with respect to major classes of depreciable assets.[16]

For natural resources, special disclosure requirements relate to the oil and gas industry. Companies engaged in these activities must disclose in their financial statements (1) the basic method of accounting for those costs incurred in oil and gas producing activities (e.g., full cost versus successful efforts) and (2) the manner of disposing of

---

[16]"Omnibus Opinion–1967," *Opinions of the Accounting Principles Board No. 12* (New York: AICPA, 1967), par. 5. Some believe that the average useful life of the assets or the range of years for asset life is significant information that should be disclosed.

costs relating to oil and gas producing activities (e.g., expensing immediately versus depreciation and depletion).[17]

The 1996 Annual Report of Boise Cascade Corporation in Illustration 11-19 illustrates an acceptable disclosure using condensed balance sheet data supplemented with details and policies in notes to the financial statements.

ILLUSTRATION 11-19
Disclosures for Property, Plant, Equipment, and Natural Resources

Go to our Web site for additional property, plant, equipment, and natural resources disclosures.

Boise Cascade Corporation

	1995	1994
	(expressed in thousands)	
Property (Note 1)		
Property and equipment		
Land and improvements	$ 39,482	$ 37,775
Buildings and improvements	459,897	439,936
Machinery and equipment	4,271,306	4,078,302
	4,770,685	4,556,013
Accumulated depreciation	(2,166,487)	(2,062,106)
	2,604,198	2,493,907
Timber, timberlands, and timber deposits	383,394	397,721
	2,987,592	2,891,628
Investments in equity affiliates	25,803	204,498
Other assets	329,623	279,687

Notes to Financial Statements

1 (In Part): Summary of Significant Accounting Policies
Property. Property and equipment are recorded at cost. Cost includes expenditures for major improvements and replacements and the net amount of interest cost associated with significant capital additions. Capitalized interest was $1,884,000 in 1995, $1,630,000 in 1994, and $1,118,000 in 1993. Substantially all of the Company's paper and wood products manufacturing facilities determine depreciation by the units-of-production method, and other operations use the straight-line method. Gains and losses from sales and retirements are included in income as they occur except at certain pulp and paper mills that use composite depreciation methods. At those facilities, gains and losses are included in accumulated depreciation. Estimated service lives of principal items of property and equipment range from 3 to 40 years.

Cost of company timber harvested and amortization of logging roads are determined on the basis of the annual amount of timber cut in relation to the total amount of recoverable timber. Timber and timberlands are stated at cost, less the accumulated total of timber previously harvested.

A portion of the Company's wood requirements are acquired from public and private sources. Except for deposits required pursuant to wood supply contracts, no amounts are recorded until such time as the Company becomes liable for the timber. At December 31, 1995, based on average prices at the time, the unrecorded amount of those contracts was estimated to be approximately $174,000,000.

Analysis of Property, Plant, Equipment, and Natural Resources

Assets may be analyzed relative to activity (turnover) and profitability. How efficiently a company uses its assets to generate sales is measured by the asset turnover ratio. This ratio is determined by dividing net sales by average total assets for the period. The resulting number is the dollars of sales produced by each dollar invested in assets. To

---

[17]Public companies, in addition to these two required disclosures, must include as supplementary information numerous schedules reporting reserve quantities; capitalized costs; acquisition, exploration, and development activities; and a standardized measure of discounted future net cash flows related to proved oil and gas reserve quantities.

"Disclosures about Oil and Gas Producing Activities," *Statement of Financial Accounting Standards Board No. 69* (Stamford, Conn.: FASB, 1982)

illustrate, we will use the following data from Campbell Soup Company's 1996 annual report:

Campbell Soup Company

	(in millions)
Net sales	$7,678
Total assets, 7/30/95	6,315
Total assets, 7/28/96	6,632
Net income	802

$$\text{Asset turnover} = \frac{\text{Net sales}}{\text{Average total assets}}$$

$$= \frac{\$7,678}{\dfrac{\$6,315 + \$6,632}{2}}$$

$$= 1.19$$

ILLUSTRATION 11-20
Asset Turnover Ratio

The asset turnover ratio shows that Campbell Soup generated sales of $1.19 per dollar of assets in the year ended July 28, 1996.

Asset turnover ratios vary considerably among industries. For example, a large utility company like Union Electric Company (St. Louis) has a ratio of 0.36 times, and a large grocery chain like Atlantic and Pacific Tea (A&P) has a ratio of 3.6 times.

Employment of the **profit margin on sales ratio** (rate of return on sales) in conjunction with the asset turnover ratio offers an interplay that leads to a **rate of return on total assets**. Using the Campbell Soup Company data in the illustration above, the profit margin on sales ratio and the rate of return on total assets are computed as follows:

$$\text{Profit margin on sales} = \frac{\text{Net income}}{\text{Net sales}}$$

$$= \frac{\$802}{\$7,678}$$

$$= 10.4\%$$

$$\text{Rate of return on total assets} = \text{Profit margin on sales} \times \text{Asset turnover}$$

$$= 10.4\% \times 1.19$$

$$= 12.4\%$$

ILLUSTRATION 11-21
Profit Margin on Sales

The profit margin on sales does not answer the question of how profitably a company uses its assets. But by relating the profit margin on sales to the asset turnover during a period of time, it is possible to ascertain how profitably the assets were used during that period of time.

The **rate of return on assets** (ROA) can be directly computed by dividing net income by average total assets. Using Campbell Soup's data the ratio is computed as follows:

$$\text{Rate of return on assets} = \frac{\text{Net income}}{\text{Average total assets}}$$

$$= \frac{\$802}{\dfrac{\$6,315 + \$6,632}{2}}$$

$$= 12.4\%$$

ILLUSTRATION 11-22
Rate of Return on Assets

The 12.4% rate of return computed in this manner is identical to the 12.4% rate computed by multiplying the profit margin on sales by the asset turnover. The rate of return on assets is a good measure of profitability because it combines the effects of profit margin and asset turnover.

SUMMARY OF LEARNING OBJECTIVES

① ***Explain the concept of depreciation.*** Depreciation is the accounting process of allocating the cost of tangible assets to expense in a systematic and rational manner to those periods expected to benefit from the use of the asset.

② ***Identify the factors involved in the depreciation process.*** Three factors involved in the depreciation process are: (1) determining the depreciation base for the asset, (2) estimating service lives, and (3) selecting a method of cost apportionment (depreciation).

③ ***Compare activity, straight-line, and decreasing charge methods of depreciation.*** (1) *Activity method:* Assumes that depreciation is a function of use or productivity instead of the passage of time. The life of the asset is considered in terms of either the output it provides, or an input measure such as the number of hours it works. (2) *Straight-line method:* Considers depreciation a function of time instead of a function of usage. This method is widely employed in practice because of its simplicity. The straight-line procedure is often the most conceptually appropriate when a decline in usefulness is constant from period to period. (3) *Decreasing charge methods:* Provide for a higher depreciation cost in the earlier years and lower charges in later periods. The main justification for this approach is that the asset suffers the greatest loss of services in those years.

④ ***Explain special depreciation methods.*** Two special depreciation methods are: (1) *Group and composite methods:* The term *group* refers to a collection of assets that are similar in nature; *composite* refers to a collection of assets that are dissimilar in nature. The group method is frequently used where the assets are fairly homogeneous and have approximately the same useful lives. The composite approach is used when the assets are heterogeneous and have different lives. (2) *Hybrid or combination methods:* A hybrid depreciation method widely used in the steel industry is a combination straight-line/activity approach referred to as the production variable method.

⑤ ***Identify reasons why depreciation methods are selected.*** The selection of a depreciation method involves factors such as the nature and uncertainty of revenue flows, matching costs and revenues, effect on income and asset book values, tax considerations, and record-keeping costs.

⑥ ***Explain the accounting issues related to asset impairment.*** The process to determine an impairment loss is as follows: (1) Review events and changes in circumstances for possible impairment. (2) If events or changes suggest impairment, determine if the sum of the expected future net cash flows from the long-lived asset is less than the carrying amount of the asset. If less, measure the impairment loss. (3) The impairment loss is the amount by which the carrying amount of the asset is greater than the fair value of the asset. After an impairment loss is recorded, the reduced carrying amount of the long-lived asset is now considered its new cost basis. Impairment losses may not be restored for assets held for use. If the asset is expected to be disposed of, the impaired asset should be reported at the lower of cost or net realizable value. It is not depreciated. It can be continuously revalued, as long as the write-up is never greater than the carrying amount before impairment.

7 ***Explain the accounting procedures for depletion of natural resources.*** The accounting procedures for depletion of natural resources are (1) establishment of depletion base, and (2) write-off of resource cost. Four factors are involved in establishing the depletion base: (a) *acquisition costs,* (b) *exploration costs,* (c) *development costs,* and (d) *restoration costs.* To write off resource cost, normally,depletion is computed on the units of production method, which means that depletion is a function of the number of units withdrawn during the period. In adopting this approach, the total cost of the natural resource less salvage value is divided by the number of units estimated to be in the resource deposit, to obtain a cost per unit of product. This cost per unit is multiplied by the number of units withdrawn to compute depletion.

8 ***Explain how property, plant, equipment, and natural resources are reported and analyzed.*** The basis of valuation for property, plant, equipment, and natural resources should be disclosed along with pledges, liens, and other commitments related to these assets. Any liability secured by property, plant, equipment, and natural resources should not be offset against these assets, but should be reported in the liability section. When assets are depreciated, a valuation account normally called Accumulated Depreciation is credited. When assets are depleted, an accumulated depletion account may be used or the depletion may be credited directly to the natural resource account. Companies engaged in significant oil and gas producing activities must provide special additional disclosures about these activities. Analysis may be performed to evaluate the asset turnover rate, the profit margin on sales, and the rate of return on assets.

Appendix 11A

Income Tax Depreciation

❖ MODIFIED ACCELERATED COST RECOVERY SYSTEM

For the most part, issues related to the computation of income taxes are not discussed in a financial accounting course. However, because the concepts of tax depreciation are similar to those of book depreciation, and because tax depreciation methods are sometimes adopted for book purposes, an overview of this subject is presented.

Objective **9**

After studying Appendix 11A, you should be able to: Describe income tax methods of depreciation.

Efforts to stimulate capital investment through faster write-offs and to bring more uniformity to the write-off period resulted in enactment of the Accelerated Cost Recovery System (ACRS) as part of the Economic Recovery Tax Act of 1981. For assets purchased in the years 1981 through 1986, ACRS and its preestablished "cost recovery periods" for various classes of assets are used.

A Modified Accelerated Cost Recovery System, known as MACRS, was enacted by Congress in the Tax Reform Act of 1986. It applies to depreciable assets placed in service in 1987 and later. The following discussion is based on these MACRS rules. Tax depreciation rules are subject to change annually.

The computation of depreciation under MACRS differs from the computation under GAAP in three respects: (1) a mandated tax life, which is generally shorter than the economic life; (2) cost recovery on an accelerated basis; and (3) an assigned salvage value of zero.

Tax Lives (Recovery Periods)

Each item of depreciable property is assigned to a property class. The recovery period (depreciable tax life) of an asset depends on the property class.[1] The MACRS property classes are presented below:

ILLUSTRATION 11A-1
MACRS Property Classes

> **3-year property**—includes small tools, horses, and assets used in research and development activities
>
> **5-year property**—includes automobiles, trucks, computers and peripheral equipment, and office machines
>
> **7-year property**—includes office furniture and fixtures, agriculture equipment, oil exploration and development equipment, railroad track, manufacturing equipment, and any property not designated by law as being in any other class
>
> **10-year property**—includes railroad tank cars, mobile homes, boilers, and certain public utility property
>
> **15-year property**—includes roads, shrubbery, and certain low-income housing
>
> **20-year property**—includes waste-water treatment plants and sewer systems
>
> **27.5-year property**—includes residential rental property
>
> **39-year property**—includes nonresidential real property

Tax Depreciation Methods

The depreciation expense is computed based on the tax basis, usually the cost, of the asset. The depreciation method depends on the life of the assets as mandated by the MACRS property class, as shown below:

ILLUSTRATION 11A-2
Depreciation Method for Various MACRS Property Classes

MACRS Property Class	Depreciation Method
3-, 5-, 7-, and 10-year property	Double-declining-balance
15- and 20-year property	150% declining-balance
27.5- and 39-year property	Straight-line

When one of the accelerated methods is used, a change is made to the straight-line method in the first year in which straight-line depreciation exceeds the accelerated depreciation. Depreciation computations for income tax purposes are based on the half-year convention; that is, a half year of depreciation is allowable in the year of acquisition and in the year of disposition.[2] An asset is depreciated to a zero value so that there is no salvage value at the end of its MACRS life.

The application of these depreciation methods is simplified by using IRS published tables as shown in illustration 11A-3.

Illustration—MACRS System

To illustrate depreciation computations under both the MACRS system and GAAP straight-line accounting, assume the following facts for a computer and peripheral equipment purchased by Denise Rode Company on January 1, 1997:

Acquisition date	January 1, 1997
Cost	$100,000
Estimated useful life	7 years
Estimated salvage value	$16,000
MACRS class life	5 years
MACRS method	200% declining-balance
GAAP method	Straight-line
Disposal proceeds—January 2, 2004	$11,000

---

[1]Tax depreciation has changed numerous times during the 1980s and 1990s. For example, since 1980, six different depreciation requirements have been enacted. The tax life of certain real property has moved from 35 years in 1980 to 15 in 1981, 18 in 1982, 19 in 1984, 31.5 in 1986, and 39 in 1993. As one writer noted, "It appears that the useful life of a depreciation law is 2.2 years."

[2]Mid-quarter and mid-month conventions are required for MACRS purposes in certain circumstances.

MACRS DEPRECIATION RATES BY CLASS OF PROPERTY						
Recovery Year	3-year (200% DB)	5-year (200% DB)	7-year (200% DB)	10-year (200% DB)	15-year (150% DB)	20-year (150% DB)
1	33.33	20.00	14.29	10.00	5.00	3.750
2	44.45	32.00	24.49	18.00	9.50	7.219
3	14.81*	19.20	17.49	14.40	8.55	6.677
4	7.41	11.52*	12.49	11.52	7.70	6.177
5		11.52	8.93*	9.22	6.93	5.713
6	....	5.76	8.92	7.37	6.23	5.285
7			8.93	6.55*	5.90*	4.888
8			4.46	6.55	5.90	4.522
9				6.56	5.91	4.462*
10				6.55	5.90	4.461
11	....			3.28	5.91	4.462
12					5.90	4.461
13					5.91	4.462
14					5.90	4.461
15					5.91	4.462
16					2.95	4.461
17						4.462
18						4.461
19						4.462
20						4.461
21						2.231

*Switchover to straight-line depreciation.

ILLUSTRATION 11A-3
IRS Table of MACRS Depreciation Rates, by Property Class

INTERNATIONAL INSIGHT

In Korea, companies are allowed to take additional depreciation (in excess of declining balance) on machinery and equipment for such reasons as energy saving, implementation of new technology, and antipollution measures. Companies that record such additional special depreciation report it as an extraordinary loss.

Using the rates from the MACRS depreciation rate schedule for a 5-year class of property, depreciation is computed as follows for tax purposes:

MACRS Depreciation			
1997	$100,000 × .20	=	$ 20,000
1998	$100,000 × .32	=	32,000
1999	$100,000 × .192	=	19,200
2000	$100,000 × .1152	=	11,520
2001	$100,000 × .1152	=	11,520
2002	$100,000 × .0576	=	5,760
	Total Depreciation		$100,000

ILLUSTRATION 11A-4
Computation of MACRS Depreciation

The depreciation under GAAP straight-line method with $16,000 of estimated salvage value and an estimated useful life of 7 years is computed as follows:

GAAP Depreciation	
($100,000 − $16,000) ÷ 7 =	$12,000 annual depreciation
	× 7 years
1/1/97–1/2/2004	$84,000 total depreciation

ILLUSTRATION 11A-5
Computation of GAAP Depreciation

The MACRS depreciation recovers the total cost of the asset on an accelerated basis. But, a taxable gain of $11,000 results from the sale of the asset at January 2, 2004. Therefore, the net effect on taxable income for the years 1997 through 2004 is $89,000 ($100,000 depreciation minus $11,000 gain).

Under GAAP, a loss on disposal of $5,000 ($16,000 book value − $11,000 disposal proceeds) is recognized. The net effect on income before income taxes for the years 1997 through 2004 is $89,000 ($84,000 depreciation plus $5,000 loss), the same as the net effect of MACRS on taxable income.

Even though the net effects are equal in amount, the deferral of income tax payments under MACRS from early in the life of the asset to later in life is desirable when considering present value concepts. The different amounts of depreciation for income tax reporting and financial GAAP reporting in each year are a matter of timing and result in temporary differences, which require interperiod tax allocation. (See Chapter 20 for an extended treatment of this topic.)

Optional Straight-line Method

An alternate MACRS method to determine depreciation deductions is based on the straight-line method. Often referred to as the optional (elective) straight-line method, it applies to the six classes of property described earlier. Under the alternate MACRS, the straight-line method is generally applied to the MACRS recovery periods. Salvage value is ignored. Under the optional straight-line method, in the first year the property is placed in service, half of the amount of depreciation that would be permitted for a full year is generally deducted (half-year convention). Use the half-year convention for homework problems.

Tax versus Book Depreciation

INTERNATIONAL INSIGHT

In Switzerland, depreciation in the financial statements must conform to that on the tax returns. As a consequence, companies may depreciate as much as 80% of the cost of assets in the first year.

GAAP requires that the cost of depreciable assets be allocated to expense over the expected useful life of the asset in a systematic and rational manner. Some argue that from a cost-benefit perspective it would be better for companies to adopt the MACRS approach to eliminate the necessity of maintaining two different sets of records. However, because the objectives of the tax laws and financial reporting are different, the adoption of one method for both tax and book purposes in all cases would be unfortunate. The purpose of taxation is to raise revenue from constituents in an equitable manner; the purpose of financial reporting is to reflect the economic substance of a transaction as closely as possible and to help predict the amounts, timing, and uncertainty of future cash flows.

KEY TERMS

Modified Accelerated
 Cost Recovery System
 (MACRS), *569*

SUMMARY OF LEARNING OBJECTIVE FOR APPENDIX 11A

⑨ ***Describe income tax methods of depreciation.*** A Modified Accelerated Cost Recovery System (MACRS) was enacted by Congress in the Tax Return Act of 1986. It applies to depreciable assets placed in service in 1987 and later. The computation of depreciation under MACRS differs from the computation under GAAP in three respects: (1) a mandated tax life, which is generally shorter than the economic life; (2) cost recovery on an accelerated basis; and (3) an assigned salvage value of zero.

Note: All **asterisked** Questions, Brief Exercises, Exercises, Problems, and Conceptual Cases relate to material contained in the appendix to each chapter.

❖ QUESTIONS ❖

❶ Distinguish between depreciation, depletion, and amortization.

❷ Identify the factors that are relevant in determining the annual depreciation charge and explain whether these factors are determined objectively or whether they are based on judgment.

❸ Recently, a trustee of a state college noted that "depreciation of assets for any college is nonsensical. We're not public companies. Forcing colleges to depreciate would

only boost our bookkeeping costs for no good reason." Do you agree? Discuss.

❹ The plant manager of a manufacturing firm suggested in a conference of the company's executives that accountants should speed up depreciation on the machinery in the finishing department because improvements were rapidly making those machines obsolete and a depreciation fund big enough to cover their replacement is needed. Discuss the accounting concept of depreciation and the effect on a business concern of the depreciation recorded for plant assets, paying particular attention to the issues raised by the plant manager.

5 For what reasons are plant assets retired? Define inadequacy, supersession, and obsolescence.

6 What basic questions must be answered before the amount of the depreciation charge can be computed?

7 Elizabeth Ashley Company purchased a machine on January 2, 1997, for $600,000. The machine has an estimated useful life of 5 years and a salvage value of $100,000. Depreciation was computed by the 150% declining-balance method. What is the amount of accumulated depreciation at the end of December 31, 1998?

8 Linda Blair Company purchased machinery for $120,000 on January 1, 1998. It is estimated that the machinery will have a useful life of 20 years, scrap value of $15,000, production of 84,000 units, and working hours of 42,000. During 1998 the company uses the machinery for 14,300 hours, and the machinery produces 20,000 units. Compute depreciation under the straight-line, units-of-output, working-hours, sum-of-the-years'-digits, and declining-balance (use 10% as the annual rate) methods.

9 What are the major factors considered in determining what depreciation method to use?

10 Under what conditions is it appropriate for a business to use the composite method of depreciation for its plant assets? What are the advantages and disadvantages of this method?

11 If Ed Asner, Inc., uses the composite method and its composite rate is 7.5% per year, what entry should it make when plant assets that originally cost $50,000 and have been used for 10 years are sold for $16,000?

12 A building that was purchased December 31, 1973, for $2,400,000 was originally estimated to have a life of 50 years with no salvage value at the end of that time. Depreciation has been recorded through 1997. During 1998 an examination of the building by an engineering firm discloses that its estimated useful life is 15 years after 1997. What should be the amount of depreciation for 1998?

13 Armand Assante, president of Flatbush Company, has recently noted that depreciation increases cash provided by operations and, therefore, depreciation is a good source of funds. Do you agree? Discuss.

14 Melanie Mayron purchased a computer for $6,000 on July 1, 1998. She intends to depreciate it over 4 years using the double-declining balance method. Salvage value is $1,000. Compute depreciation for 1999.

15 Astaire Inc. is considering the write-down of its long-term plant because of a lack of profitability. Explain to the man-agement of Astaire how to determine whether a write-off is permitted.

16 Kuga Co. has equipment with a carrying amount of $700,000. The expected future net cash flows from the equipment is $705,000 and its fair value is $590,000. The equipment is expected to be used in operations in the future. What amount (if any) should Kuga report as an impairment to its equipment?

17 It has been suggested that plant and equipment could be replaced more quickly if depreciation rates for income tax and accounting purposes were substantially increased. As a result, business operations would receive the benefit of more modern and more efficient plant facilities. Discuss the merits of this proposition.

18 Neither depreciation on replacement cost nor depreciation adjusted for changes in the purchasing power of the dollar has been recognized as generally accepted accounting practice for inclusion in the primary financial statements. Briefly present the accounting treatment that might be used to assist in the maintenance of the ability of a company to replace its productive capacity.

19 List (a) the similarities and (b) the differences in the accounting treatments of depreciation and cost depletion.

20 Describe cost depletion and percentage depletion. Why is the percentage depletion method permitted?

21 In what way may the use of percentage depletion violate sound accounting theory?

22 In the extractive industries, businesses may pay dividends in excess of net income. What is the maximum permissible? How can this practice be justified?

23 The following statement appeared in a financial magazine: "RRA—or Rah-Rah, as it's sometimes dubbed—has kicked up quite a storm. Oil companies, for example, are convinced that the approach is misleading. Major accounting firms agree." What is RRA? Why might oil companies believe that this approach is misleading?

24 Adriana Oil uses successful efforts accounting and also provides full-cost results as well. Under full-cost, Adriana Oil would have reported retained earnings of $42 million and net income of $4 million. Under successful efforts, retained earnings were $29 million and net income was $3 million. Explain the difference between full costing and successful efforts accounting.

25 McDonald's Corporation in 1995 reports net income of $1.4 billion, net sales of $9.8 billion, and average total assets of $14.5 billion. What is McDonald's asset turnover ratio? What is McDonald's rate of return on assets?

*26 What is a modified accelerated cost recovery system (MACRS)? Speculate as to why this system is now required for tax purposes.

❖ BRIEF EXERCISES ❖

BE11-1 Castlevania Corporation purchased a truck at the beginning of 1998 for $42,000. The truck is estimated to have a salvage value of $2,000 and a useful life of 160,000 miles. It was driven 23,000 miles in 1998 and 31,000 miles in 1999. Compute depreciation expense for 1998 and 1999.

BE11-2 Cheetah Company purchased machinery on January 1, 1998, for $60,000. The machinery is estimated to have a salvage value of $6,000 after a useful life of 8 years. (a) Compute 1998 depreciation expense using the straight-line method. (b) Compute 1998 depreciation expense using the straight-line method assuming the machinery was purchased on September 1, 1998.

BE11-3 Use the information for Cheetah Company given in BE11-2. (a) Compute 1998 depreciation expense using the sum-of-the-years'-digits method. (b) Compute 1998 depreciation expense using the sum-of-the-years'-digits method assuming the machinery was purchased on April 1, 1998.

BE11-4 Use the information for Cheetah Company given in BE11-2. (a) Compute 1998 depreciation expense using the double-declining balance method. (b.) Compute 1998 depreciation expense using the double-declining balance method assuming the machinery was purchased on October 1, 1998.

BE11-5 Battlesport Inc. owns the following assets:

Asset	Cost	Salvage	Estimated Useful Life
A	$70,000	$ 7,000	10 years
B	$50,000	$10,000	5 years
C	$82,000	$ 4,000	12 years

Compute the composite depreciation rate and the composite life of Battlesport's assets.

BE11-6 Myst Company purchased a computer for $7,000 on January 1, 1997. Straight-line depreciation is used, based on a 5-year life and a $1,000 salvage value. In 1999, the estimates are revised. Myst now feels the computer will be used until December 31, 2000, when it can be sold for $500. Compute the 1999 depreciation.

BE11-7 Dinoland Company owns machinery that cost $900,000 and has accumulated depreciation of $360,000. The expected future net cash flows from the use of the asset are expected to be $500,000. The fair value of the equipment is $400,000. Prepare the journal entry, if any, to record the impairment loss.

BE11-8 Genghis Khan Corporation acquires a coal mine at a cost of $400,000. Intangible development costs total $100,000. After extraction has occurred, $75,000 will be spent to restore the property, after which it can be sold for $160,000. Khan estimates that 4,000 tons of coal can be extracted. If 700 tons are extracted the first year, prepare the journal entry to record depletion.

BE11-9 In its 1995 Annual Report Chrysler Corporation reports beginning of the year total assets of $38,077 million, end of the year total assets of $40,475 million, total sales of $50,970 million, and net income of $2,025 million. (a) Compute Chrysler's asset turnover ratio. (b) Compute Chrysler's profit margin on sales. (c) Compute Chrysler's rate of return on assets (1) using asset turnover and profit margin, and (2) using net income.

***BE11-10** Timecap Corporation purchased an asset at a cost of $40,000 on March 1, 1999. The asset has a useful life of 8 years and a salvage value of $4,000. For tax purposes, the MACRS class life is 5 years. Compute tax depreciation for each year 1999–2004.

❖ EXERCISES ❖

E11-1 (Depreciation Computations—SL, SYD, DDB) Deluxe Ezra Company purchases equipment on January 1, Year 1, at a cost of $469,000. The asset is expected to have a service life of 12 years and a salvage value of $40,000.

Instructions
(a) Compute the amount of depreciation for each of Years 1 through 3 using the straight-line depreciation method.
(b) Compute the amount of depreciation for each of Years 1 through 3 using the sum-of-the-years'-digits method.
(c) Compute the amount of depreciation for each of Years 1 through 3 using the double-declining balance method. (In performing your calculations, round constant percentage to the nearest one-hundredth of a point and round answers to the nearest dollar.)

E11-2 (Depreciation—Conceptual Understanding) Rembrandt Company acquired a plant asset at the beginning of Year 1. The asset has an estimated service life of 5 years. An employee has prepared depreciation schedules for this asset using three different methods to compare the results of using one method with the results of using other methods. You are to assume that the following schedules have been correctly prepared for this asset using (1) the straight-line method, (2) the sum-of-the-years'-digits method, and (3) the double-declining balance method.

Year	Straight-line	Sum-of-the-Years'-Digits	Double-declining Balance
1	$ 9,000	$15,000	$20,000
2	9,000	12,000	12,000
3	9,000	9,000	7,200
4	9,000	6,000	4,320
5	9,000	3,000	1,480
Total	$45,000	$45,000	$45,000

Instructions
Answer the following questions:
  (a) What is the cost of the asset being depreciated?
  (b) What amount, if any, was used in the depreciation calculations for the salvage value for this asset?
  (c) Which method will produce the highest charge to income in Year 1?
  (d) Which method will produce the highest charge to income in Year 4?
  (e) Which method will produce the highest book value for the asset at the end of Year 3?
  (f) If the asset is sold at the end of Year 3, which method would yield the highest gain (or lowest loss) on disposal of the asset?

E11-3 (Depreciation Computations—SYD, DDB—Partial Periods) Judds Company purchased a new plant asset on April 1, 1998, at a cost of $711,000. It was estimated to have a service life of 20 years and a salvage value of $60,000. Judds' accounting period is the calendar year.

Instructions
  (a) Compute the depreciation for this asset for 1998 and 1999 using the sum-of-the-years'-digits method.
  (b) Compute the depreciation for this asset for 1998 and 1999 using the double-declining balance method.

E11-4 (Depreciation Computations—Five Methods) Jon Seceda Furnace Corp. purchased machinery for $315,000 on May 1, 1998. It is estimated that it will have a useful life of 10 years, scrap value of $15,000, production of 240,000 units, and working hours of 25,000. During 1999 Seceda Corp. uses the machinery for 2,650 hours, and the machinery produces 25,500 units.

Instructions
From the information given, compute the depreciation charge for 1999 under each of the following methods (round to three decimal places):
  (a) Straight-line.   **(c)** Working hours.   **(e)** Declining-balance
  (b) Units-of-output.   **(d)** Sum-of-the-years'-digits.   (use 20% as the annual rate).

E11-5 (Depreciation Computations—Four Methods) Robert Parish Corporation purchased a new machine for its assembly process on August 1, 1998. The cost of this machine was $117,900. The company estimated that the machine would have a trade-in value of $12,900 at the end of its service life. Its life is estimated at 5 years and its working hours are estimated at 21,000 hours. Year-end is December 31.

Instructions
Compute the depreciation expense under the following methods: (1) straight-line depreciation for 1998, (2) activity method for 1998, assuming that machine usage was 800 hours, (3) sum-of-the-years'-digits for 1999, and (4) double-declining balance for 1999. Each of the foregoing should be considered unrelated.

E11-6 (Depreciation Computations—Five Methods, Partial Periods) Muggsy Bogues Company purchased equipment for $212,000 on October 1, 1997. It is estimated that the equipment will have a useful life of 8 years and a salvage value of $12,000. Estimated production is 40,000 units and estimated working hours 20,000. During 1997, Bogues uses the equipment for 525 hours and the equipment produces 1,000 units.

Instructions
Compute depreciation expense under each of the following methods. Bogues is on a calendar-year basis ending December 31.
  (a) Straight-line method for 1997.   **(d)** Sum-of-the-years'-digits method for 1999.
  (b) Activity method (units of output) for 1997.   **(e)** Double-declining balance method for 1998.
  (c) Activity method (working hours) for 1997.

E11-7 (Depreciation Computation—Replacement, Nonmonetary Exchange)   George Zidek Corporation bought a machine on June 1, 1996, for $31,000, f.o.b. the place of manufacture. Freight to the point where it was set up was $200, and $500 was expended to install it. The machine's useful life was estimated at 10 years, with a scrap value of $2,500. On June 1, 1997, an essential part of the machine is replaced, at a cost of $1,980, with one designed to reduce the cost of operating the machine. On June 1, 2000, the company buys a new machine of greater capacity for $35,000, delivered, trading in the old machine which has a fair market value and trade-in allowance of $20,000. To prepare the old machine for removal from the plant cost $75, and expenditures to install the new one were $1,500. It is estimated that the new machine has a useful life of 10 years, with a scrap value of $4,000 at the end of that time.

Instructions
Assuming that depreciation is to be computed on the straight-line basis, compute the annual depreciation on the new equipment that should be provided for the fiscal year beginning June 1, 2000. (Round to the nearest dollar.)

E11-8 (Composite Depreciation)   Presented below is information related to Dell Curry Manufacturing Corporation:

Asset	Cost	Estimated Scrap	Estimated Life (in years)
A	$40,500	$5,500	10
B	33,600	4,800	9
C	36,000	3,600	9
D	19,000	1,500	7
E	23,500	2,500	6

Instructions
(a) Compute the rate of depreciation per year to be applied to the plant assets under the composite method.
(b) Prepare the adjusting entry necessary at the end of the year to record depreciation for the year.
(c) Prepare the entry to record the sale of fixed asset D for cash of $4,800. It was used for 6 years, and depreciation was entered under the composite method.

E11-9 (Depreciation Computations, SYD)   The Five Satins Company purchased a piece of equipment at the beginning of 1995. The equipment cost $430,000. It has an estimated service life of 8 years and an expected salvage value of $70,000. The sum-of-the-years'-digits method of depreciation is being used. Someone has already correctly prepared a depreciation schedule for this asset. This schedule shows that $60,000 will be depreciated for a particular calendar year.

Instructions
Show calculations to determine for what particular year the depreciation amount for this asset will be $60,000.

E11-10 (Depreciation—Change in Estimate)   Machinery purchased for $60,000 by Joe Montana Co. in 1994 was originally estimated to have a life of 8 years with a salvage value of $4,000 at the end of that time. Depreciation has been entered for 5 years on this basis. In 1999, it is determined that the total estimated life (including 1999) should be 10 years with a salvage value of $4,500 at the end of that time. Assume straight-line depreciation.

Instructions
(a) Prepare the entry to correct the prior years' depreciation, if necessary.
(b) Prepare the entry to record depreciation for 1999.

E11-11 (Depreciation Computation—Addition, Change in Estimate)   In 1971, Herman Moore Company completed the construction of a building at a cost of $2,000,000 and first occupied it in January 1972. It was estimated that the building will have a useful life of 40 years, and a salvage value of $60,000 at the end of that time.

Early in 1982, an addition to the building was constructed at a cost of $500,000. At that time it was estimated that the remaining life of the building would be, as originally estimated, an additional 30 years, and that the addition would have a life of 30 years, and a salvage value of $20,000.

In 2000, it is determined that the probable life of the building and addition will extend to the end of 2031, or 20 years beyond the original estimate.

Instructions
(a) Using the straight-line method, compute the annual depreciation that would have been charged from 1972 through 1981.
(b) Compute the annual depreciation that would have been charged from 1982 through 1999.

(c) Prepare the entry, if necessary, to adjust the account balances because of the revision of the estimated life in 2000.

(d) Compute the annual depreciation to be charged beginning with 2000.

E11-12 (Depreciation—Replacement, Change in Estimate) Orel Hershiser Company constructed a building at a cost of $2,200,000 and occupied it beginning in January 1979. It was estimated at that time that its life would be 40 years, with no salvage value.

In January 1999, a new roof was installed at a cost of $300,000, and it was estimated then that the building would have a useful life of 25 years from that date. The cost of the old roof was $160,000.

Instructions

(a) What amount of depreciation should have been charged annually from the years 1979 to 1998? (Assume straight-line depreciation.)

(b) What entry should be made in 1999 to record the replacement of the roof?

(c) Prepare the entry in January 1999, to record the revision in the estimated life of the building, if necessary.

(d) What amount of depreciation should be charged for the year 1999?

E11-13 (Error Analysis and Depreciation, SL and SYD) Mike Devereaux Company shows the following entries in its Equipment account for 1999; all amounts are based on historical cost.

Equipment						
1999				1999		
Jan. 1	Balance	134,750		June 30	Cost of equipment sold	
Aug. 10	Purchases	32,000			(purchased prior	
12	Freight on equipment				to 1999)	23,000
	purchased	700				
25	Installation costs	2,700				
Nov. 10	Repairs	500				

Instructions

(a) Prepare any correcting entries necessary.

(b) Assuming that depreciation is to be charged for a full year on the ending balance in the asset account, compute the proper depreciation charge for 1999 under each of the methods listed below. Assume an estimated life of 10 years, with no salvage value. The machinery included in the January 1, 1999, balance was purchased in 1997.

    1. Straight-line.

    2. Sum-of-the-years'-digits.

E11-14 (Depreciation for Fractional Periods) On March 10, 2000, Lost World Company sells equipment that it purchased for $192,000 on August 20, 1993. It was originally estimated that the equipment would have a life of 12 years and a scrap value of $16,800 at the end of that time, and depreciation has been computed on that basis. The company uses the straight-line method of depreciation.

Instructions

(a) Compute the depreciation charge on this equipment for 1993, for 2000, and the total charge for the period from 1994 to 1999, inclusive, under each of the six following assumptions with respect to partial periods.

    1. Depreciation is computed for the exact period of time during which the asset is owned. (Use 365 days for base.)

    2. Depreciation is computed for the full year on the January 1 balance in the asset account.

    3. Depreciation is computed for the full year on the December 31 balance in the asset account.

    4. Depreciation for one-half year is charged on plant assets acquired or disposed of during the year.

    5. Depreciation is computed on additions from the beginning of the month following acquisition and on disposals to the beginning of the month following disposal.

    6. Depreciation is computed for a full period on all assets in use for over one-half year, and no depreciation is charged on assets in use for less than one-half year. (Use 365 days for base.)

(b) Briefly evaluate the methods above, considering them from the point of view of basic accounting theory as well as simplicity of application.

E11-15 (Impairment) Presented below is information related to equipment owned by Suarez Company at December 31, 1999.

Cost	$9,000,000
Accumulated depreciation to date	1,000,000
Expected future net cash flows	7,000,000
Fair value	4,800,000

Assume that Suarez will continue to use this asset in the future. As of December 31, 1999, the equipment has a remaining useful life of 4 years.

Instructions

    (a) Prepare the journal entry (if any) to record the impairment of the asset at December 31, 1999.

    (b) Prepare the journal entry to record depreciation expense for 2000.

    (c) The fair value of the equipment at December 31, 2000, is $5,100,000. Prepare the journal entry (if any) necessary to record this increase in fair value.

E11-16 (Impairment)   Assume the same information as Exercise 11-15, except that Suarez intends to dispose of the equipment in the coming year. It is expected that the cost of disposal will be $20,000.

Instructions

    (a) Prepare the journal entry (if any) to record the impairment of the asset at December 31, 1999.

    (b) Prepare the journal entry (if any) to record depreciation expense for 2000.

    (c) The asset was not sold by December 31, 2000. The fair value of the equipment on that date is $5,300,000. Prepare the journal entry (if any) necessary to record this increase in fair value. It is expected that the cost of disposal is still $20,000.

E11-17 (Impairment)   The management of Luis Andujar Inc. was discussing whether certain equipment should be written off as a charge to current operations because of obsolescence. This equipment has a cost of $900,000 with depreciation to date of $400,000 as of December 31, 1998. On December 31, 1998, management projected its future net cash flows from this equipment to be $300,000 and its fair value to be $230,000. The company intends to use this equipment in the future.

Instructions

    (a) Prepare the journal entry (if any) to record the impairment at December 31, 1998.

    (b) Where should the gain or loss (if any) on the write-down be reported in the income statement?

    (c) At December 31, 1999, the equipment's fair value increased to $260,000. Prepare the journal entry (if any) to record this increase in fair value.

    (d) What accounting issues did management face in accounting for this write-down?

E11-18 (Depletion Computations—Timber)   Stanislaw Timber Company owns 9,000 acres of timberland purchased in 1987 at a cost of $1,400 per acre. At the time of purchase the land without the timber was valued at $400 per acre. In 1988, Stanislaw built fire lanes and roads, with a life of 30 years, at a cost of $84,000. Every year Stanislaw sprays to prevent disease at a cost of $3,000 per year and spends $7,000 to maintain the fire lanes and roads. During 1989, Stanislaw selectively logged and sold 700,000 board feet of timber, of the estimated 3,500,000 board feet. In 1990, Stanislaw planted new seedlings to replace the trees cut at a cost of $100,000.

Instructions

    (a) Determine the depreciation expense and the cost of timber sold related to depletion for 1989.

    (b) Stanislaw has not logged since 1989. If Stanislaw logged and sold 900,000 board feet of timber in 2000, when the timber cruise (appraiser) estimated 5,000,000 board feet, determine the cost of timber sold related to depletion for 2000.

E11-19 (Depletion Computations—Oil)   Diderot Drilling Company has leased property on which oil has been discovered. Wells on this property produced 18,000 barrels of oil during the past year that sold at an average sales price of $15 per barrel. Total oil resources of this property are estimated to be 250,000 barrels.

    The lease provided for an outright payment of $500,000 to the lessor before drilling could be commenced and an annual rental of $31,500. A premium of 5% of the sales price of every barrel of oil removed is to be paid annually to the lessor. In addition, the lessee is to clean up all the waste and debris from drilling and to bear the costs of reconditioning the land for farming when the wells are abandoned. It is estimated that this clean-up and reconditioning will cost $30,000.

Instructions

From the provisions of the lease agreement, you are to compute the cost per barrel for the past year, exclusive of operating costs, to Diderot Drilling Company.

E11-20 (Depletion Computations—Timber)   Forda Lumber Company owns a 7,000-acre tract of timber purchased in 1992 at a cost of $1,300 per acre. At the time of purchase the land was estimated to have a value of $300 per acre without the timber. Forda Lumber Company has not logged this tract since it was purchased. In 1999, Forda had the timber cruised. The cruise (appraiser) estimated that each acre contained 8,000 board feet of timber. In 1999, Forda built 10 miles of roads at a cost of $7,840 per mile. After the roads were completed, Forda logged and sold 3,500 trees containing 850,000 board feet.

Instructions
(a) Determine the cost of timber sold related to depletion for 1999.
(b) If Forda depreciates the logging roads on the basis of timber cut, determine the depreciation expense for 1999.
(c) If Forda plants five seedlings at a cost of $4 per seedling for each tree cut, how should Forda treat the reforestation?

E11-21 (Depletion Computations—Mining) Alcide Mining Company purchased land on February 1, 1998, at a cost of $1,190,000. It estimated that a total of 60,000 tons of mineral was available for mining. After it has removed all the natural resources, the company will be required to restore the property to its previous state because of strict environmental protection laws. It estimates the cost of this restoration at $90,000. It believes it will be able to sell the property afterwards for $100,000. It incurred developmental costs of $200,000 before it was able to do any mining. In 1998 resources removed totaled 30,000 tons. It sold 22,000 tons.

Instructions (Round to two decimals)
Compute the following information for 1998: (1) per unit material cost; (2) total material cost of 12/31/98 inventory; and (3) total material cost in cost of goods sold at 12/31/98.

E11-22 (Depletion Computations—Minerals) At the beginning of 1998, Aristotle Company acquired a mine for $970,000. Of this amount, $100,000 was ascribed to the land value and the remaining portion to the minerals in the mine. Surveys conducted by geologists have indicated that approximately 12,000,000 units of the ore appear to be in the mine. Aristotle incurred $170,000 of development costs associated with this mine prior to any extraction of minerals and estimates that it will require $40,000 to prepare the land for an alternative use when all of the mineral has been removed. During 1998, 2,500,000 units of ore were extracted and 2,100,000 of these units were sold.

Instructions
Compute (1) the total amount of depletion for 1998, and (2) the amount that is charged as an expense for 1998 for the cost of the minerals sold during 1998.

E11-23 (Ratio Analysis) The 1995 Annual Report of Microsoft Corporation contains the following information:

(in millions)	June 30,1994	June 30, 1995
Total assets	$5,363	$7,210
Total liabilities	913	1,347
Net sales	4,649	5,937
Total costs and expenses	3,503	4,484
Net income	1,146	1,453

Instructions
Compute the following ratios for Microsoft for 1995:

(a) Asset turnover ratio.
(b) Rate of return on assets.
(c) Profit margin on sales.
(d) How can the asset tunrover ratio be used to compute the rate of return on assets?

E11-24 (Book vs. Tax (MACRS) Depreciation) Futabatei Enterprises purchased a delivery truck on January 1, 1999, at a cost of $27,000. The truck has a useful life of 7 years with an estimated salvage value of $6,000. The straight-line method is used for book purposes. For tax purposes the truck, having an MACRS class life of 7 years, is classified as 5-year property; the optional MACRS tax rate tables are used to compute depreciation. In addition, assume that for 1999 and 2000 the company has revenues of $200,000 and operating expenses (excluding depreciation) of $130,000.

Instructions
(a) Prepare income statements for 1999 and 2000. (The final amount reported on the income statement should be income before income taxes.)
(b) Compute taxable income for 1999 and 2000.
(c) Determine the total depreciation to be taken over the useful life of the delivery truck for both book and tax purposes.
(d) Explain why depreciation for book and tax purposes will generally be different over the useful life of a depreciable asset.

*E11-25 (Book vs. Tax (MACRS) Depreciation)   Shimei Inc. purchased computer equipment on March 1, 1998, for $31,000. The computer equipment has a useful life of 10 years and a salvage value of $1,000. For tax purposes, the MACRS class life is 5 years.

Instructions

(a) Assuming that the company uses the straight-line method for book and tax purposes, what is the depreciation expense reported in (1) the financial statements for 1998 and (2) the tax return for 1998?

(b) Assuming that the company uses the double-declining balance method for both book and tax purposes, what is the depreciation expense reported in (1) the financial statements for 1998 and (2) t6e tax return for 1998?

(c) Why is depreciation for tax purposes different from depreciation for book purposes even if the company uses the same depreciation method to compute them both?

❖ PROBLEMS ❖

P11-1 (Depreciation for Partial Period—SL, SYD, and DDB)   Onassis Company purchased Machine #201 on May 1, 1998. The following information relating to Machine #201 was gathered at the end of May.

Price	$73,500
Credit terms	2/10, n/30
Freight-in costs	$ 970
Preparation and installation costs	$ 3,800
Labor costs during regular production operations	$10,500

It was expected that the machine could be used for 10 years, after which the salvage value would be zero. Onassis intends to use the machine for only 8 years, however, after which it expects to be able to sell it for $1,200. The invoice for Machine #201 was paid May 5, 1998. Onassis uses the calendar year as the basis for the preparation of financial statements.

Instructions

(a) Compute the depreciation expense for the years indicated using the following methods. (Round to the nearest dollar.)
   1. Straight-line method for 1998.
   2. Sum-of-the-years'-digits method for 1999.
   3. Double-declining balance method for 1998.

(b) Suppose Jackie Ari, the president of Onassis, tells you that because the company is a new organization, she expects it will be several years before production and sales reach optimum levels. She asks you to recommend a depreciation method that will allocate less of the company's depreciation expense to the early years and more to later years of the assets' lives. What method would you recommend?

P11-2 (Depreciation for Partial Periods—SL, Act., SYD, and DDB)   The cost of equipment purchased by Boris Becker, Inc., on June 1, 1998, is $67,000. It is estimated that the machine will have a $4,000 salvage value at the end of its service life. Its service life is estimated at 7 years; its total working hours are estimated at 42,000 and its total production is estimated at 525,000 units. During 1998 the machine was operated 6,000 hours and produced 55,000 units. During 1999 the machine was operated 5,500 hours and produced 48,000 units.

Instructions

Compute depreciation expense on the machine for the year ending December 31, 1998, and the year ending December 31, 1999, using the following methods: (1) straight-line; (2) units-of-output; (3) working hours; (4) sum-of-the-years'-digits; and (5) declining balance (twice the straight-line rate).

P11-3 (Depreciation—Partial Periods, Machinery)   Goran Tool Company records depreciation annually at the end of the year. Its policy is to take a full year's depreciation on all assets used throughout the year and depreciation for one-half a year on all machines acquired or disposed of during the year. The depreciation rate for the machinery is 10% applied on a straight-line basis, with no estimated scrap value.

The balance of the Machinery account at the beginning of 1999 was $172,300; the Accumulated Depreciation on Machinery account had a balance of $72,900. The following transactions affecting the machinery accounts took place during the year.

Jan. 15   Machine No. 38, which cost $9,600 when acquired June 3, 1992, was retired and sold as scrap metal for $600.

Feb. 27 Machine No. 81 was purchased. The fair market value of this machine was $12,500. It replaces Machines No. 12 and No. 27, which were traded in on the new machine. Machine No. 12 was acquired Feb. 4, 1987, at a cost of $5,500 and is still carried in the accounts although fully depreciated and not in use; Machine No. 27 was acquired June 11, 1992, at a cost of $8,200. In addition to these two used machines, $9,000 was paid in cash. (Assume exchange of similar assets.)

Apr. 7 Machine No. 54 was equipped with electric control equipment at a cost of $940. This machine, originally equipped with simple hand controls, was purchased Dec. 11, 1995, for $1,800. The new electric controls can be attached to any one of several machines in the shop.

12 Machine No. 24 was repaired at a cost of $720 after a fire caused by a short circuit in the wiring burned out the motor and damaged certain essential parts.

July 22 Machines No. 25, 26, and 41 are sold for $3,100 cash. The purchase dates and cost of these machines are:

No. 25	$4,000	May 8, 1991
No. 26	3,200	May 8, 1991
No. 41	2,800	June 1, 1993

Nov. 17 Rearrangement and reinstallation of several machines to facilitate material handling and to speed up production are completed at a cost of $13,400.

Instructions

(a) Record each transaction in general journal entry form.

(b) Compute and record depreciation for the year. No machines now included in the balance of the account were acquired before January 1, 1990.

P11-4 (Depreciation—SYD, Act., SL, and DDB) The following data relate to the Plant Asset account of Arthur Fiedler, Inc. at December 31, 1998:

Plant Asset

	A	B	C	D
Original cost	$35,000	$51,000	$80,000	$80,000
Year purchased	1993	1994	1995	1997
Useful life	10 years	15,000 hours	15 years	10 years
Salvage value	$ 3,100	$ 3,000	$ 5,000	$ 5,000
Depreciation method	Sum-of-the-years'-digits	Activity	Straight-line	Double-declining balance
Accum. Depr. through 1998[a]	$23,200	$35,200	$15,000	$16,000

[a]In the year an asset is purchased, Fiedler, Inc. does not record any depreciation expense on the asset.
In the year an asset is retired or traded in, Fiedler, Inc. takes a full year's depreciation on the asset.

The following transactions occurred during 1999:

(a) On May 5, Asset A was sold for $13,000 cash. The company's bookkeeper recorded this retirement in the following manner in the cash receipts journal:

Cash	13,000	
Asset A		13,000

(b) On December 31, it was determined that Asset B had been used 2,100 hours during 1999.

(c) On December 31, before computing depreciation expense on Asset C, the management of Fiedler, Inc. decided the useful life remaining from 1/1/99 was 10 years.

(d) On December 31, it was discovered that a plant asset purchased in 1998 had been expensed completely in that year. This asset cost $22,000 and has a useful life of 10 years and no salvage value. Management has decided to use the double-declining balance method for this asset, which can be referred to as "Asset E."

Instructions

Prepare the necessary correcting entries for the year 1999. Record the appropriate depreciation expense on the above-mentioned assets.

P11-5 (Depreciation and Error Analysis) A depreciation schedule for semitrucks of Oglala Manufacturing Company was requested by your auditor soon after December 31, 1999, showing the additions, retirements, depreciation, and other data affecting the income of the company in the 4-year period 1996 to 1999, inclusive. The following data were ascertained:

Balance of Semitrucks account, Jan. 1, 1996:	
Truck No. 1 purchased Jan. 1, 1993, cost	$18,000
Truck No. 2 purchased July 1, 1993, cost	22,000
Truck No. 3 purchased Jan. 1, 1995, cost	30,000
Truck No. 4 purchased July 1, 1995, cost	24,000
Balance, Jan. 1, 1996	$94,000

The Semitrucks-Accumulated Depreciation account previously adjusted to January 1, 1996, and duly entered in the ledger, had a balance on that date of $30,200 (depreciation on the four trucks from the respective dates of purchase, based on a 5-year life, no salvage value). No charges had been made against the account before January 1, 1996.

Transactions between January 1, 1996, and December 31, 1999, and their record in the ledger were as follows:

July 1, 1996   Truck No. 3 was traded for a larger one (No. 5), the agreed purchase price of which was $34,000. Oglala Mfg. Co. paid the automobile dealer $15,000 cash on the transaction. The entry was a debit to Semitrucks and a credit to Cash, $15,000.

Jan. 1, 1997   Truck No. 1 was sold for $3,500 cash; entry debited Cash and credited Semitrucks, $3,500.

July 1, 1998   A new truck (No. 6) was acquired for $36,000 cash and was charged at that amount to the Semitrucks account. (Assume truck No. 2 was not retired.)

July 1, 1998   Truck No. 4 was damaged in a wreck to such an extent that it was sold as junk for $700 cash. Oglala Mfg. Co. received $2,500 from the insurance company. The entry made by the bookkeeper was a debit to Cash, $3,200, and credits to Miscellaneous Income, $700, and Semitrucks, $2,500.

Entries for depreciation had been made at the close of each year as follows: 1996, $20,300; 1997, $21,100; 1998, $24,450; 1999, $27,800.

Instructions

(a) For each of the 4 years compute separately the increase or decrease in net income arising from the company's errors in determining or entering depreciation or in recording transactions affecting trucks, ignoring income tax considerations.

(b) Prepare one compound journal entry as of December 31, 1999, for adjustment of the Semitrucks account to reflect the correct balances as revealed by your schedule, assuming that the books have not been closed for 1999.

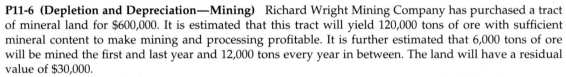

P11-6 (Depletion and Depreciation—Mining)   Richard Wright Mining Company has purchased a tract of mineral land for $600,000. It is estimated that this tract will yield 120,000 tons of ore with sufficient mineral content to make mining and processing profitable. It is further estimated that 6,000 tons of ore will be mined the first and last year and 12,000 tons every year in between. The land will have a residual value of $30,000.

The company builds necessary structures and sheds on the site at a cost of $36,000. It is estimated that these structures can serve 15 years but, because they must be dismantled if they are to be moved, they have no scrap value. The company does not intend to use the buildings elsewhere. Mining machinery installed at the mine was purchased second-hand at a cost of $48,000. This machinery cost the former owner $100,000 and was 50% depreciated when purchased. Richard Wright Mining estimates that about half of this machinery will still be useful when the present mineral resources have been exhausted but that dismantling and removal costs will just about offset its value at that time. The company does not intend to use the machinery elsewhere. The remaining machinery will last until about one-half the present estimated mineral ore has been removed and will then be worthless. Cost is to be allocated equally between these two classes of machinery.

Instructions

(a) As chief accountant for the company, you are to prepare a schedule showing estimated depletion and depreciation costs for each year of the expected life of the mine.

(b) Also compute the depreciation and depletion for the first year assuming actual production of 7,000 tons. Nothing occurred during the year to cause the company engineers to change their estimates of either the mineral resources or the life of the structures and equipment.

P11-7 (Depletion, Timber, and Extraordinary Loss)   Ted Koppel Logging and Lumber Company owns 3,000 acres of timberland on the north side of Mount St. Helens, which was purchased in 1968 at a cost of $550 per acre. In 1980, Koppel began selectively logging this timber tract. In May of 1980, Mount St. Helens erupted, burying the timberland of Koppel under a foot of ash. All of the timber on the Koppel tract was downed. In addition, the logging roads, built at a cost of $150,000, were destroyed, as well as the logging equipment, with a net book value of $300,000.

At the time of the eruption, Koppel had logged 20% of the estimated 500,000 board feet of timber. Prior to the eruption, Koppel estimated the land to have a value of $200 per acre after the timber was harvested. Koppel includes the logging roads in the depletion base.

Koppel estimates it will take 3 years to salvage the downed timber at a cost of $700,000. The timber can be sold for pulp wood at an estimated price of $3 per board foot. The value of the land is unknown, but must be considered nominal due to future uncertainties.

Instructions

(a) Determine the depletion cost per board foot for the timber harvested prior to the eruption of Mount St. Helens.

(b) Prepare the journal entry to record the depletion prior to the eruption.

(c) If this tract represents approximately half of the timber holdings of Koppel, determine the amount of the estimated loss and show how the losses of roads, machinery, and timber and the salvage of the timber should be reported in the financial statements of Koppel for the year ended December 31, 1980.

P11-8 (Comprehensive Depreciation Computations) Anjelica Huston Corporation, a manufacturer of steel products, began operations on October 1, 1997. The accounting department of Huston has started the fixed-asset and depreciation schedule presented below. You have been asked to assist in completing this schedule. In addition to ascertaining that the data already on the schedule are correct, you have obtained the following information from the company's records and personnel:

1. Depreciation is computed from the first of the month of acquisition to the first of the month of disposition.
2. Land A and Building A were acquired from a predecessor corporation. Huston paid $820,000 for the land and building together. At the time of acquisition, the land had an appraised value of $90,000, and the building had an appraised value of $810,000.
3. Land B was acquired on October 2, 1997, in exchange for 2,500 newly issued shares of Huston's common stock. At the date of acquisition, the stock had a par value of $5 per share and a fair value of $30 per share. During October 1997, Huston paid $16,000 to demolish an existing building on this land so it could construct a new building.
4. Construction of Building B on the newly acquired land began on October 1, 1998. By September 30, 1999, Huston had paid $320,000 of the estimated total construction costs of $450,000. It is estimated that the building will be completed and occupied by July 2000.
5. Certain equipment was donated to the corporation by a local university. An independent appraisal of the equipment when donated placed the fair market value at $30,000 and the salvage value at $3,000.
6. Machinery A's total cost of $164,900 includes installation expense of $600 and normal repairs and maintenance of $14,900. Salvage value is estimated at $6,000. Machinery A was sold on February 1, 1999.
7. On October 1, 1998, Machinery B was acquired with a down payment of $5,740 and the remaining payments to be made in 11 annual installments of $6,000 each beginning October 1, 1998. The prevailing interest rate was 8%. The following data were abstracted from present-value tables (rounded):

Present value of $1.00 at 8%		Present value of an ordinary annuity of $1.00 at 8%	
10 years	.463	10 years	6.710
11 years	.429	11 years	7.139
15 years	.315	15 years	8.559

Anjelica Huston Corporation
FIXED ASSET AND DEPRECIATION SCHEDULE
For Fiscal Years Ended September 30, 1998, and September 30, 1999

Assets	Acquisition Date	Cost	Salvage	Depreciation Method	Estimated Life in Years	Depreciation Expense Year Ended September 30 1998	1999
Land A	October 1, 1997	$ (1)	N/A	N/A	N/A	N/A	N/A
Building A	October 1, 1997	(2)	$40,000	Straight-line	(3)	$17,450	(4)
Land B	October 2, 1997	(5)	N/A	N/A	N/A	N/A	N/A
Building B	Under Construction	320,000 to date	—	Straight-line 150%	30	—	(6)
Donated Equipment	October 2, 1997	(7)	3,000	Declining balance	10	(8)	(9)
Machinery A	October 2, 1997	(10)	6,000	Sum-of-the-years'-digits	8	(11)	(12)
Machinery B	October 1, 1998	(13)	—	Straight-line	20	—	(14)

N/A—Not applicable

Instructions
For each numbered item on the foregoing schedule, supply the correct amount. Round each answer to the nearest dollar.

P11-9 (Depreciation for Partial Periods—SL, Act., SYD, and DDB) On January 1, 1996, a machine was purchased for $77,000. The machine has an estimated salvage value of $5,000 and an estimated useful life of 5 years. The machine can operate for 100,000 hours before it needs to be replaced. The company closed its books on December 31 and operates the machine as follows: 1996, 20,000 hrs; 1997, 25,000 hrs; 1998, 15,000 hrs; 1999, 30,000 hrs; 2000, 10,000 hrs.

Instructions

(a) Compute the annual depreciation charges over the machine's life assuming a December 31 year-end for each of the following depreciation methods:

    1. Straight-line method.   **3.** Sum-of-the-years'-digits method.

    2. Activity method.   **4.** Double-declining balance method.

(b) Assume a fiscal year-end of September 30. Compute the annual depreciation charges over the asset's life applying

    1. Straight-line method.

    2. Sum-of-the-years'-digits method.

    3. Double-declining balance method.

 ***P11-10 (Depreciation—SL, DDB, SYD, Act., and MACRS)** On January 1, 1996, Moshe Dayan Company, a small machine-tool manufacturer, acquired for $1,100,000 a piece of new industrial equipment. The new equipment had a useful life of 5 years and the salvage value was estimated to be $50,000. Dayan estimates that the new equipment can produce 12,000 machine tools in its first year. It estimates that production will decline by 1,000 units per year over the remaining useful life of the equipment.

The following depreciation methods may be used: (1) straight-line; (2) double-declining balance; (3) sum-of-the-years'-digits; and (4) units-of-output. For tax purposes, the class life is 7 years. Use the MACRS tables for computing depreciation.

Instructions

(a) Which depreciation method would maximize net income for financial statement reporting for the 3-year period ending December 31, 1998? Prepare a schedule showing the amount of accumulated depreciation at December 31, 1998, under the method selected. Ignore present value, income tax, and deferred income tax considerations.

(b) Which depreciation method (MACRS or optional straight-line) would minimize net income for income tax reporting for the 3-year period ending December 31, 1998? Determine the amount of accumulated depreciation at December 31, 1998. Ignore present value considerations.

(AICPA adapted)

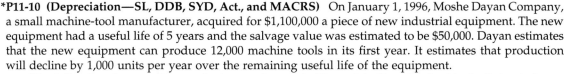 For coverage of special depreciation methods (inventory method, retirement and replacement methods, and compound interest methods) with accompanying assignment material, refer to our Web site.

❖ CONCEPTUAL CASES ❖

C11-1 (Depreciation Basic Concepts) Prophet Manufacturing Company was organized January 1, 1999. During 1999, it has used in its reports to management the straight-line method of depreciating its plant assets.

On November 8 you are having a conference with Prophet's officers to discuss the depreciation method to be used for income tax and stockholder reporting. Frank Peretti, president of Prophet, has suggested the use of a new method, which he feels is more suitable than the straight-line method for the needs of the company during the period of rapid expansion of production and capacity that he foresees. Following is an example in which the proposed method is applied to a fixed asset with an original cost of $248,000, an estimated useful life of 5 years, and a scrap value of approximately $8,000.

Year	Years of Life Used	Fraction Rate	Depreciation Expense	Accumulated Depreciation at End of Year	Book Value at End of Year
1	1	1/15	$16,000	$ 16,000	$232,000
2	2	2/15	32,000	48,000	200,000
3	3	3/15	48,000	96,000	152,000
4	4	4/15	64,000	160,000	88,000
5	5	5/15	80,000	240,000	8,000

The president favors the new method because he has heard that:

    1. It will increase the funds recovered during the years near the end of the assets' useful lives when maintenance and replacement disbursements are high.

2. It will result in increased write-offs in later years and thereby will reduce taxes.

Instructions
    (a) What is the purpose of accounting for depreciation?
    (b) Is the president's proposal within the scope of generally accepted accounting principles? In making your decision discuss the circumstances, if any, under which use of the method would be reasonable and those, if any, under which it would not be reasonable.
    (c) The president wants your advice.
        1. Do depreciation charges recover or create funds? Explain.
        2. Assume that the Internal Revenue Service accepts the proposed depreciation method in this case. If the proposed method were used for stockholder and tax reporting purposes, how would it affect the availability of funds generated by operations?

C11-2 (Unit, Group, and Composite Depreciation) The certified public accountant is frequently called upon by management for advice regarding methods of computing depreciation. Of comparable importance, although it arises less frequently, is the question of whether the depreciation method should be based on consideration of the assets as units, as a group, or as having a composite life.

Instructions
    (a) Briefly describe the depreciation methods based on treating assets as (1) units and (2) a group or as having a composite life.
    (b) Present the arguments for and against the use of each of the two methods.
    (c) Describe how retirements are recorded under each of the two methods.

                                                                         (AICPA adapted)

C11-3 (Depreciation—Strike, Units-of-Production, Obsolescence) Presented below are three different and unrelated situations involving depreciation accounting. Answer the question(s) at the end of each case situation.

Situation I
Recently, John Brown Company experienced a strike that affected a number of its operating plants. The controller of this company indicated that it was not appropriate to report depreciation expense during this period because the equipment did not depreciate and an improper matching of costs and revenues would result. She based her position on the following points:

    1. It is inappropriate to charge the period with costs for which there are no related revenues arising from production.
    2. The basic factor of depreciation in this instance is wear and tear, and because equipment was idle, no wear and tear occurred.

Instructions
Comment on the appropriateness of the controller's comments.

Situation II
Andrew Carnegie Company manufactures electrical appliances, most of which are used in homes. Company engineers have designed a new type of blender which, through the use of a few attachments, will perform more functions than any blender currently on the market. Demand for the new blender can be projected with reasonable probability. In order to make the blenders, Carnegie needs a specialized machine that is not available from outside sources. It has been decided to make such a machine in Carnegie's own plant.

Instructions
    (a) Discuss the effect of projected demand in units for the new blenders (which may be steady, decreasing, or increasing) on the determination of a depreciation method for the machine.
    (b) What other matters should be considered in determining the depreciation method? Ignore income tax considerations.

Situation III
Dorothea Dix Paper Company operates a 300-ton-per-day kraft pulp mill and four sawmills in Wisconsin. The company is in the process of expanding its pulp mill facilities to a capacity of 1,000 tons per day and plans to replace three of its older, less efficient sawmills with an expanded facility. One of the mills to be replaced did not operate for most of 1998 (current year), and there are no plans to reopen it before the new sawmill facility becomes operational.

    In reviewing the depreciation rates and in discussing the residual values of the sawmills that were to be replaced, it was noted that if present depreciation rates were not adjusted, substantial amounts of plant costs on these three mills would not be depreciated by the time the new mill came on stream.

Instructions
What is the proper accounting for the four sawmills at the end of 1998?

❖FINANCIAL REPORTING PROBLEM—INTEL CORPORATION

The financial statements of Intel Corporation appear in Appendix 5B. Refer to these financial statements and the accompanying notes to answer the following questions.

Instructions

(a) What descriptions are used by Intel in its balance sheet to classify its property, plant, and equipment?

(b) What method or methods of depreciation does Intel Corporation use to depreciate its property, plant, and equipment?

(c) Over what estimated useful lives does Intel depreciate its property, plant, and equipment?

(d) What amounts for depreciation expense did Intel charge to its income statement in 1995, 1994, and 1993?

(e) What amounts of interest expense were capitalized by Intel as part of construction costs in 1995, 1994, and 1993?

(f) What were the additions to property, plant, and equipment made by Intel in 1995, 1994, and 1993?

(g) What was the effect of Intel's 1995 adoption of SFAS No. 121 (Impairment of Assets) on its financial statements?

❖FINANCIAL STATEMENT ANALYSIS CASES

Case 1 (Boeing versus McDonnell Douglas)

Boeing and McDonnell Douglas are two leaders in the manufacture of aircraft. In 1996 Boeing announced intentions to acquire McDonnell Douglas and create one huge corporation. Its competitors, primarily Airbus of Europe, are very concerned that they will not be able to compete with such a huge rival. In addition, customers are concerned that this will reduce the number of suppliers to a point where Boeing will be able to dictate prices. Provided below are figures taken from the 1995 financial statements of Boeing and McDonnell Douglas which allow a comparison of the operations of the two corporations prior to their proposed merger.

(in millions of dollars)	Boeing	McDonnell Douglas
Total revenue	$19,515	$14,322
Net income (loss)	393	(416)
Total assets	22,098	10,466
Land	404	91
Buildings and fixtures	5,791	1,647
Machinery and equipment	7,251	2,161
Total property, plant, and equipment (at cost)	13,744	3,899
Accumulated depreciation	7,288	2,541
Depreciation expense	976	196

Instructions

(a) Based on the asset turnover ratio, which company uses its assets more effectively to generate sales? Assume that total assets reported are a reasonable average of beginning and ending balances.

(b) Which company has a better profit margin on sales?

(c) Which company has the higher rate of return on total assets?

(d) Besides an increase in size, what other factors might be motivating this merger?

Case 2 (McDonald's Corporation)

McDonald's is the largest and best-known global foodservice retailer, with more than 18,000 restaurants in 89 countries. On any day, McDonald's serves a little less than one percent of the world's population.

Presented below is information related to property and equipment.

Summary of Significant Accounting Policies Section

Property and Equipment. Property and equipment are stated at cost, with depreciation and amortization provided on the straight-line method over the following estimated useful lives: buildings–up to 40 years; leasehold improvements–lesser of useful lives of assets or lease terms including option periods; and equipment–3 to 12 years.

Accounting for the Impairment of Long-Lived Assets. In the first quarter of 1996, the Company will adopt Statement of Financial Accounting Standard No. 121, *Accounting for the Impairment of Long-Lived Assets and for Long-Lived Assets to be Disposed of.* This statement requires impairment losses be recognized for long-lived assets, whether these assets are held for disposal or continue to be used in operations, when indicators of impairment are present and the fair value of assets are estimated to be less than carrying amounts. After reviewing its assets, the Company anticipates a pre-tax charge to operating income of approximately $16 million related to restaurant sites in Mexico on adoption of this new accounting standard.

In the notes to the financial statements:

Property and Equipment

(in millions of dollars)	December 31, **1995**	1994
Land	$ 3,251.5	$ 2,950.1
Buildings and improvements on owned land	6,419.7	5,814.7
Buildings and improvements on leased land	4,986.3	4,211.2
Equipment, signs and seating	1,942.3	1,727.8
Other	537.8	480.8
	17,137.6	15,184.6
Accumulated depreciation and amortization	(4,326.3)	(3,856.2)
Net property and equipment	$12,811.3	$11,328.4

Depreciation and amortization were (in millions): 1995–$619.9; 1994–$550.5; 1993–$492.8. Contractual obligations for the acquisition and construction of property amounted to $268.2 million at December 31, 1995.

In the management discussion and analysis section, the following schedule is provided:

(Dollars in millions)	**1995**	1994	1993	1992	1991
Cash provided by operations	**$2,296**	$1,926	$1,680	$1,426	$1,423
Cash provided by operations less capital expenditures	**233**	388	363	339	294
Cash provided by operations as a percent of capital expenditures	**111**	125	128	131	126
Cash provided by operations as a percent of average total debt	**49**	48	44	33	31

Instructions

(a) What method of depreciation is used by McDonald's?

(b) Does depreciation and amortization expense cause cash flow from operations to increase? Explain.

(c) McDonald's indicates that in 1996, it will adopt Financial Accounting Standard No. 121. What criterion is McDonald's using to record an impairment loss in 1996?

(d) What does the schedule of cash flow measures indicate?

❖ COMPARATIVE ANALYSIS CASE

The Coca-Cola Company versus PepsiCo Inc.

Instructions

Go to our Web site and answer the following questions.

1. What amount is reported in the balance sheets as property, plant, and equipment (net) of Coca-Cola at December 31, 1995, and of PepsiCo at December 30, 1995? What percentage of total assets is invested in property, plant, and equipment by each company?

2. What depreciation methods are used by Coca-Cola and PepsiCo for property, plant, and equipment? How much depreciation was reported by Coca-Cola and PepsiCo in 1995, 1994, and 1993?

www.wiley.com/college/kieso

3. Compute and compare the following ratios for Coca-Cola and PepsiCo for 1995:
    (a) Asset turnover.
    (b) Profit margin on sales.
    (c) Ratio of return on assets.
4. What amount was spent in 1995 for capital expenditures by Coca-Cola and PepsiCo? What amount of interest was capitalized in 1995?
5. What references do Coca-Cola and PepsiCo make to any impairments of long-lived assets?

❖ RESEARCH CASES

Case 1

A wealth of accounting-related information is available via the Internet. For example, the Rutgers Accounting Web (http://www.rutgers.edu/accounting/raw) offers access to a great variety of sources.

Instructions

Once in the Rutgers Accounting Web, click on "internet" to arrive at the "Accounting Resources on the Internet" page. (*Note*: Once on this page, you may have to click on the "text only" box to access the available information.)

(a) List the categories of information available through the "Accounting Resources on the Internet" page.
(b) Select any one of these categories and briefly describe the types of information available.

Case 2

The December 4, 1995, issue of *Forbes ASAP* includes an article by Umberto Tosi entitled "Digital Air."

Instructions

Read the article and answer the following questions.

(a) What does "AMIS" stand for?
(b) What are the primary features of AMIS?
(c) How did deregulation in the airline industry aid in the development of AMIS?
(d) How does AMIS help reduce maintenance costs?

❖ WRITING ASSIGNMENT

As a cost accountant for San Francisco Cannery, you have been approached by Merton Miller, canning room supervisor, about the 1997 costs charged to his department. In particular, he is concerned about the line item "depreciation." Miller is very proud of the excellent condition of his canning room equipment. He has always been vigilant about keeping all equipment serviced and well oiled. He is sure that the huge charge to depreciation is a mistake: it does not at all reflect the cost of minimal wear and tear that the machines have experienced over the last year. He believes that the charge should be considerably lower.

The machines being depreciated are six automatic canning machines. All were put into use on January 1, 1997. Each cost $469,000, having a salvage value of $40,000 and a useful life of 12 years. San Francisco depreciates this and similar assets using double-declining balance. Miller has also pointed out that if you used straight-line depreciation the charge to his department would not be so great.

Instructions

Write a memo to Merton Miller to clear up his misunderstanding of the term "depreciation." Also, calculate year 1 depreciation on all machines using both methods. Explain the theoretical justification for double-declining balance and why, in the long run, the aggregate charge to depreciation will be the same under both methods.

❖ GROUP ASSIGNMENT

Selig Sporting Goods Inc. has been experiencing growth in the demand for its products over the last several years. The last two Olympic Games greatly increased the popularity of basketball around the world. As a result, a European sports retailing consortium entered into an agreement with Selig's Roundball Division to purchase basketballs and other accessories on an increasing basis over the next 5 years.

To be able to meet the quantity commitments of this agreement, Selig had to obtain additional manufacturing capacity. A real estate firm located an available factory in close proximity to Selig's Roundball manufacturing facility, and Selig agreed to purchase the factory and used machinery from Starks Athletic Equipment Company on October 1, 1997. Renovations were necessary to convert the factory for Selig's manufacturing use.

The terms of the agreement required Selig to pay Starks $50,000 when renovations started on January 1, 1998, with the balance to be paid as renovations were completed. The overall purchase price for the factory and machinery was $400,000. The building renovations were contracted to Malone Construction at $100,000. The payments made, as renovations progressed during 1998, are shown below. The factory was placed in service on January 1, 1999.

	1/1	4/1	10/1	12/31
Starks	$50,000	$100,000	$100,000	$150,000
Malone		30,000	30,000	40,000

On January 1, 1998, Selig secured a $500,000 line-of-credit with a 12% interest rate to finance the purchase cost of the factory and machinery, and the renovation costs. Selig drew down on the line-of-credit to meet the payment schedule shown above; this was Selig's only outstanding loan during 1998.

Rob Stewart, Selig's controller, will capitalize the maximum allowable interest costs for this project. Selig's policy regarding purchases of this nature is to use the appraisal value of the land for book purposes and prorate the balance of the purchase price over the remaining items. The building had originally cost Starks $300,000 and had a net book value of $50,000, while the machinery originally cost $125,000 and had a net book value of $40,000 on the date of sale. The land was recorded on Starks' books at $40,000. An appraisal, conducted by independent appraisers at the time of acquisition, valued the land at $280,000, the building at $105,000, and the machinery at $45,000.

Linda Safford, chief engineer, estimated that the renovated plant would be used for 15 years, with an estimated salvage value of $30,000. Safford estimated that the productive machinery would have a remaining useful life of five years and a salvage value of $3,000. Selig's depreciation policy specifies the 200% declining-balance method for machinery and the 150% declining-balance method for the plant. One-half year's depreciation is taken in the year the plant is placed in service and one-half year is allowed when the property is disposed of or retired. Selig uses a 360-day year for calculating interest costs.

Instructions

Your instructor will assign one member of the group to serve as a recorder and one member to serve as spokesperson. As a group, provide the information for the recorder to prepare responses to the following three requirements. Upon completion of each requirement and before moving on to the next part, the spokesperson will report the group findings to the class.

   (a) Determine the amounts to be recorded on the books of Selig Sporting Goods Inc. as of December 31, 1998, for each of the following properties acquired from Starks Athletic Equipment Company.
      1. Land.   **2.** Building.   **3.** Machinery.
   (b) Calculate Selig Sporting Goods Inc.'s 1999 depreciation expense, for book purposes, for each of the properties acquired from Starks Athletic Equipment Company.
   (c) Discuss the arguments for and against the capitalization of interest costs.

(CMA adapted)

❖ ETHICS CASE

Billy Williams, Sheffield Corporation's controller, is concerned that net income may be lower this year. He is afraid upper-level management might recommend cost reductions by laying off accounting staff, him included.

Williams knows that depreciation is a major expense for Sheffield. The company currently uses the double-declining balance for both financial reporting and tax purposes, and he's thinking of a change to the straight-line method. That, of course, would require a cumulative-effect adjustment since it is a change in accounting principle and would be reported separately in the income statement. He doesn't want to highlight the method of increasing income in this manner. He thinks, "Why don't I increase the estimated useful lives and the salvage values? That will decrease depreciation expense and since the changes are accounted for prospectively, they will not be disclosed in the income statement. I may be able to save my job and those of my staff."

Instructions

Answer the following questions:
   (a) Who are the stakeholders in this situation?
   (b) What are the ethical issues involved?
   (c) What should Williams do?

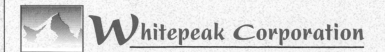 **Whitepeak Corporation**   **MODULE 6**

Whitepeak groups its long-term assets into three major categories: Buildings, Sales Equipment, and Office Equipment. Whitepeak uses three different methods to depreciate these assets. They are, respectively, the declining-balance method, the sum-of-the-years'-digits method, and the straight-line method.

Depreciation computations are more difficult this year because three groupings of long-term assets were exchanged earlier in the year. Thus you are needed to conduct a three-part analysis, as outlined below.

Section 6.1   Depreciation Computation
Instructions First, compute a full year's depreciation on all depreciable assets on Whitepeak's books as of January 1, 1997.

Section 6.2   Partial-Period Depreciation on Exchanges
Instructions Next, compute depreciation for the partial year, 1997, on all assets obtained in the previous exchanges.

Section 6.3
Instructions Finally, remove depreciation from the point of exchange to the end of the year on assets that were exchanged away earlier in the year. ■

A visit with
Gary Valenzuela

GARY VALENZUELA is chief financial officer for Yahoo!, a company that helps millions of people find what they're looking for on the Internet. Prior to joining Yahoo!, he held increasingly responsible accounting and finance positions in several other high-technology companies. Mr. Valenzuela is a CPA and holds a bachelor's degree in accounting from San Jose State University.

High-Tech Accounting

How did you get started in accounting and finance? During my sophomore year in college, I had a part-time professor at San Jose State who was a controller at a local technology company, and he mentioned that he might be hiring somebody. For about six months, I just hounded him for a position. Finally, he hired me and I spent two years working in all types of accounting jobs. In the job market immediately after college, it was an advantage to have had real-world accounting experience.

Describe the accounting phase of your career after college. After graduating in 1980, I spent two years with what is now KPMG Peat Marwick, becoming a computer auditing specialist, and receiving my CPA certificate. In 1982, I joined the internal audit staff at Syntex, a large pharmaceutical company. It was appealing to me because of the computer audit emphasis and because it involved doing operational audits throughout the Syntex worldwide network, requiring quite a bit of international travel. Then I got recruited—and this is a milestone event in my career—by Wyse Technology in 1984 and joined them six months before they went public. That was an absolute rocketship. When I joined the computer terminal maker, its sales were $17 million per year. Within three years, we were over $250 million. I started as assistant controller, and I left as controller of the customer service organization.

At what point did you begin to move from accounting to finance? When I joined minicomputer maker Pyramid Technology as corporate controller, the individual I worked for really gave me a lot of flexibility to do a lot of different things. As a result, I became involved in tax, the treasury function, some business development activities, international operations, a major systems project, and so on. Also, I got to work directly with the CEO and the entire management team, where I established a reputation as a person who would get something done. After being with the company about two and a half years, I became CFO after my mentor, the former CFO, left the company. A few years later, I joined a start-up Internet software company called TGV Software that was poised to go public. Then nine months later, I negotiated the sale of that company to Cisco Systems. We announced the acquisition by Cisco in January of 1996. I started working at Yahoo! on February 1, 1996, where I immediately began preparations to take the company public.

What was your role in Yahoo!'s initial public offering? The role of a CFO in a well-executed IPO is to be the quarterback of the IPO process. The first step is forming your IPO team—selecting investment bankers is a very key step. You go public only once, and those bankers will forever be associated with your name as having taken your company public. We selected Goldman Sachs, Montgomery Securities, and Donaldson, Lufkin & Jenrette. Forming the IPO team also includes lawyers and accountants. One of the things I had to do was switch accounting firms, because I knew I was on an incredibly fast track to take this company public, and there was no room for any potential problem on the auditing side. Next, you put together a prospectus for potential investors which is filed with the SEC. Then there's a waiting period, during which time you work on your "road show." We traveled to 15 cities in 11 days and made presentations to more than 400 investors. We went public on April 12, 1996. The initial filing range was $10 to $12 per share. The stock opened at $24 and went to $43 on the first day, closing at $33. For the first 6 months of 1996, we reported revenues of about $5 million, but a net loss, which was expected. A lot of people get mesmerized by the IPO process, but it's just one step. Right away, you start transitioning the company for the public arena. We spent a lot of time talking about legal issues, trading issues, educating all employees about the responsibilities of being insiders—what you can and cannot do.

What kinds of questions did potential investors ask you? They asked how we are going to sustain a business model long-term when the Internet is free to users and has a lot of competitors already. What we say is that yes, our service is free to users, but you need to think like broadcasters. TV broadcasts are free to users but advertising-supported. There are some advertising agencies that specialize in the Internet. They tend to be young Internet-savvy advertising types who understand the potential and power of this new medium and can go out and sell these to mainstream advertisers. Another category of question we received is what we are planning to do with the $100 million that we would raise in the public offering.

What advice do you have for college students? I would advise students to seize opportunities and not be scared off by risk. There have been some major challenges in my career. TGV Software was supposed to go public in six months. It took a year because of a downturn in the stock market. When I stepped into the role of CFO of Pyramid Technology, the company had just had one restructuring, was still losing money, and six months later I had to go back to the CEO and tell him that the restructuring was inadequate and that we had to take another $30 million restructuring charge. That was a definite career risk.

CHAPTER 12

Intangible Assets

Trying to Grasp the Intangible

In 1494, a mathematically minded Venetian monk named Luca Pacioli published his *Summa de Arithmetica, Geometrica*, the first accounting textbook. It illustrated double-entry accounting, a system that makes the modern corporation manageable, even possible. Today, half a millennium later, Pacioli's process, still pretty much intact, is being challenged like never before.

Pacioli's accounting system lets businesses keep track of changes in their assets. But this system deals primarily with *tangible assets* such as cash, inventory, investments, receivables, property, plant, and equipment. What go unrecorded are *intangible assets* such as quality of management, customer loyalty, information infrastructure, trade secrets, patents, goodwill, research, and, considered by some the ultimate intangible, *knowledge*—a company's intellectual capital. As Edmund Jenkins, an Arthur Andersen partner and chair of the AICPA Special Committee on Financial Reporting, attests, "The components of cost in a product today are largely R & D, intellectual assets, and services. The old accounting system, which tells us the cost of material and labor, isn't applicable." Argues Professor James Quinn of Dartmouth College, "Even in manufacturing, perhaps three-fourths of the value added derives from knowledge."[1]

This refrain is echoed by the managing editor of *Fortune* magazine, Walter Kiechel, who says, "To be sure, there are still industries in which the factory confers a competitive advantage. But this is changing fast, as more and more companies realize that their edge derives less from their machines, bricks, and mortar than from what we used to think of as the intangibles, like the brainpower resident in the corporation."[2]

In this emerging economy of knowledge, even some banks have concluded that "soft" assets (like computer programming know-how and information infrastructure) can be a better credit risk than "hard" assets (like buildings). But how should the "soft assets" be valued? Accountants get little solace from former FASB chairman Donald Kirk, who acknowledges, "There are arguments that balance sheets ignore certain intangibles, but the reporting issues of trying to recognize them are, in my mind, insurmountable."[3] It appears that the assets that really count are the ones accountants can't count—yet.

LEARNING OBJECTIVES
After studying this chapter, you should be able to:

1. Describe the characteristics of intangible assets.
2. Explain the procedure for valuing and amortizing intangible assets.
3. Identify the types of specifically identifiable intangible assets.
4. Explain the conceptual issues related to goodwill.
5. Describe the accounting procedures for recording goodwill.
6. Identify the conceptual issues related to research and development costs.
7. Describe the accounting procedures for research and development costs.
8. Indicate the presentation of intangibles and related items.

---

[1]Thomas Stewart, "Your Company's Most Valuable Asset: Intellectual Capital," *Fortune*, October 3, 1994, p. 68.

[2]"Searching for Nonfiction in Financial Statements," *Fortune*, December 23, 1996, p. 38.

[3]Ibid.

As the opening story indicates, the accounting and reporting of intangibles is taking on increasing importance in this information age. The purpose of this chapter is to explain the basic conceptual and reporting issues related to intangible assets. The content and organization of the chapter are as follows:

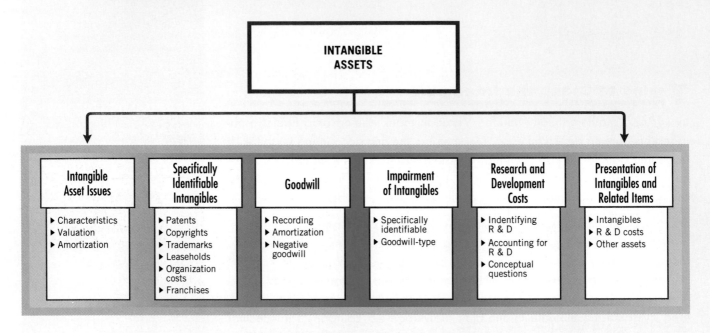

❖ INTANGIBLE ASSET ISSUES

Characteristics

Objective ❶

Describe the characteristics of intangible assets.

Intangible assets are generally characterized by a lack of physical existence and a high degree of uncertainty concerning future benefits. These criteria are not so clear-cut as they may seem. The **lack of physical existence** may not by itself be a satisfactory criterion for distinguishing a tangible from an intangible asset. Such assets as bank deposits, accounts receivable, and long-term investments lack physical substance, yet they are classified as tangible assets.

Some believe that an intangible asset's major characteristic is the **high degree of uncertainty concerning the future benefits** that are to be received from its employment. For example, many intangibles (1) have value only to a given enterprise, (2) have indeterminate lives, and (3) are subject to large fluctuations in value because their benefits are based on a competitive advantage. The determination and timing of future benefits are extremely difficult and pose serious valuation problems. True, some tangible assets possess similar characteristics but they are not so pronounced.

Others, finding the problem of defining intangibles insurmountable, prefer simply to present them in financial statements on the basis of tradition. The more common types of intangibles are patents, copyrights, franchises, goodwill, organization costs, and trademarks or trade names. Intangibles may be further subdivided on the basis of the following characteristics.

❶ *Identifiability.* Separately identifiable or lacking specific identification.
❷ *Manner of Acquisition.* Acquired singly, in groups, or in business combinations, or developed internally.
❸ *Expected Period of Benefit.* Limited by law or contract, related to human or economic factors, or indefinite or indeterminate duration.
❹ *Separability from an Entire Enterprise.* Rights transferable without title, salable, or inseparable from the enterprise or a substantial part of it.[4]

These subdivisions provide insight into how the reporting requirements for intangibles have developed.

Valuation

Purchased Intangibles

Intangibles purchased from another party are **recorded at cost**. Cost includes all costs of acquisition and expenditures necessary to make the intangible asset ready for its intended use—for example, purchase price, legal fees and other incidental expenses.

   If intangibles are acquired for stock or in exchange for other assets, **the cost of the intangible is the fair market value of the consideration given or the fair market value of the intangible received, whichever is more clearly evident**. When several intangibles, or a combination of intangibles and tangibles, are bought in a "basket purchase," the cost should be allocated on the basis of fair market values or on the basis of relative sales values. Essentially the accounting treatment for purchased intangibles closely parallels that followed for purchased tangible assets. The profession has resisted employment of some other basis of valuation, such as current replacement costs or appraisal value for intangible assets.[5]

Internally-Created Intangibles

Costs incurred internally to create intangibles are generally expensed as incurred. Thus, even though a company may incur substantial research and development costs to create an intangible, these costs are expensed. Various reasons are given for this approach. Some argue that the costs incurred internally to create intangibles bear no relationship to their real value; therefore, expensing these costs is appropriate. Others note that with a purchased intangible, a reliable number for the cost of the intangible can be determined; with internally developed intangibles, it is difficult to associate costs with specific intangible assets. And others argue that due to the underlying subjectivity related to intangibles, a conservative approach should be followed—that is, expense as incurred. As a result, the **only internal costs capitalized are direct costs** incurred in obtaining the intangible, such as legal costs.

   For subsequent discussion, we will classify intangibles into intangibles that are specifically identifiable, as contrasted to "goodwill-type" intangible assets (unidentifiable values). **Specifically identifiable** means that costs associated with obtaining a given intangible asset can be identified as a part of the cost of that intangible asset. In contrast, a **goodwill-type** intangible may create some right or privilege, but it is not specifically identifiable and it has an indeterminable life. The accounting treatments accorded these two types of intangibles are shown in Illustration 12-1.

Objective ❷

Explain the procedure for valuing and amortizing intangible assets.

UNDERLYING CONCEPTS

The basic attributes of intangibles, their uncertainty as to future benefits, and their uniqueness, have discouraged valuation in excess of cost.

INTERNATIONAL INSIGHT

In Japan the cost of intangibles can be capitalized whether they are externally purchased or internally developed.

---

[4]"Intangible Assets," *Opinions of the Accounting Principles Board No. 17* (New York: AICPA, 1970), par. 10.

[5]For example, Sprouse and Moonitz in *AICPA Accounting Research Study No. 3*, "A Tentative Set of Broad Accounting Principles for a Business Enterprise," advocate abandonment of historical cost in favor of replacement cost for most asset items, but suggest that intangibles should normally be carried at acquisition cost less amortization because valuation problems are so difficult.

ILLUSTRATION 12-1
Accounting for the Costs
of Intangibles

		Manner Acquired	
Type of Intangible	Purchased		Internally Created
Specifically Identifiable Intangibles	Capitalize		Expense, except certain costs
Goodwill-type Intangibles	Capitalize		Expense

Amortization of Intangibles

As you learned in Chapter 11, the expiration of intangible assets is called amortization. Intangible assets should be amortized by systematic charges to expense over their useful lives. *APB Opinion No. 17* lists the factors that might be considered in determining useful life:

❶ Legal, regulatory, or contractual provisions.
❷ Provisions for renewal or extension.
❸ Effects of obsolescence, demand, competition, and other economic factors.
❹ A useful life may parallel the service life expectancies of individuals or groups of employees.
❺ Expected actions of competitors and others may restrict competitive advantages.
❻ An apparently unlimited useful life may in fact be indefinite and benefits cannot be reasonably projected.
❼ An intangible asset may be a composite of many individual factors with varying effective lives.[6]

INTERNATIONAL INSIGHT

Although in many nations it is standard practice to capitalize and amortize goodwill, practice varies widely. In a few countries goodwill is capitalized but not amortized, thus remaining as a permanent asset. In other nations goodwill is written off immediately.

One problem relating to the amortization of intangibles is that some intangibles have indeterminable useful lives. In this case, **intangible assets must be amortized over a period not exceeding 40 years**.[7] The 40-year requirement is based on the premise that only a few, if any, intangibles last forever. Sometimes, because useful life is difficult to determine, a 40-year period is employed because it is practical, although admittedly arbitrary. Another reason for this 40-year limitation is simply that it ensures that companies eventually write off their intangibles. Prior to the 40-year rule, there was evidence that some companies retained their intangibles (notably goodwill) indefinitely on their balance sheet for only one reason—to avoid the charge to expense that occurs when goodwill is written off.

Intangible assets acquired from other enterprises (notably goodwill) should not be written off at acquisition. Some contend that certain intangibles should not be carried as assets on the balance sheet under any circumstances but should be written off directly to retained earnings or additional paid-in capital. However, the immediate writeoff to retained earnings and additional paid-in capital is not acceptable because this approach denies the existence of an asset that has just been purchased.

Intangible assets are generally amortized on a straight-line basis (tax practice requires a straight-line approach), although there is no reason why another systematic approach might not be employed if the firm demonstrates that another method is more appropriate. In any case the method and period of amortization should be disclosed.

When intangible assets are amortized, the charges should be shown as expenses, and the credits should be made either to the appropriate asset accounts or to separate accumulated amortization accounts.

---

[6]*APB Opinion No. 17*, op. cit., par. 27.
[7]Ibid., par. 10.

❖ SPECIFICALLY IDENTIFIABLE INTANGIBLES

Patents

Patents are granted by the U.S. Patent and Trademark Office. The two principal kinds of patents are **product patents**, which cover actual physical products, and **process patents**, which govern the process by which products are made. A patent gives the holder exclusive right to use, manufacture, and sell a product or process **for a period of 17 years** without interference or infringement by others. With this exclusive right, fortunes can be made. For example: companies such as Merck, Polaroid, and Xerox were founded on patents.[8] If a patent is purchased from an inventor (or other owner), the purchase price represents its cost. Other costs incurred in connection with securing a patent, as well as attorneys' fees and other unrecovered costs of a successful legal suit to protect the patent, can be capitalized as part of the patent cost. Research and development costs related to the **development** of the product, process, or idea that is subsequently patented **must be expensed as incurred**, however. See pages 608–612 for a more complete presentation of accounting for research and development costs.

The cost of a patent should be amortized over its legal life or its useful life (the period benefits are received), whichever is shorter. If a patent is owned from the date it is granted, and it is expected to be useful during its entire legal life, it should be amortized over 17 years. If it appears that the patent will be useful for a shorter period of time, say, for 5 years, its cost should be amortized to expense over 5 years. Changing demand, new inventions superseding old ones, inadequacy, and other factors often limit the useful life of a patent to less than the legal life. For example, the useful life of patents in the pharmaceutical and drug industry is frequently less than the legal life because of the testing and approval period that follows their issuance. A typical drug patent has 5 to 11 years knocked off its 17-year legal life because 1 to 4 years must be spent on tests on animals, 4 to 6 years on human tests, and 2 to 3 years for the Food and Drug Administration to review the tests—all after the patent is issued but before the product goes on a pharmacist's shelves.

From bioengineering to software design, battles over patents are heating up as global competition intensifies. Consider *Hughes Tool* v. *Smith International* with a judgment of $205 million against Smith which caused it to declare bankruptcy; or *Lemelson* v. *Mattel, Inc.*, in which Lemelson was awarded $71 million because Mattel infringed on his flexible track invention in marketing Hot Wheels miniature cars; or *Polaroid* v. *Kodak* with Kodak permanently withdrawing from the U.S. instant photography market and paying damages of $900 million.[9] Texas Instruments has 35 patent lawyers on its payroll, which is only one of the costs it incurs to obtain and defend its many patents. **Legal fees and other costs incurred in successfully defending a patent suit are debited to Patents**, an asset account, because such a suit establishes the legal rights of the holder of the patent. Such costs should be amortized along with acquisition cost over the remaining useful life of the patent.

Amortization of patents may be computed on a time basis or on a basis of units produced and may be credited directly to the Patents account. It is acceptable also,

---

[8]Consider the opposite result: Sir Alexander Fleming, who discovered penicillin, decided not to use a patent to protect his discovery. He hoped that companies would produce it more quickly to help save sufferers. Companies, however, refused to develop it because they did not have the patent shield and, therefore, were afraid to make the investment.

[9]In a 1988 suit, Apple Computer sued Hewlett-Packard and Microsoft, the major supplier of software for IBM desktop computers, charging that they copied the "look and feel" of the Macintosh's distinctive user-friendly programming. Determining exactly what the "look and feel" of a piece of software amounts to is a tricky legal question, but suing over patent and copyright infringement has become increasingly successful and necessary. See "New Profits from Patents," *Fortune*, April 25, 1988; "Loophole Closing Time," *Forbes*, May 4, 1987; and "The Surprising New Power of Patents," *Fortune*, June 23, 1986.

although less common, to credit an Accumulated Patent Amortization account. To illustrate, assume that Harcott Co. incurs $170,000 in legal costs on January 1, 1998, to successfully defend a patent. The patent has a useful life of 17 years, and is amortized on a straight-line basis. The entries to record the legal fees and the amortization at the end of each year are as follows:

January 1, 1998

Patents	170,000	
Cash		170,000
(To record legal fees related to patent)		

December 31, 1998

Patent Amortization Expense	10,000	
Patents (or Accumulated Patent Amortization)		10,000
(To record amortization of patent)		

Amortization on a units-of-production basis would be computed in a manner similar to that described for depreciation on property, plant, and equipment in Chapter 11, page 549.

Although a patent's useful life should not extend beyond its legal life of 17 years, small modifications or additions may lead to a new patent. The effect may be to extend the life of the old patent. In that case it is permissible to apply the unamortized costs of the old patent to the new patent if the new patent provides essentially the same benefits. Alternatively, if a patent becomes worthless (impairment) because demand drops for the product produced, the asset should be written down or written off immediately to expense.

Copyrights

A copyright is a federally granted right that all authors, painters, musicians, sculptors, and other artists have in their creations and expressions. A copyright is granted for the **life of the creator plus 50 years**, and gives the owner, or heirs, the exclusive right to reproduce and sell an artistic or published work. Copyrights are not renewable. Like patents, they may be assigned or sold to other individuals. The costs of acquiring and defending a copyright may be capitalized, but the research and development costs involved must be expensed as incurred.

Generally, the useful life of the copyright is less than its legal life (life in being plus 50 years). The costs of the copyright should be allocated to the years in which the benefits are expected to be received, not to exceed 40 years. The difficulty of determining the number of years over which benefits will be received normally encourages the company to write these costs off over a fairly short period of time.

Copyrights can be valuable. Really Useful Group is a company that consists of copyrights on the musicals of Andrew Lloyd Webber—*Cats, Phantom of the Opera, Jesus Christ-Superstar*, and others. It has little in the way of hard assets, yet it has been valued at $300 million.[10]

Trademarks and Trade Names

A trademark or trade name is a word, phrase, or symbol that distinguishes or identifies a particular enterprise or product. The right to use a trademark or trade name under common law, whether it is registered or not, rests exclusively with the original user as long as the original user continues to use it. Registration with the U.S. Patent and Trademark Office provides legal protection for an **indefinite number of renewals for periods of 20 years each**, so a business that uses an established trademark or trade name may properly consider it to have an unlimited life. Trade names like Kleenex, Pepsi-Cola, Oldsmobile, Excedrin, Wheaties, and Sunkist create immediate product identification in our minds, thereby enhancing marketability.

---

[10]Russell L. Parr, *Investing in Intangible Assets* (New York: John Wiley & Sons, Inc., 1991), p. 47.

The value of a trademark or trade name can be substantial. For example, of all Philip Morris Corporation's many assets, none surpasses in value the most intangible of intangibles, the appeal of the Marlboro Cowboy. At one time it was estimated that the value of that image was $10 billion, or ½ of the company's value.[11]

Company names themselves identify qualities and characteristics that the companies have worked hard and spent much to develop. In a recent year an estimated 1,230 companies took on new names in an attempt to forge new identities and paid over $250 million to corporate-identity consultants. Among these were Primerica (formerly American Can), Navistar (formerly International Harvester), Nissan (formerly Datsun), and USX (U.S. Steel).

If a trademark or trade name is acquired, its capitalizable cost is the purchase price. If a trademark or trade name is developed by the enterprise itself, the capitalizable cost includes attorney fees, registration fees, design costs, consulting fees, successful legal defense costs, and other expenditures directly related to securing it (excluding research and development costs). When the total cost of a trademark or trade name is insignificant, it can be expensed rather than capitalized.

Although the life of a trademark, trade name, or company name may be unlimited, for accounting purposes the cost must be amortized over the periods benefited, not to exceed 40 years. However, because of the uncertainty involved in estimating their useful life, the cost of trademarks and trade names is frequently amortized over a much shorter period of time.[12]

INTERNATIONAL INSIGHT

Traditionally, when brand names are included in the acquisition of another company, the value of the brand name has been included in goodwill. In recent years, however, a number of firms in Great Britain and Australia have begun to value brand names separately in their balance sheets. This practice is highly controversial.

Leaseholds

A **leasehold** is a contractual understanding between a lessor (owner of property) and a lessee (renter of property) that grants the lessee **the right to use specific property, owned by the lessor, for a specific period of time in return for stipulated, and generally periodic, cash payments**. In most cases, the rent is included as an expense on the books of the lessee. Special problems, however, develop in the following situations.

Lease Prepayments

If the rent for the period of the lease is paid in advance, or if a lump sum payment is made in advance in addition to periodic rental payments, it is necessary to allocate this prepaid rent to the proper periods. The lessee has purchased the exclusive right to use the property for an extended period of time. These prepayments should be reported as a prepaid expense and not as an intangible asset.

Leasehold Improvements

Long-term leases ordinarily provide that any leasehold improvements, improvements made to the leased property, revert to the lessor at the end of the life of the lease. If the lessee constructs new buildings on leased land or reconstructs and improves existing buildings, **the lessee has the right to use such facilities during the life of the lease, but they become the property of the lessor when the lease expires**.

The lessee should charge the cost of the facilities to the Leasehold Improvements account and **depreciate the cost as operating expense over the remaining life of the lease, or the useful life of the improvements, whichever is shorter**. If a building with an estimated useful life of 25 years is constructed on land leased for 35 years, the cost of the building should be depreciated over 25 years. On the other hand, if the building has an estimated life of 50 years, it should be depreciated over 35 years, the life of the lease.

UNDERLYING CONCEPTS

The treatment of leases is an example of the importance of the definition of an asset. The definition does not require ownership but it does require that the benefits of an asset flow to and be under the control of the entity.

---

[11]"Here's One Tough Cowboy," *Forbes* (February 9, 1987), p. 110.

[12]To illustrate how various intangibles might arise from a given product, consider what the creators of the highly successful game, Trivial Pursuit, did to protect their creation. First, they copyrighted the 6,000 questions that are at the heart of the game. Then they shielded the Trivial Pursuit name by applying for a registered trademark. As a third mode of protection, the creators obtained a design patent on the playing board's design because it represents a unique graphic creation.

If the lease contains an option to renew for a period of additional years and the likelihood of renewal is too uncertain to warrant apportioning the cost over the longer period of time, the leasehold improvements are generally written off over the original term of the lease (assuming that the life of the lease is shorter than the useful life of the improvements). **Leasehold improvements are generally shown in the tangible property, plant, and equipment section**, although some accountants classify them as intangible assets. The rationale for intangible asset treatment is that the improvements revert to the lessor at the end of the lease and are therefore more of a right than a tangible asset.

Capital Leases

In some cases, the lease agreement transfers substantially all of the benefits and risks incident to ownership of the property so that the economic effect on the parties is similar to that of an installment purchase. As a result, the asset value recognized when a lease is capitalized is classified as a tangible rather than an intangible asset. Such a lease is referred to as a capital lease. We will cover the accounting for leases in more detail in Chapter 22.

Organization Costs

Costs incurred in the formation of a corporation such as fees to underwriters (investment bankers) for handling stock or bond issues, legal fees, state fees of various sorts, and certain promotional expenditures are classified as organization costs.

These items are usually charged to an account called Organization Costs and may be carried as an asset on the balance sheet as expenditures that will benefit the company over its life. These costs are amortized over an arbitrary period of time (maximum 40 years), since the life of the corporation is indeterminate. However, the amortization period is frequently short (5–10 years) because of the assumption that the early years of a business benefit most from organization costs and that these costs lose their significance once the business becomes fully established. In addition, because income tax regulations require the amortization of organization costs over a period of at least 5 years, some find it convenient to use the same period for accounting purposes.

It is sometimes difficult to draw a line between organization costs, normal operating expenses, and losses. Some contend that **operating losses incurred in the start-up of a business** should be capitalized, since they are unavoidable and are a cost of starting a business. This approach seems unsound, however, since losses have no future service potential and cannot be considered an asset.

Our position that operating losses should not be capitalized during the early years is supported by *Statement of Financial Accounting Standards No. 7*, which clarifies the accounting and reporting practices for development stage enterprises. The FASB concludes that the accounting practices and reporting standards should be no different for an enterprise trying to establish a new business than they are for other enterprises. The same "generally accepted accounting principles that apply to established operating enterprises shall govern the recognition of revenue by a development stage enterprise and shall determine whether a cost incurred by a development stage enterprise is to be charged to expense when incurred or is to be capitalized or deferred."[13]

---

[13]"Accounting and Reporting by Development Stage Enterprises," *Statement of Financial Accounting Standards No. 7* (Stamford, Conn.: FASB, 1975), par. 10. A company is considered to be in the developing stages when its efforts are directed toward establishing a new business and either the principal operations have not started or no significant revenue has been earned. To evaluate the economic impact of applying the same accounting principles to development stage enterprises that apply to established operating enterprises, the FASB interviewed officers of fifteen venture capital companies. The consensus was that whether a development stage enterprise defers or expenses preoperating costs has little effect on the amount of, or the terms under which venture capital is provided. According to these officers, venture capital investors instead rely on an evaluation of potential cash flows resulting from an investigation of the technological, marketing, management, and financial aspects of the enterprise.

Franchises and Licenses

When you drive down the street in an automobile purchased from a Chrysler dealer, fill your tank at the corner Texaco station, eat lunch at McDonald's, cool off with one of Baskin-Robbins' 31 flavors, work at a Coca-Cola bottling plant, live in a home purchased through a Century 21 real estate broker, or vacation at a Holiday Inn resort, you are dealing with franchises. A franchise is a contractual arrangement under which the franchisor grants the franchisee the right to sell certain products or services, to use certain trademarks or trade names, or to perform certain functions, usually within a designated geographical area.

The franchisor, having developed a unique concept or product, protects its concept or product through a patent, copyright, or trademark or trade name. The franchisee acquires the right to exploit the franchisor's idea or product by signing a franchise agreement.

Another type of franchise is the arrangement commonly entered into by a municipality (or other governmental body) and a business enterprise that uses public property. In such cases, a privately owned enterprise is permitted to use public property in performing its services. Examples are the use of public waterways for a ferry service, the use of public land for telephone or electric lines, the use of phone lines for cable TV, the use of city streets for a bus line, or the use of the airwaves for radio or TV broadcasting. Such operating rights, obtained through agreements with governmental units or agencies, are frequently referred to as licenses or **permits**.

Franchises and licenses may be for a definite period of time, for an indefinite period of time, or perpetual. The enterprise securing the franchise or license carries an intangible asset account entitled Franchise or License on its books only when there are costs (such as a lump sum payment in advance or legal fees and other expenditures) that are identified with the acquisition of the operating right. **The cost of a franchise (or license) with a limited life should be amortized as operating expense over the life of the franchise**. A franchise with an indefinite life, or a perpetual franchise, should be carried at cost and amortized over a reasonable period not to exceed 40 years.

If a franchise is deemed to be worthless, it should be written off immediately. For example, in 1980, Congress deregulated the trucking industry and opened to competition long-protected routes covered by franchises. Because these franchise rights were substantial, approximately 15% of the trucking industry's equity was eliminated; as a result, losses instead of profits were reported in the period of write-off.[14] For example, Roadway Express wrote off all $26.8 million worth of these assets, changing a $16.4 million profit for the quarter to a $10.4 million loss.

Annual payments made under a franchise agreement should be entered as operating expenses in the period in which they are incurred. They do not represent an asset to the concern since they do not relate to future rights to use public property.

❖ GOODWILL

Goodwill is often referred to as the most "intangible" of the intangibles. It is undoubtedly one of the most complex and controversial assets presented in financial statements. Goodwill is unique because unlike receivables, inventories, and patents that can be sold or exchanged individually in the marketplace, goodwill can be identified only with the business as a whole. For example, a substantial list of regular customers and an established reputation are unrecorded assets that give the enterprise a valuation greater than the sum of the fair market value of the individual identifiable assets. Goodwill is com-

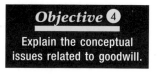

Objective **4**

Explain the conceptual issues related to goodwill.

[14]"Accounting for Intangible Assets of Motor Carriers," *Statement of Financial Accounting Standards No. 44* (Stamford, Conn.: FASB, 1980).

prised of many advantageous factors and conditions that might contribute to the value and the earning power of an enterprise:[15]

① Superior management team
② Outstanding sales organization
③ Effective advertising
④ Secret process or formula
⑤ Good labor relations
⑥ Outstanding credit rating
⑦ Top-flight training program
⑧ High standing in the community
⑨ Discovery of talents or resources
⑩ Favorable tax conditions
⑪ Favorable government regulation
⑫ Favorable association with another company
⑬ Strategic location
⑭ Weakness in management of a competitor
⑮ Unfavorable developments in the operations of a competitor[16]

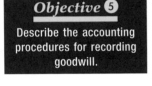

UNDERLYING CONCEPTS

Capitalizing goodwill only when it is purchased in an arm's-length transaction and not capitalizing any goodwill generated internally is another example of reliability winning out over relevance.

Goodwill is recorded only when an entire business is purchased because goodwill is a "going concern" valuation and cannot be separated from the business as a whole.[17] Goodwill generated internally should **not** be capitalized in the accounts, because measuring the components of goodwill (as listed above) is simply too complex and associating any costs with future benefits too difficult. The future benefits of goodwill may have no relationship to the costs incurred in the development of that goodwill. To add to the mystery, goodwill may even exist in the absence of specific costs to develop it. In addition, because no objective transaction with outside parties has taken place, a great deal of subjectivity—even misrepresentation—might be involved.

Recording Goodwill

Objective ⑤

Describe the accounting procedures for recording goodwill.

To record goodwill, the fair market value of the net tangible and identifiable intangible assets are compared with the purchase price of the acquired business. The difference is considered goodwill, which is why goodwill is sometimes referred to as a "plug" or "gap filler" or **"master valuation"** account. **Goodwill is the residual: the excess of cost over fair value of the identifiable net assets acquired.**

To illustrate, Multi-Diversified, Inc. decides that it needs a parts division to supplement its existing tractor distributorship. The president of Multi-Diversified is interested in buying a small concern in Chicago (Tractorling Company) that has an established reputation and is seeking a merger candidate. The balance sheet of Tractorling Company is presented in Illustration 12-2.

---

[15]George R. Catlett and Norman O. Olson, "Accounting for Goodwill," *Accounting Research Study No. 10* (New York: AICPA, 1968), pp. 17–18.

[16]Another study clustered 17 specific characteristics of goodwill into four more general categories as follows:

Increasing Short-Run Cash Flows
　Production economies
　Raise more funds
　Cash reserves
　Low cost of funds
　Reduce inventory holding cost
　Avoiding transaction cost
　Tax benefits
Exclusiveness
　Access to technology
　Brand name

Human Factor
　Managerial talent
　Good labor relations
　Good training programs
　Organizational structure
　Good public relations
Stability
　Assurance of supply
　Reducing fluctuations
　Good government relations

See Haim Falk and L. A. Gordon, "Imperfect Markets and the Nature of Goodwill," *Journal of Business Finance and Accounting* (April 1977), pp. 443–463.

[17]See "Conceptual Framework for Financial Accounting and Reporting Elements of Financial Statements and Their Measurement," *FASB Discussion Memorandum* (Stamford, Conn.: FASB, 1976), p. 235.

ILLUSTRATION 12-2
Tractorling Balance Sheet

Tractorling Co. BALANCE SHEET as of December 31, 1997			
Assets		**Equities**	
Cash	$ 25,000	Current liabilities	$ 55,000
Receivables	35,000	Capital stock	100,000
Inventories	42,000	Retained earnings	100,000
Property, plant, and equipment, net	153,000		
Total assets	$255,000	Total equities	$255,000

After considerable negotiation, Tractorling Company decides to accept Multi-Diversified's offer of $400,000. What then is the value of the goodwill, if any?

The answer is not obvious. The fair market values of Tractorling's identifiable assets are not disclosed in its historical cost-based balance sheet. Suppose, though, that as the negotiations progressed, Multi-Diversified conducted an investigation of the underlying assets of Tractorling to determine the fair market value of the assets. Such an investigation may be accomplished either through a purchase audit undertaken by Multi-Diversified's auditors in order to estimate the values of the seller's assets, or an independent appraisal from some other source. The following valuations are determined.

ILLUSTRATION 12-3
Fair Market Value of
Tractorling's Assets

Fair Market Values	
Cash	$ 25,000
Receivables	35,000
Inventories	122,000
Property, plant, and equipment, net	205,000
Patents	18,000
Liabilities	(55,000)
Fair market value of net assets	$350,000

Normally, differences between current fair market value and book value are more common among long-term assets, although significant differences can also develop in the current asset category. Cash obviously poses no problems, and receivables normally are fairly close to current valuation, although at times certain adjustments need to be made because of inadequate bad debt provisions. Liabilities usually are stated at book value, although if interest rates have changed since the liabilities were incurred, a different valuation (such as present value) might be appropriate. Careful analysis must be made to determine that no unrecorded liabilities are present.

The $80,000 difference in inventories ($122,000 − $42,000) could result from a number of factors, the most likely being that Tractorling Company uses LIFO. Recall that during periods of inflation, LIFO better matches expenses against revenues, but in doing so creates a balance sheet distortion. Ending inventory is comprised of older layers costed at lower valuations.

In many cases, the values of long-term assets such as property, plant, and equipment, and intangibles may have increased substantially over the years. This difference could be due to inaccurate estimates of useful lives, continual expensing of small expenditures (say, less than $300), inaccurate estimates of salvage values and the discovery of some unrecorded assets (as in Tractorling's case where Patents are discovered to have a fair value of $18,000). Or, replacement costs may have substantially increased.

Since the fair market value of net assets is now determined to be $350,000, why did Multi-Diversified pay $400,000? Undoubtedly, the seller pointed to an established reputation, good credit rating, top management team, well-trained employees, and so on, as factors that make the value of the business greater than $350,000.[18] At the same time, Multi-Diversified placed a premium on the future earning power of these attributes as well as the basic asset structure of the enterprise today. At this point in the negotiations, price can be a function of many factors: the most important is probably sheer skill at the bargaining table.

The difference between the purchase price of $400,000 and the fair market value of $350,000 is labeled goodwill. Goodwill is viewed as one or a group of unidentifiable values (intangible assets) the cost of which "is measured by the difference between the cost of the group of assets or enterprise acquired and the sum of the assigned costs of individual tangible and identifiable intangible assets acquired less liabilities assumed."[19] This procedure for valuation is referred to as a master valuation approach because goodwill is assumed to cover all the values that cannot be specifically identified with any identifiable tangible or intangible asset; this approach is shown in Illustration 12-4.

ILLUSTRATION 12-4
Determination of
Goodwill—Master
Valuation Approach

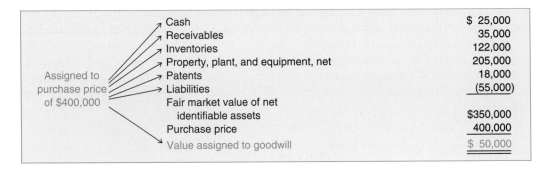

Cash	$ 25,000
Receivables	35,000
Inventories	122,000
Property, plant, and equipment, net	205,000
Patents	18,000
Liabilities	(55,000)
Fair market value of net identifiable assets	$350,000
Purchase price	400,000
Value assigned to goodwill	$ 50,000

The entry to record this transaction would be as follows:

Cash	25,000	
Receivables	35,000	
Inventories	122,000	
Property, plant, and equipment	205,000	
Patents	18,000	
Goodwill	50,000	
Liabilities		55,000
Cash		400,000

Goodwill is often identified on the balance sheet as the **excess of cost over the fair value** of the net assets acquired.

Amortization of Goodwill

Once goodwill has been recognized in the accounts, the next question is how it should be amortized (if at all). Three basic approaches have been suggested.

❶ **Charge Goodwill Off Immediately to Stockholders' Equity.** *Accounting Research Study No. 10*, "Accounting for Goodwill," takes the position that goodwill differs

---

[18]As another example of valuation criteria, the National Economic Research Associates of New York ranked "the quality of assets" of the 24 U.S.-based major league baseball teams in the early 1980s: At the high end were the Detroit Tigers at $36.2 million, Philadelphia Phillies at $35.3 million and Boston Red Sox at $34.3 million. At the low end were the Chicago Cubs and the Chicago White Sox at $20.6 million each, and the San Francisco Giants and the Oakland A's at $19 million each. Research Associates based their estimates on what the baseball franchises could be worth if they were "reasonably well managed," on the population and per capita income of the area in which a team plays, and on the number of local professional sports franchises it competes with. Surprisingly, the valuation did not include the team's recent attendance, local radio and TV revenue, and past profits.

[19]*APB Opinion No. 17*, op. cit., par. 26.

from other types of assets and demands special attention.[20] Unlike other assets, it is not separable and distinct from the business as a whole and therefore is not an asset in the same sense as cash, receivables, or plant assets. In other words, goodwill cannot be sold without selling the business.

Furthermore, say proponents of this approach, the accounting treatment for purchased goodwill and goodwill internally created should be consistent. Goodwill created internally is immediately expensed and does not appear as an asset: the same treatment should be accorded purchased goodwill. Amortization of purchased goodwill leads to double counting, because net income is reduced by amortization of the purchased goodwill as well as by the internal expenditure made to maintain or enhance the value of assets.

Perhaps the best rationale for direct writeoff is that determining the periods over which the future benefits are to be received is so difficult that immediate charging to stockholders' equity is justified.

❷ **Retain Goodwill Indefinitely Unless Reduction in Value Occurs.** Many believe that goodwill can have an indefinite life and should be maintained as an asset until a decline in value occurs. They contend that some form of goodwill should always be an asset inasmuch as internal goodwill is being expensed to maintain or enhance the purchased goodwill. In addition, without sufficient evidence that a decline in value has occurred, a writeoff of goodwill is both arbitrary and capricious and will lead to distortions in net income.

❸ **Amortize Goodwill Over Useful Life.** Still others believe that goodwill's value eventually disappears and it is proper that the asset be charged to expense over the periods affected. This procedure provides a better matching of costs and revenues.

APB Opinion No. 17 takes the position that goodwill should be written off over its useful life, which is dependent on a number of factors such as regulatory restrictions, demand, competition, and obsolescence. **The profession did note that goodwill should never be written off immediately or amortized over more than 40 years.**[21]

Immediate writeoff was not considered proper, because it would lead to the untenable conclusion that goodwill has no future service potential. The profession merely prohibits the writing off of goodwill in the period of purchase and over a period exceeding 40 years; no other mention is made regarding another period. Some believe that a 5-year period for amortization would be appropriate unless a shorter period is obviously justified.[22] Such circumstances would include continuous losses or an exodus

---

[20]Catlett and Olson, op. cit., pp. 89–95.

[21]More companies than ever before have learned recently that by classifying some or all of an acquisition's cost as "purchased research and development," they can write off immediately a large chunk of what would otherwise have been capitalized as goodwill. In some cases, they have made the entire purchase price of companies vanish from the books on the day of acquisition. *The Wall Street Journal* (December 2, 1996, p. A2) reported the following acquisition R & D write-offs:

Acquiring Company	Acquired Company	Year	Total (000,000)	R & D Write-off	% of Price
Adobe Systems	Ares Software	1996	$ 15.6	$ 14.7	94%
3 Com	Axon Networks	1996	65.3	52.4	80
H&R Block	Epry	1995	106.4	83.5	78
IBM	Lotus	1995	3,236.0	1,840.0	57
Lotus	Edge Research	1994	5.4	5.4	100
Sphinx Pharm.	Genesis Pharm.	1993	3.8	3.8	100

[22]A 1988 study of goodwill reached the following conclusion: "Thus, the 40-year amortization period used in current practice is too long and cannot be supported on either theoretical or technical grounds. Consequently, a rapid amortization (specifically if the use of the present value amortization method is permitted by the FASB) of capitalized goodwill over a relatively short period of time should occur. J. Ron Colley and Ara G. Volkan, "Accounting for Goodwill," *Accounting Horizons* (March 1988), p. 40.

of managerial talent. A single loss year or a combination of loss years does not automatically necessitate a charge-off of the goodwill.

Goodwill amortization should be computed using the straight-line method unless another method is deemed more appropriate. It should be treated as a regular operating expense. Where the amortization is material, a disclosure of the charge is necessary, as well as the method and period of amortization. Goodwill amortization is now deductible for tax purposes.

The amortization practices associated with goodwill sometimes lead to major disagreements. When Ted Turner of Turner Broadcasting attempted to take over CBS, he was required to file income statements on what a combined Turner-CBS company would look like in subsequent years. Turner assigned the difference between what he proposed to pay and the book value of CBS entirely to goodwill and amortized this amount over 40 years. CBS disagreed, noting that some of CBS's assets should have been revalued and a smaller amount assigned to goodwill. These revalued assets have a shorter life than goodwill and would lower the net income of the combined Turner-CBS Company. Thus the merger would be supposedly less attractive to stockholders of CBS. Questions of valuation and amortization of goodwill were important considerations in this takeover battle which failed.

Negative Goodwill—Badwill

Negative goodwill, **often appropriately dubbed** badwill, **or bargain purchase, arises when the fair market value of the assets acquired is higher than the purchase price of the assets.** This situation is a result of market imperfection because the seller would be better off to sell the assets individually than in total. Situations do occur in which the purchase price is less than the value of the net identifiable assets and therefore a credit develops; this credit is referred to as negative goodwill or **excess of fair value over the cost of assets acquired.** Companies that have negative goodwill are in a very interesting position because the amortization of this negative goodwill to revenue increases earnings.

APB Opinion No. 16 **takes the position that an excess of fair value over purchase price should be allocated to reduce proportionately the values assigned to noncurrent assets** of the acquired company (except long-term investments in marketable securities). If the allocation reduces the noncurrent assets to zero, the remainder of the excess over cost should be classified as a deferred credit and should be amortized systematically to revenue over the period estimated to be benefited but not in excess of 40 years. The method and period of amortization should be disclosed.[23]

❖ IMPAIRMENT OF INTANGIBLE ASSETS

The general rules that apply to **impairments of long-lived assets also apply to intangibles.** As indicated in Chapter 11, long-lived assets to be held and used by a company are to be reviewed for impairment whenever events or changes in circumstances indicate that **the carrying amount of the assets may not be recoverable.** In performing the review for recoverability, the company would estimate the future cash flows expected to result from the use of the asset and its eventual disposition. If the sum of the expected future net cash flows (undiscounted) is less than the carrying amount of the asset, an impairment loss would be measured and recognized. Otherwise, an impairment loss would not be recognized.[24]

[23]"Business Combinations," *Opinions of the Accounting Principles Board No. 16* (New York: AICPA, 1970), par. 91.

[24]"Accounting for the Impairment of Long-Lived Assets," *Statement of Financial Accounting Standards No. 121* (Norwalk, CT: FASB, 1994).

The impairment loss is the amount by which the carrying amount of the asset exceeds the fair value of the impaired asset. Illustrations of impairment for specifically identifiable and goodwill type intangibles are shown below.

Specifically Identifiable Intangibles

Assume that Lerch, Inc. has a patent on how to extract oil from shale rock. Unfortunately, reduced oil prices have made the shale oil technology somewhat unprofitable, and the patent has provided little income to date. As a result, a recoverability test is performed, and it is found that the expected net future cash flows from this patent are $35 million. Lerch's patent has a carrying amount of $60 million. Because the expected future net cash flows of $35 million are less than the carrying amount of $60 million, an impairment loss must be measured. Discounting the expected net future cash flows at its market rate of interest, Lerch determines the fair value of its patent to be $20 million. The impairment loss computation is shown in Illustration 12-5:

Carrying amount of patent	$60,000,000
Fair value (based on present value computation)	20,000,000
Loss on impairment	$40,000,000

ILLUSTRATION 12-5
Computation of Loss on Impairment of Patent

The journal entry to record this loss is:

Loss on Impairment	40,000,000	
Patents		40,000,000

After the impairment is recognized, the reduced carrying amount of the patents is its new cost basis. The patent's new cost should be amortized over its useful life or legal life, whichever is shorter. Even if oil prices increase in subsequent periods, and the value of the patent increases, **restoration of the previously recognized impairment loss is not permitted**.

Goodwill-Type Intangibles

Goodwill is a "going concern" valuation and cannot be separated from the other assets and liabilities which give it value. As a result, goodwill impairments involve a grouping of net assets.

To illustrate an impairment loss when goodwill is involved, assume that Kohlberg Corporation has three divisions in its company. One division, Pritt Products, was purchased four years ago for $2 million. Unfortunately, it has experienced operating losses over the last three quarters and management is reviewing the division for purposes of recognizing an impairment. The Pritt Division's net assets including the associated goodwill of $1,200,000 are listed in Illustration 12-6:

Cash	$ 200,000
Receivables	300,000
Inventory	400,000
Property, plant, and equipment (net)	800,000
Goodwill	1,200,000
Less: Accounts and notes payable	(500,000)
Net assets	$2,400,000

ILLUSTRATION 12-6
Pritt Division Net Assets

A recoverability test is performed and it is found that the expected net future cash flows from Pritt Division are $2,000,000. The fair value of the division is estimated to be $1,300,000, the present value of the expected future net cash flows. The impairment loss is computed as follows:

Carrying amount of Pritt Division	$2,400,000
Fair value	1,300,000
Loss on impairment	$1,100,000

ILLUSTRATION 12-7
Computation of Impairment Loss on Pritt Division

How should the impairment loss be allocated to the net assets of the Pritt Division? Various allocation approaches might be used. The FASB requires that where goodwill is associated with assets that are subject to the impairment loss, the carrying amount of the associated goodwill should be eliminated *before* the carrying amounts of impaired long-lived assets and identifiable intangibles are reduced to their fair values.

For Pritt Division, therefore, the total loss on impairment reduces only goodwill. The entry to record the impairment is:

Loss on Impairment	1,100,000	
Goodwill		1,100,000

If the impairment loss were greater than the carrying amount of goodwill, the additional loss would be used to reduce the remaining long-lived assets to fair value.[25]

❖ RESEARCH AND DEVELOPMENT COSTS

Objective ❻

Identify the conceptual issues related to research and development costs.

Research and development (R & D) costs are not in themselves intangible assets. The accounting for R & D costs is presented here, however, because research and development activities frequently result in the development of something that is patented or copyrighted (such as a new product, process, idea, formula, composition, or literary work).

Many businesses spend considerable sums of money on research and development to create new products or processes, to improve present products, and to discover new knowledge that may be valuable at some future date. The following schedule shows the outlays for R & D made by selected American companies:

ILLUSTRATION 12-8
R & D Outlays, as Percentage of Sales and Profits

Company	R & D Dollars	% of Sales	% of Profits
Amoco Corporation	$ 787,000,000	2.4%	27%
Johnson & Johnson	1,278,000,000	8.1	63
Kellogg Company	72,200,000	0.1	15
Eastman Kodak Company	935,000,000	6.0	75
Motorola, Inc.	2,197,000,000	8.1	123
PepsiCo, Inc.	96,000,000	0.03	6

🌐 INTERNATIONAL INSIGHT

Contrary to U.S. practice, in most other nations (the Netherlands, Canada, and Japan, for example) the capitalization of research and development costs is allowed under specified circumstances.

The difficulties in accounting for these research and development (R & D) expenditures are (1) identifying the costs associated with particular activities, projects, or achievements and (2) determining the magnitude of the future benefits and length of time over which such benefits may be realized. Because of these latter uncertainties, the accounting profession has standardized and simplified accounting practice in this area by requiring that **all research and development costs be charged to expense when incurred.**[26]

Identifying R & D Activities

To differentiate research and development costs from **other similar costs,** the FASB issued the following definitions:

> **RESEARCH** is planned search or critical investigation aimed at discovery of new knowledge with the hope that such knowledge will be useful in developing a new product or service . . . or a new process or technique . . . or in bringing about a significant improvement to an existing product or process.

---

[25]Once the goodwill is completely eliminated, the remaining loss would probably be allocated pro-rata, based on relative fair values, to those long-lived assets and identifiable intangible assets that had fair values less than their carrying amounts.

[26]"Accounting for Research and Development Costs," *Statement of Financial Accounting Standards No. 2* (Stamford, Conn.: FASB, 1974), par. 12.

DEVELOPMENT is the translation of research findings or other knowledge into a plan or design for a new product or process or for a significant improvement to an existing product or process whether intended for sale or use. It includes the conceptual formulation, design, and testing of product alternatives, construction of prototypes, and operation of pilot plants. It does not include routine or periodic alterations to existing products, production lines, manufacturing processes, and other on-going operations even though those alterations may represent improvements and it does not include market research or market testing activities.[27]

Many costs have characteristics similar to those of research and development costs. Examples are costs of relocation and rearrangement of facilities, start-up costs for a new plant or new retail outlet, marketing research costs, promotion costs of a new product or service, and costs of training new personnel. To distinguish between R & D and these other similar costs, the following schedule provides (1) examples of activities that typically would be **included** in research and development, and (2) examples of activities that typically would be **excluded** from research and development.[28]

❶ R & D Activities
 (a) Laboratory research aimed at discovery of new knowledge.
 (b) Searching for applications of new research findings.
 (c) Conceptual formulation and design of possible product or process alternatives.
 (d) Testing in search for or evaluation of product or process alternatives.
 (e) Modification of the design of a product or process.
 (f) Design, construction, and testing of preproduction prototypes and models.
 (g) Design of tools, jigs, molds, and dies involving new technology.
 (h) Design, construction, and operation of a pilot plant not useful for commercial production.
 (i) Engineering activity required to advance the design of a product to the manufacturing stage.

❷ Activities Not Considered R & D
 (a) Engineering follow-through in an early phase of commercial production.
 (b) Quality control during commercial production including routine testing.
 (c) Trouble-shooting breakdowns during production.
 (d) Routine, on-going efforts to refine, enrich, or improve the qualities of an existing product.
 (e) Adaptation of an existing capability to a particular requirement or customer's need.
 (f) Periodic design changes to existing products.
 (g) Routine design of tools, jigs, molds, and dies.
 (h) Activity, including design and construction engineering related to the construction, relocation, rearrangement, or start-up of facilities or equipment.
 (i) Legal work on patent applications, sale, licensing, or litigation.

Accounting for R & D Activities

The costs associated with R & D activities and the accounting treatment accorded them are as follows:

❶ *Materials, Equipment, and Facilities.* Expense the entire costs, **unless the items have alternative future uses** (in other R & D projects or otherwise), then carry as inventory and allocate as consumed, or capitalize and depreciate as used.

❷ *Personnel.* Salaries, wages, and other related costs of personnel engaged in R & D should be expensed as incurred.

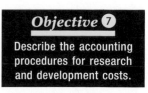

Objective ❼
Describe the accounting procedures for research and development costs.

[27]Ibid., par. 8.
[28]Ibid., pars. 9 and 10.

INTERNATIONAL INSIGHT

International accounting standards require the capitalization of appropriate development expenditures. This conflicts with U.S. GAAP.

❸ *Purchased Intangibles.* Expense the entire cost, **unless the items have alternative future uses** (in other R & D projects or otherwise), then capitalize and amortize.

❹ *Contract Services.* The costs of services performed by others in connection with the reporting company's R & D should be expensed as incurred.

❺ *Indirect Costs.* A reasonable allocation of indirect costs shall be included in R & D costs, except for general and administrative cost, which must be clearly related in order to be included and expensed.[29]

Consistent with item 1(a) above, if an enterprise owns a research facility consisting of buildings, laboratories, and equipment that conducts R & D activities and that has alternative future uses (in other R & D projects or otherwise), the facility should be accounted for as a capitalized operational asset. The depreciation and other costs related to such research facilities are accounted for as R & D expenses.[30]

Sometimes enterprises conduct R & D activities for other entities under a **contractual arrangement**. In this case, the contract usually specifies that all direct costs, certain specific indirect costs, plus a profit element, should be reimbursed to the enterprise performing the R & D work. Because reimbursement is expected, such R & D costs should be recorded as a receivable. It is the company for whom the work has been performed that reports these costs as R & D and expenses them as incurred.[31]

To illustrate the identification of R & D activities and the accounting treatment of related costs, assume that Next Century Incorporated develops, produces, and markets laser machines for medical, industrial, and defense uses. The types of expenditures related to its laser machine activities, along with the recommended accounting treatment, are listed in Illustration 12-9.

A special problem arises in distinguishing R & D costs from selling and administrative activities. The FASB's intent was that the acquisition, development, or improvement of a product or process by an enterprise **for use in its selling or administrative activities** be excluded from the definition of research and development activities. For example, the costs of software incurred by an airline in acquiring, developing, or improving its computerized reservation system, or the costs incurred during the development of a general management information system, are not research and development costs. Accounting for computer software costs is a specialized and complicated new accounting topic that is discussed and illustrated in an appendix to this chapter (Appendix 12A).

UNDERLYING CONCEPTS

The requirement that all R & D costs be expensed as incurred is an example of the conflict between relevance and reliability, with this requirement leaning strongly in support of reliability, as well as conservatism, consistency, and comparability. No attempt is made to match costs and revenues.

Conceptual Questions

The requirement that all R & D costs incurred internally be expensed immediately is a conservative, practical solution that ensures consistency in practice and uniformity among companies. But the practice of immediately writing off expenditures made in

[29]Ibid., par. 11.

[30]Costs of research, exploration, and development activities that are unique to companies in the **extractive industries** (e.g., prospecting, acquisition of mineral rights, exploration, drilling, mining, and related mineral development) and those costs discussed which are similar to but not classified as R & D costs may be:

❶ expensed as incurred,
❷ capitalized and either depreciated or amortized over an appropriate period of time, or
❸ accumulated as part of inventoriable costs.

Choice of the appropriate accounting treatment for such costs should be guided by the degree of certainty of future benefits and the principle of matching revenues and expenses.

[31]For a more complete discussion of how an enterprise should account for its obligation under an arrangement for the funding of its research and development by others, see "Research and Development Arrangements," *Statement of Financial Accounting Standards No. 68* (Stamford, Conn.: FASB, 1982).

Next Century Incorporated

Type of Expenditure	Accounting Treatment
1. Construction of long-range research facility for use in current and future projects (three-story, 400,000-square-foot building).	Capitalize and depreciate as R & D expense.
2. Acquisition of R & D equipment for use on current project only.	Expense immediately as R & D.
3. Acquisition of machinery to be used on current and future R & D projects.	Capitalize and depreciate as R & D expense.
4. Purchase of materials to be used on current and future R & D projects.	Inventory and allocate to R & D projects; expense as consumed.
5. Salaries of research staff designing new laser bone scanner.	Expense immediately as R & D.
6. Research costs incurred under contract with New Horizon, Inc., and billable monthly.	Record as a receivable (reimbursable expenses).
7. Material, labor, and overhead costs of prototype laser scanner.	Expense immediately as R & D.
8. Costs of testing prototype and design modifications.	Expense immediately as R & D.
9. Legal fees to obtain patent on new laser scanner.	Capitalize as patent and amortize to overhead as part of cost of goods manufactured.
10. Executive salaries.	Expense as operating expense (general and administrative).
11. Cost of marketing research to promote new laser scanner.	Expense as operating expense (selling).
12. Engineering costs incurred to advance the laser scanner to full production stage.	Expense immediately as R & D.
13. Costs of successfully defending patent on laser scanner.	Capitalize as patent and amortize to overhead as part of cost of goods manufactured.
14. Commissions to sales staff marketing new laser scanner.	Expense as operating expense (selling).

ILLUSTRATION 12-9
Sample R & D
Expenditures and Their
Accounting Treatment

the expectation of benefiting future periods cannot be justified on the grounds that it is good accounting theory.[32]

Defendants of immediate expensing contend that from an income statement standpoint, long-run application of this standard frequently makes little difference. They contend that the amount of R & D cost charged to expense each accounting period would be about the same whether there is immediate expensing or capitalization and subsequent amortization because of the ongoing nature of most companies' R & D activities. Critics of this practice argue that the balance sheet should report an intangible asset related to expenditures that have future benefit. To preclude capitalization of all R & D expenditures removes from the balance sheet what may be a company's most valuable asset.[33] This standard represents one of the many trade-offs made among relevance, reliability, and cost-benefit considerations.[34]

---

[32]The International Accounting Standards Committee issued a standard that is in disagreement with the FASB's standard on accounting for R & D costs. The International Committee identified certain circumstances that justify the capitalization and deferral of development costs. See "Accounting for Research and Development Activities," *International Accounting Standard No. 9* (London, England: International Accounting Standards Committee, 1978), par. 17.

[33]Bertrand Horwitz and Richard Kolodmy, "The FASB, the SEC, and R & D," *Bell Journal of Economics* (Spring 1981), who argue that expensing R & D has economic consequences.

[34]For a discussion of the position that R & D should be capitalized in certain situations, see Harold Bierman, Jr., and Roland E. Dukes, "Accounting for Research and Development Costs, *The Journal of Accountancy* (April, 1975).

❖ PRESENTATION OF INTANGIBLES AND RELATED ITEMS

Intangibles

Objective ❽

Indicate the presentation of intangibles and related items.

The reporting of intangibles differs from the reporting of property, plant, and equipment in that contra accounts are not normally shown. The amortization of intangibles is frequently credited directly to the intangible asset.[35]

The financial statements should disclose the method and period of amortization. Intangible assets shown net of amortization might appear on the balance sheet as follows:

ILLUSTRATION 12-10
Balance Sheet
Presentation
of Intangible Assets, Net
of Amortization

Intangible assets (Note 3)		
Patents	$ 98,000	
Franchises	115,000	
Goodwill	342,000	$555,000

Note 3: The patents are amortized on a unit-of-production approach over a period of 6 years. The franchises are perpetual in nature, but in accordance with *APB Opinion No. 17* are being written off over the maximum period allowable (40 years) on a straight-line basis. The goodwill arose from the purchase of Multi-Media and is being amortized over a 10-year period on a straight-line basis.

Go to our Web site for additional disclosures of intangibles

Some companies follow the practice of writing their intangibles down to $1.00 to indicate that they have intangibles of uncertain value. This practice is not good accounting. It would be much better to disclose the nature of the intangible, its original cost, and other relevant information such as competition, danger of obsolescence, and so on.

Research and Development Costs

Acceptable accounting practice requires that disclosure be made in the financial statements (generally in the notes) of the total R & D costs charged to expense in each period for which an income statement is presented. An example of an R & D disclosure in the income statement and in an accompanying note is the excerpt from the annual report of Oncogene Science, Inc.

ILLUSTRATION 12-11
Income Statement and
Note Disclosure of R & D
Costs

Oncogene Science, Inc.			
	Years Ended September 30,		
	1993	1992	1991
Expenses:			
Research and development—Note 1(d)	$10,659,806	$ 8,127,466	$4,860,226
Production	1,443,649	1,420,686	748,927
Selling, general and administrative	6,429,701	5,219,606	4,130,777
Amortization of intangibles—Note 1(c)	1,745,713	1,745,694	—
	20,278,869	16,513,452	9,739,930

**Note 1: Summary of Significant Accounting Policies
    (d) Research and Development Costs**
    Research and development costs are charged to operations as incurred and include direct costs of research scientists and equipment and an allocation of laboratory facility and central service. In fiscal years 1993, 1992, and 1991 R & D activities include approximately $3,012,000, $2,701,000, and $2,122,000 of independent R & D, respectively. Independent R & D represents those research and development activities, including research and development activities funded by government research grants, the results of which the Company retains substantially all rights. The balance of research and development represents research and development expenses under the collaborative agreements funded by Pfizer Inc., Becton Dickinson and Co., Wyeth-Ayerst, a division of American Home Products, Marion Merrell Dow Inc., and Hoechst AG.

Go to our Web site for additional disclosures of R & D expense.

---

[35]Accounting Trends and Techniques—1996 reports that the most common type of intangible is goodwill followed by patents; trademarks, brand names, and copyrights; and then noncompete covenants, licenses, franchises, memberships, technology, and customer lists.

Other Assets

Other assets (sometimes referred to as deferred charges) is a classification often used to describe a number of different items that have debit balances, among them certain types of intangibles. How do these items happen to be classified in this section and not in a separate intangible section? In truth, the other asset section serves as a dumping ground for a number of small items. Some of these items are: property held for sale, prepaid pension costs, segregated cash or securities, cash surrender value of life insurance, and deferred income taxes. In many cases, deferred income taxes are separately identified.

SUMMARY OF LEARNING OBJECTIVES

① ***Describe the characteristics of intangible assets.*** A major characteristic of intangible assets is the high degree of uncertainty concerning the *future benefits* that are to be received from their employment. Intangibles may be subdivided on the basis of the following characteristics: (1) *Identifiability:* separately identifiable or lacking specific identification. (2) *Manner of acquisition:* acquired singly, in groups, or in business combinations, or developed internally. (3) *Expected period of benefit:* limited by law or contract, related to human or economic factors, or indefinite or indeterminate duration. (4) *Separability from the enterprise:* rights transferable without title, salable, or inseparable from the enterprise or a substantial part of it.

② ***Explain the procedure for valuing and amortizing intangible assets.*** Intangibles are recorded at cost. Cost includes all costs of acquisition and expenditures necessary to make the intangible asset ready for its intended use. If intangibles are acquired for stock or in exchange for other assets, the cost of the intangible is the fair market value of the consideration given or the fair market value of the intangible received, whichever is more clearly evident. When several intangibles, or a combination of intangibles and tangibles, are bought in a "basket purchase," the cost should be allocated on the basis of fair market values or on the basis of relative sales values. Intangible assets should be amortized by systematic charges to expense over their useful lives. Intangible assets must be amortized over a period not exceeding 40 years.

③ ***Identify the types of specifically identifiable intangible assets.*** The major identifiable assets are: (1) *Patents:* give the holder exclusive right to use, manufacture, and sell a product or process for a period of 17 years without interference or infringement by others. (2) *Copyrights:* a federally granted right that all authors, painters, musicians, sculptors, and other artists have in their creations and expressions. (3) *Trademarks and trade names:* a word, phrase, or symbol that distinguishes or identifies a particular enterprise or product. (4) *Leaseholds:* a contractual understanding between a lessor (owner of property) and a lessee (renter of property) that grants the lessee the right to use specific property, owned by the lessor, for a specific period of time in return for stipulated, and generally periodic, cash payments. (5) *Organization costs:* costs incurred in the formation of a corporation such as fees to underwriters for handling stock or bond issues, legal fees, state fees of various sorts, and certain promotional expenditures. (6) *Franchises and licenses:* a contractual arrangement under which the franchisor grants the franchisee the right to sell certain products or services, to use certain trademarks or trade names, or to perform certain functions, usually within a designated geographical area.

④ ***Explain the conceptual issues related to goodwill.*** Goodwill is unique because unlike receivables, inventories, and patents that can be sold or exchanged individually in the marketplace, goodwill can be identified only with the business as a whole. Goodwill is a "going concern" valuation and is recorded only when an entire business is purchased. Goodwill generated internally should not be capi-

KEY TERMS

amortization, *596*
capital lease, *600*
copyright, *598*
deferred charges, *613*
development
  activities, *609*
development stage
  enterprises, *600*
franchise, *601*
goodwill, *601*
intangible assets, *594*
leasehold
  improvements, *599*
license, *601*
master valuation
  approach, *604*
negative goodwill
  (badwill), *606*
organization costs, *600*
patent, *597*
research activities, *608*
research and
  development (R & D)
  costs, *608*
specifically identifiable
  intangible asset, *595*
trademark, trade
  name, *598*

talized in the accounts, because measuring the components of goodwill is simply too complex and associating any costs with future benefits too difficult. The future benefits of goodwill may have no relationship to the costs incurred in the development of that goodwill. Goodwill may exist even in the absence of specific costs to develop it.

(5) *Describe the accounting procedures for recording goodwill.* To record goodwill, the fair market value of the net tangible and identifiable intangible assets are compared with the purchase price of the acquired business. The difference is considered goodwill. Goodwill is the residual—the excess of cost over fair value of the identifiable net assets acquired. Goodwill is often identified on the balance sheet as the excess of cost over the fair value of the net assets acquired.

(6) *Identify the conceptual issues related to research and development costs.* R & D costs are not in themselves intangible assets, but research and development activities frequently result in the development of something that is patented or copyrighted. The difficulties in accounting for R & D expenditures are (1) identifying the costs associated with particular activities, projects, or achievements and (2) determining the magnitude of the future benefits and length of time over which such benefits may be realized. Because of these latter uncertainties, the FASB has standardized and simplified accounting practice by requiring that all research and development costs be charged to expense when incurred.

(7) *Describe the accounting procedures for research and development costs.* The costs associated with R & D activities and the accounting treatment accorded them are as follows: (1) *Materials, equipment, and facilities:* Expense the entire costs, unless the items have alternative future uses, then carry as inventory and allocate as consumed, or capitalize and depreciate as used. (2) *Personnel:* Salaries, wages, and other related costs of personnel engaged in R & D should be expensed as incurred. (3) *Purchased intangibles:* Expense the entire cost, unless the items have alternative future uses, then capitalize and amortize. (4) *Contract services:* The costs of services performed by others in connection with the reporting company's R & D should be expensed as incurred. (5) *Indirect costs:* A reasonable allocation of indirect costs shall be included in R & D costs, except for general and administrative costs, which must be related to be included and expensed.

(8) *Indicate the presentation of intangible and related items.* The reporting of intangibles differs from the reporting of of property, plant and equipment in that contra accounts are not normally shown. Disclosure must be made in the financial statements for the total R&D costs charged to expense each period for which an income statement is presented.

Appendix 12A

Accounting for Computer Software Costs

The development of computer software products takes on increasing importance as our economy continues to change from a manufacturing process orientation (tangible outputs) to an information flow society (intangible outputs).[1] This short appendix discusses the basic issues involved in accounting for computer software.

> **Objective 9**
>
> After studying Appendix 12A, you should be able to: Identify the accounting treatment for computer software costs.

❖ DIVERSITY IN PRACTICE

Computer software may be either **purchased** or **created** by a company. It may be purchased or created for **external use** (such as spreadsheet applications like Excel or Lotus 1-2-3) or for **internal use** (e.g., to establish a better internal accounting system). Should costs incurred in developing the software be expensed immediately or capitalized and amortized in the future? Prior to 1985, some companies expensed all software costs, and others capitalized such costs. Still others differentiated such costs on the basis of whether the software was purchased or created, or whether it was used for external or internal purposes.

The issue is controversial because some companies' major assets are software programs. For example, Comserve (maker of software systems for manufacturing companies) at one time reported net income of $2.2 million. However, if Comserve were forced to expense the costs it incurred to develop software, this $2.2 million would become a loss of $1 million. And, if IBM had been forced to expense its $785 million "investment in program products" in 1985, its earnings would have been decreased by $443 million.

❖ THE PROFESSION'S POSITION

A major question is whether the costs involved in developing software are research and development costs. If they are actually R & D, then the profession requires that they be expensed as incurred. If they are not research and development costs, then a strong case can be made for capitalization. As one financial executive of a software company who argues for capitalization noted: "The key distinction between our spending and R & D is recoverability. We know we are developing something we can sell."

In an attempt to resolve this issue (at least for companies that sell computer software), the FASB issued *Statement of Financial Accounting Standards No. 86*, "Accounting for the Costs of Computer Software to Be Sold, Leased, or Otherwise Marketed."[2] The

---

[1] A major contributing factor was IBM's decision in 1969 to "unbundle" its hardware and software, that is, to state the cost of the hardware and software separately. Prior to the unbundling, most applications software was provided free with the hardware. This unbundling led to the creation of a whole new industry, the software industry, whose members began selling software to hardware users. Today, more than 4,000 U.S. companies develop software for sale.

[2] "Accounting for the Cost of Computer Software to Be Sold, Leased, or Otherwise Marketed," *Statement of Financial Accounting Standards No. 86* (Stamford, Conn.: FASB, 1985). Also see, "Accounting for Software," Robert W. McGee, Dow Jones–Irwin, Homewood, Il., 1985.

major recommendations of this pronouncement are:

❶ Costs incurred in creating a computer software product should be charged to research and development expense when incurred until **technological feasibility** has been established for the product.

❷ Technological feasibility is established upon completion of a detailed program design or working model.

In short, the FASB has taken a conservative position in regard to computer software costs. All costs must be expensed until the company has completed planning, designing, coding, and testing activities necessary to establish that the product can be produced to meet its design specifications. Subsequent costs incurred should be capitalized and amortized to current and future periods.

Two additional points should be emphasized. First, **if the software is purchased and it has alternative future uses, then it may be capitalized.** Second, **this standard applies only to the development of software that is to be sold, leased, or otherwise marketed to third parties** (i.e., for external use).

In December 1996, the American Institute of CPAs (AICPA) proposed a new rule that requires companies to capitalize and amortize the cost of software they use internally. Companies would also be permitted to capitalize and amortize the cost of upgrading or enhancing computer programs. But the rule would force companies to immediately write off any money spent on training related to the internal use of software, as well as expenses related to internally developed software that does not pan out. As of 1997, the FASB is reviewing the AICPA's proposed rule covering software purchased or created for internal use.

❖ ACCOUNTING FOR CAPITALIZED SOFTWARE COSTS

If software costs are capitalized, then a proper amortization pattern for these costs must be established. **Companies are required to use the greater of (1) the ratio of current revenues to current and anticipated revenues (percent of revenue approach) or (2) the straight-line method over the remaining useful life of the asset (straight-line approach) as a basis for amortization.** These rules can result in the use of the ratio method one year and the straight-line method in another.

To illustrate, assume that AT&T has capitalized software costs of $10 million and its current (first-year) revenues from sales of this product are $4 million. AT&T anticipates earning $16 million in additional future revenues from this product, which is estimated to have an economic life of 4 years. Using the percent of revenue approach, the current (first) year's amortization would be $2 million ($10,000,000 × $4,000,000/ $20,000,000). Using the straight-line approach, the amortization would be $2.5 million ($10,000,000/4 years). Thus the straight-line approach would be employed because it results in the greater amortization charge.

❖ REPORTING SOFTWARE COSTS

Because much concern exists about the reliability of an asset such as software, the Board indicated that capitalized software costs should be valued at the **lower of unamortized cost or net realizable value.** If net realizable value is lower, then the capitalized software costs should be written down to this value. Once written down, it **may not be written back up.** In addition to the regular disclosures for R & D costs, the following should be reported in the financial statements:

1. Unamortized software costs.

2. The total amount charged to expense and amounts, if any, written down to net realizable value.

Once again these accounting and reporting requirements apply only to software **developed for external purposes**.

An example of software development cost disclosure, taken from the annual report of Moscom Corporation, is shown below.

Moscom Corporation

Balance Sheet	1989	($000)	1988
Other Assets:			
License fees (net of accumulated amortization of $652,013 and $319,878, respectively)	501		736
Software development costs (net of accumulated amortization of $1,567,330 and $814,500, respectively) (Note D)	1,038		1,163
Excess purchase price over net assets acquired (net of accumulated amortization of $318,391, and $63,678, respectively) (Note K)	2,228		2,483
Deposits and other assets	88		84

	Year Ended December 31,		
Income Statement	1989	1988	1987
Sales	$13,619	$10,595	$8,530
Costs and Operating Expenses:			
Cost of sales	5,112	3,344	2,738
Engineering and software development (Note D)	958	855	1,498

Significant Accounting Policies

Software development costs meeting recoverability tests are capitalized under *Statement of Financial Accounting Standards No. 86.* The cost of software capitalized is amortized on a product-by-product basis over its economic life, generally three years, or the ratio of current revenues to current and anticipated revenues from such software, whichever provides the greater amortization. There were no amounts written down to net realizable value during the years ended December 31, 1989, 1988 and 1987.

Note D: Engineering and Software Development Costs

	Year Ended December 31,		
	1989	1988	1987
Total expenditures for engineering and software development	$1,750,563	$1,797,495	$1,916,428
Less:			
Amounts capitalized under Statement of Financial Accounting Standards No. 86	(792,295)	(942,470)	(418,059)
Engineering and software development expense	$ 958,268	$ 855,025	$1,498,369

Amortization expense of software development costs was approximately $917,000, $528,000 and $185,000 for the years ended December 31, 1989, 1988 and 1987, respectively.

❖ SETTING STANDARDS FOR SOFTWARE ACCOUNTING

"It's unreasonable to expense all software costs, and it's unreasonable to capitalize all software costs," says Joseph Smith, IBM's director of financial reporting. "If you subscribe to those two statements, then it follows that there is somewhere in between where development ends and capitalization begins. Now you have to define that point."[3] The FASB defined that point as "technological feasibility," which is established upon completion of a detailed program design or working model. The difficulty of applying this criterion to software is that, "there is no such thing as a real, specific, baseline design. But you could make it look like you have one as early or as late as you like," says Osman Erlop of Hambrecht & Quist.[4] That is, if you wish to capitalize, draw up a

---

[3]"When Does Life Begin?" *Forbes*, June 16, 1986, pp. 72–74.

[4]Ibid.

detailed program design quickly. If you want to expense lots of development costs, simply hold off writing a detailed program design. And, once capitalized, the costs are amortized over the useful life specified by the developer, which because of either constant redesign or supersession is generally quite short (2 to 4 years).

As another example, some companies "manage by the numbers"; that is, they are very careful to identify projects that are worthwhile and capitalize the computer software costs associated with them. They believe that good projects must be capitalized and amortized in the future; otherwise, the concept of properly matching expense and revenues is abused.

Other companies choose not to manage by the numbers and simply expense all these costs. Companies that expense all these costs have no use for a standard that requires capitalization. In their view, it would mean only that a more complex, more expensive cost accounting system would be required, one that would provide little if any benefit.

Financial analysts have reacted almost uniformly against any capitalization. They believe software costs should be expensed because of the rapid obsolescence of software and the potential for abuse that may result from capitalizing costs inappropriately. As Donald Kirk, a former chairman of the FASB, stated: "The Board is now faced with the problem of balancing what it thought was good theory with the costs for some companies of implementing a new accounting system with the concerns of users about the potential for abuse of the standard."[5]

Resolving the software accounting problem again demonstrates the difficulty of establishing reporting standards.

SUMMARY OF LEARNING OBJECTIVE FOR APPENDIX 12A

(9) *Identify the accounting treatment for computer software costs.* Costs incurred in creating a software product should be charged to R & D expense when incurred until technological feasibility has been established for the product. Subsequent costs should be capitalized and amortized to current and future periods. Software that is purchased for sale or lease to third parties and has alternative future uses may be capitalized and amortized using the greater of the percent of revenue approach or the straight-line approach.

Appendix 12B

Valuing Goodwill

Objective (10)

After studying Appendix 12B, you should be able to: Explain various approaches to valuing goodwill.

In this chapter we discussed the generally accepted method of measuring and recording goodwill as the excess of cost over fair value of the identifiable net assets acquired in a business acquisition. Accountants are frequently asked to participate in the valuation of businesses as part of a planned business acquisition.

To determine the purchase price for a business and the resulting goodwill is a difficult and inexact process. As indicated, it is often possible to determine the fair value of identifiable assets. But how does a buyer value intangible factors like good management, good credit rating, and so on?

---

[5]Donald J. Kirk, "Growing Temptation & Rising Expectation = Accelerating Regulation," *FASB Viewpoints*, June 12, 1985, p. 7.

❖ EXCESS EARNINGS APPROACH

One method is called the **excess earnings approach**. Using this approach, the total earning power that the company commands is computed. The next step is to calculate "normal earnings" by determining the normal rate of return on assets in that industry. **The difference between what the firm earns and what is normal in the industry is referred to as the excess earning power.** This extra earning power indicates that there are unidentifiable values (intangible assets) that provide this increased earning power. Finding the value of goodwill then is a matter of discounting these excess future earnings to the present.

This approach appears to be a systematic and logical way of determining goodwill. However, each factor necessary to compute a value under this approach is subject to question. Generally, the problems relate to getting answers to the following questions:

❶ What is a normal rate of return?
❷ How does one determine the future earnings?
❸ What discount rate should be applied to the excess earnings?
❹ Over what period should the excess earnings be discounted?

Finding a Normal Rate of Return

Determining the normal rate of return for tangible and identifiable intangible assets requires analysis of companies similar to the enterprise in question. An industry average may be determined by examining annual reports or data from statistical services. Suppose that a rate of 15% is decided as normal for a concern such as Tractorling (see page 603). In this case, the normal earnings are calculated in the following manner.[1]

Fair market value of Tractorling's net identifiable assets	$350,000
Normal rate of return	15%
Normal earnings	$ 52,500

ILLUSTRATION 12B-1
Calculation of Normal Earnings

Determining Future Earnings

The starting point for determining future earnings is normally the past earnings of the enterprise. Although estimates of future earnings are needed, the past often provides useful information concerning the enterprise's future earnings potential. Past earnings—generally 3 to 6 years—are also useful because estimates of the future are usually overly optimistic; the hard facts of previous periods bring a sobering reality to the negotiations.

Tractorling's net earnings for the last 5 years are as follows:

Earnings History—Tractorling

Year	Earnings	
1994	$ 60,000	Average Earnings
1995	55,000	$\dfrac{\$375,000}{5} = \$75,000$
1996	110,000[a]	
1997	70,000	
1998	80,000	
	$375,000	

[a]Includes extraordinary gain of $25,000.

ILLUSTRATION 12B-2
Calculation of Average Earnings

The average net earnings for the last 5 years is $75,000 or a rate of return of approximately 21.4% on the current value of the assets excluding goodwill ($75,000 ÷ $350,000). Before we go further, however, we need to know whether $75,000 is representative of the future earnings of this enterprise.

---

[1]The fair value of Tractorling's assets (rather than historical cost) is used to compute the normal profit, because fair value is closer to the true value of the company's assets exclusive of goodwill.

Often past earnings of a company to be acquired need to be evaluated on the basis of the acquirer's own accounting procedures. Suppose, that in determining earning power, Multi-Diversified measures earnings in relation to a FIFO inventory valuation figure rather than LIFO, which Tractorling employs, and that the use of LIFO reduced Tractorling's net income by $2,000 per year. In addition, Tractorling uses accelerated depreciation while Multi-Diversified uses straight-line. As a result, Tractorling's earnings were lower by $3,000.

Also, assets discovered on examination that might affect the earnings flow should be considered. Patent costs not previously recorded should be amortized, say, at the rate of $1,000 per period. Finally because the estimate of the future earnings is what we are attempting to determine, some items, like the extraordinary gain of $25,000, probably should not be considered. An analysis can now be made as follows:

ILLUSTRATION 12B-3
Calculation of Adjusted Net Earnings

Average net earnings per Tractorling computation		$75,000
Add		
Adjustment for switch from LIFO to FIFO	$2,000	
Adjustment for change from accelerated to straight-line approach	3,000	5,000
		80,000
Deduct		
Extraordinary gain ($25,000 ÷ 5)	5,000	
Patent amortization on straight-line basis	1,000	6,000
Adjusted average net earnings of Tractorling		$74,000

The excess earnings would be determined to be $21,500 ($74,000 − $52,500).

Choosing a Discount Rate to Apply to Excess Earnings

Determining the discount rate is a fairly subjective estimate.[2] **The lower the discount rate, the higher the value of the goodwill and vice versa.** To illustrate, assume that the excess earnings are $21,500 and that these earnings will continue indefinitely. If the excess earnings are capitalized at, say, a rate of 25% in perpetuity,[3] the results are:

---

[2]The following illustration shows how the capitalization rate might be computed for a small business:

A Method of Selecting a Capitalization Rate

Long-term U.S. government bond rate	10%
Plus: Average premium return on small stocks over U.S. government bonds	10
Expected total rate of return on small publicly held stocks	20
Plus: Premium for greater risk and illiquidity	6
Total required expected rate of return, including inflation component	26
Less: Consensus long-term inflation expectation	6
Capitalization rate to apply to current earnings	20%

From Warren Kissin and Ronald Zulli, "Valuation of a Closely Held Business," *The Journal of Accountancy* (June 1988), p. 42.

[3]Why do we divide by the capitalization rate to arrive at the goodwill amount? Recall that the present value of an ordinary annuity is equal to:

$$PV\text{-}OA_{n,i} = \frac{1 - \dfrac{1}{(1+i)^n}}{i}$$

When a number is capitalized into perpetuity, $(1+i)^n$ becomes so large that $1/(1+i)^n$ essentially equals zero, which leaves $1/i$ or, as in the case above, $21,500/.25$.

> **Capitalization at 25%**
>
> $\dfrac{\text{Excess earnings}}{\text{Capitalization rate}} \quad \dfrac{\$21{,}500}{.25} = \$86{,}000$

If the excess earnings are capitalized in perpetuity at a somewhat lower rate, say 15%, a much higher goodwill figure results.

> **Capitalization at 15%**
>
> $\dfrac{\text{Excess earnings}}{\text{Capitalization rate}} \quad \dfrac{\$21{,}500}{.15} = \$143{,}333$

Because the continuance of excess profits is uncertain, a conservative rate (higher than the normal rate) is usually employed. Factors that are considered in determining the rate are the stability of past earnings, the speculative nature of the business, and general economic conditions.

Choosing a Discounting Period for Excess Earnings

Determining the period over which excess earnings will exist is perhaps the most difficult problem associated with computing goodwill. If it is assumed that the excess earnings will last indefinitely, then goodwill is $143,333 as computed in the previous section (assuming a rate of 15%).

Another method of computing goodwill that gives the same answer, using the normal return of 15%, is to discount the total average earnings of the company and subtract the fair market value of the net identifiable assets as shown in Illustration 12B-6.

Average earnings capitalized at 15% in perpetuity	
($74,000 ÷ 15%)	$493,333
Less fair market value of net identifiable assets	350,000
Present value of estimated earnings (goodwill)	$143,333

Frequently, however, the excess earnings are assumed to last a limited number of years, say 10, and then it is necessary to discount these earnings only over that time. Assume that Multi-Diversified believes that the excess earnings of Tractorling will last 10 years and, because of the uncertainty surrounding this earning power, uses 25% as an appropriate rate of return. The present value of an annuity of $21,500 ($74,000 − $52,500) discounted at 25% for 10 years is $76,766.[4] That is the amount that Multi-Diversified should be willing to pay above the fair value of net identifiable assets.

❖ OTHER METHODS OF VALUATION[5]

Some accountants fail to discount but simply multiply the excess earnings by the number of years they believe the excess earnings will continue. This approach, often referred to as the **number of years method**, is used to provide a rough measure for the goodwill

---

[4]The present value of an annuity of one dollar received in a steady stream for 10 years in the future discounted at 25% is 3.57050 (3.57050 × $21,500 = $76,766).

[5]One article lists three "asset-based approaches" (tangible net worth, adjusted book value, and price-book value ratio methods) and three "earnings-based approaches" (capitalization of earnings, capitalization of excess earnings, and discounted cash flow methods) as the popular methods for valuing closely held businesses. See Warren Rissin and Ronald Zulli, "Valuation of a Closely Held Business," *The Journal of Accountancy* (June 1988), pp. 38–44.

factor. The approach has only the advantage of simplicity; it is sounder to recognize the discount factor.

An even simpler method is one that relies on multiples of average yearly earnings that are paid for other companies in the same industry. If Skyward Airlines was recently acquired for five times its average yearly earnings of $50 million, or $250 million, then Worldwide Airways, a close competitor, with $80 million in average yearly earnings would be worth $400 million.

Another method (similar to discounting excess earnings) is the **discounted free cash flow method**, which involves a projection of the acquired company's free cash flow over a long period, typically 10 or 20 years. The method first projects into the future a dozen or so important financial variables, including production, prices, noncash expenses (such as depreciation and amortization), taxes, and capital outlays, all adjusted for inflation. The objective is to determine the amount of cash that will accumulate over a specified number of years. The present value of the free cash flows is then computed. This amount represents the price to be paid for the business.[6]

For example, if Magnaputer Company is expected to generate $1 million a year for 20 years, and the buyer's rate-of-return objective is 15%, the buyer would be willing to pay about $6.26 million for Magnaputer Company. (The present value of $1 million to be received for 20 years discounted at 15% is $6,259,330.)

In practice, prospective buyers use a variety of methods to produce a "valuation curve" or range of prices. But the actual price paid may be more a factor of the buyer's or seller's ego and horse-trading acumen.

Valuation of goodwill is at best a highly uncertain process. The estimated value of goodwill depends on a number of factors, all of which are extremely tenuous and subject to bargaining.

SUMMARY OF LEARNING OBJECTIVE FOR APPENDIX 12B

⑩ *Explain various approaches to valuing goodwill.* One method of valuing goodwill is the excess earnings approach. Using this approach, the total earning power that the company commands is computed. The next step is to calculate "normal earnings" by determining the normal rate of return on assets in that industry. The difference between what the firm earns and what is normal in the industry is referred to as the excess earning power. This excess earning power indicates that there are unidentifiable values that provide the increased earning power. Finding the value of goodwill then is a matter of discounting these excess future earnings to the present. The number of years method of valuing goodwill, which simply multiplies the excess earnings by the number of years of expected excess earnings, is used to provide a rough measure for the goodwill factor. A third method of valuing goodwill is the discounted free cash flow method, which projects the amount of cash that will accumulate over a specified number of years and then finds the present value of that amount as today's value of the firm.

KEY TERMS

discounted free cash flow
  method, *622*
excess earnings
  approach, *619*
number of years
  method, *621*

Note: All **asterisked** Questions, Brief Exercises, Problems, and Conceptual Cases relate to material contained in the appendix to each chapter.

---

[6]Tim Metz, "Deciding How Much a Company Is Worth Often Depends on Whose Side You're On," *The Wall Street Journal*, March 18, 1981.

❖ QUESTIONS ❖

1 What are the major accounting problems related to accounting for intangibles?

2 Accounting authors and practitioners have proposed various solutions to the problems of accounting in terms of historical cost for goodwill and similar intangibles. What problems of accounting for goodwill and similar intangibles are comparable to those of accounting for plant assets? What problems are different?

3 Many accountants advocate the abandonment of historical cost for plant assets but argue that historical cost should be used in accounting for intangible assets. Are the two viewpoints inconsistent?

4 Intangible assets may be classified on a number of different bases. Indicate three different bases and illustrate how intangibles could be subdivided into these groupings.

5 What are some examples of internally created intangibles? Why does the accounting profession make a distinction between internally created "goodwill type" intangibles and other intangibles?

6 In 1998, Chris Farley Corp. spent $420,000 for "goodwill" visits by sales personnel to key customers. The purpose of these visits was to build a solid, friendly relationship for the future and to gain insight into the problems and needs of the companies served. How should this expenditure be reported?

7 State the generally accepted accounting procedures for the amortization and writedown or writeoff of capitalized intangible assets.

8 It has been argued, on the grounds of conservatism, that all intangible assets should be written off immediately after acquisition. Give the accounting arguments against this treatment.

9 Tom Hanks Company spent $190,000 developing a new process, $45,000 in legal fees to obtain a patent, and $91,000 to market the process that was patented, all in the year 1998. How should these costs be accounted for in 1998?

10 Indicate the period of time over which each of the following should be amortized.
(a) Research and development costs.
(b) Trademarks.
(c) Goodwill.
(d) A 25-year lease with payments of $80,000 per year on property with an estimated useful life of 50 years. The lessee has the option to renew the lease for 25 additional years at $5,000 per year.
(e) Franchises.
(f) Patents.
(g) Leasehold improvements.
(h) Copyrights.

11 What is a lease prepayment? What are property rights capitalized by the lessee? What are leasehold improvements?

Should any of these items be classified as an intangible asset?

12 On January 1, 1994, an intangible asset with a 35-year estimated useful life was acquired. On January 1, 1999, a review was made of the estimated useful life, and it was determined that the intangible asset had an estimated useful life of 45 more years. Assuming that the company wants to amortize this intangible over the maximum period possible, how many more years may this intangible be amortized?

13 Recently Gena Olin Corporation entered into a lease agreement with Eagle Developers, Inc. to lease some land for 25 years in southwest New Mexico. Gena Olin Corporation as lessee then built on this site a number of apartment buildings having a useful life of 35 years. The lease agreement states that the lessee has the option to renew the lease for another 20 years. Over what period should the apartments be depreciated?

14 Recently, a group of university students decided to incorporate for the purposes of selling a process to recycle the waste product from manufacturing cheese. Some of the initial costs involved were legal fees and office expenses incurred in starting the business, state incorporation fees, and stamp taxes. One student wishes to charge these costs against revenue in the current period; another wishes to defer these costs and amortize them in the future; and another believes these costs should be netted against common stock. Which student is correct?

15 What is goodwill? What is negative goodwill?

16 Under what circumstances is it appropriate to record goodwill in the accounts? How should goodwill, properly recorded on the books, be amortized in order to conform with generally accepted accounting principles?

17 In examining financial statements, financial analysts often write off goodwill immediately. Evaluate this procedure.

18 What is the nature of research and development costs? What other costs have similar characteristics?

19 Research and development activities may include (a) personnel costs, (b) materials and equipment costs, and (c) indirect costs. What is the recommended accounting treatment for these three types of R & D costs?

20 Which of the following activities should be expensed currently as R & D costs:
(a) Testing in search for or evaluation of product or process alternatives.
(b) Engineering follow-through in an early phase of commercial production.
(c) Legal work in connection with patent applications or litigation, and the sale or licensing of patents.
(d) Adaptation of an existing capability to a particular requirement or customer's need as a part of continuing commercial activity.

㉑ During the current year Reading Railroad spent $700,000 to develop a computer program that will assist in identifying and locating all of its rolling equipment. How should Reading account for this expenditure?

㉒ In 1997, Cassie Logan Corporation developed a new product that will be marketed in 1998. In connection with the development of this product, the following costs were incurred in 1997: research and development departmental costs, $420,000; materials and supplies consumed, $60,000; compensation paid to research consultants, $125,000. It is anticipated that these costs will be recovered in 2000. What is the amount of research and development costs that Cassie Logan should record in 1997 as a charge to expense?

㉓ An intangible asset with an estimated useful life of 30 years was acquired on January 1, 1988, for $450,000. On January 1, 1998, a review was made of intangible assets and their expected service lives and it was determined that this asset had an estimated useful life of 35 more years from the date of the review. What is the amount of amortization for this intangible asset for 1998?

*㉔ An article in the financial press stated "More than half of software maker Comserve's net worth is in a pile of tapes and ring-bound books. That raises some accountants' eyebrows." What is the profession's position regarding the incurrence of costs for computer software that will be sold?

*㉕ Moe Turner Inc. has incurred $6 million in developing a computer software product for sale to third parties. Of the $6 million costs incurred, $4 million is capitalized. The product produced from this development work has generated $2 million in 1998 and is anticipated to generate another $8 million in future years. The estimated useful life of the project is 4 years. How much of the capitalized costs should be amortized in 1998?

*㉖ In 1998, Hollywood Software developed a software package for assisting calculus instruction in business colleges, at a cost of $2,000,000. Although there are tens of thousands of calculus students in the market, college instructors seem to change their minds frequently on the use of teaching aids. And, not one package has yet been ordered or delivered. Prepare an argument to advocate expensing the development cost in the current year. Offer an argument for capitalizing the development cost over its estimated useful life. Which stakeholders are harmed or benefited by either approach?

*㉗ Explain how "average excess earnings" are determined. What is the justification for the use of this method of estimating goodwill?

*㉘ Discuss two methods for estimating the value of goodwill in determining the amount that should properly be paid for it.

❖ BRIEF EXERCISES ❖

BE12-1 Doom Troopers Corporation purchases a patent from Judge Dredd Company on January 1, 1999, for $64,000. The patent has a remaining legal life of 16 years. Doom Troopers feels the patent will be useful for 10 years. Prepare Doom Troopers' journal entries to record the purchase of the patent and 1999 amortization.

BE12-2 Use the information provided in BE12-1. Assume that at January 1, 2001, the carrying amount of the patent on Doom Troopers' books is $51,200. In January, Doom Troopers spends $24,000 successfully defending a patent suit. Doom Troopers still feels the patent will be useful until the end of 2008. Prepare the journal entries to record the $24,000 expenditure and 2001 amortization.

BE12-3 Dr. Robotnik's, Inc., spent $60,000 in attorney fees, registration fees, design costs, consulting fees, and other costs while developing the trade name of its new product, the Mean Bean Machine. Prepare the journal entries to record the $60,000 expenditure and the first year's amortization, using an 8-year life.

BE12-4 Incredible Hulk Corporation commenced operations in early 1999. The corporation incurred $70,000 of costs such as fees to underwriters, legal fees, state fees, and promotional expenditures during its formation. Prepare journal entries to record the $70,000 expenditure and 1999 amortization. Assume a full year's amortization based on a 5-year life.

BE12-5 Cyborg Company leased a building on July 1, 1999, for 8 years ending June 30, 2007. The building has an estimated remaining useful life of 20 years. Cyborg immediately made improvements to the building. The improvements, which cost $89,120, have a useful life of 10 years. Prepare journal entries to record the $89,120 expenditure and 1999 amortization.

BE12-6 Knuckles Corporation obtained a franchise from Sonic Hedgehog Inc. for a cash payment of $100,000 on April 1, 1999. The franchise grants Knuckles the right to sell certain products and services for a period of 8 years. Prepare Knuckles' April 1 journal entry and December 31 adjusting entry.

BE12-7 On September 1, 1999, Dungeon Corporation acquired Dragon Enterprises for a cash payment of $750,000. At the time of purchase, Dragon's balance sheet showed assets of $620,000, liabilities of $200,000, and owners' equity of $420,000. The fair value of Dragon's assets is estimated to be $800,000. (a) Compute the amount of goodwill acquired by Dungeon. (b) Prepare the December 31 entry to record amortization, based on a 10-year life.

BE12-8 Nobunaga Corporation owns a patent that has a carrying amount of $330,000. Nobunaga expects future net cash flows from this patent to total $190,000. The fair value of the patent is $110,000. Prepare Nobunaga's journal entry, if necessary, to record the loss on impairment.

BE12-9 Evander Corporation purchased Holyfield Company 3 years ago and at that time recorded goodwill of $400,000. The carrying amount of the goodwill today is $340,000. The Holyfield Division's net assets, including the goodwill, have a carrying amount of $800,000. Evander expects net future cash flows of $700,000 from the Holyfield Division. The fair value of the division is estimated to be $525,000. Prepare Evander's journal entry, if necessary, to record impairment of the goodwill.

BE12-10 Dorsett Corporation incurred the following costs in 1999:

Cost of laboratory research aimed at discovery of new knowledge	$140,000
Cost of testing in search for product alternatives	100,000
Cost of engineering activity required to advance the design of a product to the manufacturing stage	210,000
	$450,000

Prepare the necessary 1999 journal entry or entries for Dorsett.

*__BE12-11__ Earthworm Jim Corporation has capitalized software costs of $700,000, and sales of this product the first year totaled $420,000. Earthworm Jim anticipates earning $980,000 in additional future revenues from this product, which is estimated to have an economic life of 4 years. Compute the amount of software cost amortization for the first year.

*__BE12-12__ Nigel Mansel Corporation is interested in purchasing Indy Car Company. Indy's total net income during the last 5 years is $600,000. During one of those years, Indy reported an extraordinary gain of $80,000. The fair value of Indy's identifiable net assets is $560,000. A normal rate of return is 15%, and Mansel wishes to capitalize excess earnings at 20%. Compute the estimated value of Indy's goodwill.

❖ EXERCISES ❖

E12-1 (Classification Issues—Intangibles) Presented below is a list of items that could be included in the intangible asset section of the balance sheet.

1. Investment in a subsidiary company.
2. Timberland.
3. Cost of engineering activity required to advance the design of a product to the manufacturing stage.
4. Lease prepayment (6 months' rent paid in advance).
5. Cost of equipment obtained under a capital lease.
6. Retained earnings appropriation.
7. Costs incurred in the formation of a corporation.
8. Operating losses incurred in the start-up of a business.
9. Sinking fund for repayment of bonds.
10. Cost of a franchise.
11. Goodwill generated internally.
12. Cost of testing in search for product alternatives.
13. Cost of developing computer software for internal use.
14. Goodwill acquired in the purchase of a business.
15. Cost of developing a patent.
16. Cost of purchasing a patent from an inventor.
17. Legal costs incurred in securing a patent.
18. Unrecovered costs of a successful legal suit to protect the patent.
19. Cost of modifying the design of a product or process.
20. Cost of acquiring a copyright.
21. Research and development costs.
22. Long-term receivables.
23. Cost of developing a trademark.
24. Cost of securing a trademark.

Instructions

(a) Indicate which items on the list above would generally be reported as intangible assets in the balance sheet.

(b) Indicate how, if at all, the items not reportable as intangible assets would be reported in the financial statements.

E12-2 (Classification Issues—Intangibles) Presented below is selected account information related to Martin Burke Inc. as of December 31, 1998. All these accounts have debit balances.

Cable television franchises	Film contract rights
Music copyrights	Customer lists
Research and development costs	Prepaid expenses
Goodwill	Covenants not to compete
Cash	Brand names
Discount on notes payable	Notes receivable
Accounts receivable	Investments in affiliated companies
Property, plant, and equipment	Organization cost
Leasehold improvements	Land

Instructions

Identify which items should be classified as an intangible asset. For those items not classified as an intangible asset, indicate where they would be reported in the financial statements.

E12-3 (Classification Issues—Intangible Asset) Joni Hyde Inc. has the following amounts included in its general ledger at December 31, 1998:

Organization costs	$24,000
Trademarks	15,000
Discount on bonds payable	35,000
Deposits with advertising agency for ads to promote goodwill of company	10,000
Excess of cost over book value of net assets of acquired subsidiary	75,000
Cost of equipment acquired for research and development projects	90,000
Costs of developing a secret formula for a product that is expected to be marketed for at least 20 years	80,000

Instructions

(a) On the basis of the information above, compute the total amount to be reported by Hyde for intangible assets on its balance sheet at December 31, 1998. Equipment has alternative future use.

(b) If an item is not to be included in intangible assets, explain its proper treatment for reporting purposes.

E12-4 (Intangible Amortization) Presented below is selected information for Alatorre Company. Answer each of the factual situations.

1. Alatorre purchased a patent from Vania Co. for $1,000,000 on January 1, 1995. The patent is being amortized over its remaining legal life of 10 years, expiring on January 1, 2005. During 1997, Alatorre determined that the economic benefits of the patent would not last longer than 6 years from the date of acquisition. What amount should be reported in the balance sheet for the patent, net of accumulated amortization, at December 31, 1997?

2. Alatorre bought a franchise from Alexander Co. on January 1, 1996, for $400,000. It is estimated that the franchise has a useful life of 60 years. Its carrying amount on Alexander's books at January 1, 1996, was $500,000. Alatorre has decided to amortize the franchise over the maximum period permitted. What amount should be amortized for the year ended December 31, 1997?

3. On January 1, 1993, Alatorre incurred organization costs of $275,000. Alatorre is amortizing these costs on the same basis as the maximum allowable for federal income tax purposes. What amount should be reported as unamortized organization costs as of December 31, 1997?

E12-5 (Correct Intangible Asset Account) As the recently appointed auditor for William J. Bryan Corporation, you have been asked to examine selected accounts before the 6-month financial statements of June 30, 1998, are prepared. The controller for William J. Bryan Corporation mentions that only one account (shown below) is kept for Intangible Assets.

Intangible Assets

		Debit	Credit	Balance
January 4	Research and development costs	940,000		940,000
January 5	Legal costs to obtain patent	75,000		1,015,000
January 31	Payment of 7 months' rent on property leased by Bryan	91,000		1,106,000

February 1	Stock issue costs	36,000		1,142,000
February 11	Premium on common stock		250,000	892,000
March 31	Unamortized bond discount on bonds			
	due March 31, 2018	84,000		976,000
April 30	Promotional expenses related to			
	start-up of business	207,000		1,183,000
June 30	Operating losses for first 6 months	241,000		1,424,000

Instructions

Prepare the entry or entries necessary to correct this account. Assume that the patent has a useful life of 10 years, and that organization costs are being amortized over a 5-year period.

E12-6 (Recording and Amortization of Intangibles) Rolanda Marshall Company, organized in 1998, has set up a single account for all intangible assets. The following summary discloses the debit entries that have been recorded during 1999:

1/2/99	Purchased patent (8-year life)	$ 350,000
4/1/99	Goodwill purchased (indefinite life)	360,000
7/1/99	10-year franchise; expiration date 7/1/2009	450,000
8/1/99	Payment for copyright (5-year life)	156,000
9/1/99	Research and development costs	215,000
		$1,531,000

Instructions

Prepare the necessary entries to clear the Intangible Assets account and to set up separate accounts for distinct types of intangibles. Make the entries as of December 31, 1999, recording any necessary amortization and reflecting all balances accurately as of that date (straight-line amortization).

E12-7 (Accounting for Trade Name) In early January of 1998, Gayle Crystal Corporation applied for a trade name, incurring legal costs of $16,000. In January of 1999, Gayle Crystal incurred $7,800 of legal fees in a successful defense of its trade name.

Instructions

(a) Compute 1998 amortization, 12/31/98 book value, 1999 amortization, and 12/31/99 book value if the company amortizes the trade name over the maximum allowable life.

(b) Repeat part (a), assuming a useful life of 5 years.

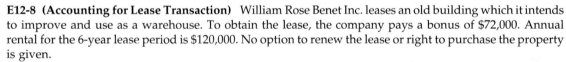 **E12-8 (Accounting for Lease Transaction)** William Rose Benet Inc. leases an old building which it intends to improve and use as a warehouse. To obtain the lease, the company pays a bonus of $72,000. Annual rental for the 6-year lease period is $120,000. No option to renew the lease or right to purchase the property is given.

After the lease is obtained, improvements costing $144,000 are made. The building has an estimated remaining useful life of 17 years.

Instructions

(a) What is the annual cost (excluding depreciation) of this lease to William Rose Benet Inc.?

(b) What amount of annual depreciation, if any, on a straight-line basis should William Rose Benet record?

E12-9 (Accounting for Organization Costs) Horace Greeley Corporation was organized in 1997 and began operations at the beginning of 1998. The company is involved in interior design consulting services. The following costs were incurred prior to the start of operations:

Attorney's fees in connection with organization of the	
company	$15,000
Improvements to leased offices prior to occupancy	25,000
Fees to underwriters for handling stock issue	4,000
Costs of meetings of incorporators to discuss	
organizational activities	7,000
State filing fees to incorporate	1,000
	$52,000

Instructions

(a) Compute the total amount of organization costs incurred by Greeley.

(b) Assuming Greeley Corporation is amortizing organization costs for financial reporting purposes on the same basis as the maximum amount allowable for federal income tax purposes, prepare the journal entry to amortize organization costs for 1998.

E12-10 (Accounting for Patents, Franchises, and R&D)   Jimmy Carter Company has provided information on intangible assets as follows:

A patent was purchased from Gerald Ford Company for $2,000,000 on January 1, 1998. Carter estimated the remaining useful life of the patent to be 10 years. The patent was carried in Ford's accounting records at a net book value of $2,000,000 when Ford sold it to Carter.

During 1999, a franchise was purchased from the Ronald Reagan Company for $480,000. In addition, 5% of revenue from the franchise must be paid to Reagan. Revenue from the franchise for 1999 was $2,500,000. Carter estimates the useful life of the franchise to be 10 years and takes a full year's amortization in the year of purchase.

Carter incurred research and development costs in 1999 as follows:

Materials and equipment	$142,000
Personnel	189,000
Indirect costs	102,000
	$433,000

Carter estimates that these costs will be recouped by December 31, 2002.

On January 1, 1999, Carter, because of recent events in the field, estimates that the remaining life of the patent purchased on January 1, 1998, is only 5 years from January 1, 1999.

Instructions
  (a) Prepare a schedule showing the intangibles section of Carter's balance sheet at December 31, 1999. Show supporting computations in good form.
  (b) Prepare a schedule showing the income statement effect for the year ended December 31, 1999, as a result of the facts above. Show supporting computations in good form.

(AICPA adapted)

E12-11 (Accounting for Patents)   Emerson Inc. has its own research department. In addition, the company purchases patents from time to time. The following statements summarize the transactions involving all patents now owned by the company.

During 1992 and 1993, $153,000 was spent developing a new process that was patented (No. 1) on March 18, 1994; additional legal and other costs were $16,490. A patent (No. 2) developed by Ralph Waldo, an inventor, was purchased for $62,500 on November 30, 1995, on which date it had 12½ years yet to run.

During 1994, 1995, and 1996, research and development activities cost $170,000. No additional patents resulted from these activities.

A patent infringement suit brought by the company against a competitor because of the manufacture of articles infringing on Patent No. 2 was successfully prosecuted at a cost of $14,200. A decision in the case was rendered in July 1996.

A competing patent (No. 3) was purchased for $57,600 on July 1, 1997. This patent had 16 years yet to run. During 1998, $60,000 has been expended on patent development: $20,000 of this amount represents the cost of a device for which a patent application has been filed, but no notification of acceptance or rejection by the Patent Office has been received. The other $40,000 represents costs incurred on uncompleted development projects.

Instructions
  (a) Compute the carrying value of these patents as of December 31, 1998, assuming that the legal life and useful life of each patent is the same and that each patent is to be amortized from the first day of the month following its acquisition.
  (b) Prepare a journal entry to record amortization for 1998.

E12-12 (Accounting for Patents)   During 1995, George Winston Corporation spent $170,000 in research and development costs. As a result, a new product called the New Age Piano was patented at additional legal and other costs of $18,000. The patent was obtained on October 1, 1995, and had a legal life of 17 years and a useful life of 10 years.

Instructions
  (a) Prepare all journal entries required in 1995 and 1996 as a result of the transactions above.
  (b) On June 1, 1997, Winston spent $9,480 to successfully prosecute a patent infringement. As a result, the estimate of useful life was extended to 12 years from June 1, 1997. Prepare all journal entries required in 1997 and 1998.
  (c) In 1999, Winston determined that a competitor's product would make the New Age Piano obsolete and the patent worthless by December 31, 2000. Prepare all journal entries required in 1999 and 2000.

E12-13 (Accounting for Goodwill) On July 1, 1998, Brigham Corporation purchased Young Company by paying $250,000 cash and issuing a $100,000 note payable to Steve Young. At July 1, 1998, the balance sheet of Young Company was as follows:

Cash	$ 50,000	Accounts payable	$200,000
Receivables	90,000	Young, capital	235,000
Inventory	100,000		$435,000
Land	40,000		
Buildings (net)	75,000		
Equipment (net)	70,000		
Trademarks	10,000		
	$435,000		

The recorded amounts all approximate current values except for land (worth $60,000), inventory (worth $125,000), and trademarks (worthless).

Instructions
(a) Prepare the July 1 entry for Brigham Corporation to record the purchase.
(b) Prepare the December 31 entry for Brigham Corporation to record amortization of goodwill. The goodwill is estimated to have a useful life of 50 years.

E12-14 (Intangible Impairment) Presented below is information related to copyrights owned by Walter de la Mare Company at December 31, 1999.

Cost	$8,600,000
Carrying amount	4,300,000
Expected future net cash flows	4,000,000
Fair value	3,200,000

Assume that Walter de la Mare Company will continue to use this copyright in the future. As of December 31, 1999, the copyright is estimated to have a remaining useful life of 10 years.

Instructions
(a) Prepare the journal entry (if any) to record the impairment of the asset at December 31, 1999. The company does not use accumulated amortization accounts.
(b) Prepare the journal entry to record amortization expense for 2000 related to the copyrights.
(c) The fair value of the copyright at December 31, 2000, is $3,400,000. Prepare the journal entry (if any) necessary to record the increase in fair value.

E12-15 (Goodwill Impairment) Presented below is net asset information (including associated goodwill of $200 million) related to the Carlos Division of Santana, Inc.

Carlos Division
NET ASSETS
as of December 31, 1999
(in millions)

Cash	$ 50
Receivables	200
Property, plant, and equipment (net)	2,600
Goodwill	200
Less: Notes payable	(2,700)
Net assets	$ 350

The purpose of this division is to develop a nuclear-powered aircraft. If successful, traveling delays associated with refueling could be substantially reduced. Many other benefits would also occur. To date, management has not had much success and is deciding whether a writedown at this time is appropriate. Management estimated its future net cash flows from the project to be $300 million. Management has also received an offer to purchase the division for $220 million.

Instructions
(a) Prepare the journal entry (if any) to record the impairment at December 31, 1999.
(b) At December 31, 2000, it is estimated that the division's fair value increased to $240 million. Prepare the journal entry (if any) to record this increase in fair value.

E12-16 (Accounting for R & D Costs) Leontyne Price Company from time to time embarks on a research program when a special project seems to offer possibilities. In 1998 the company expends $325,000 on a research project, but by the end of 1998 it is impossible to determine whether any benefit will be derived from it.

Instructions
(a) What account should be charged for the $325,000, and how should it be shown in the financial statements?
(b) The project is completed in 1999, and a successful patent is obtained. The R & D costs to complete the project are $110,000. The administrative and legal expenses incurred in obtaining patent number 472-1001-84 in 1999 total $16,000. The patent has an expected useful life of 5 years. Record these costs in journal entry form. Also, record patent amortization (full year) in 1999.
(c) In 2000, the company successfully defends the patent in extended litigation at a cost of $47,200, thereby extending the patent life to 12/31/07. What is the proper way to account for this cost? Also, record patent amortization (full year) in 2000.
(d) Additional engineering and consulting costs incurred in 2000 required to advance the design of a product to the manufacturing stage total $60,000. These costs enhance the design of the product considerably. Discuss the proper accounting treatment for this cost.

E12-17 (Accounting for R & D Costs) Josha Heifitz Company incurred the following costs during 1998:

Quality control during commercial production, including routine testing of products	$58,000
Laboratory research aimed at discovery of new knowledge	68,000
Testing for evaluation of new products	24,000
Modification of the formulation of a plastics product	26,000
Engineering follow-through in an early phase of commercial production	15,000
Adaptation of an existing capability to a particular requirement or customer's need as a part of continuing commercial activity	13,000
Trouble-shooting in connection with breakdowns during commercial production	29,000
Searching for applications of new research findings	19,000

Instructions
Compute the total amount Josha Heifitz should classify and expense as research and development costs for 1998.

E12-18 (Accounting for R & D Costs) Thomas More Company incurred the following costs during 1998 in connection with its research and development activities:

Cost of equipment acquired that will have alternative uses in future research and development projects over the next 5 years (uses straight-line depreciation)	$280,000
Materials consumed in research and development projects	59,000
Consulting fees paid to outsiders for research and development projects	100,000
Personnel costs of persons involved in research and development projects	128,000
Indirect costs reasonably allocable to research and development projects	50,000
Materials purchased for future research and development projects	34,000

Instructions
Compute the amount to be reported as research and development expense by More on its income statement for 1998. Assume equipment purchased at beginning of year.

E12-19 (Accounting for R & D Costs) Listed below are four independent situations involving research and development costs:

1. During 1999, Jake Sisco Co. incurred the following costs:

Research and development services performed by Miles Company for Sisco	$350,000
Testing for evaluation of new products	300,000
Laboratory research aimed at discovery of new knowledge	425,000

For the year ended December 31, 1999, Jake Sisco Co. should report research and development expense of how much?

2. Odo Corp. incurred the following costs during the year ended December 31, 1999:

Design, construction, and testing of preproduction prototypes and models	$290,000
Routine, on-going efforts to refine, enrich, or otherwise improve upon the qualities of an existing product	250,000
Quality control during commercial production including routine testing of products	300,000
Laboratory research aimed at discovery of new knowledge	420,000

What is the total amount to be classified and expensed as research and development for 1999?

3. Quark Company incurred costs in 1999 as follows:

Equipment acquired for use in various research and development projects	$900,000
Depreciation on the equipment above	210,000
Materials used in R & D	300,000
Compensation costs of personnel in R & D	400,000
Outside consulting fees for R & D work	220,000
Indirect costs appropriately allocated to R & D	260,000

What is the total amount of research and development that should be reported in Quark's 1999 income statement?

4. Julian Inc. incurred the following costs during the year ended December 31, 1999:

Laboratory research aimed at discovery of new knowledge	$200,000
Radical modification to the formulation of a chemical product	145,000
Research and development costs reimbursable under a contract to perform research and development for Bashir Inc.	350,000
Testing for evaluation of new products	225,000

What is the total amount to be classified and expensed as research and development for 1999?

Instructions
Provide the correct answer to each of the four situations.

*E12-20 (Accounting for Computer Software Costs) New Jersey Inc. has capitalized computer software costs of $3,600,000 on its new "Trenton" software package. Revenues from 1998 (first year) sales are $2,000,000; additional future revenues from "Trenton" for the remainder of its economic life, through 2002, are estimated to be $10,000,000.

Instructions
    (a) What method or methods of amortization are to be applied in the writeoff of capitalized computer software costs?
    (b) Compute the amount of amortization for 1998 for "Trenton."

*E12-21 (Accounting for Computer Software Costs) During 1998, Delaware Enterprises spent $5,000,000 developing its new Dover software package. Of this amount, $2,200,000 was spent before technological feasibility was established for the product, which is to be marketed to third parties. The package was completed at December 31, 1998. Delaware expects a useful life of 8 years for this product with total revenues of $16,000,000. During the first year (1999), Delaware realizes revenues of $3,200,000.

Instructions
    (a) Prepare journal entries required in 1998 for the foregoing facts.
    (b) Prepare the entry to record amortization at December 31, 1999.
    (c) At what amount should the computer software costs be reported in the December 31, 1999, balance sheet? Could the net realizable value of this asset affect your answer?
    (d) What disclosures are required in the December 31, 1999, financial statements for the computer software costs?
    (e) How would your answers for (a), (b), and (c) be different if the computer software was developed for internal use?

*E12-22 (Compute Goodwill) The net assets of Frankie Beverly Company excluding goodwill totals $800,000 and earnings for the last 5 years total $890,000. Included in the latter figure are extraordinary gains of $75,000, nonrecurring losses of $40,000, and sales commissions of $15,000. In developing a sales price for the business a 14% return on net worth is considered normal for the industry, and annual excess earnings are to be capitalized at 20% in arriving at goodwill.

Instructions
Compute estimated goodwill.

*E12-23 (Compute Normal Earnings) Cliff Barnes Petroleum Corporation's pretax accounting income for the year 1998 was $850,000 and included the following items:

Amortization of goodwill	$ 60,000
Amortization of identifiable intangibles	57,000
Depreciation on building	80,000
Extraordinary losses	44,000
Extraordinary gains	150,000
Profit-sharing payments to employees	65,000

Ewing Oil Industries is seeking to purchase Cliff Barnes Petroleum Corporation. In attempting to measure Barnes' normal earnings for 1998, Ewing determines that the fair value of the building is triple the book value and that the remaining economic life is double that used by Barnes. Ewing would continue the profit-sharing payments to employees; such payments are based on income before depreciation and amortization.

Instructions
Compute the normal earnings (for purposes of computing goodwill) of Barnes Petroleum Corporation for the year 1998.

*E12-24 (Compute Goodwill) Texas News Inc. is considering acquiring Austin Company in total as a going concern. Texas makes the following computations and conclusions:

1. The fair value of the identifiable assets of Austin Company is $720,000.
2. The liabilities of Austin Company are $380,000.
3. A fair estimate of annual earnings for the indefinite future is $120,000 per year.
4. Considering the risk and potential of Austin Company, Texas feels that it must earn a 25% return on its investment.

Instructions
(a) How much should Texas be willing to pay for Austin Company?
(b) How much of the purchase price would be goodwill?

*E12-25 (Compute Goodwill) As the president of Tennessee Recording Corp., you are considering purchasing Nashville CD Corp., whose balance sheet is summarized as follows:

Current assets	$ 300,000	Current liabilities	$ 300,000
Fixed assets (net of depreciation)	700,000	Long-term liabilities	500,000
Other assets	300,000	Common stock	400,000
		Retained earnings	100,000
Total	$1,300,000	Total	$1,300,000

The fair market value of current assets is $550,000 because of the undervaluation of inventory. The normal rate of return on net assets for the industry is 15%. The average expected annual earnings projected for Nashville CD Corp. is $140,000.

Instructions
Assuming that the excess earnings continue for 5 years, how much would you be willing to pay for goodwill? (Estimate goodwill by the present-value method.)

*E12-26 (Compute Goodwill) Net income figures for Maryland Company are as follows:

1994—$64,000	1997—$80,000
1995—$50,000	1998—$75,000
1996—$81,000	

Tangible net assets of this company are appraised at $400,000 on December 31, 1998. This business is to be acquired by Annapolis Co. early in 1999.

Instructions
What amount should be paid for goodwill if:
(a) 14% is assumed to be a normal rate of return on net tangible assets, and average excess earnings for the last 5 years are to be capitalized at 25%?
(b) 12% is assumed to be a normal rate of return on net tangible assets, and payment is to be made for excess earnings for the last 4 years?

*E12-27 (Compute Goodwill) Virginia Corporation is interested in acquiring Richmond Plastics Company. It has determined that Richmond Company's excess earnings have averaged approximately $150,000 annually over the last 6 years. Richmond Company agrees with the computation of $150,000 as the approximate excess earnings and feels that such amount should be capitalized over an unlimited period at a 20% rate. Virginia Corporation feels that because of increased competition the excess earnings of Richmond Company will continue for 7 more years at best and that a 15% discount rate is appropriate.

Instructions
  (a) How far apart are the positions of these two parties?
  (b) Is there really any difference in the two approaches used by the two parties in evaluating Richmond Company's goodwill? Explain.

*E12-28 (Compute Goodwill) West Virginia Corporation is contemplating the purchase of Charleston Industries and evaluating the amount of goodwill to be recognized in the purchase.
  Charleston reported the following net incomes:

1993	$170,000
1994	200,000
1995	240,000
1996	250,000
1997	380,000

Charleston has indicated that 1997 net income included the sale of one of its warehouses at a gain of $115,000 (net of tax). Net identifiable assets of Charleston have a total fair market value of $900,000.

Instructions
Calculate goodwill in the following cases, assuming that expected income is to be a simple average of **normal income** for the past 5 years:
  (a) Goodwill is determined by capitalizing average net earnings at 16%.
  (b) Goodwill is determined by presuming a 16% return on identifiable net assets and capitalizing excess earnings at 25%.

*E12-29 (Compute Fair Value of Identifiable Assets) Bret Harte Company bought a business that would yield exactly a 20% annual rate of return on its investment. Of the total amount paid for the business, $80,000 was deemed to be goodwill, and the remaining value was attributable to the identifiable net assets.
  Bret Harte Company projected that the estimated annual future earnings of the new business would be equal to its average annual ordinary earnings over the past 4 years. The total net income over the past 4 years was $380,000, which included an extraordinary loss of $35,000 in one year and an extraordinary gain of $115,000 in one of the other 3 years.

Instructions
Compute the fair market value of the identifiable net assets that Bret Harte Company purchased in this transaction.

❖ PROBLEMS ❖

P12-1 (Correct Intangible Asset Account) Esplanade Co., organized in 1997, has set up a single account for all intangible assets. The following summary discloses the debit entries that have been recorded during 1997 and 1998.

Intangible Assets

7/1/97	8-year franchise; expiration date 6/30/05	$ 42,000
10/1/97	Advance payment on leasehold (2-year lease)	28,000
12/31/97	Net loss for 1997 including state incorporation fee, $1,000, and related legal fees of organizing, $5,000 (all fees incurred in 1997)	16,000
1/2/98	Patent purchased (10-year life)	74,000
3/1/98	Cost of developing a secret formula (indefinite life)	75,000
4/1/98	Goodwill purchased (indefinite life)	278,400
6/1/98	Legal fee for successful defense of patent purchased above	12,650
9/1/98	Research and development costs	160,000

Instructions
Prepare the necessary entries to clear the Intangible Assets account and to set up separate accounts for distinct types of intangibles. Make the entries as of December 31, 1998, recording any necessary amortization and reflecting all balances accurately as of that date. (Assume a 40-year amortization for intangibles unless specified. Ignore income tax effects.)

P12-2 (Accounting for Patents) Ankara Laboratories holds a valuable patent (No. 758-6002-1A) on a precipitator that prevents certain types of air pollution. Ankara does not manufacture or sell the products and processes it develops; it conducts research and develops products and processes which it patents, and then assigns the patents to manufacturers on a royalty basis. Occasionally it sells a patent. The history of Ankara patent number 758-6002-1A is as follows:

Date	Activity	Cost
1988–1989	Research conducted to develop precipitator	$384,000
Jan. 1990	Design and construction of a prototype	87,600
March 1990	Testing of models	42,000
Jan. 1991	Fees paid engineers and lawyers to prepare patent application; patent granted July 1, 1991	62,050
Nov. 1992	Engineering activity necessary to advance the design of the precipitator to the manufacturing stage	81,500
Dec. 1993	Legal fees paid to successfully defend precipitator patent	35,700
April 1994	Research aimed at modifying the design of the patented precipitator	43,000
July 1998	Legal fees paid in unsuccessful patent infringement suit against a competitor	34,000

Ankara assumed a useful life of 17 years when it received the initial precipitator patent. On January 1, 1996, it revised its useful life estimate downward to 5 remaining years. Amortization is computed for a full year if the cost is incurred prior to July 1, and no amortization for the year if the cost is incurred after June 30. The company's year ends December 31.

Instructions
Compute the carrying value of patent No. 758-6002-1A on each of the following dates:
(a) December 31, 1991.
(b) December 31, 1995.
(c) December 31, 1998.

P12-3 (Accounting for Franchise, Patents, and Trade Name) Information concerning Haerhpin Corporation's intangible assets is as follows:

1. On January 1, 1999, Haerhpin signed an agreement to operate as a franchisee of Hsian Copy Service, Inc. for an initial franchise fee of $75,000. Of this amount, $15,000 was paid when the agreement was signed and the balance is payable in 4 annual payments of $15,000 each, beginning January 1, 2000. The agreement provides that the down payment is not refundable and no future services are required of the franchisor. The present value at January 1, 1999, of the 4 annual payments discounted at 14% (the implicit rate for a loan of this type) is $43,700. The agreement also provides that 5% of the revenue from the franchise must be paid to the franchisor annually. Haerhpin's revenue from the franchise for 1999 was $950,000. Haerhpin estimates the useful life of the franchise to be 10 years. (*Hint:* You may refer to Appendix 19A to determine the proper accounting treatment for the franchise fee and payments.)
2. Haerhpin incurred $65,000 of experimental and development costs in its laboratory to develop a patent which was granted on January 2, 1999. Legal fees and other costs associated with registration of the patent totaled $13,600. Haerhpin estimates that the useful life of the patent will be 8 years.
3. A trademark was purchased from Shanghai Company for $32,000 on July 1, 1996. Expenditures for successful litigation in defense of the trademark totaling $8,160 were paid on July 1, 1999. Haerhpin estimates that the useful life of the trademark will be 20 years from the date of acquisition.

Instructions
(a) Prepare a schedule showing the intangible section of Haerhpin's balance sheet at December 31, 1999. Show supporting computations in good form.
(b) Prepare a schedule showing all expenses resulting from the transactions that would appear on Haerhpin's income statement for the year ended December 31, 1999. Show supporting computations in good form.

(AICPA adapted)

P12-4 (Amortization of Various Intangibles) The following information relates to the intangible assets of Rube Goldberg Product Company:

	Organization Costs	Goodwill	Purchased Patent Costs
Original cost at 1/1/1998	$80,000	$280,000	$48,000
Useful life at 1/1/1998 (estimated)	Indefinite[a]	50 years	6 years

[a]The company has decided to write off for accounting and tax purposes the organization costs as quickly as the tax law allows.

Instructions

(a) Assuming straight-line amortization, compute the amount of the amortization of **each** item for 1998 in accordance with generally accepted accounting principles.

(b) Prepare the journal entries for the amortization of organization costs and goodwill for 1998.

(c) Assume that at January 1, 1999, Rube Goldberg Product Company incurred $6,000 of legal fees in successfully defending the rights to the patents. Prepare the entry for the year 1999 to amortize the patents.

(d) Assume that at the beginning of year 2000 the company decided that the patent costs would be applicable only for the years 2000 and 2001. (A competitor has developed a product that will eventually make Rube Goldberg Product's obsolete.) Record the amortization of the patent costs at the end of 2000.

P12-5 (Accounting for R & D Costs) During 1996, Florence Nightingale Tool Company purchased a building site for its proposed research and development laboratory at a cost of $60,000. Construction of the building was started in 1996. The building was completed on December 31, 1997, at a cost of $280,000 and was placed in service on January 2, 1998. The estimated useful life of the building for depreciation purposes was 20 years; the straight-line method of depreciation was to be employed and there was no estimated net salvage value.

Management estimates that about 50% of the projects of the research and development group will result in long-term benefits (i.e., at least 10 years) to the corporation. The remaining projects either benefit the current period or are abandoned before completion. A summary of the number of projects and the direct costs incurred in conjunction with the research and development activities for 1998 appears below.

Upon recommendation of the research and development group Florence Nightingale Tool Company acquired a patent for manufacturing rights at a cost of $80,000. The patent was acquired on April 1, 1997, and has an economic life of 10 years.

	Number of Projects	Salaries and Employee Benefits	Other Expenses (excluding Building Depreciation Charges)
Completed projects with long-term benefits	15	$ 90,000	$50,000
Abandoned projects or projects that benefit the current period	10	65,000	15,000
Projects in process—results indeterminate	5	40,000	12,000
Total	30	$195,000	$77,000

Instructions

If generally accepted accounting principles were followed, how would the items above relating to research and development activities be reported on the company's

(a) Income statement for 1998?

(b) Balance sheet as of December 31, 1998?

Be sure to give account titles and amounts, and briefly justify your presentation.

(CMA adapted)

*P12-6 (Accounting for Purchase of a Business) Anshan Inc. has recently become interested in acquiring a South American plant to handle many of its production functions in that market. One possible candidate is La Paz Inc., a closely held corporation, whose owners have decided to sell their business if a proper settlement can be obtained. La Paz's balance sheet appears as follows:

Current assets	$150,000	Current liabilities	$ 80,000
Investments	50,000	Long-term debt	100,000
Plant assets (net)	400,000	Capital stock	50,000
Total assets	$600,000	Additional paid-in capital	170,000
		Retained earnings	200,000
		Total equities	$600,000

Anshan has hired Palermo Appraisal Corporation to determine the proper price to pay for La Paz Inc. The appraisal firm finds that the investments have a fair market value of $150,000 and that inventory is understated by $80,000. All other assets and equities are properly stated. An examination of the company's income for the last 4 years indicates that the net income has steadily increased. In 1998, the company had a net operating income of $100,000, and this income should increase 20% each year over the next 4 years. Anshan believes that a normal return in this type of business is 18% on net assets. The asset investment in the South American plant is expected to stay the same for the next 4 years.

Instructions

(a) Palermo Appraisal Corporation has indicated that the fair value of the company can be estimated in a number of ways. Prepare an estimate of the value of La Paz Inc., assuming that any goodwill will be computed as:

1. The capitalization of the average excess earnings of La Paz Inc. at 18%.
2. The purchase of average excess earnings over the next 4 years.
3. The capitalization of average excess earnings of La Paz Inc. at 24%.
4. The present value of the average excess earnings over the next four years discounted at 15%.

(b) La Paz Inc. is willing to sell the business for $1,000,000. How do you believe Palermo Appraisal should advise Anshan?

(c) If Anshan were to pay $770,000 to purchase the assets and assume the liabilities of La Paz Inc., how would this transaction be reflected on Anshan's books?

P12-7 (Comprehensive Problem on Intangibles) Yuka Sato Corporation was incorporated on January 3, 1997. The corporation's financial statements for its first year's operations were not examined by a CPA. You have been engaged to audit the financial statements for the year ended December 31, 1998, and your audit is substantially completed. The corporation's trial balance appears below.

Yuka Sato Corporation TRIAL BALANCE December 31, 1998		
	Debit	Credit
Cash	$ 15,000	
Accounts Receivable	73,000	
Allowance for Doubtful Accounts		$ 1,460
Inventories	50,200	
Machinery	82,000	
Equipment	37,000	
Accumulated Depreciation		26,200
Patents	128,200	
Leasehold Improvements	36,100	
Prepaid Expenses	13,000	
Organization Costs	32,000	
Goodwill	30,000	
Licensing Agreement No. 1	60,000	
Licensing Agreement No. 2	56,000	
Accounts Payable		73,000
Unearned Revenue		17,280
Capital Stock		300,000
Retained Earnings, January 1, 1998		159,060
Sales		720,000
Cost of Goods Sold	475,000	
Selling and General Expenses	180,000	
Interest Expense	9,500	
Extraordinary Losses	20,000	
Totals	$1,297,000	$1,297,000

The following information relates to accounts that may yet require adjustment.

1. Patents for Sato's manufacturing process were acquired January 2, 1998, at a cost of $93,500. An additional $34,700 was spent in December 1998, to improve machinery covered by the patents and charged to the Patents account. Depreciation on fixed assets has been properly recorded for 1998 in accordance with Sato's practice, which provides a full year's depreciation for property on hand June 30 and no depreciation otherwise. Sato uses the straight-line method for all depreciation and amortization and the legal life on its patents.
2. On January 3, 1997, Sato purchased licensing agreement No. 1, which was believed to have an unlimited useful life. The balance in the Licensing Agreement No. 1 account includes its purchase price of $57,000 and expenses of $3,000 related to the acquisition. On January 1, 1998, Sato purchases licensing agreement No. 2, which has a life expectancy of 10 years. The balance in the Licensing Agreement No. 2 account includes its $54,000 purchase price and $6,000 in acquisition expenses, but it has been reduced by a credit of $4,000 for the advance collection of 1999 revenue from the agreement.

   In late December 1997, an explosion caused a permanent 70% reduction in the expected revenue-producing value of licensing agreement No. 1, and in January 1999, a flood caused additional damage that rendered the agreement worthless.

3. The balance in the Goodwill account includes (a) $18,000 paid December 30, 1997, for an advertising program it is estimated will assist in increasing Sato's sales over a period of 4 years following the disbursement, and (b) legal expenses of $12,000 incurred for Sato's incorporation on January 3, 1997.

4. The Leasehold Improvements account includes (a) the $15,000 cost of improvements with a total estimated useful life of 12 years, which Sato, as tenant, made to leased premises in January 1997, (b) movable assembly line equipment costing $15,000 that was installed in the leased premises in December 1998, and (c) real estate taxes of $6,100 paid by Sato in 1998, which under the terms of the lease should have been paid by the landlord. Sato paid its rent in full during 1998. A 10-year non-renewable lease was signed January 3, 1997, for the leased building that Sato used in manufacturing operations.

5. The balance in the Organization Costs account properly includes costs incurred during the organizational period. The corporation has exercised its option to amortize organization costs over a 60-month period for federal income tax purposes and wishes to amortize these for accounting purposes on the same basis.

Instructions

Prepare an 8-column worksheet to adjust accounts that require adjustment and include columns for an income statement and a balance sheet.

A separate account should be used for the accumulation of each type of amortization and for each prior period adjustment. Formal adjusting journal entries and financial statements are **not** required. (*Hint:* Make sure that Licensing Agreement No. 1 is amortized over the maximum life required in *APB Opinion No. 17* before the explosion damage loss is determined.)

(AICPA adapted)

*P12-8 (Compute Goodwill)   Presented below are financial forecasts related to Barbara Bush Company for the next 10 years.

Forecasted average earnings (per year)	$ 70,000
Forecasted market value of net assets, exclusive of goodwill (average over 10 years)	340,000

Instructions

You have been asked to compute goodwill under the following methods. The normal rate of return on net assets for the industry is 15%.

(a) Goodwill is equal to 5 years' excess earnings.

(b) Goodwill is equal to the present value of 5 years' excess earnings discounted at 12%.

(c) Goodwill is equal to the average excess earnings capitalized at 16%.

(d) Goodwill is equal to average excess earnings capitalized at the normal rate of return for the industry of 15%.

*P12-9 (Compute Goodwill)   Batman Corp., a high-flying conglomerate, has recently been involved in discussions with Robin Inc. As its CPA, you have been instructed by Batman to conduct a purchase audit of Robin's books to determine a possible purchase price for Robin's net assets. The following information is found.

Total identifiable assets of Robin's (fair market value)	$250,000
Liabilities	60,000
Average rate of return on net assets for Robin's industry	15%
Forecasted earnings per year based on past earnings figures	35,000

Instructions

(a) Batman asked you to determine the purchase price on the basis of the following assumptions:

1. Goodwill is equal to 3 years' excess earnings.

2. Goodwill is equal to the present value of excess earnings discounted at 15% for 3 years.

3. Goodwill is equal to the capitalization of excess earnings at 15%.

4. Goodwill is equal to the capitalization of excess earnings at 25%.

(b) Batman asks you which of the methods above is the most theoretically sound. Justify your answer. Any assumptions made should be clearly indicated.

❖ CONCEPTUAL CASES ❖

C12-1 (Patent Cost)   In examining the books of Annita Sorenstam Mfg. Company, you find on the December 31, 1998, balance sheet, the item, "Costs of patents, $922,000."

Referring to the ledger accounts, you note the following items regarding one patent acquired in 1995:

1995	Legal costs incurred in defending the validity of the patent	$ 55,000
1997	Legal costs in prosecuting an infringement suit	94,000
1998	Legal costs (additional expenses) in the infringement suit	44,500
1998	Cost of improvements (unpatented) on the patented device	151,200

There are no credits in the account, and no allowance for amortization has been set up on the books for any of the patents. Three other patents issued in 1992, 1994, and 1995 were developed by the staff of the client. The patented articles are currently very marketable, but it is estimated that they will be in demand only for the next few years.

Instructions

Discuss the items included in the Patent account from an accounting standpoint.

(AICPA adapted)

C12-2 (Accounting for Intangible-Type Expenditures) Missie McGeorge, Inc., is a large, publicly held corporation. Listed below are six selected expenditures made by the company during the current fiscal year ended April 30, 1998. The proper accounting treatment of these transactions must be determined in order that McGeorge's annual financial statements will be prepared in accordance with generally accepted accounting principles.

1. McGeorge, Inc. spent $3,000,000 on a program designed to improve relations with its dealers. This project was favorably received by the dealers and McGeorge's management believes that significant future benefits should be received from this program. The program was conducted during the fourth quarter of the current fiscal year.
2. A pilot plant was constructed during 1997–98 at a cost of $5,500,000 to test a new production process. The plant will be operated for approximately 5 years. At that time, the company will make a decision regarding the economic value of the process. The pilot plant is too small for commercial production, so it will be dismantled when the test is over.
3. A new product will be introduced next year. The company spent $3,400,000 during the current year for design of tools, jigs, molds, and dies for this product.
4. McGeorge, Inc. purchased Eagle Company for $6,000,000 in cash in early August 1997. The fair market value of the identifiable assets of Eagle was $5,200,000.
5. A large advertising campaign was conducted during April 1998 to introduce a new product to be released during the first quarter of the 1998–99 fiscal year. The advertising campaign cost $3,500,000.
6. During the first six months of the 1997–98 fiscal year, $400,000 was expended for legal work in connection with a successful patent application. The patent became effective November 1, 1997. The legal life of the patent is 17 years and the economic life of the patent is expected to be approximately 10 years.

Instructions

For each of the six expenditures presented, determine and justify:
 (a) The amount, if any, that should be capitalized and be included on McGeorge's statement of financial position prepared as of April 30, 1998.
 (b) The amount that should be included in McGeorge's statement of income for the year ended April 30, 1998.

(CMA adapted)

C12-3 (Accounting for Pollution Expenditure) Phil Mickelson Company operates several plants at which limestone is processed into quicklime and hydrated lime. The Eagle Ridge plant, where most of the equipment was installed many years ago, continually deposits a dusty white substance over the surrounding countryside. Citing the unsanitary condition of the neighboring community of Scales Mound, the pollution of the Galena River, and the high incidence of lung disease among workers at Eagle Ridge, the state's Pollution Control Agency has ordered the installation of air pollution control equipment. Also, the Agency has assessed a substantial penalty, which will be used to clean up Scales Mound. After considering the costs involved (which could not have been reasonably estimated prior to the Agency's action), Phil Mickelson Company decides to comply with the Agency's orders, the alternative being to cease operations at Eagle Ridge at the end of the current fiscal year. The officers of Mickelson agree that the air pollution control equipment should be capitalized and depreciated over its useful life, but they disagree over the period(s) to which the penalty should be charged.

Instructions

Discuss the conceptual merits and reporting requirements of accounting for the penalty as a:
 (a) Charge to the current period.

(b) Correction of prior periods.

(c) Capitalizable item to be amortized over future periods.

(AICPA adapted)

C12-4 (Accounting for Pre-Opening Costs) After securing lease commitments from several major stores, Lobo Shopping Center, Inc. was organized and built a shopping center in a growing suburb.

The shopping center would have opened on schedule on January 1, 1998, if it had not been struck by a severe tornado in December; it opened for business on October 1, 1998. All of the additional construction costs that were incurred as a result of the tornado were covered by insurance.

In July 1997, in anticipation of the scheduled January opening, a permanent staff had been hired to promote the shopping center, obtain tenants for the uncommitted space, and manage the property.

A summary of some of the costs incurred in 1997 and the first nine months of 1998 follows.

	1997	January 1, 1998 through September 30, 1998
Interest on mortgage bonds	$720,000	$540,000
Cost of obtaining tenants	300,000	360,000
Promotional advertising	540,000	557,000

The promotional advertising campaign was designed to familiarize shoppers with the center. Had it been known in time that the center would not open until October 1998, the 1997 expenditure for promotional advertising would not have been made. The advertising had to be repeated in 1998.

All of the tenants who had leased space in the shopping center at the time of the tornado accepted the October occupancy date on condition that the monthly rental charges for the first 9 months of 1998 be canceled.

Instructions
Explain how each of the costs for 1997 and the first 9 months of 1998 should be treated in the accounts of the shopping center corporation. Give the reasons for each treatment.

(AICPA adapted)

C12-5 (Accounting for Patents) On June 30, 1998, your client, Bearcat Company, was granted two patents covering plastic cartons that it has been producing and marketing profitably for the past 3 years. One patent covers the manufacturing process and the other covers the related products.

Bearcat executives tell you that these patents represent the most significant breakthrough in the industry in the past 30 years. The products have been marketed under the registered trademarks Evertight, Duratainer, and Sealrite. Licenses under the patents have already been granted by your client to other manufacturers in the United States and abroad and are producing substantial royalties.

On July 1, Bearcat commenced patent infringement actions against several companies whose names you recognize as those of substantial and prominent competitors. Bearcat's management is optimistic that these suits will result in a permanent injunction against the manufacture and sale of the infringing products and collection of damages for loss of profits caused by the alleged infringement.

The financial vice-president has suggested that the patents be recorded at the discounted value of expected net royalty receipts.

Instructions
(a) What is the meaning of "discounted value of expected net receipts"? Explain.

(b) How would such a value be calculated for net royalty receipts?

(c) What basis of valuation for Bearcat's patents would be generally accepted in accounting? Give supporting reasons for this basis.

(d) Assuming no practical problems of implementation and ignoring generally accepted accounting principles, what is the preferable basis of valuation for patents? Explain.

(e) What would be the preferable theoretical basis of amortization? Explain.

(f) What recognition, if any, should be made of the infringement litigation in the financial statements for the year ending September 30, 1998? Discuss.

(AICPA adapted)

C12-6 (Accounting for Goodwill) Ecco Co., a retail propane gas distributor, has increased its annual sales volume to a level three times greater than the annual sales of a dealer it purchased in 1995 in order to begin operations.

The Board of Directors of Ecco Co. recently received an offer to negotiate the sale of Ecco to a large competitor. As a result, the majority of the Board wants to increase the stated value of goodwill on the balance sheet to reflect the larger sales volume developed through intensive promotion and the current market price of sales gallonage. A few of the Board members, however, would prefer to eliminate goodwill altogether from the balance sheet in order to prevent "possible misinterpretations." Goodwill was recorded properly in 1995.

Instructions

(a) Discuss the meaning of the term "goodwill."

*(b) List the techniques used to calculate the tentative value of goodwill in negotiations to purchase a going concern.

(c) Why are the book and market values of the goodwill of Ecco Co. different?

(d) Discuss the propriety of
   1. Increasing the stated value of goodwill prior to the negotiations.
   2. Eliminating goodwill completely from the balance sheet prior to negotiations.

(AICPA adapted)

C12-7 (Accounting for Research and Development Costs)   Indiana Jones Co. is in the process of developing a revolutionary new product. A new division of the company was formed to develop, manufacture, and market this new product. As of year-end (December 31, 1998) the new product has not been manufactured for resale; however, a prototype unit was built and is in operation.

Throughout 1998 the new division incurred certain costs. These costs include design and engineering studies, prototype manufacturing costs, administrative expenses (including salaries of administrative personnel), and market research costs. In addition, approximately $900,000 in equipment (estimated useful life—10 years) was purchased for use in developing and manufacturing the new product. Approximately $315,000 of this equipment was built specifically for the design development of the new product; the remaining $585,000 of equipment was used to manufacture the pre-production prototype and will be used to manufacture the new product once it is in commercial production.

Instructions

(a) How are "research" and "development" defined in *Statement of Financial Accounting Standards No. 2*?

(b) Briefly indicate the practical and conceptual reasons for the conclusion reached by the Financial Accounting Standards Board on accounting and reporting practices for research and development costs.

(c) In accordance with *Statement of Financial Accounting Standards No. 2*, how should the various costs of Indiana Jones described above be recorded on the financial statements for the year ended December 31, 1998?

(AICPA adapted)

*C12-8 (Computer Software Costs)   During the examination of the financial statements of El Viento Corp., your assistant calls attention to significant costs incurred in the development of the computer software for major segments of the sales and inventory scheduling systems (internal use).

The computer software development costs will benefit future periods to the extent that the systems change slowly and the program instructions are compatible with new equipment acquired at 3- to 6-year intervals. The service value of the software is affected almost entirely by changes in the technology of systems and EDP equipment and does not decline with the number of times the program is used. Because many system changes are minor, program instructions frequently can be modified with only minor losses in program efficiency. The frequency of such changes tends to increase with the passage of time.

Instructions

(a) Discuss the propriety of classifying the unamortized computer software development costs as
   1. A prepaid expense.
   2. An intangible asset.
   3. A tangible fixed asset.

(b) Discuss the propriety of amortizing the computer software development costs by means of
   1. The straight-line method.
   2. A decreasing-charge method (e.g., the sum-of-the-years'-digits method).
   3. A variable-charge method (e.g., the units-of-production method).

(c) If the computer software had been developed for sale (external use), how should the development cost be accounted for and amortized?

(AICPA adapted)

❖USING YOUR JUDGMENT❖

❖ FINANCIAL REPORTING PROBLEM—INTEL CORPORATION

Refer to the financial statements and accompanying notes and discussion of Intel Corporation presented in Appendix 5B and answer the following questions:

Instructions
1. Does Intel report any intangible assets, especially goodwill, in its 1995 financial statements and accompanying notes?
2. How much research and development (R&D) cost was expensed by Intel in 1995 and in 1994? What percentage of sales revenue and net income did Intel spend on R&D in 1995 and 1994? How much does Intel expect to spend on R&D in 1996?

❖ FINANCIAL STATEMENT ANALYSIS CASES

*Case 1 (Microsoft versus Oracle)

As noted in the chapter, most expenditures for research and development must be expensed. One exception is that computer software companies are allowed to capitalize some software development costs and record them as assets on their books. Any capitalized software costs are then amortized over the life of the software. The implementation of this rule differs across companies, with some capitalizing many costs, while others expense nearly all of their costs. For example, in 1995 Microsoft incurred research and development costs of $860 million, and capitalized none of these costs. Oracle incurred research and development costs of $301 million, and capitalized $48 million during 1995.

The following additional facts are also available for 1995.

(all dollars in millions)	Company	
	Microsoft	Oracle
Total revenue	$5,937	$2,966
Net income	$1,453	$ 442

Instructions
(a) If you are evaluating the performance of Microsoft versus that of Oracle, what implications do their different policies on capitalization of software development expenditures have on your analysis?
(b) Which company spends a greater percentage of its revenue on developing new products? What implications might this have for the future performance of the companies?
(c) SoftKey International Inc., headquartered in Cambridge, Massachusetts, noted in its 1994 report that, beginning in 1994, it changed the estimated life of its computer software for amortization purposes from a 3 year life to a 12 year life. What implications does this have for analysis of SoftKey's results?

Case 2 (Merck and Johnson & Johnson)

Merck and Co., Inc. and Johnson & Johnson are two leading producers of health care products. Each has considerable assets, as well as expending considerable funds each year toward the development of new products. The development of a new health care product is often very expensive, and risky. New products frequently must undergo considerable testing before approval for distribution to the public. For example, it took Johnson & Johnson 4 years and $200 million to develop its 1-DAY ACUVUE contact lenses. Below are some basic data compiled from the 1994 financial statements of these two companies.

(all dollars in millions)	Johnson & Johnson	Merck
Total assets	$15,668	$21,857
Total revenue	15,734	14,970
Net income	2,006	2,997
Research and development expense	1,278	1,230
Intangible assets	2,403	7,212

Instructions

(a) What kinds of intangible assets might a health care products company have? Does the composition of these intangibles matter to investors—that is, would it be perceived differently if all of Merck's intangibles were goodwill, than if all of its intangibles were patents?

(b) By employing the total asset turnover ratio, determine which company is using its assets more effectively. (Note, 1993 total assets were $19,928 million for Merck and $12,242 million for Johnson & Johnson.)

(c) Suppose the president of Merck has come to you for advice. He has noted that by eliminating research and development expenditures the company could have reported $1.3 billion more in net income in 1994. He is frustrated because much of the research never results in a product, or the products take years to develop. He says shareholders are eager for higher returns, so he is considering eliminating research and development expenditures for at least a couple of years. What would you advise?

(d) The notes to Merck's financial statements note that Merck has goodwill of $4.1 billion. Where does recorded goodwill come from? Is it necessarily a good thing to have a lot of goodwill on your books?

❖ COMPARATIVE ANALYSIS CASE

The Coca-Cola Company versus PepsiCo, Inc.

Instructions

Go to our Web site and, using The Coca-Cola Company and PepsiCo, Inc. annual report information, answer the following questions.

1. (a) What amounts for intangible assets were reported in their respective balance sheets by Coca-Cola and PepsiCo? (b) What percentage of total assets is each of these reported amounts? (c) What was the change in the amount of intangibles from 1994 to 1995 for Coca-Cola and PepsiCo?

2. (a) On what basis and over what periods of time did Coca-Cola and PepsiCo amortize their intangible assets? (b) What were the amounts of accumulated amortization reported by Coca-Cola and PepsiCo at December 31, 1995, and at December 31, 1994? (c) What was the composition of identifiable and unidentifiable intangible assets reported by Coca-Cola and PepsiCo at December 31, 1995? (d) What was the effect of the adoption of FASB No. 121 on impairments of long-lived assets (intangibles) by Coca-Cola and PepsiCo?

❖ RESEARCH CASES

Case 1

Instructions

Examine the financial statements and related footnotes for three companies of your choice and answer the following questions with respect to each company.

(a) Identify any intangible assets included on the balance sheet.

(b) What is the useful life over which the intangibles are being amortized?

(c) Does the company utilize an Accumulated Amortization account?

(d) What were the company's research and development expenses in the most recent two years?

Case 2

The February 19, 1996, issue of *Fortune* includes an article by Thomas A. Stewart, entitled "The Coins in the Knowledge Bank."

Instructions

Read the article and answer the following questions.

(a) What is the rationale for estimating the "knowledge bank" and reporting it on the balance sheet?

(b) What is the purpose of income measurement under the proposed approach?

(c) Why should capital spending be treated as an expense?

(d) What items treated as expenses under GAAP should be capitalized on the balance sheet?

(e) While the article admits that the method is subjective, why might it still be appropriate for financial reporting?

❖ WRITING ASSIGNMENT

The president of Dane Co., Mrs. Joyce Pollachek, is considering purchasing Balloon Bunch Company. She thinks that the offer sounds pretty good, but she wants to consult a certified public accountant to be sure. Balloon Bunch Company is asking $78,000 over the fair market value of the net identifiable assets. Balloon Bunch's net income figures for the last 5 years are as follows:

1994—$64,000	1997—$80,000
1995—$50,000	1998—$70,000
1996—$81,000	

The tangible net assets of this company were appraised at $400,000 on December 31, 1998.

You have done some initial research on the balloon industry and discovered that the normal rate of return on net tangible assets is 13%. After analyzing variables such as stability of past earnings, the nature of the business, and general economic conditions, you have decided that the average excess earnings for the last 5 years should be capitalized at 25% and that the excess earnings will continue for about 5 more years. Further research led you to discover that the Happy Balloon Company, a competitor of similar size and profitability, was recently sold for six times its average yearly earnings ($90,000) for $540,000.

Instructions

(a) Prepare a schedule that includes the computation of Balloon Bunch Company's goodwill and purchase price under at least three methods.

(b) Write a letter to Mrs. Pollachek that includes:
   (1) An explanation of the nature of goodwill.
   (2) An explanation of the different acceptable methods of determining its fair value. (Include with your explanation of the different methods the rationale of how each method arrives at a goodwill value.)
   (3) Advice for Mrs. Pollachek on how to determine her purchase price.

❖ GROUP ASSIGNMENT

(Accounting for Various Intangible Assets and R & D Costs)   The following situations relate to the accounting for intangible assets and research and development costs.

1. Warfield Corporation, a development stage company, deferred all its preoperating and R & D costs. Its 1995 financial statements consisted only of statements of cash receipts and disbursements, capital shares, and assets and unrecovered preoperating costs and liabilities. The officers indicate that operations should start June 30, 1996, and complete financials will be issued December 31, 1996.
2. Hanson Components Corp. develops computer software to be used internally for its management information systems. The corporation incurred $290,000 in developing this new software package.
3. Williams Research Company is developing a new space station under contract for Star Search Corp. The contract, signed January 4, requires payments to Williams Research of $600,000 on December 31 and $1,000,000 at the completion of the project. At December 31, Williams has recorded an account receivable of $600,000 and has deferred R & D costs of $400,000.
4. Wild Co. purchased two patents directly from the inventors. Patent No. 1 can be used only in its listening device development research project. Patent No. 2 can be used in many different projects and currently is being used in a research project.
5. Green Golf Company deferred all of its 1994 R & D costs, which totaled $360,000. In November 1995, you are hired as controller and informed that an additional $450,000 has been deferred thus far in 1995. The company wants to issue comparative financial statements in accordance with generally accepted accounting principles for the first time this year.

Instructions

Your instructor will assign one member of the group to serve as a recorder and one member to serve as spokesperson. As a group, provide the information for the recorder to prepare a recommended accounting treatment for each of the items above (you may wish to divide the parts among the members). Upon completion, the spokesperson will report the group findings to the class and be prepared to provide justifications for the recommendations.

❖ETHICS CASE

Waveland Corporation's research and development department has an idea for a project it believes will culminate in a new product that would be very profitable for the company. Because the project will be very expensive, the department requests approval from Waveland Corporation's controller, Ron Santo.

Santo recognizes that corporate profits have been down lately and is hesitant to approve a project that will incur significant expenses that cannot be capitalized due to the requirement of *FASB Statement #2, Accounting for Research and Development Costs*. He knows that if they hire an outside firm that does the work and obtains a patent for the process, Waveland Corporation can purchase the patent from the outside firm and record the expenditure as an asset. Santo knows that the company's own R&D department is first-rate, and he is confident they can do the work well.

Instructions
Answer the following questions:

(a) Who are the stakeholders in this situation?
(b) What are the ethical issues involved?
(c) What should Santo do?

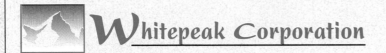 **W** hitepeak Corporation   MODULE 7

Section 7.1   Underpayments for Purchased Assets

During 1997, Whitepeak purchased the net assets of a small retail clothing store in downtown Colorado Springs known as Pike's Clothing, Esquire. An analysis of the transaction determines that Whitepeak paid less than fair market value for Pike's net assets. Whitepeak did not adjust for this event in recording the transaction.

Instructions Correct this error and the others that have followed in 1997 because of this misrecording.

Section 7.2   Research and Development

During 1997, Whitepeak has been involved in a number of transactions that it is unable to classify properly.

Instructions Determine whether these events should be recorded as Research & Development or as Intangible Assets. Make the appropriate journal entry for each transaction. ■

CHAPTER 13

Current Liabilities and Contingencies

Drowning in Debt!

A consumer spending party, three years in duration, has taken on the proportions of a binge. Credit card debt has been the stimulant that's kept the party hearty. Up to now, purveyors of plastic have had an easy time signing up consumers whose wants and needs have grown faster than their incomes.

For over three years banks have been tripping over each other, stuffing our mail boxes, to see how fast they could give someone, anyone, a credit card. Even people long dead (unquestionably good risks) received pre-approved card offers. Children and animals? No problem. In the headlong rush to generate revenues, low teaser rates became common and annual fees disappeared. Nobody has been too much of a risk to be denied.

As consumer credit card expert Charlene Sullivan noted, "There's more credit in the hands of more people than we've ever seen before, and they're using it in more ways. They're using credit cards to start a business, to invest in the stock market, to gamble, and to pay for medical care. More people are operating with less margin of error."

Outstanding credit card balances mushroomed 40% from 1994 to 1996, to more than $380 billion. How big a number is that? So big that consumers are devoting nearly 11% of their income to servicing just consumer debt. And, what has been the fallout from their personal debt binge?

Personal bankruptcies are running at record levels, posting the biggest increases in a decade, and topping the one million mark for the first time ever in 1996. Looked at another way, experts say that one in every 100 households filed for personal bankruptcy in 1996. In short, bankruptcy, once viewed as shameful, has become an accepted part of the American way of life and debt. According to bankers, lawyers, and bankruptcy clerks, there's one characteristic common to all individuals filing for bankruptcy: "They're in hock up to their eyeballs, in most cases maxxed out on credit card debt."[1]

LEARNING OBJECTIVES

After studying this chapter, you should be able to:

① Define current liabilities and describe how they are valued.

② Identify the nature and types of current liabilities.

③ Explain the classification issues of short-term debt expected to be refinanced.

④ Identify types of employee-related liabilities.

⑤ Identify the criteria used to account for and disclose gain and loss contingencies.

⑥ Explain the accounting for different types of contingent liabilities.

⑦ Indicate how current liabilities and contingencies are presented and analyzed.

---

[1]Adapted from an article by Joseph Spiers, "Watch Out! A Debt Bomb is Ticking," *Fortune*, November 27, 1995.

Preview of Chapter 13

As the opening story indicates, more and more individuals are overextended financially and amassing significant debt. Fortunately, companies appear to be taking a more conservative approach and generally have reduced their debt to acceptable levels. The purpose of this chapter is to explain the basic principles regarding accounting and reporting for current and contingent liabilities. Chapter 14 addresses issues related to long-term liabilities. The content and organization of this chapter are as follows:

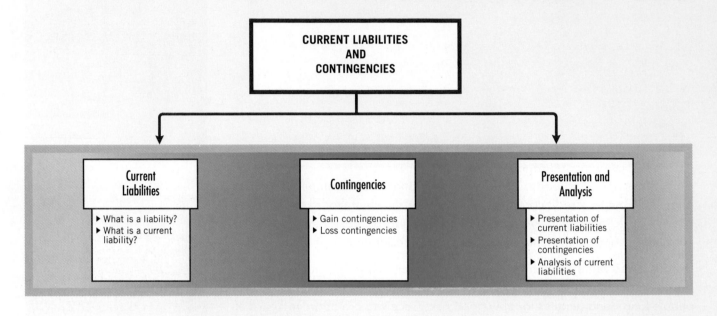

SECTION 1   *CURRENT LIABILITIES*

❖ WHAT IS A LIABILITY?

The question, "What is a liability?" is not easy to answer. For example, one might ask whether preferred stock is a liability or an ownership claim. The first reaction is to say that preferred stock is in fact an ownership claim and should be reported as part of stockholders' equity. In fact, preferred stock has many elements of debt as well.[2] The issuer (and in some cases the holder) often has the right to call the stock within a specific period of time—making it similar to a repayment of principal. The dividend is in many

---

[2]It should be noted that this illustration is not just a theoretical exercise. In practice, there are a number of preferred stock issues that have all the characteristics of a debt instrument, except that they are called and legally classified preferred stock. In some cases, the IRS has even permitted the dividend payments to be treated as interest expense for tax purposes. This issue is discussed further in Chapter 15.

cases almost guaranteed (cumulative provision)—making it look like interest. And preferred stock is but one of many financial instruments that are difficult to classify.[3]

To help resolve some of these controversies, the FASB, as part of its conceptual framework study, defined liabilities as **"probable future sacrifices of economic benefits arising from present obligations of a particular entity to transfer assets or provide services to other entities in the future as a result of past transactions or events."**[4] In other words, a liability has three essential characteristics:

UNDERLYING CONCEPTS

To determine the appropriate classification of specific financial instruments, proper definitions of assets, liabilities, and equities are needed. The conceptual framework definitions are often used as the basis for resolving controversial classification issues.

❶ It is a present obligation that entails settlement by probable future transfer or use of cash, goods, or services.
❷ It is an unavoidable obligation.
❸ The transaction or other event creating the obligation has already occurred.

Because liabilities involve future disbursements of assets or services, one of their most important features is the date on which they are payable. Currently maturing obligations must be satisfied promptly and in the ordinary course of business if operations are to be continued. Liabilities with a more distant due date do not, as a rule, represent a claim on the enterprise's current resources and are therefore in a slightly different category. This feature gives rise to the basic division of liabilities into (1) current liabilities and (2) long-term debt.

❖ WHAT IS A CURRENT LIABILITY?

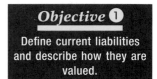

Objective ❶

Define current liabilities and describe how they are valued.

Current assets are cash or other assets that can reasonably be expected to be converted into cash, sold, or consumed in operations within a single operating cycle or within a year if more than one cycle is completed each year. Current liabilities are **"obligations whose liquidation is reasonably expected to require use of existing resources properly classified as current assets, or the creation of other current liabilities."**[5] This definition has gained wide acceptance because it recognizes operating cycles of varying lengths in different industries and takes into consideration the important relationship between current assets and current liabilities. [6]

The operating cycle is the period of time elapsing between the acquisition of goods and services involved in the manufacturing process and the final cash realization resulting from sales and subsequent collections. Industries that manufacture products requiring an aging process and certain capital-intensive industries have an operating

INTERNATIONAL INSIGHT

In France, the balance sheet does not show current liabilities in a separate category. Rather, debts are disclosed separately by maturity in the notes.

---

[3]As examples of the diversity within preferred stock, companies now issue (1) mandatorily redeemable preferred stock (redeemable at a specified price and time), (2) Dutch auction preferred stock (holders have the right to change the rate at defined intervals through a bidding process), (3) increasing rate (exploding rate) preferred stock (holder receives an increasing dividend rate each period with the issuer having the right to call the stock at a certain date in the future). In all three cases the issuer either has to redeem the stock per the contract or has a strong economic reason for calling the stock. These securities are more like debt than equity. The FASB has issued a discussion memorandum addressing these issues: "Distinguishing between Liability and Equity Instruments and Accounting for Instruments with Characteristics of Both," Discussion Memorandum (Norwalk, Conn.: FASB, 1990).

[4]"Elements of Financial Statements of Business Enterprises," *Statement of Financial Accounting Concepts No. 6* (Stamford, Conn.: FASB, 1980).

[5]Committee on Accounting Procedure, American Institute of Certified Public Accountants, "Accounting Research and Terminology Bulletins," Final Edition (New York: AICPA, 1961), p. 21.

[6]The FASB affirmed this concept of "maturity within one year or the operating cycle whichever is longer" in its definition of short-term obligations in *Statement No. 6*. "Classification of Short-term Obligations Expected to Be Refinanced," *Statement of Financial Accounting Standards No. 6* (Stamford, Conn.: FASB, 1975), par. 2.

cycle of considerably more than one year. On the other hand, most retail and service establishments have several operating cycles within a year.

There are many different types of current liabilities. The following ones are covered in this chapter in this order.

❶ Accounts payable.
❷ Notes payable.
❸ Current maturities of long-term debt.
❹ Short-term obligations expected to be refinanced.
❺ Dividends payable.

❻ Returnable deposits.
❼ Unearned revenues.
❽ Sales taxes payable.
❾ Property taxes payable.
❿ Income taxes payable.
⓫ Employee related liabilities.

Accounts Payable

Accounts payable, or trade accounts payable, are balances owed to others for goods, supplies, or services purchased on open account. Accounts payable arise because of the time lag between the receipt of services or acquisition of title to assets and the payment for them. This period of extended credit is usually found in the terms of the sale (e.g., 2/10, n/30 or 1/10, E.O.M.) and is commonly 30 to 60 days.

Most accounting systems are designed to record liabilities for purchases of goods when the goods are received or, practically, when the invoices are received. Frequently there is some delay in recording the goods and the related liability on the books. If title has passed to the purchaser before the goods are received, the transaction should be recorded at the time of title passage. Attention must be paid to transactions occurring near the end of one accounting period and at the beginning of the next to ascertain that the record of goods received (the inventory) is in agreement with the liability (accounts payable) and that both are recorded in the proper period.

Measuring the amount of an account payable poses no particular difficulty because the invoice received from the creditor specifies the due date and the exact outlay in money that is necessary to settle the account. The only calculation that may be necessary concerns the amount of cash discount. See Chapter 8 for illustrations of entries related to accounts payable and purchase discounts.

Notes Payable

Notes payable are written promises to pay a certain sum of money on a specified future date and may arise from sales, financing, or other transactions. In some industries, notes (often referred to as trade notes payable) are required as part of the sales/purchases transaction in lieu of the normal extension of open account credit. Notes payable to banks or loan companies generally arise from cash loans. Notes may be classified as short-term or long-term, depending upon the payment due date. Notes may also be interest-bearing or zero-interest-bearing.

Interest-Bearing Note Issued

Assume that the Castle National Bank agrees to lend $100,000 on March 1, 1998, to Landscape Co. if Landscape Co. signs a $100,000, 12%, 4-month note. The entry to record the cash received by Landscape Co. on March 1 is:

March 1

Cash	100,000	
Notes Payable		100,000
(To record issuance of 12%, 4-month note to Castle National Bank)		

If Landscape Co. prepares financial statements semiannually, an adjusting entry is required to recognize interest expense and interest payable of $4,000 ($100,000 × 12% × 4/12) at June 30. The adjusting entry is:

June 30

Interest Expense	4,000	
Interest Payable		4,000
(To accrue interest for 4 months on Castle National Bank note)		

If Landscape prepared financial statements monthly, the adjusting entry at the end of each month would have been $1,000 ($100,000 × 12% × 1/12).

At maturity (July 1), Landscape Co. must pay the face value of the note ($100,000) plus $4,000 interest ($100,000 × 12% × 4/12).

The entry to record payment of the note and accrued interest is as follows:

July 1

Notes Payable	100,000	
Interest Payable	4,000	
Cash		104,000
(To record payment of Castle National Bank interest-bearing note and accrued interest at maturity)		

Zero-Interest-Bearing Note Issued

A zero-interest-bearing note may be issued instead of an interest-bearing note. A zero-interest-bearing note does not explicitly state an interest rate on the face of the note. Interest is still charged, however, because the borrower is required at maturity to pay back an amount greater than the cash received at the issuance date. In other words, the borrower receives in cash the present value of the note. The present value equals the face value of the note at maturity minus the interest or discount charged by the lender for the term of the note. In essence, the bank takes its fee "up front" rather than on the date the note matures.

To illustrate, we will assume that Landscape Co. issues a $104,000 4-month, zero-interest-bearing note to the Castle National Bank. The present value of the note is $100,000.[7] The entry to record this transaction for Landscape Co. is as follows:

March 1

Cash	100,000	
Discount on Notes Payable	4,000	
Notes Payable		104,000
(To record issuance of 4-month, zero-interest-bearing note to Castle National Bank)		

The Notes Payable account is credited for the face value of the note, which is $4,000 more than the actual cash received. The difference between the cash received and the face value of the note is debited to Discount on Notes Payable. **Discount on Notes Payable is a contra account to Notes Payable and therefore is subtracted from Notes Payable on the balance sheet.** The balance sheet presentation on March 1 is as follows:

Current liabilities		
Notes Payable	104,000	
Less: Discount on notes payable	4,000	100,000

ILLUSTRATION 13-1
Balance Sheet
Presentation of Discount

The amount of the discount, $4,000 in this case, represents the cost of borrowing $100,000 for 4 months. Accordingly, the discount is charged to interest expense over the life of the note. That is, the Discount on Notes Payable balance **represents interest expense chargeable to future periods.** Thus, it would be incorrect to debit Interest Expense for $4,000 at the time the loan is obtained. Additional accounting issues related to notes payable are discussed in Chapter 14.

Current Maturities of Long-Term Debt

The portion of bonds, mortgage notes, and other long-term indebtedness that matures within the next fiscal year—**current maturities of long-term debt**—is reported as a current liability. When only a part of a long-term debt is to be paid within the next 12

---

[7]The bank discount rate used in this example to find the present value is 11.538%.

months, as in the case of serial bonds that are to be retired through a series of annual installments, **the maturing portion of long-term debt is reported as a current liability**, the balance as a long-term debt.

Long-term debts maturing currently should not be included as current liabilities if they are to be:

❶ retired by assets accumulated for this purpose that properly have not been shown as current assets,

❷ refinanced, or retired from the proceeds of a new debt issue (see next topic), or

❸ converted into capital stock.

In these situations, the use of current assets or the creation of other current liabilities does not occur. Therefore, classification as a current liability is inappropriate. The plan for liquidation of such a debt should be disclosed either parenthetically or by a note to the financial statements.

However, a liability that is **due on demand** (callable by the creditor) or will be due on demand within a year (or operating cycle, if longer) should be classified as a current liability. Liabilities often become callable by the creditor when there is a violation of the debt agreement. For example, most debt agreements specify a given level of equity to debt be maintained, or specify that working capital be of a minimum amount. If an agreement is violated, classification of the debt as current is required because it is a reasonable expectation that existing working capital will be used to satisfy the debt. Only if it can be shown that it is **probable** that the violation will be cured (satisfied) within the grace period usually given in these agreements can the debt be classified as noncurrent.[8]

Short-Term Obligations Expected to Be Refinanced

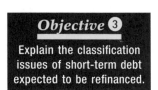

Objective ❸

Explain the classification issues of short-term debt expected to be refinanced.

Short-term obligations are those debts that are scheduled to mature within one year after the date of an enterprise's balance sheet or within an enterprise's operating cycle, whichever is longer. Some short-term obligations are expected to be refinanced on a long-term basis and, therefore, are not expected to require the use of working capital during the next year (or operating cycle).[9]

At one time, the accounting profession generally supported the exclusion of short-term obligations from current liabilities if they were "expected to be refinanced." Because the profession provided no specific guidelines, however, determining whether a short-term obligation was "expected to be refinanced" was usually based solely on management's **intent** to refinance on a long-term basis. A company may obtain a 5-year bank loan but, because the bank prefers it, handle the actual financing with 90-day notes, which it must keep turning over (renewing). So what is the loan—a long-term debt or a current liability? Another example of this problem of classification was the Penn Central Railroad before it went bankrupt. The railroad was deep into short-term debt and commercial paper but classified it as long-term debt. Why? Because the railroad believed it had commitments from lenders to keep refinancing the short-term debt. When those commitments suddenly disappeared, it was good-bye Pennsy. As the Greek philosopher Epictetus once said, "Some things in this world are not and yet appear to be."

Refinancing Criteria

As a result of these classification problems, the profession set forth authoritative criteria for determining the circumstances under which short-term obligations may properly

---

[8]"Classification of Obligations That Are Callable by the Creditor," *Statement of Financial Accounting Standards No. 78* (Stamford, Conn.: FASB, 1983).

[9]*Refinancing a short-term obligation on a long-term basis* means either replacing it with a long-term obligation or with equity securities, or renewing, extending, or replacing it with short-term obligations for an uninterrupted period extending beyond one year (or the operating cycle, if longer) from the date of the enterprise's balance sheet.

be excluded from current liabilities. An enterprise is required to exclude a short-term obligation from current liabilities only if **both** of the following conditions are met:

❶ It must **intend to refinance** the obligation on a long-term basis, and
❷ It must **demonstrate an ability** to consummate the refinancing.[10]

Intention to refinance on a long-term basis means the enterprise intends to refinance the short-term obligation so that the use of working capital will not be required during the ensuing fiscal year or operating cycle, if longer. The **ability** to consummate the refinancing may be demonstrated by:

(a) **Actually refinancing** the short-term obligation by issuing a long-term obligation or equity securities after the date of the balance sheet but before it is issued; or
(b) Entering into a **financing agreement** that clearly permits the enterprise to refinance the debt on a long-term basis on terms that are readily determinable.

If an actual refinancing occurs, the portion of the short-term obligation to be excluded from current liabilities may not exceed the proceeds from the new obligation or equity securities that are applied to retire the short-term obligation. For example, Montavon Winery with $3,000,000 of short-term debt issued 100,000 shares of common stock subsequent to the balance sheet date but before the balance sheet was issued, intending to use the proceeds to liquidate the short-term debt at its maturity. If the net proceeds from the sale of the 100,000 shares totaled $2,000,000, only that amount of the short-term debt could be excluded from current liabilities.

An additional question relates to whether a short-term obligation should be excluded from current liabilities if it is paid off after the balance sheet date and subsequently replaced by long-term debt before the balance sheet is issued. To illustrate, Marquardt Company pays off short-term debt of $40,000 on January 17, 1999, and issues long-term debt of $100,000 on February 3, 1999. Marquardt's financial statements dated December 31, 1998, are to be issued March 1, 1999. Because repayment of the short-term obligation **before** funds were obtained through long-term financing required the use of **existing** current assets, the profession requires that the short-term obligation be included in current liabilities at the balance sheet date (see graphical presentation below).

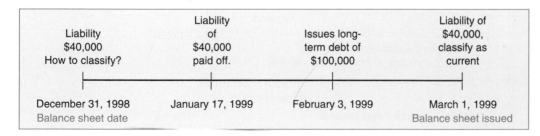

ILLUSTRATION 13-2
Short-Term Debt Paid Off after Balance Sheet Date and Later Replaced by Long-Term Debt

Dividends Payable

A **cash dividend payable** is an amount owed by a corporation to its stockholders as a result of board of directors' authorization. At the date of declaration the corporation assumes a liability that places the stockholders in the position of creditors in the amount of dividends declared. Because cash dividends are always paid within one year of declaration (generally within 3 months), they are classified as current liabilities.

Accumulated but undeclared dividends on cumulative preferred stock are not a recognized liability because **preferred dividends in arrears** are not an obligation until formal action is taken by the board of directors authorizing the distribution of earnings. Nevertheless, the amount of cumulative dividends unpaid should be disclosed in a note or it may be shown parenthetically in the capital stock section.

---

[10]"Classification of Short-term Obligations Expected to Be Refinanced," *Statement of Financial Accounting Standards No. 6* (Stamford, Conn.: FASB, 1975), pars. 10 and 11.

Dividends payable in the form of additional shares of stock are not recognized as a liability. Such **stock dividends** (as discussed in Chapter 16) do not require future outlays of assets or services and are revocable by the board of directors at any time prior to issuance. Even so, such undistributed stock dividends are generally reported in the stockholders' equity section because they represent retained earnings in the process of transfer to paid-in capital.

Returnable Deposits

Current liabilities of a company may include returnable cash deposits received from customers and employees. Deposits may be received from customers to guarantee performance of a contract or service or as guarantees to cover payment of expected future obligations. For example, telephone companies often require a deposit upon installation of a phone. Deposits may also be received from customers as guarantees for possible damage to property left with the customer. Some companies require their employees to make deposits for the return of keys or other company property. The classification of these items as current or noncurrent liabilities is dependent on the time between the date of the deposit and the termination of the relationship that required the deposit.

Unearned Revenues

A magazine publisher such as Golf Digest may receive a customer's check when magazines are ordered, and an airline company, such as American Airlines, often sells tickets for future flights. Restaurants may issue meal tickets that can be exchanged or used for future meals. Who hasn't received or given a McDonald's gift certificate? Retail stores issue gift certificates that are redeemable in merchandise. How do these companies account for unearned revenues that are received before goods are delivered or services are rendered?

❶ When the advance is received, Cash is debited, and a current liability account identifying the source of the unearned revenue is credited.

❷ When the revenue is earned, the unearned revenue account is debited, and an earned revenue account is credited.

To illustrate, assume that Allstate University sells 10,000 season football tickets at $50 each for its five-game home schedule. The entry for the sales of season tickets is:

August 6

Cash	500,000	
Unearned Football Ticket Revenue		500,000
(To record sale of 10,000 season tickets)		

As each game is completed, the following entry is made:

September 7

Unearned Football Ticket Revenue	100,000	
Football Ticket Revenue		100,000
(To record football ticket revenues earned)		

Unearned Football Ticket Revenue is, therefore, unearned revenue and is reported as a current liability in the balance sheet. As revenue is earned, a transfer from unearned revenue to earned revenue occurs. Unearned revenue is material for some companies: In the airline industry, tickets sold for future flights represent almost 50% of total current liabilities. At United Air Lines, unearned ticket revenue is the largest current liability, recently amounting to over $882 million.

Illustration 13-3 shows specific unearned and earned revenue accounts used in selected types of businesses.

ILLUSTRATION 13-3
Unearned and Earned Revenue Accounts

Type of Business	Account Title	
	Unearned Revenue	Earned Revenue
Airline	Unearned Passenger Ticket Revenue	Passenger Revenue
Magazine Publisher	Unearned Subscription Revenue	Subscription Revenue
Hotel	Unearned Rental Revenue	Rental Revenue
Auto Dealer	Unearned Warranty Revenue	Warranty Revenue

The balance sheet should report obligations for any commitments that are redeemable in goods and services; the income statement should report revenues earned during the period.

Sales Taxes Payable

Sales taxes on transfers of tangible personal property and on certain services must be collected from customers and remitted to the proper governmental authority. A liability is set up to provide for taxes collected from customers but not yet remitted to the tax authority. The Sales Taxes Payable account should reflect the liability for sales taxes due various governments. The entry below is the proper one for a sale of $3,000 when a 4% sales tax is in effect.

Cash or Accounts Receivable	3,120	
Sales		3,000
Sales Taxes Payable		120

When the sales tax collections credited to the liability account are not equal to the liability as computed by the governmental formula, an adjustment of the liability account may be made by recognizing a gain or a loss on sales tax collections.

In many companies, however, the sales tax and the amount of the sale are not segregated at the time of sale; both are credited in total in the Sales account. In that case, to reflect correctly the actual amount of sales and the liability for sales taxes, the Sales account must be debited for the amount of the sales taxes due the government on these sales and the Sales Taxes Payable account credited for the same amount. As an illustration, assume that the Sales account balance of $150,000 includes sales taxes of 4%. Because the amount recorded in the Sales account is equal to sales plus 4% of sales, or 1.04 times the sales total, sales are $150,000 ÷ 1.04, or $144,230.77. The sales tax liability is $5,769.23 ($144,230.77 × 0.04; or $150,000 − $144,230.77), and the following entry would be made to record the amount due the taxing unit:

Sales	5,769.23	
Sales Taxes Payable		5,769.23

Property Taxes Payable

Local governmental units generally depend on property taxes as their primary source of revenue. Such taxes are based on the assessed value of both real and personal property and become a lien against the property at a date determined by law. This lien is a liability of the property owner and is a cost of the services of such property. The accounting questions that arise from property taxes are:

① When should property owners record the liability?
② To which accounting period should the cost be charged?

The accounting profession, in considering the various periods to which property taxes might be charged and how the liability should be reported, contends that generally, the most acceptable basis of providing for property taxes is monthly accrual on the taxpayer's books during the fiscal period of the taxing authority for which the taxes are paid. Charging the taxes to the period subsequent to the lien date **relates the expense to the period in which the taxes are used by the governmental unit to provide benefits to the property owner.**[11]

---

[11]Possible alternatives are: (a) year in which paid, (b) year ending on assessment (or lien) date, (c) year beginning on assessment (or lien) date, (d) calendar or fiscal year of taxpayer prior to assessment (or lien) date, (e) calendar or fiscal year of taxpayer including assessment (or lien) date, (f) calendar or fiscal year of taxpayer prior to payment date, (g) fiscal year of governing body levying the tax, and (h) year appearing on tax bill. Committee on Accounting Procedure, American Institute of Certified Public Accountants, *Accounting Research and Terminology Bulletin, Final Edition* (New York: AICPA, 1961), ch. 10, sec. A, par. 10.

Assume that Seaboard Company, which closes its books each year on December 31, receives its property tax bill in May each year. The fiscal year for the city and county in which Seaboard Company is located begins on May 1 and ends on the following April 30. Property taxes of $36,000 are assessed against Seaboard Company property on January 1, 1998, and become a lien on May 1, 1998. Tax bills are sent out in May and are payable in equal installments on July 1 and September 1.

Entries to record the liability, monthly tax charges, and the tax payments for taxes becoming a lien on May 1, 1998 are shown below.

❶ Entry, if any, on May 1, 1998 (lien date):

No entry

❷ Monthly expense accrual for May 31 and June 30, 1998:

Property Tax Expense	3,000	
Property Taxes Payable		3,000

❸ First tax payment on July 1, 1998:

Property Taxes Payable	6,000	
Prepaid Property Taxes	12,000	
Cash		18,000

❹ Monthly expense accrual for July 31 and August 31, 1998:

Property Tax Expense	3,000	
Prepaid Property Taxes		3,000

❺ Second tax payment on September 1, 1998:

Prepaid Property Taxes	18,000	
Cash		18,000

❻ Monthly expense accrual for Sept. 30, 1998, through April 30, 1999:

Property Tax Expense	3,000	
Prepaid Property Taxes		3,000

Prepaid Property Taxes of $12,000 on July 1 represents a 4-month prepayment and $18,000 on September 1 represents a 6-month prepayment. At December 31, the account has 4 months of unexpired tax.[12]

Some advocate accruing property taxes by charges to expense during the fiscal year **ending on the lien date,** rather than during the fiscal year beginning on the lien date (the fiscal year of the tax authority). In such instances the property tax for the coming fiscal year must be estimated and charged monthly to Property Tax Expense and must be credited to Property Tax Payable. Under this method the entire amount of the tax is accrued by the lien date and the expense is therefore charged to the fiscal period preceding payment of the tax. Justification for this method exists when the assessment date precedes the lien date by a year or more, as is the case in some taxing units. In such instances, the amount is estimated and accrued by the property owner before receipt of the tax bill.

Recognizing that special circumstances can suggest the use of alternative accrual periods, the profession supports the view that **"consistency of application from year**

---

[12]Some argue that the entire liability of $36,000 should be recorded on the lien date with a related debit to a Deferred Charge account. These individuals contend that the company has a legal liability at that date and therefore the full amount of the liability should be reported. We disagree. To report the full liability at the lien date necessitates the recording of a Deferred Property Tax Asset for unpaid property taxes—a dubious asset. In addition, the liability accrues as the property is used—if the property is sold, the buyer has the responsibility for the property taxes subsequent to purchase—not the seller.

to year is the important consideration and selection of any of the periods mentioned is a matter for individual judgment."[13]

Income Taxes Payable

Any federal or state income tax varies in proportion to the amount of annual income. Some consider the amount of income tax on annual income as an estimate because the computation of income (and the tax thereon) is subject to IRS review and approval. The meaning and application of numerous tax rules, especially new ones, are debatable and often dependent on a court's interpretation. Using the best information and advice available, a business must prepare an income tax return and compute the income tax payable resulting from the operations of the current period. The taxes payable on the income of a corporation, as computed per the tax return, should be classified as a current liability.[14]

Unlike the corporation, the proprietorship and the partnership are not taxable entities. Because the individual proprietor and the members of a partnership are subject to personal income taxes on their share of the business's taxable income, income tax liabilities do not appear on the financial statements of proprietorships and partnerships.

Most corporations must make periodic tax payments in an authorized bank depository or a Federal Reserve bank throughout the year. These payments are based upon estimates of the total annual tax liability. As the estimated total tax liability changes, the periodic contributions also change. If in a later year an additional tax is assessed on the income of an earlier year, Income Taxes Payable should be credited. The related debit should be charged to current operations.

Differences between taxable income under the tax laws and accounting income under generally accepted accounting principles sometimes occur. Because of these differences, the amount of income tax payable to the government in any given year may differ substantially from income tax expense, as reported on the financial statements. Chapter 20 is devoted solely to income tax matters and presents an extensive discussion of this complex and controversial problem.

Employee-Related Liabilities

Amounts owed to employees for salaries or wages at the end of an accounting period are reported as a current liability. In addition, the following items related to employee compensation are often reported as current liabilities:

Objective 4

Identify types of employee-related liabilities.

❶ Payroll deductions.
❷ Compensated absences.
❸ Postretirement benefits.
❹ Bonuses. (Accounting for bonuses is covered in Appendix 13A.)

Payroll Deductions

The most common types of payroll deductions are taxes and miscellaneous items such as insurance premiums, employee savings, and union dues. To the extent the amounts

---

[13]*Accounting Research and Terminology Bulletin*, Final Edition, par. 3.

[14]The four-step progressive tax rate structure on corporate income applies:

Corporate Taxable Income	1997 Tax Rate
$50,000 or less	15%
$50,001–$75,000	25%
$75,001–$10,000,000	34%
Above $10,000,000	35%

If a corporation has taxable income in excess of $100,000 for any taxable year, the amount of tax is increased by the lesser of 5% of such excess or $11,750. This surtax phases out the benefits of the 15% and 25% rates. A similar phaseout applies for taxable incomes above $15,000,000. In such cases, a 3% surtax is imposed, up to a maximum tax of $100,000.

deducted have not been remitted to the proper authority at the end of the accounting period, they should be recognized as current liabilities.

Social Security Taxes. Since January 1, 1937, social security legislation has provided federal old-age, survivor, and disability insurance (O.A.S.D.I.) benefits for certain individuals and their families through taxes levied on both the employer and the employee. All employers covered are required to collect the employee's share of this tax, by deducting it from the employee's gross pay, and to remit it to the government along with the employer's share. Both the employer and the employee are taxed at the same rate, currently 6.2% (1997) based on the employee's gross pay up to a $65,400 annual limit.

In 1965 Congress passed the first federal health insurance program for the aged—popularly known as Medicare. It is a two-part program designed to alleviate the high cost of medical care for those over age 65. The Basic Plan, which provides hospital and other institutional services, is financed by a separate Hospital Insurance tax paid by both the employee and the employer at the rate of 1.45% on the employee's total compensation. The Voluntary Plan takes care of the major part of doctors' bills and other medical and health services and is financed by monthly payments from all who enroll plus matching funds from the federal government.

The combination of the O.A.S.D.I. tax, often called Federal Insurance Contribution Act (F.I.C.A.) tax, and the federal Hospital Insurance Tax is commonly referred to as the **social security tax**. The combined rate for these taxes, 7.65% on an employee's wages to $65,400 and 1.45% in excess of $65,400, is changed intermittently by acts of Congress. The amount of unremitted employee and employer social security tax on gross wages paid should be reported by the employer as a current liability.

Unemployment Taxes. Another payroll tax levied by the federal government in cooperation with state governments provides a system of unemployment insurance. All employers who (1) paid wages of $1,500 or more during any calendar quarter in the year or preceding year or (2) employed at least one individual on at least one day in each of 20 weeks during the current or preceding calendar year are subject to the Federal Unemployment Tax Act (F.U.T.A.). This tax is levied only on the employer at a rate of 6.2% (1997) on the first $7,000 of compensation paid to each employee during the calendar year. The employer is allowed a tax credit not to exceed 5.4% for contributions paid to a state plan for unemployment compensation. Thus, if an employer is subject to a state unemployment tax of 5.4% or more, only 0.8% tax is due the federal government.

State unemployment compensation laws differ from the federal law and differ among various states. Therefore, employers must be familiar with the unemployment tax laws in each state in which they pay wages and salaries. Although the normal state tax may range from 3% to 7% or higher, all states provide for some form of merit rating under which a reduction in the state contribution rate is allowed. Employers who display by their benefit and contribution experience that they have provided steady employment may be entitled to this reduction—if the size of the state fund is adequate to provide the reduction. In order not to penalize an employer who has earned a reduction in the state contribution rate, the federal law allows a credit of 5.4% even though the effective state contribution rate is less than 5.4%.

To illustrate, Appliance Repair Co., which has a taxable payroll of $100,000, is subject to a federal rate of 6.2% and a state contribution rate of 5.7%. But because of stable employment experience, the company's state rate has been reduced to 1%. The computation of the federal and state unemployment taxes for Appliance Repair Co. is:

ILLUSTRATION 13-4
Computation of
Unemployment Taxes

State unemployment tax payment (1%)($100,000)	$1,000
Federal unemployment tax (6.2% − 5.4%)($100,000)	800
Total federal and state unemployment tax	$1,800

The federal unemployment tax is paid quarterly with a tax form filed annually. State contributions generally are required to be paid quarterly. Because both the federal and the state unemployment taxes accrue on earned compensation, the amount of accrued but unpaid employer contributions should be recorded as an operating expense and as a current liability when financial statements are prepared at year-end.

Income Tax Withholding. Federal and some state income tax laws require employers to withhold from the pay of each employee the applicable income tax due on those wages. The amount of income tax withheld is computed by the employer according to a government-prescribed formula or withholding tax table. That amount depends on the length of the pay period and each employee's taxable wages, marital status, and claimed dependents.

If the income tax withheld plus the employee and the employer social security taxes exceeds specified amounts per month, the employer is required to make remittances to the government during the month. Monthly deposits are not required if the employer's liability for the calendar quarter is less than $500. Instead, the tax liability is remitted with the employer's quarterly payroll tax return.

Illustration. Assume a weekly payroll of $10,000 entirely subject to F.I.C.A. and Medicare (7.65%), federal (0.8%) and state (4%) unemployment taxes with income tax withholding of $1,320 and union dues of $88 deducted.

The entry to record the wages and salaries paid and the employee payroll deductions would be:

Wages and Salaries Expense	10,000	
Withholding Taxes Payable		1,320
F.I.C.A. Taxes Payable		765
Union Dues Payable to Local No. 257		88
Cash		7,827

The entry to record the employer payroll taxes would be:

Payroll Tax Expense	1,245	
F.I.C.A. Taxes Payable		765
Federal Unemployment Tax Payable		80
State Unemployment Tax Payable		400

The employer is required to remit to the government its share of F.I.C.A. tax along with the amount of F.I.C.A. tax deducted from each employee's gross compensation. All unremitted employer F.I.C.A. taxes should be recorded as payroll tax expense and payroll tax payable. In a manufacturing enterprise, all of the payroll costs (wages, payroll taxes, and fringe benefits) are allocated to appropriate cost accounts such as Direct Labor, Indirect Labor, Sales Salaries, Administrative Salaries, and the like. This abbreviated and somewhat simplified discussion of payroll costs and deductions is not indicative of the volume of records and clerical work that may be involved in maintaining a sound and accurate payroll system.

Compensated Absences

Compensated absences are absences from employment—such as vacation, illness, and holidays—for which employees are paid anyway. A liability should be accrued for the cost of compensation for future absences if **all** of the following conditions are met:[15]

(a) The employer's obligation relating to employees' rights to receive compensation for future absences is attributable to employees' services **already rendered**,
(b) The obligation relates to the rights that **vest or accumulate**,

UNDERLYING CONCEPTS

When these four conditions exist, all elements in the definition of a liability exist. In addition, the matching concept requires that the period receiving the services also should report the related expense.

[15]"Accounting for Compensated Absences," *Statement of Financial Accounting Standards No. 43* (Stamford, Conn.: FASB, 1980), par. 6.

(c) Payment of the compensation is **probable**, and
(d) The amount can be **reasonably estimated**.[16]

An example of an accrual for compensated absences is shown below in an excerpt from the balance sheet of Clarcor Inc. presented in its Annual Report.

ILLUSTRATION 13-5
Balance Sheet
Presentation of Accrual
for Compensated
Absences

Clarcor Inc.	
Current Liabilities	
Accounts payable	$ 6,308
Accrued salaries, wages and commissions	2,278
Compensated absences	2,271
Accrued pension liabilities	1,023
Other accrued liabilities	4,572
	$16,452

If an employer meets conditions (a), (b), and (c) but does not accrue a liability because of a failure to meet condition (d), that fact should be disclosed. An example of such a disclosure is the following note from the financial statements of Gotham Utility Company:

ILLUSTRATION 13-6
Disclosure of Policy for
Compensated Absences

> **Gotham Utility Company**
>
> Employees of the Company are entitled to paid vacation, personal, and sick days off, depending on job status, length of service, and other factors. Due to numerous differing union contracts and other agreements with nonunion employees, it is impractical to estimate the amount of compensation for future absences, and, accordingly, no liability has been reported in the accompanying financial statements. The Company's policy is to recognize the cost of compensated absences when actually paid to employees; compensated absence payments to employees totaled $2,786,000.

Vested rights exist when an employer has an obligation to make payment to an employee even if his or her employment is terminated; thus, vested rights are not contingent on an employee's future service. **Accumulated rights** are those that can be carried forward to future periods if not used in the period in which earned. For example, assume that you have earned 4 days of vacation pay as of December 31, the end of your employer's fiscal year, and that you will be paid for this vacation time even if you terminate employment. In this situation, your 4 days of vacation pay are considered vested and must be accrued. Now assume that your vacation days are not vested, but that you can carry the 4 days over into later periods. Although the rights are not vested, they are accumulated rights for which the employer must provide an accrual, allowing for estimated forfeitures due to turnover.

A modification of the general rules relates to the issue of **sick pay**. If sick pay benefits vest, accrual is required. If sick pay benefits accumulate but do not vest, accrual is permitted but not required. The reason for this distinction is that compensation that is designated as sick pay may be administered in one of two ways. In some companies, employees receive sick pay only if they are absent because of illness. Accrual of a liability is permitted but not required because its payment is contingent upon future employee illness. In other companies, employees are allowed to accumulate unused sick pay and take compensated time off from work even though they are not ill. For this type of sick pay, a liability must be accrued because it will be paid whether or not employees ever become ill.

---

[16]These same four conditions are to be applied to accounting for **postemployment benefits. Postemployment benefits** are benefits provided by an enterprise to past or inactive employees **after employment but prior to retirement**. Examples include salary continuation, supplemental unemployment benefits, severance pay, job training, and continuation of health and life insurance coverage. The FASB recently issued *Statement No. 112*, "Employers' Accounting for Postemployment Benefits" which requires that the accounting treatment for compensated absences described in *FASB Statement No. 43* should be applied to postemployment benefits. "Employers' Accounting for Postemployment Benefits," *Statement of Financial Accounting Standards No. 112* (Norwalk, Conn.: FASB, November 1992), par. 18.

The expense and related liability for compensated absences should be recognized in the year earned by employees. For example, if new employees receive rights to 2 weeks' paid vacation at the beginning of their second year of employment, the vacation pay is considered to be earned during the first year of employment.

What rate should be used to accrue the compensated absence cost—the current rate or an estimated future rate? *FASB Statement No. 43* is silent on this subject; therefore, it is likely that companies will use the current rather than future rate. The future rate is less certain and raises issues concerning the time value of money. To illustrate, assume that Amutron Inc. began operations on January 1, 1997. The company employs 10 individuals who are paid $480 per week. Vacation weeks earned by all employees in 1997 were 20 weeks, but none were used during this period. In 1998, the vacation weeks were used when the current rate of pay was $540 per week for each employee. The entry at December 31, 1997 to accrue the accumulated vacation pay is as follows:

Wages Expense	9,600	
Vacation Wages Payable ($480 × 20)		9,600

At December 31, 1997 the company would report on its balance sheet a liability of $9,600. In 1998, the vacation pay related to 1997 would be recorded as follows:

Vacation Wages Payable	9,600	
Wages Expense	1,200	
Cash ($540 × 20)		10,800

In 1998 the vacation weeks were used; therefore, the liability is extinguished. Note that the difference between the amount of cash paid and the reduction in the liability account is recorded as an adjustment to Wages Expense in the period when paid. This difference arises because the liability account was accrued at the rates of pay in effect during the period when compensated time was earned. The cash paid, however, is based on the rates in effect during the period when compensated time is used. If the future rates of pay had been used to compute the accrual in 1997, then the cash paid in 1998 would have been equal to the liability.

Postretirement Benefits

The accounting and reporting standards for postretirement benefit payments are complex. These standards relate to two different types of **postretirement benefits**: (1) pensions and (2) postretirement health care and life insurance benefits. These issues are discussed extensively in Chapter 21.

Bonus Agreements

For various reasons, many companies give a **bonus** to certain or all officers and employees in addition to their regular salary or wage. Frequently the bonus amount is dependent on the company's yearly profit. For example, Ford Motor Company has a plan whereby employees share in the success of the company's operations on the basis of a complicated formula using net income as its primary basis for computation. From the standpoint of the enterprise, **bonus payments to employees** may be considered additional wages and should be included as a deduction in determining the net income for the year.

To illustrate the entries for an employee bonus, assume a company whose income for the year 1998 is $100,000 will pay out bonuses of $10,714.29 in January 1999. (Computations of this and other bonuses are illustrated in Appendix 13A.) An adjusting entry dated December 31, 1998, is made to record the bonus as follows:

Employees' Bonus Expense	10,714.29	
Profit-Sharing Bonus Payable		10,714.29

In January 1999, when the bonus is paid, the journal entry would be:

Profit-Sharing Bonus Payable	10,714.29	
Cash		10,714.29

INTERNATIONAL INSIGHT

In Japan, bonuses to members of the Board of Directors and to the Commercial Code auditors are not treated as expenses. They are considered to be a distribution of profits and charged against retained earnings.

The expense account should appear in the income statement as an operating expense. The liability, profit-sharing bonus payable, is usually payable within a short period of time and should be included as a current liability in the balance sheet.

Similar to bonus arrangements are contractual agreements covering rents or royalty payments conditional on the amount of revenues earned or the quantity of product produced or extracted. Conditional expenses based on revenues or units produced are usually less difficult to compute than bonus arrangements. For example, if a lease calls for a fixed rent payment of $500 per month and 1% of all sales over $300,000 per year, the annual rent obligation would amount to $6,000 plus $.01 of each dollar of revenue over $300,000. Or, a royalty agreement may accrue to the patent owner $1.00 for every ton of product resulting from the patented process, or accrue to the mineral rights owner $.50 on every barrel of oil extracted. As each additional unit of product is produced or extracted, an additional obligation, usually a current liability, is created.

SECTION 2	*CONTINGENCIES*

A **contingency** is defined in *FASB Statement No. 5* "as an existing condition, situation, or set of circumstances involving uncertainty as to possible gain (**gain contingency**) or loss (**loss contingency**) to an enterprise that will ultimately be resolved when one or more future events occur or fail to occur."[17]

❖ GAIN CONTINGENCIES

Objective ❺

Identify the criteria used to account for and disclose gain and loss contingencies.

Gain contingencies are claims or rights to receive assets (or have a liability reduced) whose existence is uncertain but which may become valid eventually.

The typical gain contingencies are:

❶ Possible receipts of monies from gifts, donations, bonuses, and so on.
❷ Possible refunds from the government in tax disputes.
❸ Pending court cases where the probable outcome is favorable.
❹ Tax loss carryforwards (discussed in Chapter 20).

Accountants have adopted a conservative policy in this area. Gain contingencies are not recorded. They are disclosed in the notes only when the probabilities are high that a gain contingency will become reality. As a result, it is unusual to find information about contingent gains in the financial statements and the accompanying notes. An example of a disclosure of a gain contingency is as follows:

ILLUSTRATION 13-7
Disclosure of Gain
Contingency

BMC Industries, Inc.

Note 13: Legal Matters.   In January 1995, a U.S. District Court in Miami, Florida, awarded the Company a $5.1 million judgment against Barth Industries (Barth) of Cleveland, Ohio and its parent, Nesco Holdings, Inc. (Nesco). The judgment relates to an agreement under which Barth and Nesco were to help automate the plastic lens production plant in Fort Lauderdale, Florida. The Company has not recorded any income relating to this judgment because Barth and Nesco have filed an appeal.

❖ LOSS CONTINGENCIES

Loss contingencies are situations involving uncertainty as to possible loss. A liability incurred as a result of a loss contingency is by definition a **contingent liability**. **Contingent liabilities** are obligations that are dependent upon the occurrence or non-

---

[17]"Accounting for Contingencies," *Statement of Financial Accounting Standards No. 5* (Stamford, Conn.: FASB, 1975), par. 1.

occurrence of one or more future events to confirm either the amount payable, the payee, the date payable, or its existence. That is, one or more of these factors depend upon a contingency.

When a loss contingency exists, the likelihood that the future event or events will confirm the incurrence of a liability can range from probable to remote. The FASB uses the terms **probable**, **reasonably possible**, and **remote** to identify three areas within that range and assigns the following meanings:

Probable. The future event or events are likely to occur.

Reasonably Possible. The chance of the future event or events occurring is more than remote but less than likely.

Remote. The chance of the future event or events occurring is slight.

An estimated loss from a loss contingency should be accrued by a charge to expense and a liability recorded only if **both** of the following conditions are met:[18]

❶ Information available prior to the issuance of the financial statements indicates that it is **probable that a liability has been incurred** at the date of the financial statements.
❷ The amount of the loss can be **reasonably estimated**.

Neither the exact payee nor the exact date payable need be known to record a liability. **What must be known is whether it is probable that a liability has been incurred.**

The second criterion indicates that an amount for the liability can be reasonably determined; otherwise, it should not be accrued as a liability. Evidence to determine a reasonable estimate of the liability may be based on the company's own experience, experience of other companies in the industry, engineering or research studies, legal advice, or educated guesses by personnel in the best position to know. The following excerpt from the annual report of Quaker State Oil Refining Corp. is an example of an accrual recorded for a loss contingency.

Quaker State Oil Refining Corp.

Note 5: Contingencies. During the period from November 13 to December 23, a change in an additive component purchased from one of its suppliers caused certain oil refined and shipped to fail to meet the Company's low-temperature performance requirements. The Company has recalled this product and has arranged for reimbursement to its customers and the ultimate consumers of all costs associated with the product. Estimated cost of the recall program, net of estimated third party reimbursement, in the amount of $3,500,000 has been charged to current operations.

ILLUSTRATION 13-8
Disclosure of Accrual for Loss Contingency

Use of the terms probable, reasonably possible, and remote as guidelines for classifying contingencies involves judgment and subjectivity. The items in Illustration 13-9 are examples of loss contingencies and the general accounting treatment accorded them.

Practicing accountants express concern over the diversity that now exists in the interpretation of "probable," "reasonably possible," and "remote." Current practice relies heavily on the exact language used in responses received from lawyers (such language is necessarily biased and protective rather than predictive). As a result, accruals and disclosures of contingencies vary considerably in practice. Some of the more common loss contingencies discussed in this chapter are:[19]

❶ Litigation, claims, and assessments.
❷ Guarantee and warranty costs.

 **INTERNATIONAL INSIGHT**

In Germany, company law allows firms to accrue losses for contingencies as long as they are possible and reasonable. Such provisions are one means of smoothing income.

---

[18]Those loss contingencies that result in the incurrence of a liability are most relevant to the discussion in this chapter. Loss contingencies that result in the impairment of an asset (e.g., collectibility of receivables or threat of expropriation of assets) are discussed more fully in other sections of this textbook.

[19]*Accounting Trends and Techniques—1996* reports that of the 600 companies surveyed, loss contingencies of the following nature and number were reported: litigation, 422; environmental, 291; insurance, 64; possible tax assessments, 61; governmental investigation, 34; and others, 69.

ILLUSTRATION 13-9
Accounting Treatment
of Loss Contingencies

Loss Related to	Usually Accrued	Not Accrued	May Be Accrued*
1. Collectibility of receivables	X		
2. Obligations related to product warranties and product defects	X		
3. Premiums offered to customers	X		
4. Risk of loss or damage of enterprise property by fire, explosion, or other hazards		X	
5. General or unspecified business risks		X	
6. Risk of loss from catastrophes assumed by property and casualty insurance companies including reinsurance companies		X	
7. Threat of expropriation of assets			X
8. Pending or threatened litigation			X
9. Actual or possible claims and assessments**			X
10. Guarantees of indebtedness of others			X
11. Obligations of commercial banks under "standby letters of credit"			X
12. Agreements to repurchase receivables (or the related property) that have been sold			X

*Should be accrued when both criteria are met (probable and reasonably estimable).
**Estimated amounts of losses incurred prior to the balance sheet date but settled subsequently should be accrued as of the balance sheet date.

❸ Premiums and coupons.
❹ Environmental liabilities.
❺ Self-insurance risks.

Note that general risk contingencies that are inherent in business operations, such as the possibility of war, strike, uninsurable catastrophes, or a business recession, are not reported in the notes to the financial statements.

Litigation, Claims, and Assessments

Objective ❻

Explain the accounting for different types of loss contingencies.

The following factors, among others, must be considered in determining whether a liability should be recorded with respect to **pending or threatened** litigation and actual or possible **claims** and **assessments**:

❶ The **time period** in which the underlying cause for action occurred.
❷ The **probability** of an unfavorable outcome.
❸ The ability to make a **reasonable estimate** of the amount of loss.

To report a loss and a liability in the financial statements, the cause for litigation must have occurred on or before the date of the financial statements. It does not matter that the company did not become aware of the existence or possibility of the lawsuit or claims until after the date of the financial statements but before they are issued. To evaluate the probability of an unfavorable outcome, consider: the nature of the litigation; the progress of the case; the opinion of legal counsel; the experience of your company and others in similar cases; and any management response to the lawsuit.

The outcome of pending litigation, however, can seldom be predicted with any assurance. And, even if the evidence available at the balance sheet date does not favor the defendant, it is hardly reasonable to expect the company to publish in its financial statements a dollar estimate of the probable negative outcome. Such specific disclosures could weaken the company's position in the dispute and encourage the plaintiff to intensify its efforts. A typical example of the wording of such a disclosure is the note to the financial statements of Apple Computer, Inc., relating to its litigation concerning repetitive stress injuries as shown in Illustration 13-10.

ILLUSTRATION 13-10
Disclosure of Litigation

> ### Apple Computer, Inc.
>
> **"Repetitive Stress Injury" Litigation.** The Company is named in numerous lawsuits (fewer than 100) alleging that the plaintiff incurred so-called "repetitive stress injury" to the upper extremities as a result of using keyboards and/or mouse input devices sold by the Company. On October 4, 1996, in a trial of one of these cases (*Dorsey v. Apple*) in the United States District Court for the Eastern District of New York, the jury rendered a verdict in favor of the Company, and final judgment in favor of the Company has been entered. The other cases are in various stages of pretrial activity. These suits are similar to those filed against other major suppliers of personal computers. Ultimate resolution of the litigation against the Company may depend on progress in resolving this type of litigation in the industry overall.

With respect to **unfiled suits** and **unasserted claims and assessments**, a company must determine (1) the degree of **probability** that a suit may be filed or a claim or assessment may be asserted and (2) the **probability** of an unfavorable outcome. For example, assume that Nawtee Company is being investigated by the Federal Trade Commission for restraint of trade, and enforcement proceedings have been instituted. Such proceedings are often followed by private claims of triple damages for redress. In this case, Nawtee Company must determine the probability of the claims being asserted **and** the probability of triple damages being awarded. If both are probable, if the loss is reasonably estimable, and if the cause for action is dated on or before the date of the financial statements, then the liability should be accrued.[20]

Guarantee and Warranty Costs

A warranty **(product guarantee)** is a promise made by a seller to a buyer to make good on a deficiency of quantity, quality, or performance in a product. It is commonly used by manufacturers as a sales promotion technique. Automakers, for instance, recently "hyped" their sales by extending their new-car warranty to 7 years or 70,000 miles. For a specified period of time following the date of sale to the consumer, the manufacturer may promise to bear all or part of the cost of replacing defective parts, to perform any necessary repairs or servicing without charge, to refund the purchase price, or even to "double your money back."

Warranties and guarantees entail future costs, frequently significant additional costs, which are sometimes called "after costs" or "post-sale costs." Although the future cost is indefinite as to amount, due date, and even customer, a liability is probable in most cases and should be recognized in the accounts if it can be reasonably estimated. The amount of the liability is an estimate of all the costs that will be incurred after sale and delivery and that are incident to the correction of defects or deficiencies required under the warranty provisions. Warranty costs are a classic example of a loss contingency. There are two basic methods of accounting for warranty costs: (1) the cash basis method and (2) the accrual method.

Cash Basis

Under the **cash basis method**, warranty costs are charged to expense as they are incurred. In other words, **warranty costs are charged to the period in which the seller or manufacturer complies with the warranty**. No liability is recorded for future costs arising from warranties, nor is the period in which the sale is recorded necessarily charged with the costs of making good on outstanding warranties. Use of this method, the only one recognized for income tax purposes, is frequently justified for accounting on the basis of expediency when warranty costs are immaterial or when the warranty period is relatively short. The cash basis method is required when a warranty liability is not accrued in the year of sale either because

❶ It is not probable that a liability has been incurred; or
❷ The amount of the liability cannot be reasonably estimated.

---

[20]Contingencies involving an unasserted claim or assessment need not be disclosed when no claimant has come forward unless (1) it is considered probable that a claim will be asserted and (2) there is a reasonable possibility that the outcome will be unfavorable.

Accrual Basis

If it is probable that customers will make claims under warranties relating to goods or services that have been sold and a reasonable estimate of the costs involved can be made, the accrual method must be used. Under the **accrual method**, warranty costs are charged to operating expense **in the year of sale.** It is the generally accepted method and should be used whenever the warranty is an integral and inseparable part of the sale and is viewed as a loss contingency. We refer to this approach as the expense warranty approach.

Illustration of Expense Warranty Approach. To illustrate the expense warranty method, assume that the Denson Machinery Company begins production on a new machine in July 1998, and sells 100 units at $5,000 each by its year-end, December 31, 1998. Each machine is under warranty for one year and the company has estimated, from past experience with a similar machine, that the warranty cost will probably average $200 per unit. Further, as a result of parts replacements and services rendered in compliance with machinery warranties, the company incurs $4,000 in warranty costs in 1998 and $16,000 in 1999.

❶ Sale of 100 machines at $5,000 each, July through December 1998

Cash or Accounts Receivable	500,000	
Sales		500,000

❷ Recognition of warranty expense, July through December 1998

Warranty Expense	4,000	
Cash, Inventory, or Accrued Payroll		4,000
(Warranty costs incurred)		
Warranty Expense	16,000	
Estimated Liability under Warranties		16,000
(To accrue estimated warranty costs)		

The 12/31/98 balance sheet would report Estimated Liability Under Warranties as a current liability of $16,000, and the income statement for 1998 would report Warranty Expense of $20,000.

❸ Recognition of warranty costs incurred in 1999 (on 1998 machinery sales)

Estimated Liability under Warranties	16,000	
Cash, Inventory, or Accrued Payroll		16,000
(Warranty costs incurred)		

If the cash basis method were applied to the facts in the Denson Machinery Company example, $4,000 would be recorded as warranty expense in 1998 and $16,000 as warranty expense in 1999 with all of the sale price being recorded as revenue in 1998. In many instances, application of the cash basis method does not match the warranty costs relating to the products sold during a given period with the revenues derived from such products, and therefore it violates the matching principle. Where ongoing warranty policies exist year after year, the differences between the cash and the expense warranty basis probably would not be so great.

Sales Warranty Approach. A warranty is sometimes **sold separately from the product.** For example, when you purchase a television set or VCR, you will be entitled to the manufacturer's warranty. You also will undoubtedly be offered an extended warranty on the product at an additional cost.[21]

In this case, the seller should recognize separately the sale of the television or VCR with the manufacturer's warranty and the sale of the extended warranty.[22] This ap-

---

[21]A contract is separately priced **if the customer has the option to purchase** the services provided under the contract for an expressly stated amount separate from the price of the product. An extended warranty or product maintenance contract usually meets these conditions.

[22]"Accounting for Separately Extended Warranty and Product Maintenance Contracts," *FASB Technical Bulletin No. 90–1* (Stamford, Conn.: FASB, 1990).

proach is referred to as the **sales warranty approach**. **Revenue on the sale of the extended warranty is deferred** and is generally recognized on a straight-line basis over the life of the contract. Revenue is deferred because the seller of the warranty has an obligation to perform services over the life of the contract. Only costs that vary with and are directly related to the sale of the contracts (mainly commissions) should be deferred and amortized. Costs such as employees' salaries, advertising, and general and administrative expenses that would have been incurred even if no contract were sold should be expensed as incurred.

To illustrate, assume you have just purchased a new automobile from Hanlin Auto for $20,000. In addition to the regular warranty on the auto (all repairs will be paid by the manufacturer for the first 36,000 miles or 3 years, whichever comes first), you purchase at a cost of $600 an extended warranty that protects you for an additional 3 years or 36,000 miles. The entry to record the sale of the automobile (with the regular warranty) and the sale of the extended warranty on January 2, 1998, on Hanlin Auto's books is:

Cash	20,600	
Sales		20,000
Unearned Warranty Revenue		600

The entry to recognize revenue at the end of the fourth year (using straight-line amortization) would be as follows:

Unearned Warranty Revenue	200	
Warranty Revenue		200

Because the extended warranty contract does not start until after the regular warranty expires, revenue is not recognized until the fourth year. If the costs of performing services under the extended warranty contract are incurred on other than a straight-line basis (as historical evidence might indicate), revenue should be recognized over the contract period in proportion to the costs expected to be incurred in performing services under the contract.[23]

Premiums and Coupons

Numerous companies offer (either on a limited or continuing basis) premiums to customers in return for boxtops, certificates, coupons, labels, or wrappers. The **premium** may be silverware, dishes, a small appliance, a toy, other goods, or free transportation.[24]

---

[23]Ibid, par. 3.

[24]Recent premium plans that have gained momentum and widespread adoption are the **frequent-flier programs** used by nearly every major airline. On the basis of mileage accumulated, frequent-flier members are awarded discounted or free airline tickets. Although the frequent-flier concept, begun in 1981 by American Airlines, was little more than a takeoff on green stamps, its success in generating repeat business stunned the airline industry. Today, especially with the advent of triple-mileage bonuses, frequent-flier programs are so popular that airlines now owe participants more than 3 million round-trip domestic tickets. That's enough to fly at least 5.4 billion miles—free. And therein lies the accounting problem. Those free tickets represent an enormous potential liability because people using them may displace paying passengers.

When airlines first started offering frequent-flier bonuses, everyone assumed that they could accommodate the free-ticket holders with otherwise-empty seats. That made the additional cost of the program so minimal that airlines didn't accrue it or report the small liability. But, as more and more paying passengers have been crowded off of flights by frequent-flier awardees, the loss of revenues has grown enormously. One investment analyst estimated in a recent year the loss in airline profits due to the frequent-flier plan at $150 million.

Although the accounting for this transaction has been studied by the profession, no authoritative guidelines have been issued.

Also, **printed coupons** that can be redeemed for a cash discount on items purchased are extremely popular.[25] A more recent marketing innovation is the **cash rebate**, which the buyer can obtain by returning the store receipt, a rebate coupon, and Universal Product Code (UPC label) or "bar code" to the manufacturer. These premiums, coupon offers, and rebates are made to stimulate sales, and their **costs should be charged to expense in the period of the sale** that benefits from the premium plan. At the end of the accounting period many of these premium offers may be outstanding and, when presented in subsequent periods, must be redeemed. **The number of outstanding premium offers that will be presented for redemption must be estimated in order to reflect the existing current liability and to match costs with revenues.** The cost of premium offers should be charged to Premium Expense, and the outstanding obligations should be credited to an account titled Estimated Liability for Premiums.

Although the FASB did not include premium offers in its list of loss contingencies, the authors believe that **premium offers result in the probable existence of a liability at the date of the financial statements, can be reasonably estimated in amount, are contingent upon the occurrence of a future event (redemption), and, therefore, are a loss contingency** within the guidelines of *FASB Statement No. 5*.

The following example illustrates the accounting treatment accorded a premium offer. Fluffy Cakemix Company offered its customers a large nonbreakable mixing bowl in exchange for 25 cents and 10 boxtops. The mixing bowl costs Fluffy Cakemix Company 75 cents, and the company estimates that 60% of the boxtops will be redeemed. The premium offer began in June 1998 and resulted in the following transactions and entries during 1998.

❶ To record purchase of 20,000 mixing bowls at 75 cents each:

Inventory of Premium Mixing Bowls	15,000	
Cash		15,000

❷ To record sales of 300,000 boxes of cake mix at 80 cents:

Cash	240,000	
Sales		240,000

❸ To record the actual redemption of 60,000 boxtops, the receipt of 25 cents per 10 boxtops, and the delivery of the mixing bowls:

Cash [(60,000 ÷ 10) × $0.25]	1,500	
Premium Expense	3,000	
Inventory of Premium Mixing Bowls		4,500
(Computation: [60,000 ÷ 10] × $0.75 = $4,500)		

❹ To record end-of-period adjusting entry for estimated liability for outstanding premium offers (boxtops):

Premium Expense	6,000	
Estimated Liability for Premiums		6,000

Computation:

Total boxtops sold in 1998	300,000
Total estimated redemptions (60%)	180,000
Boxtops redeemed in 1998	60,000
Estimated future redemptions	120,000

Cost of estimated claims outstanding
(120,000 ÷ 10) × ($0.75 − $0.25) = $6,000

UNDERLYING CONCEPTS

Warranties and coupons are loss contingencies that satisfy the conditions necessary for a liability. Regarding the income statement, the *matching principle* requires that the related expense be reported in the period that the sale occurs.

---

[25]Approximately 4% of coupons are redeemed. Redeemed coupons eventually make their way to the corporate headquarters of the stores that accept them. From there they are shipped in 50-pound boxes to Mexico's border towns (Juárez, Tijuana, Nuevo Laredo), where clearinghouses operated by A. C. Nielsen Company (of TV rating fame) count them and report back to the manufacturers who, in turn, reimburse the stores.

The December 31, 1998, balance sheet of Fluffy Cakemix Company will report an Inventory of Premium Mixing Bowls of $10,500 as a current asset and Estimated Liability for Premiums of $6,000 as a current liability. The 1998 income statement will report a $9,000 Premium Expense among the selling expenses.

Environmental Liabilities

Estimates to clean up existing toxic waste sites run to upward of $752 billion over a 30-year period. In addition, the cost of cleaning up our air and preventing future deterioration of the environment is estimated to cost even more. The average environmental cost per firm in various industries is: high-tech firms, $2 million (6.1% of revenues); utilities, $340 million (6.1% of revenues); steel and metals, $50 million (2.9% of revenues); and oil companies, $430 million (1.9% of revenues). Given that the average pretax profit of the 500 largest U.S. manufacturing companies recently was 7.7 percent of sales, these figures are staggering!

These costs will only grow when one considers "superfund legislation": it provides not only a government-supported fund to clean up pollution, but a mandate to clean up existing waste sites. Further it provided the Environmental Protection Agency (EPA) with the power to clean up waste sites and charge the clean-up costs to parties the EPA deems responsible for contaminating the site. These potentially responsible parties have an onerous liability. The EPA estimates that it will likely cost an average of $25 million to clean up each polluted site. For the most troublesome sites, the cost could easily reach $100 million or more. It is estimated that $65 billion will be required nationwide by the year 2000 to clean up contaminated land.

Presently **companies infrequently record any liability for these potential costs.** They note that the liability is a contingent liability that is not estimable. As a result, generally only a description regarding the possible liability is disclosed in the financial statements. An example of one company that did report a liability is provided in Illustration 13-11.

More extensive disclosure is needed regarding environmental liabilities. In addition, more of these liabilities should be recorded. The SEC believes that managements should not delay recognition of a liability due to significant uncertainty. The SEC argues that if the liability is within a range and no amount within the range is the best estimate, then management should recognize the minimum amount of the range; that is in accordance with *FASB Interpretation No. 14*, "Reasonable Estimation of a Loss." The SEC also believes that environmental liabilities should be reported in the balance sheet independent of recoveries from third parties. Thus, possible insurance recoveries are not permitted to be netted against liabilities but must be shown separately. Because there is much litigation regarding recovery of insurance proceeds, these "assets" appear to be gain contingencies and, therefore, companies will not be reporting these on the balance sheet.[26]

Self-Insurance

A company may insure against many contingencies such as fire, flood, storm, and accident by taking out insurance policies and paying premiums to insurance companies. Some contingencies are, however, not insurable, or the insurance rates are prohibitive (e.g., earthquakes and riots). For such contingencies, even though insurance may be available, some businesses adopt a policy of self-insurance.

> **UNDERLYING CONCEPTS**
>
> Even if the amount of losses is estimable with a high degree of certainty, the losses are not liabilities because they result from a future event and not from a past event.

---

[26]As indicated earlier, the FASB pronouncements on this topic require that, when some amount within the range appears at the time to be a better estimate than any other amount within the range, that amount is accrued. When no amount within the range is a better estimate than any other amount, the dollar amount at the low end of the range is **accrued** and the dollar amount of the high end of the range is **disclosed.** See *FASB Interpretation No. 14*, "Reasonable Estimation of the Amount of a Loss" (Stamford, Conn.: FASB, 1976), par. 3, and *FASB Statement No. 5*, "Accounting for Contingencies" (Stamford, Conn.: FASB, 1975).

ILLUSTRATION 13-11
Disclosure of a Recorded
Liability for
Environmental Costs

> ### Crown Central Petroleum Corporation
>
> **Note G (in part): Contingencies—Environmental.** Like other petroleum refiners and marketers, the Company's operations are subject to extensive and rapidly changing federal and state environmental regulations governing air emissions, waste water discharges, and solid and hazardous waste management activities. The Company's policy is to accrue environmental and clean-up related costs of a noncapital nature when it is both probable that a liability has been incurred and the amount can be reasonably estimated. While it is often extremely difficult to reasonably quantify future environmental related expenditures, the Company anticipates a substantial capital investment will be required over the next several years to comply with existing regulations. The Company had recorded a liability of approximately $10,485,000 to cover the estimated costs of compliance with environmental regulations which are not anticipated to be of a capital nature.

🌐 **INTERNATIONAL INSIGHT**

In Switzerland, companies may make provisions for general (non-specified) contingencies to the extent allowed by tax regulations.

Despite its name, self-insurance is **not insurance, but risk assumption,** and any company that assumes its own risks puts itself in the position of incurring expenses or losses as they occur. There is little theoretical justification for the establishment of a liability based on a hypothetical charge to insurance expense. This is "as if" accounting. The conditions for accrual stated in *FASB Statement No. 5* are not satisfied prior to the occurrence of the event; until that time there is no diminution in the value of the property. And unlike an insurance company, which has contractual obligations to reimburse policyholders for losses, a company can have no such obligation to itself and, hence, no liability either before or after the occurrence of damage.[27]

The following note from the annual report of Adolph Coors Company is typical of the self-insurance disclosure.

ILLUSTRATION 13-12
Disclosure of Self-
Insurance

> ### Adolph Coors Company
>
> **Notes to Financial Statements**
>
> **Note 4: Commitments and Contingencies.** It is generally the policy of the Company to act as a self-insurer for certain insurable risks consisting primarily of physical loss to corporate property, business interruption resulting from such loss, employee health insurance programs, and workmen's compensation. Losses and claims are accrued as incurred.

Exposure to **risks of loss resulting from uninsured past injury to others,** however, is an existing condition involving uncertainty about the amount and timing of losses that may develop, in which case a contingency exists. A company with a fleet of vehicles would have to accrue uninsured losses resulting from injury to others or damage to the property of others that took place prior to the date of the financial statements (if the experience of the company or other information enables it to make a reasonable estimate of the liability). However, it should not establish a liability for **expected future injury** to others or damage to the property of others even if the amount of losses is reasonably estimable.

❖ PRESENTATION AND ANALYSIS

Objective ❼

Indicate how current liabilities and contingencies are presented and analyzed.

Presentation of Current Liabilities

In practice, **current liabilities are usually recorded in accounting records and reported in financial statements at their full maturity value.** Because of the short time periods involved, frequently less than one year, the difference between the present value of a current liability and the maturity value is not usually large. The slight overstatement

---

[27]"Accounting for Contingencies," *FASB Statement No. 5,* op. cit., par. 28. A commentary in *Forbes* (June 15, 1974, p. 42) stated its position on this matter quite succinctly: "The simple and unqestionable fact of life is this: Business is cyclical and full of unexpected surprises. Is it the role of accounting to disguise this unpleasant fact and create a fairyland of smoothly rising earnings? Or, should accounting reflect reality, warts and all—floods, expropriations and all manner of rude shocks?"

of liabilities that results from carrying current liabilities at maturity value is accepted as immaterial. *APB Opinion No. 21,* "Interest on Receivables and Payables," specifically exempts from present value measurements those payables arising from transactions with suppliers in the normal course of business that do not exceed approximately one year.[28]

The current liability accounts are commonly presented as the first classification in the liabilities and stockholders' equity section of the balance sheet. Within the current liability section the accounts may be listed in order of maturity, in descending order of amount, or in order of liquidation preference. Presented in Illustration 13-13 is an excerpt of the Tyson Foods, Inc., published financial statements, which is a representative presentation of the current liabilities as found in the reports of large corporations:

ILLUSTRATION 13-13
Balance Sheet
Presentation of Current
Liabilities

Tyson Foods, Inc.

(In millions)	1995	1994
Current liabilities		
Notes payable	$ 95.2	$ 49.4
Current portion of long-term debt	269.0	24.2
Trade accounts payable	274.7	258.6
Accrued salaries and wages	74.6	71.8
Federal and state income taxes payable	14.6	19.7
Accrued interest payable	7.9	4.2
Other current liabilities	129.8	111.9
Total current liabilities	$865.8	$539.8

Go to our Web site for additional disclosures of current liability sections.

Detail and supplemental information concerning current liabilities should be sufficient to meet the requirement of full disclosure. Secured liabilities should be identified clearly, and the related assets pledged as collateral indicated. If the due date of any liability can be extended, the details should be disclosed. Current liabilities should not be offset against assets that are to be applied to their liquidation. Current maturities of long-term debt should be classified as current liabilities.

A major exception exists when a currently maturing obligation is to be paid from assets classified as long-term. For example, if payments to retire a bond payable are made from a bond sinking fund classified as a long-term asset, the bonds payable should be reported in the long-term liability section. Presentation of this debt in the current liability section would distort the working capital position of the enterprise.

If a short-term obligation is excluded from current liabilities because of refinancing, the note to the financial statements should include:

INTERNATIONAL INSIGHT

In Brazil, material current liabilities due in foreign currencies are presented separately.

❶ A general description of the financing agreement.
❷ The terms of any new obligation incurred or to be incurred.
❸ The terms of any equity security issued or to be issued.

When refinancing on a long-term basis is expected to be accomplished through the issuance of equity securities, it is not appropriate to include the short-term obligation in owners' equity. At the date of the balance sheet, the obligation is a liability and not owners' equity. The disclosure requirements are shown in Illustration 13-14 for an actual refinancing situation.

Presentation of Contingencies

A loss contingency and a liability is recorded if the loss is both probable and estimable. But, if the loss is **either probable or estimable but not both** and if there is at least a **reasonable possibility** that a liability may have been incurred, the following disclosure in the notes is required:

❶ The nature of the contingency.

---

[28]"Interest on Receivables and Payables," *Opinions of the Accounting Principles Board No. 21* (New York: AICPA, 1971), par. 3.

ILLUSTRATION 13-14
Actual Refinancing of
Short-Term Debt

	December 31, 1997
Current liabilities:	
Accounts payable	$ 3,600,000
Accrued payables	2,500,000
Income taxes payable	1,100,000
Current portion of long-term debt	1,000,000
Total current liabilities	$ 8,200,000
Long-term debt:	
Notes payable refinanced in January 1998 (Note 1)	$ 2,000,000
11% bonds due serially through 2008	15,000,000
Total long-term debt	$17,000,000

Note 1: On January 19, 1998, the Company issued 50,000 shares of Common Stock and received proceeds totaling $2,385,000 of which $2,000,000 was used to liquidate notes payable that matured on February 1, 1998. Accordingly, such notes payable have been classified as long-term debt at December 31, 1997.

Go to our Web site for additional
disclosures of contingencies.

❷ An estimate of the possible loss or range of loss or a statement that an estimate cannot be made.

Presented in Illustration 13-15 is an extensive litigation disclosure note (taken from the financial statements of Raymark Corporation), which shows that although actual losses have been charged to operations and further liability possibly exists, no estimate of this liability is possible.

ILLUSTRATION 13-15
Disclosure of Loss
Contingency through
Litigation

**INTERNATIONAL
INSIGHT**

U.S. GAAP provides more
guidance on the content of
disclosures about contingencies
than IASC standards

Raymark Corporation

Note I: Litigation. Raymark is a defendant or co-defendant in a substantial number of lawsuits alleging wrongful injury and/or death from exposure to asbestos fibers in the air. The following table summarizes the activity in these lawsuits:

Claims	
Pending at beginning of year	8,719
Received during year	4,494
Settled or otherwise disposed of	(1,445)
Pending at end of year	11,768
Average indemnification cost	$3,364
Average cost per case, including defense costs	$6,499
Trial activity	
Verdicts for the Company	23
Total trials	36

The following table presents the cost of defending asbestos litigation, together with related insurance and workers' compensation expenses.

Included in operating profit	$ 1,872,000
Nonoperating expense	9,077,000
Total	$10,949,000

The Company is seeking to reasonably determine its liability. However, it is not possible to predict which theory of insurance will apply, the number of lawsuits still to be filed, the cost of settling and defending the existing and unfiled cases, or the ultimate impact of these lawsuits on the Company's consolidated financial statements.

Certain other contingent liabilities that should be disclosed even though the possibility of loss may be remote are the following:

❶ Guarantees of indebtedness of others.
❷ Obligations of commercial banks under "stand-by letters of credit."
❸ Guarantees to repurchase receivables (or any related property) that have been sold or assigned.

Disclosure should include the nature and amount of the guarantee and, if estimable, the amount that could be recovered from outside parties. Cities Service Company disclosed its guarantees of indebtedness of others in the following note:

ILLUSTRATION 13-16
Disclosure of Guarantees
of Indebtedness

Cities Service Company

Note 10: Contingent Liabilities. The Company and certain subsidiaries have guaranteed debt obligations of approximately $62 million of companies in which substantial stock investments are held. Also, under long-term agreements with certain pipeline companies in which stock interests are held, the Company and its subsidiaries have agreed to provide minimum revenue for product shipments. The Company has guaranteed mortgage debt ($80 million) incurred by a 50 percent owned tanker affiliate for construction of tankers which are under long-term charter contracts to the Company and others. It is not anticipated that any loss will result from any of the above described agreements.

Analysis of Current Liabilities

The distinction between current liabilities and long-term debt is important because it provides information about the liquidity of the company. Liquidity regarding a liability is the time that is expected to elapse until a liability has to be paid. In other words, a liability soon to be paid is a current liability. A liquid company is better able to withstand a financial downturn. Also, it has a better chance of taking advantage of investment opportunities that develop.

As indicated, certain basic ratios such as net cash flow provided by operating activities to current liabilities, and the turnover ratios for receivables and inventory, are used to assess liquidity. Two other ratios used to examine liquidity are the current ratio and the acid-test ratio.

The current ratio is the ratio of total current assets to total current liabilities. The formula is shown below.

$$\text{Current ratio} = \frac{\text{Current assets}}{\text{Current liabilities}}$$

ILLUSTRATION 13-17
Formula for Current
Ratio

It is frequently expressed as a coverage of so many times. Sometimes it is called the working capital ratio because working capital is the excess of current assets over current liabilities.

A satisfactory current ratio does not disclose that a portion of the current assets may be tied up in slow-moving inventories. With inventories, especially raw materials and work in process, there is a question of how long it will take to transform them into the finished product and what ultimately will be realized in the sale of the merchandise. Elimination of the inventories, along with any prepaid expenses from the current assets, might provide better information for the short-term creditors. Many analysts favor a quick or acid-test ratio that relates total current liabilities to cash, marketable securities, and receivables. The formula for this ratio is shown below:

$$\text{Acid-test ratio} = \frac{\text{Cash} + \substack{\text{marketable} \\ \text{securities}} + \substack{\text{net} \\ \text{receivables}}}{\text{Current liabilities}}$$

ILLUSTRATION 13-18
Formula for Acid-test
Ratio

To illustrate the computation of these two ratios, the following information for W. H. Brady Company is provided:

ILLUSTRATION 13-19
Current Asset Section of
W. H. Brady Company

W. H. Brady

Current assets	1996
Cash and cash equivalents	$49,281,000
Accounts receivable less allowance	53,679,000
Inventories	
Finished products	28,732,000
Work in process	3,173,000
Raw materials and supplies	8,792,000
Prepaid expenses	12,454,000
Total current assets	$156,111,000

The total current liabilities for W. H. Brady Company were $46,423,000. The computation of the current and acid-test ratios for W. H. Brady Company are as follows:

ILLUSTRATION 13-20
Computation of Current
and Acid-test Ratios

$$\text{Current ratio} = \frac{\text{Current assets}}{\text{Current liabilities}} = \frac{\$156,111,000}{\$46,423,000} = 3.36 \text{ times}$$

$$\text{Acid-test ratio} = \frac{\text{Cash and cash equivalents + net receivables}}{\text{Current liabilities}} = \frac{\$102,960,000}{\$46,423,000} = 2.22 \text{ times}$$

From this information, it appears that W. H. Brady Company's liquidity is excellent.

KEY TERMS

accumulated rights, 658
acid-test ratio, 671
assessments, 662
bonus, 659
claims, 662
compensated absences, 657
contingency, 660
contingent liabilities, 660
current liabilities, 647
current maturities of long-term debt, 649
current ratio, 671
expense warranty approach, 664
gain contingencies, 660
liabilities, 647
litigation, claims, and assessments, 662
loss contingencies, 660
notes payable (trade notes payable), 648
operating cycle, 647
postretirement benefits, 659
premiums, 665
probable (contingency), 661
reasonably possible (contingency), 661
remote (contingency), 661
returnable cash deposits, 652
sales warranty approach, 665
self-insurance, 668
short-term obligations expected to be refinanced, 650
social security tax, 656
trade accounts payable, 648
trade notes payable, 648
unearned revenues, 652
vested rights, 658
warranty, 664

SUMMARY OF LEARNING OBJECTIVES

① *Define current liabilities and describe how they are valued.* Current liabilities are obligations whose liquidation is reasonably expected to require the use of current assets or the creation of other current liabilities. Theoretically, liabilities should be measured by the present value of the future outlay of cash required to liquidate them. In practice, current liabilities are usually recorded in accounting records and reported in financial statements at their full maturity value.

② *Identify the nature and types of current liabilities.* There are several types of liabilities: (1) accounts payable, (2) notes payable, (3) current maturities of long-term debts, (4) dividends payable, (5) returnable deposits, (6) unearned revenues, (7) taxes payable, and (8) employee-related liabilities.

③ *Explain the classification issues of short-term debt expected to be refinanced.* An enterprise is required to exclude a short-term obligation from current liabilities if both of the following conditions are met: (1) It must intend to refinance the obligation on a long-term basis, *and* (2) it must demonstrate an ability to consummate the refinancing.

④ *Identify types of employee-related liabilities.* The employee-related liabilities are: (1) payroll deductions; (2) compensated absences; (3) postretirement benefits, which consist of pensions and postretirement health care and life insurance benefits; and (4) bonus agreements.

⑤ *Identify the criteria used to account for and disclose gain and loss contingencies.* Gain contingencies are not recorded. They are disclosed in the notes only when the probabilities are high that a gain contingency will become a reality. An estimated loss from a loss contingency should be accrued by a charge to expense and a liability recorded only if both of the following conditions are met: (1) Information available prior to the issuance of the financial statements indicates that it is probable that a liability has been incurred at the date of the financial statements, and (2) the amount of the loss can be reasonably estimated.

⑥ *Explain the accounting for different types of loss contingencies.* (1) The following factors must be considered in determining whether a liability should be recorded with respect to pending or threatened litigation and actual or possible claims and assessments: (a) the time period in which the underlying cause for action occurred; (b) the probability of an unfavorable outcome; and (c) the ability to make a reasonable estimate of the amount of loss.

(2) If it is probable that customers will make claims under warranties relating to goods or services that have been sold and a reasonable estimate of the costs involved can be made, the accrual method must be used. Warranty costs under the accrual basis are charged to operating expense in the year of sale.

(3) Premiums, coupon offers, and rebates are made to stimulate sales, and their costs should be charged to expense in the period of the sale that benefits from the premium plan.

DARIAN GRIFFIN works for S.C. Johnson Wax in Racine, Wisconsin. The company is a leading maker of chemical specialty products for home, personal care, and insect control. Mr. Griffin is a graduate of the University of Wisconsin at Madison, with a major in accounting.

Why did you choose industry over public accounting? During the summer before graduation, I interned at Johnson Wax. I really liked the people that I worked with and the diversity of their backgrounds in such fields as marketing, sales, R&D, etc. I also liked the idea of working with a product—actually making something. My first job was in the home care division, which is one of our consumer products businesses. The products include Pledge and Glade air fresheners. My job was to prepare the financial schedules for the business, which included the division's profit and loss statement. Early on, I had to refer back to Intermediate Accounting to set up accruals for our coupon programs. We have to take the estimated redemption and multiply it times the face value of the coupon, plus a handling fee per coupon to come up with the accrual. In my next job, I went into consolidation accounting, where I was responsible for making sure that the trial balances from overseas subsidiaries fit together. I was also responsible for making the various consolidation entries for our worldwide balance sheet.

How would you compare the working world to the college world? In school, you'll go to class and know what chapters are going to be covered. But at work, you have no idea what the hot topic will be that day. You'd better be sharp because the head of your division might show up and want to ask you questions—and you'd better be prepared to answer them. There are a ton of things that have to be dealt with in the morning that you might not be expecting, so the idea of being sharp right when you walk in the door is important.

What is your current job at Johnson Wax? In my current job, I'm a general ledger accountant for the polymer division. I produce P&L, the balance sheet, and the cash flow statement on a monthly basis. We have a business model that we run for the marketing department which produces the net present value of cash flows on pro-forma P&Ls and balance sheets for new business proposals. I manage the inputs into the model and make sure the outputs make sense. The goal of most people here is to become a controller or director of finance for a division. There's also a career track for people to leave finance and go into marketing because, after all, this is a marketing-driven company. Accounting gives you a very good overall business background to see how the various parts of the company fit together.

Indicate how current liabilities and contingencies are presented and analyzed. The current liability accounts are commonly presented as the first classification in the liabilities and stockholders' equity section of the balance sheet. Within the current liability section the accounts may be listed in order of maturity, in descending order of amount, or in order of liquidation preference. Detail and supplemental information concerning current liabilities should be sufficient to meet the requirement of full disclosure. If the loss is either probable or estimable but not both, and if there is at least a reasonable possibility that a liability may have been incurred, disclosure should be made in the notes of the nature of the contingency and an estimate given of the possible loss. Two ratios used to analyze liquidity are the current and acid-test ratios.

Appendix 13A

Computation of Employees' Bonuses

Objective 8

After studying Appendix 13A, you should be able to: Compute employee bonuses under differing arrangements.

Because the amount of a bonus is an expense of the business, the problem of computing the amount of bonus based on income becomes more difficult. Say a company has income of $100,000 determined before considering the bonus expense. According to the terms of the bonus agreement, 20% of the income is to be set aside for distribution among the employees. If the bonus were not itself an expense to be deducted in determining net income, the amount of the bonus could be computed very simply as 20% of the income before bonus of $100,000. However, the bonus itself is an expense that must be deducted in arriving at the amount of income on which the bonus is to be based. Hence, $100,000 reduced by the bonus is the figure on which the bonus is to be computed. That is, the bonus is equal to 20% of $100,000 less the bonus. Stated algebraically:

$$B = 0.20\ (\$100{,}000 - B)$$
$$B = \$20{,}000 - 0.2B$$
$$1.2B = \$20{,}000$$
$$B = \$16{,}666.67$$

A similar problem results from the relationship of bonus payments to federal income taxes. Assume income of $100,000 computed without subtracting either the employees' bonus or taxes on income. The bonus is to be based on income **after deducting income taxes but before deducting the bonus**. The rate of income tax is 40% and the bonus of 20% is a deductible expense for tax purposes. The bonus is, therefore, equal to 20% of $100,000 minus the tax, and the tax is equal to 40% of $100,000 minus the bonus. Thus we have two simultaneous equations that, using B as the symbol for the bonus and T for the tax, may be stated algebraically as follows:

$$B = 0.20\ (\$100{,}000 - T)$$
$$T = 0.40\ (\$100{,}000 - B)$$

These may be solved by substituting the value of T as indicated in the second equation for T in the first equation.

$$B = 0.20\ [\$100,000 - 0.40(\$100,000 - B)]$$
$$B = 0.20\ (\$100,000 - \$40,000 + 0.4B)$$
$$B = 0.20\ (\$60,000 + 0.4B)$$
$$B = \$12,000 + 0.08B$$
$$0.92B = \$12,000$$
$$B = \$13,043.48$$

Substituting this value for B into the second equation allows us to solve for T:

$$T = 0.40\ (\$100,000 - \$13,043.48)$$
$$T = 0.40\ (\$86,956.52)$$
$$T = \$34,782.61$$

To prove these amounts, both should be worked back into the original equation.

$$B = 0.20\ (\$100,000 - T)$$
$$\$13,043.48 = 0.20\ (\$100,000 - \$34,782.61)$$
$$\$13,043.48 = 0.20\ (\$65,217.39)$$
$$\$13,043.48 = \$13,043.48$$

If the terms of the agreement provide for deducting both the tax and the bonus to arrive at the income figure on which the bonus is computed, the equations would be:

$$B = 0.20\ (\$100,000 - B - T)$$
$$T = 0.40\ (\$100,000 - B)$$

Substituting the value of T from the second equation into the first equation enables us to solve for B:

$$B = 0.20\ [\$100,000 - B - 0.40\ (\$100,000 - B)]$$
$$B = 0.20\ (\$100,000 - B - \$40,000 + 0.4B)$$
$$B = 0.20\ (\$60,000 - 0.6B)$$
$$B = \$12,000 - 0.12B$$
$$1.12B = \$12,000$$
$$B = \$10,714.29$$

The value for B may then be substituted in the second equation above, and that equation solved for T:

$$T = 0.40\ (\$100,000 - \$10,714.29)$$
$$T = 0.40\ (\$89,285.71)$$
$$T = \$35,714.28$$

If these values are then substituted in the original bonus equation, they prove themselves as follows:

$$B = 0.20\ (\$100,000 - B - T)$$
$$\$10,714.29 = 0.20\ (\$100,000 - \$10,714.29 - \$35,714.28)$$
$$\$10,714.29 = 0.20\ (\$53,571.43)$$
$$\$10,714.29 = \$10,714.29$$

Drawing up a legal document such as a bonus agreement is a task for a lawyer, not an accountant, although accountants are frequently called on to express an opinion on the agreement's feasibility. In this respect, one should always insist that the agreement state specifically whether income taxes and the bonus itself are expenses deductible in determining income for purposes of the bonus computation.

SUMMARY OF LEARNING OBJECTIVE FOR APPENDIX 13A

⑧ *Compute employee bonuses under differing arrangements.* Because the bonus is based on net income and is deductible in determining net income, the bonus may have to be determined algebraically. Its computation is made more difficult by the bonus being deductible for tax purposes and the taxes being deductible from the income on which the bonus is based.

Note: All **asterisked** Questions, Brief Exercises, Exercises, Problems, and Conceptual Cases relate to material contained in the appendix to each chapter.

❖ QUESTIONS ❖

❶ Distinguish between a current liability and a long-term debt.

❷ Assume that your friend Michael W. Smith, who is a music major, asks you to define and discuss the nature of a liability. Assist him by preparing a definition of a liability and by explaining to him what you believe are the elements or factors inherent in the concept of a liability.

❸ Why is the liability section of the balance sheet of primary significance to bankers?

❹ How are current liabilities related by definition to current assets? How are current liabilities related to a company's operating cycle?

❺ How is present value related to the concept of a liability?

❻ What is the nature of a "discount" on notes payable?

❼ How should a debt callable by the creditor be reported in the debtor's financial statements?

❽ Under what conditions should a short-term obligation be excluded from current liabilities?

❾ What evidence is necessary to demonstrate the ability to consummate the refinancing of short-term debt?

❿ Discuss the accounting treatment or disclosure that should be accorded a declared but unpaid cash dividend; an accumulated but undeclared dividend on cumulative preferred stock; a stock dividend distributable.

⓫ How does deferred or unearned revenue arise? Why can it be classified properly as a current liability? Give several examples of business activities that result in unearned revenues.

⓬ What are compensated absences?

⓭ Under what conditions must an employer accrue a liability for the cost of compensated absences?

⓮ What are postretirement benefits?

⓯ Under what conditions is an employer required to accrue a liability for sick pay? Under what conditions is an employer permitted but not required to accrue a liability for sick pay?

⓰ Over which two periods of time is the property tax most commonly allocated? Under what circumstances might each of these periods be justified as the period of expense?

⓱ Define (a) a contingency and (b) a contingent liability.

⓲ Under what conditions should a contingent liability be recorded?

⓳ Distinguish between a "current liability" and a "contingent liability." Give two examples of each type.

⓴ How are the terms "probable," "reasonably possible," and "remote" related to contingent liabilities?

㉑ Contrast the cash basis method and the accrual method of accounting for warranty costs.

㉒ How does the expense warranty approach differ from the sales warranty approach?

㉓ Zucker-Abrahams Airlines Inc. awards members of its Flightline program a second ticket at half price, valid for 2 years anywhere on its flight system, when a full-price ticket is purchased. How would you account for the full-fare and half-fare tickets?

㉔ Robert Hays Airlines Co. awards members of its Frequent Fliers Club one free round-trip ticket, anywhere on its flight system, for every 50,000 miles flown on its planes. How would you account for the free ticket award?

㉕ Should a liability be recorded for risk of loss due to lack of insurance coverage? Discuss.

㉖ What factors must be considered in determining whether or not to record a liability for pending litigation? For threatened litigation?

㉗ Within the current liability section, how do you believe the accounts should be listed? Defend your position.

㉘ How does the acid-test ratio differ from the current ratio? How are they similar? Of what benefit is the defensive interval ratio?

29 When should liabilities for each of the following items be recorded on the books of an ordinary business corporation?

(a) Acquisition of goods by purchase on credit.

(b) Officers' salaries.

(c) Special bonus to employees.

(d) Dividends.

(e) Purchase commitments.

❖ BRIEF EXERCISES ❖

BE13-1 Congo Corporation uses a periodic inventory system and the gross method of accounting for purchase discounts. On July 1, Congo purchased $40,000 of inventory, terms 2/10, n/30, FOB shipping point. Congo paid freight costs of $1,200. On July 3, Congo returned damaged goods and received credit of $6,000. On July 10, Congo paid for the goods. Prepare all necessary journal entries for Congo.

BE13-2 Desert Storm Company borrowed $50,000 on November 1, 1998, by signing a $50,000, 9%, 3-month note. Prepare Desert Storm's November 1, 1998, entry; the December 31, 1998, annual adjusting entry; and the February 1, 1999, entry.

BE13-3 Kawasaki Corporation borrowed $50,000 on November 1, 1998, by signing a $51,125, 3-month, zero-interest-bearing note. Prepare Kawasaki's November 1, 1998, entry; the December 31, 1998, annual adjusting entry; and the February 1, 1999, entry.

BE13-4 At December 31, 1998, Fifa Corporation owes $500,000 on a note payable due February 15, 1999. (a) If Fifa refinances the obligation by issuing a long-term note on February 14 and using the proceeds to pay off the note due February 15, how much of the $500,000 should be reported as a current liability at December 31, 1998? (b) If Fifa pays off the note on February 15, 1998, and then borrows $1,000,000 on a long-term basis on March 1, how much of the $500,000 should be reported as a current liability at December 31, 1998?

BE13-5 Game Pro Magazine sold 10,000 annual subscriptions on August 1, 1998, for $18 each. Prepare Game Pro's August 1, 1998, journal entry and the December 31, 1998, annual adjusting entry.

BE13-6 Flintstones Corporation made credit sales of $30,000 which are subject to 6% sales tax. The corporation also made cash sales which totaled $19,610 including the 6% sales tax. (a) Prepare the entry to record Flintstones' credit sales. (b) Prepare the entry to record Flintstones' cash sales.

BE13-7 Final Fantasy Inc. receives its property tax bill from Jidoor County in December each year. The county uses the tax receipts to provide services from January through the following December. Tax payments are due February 1 and August 1. In December 1997, Final Fantasy received a tax bill of $14,760 for 1998. At January 31, the company recorded property tax expense and property taxes payable of $1,230 (1/12 of $14,760). Prepare Final Fantasy's February 1 entry (when half of the taxes are due), and the February 28 adjusting entry.

BE13-8 Future Zone Corporation's weekly payroll of $23,000 included FICA taxes withheld of $1,426, federal taxes withheld of $2,990, state taxes withheld of $920, and insurance premiums withheld of $250. Prepare the journal entry to record Future Zone's payroll.

BE13-9 Tale Spin Inc. provides paid vacations to its employees. At December 31, 1998, 30 employees have each earned 2 weeks of vacation time. The employees' average salary is $600 per week. Prepare Tale Spin's December 31, 1998, adjusting entry.

BE13-10 Gargoyle Corporation provides its officers with bonuses based on income. For 1998, the bonuses total $450,000 and are paid on February 15, 1999. Prepare Gargoyle's December 31, 1998, adjusting entry and the February 15, 1999, entry.

BE13-11 Justice League Inc. is involved in a lawsuit at December 31, 1998. (a) Prepare the December 31 entry assuming it is probable that Justice League will be liable for $700,000 as a result of this suit. (b) Prepare the December 31 entry, if any, assuming it is *not* probable that Justice League will be liable for any payment as a result of this suit.

BE13-12 Frantic Factory provides a 2-year warranty with one of its products which was first sold in 1998. In that year, Frantic spent $70,000 servicing warranty claims. At year-end, Frantic estimates that an additional $500,000 will be spent in the future to service warranty claims related to 1998 sales. Prepare Frantic's journal entry to record the $70,000 expenditure, and the December 31 adjusting entry.

BE13-13 Herzog Zwei Corporation sells VCRs. The corporation also offers its customers a 2-year warranty contract. During 1998, Herzog Zwei sold 15,000 warranty contracts at $99 each. The corporation spent $180,000 servicing warranties during 1998, and it estimates that an additional $900,000 will be spent in the future to service the warranties. Prepare Herzog Zwei's journal entries for (a) the sale of contracts, (b) the cost of servicing the warranties, and (c) the recognition of warranty revenue.

BE13-14 Klax Company offers a set of building blocks to customers who send in 3 UPC codes from Klax cereal, along with 50¢. The blocks sets cost Klax $1.10 each to purchase and 60¢ each to mail to customers. During 1998, Klax sold 1,000,000 boxes of cereal. The company expects 30% of the UPC codes to be sent in. During 1998, 120,000 UPC codes were redeemed. Prepare Klax's December 31, 1998, adjusting entry.

*BE13-15 Locke Company provides its president, Cyan Garamonde, with a bonus equal to 10% of income after deducting income tax and bonus. Income *before* deducting income tax and bonus is $265,000, and the tax rate is 40%. Compute the amount of Cyan Garamonde's bonus.

❖ EXERCISES ❖

E13-1 (Balance Sheet Classification of Various Liabilities) How would each of the following items be reported on the balance sheet?

(a) Accrued vacation pay.
(b) Estimated taxes payable.
(c) Service warranties on appliance sales.
(d) Bank overdraft.
(e) Employee payroll deductions unremitted.
(f) Unpaid bonus to officers.
(g) Deposit received from customer to guarantee performance of a contract.
(h) Sales taxes payable.
(i) Gift certificates sold to customers but not yet redeemed.
(j) Premium offers outstanding.
(k) Discount on notes payable.
(l) Personal injury claim pending.
(m) Current maturities of long-term debts to be paid from current assets.
(n) Cash dividends declared but unpaid.
(o) Dividends in arrears on preferred stock.
(p) Loans from officers.

E13-2 (Accounts and Notes Payable) The following are selected 1998 transactions of Sean Astin Corporation:

Sept. 1   Purchased inventory from Encino Company on account for $50,000. Astin records purchases gross and uses a periodic inventory system.
Oct. 1   Issued a $50,000, 12-month, 12% note to Encino in payment of account.
Oct. 1   Borrowed $50,000 from the Shore Bank by signing a 12-month, noninterest-bearing $56,000 note.

Instructions

(a) Prepare journal entries for the selected transactions above.
(b) Prepare adjusting entries at December 31.
(c) Compute the total net liability to be reported on the December 31 balance sheet for:
(1) the interest-bearing note.
(2) the noninterest-bearing note.

E13-3 (Refinancing of Short-Term Debt) On December 31, 1998, Hattie McDaniel Company had $1,200,000 of short-term debt in the form of notes payable due February 2, 1999. On January 21, 1999, the company issued 25,000 shares of its common stock for $38 per share, receiving $950,000 proceeds after brokerage fees and other costs of issuance. On February 2, 1999, the proceeds from the stock sale, supplemented by an additional $250,000 cash, are used to liquidate the $1,200,000 debt. The December 31, 1998, balance sheet is issued on February 23, 1999.

Instructions

Show how the $1,200,000 of short-term debt should be presented on the December 31, 1998, balance sheet, including note disclosure.

E13-4 (Refinancing of Short-Term Debt) On December 31, 1998, Chris Atkins Company has $7,000,000 of short-term debt in the form of notes payable to Blue Lagoon State Bank due periodically in 1999. On January 28, 1999, Atkins enters into a refinancing agreement with Blue Lagoon that will permit it to borrow up to 60% of the gross amount of its accounts receivable. Receivables are expected to range between a low of $6,000,000 in May to a high of $8,000,000 in October during the year 1999. The interest cost of the maturing short-term debt is 15%, and the new agreement calls for a fluctuating interest at 1% above the prime rate on notes due in 2003. Atkin's December 31, 1998, balance sheet is issued on February 15, 1999.

Instructions

Prepare a partial balance sheet for Atkins at December 31, 1998, showing how its $7,000,000 of short-term debt should be presented, including footnote disclosures.

E13-5 (Compensated Absences) Zero Mostel Company began operations on January 2, 1997. It employs 9 individuals who work 8-hour days and are paid hourly. Each employee earns 10 paid vacation days and 6 paid sick days annually. Vacation days may be taken after January 15 of the year following the year in which they are earned. Sick days may be taken as soon as they are earned; unused sick days accumulate. Additional information is as follows:

Actual Hourly Wage Rate		Vacation Days Used by Each Employee		Sick Days Used by Each Employee	
1997	1998	1997	1998	1997	1998
$10	$11	0	9	4	5

Zero Mostel Company has chosen to accrue the cost of compensated absences at rates of pay in effect during the period when earned and to accrue sick pay when earned.

Instructions
(a) Prepare journal entries to record transactions related to compensated absences during 1997 and 1998.
(b) Compute the amounts of any liability for compensated absences that should be reported on the balance sheet at December 31, 1997 and 1998.

E13-6 (Compensated Absences) Assume the facts in the preceding exercise, except that Zero Mostel Company has chosen not to accrue paid sick leave until used, and has chosen to accrue vacation time at expected future rates of pay without discounting. The company used the following projected rates to accrue vacation time:

Year in Which Vacation Time Was Earned	Projected Future Pay Rates Used to Accrue Vacation Pay
1997	$10.75
1998	11.60

Instructions
(a) Prepare journal entries to record transactions related to compensated absences during 1997 and 1998.
(b) Compute the amounts of any liability for compensated absences that should be reported on the balance sheet at December 31, 1997, and 1998.

E13-7 (Adjusting Entry for Sales Tax) During the month of June, R. Attenborough Boutique had cash sales of $233,200 and credit sales of $153,700, both of which include the 6% sales tax that must be remitted to the state by July 15.

Instructions
Prepare the adjusting entry that should be recorded to fairly present the June 30 financial statements.

E13-8 (Payroll Tax Entries) The payroll of Rene Auber Company for September 1997 is as follows:
Total payroll was $480,000, of which $110,000 is exempt from social security tax because it represented amounts paid in excess of $65,400 to certain employees. The amount paid to employees in excess of $7,000 was $400,000. Income taxes in the amount of $90,000 were withheld, as was $9,000 in union dues. The state unemployment tax is 3.5%, but Auber Company is allowed a credit of 2.3% by the state for its unemployment experience. Also, assume that the current F.I.C.A. tax is 7.65% on an employee's wages to $65,400 and 1.45% in excess of $65,400. No employee for Auber makes more than $125,000. The federal unemployment tax rate is .8% after state credit.

Instructions
Prepare the necessary journal entries if the wages and salaries paid and the employer payroll taxes are recorded separately.

E13-9 (Payroll Tax Entries) Green Day Hardware Company's payroll for November 1998 is summarized below.

Payroll	Wages Due	F.I.C.A.	Amount Subject to Payroll Taxes	
			Unemployment Tax	
			Federal	State
Factory	$120,000	$120,000	$40,000	$40,000
Sales	44,000	32,000	4,000	4,000
Administrative	36,000	36,000	—	—
Total	$200,000	$188,000	$44,000	$44,000

At this point in the year some employees have already received wages in excess of those to which payroll taxes apply. Assume that the state unemployment tax is 2.5%. The F.I.C.A. rate is 7.65% on an employee's wages to $65,400 and 1.45% in excess of $65,400. Of the $188,000 wages subject to F.I.C.A. tax, $20,000 is in excess of $65,400 related to the sales wages. Federal unemployment tax rate is .8% after credits. Income tax withheld amounts to $16,000 for factory, $7,000 for sales, and $6,000 for administrative.

Instructions
(a) Prepare a schedule showing the employer's total cost of wages for November by function. (Round all computations to nearest dollar.)
(b) Prepare the journal entries to record the factory, sales, and administrative payrolls including the employer's payroll taxes.

E13-10 (Warranties) Dookie Company sold 200 copymaking machines in 1998 for $4,000 apiece, together with a one-year warranty. Maintenance on each machine during the warranty period averages $330.

Instructions
(a) Prepare entries to record the sale of the machines and the related warranty costs, assuming that the accrual method is used. Actual warranty costs incurred in 1998 were $17,000.
(b) On the basis of the data above, prepare the appropriate entries, assuming that the cash basis method is used.

E13-11 (Warranties) The Sheryl Crow Equipment Company sold 500 Rollomatics during 1998 at $6,000 each. During 1998, Crow spent $20,000 servicing the 2-year warranties that accompany the Rollomatic. All applicable transactions are on a cash basis.

Instructions
(a) Prepare 1998 entries for Crow using the expense warranty approach. Assume that Crow estimates the total cost of servicing the warranties will be $120,000 for 2 years.
(b) Prepare 1998 entries for Crow assuming that the warranties are not an integral part of the sale. Assume that of the sales total, $150,000 relates to sales of warranty contracts. Crow estimates the total cost of servicing the warranties will be $120,000 for 2 years. Estimate revenues earned on the basis of costs incurred and estimated costs.

E13-12 (Liability for Returnable Containers) Candlebox Company sells its products in expensive, re-usable containers. The customer is charged a deposit for each container delivered and receives a refund for each container returned within two years after the year of delivery. Candlebox accounts for the containers not returned within the time limit as being sold at the deposit amount. Information for 1998 is as follows:

Containers held by customers at December 31, 1997, from deliveries in:	1996	$170,000	
	1997	480,000	$650,000
Containers delivered in 1998			860,000
Containers returned in 1998 from deliveries in:	1996	$115,000	
	1997	280,000	
	1998	314,000	709,000

Instructions
(a) Prepare all journal entries required for Candlebox Company during 1998 for the returnable containers.
(b) Compute the total amount Candlebox should report as a liability for returnable containers at December 31, 1998.
(c) Should the liability computed in (b) above be reported as current or long-term?

(AICPA adapted)

E13-13 (Premium Entries) Yanni Company includes 1 coupon in each box of soap powder that it packs, and 10 coupons are redeemable for a premium (a kitchen utensil). In 1998, Yanni Company purchased 8,800 premiums at 80 cents each and sold 110,000 boxes of soap powder @ $3.30 per box; 44,000 coupons were presented for redemption in 1998. It is estimated that 60% of the coupons will eventually be presented for redemption.

Instructions
Prepare all the entries that would be made relative to sales of soap powder and to the premium plan in 1998.

E13-14 (Contingencies) Presented below are three independent situations. Answer the question at the end of each situation.

1. During 1998, Salt-n-Pepa Inc. became involved in a tax dispute with the IRS. Salt-n-Pepa's attorneys have indicated that they believe it is probable that Salt-n-Pepa will lose this dispute. They also believe that Salt-n-Pepa will have to pay the IRS between $900,000 and $1,400,000. After the 1998 financial statements were issued, the case was settled with the IRS for $1,200,000. What amount, if any, should be reported as a liability for this contingency as of December 31, 1998?

2. On October 1, 1998, Alan Jackson Chemical was identified as a potentially responsible party by the Environmental Protection Agency. Jackson's management along with its counsel have concluded that it is probable that Jackson will be responsible for damages, and a reasonable estimate of these damages is $5,000,000. Jackson's insurance policy of $9,000,000 has a deductible clause of $500,000. How should Alan Jackson Chemical report this information in its financial statements at December 31, 1998?

3. Melissa Etheridge Inc. had a manufacturing plant in Kuwait, which was destroyed in the Gulf War. It is not certain who will compensate Etheridge for this destruction, but Etheridge has been assured by governmental officials that it will receive a definite amount for this plant. The amount of the compensation will be less than the fair value of the plant, but more than its book value. How should the contingency be reported in the financial statements of Etheridge Inc.?

E13-15 (Premiums)   Presented below are three independent situations.

1. Luc Longley Stamp Company records stamp service revenue and provides for the cost of redemptions in the year stamps are sold to licensees. Longley's past experience indicates that only 80% of the stamps sold to licensees will be redeemed. Longley's liability for stamp redemptions was $13,000,000 at December 31, 1997. Additional information for 1998 is as follows:

Stamp service revenue from stamps	
sold to licensees	$9,500,000
Cost of redemptions (stamps	
sold prior to 1/1/98)	6,000,000

If all the stamps sold in 1998 were presented for redemption in 1999, the redemption cost would be $5,200,000. What amount should Longley report as a liability for stamp redemptions at December 31, 1998?

2. In packages of its products, Michael Jordan Inc. includes coupons that may be presented at retail stores to obtain discounts on other Jordan products. Retailers are reimbursed for the face amount of coupons redeemed plus 10% of that amount for handling costs. Jordan honors requests for coupon redemption by retailers up to 3 months after the consumer expiration date. Jordan estimates that 60% of all coupons issued will ultimately be redeemed. Information relating to coupons issued by Jordan during 1998 is as follows:

Consumer expiration date	12/31/98
Total face amount of coupons issued	$800,000
Total payments to retailers as of 12/31/98	330,000

What amount should Jordan report as a liability for unredeemed coupons at December 31, 1998?

3. Steve Kerr Company sold 700,000 boxes of pie mix under a new sales promotional program. Each box contains one coupon, which submitted with $4.00, entitles the customer to a baking pan. Kerr pays $6.00 per pan and $0.50 for handling and shipping. Kerr estimates that 70% of the coupons will be redeemed, even though only 250,000 coupons had been processed during 1998. What amount should Kerr report as a liability for unredeemed coupons at December 31, 1998?

(AICPA adapted)

E13-16 (Financial Statement Impact of Liability Transactions)   Presented below is a list of possible transactions.

1. Purchased inventory for $80,000 on account (assume perpetual system is used).
2. Issued an $80,000 note payable in payment on account (see item 1 above).
3. Recorded accrued interest on the note from item 2 above.
4. Borrowed $100,000 from the bank by signing a 6-month, $112,000 noninterest-bearing note.
5. Recognized four months' interest expense on the note from item 4 above.
6. Recorded cash sales of $75,260, which includes 6% sales tax.
7. Recorded wage expense of $35,000. The cash paid was $25,000; the difference was due to various amounts withheld.
8. Recorded employer's payroll taxes.
9. Accrued accumulated vacation pay.
10. Recorded accrued property taxes payable.
11. Recorded bonuses due to employees.
12. Recorded a contingent loss on a lawsuit that the company will probably lose.

13. Accrued warranty expense (assume expense warranty approach).
14. Paid warranty costs that were accrued in item 13 above.
15. Recorded sales of product and related warranties (assume sales warranty approach).
16. Paid warranty costs under contracts from item 15 above.
17. Recognized warranty revenue (see item 15 above).
18. Recorded estimated liability for premium claims outstanding.

Instructions

Set up a table using the format shown below and analyze the effect of the 18 transactions on the financial statement categories indicated.

#	Assets	Liabilities	Owners' Equity	Net Income
1				

Use the following code:

I: Increase   D: Decrease   NE: No net effect

E13-17 (Ratio Computations and Discussion)   Sprague Company has been operating for several years, and on December 31, 1998, presented the following balance sheet:

Sprague Company
BALANCE SHEET
December 31, 1998

Cash	$ 40,000	Accounts payable	$ 80,000
Receivables	75,000	Mortgage payable	140,000
Inventories	95,000	Common stock ($1.00 par)	150,000
Plant assets (net)	220,000	Retained earnings	60,000
	$430,000		$430,000

The net income for 1998 was $25,000. Assume that total assets are the same in 1997 and 1998.

Instructions

Compute each of the following ratios. For each of the four indicate the manner in which it is computed and its significance as a tool in the analysis of the financial soundness of the company.

(a) Current ratio.
(b) Acid-test ratio.
(c) Debt to total assets.
(d) Rate of return on assets.

E13-18 (Ratio Computations and Analysis)   Hood Company's condensed financial statements provide the following information:

BALANCE SHEET

	Dec. 31, 1998	Dec. 31, 1997
Cash	$ 52,000	$ 60,000
Accounts receivable (net)	198,000	80,000
Marketable securities (short-term)	80,000	40,000
Inventories	440,000	360,000
Prepaid expenses	3,000	7,000
Total current assets	$ 773,000	$ 547,000
Property, plant, and equipment (net)	857,000	853,000
Total assets	$1,630,000	$1,400,000
Current liabilities	240,000	160,000
Bonds payable	400,000	400,000
Common stockholders' equity	990,000	840,000
Total liabilities and stockholders' equity	$1,630,000	$1,400,000

INCOME STATEMENT
For the Year Ended 1998

Sales	$1,640,000
Cost of goods sold	(800,000)
Gross profit	840,000
Selling and administrative expense	(440,000)
Interest expense	(40,000)
Net income	$ 360,000

Instructions

(a) Determine the following:
1. Current ratio at December 31, 1998.
2. Acid-test ratio at December 31, 1998.
3. Accounts receivable turnover for 1998.
4. Inventory turnover for 1998.
5. Rate of return on assets for 1998.
6. Profit margin on sales.

(b) Prepare a brief evaluation of the financial condition of Hood Company and of the adequacy of its profits.

E13-19 (Ratio Computations and Effect of Transactions) Presented below is information related to Carver Inc.:

Carver Inc.
BALANCE SHEET
December 31, 1998

Cash		$ 45,000	Notes payable (short-term)	$ 50,000
Receivables	$110,000		Accounts payable	32,000
less allowance	15,000	95,000	Accrued liabilities	5,000
Inventories		170,000	Capital stock (par $5)	260,000
Prepaid insurance		8,000	Retained earnings	141,000
Land		20,000		
Equipment (net)		150,000		
		$488,000		$488,000

INCOME STATEMENT
For the Year Ended December 31, 1998

Sales		$1,400,000
Cost of Goods Sold		
Inventory, Jan. 1, 1998	$200,000	
Purchases	790,000	
Cost of goods available for sale	990,000	
Inventory, Dec. 31, 1998	170,000	
Cost of goods sold		820,000
Gross Profit on Sales		580,000
Operating Expenses		170,000
Net Income		$ 410,000

Instructions

(a) Compute the following ratios or relationships of Carver Inc. Assume that the ending account balances are representative unless the information provided indicates differently.
1. Current ratio.
2. Inventory turnover.
3. Receivables turnover.

4. Earnings per share.
5. Profit margin on sales.
6. Rate of return on assets on December 31, 1998.

(b) Indicate for each of the following transactions whether the transaction would improve, weaken, or have no effect on the current ratio of Carver Inc. at December 31, 1998.

1. Write off an uncollectible account receivable, $2,200.
2. Purchase additional capital stock for cash.
3. Pay $40,000 on notes payable (short-term).
4. Collect $23,000 on accounts receivable.
5. Buy equipment on account.
6. Give an existing creditor a short-term note in settlement of account.

*E13-20 (Bonus Computation) Jud Buechler, president of the Supporting Cast Company, has a bonus arrangement with the company under which he receives 15% of the net income (after deducting taxes and bonuses) each year. For the current year, the net income before deducting either the provision for income taxes or the bonus is $299,750. The bonus is deductible for tax purposes, and the effective tax rate may be assumed to be 40%.

Instructions

(a) Compute the amount of Jud Buechler's bonus.
(b) Compute the appropriate provision for federal income taxes for the year.
(c) Prepare the December 31 journal entry to record the bonus (which will not be paid until next year).

*E13-21 (Bonus Computation and Income Statement Preparation) The incomplete income statement of Scottie Pippen Company appears below:

Scottie Pippen Company
INCOME STATEMENT
For the Year 1998

Revenue		$10,000,000
Cost of goods sold		7,000,000
Gross profit		3,000,000
Administrative and selling expenses	$1,000,000	
Profit-sharing bonus to employees	?	?
Income before income taxes		?
Income taxes		?
Net income		$?

The employee profit-sharing plan requires that 20% of all profits remaining after the deduction of the bonus and income taxes be distributed to the employees by the first day of the fourth month following each year-end. The federal income tax is 45%, and the bonus is tax-deductible.

Instructions

Complete the condensed income statement of Scottie Pippen Company for the year 1998.

*E13-22 (Bonus Compensation) Bill Wennington Company has a profit-sharing agreement with its employees that provides for deposit in a pension trust for the benefit of the employees of 25% of the net income after deducting (1) federal taxes on income, (2) the amount of the annual pension contribution, and (3) a return of 10% on the stockholders' equity as of the end of the year 1998.

Instructions

Compute the amount of the pension contribution under the assumption that the stockholders' equity at the end of the year before adding the net income for the year is $700,000; that net income for the year before either the pension contribution or tax is $300,000; and that the pension contribution is deductible for tax purposes. Use 40% as the applicable rate of tax.

❖ PROBLEMS ❖

P13-1 (Current Liability Entries and Adjustments) Described below are certain transactions of James Edwards Corporation.

1. On February 2, the corporation purchased goods from Jack Haley Company for $50,000 subject to cash discount terms of 2/10, n/30. Purchases and accounts payable are recorded by the corporation at net amounts after cash discounts. The invoice was paid on February 26.
2. On April 1, the corporation bought a truck for $40,000 from General Motors Company, paying $4,000 in cash and signing a one-year, 12% note for the balance of the purchase price.
3. On May 1, the corporation borrowed $80,000 from Chicago National Bank by signing a $92,000 noninterest-bearing note due one year from May 1.
4. On August 1, the Board of Directors declared a $300,000 cash dividend that was payable on September 10 to stockholders of record on August 31.

Instructions
(a) Make all the journal entries necessary to record the transactions above using appropriate dates.
(b) James Edwards Corporation's year-end is December 31. Assuming that no adjusting entries relative to the transactions above have been recorded, prepare any adjusting journal entries concerning interest that are necessary to present fair financial statements at December 31. Assume straight-line amortization of discounts.

P13-2 (Current Liability Entries and Adjustments) Listed below are selected transactions of Dennis Rodman Department Store for the current year ending December 31.

1. On December 5, the store received $500 from the Phil Jackson Players as a deposit to be returned after certain furniture to be used in stage production was returned on January 15.
2. During December, cash sales totaled $834,750, which includes the 5% sales tax that must be remitted to the state by the fifteenth day of the following month.
3. On December 10, the store purchased for cash three delivery trucks for $99,000. The trucks were purchased in a state that applies no sales tax, but the store is located in and must register the trucks in a state that applies a use tax of 5% to nonsalable goods bought outside of its sales tax authority.
4. The store follows the practice of accruing its property tax liability from the lien date. Property taxes of $66,000 became a lien on May 1 and were paid in two equal installments on July 1 and October 1.

Instructions
Prepare all the journal entries necessary to record the transactions noted above as they occurred and any adjusting journal entries relative to the transactions that would be required to present fair financial statements at December 31. Date each entry. For simplicity, assume that adjusting entries are recorded only once a year on December 31.

P13-3 (Payroll Tax Entries) Star Wars Company pays its office employee payroll weekly. Below is a partial list of employees and their payroll data for August. Because August is their vacation period, vacation pay is also listed.

Employee	Earnings to July 31	Weekly Pay	Vacation Pay to Be Received in August
Mark Hamill	$4,200	$180	—
Carrie Fisher	3,500	150	$300
Harrison Ford	2,700	110	220
Alec Guinness	7,400	250	—
Peter Cushing	8,000	290	580

Assume that the federal income tax withheld is 10% of wages. Union dues withheld are 2% of wages. Vacations are taken the second and third weeks of August by Fisher, Ford, and Cushing. The state unemployment tax rate is 2.5% and the federal is .8%, both on a $7,000 maximum. The F.I.C.A. rate is 7.65% on employee and employer on a maximum of $65,400 per employee. In addition, a 1.45% rate is charged both employer and employee for an employee's wage in excess of $65,400.

Instructions
Make the journal entries necessary for each of the four August payrolls. The entries for the payroll and for the company's liability are made separately. Also make the entry to record the monthly payment of accrued payroll liabilities.

P13-4 (Payroll Tax Entries) Below is a payroll sheet for Empire Import Company for the month of September 1998. The company is allowed a 1% unemployment compensation rate by the state; the federal unemployment tax rate is .8% and the maximum for both is $7,000. Assume a 10% federal income tax rate for all employees and a 7.65% F.I.C.A. tax on employee and employer on a maximum of $65,400. In addition, 1.45% is charged both employer and employee for an employee's wage in excess of $65,400 per employee.

Name	Earnings to Aug. 31	September Earnings	Income Tax Withholding	F.I.C.A.	State U.C.	Federal U.C.
B.D. Williams	$ 6,800	$ 800				
D. Prowse	6,300	700				
K. Baker	7,600	1,100				
F. Oz	13,600	1,900				
A. Daniels	105,000	15,000				
P. Mayhew	112,000	16,000				

Instructions

(a) Complete the payroll sheet and make the necessary entry to record the payment of the payroll.
(b) Make the entry to record the payroll tax expenses of Empire Import Company.
(c) Make the entry to record the payment of the payroll liabilities created. Assume that the company pays all payroll liabilities at the end of each month.

P13-5 (Warranties, Accrual, and Cash Basis) John Paxson Corporation sells portable computers under a 2-year warranty contract that requires the corporation to replace defective parts and to provide the necessary repair labor. During 1998 the corporation sells for cash 300 computers at a unit price of $3,500. On the basis of past experience, the 2-year warranty costs are estimated to be $155 for parts and $185 for labor per unit. (For simplicity, assume that all sales occurred on December 31, 1998.) The warranty is not sold separately from the computer.

Instructions

(a) Record any necessary journal entries in 1998, applying the cash basis method.
(b) Record any necessary journal entries in 1998, applying the expense warranty accrual method.
(c) What liability relative to these transactions would appear on the December 31, 1998, balance sheet and how would it be classified if the cash basis method is applied?
(d) What liability relative to these transactions would appear on the December 31, 1998, balance sheet and how would it be classified if the expense warranty accrual method is applied?

In 1999 the actual warranty costs to John Paxson Corporation were $21,400 for parts and $24,900 for labor.

(e) Record any necessary journal entries in 1999, applying the cash basis method.
(f) Record any necessary journal entries in 1999, applying the expense warranty accrual method.

P13-6 (Extended Warranties) Brett Perriman Company sells televisions at an average price of $750 and also offers to each customer a separate 3-year warranty contract for $75 that requires the company to perform periodic services and to replace defective parts. During 1998, the company sold 300 televisions and 270 warranty contracts for cash. It estimates the 3-year warranty costs as $20 for parts and $40 for labor and accounts for warranties separately. Assume sales occurred on December 31, 1998, income is recognized on the warranties, and straight-line recognition of warranty revenues occurs.

Instructions

(a) Record any necessary journal entries in 1998.
(b) What liability relative to these transactions would appear on the December 31, 1998, balance sheet and how would it be classified?

In 1999, Brett Perriman Company incurred actual costs relative to 1998 television warranty sales of $2,000 for parts and $3,000 for labor.

(c) Record any necessary journal entries in 1999 relative to 1998 television warranties.
(d) What amounts relative to the 1998 television warranties would appear on the December 31, 1999, balance sheet and how would they be classified?

P13-7 (Warranties, Accrual, and Cash Basis) Albert Belle Company sells a machine for $7,400 under a 12-month warranty agreement that requires the company to replace all defective parts and to provide the repair labor at no cost to the customers. With sales being made evenly throughout the year, the company sells 650 machines in 1999 (warranty expense is incurred half in 1999 and half in 2000). As a result of product testing, the company estimates that the warranty cost is $370 per machine ($170 parts and $200 labor).

Instructions

Assuming that actual warranty costs are incurred exactly as estimated, what journal entries would be made relative to these facts:

(a) Under application of the expense warranty accrual method for:
  1. Sale of machinery in 1999?
  2. Warranty costs incurred in 1999?
  3. Warranty expense charged against 1999 revenues?
  4. Warranty costs incurred in 2000?

(b) Under application of the cash basis method for:
  1. Sale of machinery in 1999?
  2. Warranty costs incurred in 1999?
  3. Warranty expense charged against 1999 revenues?
  4. Warranty costs incurred in 2000?

(c) What amount, if any, is disclosed in the balance sheet as a liability for future warranty cost as of December 31, 1999, under each method?

(d) Which method best reflects the income in 1999 and 2000 of Albert Belle Company? Why?

P13-8 (Premium Entries) To stimulate the sales of its Alladin breakfast cereal, the Khamsah Company places 1 coupon in each box. Five coupons are redeemable for a premium consisting of a children's hand puppet. In 1999, the company purchases 40,000 puppets at $1.50 each and sells 440,000 boxes of Alladin at $3.75 a box. From its experience with other similar premium offers, the company estimates that 40% of the coupons issued will be mailed back for redemption. During 1999, 105,000 coupons are presented for redemption.

Instructions

Prepare the journal entries that should be recorded in 1999 relative to the premium plan.

P13-9 (Premium Entries and Financial Statement Presentation) Roberto Hernandez Candy Company offers a CD single as a premium for every five candy bar wrappers presented by customers together with $2.00. The candy bars are sold by the company to distributors for 30 cents each. The purchase price of each CD to the company is $1.80; in addition it costs 30 cents to mail each record. The results of the premium plan for the years 1998 and 1999 are as follows (all purchases and sales are for cash):

	1998	1999
CDs purchased	250,000	330,000
Candy bars sold	2,895,400	2,743,600
Wrappers redeemed	1,200,000	1,500,000
1998 wrappers expected to be redeemed in 1999	290,000	
1999 wrappers expected to be redeemed in 2000		350,000

Instructions

(a) Prepare the journal entries that should be made in 1998 and 1999 to record the transactions related to the premium plan of the Roberto Hernandez Candy Company.

(b) Indicate the account names, amounts, and classifications of the items related to the premium plan that would appear on the balance sheet and the income statement at the end of 1998 and 1999.

P13-10 (Loss Contingencies: Entries and Essay) On November 24, 1998, 26 passengers on Tom Paris Airlines Flight No. 901 were injured upon landing when the plane skidded off the runway. Personal injury suits for damages totaling $5,000,000 were filed on January 11, 1999, against the airline by 18 injured passengers. The airline carries no insurance. Legal counsel has studied each suit and advised Paris that it can reasonably expect to pay 60% of the damages claimed. The financial statements for the year ended December 31, 1998, were issued February 27, 1999.

Instructions

(a) Prepare any disclosures and journal entries required by the airline in preparation of the December 31, 1998, financial statements.

(b) Ignoring the Nov. 24, 1998, accident, what liability due to the risk of loss from lack of insurance coverage should Tom Paris Airlines record or disclose? During the past decade the company has experienced at least one accident per year and incurred average damages of $3,200,000. Discuss fully.

P13-11 (Loss Contingencies: Entries and Essays) Shoyo Corporation, in preparation of its December 31, 1998, financial statements, is attempting to determine the proper accounting treatment for each of the following situations:

1. As a result of uninsured accidents during the year, personal injury suits for $350,000 and $60,000 have been filed against the company. It is the judgment of Shoyo's legal counsel that an unfavorable

outcome is unlikely in the $60,000 case but that an unfavorable verdict approximating $225,000 will probably result in the $350,000 case.

2. Shoyo Corporation owns a subsidiary in a foreign country that has a book value of $5,725,000 and an estimated fair value of $8,700,000. The foreign government has communicated to Shoyo its intention to expropriate the assets and business of all foreign investors. On the basis of settlements other firms have received from this same country, Shoyo expects to receive 40% of the fair value of its properties as final settlement.

3. Shoyo's chemical product division consisting of five plants is uninsurable because of the special risk of injury to employees and losses due to fire and explosion. The year 1998 is considered one of the safest (luckiest) in the division's history because no loss due to injury or casualty was suffered. Having suffered an average of three casualties a year during the rest of the past decade (ranging from $60,000 to $700,000), management is certain that next year the company will probably not be so fortunate.

Instructions

(a) Prepare the journal entries that should be recorded as of December 31, 1998, to recognize each of the situations above.

(b) Indicate what should be reported relative to each situation in the financial statements and accompanying notes. Explain why.

 P13-12 (Warranties and Premiums) Gloria Estefan's Music Emporium carries a wide variety of musical instruments, sound reproduction equipment, recorded music, and sheet music. Estefan's uses two sales promotion techniques—warranties and premiums—to attract customers.

Musical instruments and sound equipment are sold with a one-year warranty for replacement of parts and labor. The estimated warranty cost, based on past experience, is 2% of sales.

The premium is offered on the recorded and sheet music. Customers receive a coupon for each dollar spent on recorded music or sheet music. Customers may exchange 200 coupons and $20 for a cassette player. Estefan's pays $34 for each cassette player and estimates that 60% of the coupons given to customers will be redeemed.

Estefan's total sales for 1998 were $7,200,000—$5,400,000 from musical instruments and sound reproduction equipment and $1,800,000 from recorded music and sheet music. Replacement parts and labor for warranty work totaled $164,000 during 1998. A total of 6,500 cassette players used in the premium program were purchased during the year and there were 1,200,000 coupons redeemed in 1998.

The accrual method is used by Estefan's to account for the warranty and premium costs for financial reporting purposes. The balances in the accounts related to warranties and premiums on January 1, 1998, were as shown below.

Inventory of Premium Cassette Players	$39,950
Estimated Premium Claims Outstanding	44,800
Estimated Liability from Warranties	136,000

Instructions

Gloria Estefan's Music Emporium is preparing its financial statements for the year ended December 31, 1998. Determine the amounts that will be shown on the 1998 financial statements for the following:

1. Warranty Expense.
2. Estimated Liability from Warranties.
3. Premium Expense.
4. Inventory of Premium Cassette Players.
5. Estimated Premium Claims Outstanding.

(CMA adapted)

*P13-13 (Bonus Computation) Henryk Inc. has a contract with its president, Nathalie Sarraute, to pay her a bonus during each of the years 1997, 1998, 1999, and 2000. The federal income tax rate is 40% during the 4 years. The profit before deductions for bonus and federal income taxes was $250,000 in 1997, $308,000 in 1998, $350,000 in 1999, and $380,000 in 2000. The president's bonus of 12% is deductible for tax purposes in each year and is to be computed as follows:

(a) In 1997 the bonus is to be based on profit before deductions for bonus and income tax.

(b) In 1998 the bonus is to be based on profit after deduction of bonus but before deduction of income tax.

(c) In 1999 the bonus is to be based on profit before deduction of bonus but after deduction of income tax.

(d) In 2000 the bonus is to be based on profit after deductions for bonus and income tax.

Instructions

Compute the amounts of the bonus and the income tax for each of the 4 years.

P13-14 (Warranty, Bonus, and Coupon Computation) Victor Hugo Company must make computations and adjusting entries for the following independent situations at December 31, 1998:

1. Its line of amplifiers carries a 3-year warranty against defects. On the basis of past experience the estimated warranty costs related to dollar sales are: first year after sale—2% of sales; second year after sale—3% of sales; and third year after sale—4% of sales. Sales and actual warranty expenditures for the first 3 years of business were:

	Sales	Warranty Expenditures
1996	$ 800,000	$ 6,500
1997	1,100,000	17,200
1998	1,200,000	62,000

Instructions
Compute the amount that Hugo Company should report as a liability in its December 31, 1998, balance sheet. Assume that all sales are made evenly throughout each year with warranty expenses also evenly spaced relative to the rates above.

*2. Hugo Company's profit-sharing plan provides that the company will contribute to a fund an amount equal to one-fourth of its net income each year. Income before deducting the profit-sharing contribution and taxes for 1998 is $1,035,000. The applicable income tax rate is 40%, and the profit-sharing contribution is deductible for tax purposes.

Instructions
Compute the amount to be contributed to the profit-sharing fund for 1998.

3. With some of its products, Hugo Company includes coupons that are redeemable in merchandise. The coupons have no expiration date and, in the company's experience, 40% of them are redeemed. The liability for unredeemed coupons at December 31, 1997, was $9,000. During 1998, coupons worth $25,000 were issued, and merchandise worth $8,000 was distributed in exchange for coupons redeemed.

Instructions
Compute the amount of the liability that should appear on the December 31, 1998, balance sheet.

(AICPA adapted)

❖ CONCEPTUAL CASES ❖

C13-1 (Nature of Liabilities) Presented below is the current liability section of Nizami Corporation.

	($000)	
	1996	1995
Current Liabilities		
Notes payable	$ 68,713	$ 7,700
Accounts payable	179,496	101,379
Compensation to employees	60,312	31,649
Accrued liabilities	158,198	77,021
Income taxes payable	10,486	26,491
Current maturities of long-term debt	16,592	6,649
Total current liabilities	$493,797	$251,489

Instructions
Answer the following questions.
  (a) What are the essential characteristics that make an item a liability?
  (b) How does one distinguish between a current liability and a long-term liability?
  (c) What are accrued liabilities? Give three examples of accrued liabilities that Nizami might have.
  (d) What is the theoretically correct way to value liabilities? How are current liabilities usually valued?
  (e) Why are notes payable reported first in the current liability section?
  (f) What might be the items that comprise Nizami's liability for "Compensation to employees"?

C13-2 (Current versus Noncurrent Classification) D'Annunzio Corporation includes the following items in their liabilities at December 31, 1998:

1. Notes payable, $25,000,000, due June 30, 1999.
2. Deposits from customers on equipment ordered by them from D'Annunzio, $6,250,000.
3. Salaries payable, $3,750,000, due January 14, 1999.

Instructions
Indicate in what circumstances, if any, each of the three liabilities above would be excluded from current liabilities.

C13-3 (Current versus Noncurrent Classification) The following items are listed as liabilities on the balance sheet of Eleutherios Company on December 31, 1998:

Accounts payable	$ 420,000
Notes payable	750,000
Bonds payable	2,250,000

The accounts payable represent obligations to suppliers that were due in January 1999. The notes payable mature on various dates during 1999. The bonds payable mature on July 1, 1999.

These liabilities must be reported on the balance sheet in accordance with generally accepted accounting principles governing the classification of liabilities as current and noncurrent.

Instructions
(a) What is the general rule for determining whether a liability is classified as current or noncurrent?
(b) Under what conditions may any of Eleutherios Company's liabilities be classified as noncurrent? Explain your answer.

(CMA adapted)

C13-4 (Refinancing of Short-Term Debt) Levi Eshkol Corporation reports in the current liability section of its balance sheet at December 31, 1998 (its year-end), short-term obligations of $15,000,000, which includes the current portion of 12% long-term debt in the amount of $11,000,000 (matures in March 1999). Management has stated its intention to refinance the 12% debt whereby no portion of it will mature during 1999. The date of issuance of the financial statements is March 25, 1999.

Instructions
(a) Is management's intent enough to support long-term classification of the obligation in this situation?
(b) Assume that Eshkol Corporation issues $13,000,000 of 10-year debentures to the public in January 1999 and that management intends to use the proceeds to liquidate the $11,000,000 debt maturing in March 1999. Furthermore, assume that the debt maturing in March 1999 is paid from these proceeds prior to the issuance of the financial statements. Will this have any impact on the balance sheet classification at December 31, 1998? Explain your answer.
(c) Assume that Eshkol Corporation issues common stock to the public in January and that management intends to entirely liquidate the $11,000,000 debt maturing in March 1999 with the proceeds of this equity securities issue. In light of these events, should the $11,000,000 debt maturing in March 1999 be included in current liabilities at December 31, 1998?
(d) Assume that Eshkol Corporation, on February 15, 1999, entered into a financing agreement with a commercial bank that permits Eshkol Corporation to borrow at any time through 2000 up to $15,000,000 at the bank's prime rate of interest. Borrowings under the financing agreement mature three years after the date of the loan. The agreement is not cancelable except for violation of a provision with which compliance is objectively determinable. No violation of any provision exists at the date of issuance of the financial statements. Assume further that the current portion of long-term debt does not mature until August 1999. In addition, management intends to refinance the $11,000,000 obligation under the terms of the financial agreement with the bank, which is expected to be financially capable of honoring the agreement.
  1. Given these facts, should the $11,000,000 be classified as current on the balance sheet at December 31, 1998?
  2. Is disclosure of the refinancing method required?

C13-5 (Refinancing of Short-Term Debt) Medvedev Inc. issued $10,000,000 of short-term commercial paper during the year 1997 to finance construction of a plant. At December 31, 1997, the corporation's year-end, Medvedev intends to refinance the commercial paper by issuing long-term debt. However, because the corporation temporarily has excess cash, in January 1998 it liquidates $4,000,000 of the commercial paper as the paper matures. In February 1998, Medvedev completes an $18,000,000 long-term debt offering. Later during the month of February, it issues its December 31, 1997, financial statements. The proceeds of the long-term debt offering are to be used to replenish $4,000,000 in working capital, to pay $6,000,000 of commercial paper as it matures in March 1998, and to pay $8,000,000 of construction costs expected to be incurred later that year to complete the plant.

Instructions
(a) How should the $10,000,000 of commercial paper be classified on the December 31, 1997, January 31, 1998, and February 28, 1998, balance sheets? Give support for your answer and also consider the cash element.

(b) What would your answer be if, instead of a refinancing at the date of issuance of the financial statements, a financing agreement existed at that date?

C13-6 (Loss Contingencies) Animaniacs Company is a manufacturer of toys. During the year, the following situations arose:

1. A safety hazard related to one of its toy products was discovered. It is considered probable that liabilities have been incurred. On the basis of past experience, a reasonable estimate of the amount of loss can be made.
2. One of its small warehouses is located on the bank of a river and could no longer be insured against flood losses. No flood losses have occurred after the date that the insurance became unavailable.
3. This year, Animaniacs began promoting a new toy by including a coupon, redeemable for a movie ticket, in each toy's carton. The movie ticket, which cost Animaniacs $3, is purchased in advance and then mailed to the customer when the coupon is received by Animaniacs. Animaniacs estimated, based on past experience, that 60% of the coupons would be redeemed. Forty-five percent of the coupons were actually redeemed this year, and the remaining 15% of the coupons are expected to be redeemed next year.

Instructions

(a) How should Animaniacs report the safety hazard? Why? Do not discuss deferred income tax implications.
(b) How should Animaniacs report the noninsurable flood risk? Why?
(c) How should Animaniacs account for the toy promotion campaign in this year?

C13-7 (Loss Contingencies) On February 1, 1998, one of the huge storage tanks of Paunee Manufacturing Company exploded. Windows in houses and other buildings within a one-mile radius of the explosion were severely damaged, and a number of people were injured. As of February 15, 1998 (when the December 31, 1997, financial statements were completed and sent to the publisher for printing and public distribution), no suits had been filed or claims asserted against the company as a consequence of the explosion. The company fully anticipates that suits will be filed and claims asserted for injuries and damages. Because the casualty was uninsured and the company considered at fault, Paunee Manufacturing will have to cover the damages from its own resources.

Instructions

Discuss fully the accounting treatment and disclosures that should be accorded the casualty and related contingent losses in the financial statements dated December 31, 1997.

C13-8 (Loss Contingency) Presented below is a note disclosure for Ralph Ellison Corporation:

Litigation and Environmental: The Company has been notified, or is a named or a potentially responsible party in a number of governmental (federal, state and local) and private actions associated with environmental matters, such as those relating to hazardous wastes, including certain sites which are on the United States EPA National Priorities List ("Superfund"). These actions seek cleanup costs, penalties and/or damages for personal injury or to property or natural resources.

In 1996, the Company recorded a pre-tax charge of $56,229,000, included in the "Other Expense (Income)—Net" caption of the Company's Consolidated Statements of Income, as an additional provision for environmental matters. These expenditures are expected to take place over the next several years and are indicative of the Company's commitment to improve and maintain the environment in which it operates. At December 31, 1996, environmental accruals amounted to $69,931,000, of which $61,535,000 are considered noncurrent and are included in the "Deferred Credits and Other Liabilities" caption of the Company's Consolidated Balance Sheets.

While it is impossible at this time to determine with certainty the ultimate outcome of environmental matters, it is management's opinion, based in part on the advice of independent counsel (after taking into account accruals and insurance coverage applicable to such actions) that when the costs are finally determined they will not have a material adverse effect on the financial position of the Company.

Instructions

Answer the following questions.
(a) What conditions must exist before a loss contingency can be recorded in the accounts?
(b) Suppose that Ralph Ellison Corporation could not reasonably estimate the amount of the loss, although it could establish with a high degree of probability the minimum and maximum loss possible. How should this information be reported in the financial statements?
(c) If the amount of the loss is uncertain, how would the loss contingency be reported in the financial statements?

C13-9 (Loss Contingencies) The following three independent sets of facts relate to (1) the possible accrual or (2) the possible disclosure of a loss contingency.

Situation I

Subsequent to the date of a set of financial statements, but prior to the issuance of the financial statements, a company enters into a contract that will probably result in a significant loss to the company. The amount of the loss can be reasonably estimated.

Situation II

A company offers a one-year warranty for the product that it manufactures. A history of warranty claims has been compiled and the probable amount of claims related to sales for a given period can be determined.

Situation III

A company has adopted a policy of recording self-insurance for any possible losses resulting from injury to others by the company's vehicles. The premium for an insurance policy for the same risk from an independent insurance company would have an annual cost of $4,000. During the period covered by the financial statements, there were no accidents involving the company's vehicles that resulted in injury to others.

Instructions

Discuss the accrual or type of disclosure necessary (if any) and the reason(s) why such disclosure is appropriate for each of the three independent sets of facts above.

(AICPA adapted)

C13-10 (Warranties and Loss Contingencies) The following two independent situations involve loss contingencies:

Part 1

Clarke Company sells two products, John and Henrick. Each carries a one-year warranty.

1. Product John—Product warranty costs, based on past experience, will normally be 1% of sales.
2. Product Henrick—Product warranty costs cannot be reasonably estimated because this is a new product line. However, the chief engineer believes that product warranty costs are likely to be incurred.

Instructions

How should Clarke report the estimated product warranty costs for each of the two types of merchandise above? Discuss the rationale for your answer. Do not discuss deferred income tax implications, or disclosures that should be made in Clarke's financial statements or notes.

Part 2

Toni Morrison Company is being sued for $4,000,000 for an injury caused to a child as a result of alleged negligence while the child was visiting the Toni Morrison Company plant in March 1998. The suit was filed in July 1998. Toni Morrison's lawyer states that it is probable that Toni Morrison will lose the suit and be found liable for a judgment costing anywhere from $400,000 to $2,000,000. However, the lawyer states that the most probable judgment is $800,000.

Instructions

How should Toni Morrison report the suit in its 1998 financial statements? Discuss the rationale for your answer. Include in your answer disclosures, if any, that should be made in Toni Morrison's financial statements or notes.

(AICPA adapted)

❖ FINANCIAL REPORTING PROBLEM—INTEL CORPORATION

Instructions

Refer to the financial statements and other documents of Intel Corporation presented in Appendix 5A and answer the following questions:

1. What was Intel Corporation's short-term debt and related weighted average interest rate in this debt?
2. What was Intel's working capital, acid-test ratio, and current ratio? Comment on Intel's liquidity.
3. What types of commitments and contingencies has Intel reported in its financial statements? What is management's reaction to these contingencies?
4. Explain the nature of the current liability identified as "Deferred Income on Shipments to Distributors."

❖ FINANCIAL STATEMENT ANALYSIS CASES

Case 1 (Northland Cranberries)

Despite only being a publicly traded company since 1987, Northland Cranberries of Wisconsin Rapids, Wisconsin, is the world's largest cranberry grower. Despite its short life as a publicly traded corporation, it has engaged in an aggressive growth strategy. As a consequence, the company has taken on significant amounts of both short-term and long-term debt. The following information is taken from recent annual reports of the company.

	1995	1994
Current assets	$ 6,745,759	$ 5,598,054
Total assets	107,744,751	83,074,339
Current liabilities	10,168,685	4,484,687
Total liabilities	73,118,204	49,948,787
Stockholders' equity	34,626,547	33,125,552
Net sales	21,783,966	18,051,355
Cost of goods sold	13,057,275	8,751,220
Interest expense	3,654,006	2,393,792
Income tax expense	1,051,000	1,917,000
Net income	1,581,707	2,942,954

Instructions

(a) Evaluate the company's liquidity by calculating and analyzing working capital and the current ratio.

(b) The following discussion of the company's liquidity was provided by the company in the Management Discussion and Analysis section of the company's 1995 annual report. Comment on whether you agree with management's statements, and what might be done to remedy the situation.

The lower comparative current ratio at March 31, 1995, was due to $3 million of short-term borrowing then outstanding which was incurred to fund the Company's September 1994 Yellow River Marsh acquisitions. As a result of the extreme seasonality of its business, the company does not believe that its current ratio or its underlying stated working capital at its March 31, 1995, fiscal year end is a meaningful indication of the Company's liquidity. As of March 31 of each fiscal year, the Company has historically carried no significant amounts of inventories and by such date all of the Company's accounts receivable from its crop sold for processing under the supply agreements have been paid in cash, with the resulting cash received from such payments used to reduce indebtedness. The Company utilizes its revolving bank credit facility, together with cash generated from operations, to fund its working capital requirements throughout its growing season.

Case 2 (Mohican Company)

Presented below is the current liability section and related note of the Mohican Company.

	1996	1995
	(dollars in thousands)	
Current Liabilities		
Current portion of long-term debt	$ 15,000	$ 10,000
Short-term debt	2,668	405
Accounts payable	29,495	42,427
Accrued warranty	16,843	16,741
Accrued marketing programs	17,512	16,585
Other accrued liabilities	35,653	33,290
Accrued and deferred income taxes	16,206	17,348
Total current liabilities	$133,377	$136,796

Notes to Consolidated Financial Statements

1(in part): Summary of Significant Accounting Policies and Related Data

Accrued Warranty—The company provides an accrual for future warranty costs based upon the relationship of prior years' sales to actual warranty costs.

Instructions

Answer the following questions.

(a) What is the difference between the cash basis and the accrual basis of accounting for warranty costs?

(b) Under what circumstance, if any, would it be appropriate for Mohican Company to recognize deferred revenue on warranty contracts?

(c) If Mohican Company recognized deferred revenue on warranty contracts, how would it recognize this revenue in subsequent periods?

❖ COMPARATIVE ANALYSIS CASE

The Coca-Cola Company versus PepsiCo Inc.

Instructions

Go to our Web site and answer the following questions:

1. How much working capital do each of these companies have at the end of 1995? Comment on the appropriateness of the working capital they maintain.

2. Compute both company's (a) current cash debt coverage ratio, (b) cash debt coverage ratio, (c) current ratio, (d) acid-test ratio, (e) receivable turnover ratio and (f) inventory turnover ratio for 1995. Comment on each company's overall liquidity.

3. In PepsiCo's financial statements, it reports in the long-term debt section "short-term borrowings, reclassified." How can short-term borrowings be classified as long-term debt? What is the weighted average cost of short-term borrowing for PepsiCo, and does it pay variable or fixed rate interest on this debt?

4. What types of loss or gain contingencies do these two companies have at December 31, 1995?

❖ RESEARCH CASES

Case 1

Instructions

Obtain the most recent edition of *Accounting Trends and Techniques*. Examine the disclosures included under the section regarding gain contingencies and answer the following questions.

(a) Determine the nature of each of the disclosed gain contingencies. Are there any common themes?
(b) How many of the footnotes include dollar amounts?
(c) What are the smallest and largest amounts disclosed?

Case 2

The December 1995 issue of *Management Accounting* includes a reprint of an article by Glenn Cheney, entitled "It's Not Easy Being Green But Top Companies Are Trying."

Instructions
Read the article and answer the following questions.

(a) What portion of the Fortune 500 companies disclose their position on the environment? What type of information is included in these disclosures?
(b) How can companies save money by "being green"?
(c) What is the "take-back principle"?
(d) What is the role of public accountants in this area?

❖ WRITING ASSIGNMENT

You are the independent auditor engaged to audit Christine Agazzi Corporation's December 31, 1997, financial statements. Christine Agazzi manufactures household appliances. During the course of your audit, you discovered the following contingent liabilities:

1. Christine Agazzi began production on a new dishwasher in June 1997 and, by December 31, 1997, sold 100,000 to various retailers for $500 each. Each dishwasher is under a one-year warranty. The company estimates that its warranty expense per dishwasher will amount to $25. At year-end, the company had already paid out $1,000,000 in warranty expenses. Christine Agazzi's income statement shows warranty expenses of $1,000,000 for 1997. Agazzi accounts for warranty costs on the accrual basis.

2. In response to your attorney's letter, Robert Sklodowski, Esq., has informed you that Agazzi has been cited for dumping toxic waste into the Kishwaukee River. Clean-up costs and fines amount to $3,330,000. Although the case is still being contested, Sklodowski is certain that Agazzi will most probably have to pay the fine and clean-up costs. No disclosure of this situation was found in the financial statements.

3. Christine Agazzi is the defendant in a patent infringement lawsuit by Heidi Goldman over Agazzi's use of a hydraulic compressor in several of its products. Sklodowski claims that, if the suit goes against Agazzi, the loss may be as much as $5,000,000; however, Sklodowski believes the loss of this suit to be only reasonably possible. Again, no mention of this suit occurs in the financial statements.

As presented, these contingencies are not reported in accordance with GAAP which may create problems in issuing a clean audit report. You feel the need to note these problems in the work papers.

Instructions
Heading each page with the name of the company, balance sheet date, and a brief description of the problem, write a brief narrative for each of the above issues in the form of **a memorandum** to be incorporated in the audit work papers. Explain what led to the discovery of each problem, what the problem really is, and what you advised your client to do (along with any appropriate journal entries) in order to bring these contingencies in accordance with GAAP.

❖ GROUP ASSIGNMENT

Alex Rodriguez Inc., a publishing company, is preparing its December 31, 1997, financial statements and must determine the proper accounting treatment for the following situations; they have retained your group to assist them in this task.

1. Rodriguez sells subscriptions to several magazines for a 1-year, 2-year, or 3-year period. Cash receipts from subscribers are credited to magazine subscriptions collected in advance, and this account had a balance of $2,300,000 at December 31, 1997. Outstanding subscriptions at December 31, 1997, expire as follows:

During 1998—$600,000
During 1999— 500,000
During 2000— 800,000

2. On January 2, 1997, Rodriguez discontinued collision, fire, and theft coverage on its delivery vehicles and became self-insured for these risks. Actual losses of $50,000 during 1997 were charged to delivery expense. The 1996 premium for the discontinued coverage amounted to $80,000 and the controller wants to set up a reserve for self-insurance by a debit to delivery expense of $30,000 and a credit to the reserve for self-insurance of $30,000.

3. A suit for breach of contract seeking damages of $1,000,000 was filed by an author against Rodriguez on July 1, 1997. The company's legal counsel believes that an unfavorable outcome is probable. A reasonable estimate of the court's award to the plaintiff is in the range between $300,000 and $700,000. No amount within this range is a better estimate of potential damages than any other amount.

4. During December 1997, a competitor company filed suit against Rodriguez for industrial espionage claiming $1,500,000 in damages. In the opinion of management and company counsel, it is reasonably possible that damages will be awarded to the plaintiff. However, the amount of potential damages awarded to the plaintiff cannot be reasonably estimated.

Instructions

Your instructor will assign one group member to serve as a recorder and one member to serve as spokesperson. As a group, provide the information for the recorder to prepare, for each of the above situations, the journal entry that should be recorded as of December 31, 1997, or explain why an entry should not be recorded (you may wish to divide the parts among the members). Upon completion, the spokesperson will report the group findings to the class and be prepared to show supporting computations in good form.

(AICPA adapted)

❖ETHICS CASES

Case 1

The WGN Company has a bonus arrangement which grants the financial vice president and other executives a $15,000 bonus if net income exceeds the previous year's by $1,000,000. Noting that the current financial statements report an increase of $950,000 in net income, Vice President Jack Brickhouse asks Louise Boudreau, the controller, to reduce the estimate of warranty expense by $60,000. The present estimate of warranty expense is $500,000 and is known by both Brickhouse and Boudreau to be a fairly "soft" amount.

Instructions
Answer the following questions:
   (a) Should Boudreau lower her estimate?
   (b) What ethical issue is at stake? Would anyone be harmed by the change in estimate?
   (c) Is Brickhouse acting ethically?

Case 2

The Ray Company, owner of Bleacher Mall, charges Creighton Clothing Store a rental fee of $600 per month plus 5% of yearly profits over $500,000. Harry Creighton, the owner of the store, directs his accountant, Burt Wilson, to increase the estimate of bad debt expense and warranty costs in order to keep profits at $475,000.

Instructions
Answer the following questions:

   (a) Should Wilson follow his boss's directive?
   (b) Who is harmed if the estimates are increased?
   (c) Is Creighton's directive ethical?

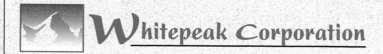

Whitepeak Corporation   Module 8

For the most part, Whitepeak has kept good track of its current liabilities for 1997. However, the company does need help on a few issues, as described below.

Section 8.1   Purchases of Inventory

An inventory purchase was recorded using the *net* method. However, Whitepeak uses the *gross* method.

Instructions Correct the journal entry so that it shows the inventory purchase under the gross method.

Section 8.2   Payroll

Payroll and related employee and employer taxes for some of Whitepeak's sales staff have not yet been made for 1997.

Instructions Record the payroll and related taxes.

Section 8.3   Contingencies

Whitepeak is involved in one patent infringement case with a firm called Tri-Peak. Tri-Peak claims that Whitepeak copied part of its patented unique quad-edged cross-country ski blade design. Whitepeak has countersued to establish its innocence and to claim counter-damages from wrongful charges.

Instructions Determine whether any reporting is necessary regarding these contingencies.

Section 8.4   Warranties

Whitepeak is also facing another possible contingency in relation to warranties extended on its cartop skicarrier. Whitepeak began manufacturing these carriers last year. However, by the end of 1997 warranty repair costs were increasing, and a recall of the carriers may be needed.

Instructions Determine what type of adjustment or possible write-down (if any) is needed in this situation. ■

CHAPTER 14

Long-Term Liabilities

Long-Term Debt and a War Won!

If companies want to obtain large amounts of funds to support expansion, they will generally issue bonds—long-term debt—or use stock financing. The advantages of issuing debt are: debt is often cheaper than stock financing, interest on debt is tax-deductible, and debtholders don't have voting rights.

A fact that few people know about long-term debt is that it changed the course of history, by aiding Britain's dramatic victory over the French in their long struggle for supremacy in the eighteenth and early nineteenth centuries. How did Britain, a small island nation with only a fraction of the population and wealth of France, ultimately humble its mightier foe? Many believe it was accomplished through the use of long-term debt. By pioneering a central bank and a fair system of collecting taxes, Britain developed the capital markets that enabled its government to issue bonds and thereby raise funds for military purposes. Skeptics regarded bonds—and the people who issued them—with both fear and contempt. But Britain, through the issuance of bonds, was able to borrow money at almost half the cost that France could and to incur indebtedness far greater, as a proportion of the economy, than the French could. Thus Britain could more than match the French navy, raise an army of its own, and lavishly subsidize other armies, eventually destroying Napoleon.[1]

LEARNING OBJECTIVES

After studying this chapter, you should be able to:

1. Describe the formal procedures associated with issuing long-term debt.
2. Identify various types of bond issues.
3. Describe the accounting valuation for bonds at date of issuance.
4. Apply the methods of bond discount and premium amortization.
5. Describe the accounting procedures for the extinguishment of debt.
6. Explain the accounting procedures for long-term notes payable.
7. Explain the reporting of off-balance-sheet financing arrangements.
8. Indicate how long-term debt is presented and analyzed.

[1]Adapted from "How British Bonds Beat Back Bigger France," *Forbes*, March 13, 1995, p. 26.

As indicated in the opening story, long-term debt played a decisive role in enabling Britain to obtain resources to defeat France in the eighteenth and nineteenth centuries. Long-term debt continues to play an important role today in our capital markets because companies—and governments—need large amounts of capital to finance their growth. In many cases, the most effective way to obtain the capital is through the issuance of long-term debt. The purpose of this chapter is to explain the accounting issues related to long-term debt. The content and organization of the chapter are as follows:

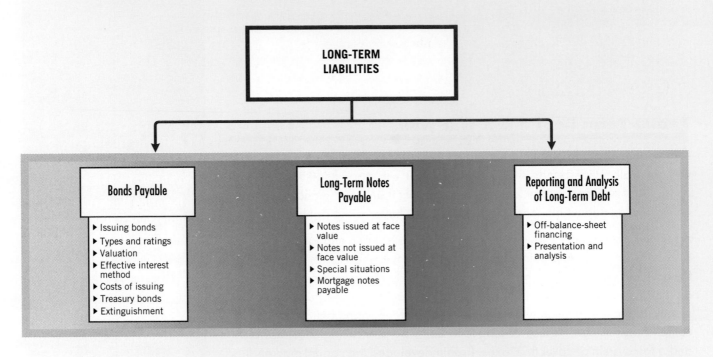

LONG-TERM LIABILITIES

Bonds Payable
- Issuing bonds
- Types and ratings
- Valuation
- Effective interest method
- Costs of issuing
- Treasury bonds
- Extinguishment

Long-Term Notes Payable
- Notes issued at face value
- Notes not issued at face value
- Special situations
- Mortgage notes payable

Reporting and Analysis of Long-Term Debt
- Off-balance-sheet financing
- Presentation and analysis

SECTION 1 *BONDS PAYABLE*

Long-term debt consists of probable future sacrifices of economic benefits arising from present obligations that are not payable within a year or the operating cycle of the business, whichever is longer. Bonds payable, long-term notes payable, mortgages payable, pension liabilities, and lease liabilities are examples of long-term liabilities.

Incurring long-term debt is often accompanied by considerable formality. For example, the bylaws of corporations usually require approval by the board of directors and the stockholders before bonds can be issued or other long-term debt arrangements can be contracted.

Generally, long-term debt has various **covenants or restrictions** for the protection of both lenders and borrowers. The covenants and other terms of the agreement between the borrower and the lender are stated in the bond indenture or note agreement. Items often mentioned in the indenture or agreement include the amounts authorized to be issued, interest rate, due date or dates, call provisions, property pledged as se-

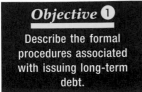

curity, sinking fund requirements, working capital and dividend restrictions, and limitations concerning the assumption of additional debt. Whenever these stipulations are important for a complete understanding of the financial position and the results of operations, they should be described in the body of the financial statements or the notes thereto.

Although it would seem that these covenants provide adequate protection to the long-term debt holder, many bondholders suffer considerable losses when additional debt is added to the capital structure. Consider what happened to bondholders in the leveraged buyout of RJR Nabisco. Solidly rated 9⅜% bonds due in 2016 plunged 20% in value when management announced the leveraged buyout. Such a loss in value occurs because the additional debt added to the capital structure increases the likelihood of default. Although bondholders have covenants to protect them, they often are written in a manner that can be interpreted in a number of different ways.

❖ ISSUING BONDS

Bonds are the most common type of long-term debt reported on a company's balance sheet. The main purpose of bonds is to borrow for the long term when the amount of capital needed is too large for one lender to supply. By issuing bonds in $100, $1,000, or $10,000 denominations, a large amount of long-term indebtedness can be divided into many small investing units, thus enabling more than one lender to participate in the loan.

A bond arises from a contract known as a **bond indenture** and represents a promise to pay: (1) a sum of money at a designated maturity date, plus (2) periodic interest at a specified rate on the maturity amount (face value). Individual bonds are evidenced by a paper certificate and typically have a $1,000 face value. Bond interest payments usually are made semiannually, although the interest rate is generally expressed as an annual rate.

An entire bond issue may be sold to an investment banker who acts as a selling agent in the process of marketing the bonds. In such arrangements, investment bankers may either underwrite the entire issue by guaranteeing a certain sum to the corporation, thus taking the risk of selling the bonds for whatever price they can get (firm underwriting), or they may sell the bond issue for a commission to be deducted from the proceeds of the sale (best efforts underwriting). Alternatively, the issuing company may choose to place privately a bond issue by selling the bonds directly to a large institution, financial or otherwise, without the aid of an underwriter (private placement).

❖ TYPES AND RATINGS OF BONDS

Some of the more common types of bonds found in practice are:

Objective ❷

Identify various types of bond issues.

❖ TYPES OF BONDS ❖

Secured and Unsecured Bonds. **Secured bonds** are backed by a pledge of some sort of collateral. Mortgage bonds are secured by a claim on real estate. Collateral trust bonds are secured by stocks and bonds of other corporations. Bonds not backed by collateral are **unsecured**. A **debenture bond** is unsecured. A "junk bond" is unsecured and also very risky, and therefore pays a high interest rate. These bonds are often used to finance leveraged buyouts.

Term, Serial Bonds, and Callable Bonds. Bond issues that mature on a single date are called **term bonds**, and issues that mature in installments are called **serial bonds**. Serially maturing bonds are frequently used by school or sanitary districts, municipalities, or other local taxing bodies that borrow money through a special levy. **Callable bonds** give the issuer the right to call and retire the bonds prior to maturity.

Convertible, Commodity-Backed, and Deep Discount Bonds.   If bonds are convertible into other securities of the corporation for a specified time after issuance, they are called convertible bonds. Accounting for bond conversions is discussed in Chapter 17. Two new types of bonds have been developed in an attempt to attract capital in a tight money market—commodity-backed bonds and deep discount bonds.

Commodity-backed bonds (also called **asset-linked bonds**) are redeemable in measures of a commodity, such as barrels of oil, tons of coal, or ounces of rare metal. To illustrate, Sunshine Mining, a silver mining producer, sold two issues of bonds redeemable with either $1,000 in cash or 50 ounces of silver, whichever is greater at maturity, and that have a stated interest rate of 8½%. The accounting problem is one of projecting the maturity value, especially since silver has fluctuated between $4 and $40 an ounce since issuance.

J. C. Penney Company sold the first publicly marketed long-term debt securities in the United States that do not bear interest. These deep discount bonds, also referred to as zero interest debenture bonds, are sold at a discount that provides the buyer's total interest payoff at maturity. Caesar's World Inc., a Las Vegas/Lake Tahoe gambling casino operator, proposed a unique version of the zero interest bond.[2] Caesar's World proposed to issue 5,000 of $15,000 face amount bonds that would entitle each bondholder to spend two weeks a year at its Lake Tahoe resort in lieu of interest.

Registered and Bearer (Coupon) Bonds.   Bonds issued in the name of the owner are registered bonds and require surrender of the certificate and issuance of a new certificate to complete a sale. A bearer or coupon bond, however, is not recorded in the name of the owner and may be transferred from one owner to another by mere delivery.

Income and Revenue Bonds.   Income bonds pay no interest unless the issuing company is profitable. Revenue bonds, so called because the interest on them is paid from specified revenue sources, are most frequently issued by airports, school districts, counties, toll-road authorities, and governmental bodies.

Two major investment publication companies, Moody's Investors Service and Standard & Poor's Corporation, issue quality ratings on every public bond issue. The bond quality designations and rating symbols of these two firms are as follows:

ILLUSTRATION 14-1
Bond Quality Ratings

Quality	Symbols	
	Moody's	Standard & Poor's
Prime	Aaa	AAA
Excellent	Aa	AA
Upper medium	A	A
Lower medium	Baa	BBB
Marginally speculative	Ba	BB
Very speculative	B, Caa	B
Default	Ca, C	D

A quality rating is assigned to each new public bond issue and is a current assessment of the company's ability to pay with respect to a specific borrowing. The rating may be

---

[2]"Caesar's World May Try Bond Issue Paying in Vacations," *The Wall Street Journal* (January 22, 1982), p. 32.

changed up or down during the issue's outstanding life because the quality is constantly monitored. The debt rating is not a recommendation to purchase, sell, or hold a security, because it does not comment on market prices or suitability for particular investors.[3]

❖ VALUATION OF BONDS PAYABLE— DISCOUNT AND PREMIUM

The issuance and marketing of bonds to the public does not happen overnight. It usually takes weeks or even months. Underwriters must be arranged, Securities and Exchange Commission approval must be obtained, audits and issuance of a prospectus may be required, and certificates must be printed. Frequently, the terms in a bond indenture are established well in advance of the sale of the bonds. Between the time the terms are set and the bonds are issued, the market conditions and the financial position of the issuing corporation may change significantly. Such changes affect the marketability of the bonds and thus their selling price.

The selling price of a bond issue is set by such familiar phenomena as supply and demand of buyers and sellers, relative risk, market conditions, and the state of the economy. The investment community values a bond at the present value of its future cash flows, which consist of (1) interest and (2) principal. The rate used to compute the present value of these cash flows is the interest rate that provides an acceptable return on an investment commensurate with the issuer's risk characteristics.

The interest rate written in the terms of the bond indenture (and ordinarily printed on the bond certificate) is known as the **stated, coupon,** or **nominal rate**. This rate, which is set by the issuer of the bonds, is expressed as a percentage of the **face value**, also called the **par value, principal amount,** or **maturity value**, of the bonds. If the rate employed by the investment community (buyers) differs from the stated rate, the present value of the bonds computed by the buyers (and the current purchase price) will differ from the face value of the bonds. The difference between the face value and the present value of the bonds is either a discount or premium.[4] If the bonds sell for less than face value, they are sold at a **discount**. If the bonds sell for more than face value, they are sold at a **premium**.

The rate of interest actually earned by the bondholders is called the **effective yield**, or **market rate**. If bonds sell at a discount, the effective rate is higher than the stated rate. Conversely, if bonds sell at a premium, the effective rate or yield is lower than the stated rate. While the bond is outstanding, its price is affected by several variables, most notably the market rate of interest. There is an inverse relationship between the market interest rate and the price of the bond. The proof of this is graphically portrayed in Illustration 14-2. These huge bond principal losses were due primarily to the Federal Reserve's 1.5% increase in the short-term interest rate in the mid-1990s.

Objective ❸

Describe the accounting valuation for bonds at date of issuance.

🌐 **INTERNATIONAL INSIGHT**

Valuation of long-term debt varies internationally. In the U.S., discount and premium are booked and amortized over the life of the debt. In some countries (e.g., Sweden, Japan, Belgium), it is permissible to write off the discount and premium immediately.

---

[3]Moody's, a credit-rating agency, noted in late 1996 that the U.S. corporate bond market is in good health. Upgrades related to credit quality have outpaced downgrades by 80 percent. The reasons: heavy cost-cutting and corporate restructuring of the past 5 years, coupled with continued earnings growth. In addition, mergers (which often have high risk) have tended in recent years to be financed by equity, not debt.

[4]Until the 1950s it was common for corporations to issue bonds with low, even-percentage coupons (such as 4%) to demonstrate their financial solidity. Frequently, the result was large discounts. More recently, it has become acceptable to set the stated rate of interest on bonds in rather precise fractions (such as 10⅞%). Companies usually attempt to align the stated rate as closely as possible with the market or effective rate at the time of issue. While discounts and premiums continue to occur, their absolute magnitude tends to be much smaller; many times it is immaterial. Professor Bill N. Schwartz (Virginia Commonwealth University) studied the 685 new debt offerings in 1985. Of these, none were issued at a premium. Approximately 95% were issued either with no discount or at a price above 98. Now, however, zero interest (deep discount) bonds are more popular which cause substantial discounts.

ILLUSTRATION 14-2
Effects of Interest Rate
Change on Various
Types of Outstanding
Bonds

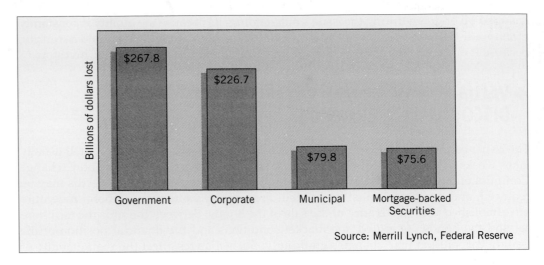

To illustrate the computation of the **present value of a bond issue**, consider ServiceMaster which issues $100,000 in bonds, due in 5 years with 9% interest payable annually at year-end. At the time of issue, the market rate for such bonds is 11%. The following time diagram depicts both the interest and the principal cash flows:

The actual principal and interest cash flows are discounted at an 11% rate for 5 periods as follows:

ILLUSTRATION 14-3
Present Value
Computation of Bond
Selling at a Discount

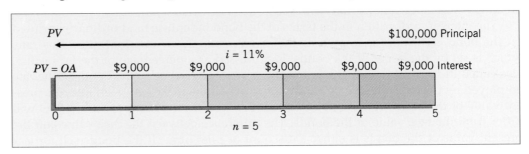

By paying $92,608.10 at the date of issue, the investors will realize an effective rate or yield of 11% over the 5-year term of the bonds. These bonds would sell at a discount of $7,391.90 ($100,000–$92,608.10). The price at which the bonds sell is typically stated as a percentage of the face or par value of the bonds. For example, the ServiceMaster bonds sold for 92.6 (92.6% of par). If ServiceMaster had received $102,000, we would say the bonds sold for 102 (102% of par).

When bonds sell below face value, it means that investors demand a rate of interest higher than the stated rate. The investors are not satisfied with the stated rate because they can earn a greater rate on alternative investments of equal risk. They cannot change the stated rate, so they refuse to pay face value for the bonds. Thus, by changing the amount invested they alter the effective rate of interest. The investors receive interest at the stated rate computed on the face value, but they are earning at **an effective rate that is higher than the stated rate because they paid less than face value for the bonds**. (An illustration of a bond that sells at a premium is shown in Illustrations 14-7 and 14-8.)

Bonds Issued at Par on Interest Date

When bonds are issued on an interest payment date at par (face value), no interest has accrued and no premium or discount exists. The accounting entry is made simply for the cash proceeds and the face value of the bonds. To illustrate, if 10-year term bonds with a par value of $800,000, dated January 1, 1998, and bearing interest at an annual rate of 10% payable semiannually on January 1 and July 1, are issued on January 1 at par, the entry on the books of the issuing corporation would be:

Cash	800,000	
Bonds Payable		800,000

The entry to record the first semiannual interest payment of $40,000 ($800,000 × .10 × 1/2) on July 1, 1998, would be as follows:

Bond Interest Expense	40,000	
Cash		40,000

The entry to record accrued interest expense at December 31, 1998 (year-end) would be as follows:

Bond Interest Expense	40,000	
Bond Interest Payable		40,000

Bonds Issued at Discount or Premium on Interest Date

If the $800,000 of bonds illustrated above were issued on January 1, 1998, at 97 (meaning 97% of par), the issuance would be recorded as follows:

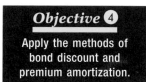

Cash ($800,000 × .97)	776,000	
Discount on Bonds Payable	24,000	
Bonds Payable		800,000

Because of its relation to interest, as previously discussed, **the discount is amortized and charged to interest expense over the period of time that the bonds are outstanding.** Under the straight-line method,[5] the amount amortized each year is a constant amount. For example, using the bond discount above of $24,000, the amount amortized to interest expense each year for 10 years is $2,400 ($24,000 ÷ 10 years) and, if amortization is recorded annually, it is recorded as follows:

Bond Interest Expense	2,400	
Discount on Bonds Payable		2,400

At the end of the first year, 1998, as a result of the amortization entry above, the un-amortized balance in Discount on Bonds Payable is $21,600, ($24,000–$2,400).

If the bonds were dated and sold on October 1, 1998, and if the fiscal year of the corporation ended on December 31, the discount amortized during 1998 would be only 3/12 of 1/10 of $24,000, or $600. Three months of accrued interest must also be recorded on December 31.

Premium on Bonds Payable is accounted for in a manner similar to that for Discount on Bonds Payable. If the 10-year bonds of a par value of $800,000 are dated and sold on January 1, 1998, at 103, the following entry is made to record the issuance:

Cash ($800,000 × 1.03)	824,000	
Premium on Bonds Payable		24,000
Bonds Payable		800,000

---

[5]Although the effective interest method is preferred for amortization of discount or premium, to keep these initial illustrations simple, we have chosen to use the straight-line method (which is acceptable if the results obtained are not materially different from those produced by the effective interest method).

At the end of 1998 and for each year the bonds are outstanding, the entry to amortize the premium on a straight-line basis is:

Premium on Bonds Payable	2,400	
Bond Interest Expense		2,400

Bond interest expense is increased by amortization of a discount and decreased by amortization of a premium. Amortization of a discount or premium under the effective interest method is discussed later.

Some bonds are callable by the issuer after a certain date at a stated price so that the issuing corporation may have the opportunity to reduce its bonded indebtedness or take advantage of lower interest rates. **Whether callable or not, any premium or discount must be amortized over the life to maturity date because early redemption (call of the bond) is not a certainty.**

Bonds Issued between Interest Dates

Bond interest payments are usually made semiannually on dates specified in the bond indenture. When bonds are issued on other than the interest payment dates, **buyers of the bonds will pay the seller the interest accrued from the last interest payment date to the date of issue.** The purchasers of the bonds, in effect, pay the bond issuer in advance for that portion of the full 6-months' interest payment to which they are not entitled, not having held the bonds during that period. **The purchasers will receive the full 6-months' interest payment on the next semiannual interest payment date.**

To illustrate, if 10-year bonds of a par value of $800,000, dated January 1, 1998, and bearing interest at an annual rate of 10% payable semiannually on January 1 and July 1, are issued on March 1, 1998, at **par plus accrued interest**, the entry on the books of the issuing corporation is:

Cash	813,333	
Bonds Payable		800,000
Bond Interest Expense ($800,000 × .10 × 2/12)		13,333
(Interest Payable might be credited instead)		

The purchaser advances 2 months' interest, because on July 1, 1998, 4 months after the date of purchase, 6 months' interest will be received from the issuing company. The company makes the following entry on July 1, 1998:

Bond Interest Expense	40,000	
Cash		40,000

The expense account now contains a debit balance of $26,667, which represents the proper amount of interest expense, 4 months at 10% on $800,000.

The illustration above was simplified by having the January 1, 1998, bonds issued on March 1, 1998, **at par**. If, however, the 10% bonds were issued at 102, the entry on March 1 on the books of the issuing corporation would be:

Cash [($800,000 × 1.02) + ($800,000 × .10 × 2/12)]	829,333	
Bonds Payable		800,000
Premium on Bonds Payable ($800,000 × .02)		16,000
Bond Interest Expense		13,333

The premium would be amortized **from the date of sale**, March 1, 1998, not from the date of the bonds, January 1, 1998.

❖ EFFECTIVE INTEREST METHOD

The profession's preferred procedure for amortization of a discount or premium is the effective interest method (also called **present value amortization**). Under the effective interest method:

❶ Bond interest expense is computed first by multiplying the carrying value[6] of the bonds at the beginning of the period by the effective interest rate.
❷ The bond discount or premium amortization is then determined by comparing the bond interest expense with the interest to be paid.

The computation of the amortization is depicted graphically as follows:

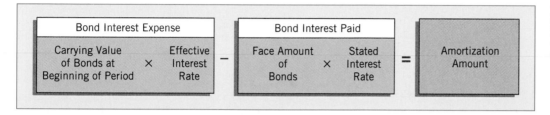

ILLUSTRATION 14-4
Bond Discount and
Premium Amortization
Computation

The effective interest method produces a periodic interest expense equal to **a constant percentage of the carrying value of the bonds**. Since the percentage is the effective rate of interest incurred by the borrower at the time of issuance, the effective interest method results in a better matching of expenses with revenues than the straight-line method.

Both the effective interest and straight-line methods result in the **same total amount of interest expense over the term of the bonds**, and the annual amounts of interest expense are generally quite similar. However, **when the annual amounts are materially different, the effective interest method is required under generally accepted accounting principles**.

 **INTERNATIONAL INSIGHT**

The U.S. generally requires that discount (premium) be amortized using the effective interest method. Some countries prefer straight-line amortization, and Brazil requires it.

Bonds Issued at a Discount

To illustrate amortization of a discount, Evermaster Corporation issued $100,000 of 8% term bonds on January 1, 1998, due on January 1, 2003, with interest payable each July 1 and January 1. Because the investors required an effective interest rate of 10%, they paid $92,278 for the $100,000 of bonds, creating a $7,722 discount. The $7,722 discount is computed as follows:[7]

Maturity value of bonds payable		$100,000
Present value of $100,000 due in 5 years at 10%, interest payable		
semiannually (Table 6-2); $FV(PVF_{10,5\%})$; ($100,000 × .61391)	$61,391	
Present value of $4,000 interest payable semiannually for 5 years at		
10% annually (Table 6-4); $R(PVF\text{-}OA_{10,5\%})$; ($4,000 × 7.72173)	30,887	
Proceeds from sale of bonds		92,278
Discount on bonds payable		$ 7,722

ILLUSTRATION 14-5
Computation of Discount
on Bonds Payable

---

[6]The **book value**, also called the **carrying value**, equals the face amount minus any unamortized discount or plus any unamortized premium.

[7]Because interest is paid semiannually, the interest rate used is 5% (10% × %₁₂). The number of periods is 10 (5 years × 2).

The 5-year amortization schedule appears below.

ILLUSTRATION 14-6
Bond Discount
Amortization Schedule

SCHEDULE OF BOND DISCOUNT AMORTIZATION
EFFECTIVE INTEREST METHOD—SEMIANNUAL INTEREST PAYMENTS
5-YEAR, 8% BONDS SOLD TO YIELD 10%

Date	Cash Paid	Interest Expense	Discount Amortized	Carrying Amount of Bonds
1/1/98				$ 92,278
7/1/98	$ 4,000[a]	$ 4,614[b]	$ 614[c]	92,892[d]
1/1/99	4,000	4,645	645	93,537
7/1/99	4,000	4,677	677	94,214
1/1/00	4,000	4,711	711	94,925
7/1/00	4,000	4,746	746	95,671
1/1/01	4,000	4,783	783	96,454
7/1/01	4,000	4,823	823	97,277
1/1/02	4,000	4,864	864	98,141
7/1/02	4,000	4,907	907	99,048
1/1/03	4,000	4,952	952	100,000
	$40,000	$47,722	$7,722	

[a]$4,000 = $100,000 × .08 × 6/12
[b]$4,614 = $92,278 × .10 × 6/12
[c]$614 = $4,614 − $4,000
[d]$92,892 = $92,278 + $614

The entry to record the issuance of Evermaster Corporation's bonds at a discount on January 1, 1998, is:

Cash	92,278	
Discount on Bonds Payable	7,722	
Bonds Payable		100,000

The journal entry to record the first interest payment on July 1, 1998, and amortization of the discount is:

Bond Interest Expense	4,614	
Discount on Bonds Payable		614
Cash		4,000

The journal entry to record the interest expense accrued at December 31, 1998 (year-end) and amortization of the discount is:

Bond Interest Expense	4,645	
Bond Interest Payable		4,000
Discount on Bonds Payable		645

Bonds Issued at a Premium

If the market had been such that the investors were willing to accept an effective interest rate of 6% on the bond issue described above, they would have paid $108,530 or a premium of $8,530, computed as follows:

ILLUSTRATION 14-7
Computation of Premium
on Bonds Payable

Maturity value of bonds payable		$100,000
Present value of $100,000 due in 5 years at 6%, interest payable semiannually (Table 6-2); $FV(PVF_{10,3\%})$; ($100,000 × .74409)	$74,409	
Present value of $4,000 interest payable semiannually for 5 years at 6% annually (Table 6-4); $R(PVF\text{-}OA_{10,3\%})$; ($4,000 × 8.53020)	34,121	
Proceeds from sale of bonds		108,530
Premium on bonds payable		$ 8,530

The 5-year amortization schedule appears below.

ILLUSTRATION 14-8
Bond Premium
Amortization Schedule

	SCHEDULE OF BOND PREMIUM AMORTIZATION EFFECTIVE INTEREST METHOD—SEMIANNUAL INTEREST PAYMENTS 5-YEAR, 8% BONDS SOLD TO YIELD 6%			
Date	Cash Paid	Interest Expense	Premium Amortized	Carrying Amount of Bonds
1/1/98				$108,530
7/1/98	$ 4,000[a]	$ 3,256[b]	$ 744[c]	107,786[d]
1/1/99	4,000	3,234	766	107,020
7/1/99	4,000	3,211	789	106,231
1/1/00	4,000	3,187	813	105,418
7/1/00	4,000	3,162	838	104,580
1/1/01	4,000	3,137	863	103,717
7/1/01	4,000	3,112	888	102,829
1/1/02	4,000	3,085	915	101,914
7/1/02	4,000	3,057	943	100,971
1/1/03	4,000	3,029	971	100,000
	$40,000	$31,470	$8,530	

[a]$4,000 = $100,000 × .08 × 6/12   [c]$744 = $4,000 − $3,256
[b]$3,256 = $108,530 × .06 × 6/12   [d]$107,786 = $108,530 − $744

The entry to record the issuance of Evermaster bonds at a premium on January 1, 1998, is:

Cash	108,530	
Premium on Bonds Payable		8,530
Bonds Payable		100,000

The journal entry to record the first interest payment on July 1, 1998, and amortization of the premium is:

Bond Interest Expense	3,256	
Premium on Bonds Payable	744	
Cash		4,000

The discount or premium should be amortized as an adjustment to interest expense over the life of the bond in such a way as to result in a **constant rate of interest** when applied to the carrying amount of debt outstanding at the beginning of any given period.[8] Although the effective interest method is recommended, the straight-line method is permitted if the results obtained are not materially different from those produced by the effective interest method.

Accruing Interest

In our previous examples, the interest payment dates and the date the financial statements were issued were the same. For example, when Evermaster sold bonds at a premium (page 708), the two interest payment dates coincided with the financial reporting dates. However, what happens if Evermaster wishes to report financial statements at the end of February 1998? In this case, the premium is prorated by the appropriate number of months to arrive at the proper interest expense as follows:

ILLUSTRATION 14-9
Computation of Interest
Expense

Interest accrual ($4,000 × 2/6)	$1,333.33
Premium amortized ($744 × 2/6)	(248.00)
Interest expense (Jan.–Feb.)	$1,085.33

---

[8]"Interest on Receivables and Payables," *Opinions of the Accounting Principles Board No. 21* (New York: AICPA, 1971), par. 16.

The journal entry to record this accrual is as follows:

Interest Expense	1,085.33	
Premium on Bonds Payable	248.00	
Interest Payable		1,333.33

If the company prepares financial statements 6 months later, the same procedure is followed; that is, the premium amortized would be as follows:

ILLUSTRATION 14-10
Computation of Premium
Amortization

Premium amortized (March–June) ($744 × 4/6)	$496.00
Premium amortized (July–August) ($766 × 2/6)	255.33
Premium amortized (March–August, 1998)	$751.33

The computation is much simpler if the straight-line method is employed. For example, in the Evermaster situation, the total premium is $8,530, which is allocated evenly over the 5-year period. Thus, premium amortization per month is $142.17 ($8,530 ÷ 60 months).

Classification of Discount and Premium

Discount on bonds payable is **not an asset** because it does not provide any future economic benefit. The enterprise has the use of the borrowed funds, but for that use it must pay interest. A bond discount means that the company borrowed less than the face or maturity value of the bond and therefore is faced with an actual (effective) interest rate higher than the stated (nominal) rate. Conceptually, discount on bonds payable is a liability valuation account; that is, it is a reduction of the face or maturity amount of the related liability.[9] This account is referred to as a **contra** account.

Premium on bonds payable has no existence apart from the related debt. The lower interest cost results because the proceeds of borrowing exceed the face or maturity amount of the debt. Conceptually, premium on bonds payable is a liability valuation account; that is, it is an addition to the face or maturity amount of the related liability.[10] This account is referred to as an **adjunct** account. As a result, the profession requires that **bond discount and bond premium be reported as a direct deduction from or addition to the face amount of the bond.**

❖ COSTS OF ISSUING BONDS

The issuance of bonds involves engraving and printing costs, legal and accounting fees, commissions, promotion costs, and other similar charges. According to *APB Opinion No. 21*, these items should be debited to a **deferred charge** account (asset) for Unamortized Bond Issue Costs and amortized over the life of the debt, in a manner similar to that used for discount on bonds.[11]

The FASB, however, in *Concepts Statement No. 3* takes the position that debt issue cost can be treated as either an expense or a reduction of the related debt liability. Debt issue cost is not considered an asset because it provides no future economic benefit. The cost of issuing bonds in effect reduces the proceeds of the bonds issued and increases the effective interest rate and thus may be accounted for the same as the unamortized discount.

There is an obvious difference between GAAP and *Concepts Statement No. 3*'s view of debt issue costs. Until a standard is issued to supersede *Opinion No. 21*, however, **acceptable GAAP for debt issue costs is to treat them as a deferred charge and amortize them over the life of the debt.**

---

[9]"Elements of Financial Statements of Business Enterprises," *Statement of Financial Accounting Concepts No. 3* (Stamford, Conn.: FASB, 1980), par. 160.

[10]Ibid., par. 162.

[11]"Interest on Receivables and Payables," op. cit., par. 15.

To illustrate the accounting for costs of issuing bonds, assume that Microchip Corporation sold $20,000,000 of 10-year debenture bonds for $20,795,000 on January 1, 1999 (also the date of the bonds). Costs of issuing the bonds were $245,000. The entries at January 1, 1999, and December 31, 1999, for issuance of the bonds and amortization of the bond issue costs would be as follows:

January 1, 1999

Cash	20,550,000	
Unamortized Bond Issue Costs	245,000	
Premium on Bonds Payable		795,000
Bonds Payable		20,000,000
(To record issuance of bonds)		

December 31, 1999

Bond Issue Expense	24,500	
Unamortized Bond Issue Costs		24,500
(To amortize one year of bond issue		
costs—straight-line method)		

While the bond issue costs should be amortized using the effective interest method, the straight-line method is generally used in practice because it is easier and the results are not materially different.

❖ TREASURY BONDS

Bonds payable that have been reacquired by the issuing corporation or its agent or trustee and have not been canceled are known as treasury bonds. They should be shown on the balance sheet at par value—as a deduction from the bonds payable issued to arrive at a net figure representing bonds payable outstanding. When they are sold or canceled, the Treasury Bonds account should be credited.

❖ EXTINGUISHMENT OF DEBT

How is the payment of debt—often referred to as extinguishment of debt—recorded? If the bonds (or any other form of debt security) are held to maturity, the answer is straightforward—no gain or loss is computed. Any premium or discount and any issue costs will be fully amortized at the date the bonds mature. As a result, the carrying amount will be equal to the maturity (face) value of the bond. As the maturity or face value is also equal to the bond's market value at that time, no gain or loss exists.

In some cases, debt is extinguished before its maturity date.[12] The amount paid on extinguishment or redemption before maturity, including any call premium and expense of reacquisition, is called the **reacquisition price**. On any specified date, the **net carrying amount** of the bonds is the amount payable at maturity, adjusted for unamortized premium or discount, and cost of issuance. Any excess of the net carrying amount over the reacquisition price is a **gain from extinguishment**, whereas the excess of the reacquisition price over the net carrying amount is a **loss from extinguishment**. At the time of reacquisition, **the unamortized premium or discount, and any costs of issue applicable to the bonds, must be amortized up to the reacquisition date**.

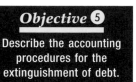

Objective 5

Describe the accounting procedures for the extinguishment of debt.

INTERNATIONAL INSIGHT

In several nations (e.g., Germany, Hong Kong, Korea, Spain), there are no specific accounting principles covering debt extinguishment.

---

[12]Some companies have attempted to extinguish debt through an in-substance defeasance. **In-substance defeasance** is an arrangement whereby a company provides for the future repayment of one or more of its long-term debt issues by placing purchased securities in an irrevocable trust, the principal and interest of which are pledged to pay off the principal and interest of its own debt securities as they mature. The company, however, is not legally released from being the primary obligor under the debt that is still outstanding. In some cases, debt holders are not even aware of the transaction and continue to look to the company for repayment. This practice is not considered an extinguishment of debt and, therefore, no gain or loss is recorded.

To illustrate, assume that on January 1, 1988, General Bell Corp. issued bonds with a par value of $800,000 at 97, due in 20 years. Bond issue costs totaling $16,000 were incurred. Eight years after the issue date, the entire issue is called at 101 and canceled. The loss on redemption (extinguishment) is computed as follows (straight-line amortization is used for simplicity):

ILLUSTRATION 14-11
Computation of Loss on
Redemption of Bonds

Reacquisition price ($800,000 × 1.01)		$808,000
Net carrying amount of bonds redeemed:		
Face value	$800,000	
Unamortized discount ($24,000* × 12/20)	(14,400)	
Unamortized issue costs ($16,000 × 12/20)		
(both amortized using straight-line basis)	(9,600)	776,000
Loss on redemption		$ 32,000

*[$800,000 × (1 − .97)]

The entry to record the reacquisition and cancellation of the bonds is:

Bonds Payable	800,000	
Loss on Redemption of Bonds (Extraordinary)	32,000	
Discount on Bonds Payable		14,400
Unamortized Bond Issue Costs		9,600
Cash		808,000

Note that it is often advantageous for the issuing corporation to acquire the entire outstanding bond issue and replace it with a new bond issue bearing a lower rate of interest. The replacement of an existing issuance with a new one is called **refunding**. Whether the early redemption or other extinguishment of outstanding bonds is a nonrefunding or a refunding situation, the difference (gain or loss) between the reacquisition price and the net carrying amount of the redeemed bonds should be recognized currently in income of the period of redemption, and **classified as an extraordinary item**.

The issuer of callable bonds is generally required to exercise the call on an interest date. Therefore, the amortization of any discount or premium will be up to date and there will be no accrued interest. However, early extinguishments through purchases of bonds in the open market are more likely to be on other than an interest date. If the purchase is not made on an interest date, the discount or premium must be amortized and the interest payable must be accrued from the last interest date to the date of purchase.

SECTION 2 *LONG-TERM NOTES PAYABLE*

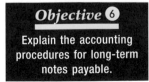

Objective ❻

Explain the accounting procedures for long-term notes payable.

The difference between current notes payable and long-term notes payable is the maturity date. As discussed in Chapter 13, short-term notes payable are expected to be paid within a year or the operating cycle—whichever is longer. Long-term notes are similar in substance to bonds in that both have fixed maturity dates and carry either a stated or implicit interest rate. However, notes do not trade as readily as bonds in the organized public securities markets. Noncorporate and small corporate enterprises issue notes as their long-term instruments, whereas larger corporations issue both long-term notes and bonds.

Accounting for notes and bonds is quite similar. **Like a bond, a note is valued at the present value of its future interest and principal cash flows, with any discount** or premium being similarly amortized over the life of the note.[13] The computation of the present value of an **interest-bearing note**, the recording of its issuance, and the amortization of any discount or premium and accrual of interest are as shown for bonds on pages 703–710 of this chapter.

INTERNATIONAL INSIGHT

In Italy, debt instruments are valued at their face value.

As you might expect, accounting for long-term notes payable parallels accounting for long-term notes receivable as was presented in Chapter 7.

❖ NOTES ISSUED AT FACE VALUE

In Chapter 7, we discussed the recognition of a $10,000, 3-year note issued at face value by Scandinavian Imports to Bigelow Corp. In this transaction, the stated rate and the effective rate were both 10%. The time diagram and present value computation on page 345 of Chapter 7 (see Illustration 7-9) for Bigelow Corp. would be the same for the issuer of the note, Scandinavian Imports, in recognizing a note payable. Because the present value of the note and its face value are the same, $10,000, no premium or discount is recognized. The issuance of the note is recorded by Scandinavian Imports as follows:

Cash	10,000	
Notes Payable		10,000

Scandinavian Imports would recognize the interest incurred each year as follows:

Interest Expense	1,000	
Cash		1,000

❖ NOTES NOT ISSUED AT FACE VALUE

Zero-Interest-Bearing Notes

If a zero-interest-bearing (noninterest-bearing) note[14] is issued solely for cash, its present value is measured by the cash received by the issuer of the note. The implicit interest rate is the **rate that equates the cash received with the amounts received in the future**. The difference between the face amount and the present value (cash received) is recorded as **a discount and amortized to interest expense over the life of the note**.

An example of such a transaction is Beneficial Corporation's offering of $150 million of zero-coupon notes (deep discount bonds) having an 8-year life. With a face value of $1,000 each, these notes sold for $327—a deep discount of $673 each. The present value of each note is the cash proceeds of $327. The interest rate can be calculated by determining the interest rate that equates the amount currently paid by the investor with those amounts to be received in the future. Thus, Beneficial amortized the discount over the 8-year life of the notes using an effective interest rate of 15%.[15]

---

[13]According to *APB Opinion No. 21*, all payables that represent commitments to pay money at a determinable future date are subject to present value measurement techniques, except for the following specifically excluded types:
1. Normal accounts payable due within one year.
2. Security deposits, retainages, advances, or progress payments.
3. Transactions between parent and subsidiary.
4. Convertible debt securities.
5. Obligations payable at some indeterminable future date.

[14]Although the term "note" is used throughout this discussion, the basic principles and methodology are equally applicable to other long-term debt instruments, such as bonds.

[15]$327 = $1,000 $(PVF_{8,i})$

$$PVF_{8,i} = \frac{\$327}{\$1,000} = .327$$

.327 = 15% (in Table 6-2 locate .32690).

To illustrate the entries and the amortization schedule, assume that your company is the one that issued the 3-year, $10,000, zero interest-bearing note to Jeremiah Company as illustrated on page 345 of Chapter 7 (notes receivable). The implicit rate that equated the total cash to be paid ($10,000 at maturity) to the present value of the future cash flows ($7,721.80 cash proceeds at date of issuance) was 9%. (The present value of $1 for 3 periods at 9% is $.77218.) The time diagram depicting the one cash flow is shown below:

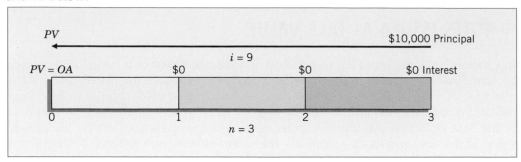

Your entry to record issuance of the note is as follows:

Cash	7,721.80	
Discount on Notes Payable	2,278.20	
Notes Payable		10,000.00

The discount is amortized and interest expense is recognized annually using the **effective interest method**. The 3-year discount amortization and interest expense schedule is shown in Illustration 14-12. (This schedule is similar to the note receivable schedule of Jeremiah Company in Illustration 7-10.)

ILLUSTRATION 14-12
Schedule of Note
Discount Amortization

	Schedule of Note Discount Amortization Effective Interest Method 0% Note Discounted at 9%			
	Cash Paid	Interest Expense	Discount Amortized	Carrying Amount of Note
Date of issue				$ 7,721.80
End of year 1	$-0-	$ 694.96[a]	$ 694.96[b]	8,416.76[c]
End of year 2	-0-	757.51	757.51	9,174.27
End of year 3	-0-	825.73[d]	825.73	10,000.00
	$-0-	$2,278.20	$2,278.20	

[a]$7,721.80 × .09 = $694.96   [c]$7,721.80 + $694.96 = $8,416.76
[b]$694.96 − 0 = $694.96   [d]5¢ adjustment to compensate for rounding

Interest expense at the end of the first year using the effective interest method is recorded as follows:

Interest Expense ($7,721.80 × 9%)	694.96	
Discount on Notes Payable		694.96

The total amount of the discount, $2,278.20 in this case, represents the expense to be incurred on the note over the 3 years.

Interest-Bearing Notes

The zero-interest-bearing note above is an example of the extreme difference between the stated rate and the effective rate. In many cases, the difference between these rates is not so great. Take, for example, the illustration from Chapter 7 where Marie Co. issued a $10,000, 3-year note bearing interest at 10% to Morgan Corp. for cash. The market rate of interest for a note of similar risk is 12%. The time diagram depicting the cash flows and the computation of the present value of this note are shown on page 346 (Illustration 7-11). In this case, because the effective rate of interest (12%) is greater than the stated rate (10%), the present value of the note is less than the face value; that is, the note is exchanged at a **discount**. The issuance of the note is recorded by Marie Co. as follows:

Cash	9,520	
Discount on Notes Payable	480	
Notes Payable		10,000

The discount is then amortized and interest expense is recognized annually using the **effective interest method.** The 3-year discount amortization and interest expense schedule is shown in Illustration 14-13.

ILLUSTRATION 14-13
Schedule of Note
Discount Amortization

Schedule of Note Discount Amortization
Effective Interest Method
10% Note Discounted at 12%

	Cash Paid	Interest Expense	Discount Amortized	Carrying Amount of Note
Date of issue				$ 9,520
End of year 1	$1,000[a]	$1,142[b]	$142[c]	9,662[d]
End of year 2	1,000	1,159	159	9,821
End of year 3	1,000	1,179	179	10,000
	$3,000	$3,480	$480	

[a]$10,000 × 10% = $1,000
[b]$9,520 × 12% = $1,142
[c]$1,142 − $1,000 = $142
[d]$9,520 + $142 = $9,662

Payment of the annual interest and amortization of the discount for the first year are recorded by Marie Co. as follows (amounts per amortization schedule):

Interest Expense	1,142	
Discount on Bonds Payable		142
Cash		1,000

When the present value exceeds the face value, the note is exchanged at a premium. The premium on a note payable is recorded as a credit and amortized using the effective interest method over the life of the note as annual reductions in the amount of interest expense recognized.

❖ SPECIAL NOTE PAYABLE SITUATIONS

The note payable transactions just discussed are the common types of transactions encountered in practice. Three special situations are as follows:

❶ Notes issued for cash and other rights.
❷ Notes issued for property, goods, and services.
❸ Imputed interest.

Notes Issued for Cash and Other Rights

Sometimes when a note is issued, additional rights or privileges are given to the recipient of the note. For example, a corporation issues at face value a zero-interest-bearing note payable that is to be repaid over 5 years with no stated interest. In exchange it agrees to sell merchandise to the lender at less than prevailing prices. In this circumstance, the difference between the present value of the payable and the amount of **cash** received should be recorded by the issuer of the note (borrower/supplier) simultaneously as a discount (debit) on the note and an unearned revenue (credit) on the future sales. The discount should be amortized as a charge to interest expense over the life of the note. The unearned revenue, equal in amount to the discount, reflects a partial prepayment for sales transactions that will occur over the next 5 years. This unearned revenue should be recognized as revenue when sales are made to the lender over the next 5 years.

To illustrate, assume that the face or maturity value of a 5-year, zero-interest-bearing note is $100,000, that it is issued at face value, and that the appropriate rate of interest is 10%. The conditions of the note provide that the recipient of the note (lender/customer) can purchase $500,000 of merchandise from the issuer of the note (borrower/supplier) at something less than regular selling price over the next 5 years. To record the loan, the issuer of the note records a discount of $37,908, the difference between the $100,000 face amount of the loan and its present value of $62,092 ($100,000 $\times$ $PVF_{5,10\%}$ = $100,000 x .62092); as the supplier of the merchandise, the issuer also records a credit to unearned revenue of $37,908. The issuer's journal entry is:

Cash	100,000	
Discount on Notes Payable	37,908	
Notes Payable		100,000
Unearned Revenue		37,908

The Discount on Notes Payable is subsequently amortized to interest expense using the effective interest method. The Unearned Revenue is recognized as revenue from the sale of merchandise and is prorated on the same basis that each period's sales to the lender-customer bear to the total sales to that customer for the term of the note. In this situation the writeoff of the discount and the recognition of the unearned revenue are at different rates.

Notes Issued for Property, Goods, and Services

The second type of situation involves the issuance of a note for some noncash consideration such as property, goods, or services. When the debt instrument is exchanged for property, goods, or services in a bargained transaction entered into at arm's length, the stated interest rate is presumed to be fair unless:

❶ No interest rate is stated, or
❷ The stated interest rate is unreasonable, or
❸ The stated face amount of the debt instrument is materially different from the current cash sales price for the same or similar items or from current market value of the debt instrument.

In these circumstances the present value of the debt instrument is measured by the fair value of the property, goods, or services or by an amount that reasonably approximates the market value of the note.[16] **The interest element other than that evidenced by any stated rate of interest is the difference between the face amount of the note and the fair value of the property.**

For example, assume that Scenic Development Company sold land having a cash sale price of $200,000 to Health Spa, Inc. in exchange for Health Spa's 5-year, $293,860 zero-interest-bearing note. The $200,000 cash sale price represents the present value of the $293,860 note discounted at 8% for 5 years. If the transaction is recorded on the sale date at the face amount of the note, $293,860, by both parties, Health Spa's Land account and Scenic's sales would be overstated by $93,860, because the $93,860 represents the interest for 5 years at an effective rate of 8%. Interest revenue to Scenic and interest expense to Health Spa for the 5-year period correspondingly would be understated by $93,860.

---

[16]"Interest on Receivables and Payables," op. cit., par. 12.

Because the difference between the cash sale price of $200,000 and the face amount of the note, $293,860, represents interest at an effective rate of 8%, the transaction is recorded at the exchange date as follows:

Health Spa, Inc. Books			Scenic Development Company Books		
Land	200,000		Notes Receivable	293,860	
Discount on Notes Payable	93,860		Discount on Notes Rec.		93,860
Notes Payable		293,860	Sales		200,000

ILLUSTRATION 14-14
Entries for Noncash Note Transactions

During the 5-year life of the note, Health Spa amortizes annually a portion of the discount of $93,860 as a charge to interest expense. Scenic Development records interest revenue totaling $93,860 over the 5-year period by also amortizing the discount. The effective interest method is required, although other approaches to amortization may be used if the results obtained are not materially different from those that result from the effective interest method.

Imputed Interest

In instances when the stated rate is known to be unreasonable, the effective rate must be imputed (as explained in Chapter 7). Whenever the imputed interest rate is different from the stated rate at the date the note is issued, a discount or premium must be recognized and amortized in subsequent periods. Using the illustration from Chapter 7, assume that on December 31, 1998, Wunderlich Company issued a promissory note to Brown Interiors Company for architectural services. The note has a face value of $550,000, a due date of December 31, 2003, and bears a stated interest rate of 2%, payable at the end of each year. The fair value of the architectural services is not readily determinable, nor is the note readily marketable. On the basis of the credit rating of Wunderlich Company, the absence of collateral, the prime interest rate at that date, and the prevailing interest on Wunderlich's other outstanding debt, an 8% interest rate is imputed as appropriate in this circumstance. The time diagram depicting both cash flows is shown as follows.

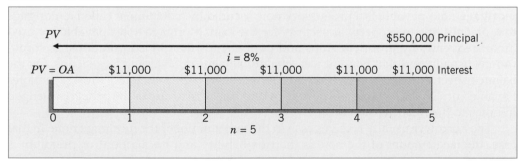

The present value of the note and the imputed fair value of the architectural services are determined as follows:

Face value of the note		$550,000
Present value of $550,000 due in 5 years at 8% interest payable annually (Table 6-2); $FV(PVF_{5,8\%})$; ($550,000 × .68058)	$374,319	
Present value of $11,000 interest payable annually for 5 years at 8%; $R(PVF\text{-}OA_{5,8\%})$; ($11,000 × 3.99271)	43,920	
Present value of the note		418,239
Discount on notes payable		$131,761

ILLUSTRATION 14-15
Computation of Imputed Fair Value and Note Discount

The issuance of the note and receipt of the architectural services are recorded as follows:

December 31, 1998

Building (or Construction in Process)	418,239	
Discount on Notes Payable	131,761	
Notes Payable		550,000

The 5-year amortization schedule appears below.

ILLUSTRATION 14-16
Schedule of Discount
Amortization Using
Imputed Interest Rate

Date	Cash Paid (2%)	Interest Expense (8%)	Discount Amortized	Carrying Amount of Note
12/31/98				$418,239
12/31/99	$11,000[a]	$ 33,459[b]	$ 22,459[c]	440,698[d]
12/31/00	11,000	35,256	24,256	464,954
12/31/01	11,000	37,196	26,196	491,150
12/31/02	11,000	39,292	28,292	519,442
12/31/03	11,000	41,558[e]	30,558	550,000
	$55,000	$186,761	$131,761	

**SCHEDULE OF NOTE DISCOUNT AMORTIZATION
EFFECTIVE INTEREST METHOD
2% NOTE DISCOUNTED AT 8% (IMPUTED)**

[a]$550,000 × 2% = $11,000
[b]$418,239 × 8% = $33,459
[c]$33,459 − $11,000 = $22,459
[d]$418,239 + $22,459 = $440,698
[e]$3 adjustment to compensate for rounding.

Payment of the first year's interest and amortization of the discount is recorded as follows:

December 31, 1999

Interest Expense	33,459	
Discount on Notes Payable		22,459
Cash		11,000

❖ MORTGAGE NOTES PAYABLE

The most common form of long-term notes payable is a mortgage note payable. A mortgage note payable is a promissory note secured by a document called a mortgage that pledges title to property as security for the loan. Mortgage notes payable are used more frequently by proprietorships and partnerships than by corporations, as corporations usually find that bond issues offer advantages in obtaining large loans. On the balance sheet, the liability should be reported using a title such as "Mortgage Notes Payable" or "Notes Payable—Secured," with a brief disclosure of the property pledged in notes to the financial statements.

The borrower usually receives cash in the face amount of the mortgage note. In that case, the face amount of the note is the true liability and no discount or premium is involved. When "points" are assessed by the lender, however, the total amount paid by the borrower exceeds the face amount of the note.[17] Points raise the effective interest rate above the rate specified in the note. A point is 1% of the face of the note. For example, assume that a 20-year mortgage note in the amount of $100,000 with a stated interest rate of 10.75% is given by you to Local Savings and Loan Association as part of the financing of your new house. If Local Savings demands 4 points to close the financing, you will receive 4% less than $100,000—or $96,000—but you will be obligated to repay the entire $100,000 at the rate of $1,015 per month. Because you received only $96,000, and must repay $100,000, your effective interest rate is increased to approximately 11.3% on the money you actually borrowed.

Mortgages may be payable in full at maturity or in installments over the life of the loan. If payable at maturity, the mortgage payable is shown as a long-term liability on the balance sheet until such time as the approaching maturity date warrants showing it as a current liability. If it is payable in installments, the current installments due are shown as current liabilities, with the remainder shown as a long-term liability.

---

[17]Points, in mortgage financing, are analogous to the original issue discount of bonds.

Because of unusually high, unstable interest rates and a tight money supply, the traditional **fixed-rate mortgage** recently has been partially supplanted with new and unique mortgage arrangements. Most lenders offer **variable-rate mortgages** (also called floating-rate or adjustable rate mortgages) featuring interest rates tied to changes in the fluctuating market rate. Generally the variable-rate lenders adjust the interest rate at either 1- or 3-year intervals, pegging the adjustments to changes in the prime rate or the U.S. Treasury bond rate.

REPORTING AND ANALYSIS OF LONG-TERM DEBT   SECTION 3

Reporting of long-term debt is one of the most controversial areas in financial reporting. Because long-term debt has significant impact on the cash flows of the company, reporting requirements must be substantive and informative. One problem is that the definition of a liability established in *Concepts Statement No. 6* and the recognition criteria established in *Concepts Statement No. 5* are sufficiently imprecise that arguments can still be made that certain obligations need not be reported as debt.

❖ OFF-BALANCE-SHEET FINANCING

Off-balance-sheet financing is an attempt to borrow monies in such a way that the obligations are not recorded. It is an issue of extreme importance to accountants (as well as general management). As one writer noted, "The basic drives of humans are few: to get enough food, to find shelter, and to keep debt off the balance sheet."

> *Objective* ❼
> Explain the reporting of off-balance-sheet financing arrangements.

Illustration

One form of off-balance-sheet financing occurs with **project financing arrangements**. These arrangements arise when (1) two or more entities form a new entity to construct an operating plant that will be used by both parties; (2) the new entity borrows funds to construct the project and repays the debt from the proceeds received from the project; (3) payment of the debt is guaranteed by the companies that formed the new entity. The advantage of such an arrangement is that **the companies that formed the new entity do not have to report the liability on their books**. To illustrate, assume that Dow Chemical and Mobil Oil each put up $1 million and form a separate company to build a chemical plant to be used by both companies. The newly formed company borrows $48 million to construct the plant. The arrangement is illustrated below:

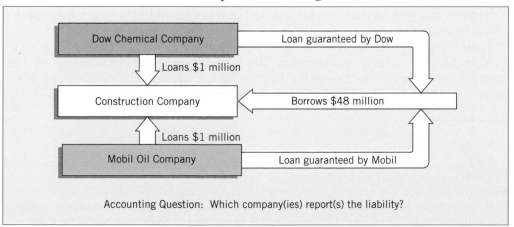

ILLUSTRATION 14-17
Project Financing
Arrangement

The answer is that each needs to disclose only that they guarantee debt repayment if the project's proceeds are inadequate to pay off the loan.[18]

In some cases, project financing arrangements become more formalized through the use of a variety of contracts. In a simple take-or-pay contract, a purchaser of goods signs an agreement with a seller to pay specified amounts periodically in return for an option to receive products. The purchaser must make specified minimum payments even if delivery of the contracted products is not taken. Often these take-or-pay contracts are associated with project financing arrangements. For example, in Illustration 14-17, Dow Chemical and Mobil Oil sign an agreement that they will purchase products from this new plant and that they will make certain minimum payments **even if they do not take delivery of the goods.**

Through-put agreements are similar in concept to take-or-pay contracts, except that a service instead of a product is provided by the asset under construction. Assume that Dow and Mobil become involved in a project financing arrangement to build a pipeline to transport their various products. They sign an agreement that requires them to pay specified amounts in return for the transportation of the product. In addition, these companies are required to make cash payments **even if they do not provide the minimum quantities to be transported**.

Inconsistent methods have been used in practice to account for and disclose the unconditional obligation in a take-or-pay or through-put contract involved in a project financing arrangement. In general, most companies have attempted to develop these types of contracts to "get the debt off the balance sheet."

Rationale

Companies attempt to arrange off-balance-sheet financing for several reasons. First, many believe that removing debt enhances the quality of the balance sheet and permits credit to be obtained more readily and at less cost.

Second, loan covenants often impose a limitation on the amount of debt a company may have. As a result, off-balance-sheet financing is used because these types of commitments might not be considered in computing the debt limitation.

Third, it is argued by some that the asset side of the balance sheet is severely understated. For example, companies that use LIFO costing for inventories and depreciate assets on an accelerated basis will often have carrying amounts for inventories and property, plant, and equipment that are much lower than their current values. As an offset to these lower values, some managements believe that part of the debt does not have to be reported. In other words, if assets were reported at current values, less pressure would undoubtedly exist for off-balance-sheet financing arrangements.

Whether the arguments above have merit is debatable. The general idea "out of sight, out of mind" may not be true in accounting. Many users of financial statements indicate that they factor these off-balance-sheet financing arrangements into their computations when assessing debt to equity relationships. Similarly, many loan covenants also attempt to take these complex arrangements into account. Nevertheless, many companies still believe that benefits will accrue if certain obligations are not reported on the balance sheet.

The FASB response to these off-balance-sheet financing arrangements has been increased disclosure (note) requirements. This response is consistent with an "efficient markets" philosophy: the important question is not whether the presentation is off-balance sheet or not, but whether the items are disclosed at all.[19] The authors believe

---

[18]"Accounting for Contingencies," *Statement of Financial Accounting Standards No. 5* (Stamford, Conn.: FASB, 1975), par. 12.

[19]It is unlikely that the FASB will be able to stop all types of off-balance-sheet transactions. Financial information is the Holy Grail of Wall Street. Developing new financial instruments and arrangements to sell and market to customers is not only profitable, but also adds to the prestige of the investment firms that create them. Thus, new financial products will continue to appear that will test the ability of the FASB to develop appropriate accounting standards for them.

that financial reporting would be enhanced if more obligations were recorded on the balance sheet instead of merely described in the notes to the financial statements.[20]

❖ PRESENTATION AND ANALYSIS OF LONG-TERM DEBT

Income Statement Presentation

Gains and losses from extinguishment of debt should be aggregated and, if material, classified in the income statement as an extraordinary item, net of related income tax effect.[21] Extraordinary item treatment applies whether an extinguishment is early or at a scheduled maturity date or later, without regard to the criteria of "unusual in nature" and "infrequency of occurrence." These gains and losses are reported as extraordinary items in such a way that readers of the financial statements can evaluate their significance.[22] The following disclosures are required:

Objective ❽
Indicate how long-term debt is presented and analyzed.

❶ A description of the extinguishment transactions, including the sources of any funds used to extinguish debt if it is practicable to identify the sources.
❷ The income tax effect in the period of extinguishment.
❸ The per share amount of the aggregate gain or loss, net of related tax effect.[23]

The preceding information, to the extent that it is not shown separately on the face of the income statement, must be disclosed in a single note or adequately cross-referenced if in more than one note. The following illustration presents disclosure on the face of the income statement and in a note to the financial statements.

Digital Computer Corp. purchased for $5,000,000 cash its outstanding 5% debenture bonds having a face or maturity value, as well as net carrying amount, of $6,000,000. Disclosure was appropriately made in its annual report as follows:

Digital Computer Corp.	
Income before extraordinary item	$4,200,000
Extraordinary item—gain from liquidation of debt, net of income tax effect of $480,000—Note 3	520,000
Net income	$4,720,000
Per share of common stock:	
Income before extraordinary item	$1.62
Extraordinary item, net of tax	.20
Net income	$1.82

Note 3: Extraordinary Item. The extraordinary item represents a gain of $1,000,000 less related income tax effect from the redemption and retirement of the company's outstanding 5% debenture bonds pursuant to an offer made by the company. The funds used to purchase the debentures represent a portion of the proceeds from the sale of 300,000 shares of the company's common stock.

ILLUSTRATION 14-18
Disclosure of Debt Extinguishment

---

[20]The FASB's recent efforts to report financial instrument derivatives on the balance sheet is a major breakthrough in this area. See the appendix to Chapter 18 for discussion of the reporting issues related to these complex transactions.

[21]"Reporting Gains and Losses from Extinguishment of Debt," *Statement of Financial Accounting Standards No. 4* (Stamford, Conn.: FASB, 1975), par. 8.

[22]Two types of extinguishment that are not reported as extraordinary items are (1) gains and losses that result from a conversion agreement that is part of the original debt covenant and (2) gains and losses from cash purchases of debt made to satisfy current or future sinking fund requirements.

[23]*FASB Statement No. 4* requires disclosure of the per-share effect of gains and losses from extinguishment of debt.

Balance Sheet Presentation

Companies that have large amounts and numerous issues of long-term debt frequently report only one amount in the balance sheet and support this with comments and schedules in the accompanying notes. These note disclosures generally indicate the nature of the liabilities, maturity dates, interest rates, call provisions, conversion privileges, restrictions imposed by the borrower, and assets designated or pledged as security. Any assets pledged as security for the debt should be shown in the asset section of the balance sheet.

Long-term debt that matures within one year should be reported as a current liability, unless retirement is to be accomplished with other than current assets. If the debt is to be refinanced, converted into stock, or is to be retired from a bond retirement fund, it should continue to be reported as noncurrent and accompanied with a note explaining the method to be used in its liquidation.[24]

Note Disclosure

Disclosure is required of future payments for sinking fund requirements and maturity amounts of long-term debt during each of the next 5 years.[25] The purpose of the disclosures is to aid financial statement users in evaluating the amounts and timing of future cash flows. For example, assume that Percy Corporation has two long-term borrowings outstanding at December 31, 1998. The first borrowing is a $50 million sinking fund debenture with annual sinking fund payments of $5 million in 1999, 2000, and 2001, $10 million in 2002 and 2003, and $15 million in 2004. The second borrowing is a $75 million bond issue that matures in 2001. Percy's disclosures would be as follows:

ILLUSTRATION 14-19
Disclosure of Long-Term
Debt Maturing in Next 5
Years

Maturities and sinking fund requirements on long-term debt for the next 5 years are as follows:	
1999	$ 5,000,000
2000	5,000,000
2001	80,000,000
2002	10,000,000
2003	10,000,000

In addition, any unconditional long-term obligations (such as project financing arrangements) must be disclosed.

For **unconditional purchase obligations** recorded on the purchaser's balance sheet, disclosure must be made of the payments to be made under the obligation for each of the next 5 years. In addition, the following disclosures are required for those unconditional purchase obligations **not recorded** on the purchaser's balance sheet:

➊ The nature and term of the obligations.
➋ The total amount of the fixed and determinable portion of the obligations at the balance sheet date and for each of the next 5 years.
➌ The nature of any variable portions of the obligations.
➍ The amounts purchased under the obligations (as in take-or-pay contracts or through-put contracts) for each period for which an income statement is presented.

With respect to requirement (2) above, it is recommended, but not required, that the amount of imputed interest necessary to reduce the total amount of the obligation to its present value be disclosed.[26] The discount rate to be used should be the effective interest rate, if known, of the borrowings that financed the facility that will provide the

---

[24]"Balance Sheet Classification of Short-Term Obligations Expected to Be Refinanced," *FASB Statement of Financial Accounting Standards No. 6* (Stamford, Conn.: FASB, 1975), par. 15. See also "Disclosure of Information about Capital Structure," *FASB Statement of Financial Accounting Standards No. 129* (Norwalk, Conn.: FASB, 1997), par. 4.

[25]"Disclosure of Long-Term Obligations," *Statement of Financial Accounting Standards No. 47* (Stamford, Conn.: FASB, 1981), par. 10.

[26]Ibid., par. 7.

Presentation and Analysis of Long-Term Debt • **723**

contracted goods or services. If not known, the discount rate should be the purchaser's incremental borrowing rate when the obligation is entered into—the rate the purchaser would have incurred to borrow the funds necessary to discharge the unconditional purchase obligation. An example of a through-put agreement involving a project financing arrangement is reported below for Hewlett Chemical Company:

Hewlett Chemical Company	
To secure access to facilities to process the chemical phenoxyethanol, the company has signed a processing agreement with a chemical company allowing Hewlett to submit 100,000 tons for processing annually for 15 years. Under the terms of the agreement, Hewlett may be required to advance funds if the chemical company is unable to meet its financial obligations. The aggregate amount of required payments at December 31, 1993, is as follows:	
1994	$ 20,000,000
1995	15,000,000
1996	10,000,000
1997	9,000,000
1998	8,000,000
Later years	78,000,000
Total	140,000,000
Less: Amount representing interest	(79,791,510)
Total at present value	$ 60,208,490
In addition, the company is required to pay a proportional share of the variable operating expenses of the plant. The company's total processing charges under the agreement for each of the preceding 5 years were: 1989 and 1990, $27,000,000; 1991 and 1992, $29,000,000; and 1993, $28,000,000.	

ILLUSTRATION 14-20
Disclosure of a Project Financing Arrangement

Go to Web site for additional disclosures of off-balance-sheet financing arrangements.

Analysis of Long-Term Debt

Long-term creditors and stockholders are interested in a company's long-run solvency, particularly its ability to pay interest as it comes due and to repay the face value of the debt at maturity. Debt to total assets and times interest earned are two ratios that provide information about debt-paying ability and long-run solvency.

The **debt to total assets ratio** measures the percentage of the total assets provided by creditors. It is computed as shown in the following formula by dividing total debt (both current and long-term liabilities) by total assets:

$$\text{Debt to total assets} = \frac{\text{Total debt}}{\text{Total assets}}$$

ILLUSTRATION 14-21
Computation of Debt to Total Assets Ratio

The higher the percentage of debt to total assets, the greater the risk that the company may be unable to meet its maturing obligations.

The **times interest earned ratio** indicates the company's ability to meet interest payments as they come due. It is computed by dividing income before interest expense and income taxes by interest expense:

$$\text{Times interest earned} = \frac{\text{Income before income taxes and interest expense}}{\text{Interest expense}}$$

ILLUSTRATION 14-22
Computation of Times Interest Earned Ratio

To illustrate these ratios, we will use data from Hershey Foods Company's 1995 Annual Report, which disclosed total liabilities of $1,748 million, total assets of $2,831 million, interest expense of $45 million, income taxes of $184 million, and net income of $282 million. Hershey Foods' debt to total assets ratio is computed as follows:

$$\text{Debt to total assets} = \frac{\$1,748}{\$2,831} = 61.7\%$$

Hershey Foods' times interest earned ratio is computed as follows:

$$\text{Times interest earned} = \frac{(\$282 + \$45 + \$184)}{\$45} = 11.4 \text{ times}$$

Even though Hershey Foods has a relatively high debt to total assets percentage of 61.7%, its interest coverage of 11.4 times appears very safe.

SUMMARY OF LEARNING OBJECTIVES

① *Describe the formal procedures associated with issuing long-term debt.* Incurring long-term debt is often a formal procedure. The bylaws of corporations usually require approval by the board of directors and the stockholders before bonds can be issued or other long-term debt arrangements can be contracted. Generally, long-term debt has various convenants or restrictions. The covenants and other terms of the agreement between the borrower and the lender are stated in the bond indenture or note agreement.

② *Identify various types of bond issues.* (1) Secured and unsecured bonds. (2) Term, serial bonds, and callable bonds. (3) Convertible, commodity-backed, and deep discount bonds. (4) Registered and bearer (coupon) bonds. (5) Income and revenue bonds. The variety in the types of bonds is a result of attempts to attract capital from different investors and risk takers and to satisfy the cash flow needs of the issuers.

③ *Describe the accounting valuation for bonds at date of issuance.* The investment community values a bond at the present value of its future cash flows, which consist of interest and principal. The rate used to compute the present value of these cash flows is the interest rate that provides an acceptable return on an investment commensurate with the issuer's risk characteristics. The interest rate written in the terms of the bond indenture and ordinarily appearing on the bond certificate is the stated, coupon, or nominal rate. This rate, which is set by the issuer of the bonds, is expressed as a percentage of the face value, also called the par value, principal amount, or maturity value, of the bonds. If the rate employed by the buyers differs from the stated rate, the present value of the bonds computed by the buyers will differ from the face value of the bonds. The difference between the face value and the present value of the bonds is either a discount or premium.

④ *Apply the methods of bond discount and premium amortization.* The discount (premium) is amortized and charged (credited) to interest expense over the period of time that the bonds are outstanding. Bond interest expense is increased by amortization of a discount and decreased by amortization of a premium. The profession's preferred procedure for amortization of a discount or premium is the effective interest method. Under the effective interest method, (1) bond interest expense is computed by multiplying the carrying value of the bonds at the beginning of the period by the effective interest rate, and (2) the bond discount or premium amortization is then determined by comparing the bond interest expense with the interest to be paid.

⑤ *Describe the accounting procedures for the extinguishment of debt.* At the time of reacquisition, the unamortized premium or discount and any costs of issue applicable to the debt must be amortized up to the reacquisition date. The amount paid on extinguishment or redemption before maturity, including any call premium and expense of reacquisition, is the reacquisition price. On any specified date, the net carrying amount of the debt is the amount payable at maturity, adjusted for unamortized premium or discount, and cost of issuance. Any excess of the net carrying amount over the reacquisition price is a gain from extinguishment, whereas the excess of the reacquisition price over the net carrying amount is a loss from extinguishment.

6 ***Explain the accounting procedures for long-term notes payable.*** Accounting procedures for notes and bonds are quite similar. Like a bond, a note is valued at the present value of its future interest and principal cash flows, with any discount or premium being similarly amortized over the life of the note. Whenever the face amount of the note does not reasonably represent the present value of the consideration given or received in the exchange, the entire arrangement must be evaluated to properly record the exchange and the subsequent interest.

7 ***Explain the reporting of off-balance-sheet financing arrangements.*** Off-balance-sheet financing is an attempt to borrow funds in such a way that the obligations are not recorded. One type of off-balance-sheet financing occurs with project financing arrangements that may take the form of take-or-pay contracts or through-put agreements.

8 ***Indicate how long-term debt is presented and analyzed.*** Companies that have large amounts and numerous issues of long-term debt frequently report only one amount in the balance sheet and support this with comments and schedules in the accompanying notes. Any assets pledged as security for the debt should be shown in the asset section of the balance sheet. Long-term debt that matures within one year should be reported as a current liability, unless retirement is to be accomplished with other than current assets. If the debt is to be refinanced, converted into stock, or is to be retired from a bond retirement fund, it should continue to be reported as noncurrent and accompanied with a note explaining the method to be used in its liquidation. Disclosure is required of future payments for sinking fund requirements and maturity amounts of long-term debt during each of the next 5 years. Debt to total assets and times interest earned are two ratios that provide information about debt-paying ability and long-run solvency.

Appendix 14A

Accounting for Troubled Debt

During periods of depressed economic conditions or other financial hardship, some debtors have difficulty meeting their financial obligations. For example, owing to rising interest rates and corporate mismanagement, the savings and loan industry experienced a decade of financial crises. The banking industry also faced credit concerns: During the late 1980s bad energy loans and the rescheduling of loans between "less developed countries," such as Argentina, Brazil, and Mexico, and major U.S. banks created considerable uncertainty about the soundness of our banking system. Electric utilities with large nuclear plant construction programs suffered from the financial strains of illiquidity. Companies such as Public Service of New Hampshire, Continental Illinois Bank, Lions Capital, and Braniff Airlines had to restructure their debts or in some other way be bailed out of negative cash flow situations.

> **Objective 9**
>
> After studying Appendix 14A, you should be able to: Distinguish between and account for (1) a loss on loan impairment, (2) a troubled debt restructuring that results in the settlement of a debt, and (3) a troubled debt restructuring that results in a continuation of debt with modification of terms.

❖ ACCOUNTING ISSUES

The major accounting issues related to troubled debt situations involve recognition and measurement. In other words, when should a loss be recognized and at what amount?

To illustrate the major issue related to recognition, assume that Citicorp has a

$10,000,000, 5-year, 10% loan to Brazil with interest receivable annually. At the end of the third year, Citicorp has determined that it probably will be able to collect $7,000,000 of this loan at maturity. Should it wait until the loan becomes uncollectible, or should it record a loss immediately? The general recognition principle is: **Losses should be recorded immediately if it is probable that the loss will occur.**

Assuming that Citicorp decides to record a loss, at what amount should the loss be recorded? Three alternatives are:

❶ *Aggregate Cash Flows.* Some argue that a loss should not be recorded unless the aggregate cash flows from the loan are less than its carrying amount. In the Citicorp example, the aggregate cash flows expected are $7,000,000 of principal and $2,000,000 of interest ($10,000,000 × 10% × 2), for a total of $9,000,000. Thus, a loss of only $1,000,000 ($10,000,000 − $9,000,000) would be reported.

Advocates of this position argue that Citicorp will recover $9,000,000 of the $10,000,000 and, therefore, its loss is only $1,000,000. Others disagree, noting that this approach ignores present values. That is, the present value of the future cash flows is much less than $9,000,000 and, therefore, the loss is much greater than $1,000,000.

❷ *Present Value—Historical Effective Rate.* Those who argue for the use of present value, however, disagree about the interest rate to use to discount the expected future cash flows. The two rates discussed are the historical (original) effective rate and the market rate at the time the loan is recognized as troubled. Those who favor the historical effective rate believe that losses should reflect only a deterioration in credit quality. When the historical effective loan rate is used, the value of the investment will change only if some of the legally contracted cash flows are reduced. A loss in this case is recognized because the expected future cash flows have changed. Interest rate changes caused by current economic events that affect the fair value of the loan are ignored.

❸ *Present Value—Market Rate.* Others believe that expected future cash flows of a troubled loan should be discounted at market interest rates, which reflect current economic events and conditions that are commensurate with the risks involved. The historical effective interest rate reflects the risk characteristics of the loan at the time it was originated or acquired, but not at the time it is troubled. In short, proponents of the market rate believe that a fair value measure should be used.

This appendix addresses issues concerning the accounting by debtors and creditors for troubled debt. Two different types of situations result with troubled debt:

❶ Impairments.
❷ Restructurings:
  a. Settlements.
  b. Modification of terms.

In a troubled debt situation, the creditor usually first recognizes a loss on impairment. Subsequently either the terms of the loan are modified or the loan is settled on terms unfavorable to the creditor. In unusual cases, the creditor forces the debtor into bankruptcy in order to ensure the highest possible collection on the loan. Illustration 14A-1 shows this continuum:

ILLUSTRATION 14A-1
Usual Progression in
Troubled Debt Situations

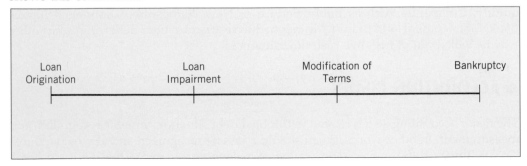

| Loan | Loan | Modification of | Bankruptcy |
| Origination | Impairment | Terms | |

❖ IMPAIRMENTS

A loan[1] is considered **impaired** when it is **probable**,[2] based on current information and events, that the creditor will be unable to collect all amounts due (both principal and interest) according to the contractual terms of the loan. Creditors should apply their normal review procedures in making the judgment as to the probability of collection.[3] If a loan is considered impaired, the loss due to the impairment should be measured as the difference between the investment in the loan (generally the principal plus accrued interest) and the expected future cash flows discounted at the loan's historical effective interest rate.[4] In estimating future cash flows the creditor should employ all reasonable and supportable assumptions and projections.[5]

Illustration of Loss on Impairment

On December 31, 1998, Prospect Inc. issued a $500,000, 5-year, zero-interest-bearing note to Community Bank. The note was issued to yield 10% annual interest. As a result, Prospect received and Community Bank paid $310,460 ($500,000 × .62092) on December 31, 1998.[6] A time diagram illustrates the factors involved:

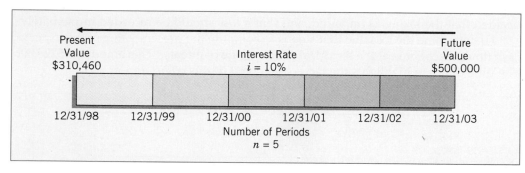

The entries to record this transaction on the books of Community Bank (creditor) and Prospect Inc. (debtor) are as follows:

ILLUSTRATION 14A-2
Creditor and Debtor
Entries to Record Note

December 31, 1998				
Community Bank (Creditor)		**Prospect Inc. (Debtor)**		
Notes Receivable	500,000	Cash	310,460	
Discount on Notes Receivable	189,540	Discount on Notes		
Cash	310,460	Payable	189,540	
		Notes Payable		500,000

Assuming that Community Bank and Prospect Inc. use the effective interest method to amortize discounts, Illustration 14A-3 shows the amortization of the discount and the increase in the carrying amount of the note over the life of the note.

---

[1]*FASB Statement No. 114*, "Accounting by Creditors for Impairment of a Loan," (Norwalk, Conn.: FASB, May 1993), defines a loan as "a contractual right to receive money on demand or on fixed and determinable dates that is recognized as an asset in the creditor's statement of financial position." For example, accounts receivable with terms exceeding one year are considered loans.

[2]Recall the definitions of probable, reasonably possible, and remote with respect to contingencies, as defined in *FASB Statement No. 5*.

[3]Normal review procedures include examination of "watch lists," review of regulatory reports of examination, and examination of management reports of total loan amounts by borrower.

[4]The creditor may also, for the sake of expediency, use the market price of the loan (if such a price is available) or the fair value of collateral if it is a collateralized loan. *FASB Statement No. 114*, par. 13.

[5]*FASB Statement No. 114*, par. 15.

[6]Present value of $500,000 due in 5 years at 10%, annual compounding (Table 6-2) equals $500,000 × .62092.

ILLUSTRATION 14A-3
Schedule of Interest and
Discount Amortization
(Before Impairment)

	Community Bank			
Date	Cash Received (0%)	Interest Revenue (10%)	Discount Amortized	Carrying Amount of Note
12/31/98				$310,460
12/31/99	$0	$ 31,046ᵃ	$ 31,046	341,506ᵇ
12/31/00	0	34,151	34,151	375,657
12/31/01	0	37,566	37,566	413,223
12/31/02	0	41,322	41,322	454,545
12/31/03	0	45,455	45,455	500,000
Total	$0	$189,540	$189,540	

ᵃ$31,046 = $310,460 × .10
ᵇ$341,506 = $310,460 + $31,046

Unfortunately, during 2000 Prospect's business deteriorated due to increased competition and a faltering regional economy. After reviewing all available evidence at December 31, 2000, Community Bank determined that it was probable that Prospect would pay back only $300,000 of the principal at maturity. As a result, Community Bank decided that the loan was impaired, and that a loss should be recorded immediately.

To determine the loss, the first step is to compute the present value of the expected cash flows discounted at the historical effective rate of interest. This amount is $225,396. The time diagram highlights the factors involved in this computation.

ILLUSTRATION 14A-4
Time Diagram, Factors
for Loss on Note

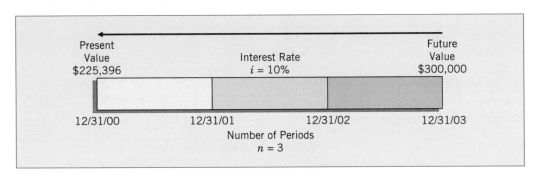

The loss due to impairment is equal to the difference between the present value of the expected future cash flows and the recorded carrying amount of the investment in the loan. The calculation of the loss is shown in Illustration 14A-5:

ILLUSTRATION 14A-5
Computation of Loss Due
to Impairment

Carrying amount of investment (12/31/00)—Illustration 14A-3	$375,657
Less: Present value of $300,000 due in 3 years at 10% interest compounded annually (Table 6-2); $FV(PVF_{3,10\%})$; ($300,000 × .75132)	225,396
Loss due to impairment	$150,261

The loss due to the impairment is $150,261 not $200,000 ($500,000 − $300,000). The reason is that the loss is measured at a present value amount, not an undiscounted amount, at the time the loss is recorded.

The entry to record the loss is as follows:

ILLUSTRATION 14A-6
Creditor and Debtor
Entries to Record Loss
on Note

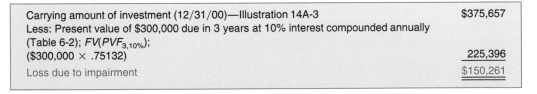

December 31, 2000			
Community Bank (Creditor)			**Prospect Inc. (Debtor)**
Bad Debt Expense	150,261		No entry
Allowance for Doubtful Accounts		150,261	

Community Bank (creditor) debits Bad Debt Expense for the expected loss. At the same time, it reduces the overall value of its loan receivable by crediting Allowance for Doubtful Accounts.[7] On the other hand, Prospect Inc. (debtor) makes no entry because it still legally owes $500,000.[8]

❖ TROUBLED DEBT RESTRUCTURINGS

A **troubled debt restructuring** occurs when a creditor "for economic or legal reasons related to the debtor's financial difficulties grants a concession to the debtor that it would not otherwise consider."[9] Thus a **troubled** debt restructuring does not apply to modifications of a debt obligation that reflect general economic conditions that dictate a reduction in interest rates. Nor does it apply to the refunding of an old debt with new debt having an effective interest rate approximately equal to that of similar debt issued by nontroubled debtors.

A troubled debt restructuring involves one of two basic types of transactions:

❶ Settlement of debt at less than its carrying amount.
❷ Continuation of debt with a modification of terms.

Settlement of Debt

A transfer of noncash assets (real estate, receivables, or other assets) or the issuance of the debtor's stock can be used to settle a debt obligation in a troubled debt restructuring. In these situations, **the noncash assets or equity interest given should be accounted for at their fair market value.** The debtor is required to determine the excess of the carrying amount of the payable over the fair value of the assets or equity transferred (gain). Likewise, the creditor is required to determine the excess of the receivable over the fair value of those same assets or equity interests transferred (loss). The debtor recognizes an extraordinary gain equal to the amount of the excess, and the creditor normally would charge the excess (loss) against Allowance for Doubtful Accounts. In addition, the debtor recognizes a gain or loss on disposition of assets to the extent that the fair value of those assets differs from their carrying amount (book value).

To illustrate a transfer of assets, assume that American City Bank has loaned $20,000,000 to Union Mortgage Company. Union Mortgage in turn has invested these monies in residential apartment buildings, but because of low occupancy rates it cannot meet its loan obligations. American City Bank agrees to accept from Union Mortgage real estate with a fair market value of $16,000,000 in full settlement of the $20,000,000 loan obligation. The real estate has a recorded value of $21,000,000 on the books of Union Mortgage Company. The entry to record this transaction on the books of American City Bank (creditor) is as follows:

Real Estate	16,000,000	
Allowance for Doubtful Accounts	4,000,000	
Note Receivable from Union Mortgage Company		20,000,000

The real estate is recorded at fair market value, and a charge is made to the Allowance for Doubtful Accounts to reflect the bad debt writeoff. If no allowance were available to absorb the charge of $4,000,000, the debit would be to a loss (ordinary) account.

The entry to record this transaction on the books of Union Mortgage Company (debtor) is as follows:

---

[7]In the event that the loan is written off, the loss is charged against the allowance. In subsequent periods, if the estimated expected cash flows are revised based on new information, the allowance account and loss account would be adjusted (either increased or decreased depending whether conditions improved or worsened) in the same fashion as the original impairment.

[8]Many alternatives are permitted to recognize income in subsequent periods. See *FASB Statement No. 118*, "Accounting by Creditors for Impairment of a Loan—Income Recognition and Disclosures," (Norwalk, Conn.: FASB, October 1994) for appropriate methods.

[9]"Accounting by Debtors and Creditors for Troubled Debt Restructurings," *FASB Statement No. 15* (Norwalk, Conn.: FASB, June, 1977), par. 1.

Note Payable to American City Bank	20,000,000	
Loss on Disposition of Real Estate	5,000,000	
Real Estate		21,000,000
Gain on Restructuring of Debt (Extraordinary)		4,000,000

Union Mortgage Company has a loss on the disposition of real estate in the amount of $5,000,000 (the difference between the $21,000,000 book value and the $16,000,000 fair market value), which should be shown as an ordinary loss on the income statement. In addition, it has a gain on restructuring of debt of $4,000,000 (the difference between the $20,000,000 carrying amount of the note payable and the $16,000,000 fair market value of the real estate). **The gain on restructuring should be shown as an extraordinary item**.

To illustrate the granting of an equity interest, assume that American City Bank had agreed to accept from Union Mortgage Company 320,000 shares of Union's common stock ($10 par) that has a fair market value of $16,000,000 in full settlement of the $20,000,000 loan obligation. The entry to record this transaction on the books of American City Bank (creditor) is as follows:

Investment	16,000,000	
Allowance for Doubtful Accounts	4,000,000	
Note Receivable from Union Mortgage Company		20,000,000

The stock received by American City Bank is recorded as an investment at the fair market value at the date of restructure.

The entry to record this transaction on the books of Union Mortgage Company (debtor) is as follows:

Note Payable to American City Bank	20,000,000	
Common Stock		3,200,000
Additional Paid-in Capital		12,800,000
Gain on Restructuring of Debt (Extraordinary)		4,000,000

The stock issued by Union Mortgage Company is recorded in the normal manner with the difference between the par value and the fair value of the stock recorded as additional paid-in capital.

Modification of Terms

In some cases, a debtor will have serious short-run cash flow problems that lead it to request one or a combination of the following modifications:

❶ Reduction of the stated interest rate.
❷ Extension of the maturity date of the face amount of the debt.
❸ Reduction of the face amount of the debt.
❹ Reduction or deferral of any accrued interest.

Prior to *FASB Statement No. 114*, debtors and creditors computed the gain or loss on restructuring based upon the undiscounted restructured cash flows. Under *FASB Statement No. 114*, the creditor's loss is based upon cash flows discounted at the historical effective rate of the loan. The FASB concluded that, "because loans are recorded originally at discounted amounts, the ongoing assessment for impairment should be made in a similar manner."[10] The debtor's gain will continue to be calculated based upon **undiscounted amounts**, as described in *FASB Statement No. 15*. As a consequence, **the gain recorded by the debtor will not equal the loss recorded by the creditor under many circumstances**.[11]

Two illustrations demonstrate the accounting for a troubled debt restructuring by debtors and creditors:

---

[10]*FASB Statement No. 114*, par. 42.

[11]In response to concerns expressed about this nonsymmetric treatment, the FASB stated that *Statement No. 114* does not address debtor accounting because the FASB was concerned that expansion of the scope of the statement would delay its issuance.

❶ The debtor does not record a gain.
❷ The debtor does record a gain.

In both instances the creditor has a loss.

Illustration 1—No Gain for Debtor

This illustration demonstrates a restructuring in which no gain is recorded by the debtor.[12] On December 31, 1998, Morgan National Bank enters into a debt restructuring agreement with Resorts Development Company, which is experiencing financial difficulties. The bank restructures a $10,500,000 loan receivable issued at par (interest paid to date) by:

❶ Reducing the principal obligation from $10,500,000 to $9,000,000,
❷ Extending the maturity date from December 31, 1998, to December 31, 2002, and
❸ Reducing the interest rate from 12% to 8%.

Debtor Calculations. The total future cash flow after restructuring of $11,880,000 ($9,000,000 of principal plus $2,880,000 of interest payments[13]) exceeds the total pre-restructuring carrying amount of the debt of $10,500,000. Consequently, **no gain is recorded and no adjustment is made by the debtor** to the carrying amount of the payable. As a result, no entry is made by Resorts Development Co. (debtor) at the date of restructuring.

A new effective interest rate must be computed by the debtor in order to record interest expense in future periods. The new effective interest rate equates the present value of the future cash flows specified by the new terms with the pre-restructuring carrying amount of the debt. In this case, the new rate is computed by relating the pre-restructure carrying amount ($10,500,000) to the total future cash flow ($11,880,000). The rate necessary to discount the total future cash flow ($11,880,000) to a present value equal to the remaining balance ($10,500,000) is 3.46613%.[14]

On the basis of the effective rate of 3.46613%, the schedule shown in Illustration 14A-7 is prepared:

	Resorts Development Co. (Debtor)			
Date	Interest Paid (8%)	Interest Expense (3.46613%)	Reduction of Carrying Amount	Carrying Amount of Note
12/31/98				$10,500,000
12/31/99	$ 720,000[a]	$ 363,944[b]	$ 356,056[c]	10,143,944
12/31/00	720,000	351,602	368,398	9,775,546
12/31/01	720,000	338,833	381,167	9,394,379
12/31/02	720,000	325,621	394,379	9,000,000
	$2,880,000	$1,380,000	$1,500,000	

[a]$720,000 = $9,000,000 × .08
[b]$363,944 = $10,500,000 × 3.46613%
[c]$356,056 = $720,000 − $363,944

ILLUSTRATION 14A-7
Schedule Showing Reduction of Carrying Amount of Note

---

[12]Note that the examples given for restructuring assume no previous entries were made by the creditor for impairment. In actuality it is likely that, in accordance with *Statement No. 114*, the creditor would have already made an entry when the loan initially became impaired, and restructuring would simply require an adjustment of the initial estimated loss by the creditor. Recall, however, that the debtor makes no entry upon impairment.

[13]Total interest payments are: $9,000,000 × .08 × 4 years = $2,880,000.

[14]An accurate interest rate i can be found by using the formulas given at the tops of Tables 6-2 and 6-4 to set up the following equation:

$$\$10,500,000 = \underbrace{\frac{1}{(1 + i)^4} \times \$9,000,000}_{\text{(from Table 6-2)}} + \underbrace{\frac{1 - \frac{1}{(1 + i)^4}}{i} \times \$720,000}_{\text{(from Table 6-4)}}$$

Solving algebraically for i, we find that i = 3.46613%.
In practice a computer program is frequently used to find the implicit interest rate.

Thus, on December 31, 1999 (date of first interest payment after restructure), the debtor makes the following entry:

December 31, 1999

Notes Payable	356,056	
Interest Expense	363,944	
Cash		720,000

A similar entry (except for different amounts for debits to Notes Payable and Interest Expense) is made each year until maturity. At maturity, the following entry is made:

December 31, 2002

Notes Payable	9,000,000	
Cash		9,000,000

Creditor Calculations. Morgan National Bank (creditor) is required to calculate its loss based upon the expected future cash flows discounted at the historical effective rate of the loan. This loss is calculated as follows:

ILLUSTRATION 14A-8
Computation of Loss to
Creditor on Restructuring

Pre-restructure carrying amount		$10,500,000
Present value of restructured cash flows:		
Present value of $9,000,000 due in 4 years at 12%, interest payable annually (Table 6-2); $FV(PVF_{4,12\%})$; ($9,000,000 × .63552).	$5,719,680	
Present value of $720,000 interest payable annually for 4 years at 12% (Table 6-4); $R(PVF\text{-}OA_{4,12\%})$; ($720,000 × 3.03735).	2,186,892	
Present value of restructured cash flows		7,906,572
Loss on restructuring		$ 2,593,428

As a result, Morgan National Bank records a bad debt expense account as follows (assuming no allowance balance has been established from recognition of an improvement):

Bad Debt Expense	2,593,428	
Allowance for Doubtful Accounts		2,593,428

In subsequent periods, interest revenue is reported based on the historical effective rate. Illustration 14A-9 provides the following interest and amotization information:

ILLUSTRATION 14A-9
Schedule of Interest and
Amortization after Debt
Restructuring

Morgan National Bank (Creditor)				
Date	Interest Received (8%)	Interest Revenue (12%)	Increase in Carrying Amount	Carrying Amount of Note
12/31/98				$7,906,572
12/31/99	$ 720,000[a]	$ 948,789[b]	$ 228,789[c]	8,135,361
12/31/00	720,000	976,243	256,243	8,391,604
12/31/01	720,000	1,006,992	286,992	8,678,596
12/31/02	720,000	1,041,404[d]	321,404[d]	9,000,000
Total	$2,880,000	$3,973,428	$1,093,428	

[a]$720,000 = $9,000,000 × .08
[b]$948,789 = $7,906,572 × .12
[c]$228,789 = $948,789 − $720,000
[d]$28 adjustment to compensate for rounding.

On December 31, 1999, Morgan National Bank would make the following entry:

December 31, 1999

Cash	720,000	
Allowance for Doubtful Accounts	228,789	
Interest Revenue		948,789

A similar entry (except for different amounts debited to Allowance for Doubtful Accounts and credited to Interest Revenue) is made each year until maturity. At maturity, the following entry is made:

December 31, 2002

Cash	9,000,000	
Notes Receivable		9,000,000

Illustration 2—Gain for Debtor

If the pre-restructure carrying amount exceeds the total future cash flows as a result of a modification of the terms, the debtor records a gain. To illustrate, assume the facts in the previous example except that Morgan National Bank reduced the principal to $7,000,000 (and extended the maturity date to December 31, 2002, and reduced the interest from 12% to 8%). The total future cash flow is now $9,240,000 ($7,000,000 of principal plus $2,240,000 of interest[15]), which is $1,260,000 less than the pre-restructure carrying amount of $10,500,000. Under these circumstances, Resorts Development Company (debtor) would reduce the carrying amount of its payable $1,260,000 and record an extraordinary gain of $1,260,000. On the other hand, Morgan National Bank (creditor) would debit its Bad Debt Expense for $4,350,444. This computation is shown in Illustration 14A-10.

Pre-restructure carrying amount		$10,500,000
Present value of restructured cash flows:		
Present value of $7,000,000 due in 4 years at 12%, interest payable annually (Table 6-2); $FV(PVF_{4,12\%})$; ($7,000,000 × .63552).	$4,448,640	
Present value of $560,000 interest payable annually for 4 years at 12% (Table 6-4); $R(PVF\text{-}OA_{4,12\%})$; ($560,000 × 3.03735).	1,700,916	6,149,556
Creditor's loss on restructuring		$ 4,350,444

ILLUSTRATION 14A-10
Computation of Loss to Creditor on Restructuring

Entries to record the gain and loss on the debtor's and creditor's books at the date of restructure, December 31, 1998, are as follows:

ILLUSTRATION 14A-11
Debtor and Creditor Entries to Record Gain and Loss on Note

December 31, 1998 (date of restructure)

Resorts Development Co. (Debtor)			Morgan National Bank (Creditor)		
Notes Payable	1,260,000		Bad Debt Expense	4,350,444	
Gain on Restructuring of Debt (Extraordinary)		1,260,000	Allowance for Doubtful Accounts		4,350,444

For Resorts Development (debtor), because the new carrying value of the note ($10,500,000 − $1,260,000 = $9,240,000) equals the sum of the undiscounted cash flows ($9,240,000), the imputed interest rate is 0%. Consequently, all of the future cash flows reduce the principal balance, and no interest expense is recognized. For Morgan National the interest revenue would be reported in the same fashion as the previous example, that is, using the historical effective interest rate applied toward the newly discounted value of the note. Interest computations are shown in Illustration 14A-12.

---

[15]Total interest payments are: $7,000,000 × .08 × 4 years = $2,240,000.

ILLUSTRATION 14A-12
Schedule of Interest and
Amortization after Debt
Restructuring

	Morgan National Bank (Creditor)			
Date	Cash Received 8%	Interest Revenue 12%	Increase in Carrying Amount	Carrying Amount of Note
12/31/98				$6,149,556
12/31/99	$ 560,000ᵃ	$ 737,947ᵇ	$177,947ᶜ	6,327,503
12/31/00	560,000	759,300	199,300	6,526,803
12/31/01	560,000	783,216	223,216	6,750,019
12/31/02	560,000	809,981ᵈ	249,981ᵈ	7,000,000
Total	$2,240,000	$3,090,444	$850,444	

ᵃ$560,000 = $7,000,000 × .08
ᵇ$737,947 = $6,149,556 × .12
ᶜ$177,947 = $737,947 − $560,000
ᵈ$21 adjustment to compensate for rounding

ILLUSTRATION 14A-13
Debtor and Creditor
Entries to Record
Periodic Interest and
Final Principal Payments

The following journal entries illustrate the accounting by debtor and creditor for periodic interest payments and final principal payment:

Resorts Development Co. (Debtor)			Morgan National Bank (Creditor)		
December 31, 1999 (date of first interest payment following restructure):					
Notes Payable	560,000		Cash	560,000	
Cash		560,000	Allowance for Doubtful Accounts	177,947	
			Interest Revenue		737,947
December 31, 2000, 2001, and 2002 (dates of 2nd, 3rd, and last interest payments.)					
	(Debit and credit same accounts as 12/31/99 using applicable amounts from appropriate amortization schedules.)				
December 31, 2002 (date of principal payment):					
Notes Payable	7,000,000		Cash	7,000,000	
Cash		7,000,000	Notes Receivable		7,000,000

Evaluation

Under *Statement No. 15,* the FASB justified accounting for troubled debt restructurings at undiscounted values by saying that a restructuring involving a modification of terms is a continuation of an existing debt and is not a business transaction involving transfers of resources and obligations. Many challenged this approach. If a company has a $1,000,000 loan receivable earning interest at 10% and the interest rate is lowered to 5% because the debtor has financial problems, they believed that a loss should be recognized immediately to reflect the change in the economic relationship between the debtor and the creditor. The FASB contended that the creditor's primary objective is to recover its investment—as long as this is accomplished a loss should not be recognized.

The position taken by the FASB under *Statement No. 15* was the position lobbied for by financial institutions. They argued that the economic consequences of loss recognition would be devastating to their industry. During the troubled economic times of the early and mid-1970s and the late 1980s, many financial institutions would have had to take substantial losses if the usual present value techniques had been employed. They argued that the recognition of these losses might cause individuals to lose confidence in the financial system, which would make it more difficult for financial institutions to raise capital and to grant credit to marginal or small borrowers. They argued that some bankruptcies, perhaps even a recession, would result.

With the gift of hindsight, in light of the savings-and-loan crisis, it appears that the nonrecognition of losses under *Statement No. 15* hid the extent to which financial institutions had many bad loans on their books. In the aftermath of the savings-and-loan clean-up, bank regulators and accounting regulators have taken considerable steps toward improving the accounting and disclosure for loans.

❖ SUMMARY OF ACCOUNTING FOR IMPAIRMENT AND TROUBLED DEBT RESTRUCTURINGS

Event	Accounting Procedure
1. Impairment	**Creditor:** Loss based upon difference between present value of future cash flows discounted at historical effective interest rate and carrying amount of note. Recognize interest revenue based upon new carrying amount and original effective rate. **Debtor:** No recognition.
2. Restructurings—Settlement of Debt a. Transfer of noncash assets.	**Creditor:** Recognize loss on restructure. **Debtor:** Recognize gain on restructure and recognize gain or loss on asset transfer.
b. Granting of equity interest.	**Creditor:** Recognize loss on restructure. **Debtor:** Recognize gain on restructure.
3. Restructurings—Continuation of Debt with Modified Terms a. Carrying amount of debt is less than future cash flows (no gain for debtor).	**Creditor:** Recognize loss based upon present value of restructured cash flows. Recognize interest revenue based upon new recorded value and original effective rate. **Debtor:** Recognize no gain on restructure. Determine new effective interest rate to be used in recording interest expense.
b. Carrying amount of debt is greater than total future cash flows (gain for debtor).	**Creditor:** Recognize loss based upon present value of restructured cash flows. Recognize interest revenue based upon new recorded value and original effective rate. **Debtor:** Recognize gain on restructure and reduce carrying amount to the sum of the undiscounted cash flows. Recognize no interest expense over the remaining life of the debt.

ILLUSTRATION 14A-14
Procedures for Impairments and Troubled Debt Restructurings

The following disclosures for loan impairment and restructurings are required of creditors:[16]

DISCLOSURES OF CREDITORS

1. As of the date of each balance sheet presented, the total recorded investment in the impaired loans at the end of each period and (1) the amount of that recorded investment for which there is a related allowance for doubtful accounts determined in accordance with this Statement and the amount of that allowance and (2) the amount of that recorded investment for which there is no related allowance for doubtful accounts determined in accordance with this Statement

2. The creditor's policy for recognizing interest revenue on impaired loans, including how cash receipts are recorded

3. For each period for which results of operations are presented, the average recorded investment in the impaired loans during each period, the related amount of interest revenue recognized during the time within that period that the loans were impaired, and, unless not practicable, the amount of interest revenue recognized using a cash-basis method of accounting during the time within that period that the loans were impaired.

4. Activity in allowance for doubtful accounts, including beginning and ending balances.

ILLUSTRATION 14A-15
Disclosures of Creditors for Loan Impairment and Restructurings

---

[16]*FASB Statement No. 118*, par. 6.i.

The following disclosures for troubled debt restructures as of the date of each balance sheet presented are required of debtors:

ILLUSTRATION 14A-16
Disclosures of Debtors for Restructurings

DISCLOSURES OF DEBTORS
1. A description of the changes in terms or major features of settlement.
2. The aggregate gain on restructuring and the related tax effect.
3. The per-share amount of the aggregate gain on restructuring.
4. The aggregate gain or loss on transfers of assets.
5. Information on any contingent payments.

SUMMARY OF LEARNING OBJECTIVE FOR APPENDIX 14A

❾ Distinguish between and account for (1) a loss on loan impairment, (2) a troubled debt restructuring that results in the settlement of a debt, and (3) a troubled debt restructuring that results in a continuation of debt with modification of terms. An impairment loan loss is based on the difference between the present value of the future cash flows and the carrying amount of the note. There are two types of settlement of debt restructurings: (1) transfer of noncash assets and (2) granting of equity interest. For accounting purposes there are also two types of restructurings with continuation of debt with modified terms: (1) the carrying amount of debt is less than the future cash flows, and (2) the carrying amount of debt is greater than the total future cash flows.

KEY TERMS

impairments, 727
troubled debt
   restructuring, 729

Note: All **asterisked** Questions, Brief Exercises, Exercises, Problems, and Conceptual Cases relate to material contained in the appendix to each chapter.

❖ QUESTIONS ❖

❶ (a) From what sources might a corporation obtain funds through long-term debt? (b) What is a bond indenture? What does it contain? (c) What is a mortgage?

❷ Differentiate between term bonds, mortgage bonds, collateral trust bonds, debenture bonds, income bonds, callable bonds, registered bonds, bearer or coupon bonds, convertible bonds, commodity-backed bonds, and deep discount bonds.

❸ (a) What is the typical denomination of corporate bonds? (b) How often is bond interest typically payable?

❹ Distinguish between the following interest rates for bonds payable:
(a) yield rate   (d) market rate
(b) nominal rate   (e) effective rate
(c) stated rate

❺ Distinguish between the following values relative to bonds payable:
(a) maturity value   (c) market value
(b) face value   (d) par value

❻ Under what conditions of bond issuance does a discount on bonds payable arise? Under what conditions of bond issuance does a premium on bonds payable arise?

❼ How should unamortized discount on bonds payable be reported on the financial statements? Unamortized premium on bonds payable?

❽ What are the two methods of amortizing discount and premium on bonds payable? Explain each.

❾ Stone Temple Company sells its bonds at a premium and applies the effective interest method in amortizing the premium. Will the annual interest expense increase or decrease over the life of the bonds? Explain.

❿ How should the costs of issuing bonds be accounted for and classified in the financial statements?

⓫ Where should treasury bonds be shown on the balance sheet? Should treasury bonds be carried at par or at reacquisition cost?

⓬ What is the "call" feature of a bond issue? How does the call feature affect the amortization of bond premium or discount?

⓭ Why would a company wish to reduce its bond indebtedness before its bonds reach maturity? Indicate how this can be done and the correct accounting treatment for such a transaction.

14 How are gains and losses from extinguishment of debt classified in the income statement? What disclosures are required of such transactions by *FASB Statement No. 4*?

15 What must the accountant do to record properly a transaction involving the issuance of a noninterest-bearing long-term note in exchange for property?

16 How is the present value of a noninterest-bearing note computed?

17 When is the stated interest rate of a debt instrument presumed to be fair?

18 What types of payables are exempted from the provisions of *APB Opinion No. 21*?

19 What are the considerations in imputing an appropriate interest rate?

20 Differentiate between a fixed-rate mortgage and a variable-rate mortgage.

21 According to *FASB Statement No. 47*, "Disclosure of Long-Term Obligations," what disclosures are required relative to long-term debt and sinking fund requirements?

22 What are project financing arrangements?

23 What are take-or-pay contracts and through-put contracts?

24 What conditions must be met in order for a contractual obligation to be disclosed as an unconditional purchase obligation?

25 What disclosures are required relative to unconditional purchase obligations that have been recognized as balance sheet liabilities?

26 What disclosures are required relative to unconditional purchase obligations that have been disclosed only in the notes to the financial statements?

*27 What are three measurement bases that might be used to value troubled debt? What are the advantages of each method?

*28 What are the general rules for measuring and recognizing gain or loss by both the debtor and the creditor in an impairment?

*29 What are the general rules for measuring gain or loss by both creditor and debtor in a troubled debt restructuring involving a settlement?

*30 (a) In a troubled debt situation, why might the creditor grant concessions to the debtor?

(b) What type of concessions might a creditor grant the debtor in a troubled debt situation?

(c) What is meant by "impairment" of a loan? Under what circumstances should a creditor or debtor recognize an impaired loan?

*31 What are the general rules for measuring and recognizing gain or loss by both the debtor and the creditor in a troubled debt restructuring involving a modification of terms?

*32 What is meant by "accounting symmetry" between the entries recorded by the debtor and creditor in a troubled debt restructuring involving a modification of terms? In what ways is the accounting for troubled debt restructurings and impairments non-symmetrical?

*33 Under what circumstances would a transaction be recorded as a troubled debt restructuring by only one of the two parties to the transaction?

*34 DC Bank agrees to restructure Talk Company's troubled debt situation by reducing the interest rate from 14% to 8% and extending the maturity date of the debt 5 additional years. Explain how Talk Company should account for this modification of terms in the restructuring of its debt to DC Bank.

*35 What is the major difference between *FASB Statement No. 114* and *No. 15* when debtors and creditors want to compute the gain or loss on debt restructuring?

*36 Assume that on January 1, 1997, the First Bank of Blackhawk enters into a debt restructuring agreement with Arista Sports Co., which is experiencing financial difficulties. The bank agrees to reduce both the principal obligation and interest rate. In this situation, what are the general rules for both debtor and creditor to measure and recognize gain or loss resulting from the debt restructuring?

*37 Assume that Toni Braxton Company has recently fallen into financial difficulties. By reviewing all available evidence on December 31, 1997, one creditor of Toni Braxton, the National American Bank, determined that Toni Braxton would pay back only 65% of the principal at maturity. As a result, the bank decided that the loan was impaired. If the loss is estimated to be $225,000, what entries should both Toni Braxton and National American Bank make to record this loss?

❖ BRIEF EXERCISES ❖

BE14-1 Ghostbusters Corporation issues $300,000 of 9% bonds, due in 10 years, with interest payable semiannually. At the time of issue, the market rate for such bonds is 10%. Compute the issue price of the bonds.

BE14-2 The Goofy Company issued $200,000 of 10% bonds on January 1, 1999. The bonds are due January 1, 2004, with interest payable each July 1 and January 1. The bonds are issued at face value. Prepare Goofy's journal entries for (a) the January issuance, (b) the July 1 interest payment, and (c) the December 31 adjusting entry.

BE14-3 Assume the bonds in BE14-2 were issued at 98. Prepare the journal entries for (a) January 1, (b) July 1, and (c) December 31. Assume The Goofy Company records straight-line amortization annually on December 31.

BE14-4 Assume the bonds in BE14-2 were issued at 103. Prepare the journal entries for (a) January 1, (b) July 1, and (c) December 31. Assume The Goofy Company records straight-line amortization annually on December 31.

BE14-5 Toy Story Corporation issued $500,000 of 12% bonds on May 1, 1999. The bonds were dated January 1, 1999, and mature January 1, 2004, with interest payable July 1 and January 1. The bonds were issued at face value plus accrued interest. Prepare Toy Story's journal entries for (a) the May 1 issuance, (b) the July 1 interest payment, and (c) the December 31 adjusting entry.

BE14-6 On January 1, 1999, Qix Corporation issued $400,000 of 7% bonds, due in 10 years. The bonds were issued for $372,816, and pay interest each July 1 and January 1. Qix uses the effective interest method. Prepare the company's journal entries for (a) the January 1 issuance, (b) the July 1 interest payment, and (c) the December 31 adjusting entry. Assume an effective interest rate of 8%.

BE14-7 Assume the bonds in BE14-6 were issued for $429,757 and the effective interest rate is 6%. Prepare the company's journal entries for (a) the January 1 issuance, (b) the July 1 interest payment, and (c) the December 31 adjusting entry.

BE14-8 Izzy Corporation issued $400,000 of 7% bonds on November 1, 1999, for $429,757. The bonds were dated November 1, 1999, and mature in 10 years, with interest payable each May 1 and November 1. Izzy uses the effective interest method with an effective rate of 6%. Prepare Izzy's December 31, 1999, adjusting entry.

BE14-9 At December 31, 1999, Treasure Land Corporation has the following account balances:

Bonds payable, due January 1, 2007	$2,000,000
Discount on bonds payable	98,000
Bond interest payable	80,000

Show how the above accounts should be presented on the December 31, 1999, balance sheet, including the proper classifications.

BE14-10 James Bond 007 Corporation issued 10-year bonds on January 1, 1999. Costs associated with the bond issuance were $180,000. Bond uses the straight-line method to amortize bond issue costs. Prepare the December 31, 1999, entry to record 1999 bond issue cost amortization.

BE14-11 On January 1, 1999, Uncharted Waters Corporation retired $600,000 of bonds at 99. At the time of retirement, the unamortized premium was $15,000 and unamortized bond issue costs were $5,250. Prepare the corporation's journal entry to record the reacquisition of the bonds.

BE14-12 Jennifer Capriati, Inc. issued a $100,000, 4-year, 11% note at face value to Forest Hills Bank on January 1, 1999, and received $100,000 cash. The note requires annual interest payments each December 31. Prepare Capriati's journal entries to record (a) the issuance of the note and (b) the December 31 interest payment.

BE14-13 Joe Montana Corporation issued a 4-year, $50,000, zero-interest-bearing note to John Madden Company on January 1, 1999, and received cash of $31,776. The implicit interest rate is 12%. Prepare Montana's journal entries for (a) the January 1 issuance and (b) the December 31 recognition of interest.

BE14-14 Larry Byrd Corporation issued a 4-year, $50,000, 5% note to Magic Johnson Company on January 1, 1999, and received a computer that normally sells for $39,369. The note requires annual interest payments each December 31. The market rate of interest for a note of similar risk is 12%. Prepare Larry Byrd's journal entries for (a) the January 1 issuance and (b) the December 31 interest.

BE14-15 King Corporation issued a 4-year, $50,000, zero-interest-bearing note to Salmon Company on January 1, 1999, and received cash of $50,000. In addition, King agreed to sell merchandise to Salmon at an amount less than regular selling price over the 4-year period. The market rate of interest for similar notes is 12%. Prepare King Corporation's January 1 journal entry.

❖ EXERCISES ❖

E14-1 (Classification of Liabilities) Presented below are various account balances of K.D. Lang Inc.:

1. Unamortized premium on bonds payable, of which $3,000 will be amortized during the next year.
2. Bank loans payable of a winery, due March 10, 2002. (The product requires aging for 5 years before sale.)
3. Serial bonds payable, $1,000,000, of which $200,000 are due each July 31.
4. Dividends payable in shares of stock on January 20, 2000.
5. Amounts withheld from employees' wages for income taxes.
6. Notes payable due January 15, 2001.
7. Credit balances in customers' accounts arising from returns and allowances after collection in full of account.
8. Bonds payable of $2,000,000 maturing June 30, 2000.
9. Overdraft of $1,000 in a bank account. (No other balances are carried at this bank.)
10. Deposits made by customers who have ordered goods.

Instructions

Indicate whether each of the items above should be classified on December 31, 1999, as a current liability, a long-term liability, or under some other classification. Consider each one independently from all others; that is, do not assume that all of them relate to one particular business. If the classification of some of the items is doubtful, explain why in each case.

E14-2 (Classification) The following items are found in the financial statements:

(a) Discount on bonds payable
(b) Interest expense (credit balance)
(c) Unamortized bond issue costs
(d) Gain on repurchase of debt
(e) Mortgage payable (payable in equal amounts over next 3 years)
(f) Debenture bonds payable (maturing in 5 years)
(g) Notes payable (due in 4 years)
(h) Premium on bonds payable
(i) Treasury bonds
(j) Income bonds payable (due in 3 years)

Instructions

Indicate how each of these items should be classified in the financial statements.

E14-3 (Entries for Bond Transactions) Presented below are two independent situations:

1. On January 1, 1998, Paul Simon Company issued $200,000, of 9%, 10-year bonds at par. Interest is payable quarterly on April 1, July 1, October 1, and January 1.
2. On June 1, 1998, Graceland Company issued $100,000 of 12%, 10-year bonds dated January 1 at par plus accrued interest. Interest is payable semiannually on July 1 and January 1.

Instructions

For each of these two independent situations, present journal entries to record:

(a) The issuance of the bonds.
(b) The payment of interest on July 1.
(c) The accrual of interest on December 31.

E14-4 (Entries for Bond Transactions) Celine Dion Company issued $600,000 of 10%, 20-year bonds on January 1, 1999, at 102. Interest is payable semiannually on July 1 and January 1. Dion Company uses the straight-line method of amortization for bond premium or discount.

Instructions

(a) Prepare the journal entries to record
   1. The issuance of the bonds.
   2. The payment of interest and the related amortization on July 1, 1999.
   3. The accrual of interest and the related amortization on December 31, 1999.
(b) If the effective interest method of amortization was used, what would be the (1) interest expense recorded on July 1, 1999; (2) premium or discount amortization for the 6-month period July 1 to December 31, 1999. Assume an effective yield of 9.75%.

E14-5 (Determine Proper Amounts in Account Balances) Presented below are three independent situations:

(a) CeCe Winans Corporation incurred the following cost in connection with the issuance of bonds: (1) printing and engraving costs, $12,000; (2) legal fees, $49,000, and (3) commissions paid to underwriter, $60,000. What amount should be reported as Unamortized Bond Issue Costs and where should this amount be reported on the balance sheet?

(b) George Gershwin Co. sold $2,000,000 of 10%, 10-year bonds at 104 on January 1, 1998. The bonds were dated January 1, 1998, and pay interest on July 1 and January 1. If Gershwin uses the straight-line method to amortize bond premium or discount, determine the amount of interest expense to be reported on July 1, 1998, and December 31, 1998.

(c) Ron Kenoly Inc. issued $600,000 of 9%, 10-year bonds on June 30, 1998, for $562,500. This price provided a yield of 10% on the bonds. Interest is payable semiannually on December 31 and June 30. If Kenoly uses the effective interest method, determine the amount of interest expense to record if financial statements are issued on October 31, 1998.

E14-6 (Entries and Questions for Bond Transactions) On June 30, 1999, Mischa Auer Company issued $4,000,000 face value of 13%, 20-year bonds at $4,300,920, a yield of 12%. Auer uses the effective interest method to amortize bond premium or discount. The bonds pay semiannual interest on June 30 and December 31.

Instructions

(a) Prepare the journal entries to record the following transactions.
1. The issuance of the bonds on June 30, 1999.
2. The payment of interest and the amortization of the premium on December 31, 1999.
3. The payment of interest and the amortization of the premium on June 30, 2000.
4. The payment of interest and the amortization of the premium on December 31, 2000.

(b) Show the proper balance sheet presentation for the liability for bonds payable on the December 31, 2000, balance sheet.

(c) Provide the answers to the following questions.
1. What amount of interest expense is reported for 2000?
2. Will the bond interest expense reported in 2000 be the same as, greater than, or less than the amount that would be reported if the straight-line method of amortization were used?
3. Determine the total cost of borrowing over the life of the bond.
4. Will the total bond interest expense for the life of the bond be greater than, the same as, or less than the total interest expense if the straight-line method of amortization were used?

E14-7 (Entries for Bond Transactions) On January 1, 1998, Aumont Company sold 12% bonds having a maturity value of $500,000 for $537,907.37, which provides the bondholders with a 10% yield. The bonds are dated January 1, 1998, and mature January 1, 2003, with interest payable December 31 of each year. Aumont Company allocates interest and unamortized discount or premium on the effective interest basis.

Instructions

(a) Prepare the journal entry at the date of the bond issuance.
(b) Prepare a schedule of interest expense and bond amortization for 1998–2000.
(c) Prepare the journal entry to record the interest payment and the amortization for 1998.
(d) Prepare the journal entry to record the interest payment and the amortization for 2000.

E14-8 (Information Related to Various Bond Issues) Karen Austin Inc. has issued three types of debt on January 1, 1998, the start of the company's fiscal year.

1. $10 million, 10-year, 15% unsecured bonds, interest payable quarterly. Bonds were priced to yield 12%.
2. $25 million par of 10-year zero-coupon bonds at a price to yield 12% per year.
3. $20 million, 10-year, 10% mortgage bonds, interest payable annually to yield 12%.

Instructions

Prepare a schedule that identifies the following items for each bond: (1) maturity value, (2) number of interest periods over life of bond, (3) stated rate per each interest period, (4) effective interest rate per each interest period, (5) payment amount per period, and (6) present value of bonds at date of issue.

E14-9 (Entry for Retirement of Bond; Bond Issue Costs) On January 2, 1993, Yoshimitu Banno Corporation issued $1,500,000 of 10% bonds at 97 due December 31, 2002. Legal and other costs of $24,000 were incurred in connection with the issue. Interest on the bonds is payable annually each December 31. The $24,000 issue costs are being deferred and amortized on a straight-line basis over the 10-year term of the bonds. The discount on the bonds is also being amortized on a straight-line basis over the 10 years. (Straight-line is not materially different in effect from the preferable "interest method".)

The bonds are callable at 101 (i.e., at 101% of face amount), and on January 2, 1998, Banno called $900,000 face amount of the bonds and retired them.

Instructions
Ignoring income taxes, compute the amount of loss, if any, to be recognized by Banno as a result of retiring the $900,000 of bonds in 1998 and prepare the journal entry to record the retirement.

(AICPA adapted)

E14-10 (Entries for Retirement and Issuance of Bonds) Larry Hagman, Inc. had outstanding $6,000,000 of 11% bonds (interest payable July 31 and January 31) due in 10 years. On July 1, it issued $9,000,000 of 10%, 15-year bonds (interest payable July 1 and January 1) at 98. A portion of the proceeds was used to call the 11% bonds at 102 on August 1. Unamortized bond discount and issue cost applicable to the 11% bonds were $120,000 and $30,000, respectively.

Instructions
Prepare the journal entries necessary to record issue of the new bonds and the refunding of the bonds.

E14-11 (Entries for Retirement and Issuance of Bonds) On June 30, 1990, Gene Autry Company issued 12% bonds with a par value of $800,000 due in 20 years. They were issued at 98 and were callable at 104 at any date after June 30, 1998. Because of lower interest rates and a significant change in the company's credit rating, it was decided to call the entire issue on June 30, 1999, and to issue new bonds. New 10% bonds were sold in the amount of $1,000,000 at 102; they mature in 20 years. Autry Company uses straight-line amortization. Interest payment dates are December 31 and June 30.

Instructions
(a) Prepare journal entries to record the retirement of the old issue and the sale of the new issue on June 30, 1999.
(b) Prepare the entry required on December 31, 1999, to record the payment of the first 6 months' interest and the amortization of premium on the bonds.

E14-12 (Entries for Retirement and Issuance of Bonds) Linda Day George Company had bonds outstanding with a maturity value of $300,000. On April 30, 1999, when these bonds had an unamortized discount of $10,000, they were called in at 104. To pay for these bonds, George had issued other bonds a month earlier bearing a lower interest rate. The newly issued bonds had a life of 10 years. The new bonds were issued at 103 (face value $300,000). Issue costs related to the new bonds were $3,000.

Instructions
Ignoring interest, compute the gain or loss and record this refunding transaction.

(AICPA adapted)

E14-13 (Entries for Noninterest-Bearing Debt) On January 1, 1999, Ellen Greene Company makes the two following acquisitions:

1. Purchases land having a fair market value of $200,000 by issuing a 5-year noninterest-bearing promissory note in the face amount of $337,012.
2. Purchases equipment by issuing a 6%, 8-year promissory note having a maturity value of $250,000 (interest payable annually).

The Company has to pay 11% interest for funds from its bank.

Instructions
(a) Record the two journal entries that should be recorded by Ellen Greene Company for the two purchases on January 1, 1999.
(b) Record the interest at the end of the first year on both notes using the effective interest method.

E14-14 (Imputation of Interest) Presented below are two independent situations:
(a) On January 1, 1999, Robin Wright Inc. purchased land that had an assessed value of $350,000 at the time of purchase. A $550,000 noninterest-bearing note due January 1, 2002, was given in exchange. There was no established exchange price for the land, nor a ready market value for the note. The interest rate charged on a note of this type is 12%. Determine at what amount the land should be recorded at January 1, 1999, and the interest expense to be reported in 1999 related to this transaction.
(b) On January 1, 1999, Sally Field Furniture Co. borrowed $5,000,000 (face value) from Gary Sinise Co., a major customer, through a noninterest-bearing note due in 4 years. Because the note was noninterest-bearing, Sally Field Furniture agreed to sell furniture to this customer at lower than market price. A 10% rate of interest is normally charged on this type of loan. Prepare the journal entry to record this transaction and determine the amount of interest expense to report for 1999.

E14-15 (Imputation of Interest with Right)   On January 1, 1997, Margaret Avery Co. borrowed and received $400,000 from a major customer evidenced by a noninterest-bearing note due in 3 years. As consideration for the noninterest-bearing feature, Avery agrees to supply the customer's inventory needs for the loan period at lower than the market price. The appropriate rate at which to impute interest is 12%.

Instructions

(a) Prepare the journal entry to record the initial transaction on January 1, 1997. (Round all computations to the nearest dollar.)

(b) Prepare the journal entry to record any adjusting entries needed at December 31, 1997. Assume that the sales of Avery's product to this customer occur evenly over the 3-year period.

E14-16 (Long-Term Debt Disclosure)   At December 31, 1997, Helen Reddy Company has outstanding three long-term debt issues. The first is a $2,000,000 note payable which matures June 30, 2000. The second is a $6,000,000 bond issue which matures September 30, 2001. The third is a $17,500,000 sinking fund debenture with annual sinking fund payments of $3,500,000 in each of the years 1999 through 2003.

Instructions

Prepare the note disclosure required by *FASB Statement No. 47*, "Disclosure of Long-term Obligations," for the long-term debt at December 31, 1997.

E14-17 (Long-Term Debt Disclosure)   To secure a long-term supply, Awashima Company entered into a take-or-pay contract with an aluminum recycling plant on January 1, 1997. Awashima is obligated to purchase 40% of the output of the plant each period while the debt incurred to finance the plant remains outstanding. The annual cost of the aluminum to Awashima will be the sum of 40% of the raw material costs, operating expenses, depreciation, interest on the debt used to finance the plant, and return on the owner's investment. The minimum amount payable to the plant under the contract, whether or not Awashima is able to take delivery, is $7 million annually through December 31, 2016. Awashima's total purchases under the agreement were $8 million in 1997 and $8.5 million in 1998. Funds to construct the plant were borrowed at an effective interest rate of 9%. Awashima's incremental borrowing rate was 10% at January 1, 1997, and is 11% at December 31, 1998. Awashima intends to disclose the contract in the footnotes to its financial statements at December 31, 1998.

Instructions

Assuming that the contract is an "unconditional purchase obligation" as specified by *FASB Statement No. 47*, "Disclosure of Long-term Obligations," prepare the note disclosure required for the contract at December 31, 1998.

*E14-18 (Settlement of Debt)   Larisa Nieland Company owes $200,000 plus $18,000 of accrued interest to First State Bank. The debt is a 10-year, 10% note. During 1998, Larisa Nieland's business deteriorated due to a faltering regional economy. On December 31, 1998, First State Bank agrees to accept an old machine and cancel the entire debt. The machine has a cost of $390,000, accumulated depreciation of $221,000, and a fair market value of $190,000.

Instructions

(a) Prepare journal entries for Larisa Nieland Company and First State Bank to record this debt settlement.

(b) How should Larisa Nieland report the gain or loss on the disposition of machine and on restructuring of debt in its 1998 income statement?

(c) Assume that, instead of transferring the machine, Larisa Nieland decides to grant 15,000 shares of its common stock ($10 par) which has a fair market value of $190,000 in full settlement of the loan obligation. If First State Bank treats Larisa Nieland's stock as a trading investment, prepare the entries to record the transaction for both parties.

*E14-19 (Term Modification without Gain—Debtor's Entries)   On December 31, 1998, the Firstar Bank enters into a debt restructuring agreement with Nicole Bradtke Company, which is now experiencing financial trouble. The bank agrees to restructure a 12%, issued at par, $2,000,000 note receivable by the following modifications:

1. Reducing the principal obligation from $2,000,000 to $1,600,000.
2. Extending the maturity date from December 31, 1998, to December 31, 2001.
3. Reducing the interest rate from 12% to 10%.

Bradtke pays interest at the end of each year. On January 1, 2002, Bradtke Company pays $1,600,000 in cash to Firstar Bank.

Instructions

(a) Based on *FASB Statement No. 114*, will the gain recorded by Bradtke be equal to the loss recorded by Firstar Bank under the debt restructuring?

(b) Can Bradtke Company record a gain under the term modification mentioned above? Explain.

(c) Assuming that the interest rate Bradtke should use to compute interest expense in future periods is 1.4276%, prepare the interest payment schedule of the note for Bradtke Company after the debt restructuring.

(d) Prepare the interest payment entry for Bradtke Company on December 31, 2000.

(e) What entry should Bradtke make on January 1, 2002?

***E14-20 (Term Modification without Gain—Creditor's Entries)** Using the same information as in E14-19 above, answer the following questions related to Firstar Bank (creditor).

Instructions

(a) What interest rate should Firstar Bank use to calculate the loss on the debt restructuring?

(b) Compute the loss that Firstar Bank will suffer from the debt restructuring. Prepare the journal entry to record the loss.

(c) Prepare the interest receipt schedule for Firstar Bank after the debt restructuring.

(d) Prepare the interest receipt entry for Firstar Bank on December 31, 2000.

(e) What entry should Firstar Bank make on January 1, 2002?

***E14-21 (Term Modification with Gain—Debtor's Entries)** Use the same information as in E14-19 above except that Firstar Bank reduced the principal to $1,300,000 rather than $1,600,000. On January 1, 2002, Bradtke pays $1,300,000 in cash to Firstar Bank for the principal.

Instructions

(a) Can Bradtke Company record a gain under this term modification? If yes, compute the gain for Bradtke Company.

(b) Prepare the journal entries to record the gain on Bradtke's books.

(c) What interest rate should Bradtke use to compute its interest expense in future periods? Will your answer be the same as in E14-19 above? Why or why not?

(d) Prepare the interest payment schedule of the note for Bradtke Company after the debt restructuring.

(e) Prepare the interest payment entries for Bradtke Company on December 31 of 1999, 2000, and 2001.

(f) What entry should Bradtke make on January 1, 2002?

***E14-22 (Term Modification with Gain—Creditor's Entries)** Using the same information as in E14-19 and E14-21 above, answer the following questions related to Firstar Bank (creditor).

Instructions

(a) Compute the loss Firstar Bank will suffer under this new term modification. Prepare the journal entry to record the loss on Firstar's books.

(b) Prepare the interest receipt schedule for Firstar Bank after the debt restructuring.

(c) Prepare the interest receipt entry for Firstar Bank on December 31, 1999, 2000, and 2001.

(d) What entry should Firstar Bank make on January 1, 2002?

***E14-23 (Debtor/Creditor Entries for Settlement of Troubled Debt)** Petra Langrova Co. owes $199,800 to Mary Joe Fernandez Inc. The debt is a 10-year, 11% note. Because Petra Langrova Co. is in financial trouble, Mary Joe Fernandez Inc. agrees to accept some property and cancel the entire debt. The property has a book value of $80,000 and a fair market value of $120,000.

Instructions

(a) Prepare the journal entry on Langrova's books for debt restructure.

(b) Prepare the journal entry on Fernandez's books for debt restructure.

***E14-24 (Debtor/Creditor Entries for Modification of Troubled Debt)** Steffi Graf Corp. owes $225,000 to First Trust. The debt is a 10-year, 12% note due December 31, 1998. Because Graf Corp. is in financial trouble, First Trust agrees to extend the maturity date to December 31, 2000, reduce the principal to $200,000, and reduce the interest rate to 5%, payable annually on December 31.

Instructions

(a) Prepare the journal entries on Graf's books on December 31, 1998, 1999, 2000.

(b) Prepare the journal entries on First Trust's books on December 31, 1998, 1999, 2000.

***E14-25 (Impairments)** On December 31, 1997, Iva Majoli Company borrowed $62,092 from Paris Bank, signing a 5-year, $100,000 noninterest bearing note. The note was issued to yield 10% interest. Unfortunately, during 1999, Majoli began to experience financial difficulty. As a result, at December 31, 1999, Paris Bank determined that it was probable that it would receive back only $75,000 at maturity. The market rate of interest on loans of this nature is now 11%.

Instructions

(a) Prepare the entry to record the issuance of the loan by Paris Bank on December 31, 1997.

(b) Prepare the entry (if any) to record the impairment of the loan on December 31, 1999, by Paris Bank.

(c) Prepare the entry (if any) to record the impairment of the loan on December 31, 1999, by Majoli Company.

*E14-26 (Impairments) On December 31, 1996, Conchita Martinez Company signed a $1,000,000 note to Sauk City Bank. The market interest rate at that time was 12%. The stated interest rate on the note was 10%, payable annually. The note matures in 5 years. Unfortunately, because of lower sales, Conchita Martinez's financial situation worsened. On December 31, 1998, Sauk City Bank determined that it was probable that the company would pay back only $600,000 of the principal at maturity. However, it was considered likely that interest would continue to be paid, based on the $1,000,000 loan.

Instructions

(a) Determine the amount of cash Conchita Martinez received from the loan on December 31, 1996.

(b) Prepare a note amortization schedule for Sauk City Bank up to December 31, 1998.

(c) Determine the loss on impairment that Sauk City Bank should recognize on December 31, 1998.

❖ PROBLEMS ❖

P14-1 (Analysis of Amortization Schedule and Interest Entries) The following amortization and interest schedule reflects the issuance of 10-year bonds by Terrel Brandon Corporation on January 1, 1991, and the subsequent interest payments and charges. The company's year-end is December 31, and financial statements are prepared once yearly.

AMORTIZATION SCHEDULE

Year	Cash	Interest	Amount Unamortized	Book Value
1/1/91			$5,651	$ 94,349
1991	$11,000	$11,322	5,329	94,671
1992	11,000	11,361	4,968	95,032
1993	11,000	11,404	4,564	95,436
1994	11,000	11,452	4,112	95,888
1995	11,000	11,507	3,605	96,395
1996	11,000	11,567	3,038	96,962
1997	11,000	11,635	2,403	97,597
1998	11,000	11,712	1,691	98,309
1999	11,000	11,797	894	99,106
2000	11,000	11,894		100,000

Instructions

(a) Indicate whether the bonds were issued at a premium or a discount and how you can determine this fact from the schedule.

(b) Indicate whether the amortization schedule is based on the straight-line method or the effective interest method and how you can determine which method is used.

(c) Determine the stated interest rate and the effective interest rate.

(d) On the basis of the schedule above, prepare the journal entry to record the issuance of the bonds on January 1, 1991.

(e) On the basis of the schedule above, prepare the journal entry or entries to reflect the bond transactions and accruals for 1991. (Interest is paid January 1.)

(f) On the basis of the schedule above, prepare the journal entry or entries to reflect the bond transactions and accruals for 1998. (Prepare reversing entry.)

P14-2 (Amortization Schedules; Straight-line and Effective Interest) Dan Majerle Company sells 10% bonds having a maturity value of $2,000,000 for $1,855,816. The bonds are dated January 1, 1998, and mature January 1, 2003. Interest is payable annually on January 1. (*Hint:* The effective interest rate must be computed.)

Instructions

(a) Set up a schedule of interest expense and discount amortization under the straight-line method.

(b) Set up a schedule of interest expense and discount amortization under the effective interest method.

P14-3 (Entries for Bonds Issued at Discount; Bond Issued at Par with Premium at Maturity Provision)
In 1998, Bobby Phills Co. was considering the issuance of bonds as of January 1, 1999, as follows:

Plan 1:
$2,000,000 par value 11%, first mortgage, 20-year bonds, due Dec. 31, 2018, at 96, with interest payable annually, or

Plan 2:
$2,000,000 par value 11%, first mortgage, 20-year bonds, due Dec. 31, 2018, at 100, with provision for payment of a 4% ($80,000) premium at maturity, interest payable annually.

Costs of issue such as printing and lawyers' fees may be ignored for the purpose of answering this question. Discount and premium are to be allocated to accounting periods on a straight-line basis.

Instructions
Give two separate sets of journal entries with appropriate explanations showing the accounting treatment that the foregoing bond issues would necessitate, respectively:
- **(a)** At time of issue.
- **(b)** Yearly thereafter.
- **(c)** On payment at date of maturity.

P14-4 (Issuance and Retirement of Bonds; Income Statement Presentation) Chris Mills Company issued its 9%, 25-year mortgage bonds in the principal amount of $5,000,000 on January 2, 1984, at a discount of $250,000, which it proceeded to amortize by charges to expense over the life of the issue on a straight-line basis. The indenture securing the issue provided that the bonds could be called for redemption in total but not in part at any time before maturity at 104% of the principal amount, but it did not provide for any sinking fund.

On December 18, 1998, the company issued its 11%, 20-year debenture bonds in the principal amount of $6,000,000 at 102, and the proceeds were used to redeem the 9%, 25-year mortgage bonds on January 2, 1999. The indenture securing the new issue did not provide for any sinking fund or for retirement before maturity.

Instructions
- **(a)** Prepare journal entries to record the issuance of the 11% bonds and the retirement of the 9% bonds.
- **(b)** Indicate the income statement treatment of the gain or loss from retirement and the note disclosure required. Assume 1999 income before extraordinary items of $3,200,000, a weighted number of shares outstanding of 1,500,000, and an income tax rate of 40%.

P14-5 (Comprehensive Bond Problem) In each of the following independent cases the company closes its books on December 31.

1. Danny Ferry Co. sells $250,000 of 10% bonds on March 1, 1998. The bonds pay interest on September 1 and March 1. The due date of the bonds is September 1, 2001. The bonds yield 12%. Give entries through December 31, 1999.
2. Brad Dougherty Co. sells $600,000 of 12% bonds on June 1, 1998. The bonds pay interest on December 1 and June 1. The due date of the bonds is June 1, 2002. The bonds yield 10%. On October 1, 1999, Dougherty buys back $120,000 worth of bonds for $126,000 (includes accrued interest). Give entries through December 1, 2000.

Instructions
(Round to the nearest dollar.)
For the two cases above prepare all of the relevant journal entries from the time of sale until the date indicated. Use the effective interest method for discount and premium amortization (construct amortization tables where applicable). Amortize premium or discount on interest dates and at year-end. (Assume that no reversing entries were made.)

P14-6 (Issuance of Bonds between Interest Dates, Straight-line, Retirement) Presented below are selected transactions on the books of Michael Cage Powerglide Corporation.

May 1, 1998	Bonds payable with a par value of $700,000, which are dated January 1, 1998, are sold at 106 plus accrued interest. They are coupon bonds, bear interest at 12% (payable annually at January 1), and mature January 1, 2008. (Use interest expense account for accrued interest.)
Dec. 31	Adjusting entries are made to record the accrued interest on the bonds, and the amortization of the proper amount of premium. (Use straight-line amortization.)
Jan. 1, 1999	Interest on the bonds is paid.
April 1	Bonds of par value of $420,000 are purchased at 102 plus accrued interest, and retired. (Bond premium is to be amortized only at the end of each year.)

Dec. 31   Adjusting entries are made to record the accrued interest on the bonds, and the proper amount of premium amortized.

Instructions
Prepare journal entries for the transactions above.

P14-7 (Entries for Life Cycle of Bonds) On April 1, 1998, Jerry Fontenot Company sold 12,000 of its 11%, 15-year, $1,000 face value bonds at 97. Interest payment dates are April 1 and October 1, and the company uses the straight-line method of bond discount amortization. On March 1, 1999, Fontenot took advantage of favorable prices of its stock to extinguish 3,000 of the bonds by issuing 100,000 shares of its $10 par value common stock. At this time, the accrued interest was paid in cash. The company's stock was selling for $31 per share on March 1, 1999.

Instructions
Prepare the journal entries needed on the books of Fontenot Company to record the following:
  (a) April 1, 1998: issuance of the bonds.
  (b) October 1, 1998: payment of semiannual interest.
  (c) December 31, 1998: accrual of interest expense.
  (d) March 1, 1999: extinguishment of 3,000 bonds. (No reversing entries made.)

P14-8 (Entries for Noninterest-Bearing Debt) On December 31, 1998, Jose Luis Company acquired a computer from Cuevas Corporation by issuing a $400,000 noninterest-bearing note, payable in full on December 31, 2002. Jose Luis Company's credit rating permits it to borrow funds from its several lines of credit at 10%. The computer is expected to have a 5-year life and a $50,000 salvage value.

Instructions
  (a) Prepare the journal entry for the purchase on December 31, 1998.
  (b) Prepare any necessary adjusting entries relative to depreciation (use straight-line) and amortization (use effective interest method) on December 31, 1999.
  (c) Prepare any necessary adjusting entries relative to depreciation and amortization on December 31, 2000.

P14-9 (Entries for Noninterest-Bearing Debt; Payable in Installments) Sun Yat-sen Cosmetics Co. purchased machinery on December 31, 1997, paying $40,000 down and agreeing to pay the balance in four equal installments of $30,000 payable each December 31. An assumed interest of 12% is implicit in the purchase price.

Instructions
Prepare the journal entries that would be recorded for the purchase and for the payments and interest on the following dates:
  (a) December 31, 1997.   (d) December 31, 2000.
  (b) December 31, 1998.   (e) December 31, 2001.
  (c) December 31, 1999.

P14-10 (Comprehensive Problem; Issuance, Classification, Reporting) Presented below are five independent situations:
  (a) On March 1, 1999, Wladyslaw Co. issued at 103 plus accrued interest $3,000,000, 9% bonds. The bonds are dated January 1, 1999, and pay interest semiannually on July 1 and January 1. In addition, Wladyslaw Co. incurred $27,000 of bond issuance costs. Compute the net amount of cash received by Wladyslaw Co. as a result of the issuance of these bonds.
  (b) On January 1, 1998, Reymont Co. issued 9% bonds with a face value of $500,000 for $469,280 to yield 10%. The bonds are dated January 1, 1998, and pay interest annually. What amount is reported for interest expense in 1998 related to these bonds, assuming that Reymont used the effective interest method for amortizing bond premium and discount?
  (c) Czeslaw Building Co. has a number of long-term bonds outstanding at December 31, 1999. These long-term bonds have the following sinking fund requirements and maturities for the next 6 years.

	Sinking Fund	Maturities
2000	$300,000	$100,000
2001	100,000	250,000
2002	100,000	100,000
2003	200,000	—
2004	200,000	150,000
2005	200,000	100,000

Indicate how this information should be reported in the financial statements at December 31, 1999.

(d) In the long-term debt structure of Marie Curie Inc., the following three bonds were reported: mortgage bonds payable $10,000,000; collateral trust bonds $5,000,000; bonds maturing in installments, secured by plant equipment $4,000,000. Determine the total amount, if any, of debenture bonds outstanding.

P14-11 (Comprehensive Liability Problem; Balance Sheet Presentation) Honoré de Balzac Inc. has been producing quality children's apparel for more than 25 years. The company's fiscal year runs from April 1 to March 31. The following information relates to the obligations of Balzac as of March 31, 1999.

Bonds Payable
Balzac issued $5,000,000 of 11% bonds on July 1, 1993, at 96 which yielded proceeds of $4,800,000. The bonds will mature on July 1, 2003. Interest is paid semiannually on July 1 and January 1. Balzac uses the straight-line method to amortize the bond discount.

Notes Payable
Balzac has signed several long-term notes with financial institutions and insurance companies. The maturities of these notes are given in the schedule below. The total unpaid interest for all of these notes amounts to $210,000 on March 31, 1999.

Due Date	Amount Due
April 1, 1999	$ 200,000
July 1, 1999	300,000
October 1, 1999	150,000
January 1, 2000	150,000
April 1, 2000–March 31, 2001	600,000
April 1, 2001–March 31, 2002	500,000
April 1, 2002–March 31, 2003	700,000
April 1, 2003–March 31, 2004	400,000
April 1, 2004–March 31, 2005	500,000
	$3,500,000

Estimated Warranties
Balzac has a one-year product warranty on some selected items in its product line. The estimated warranty liability on sales made during the 1997–98 fiscal year and still outstanding as of March 31, 1998 amounted to $84,000. The warranty costs on sales made from April 1, 1998, through March 31, 1999, are estimated at $210,000. The actual warranty costs incurred during the current 1998–99 fiscal year are as follows:

Warranty claims honored on 1997–98 sales	$ 84,000
Warranty claims honored on 1998–99 sales	95,000
Total warranty claims honored	$179,000

Other Information
1. *Trade payables.* Accounts payable for supplies, goods and services purchased on open account amount to $370,000 as of March 31, 1999.
2. *Payroll related items.* Outstanding obligations related to Balzac's payroll as of March 31, 1999, are:

Accrued salaries and wages	$150,000
FICA taxes	22,000
State and federal income taxes withheld from employees	25,000
Other payroll deductions	5,000

3. *Taxes.* The following taxes incurred but not due until the next fiscal year are:

State and federal income taxes	$310,000
Property taxes	125,000
Sales and use taxes	182,000

4. *Miscellaneous accruals.* Other accruals not separately classified amount to $75,000 as of March 31, 1999.
5. *Dividends.* On March 15, 1999, Balzac's board of directors declared a cash dividend of $.40 per common share and a 10% common stock dividend. Both dividends were to be distributed on April 12, 1999, to the common stockholders of record at the close of business on March 31, 1999. Data regarding Balzac common stock are as follows:

Par value	$5 per share
Number of shares issued and outstanding	3,000,000 shares

Market values of common stock:

March 15, 1999	$22.00 per share
March 31, 1999	21.50 per share
April 12, 1999	22.50 per share

Instructions

Prepare the liability section of the balance sheet and appropriate notes to the statement for Balzac Inc. as of March 31, 1999, as they should appear in its annual report to the stockholders.

(CMA adapted)

*P14-12 **(Loan Impairment Entries)**   On January 1, 1998, Bostan Company issued a $1,200,000, 5-year, zero-interest-bearing note to National Organization Bank. The note was issued to yield 8% annual interest. Unfortunately, during 1999, Bostan fell into financial trouble due to increased competition. After reviewing all available evidence on December 31, 1999, National Organization Bank decided that the loan was impaired. Bostan will probably pay back only $800,000 of the principal at maturity.

Instructions

(a) Prepare journal entries for both Bostan Company and National Organization Bank to record the issuance of the note on January 1, 1998.

(b) Assuming that both Bostan Company and National Organization Bank use the effective interest method to amortize the discount, prepare the amortization schedule for the note.

(c) Under what circumstances can National Organization Bank consider Bostan's note to be "impaired"?

(d) Compute the loss National Organization Bank will suffer from Bostan's financial distress on December 31, 1999. What journal entries should be made to record this loss?

*P14-13 **(Debtor/Creditor Entries for Continuation of Troubled Debt)**   Jeremy Hillary is the sole shareholder of Hillary Inc., which is currently under protection of the U.S. bankruptcy court. As a "debtor in possession," he has negotiated the following revised loan agreement with Valley Bank. Hillary Inc.'s $400,000, 12%, 10-year note was refinanced with a $400,000, 5%, 10-year note. *[handwritten: legal/economic matter. Company is in trouble.]*

Instructions

(a) What is the accounting nature of this transaction?

(b) Prepare the journal entry to record this refinancing:
   1. On the books of Hillary Inc.
   2. On the books of Valley Bank.

(c) Discuss whether generally accepted accounting principles provide the proper information useful to managers and investors in this situation.

*P14-14 **(Restructure of Note under Different Circumstances)**   Sandro Corporation is having financial difficulty and therefore has asked Botticelli National Bank to restructure its $3 million note outstanding. The present note has 3 years remaining and pays a current rate of interest of 10%. The present market rate for a loan of this nature is 12%. The note was issued at its face value.

Instructions

Presented below are four independent situations. Prepare the journal entry that Sandro and Botticelli National Bank would make for each of these restructurings.

(a) Botticelli National Bank agrees to take an equity interest in Sandro by accepting common stock valued at $2,200,000 in exchange for relinquishing its claim on this note. The common stock has a par value of $1,000,000.

(b) Botticelli National Bank agrees to accept land in exchange for relinquishing its claim on this note. The land has a book value of $1,950,000 and a fair value of $2,400,000.

(c) Botticelli National Bank agrees to modify the terms of the note, indicating that Sandro does not have to pay any interest on the note over the 3-year period.

(d) Botticelli National Bank agrees to reduce the principal balance due to $2,500,000 and require interest only in the second and third year at a rate of 10%.

*P14-15 **(Debtor/Creditor Entries for Continuation of Troubled Debt)**   Dionysus Inc. owes Solomos Bank a 10-year, 15% note in the amount of $250,000. The note is due today, 12/31/98. Because Dionysus Inc. is in financial trouble, Solomos agrees to accept 60,000 shares of Dionysus's $1.00 par value common stock, which is selling for $1.40, reduce the face amount of the note to $150,000, extend the maturity date to 12/31/02, and reduce the interest rate to 6%. Interest will continue to be due on December 31 each year.

Instructions

(a) Prepare all the necessary journal entries on the books of Dionysus Inc. from restructure through maturity.

(b) Prepare all the necessary journal entries on the books of Solomos Bank from restructure through maturity.

*P14-16 (Entries for Troubled Debt Restructurings) At December 31, 1997, Sioux Manufacturing Company had outstanding a $300,000, 12% note payable to Teton National Bank. Dated January 1, 1995, the note was due December 31, 1998, with interest payable each December 31. During 1998, Sioux notified Teton that it might be unable to meet the scheduled December 31, 1998, payment of principal and interest because of financial difficulties. On September 30, 1998, Teton sold the note, including interest accrued since December 31, 1997, for $280,000 to Osage Foundry, one of Sioux's oldest and largest customers. On December 31, 1998, Osage agreed to accept inventory costing $240,000 and worth $315,000 from Sioux in full settlement of the note.

Instructions

(a) Prepare the journal entry to record the September 30, 1998, transaction on the books of Teton, Sioux, and Osage. For each, indicate whether the transaction is a troubled debt restructuring.

(b) Prepare the journal entries to record the December 31, 1998, transaction on the books of Sioux and Osage. For each, indicate whether the transaction is a troubled debt restructuring.

*P14-17 (Debtor/Creditor Entries for Continuation of Troubled Debt with New Effective Interest) Mildred Corp. owes D. Taylor Corp. a 10-year, 10% note in the amount of $110,000 plus $11,000 of accrued interest. The note is due today, December 31, 1998. Because Mildred Corp. is in financial trouble, D. Taylor Corp. agrees to forgive the accrued interest, $10,000 of the principal, and to extend the maturity date to December 31, 2001. Interest at 10% of revised principal will continue to be due on 12/31 each year.

Assume the following present value factors for 3 periods:

	2¼%	2⅜%	2½%	2⅝%	2¾%	3%
Single sum	.93543	.93201	.92859	.92521	.92184	.91514
Ord. Annuity of 1	2.86989	2.86295	2.85602	2.84913	2.84226	2.82861

Instructions

(a) Compute the new effective interest rate for Mildred Corp. following restructure. (*Hint:* Find the interest rate that establishes approximately $121,000 as the present value of the total future cash flows.)

(b) Prepare a schedule of debt reduction and interest expense for the years 1998 through 2001.

(c) Compute D. Taylor Corp. gain or loss and prepare a schedule of receivable reduction and interest revenue for the years 1998 through 2001.

(d) Prepare all the necessary journal entries on the books of Mildred Corp. for the years 1998, 1999, and 2000.

(e) Prepare all the necessary journal entries on the books of D. Taylor Corp. for the years 1998, 1999, and 2000.

❖ CONCEPTUAL CASES ❖

C14-1 (Bond Theory: Balance Sheet Presentations, Interest Rate, Premium) On January 1, 1999, Branagh Company issued for $1,075,230 its 20-year, 13% bonds that have a maturity value of $1,000,000 and pay interest semiannually on January 1 and July 1. Bond issue costs were not material in amount. Below are three presentations of the long-term liability section of the balance sheet that might be used for these bonds at the issue date:

1. Bonds payable (maturing January 1, 2019)	$1,000,000
Unamortized premium on bonds payable	75,230
Total bond liability	$1,075,230
2. Bonds payable—principal (face value $1,000,000 maturing January 1, 2019)	$ 97,220[a]
Bonds payable—interest (semiannual payment $65,000)	978,010[b]
Total bond liability	$1,075,230

3. Bonds payable—principal (maturing January 1, 2019) $1,000,000

Bonds payable—interest ($65,000 per period for 40 periods)   2,600,000

         Total bond liability $3,600,000

^aThe present value of $1,000,000 due at the end of 40 (6-month) periods at the yield rate of 6% per period.

^bThe present value of $65,000 per period for 40 (6-month) periods at the yield rate of 6% per period.

Instructions

(a) Discuss the conceptual merit(s) of each of the date-of-issue balance sheet presentations shown above for these bonds.

(b) Explain why investors would pay $1,075,230 for bonds that have a maturity value of only $1,000,000.

(c) Assuming that a discount rate is needed to compute the carrying value of the obligations arising from a bond issue at any date during the life of the bonds, discuss the conceptual merit(s) of using for this purpose:

1. The coupon or nominal rate.

2. The effective or yield rate at date of issue.

(d) If the obligations arising from these bonds are to be carried at their present value computed by means of the current market rate of interest, how would the bond valuation at dates subsequent to the date of issue be affected by an increase or a decrease in the market rate of interest?

(AICPA adapted)

C14-2 (Various Long-Term Liability Conceptual Issues) The Emma Thompson Company has completed a number of transactions during 1998. In January the company purchased under contract a machine at a total price of $1,200,000, payable over 5 years with installments of $240,000 per year. The seller has considered the transaction as an installment sale with the title transferring to Thompson at the time of the final payment.

On March 1, 1998, Thompson issued $10 million of general revenue bonds priced at 99 with a coupon of 10% payable July 1 and January 1 of each of the next 10 years. The July 1 interest was paid and on December 30 the company transferred $1,000,000 to the trustee, Hollywood Trust Company, for payment of the January 1, 1999, interest.

Due to the depressed market for the company's stock, Thompson purchased $500,000 par value of their 6% convertible bonds for a price of $455,000. They expect to resell the bonds when the price of their stock has recovered.

As the accountant for Emma Thompson Company, you have prepared the balance sheet as of December 31, 1998, and have presented it to the president of the company. You are asked the following questions about it:

1. Why has depreciation been charged on equipment being purchased under contract? Title has not passed to the company as yet and, therefore, they are not our assets. Why should the company not show on the left side of the balance sheet only the amount paid to date instead of showing the full contract price on the left side and the unpaid portion on the right side? After all, the seller considers the transaction an installment sale.

2. What is bond discount? As a debit balance, why is it not classified among the assets?

3. Bond interest is shown as a current liability. Did we not pay our trustee, Hollywood Trust Company, the full amount of interest due this period?

4. Treasury bonds are shown as a deduction from bonds payable issued. Why should they not be shown as an asset, since they can be sold again? Are they the same as bonds of other companies that we hold as investments?

Instructions

Outline your answers to these questions by writing a brief paragraph that will justify your treatment.

C14-3 (Bond Theory: Price, Presentation, and Retirement) On March 1, 1999, Chuck Norris Company sold its 5-year, $1,000 face value, 9% bonds dated March 1, 1999, at an effective annual interest rate (yield) of 11%. Interest is payable semiannually, and the first interest payment date is September 1, 1999. Norris uses the interest method of amortization. Bond issue costs were incurred in preparing and selling the bond issue. The bonds can be called by Norris at 101 at any time on or after March 1, 2000.

Instructions

(a) 1. How would the selling price of the bond be determined?

2. Specify how all items related to the bonds would be presented in a balance sheet prepared immediately after the bond issue was sold.

(b) What items related to the bond issue would be included in Norris' 1999 income statement, and how would each be determined?

(c) Would the amount of bond discount amortization using the effective interest method of amortization be lower in the second or third year of the life of the bond issue? Why?

(d) Assuming that the bonds were called in and retired on March 1, 2000, how should Norris report the retirement of the bonds on the 2000 income statement?

(AICPA adapted)

C14-4 (Bond Theory: Amortization and Gain or Loss Recognition) **Part I.** The appropriate method of amortizing a premium or discount on issuance of bonds is the effective interest method.

Instructions

(a) What is the effective interest method of amortization and how is it different from and similar to the straight-line method of amortization?

(b) How is amortization computed using the effective interest method, and why and how do amounts obtained using the effective interest method differ from amounts computed under the straight-line method?

Part II. Gains or losses from the early extinguishment of debt that is refunded can theoretically be accounted for in three ways:

1. Amortized over remaining life of old debt.
2. Amortized over the life of the new debt issue.
3. Recognized in the period of extinguishment.

Instructions

(a) Develop supporting arguments for each of the three theoretical methods of accounting for gains and losses from the early extinguishment of debt.

(b) Which of the methods above is generally accepted and how should the appropriate amount of gain or loss be shown in a company's financial statements?

(AICPA adapted)

C14-5 (Off-Balance Sheet Financing) The Brad Pitt Corporation is interested in building its own soda can manufacturing plant adjacent to its existing plant in Partyville, Kansas. The objective would be to ensure a steady supply of cans at a stable price and to minimize transportation costs. However, the company has been experiencing some financial problems and has been reluctant to borrow any additional cash to fund the project. The company is not concerned with the cash flow problems of making payments, but rather with the impact of adding additional long-term debt to their balance sheet.

The president of Pitt, Aidan Quinn, approached the president of the Aluminum Can Company (ACC), their major supplier, to see if some agreement could be reached. ACC was anxious to work out an arrangement, since it seemed inevitable that Pitt would begin their own can production. The Aluminum Can Company could not afford to lose the account.

After some discussion a two part plan was worked out. First ACC was to construct the plant on Pitt's land adjacent to the existing plant. Second, Pitt would sign a 20-year purchase agreement. Under the purchase agreement, Pitt would express its intention to buy all of its cans from ACC, paying a unit price which at normal capacity would cover labor and material, an operating management fee, and the debt service requirements on the plant. The expected unit price, if transportation costs are taken into consideration, is lower than current market. If Pitt did not take enough production in any one year and if the excess cans could not be sold at a high enough price on the open market, Pitt agrees to make up any cash shortfall so that ACC could make the payments on its debt. The bank will be willing to make a 20-year loan for the plant, taking the plant and the purchase agreement as collateral. At the end of 20 years the plant is to become the property of Pitt.

Instructions

1. What are project financing arrangements?
2. What are take-or-pay contracts?
3. What conditions must be met in order for a contractual obligation to be disclosed as an unconditional purchase obligation?
4. Should Pitt record the plant as an asset together with the related obligation?
5. If not, should Pitt record an asset relating to the future commitment?
6. What is meant by off-balance-sheet financing?

❖ **FINANCIAL REPORTING PROBLEM—INTEL CORPORATION**

Refer to the financial statements and other documents of Intel Corporation presented in Appendix 5B and answer the following questions.

Instructions

(a) What are put warrants and why have they been reclassified from stockholders' equity to put warrants?

(b) What cash outflow obligations related to the repayment of long-term debt does Intel Corporation have over the next five years?

(c) Intel indicates that it believes that it has the ability to meet business requirements in the forseeable future, including capital expenditures for the recently announced expansion of international manufacturing sites, working capital requirements, the potential put obligation, and the dividend program. Prepare an assessment of its solvency and financial flexibility using ratio analysis.

❖ **FINANCIAL STATEMENT ANALYSIS CASES**

Case 1 (Commonwealth Edison Co.)

The following article appeared in *The Wall Street Journal*:

Bond Markets

Giant Commonwealth Edison Issue Hits Resale Market With $70 Million Left Over

NEW YORK—Commonwealth Edison Co.'s slow-selling new 9¼% bonds were tossed onto the resale market at a reduced price with about $70 million still available from the $200 million offered Thursday, dealers said.

The Chicago utility's bonds, rated double-A by Moody's and double-A-minus by Standard & Poor's, originally had been priced at 99.803, to yield 9.3% in 5 years. They were marked down yesterday the equivalent of about $5.50 for each $1,000 face amount, to about 99.25, where their yield jumped to 9.45%.

Instructions

(a) How will the development above affect the accounting for Commonwealth Edison's bond issue?

(b) Provide several possible explanations for the markdown and the slow sale of Commonwealth Edison's bonds.

Case 2 (PepsiCo, Inc.)

PepsiCo, Inc. based in Purchase, New York, was founded 32 years ago and today is the third largest employer in the world with 480,000 employees.

Assume that the following events occurred relating to PepsiCo's long-term debt during 1997:

1. The company decided on February 1 to refinance $3.5 billion in short-term 8% debt to make it long-term 6%.

2. $780 million of long-term zero-coupon bonds with an effective interest rate of 14.4% matured July 1 and were paid.

3. On October 1, the company issued $200 million in Australian dollar 6.3% bonds at 102 and $95 million in Italian lira 11.4% bonds at 99.

4. The company holds $400 million in perpetual Foreign Interest Payment bonds that were issued in 1986, and presently have a rate of interest of 7.5%. These bonds are called perpetual because they have no stated due date. Instead, at the end of every 10-year period after the bond's issuance, the bondholders and PepsiCo have the option of redeeming the bonds. If either party desires to redeem the bonds, the bonds must be redeemed. If the bonds are not redeemed, a new interest rate is set, based on the then-prevailing interest rate for 10-year bonds. The company does not intend to cause

redemption of the bonds, but will reclassify this debt to current in 1996, since the bondholders could decide to redeem the bonds.

Instructions

(a) Consider event 1. What are some of the reasons the company may have decided to refinance this short-term debt, besides lowering the interest rate?

(b) What do you think are the benefits to the investor in purchasing zero-coupon bonds, such as those described in event 2? What journal entry would be required to record the payment of these bonds? If financial statements are prepared each December 31, in which year would the bonds have been included in short-term liabilities?

(c) Make the journal entry to record the bond issue described in event 3. Note that the bonds were issued on the same day, yet one was issued at a premium and the other at a discount. What are some of the reasons that this may have happened?

(d) What are the benefits to PepsiCo in having perpetual bonds as described in event 4? Suppose that in 1996 the bonds are not redeemed and the interest rate is adjusted to 6% from 7.5%. Make all necessary journal entries to record the renewal of the bonds and the change in rate.

❖ COMPARATIVE ANALYSIS CASE

The Coca-Cola Company versus PepsiCo, Inc.
Instructions
Go to our Web site and answer the following questions.

(a) Compute the debt to total assets ratio and the times interest earned ratio for these two companies. Comment on the quality of these two ratios for both Coca-Cola and PepsiCo.

(b) What financial measurements does the Coca-Cola Company use to manage its debt levels? What financial measures does PepsiCo use as a basis to assess its level of long-term debt?

(c) What is the difference between the fair value and the historical cost (carrying amount) of each company's debt at year-end 1995? Why might a difference exist in these two amounts?

(d) Both companies have debt issued in foreign countries. Speculate as to why these companies may use foreign debt to finance their operations. What risks are involved in this strategy, and how might they adjust for this risk?

❖ RESEARCH CASES

Case 1
Instructions
Use an appropriate source (such as those identified in the chapter 2 research case) to identify a firm that recently had its bond rating changed. Answer the following questions.

(a) Which rating agency(ies) changed the rating?

(b) What was the bond rating before and after the change?

(c) What reasons did the rating agency give in support of its action? What accounting data was used as support?

(d) Are additional changes possible?

Case 2
The November 6, 1995, edition of *The Wall Street Journal* includes an article by Linda Sandler, entitled "Kmart Is Pressured Over Obscure Bond 'Puts', Which Stir Worries Amid Tough Retail Times."

Instructions
Read the article and answer the following questions.

(a) What is the total dollar amount of the bond issue in question? Who purchased these bonds?

(b) What right does the "put option" give to bondholders?

(c) What amount is available under Kmart's bank lines? Why can't Kmart borrow under these lines to purchase the bonds? What is the most likely solution to the problem?

(d) Were the terms of the put bonds adequately disclosed?

❖ WRITING ASSIGNMENT

Mathilda B. Reichenbacher, an intermediate accounting student, is having difficulty amortizing bond premiums and discounts using the effective interest method. Furthermore, she cannot understand why the accountancy profession prefers that this method be used instead of the straight-line method. She has come to you with the following problem, looking for help.

On June 30, 1997, Joan Elbert Company issued $3,000,000 face value of 13%, 20-year bonds at $3,225,690, a yield of 12%. Elbert Company uses the effective interest method to amortize bond premiums or discounts. The bonds pay semiannual interest on June 30 and December 31. Compute the amortization schedule for four periods.

Instructions

Write a short paper (1-1.5 pages double-spaced) to Mathilda, explaining what the effective interest method is, why it is preferable, and how it is computed. As an illustration, use the data from the foregoing problem. (Do not forget to include an amortization schedule, referring to it whenever necessary.)

❖ GROUP ASSIGNMENT

Use the data below to work this group project. Your instructor will assign one group member to serve as recorder and one member to serve as spokesperson. As a group, provide the information for the recorder to prepare responses for each of the requirements below. (You may wish to divide the parts among the members.) Upon completion, the spokesperson will report the group findings to the class and be prepared to show supporting computations in good form (round answers to the nearest dollar or percent).

On January 1, 1998, Dewey Yaeger Co. sold $150,000 (face value) of bonds. The bonds are dated January 1, 1998, and will mature on January 1, 2003. Interest is paid annually on December 31. The bonds are callable after December 31, 2000, at 102. Issue costs related to these bonds amounted to $4,000, and these costs are being amortized by the straight-line method. The following amortization schedule was prepared by the accountant for the first 2 years of the life of the bonds:

Date	Cash	Interest	Amortization	Carrying Value of Bonds
1/1/98				$139,186
12/31/98	$15,000	$16,702	$1,702	140,888
12/31/99	15,000	16,907	1,907	142,795

Instructions

On the basis of the information above, answer the following questions (round your answers to the nearest dollar or percent).

- **(a)** What is the nominal or stated rate of interest for this bond issue?
- **(b)** What is the effective or market rate of interest for this bond issue?
- **(c)** Present the journal entry to record the sale of the bond issue, including the issue costs.
- **(d)** Present the appropriate entry(ies) at December 31, 2000.
- **(e)** Present the disclosure of this bond issue on the December 31, 2000, balance sheet. Proper balance sheet subheadings must be indicated.
- **(f)** On June 30, 2001, $100,000 of the bond issue was redeemed at the call price. Present the journal entry for this redemption. Amortization of the discount is recorded ony at the end of the year.
- **(g)** Present the effects of the bond redemption on the 2001 income statement and proper note disclosure. Proper income statement subheadings must be indicated. The income tax rate is 40%; 2001 income before extraordinary items is $30,000 with a weighted number of common shares outstanding during the year of 10,000. Working capital funds were used to redeem the bonds.

❖ ETHICS CASE

Roland Carlson is the president, founder, and majority owner of Thebeau Medical Corporation, an emerging medical technology products company. Thebeau is in dire need of additional capital to keep operating and to bring several promising products to final development, testing, and production. Roland, as owner of 51% of the outstanding stock, manages the company's operations. He places heavy emphasis on research and development and long-term growth. The other principal stockholder is Jana Kingston who, as a nonemployee investor, owns 40% of the stock. Jana would like to deemphasize the R&D functions and emphasize the marketing function to maximize short-run sales and profits from existing products. She believes this strategy would raise the market price of Thebeau's stock.

All of Roland's personal capital and borrowing power is tied up in his 51% stock ownership. He knows that any offering of additional shares of stock will dilute his controlling interest because he won't be able to participate in such an issuance. But, Jana has money and would likely buy enough shares to gain control of Thebeau. She then would dictate the company's future direction, even if it meant replacing Roland as president and CEO.

The company already has considerable debt. Raising additional debt will be costly, will adversely affect Thebeau's credit rating, and will increase the company's reported losses due to the growth in interest expense. Jana and the other minority stockholders express opposition to the assumption of additional debt, fearing the company will be pushed to the brink of bankruptcy. Wanting to maintain his control and to preserve the direction of "his" company, Roland is doing everything to avoid a stock issuance and is contemplating a large issuance of bonds, even if it means the bonds are issued with a high effective-interest rate.

Instructions
    (a) Who are the stakeholders in this situation?
    (b) What are the ethical issues in this case?
    (c) What would you do if you were Roland?

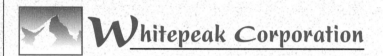 **W**hitepeak Corporation   **MODULE 9**

Sections 9.1 and 9.2 Bond Issuance

On January 1, 1997, Whitepeak issued $150,000 of 11% convertible bonds not at face value. Additionally, these bonds were issued between interest payment dates. The issue was incorrectly recorded. Then on November 1, 1997, also between interest dates, the bonds were retired early.

Instructions Make corrections and update all adjustments related to the bonds, assuming that Whitepeak uses the effective interest method. ■

MODULE 10

Section 10.1 Impaired Loan

In January 1995, Whitepeak loaned funds to one of its subsidiaries, Pueblo Peaks, with a $100,000, 5-year, non-interest-bearing note. Whitepeak has correctly accounted for this asset up to and including December 31, 1996. On December 31, 1996, however, Whitepeak determined that only $40,000 of this amount would be collected at maturity and the note was impaired. Whitepeak incorrectly recorded the write down of the receivable.

Instructions Make any necessary corrections and entries related to the note for 1997. ■

Date Issued		No.	Title
Dec.	1992	No. 113	Accounting and Reporting for Reinsurance of Short-Duration and Long-Duration Contracts
May	1993	No. 114	Accounting by Creditors for Impairment of a Loan
May	1993	No. 115	Accounting for Certain Investments in Debt and Equity Securities
June	1993	No. 116	Accounting for Contributions Received and Contributions Made
June	1993	No. 117	Financial Statements of Not-for-Profit Organizations
Oct.	1994	No. 118	Accounting by Creditors for Impairments of a Loan—Income Recognition and Disclosures
Oct.	1994	No. 119	Disclosure about Derivative Financial Instruments and Fair Value of Financial Instruments
Jan.	1995	No. 120	Accounting and Reporting by Mutual Life Insurance Enterprises
Mar.	1995	No. 121	Accounting for the Impairment of Long-Lived Assets
May	1995	No. 122	Accounting for Mortgage Servicing Rights
Oct.	1995	No. 123	Accounting for Stock-Based Compensation
Nov.	1995	No. 124	Accounting for Certain Investments Held by Not-for-Profit Organizations
June	1996	No. 125	Accounting for Transfers and Servicing of Financial Assets and Extinguishment of Liabilities
Dec.	1996	No. 126	Exemption from Certain Required Disclosures about Financial Instruments for Certain Nonpublic Entities
Dec.	1996	No. 127	Deferral of the Effective Date of Certain Provisions of FASB Statement No. 125
Feb.	1997	No. 128	Earnings per Share
Feb.	1997	No. 129	Disclosure of Information about Capital Structure
June	1997	No. 130	Reporting Comprehensive Income
June	1997	No. 131	Reporting Disaggregated Information about a Business Enterprise

Financial Accounting Standards Board (FASB),
Interpretations (1974–1997)

Date Issued		No.	Title
June	1974	No. 1	Accounting Changes Related to the Cost of Inventory (APB Opinion No. 20)
June	1974	No. 2	Imputing Interest on Debt Arrangements Made Under the Federal Bankruptcy Act (APB Opinion No. 21) (superseded)
Dec.	1974	No. 3	Accounting for the Cost of Pension Plans Subject to the Employee Retirement Income Security Act of 1974 (APB Opinion No. 8)
Feb.	1975	No. 4	Applicability of FASB Statement No. 2 to Purchase Business Combinations
Feb.	1975	No. 5	Applicability of FASB St. No. 2 to Development Stage Enterprises (superseded)
Feb.	1975	No. 6	Applicability of FASB Statement No. 2 to Computer Software
Oct.	1975	No. 7	Applying FASB Statement No. 7 in Statements of Established Enterprises
Jan.	1976	No. 8	Classification of a Short-Term Obligation Repaid Prior to Being Replaced by a Long-Term Security (FASB Std. No. 6)
Feb.	1976	No. 9	Applying APB Opinions No. 16 and 17 when a Savings and Loan or Similar Institution is Acquired in a Purchase Business Combination (APB Op. No. 16 & 17)
Sept.	1976	No. 10	Application of FASB Statement No. 12 to Personal Financial Statements (FASB Std. No. 12)
Sept.	1976	No. 11	Changes in Market Value after the Balance Sheet Date (FASB Std. No. 12)
Sept.	1976	No. 12	Accounting for Previously Established Allowance Accounts (FASB Std. No. 12)
Sept.	1976	No. 13	Consolidation of a Parent and Its Subsidiaries Having Different Balance Sheet Dates (FASB Std. No. 12)
Sept.	1976	No. 14	Reasonable Estimation of the Amount of a Loss (FASB Std. No. 5)
Sept.	1976	No. 15	Translation of Unamortized Policy Acquisition Costs by Stock Life Insurance Company (FASB Std. No. 8) (amended and partially superseded)
Feb.	1977	No. 16	Clarification of Definitions and Accounting for Marketable Equity Securities That Become Nonmarketable (FASB Std. No. 12)
Feb.	1977	No. 17	Applying the Lower of Cost or Market Rule in Translated Financial Statements (FASB Std. No. 8) (superseded)
Mar.	1977	No. 18	Accounting for Income Taxes in Interim Periods (APB Op. No. 28)
Oct.	1977	No. 19	Lessee Guarantee of the Residual Value of Leased Property (FASB Std. No. 13)
Nov.	1977	No. 20	Reporting Accounting Changes under AICPA Statements of Position (APB Op. No. 20)
April	1978	No. 21	Accounting for Leases in a Business Combination (FASB Std. No. 13)
April	1978	No. 22	Applicability of Indefinite Reversal Criteria to Timing Differences (APB Op. No. 11 and 23)
Aug.	1978	No. 23	Leases of Certain Property Owned by a Governmental Unit or Authority (FASB Std. No. 13)
Sept.	1978	No. 24	Leases Involving Only Part of a Building (FASB Std. No. 13)
Sept.	1978	No. 25	Accounting for an Unused Investment Tax Credit (APB Op. No. 2, 4, 11, and 16)
Sept.	1978	No. 26	Accounting for Purchase of a Leased Asset by the Lessee During the Term of the Lease (FASB Std. No. 13)
Nov.	1978	No. 27	Accounting for a Loss on a Sublease (FASB Std. No. 13 and APB Op. No. 30)
Dec.	1978	No. 28	Accounting for Stock Appreciation Rights and Other Variable Stock Option or Award Plans (APB Op. No. 15 and 25) (amended)
Feb.	1979	No. 29	Reporting Tax Benefits Realized on Disposition of Investments in Certain Subsidiaries and Other Investees (APB Op. No. 23 and 24)
Sept.	1979	No. 30	Accounting for Involuntary Conversions of Nonmonetary Assets to Monetary Assets (APB Op. No. 29)

Refer to Index for page citations

Date Issued		No.	Title
Feb.	1980	No. 31	Treatment of Stock Compensation Plans in EPS Computations (APB Op. No. 15 and Interp. 28)
Mar.	1980	No. 32	Application of Percentage Limitations in Recognizing Investment Tax Credit (APB Op. No. 2, 4, and 11)
Aug.	1980	No. 33	Applying FASB Statement No. 34 to Oil and Gas Producing Operations (FASB Std. No. 34)
Mar.	1981	No. 34	Disclosure of Indirect Guarantees of Indebtedness of Others (FASB Std. No. 5)
May	1981	No. 35	Criteria for Applying the Equity Method of Accounting for Investments in Common Stock (APB Op. No. 18)
Oct.	1981	No. 36	Accounting for Exploratory Wells in Progress at the End of a Period
July	1983	No. 37	Accounting for Translation Adjustments upon Sale of Part of an Investment in a Foreign Entity (Interprets FASB Statement No. 52)
Aug.	1984	No. 38	Determining the Measurement Date for Stock Option, Purchase, and Award Plans Involving Junior Stock (Interprets APB Opinion No. 25)
Mar.	1992	No. 39	Offsetting of Amounts Related to Certain Contracts (Interprets APB Opinion No. 10 and FASB Statement No. 105)
Apr.	1993	No. 40	Applicability of Generally Accepted Accounting Principles to Mutual Life Insurance and Other Enterprises (Interprets FASB Statements No. 12, 60, 97, and 113)
Dec.	1994	No. 41	Offsetting of Amounts Related to Certain Repurchase and Reverse Repurchase Agreements
Sept.	1996	No. 42	Accounting for Transfers of Assets in Which a Not-for-Profit Organization is Granted Variance Power

Financial Accounting Standards Board
(FASB), Technical Bulletins (1979–1997)

Date Issued		No.	Title
Dec.	1979	No. 79-1	Purpose and Scope of FASB Technical Bulletins and Procedures for Issuance
Dec.	1979	No. 79-2	Computer Software Costs
Dec.	1979	No. 79-3	Subjective Acceleration Clauses in Long-Term Debt Agreements
Dec.	1979	No. 79-4	Segment Reporting of Puerto Rican Operations
Dec.	1979	No. 79-5	Meaning of the Term 'Customer' as it Applies to Health Care Facilities under FASB Statement No. 14
Dec.	1979	No. 79-6	Valuation Allowances Following Debt Restructuring
Dec.	1979	No. 79-7	Recoveries of a Previous Writedown under a Troubled Debt Restructuring Involving a Modification of Terms
Dec.	1979	No. 79-8	Applicability of FASB Statements 21 and 33 to Certain Brokers and Dealers in Securities
Dec.	1979	No. 79-9	Accounting in Interim Periods for Changes in Income Tax Rates
Dec.	1979	No. 79-10	Fiscal Funding Clauses in Lease Agreements
Dec.	1979	No. 79-11	Effect of a Penalty on the Term of a Lease
Dec.	1979	No. 79-12	Interest Rate Used in Calculating the Present Value of Minimum Lease Payments
Dec.	1979	No. 79-13	Applicability of FASB Statement No. 13 to Current Value Financial Statements
Dec.	1979	No. 79-14	Upward Adjustment of Guaranteed Residual Values
Dec.	1979	No. 79-15	Accounting for Loss on a Sublease Not Involving the Disposal of a Segment
Dec.	1979	No. 79-16	Effect on a Change in Income Tax Rate on the Accounting for Leveraged Leases
Dec.	1979	No. 79-17	Reporting Cumulative Effect Adjustment from Retroactive Application of FASB No. 13
Dec.	1979	No. 79-18	Transition Requirements of Certain FASB Amendments and Interpretations of FASB Statement No. 13
Dec.	1979	No. 79-19	Investor's Accounting for Unrealized Losses on Marketable Securities Owned by an Equity Method Investee
Dec.	1980	No. 80-1	Early Extinguishment of Debt through Exchange for Common or Preferred Stock
Dec.	1980	No. 80-2	Classification of Debt Restructuring by Debtors and Creditors
Feb.	1981	No. 81-1	Disclosure of Interest Rate Futures Contracts and Forward and Standby Contracts
Feb.	1981	No. 81-2	Accounting for Unused Investment Tax Credits Acquired in a Business Combination Accounted for by the Purchase Method
Feb.	1981	No. 81-3	Multiemployer Pension Plan Amendments Act of 1980
Feb.	1981	No. 81-4	Classification as Monetary or Nonmonetary Items
Feb.	1981	No. 81-5	Offsetting Interest Cost to be Capitalized with Interest Income
Nov.	1981	No. 81-6	Applicability of Statement 15 to Debtors in Bankruptcy Situations
Jan.	1982	No. 82-1	Disclosure of the Sale or Purchase of Tax Benefits through Tax Leases
Mar.	1982	No. 82-2	Accounting for the Conversion of Stock Options into Incentive Stock Options as a Result of the Economic Recovery Tax Act of 1981
July	1983	No. 83-1	Accounting for the Reduction in the Tax Basis of an Asset Caused by the Investment Tax Credit (ITC)
Mar.	1984	No. 84-1	Accounting for Stock Issued to Acquire the Results of a Research and Development Arrangement
June	1984	No. 79-1	Purpose and Scope of FASB Technical Bulletins and Procedures for Issuance (Revised)
Sept.	1984	No. 84-2	Accounting for the Effects of the Tax Reform Act of 1984 on Deferred Income Taxes Relating to Domestic International Sales Corporations

Refer to Index for page citations